ENCYCLOPEDIA
of AMERICAN
FOREIGN POLICY

ADVISORY BOARD

ENCYCLOPEDIA
of AMERICAN
FOREIGN POLICY

Second Edition

VOLUME 3

O – W
Index

*Alexander DeConde, Richard Dean Burns,
and Fredrik Logevall, Editors in Chief*

Louise B. Ketz, Executive Editor

CHARLES SCRIBNER'S SONS

GALE GROUP

THOMSON LEARNING

*New York • Detroit • San Diego • San Francisco
Boston • New Haven, Conn. • Waterville, Maine
London • Munich*

Copyright © 2002 by Charles Scribner's Sons

Charles Scribner's Sons
An imprint of the Gale Group
300 Park Avenue South
New York, NY 10010

1 3 5 7 9 11 13 15 17 19 20 18 16 14 12 10 8 6 4 2

Printed in the United States of America

Library of Congress Cataloging-in-Publication Data

Encyclopedia of American Foreign Policy : studies of the principal movements and ideas / editors, Alexander DeConde ... [et al.]--2nd ed.
    p. cm.
Includes bibliographical references and index.
ISBN 0-684-80657-6 (set : alk. paper) -- ISBN 0-684-80658-4 (v. 1) -- ISBN 0-684-80659-2 (v. 2) -- ISBN 0-684-80660-6 (v. 3)
    1. United States--Foreign relations--Encyclopedias. 2. United States--Foreign relations--Philosophy--Encyclopedias. I. DeConde, Alexander.

E183.7 .E52 2002
327.73'003--dc21   2001049800

The paper used in this publication meets the requirements of ANSI/NISO Z3948-1992 (Permanence of Paper)

CONTENTS

★ ★ ★ ★

CONTENTS OF OTHER VOLUMES

VOLUME 2

CONTENTS

ENCYCLOPEDIA
of AMERICAN
FOREIGN POLICY

OIL

★ ★ ★ ★

David S. Painter

Oil was an integral part of U.S. foreign policy in the twentieth century, and its influence has shown no sign of diminishing in the twenty-first century. Oil has been and continues to be central to military power and to modern industrial society, and possession of ample domestic oil supplies and control over access to foreign oil reserves is a significant, and often overlooked, element in the power position of the United States relative to its rivals. While demand for oil is worldwide, for most of the twentieth century the major industrial powers, with the significant exceptions of the United States and the Soviet Union, had meager domestic oil production, and, with the same two exceptions, the major oil producers were not industrial powers. Because of this disparity, struggles over access to oil have been an important focus of rivalry among the great powers and a significant source of conflict between oil-consuming industrial countries and oil-producing nonindustrial nations.

Control of oil has been intimately linked to broader political, military, and economic objectives. These larger foreign policy concerns have shaped the issue of control and have, in turn, been shaped by it. For example, all the major postwar doctrines of U.S. foreign policy—the Truman, Eisenhower, Nixon, Carter, and Reagan doctrines—relate, either directly or indirectly, to the Middle East and its oil.

The history of oil and foreign policy also provides important insights into the relationship between private power and public policy that are crucial to understanding the nature and development of U.S. foreign policy in the twentieth century. Finally, the impact of oil use on the environment has become almost as important an issue as access to oil.

OIL AND WORLD POWER

The United States dominated world oil production in the first half of the twentieth century. U.S. fields accounted for slightly more than 70 percent of world oil production in 1925, around 63 percent in 1941, and over 50 percent in 1950. The U.S. oil industry operated in a unique regulatory environment that included a permissive legal regime, generous tax treatment, and a cooperative system of national production control centered on the state of Texas, which accounted for almost half of total U.S. production. During the Great Depression, the federal government, several state governments, and the oil companies worked out a control system that placed a ceiling on total output and allocated production so that marginal producers could survive in the face of considerable excess capacity. Although Texas authorities refused to require producers to pool their extractive activities in each oil field, thereby allowing wasteful extractive processes to continue, the system allowed high-cost marginal wells to continue to produce, thus preserving lower-cost fields for future use. Higher prices also somewhat reduced consumption. With the Texas Railroad Commission as a balance wheel, the system remained in place until the early 1970s, when domestic production alone could no longer fill national demand.

In addition to being blessed with a thriving and productive domestic oil industry, five of the seven great oil corporations (the so-called Seven Sisters) that dominated the international oil industry from the 1920s to the 1970s were American companies. U.S. oil companies, along with British firms, dominated the oil industries of the two main producing countries in Latin America, Mexico and Venezuela, and had smaller holdings throughout the region. During the 1920s and early 1930s, the United States successfully supported efforts by U.S. oil companies to gain oil concessions in the Middle East. U.S. companies were also involved in regionally significant oil fields in the Netherlands East Indies. By the eve of World War II, U.S. companies accounted for nearly 40 percent of oil production outside the United States and the Soviet Union.

★ ★ ★ ★
★

THE SEVEN SISTERS

Seven large, vertically integrated oil companies dominated the world oil industry from the 1920s to the 1970s. With annual sales in the billions of dollars, the so-called "seven sisters" have consistently ranked among the largest industrial companies in the world. The five American international major oil companies were Standard Oil Company (New Jersey), which became Exxon in 1972; Socony-Vacuum Oil Company, which became Socony Mobil in 1955 and Mobil in 1966; Standard Oil Company of California, later Chevron; the Texas Company, which became Texaco in 1959; and Gulf Oil Company. Chevron bought Gulf in 1984, and in 1998 Exxon and Mobil merged to form Exxon-Mobil.

The other two international majors were Anglo-Persian Oil Company, which changed its name to Anglo-Iranian in 1935 and to British Petroleum in 1954, and the Royal Dutch/Shell group. The British government held a majority share in British Petroleum from 1914 to the 1980s, when Margaret Thatcher's government sold its shares to private investors. Although ownership was divided between Dutch (60 percent) and British (40 percent) interests, Shell had its operating and commercial headquarters in London and was regarded as a British company.

More importantly, the United States possessed the means to ensure the stability of the producing regions and gain access to their oil. The United States Navy had emerged from World War I second to none, thus providing the United States with the capability of securing access to overseas oil-producing areas. The United States was already firmly entrenched in the oil-rich Gulf of Mexico–Caribbean region before World War I for security reasons that predated oil's emergence as a strategic commodity. World War II and the Cold War reinforced traditional U.S. determination to maintain an economic and strategic sphere of influence in Latin America. Securing the Persian Gulf, which emerged as the center of the world oil industry following World War II, was more difficult for several reasons, including the region's distance from the United States, the involvement of rival great powers, and the dynamics of regional

politics. Great Britain had emerged as the leading power in the Middle East following World War I. Following World War II, the United States gradually assumed Britain's role as the main guarantor of Western interests in the Middle East.

Oil became an important element in military power in the decade before World War I when the navies of the great powers, led by Great Britain and the United States, began to switch from coal to oil as their source of power. In addition, the major military innovations of World War I—the submarine, the airplane, the tank, and motorized transport—were all oil-powered. Although the surface fleets of the great powers played a relatively minor part in the fighting, German submarines wreaked havoc on British and French shipping and helped bring the United States into the war. In addition, oil carved out a role in the manufacture of munitions when the British, using a process developed by Royal Dutch/Shell, began extracting toluol, an essential ingredient in the explosive TNT, from oil. Access to oil became more important toward the end of the war with the transition from static trench warfare, with its limited demand for oil-powered machinery, to a more fluid operational environment in which tanks, motorized transport, and aircraft played a larger role.

Britain and France were able to draw on overseas sources of supply from Iran, Mexico, and the United States, while the Germans were limited to oil from Romania. By the last year of the war, the United States was supplying more than 80 percent of Allied oil requirements, and the American navy was playing a key role in supplying and protecting tanker transport of oil to Europe. Although Lord Curzon's boast that the Allied cause had floated to victory on a wave of oil was an overstatement, severe shortages of oil in 1917 and 1918 threatened to immobilize the Royal Navy and the French army. In both cases, urgent requests to the United States for help led to the provision of the needed supplies. In contrast, without such external assistance, oil shortages hindered German military operations at critical points.

In addition to being a tremendous military asset, access to ample supplies of oil provided the United States with important advantages in the industrial transformation of the first half of the twentieth century. By the 1890s, the United States had overtaken Great Britain as the leading industrial power in the world, and by the 1920s, the U.S. economy was larger than the combined economies of the next six great powers (Great

Britain, France, Germany, Italy, Soviet Union, and Japan).

Cheap and plentiful supplies of oil were a prerequisite for the automobile industry, which played a central role in the U.S. economy from the 1920s to the 1960s. Oil became the fuel of choice in land and sea transport as well as the only fuel for air transport, and challenged coal as the main source of energy for industry. Oil also played an important, if somewhat less crucial, role in heating and electricity generation, but oil-powered machinery became crucial to modern agriculture, and oil became an important feedstock for fertilizers and pesticides. Indeed, with the development of the petrochemical industry, oil reached into almost every area of modern life. Already almost one-fifth of U.S. energy consumption by 1925, oil accounted for around one-third of U.S. energy use by World War II. Outside the United States, in contrast, oil was a secondary fuel reserved mainly for transportation and military uses and accounted for less than 10 percent of energy consumption in western Europe and Japan before World War II.

The Soviet Union was the only other great power that possessed significant quantities of oil within its borders. The Russian empire had been the world's leading oil producer in 1900, accounting for more than half of world production. Soon thereafter a combination of geological and political problems caused output to plummet. Soviet oil production recovered rapidly in the 1920s, and by 1939 the Soviet Union was the second-largest oil producer in the world, far behind the United States and slightly ahead of Venezuela. Although the Soviets reentered exports markets briefly in the late 1920s, by the end of the 1930s almost all Soviet oil production was being devoted to internal uses.

The other great powers (Great Britain, France, Germany, and Japan) lacked indigenous oil reserves and were therefore dependent on foreign sources. Although British companies held concessions in Latin America, the Middle East, and Asia, maintaining access to this oil required stability in the oil-producing areas and control of the sea routes linking the oil-producing areas to Britain. British security policy called for the Mediterranean and the Middle East to be defended because they lay athwart land, sea, and air routes to India, the Far East, and the Pacific dominions. If the Mediterranean were closed, a prospect that seemed increasingly likely as Britain's relative power declined in the 1930s, access to Middle East oil would be very difficult,

assuming that the oil fields and other facilities could be defended. Production in the Far East was not great, and access to its oil would be even more difficult to defend in wartime. Wartime access to Western Hemisphere oil would be dependent on the acquiescence and probably the assistance of the United States, to which Britain had conceded regional supremacy shortly after 1900 and whose help would be needed to transport the oil safely across the Atlantic. This dependence on the United States for vital oil supplies was a critical weakness in Great Britain's power position.

During the 1930s, the British government studied the possibility of reducing its reliance on imported oil by using Britain's ample coal supplies as a source of synthetic oil. It rejected this alternative on security grounds, concluding that, given the British position in the major oil producing areas and the strength of the Royal Navy, reliance on imported oil would be less vulnerable to interdiction than large synthetic oil plants that would be conspicuous targets for air attack.

France's stake in foreign oil was largely limited to a share in Iraqi oil production and a few holdings in Romania. Access to Iraq, which by 1939 supplied almost half of France's oil imports, was dependent on British assistance to keep the Mediterranean open and the Middle East secure. Romania was able to fill only a small portion of French oil requirements, and access to Romanian oil would be unreliable in the event of a conflict with Germany. Access to Western Hemisphere oil, the other source of French imports, was dependent on U.S. goodwill and assistance. The French also explored extracting oil from coal and using alcohol as a motor fuel, but neither alternative provided sufficient supplies to relieve France's dependence on imported oil. France was thus doubly dependent, needing British and U.S. cooperation to ensure access to oil.

German and Japanese oil companies had been shut out of the major foreign oil-producing areas, leaving both nations dependent on foreign companies for necessary supplies and thus vulnerable to economic and political pressure. Moreover, their access to oil in the Middle East and the Western Hemisphere was threatened by British and U.S. control of the oil-producing areas and Anglo-American command of the sea routes to these regions.

Convinced that oil was essential to fuel his ambitions, Nazi leader Adolf Hitler moved to promote the development of a synthetic fuel industry in Germany shortly after taking power in 1933.

By the outbreak of World War II, coal-derived synfuels accounted for nearly half of Germany's peacetime oil needs. The process of extracting oil from coal was complicated and expensive, and the huge installations required massive amounts of steel and were very vulnerable to air attack. Therefore, obtaining access to oil that did not depend on sea routes subject to interdiction by enemies remained an important part of Nazi expansionist strategy.

Germany received large quantities of oil from the Soviet Union under the terms of the 1939 Nazi-Soviet Pact, and in November 1940 gained assured access to Romanian oil when Romania was forced to adhere to the Tripartite Pact. These supplies were inadequate for Germany's needs, leading Hitler to look to the conquest of the rich oil fields of the Caucasus as a way to gain oil for Germany's highly mechanized military machine. Thus, the desire to gain assured access to oil was an important factor in Hitler's decision to invade the Soviet Union in June 1941.

Obtaining access to oil was also a key factor behind Japan's decision to attack the United States. By the end of the 1930s, Japan was dependent on the United States for 80 percent of its oil needs. Most of the rest came from the Netherlands East Indies, where Shell and the Standard-Vacuum Oil Company, a jointly owned subsidiary of Standard Oil (New Jersey) and Socony-Vacuum, controlled production. The Netherlands East Indies possessed the largest reserves in East Asia, and control over its oil would go a long way toward meeting Japan's oil needs. On the other hand, seizing the Netherlands East Indies would lead to conflict with Great Britain and the United States. Nevertheless, the Japanese chose this course after the United States, Britain, and the Netherlands imposed an oil embargo on Japan in the late summer of 1941 in response to Japan's decision to take control of all Indochina.

World War II marked the apogee of oil's direct military importance, and the role of oil-powered weapons systems demonstrated that oil had become the lifeblood of the modern military machine. All the key weapons systems of World War II were oil-powered: surface warships (including aircraft carriers), submarines, airplanes (including long-range bombers), tanks, and a large portion of sea and land transport. Oil continued to play an important role in the manufacture of munitions, and the development of petroleum-based synthetic rubber helped relieve Allied dependence on Southeast Asian natural rubber supplies, most of which were in the hands of the Japanese for much of the war.

The United States entered World War II with a surplus production capacity of over one million barrels per day, almost one-third of U.S. production in 1941. This margin enabled the United States, almost single-handedly, to fuel not only its own war effort but that of its Allies, once the logistics of transporting the oil safely across the Atlantic had been mastered. In addition, U.S. leadership in oil-refining technology provided the U.S. military with such advantages as 100-octane aviation gasoline and specialty lubricants needed for high performance aircraft engines.

The Soviet Union also benefited from having indigenous oil supplies. The Soviets were able to retain control of the vital Caucasian oil fields, and rushed new fields in the Volga-Urals region, safely removed from the fighting, into production. These successes helped Soviet forces attain the mobility necessary to repel the German invaders and go on the offensive.

German and Japanese failure to gain secure access to sufficient oil supplies was an important factor in their defeat. German synthetic fuel production proved barely adequate for wartime requirements, and failure to gain control of the rich oil fields in the Caucasus, coupled with setbacks in the Middle East and North Africa, left the German military vulnerable to oil shortages throughout the war. Indeed, Germany was able to hang on as long as it did only because the absence of a second front until the summer of 1944 kept oil requirements at manageable levels. In the late summer of 1944, the Allied bombing campaign began belatedly targeting synthetic fuel plants. By the end of the war, the German war machine was running on empty.

The Japanese gained control of the Netherlands East Indies in 1942, but many of the oil facilities had been sabotaged and took time to restore to full production. More importantly, transporting oil from the East Indies to Japan proved increasingly difficult owing to the remarkable success of U.S. submarines in interdicting Japanese shipping. By late 1944, Japan faced serious oil shortages, with crippling military consequences.

With the exception of the jet engine, the major military innovations of World War II—radar, ballistic missiles, and the atomic bomb—were not oil-powered. Nevertheless, oil remained central to the mobility of land, sea, and air forces. Despite the development of nuclear-powered warships (mainly aircraft carriers and submarines), most of the world's warships remained oil-powered, as did aircraft, armor, and transport. In addition, each new generation of weapons required more oil than its predecessors. Thus, while the advent of the atomic age meant that access to oil would not have been a key factor in a full-scale war between the United States and the Soviet Union, which presumably would have been fought primarily with nuclear weapons and ballistic missiles, such conflicts as the wars in Korea, Vietnam, and the Persian Gulf were fought with conventional, largely oil-powered weapons, thus demonstrating the continued centrality of oil-powered forces, and hence oil, to military power.

Oil's economic importance increased after World War II as the United States intensified its embrace of patterns of socioeconomic organization premised on high levels of oil use, and western Europe and Japan made the transition from coal to oil as their main source of energy. U.S. and world oil consumption skyrocketed in the 1950s and 1960s. Between 1950 and 1972, total world energy consumption increased 179 percent, much faster than population growth, resulting in a doubling of per capita energy consumption. Oil accounted for much of this increase, rising from 29 percent of world energy consumption in 1950 to 46 percent in 1972. By 1973, oil accounted for 47 percent of U.S. energy consumption. Western Europe and Japan were even more dependent on oil for meeting their energy needs; by 1973 oil accounted for 64 percent of west European energy consumption and 80 percent of Japanese energy consumption.

Control of oil played a vital role in establishing and maintaining U.S. preeminence in the postwar international system. Adding to its domestic power base, the United States consolidated its control of world oil in the decade following World War II. By the mid-1950s, U.S. oil companies were firmly entrenched in the great oil-producing areas outside the Soviet Union. Equally, if not more important, the United States, as the dominant power in the Western Hemisphere, controlled access to the region's oil, and the United States alone had the economic and military power to secure Western access to Middle East oil.

The Soviet Union also possessed a powerful domestic oil industry, but despite geographical proximity, extensive efforts, and widespread anti-Western sentiment in Iran and the Arab world, the Soviets failed to achieve a secure foothold in the Persian Gulf and had little impact on the region's oil industry. The Soviets had even less influence over the Western Hemisphere's oil producers. Indeed, the U.S.-led economic boycott of Cuba forced the Soviets to supply the one foothold they possessed in the Western Hemisphere with oil at subsidized prices.

The strong position of the United States in world oil provided multiple advantages. In addition to being central to military power and economic prosperity, control of oil gave the United States leverage over its allies and its former and prospective enemies. U.S. policymakers saw economic growth as essential to preventing the recurrence of the divisive ideological and social conflicts of the interwar years. Soviet expansion into eastern and central Europe as a result of World War II left the Soviet Union in control of almost all of Europe's known indigenous oil reserves as well as important sources of coal in Poland and the Soviet zone of Germany. Making matters worse, postwar western Europe faced a coal shortage of alarming proportions owing to wartime overproduction and destruction and postwar food, transportation, and other problems.

To fuel economic recovery and to prevent western Europe from becoming dependent on the Soviets for energy, the United States sought to ensure that this critical area received the oil it needed. Economic growth, in turn, was crucial to mitigating the divisive class conflicts that had divided European and Japanese society in the first half of the century. Economic growth and prosperity undercut the appeal of leftist parties, financed the welfare state, perpetuated the ascendancy of moderate elites, and sustained the cohesion of the Western alliance. By controlling access to essential oil supplies, the United States was able to reconcile its aim of German and Japanese economic recovery and integration into a Western alliance with that of ensuring against the recurrence of German and Japanese aggression.

Economic growth in western Europe and Japan was central to the containment of Soviet power and influence during the Cold War because it helped prevent these areas from falling to communism through internal processes. Finally, for many years after World War II the Soviets lacked sufficient oil to fight a major war. Hit hard by wartime damage, disruption, transportation problems, equipment shortages, and overuse, Soviet oil production dropped after the war, and the Soviet Union was a net importer of oil (mostly from Romania) until 1954. Exclusion of the Soviets from the Middle East retained oil for Western recovery, and kept the Soviets short of oil. In addition, U.S. and British strategic planners wanted to keep the Soviets out of the Middle East because the region contained the most defensible locations for launching a strategic air offensive against the Soviet Union in the event of a global war. Throughout the Cold War, ensuring Western access to Middle East oil was a basic objective of U.S. foreign policy.

THE ORIGINS OF U.S. FOREIGN OIL POLICY

Access to foreign oil first emerged as an issue in U.S. foreign policy following World War I, because of the growing importance of oil to modern industrial society and modern warfare, fear of exhaustion of U.S. domestic reserves, and the need of U.S. companies with foreign markets for additional sources of supply. Although U.S. oil production quickly rebounded with several new oil finds, culminating in the discovery of the great East Texas oil field in 1930, increasing the presence of U.S. companies in foreign oil fields allowed U.S. companies to supply their foreign markets from overseas sources. Not only was foreign oil usually cheaper to produce and transport, thus boosting company profits, but utilizing overseas oil to meet foreign demand reduced the potential drain on U.S. reserves.

Rejecting such alternatives as government ownership of oil reserves or the division of the world into exclusive spheres of influence, the United States insisted instead on the Open Door policy of equal opportunity for U.S. oil companies to gain access to foreign oil. A clash with the British over access to Middle East oil was averted when the U.S. government threw its support behind private cooperative arrangements between U.S. and British oil corporations. A multinational consortium, the Iraq Petroleum Company, established in 1928, allowed selected U.S. oil companies access to Iraq's oil along with British and French companies. To ensure that the development of the region's oil took place in a cooperative manner, the consortium agreement contained a self-denying ordinance that prohibited its members from engaging in oil development within the area of the old Ottoman Empire, which was marked on a map with a red line. In addition to the Red Line Agreement, the major British and U.S. oil companies sought to manage the world oil economy through a series of agreements between 1928 and 1934 that allocated markets, fixed prices, eliminated competition, and avoided duplication of facilities.

The U.S. government successfully supported subsequent efforts by other U.S. oil companies to gain concessions in the Middle East. In 1930, Standard Oil of California (SOCAL), which had not been party to the cooperative agreements, obtained a concession on the island of Bahrain, off the coast of Saudi Arabia, and in 1933 obtained extensive concession rights in Saudi Arabia. The Texas Company joined forces with SOCAL in Bahrain and Saudi Arabia in 1936. Meanwhile, Gulf Oil Company, in partnership with Anglo-Persian, had gained access to Kuwait, which was not within the Red Line.

U.S. and British companies also worked together to control Latin American oil. U.S. and British oil companies had been active in Mexico since the turn of the century, drawn by the rich deposits along the Gulf of Mexico coast and the generous terms offered by Mexican dictator Porfirio Díaz. Production continued during the revolution (1910–1920), and Mexico was briefly the world's leading oil exporter during World War I and the early 1920s.

One of the chief goals of the Mexican revolution was to reassert national control over the nation's economic life. The revolutionary constitution of 1917 reserved subsoil rights to the state, leading to almost a decade of conflict with the foreign oil companies, who had convinced Díaz to go against Spanish law and grant them ownership of subsoil rights. Private ownership of subsoil rights would make it difficult for Mexico to share in the profits generated by oil exports since the oil companies, as owners of the oil, would not have to pay royalties to the Mexican government. Although the United States and Mexico were able to work out a compromise that protected the position of companies already operating in Mexico, Mexican oil production declined sharply during the 1920s as the major oil companies remained concerned over the course of the revolution and shifted their investment to Venezuela. By the eve of World War II, Venezuela had become the third leading oil producer in the world and the leading exporter.

In March 1938, a labor dispute between the major oil companies and Mexican oil workers resulted in government intervention and the nationalization of the main U.S. and British oil companies operating in Mexico. Not only did the companies lose their properties, but henceforth foreign capital was denied access to a basic sector of the Mexican economy. Moreover, the resource in question was an exportable commodity in great demand by the developed countries. Thus, the Mexican action challenged not only the position of the international oil companies but also the role of multinational corporations in the economic development of what would become known as the Third World.

The oil companies reacted strongly to nationalization, instituting a boycott of Mexican oil and pressuring oil equipment manufacturers not to sell equipment to Petróleos Mexicanos (Pemex), the state-owned oil company that took over the nationalized properties. Concerned about the impact of nationalization on U.S. investment abroad, the Department of State supported the companies' demands for full and immediate compensation. Although President Franklin D. Roosevelt softened "immediate" compensation to "prompt," Mexico could only raise the funds to pay compensation through the long-term operation of the industry. Since the companies, with the support of the U.S. government, were working to prevent Mexico from selling its oil abroad, the demand for full and prompt compensation amounted to denying Mexico the means of carrying out nationalization.

The Mexicans refused to give in, however, and Pemex turned to Germany, Italy, and Japan for markets and equipment. In addition to oil, U.S. economic interests in Mexico included mining, ranching, and manufacturing firms, and the worsening international situation provided further impetus for a shift in U.S. strategy. In November 1941, with war imminent, the U.S. government reached agreement with Mexico on compensation. Contrary to the views of some scholars, the settlement of the oil controversy did not constitute acceptance of nationalization or abandonment of the oil companies. The U.S. government remained opposed to nationalization and viewed settlement of the compensation issue not only as necessary to ensure Mexico's cooperation in international affairs but also as a way to keep the door open for U.S. companies to return to Mexico in the future. The agreement was limited to the issue of compensation for the expropriated properties and was significantly silent on the question of the future status of foreign participation in the Mexican oil industry. For the rest of the 1940s, the United States sought, albeit unsuccessfully, to convince the Mexican government to reverse nationalization.

Concerned not to repeat the Mexican experience, the U.S. government played a major role in facilitating a settlement between the Venezuelan government and the major oil companies that resulted in a fifty-fifty profit-sharing agreement in early 1943. Although some scholars see the oil settlement as evidence of the subordination of the interests of U.S. corporations to larger foreign policy goals, those goals and the interests of the U.S. oil companies involved did not conflict but were complementary. Both aimed at ensuring the continuation of the companies' control and continued U.S. and British access to Venezuelan oil. In addition to profit sharing, the settlement included confirmation of the companies' existing concession rights, their extension for forty years, and the opening of new areas to the companies. Venezuelan oil production increased substantially, and Venezuelan oil played an important role in fueling the British and U.S. war efforts.

Although the United States was able to fuel its own war effort and that of its allies from domestic oil production during World War II, the increased consumption strained U.S. oil reserves. The possibility of running short of oil led to concerns over the long-term adequacy of U.S. reserves. Policymakers in the U.S. government soon focused their attention on the Middle East, especially on Saudi Arabia. The Middle East not only contained one-third of the world's known reserves; it also offered better geological prospects for the discovery of additional reserves than any other area.

Believing that government ownership was necessary to protect the national interest and to ensure public support for whatever measures might be necessary to secure access to Saudi Arabia's oil, the Roosevelt administration contemplated creating a government-owned national oil company to take over the concession rights in Saudi Arabia held by the Arabian American Oil Company (ARAMCO), a jointly owned subsidiary of Standard Oil of California and the Texas Company. It also proposed having the U.S. government construct and own an oil pipeline stretching from the Persian Gulf to the Mediterranean as a means of demonstrating and securing the U.S. stake in Middle East oil. By war's end, the U.S. government had also worked out the text of an oil agreement with Great Britain that called for guarantees of existing concessions, equality of opportunity to compete for new concessions, and a binational petroleum commission to allocate production among the various producing countries in order to integrate Middle East oil into world markets with minimal disruption. Expansion of Middle East production would enhance U.S. security by reducing the drain on U.S. and other Western Hemisphere reserves.

Divisions within the U.S. oil industry, coupled with the strong ideological opposition of American business and politicians to government involvement in corporate affairs, derailed these initiatives. In the case of the plan to purchase ARAMCO, the company's owners, while willing to accept some government involvement to secure their position and provide capital for further development of their potentially rich concession, were not willing to sell out entirely. The rest of the oil industry, ideologically and pragmatically opposed to government involvement in corporate affairs, vigorously opposed the plan, forcing its abandonment.

Similarly, while the companies that would benefit from the proposed pipeline supported the plan, the other major oil companies opposed it because it would give their competitors significant advantages. Domestic producers, fearing that the pipeline would allow Middle East oil to push Venezuelan oil from European markets into the United States, also opposed the plan. Congress, increasingly conservative and ever receptive to appeals cast in terms of defense of free enterprise, joined the opponents to defeat the pipeline plan.

The Anglo-American Oil Agreement was compatible with the interests of the major U.S. oil companies. All the U.S. majors held concessions in the Middle East, and all initially believed that an international allocation mechanism was needed to assimilate growing Middle East production without disrupting markets. The domestic oil industry, on the other hand, had worked out a system of production control in the 1930s, which protected the interests of smaller companies. Domestic producers feared that the proposed petroleum commission would allow cheap foreign oil to flood the U.S. market. While the U.S. government had no intention of destroying the domestic oil industry, it did intend to use the proposed commission to increase Middle East oil production and conserve U.S. oil supplies for future defense needs. The concerns of the independent oil companies were heard in Congress, and the Anglo-American Oil Agreement never came to a vote.

The only foreign oil policy on which all segments of the industry could agree was that the government should limit its involvement in foreign oil matters to providing and maintaining an international environment in which private enterprise could operate with security and profit. Thus, in the end, the United States, as it had in the 1920s, turned to the major oil companies to secure the national interest in foreign sources of oil. Even though oil industry divisions limited some types of government assistance to the major oil companies, reliance on the major oil companies as vehicles of the national interest in foreign oil enhanced the influence of the oil industry and facilitated control of the world oil economy by the most powerful private interests.

In a series of private deals in 1946 and 1947, the major U.S. oil companies managed to secure their position in the Middle East by joining forces with each other and their British counterparts. The centerpiece of the so-called "great oil deals" was the expansion of ARAMCO's ownership to include Standard Oil of New Jersey and Socony-Vacuum. The result was a private system of worldwide production management that facilitated the development of Middle East oil and its integration into world markets, thus reducing the drain on Western Hemisphere reserves. To help consolidate this system, the U.S. government supported fifty-fifty profit-sharing arrangements between the major oil companies and host governments. Owing to provisions in the U.S. tax code granting U.S. corporations credits for taxes paid overseas, this solution to host-country demands for higher revenues transferred the cost of higher payments from the oil companies to the U.S. Treasury.

Utilizing private oil companies as vehicles of the national interest in foreign oil did not mean that the government had no role to play. On the contrary, the policy required the United States to take an active interest in the security and stability of the Middle East. This was especially the case in Iran, where fear of Soviet expansion and determination to maintain access to the region's resources transformed U.S. policy from relative indifference to deep concern for Iranian independence and territorial integrity. To secure Iran's role as a buffer between the Soviet Union and the oil fields of the Persian Gulf, the United States provided economic and military assistance and gradually assumed Britain's role as a barrier to the expansion of Russian influence in the Middle East. U.S. support came at a price, however. During this period, the United States began looking to the shah of Iran as the main guarantor of Western interests in Iran. U.S. support for the shah and the Iranian military was crucial to the young shah in his struggle with internal rivals for power.

Although mention of oil was deliberately deleted from President Harry Truman's address, the Truman Doctrine (1947), with its call for the

★ ★ ★ ★
★

OIL AND THE AMERICAN WAY OF LIFE

The history of oil and foreign policy provides many examples of the links between the internal organization of the United States and its external behavior. Oil and the automobile have been potent symbols of the American way of life since the second decade of the twentieth century, and American popular culture has come to equate the private automobile and personal mobility with individual freedom. Thus, when it became clear in the 1940s that U.S. domestic oil production would soon no longer be able to meet domestic demand, American leaders looked abroad for additional sources of oil. The alternative of reducing, or at least slowing, the growth of rapidly rising consumption was not considered.

Remarks by Secretary of Defense James Forrestal in early January 1948 illustrate this tendency to look to external expansion to solve internal problems rather than confronting them directly. Meeting with the head of the Socony-Vacuum Oil Company to discuss the impact of turmoil over Palestine on access to Middle East oil, Forres-

tal stated that he "was deeply concerned about the future supply of oil for this country, not merely for the possible use in war but for the needs of peace." He then warned that unless we had access to Middle East oil, American motor-car companies would have to design a four-cylinder motor-car sometime within the next five years." Annual per capita oil consumption in the United States in 1948 was 14.4 barrels. Had U.S. public policy, through the preservation of public transportation, the promotion of efficiency, and other measures (including four-cylinder motorcars), maintained this level of oil use, the United States would have consumed significantly less oil over the following half century, with consequent benefits for the environment, the quality of life, and U.S. oil security. Instead, U.S. oil consumption climbed steadily, reaching an annual per capita level of 31 barrels in 1978. Although it declined sharply for a brief period in the early 1980s, annual per capita oil consumption soon renewed its upward trend, reaching 26.1 barrels in 1999.

global containment of communism, provided a political basis for an active U.S. role in maintaining the security and stability of the Middle East. The Marshall Plan also helped solidify the U.S. position in the region by providing dollars for western Europe to buy oil produced by U.S. companies from their holdings in the Middle East. Fully 10 percent of Marshall Plan aid went to finance oil imports.

U.S. support for a Jewish homeland in Palestine complicated but did not nullify U.S. efforts to maintain access to Middle East oil. The apparent conflict between U.S. economic and strategic interests in Middle East oil on one hand, and its emotional support for a Jewish homeland in Palestine on the other, led the United States to follow a policy of minimal involvement. Although the United States voted for the United Nations resolution calling for the creation of Israel in November 1947 and recognized the new country immediately in May 1948, it refrained from sending troops, arms, or extensive economic assistance to enforce the UN decision for fear of alienating the Arab states and providing an opening for Soviet influence in the Middle East. Ironically, the Palestine problem

enhanced the status of the major oil companies as vehicles of the national interest in Middle East oil. While official relations with the Arab states suffered somewhat because of U.S. support for Israel, the oil companies managed to maintain a degree of distance from government policy and thus escaped the burden of Arab displeasure. On the other hand, failure to enforce the UN decision led to the issue being decided through arms, with results that still haunt the region.

The policy of public support for private control of the world's oil reinforced traditional U.S. opposition to economic nationalism, especially when it affected U.S. companies and threatened to reduce oil production for export to world markets. U.S. security interests called for the rapid and extensive development of Mexico's nearby reserves, but U.S. assistance to Mexico to achieve that goal could be seen as a reward for nationalization and thus encourage other nations to take over their oil industries. Unable to convince the Mexican government to reverse nationalization, the United States maintained its policy of providing no assistance to Pemex, and, as it had before the war, focused instead on Venezuela. Although willing to work with the nationalist government that ruled Venezuela between 1945 and 1948 as long as it did not challenge corporate control of the oil industry, the United States stood by when the democratically elected government was ousted in a November 1948 military coup, and worked closely with the brutal dictatorship that ruled Venezuela for the next decade.

The Truman administration also sought a solution to the problem of oil security by undertaking a large-scale program of synthetic fuel production as a way of obtaining oil from domestic sources. Synthetic fuel production required massive amounts of steel, produced millions of tons of waste products, and cost more than natural petroleum. Although a potential boon to the ailing coal industry, the oil industry opposed the development of competition at public expense, and convinced the Eisenhower administration to cancel the government's synthetic fuel program in 1954.

The U.S. response to the nationalization of the Iranian oil industry highlighted the main elements of U.S. foreign oil policy—opposition to economic nationalism, an activist role in maintaining the stability and Western orientation of the Middle East, and public support for and nonintervention in the operations of the major oil industry. The Iranian crisis of 1951–1954 grew out of Iran's nationalization of the British-owned Anglo-Iranian Oil Company (AIOC) in the spring of 1951. AIOC's Iranian operations were Britain's most valuable overseas asset, and the British feared that if Iran succeeded in taking over the company all of Britain's overseas investments would be jeopardized. Although the United States shared British concerns about the impact of nationalization on foreign investment, it also feared that British use of force to reverse nationalization could result in turmoil in Iran that could undercut the position of the shah, boost the prospects of the pro-Soviet Tudeh party, and might even result in intervention by the Soviets at Iranian invitation. The crisis broke out in the midst of the Korean War, making U.S. policymakers extremely reluctant to risk another confrontation. Therefore, the United States urged the British to try to reach a negotiated settlement that preserved as much of their position as possible. The British, however, preferred to stand on their rights and force Iran to give in by organizing an international boycott of Iranian oil and attempting to manipulate Iranian politics.

U.S. efforts to mediate a settlement failed, as did less public attempts to convince the shah to

remove nationalist Prime Minister Mohammad Mossadeq. By 1953 the oil boycott had sharply reduced Iran's export earnings and decimated government revenues, and British and U.S. involvement in Iranian internal affairs had exacerbated the polarization of Iranian politics. Moreover, the end of the Korean War and the completion of the U.S. military buildup allowed a more aggressive posture toward Iran. Fearing that Mossadeq might displace the shah and that Tudeh influence was increasing, the United States and Britain organized, financed, and directed a coup that removed Mossadeq and installed a government willing to reach an oil settlement on Western terms.

Following the coup, the United States enlisted the major U.S. oil companies in an international consortium to run Iran's oil industry. Cooperation of all the majors was necessary in order to fit Iranian oil, which had been shut out of world markets during the crisis, back into world markets without disruptive price wars and destabilizing cutbacks in other oil-producing countries. The antitrust exemption required for this strategy undercut efforts by the Department of Justice to challenge the major oil companies' control of the world oil industry on antitrust grounds and strengthened the hand of the major oil companies, whose cooperation was needed to ensure Western access to the region's oil.

The U.S. role in the coup and the subsequent inclusion of U.S. oil companies in the Iranian consortium mark important milestones in the gradual process by which the United States replaced Great Britain as the main guardian of Western interests in the Middle East. The experience also reinforced the U.S. tendency to see the shah as the best guarantor of Western interests in Iran. U.S. security and economic assistance helped the shah establish a royal dictatorship, ending the progress Iran had been making toward more representative government. Iranian nationalism, in turn, veered from liberalism and secularism, laying the groundwork for the fundamental rupture in Iranian-American relations that followed the Iranian revolution of 1978–1979. Finally, the short-term success of the Iranian model of covert intervention influenced subsequent U.S. actions in the Middle East, Latin America, and Asia.

COPING WITH CHANGE

With Mossadeq's fate serving as a warning to those who might challenge the international oil companies and their sponsors, the 1950s and 1960s were the golden age of the postwar oil regime. At the peak of their influence in the 1950s, the seven major oil companies controlled over 90 percent of the oil reserves and accounted for almost 90 percent of oil production outside the United States, Mexico, and the centrally planned economies. Moreover, they owned almost 75 percent of world refining capacity and provided around 90 percent of the oil traded in international markets.

Despite these strengths, the system contained the seeds of its own demise. The Iranian crisis demonstrated that threats to Western access to Middle East oil could come from within the region. Although the United States did not rule out the possibility of Soviet military intervention in the Middle East, U.S. threat assessments increasingly focused on the decline of British power, instability within the countries of the region, the anti-Western cast of Middle Eastern nationalism, and turmoil resulting from the Arab-Israeli conflict.

The Suez crisis grew out of the nationalization of the British- and French-owned Suez Canal Company by Egyptian nationalist leader Gamal Abdel Nasser in July 1956. The Suez Canal was an important symbol of the Western presence in the Middle East and a major artery of international trade; two-thirds of the oil that went from the Persian Gulf to western Europe traveled through the canal. Viewing Nasser's action as an intolerable challenge to their position in the region, the British, together with the French, who resented Nasser's support for the Algerian revolution, and the Israelis, who felt threatened by Egyptian support for guerrilla attacks on their territory, developed a complex scheme to recapture control of the canal and topple Nasser through military action.

The plan, which they put into action in late October, depended on U.S. acquiescence and cooperation in supplying them with oil if the canal were closed. The Egyptians closed the canal by sinking ships in it. In addition, Saudi Arabia embargoed oil shipments to Britain and France, and Syria shut down the oil pipeline from Iraq to the Mediterranean. Incensed by his allies' deception, concerned about the impact of their actions on the Western position in the Middle East, and embarrassed by the timing of the attack—just before the U.S. presidential election and in the midst of the Soviet suppression of the Hungarian revolt—President Dwight D. Eisenhower put pressure on the British, French, and Israelis to withdraw. The United States refused to provide Britain and France with oil, blocked British attempts to stave off a run on the pound, and threatened to cut off economic aid to Israel. The pressure worked. Following the withdrawal of Anglo-French forces, the U.S. government and the major oil companies cooperated to supply Europe with oil until the canal was reopened and oil shipments from the Middle East to Europe restored.

In the wake of the Suez crisis, President Eisenhower pledged to protect Middle East states from the Soviet Union and its regional and local allies. In addition, the United States sought to bolster its friends in the region through economic and military assistance. With the exception of Lebanon, where fourteen thousand U.S. troops landed in July 1958 to shore up a pro-Western regime, most of these friends were authoritarian monarchies, demonstrating that despite its rhetoric about democracy, the United States was primarily interested in access to oil. Israel presented the United States with an additional dilemma. On one hand, it was pro-Western and militarily the most powerful country in the region. On the other hand, U.S. support for Israel was a major irritant in relations with the Arab states of the Middle East, including the key oil-producing countries in the Persian Gulf.

The Suez crisis highlighted the growing importance of Middle East oil for western Europe. During the 1950s and the first half of the 1960s, the United States was capable of supplying its oil needs from domestic sources, and Middle East oil went mainly to western Europe and Japan. Some Middle East oil made its way into the United States, and, more importantly, Middle East oil displaced Venezuelan oil from European markets and led to an increase in U.S. oil imports with consequent pressure on prices and high-cost domestic producers.

The question of oil imports presented U.S. policymakers with a strategic dilemma. If what would be needed in an emergency was a rapid increase in production, oil in the ground was of little use, and even proved reserves would not be particularly helpful. The need could only be filled by spare productive capacity. Too high a level of imports would undercut such capacity by driving out all but the lowest cost producers. Moreover, reliance on imports, especially from the Middle East, was risky from a security standpoint because of the chronic instability of the region and its vulnerability to Soviet attack. However, restricting imports and encouraging the increased use of a nonrenewable resource would eventually undermine the goal of maintaining spare productive capacity and preserving a national defense reserve.

Rising oil imports led to demands by domestic producers and the coal industry for protection against cheaper foreign oil. In contrast, the President's Materials Policy Commission, appointed by President Truman in January 1951 and headed by the chairman of the Columbia Broadcasting System, William S. Paley, had called for a policy of ensuring access to the lowest cost sources of supply wherever located. The commission's report, issued in June 1952, rejected national self-sufficiency in favor of interdependence, arguing that the United States had to be concerned about the needs of its allies for imported raw materials and about the needs of pro-Western less developed countries for markets for their products. Although the commission admitted that self-sufficiency in oil and other vital raw materials was possible, it argued that it would be very expensive, that the controls necessary to make it possible would interfere with trade, that it would undercut the goal of rebuilding and integrating western Europe and Japan under U.S. auspices, and that it would increase instability in the Third World by limiting export earnings.

Nevertheless, after attempts to implement voluntary oil import restrictions failed, the Eisenhower administration, in March 1959, imposed mandatory import quotas, with preferences given to Western Hemisphere sources. Although the Mandatory Oil Import Program (MOIP) seemed to be a victory for advocates of national self-sufficiency, the result, ironically, was to make the United States more dependent on oil imports in the long run because the restrictions meant that increases in U.S. consumption were met mainly by domestic production.

High levels of oil use were built into the U.S. economy in several ways. Following World War II, the U.S. transportation sector was transformed as automobiles, trucks, buses, airplanes, and diesel-powered locomotives replaced steam and electric-powered modes of transportation. Between 1945 and 1973, U.S. car registrations increased from 25 million to over 100 million, and per capita gasoline consumption in the same period skyrocketed as fuel efficiency fell and gas-guzzling car models grew more popular. Neglect of public transportation and dispersed housing patterns fostered by increasing suburbanization further fueled increased automobile use. In addition, the nation's

truck population grew from 6 million in 1945 to around 21 million in 1973, and trucks increased their share of intercity freight traffic from 16 percent in 1950 to 21 percent in 1970.

Public policy aided and abetted these changes. Since the early 1930s, the so-called highway lobby had been promoting public expenditures for highway construction. Between 1956 and 1970, the federal government spent approximately $70 billion on highways, as contrasted with less than $1 billion on rail transit.

The dramatic rise in U.S. oil consumption, coupled with a shift in investment to more profitable overseas areas, decimated the U.S. reserve position. By 1965, the U.S. share of world production had fallen to about a quarter and by 1972 to a fifth. The U.S. share of world oil reserves declined even more drastically, from around 46 percent on the eve of World War II to a little more than 6 percent in 1972. With U.S. oil consumption continuing to climb, domestic production was no longer able to meet demand, and oil imports rose from 9 percent of U.S. consumption in 1954 to 36 percent by 1973.

U.S. oil import restrictions also put downward pressure on world oil prices by limiting U.S. demand for foreign oil. Beginning in the mid-1950s, increasing numbers of smaller, mostly U.S.-owned companies challenged the majors' control over the world oil economy by obtaining concessions in Venezuela, the Middle East, and North Africa. Drawn by the lure of high profits, aided by the increasing standardization and diffusion of basic technology and the security provided by the Pax Americana, and unconcerned about reducing the generous profit margins available in international markets, the newcomers cut prices in order to sell their oil. Pressure from the production of these companies, coupled with the reentry of Soviet oil into world markets in the late 1950s, exerted a steady downward pressure on world oil prices.

Declining oil prices led to a resurgence of economic nationalism in the producing countries, whose incomes were reduced. In September 1960, following cuts in posted prices (the price on which government revenues were calculated) by the major oil companies, the oil ministers of Iran, Iraq, Kuwait, Saudi Arabia, and Venezuela met in Baghdad and formed the Organization of the Petroleum Exporting Countries. OPEC was able to prevent further declines in posted prices, and a strong increase in world demand in the 1960s allowed the companies to increase production, thereby maintaining their overall level of profits. As new sources of African production entered the market later in the decade, however, market prices resumed their downward trend.

Despite falling prices, the spectacular increases in oil consumption enhanced the position of Middle East oil in the world oil economy. At the same time the U.S. oil position was eroding, the Middle East and North Africa were becoming the center of the world oil industry. By 1972 these areas accounted for 41 percent of world oil production and contained almost two-thirds of the world's proved reserves. Reacting to the changing circumstances, the region's oil producers, along with other OPEC members, began to pressure the oil companies to gain control of pricing and production decisions.

The profound political, economic, and strategic consequences of the U.S. involvement in the Vietnam War and the overall course of the Cold War reinforced the geological and economic factors that gave Middle East oil increased importance. By the early 1970s, the Soviet Union had achieved rough strategic parity with the United States, which raised the risks involved in U.S. intervention in the Middle East. Moreover, in the midst of the Vietnam War, the British decided to end their military commitments "east of Suez." To make matters worse, U.S. relations with the Arab oil producers, including Saudi Arabia, were becoming increasingly strained owing to U.S. support for Israel following the 1967 Arab-Israeli war, which left most of Palestine under Israeli control.

When the United States moved to airlift arms to Israel during the 1973 Arab-Israeli War, the Arab members of OPEC imposed an embargo on oil shipments to the United States and the Netherlands and reduced shipments to other countries, depending on their position in the Arab-Israeli dispute. The oil companies carried out the embargo, though they undercut its political purpose by shifting non-Arab oil to the embargoed countries and distributing the cutbacks so that both embargoed and nonembargoed countries had their oil imports cut by about 15 percent. Arab OPEC members unilaterally raised the price of oil by 70 percent in October, and by December the price had quadrupled from its level before the embargo. Although Iran and other non-Arab OPEC members did not join the embargo and cut back production and exports, they were happy to go along with the price increases spurred by the embargo and production cutbacks.

Differences among the United States and its allies on higher oil prices and on the Arab-Israeli conflict undercut attempts at a unified response to the embargo. Although there was some tough talk about military action to regain control of the Middle East oil fields, the reality of the Cold War and fears during the Gulf War of 1991 (later borne out), that use of force would lead to the destruction of the oil fields, prevented such action. U.S. allies, noting that higher international oil prices could provide the United States, which was much less dependent on imported oil than they were, with a means of reversing the decline in its share of world production, doubted the U.S. commitment to lowering oil prices, further complicating a unified response.

The United States sought to salvage the old oil order by organizing the Western consuming nations in a united front against OPEC. In February 1974 the U.S.-initiated Washington Energy Conference laid the groundwork for the establishment later in the year of the International Energy Agency. The IEA called on member states to reduce their reliance on Middle East oil by diversifying their sources of energy and adopting policies promoting reductions in oil consumption.

The United States also moved to shore up its position with the oil-producing countries. In 1969, President Richard Nixon had announced that the United States could no longer intervene directly in all parts of the world, but rather would rely on regional allies, which it would provide with arms and other assistance to carry out their tasks. In the Middle East, the United States looked to Iran and Saudi Arabia as the "twin pillars" of pro-Western stability in the region, and rewarded the two monarchies with almost unlimited access to the latest U.S. military equipment. Between 1970 and 1978, for example, the United States sold Iran over $20 billion worth of military equipment and training. The United States also provided massive military and economic assistance to Israel following the 1973 war, viewing the Jewish state as a strategic asset and counter to Soviet client-states such as Syria and Iraq. Egypt (after 1973) and Turkey also received large amounts of U.S. aid.

The Arab oil embargo had a major economic impact. Higher oil prices intensified the economic problems faced by the United States and the other Western industrial countries in the 1970s, especially inflation, which was now accompanied by stagnation and increased unemployment. Non–oil-producing developing countries were also hit hard as they had to pay higher prices for products from the developed countries as well as for oil. Many countries borrowed large sums from Western banks to cover their costs, a move that contributed to the Third World debt crisis of the 1980s when the United States sharply raised interest rates in late 1979.

In contrast, higher prices enabled the Soviets, who were in the process of developing new oil and gas fields in Siberia, to increase their export earnings. While allowing the Soviets to import large amounts of Western grain and machinery, most of the exports came from new areas east of the Urals, and the cost of developing the necessary transportation infrastructure drained scarce capital from other sectors of the economy. Oil earnings also tended to mask the Soviet Union's increasingly severe economic problems and to reduce incentives for undertaking sorely needed structural reforms. The oil crisis may also have contributed to Soviet decisions to increase their involvement in the Third World in the 1970s, decisions that proved costly not only in terms of resources but also in their negative impact on détente.

The first oil shock also accelerated efforts by oil-producing countries to gain control of their oil industries. While the timing and extent of nationalization differed, most OPEC nations effectively nationalized their oil industries during the 1970s. The equity participation of the international oil companies in OPEC production fell from about 94 percent in 1970 to about 12 percent in 1981. Although they lost control of production and their ability to set prices, the major oil companies received generous compensation. In most cases, the companies maintained access to the oil they had previously owned through long-term contracts and were retained to manage the newly nationalized industries. Moreover, higher oil prices provided the major oil companies with windfall profits, easing the pain of losing formal control of their concessions.

Because it was both a major oil producer as well as the leading oil consumer, higher oil prices posed a dilemma for the United States. On one hand, higher prices could provide U.S. domestic producers with incentives for increased exploration and development, making the nation more self-sufficient in oil. On the other hand, higher prices fed inflation and slowed economic growth. The fact that the oil companies profited from higher oil prices and oil shortages prompted suspicions that the companies had colluded with OPEC to produce such an outcome. These suspi-cions made it impossible for the U.S. government to remove oil price controls, initially imposed in August 1971 as part of a larger package of wage and price controls. Although lower domestic oil prices lessened the impact of the rise in international oil prices on the U.S. economy, they also encouraged consumption and led to increased demand being met mainly by imported oil. When the second oil shock hit in 1979, the United States was more dependent on oil imports than in 1973.

The overthrow of the shah of Iran in early 1979 provoked this second oil shock, disrupting markets and causing prices to double. The fall of the shah and fears of internal unrest in Saudi Arabia convinced U.S. policymakers that the previous policy of reliance on regional surrogates to guard Western interests in the Middle East was no longer viable. While Israel was useful to counter Soviet clients, too great a reliance on Israel could prove counterproductive by alienating the Arab states. Therefore, the United States began to explore the possibility of introducing U.S. military forces into the region. These plans received a boost from the Soviet intervention in Afghanistan in December 1979, which revived fears of direct Soviet encroachment in the region. In addition, the United States was concerned that Soviet and Cuban involvement in the Horn of Africa, an area in the northeast part of the continent close to the Middle East, could threaten Western access to Middle East oil.

The prospect of losing access to Middle East oil led President James Earl Carter to announce in January 1980 that "an attempt by any outside force to gain control of the Persian Gulf region will be regarded as an assault on the vital interests of the United States of America, and such assault will be repelled by any means necessary, including military force." The Carter administration followed up soon thereafter with steps to create the long-discussed rapid deployment forces for possible use in the region. Planned from the time of the collapse of the shah's regime, the move reflected U.S. belief that local forces were not sufficient to protect Western interests in the Middle East from either Soviet aggression or internal instability. The Carter administration also sought to strengthen the "special relationship" between the United States and Saudi Arabia by continuing to sell sophisticated arms to the desert kingdom and by allowing the Saudis to buy massive amounts of U.S. Treasury securities outside normal channels.

The administration of Ronald Reagan (1981–1989) built on these initiatives, forging a foreign oil policy based on market forces and military power. Reagan began by ending oil price controls, allowing U.S. prices to rise to international levels in the hope that this would provide incentives to domestic producers and spur conservation. The Reagan administration continued the buildup of U.S. forces in the Middle East, transforming the Rapid Deployment Force into the Central Command. The Reagan administration also stressed close relations with Saudi Arabia, and worked with the Saudis and other conservative Persian Gulf producers to drive down international oil prices. Lower oil prices would not only help Western consumers but would also cut Soviet oil earnings. Finally, the United States began filling the Strategic Petroleum Reserve (SPR), established in 1977 to reduce the nation's vulnerability to oil supply interruptions. By 1990 the SPR held almost 600 million barrels of oil, somewhere between eighty and ninety days of net oil imports at then prevailing import levels. The other industrial nations also built up similar, and in some cases higher, levels of strategic reserves. Strategic reserves, although expensive to create and maintain, functioned as a substitute for the spare production capacity that the United States had once possessed.

Higher oil prices worked their way through the economies of the Western industrial nations and Japan to encourage significant increases in energy efficiency. The amount of energy required to produce a dollar of real gross national product declined 26 percent between 1972 and 1986. The gains in efficiency in oil use were even more dramatic: by 1990, 40 percent less oil was used in producing a dollar of real GNP than in 1973. As a result, by 1990 oil played a less significant role in the economies of the Western industrial nations than it had before the two oil shocks of the 1970s.

Higher oil prices also encouraged consumers to switch to other energy sources. While the use of coal and nuclear power increased, both turned out to have significant drawbacks, particularly those relating to the environment, and neither addressed the transportation sector, which accounted for the bulk of oil use. Although U.S. automobile fuel efficiency almost doubled between 1970 and 1990, this gain was partly eroded by a 40 percent rise in total motor vehicle use in the same period. In addition, the number of trucks on U.S. roads tripled between 1970 and 1990, and their fuel consumption doubled.

Higher oil prices also encouraged the development of alternative sources of oil. With higher prices and improving technologies of exploration and development, new sources of oil came on line in Alaska, Mexico, the North Sea, and the Soviet Union. U.S. production increased only briefly, however, and soon leveled off at around seven million barrels a day. Middle East oil production, which had accounted for 41 percent of world output in 1973 and 37 percent in 1977, fell to 19 percent by 1985. In 1986, with supply increasing and demand dropping, oil prices collapsed.

The collapse of oil prices provided a boost to Western economies but it also decimated the U.S. domestic oil industry, forcing the closure of high-cost wells. All producers experienced huge declines in export earnings. The Soviet Union was especially hard hit, and the collapse of oil earnings undercut Soviet leader Mikhail Gorbachev's hopes to use oil revenues to cushion the shock of economic reform. By the end of the decade, the Soviet oil industry was suffering from the same problems affecting the nation as a whole, and production and exports declined sharply.

Although lower prices led to increased demand for oil, producers in the Middle East captured most of the increase because they controlled the lowest cost fields. By 1990, oil imports were making up nearly half of U.S. oil supply, around 70 percent of western Europe's oil supply, and over 90 percent of Japan's oil supply; and 25 percent of U.S. imports, 41 percent of western Europe's imports, and 68 percent of Japan's imports originated in the Middle East.

Nevertheless, after rising sharply in the aftermath of the Iraqi invasion of Kuwait in August 1990, oil prices soon returned to preinvasion levels. The IEA contributed to stability by calling on member countries to make simultaneous use of their respective stockpiles. The success of U.S. diplomacy and military forces in the 1991 Gulf War demonstrated that with the end of the Cold War and the resulting retreat of the Soviet Union from a world role, the ability of the United States to intervene in the Middle East had increased significantly.

Low prices prevailed throughout most of the 1990s despite Iraq's exclusion from world oil markets. Russian oil exports recovered owing to Russia's need for export earnings and the drastic drop in domestic demand because of widespread deindustrialization. The Asian financial crisis of 1997 also kept demand down despite China's increasing imports. In the United States, lower oil prices led to increased consumption, as the number of private motor vehicles, especially gas-guzzling sport-utility vehicles and light trucks, continued to climb. By the end of the decade, the fuel efficiency gains of the 1980s had been lost. Rising consumption and OPEC production cuts led to sharp price increases in 2000 and 2001. What happened in the 1990s may foreshadow a pattern whereby lower prices lead to greater consumption which leads to higher prices which lead to lower consumption which leads to lower prices and the repeat of the cycle. Thus, a foreign oil policy based on market forces and military power has its own set of problems.

THE POLITICAL ECONOMY OF FOREIGN OIL POLICY

Oil has been unique as a vital resource owing to its pervasiveness in the civilian economy and its continuing centrality to military power, and maintaining access to the great oil-producing areas of the world has been a key goal of U.S. foreign policy since World War I. The objective of maintaining access to economically vital overseas areas resonated with the global conception of U.S. national security interests that emerged during World War II and dominated U.S. policy throughout the Cold War. U.S. leaders sought to prevent any power or coalition of powers from dominating Europe and/or Asia, to maintain U.S. strategic supremacy, to fashion an international economic environment open to U.S. trade and investment, and to maintain the integration of the Third World in the world economy.

Control of oil helped the United States contain the Soviet Union, end destructive political, economic, and military competition among the core capitalist states, mitigate class conflict within the capitalist core by promoting economic growth, and retain access to the raw materials, markets, and labor of the periphery in an era of decolonization and national liberation. Moreover, the strategic forces necessary for maintaining access to overseas oil were fungible; that is, they could, and were, used for other purposes in other parts of the world. Likewise, as the Gulf War demonstrated, strategic forces from other parts of the world could be used to help maintain access to oil. Thus, there has been a symbiotic relationship between maintaining power projection capabilities in general and relying on strategic forces to maintain access to overseas oil. In short, control of oil has been a key component of American hegemony.

While national security concerns have been an important source of foreign oil policy, defini-tions of national security and national interest have not been shaped in isolation from the nature of the society they were designed to defend. Arguments that claim a noncapitalist United States would have followed the same policies, even when sincere, assume no changes in domestic economic, social, and political structures, and thus miss the point entirely. They also ignore the constraints, opportunities, and contradictions that the structure of society, and in particular the operation of the economic system, impose on public policy.

The expansion of U.S. business abroad beginning in the late nineteenth century increasingly linked the health and survival of the U.S. political economy to developments abroad. These concerns were not restricted to fears for the nation's physical security or to the well-being of specific companies or sectors but rather were linked to concerns about the survival of a broadly defined "American way of life" in what was seen as an increasingly dangerous and hostile world.

U.S. oil companies were among the pioneers in foreign involvement, looking abroad initially for markets and increasingly for sources of oil. The U.S. government facilitated this expansion by insisting on the Open Door policy of equal opportunity for U.S. companies. Although the United States became a net importer of oil in the late 1940s, it was able to meet its oil needs from domestic resources until the late 1960s. Still, U.S. leaders were aware as early as World War II that one day the nation would no longer be able to supply its growing consumption from domestic oil production. This realization led to a determination to maintain access to the great producing areas abroad, especially in the Middle East.

Once the issue was defined in terms of access to additional oil, the interests of the major oil companies, which possessed the means to discover, develop, and deliver this oil, coincided with the national interest. In these circumstances, the major international oil companies have been vehicles of the national interest in foreign oil, not just another interest group. To maintain an international environment in which private corporations could operate with security and profit, the U.S. government became actively involved in maintaining the stability and pro-Western orientation of the Middle East, in containing economic nationalism, and in supporting private arrangements for controlling the world's oil.

Although there was a broad consensus in favor of policies aimed at ensuring U.S. control of world oil, the structure of the U.S. oil industry significantly shaped specific struggles over foreign oil policy. Like much of U.S. industry, the oil industry was divided between a mass of small- and medium-sized companies and a handful of large multinational firms. Within these divisions the competing strategies of different firms often led to intense conflict and to efforts to enlist government agencies as allies in the competitive struggle. Any public policy that seemed to favor one group of companies was certain to be opposed by the rest of the industry. Divisions within the industry were at the base of much of the oil companies' ideological opposition to government involvement in oil matters. In addition, oil companies shared the general distrust of the democratic state that prevailed throughout American business.

There were also conflicts with other energy producers, especially the coal industry, though these were somewhat muted owing to oil's near monopoly position in the transportation sector. Coal, in contrast, was used mainly for heating and electricity generation, as was natural gas, which increased its share of overall U.S. energy consumption, largely at the expense of coal. There was less conflict with industries that were themselves heavy oil users, in part because most of them were able to pass increased costs along to consumers. The automobile industry, in particular, has been heavily dependent on inexpensive oil for its very existence, and thus has shared the oil industry's interest in continued and growing use of its products.

The U.S. government was also frequently divided over foreign oil policy. Competing bureaucracies and institutions, each with their own set of organizational interests, supported different policies. While these divisions often influenced the specific contours of foreign oil policy, they generally reflected the divisions in the U.S. oil industry. For both organizational and ideological reasons, the Department of State has represented the interests of the major oil companies whose actions can have a great impact on U.S. foreign policy. Congress, in contrast, has played its traditional role as the protector of small business and often backed the numerically dominant independent oil companies and the coal industry, whose interests have been mostly within the United States. Presidents have tried to mediate the conflicts among government agencies, with Congress, and among competing industry groups, and craft compromises acceptable to the greatest number of groups possible.

Even though industry and government divisions effectively blocked some types of government actions, the splits did not reduce the oil industry's influence on U.S. foreign policy. Almost all segments of the oil industry agreed on policies aimed at creating and maintaining an international environment in which all U.S. companies could operate with security and profit. Thus, the impact of business conflict was not a free hand for government agencies but rather strict limits on government actions and control of the world oil economy by the most powerful private interests.

Foreign oil policy has been shaped not only by the structure of the oil industry, which has changed over time, but also by the privileged position of business in the United States. The oil industry has operated in a political culture that favored private interests and put significant limits on public policy. Thus, the fact that business interests were often divided and that specific business interests at times did not prevail does not mean, as some analysts argue, that the oil industry and other business sectors had little influence on U.S. foreign policy. On the contrary, the overall structure of power within the United States had a profound impact on U.S. foreign oil policy.

Corporate power not only influenced the outcome of specific decisions but more importantly, significantly shaped the definitions of policy objectives. The realization that U.S. oil consumption threatened to outpace domestic production led to plans to ensure access to foreign oil reserves. The alternative of reducing, or at least slowing, the growth of rapidly rising consumption has only rarely been seriously considered.

Part of the reason for a supply side focus has been the obvious strategic and economic advantages of controlling world oil. Nevertheless, the degree to which U.S. public policy has ignored conservation cannot be explained solely by foreign policy considerations. The consideration and adoption of alternative policies limiting the consumption of oil has also clashed with well-organized political and economic interests, deep-seated ideological beliefs, and the structural weight of an economic system in which almost all investment decisions are in private hands.

The oil industry has been one of the most modern and best-organized sectors of the U.S. economy, and both domestic and international companies have opposed policies that reduce the demand for their products. Domestic producers have argued that greater incentives for domestic production are the answer to U.S. oil needs, while companies with interests overseas have argued that they can supply U.S. oil needs, provided they receive government protection and support.

Demand-side planning, in contrast, involves end-use and other restrictions that clash with the interests of the oil industry and other industries using oil. Planning for publicly defined purposes, such as limiting demand for oil products, requires a role for public authority—supplanting the market in some areas—that has been unacceptable to the dominant political culture of the United States. In addition, the patterns of social and economic organization, in particular the availability of inexpensive private automobiles, the consequent deterioration of public transportation, and the continuing trend toward increased suburbanization, all of which were premised upon high oil consumption, have been regarded as natural economic processes not subject to conscious control, rather than as the results of identifiable, and reversible, social, economic, and political decisions. Conservation also goes against the ideology of growth and the desire, reinforced by the experiences of depression and war, to escape redistributionist conflicts by expanding production and the absolute size of the economic "pie." Finally, decisions to look to external expansion to solve internal problems rather than confront them directly has been characteristic of U.S. foreign policy throughout the nation's existence.

The structure of power within the United States has also deeply affected the U.S. response to the environmental impact of oil use. While abundant oil has helped fuel American power and prosperity, it also helped entrench social and economic patterns dependent on ever-higher levels of energy use. Whether or not these patterns are sustainable on the basis of world oil resources, it has become increasingly clear that they are not sustainable ecologically, either for the United States or as a model of development for the rest of the world.

At the beginning of the twenty-first century, oil accounted for 40 percent of world energy demand, and energy use was the primary source of carbon dioxide, the main greenhouse gas. For this reason, environmental scientists considered air pollution associated with energy use to be the main threat to the earth's climate. Increased energy demand will only make the situation worse. In short, there are environmental limits to continuing, let alone expanding, the high production–high consumption lifestyle associated with the U.S. model of development. Therefore, the most important question facing the United States in regard to oil in the twenty-first century may not be how to ensure access to oil to meet growing demands, but rather how to move away from what is clearly an unsustainable development path.

BIBLIOGRAPHY

Adelman, M. A. *The World Petroleum Market.* Baltimore, 1972. Attempt to apply neoclassical economics to world oil markets.

———. *The Genie Out of the Bottle: World Oil Since 1970.* Cambridge, Mass., 1995. Continues the analysis to the 1990s.

Anderson, Irvine H. *The Standard-Vacuum Oil Company and United States East Asian Policy, 1933–1941.* Princeton, N.J., 1975. Oil and Pearl Harbor.

———. *Aramco, the United States, and Saudi Arabia: A Study in the Dynamics of Foreign Oil Policy, 1933–1950.* Princeton, N.J., 1981. Stimulating combination of business history and foreign policy analysis from a perspective that plays down industry influence.

Blair, John M. *The Control of Oil.* New York, 1976. Classic study of the oligopolistic organization of the oil industry.

Bromley, Simon. *American Hegemony and World Oil: The Industry, the State System, and the World Economy.* University Park, Pa., 1991. Critical account of the role of oil in underpinning U.S. hegemony within the global system.

Clark, John G. *The Political Economy of World Energy: A Twentieth-Century Perspective.* Chapel Hill, N.C., 1990. Full of useful information and statistics.

Eckes, Alfred E., Jr. *The United States and the Global Struggle for Minerals.* Austin, Texas, 1979. Study of oil and other minerals as sources of conflict.

Engler, Robert. *The Politics of Oil: A Study of Private Power and Democratic Directions.* New York, 1961. Classic study of the impact of private power on American democracy.

Goode, James. *The United States and Iran: In the Shadow of Mussaddiq.* New York, 1997. Perceptive account of the oil nationalization crisis.

Heiss, Mary Ann. *Empire and Nationhood: The United States, Great Britain, and Iranian Oil, 1950–1954.* New York, 1997. Solid study, focusing on Anglo-American relations.

Kapstein, Ethan B. *The Insecure Alliance: Energy Crises and Western Politics Since 1944*. New York, 1990. Solid study of oil and the Western alliance.

Koppes, Clayton R. "The Good Neighbor Policy and the Nationalization of Mexican Oil: A Reinterpretation." *Journal of American History* 69 (June 1982): 62–81.

Lesser, Ian O. *Resources and Strategy*. London and New York, 1989.

Levy, Walter J. *Oil Strategy and Politics, 1941–1981*. Edited by Melvin A. Conant. Boulder, Colo., 1982. Collection of papers by a leading oil consultant compiled by another leading industry analyst.

Lieber, Robert J. *The Oil Decade: Conflict and Cooperation in the West*. New York, 1983. Astute account of the oil crises of the 1970s and alliance politics.

Meyer, Lorenzo. *Mexico and the United States in the Oil Controversy, 1917–1942*. Translated by Muriel Vasconcellos. Austin, Texas, 1977. Oil and U.S.–Mexican relations as seen by a leading Mexican scholar.

Miller, Aaron David. *Search for Security: Saudi Arabian Oil and American Foreign Policy, 1939–1949*. Chapel Hill, N.C., 1980. Pioneering study of the origins of the special relationship between the United States and Saudi Arabia; very informative on security issues and the Palestine question.

Nye, David E. *Consuming Power: A Social History of American Energies*. Cambridge, Mass., 1998. Valuable for long-term perspective.

Painter, David S. *Oil and the American Century: The Political Economy of U.S. Foreign Oil Policy, 1941–1953*. Baltimore, 1986. Detailed examination of U.S. foreign oil policy during the critical transition years of World War II and the early Cold War and an important source for this essay.

———. "International Oil and National Security." *Daedalus* 120 (fall 1991): 183–206.

———. "Oil and World Power." *Diplomatic History* 17 (winter 1993): 159–170. Analysis of oil's contribution to U.S. power based on a critical review of Yergin and Bromley and a source for this essay.

Palmer, Michael A. *Guardians of the Gulf: A History of America's Expanding Role in the Persian Gulf, 1833–1992*. New York, 1992. Useful overview.

Patterson, Matthew. "Car Culture and Global Environmental Politics." *Review of International Studies* 26 (2000): 253–270. Insightful on the symbiosis between the automobile and oil use.

Penrose, Edith T. *The Large International Firm in Developing Countries: The International Petroleum Industry*. Cambridge, Mass., 1969. Indispensable to understanding the operations of vertically integrated corporations.

Philip, George. *The Political Economy of International Oil*. Edinburgh, 1994. Concise and analytical historical account focusing on relations between the oil companies and Third World oil producers.

Rabe, Stephen G. *The Road to OPEC: United States Relations with Venezuela, 1919–1976*. Austin, Texas, 1982. Solid study of relations with important Latin American producer.

Randall, Stephen J. *United States Foreign Oil Policy, 1919–1948: For Profits and Security*. Kingston, Ontario, 1985. Especially strong on Latin America.

Sampson, Anthony. *The Seven Sisters: The Great Oil Companies and the World They Shaped*. New York, 1975. Colorful and insightful study of the major oil companies.

Schneider, Steven A. *The Oil Price Revolution*. Baltimore, 1983. Detailed examination of the origins and consequences of the oil shocks of the 1970s.

Skeet, Ian. *OPEC: Twenty-Five Years of Prices and Politics*. New York, 1988. Dispassionate and well-informed.

Skeet, Ian, ed. *Paul Frankel, Common Carrier of Common Sense: A Selection of His Writings, 1946–1988*. New York, 1989. Includes Frankel's classic *Essentials of Petroleum* (1946), a basic work for understanding the oil industry.

Stivers, William. *Supremacy and Oil: Iraq, Turkey, and the Anglo-American World Order, 1918–1930*. Ithaca, N.Y., 1982. Analysis of oil and Anglo-American relations in the 1920s.

Stoff, Michael B. *Oil, War, and American Security: The Search for a National Policy on Foreign Oil, 1941–1947*. New Haven, Conn., 1980. Examines oil and Anglo-American relations during World War II.

United States Senate, Subcommittee on Multinational Corporations. *Multinational Oil Corporations and U.S. Foreign Policy*. Washington, D.C., 1975. Critical report based on the invaluable work of the Church Committee in the mid-1970s.

Venn, Fiona. *Oil Diplomacy in the Twentieth Century.* New York, 1986. Pioneering study stressing oil's strategic importance.

Vernon, Raymond, ed. *The Oil Crisis.* New York, 1976. Still the best study of the 1973–1974 oil crisis.

Vietor, Richard H. K. *Energy Policy in America Since 1945: A Study of Business-Government Relations.* New York, 1984. Useful account of energy policy from a pluralist perspective.

Yergin, Daniel. *The Prize: The Epic Quest for Oil, Money, and Power.* New York, 1991. Anecdotal but comprehensive and informative, a treasure-trove of information with an extensive bibliography.

See also COLLECTIVE SECURITY; ENVIRONMENTAL DIPLOMACY; GLOBALIZATION; MULTINATIONAL CORPORATIONS; THE NATIONAL INTEREST.

OPEN DOOR INTERPRETATION

★ ★ ★ ★

William Appleman Williams

A significant number of historians and other commentators have viewed the Open Door Notes of 1899 and 1900 as the culmination of earlier attitudes, objectives, and policies, and as a coherent and decisive formulation of the major forces affecting American diplomacy during the century after 1865. But such people are too different (and too separated in time) to be jumbled together as a school. They are not, for example, defined by the ideological, institutional, personal, generational, and political affinities that characterized the Frankfurt School of Marxist sociologists that flourished from the 1930s through the 1960s and that produced a clearly defined body of analysis and interpretation. Hence, it is more helpful to speak of an Open Door interpretation of American foreign relations that has been advanced, from the 1890s to the present, by a disparate group of policymakers and politicians, bureaucrats, nonacademic intellectuals, and university and college teachers.

That odd assortment of people has nevertheless shared, however obliquely, the conviction that the Open Door policy is the keystone of twentieth-century American diplomacy. Elected policymakers, for example, as well as the bureaucrats they ushered into positions of influence, have used it as the intellectual vantage point from which to view and deal with the world. Such people have defined the policy as the touchstone of their dialogues—and confrontation—with the American public and other countries. The Open Door policy has been their idiom of thought, discourse, and action: it defines American perceptions and objectives, and hence, those who criticize or oppose the policy have been viewed as problems if not enemies. Germany was thus a troublemaker long before Adolf Hitler, Japan long before Hideki Tojo, and Russia long before Joseph Stalin.

Elihu Root and Henry L. Stimson operated within the framework of the Open Door policy when they served as secretaries of war, as well as during their tenures as secretaries of state. William Jennings Bryan thought within that framework prior to World War I just as surely as Charles Evans Hughes, Cordell Hull, and James S. Byrnes did in later years. And Presidents Theodore Roosevelt and Woodrow Wilson (and others) worked within the idiom that had been stated by President William McKinley even before Secretary of State John Hay announced it to the chancelleries and the publics of the world. The historian A. Whitney Griswold made the central point very neatly in his study *The Far Eastern Policy of the United States* (1938): "It is wrong, perhaps, to say that Hughes stole Wilson's thunder, for Wilson himself had stolen Hay's."

The contextual persuasiveness of the Open Door outlook among American bureaucrats becomes apparent during a routine survey of the volumes in the State Department's published record, as offered in its *Bulletin* and *Papers Relating to the Foreign Relations of the United States*. Indeed, the student grows weary of the references to the Open Door policy: he or she is inclined to consider it a meaningless ritual save for the seriousness with which it is repeatedly used to explain and justify American actions. Another kind of evidence is provided by the testimony (before congressional committees, as well as in memoirs) of such influential bureaucrats as William S. Culbertson, John Van Antwerp MacMurray, Joseph Clark Grew, and George F. Kennan.

Kennan, an influential foreign service officer and scholar, provides a particularly striking example of the power of the *Weltanschauung* of the Open Door. Writing as a historian in *American Diplomacy: 1900–1950* (1951), he damned the Open Door policy (and its underlying outlook) as idealistic, moralistic, legalistic, unrealistic, and ineffective. But his own zealous proposal to contain, and thereby drastically change, the Soviet Union through the global deployment of American moral, economic, political, and military power was designed to realize the objectives of Secretary Hay's original notes: a world open to American ideals and influence. Kennan was initially proposing—whatever his later denials, caveats, and remorse—an exponential escalation of President McKinley's deployment of American power against the Boxer Rebellion in China.

Because China was the initial subject of the Open Door Notes, the early commentators focused their analyses of the policy upon its operation in Asia. While some observers (and participants) felt that the government ought to act more vigorously against what they considered to be the more restrictive policies of Japan, Russia, and Germany (and even China), they generally agreed that Secretary Hay's integration of moralism, ideology, political strategy, and economic expansion provided a definitive statement of the need and the wisdom of extending the area of Anglo-American freedom and enlarging the American marketplace without war. Even leading Populists, otherwise bitterly critical of the McKinley administration, admitted that the policy addressed the basic issues. The editors of the *Prairie Farmer,* for example, urged their readers in 1900 to elect expansionist politicians. And *Wallace's Farmer* was enthusiastic about the prospect of using "our moral advantage" to expand a "valuable" trade.

Three very different people—Brooks Adams, Theodore Roosevelt, and Woodrow Wilson—promptly placed the Open Door policy within a broader—and even more dynamic—intellectual context. Adams, the grandson of President John Quincy Adams (and the brother of Charles Francis and Henry Adams), was the most original—and eccentric—of that unusual group. He suffered from those differences in two ways: he never became famous, and his major idea became associated with another person.

From the late 1880s to the publication of *The Law of Civilization and Decay* in 1894, Adams developed an explanation of world civilization that defined westward expansion as the key to progress, prosperity, and culture. The centers of civilization had moved ever westward until, in the 1890s, the scepter was passing from Paris and London to New York. That meant to Adams that the United States, if it was to seize its hour, had to move westward across the Pacific to dominate Asia. Otherwise Russia or another country would become the next center of world power and civilization. Adams then published a series of magazine articles on foreign policy, collected in 1900 as *America's Economic Supremacy,* in which he

praised Hay's Open Door Notes as a basic strategy for the United States and advocated a vigorous imperial policy—including the containment of Russia. In his view, Hay was "the only minister of foreign affairs in the whole world who grasped the situation."

Adams and his history-on-the-spot exerted a significant influence on Theodore Roosevelt (even though the latter did once remark that he thought Adams was "half-crazy"); but, in the larger arena, Adams lost out to the formulation of a similar idea offered by Frederick Jackson Turner. Adams was a disillusioned and acerbic Boston Brahmin writing history in the petulant frustration of having lost power, while Turner was an excited and romantic midwestern poet-historian who stirred the mind of the public. In December 1893, Turner offered "The Significance of the Frontier in American History," a dramatic reinterpretation of American history that explained the nation's democracy and prosperity in terms of westward expansion from Virginia and Boston to Oregon, Alaska, and Hawaii.

Turner was not as overtly imperial as Adams. He even seemed sometimes to imply that a native form of socialism was as appropriate to the end of continental frontier expansionism as overseas expansion into Asia and other regions. But his stress on past expansion, and his interpretation of the outward push from 1897 to 1901 as a natural continuation of the earlier rush across the continent, left his readers with the idea that the Open Door policy was the new frontier. Certainly Theodore Roosevelt and Woodrow Wilson read that message in his essays and took that idea from their correspondence and conversations with him.

Roosevelt was primed for Turner by Adams (and by his romantic cowboy interludes in the Dakota Territory), and his role in acquiring the Philippines and Cuba completed this transformation into what a psychologist might call a true believer. American expansion was a crusade for the Open Door virtues of peace, democracy, and prosperity. Roosevelt was sometimes discouraged by the difficulties of implementing the outlook in the face of opposition by other nations, or by the reluctance of the public to support the measures he considered desirable; but his commitment to the *Weltanschauung* remained firm: "We advocate the 'open door' with all that it implies."

Not only did Roosevelt view the Open Door policy as the extension of the Monroe Doctrine to Asia; he moved in 1905–1906 to extend the policy to Africa. His discussions with Secretary of State

Elihu Root led to one of the clearest expressions of the way in which the open door interpretation guided such policymakers. Seeking to prevent either France or Germany from establishing exclusive control over Morocco, Root advised American negotiators that "here, again, the 'open door' seems to be the sound policy to advocate." He then emphasized that it was vital "that the door, being open, shall lead to something; that the outside world shall benefit by assured opportunities, and that the Moroccan people shall be made in a measure fit and able to profit by the advantages of the proposed reform."

A very similar view was held and acted upon by President Wilson. During the late 1880s he had met and talked with Turner at Johns Hopkins University, and the results were impressive. As a historian and political scientist on his way to the White House, Wilson used Turner's frontier thesis to explain much of American history. "All I ever wrote on the subject," he once commented, "came from him." That remark qualifies as one of Wilson's unusual acts of intellectual generosity, and therefore mirrors his usual arrogance by giving Turner too much credit. Wilson was an idealistic missionary crusader on behalf of American virtues and economic supremacy in his own right, and added his particular insights to the American political system.

Even so, Wilson-as-historian leaned very heavily on Turner. "The days of glad expansion are gone, our life grows tense and difficult," he wrote in 1896 in explaining the crisis of the 1890s. Five years later, after Hay's Open Door Notes, he considered such expansion a "natural and wholesome impulse." "Who shall say," he added, "where it will end?" In 1902 he published the four-volume *History of the American People,* which made it clear that the historian-as-politician-as-would-be-world-leader viewed economic expansion as the frontier to replace the continent that had been occupied. A section in volume 5 (which reads like a close paraphrase of some essays written by Brooks Adams) recommended increased efficiency in government so that the United States "might command the economic fortunes of the world." He concluded his analysis by stressing the need for markets—markets "to which diplomacy, and if need be power, must make an open way."

Wilson classically revealed his involvement with the Open Door *Weltanschauung* during the 1915 confrontation with Japan over its Twenty-one Demands on China. He explained to Secre-tary of State William Jennings Bryan that the basic objective was "the maintenance of the policy of an open door to the world." Thereafter, Bryan periodically reminded various individuals and groups that the president's policy was to "open the doors of all the weaker countries to an invasion of American capital and enterprise." The principal importance of these and earlier quotations in this historiographical context lies not in revealing the policy per se but in suggesting how early policymakers were intellectuals developing and applying an Open Door interpretation of American foreign relations.

Moreover, even before Wilson was elected, a few historians and political scientists had recognized the importance of the policy in that sense. Archibald C. Coolidge, for example, in *The United States as a World Power* (1908), called the Open Door outlook "one of the cardinal principles of American policy." John A. Hobson, the perceptive English liberal who initiated the critical Western study of imperialism (1902), was the first scholar to recognize the pervasive nature of the Open Door *Weltanschauung*. Viewing it as the key to American policy, and reacting with a favorable judgment, he argued in an essay in *Towards a Lasting Peace* (1916) that the policy and its underlying outlook provided the basis for lasting peace and prosperity.

That statement was almost a prediction, for in January 1918 President Wilson presented in his Fourteen Points a program that was clearly a product of the Open Door *Weltanschauung*. He not only used (consciously or unconsciously) phrases from Hay's original notes, but the encompassing idiom of what he called "the only possible program" for peace was clearly an Open Door view of the world. The historian-become-policymaker and the historian as analyst-turned-public-commentator had reached an unplanned consensus.

The ensuing debates over Wilson's program, and the causes of the war and American intervention, buried Hobson's insight. His approach was ignored and unexplored for many years; and even when it was revived, it was done without any overt recognition of his pioneering effort. That did not mean, however, that the Open Door policy and its underlying outlook were wholly neglected. But that is the essence of the historiographical question: the issue involved whether or not historians (and other commentators) recognized that the Open Door policy was in truth the expression of a broad understanding of America and its relationship with the world.

Defined more formally in philosophical terms, the problem concerned a choice between a Cartesian world and a Spinozan world. Most American historians who came to maturity between 1895 and 1950 were Cartesians; they accepted a world composed of discrete atomistic units, some of which sometimes interacted with each other much as various billiard balls hit this time one ball and next time another ball. This led to what came to be known as the interest-group approach: individual A or P, or association D or S, exerted a determining influence upon decision F or Z.

Such an approach produced in history, as it did in science, some stimulating—if limited—research and analysis. Thus, in *Americans in Eastern Asia* (1922), Tyler Dennett could perceive "the Reassertion of the Open Door Policy" during the McKinley administration, but within a few pages assert that it was all "a purely temporary expedient." But Alfred L. P. Dennis's "The Open Door in China," in his *Adventures in American Diplomacy* (1928), used Dennett to suggest the long-term development of a guiding outlook. He cited Dennett's summary of the situation in 1858: the United States "desired for its citizens an open door to trade." Then he, too, retreated to call it all "an expedient." Revealing the ambivalence of early postwar scholarship, Dennis next quoted a comment that reminds one of Root and Wilson: "The policy of the Open Door . . . is the one and only policy. . . . Neither is it any use keeping the door open without insuring that the room on the other side of the door is in order."

Dennett was at his best on the broader nature of the Open Door policy a few years later when, in *John Hay: From Poetry to Politics* (1933), he was the first historian to sense the role of Brooks Adams in developing a worldview that guided Hay and other policymakers. But the key figure of the interwar years was Charles Austin Beard. The magnificent study *The Rise of American Civilization* that he and Mary Ritter Beard first published in 1927 talked candidly about the turn-of-the-century expansion as "Imperial America," and they hinted at the development of an imperial *Weltanschauung* that was crystallized in the Open Door policy.

The Beards perceptively saw the origins of that outlook in Secretary of State William H. Seward's mid-nineteenth-century vision of a global American empire. Their description of the Open Door policy made the point that it integrated three elements—while "designed with realistic and practical ends in mind, the policy of the open door also had a lofty moral flavor"—but they did not develop it as a *Weltanschauung*. They said nothing of Theodore Roosevelt's extension of the policy to Africa, for example, and barely mentioned it in dealing with the later diplomacy of Secretary of State Charles Evans Hughes.

That curiously titillating performance can be explained by two considerations: the Beards were writing a sweeping essay rather than a study of foreign policy per se, and Charles Beard was in the process of modifying his theory of knowledge and causation. His early work was grounded in an orthodox scientific-atomistic conception of reality that led him into a sophisticated interest-group analysis of history and politics, as in *The Economic Basis of Politics* (1916) and *An Economic Interpretation of the Constitution* (1913). There is strong evidence, however, that even as those books were being published, Beard was turning away from his methodology. That became apparent between 1928 and 1937, when he wrote a great deal about the problem. Beard had referred to various German antipositivists as early as 1913, and their influence reappeared in *The American Party Battle* (1928), in which he discussed the weaknesses of his earlier theory. He then opened a direct confrontation with the issue in two books and an article in 1934: *The Idea of National Interest, The Open Door at Home,* and "Written History as an Act of Faith" (*American Historical Review*).

Beard did not break completely free of the atomistic, interest-group theory of reality in *The Idea of National Interest,* but he did place the conflict between urban and agrarian interests in a much broader context. He spoke most directly about the question near the end of the book, remarking that the danger of the atomistic, Cartesian view of the world was in "limiting the understanding of the whole." That enriched the meaning of his earlier references to such intellectual heirs of Spinoza as Georg Wilhelm Hegel, Karl Marx, Max Weber, Frederich Meinecke, Karl Huessi, Karl Mannheim, Wilhelm Dilthey—and even Albert Schweitzer.

The issue was the ongoing dialogue between Descartes and Spinoza: the discrete, atomistic conception of reality versus the view that all things are related to each other. Given the American intellectual environment of those years, Beard was engaged in a lonely, courageous, and difficult task of reexamining his *Weltanschauung* in his middle years (see Lloyd Sorenson, "Charles Beard and German Historiographical Thought," *Mississippi Valley Historical Review* [September 1955]).

* * * *

WILLIAM APPLEMAN WILLIAMS

"Williams displayed great intellectual courage. Reflecting on the prerequisites for achieving individual or collective change, at least in our understanding of the world but also ideally in our actions to change it. Williams liked to pair 'intelligence and courage.' . . . His own record of intellectual courage is more complicated than it appears at first glance. Clearly he risked—and received—much criticism for challenging the intellectual orthodoxies of the 1950s, including what is usually called 'consensus' history. . . . Yet Williams was also intelligent and courageous enough to look beyond radical cant. . . .

"When attempting to categorize Williams as a critic of U.S. foreign policy, it is easiest to say what he was not. He was not a Wilsonian. Since Wilsonians have dominated discussion of foreign policy since World War II, this stance left Williams vulnerable to another epithet. Because he dissented from the Wilsonian 'imperialism of idealism,' he was stigmatized as an *isolationist* economic determinist and conspiracy theorist.

"Williams's relationship to what is usually called 'isolationism' is very complex. One of his greatest contributions was to deny over and over and over again that the United States was an isolationist nation until world power was thrust upon it in 1898 or 1917 or 1941 or 1945. On the contrary, the United States was expansion- ist from the outset, and the British, Spanish, French, Mexicans, and Native Americans certainly did not think the country isolationist. . . . Unfortunately, Wilsonian diplomatic historians, pundits, and officials still seem to think that the continent was more or less empty at the end of the eighteenth century and destined to be absorbed by the small country on the Atlantic coast (though, less candid than their forebears, they shun the term 'Manifest Destiny'). Accordingly, they presume that significant foreign policy only began in fits and starts during the 1890s.

"While repeatedly repudiating two centuries of American expansionism, Williams also criticized the United States for trying to be a 'world unto itself.' In his view, the internationalists' definition of internationalism was narrow and self-serving. They continually offered and often forced American solutions onto other nations yet only rarely acknowledged that the United States could learn lessons from abroad. This provincial internationalism was neither intelligent nor courageous."

—From Leo P. Ribuffo, "What Is Still Living in the Ideas and Example of William Appleman Williams? A Comment," Diplomatic History 25, *no. 2 (spring 2001): 310, 312–313 —*

He did not, however, develop and use the new approach in a rigorous manner. The results can be seen in *The Discussion of Human Affairs* (1936), "Currents of Thought in Historiography" (*American Historical Review* [April 1937]), and *The American Spirit* (1942).

Instead, Beard veered off into a quasi-biographical approach, interpreting foreign policy after 1934 as largely the result of Franklin Delano Roosevelt's power drive and inability to deal with the domestic crisis. Those books, *American Foreign Policy in the Making, 1932–1940* (1946) and *President Roosevelt and the Coming of the War* (1948), raised troublesome questions, but Beard's personalizing of policy neglected broader issues. Hence, his methodological explorations were ultimately developed by others who returned to Beard after they had come to the concept of an Open Door *Weltanschauung* along different lines.

In the meantime, however, the study of the Open Door policy was dominated by A. Whitney Griswold's *The Far Eastern Policy of the United States* (1938). Sensing that the Open Door was more than just a policy, he offered, for example, the suggestion that President Wilson and Secretary of State Charles Evans Hughes had transformed Hay's notes into a way of perceiving and thinking about foreign relations, and indicated that Cordell Hull's dedication to that outlook had more than a little to do with the subsequent confrontations with Germany and Japan. But all he said explicitly was that the Open Door was a "time honored American principle."

The concept of a principle emerging from the pragmatic needs and demands of various interest groups, and then becoming a *Weltanschauung*, was the analytical and interpretive tool that Beard had tried to forge between 1925 and

1935. Although they did not reveal his consciousness of purpose, three historians did advance that work during the decade after Griswold. Fred Harvey Harrington was the most intelligent and sophisticated interest-group historian of his generation, and if he had remained a historian, he would probably have gone beyond Beard in the application of a more subtle methodology. Harrington, along with William Best Hesseltine, his friend and colleague at the University of Wisconsin, had a genius for integrating biography and policy in a way that implicitly transcended interest-group analysis.

Harrington's study of American policy in Korea, *God, Mammon, and the Japanese* (1944), culminated in a three-page passage that implicitly revealed the broad outlook of Theodore Roosevelt and other early architects of the Open Door *Weltanschauung*. Sylvester K. Stevens provided a related approach in *American Expansion in Hawaii, 1842–1898* (1945). A third book, Edward H. Zabriskie's *American-Russian Rivalry in the Far East, 1895–1914* (1946), displayed the post-Beardian ambivalence in American historiography. Zabriskie (like Harrington) placed the protagonists in a broad framework and even suggested that they operated within an encompassing overview, but he never delineated that outlook.

At the end of the war, therefore, Beard's methodological explorations had neither been exploited directly nor reinforced by parallel investigations. The account of what happened next is complicated, as with all intellectual history, but the essentials are reasonably clear. To speak in the idiom of nuclear physics, a highly charged field was penetrated by highly charged particles. The environment was defined primarily by the history department of the University of Wisconsin: a great tradition was reinvigorated by the stimulating and contrasting minds of such scholars as Paul Knaplund, Paul Farmer, Robert Reynolds, and Gaines Post in European history, and Merrill Jensen, Hesseltine, and Harrington in American history. But other scholars in related fields, such as Hans Gerth in sociology and Frederick J. Hoffman in literature, were also a vital part of the ensuing nuclear reaction that was triggered by the arrival in 1946–1947 of hundreds of excited and hungry veterans who wanted to become excellent historians.

An unusually large number of them achieved that objective during the next four years and went on to make important contributions in every field of American history. The major elements involved in the part of that process that produced what came to be known as the Open Door interpretation can be defined as follows: the ongoing intellectual interaction among the professors, among the students, and between those groups; the broad training in European as well as in American history, and in related disciplines; and the particular genius of Harrington. Thus, what emerged is best understood as the result of a true community that flowered for most of two decades.

The story can be told through focus on William Appleman Williams, although he explicitly insists that the result was a communal product and, furthermore, that it involved the work of scholars who are not usually identified as part of the Wisconsin School of diplomatic history. Given his exposure to the history faculty, the vital elements in Williams's development were his previous training in mathematics and science and his work with Gerth. Gerth gave Williams a broad knowledge of the methodology of *Weltanschauung* (including the serious study of Marx) and helped him to begin developing it as a tool for the study of foreign relations. Williams thus came to Beard twice: first as a beginning graduate student who read him as an interest-group historian and later, educated by Gerth, viewing him as a man struggling briefly with the concept of *Weltanschauung*.

Williams first experimented with that methodology in *American-Russian Relations, 1784–1947* (1952), as in his discussion of the influence of Brooks Adams; but he was not fully in command of the approach, and the effort to open the orthodox form of the monograph to include such analysis posed severe additional difficulties. The next phase of his work cannot be fully understood outside his friendship with Charles Vevier, a fellow student in Harrington's seminar, for they often did primary research together over the next three years and exchanged notes and ideas on a regular basis. Vevier's *The United States and China, 1906–1913* (1955) interpreted the specific events of those years within the broad framework of a knowing effort by decision makers to act upon the Open Door view of the world.

Also in 1955, Williams provided a clear example of how he was developing and using the concept of *Weltanschauung* in his study of the way that Frederick Jackson Turner's frontier thesis and John Hay's Open Door Notes were related parts of the same overview ("The Frontier Thesis and American Foreign Policy," *Pacific Historical Review* [November 1955]). He next used the methodology in dealing with contemporary foreign policy ("The American Century: 1941–1957," *Nation* [November 1957]) and in offering a broad analysis of the revolutionary and early national period ("The Age of Mercantilism: An Interpretation of the American Political Economy," *William and Mary Quarterly* [October 1958]).

Shortly after he returned to Wisconsin as a member of the faculty, Williams published *The Tragedy of American Diplomacy* (1959), an interpretive essay on twentieth-century foreign policy. Although it came to be viewed rather narrowly as the basis for the "Open Door interpretation," and as a critique of policy after 1944, the book actually dealt with the development of a *Weltanschauung* through the interaction and integration of ideas, interest-group pressures, and the dynamic processes of marketplace capitalism. That more complicated nature of the approach was shortly underscored by Verier, just before he left history to help build the University of Wisconsin at Milwaukee. His "American Continentalism: An Idea of Expansion, 1845–1910" (*American Historical Review* [January 1960]) was a subtle interpretation of the shift from continental conquest to overseas expansion.

As Williams has repeatedly pointed out, he and others working in the idiom of an Open Door *Weltanschauung* learned much from other scholars who favored a different approach. Charles C. Campbell's *Special Business Interests and the Open Door Policy* (1951), for example, made it clear that the Open Door policy was an idea—and an ideal—that embraced the practical demands of many different groups. And Paul Schroeder's early and perceptive *The Axis Alliance and Japanese-American Relations* (1958) remains a revealing analysis of the way that Secretary of State Cordell Hull's intense commitment to the Open Door outlook defined the ultimately violent confrontation with Japan.

Williams continued his own work in *The Contours of American History* (1961), a broad interpretation of American history based on the argument that the United States has developed under three major worldviews, and in *The Roots of the Modern American Empire* (1969), an effort to provide a quasi-monographic history of how one *Weltanschauung* matures and then infuses and influences its successor. But the methodology and the interpretation took on lives of their own as the people who participated in Williams's seminar at Wisconsin began to produce their own articles and books.

As a teacher, Williams was graced with an unusual number of exceptional students, the legacy of the department's preeminence during the late 1940s and early 1950s. Perhaps his most important contribution was to give them their heads, to encourage them to explore the great resources of the university faculty, and to push them to realize the very best that was within themselves. The way that some of them received and used his version of the methodological tool of *Weltanschauung* makes the point. Martin J. Sklar, for example, produced the striking essay "Woodrow Wilson and the Political Economy of Modern United States Liberalism" (*Studies on the Left* [1960]). And James Weinstein, one of Richard Hofstadter's most perceptive students, who entered and was influenced by the Wisconsin milieu, wrote the excellent *The Corporate Ideal in the Liberal State, 1900–1968* (1968).

If Williams had operated more traditionally, directing and controlling his seminar in a narrow and orthodox manner, then the subsequent professional discussion (and gossip) about a "Wisconsin School" would have more substance. As it happened, however, the students—and their students—went their own ways. One need only consider the impressive trio who worked with Harrington as well as Williams. Walter LaFeber's first book, *The New Empire: An Interpretation of American Expansion, 1860–1898* (1963), dealt with intellectuals (and other ideamongers) more as an interest group than as craftsmen of a *Weltanschauung*. In a later study, *America, Russia, and the Cold War, 1945–1960* (1967), he further refined that process. But one of his students, David Green (*The Containment of Latin America* [1971]), did more in the way of using a worldview to explain a regional policy.

Thomas J. McCormick offered an imaginative marriage, so to speak, of Harrington and Williams in an exquisite study, *China Market: America's Quest for Informal Empire, 1893–1901* (1967). McCormick was deceptively empirical, for while his pages were filled with facts that no one else had uncovered, and his style was almost arid, he nevertheless constructed an account of how an expansionist *Weltanschauung* (in his own idiom, "informal empire") came into being at the turn of the century.

Lloyd C. Gardner's initial study, *Economic Aspects of New Deal Diplomacy* (1964), seemed more interest-group-oriented than it was: his climactic chapter, "Restoring an Open World," made the point about the power of Secretary of State

Hull's worldview with an almost fey sense of humor. He quoted Harry Hopkins telling President Roosevelt that Prime Minister Churchill ought to be "disabuse[d]" of the idea that Hull's persistence about the Open Door policy was only "a pet hobby." In a later and unusually sophisticated volume, *Architects of Illusion: Men and Ideas in American Foreign Policy, 1941–1949* (1970), Gardner transcended Beard by using the intellectual biography to explain the development of a worldview shared by many top policymakers. Gardner's students used that approach with great effectiveness in dealing with the various aspects of the origins of the outlook and its later manifestations.

The ahistorical mistake involved in personalizing the Open Door interpretation—and the methodology of Spinoza, Marx, and Dilthey—around Williams is revealed in the work of many other historians. Robert Freeman Smith, for example, demonstrated in *What Happened in Cuba* (1963) that Harrington produced many students who moved beyond the interest-group methodology. And Stephen E. Ambrose made it clear, in *Rise to Globalism: American Foreign Policy, 1938–1970* (1971), that Hesseltine was a key figure in that milieu.

Finally, the approach also attracted younger European historians who knew independently, and perhaps better, the philosophical roots in Spinoza, Marx, Dilthey, George Lukacs, and the Frankfurt School. Perhaps the most stimulating work has been done by Hans-Ulrich Wehler, as in *Der Aufsteig des amerikanischen Imperialismus* (1974). With enviable finesse he treats the process through which interests, problems, and ideas produce a *Weltanschauung*.

Given their variations on a theme, and their energy, it is not surprising that the protagonists of the Open Door interpretation have provoked much comment. Many of those who have responded favorably, however, have been as inattentive to the essentials of the methodology as have the critics—who have also overemphasized the influence of Williams and who have not differentiated and discussed the primary issues. An excellent example of the latter failure is provided by Arthur S. Link's commentary (in *The Higher Realism of Woodrow Wilson and Other Essays* [1971]) on Carl P. Parrini's *Heir to Empire: United States Diplomacy, 1916–1923* (1969).

Link acknowledges that Parrini (a member of the Williams seminar) is correct in arguing that Wilson advocated Open Door expansionism, but then comments that Wilson's motives were the best—"the slow and steady improvement of mankind through the spread of a reformed and socially responsible democratic capitalism." Link not only misses the integration of economic and idealistic elements in Wilson's outlook that is stressed by Williams, Sklar, and Parrini, but further confuses their description and analysis of the consequences of that worldview with the attribution of evil motives to Wilson. He also fails to credit Wilson, his own hero, with being a perceptive capitalist who understood the system's need for imperial expansion.

A few scholars have discussed the issues with greater insight and balance. Warren F. Kimball's "The Cold War Warmed Over" (*American Historical Review* [October 1974]) ranges far beyond his announced subject. And Joan Hoff Wilson's exploration of the subject in *Ideology and Economics: United States Relations with the Soviet Union, 1918–1933* (1974) is an example of her discerning insight into the primary problems of post-Beardian historiography. Such keen commentary underscores the judgment of Melvyn Leffler in "The Origins of Republican War Debt Policy, 1921–1923: A Case Study in the Applicability of the Open Door Interpretation" (*Journal of American History* [December 1972]). Williams and other advocates of his approach have "compelled all diplomatic historians to grapple with a complex set of criteria that heretofore had been frequently minimized."

See also CONTINENTAL EXPANSION; IMPERIALISM; OPEN DOOR POLICY; WILSONIANISM; WILSONIAN MISSIONARY DIPLOMACY.

OPEN DOOR POLICY

★ ★ ★ ★

Mark Atwood Lawrence

As he surveyed East Asian affairs in the first months of 1899, Secretary of State John Hay saw few reasons for optimism. America's main rivals for influence in that part of the world—Russia, Japan, Germany, France, and Great Britain—bristled with imperial ambition as China, weakened by war and rebellion, steadily lost its capacity to resist them. The great powers laid claim to special privileges in various parts of the country, a process that recalled the subjugation of Africa and suggested that China might be similarly partitioned. What worried Hay most was the prospect that the United States would be shut out of this new scramble as the Europeans and Japanese, with strong footholds in the area and a far greater taste for territorial conquest, divided up China and protected their new possessions with impenetrable barriers to American trade. Like many of his contemporaries, Hay imagined China as a vital and nearly limitless market for the burgeoning output of America's rapidly industrializing economy. By 1899 the United States had made little progress toward realizing that dream, but the vision beckoned powerfully. Preserving access to the China market ranked high on the McKinley administration's foreign policy agenda even as the prospects seemed to dim.

In a bold move to reverse this alarming trend, Hay dispatched his famous Open Door Notes to the leading imperial powers. Buoyed by his country's victory over Spain the previous year, Hay demanded that each of the powers respect the principle of equal commercial opportunity in the spheres of influence they were consolidating in China. The notes neither challenged the spheres' existence nor demanded equal access for American investment. Hay's dispatches stood firm, however, on the matter about which Americans cared most—the transport and selling of American goods. "Earnestly desirous to remove any cause for irritation," the United States insisted on "perfect equality of treatment for . . . commerce and navigation with such 'spheres.'" Washington asked each power to give "formal assurances" that it would charge uniform harbor dues and railway rates and leave the job of levying and collecting import duties to Chinese authorities. The door to trade, in other words, must remain open to everyone who wished to pass through.

Hay's proclamation of the Open Door policy was a landmark moment in the history of U.S. foreign relations. For one thing, it reflected the rise of the United States as a major power prepared to assert its interests in a distant part of the world where Europeans had reigned supreme. Hay set in motion a process that led ineluctably if fitfully to America's emergence as the predominant outside power attempting to shape Asia's economic and political destiny. Hay's policy also established a pattern of U.S. behavior that had long-term consequences far beyond Asia. With its annexations of Hawaii, Puerto Rico, and the Philippines in 1898, the United States had demonstrated a clear interest in territorial acquisition as the means of satisfying its expansionist impulse. But Hay's notes indicated a shift toward a different approach: The United States would expand its influence through economic hegemony rather than imperial control. The idea proved to have enormous staying power, partly because it fit with America's self-conception as a nation founded on the twin principles of anticolonialism and individual opportunity. Over the following century, Americans scorned the imperial intentions of others even as their own leaders made ambitious efforts to secure economic opportunity abroad. So characteristic was this pattern that some scholars regard it as the dominant attribute of U.S. foreign policy across the twentieth century. Beginning with William Appleman Williams in the late 1950s, a controversial but highly influential group of materialist historians elaborated the "open door interpretation" to explain America's extraordinary record of international activism since the 1890s. In the view of these scholars, Hay's initiative epitomized a quintessentially American approach to foreign policy. On the one hand, Hay invoked high-minded principles such as anticolonialism, self-determination, and equal opportunity to advance his proposals. On the other hand, he showed a hardheaded determination to protect the interests of American capitalists by promoting access to overseas markets. Advocates of the open door interpretation argue that a similar blend of proclaimed selflessness and relentless self-interest runs through the history of American diplomacy. From 1899 through the Cold War, these scholars assert, the U.S. government persistently invoked universal principles even as it intervened abroad in an unceasing effort to order the world to serve the interests of American capitalism.

Ironically, for all its indisputable importance as a watershed, an idea, and an interpretive tool, the Open Door policy produced scant results in practice. Through the period of the Open Door policy, the United States never obtained the markets about which late-nineteenth-century politicians and businessmen dreamed. Between 1899 and 1931 exports to China never exceeded 4 percent of the value of America's total annual exports and more often hovered around 1 percent. Nor did the Open Door policy discourage other powers from grabbing new chunks of Chinese territory or excluding American trade. Indeed, international compliance with American demands was always grudging and tenuous at best before collapsing completely in the 1930s as Japan unilaterally shattered Hay's vision. Even during its heyday in the early twentieth century, the Open Door proved more an illusion maintained by its promoters than a policy with real force and meaning. Moreover, the Open Door policy failed the United States by fueling resistance against foreign meddling in China. Americans clung devoutly to the belief that their policy, in contrast to European imperialism, would benefit China by preserving its integrity and bringing American know-how to its benighted masses. From the Chinese standpoint, however, the United States was often just another foreign country determined to prevent China from controlling the terms of its relations with the outside world. Chinese leaders sometimes attempted to manipulate the United States to serve their interests but rarely proved willing to play the passive and cooperative role arrogantly scripted for them by Washington.

THE ORIGINS OF THE POLICY

The Open Door policy originated in the treaty port system that emerged in China during the 1840s. For centuries, China had resisted the efforts of Western traders to penetrate the country, restricting their activities to the port of Canton (Guangzhou) and subjecting them to severe punishment for violation of Chinese law. Following Britain's sweeping military victory over China in the First Opium War from 1839 to 1842, however, the Qing dynasty had no choice but to grant major concessions. The British government forced China to open four new ports to foreign trade: Amoy (Xiamen), Foochow (Fuzhou), Ningpo (Ningbo), and Shanghai. British negotiators also insisted upon two privileges that would become hallmarks of Western imperialism in China. First, they demanded extraterritoriality, the right to subject British offenders to British rather than Chinese law. Second, they demanded most-favored-nation status, meaning that Britain would automatically benefit from concessions that China granted to any other country. In fact, as the historian Warren I. Cohen has observed, this demand for equal opportunity meshed well with Chinese calculations at the time. The imperial government, hoping to garner the goodwill of other Western powers to resist further British pressure, declared that all nations would have equal privileges in the treaty ports. "Now that the English barbarians have been allowed to trade," declared the Daoguang emperor, "whatever other countries there are, the United States and others, should naturally be permitted to trade without discrimination." In this way the United States, without firing a shot, came to enjoy the benefits that Britain had extracted through military intervention.

The treaty system became more elaborate in the following years as Qing authority continued to deteriorate amid civil wars and new military humiliations by Britain and France. What had been a trickle of Chinese concessions to the imperial powers grew into a torrent with the Treaties of Tientsin in 1858. Under those agreements China opened eleven new ports and for the first time permitted foreigners to navigate the Yangtze River and to travel throughout China's interior. The agreements also dictated a low tariff on foreign goods entering China, essentially robbing the Chinese government of the right to set its own trade policy. As in the 1840s, Americans were well placed to benefit from these concessions. The United States maintained a minimal diplomatic staff in China and had no military presence whatsoever. Yet under most-favored-nation provisions reaffirmed in the new treaties, American merchants received all of the advantages extracted by Britain and France. Historians have labeled Americans "hitchhiking" imperialists or, in a different formulation, "jackals" fattening up thanks to the British lion and other European predators.

The scavenger's role served American merchants well for half a century. In relative terms, U.S. exports to China remained tiny—just 0.5 percent of all U.S. exports as late as 1895. But American merchants managed to gain a significant toehold in a period when the U.S. government, with its commitment to laissez-faire economic principles, denied them the kind of backing their European rivals received from elaborate diplomatic and military establishments. By the early 1850s Americans operated about twenty-five of the two hundred Western firms doing business in China, and American ships carried one-third of all Western trade with the country. American shipping boomed, especially in Shanghai, the busiest treaty port, where U.S. bottoms carried about one-half of all Western trade. Over time, American merchants obtained important shares of the Chinese market for textiles, oil, metals, and tobacco, all by exploiting what the Europeans made possible.

Two developments in the 1890s—one in the United States, the other in the Far East—drove Washington to seek far more formal assurances of American trading rights. In the United States, the staggering economic collapse of 1893 led to a surge of interest in China as a market for American goods. The depression bankrupted more than fifteen thousand businesses, sent commodity prices plummeting to new lows, and fed unemployment rates as high as 25 percent in many American cities. Most alarming to the political and economic elite, the crisis touched off a wave of strikes and protests that shook the foundations of the freewheeling Gilded Age economy. Industrialists, politicians, and intellectuals naturally sought to explain the cause of such a cataclysm, and by the mid-1890s most had their answer: overproduction. The United States, they believed, simply produced more than its population could absorb and was choking on the surplus. The closing of the Western frontier left these men with little hope of expanding the domestic market, and none of them entertained demands from organized labor to increase the purchasing power of ordinary Americans. The only solution seemed to lie in exporting more to new markets abroad. "Our manufacturers have outgrown or are outgrowing the home market," the National Association of Manufacturers proclaimed in a characteristic claim of the day. "Expansion of our foreign trade," it added, was the "only promise of relief."

Few potential markets appealed as strongly as China. Since the eighteenth century Americans had commonly imagined China as a vast market peopled by millions of consumers eager for American goods. Along with India, China represented "an extensive field for the enterprise of our merchants and mariners," Alexander Hamilton wrote as far back as 1791 in his *Report on Manufactures*, proclaiming the distant Asian lands "an additional outlet for the commodities of the country." Following the events of 1893, the hyperbole soared to new heights amid a general outpouring of enthusiasm for an expansionist foreign policy. "In China there are 400 millions of people, more than five times as many as exist in the United States," marveled one business journal. "The wants of those 400 million people are increasing every year. What a market!" Other currents of the time reinforced purely commercial motives for intensified American interest in China. Social Darwinists stressed that China was an ideal stage on which the United States could demonstrate its competitive vigor. "Our geographical position, our wealth, and our energy pre-eminently fit us to enter upon the development of eastern Asia and to reduce it to part of our economic system," wrote the economic theorist Brooks Adams. Widespread fretting about national stagnation following the end of continental expansion also encouraged Americans to view China as a vast new frontier to absorb American energies. "What was once the old Far East," asserted one cotton seller, "is now our new Far West." Missionaries and social reformers, meanwhile, embraced American traders as potentially powerful allies in their efforts to penetrate China and convert its people—"a vast inert mass of humanity," in Secretary of State Walter Gresham's characteristic phrase—to American ways.

The second event that altered American thinking about China was the Sino-Japanese War of 1894–1895. Tension between China and Japan had mounted for several years amid obvious Japanese designs on Korea, which maintained an ambiguous tributary relationship with the Qing court. A political crisis in Korea sparked war in 1894. Within six months Japan dealt the crumbling Qing dynasty yet another humiliating defeat, destroying the Chinese military on land

and at sea. The lopsided settlement awarded Japan a sphere of influence in Korea and outright possession of Taiwan and the Pescadores, major gains for a rapidly industrializing power that, like the United States, sought new markets and influence abroad. At first many Americans sympathized with Japanese demands, hoping that a badly defeated China would open more treaty ports and seek Western goods and expertise in a desperate attempt at modernization. Before long, however, Americans came to see the Japanese victory in a much different light. By further weakening Chinese authority, the Japanese victory, far from creating new opportunity, set off an intense three-year period of great-power jockeying that threatened to partition China and close off American opportunities once and for all.

With a newly wounded China floundering as never before, the smell of blood was in the water. The sharks—imperial powers hoping to take a bite of Chinese territory—gathered quickly. Russia made the first in a complicated series of moves. The Sino-Japanese War had exposed Japanese designs on Manchuria, where the Russian government also harbored long-standing economic and political ambitions. Playing skillfully on Chinese vulnerabilities, Moscow extracted extensive concessions in a treaty signed in May 1896. In return for a Russian guarantee to aid China against Japanese or other foreign aggression, the Qing rulers granted Russia permission to extend its transcontinental railway through northern Manchuria. Furthermore, China awarded Russia political authority along the rail line, free right of public domain, and a tariff reduction on goods entering China along the railroad. Jealous of Russia's gains, Germany made a far more dramatic move in 1897, seizing the port of Tsingtao (Qingdao) on Kiaochow (Jiaozhou) Bay and demanding exclusive railroad-building and mining rights in Shandong province. China had little choice but to accede, spurring further exactions. Russia moved again, forcing China to concede a leasehold over Port Arthur (Lüshun) and its hinterland on the Liaodong Peninsula in early 1898. In southern China, meanwhile, France extracted a lease for Kwangchow (Guangzhou) Bay on the Leizhou Peninsula.

This feeding frenzy confronted the United States with an ominous situation. With American leaders increasingly convinced of China's importance to the American economy, the country seemed in serious jeopardy of being entirely consumed by the imperial powers. To be sure, few of the concessions granted to Japan, Russia, Germany, or France immediately infringed upon American commercial privileges; for the moment, at least, the most-favored-nation principle remained intact. But the situation was agonizingly unsettled, and heightened competition for privileges raised the prospect that the imperial powers would soon transform relatively porous spheres of influence into exclusive possessions. Intense concession-hunting also raised the specter of a great-power war in the Far East, another scenario that boded nothing but ill for U.S. interests. American merchants worried especially that imperial rivalries were concentrated in northern China and Manchuria, regions that absorbed a high percentage of U.S. exports to China. With key ports under their control, Germany or Russia could easily impose new tariffs and railroad rates that would discriminate against American goods. But it was not the threat to any particular port or railroad that alarmed Americans so much as the apparent challenge to the whole principle of equal opportunity enshrined in the treaty port system. American industrialists, after all, wished to retain access to all of China on a permanent basis. If this principle collapsed, the United States, with no sphere of its own and no capacity for obtaining one, would be in a dire position.

LAYING DOWN THE POLICY

Two sets of voices insisted that the United States abandon its passive approach in China and take the lead to shore up the principle of equal privilege. One set came from Britain. Although not averse to securing special privileges of its own, it remained the principal great-power champion of the Open Door idea. In fact, the British-controlled Shanghai Chamber of Commerce may have been the first to hit upon the phrase in expressing the view that the whole of China should be opened to foreign trade. In any case, the scramble for concessions precipitated a sense of crisis in Britain, whose dominance in the China trade was threatened just as much as the far smaller U.S. stake. A lengthy debate on the situation took place in the House of Commons in January 1898, during the course of which two government speakers invoked the Open Door by name as the desirable alternative to partition. Three months later the British government proposed a joint Anglo-American declaration calling for equal commercial opportunity in China.

The other voices demanding that Washington take bold action to protect American interests came from within the United States. By 1898, as the historian Thomas J. McCormick has documented, a chorus of trade associations, publications, jingoistic politicians, and activist diplomats urged the McKinley administration to set aside old laissez-faire notions and actively defend American interests. "We must make our plans to secure our full share of the great trade which is coming out of the Orient," the National Association of Manufacturers demanded in 1897. Early the following year, the New York Chamber of Commerce sent McKinley a petition urging "proper steps" for the "preservation and protection of . . . important commercial interest in the [Chinese] Empire." The press took a similar view. With Moscow apparently threatening to absorb Manchuria into the Russian customs area, the *Commercial and Financial Chronicle* demanded a "strong representation in favor of keeping open the trade on equal terms to all nations." Meanwhile the *New York Tribune* asserted that "commercial interests, which are now great and which promise one day to be enormous," demanded that the U.S. government be "deeply involved in China." Activism was essential, it insisted, contending that "without strenuous insistence by this Government the indisputable treaty rights of the United States are likely to be ignored and violated by the more aggressive European powers."

Washington responded cautiously to this pressure, only gradually accepting the notion that it should play an active role in promoting American economic interests abroad. The possibility clashed with laissez-faire notions of economics and governance, ideas that remained influential with many Americans even in the 1890s. Only the Spanish-American War resolved the issue in favor of the industrialists and others who advocated bold action abroad. Following its crushing victory over Spain in the spring of 1898, the United States became the scene of a vast public debate over whether to annex the Philippines, the former Spanish colony ripe for the taking if the United States was willing to become a colonial power. The debate concerned not only the Philippines themselves, of course, but also the role that the U.S. government would play in the Far East generally, including China. Advocates of annexation argued that possession of the Philippines would greatly facilitate American exploitation of the China market by providing an insular "stepping stone" to the mainland—a coaling station, naval base, cable relay station, and observation post that would enhance America's capacity to keep the door to China open. Although U.S. behavior in the Philippines smacked of naked colonialism, Americans, including McKinley himself, disavowed any such intention in China. The United States, McKinley said, desired "no advantages in the Orient which are not common to all." Still, in accepting the administrative and military burdens of empire in the Philippines, the United States signaled a new era of activism on the Asian mainland.

Hay's Open Door Notes thus formed part of a package of policy decisions taken in 1898 and 1899, the foremost being the Philippines annexation, aimed at promoting American commerce in China. The delay between McKinley's decision and Hay's issuing of the notes owed mainly to the secretary of state's fears that the other powers would reject any U.S. initiative that he did not time carefully. New great-power maneuvering in China during the first months of 1899 kept the notoriously cautious Hay from acting. But imperial rivalries eased in the summer, leading Hay to believe that Britain, Japan, Germany, and probably even Russia would respond favorably to a diplomatic démarche on behalf of the Open Door. Hay ordered his chief adviser on Far Eastern affairs, William W. Rockhill, to prepare a statement of U.S. policy. Rockhill, a champion of the Open Door with a strong sense of the dangers that would flow from China's disintegration, was only too happy to oblige. With Alfred Hippisley, an English friend who had served in the Chinese customs service, Rockhill prepared the six memoranda that Hay sent to the governments of Britain, Germany, Russia, Japan, Italy, and France beginning on 6 September. With the proclamation of the new U.S. policy, the "scepter of Open Door champion," in McCormick's words, passed from Great Britain to the United States.

The Open Door policy appeared a natural course of action for the United States for a variety of reasons. For one thing, proponents were confident that the United States would be the winner on a level commercial playing field. U.S. exports to China in 1899 amounted to a bare 1.1 percent of all U.S. exports, but in absolute terms the China trade was booming, with the value of U.S. goods shipped to China climbing to $14 million from just $6 million five years earlier. American textiles and oil companies especially profited, and further growth seemed certain as the U.S. economy revived in 1897. "In the field of trade and commerce," Hay proclaimed in 1899, "we shall be

AN EXCERPT FROM THE FIRST OPEN DOOR NOTE

"Earnestly desirous to remove any cause of irritation and to insure at the same time to the commerce of all nations in China the undoubted benefits which should accrue from a formal recognition by the various powers claiming 'spheres of interest' that they shall enjoy perfect equality of treatment for their commerce and navigation within such 'spheres,' the Government of the United States would be pleased to see His German Majesty's Government give formal assurances, and lend its cooperation in securing like assurances from the other interested powers, that each, within its respective sphere of whatever influence—

"First. Will in no way interfere with any treaty port or any vested interest within any so-called 'sphere of interest' or leased territory it may have in China.

"Second. That the Chinese treaty tariff of the time being shall apply to all merchandise landed or shipped to all such ports as are within said 'sphere of interest' . . . , no matter to what nationality it may belong, and that duties so leviable shall be collected by the Chinese Government.

"Third, that it will levy no higher harbor dues on vessels of another nationality frequenting any sport in such 'sphere' than shall be levied on vessels of its nationality, and no higher railroad charges over lines built, controlled, or operated within its 'sphere' on merchandise belonging to citizens or subjects of other nationalities transported through such 'sphere' than shall be levied on similar merchandise belonging to its own nationals transported over equal distances."

the keen competitors of the richest and greatest powers, and they need no warning to be assured that in that struggle, we shall bring the sweat to their brows." *Banker's Magazine* predicted that "without wars and without military aggression that nation will secure the widest and best markets which can offer the cheapest and best goods"; only British wares, it continued, could rival those of the United States. Some Americans predicted that their exports would balloon to billions of dollars a year if the U.S. government could keep the door open.

If the Open Door suited supposed American commercial supremacy, it also suited U.S. military weakness and aversion to great-power politics. In Central America and the Caribbean, where the United States towered over any potential rival, the United States eagerly pursued exclusive economic privileges. In the Far East, however, the situation was very different. The Spanish-American War signaled the emergence of the United States as a major world power with the capacity to project force as far away as the western Pacific, but it could hardly rival the capabilities of Japan, Russia, and even the European powers already well-ensconced in China. If great-power relations in China developed into a game of coercion and partition, the United States would inevitably lose. The Open Door policy promised to remove force

from the equation and to limit competition to fields where the United States would likely prevail. The policy, with its multilateral aspect and emphasis on universal principles, also carried the advantage of keeping the United States clear of international alliances as an alternative method of protecting American interests. Even as the United States emerged as a major power, the vast majority of Americans opposed foreign entanglements, and the McKinley administration saw no reason to risk its popularity. An alliance with Britain, the most likely candidate based on shared interests, was out of the question because of widespread Anglophobia. The other good possibility, Japan, showed an off-putting inconsistency and opportunism in China. The Open Door policy, by contrast, promised to win the cooperation of the other powers without sacrificing the administration's political standing, reducing American freedom of action, or creating military burdens that Washington was unwilling to assume.

Perhaps most importantly, the Open Door policy suited Americans ideologically by sustaining their traditional aversion to colonialism and their commitment to liberal principles. Although the United States repeatedly violated its own supposed anticolonial commitments in the late nineteenth century and maintained quasi-imperial control over Latin America, a substantial portion of congressional and public opinion abided by a perception of the United States as a fundamentally anticolonial country. The resistance that the McKinley administration confronted during the debate over Philippine annexation in mid-1898 attested to the strength of anti-imperial opinion. The Open Door offered an ideal solution because it permitted the United States to obtain markets in China while assuming the moral high ground. The notes, in the words of historian Matthew Frye Jacobson, represented "an imperialist economics in the guise of anticolonialism." Both avid expansionists and old-guard devotees of laissez-faire could unite behind the Open Door idea. The policy also appealed because it promised to sustain Chinese unity and give the Chinese access to the most modern goods and ideas that Westerners had to offer. The policy thus meshed well with Americans' self-perception as a force for modernization and enlightenment in backward areas of the world. One of the foremost promoters of the Open Door in the United States, the English author and lecturer Lord Charles Beresford, struck the theme in characteristic terms a few months before Hay's notes. Proclaiming that the Open Door represented a "grand, chivalrous, [and] noble sentiment in regard to what should be done with weaker nations," he asserted that such an approach would not only advance "the interests of trade and commerce, but it will push the interests of humanity and of Christianity."

For all these reasons, the Open Door policy was popular in the United States. In China, however, the policy encountered serious obstacles from the start. The problem was not so much the response of the great powers. Although none of them was particularly pleased with Hay's initiative, they were fearful that partition would lead to war and impressed that Washington demanded nothing more than simple equality of commercial access. One by one they grudgingly went along with Hay's demands—or at least displayed enough ambivalence so that Americans could assume acquiescence. By far the greater problem was mounting resentment among the Chinese people, whose real attitudes contradicted the ethnocentric American fantasy of a docile population that would welcome modernization from the West. The Boxer Rebellion, the most serious antiforeign uprising of the period, broke out in 1898 and grew more serious over the following two years. Armed insurgents slaughtered hundreds of missionaries and thousands of their Chinese converts and destroyed foreign property,

including the railways and communication lines integral to Western commerce. In 1900 the Boxers marched on Peking, killing foreign diplomats and missionaries and, for nearly two months, laying siege to the foreign legations. To meet the emergency, the McKinley administration dispatched five thousand U.S. troops from the Philippines to join the international expeditionary force that raised the siege in mid-August.

The fighting threw the Open Door policy into disarray. Not only did the upheaval make a mockery of American insistence that China should be regarded as an integral, sovereign nation, but the intervention of foreign troops also presented the possibility that one or more of the imperial powers would try to exploit the chaotic situation by seizing new parts of China. "Your Open Door is already off its hinges, not six months old," the author Henry Adams complained to Hay as the crisis unfolded. "What kind of door can you rig up?" Hay, once again relying on Rockhill and Hippisley, responded with his second Open Door Note on 3 July. The new circular restated American commitments from the year before and asked the powers to affirm that they supported China's "territorial and administrative integrity." U.S. policy, Hay asserted, "is to seek a solution which may bring about permanent safety and peace to China . . . and safeguard for the world the principle of equal and impartial trade with all parts of the Chinese Empire." Meanwhile, American diplomats went to work shoring up the authority of local rulers in China's center and south to minimize the temptation for any of the great powers to move in on the pretext of restoring order.

As in the previous year, American policy succeeded superficially. In 1901 all the powers withdrew from Peking and, unwilling to risk shattering the status quo, indicated at least tolerance for the Open Door principle. That result came slowly and reluctantly, however, and various developments along the way suggested trouble for the Open Door policy over the long term. First, Russia threatened to exploit the presence of its troops in China to force the Qing to yield further privileges in Manchuria. Then American support for the Open Door policy tottered as President McKinley toyed with the idea of abandoning the policy altogether. Under fierce election-year criticism for his overseas adventures and frustrated with great-power maneuvering, McKinley considered withdrawing U.S. troops from the international force in China, a move that would have destroyed the concert of powers that Washington had worked hard to maintain. As McKinley recognized, the move also would have freed the United States to participate in the partitioning of China by carving out a sphere of its own, a prospect that gained sudden support among a number of policymakers. From Peking, U.S. minister E. H. Conger made a startling proposal to acquire a lease over Zhili province, including apparently the Chinese capital itself. More modest in its aims, the U.S. Navy called for the establishment of a base on the Chinese coast, preferably Samsah (Sansha) Bay in Fujian province. McKinley and even Hay endorsed that proposal, but China, in an unusual gesture of defiance, rejected it out of hand, quoting from America's own cherished Open Door principles.

Before 1900 was out, the administration had retreated to the Open Door policy. The American flirtation with empire in China ended amid grudging acceptance that exerting influence within the concert of powers—rather than breaking out on its own—remained the best course for the United States. But events left Hay keenly aware of the many problems that beset his policy. There was not, he wrote in late 1900, "a single power we can rely on for our policy of abstention from plunder and the Open Door." Nor, he recognized, did the United States have the military or moral authority to control events in China if any of the powers chose to oppose American preferences. In a remarkably candid assessment of the limits of U.S. influence, Hay asserted:

> The inherent weakness of our position is this: we do not want to rob China ourselves, and our public opinion will not permit us to interfere, with an army, to prevent others from robbing her. Besides, we have no army. The talk of the papers about "our preeminent moral position giving us the authority to dictate to the world" is mere flap-doodle.

American impotence was on display in 1901 as the imperial powers ignored U.S. protests and demanded that China pay a debilitating $300 million indemnity to cover foreign property destroyed in the Boxer uprising. When Japan and the Europeans chose to ignore it, the Open Door policy counted for little.

THREE APPROACHES TO THE OPEN DOOR

The weakness of American policy would be further borne out over the next two decades as three U.S. administrations, each in its own way, struggled to keep the door open. At first, the main challenger to U.S. policy was Russia, which continued to tighten its grip on Manchuria in ways that directly threatened American market access. Although American trade with China remained modest (accounting for less than 1 percent of all U.S. exports in 1904), Manchuria was increasingly critical to American merchants, absorbing about 90 percent of all U.S. exports to China. As the historian Michael H. Hunt has shown, American success resulted partly from Chinese encouragement of American trade as a way to offset Russian domination. The Chinese strategy worked fairly well. The administration of Theodore Roosevelt registered vigorous protests with the Russian government and even threatened to join an emerging military alliance between Japan and Britain if Moscow did not respect American prerogatives. "I wish, in Manchuria, to go to the very limit I think our people will stand," Roosevelt wrote to Hay. In fact, war in China remained an impossibility for the United States, which was even more averse to military commitments there during the Roosevelt administration than it had been earlier. When Japan proposed cooperation against Russia in 1901, the United States indicated no interest whatsoever. As before, domestic political constraints and sheer lack of military capacity in the Far East left the United States with no alternative but to pursue its goals diplomatically. Washington gave its quiet support to the British-Japanese alliance formed in 1902, practicing the time-honored weak nation's strategy of putting other nations' power to work on its behalf.

Japan, by contrast, had enormous interests in Manchuria and military power to match. When Russia refused to permit foreign settlement of newly established treaty ports in Manchuria, Japan declared war in February 1904, smashing the Russian fleet at Tsushima Strait fifteen months later. The overwhelming Japanese victory reverberated around the world, signaling the emergence of a non-Western great power and inspiring a generation of Asian nationalists to challenge Western hegemony. It also dramatically altered the situation in China, catapulting Japan into the role of the most formidable and, from Washington's standpoint, potentially most threatening power. If the European powers necessarily had "divided interests, divided cares, double burdens" as they looked to their affairs in both Europe and the Far East, Roosevelt recognized that Japan could concentrate entirely on China. It had, as

Roosevelt wrote, "but one care, one interest, one burden." From that moment forward, the challenge of maintaining the Open Door would be mainly the challenge of managing Japanese power—a task that ultimately proved impossible.

Initially, though, the United States showed little of the alarm that Hay or Rockhill might have displayed a few years earlier. In the years following the Russo-Japanese War, China—and with it the Open Door policy—lost much of its importance for U.S. policymakers. One reason lay in Roosevelt's basic approach to foreign policy. A realist with a clear sense of the limits of American power, the president opted to appease Japan rather than to risk conflict in a part of the world where he understood Japanese interests and power were vastly superior. U.S.–Japanese tensions already simmered because of violence and discrimination against Japanese immigrants in California, and Roosevelt saw no reason to stir the pot further by insisting upon anything more than minimal toleration of American trade. A bland 1908 agreement, signed by Secretary of State Elihu Root and the Japanese ambassador in Washington, Takahira Kogoro, restated the Open Door principle but contained no new provisions to shore it up. Roosevelt may have believed that conflict with Japan was inevitable, but he was only too happy to postpone the day of reckoning into the indefinite future.

Another reason for declining U.S. interest in actively defending the Open Door was fading American enthusiasm for the China market. Following the burst of American interest in the 1890s, many U.S. businessmen began to lose faith in the vision of vast profits. Chinese nationalists helped dampen American hopes in 1905 by organizing a boycott of U.S. goods to protest Washington's indefinite extension of an 1882 law barring Chinese laborers from entering the United States. Hay, now out of office, blamed the Chinese for failing to exploit the Open Door to their advantage. "We have done the Chinks a great service which they don't seem inclined to recognize," Hay complained in 1903, revealing the scorn beneath supposedly beneficent American policy. If many Chinese lacked the desire for American goods, it also became clear that China lacked the purchasing power and infrastructure to furnish the market about which Americans fantasized. As the U.S. consul general in Hong Kong had written in 1899, "99 percent of China is still closed to the world. When the magazine writer refers in glowing terms to the 400,000,000 inhab-

itants of China, he forgets that 350,000,000 are a dead letter so far as commerce is concerned." The statistics sustained that judgment: in the first two decades of the twentieth century, U.S. exports to China continued to hover around a meager 1 percent of the value of all U.S. exports.

China hardly faded away, however, as a matter of American concern. Paradoxically, as policymakers and businessmen lost interest during the Roosevelt years, the Open Door policy became increasingly intertwined with—and sustained by—the powerful reform movement that captured the imagination of Americans as the country struggled to cope with the effects of industrialization, immigration, and other massive social transformations of the preceding quarter century. For decades, of course, Americans had assumed a special responsibility for China and viewed their efforts to exploit the China market in an altruistic light: The United States would profit, Americans believed, but so too would the Chinese, who would gain access to Christianity and modernizing ideas as well as American goods. In the Progressive era, American reformers expanded on this connection between material and moral progress and helped preserve, and even extend, American faith in the Open Door policy as the actual material basis of the policy stagnated. As the historian Jerry Israel demonstrates, Progressives were among the most important advocates of preserving the American access to China and maintaining the integrity of the Chinese state. However disappointing China had proved so far, the reformers held boundless confidence in its potential for both moral and material progress, which were indistinguishable in their minds. For the Progressives, Israel argues, China was an extension of the United States, and to admit failure there would have been tantamount to admitting failure of the reformist vision at home.

Mining engineer Herbert Hoover, Red Cross worker Mabel Boardman, education reformer John Dewey, sociologist Edward A. Ross, and many other leading Progressive figures focused their attention on China at one time or another. Ross's 1912 book, *The Changing Chinese: The Conflict of Oriental and Western Culture in China,* was typical of the Progressives' optimism about China's potential for modernization under Western tutelage. The apparent inertness of Chinese society was not, he wrote, the result of a "horror of the new." Rather, it resulted from the stultifying weight of millennia-old traditions that needed to be cracked. Among the reforms Ross advocated were "dropping ancestor worship, dissolving the clan, educating girls, elevating women, postponing marriage, introducing compulsive education, restricting child labor, and otherwise individualizing the members of the family"—all changes that Americans were ideally suited to help bring about. With similar goals, Yale University established Yale-in-China, an overseas philanthropic program for the education and "uplifting of leading Chinese young men toward civilization." Meanwhile, the Young Men's Christian Association set itself the multiple purposes of providing living quarters for visiting American businessmen, sponsoring lectures on industrial education, working to ameliorate slum conditions, combating prostitution, and spreading the Christian gospel. In a revealing quip, Mark Twain poked fun at these reformers, with their blend of material and moral objectives, as the "blessings of civilization trust."

If the door was wide open in the American imagination, William Howard Taft perceived that it was in fact creaking shut because of continued encroachment by the other powers, especially Japan. As he assumed the presidency in 1909, Taft rejected his predecessor's practice of appeasing Tokyo and advocated a major expansion of American economic activity in the Far East as part of his broader practice of "dollar diplomacy." The new administration, led by its top Far Eastern specialist, Willard Straight, not only hoped to invigorate U.S. exports but also wished to promote American investment in China, an activity that Washington had not previously emphasized. The response from the other powers indicated that the Open Door policy was becoming a fond illusion. When Taft asked the Chinese government to grant part of a major railroad-construction loan to the United States, he discovered that the decision belonged to Britain, France, and Germany, members of the banking consortium that controlled China's finances. The consortium grudgingly admitted the United States, but before long Washington's aspirations ran up against another roadblock when it sought the opportunity to invest in railroad construction in Manchuria. Peking favored the scheme, hoping to use the United States to offset Japanese and Russian influence in the region. But Chinese approval hardly mattered. Faced with great-power hostility, Taft's secretary of state, Philander Knox, resorted to a proposal that came straight from the heart of the Open Door ideal: all railroads in Manchuria, Knox suggested, should be internationalized, thus easing the com-

petition for concessions and permitting all of the powers equal opportunity. In one fell swoop, the scheme aimed to bolster Chinese autonomy, benefit American investors, and deal a blow against imperialism. Russian indebtedness made Knox optimistic of gaining Moscow's consent, but Tokyo predictably would have none of it. The scheme died quickly.

Roosevelt and Taft thus offer a study in contrasts in their conceptions of the Open Door policy. While Roosevelt attached a low priority to the policy and chose not to antagonize Japan by insisting on it too strongly, the Taft administration was determined to prop the door open firmly and went further than even Hay had thought wise in promoting U.S. economic activity in China. Woodrow Wilson offered a third alternative when he ascended to the White House in 1913. By that time, the Chinese Revolution of 1911–1912 had toppled the Qing dynasty, an inspiring development for Americans like Wilson who fancied themselves champions of democracy and progress. Wilson and his secretary of state, William Jennings Bryan, immediately distanced the United States from both Roosevelt's solicitude for power and Taft's solicitude for bankers, embracing instead a more principled variant of the Open Door based on strict anticolonialism. Far more than either of his predecessors, Wilson had imbibed the moralistic rhetoric about America's mission in China. First, he withdrew the United States from the international lending consortium in China, an enterprise of Taft's that, in the new administration's view, put Washington in league with the imperial powers. China, Wilson believed, should be permitted to obtain financial aid that did not entail dependency on the great powers. Then the administration, in a self-conscious display of support for the principle of self-determination, leaped ahead of the other powers to grant diplomatic recognition to the Republic of China.

Wilson's gestures of solidarity with America's "sister republic" were no more successful than earlier U.S. efforts to protect the Open Door policy. The new U.S. approach simply had no capacity to resolve the two problems that plagued American policy: the chronic weakness of Chinese central authority and mounting Japanese ambition. The Chinese Revolution failed to install a central government capable of unifying the country or resisting foreign exactions. Instead, political authority soon fell to an assortment of local politicians and warlords who generally accommodated themselves to the demands of the great powers. Japan was ideally positioned to profit from this situation, all the more so after the outbreak of World War I. With the other powers preoccupied in Europe, the Japanese government saw a golden opportunity to expand its grip on the mainland with minimal risk of opposition. Japan quickly seized German territories in the Far East, including those in the Shandong Peninsula. But the boldest stroke came in January 1915, when Japan presented the enfeebled Chinese government with the infamous Twenty-One Demands. The document demanded that China regularize Japanese gains in Shandong and elsewhere and surrender new concessions in Manchuria. Still more damagingly, it required that China grant no new leaseholds to other powers along the Chinese coast, allow Japan to control most of China's key natural resources, buy at least half its armaments from Japan, allow Japanese police to operate in various key locations, and accept Japanese advisers in administering domestic affairs—arrangements that would have given Japan a virtual protectorate over China.

The Japanese démarche left American officials stunned and uncertain. Initially, amid major distractions in Europe, Washington had little interest in tangling with Japan in a part of the world that was decidedly of secondary importance. After a few weeks, however, the affair caught Wilson's attention. The president brought U.S. policy back in line with his anticolonial instincts, instructing Bryan to be "as active as the circumstances permit in showing ourselves to be the champions of the sovereign rights of China." Faced with opposition from the United States and even its close ally Britain, Japan backed down on the most extreme of its demands. But Tokyo clearly understood that there was little the Western nations could do in the matter and pressed ahead with all terms that centered on economic privileges. Under the threat of force, China yielded with little delay. U.S. policy had clearly suffered a major blow, although the Wilson administration would not admit it at the time. Bryan put the best face on the episode by declaring that the United States would not recognize any agreement that violated Chinese sovereignty or conflicted with the Open Door.

In an effort to give substance to such pledges, the Wilson administration slid back toward Taft's old approach. In 1916, under the guidance of the U.S. minister in Peking, Paul Reinsch, the United States rejoined the banking consortium that Wilson had so brusquely abandoned three years earlier. American investment, the administration concluded, was the only avenue open to Washington for bolstering Chinese unity and checking Japanese influence, which otherwise would go virtually unopposed. Working within the consortium, American thinking went, would enable the United States at least to sit at the table with Japan as equals in discussions of the crucial matter of foreign lending. Wilson also tried direct negotiations with Japan in 1917. Under an agreement signed by Secretary of State Robert Lansing and the Japanese ambassador in Washington, the United States acknowledged Japan's "special interests" in China in exchange for a promise to respect the principles of Chinese sovereignty and the Open Door. These steps changed nothing, however, about the basic problem that confronted the United States in China: if Japan chose not to cooperate, there was nothing Washington could do about it. That underlying reality came to the fore in 1919 at the Versailles Conference, where Wilson, armed with his rhetoric of self-determination, proposed to roll back foreign privileges in China and affirm Chinese sovereignty. Japanese control over Shandong province became the symbolic test case for Wilson's ideas. The president demanded the restoration of Chinese sovereignty; Japan refused. When Japanese representatives threatened to leave the peace conference rather than concede the point, Wilson backed down.

THE END OF THE OPEN DOOR

Wilson's capitulation provoked fierce criticism in China, where irate students took to the streets. It also fed Wilson's growing problems at home with Congress, where opposition to the president's cherished League of Nations mounted amid accusations that the administration had sold out its own principles. But Wilson's calculation was plain: it was better to stay on Japan's good side and ensure the country's participation in the League of Nations, which would inevitably take up the China question later on. Things might, then, turn out well in the long run. Wilson's ambitious vision of an international solution in China came to naught, of course, when Congress rejected the league in 1920. Ironically, however, his successor, the notoriously unambitious Warren Harding, followed Wilson's reasoning quite closely, opting to deal with rivalries in China by gathering all of the great powers together to work out their differences and establish new principles of conduct in the Far East. The result, the Washington Conference of 1921–1922, was an important diplomatic victory for the United States and a major—if temporary—breath of life for the Open Door policy.

Following World War I, Japanese power in the Far East continued to mount. In the 1920s Japan accounted for about 90 percent of all new foreign investment in China, while a quarter of all Japanese exports went there. In many ways, Japan's relationship with the mainland resembled the economic and political stranglehold the United States held over the Caribbean and Central America. The Chinese economy was increasingly locked in to Japanese needs, as both recipient of Japanese investment and manufactured goods and as supplier of food and raw materials. The dramatic growth of Japan's naval power also alarmed American observers by raising the specter of a Japanese challenge to Anglo-American control of Pacific commerce. By 1921 warship construction consumed fully one-third of Japan's budget. Fearing a naval arms race, Secretary of State Charles Evans Hughes invited the foreign ministers of eight maritime nations to Washington to reduce tensions in the Far East. The Japanese government, content to pursue its aims peacefully, entered into all three of the resulting treaties. A four-power nonaggression pact committed Japan, the United States, Britain, and France to consult in the case of future controversies. Meanwhile, a five-power agreement, which included Italy, checked the naval arms race by fixing limits on the size of each navy. By far the most important treaty for the future of the Open Door policy was the Nine-Power Treaty that called for noninterference in China's internal affairs and respect for the Open Door principle. In words that John Hay himself might have written, the agreement bound signatories "to respect the sovereignty, the independence, and the territorial and administrative integrity of China."

The treaty was the most promising assertion of the Open Door policy since Hay's notes. In contrast to the halting and piecemeal promises of the various powers over the previous two decades to uphold the principle of equal economic opportunity, the Washington agreements solemnly bound all of the principal powers (except the excluded Soviet Union) and even reflected input from a full-fledged Chinese delegation. Moreover, the agreements had the strength of acknowledging, rather than resisting as so often in the past,

Japan's emergence as the dominant power in the Far East. As a strategy for maintaining the Open Door, the international approach outshined Roosevelt's appeasement, Taft's dollar diplomacy, or Wilson's early dedication to principle. To be sure, underlying problems remained. For one thing, the agreements contained no enforcement mechanism. Nor did they challenge the existing Japanese position in China. In fact, Elihu Root assured Japan early in the negotiations that the United States would not challenge Tokyo's special privileges. All the Chinese government obtained from the powers was permission to raise its import tariff by 5 percent and a promise to study ways of ending extraterritoriality. Most importantly, the agreements held little promise for slowing Japan's economic penetration of China and preserving a truly fair field for American goods. So strong had Japan's economic grip over China become that it no longer had much reason to fear American competition. To a considerable degree, Japan had achieved the dominant commercial position in China that Americans believed would naturally fall to them if the door were kept open.

Those underlying problems remained submerged, however, during the hopeful years that followed the Washington Conference. In Tokyo, a relatively democratic and progressive Japanese government abided by the conciliatory stance adopted at the meeting. Although overpopulation, resource shortages, and old dreams of empire on the mainland continued to drive Japanese policy, the government displayed little appetite for bold moves that would arouse the other powers. Meanwhile, U.S.–Japanese relations warmed dramatically amid a burst of American enthusiasm for Japan's economic efficiency and administrative reliability, which stood in sharp contrast to ongoing chaos in China. World War I had witnessed a vast expansion of U.S.–Japanese commerce, and during the 1920s the United States confirmed its position as Japan's most important trading partner.

If improved relations with Japan gave Americans reason to think the Open Door policy was safe from its most likely opponent, the shifting situation in China gave them hope that their ultimate dream—a unified China freed from foreign constraints and providing stable access for American goods—might be coming true. After years of political turmoil, the nationalist movement of Sun Yat-sen and Chiang Kai-shek began to make headway in the mid-1920s toward unifying the country under a viable central government. Among the nationalists' foremost objectives was the abolition of the "unequal treaties" that enshrined foreign privileges on Chinese soil. At first, U.S. officials resisted Chinese pressure to end the privileges it had obtained. Indeed, when Sun overstepped treaty provisions in 1923 by claiming surplus customs receipts, U.S. warships joined an international fleet to deter him. But Americans were hardly unified behind that approach, and an increasing number were horrified by practices that suggested colonial designs against a vigorous young republic. While some diplomats prized U.S. treaty privileges and backed gunboat diplomacy to maintain them, most Americans returned to the old vision of a wholly sovereign and administratively competent China as the key to realizing the bounty of the China market. The latter group gained the upper hand in 1928 after Chiang successfully concluded his Northern Expedition, a moment Americans chose to interpret as signaling the arrival of a united China under Kuomintang rule. On 25 July, the United States unilaterally granted tariff autonomy to China in exchange for a new guarantee of most-favored-nation status.

The American move ended one of the most humiliating aspects of the foreign presence in China and marked a moment of triumph for those Americans who had never lost faith that the United States would be China's savior. But it also provoked a powerful Japanese response against which the United States was powerless. It is one of the instructive ironies of the Open Door policy that its final downfall followed so closely on the heels of its apparent heyday. Even at its high point, the policy was more illusion than reality, riddled with so many flaws that it could be demolished once Japan decided to act. Japanese policy began to turn in the late 1920s, when Chiang challenged Japanese privileges in Manchuria. That Chiang did so with the clear support of the United States meant that American economic interests would inevitably gain at Japanese expense. As Tokyo feared, Japanese exports dropped by one-half between 1929 and 1931. The threat to Japan's prestige and its hard-won privileges on the mainland was more than the Japanese military and hard-line nationalists could abide. On 18 September 1931, mid-ranking Japanese army officers acted boldly to reverse this trend, blowing up a section of railway in Manchuria and then blaming Chinese nationalists for the act. The episode, known as the Mukden Incident, became the pretext for Japan to occupy the entire region. Less than a year later, Japan's Kwantung army succeeded in detaching Manchuria from the rest of China and creating the puppet state of Manchukuo.

The timid U.S. response pointed up the weaknesses that had riddled the Open Door policy since its inception. The Hoover administration answered not with economic sanctions but with an ineffective declaration of "nonrecognition" of Japanese aggression. Secretary of State Henry L. Stimson informed the Japanese government that the United States would not recognize any "treaty or agreement" brought about by force or coercion. The U.S. response partly reflected the administration's domestic preoccupations and the unwillingness of the American public to take on foreign commitments as the Great Depression worsened. But other deterrents to bold American action had existed long before the global economic crisis. First of all, the United States, just as in 1898, lacked the ability to back up any diplomatic démarche with force. The U.S. Navy was the world's second largest by 1930, but it still could not hope to challenge Japan in Far Eastern waters. Also discouraging any bold American reply was the longstanding problem, recognized by Theodore Roosevelt two decades before, that China just did not matter very much. Despite all of the hype about the China market and America's special role, China still played a relatively insignificant role in the U.S. economy. Through the 1920s and 1930s, China accounted for only about 2 percent of total U.S. exports each year. In the same period, by contrast, Japan absorbed between 8 and 10 percent of U.S. exports. There was thus little incentive to challenge Japan on behalf of China.

When exactly the demise of the Open Door policy should be dated is open to debate. Certainly, 1931 qualifies as a leading contender. In that year, after all, the partition of China, the development that the Open Door policy had been designed to avoid, came about with breathtaking decisiveness. Moreover, Japan's 1932 attack on Shanghai signaled that Tokyo's ambitions extended far beyond Manchuria. Another possible end point is 1937, the beginning of a full-fledged Sino-Japanese war that quickly resulted in Japanese control over virtually all of the ports, railroads, and other industrial facilities throughout China. A third contender is 1950, when Mao Zedong, having completed the communist conquest of China, slammed the door shut against the United States. Only then, perhaps, did Americans finally give up on the idea that the United

States could reopen the door after Japan's defeat. Indeed, during the mid-1940s U.S. leaders had clearly entertained notions of reestablishing a major American presence, only to see their hopes crushed by a movement that, more than any other, reflected a century of Chinese resentment over foreign intervention. The communists' special wrath for the United States illuminates more clearly than anything else the delusion of exceptionalism that had underpinned American policy for half a century.

THE POLICY AND THE INTERPRETATION

Measured in one way, the Open Door policy might be evaluated as a success. Considering what a weak hand the United States actually held in China between the 1890s and the 1930s, it arguably played the game well, constantly manipulating its rivals into paying at least lip service to American policy and helping to prevent an all-out scramble for China. Even if Americans failed to achieve the market of which they dreamed, 1 or 2 percent of U.S. exports still represented an enormous amount of trade. Measured against the aspirations of its most ardent supporters, however, the Open Door policy rates as a failure. While American businessmen and social reformers elaborated a vision of China as a protégé nation offering boundless opportunity for profit and good deeds, the reality was something else entirely. From the very moment when the Open Door was conceived and identified as a distinctive American policy, powerful forces went to work against it: the treaty port colonialism of the European powers, the rise of a robust Japan eager for control of the mainland, and mounting resistance within China itself.

If these forces destroyed American policy in China, they hardly demolished the idea of the Open Door. On the contrary, the architects of the Open Door policy, whatever their achievements—or lack thereof—in China, helped to establish an attitude toward the non-Western world that would persist powerfully in the Cold War era and beyond. The problem that confronted John Hay in 1899 had called for a decision of epoch-making importance. By what means would the nation extend its reach overseas? The emerging industrial economy seemed to demand bold steps to acquire new markets abroad, but ideological and political traditions made Americans, outside of a brief fascination with territorial acquisition at the time of the Spanish-

American War, averse to formal colonialism. The principal contribution of Hay, Rockhill, Knox, Straight, Reinsch, Hughes, and the other guardians of the door was to resolve the dilemma through a formula that enabled the United States to pursue an aggressively expansionist economic policy, while avoiding the taint of political domination and the burdens of territorial administration. It was a clever solution that, whatever its immediate failures in China, established the pattern for many decades of American foreign policy.

William Appleman Williams and his followers recognized the pattern and elaborated an "open door interpretation" of U.S. foreign policy that remains strongly influential more than forty years after Williams published the foundational text *The Tragedy of American Diplomacy*. In the writings of these scholars, the open door metaphor not only survived its eclipse in the 1930s Far East, it emerged as one of the most enduring interpretive concepts in the study of U.S. foreign relations. The interpretation remains powerful mainly because it provides a persuasive answer to one of the questions at the heart of the study of American foreign relations: How is it that the United States could be the world's most vociferous opponent of colonialism yet also a remarkably interventionist nation that would, in the second half of the twentieth century, control one of the largest empires, albeit of a new and different sort, that the world had ever known? Williams, Walter LaFeber, Thomas McCormick, and others suggest that the promotion of free trade enabled American capitalists to have it both ways. Under the banner of high-minded principles that supposedly enhanced the interests of all nations, they could justify all sorts of political, economic, and military action to prop up a system that in practice enabled the United States to reap more than its proportionate share of the profits.

The open door interpretation remains influential for two additional reasons. First, it provides a neat, totalizing explanation for more than a century of American history stretching back into the period of continental expansion. For advocates of the open door interpretation, the quest for overseas economic opportunity was simply an extension of the westward push that extended the U.S. market to the Pacific Ocean. With the closure of the frontier in the 1890s, the interpretation suggests, U.S. businesses turned their attention to overseas markets and justified the expansion of American influence through the same ideology of open markets and individual opportunity that had prevailed at home. Constant penetration of new markets was, in this view, essential to the health of an American capitalist system that depended on an ever-expanding economy to preserve social harmony in a nation characterized by vast inequities of wealth. According to the open door interpretation, American expansion in the 1890s, Wilson's appeals for an open global economy, and American determination to prevent the Sovietization of Eastern Europe in the late 1940s all stemmed from the same impulse to find and preserve markets for American industry and preserve domestic tranquility.

Second, the open door interpretation remains influential because it helps explain one of the most salient characteristics of twentieth-century international affairs, the tense relationship between the United States and much of the nonindustrial world. Americans, Williams and other argue, have persistently viewed their liberal principles as conducive to the development of the Third World. In practice, however, free trade has tended to concentrate wealth in industrial nations and to deprive poor countries on the periphery of control over their own economic circumstances. Increasingly, Third World peoples found themselves locked into subordinate roles as suppliers of raw materials and consumers of good manufactured elsewhere. "To many through the world," wrote Williams, "the Open Door Policy appeared to confront them with a door closed to their own progress." When nations attempted to break out of this unfavorable relationship and claim control over their own economies, the open door interpretation suggests, they confronted counterrevolutionary U.S. intervention aimed at restoring them to the integrated international economy dominated by Washington. During the Cold War, the pattern repeated itself in Iran, Guatemala, Cuba, Vietnam, Chile, Nicaragua, and many other places where the United States resisted the emergence of nationalist or leftist governments that threatened American economic privileges. The open door interpretation offers a power explanation for the trail of repression and blood left by American activity across the Third World.

BIBLIOGRAPHY

Buckley, Thomas H. *The United States and the Washington Conference, 1921–1922.* Knoxville, Tenn., 1970.

Cohen, Warren I. *America's Response to China: A History of Sino-American Relations.* 4th ed. New York, 2000. Outstanding survey that sets the Open Door period in a broad context.

Fairbank, John King. *The United States and China.* 4th ed. Cambridge, Mass., 1979.

Goldstein, Jonathan, Jerry Israel, and Hilary Conroy, eds. *America Views China: American Images of China Then and Now.* Bethlehem, Pa., 1991.

Hunt, Michael H. *Frontier Defense and the Open Door: Manchuria in Chinese-American Relations, 1895–1911.* New Haven, Conn., 1973. One of the first scholars to use Chinese sources, Hunt stresses China's attempts to manipulate the Open Door policy to its advantage.

———. *The Making of a Special Relationship: The United States and China to 1914.* New York, 1983.

Iriye, Akira. *Pacific Estrangement: Japanese and American Expansion, 1897–1911.* Cambridge, Mass., 1972. The best work comparing U.S. and Japanese ideas about expansionism in China.

———. *After Imperialism: The Search for a New Order in the Far East, 1921–1931.* Chicago, 1990. Useful survey of the Open Door's final years.

———. *The Globalizing of America, 1913–1945.* Cambridge, 1993.

Israel, Jerry. *Progressivism and the Open Door: America and China, 1905–1921.* Pittsburgh, 1971. Links domestic reformism with American ambitions in China.

Jacobson, Matthew Frye. *Barbarian Virtues: The United States Encounters Foreign Peoples at Home and Abroad, 1876–1917.* New York, 2000. Outstanding work that sets the Open Door within the broad flow of U.S. foreign policy and hostility to foreign workers.

Jesperson, T. Christopher. *American Images of China, 1931–1949.* Stanford, 1996.

LaFeber, Walter. *The American Search for Opportunity, 1815–1913.* Cambridge, 1993. With his *The New Empire,* elaborates the Open Door interpretation.

———. *The New Empire: An Interpretation of American Expansion, 1860–1898.* New ed. Ithaca, N.Y., 1998.

May, Ernest R., and John Fairbank, eds. *America's China Trade in Historical Perspective: The Chinese and American Performance.* Cambridge, Mass., 1986. Refines McCormick's account in important ways.

McCormick, Thomas J. *China Market: America's Quest for Informal Empire, 1893–1901.* Chicago, 1967. Remains an authoritative account of the Open Door policy's origins.

McKee, Delber L. *Chinese Exclusion Versus the Open Door Policy, 1900–1906: Clashes over China Policy in the Roosevelt Era.* Detroit, Mich., 1977. Analyses one of the most striking paradoxes of American behavior toward China.

Minger, Ralph Eldin. *William Howard Taft and United States Foreign Policy: The Apprenticeship Years, 1900–1908.* Urbana, Ill., 1975.

Ninkovich, Frank. *The United States and Imperialism.* Malden, Mass., 2001. An excellent survey that sets the Open Door in a broad context.

Rosenberg, Emily S. *Spreading the American Dream: American Economic and Cultural Expansion, 1890–1945.* New York, 1982. Brilliant analysis of the Open Door, especially valuable for contrasting U.S. policies in the Far East and Latin America.

Ross, Edward A. *The Changing Chinese: The Conflict of Oriental and Western Culture in China.* New York, 1911.

Scully, Eileen. "Taking the Low Road in Sino-American Relations: 'Open Door' Expansionists and the Two China Markets." *Journal of American History* 82 (June 1995): 62–83.

Spence, Jonathan D. *The Search for Modern China.* New York, 1990.

Thomson, James C., Jr., Peter W. Stanley, and John Curtis Perry. *Sentimental Imperialists: The American Experience in East Asia.* New York, 1981.

Varg, Paul A. *The Making of a Myth: The United States and China, 1897–1912.* East Lansing, Mich., 1968.

Williams, William Appleman. *The Tragedy of American Diplomacy.* New ed. New York, 1988. The classic formulation of the Open Door interpretation.

Young, Marilyn B. *The Rhetoric of Empire: American China Policy, 1895–1901.* Cambridge, Mass., 1968. Influential revisionist work that highlights the activities of U.S. business groups in promoting the Open Door.

See also ANTI-IMPERIALISM; THE CHINA LOBBY; CONSORTIA; DOLLAR DIPLOMACY; EXTRATERRITORIALITY; IMPERIALISM; MOST-FAVORED-NATION PRINCIPLE; OPEN DOOR INTERPRETATION.

ORGANIZED LABOR

★ ★ ★ ★

Elizabeth McKillen

An oft-quoted blue collar worker, questioned about international issues by pollsters in the 1940s, quipped: "Foreign Affairs! That's for people who don't have to work for a living." Given the complexity of the world order that emerged in the aftermath of World War II and the long hours that most working people labored, such sentiments are easy to understand. Yet since the mid-nineteenth century, when national labor unions emerged in the United States, many workers, grassroots labor activists, and trade union leaders have believed that political relations among nation states, transnational economic developments, and international labor migrations should be of vital concern to the American working class. U.S. labor groups and trade unions have sometimes sought to exercise international influence through international labor organizations or by encouraging transnational forms of collective action among workers. At other times, they have focused primarily on influencing U.S. foreign policy and economic expansion. In an effort to wield power in Washington, D.C., labor groups have typically engaged either in traditional forms of interest group lobbying or have participated in evolving corporatist power-sharing arrangements among business, trade union, and government leaders within the executive branch of government. Dominant trade union groups such as the American Federation of Labor and Congress of Industrial Organizations that pursued international influence both by participating in international labor organizations and by trying to forge a corporatist partnership with business and state representatives in promoting U.S. foreign policy goals often discovered that these two avenues to power led in different directions.

THE EARLY LABOR MOVEMENT AND INTERNATIONAL LABOR ORGANIZING

The first systematic efforts to encourage international cooperation between trade unions most likely occurred in Europe in the 1830s and 1840s. Labor leaders there sought to develop alliances with trade unions from other countries for reasons that would be familiar to workers today. In part, suggests Lewis Lorwin in his pioneering work *The International Labor Movement* (1953), they sought to prevent the importation of strikebreakers from other countries. They also feared competition from foreign sweatshop labor and believed it was in their best interest to try to raise workers' wages throughout Europe. Some anticipated the increasing concentration of international capital and sought to develop alliances with foreign workers in the same industry so as to prevent international financiers and capitalists from playing workers in one country against those in another. Finally, some unions initiated contacts with unions from other countries for the practical reason that they needed financial assistance for their organizing or strike activities.

Most of these early efforts at international labor cooperation were suppressed by European governments or came to naught. It was only in 1864 that European workers successfully formed the International Working Men's Association, later known as the First International. Among the most influential members of the organization was Karl Marx, who wrote the preamble and rules, as well as an inaugural address that included the now famous appeal "Workmen of all countries, unite!" The organization grew slowly at first, and national delegates expressed a wide variety of viewpoints about questions of capitalism and collective ownership. As the organization expanded, however, it became increasingly dominated by Marxists. Eventually, an internal struggle developed between Marx and the Russian revolutionary and writer Michael Bakunin. After Bakunin was expelled, the First International's headquarters were transferred to New York City, where it declined rapidly and was finally dissolved at a meeting of the General Council in Philadelphia in 1876.

How American workers responded to these early European efforts at international labor cooperation is not entirely clear. The First International boasted some twenty-seven American sections representing several hundred U.S. workers, mostly immigrants. The short-lived National Labor Union, under the leadership of William Sylvis, also announced its attention to affiliate with the First International and to adhere to its principles. But no record has been unearthed of an official relationship between the First International and the more predominant Knights of Labor, which was created in 1869 and reached a peak membership of some 750,000 workers in the mid-1880s. Indeed, some Knights of Labor activists and leaders adopted a hostile attitude toward socialists like those who dominated the First International. Thus, historians have often treated the Knights as a uniquely American organization that developed in relative isolation from the European labor movement. They emphasize the importance of an ideology of labor republicanism within the Knights of Labor that drew on American political traditions rather than on European socialist and Marxist doctrines emphasizing international labor solidarity.

But the Knights may not have been as isolated from European political currents and internationalist activities as previously assumed. Leon Fink and Kim Voss note parallels between the Knights of Labor's condemnations of wage labor and emphasis on worker cooperatives, and the socialist critiques and programs promoted by European labor activists. They suggest that the Knights' emphasis on inclusive membership and broad-based, working-class solidarity across nationality lines was similar to that of other industrial labor organizations developing in Britain and France at the time. Eric Foner notes the importance of immigrants within local chapters of the Knights of Labor and illuminates their role in promoting an ethos of international labor solidarity upon which future generations could draw.

Particularly important, suggests Foner, was the influence of Irish-Americans within the Knights of Labor, for they brought with them an interest in the land question in Ireland. When Knights of Labor chapters faced opposition from hostile clergy and local governments in areas such as the anthracite coal regions of Pennsylvania, Knights of Labor activists often met covertly under the guise of local Irish Land League chapters. A creative cross-breeding of Irish nationalist and American labor reform ideas resulted and frequently led workers to conceptualize their local trade union struggles as part of a worldwide struggle between the owning and producing classes. Terence Powderly, Knights of Labor "Grand Master Workman," embodied the interconnections between class and ethnicity in shaping the international orientation of some Knights of Labor activists. Born in Carbondale, Pennsylvania, of Irish immigrant parents, Powderly became active in both Irish and labor activities as a young man. During his tenure as grand master of the Knights of Labor, Powderly also served as vice president of the Irish Land League Council. Inevitably, the two causes became intertwined as Powderly used Knights conventions to publicize the linkages between the Irish land struggle and the class struggle in the United States. Although Knights of Labor activists advanced few actual international programs and developed few substantial ties with foreign labor movements, they thus sowed fertile ground for future immigrant labor activists who would develop an international labor vision that clashed fundamentally with that of the American Federation of Labor.

EARLY INTERNATIONAL POLICIES OF THE AMERICAN FEDERATION OF LABOR

Founded in 1886, the American Federation of Labor (AFL) was comprised predominantly of craft unions—many of whom had fled the Knights of Labor—that emphasized improving economic conditions for workers rather than eliminating or fundamentally transforming industrial capitalism. Although the national organization claimed to represent all workers, many constituent unions were quite exclusionary in practice, primarily made up of skilled, white male workers. Despite its narrow focus and membership base, the fledgling AFL was not opposed to international labor cooperation. When an international conference of labor leaders convened in Paris in 1889 to create the Second International, AFL President Samuel Gompers solicited its support for the AFL's campaigns on behalf of an eight-hour day. The congress responded favorably and organized May Day labor demonstrations in conjunction with the AFL's eight-hour-day rallies in the United States. The demonstrations marked the beginning of the international trade union tradition of May Day labor celebrations and rallies.

But in the decade following the Paris Congress, the AFL remained largely aloof from the Second International. In part, the AFL failed to develop a relationship with the Second International for pragmatic reasons. Still in its infancy, the AFL could not always afford to send delegates to European conferences. The organization was also preoccupied during its early years with strike activity. Perhaps most importantly, both American and European socialists became increasingly critical of the AFL's conservative orientation. When Gompers tried to arrange an international labor conference at the World's Columbian Exposition in Chicago in 1893, only the British Trades Union Congress responded favorably. Gompers subsequently canceled the conference and, while encouraging the exchange of fraternal delegates between the British Trades Union Congress and the AFL, largely eschewed contacts with European socialist and labor leaders.

AFL interest in European labor affairs revived only after 1904, when many individual unions within the AFL began to affiliate with international trade secretariats. These organizations were comprised of national trade unions from the same industry that came together to promote their international interests. For example, miners from France, Germany, and Austria created the International Miners' Federation in 1890. Constituent AFL unions became interested in these secretariats when they realized they could provide valuable information about international conditions in their industries and coordinate activities that would prevent businessmen from importing strikebreakers from other countries. Among the AFL unions that joined secretariats between 1904 and 1908 were the miners, molders, painters, shoemakers, lithographers, bakers, and brewers.

As more AFL unions joined their secretariats, Gompers in turn became more interested in joining the International Secretariat of National Trade Union Centers, which had been formed in 1903 at the behest of leaders of the international secretariats who sought an international trade union organization that would be independent of the Second International. Gompers attended one of its conferences in 1908, and the AFL convention subsequently voted to affiliate with the organization. The AFL was an active member of the International Secretariat of National Trade Union Centers between 1910 and 1913 and successfully promoted an initiative to have the organization's name changed to the International Federation of Trade Unions (IFTU). After failing in their efforts to use international labor organizations to prevent war in 1914, Gompers and other AFL leaders confidently waited for an end to the conflict, assuming that the AFL would play a predominant role in international labor organizations following the armistice.

The AFL's influence in postwar labor organizations, however, would ultimately be undermined by the corporatist role it had tried to carve for itself in shaping U.S. foreign policy during the previous two decades. The first U.S. foreign policy issue in which the AFL took a systematic interest was the McKinley administration's policies toward the Cuban rebellion against Spain in the 1890s. Like many groups in the United States, the AFL lobbied Congress to recognize Cuban belligerency. A majority of representatives from the constituent unions of the AFL apparently believed it was their responsibility to promote liberty for fellow workingmen. In the minority within the AFL, suggests Delber McKee, were those who warned that labor should avoid committing itself on the question because it might be encouraging a U.S. war with Spain. War, they argued, always disproportionately hurt the workingman, because they were the ones who fought and died. Fewer still were labor leaders like Andrew Furuseth of the Seamen's Union, who questioned whether business and government leaders supporting the Cubans might have imperialist motives of their own. As Furuseth explained, the question over whether to support Cuban belligerency was one of "whether the New York speculator or the Spanish capitalist should skin the Cuban workingman."

AFL President Gompers, for his part, supported proposals to recognize Cuban belligerency but opposed McKinley's decision to declare war against Spain. Yet the AFL did nothing to oppose U.S. mobilization for war. Instead, Gompers focused on opposing annexation of Spanish territories at war's end. Gompers highlighted his reasons for opposing empire in an article entitled "To Free Cuba, Not to Chineize [sic] America Was the War Begun." In part, as McKee has demonstrated, Gompers shared the racial assumptions of many white trade unionists of his day and feared that annexing territories would enable "semibarbaric laborers" to immigrate to the United States and undermine American labor standards. As a former cigar maker, Gompers also sought to prevent goods like cigars produced by sweatshop labor in Cuba and the Philippines from competing with American products in the U.S. market. Finally, the AFL president also hoped to preempt possible American business flight to these low-wage areas by stopping U.S. annexation.

But after the Senate approved a peace treaty with Spain that resulted in the formal annexation of the Philippines, Gompers came to what McKee calls a "tacit compromise" with the State Department. The AFL president toned down his opposition to U.S. imperial policies and even endorsed temporary ward status for the Philippines and Puerto Rico in return for government and business acquiescence in an AFL campaign to build labor unions in these areas. In rationalizing his policies, Gompers argued, "We realized that in order to protect our standards within the states we must help the Island workers to develop their own higher political, social and industrial problems [sic]."

Gompers and the AFL thus began to move away from a policy of opposing government and business imperialism and toward a corporatist partnership between business, labor, and the state in promoting American economic expansion. Gompers and other AFL leaders reasoned that if they could raise labor standards in the new island protectorates, then U.S. imperial control over them might actually benefit U.S. workers. Goods produced there would not undersell those made by U.S. workers for domestic markets and American businessmen would not be tempted to establish low-wage factories on the islands. On the other hand, wealthier island workers might welcome consumer goods from the United States, thereby promoting American economic growth in ways that benefited U.S. business and U.S. workers alike. The islands might also prove to be important strategic outposts for securing access to other markets or raw materials deemed vital to the health of U.S. industry. Lost in such reasoning, of course, were the aspirations of indigenous working-class populations in the islands for economic, political, and cultural independence.

Meanwhile, a more amicable alliance had evolved among labor, business, and state leaders to resolve domestic economic problems during the early twentieth century. In 1900 the National Civic Federation was formed to encourage a "community of interest" among the three groups that would reduce industrial strife and promote the development of a healthy capitalist economic system in the United States. Upon assuming office, President Woodrow Wilson built on the initiatives of the National Civic Federation by creating the Department of Labor and the Commission on Industrial Relations to oversee industrial arbitration and to make recommendations for promoting harmony and efficiency in industry.

But this cooperative agenda—to encourage industrial peace at home and American expansion and hegemony abroad—would fully blossom only during World War I.

WORLD WAR I

For the first several months of the war, the American Federation of Labor—like most of the American public—remained adamantly opposed to U.S. intervention in the conflict. But in 1916, Gompers began to actively support the Wilson administration's preparedness campaigns. Gompers, like Wilson, was alarmed by Germany's use of submarine warfare and believed the United States might need to enter the war to stop German aggression. Equally significant, Gompers had watched with fascination the evolving wartime partnership between British labor and the government during the early months of the war. He anticipated that by supporting Wilson's preparedness policies he might gain a voice for the AFL in executive branch defense councils comparable to that which British labor had won for itself. Gompers's reasoning proved correct: in 1917 he was appointed to the Council of National Defense, an organization created to prepare the country for possible involvement in the war. Gompers subsequently formed a labor subcommittee within the council that brought together representatives from business, labor, and the government to study questions of industrial coordination and to draw up guidelines on wages, hours, and mediation in war-related industries.

When a U.S. declaration of war against Germany seemed likely in March 1917, Gompers called a special labor assembly of the leaders of the AFL's constituent unions and secured its support for an AFL pledge to support any future U.S. war effort. The assembly was widely criticized by local AFL activists, socialists, and some members of the syndicalist Industrial Workers of the World, who charged that the labor assembly was not democratically constituted. They demanded that the AFL have a referendum vote of its entire membership to determine if workers actually favored a U.S. declaration of war against Germany. But Gompers ignored such militant proposals and instead used the AFL's patriotic pledge of support for the government as a bargaining chip to gain more representation for AFL leaders within emerging wartime agencies and councils created to mobilize the country for war. He anticipated that the defense agencies, far from being temporary, would lay the basis for a new bureaucratic order in Washington after the war in which the AFL would play a prominent role.

Gompers also sought to use his new leverage within the Wilson adminstration to expand the AFL's diplomatic influence. He obtained AFL representation on the Root Commission, a council of emissaries whose purpose was to travel to Russia to encourage it to stay in the war. He also secured the Wilson administration's support for two AFL labor commissions to go to Europe to win support among discontented European labor movements for Wilsonian war aims and to thwart European trade union efforts to plan an interbelligerent labor conference designed to negotiate an early end to the war. The AFL labor missions, as Elizabeth McKillen has shown, were greeted with hostility by European labor leaders who complained that its members behaved "as if their mission was to convince the misguided foreigners how wrong it is to differ with Americans." Labor and socialist leaders, moreover, continued to promote an interbelligerent labor conference despite the AFL's opposition. Although their plans would ultimately be stymied by their own governments, the issue provoked a profound split between the AFL and European labor movements.

That chasm widened during the Paris Peace Conference. Both European labor groups and the AFL at first supported a plan for an international labor congress to be held at the same time and place as the conference. But when France's premier, Georges Clemenceau, refused to allow labor leaders from the defeated countries on French soil, European labor leaders changed the location of their meeting to Bern, Switzerland. Gompers and other AFL leaders boycotted the Bern meeting and instead traveled to Paris to be in close contact with the leaders of the Paris Peace Conference. In return for his loyalty, Wilson appointed Gompers to head the International Labor Legislation Commission, which in turn created the International Labor Organization, a labor adjunct to the League of Nations. The organization clearly bore the imprint of Gompers's corporatist thinking about labor's role in international affairs. Far from being purely an organization of trade union representatives, the International Labor Organization was designed to consist of national delegations comprised of representatives from business, labor, and government. The organization was empowered to create international labor legislation governing such issues as hours,

working conditions, and the protection of women and child workers, which individual states could either accept or reject.

Not surprisingly, the Bern labor conference reacted with hostility to the creation of the International Labor Organization and drafted their own international labor charter. However, in an ironic twist of fate, European labor activists became dominant in the International Labor Organization after the U.S. Senate rejected the Treaty of Versailles, thereby preventing U.S. membership in the League of Nations or its adjuncts. Meanwhile, the AFL distanced itself from the newly reconstituted International Federation of Trade Unions, which committed itself to international collective labor action after the war. The AFL also bitterly opposed the activities of the Red International of Trade Unions, created by Russian communists and their allies to promote world revolution. By the early 1920s, Gompers's vision of the AFL as a partner with business and government in promoting U.S. foreign policy had thus produced a seemingly irreconcilable split between American and European labor.

The AFL's diplomatic programs also spurred profound divisions within the ranks of labor at home. The greatest opposition to the AFL's postwar international agenda came not from the Socialist Party or the Industrial Workers of the World, both of which had been greatly weakened by wartime persecution and were ridden with factionalism at war's end, but from militant AFL-affiliated city labor councils and local unions with strong ties to immigrant communities. Leading the rebellion was the Irish immigrant John Fitzpatrick, president of the powerful Chicago Federation of Labor (CFL) and the Labor Bureau of the American Commission on Irish Independence. Following in the tradition of Terence Powderly of the Knights of Labor, Fitzpatrick drew on the intellectual heritages of both the American labor movement and Irish nationalist movement in trying to understand the global condition of workers. In contrast to Gompers, Fitzpatrick bitterly opposed all forms of imperialism, arguing that imperial control by industrially developed countries of underdeveloped hinterlands buoyed the power of the capitalist class at the expense of workers. Fitzpatrick and his colleagues also believed that war was the inevitable by-product of the capitalist quest for markets and natural resources. They energetically opposed U.S. intervention in World War I until 1917, when the AFL's declaration of labor loyalty made continued

WORKING-CLASS SUBCULTURES AND LABOR INTERNATIONALISM

In 1917, when AFL President Samuel Gompers staged a meeting to secure approval of a labor declaration of loyalty to the government during wartime, he purposely excluded representatives from local labor councils, correctly suggesting to advisers that many were centers of pacifism. City labor councils often became hotbeds of antiwar and anti-imperialist sentiment during World War I because they were more organically connected to local working-class subcultures than to the AFL leadership. Chicago boasted one of the most oppositional labor subcultures of the World War I era. It was one of those rare places, suggests James Barrett, "where it was easier to be a union member than to be nonunion" in the early twentieth century. Disillusionment with President Woodrow Wilson's war policies in the city's teeming immigrant working-class neighborhoods inspired a labor party that raised critical questions about the AFL's unwavering support for Wilsonian foreign policy. Similar labor parties erupted in some forty-five other cities in the immediate postwar period and eventually culminated in the Farmer-Labor Party of 1920, a party with a strongly anti-Wilsonian agenda. Local, regional, or ethnic working-class subcultures could thus sometimes inspire alternative visions of labor internationalism that impeded AFL attempts to win working-class support for its international policies.

Other forms of oppositional working-class subcultures sometimes developed within particular industries or vocations. For example, maritime workers, by virtue of their travel, often came in contact with other cultures and ideas that instinctively bred a sense of internationalism. Yet the conditions of a seaman's life, suggests Bruce Nelson, were also characterized by "raw exploitation"

and "a legendary rootlessness and transiency that led to a persistent isolation from the main integrative institutions of American society." Such a subculture lent itself to militant and sometimes violent displays of international labor solidarity. Seamen and other maritime workers were particularly aggressive in opposing fascism during the 1930s. One typical incident occurred when crew members from American and Danish merchant ships joined together to pull a swastika from a German ship trying to enter Olympia Harbor in Washington State in July 1933. Such seamen were aware well in advance of most Americans that Nazism posed a danger to the rights of democratic trade unions. In another instance, in 1935, seven thousand longshoremen, machinists, and scalers in San Francisco struck to protest a German ship entering San Francisco Harbor with swastika flying. Maritime workers also mobilized to protest Mussolini's invasion of Ethiopia and refused to load cargo bound for Italian soldiers participating in the campaign. The militancy of the maritime workers proved difficult for either the AFL or CIO to contain.

Oppositional labor subcultures also proved critical in stimulating an independent labor internationalism during the Vietnam War. Despite the AFL-CIO's unwavering support for the nation's war effort, a host of local labor groups such as the Cleveland Federation of Labor—with strong community support—opposed U.S. government policy in Vietnam. Such examples suggest the need for historians to examine the dynamic interaction between labor leadership and oppositional subcultures within the labor movement when exploring questions of labor internationalism.

agitation strategically unwise. The CFL, however, remained critical of the AFL's wartime partnership with the Wilson administration, believing it hindered labor's advancement both at home and abroad, and launched the Farmer-Labor Party movement following the armistice.

Although an electoral failure, the Farmer-Labor movement, as McKillen has shown, served as a haven for AFL dissidents from city labor councils and trade union locals across the country that opposed Gompers's and Wilson's international programs. Along with the powerful Chicago Fed-

eration of Labor, particularly important in shaping the movement were the Seattle Central Labor Council, New York Labor Union, delegates from locals of the United Mine Workers and the railway brotherhoods, and representatives from a host of small-town labor councils that had created local labor parties in the aftermath of war. In contrast to Gompers and the AFL executive council, party advocates bitterly attacked the Versailles peace treaty, arguing that its terms were dictated by the leading imperialist powers on behalf of international capital. Labor Party leaders opposed the

League of Nations on the grounds that it would "not be satisfied with a league of imperialist governments dominated by an international league of money bosses to cement an international control of industry by a small group of men who manipulate the bulk of the world's wealth." Rather than seeking token representation for labor in the league-sponsored International Labor Organization, Labor Party advocates sought representation for workers in international tribunals "in proportion to their numbers in the armies, navies, and workshops of the world." Representatives from the Farmer-Labor Party also expressed sympathy with the Irish, Mexican, and Russian revolutions and promoted an anti-imperialist agenda for the United States in Latin America and Asia.

Since many of the activists within the Farmer-Labor Party also belonged to immigrant nationalist groups, their ideas received wide circulation and swelled the tide of opposition to the peace treaty and to the Wilson administration. That Gompers viewed such a rebellion within the ranks as a threat to his efforts to promote both a corporatist international role for labor and a Wilsonian blueprint for a new world order was evidenced by the energy he devoted to suppressing the movement. Yet it was not Gompers who succeeded in destroying the movement but communist activists within the Chicago Federation of Labor such as William Z. Foster, who outmaneuvered Fitzpatrick and won control of the executive council of the Farmer-Labor Party. Subsequently, Fitzpatrick and most other local AFL activists disavowed the party and officially renewed their commitment to the AFL's supposedly nonpartisan politics. With the Farmer-Labor Party died a unique vision of U.S. labor's international role that emphasized the responsibility of U.S. workers—as heirs to traditions of American labor republicanism and a diverse array of immigrant labor ideologies—to lead in the battle against international capitalism and international organizations that reified imperial forms of control by industrial-creditor nations over their less economically developed counterparts.

THE INTERWAR YEARS

With internal critics silenced, Gompers and his successor, William Green, were free to devote the AFL's international energies in the 1920s to developing a leadership role for U.S. labor in the Western Hemisphere—a renewed interest that in part was inspired by the AFL's alienation from European labor diplomacy. Unable to shape either the International Federation of Trade Unions or International Labor Organization in ways it deemed constructive, the AFL instead chose to concentrate after 1920 on exercising influence over its immediate neighbors. Economic issues also played a role: AFL leaders recognized that American business was expanding rapidly throughout the hemisphere and that immigrants from Canada and Latin America were swelling the U.S. workforce. Since many AFL unions had already established strong footholds in Canada by World War I, AFL leaders primarily focused on encouraging better relations with Latin American labor movements. Their avenue to influence was the Pan American Federation of Labor, created in 1918 with secret financial aid from the Wilson administration. The Pan American Federation sought to raise labor standards in Latin America, curb abuses of labor by international capitalists, and promote the growth of unions in the Americas. Gompers and the AFL also wanted to use the organization to resolve immigration problems between Mexico and the United States and to give legitimacy to corporatist-oriented labor organizations such as the Confederación Regional Obrera Mexicana at the expense of the Industrial Workers of the World and other anarchist, communist, or socialist labor movements and organizations, which were winning converts in Latin America and within the Mexican-American community in the U.S. Southwest.

Although the Pan American Federation and the AFL sometimes condemned U.S. military interventionism within Latin America, AFL delegates often asserted that the U.S. presence in Latin America was primarily a beneficial one. Significant within the Pan American Federation conventions, as Sinclair Snow has shown, were debates over the Monroe Doctrine, with delegates from the AFL defending the doctrine as one that protected Latin American countries from greedy European powers, and many Latin American trade unionists condemning it as an instrument of U.S. imperialism. The AFL's frequent support for U.S. foreign policy and predominant role in the Pan American Federation fostered much criticism among radical Latin American trade unionists, who came to view it as a tool of U.S. imperialism. The organization declined rapidly as more left-leaning labor organizations gained influence in Mexico and Latin America in the mid- and late 1920s.

Largely isolated from their European and Latin American counterparts, the AFL at first promoted a nationalist response to the Great Depression. The organization resisted Franklin D. Roosevelt's efforts to expand trade through reciprocal agreements with other countries and instead suggested that the best way to end the depression was by implementing a thirty-hour work week. Mandated shorter hours, argued AFL leaders, would force employers to hire unemployed workers and lead to increased spending. To further stimulate the economy, many AFL unions recommended increased tariff protection for some industries and even promoted William Randolph Hearst's "Buy American" campaigns. Yet the AFL's isolationist impulse proved temporary. German and Japanese aggression in the 1930s, as well as challenges from the newly created Congress of Industrial Organizations (CIO), forced the AFL to take a renewed interest in international affairs. In 1933 the AFL instituted a boycott of German goods and supported Roosevelt's ban on strategic materials to Italy. Although AFL leaders continued to support the neutrality laws and to oppose U.S. military involvement overseas throughout the 1930s, it reaffiliated with the International Federation of Trade Unions in 1937. In part, the AFL sought to support antifascist forces in Europe. But equally important it hoped to prevent the organization from admitting either the CIO or labor delegates from the Soviet Union.

The symbolic origins of the CIO lay in United Mine Workers President John L. Lewis's historic right-cross punch to the chin of William Hutcheson of the Carpenters Union during an AFL convention in 1935. The fistfight occurred following a heated debate in which Lewis attacked the AFL for failing to take advantage of the depression and Roosevelt's labor policies to organize the unorganized. Following the 1935 convention, Lewis met with other disaffected leaders to create the Committee for Industrial Organization, which would spawn the Congress of Industrial Organizations. Although the AFL had many semi-industrial unions by the 1930s, leaders of the new CIO objected to the slow rate at which the AFL organized unskilled workers and to the continued dominance of craft unions within the organization. Capitalizing on rank-and-file labor militance in industries like rubber, automobiles, and steel, the CIO organized mass industrial unions that incorporated most grades of workers within particular industries. The CIO became famous for its militant tactics, scored decisive victories for workers in numerous industries, and vied with the AFL for leadership of the American labor movement.

Less well known than the domestic quarrels between the AFL and CIO were their conflicts over foreign policy. In contrast to the AFL's heavy-handed "Monroe Doctrine" for labor, CIO leaders preached nonintervention in the internal affairs of Latin American unions. When pursuing negotiations over labor issues, moreover, the CIO chose to bargain with leftist and often communist-led organizations like the Confederación de Trabajadores de América Latina rather than with AFL-inspired organizations such as the Inter-American Labor Union. Such activities won the CIO much goodwill among Latin American trade unionists, as did its decision to endorse Mexican President Lazaro Cardenas's decision to expropriate British and American oil fields in 1938. By contrast, AFL leaders argued that Cardenas's nationalization programs were a violation of the right to private property. The CIO also parted ways with the AFL in its willingness to envision the Soviet trade union movement as a part of future international labor organizations.

The top leaders of the CIO hierarchy, such as Sidney Hillman, Philip Murray, James Carey, and Walter Reuther, were all noncommunists who had battled communists during their ascent to power. Yet all were willing to work with communists at home when it supported their purposes and to negotiate with communist labor leaders abroad because they believed their support to be critical to the defeat of fascism and to future international labor cooperation. Such sentiments were comparable to those of the European leaders of the International Federation of Trade Unions, who had battled the Red International Labor Union in the 1920s but who saw the need for a popular front against fascism in the 1930s. By contrast, the AFL remained vehemently anticommunist throughout the 1930s and strongly opposed Soviet participation in the International Federation of Trade Unions. AFL leaders argued that only "free" trade unions, unattached to government parties or institutions, should be allowed to join international labor organizations. Soviet supporters countered that Western labor movements—including the AFL—were not entirely free of state interference either. A full debate on the issue of Soviet participation in the International Federation of Trade Unions was postponed in 1939 because of the Nazi-Soviet Pact. But the success of the Grand Alliance during World War

II again led western European and CIO union leaders to speculate about the value of a postwar labor organization that would include the communist world.

WORLD WAR II AND THE WORLD FEDERATION OF TRADE UNIONS

Replicating a pattern that developed during World War I, many European labor movements as well as the AFL and CIO worked closely with their respective governments to promote efficient wartime economic planning and aid their countries' war efforts. The British Trades Union Congress also sought to promote the war effort (and to preempt British communists) by forming the Anglo-Soviet Trade Union Committee, designed to encourage cooperation and solidarity between unionists in the two countries. The British Trades Union Congress subsequently invited the Americans to join the Anglo-Soviet Trade Union Committee, but these efforts failed because of the unwillingness of the AFL to work with either the Soviets or the CIO. In early 1945, however, the British trade union leaders hosted a labor conference designed to create a new international labor organization that would include the Soviets. The AFL refused to attend, but the CIO eagerly sent delegates, and in October 1945 the new World Federation of Trade Unions (WFTU) was created.

This new federation embodied the hopes of a generation of trade union leaders for a substantive role for labor in international affairs. Most did not foresee for it a revolutionary role comparable to that sometimes espoused by the International Federation of Trade Unions. Rather, suggests Victor Silverman in *Imagining Internationalism* (2000), the leaders of the World Federation were labor bureaucrats who "envisioned a corporative world—one ruled by global institutions that would represent all elements of society." Yet the corporatist vision of these leaders differed in important ways from that of Samuel Gompers during World War I. Gompers had envisioned the International Labor Organization comprised of national delegations representing equal numbers of business, labor, and government officials. By contrast, World Federation leaders believed it was vital that labor have its own organization that could speak independently for world labor and represent the world's working classes within the United Nations.

The drive for a powerful labor international that included all significant elements of world labor was apparently given momentum by an increased spirit of internationalism that pervaded working-class life in the major democracies after 1941. Silverman suggests that in Britain the war fostered a greatly increased awareness and concern for foreign relations among workers and argues that a "vague sympathy for the Soviet 'experiment' grew into tremendous enthusiasm for cooperation in reordering the world." Because the working-class population in the United States was more diverse than that of Britain, it failed to develop a comparable consensus on internationalism or on cooperation with the Soviets. Nonetheless, many American workers had come to feel vaguely sympathetic toward a new labor internationalism by war's end. As one union carpenter cited in Silverman explained, "We can't stay on our side of the pond anymore. It's one world now and we got to go in and do our share. The Union's taught me that. Workers everywhere want it fair for all." In contrast to their British counterparts, however, many American workers—especially first- or second-generation immigrants from Eastern Europe—were distrustful of the Soviets. Yet perhaps because of their long experience with red-baiting in the unions, workers were initially slower to embrace the Cold War than wealthier Americans. The lack of a Cold War consensus about America's postwar role within the working class in turn bought time for CIO leaders to experiment with a reordering of international labor politics within the World Federation.

In addition to supporting the federation's major efforts to gain a role for itself within the United Nations and to encourage cooperation between communist and noncommunist trade unions, the CIO took the lead in developing the federation's colonial department. In contrast to many European trade union leaders, the CIO promoted independent trade unions in colonial areas and supported their efforts to gain representation in the federation. Even French communists within the organization, for example, battled CIO representatives over the question of representation for African labor, insisting that the French trade union delegates to the federation already represented workers from French possessions in Africa. Of course, CIO leaders could sometimes be naive about their own country's imperial record, as when James Carey insisted that U.S. rule in the Philippines had been entirely benevolent and designed to give democracy to the Filipinos. CIO leaders, moreover, embraced a Rooseveltian faith in the virtues of free trade that sometimes blinded them to the dangers of economic imperialism. Nonetheless, Silverman suggests that the CIO's defense of colonial rights within the federation earned it popularity in much of the underdeveloped world and offered hope that the new organization might serve the interests of Third World labor.

But several factors ultimately undermined the federation. The AFL's Free Trade Union Committee collaborated with the State Department to weaken the organization by sowing discord between communist and noncommunist unions in Europe. As Peter Weiler has shown, the AFL also successfully worked to prevent international trade secretariats from affiliating with it. Without the trade secretariats, the task of coordinating labor activities within individual industries proved impossible. Meanwhile, both the CIO and AFL became increasingly vulnerable at home following passage of the Taft-Hartley Act in 1947, which required that all union leaders sign affidavits pledging that they were not Communist Party members. The predominantly noncommunist CIO leadership at first resisted but soon chose to purge communists and communist-led unions from their ranks. Their support for purges was likely motivated both by a desire to consolidate their own leadership positions within their unions and to safeguard their unions from government persecution. Desperate to appear loyal in the face of the anticommunist hysteria sweeping the nation, the CIO also embraced the Marshall Plan and, along with other Western unions, asked the World Federation to endorse it. As Weiler wrote, the "introduction of the Marshall Plan into the WFTU brought the Cold War directly into the international trade union movement." Predictably, the Soviets opposed an endorsement of the Marshall Plan and instead advocated neutrality on the issue. Leading Western union movements with the exception of the French Confédération Générale du Travail and Italian Confederazione Generale Italiana del Lavoro then withdrew from the federation in 1949 and, in concert with the AFL, created the International Confederation of Free Trade Unions.

COLD WAR IN THE INTERNATIONAL LABOR MOVEMENT

One of the primary goals of the International Confederation of Free Trade Unions (ICFTU) was to support people trying to free themselves from totalitarianism. Silverman has revealed that CIO leaders, in joining the new international, expressed hope that the organization would support neither "Stalin" nor "Standard Oil" but a "broad democratic middle where people may fight to have both bread and freedom." The CIO placed faith, in particular, in the capacity of the organization to assist in implementing the Marshall Plan in ways that would benefit European workers. True to their New Deal roots, many CIO leaders anticipated that the Keynesian spending fostered by the Marshall Plan would stimulate European economies. The ICFTU, meanwhile, would encourage labor-management cooperation in increasing productivity and presumably both European workers and business owners would benefit.

Workers in many European countries, however, failed to profit from the Marshall Plan to the extent that AFL and CIO leaders envisioned. The activities of the AFL, and to some degree the CIO, in undermining communist-led unions and in encouraging splits within them, helped to weaken the labor movements in many countries and prevented them from claiming an increased share of their nation's wealth in the postwar era. For example, Ronald Filippelli and Federico Romero have demonstrated that in Italy the AFL worked in collaboration with the U.S. State Department to encourage discord between communists and noncommunists within the Confederacion Generale Italiana del Lavoro, or Italian General Confederation of Labor. Subsequently, both the AFL and CIO supported the formation of rival free trade union organizations in Italy that were devoid of communist influence. While some divisiveness within Italian labor circles would likely have occurred regardless of American meddling, the AFL and CIO nonetheless played some role in making the Italian labor movement one of the most faction-ridden and weakest in Europe by the 1950s. Thus, while Italy experienced the *miracalo italiano,* or the Italian economic miracle, in the aftermath of Marshall Plan spending, Italian workers remained among the lowest paid in the developed world. As European workers became increasingly dissatisfied with the fruits of the Marshall Plan, European trade union leaders within the ICFTU challenged many American initiatives and a greater balance emerged between the Europeans and Americans in the organization. (In 1969, the by-then merged AFL-CIO withdrew from the ICFTU because it believed that Europeans within the organization had become soft on communism. The AFL-CIO rejoined the ICFTU only in 1984).

The AFL and CIO's early Cold War foreign policy activities also produced mixed results in occupied Japan and in Latin America. As Howard Schonberger has demonstrated, American labor officials played an important role in the U.S. occupation of Japan because U.S. policymakers hoped to build a strong AFL-styled union movement there to check the power of traditional business and political elites whom they believed responsible for Japanese aggression during World War II. A powerful Japanese trade union movement, moreover, would force Japanese Zaibatsu corporations to share some of their profits with workers and lead them to redirect some trade exports toward their domestic markets and away from other markets where they might compete with U.S. goods. In 1945 occupation officials sponsored a trade union law that established the legal framework for Japanese workers to organize unions, bargain collectively, and strike. The Japanese labor movement subsequently grew exponentially and by 1949 represented more than half of all Japanese workers.

Charged with directing the growth of the Japanese labor movement in ways the U.S. government deemed constructive was the Labor Division of the occupation bureaucracy. The Labor Division always contained AFL representatives, and in 1947, James Killen, vice president of the International Brotherhood of Pulp, Sulphite, and Paper Mill Workers within the AFL, was appointed chief of the division. Occupation leaders sought Killen's help because they feared the Japanese labor movement was drifting to the left and were concerned about the militant tactics adopted by Japanese unions. Killen sought to counter the influence of communists by establishing anticommunist cells called *mindo* within Japanese unions. Yet Killen was also critical of the occupation bureaucracy for not stemming the tide of inflation, which undermined any gains workers achieved, and for its decision to remove government workers from the trade union movement. Eventually, convinced that occupation leaders were more concerned with weakening the Japanese labor movement than with eliminating communist influence, Killen resigned, as did several members of his staff.

Nonetheless, AFL and CIO leaders cooperated with occupation officials in 1949 and 1950 in encouraging the development of an anticommunist labor federation in Japan called Sohyo, which they hoped would affiliate with the International Confederation of Free Trade Unions. But much to the chagrin of AFL and CIO leaders, Sohyo did not affiliate with the ICFTU en bloc but instead allowed individual unions to choose whether or not to affiliate. Thus, by 1954 only one-third of Japanese union members belonged to organizations that affiliated with the ICFTU. Even more problematic, Sohyo became one of the leading critics of U.S. foreign policy in Asia. Sohyo leaders, for example, persistently criticized the peace and security treaties proposed by the Americans for terminating the Japanese occupation because they did not include Russia and the People's Republic of China and because they did not remove U.S. military bases from Japan. Sohyo leaders also opposed the Korean War. By the spring of 1953, the AFL's Free Trade Union Committee had concluded that Sohyo was a puppet of the Kremlin.

Although its independent positions on foreign policy issues and increasingly militant tactics won it the admiration of many Japanese workers, Sohyo nonetheless failed to develop into a sufficiently strong and unified organization to act as a formidable counterweight to the power of Japan's large Zaibatsu corporations. Enterprise unions, or unions within one company, continued to flourish, helping to cement the loyalty of permanent workers to their companies. Meanwhile, many temporary workers remained without union representation altogether. The fragmented nature of Japan's labor movement undermined Japanese workers' efforts to gain a larger portion of business profits, thereby undermining domestic consumption and propelling the Japanese economy along an export-driven path. Thus, American labor's goals for postwar Japan were largely frustrated.

The AFL and CIO, meanwhile, also became very active in Latin America during the early Cold War. The interest of AFL and CIO leaders in Latin America stemmed not just from their anticommunist animus but from their belief that Latin America was a vital source of raw materials for the United States and an important market for U.S. industrial products. Thus, despite their early differences on Latin American policy, both AFL and CIO leaders supported a plan proposed by Secretary of State William Clayton in 1945 that called on Latin American nations to lower tariff barriers on U.S. goods in return for greater U.S. investment in extractive and agricultural industries. Ronald Radosh has demonstrated that many Latin American labor leaders, by contrast, opposed the plan, which they argued would result in "uncontrolled foreign capital investment in Latin America [which] will cause the deterioration of programs which look to the industrialization of the countries of Latin America, aggravating their great dependence on one crop culture and exports." AFL and CIO leaders believed that communist labor leaders posed a particular threat to American economic expansion and in 1951 developed a Latin-American affiliate of the ICFTU known as the Inter-American Regional Workers' Organization (ORIT). This organization was designed to promote anticommunism within the labor force of Latin America and to undermine support for the communist-led Confederation of Latin American Unions.

The AFL and ORIT became particularly involved in Honduras and Guatemala during the early 1950s. The U.S.-based company United Fruit played a dominant role in the economies of both countries. When impoverished Honduran workers struck United Fruit in 1954, demanding a 50 percent wage increase, the AFL and ORIT intervened. According to a Senate study cited by Al Weinrub, they soon "gained the leadership of the strike." AFL President George Meany encouraged mediation by the State Department and the company quickly chose to settle. Honduran labor activists complained: "After the strike, the AFL-CIO, the U.S. Embassy and ORIT" descended upon them "like a plague," gaining them special favors with employers in return for embracing AFL principles of collective bargaining. Meanwhile, left-leaning Jacobo Arbenz Guzman was elected president of Guatemala in 1950 and began a process of land reform that involved expropriating hundreds of thousands of acres of unused United Fruit Company land. Arbenz also enacted a generous labor code that gave trade unions unprecedented rights. Yet AFL President Meany protested the Guatemalan leader's toleration of communists in the labor movement and the AFL and ORIT tried to establish a rival free trade union confederation in Guatemala. Arbenz's government, however, arrested or deported many of the leaders of the new organization.

Following a private conference between Central Intelligence Agency Director Allen Dulles and Meany, the AFL president announced that U.S. labor supported a plan to come to a showdown with communists in Guatemala. In June 1954 an invasion force that included members of the free trade union confederation created by the AFL and ORIT crossed the border from Honduras

and toppled the Arbenz government. As subsequent scholars would reveal, the coup was financed and carried out under the direction of the Central Intelligence Agency. The AFL immediately hailed the coup as a victory for democracy. By contrast, some CIO leaders initially opposed the coup, suggesting that communist penetration in Latin America had been greatly exaggerated and that State Department policy was really driven by its desire to give aid to the United Fruit Company. After Carlos Castillo Armas took power in Guatemala, AFL, CIO, and ORIT members traveled to Guatemala to reorganize the labor movement along anticommunist lines. Yet his government proved quite hostile to labor and thousands of unions were dissolved by the military regime. Union membership plummeted and Guatemalan workers remained impoverished. The Armas government, however, satisfied the U.S. government and corporate interests by returning expropriated United Fruit land. Activities like these helped to discredit ORIT. As the U.S. Senate conceded, "To many Latin Americans . . . ORIT is an instrument of the U.S. State Department."

The AFL and CIO merged in 1955, and during the 1960s, to overcome its increasingly bankrupt image in Latin America and other underdeveloped regions, the AFL-CIO created three new labor centers: the American Institute for Free Labor Development (Latin America), the African-American Labor Center, and the Asian-American Free Labor Institute. The organizations' goals were to provide education and training for trade unionists from underdeveloped countries. Yet some charged that paternalistic assumptions permeated the centers' educational programs. As Nathan Godfried writes, American labor leaders active in the centers tended to assume a stage theory of trade union development comparable to the stages of economic development posited by Western economic theorists for developing countries. Trade union movements in the Third World were allegedly in a "primitive" stage of development and thus were preoccupied with unrealistic political and radical agendas. By contrast, mature unions from the developed world focused on plausible economic goals that could be obtained through peaceful collective bargaining. Thus, Everett Kassalow, director of the AFL-CIO's Industrial Union Department, argued that American labor-education efforts would enable unions in the Third World to skip "long years of struggle which molded Western union leadership and membership." But critics from Africa, Asia, and

Latin America countered that U.S. models were often unsuitable for conditions existing in other areas of the world.

More troubling than criticisms of the content of the centers' educational programs were charges that the institutes worked with the Central Intelligence Agency and other U.S. government operatives to undermine democratically elected but left-leaning governments in Third World areas. The American Institute for Free Labor Development, in particular, was implicated in U.S. efforts to undermine the governments of Joao Goulart in Brazil in 1964 and of Salvador Allende in Chile in 1973. In both cases, the institute channeled money to conservative union groups that staged disruptive protests and strikes designed to paralyze their governments. Both Goulart and Allende were eventually overthrown in military coups supported by the United States. Former CIA agents such as Philip Agee subsequently disclosed that the institute was riddled with CIA operatives during these years and was a conduit for the agency. In contrast to the early Cold War period, the institute's activities provoked dissension within the U.S. labor movement as critics like Victor Reuther of the United Auto Workers concluded that it represented "an exercise in trade union colonialism." By the 1980s many grassroots labor councils had also emerged to oppose U.S. policy in Central America and to criticize the AFL-CIO's collaboration in these policies. The African-American Labor Center and Asian-American Labor Center operated in greater obscurity, but they too faced increasing criticism for allegedly collaborating with the CIA and other government agencies to promote U.S. Cold War objectives.

The Vietnam War also provoked opposition to the AFL-CIO's international agenda during the 1960s and 1970s. George Meany, president of the organization during these years of turmoil, unstintingly supported the policies of the Lyndon Johnson administration, as did the regular yearly conventions of the AFL-CIO. The executive council, in defending the AFL-CIO's hawkish position on the war, argued that to undermine support for U.S. military forces in Vietnam would be aiding the "communist enemy." Newscasts left an indelible imprint on the American memory by featuring demonstrations of "hard hat unionists" supporting the war and sometimes attacking antiwar demonstrators. Yet opposition to the war within the labor movement began to build from at least 1967, when a National Labor Leadership Assembly for Peace met in Chicago. Chapters of the assembly spread to at least fifteen cities. Following the bombing of Cambodia, United Auto Workers President Walter Reuther condemned the widening of the war, as did a host of other labor unions and local and regional labor bodies. The dissenters ultimately failed to alter the prowar policies of the AFL-CIO, but they set the stage for revival of debate within the labor movement over the proper direction of the AFL's international policies in an increasingly global economy.

LABOR AND THE GLOBAL ECONOMY IN THE LATE TWENTIETH CENTURY

Confronted with economic stagnation in the 1970s and 1980s, many labor activists began to question not only the morality of the AFL-CIO's Cold War policies but also whether they protected the economic interests of American workers. Undergirding the AFL-CIO's international agenda during the early Cold War lay the assumptions that a freer international marketplace would enable American capitalism to flourish and that some of the profits would trickle down to U.S. workers. Yet as industrial products from other countries—such as Japanese cars—flooded U.S. markets, many American workers faced layoffs and concessions and began to question whether a freer marketplace was really in their best interest. Thus, activists from the United Auto Workers launched a "Buy American" campaign and staged demonstrations at which they bashed Japanese cars with sledgehammers to demonstrate their point. UAW leaders sought to discourage the racism that surfaced in these campaigns but nonetheless jumped on the bandwagon of economic nationalism by promoting domestic content legislation. Such legislation took into account the global assembly line, recognizing that even cars bearing an American logo were often partly or wholly produced abroad, while some foreign companies had plants in the United States. The solution, believed UAW leaders, was to legislatively mandate that most cars sold in the United States have a 25 percent U.S. domestic content. Faced with widespread discontent among constituent unions, even the national leadership of the AFL-CIO began—in seeming contradiction to its earlier Cold War advocacy of a freer marketplace—to promote protectionist legislation.

Other labor activists, however, eschewed economic nationalism and believed that globalization instead called for a new kind of labor internationalism. The reform initiatives of these activists were given momentum by the fall of communism in the former Soviet Union and Eastern Europe.

With no Cold War to give legitimacy to their policies, Lane Kirkland and his advisers within the AFL-CIO increasingly found it difficult to defend the organization's international strategies. The AFL-CIO hierarchy temporarily joined hands with reformers in 1992 and opposed the North American Free Trade Agreement. But as union membership continued to plummet and U.S. workers continued to feel themselves at the mercy of globalization, reformers gained ascendency within the AFL-CIO and in 1995 elected as president John Sweeney of the Service Employees International Union.

Sweeney revamped the AFL-CIO's foreign policy apparatus, shutting down many of its existing overseas operations—including the CIA-linked American Institute for Free Labor Development. In its place the new American Center for International Labor Solidarity was created. The AFL-CIO's International Affairs Department was placed under the direction of the reformer Barbara Shailor of the International Association of Machinists, an experienced transnational strategist in labor solidarity. Many credited the AFL-CIO's new foreign policy team with helping to defeat the Clinton administration's efforts to gain congressional ratification for special presidential authority to "fast-track" North American trade agreements in 1997.

Also propelling the U.S. labor movement along a new international track in the 1980s and 1990s were individual AFL-CIO unions that initiated negotiations and forged ties with Canadian and Latin American unions representing workers in comparable industries. The case of the United Mine Workers of America is one of the most striking. When the Exxon Corporation closed a coal mine in West Virginia in 1983 and instead invested in one in El Cerrejon, Colombia, the United Mine Workers eschewed economic nationalism and chose to help the Colombian miners union, SINTERCOR, in its fight for better wages for Colombia miners. Perhaps most notably, the United Mine Workers filed a protest in the early 1990s under the Generalized System of Preferences, a U.S. tariff system, which charged Exxon with violating internationally recognized workers' rights. It also joined the International Metalworkers Federation in publicizing the plight of Colombian miners throughout the world. Significantly, SINTERCOR won substantial wage increases for Colombian miners in 1992 and 1993

without resorting to a strike. The United Mine Workers president, Richard Trumka, defended his union's activities on behalf of Colombian miners by arguing that if the American labor movement did not help strengthen unions and improve working conditions in low-wage countries, then "the multinational corporations will attempt to lower our standards to the lowest international common denominator."

Trumka's arguments suggested that the American labor movement had come full circle in its approach to international affairs. During its earliest years, the AFL-CIO had tried to foster international labor cooperation in an effort to gain some influence for workers over global economic and political developments. Yet for most of the twentieth century, the AFL, and later the AFL-CIO, seemed to place greater priority on promoting national economic expansion and U.S. foreign policy goals than on fostering international labor solidarity through international labor organizations. The dangers of the AFL-CIO's nationalist approach became particularly apparent during the Cold War, when AFL leaders engineered the destruction of the World Federation of Trade Unions and often joined government officials, U.S. businesspersons, and CIA operatives in undermining left-leaning and communist labor movements and governments abroad. Such activities often had the long-term effect of weakening foreign labor movements and helping create low-wage economies that invited capital flight and encouraged a loss of U.S. jobs. As the twenty-first century dawned, however, many labor activists seemed reawakened to the need to continue the task of building a strong international labor movement that European workers had begun early in the nineteenth century.

BIBLIOGRAPHY

Andrews, Gregg. *Shoulder to Shoulder? The American Federation of Labor, the United States, and the Mexican Revolution, 1910–1924.* Berkeley, Calif., 1991. The best account of U.S.–Mexican labor relations in the early twentieth century.

Babcock, Robert H. *Gompers in Canada: A Study in American Continentalism Before the First World War.* Toronto and Buffalo, N.Y., 1974.

Barrett, James R. *Work and Community in the Jungle: Chicago's Packinghouse Workers, 1894–1922.* Urbana, Ill., 1987.

Berger, Henry W. "Union Diplomacy: American Labor's Foreign Policy in Latin America, 1932–1955." Ph.D. diss. University of Wisconsin, Madison, Wis., 1966.

Brundage, David. "Denver's New Departure: Irish Nationalism and the Labor Movement in the Gilded Age." *Southwest Economy and Society* 5 (winter 1981): 10–23.

———. "Knights of Labor." In Mari Jo Buhle, Paul Buhle, and Dan Georgakas, eds. *Encyclopedia of the American Left.* 2d ed. New York, 1998.

Buhle, Paul. *From the Knights of Labor to the New World Order: Essays on Labor and Culture.* New York, 1997.

Busch, Gary K. *The Political Role of International Trades Unions.* New York and London, 1983.

DeConde, Alexander. *Ethnicity, Race, and American Foreign Policy: A History.* Boston, 1992.

Eisenberg, Carolyn. "Working-Class Politics and the Cold War: American Intervention in the German Labor Movement, 1945–1949." *Diplomatic History* 7 (fall 1983): 283–306.

Filippelli, Ronald L. *American Labor and Postwar Italy, 1943–1953: A Study of Cold War Politics.* Stanford, Calif., 1989.

Fink, Leon. *Workingmen's Democracy: The Knights of Labor and American Politics.* Urbana, Ill., 1983.

Frank, Dana. *Buy American: The Untold Story of Economic Nationalism.* Boston, 1999. A fascinating study of impulses toward economic nationalism within American society from the Revolution to the present.

Foner, Eric. "Class, Ethnicity, and Radicalism in the Gilded Age: The Land League and Irish-America." *Marxist Perspectives* 1 (summer 1978): 6–55. A pathbreaking article on the linkages between ethnicity, class, and international attitudes.

Foner, Philip S. *U.S. Labor and the Vietnam War.* New York, 1989.

Godfried, Nathan. "Spreading American Corporatism: Trade Union Education for Third World Labour." *Review of African Political Economy* 39 (September 1987): 51–63. An insightful article exploring the activities of the African-American Labor Center.

Gompers, Samuel. *Seventy Years of Life and Labor: An Autobiography.* New York, 1925.

Gordon, Jerry. *Cleveland Labor and the Vietnam War.* Cleveland, Ohio, 1990.

Grubbs, Frank L., Jr. *The Struggle for Labor Loyalty: Gompers, the A.F. of L., and the Pacifists, 1917–1920.* Durham, N.C., 1968.

Larson, Simeon. *Labor and Foreign Policy: Gompers, the AFL, and the First World War, 1914–1918.* London and Rutherford, N.J., 1975.

Levenstein, Harvey. *Labor Organizations in the United States and Mexico: A History of Their Relations.* Westport, Conn., 1971.

Lichtenstein, Nelson. *Labor's War at Home: The CIO in World War II.* New York, 1982.

Lorwin, Lewis Levitski. *The International Labor Movement: History, Politics, Outlook.* New York, 1953. One of the few books that covers U.S. labor groups and their involvement in early international labor activities.

McKee, Delber Lee. "The American Federation of Labor and American Foreign Policy, 1886–1912." Ph.D. diss. Stanford University. Stanford, Calif., 1952.

McKillen, Elizabeth. *Chicago Labor and the Quest for a Democratic Diplomacy, 1914–1924.* Ithaca, N.Y., 1995.

———. "Ethnicity, Class, and Wilsonian Internationalism Reconsidered: The Mexican-American and Irish-American Immigrant Left and U.S. Foreign Relations, 1914–1922." *Diplomatic History* 25 (fall 2001): 553–587.

McShane, Denis. *International Labour and the Origins of the Cold War.* New York, 1992.

Moody, Kim. *Workers in a Lean World: Unions in the International Economy.* London and New York, 1997.

Nelson, Bruce. *Workers on the Waterfront: Seamen, Longshoremen, and Unionism in the 1930s.* Urbana, Ill., 1988. Examines the international orientation of maritime workers in addition to domestic issues.

Radosh, Ronald. *American Labor and United States Foreign Policy.* New York, 1969.

Roberts, John W. *Putting Foreign Policy to Work: The Role of Organized Labor in American Foreign Relations, 1932–1941.* New York, 1995.

Romero, Frederico. *The United States and the European Trade Union Movement, 1944–1951.* 2d ed. Translated by Harvey Fergusson. Chapel Hill, N.C., 1992.

Schonberger, Howard B. *Aftermath of War: Americans and the Remaking of Japan, 1945–1952.* Kent, Ohio, 1989. Includes an excellent chapter on U.S. labor's participation in the occupation of Japan.

Silverman, Victor. *Imagining Internationalism in American and British Labor, 1939–1949.* Urbana, Ill., 2000. A fresh approach to the history of labor internationalism in the postwar era that includes much fascinating material on working-class attitudes toward international issues in Britain and the United States.

Sims, Beth. *Workers of the World Undermined: American Labor's Role in U.S. Foreign Policy.* Boston, 1992.

Snow, Sinclair. *The Pan-American Federation of Labor.* Durham, N.C., 1964.

Voss, Kim. *The Making of American Exceptionalism: The Knights of Labor and Class Formation in the Nineteenth Century.* Ithaca, N.Y., 1993.

Weiler, Peter. "The United States, International Labor, and the Cold War: The Breakup of the World Federation of Trade Unions." *Diplomatic History* 5 (winter 1981): 1–22.

Weinrub, Al, and William Bollinger. *The AFL-CIO in Central America.* Oakland, Calif., 1987.

See also ECONOMIC POLICY AND THEORY; INTERNATIONALISM; MULTINATIONAL CORPORATIONS; RACE AND ETHNICITY; TARIFF POLICY; WILSONIANISM.

OUTER SPACE

Roger Launius

For years the issue of international competition and cooperation in space has dominated much space exploration policy. Indeed, it is impossible to write the history of spaceflight without discussing these themes in detail. The early U.S. space exploration program was dominated by international rivalry and world prestige, and international relations have remained a powerful shaper of the program since. From the time of the creation of the National Aeronautics and Space Administration (NASA), all of its human spaceflight projects—the Apollo program, the space shuttle, and the space station—have been guided in significant part by foreign relations considerations.

In the 1950s and 1960s the United States and the Soviet Union were locked in the "Moon race," an intensely competitive Cold War struggle in which each sought to outdo the other. No cost seemed too high; no opportunity to best the rival seemed too slight. U.S. astronauts planted the American flag on the surface of the Moon when the great moment came in 1969. The irony of planting that flag, coupled with the statement that "we came in peace for all mankind," was not lost on the leaders of the Soviet Union, who realized that they were not considered a part of "all mankind" in this context.

THE FREEDOM OF SPACE DOCTRINE

From before the beginning of the space age, U.S. leaders sought to ensure the rights of free passage of spacecraft anywhere in the world. In a critical document, "Meeting the Threat of Surprise Attack," issued on 14 February 1955, a group of academics, industrialists, and the military, working at the request of President Dwight D. Eisenhower, raised the question of the international law of territorial waters and airspace, in which individual nations controlled those territories as if they were their own soil. That international cus-

tom allowed nations to board and confiscate vessels within territorial waters near their coastlines and to force down aircraft flying in their territorial airspace. But outer space was a territory not yet defined, and the United States called for it to be recognized as free territory not subject to the normal confines of territorial limits.

"Freedom of space" was extremely significant to those concerned with orbiting satellites, because the imposition of territorial prerogatives outside the atmosphere could legally restrict any nation from orbiting satellites without the permission of those nations that might be overflown. U.S. leaders thought that the Soviet Union might clamor for a closed-access position if the United States was the first to orbit a satellite. President Dwight D. Eisenhower, committed as he was to development of an orbital reconnaissance capability to spy on the Soviet Union as a national defense initiative, worked to ensure that no international bans on satellite overflights occurred.

Eisenhower tried to obtain a "freedom of space" decision on 21 July 1955 when he attended a summit conference in Geneva, Switzerland. The absence of trust among states and the presence of "terrible weapons," he argued, provoked throughout the world "fears and dangers of surprise attack." He proposed a joint agreement "for aerial photography of the other country," adding that the United States and the Soviet Union had the capacity to lead the world with mutually supervised reconnaissance overflights. The Soviets promptly rejected the proposal, saying that it was an obvious American attempt to "accumulate target information."

Eisenhower bided his time and approved the development of reconnaissance satellites under the strictest security considerations. Virtually no one, even those in high national defense positions, knew of this effort. The WS-117L program was the prototype reconnaissance satellite effort of the United States. Built by Lockheed's Missile Systems

Division in Sunnyvale, California, the project featured the development of a two-stage booster known as the Agena and a highly maneuverable satellite that took photographs with a wide array of natural, infrared, and other invisible light cameras. This early military space effort, while a closely guarded secret for years, proved critical to the later development of the overall U.S. space program.

The Soviets proved singularly inhospitable to Eisenhower's entreaties for "freedom of space," but that changed in a rather ironic way on 4 October 1957 when *Sputnik 1* was launched and ushered in the space age. Since the Soviet Union was the first nation to orbit a satellite, flying as it did over a multitude of nations, including the United States, it established the precedent of "freedom of space." It overflew international boundaries numerous times without provoking a single diplomatic protest. On 8 October 1957, knowing the president's concern over the legality of reconnaissance satellites flying over the Soviet Union, Deputy Secretary of Defense Donald Quarles told the president: "The Russians have . . . done us a good turn, unintentionally, in establishing the concept of freedom of international space." Eisenhower immediately grasped this as a means of pressing ahead with the launching of a reconnaissance satellite. The precedent held for *Explorer 1* and *Vanguard 1,* and the end of 1958 saw established the tenuous principle of "freedom of space."

LAUNCHING NASA

Sputnik kicked off an intensely competitive space race in which the two superpowers sought to outdo each other for the world's accolades. At a fundamental level a primary reason for NASA's emergence was because of U.S. rivalry during the Cold War with the Soviet Union—a broad contest over the ideologies and allegiances of the nonaligned nations of the world in which space exploration emerged as a major area of contest. From the latter 1940s the Department of Defense had pursued research in rocketry and upper atmospheric sciences as a means of assuring American hegemony. A part of the strategy required not only developing the technology for war, but also pursuing peaceful scientific activities as a means of demonstrating U.S. leadership worldwide. A major step forward came in 1955 when Eisenhower approved a plan to orbit a scientific satellite as part of the International Geophysical Year (IGY) for the period 1 July 1957 to 31 December 1958, a cooperative effort to gather scientific data about the Earth. The Soviet Union quickly followed suit, announcing plans to orbit its own satellite.

The Naval Research Laboratory's Project Vanguard was chosen on 9 September 1955 to support the IGY effort. The Eisenhower administration did so largely because the Vanguard program did not interfere with high-priority ballistic missile development programs—it used the nonmilitary Viking rocket as its basis—while a U.S. Army proposal to use the Redstone ballistic missile as the launch vehicle waited in the wings. The Redstone was being developed by Wernher von Braun and a team of engineers as a response to ballistic missile advances by the Soviet Union and was designed to carry a warhead a distance of two hundred miles on a preplanned trajectory. Project Vanguard enjoyed exceptional publicity throughout the second half of 1955 and all of 1956, but the technological demands upon the program were too great and the funding levels too small to ensure success.

A full-scale crisis resulted when the Soviets launched *Sputnik 1,* the world's first artificial satellite, as its IGY entry. This had a "Pearl Harbor" effect on American public opinion, creating an illusion of a technological gap and providing the impetus for increased spending for aerospace endeavors, technical and scientific educational programs, and the chartering of new federal agencies to manage air and space research and development.

Sputnik led directly to several critical efforts aimed at "catching up" to the Soviet Union's space achievements, among them: (1) a wide-ranging review of the civil and military space programs of the United States (scientific satellite efforts and ballistic missile development); (2) establishment of a presidential science adviser in the White House who had responsibility for overseeing the activities of the federal government in science and technology; (3) creation of the Advanced Research Projects Agency in the Department of Defense and consolidation of several space activities under centralized management; (4) creation of the National Aeronautics and Space Administration to manage civil space operations for the benefit "of all mankind" by means of the National Aeronautics and Space Act of 1958; and (5) passage of the National Defense Education Act of 1958 to provide federal funding for education in scientific and technical disciplines.

More immediately, the United States launched its first Earth satellite on 31 January 1958, when *Explorer 1* documented the existence of radiation zones encircling the Earth. Shaped by the Earth's magnetic field, what came to be called the Van Allen radiation belt partially dictates the electrical charges in the atmosphere and the solar radiation that reaches Earth. The *Explorer 1* launch also began a series of scientific missions to the Moon and planets in the latter 1950s and early 1960s.

As a direct result of this crisis, NASA began operations on 1 October 1958, absorbing the resources of the National Advisory Committee for Aeronautics intact, including its 8,000 employees, an annual budget of $100 million, three major research laboratories—Langley Aeronautical Laboratory, Ames Aeronautical Laboratory, and Lewis Flight Propulsion Laboratory—and two smaller test facilities. NASA quickly incorporated other organizations into the new agency. These included the space science group of the Naval Research Laboratory in Maryland, the Jet Propulsion Laboratory managed by the California Institute of Technology for the U.S. Army, and the Army Ballistic Missile Agency in Huntsville, Alabama. Eventually NASA created several other centers and by the early 1960s had ten located around the country.

NASA began to conduct space missions within months of its creation, and during its first twenty years NASA carried out several major programs:

1. Human space-flight initiatives: Mercury's single astronaut program (flights during 1961 to 1963) to ascertain if a human could survive in space; Project Gemini (flights 1965–1966) with two astronauts to practice space operations, especially rendezvous and docking of spacecraft and extravehicular activity (EVA); and Project Apollo (flights 1968–1972) to explore the Moon.
2. Robotic missions to the Moon (Ranger, Surveyor, and Lunar Orbiter), Venus (*Pioneer Venus*), Mars (*Mariner 4, Viking 1* and *2*), and the outer planets (*Pioneer 10* and *11, Voyager 1* and *2*).
3. Aeronautics research to enhance airplane safety, reliability, efficiency, and speed (X-15 hypersonic flight, lifting body flight research, avionics and electronics studies, propulsion technologies, structures research, aerodynamics investigations).
4. Remote-sensing Earth satellites for information gathering (Landsat satellites for environmental monitoring).
5. Applications satellites for communications (*Echo 1, TIROS,* and *Telstar*) and weather monitoring.
6. *Skylab*, an orbital workshop for astronauts.

In no case were these cooperative ventures with other nations, because the Cold War patina that overlay everything done by NASA during its first thirty years necessitated that the United States demonstrate its unique technological capability vis-à-vis the Soviet Union.

THE LUNAR LANDING PROGRAM

When U.S. astronauts planted the flag on the surface of the Moon in 1969 it signaled the final triumph of the United States over the Soviet Union in the space race, nothing more nor less. Indeed, this singular achievement of Project Apollo during NASA's early years—one that was particularly focused on demonstrating American preeminence as a spacefaring nation to the people of the world—made possible the cooperative ventures that followed.

The effort to land Americans on the Moon came about because of a unique confluence of political necessity, personal commitment and activism, scientific and technological ability, economic prosperity, and public mood. When President John F. Kennedy announced on 25 May 1961 his intention to carry out a lunar landing program before the end of the decade, he did so as a means of demonstrating U.S. technological virtuosity. In so doing Kennedy responded to perceived challenges to U.S. world leadership not only in science and technology but also in political, economic, and especially military capability.

For the next eleven years Project Apollo consumed NASA's every effort. It required significant expenditures, costing $25.4 billion in 1960s dollars over the life of the program to make it a reality. Only the building of the Panama Canal rivaled the Apollo program's size as the largest nonmilitary technological endeavor ever undertaken by the United States; only the Manhattan Project was comparable in a wartime setting.

The first mission to capture public attention was the flight of *Apollo 8*. On 21 December 1968 it took off atop a Saturn V booster from the Kennedy Space Center in Florida. Three astronauts were aboard—Frank Borman, James A. Lovell, Jr., and William A. Anders—for a historic mission to orbit the Moon. After *Apollo 8* made one and a half Earth orbits, its third stage began a burn to put the spacecraft on a lunar trajectory. It orbited the Moon on Christmas Eve and then fired the boosters for a return flight. It splashed down safely in the Pacific Ocean on 27 December. Two more Apollo missions occurred before the climax of the program, but they did little more than confirm that the time had come for a lunar landing.

That landing came during the flight of *Apollo 11,* which lifted off on 16 July 1969 and, after confirmation that the hardware was working well, began the three-day trip to the Moon. Then, on 20 July 1969 the lunar module—with astronauts Neil A. Armstrong and Edwin E. "Buzz" Aldrin aboard—landed on the lunar surface while Michael Collins orbited overhead in the command module. After checkout, Armstrong set foot on the surface, telling millions who saw and heard him on Earth that it was "one small step for [a] man— one giant leap for mankind." Aldrin soon followed him out and the two explored their surroundings and planted an American flag but omitted claiming the land for the United States, as had been routinely done during European exploration of the Americas. They collected soil and rock samples and set up scientific experiments. The next day they rendezvoused with the *Apollo* capsule orbiting overhead and began the return trip to Earth, splashing down in the Pacific Ocean on 24 July.

Five more landing missions followed at approximately six-month intervals through December 1972, each of them increasing the time spent on the Moon. The scientific experiments placed on the Moon and the lunar soil samples returned have provided grist for scientists' investigations ever since. The scientific return was significant, but the program did not answer conclusively the age-old questions of lunar origins and evolution. Three of the latter Apollo missions also used a lunar rover vehicle to travel in the vicinity of the landing site, but despite their significant scientific return none equaled the public excitement of *Apollo 11.*

Even as Project Apollo proceeded, the United States and the Soviet Union—as well as other nations—crafted in 1967 the Treaty on Principles Governing the Activities of States in the Exploration and Use of Outer Space, commonly known as the Outer Space Treaty. Its concepts and some of its provisions were modeled on its predecessor, the Antarctic Treaty. Like that document it sought to prevent "a new form of colonial competition" and the possible damage

that self-seeking exploitation might cause.

After years of discussion this treaty became a possibility on 16 June 1966 when both the United States and the Soviet Union submitted proposals to the United Nations. While there were some differences in the two texts, these were satisfactorily resolved by December 1966 in private consultations during the General Assembly. This allowed the signature of the treaty at Washington, London, and Moscow on 27 January 1967. On 25 April the U.S. Senate gave unanimous consent to its ratification, and the treaty entered into force on 10 October 1967. This treaty has remained in force and both provides for the nonmilitarization of space and directs use of the Moon and other celestial bodies exclusively for peaceful purposes. It expressly prohibits their use for establishing military bases, installations, or fortifications; for testing weapons of any kind; or for conducting military maneuvers. After the treaty entered into force, the United States and the Soviet Union began to collaborate in several joint space enterprises.

TOWARD A TRAJECTORY FOR COOPERATIVE EFFORTS IN THE 1970S

With the successful completion of the Apollo program, everyone realized that the United States was the unquestioned world leader in scientific and technological virtuosity, and continued international competition seemed pointless. President Richard M. Nixon, who took office in January 1969, made it clear that there would be during his leadership no more Apollo-like space efforts. Coupled with this was the desire of those working for a continuation of an aggressive space exploration effort, and the result, predictably, was the search for a new model. While successfully continuing to tie space exploration to foreign relations objectives, now the linkage would be based more on cooperation with allies rather than competition with the nation's Cold War rival. From the 1970s NASA leaders increasingly emphasized visible and exacting international programs. All of the major human space flight efforts, and increasingly as time progressed minor projects, have been identified with international partnerships, particularly with America's European allies.

The European Space Agency was created in 1975 after the space race of the Cold War gave way to worldwide cooperation. Its aims are to provide cooperation in space research and technology. Its ten founding members were France,

Germany, Italy, Spain, the United Kingdom, Belgium, Denmark, the Netherlands, Sweden, and Switzerland. Ireland, Austria, Norway, Finland, and Portugal joined later, and Canada is considered a cooperating state. The agency acts for Europe in a global way by promoting creative interaction and collaboration with other global space agencies, aerospace industries, and civilian space activities. In addition, there is a cooperation of international space law and a practical sharing of resources, research, and personnel.

The Cold War context in which the U.S. civil space program arose in 1958 ensured that foreign policy objectives dominated the nature of the activity. This led to the need for cooperative ventures with U.S. allies. The U.S. Congress said as much in the National Aeronautics and Space Act of 1958, the legislation creating NASA. In this chartering legislation Congress inserted a clause mandating the new space agency to engage in international cooperation with other nations for the betterment of all humankind. This legislation provided authority for international agreements in the broad range of projects essential for the development of space science and technology in a naturally international field. NASA's charter provided the widest possible latitude to the agency in undertaking international activities as the means by which the agreed goal could be reached. The scope of NASA's international program has been fortified since that time by repeated involvement with the United Nations, bilateral and multilateral treaties, and a host of less formal international agreements.

The central question for the United States has always been how best to use space exploration as a meaningful foreign policy instrument. At times an odd assemblage of political, economic, and scientific-technological objectives emerged to guide the development of international programs. The most fundamental of these objectives were the overarching geopolitical considerations, without which there would have been no space exploration program at all, much less a cooperative effort. Cooperative projects in space were thought to create a positive image of the United States in the international setting, an image that in the early years of the space age was related to the greater battle to win the "hearts and minds" of the world to the democratic-capitalistic agenda, and after the Cold War to ensure continued goodwill between the United States and the European community. Such cooperation also was thought to encourage both European unity and

American relations to collective European entities.

Equally important, the United States pursued two overarching economic objectives with its cooperative space efforts. First, cooperative projects expanded the investment for any space project beyond that committed by the United States. (Kenneth S. Pedersen, NASA director of international programs in the early 1980s, opined that "by sharing leadership for exploring the heavens with other qualified spacefaring nations, NASA stretched its own resources and was free to pursue projects which, in the absence of such sharing and cooperation, might not be initiated.") Second, cooperative projects might also help to improve the balance of trade by creating new markets for U.S. aerospace products. Finally, a set of important scientific and technological objectives have motivated U.S. international cooperative efforts in space, including the idea that such efforts enhance the intellectual horsepower applied to any scientific question, thereby increasing the likelihood of reaching fuller understanding in less time. These initiatives also have helped to shape European space projects along lines compatible with American goals, encourage the development of complementary but different experiments from European scientists, and ensure that multiple investigators throughout the international partnership make observations that contribute to a single objective.

In light of these macro-national priorities, NASA has always wrestled with how best to implement the broad international prospects mandated in legislation and polity in line with its own specific history and goals. NASA leadership developed very early, and it remained in place until an international partnership was required to build the International Space Station (ISS) in the early 1990s. As a result of that history, a set of essential features have guided the agency's international arrangements with European partners, among them, that cooperation is undertaken on a project-by-project basis, not on an ongoing basis for a specific discipline or general effort; that each cooperative project must be both mutually beneficial and scientifically valid; that scientific-technical agreement must precede any political commitment; that funds transfers will not take place between partners, but each will be responsible for its own contribution to the project; that all partners will carry out their part of the project without technical or managerial expertise provided by the other; and that scientific data will be made available to researchers of all nations involved in the project for early analysis.

From the NASA leadership's point of view, moreover, cooperative projects offered two very significant advantages in the national political arena. First, at least by the time of the lunar landings, the leadership recognized that every international partnership brought greater legitimacy to the overall project. This important fact was not lost on NASA Administrator Thomas O. Paine in 1970, for instance, when he was seeking outside sponsorship of the space shuttle program and negotiating international agreements for parts of the effort. Second, although far from being a coldly calculating move, agreements with foreign nations could also help to insulate space projects from drastic budgetary and political changes. American politics, which are notoriously rambunctious and shortsighted, are also enormously pragmatic. Dealing with what might be a serious international incident resulting from some technological program change is something neither U.S. diplomats nor politicians relish, and that fact could be the difference between letting the project continue as previously agreed or to dicker over it in Congress and thereby change funding, schedule, or other factors in response to short-term political or budgetary needs. The international partners, then, could be a stabilizing factor for any space project, in essence a bulwark to weather difficult domestic storms.

Perhaps the physicist Fritjof Capra's representative definition of a social paradigm is appropriate when considering the requirements for space projects in the United States in the aftermath of the Apollo Moon landings. While Apollo was seen as an enormous success from a geopolitical and technological standpoint, NASA had to contend with a new set of domestic political realities for its projects thereafter, and a radical alteration had taken place in what Capra described as the "constellation of concepts, values, perceptions and practices shared by a community, which forms a particular vision of reality that is the basis of the way the community organizes itself." International cooperative projects helped NASA cope with that changing social paradigm.

IMPEDIMENTS TO INTERNATIONAL COOPERATION IN SPACE

At the same time that critical objectives at both the national and agency levels might be achieved through cooperative space projects both individually and collectively, there were genuine and not inconsiderable impediments to undertaking international programs. The most important was that NASA would lose some of its authority to execute the cooperative program as it saw fit. Throughout its history the space agency had never been very willing to deal with partners, either domestic or international, as equals. It tended to see them more as hindrance than help, especially when they might get in the way of the "critical path" toward any technological goal. R. Buckminster Fuller in his 1982 book *Critical Path* discussed the evolution of technology involving project scheduling and resource allocation. Assigning an essentially equal-partnership responsibility for the development of some critical system or instrument meant giving up the power to make changes, dictate solutions, and control schedules and other factors. Partnership, furthermore, was not a synonym for contractor management— something agency leaders understood very well— and NASA was not very accepting of full partners unless they were essentially silent or at least deferential. Such an attitude mitigated against significant international cooperation in space efforts, and difficulties arose whenever any project was undertaken.

In addition to this concern, some technologists at NASA, but even more so at the U.S. Department of State, expressed fears that bringing foreign nations into any significant space project really meant giving those nations technical knowledge that only the United States held. Only a few nations were spacefaring at all, and only a subset of those had launch capabilities. Many American leaders voiced reservations about the advisability of ending technological monopolies. The prevention of technology transfer in the international arena was an especially important issue to be considered.

NASA officials understood that European space leaders were aware of these issues and that the latter understandably took a guarded approach toward dealing with American overtures in space. They also believed that this watch-and-wait attitude was not solely due to the United States, although it may have been the deciding factor, but also related to the unique difficulties of European space activities. Senior NASA officials were also convinced that the history of European involvement in space had been marked by difficulties in obtaining long-term commitments to specific programs in which participating nations had a reasonable part. And long-term, highly focused projects required centralized management capable of enforcing order on a diverse set of interests. Americans recognized that NASA had its own difficulties on this score, but with national and language barriers added in, the demands were daunting. Finally, the costs of involvement in such endeavors with the United States were not inconsiderable. The financial, organizational, and political issues of European space activity had long been understood by leaders in the field, but they had not been fully resolved. Unfortunately, NASA's efforts have long been insufficient to fully resolve them.

THE RECORD OF INTERNATIONAL COOPERATION IN SPACE

From its inception in 1958 to 2000, NASA concluded nearly 2,000 cooperative agreements with other nations for the conduct of international space projects. While most of these were bilateral in focus—such as the very first, which led to the Alouette mission with Canada in 1962—some, and increasingly so, have been multinational efforts. These agreements resulted in 139 cooperative science projects with European nations between 1962 and 1997: 29 in the earth sciences, 23 in microgravity and life sciences, and 87 in space sciences.

When this development is explored over time there are some interesting trends. First, there were small numbers of projects in the 1960s—something to be expected—but they began to rise precipitously during the late 1960s and peak in the first third of the 1970s. This coincided with the downturn in the NASA budget from a high in 1965 to a low in 1973. In the 1980s and 1990s this trend also accelerated in relation to the political realities of the era.

Is there a correlation between the demise of the NASA budget and increased international cooperative ventures with other nations? Probably, but it is also related to the emphasis on détente and international relations of the Nixon administration in the late 1960s through mid-1970s. This seemed to collapse in the early 1980s, perhaps in relation to the rise of the NASA budget during the Reagan buildup and the renewal of Cold War hostilities. If this is a correct analysis, one would expect the number of cooperative efforts to rise in response to the drastic cuts in the NASA budget undertaken by the Clinton adminis-

tration in the 1990s. Such was indeed the case, but more in relation to the former Soviet Union than with international partners.

THE INTERNATIONAL SPACE STATION

In 1984, as part of its interest in reinvigorating the space program, the Reagan administration called for the development of a space station. In a "Kennedyesque" moment, Reagan declared in his 1984 State of the Union address that "America has always been greatest when we dared to be great. We can reach for greatness again. We can follow our dreams to distant stars, living and working in space for peaceful, economic, and scientific gain. Tonight I am directing NASA to develop a permanently manned space station and to do it within a decade."

The dream of a space station had been omnipresent within NASA since the 1950s, when a station had been envisioned as a necessary outpost in the new frontier of space. The station, however, had been forced to the bottom of the priorities heap in the 1960s and 1970s as NASA raced to the Moon and then went on to build the space shuttle. When the shuttle first flew in April 1981, the space station reemerged as the priority in human space flight. Within three years space policymakers had persuaded Reagan of its importance, and NASA began work on it in earnest.

From the outset both the Reagan administration and NASA intended space station *Freedom* to be an international program. Although a range of international cooperative activities had been carried out in the past, the station offered an opportunity for a truly integrated effort. The inclusion of international partners, many with rapidly developing spaceflight capabilities, could enhance the effort. In addition, every partnership brought greater legitimacy to the overall program and might help insulate it from drastic budgetary and political changes. Inciting an international incident because of a change to the station was something neither U.S. diplomats nor politicians relished, and that fact, it was thought, could help stabilize funding, schedule, or other factors that might otherwise be changed in response to short-term political needs.

NASA officials pressed forward with international agreements among thirteen nations to take part in the space station *Freedom* program. Japan, Canada, and the nations pooling their resources in the European Space Agency agreed in the spring of 1985 to participate. Canada, for instance, decided to build a remote servicing system. The European Space Agency agreed to build an attached pressurized science module and an astronaut-tended free-flyer, a vehicle to transport an astronaut and equipment away from a spacecraft. Japan's contribution was the development and commercial use of an experiment module for materials processing, life sciences, and technology development. These separate components, with their "plug-in" capacity, eased somewhat the overall management (and congressional) concerns about unwanted technology transfer.

Almost from the outset, the space station program was controversial. Most of the debate centered on its costs versus its benefits. One NASA official remembered that "I reached the scream level at about $9 billion," referring to how much U.S. politicians appeared willing to spend on the station. To stay within budget, NASA pared away at station capabilities, in the process eliminating functions that some of its constituencies wanted. This led to a rebellion among some former supporters. For instance, the space science community began complaining that the space station configuration under development did not provide sufficient experimental opportunity. Thomas M. Donahue, an atmospheric scientist from the University of Michigan and chair of the National Academy of Science's Space Science Board, commented in the mid-1980s that he thought the government should be honest about the goals of the station, and "if the decision to build a space station is political and social, we have no problem with that . . . but don't call it a scientific program."

Because of the cost challenges, redesigns of space station *Freedom* followed in 1990, 1991, 1992, and 1993. Each time, the project got smaller, less capable of accomplishing the broad projects envisioned for it, less costly, and more controversial. As costs were reduced, capabilities also had to diminish, and increasingly political leaders who once supported the program questioned its viability. It was a seemingly endless circle, and some leaders suggested that the United States, the international partners, and the overall space exploration effort would be better off if the space station program were terminated.

In the latter 1980s and early 1990s a parade of space station managers and NASA administrators, each of them honest in their attempts to rescue the program, wrestled with *Freedom* and lost. They faced on one side politicians who demanded

that the jobs aspect of the project—itself a major cause of the overall cost growth—be maintained, with station users on the other demanding that *Freedom's* capabilities be maintained, and with people on all sides demanding that costs be reduced. The incompatibility of these various demands ensured that station program management was a task not without difficulties.

Just as the Cold War was the driving force behind big NASA budgets in the 1960s, its end was a critical component in the search for a new space policy in the 1990s. Cold War rivalries no longer held real attraction as a selling point for an aggressive space exploration program at least by the mid-1980s. Accordingly, when he became NASA administrator in 1992, Daniel S. Goldin worked to salvage the space station effort with a total redesign that brought the significant space capabilities of the former Soviet Union into the effort. The demise of the Cold War, and the collapse of the Soviet Union, created a dramatically changed international situation that allowed NASA to negotiate a landmark decision to include Russia in the building of an international space station. On 7 November 1993 the United States and Russia agreed to work together with the other international partners to build an International Space Station for the benefit of all.

This strikingly new spin on international relations regalvanized support for the program, and for the next eight years building the ISS dominated the efforts of all the spacefaring nations. In the post–Cold War era this decision provided an important linkage for the continuation of the space station at a time when many were convinced that for other reasons—cost, technological challenge, return on investment—it was an uninviting endeavor.

As a lead-in to the ISS, twenty years after the world's two greatest spacefaring nations and Cold War rivals staged a dramatic docking in the Apollo-Soyuz Test Project during the summer of 1975, the space programs of the United States and Russia again met in Earth orbit when the space shuttle *Atlantis* docked to the aging Russian *Mir* space station in June-July 1995. "This flight heralds a new era of friendship and cooperation between our two countries," said NASA's Goldin. "It will lay the foundation for construction of an International Space Station later this decade."

The docking missions conducted through 1998 represented a major alteration in the history of space exploration. They also portended considerable controversy. For example, several accidents took place aboard the aging Russian space station that called into question the validity of American involvement in a Russian program that might compromise the safety of American astronauts aboard. Mishaps on *Mir* in 1996–1998 included a fire inside the station, failure of an oxygen generator, leaks in the cooling system, a docking accident that damaged both the station and the spacecraft to be docked to it, and the temporary malfunction of an attitude control system.

These accidents triggered criticism of U.S.–Russian cooperation in the shuttle-*Mir* program. That criticism emphasized the safety of the astronauts and the aging character of *Mir*, noting it was in such bad shape that no meaningful scientific results could be achieved aboard the station. Most asked that Russia deorbit *Mir* and thereby bring it to "an honorable end," something that finally took place in the spring of 2001. Only with the launch of the first elements of the International Space Station in the autumn of 1998 did public criticism subside on the role of the shuttle-*Mir* missions in the American space program.

Other questions about the International Space Station program, however, did not subside even with first-element launches in 1998. In addition to schedule and budget concerns, many complained about the integral part played by Russia in building the International Space Station. Most observers agreed that the fundamental problems associated with Russian participation in the space station program could be reduced to a few fine points, as stated by Representative F. James Sensenbrenner, Jr., chair of the House Committee on Science, in 1998: "One, the Russians failed to follow through on their funding commitments, and two, the Clinton administration brought the Russians into the project for the wrong reasons, placed the Russians in the critical path, and routinely let them off the hook for their failures."

Some warned of complications with Russian involvement as early as September 1993, when President Clinton formally invited the Russian government to join the project, ostensibly as a gesture of goodwill to the former Cold War enemy. In reality, the invitation to the Russians involved gaining Russian compliance with the Missile Technology Control Regime, a voluntary arrangement among twenty-seven countries to control the export of weapons of mass destruction. The Clinton administration admitted as much to Congress on 20 April 1994, when the U.S. ambassador to Russia James Collins was asked by Representative Ralph M. Hall, "Give me a 1 to 10 on whether or not we are building the space station with Russia to achieve a particular foreign policy objective such as Russian compliance with the Missile Technology Control Regime." Ambassador Collins replied, "Getting Russia into the Missile Technology Control Regime and bringing it into willingness to comply with those guidelines is a very important objective." This proved unsuccessful, however, as the Russian Space Agency continued selling missile technology to so-called rogue nations. According to Sensenbrenner, American "nonproliferation goals for cooperating with the Russians in the civil space area have not been realized."

Even more than this, the Russians were integrated deeply into the critical path of International Space Station assembly. If they failed to deliver their modules on schedule, ISS assembly had to wait, and every slippage on the part of the Russian Space Agency stretched out the overall station schedule. NASA had assumed a position of complete reliance on Russia for the service module—sole provider of oxygen, avionics, reboost, and sanitary facilities—until much later in the assembly process. This meant, in simple terms, that the entire program was held hostage pending resolution of Russia's internal economic and political problems and external goodwill.

With the belated launch of the Russian service module in July 2000, however, it became clear that international competition had been firmly replaced with cooperation as the primary reason behind huge expenditures for space operations. As the dean of space policy analysts John M. Logsdon concluded, "there is little doubt, then, that there will be an international space station, barring major catastrophes like another shuttle accident or the rise to power of a Russian government opposed to cooperation with the West."

While the challenges of completing the ISS remained quite real, as the twenty-first century dawned the dream of a permanent presence in space seemed on the verge of reality. Before the end of 2000 the first ISS crew inhabited the station. Furthermore, the spacefaring nations of the world had accepted ISS as the raison d'être of their space efforts. Only through its successful achievement, space advocates insisted, would a vision of space exploration that includes all nations venturing into the unknown be ultimately realized. This scenario makes eminent sense if one is interested in developing an expansive space exploration effort, one that leads to the permanent colonization of humans on other planets. At the end of the century, that debate continued. What no one was sure of was how this would unfold in the next century.

TWENTY-FIRST-CENTURY ISSUES IN SPACE COOPERATION

In the last decade of the twentieth century U.S. space policy entered an extended period of transition. This was true for several reasons. For one thing, U.S. preeminence in space technology was coming to an end as the European Space Agency developed and made operational its superb Ariane launcher, and the agency's ancillary space capabilities made it increasingly possible for Europe to "go it alone." At the same time, U.S. commitment to sustained leadership in space activities overall waned, and significantly less public monies went into NASA missions. U.S. political commitment to cooperative projects seemingly lessened as well: for example, the United States refrained from developing a probe for the international armada of spacecraft that was launched toward Comet Halley in 1984–1985 and withdrew part of its support from the controversial International Solar Polar Mission to view the Sun from a high altitude, renamed Ulysses and launched in 1990. Of those cooperative projects that remained, NASA increasingly acceded to the demands of international collaborators to develop critical systems and technologies. This overturned the policy of not allowing partners into the critical path—something that had not been accepted in earlier development projects—and was in large measure a pragmatic decision on the part of American officials. Because of the increasing size and complexity of projects, according to Kenneth Pedersen, more recent projects had produced "numerous critical paths whose upkeep costs alone will defeat U.S. efforts to control and supply them." He added, "It seems unrealistic today to believe that other nations possessing advanced technical capabilities and harboring their own economic competitiveness objectives will be amenable to funding and developing only ancillary systems."

In addition to these important developments, in the 1990s the rise of competitive economic activities in space mitigated the prospects for future activities. The brutal competition for launch business, the cutthroat nature of space applications, and the rich possibilities for future space-based economic activities such as asteroid mining were rapidly creating a climate in which international ventures might once again become the exception rather than the rule. John Krige astutely commented in 1997 that "collaboration has worked most smoothly when the science or technology concerned is not of direct strategic (used here to mean commercial or military) importance. As soon as a government feels that its national interests are directly involved in a field of R&D, it would prefer to go it alone." He also noted that the success of cooperative projects may take as their central characteristic that they have "no practical application in at least the short to medium term."

The sole exception to this perspective might be when nations decide that for prestige or diplomatic purposes it is appropriate to cooperate in space. A concern existed that in the United States, where economic competitiveness in space was such a powerful motivation for "going it alone," and where prestige and diplomacy seemed to have taken a backseat to nationalistic hyperbole, that with every passing year there would be less tolerance for large-scale cooperative, and by extension difficult, projects in space. Indeed, there was a constant reduction under way in government spending for space exploration and open discussions of strategies on how to shift the thrust of space flight to the private sector. That would, of necessity, curtail international space exploration activities, with less funding available for scientific space missions, the very missions that are natural candidates for cooperative work. Corporations, that may well provide the greatest share of investment for space flight in the United States in the twenty-first century would be loathe to engage in partnerships in which their technological advantages might be compromised. The proliferation of space technology throughout the world, especially to those nations perceived as rogue states, may well prompt U.S. leaders to clamp down on anything that smacks of technology transfer. (This has already been seen in relation to the supposed satellite technology transferred inadvertently to the People's Republic of China through Hughes Aerospace Corp.) Finally, the disagreeable experiences of such cooperative projects as the International Space Station might sour both national and NASA officials on future endeavors. It is certain, for example, that it will be a long time before anyone in authority in the United States will sign on to an international project of similar complexity.

CONCLUSIONS

One of the key conclusions that we might reach about both the course of international cooperation between the United States and other international partners is that it has been an enormously difficult process. Apropos is a quote from Wernher von Braun, that "we can lick gravity, but sometimes the paperwork is overwhelming." Perhaps the hardest part of spaceflight is not the scientific and technological challenges of operating in an exceptionally foreign and hostile environment but in the down-to-earth environment of rough-and-tumble international and domestic politics. But even so, cooperative space endeavors have been richly rewarding and overwhelmingly useful, from all manner of scientific, technical, social, and political perspectives.

Kenneth Pedersen observed in a public forum in 1983 that "international space cooperation is not a charitable enterprise; countries cooperate because they judge it in their interest to do so." For continued cooperative efforts in space to proceed into the twenty-first century it is imperative that those desiring them define appropriate projects and ensure that enough national leaders judge those projects as being of interest and worthy of making them cooperative. Since the 1960s space-exploration proponents have gained a wealth of experience in how to define, gain approval for, and execute the simplest of cooperative projects. Even those have been conducted only with much trial and considerable force of will. For those involved in space exploration it is imperative that a coordinated approach to project definition, planning, funding, and conduct of future missions be undertaken. Only then will people be able to review the history of international programs and speak with pride about all of their many accomplishments while omitting the huge "but" that must follow in considering all of the difficulties encountered.

BIBLIOGRAPHY

Bonnet, Roger M., and Vittorio Manno. *International Cooperation in Space: The Example of the European Space Agency.* Cambridge, Mass., 1994. A prize-winning study of the philosophy and inner workings of internationally supported space exploration projects.

Bulkeley, Rip. *The Sputnik Crisis and Early United States Space Policy: A Critique of the Historiography of Space.* Bloomington, Ind., 1991. An important discussion of early efforts to develop civil space policy in the aftermath of *Sputnik.* It contains much information relative to the rivalry between the United States and the Soviet Union.

Divine, Robert. *The Sputnik Challenge.* New York, 1993. Contains insights into the space program as promoted by the Eisenhower administration.

European Science Foundation and National Research Council. *U.S.–European Collaboration in Space Science.* Washington, D.C., 1998. An official research report on collaborative issues in space science.

Frutkin, Arnold W. *International Cooperation in Space.* Englewood Cliffs, N.J., 1965. An interesting early discussion of the possibilities and problems of international cooperation written during the height of the Cold War by NASA's head of international relations.

Handberg, Roger, and Joan Johnson-Freese. *The Prestige Trap: A Comparative Study of the U.S., European, and Japanese Space Programs.* Dubuque, Iowa, 1994. An interesting study of the various programs and their development.

Harvey, Brian. *The New Russian Space Programme: From Competition to Collaboration.* Chichester, England, and New York, 1996. A solid history of the development of the Soviet space program through the mid-1980s. It has several chapters on the race to the Moon, describing what information was available before the end of the Cold War.

Harvey, Dodd L., and Linda C. Ciccoritti. *U.S.–Soviet Cooperation in Space.* Miami, Fla. 1974. A detailed exploration of the competition and cooperation in space exploration by the two superpowers of the Cold War era through the détente that led to the joint Apollo-Soyuz Test Project.

Johnson-Freese, Joan. *Changing Patterns of International Cooperation in Space.* Malabar, Fla., 1990. An interesting exploration of the movement from competition to cooperation in space exploration.

Kay, W. D. "Space Policy Redefined: The Reagan Administration and the Commercialization of Space." *Business and Economic History* 27 (fall 1998): 237–247. A reassessment of the space policy of the Reagan administration.

Krige, John. "The Politics of European Collaboration in Space." *Space Times: Magazine of the*

American Astronautical Society 36 (September–October 1997): 4–9. A lucid analysis of the difficult political issues involved in international collaboration in space.

Kuhn, Thomas S. *The Structure of Scientific Revolutions*. Chicago, 1970. A classic analysis of how science changes perspective using the Copernican revolution as a case.

Launius, Roger D. *NASA: A History of the U.S. Civil Space Program*. Malabar, Fla., 2000. A short history of the U.S. civilian space efforts with documents.

Launius, Roger D., John M. Logsdon, and Robert W. Smith, eds. *Reconsidering Sputnik: Forty Years Since the Soviet Satellite*. Amsterdam, 2000. A collection of essays on various aspects of the Sputnik crisis of 1957.

Launius, Roger D., and Howard E. McCurdy, eds. *Spaceflight and the Myth of Presidential Leadership*. Urbana, Ill., 1997. A collection of essays on presidents Eisenhower, Kennedy, Johnson, Nixon, Ford, and Carter with addition discussions of international cooperation and the role of the presidency in shaping space policy.

Logsdon, John M. "The Development of International Space Cooperation." In John M. Logsdon, ed. *Exploring the Unknown: Selected Documents in the History of the U.S. Civil Space Program*. Vol. 2. *External Relationships*. Washington, D.C., 1996. An essential reference work with key documents in space policy and its development.

———. *Together in Orbit: The Origins of International Participation in Space Station Freedom*. Washington, D.C., 1998. An excellent short account of the international coordination for the space station.

McDougall, Walter A. *"The Heavens and the Earth": A Political History of the Space Age*. New York, 1985. A Pulitzer Prize–winning book that analyzes the space race to the Moon in the 1960s.

Pedersen, Kenneth S. "Thoughts on International Space Cooperation and Interests in the Post–Cold War World." *Space Policy* 8 (August 1992): 215–224. A fine discussion of the problems of international collaboration in space.

Shaffer, Stephen M., and Lisa Robock Shaffer. *The Politics of International Cooperation: A Comparison of U.S. Experience in Space and Security*. Denver, Colo., 1980. A political science study of the subject.

See also SCIENCE AND TECHNOLOGY.

PACIFISM

Charles Chatfield

The meaning of "pacifism" was altered in Anglo-American usage during World War I. Before 1914 the word was associated with the general advocacy of peace, a cause that had enlisted leaders among the Western economic and intellectual elite and socialist leadership. In wartime, "pacifism" was used to denote the principled refusal to sanction or participate in war at all. This doctrine was associated with the nonresistance of the early Christian church or the traditional "peace" churches, such as the Mennonites, Quakers, and Brethren. During and after World War I, absolute opposition to war was joined with support for peace and reform programs to produce modern, liberal pacifism. The earlier broad usage is still current in Europe and, to some extent, in the United States; and so the significance of changes in the concept is somewhat lost.

The shift in conceptualization of pacifism early in the twentieth century is the key to its significance for American foreign policy, however. Once this is understood, it is possible to interpret pacifism as simultaneously the core of several modern peace movements and, ironically, a source of factionalism among peace workers; it is also possible to appreciate the contributions of pacifism to the foreign policymaking process.

THE ORIGINS OF MODERN PACIFISM

Pacifism, although absolutely opposed to war, never has been confined to antiwar movements. It has been a way of life for individuals and religious sects, and it has characterized peace organizations founded in the wake of wars. Thus, pacifism contributed to the formation of the first peace groups after the Napoleonic wars, notably the American Peace Society (1828). It was the basis of the Garrisonian New England Non-Resistance Society, founded in 1838 by abolitionists and others dissatisfied with the moderate position of the American

Peace Society, and of the Universal Peace Union, founded in 1866 by Alfred A. Love, following the collapse of peace societies during the Civil War.

The modern conceptualization of pacifism draws upon the doctrinal sacredness of life and abrogation of violence in the Christian religion, strains of philosophical anarchism and socialism, nineteenth-century internationalism, and a religious principle of social responsibility. These were the basic elements that were brought together in the context of World War I.

The oldest element of modern pacifism is the tradition of religious nonresistance that was formed in the first three centuries of the Christian church, under Roman rule. Abandoned for the concept of just war, in fact by the time of Constantine I and in theory Saint Augustine, nonresistance pacifism appeared again with Christian sects in the medieval era. It emerged in the Protestant Reformation, notably under Peter Chelčický and the Unity of the Brethren (Bohemian Brethren) in the fifteenth century and among the Anabaptists. From the sixteenth through the eighteenth centuries, it was institutionalized in the writings and practice of so-called peace churches: the Mennonites, the Quakers, and the Brethren.

Nonresistance characterized the thought of leaders in the early-nineteenth-century peace societies of the United States. It was officially recognized as ground for exemption under the conscription systems of the Civil War and World War I. Many of the Mennonites and Brethren who immigrated to the United States late in the nineteenth century at least partly sought to escape conscription abroad. Traditional nonresistance implied not only the repudiation of violence and warfare but, frequently, dissociation from government, based as it seemed to be on physical force.

In the second half of the nineteenth century, traditional nonresistance was supplemented by anarchism deriving from the religious inspiration of Leo Tolstoy and from those philosophical anarchists who repudiated violence. In addition, some leading European socialists took the position that national wars were instruments of class action that should be boycotted by workers. In the United States during World War I these elements of pacifism brought objectors into conflict with American law, which provided for conscientious objection based only on religious opposition to fighting and not that which derived from secular or political principles or was directed against conscription itself. Furthermore, the majority position of the Socialist Party then condemned American involvement, thus bringing socialists to the antiwar cause.

Also during the second half of the nineteenth century, nonresistance as a force motivating peace advocacy was supplemented by organized internationalism. In some measure this derived from the humanistic traditions of Hugo Grotius and Immanuel Kant, and it evolved into programs for international law, international arbitration, and even international organization. In some measure, too, internationalism derived from classical economists who, like Jeremy Bentham, repudiated mercantilism and advocated free trade. In the United States, internationalism was buttressed by Americans' tendency to assume that their institutions would produce harmonious progress if written on a world scale, and it garnered enthusiastic support from men of means and prestige in the years before World War I. It is important in the development of modern pacifism because its institutional and world views, and even some of its programs, were incorporated into the encompassing policy platforms of pacifists.

A fourth element of modern pacifism was the sense of social responsibility that derived from antebellum evangelical religion and especially from religious analyses of industrialism and urbanism about the turn of the century. The reform spirit, the transnational outlook, and the political philosophy of liberal pacifism were rooted in two decades of Social Gospel and Progressive activity that preceded World War I.

Upon the outbreak of that conflict, most traditional internationalists supported the Allied cause and became reconciled to American intervention. When the United States entered the war, they viewed the crusade as the vehicle of international organization and tried to write their views into the Allied war aims, notably in the case of the League of Nations.

Meanwhile, between 1914 and 1917 several organizations were formed to oppose Woodrow Wilson's preparedness program and intervention, and to support conscientious objectors: the American Union Against Militarism (1915–1921), which was succeeded by the National Council for Prevention of War; the Women's Peace Party (1915), which was succeeded by the United States Section of the Women's International League for Peace and Freedom; the Fellowship of Reconciliation (1915), which was supplemented in 1923 by the War Resisters' League; and the American Friends Service Committee (1917). In wartime these groups were sifted of nearly all but pacifists, and they became the institutional base of modern pacifism in the United States.

The leaders of these and other wartime pacifist organizations were predominantly Progressives, often women, and with few exceptions were religious. They included Jane Addams and Emily Balch, directors of Hull House and Denison House settlements; Crystal Eastman, an ardent suffragist and expert on the legal aspects of industrial accidents; her brother Max Eastman, who edited two radical literary journals, *Masses* and *Liberator;* Norman Thomas, later the leader of the Socialist Party; Roger Baldwin, longtime director of the American Civil Liberties Union; Rufus Jones, a Quaker historian; Paul Jones, an Episcopal bishop; Jessie Wallace Hughan, founder of the War Resisters' League; John Nevin Sayre, interwar stalwart of the Fellowship of Reconciliation; and John Haynes Holmes, a Unitarian pastor. They identified with transnational ideologies, whether religious, humanitarian, or socialist; but politically they were pragmatists in the Progressive tradition. They believed in the ultimate worth of the individual, but they appreciated the influence of social institutions upon personal development.

They associated with antiwar radicals, with whom they were often persecuted. Indeed, pacifists formed the American Civil Liberties Bureau in 1917 for the defense of conscientious objectors and radicals during the war. Leading pacifists identified force as an instrument of social control and associated violence with authoritarianism. They therefore associated their own quest for peace with a commitment to social justice, so that they combined complete opposition to war with the spirit of reform and internationalism. Their organized expression of this belief during World War I marks the beginning of modern liberal pacifism and the development of an activist core of the peace movements in recent American history.

Traditional religious pacifism as documented by Peter Brock and colleagues has been a vital, often poignant part of the twentieth-century experience in Europe and North America. It was the liberal and activist strand of pacifism, however, that became most relevant to American foreign relations.

THE PACIFIST ROLES IN POLICYMAKING

Peace and antiwar movements can be viewed, institutionally, as a single element of the foreign policy-making process. To draw a distinction between them is legitimate with regard to specific foreign policy issues—that is, specific wars—but not with regard to the process of policy formation. Taken together, peace and antiwar movements in all periods of U.S. history have been coalitions of separate groups aligned variously with regard to different policy issues. These constituencies have combined to influence public policy either directly through the professional expertise of peace advocates (as in the case of numerous projects of the Carnegie Endowment) or through political lobbying, or indirectly through public opinion. In any case, pacifists have been relevant to the policymaking process in terms of the broader peace movements, and they cannot be evaluated apart from them.

CONSCRIPTION AND CONSCIENTIOUS OBJECTION

There is one possible exception to this observation: the contribution made by pacifist pressure groups to the administration of conscription and the treatment of conscientious objectors. In this case pacifist pressure groups acted directly upon government agencies and substantially affected policy formation.

Efforts on behalf of conscientious objectors have taken essentially three forms. First, pacifists representing the peace churches—the ecumenical Fellowship of Reconciliation and, prior to World War II, the secular War Resisters' League—lobbied to broaden the basis of exemption. At the outset of World War I objectors were exempted only if they belonged to churches with doctrinal positions against military service, and even then they were legally exempted only from fighting. Provisions were broadened administratively during the war to include all religious objectors. Subsequently, exemption was expanded by court decision to include philosophical authority embodying a universal principle, and leading churchmen and

church bodies later endorsed the principle of selective objection to war on political grounds.

Second, pacifists have lobbied in support of administrative agencies that would remove objectors from military jurisdiction, in recognition of those who object to conscription per se. The Civilian Public Service of World War II was the result of such pressure, although it proved to be an unsatisfactory solution. Various forms of exemption for civilian jobs since that time represent attempts to accommodate pressure from pacifists, buttressed as it often is by church bodies and liberals who recognize conscientious objection as an authentic ethical choice even when they do not endorse it as a preferred one.

Third, pacifists lobbied for amnesty for conscientious objectors following each war of the twentieth century. The basic rationale for amnesty has been that objectors are really political prisoners, although the laws of the United States do not recognize political crimes and treat objectors as criminals. During the Vietnam War the number of men who publicly deserted from the military or fled the country to escape the draft created a situation in which pacifists found themselves joined in their demand for amnesty by nonpacifists interested in political and social reconciliation. Insofar as conscientious objection has become recognized as a legitimate ethical option and a form of protest, it has ceased to become the exclusive concern of pacifists.

Even with regard to conscientious objection, therefore, the influence of pacifists must now be evaluated in relation to that of the general peace movements. Indeed, as John Chambers and Charles Moskos have shown, the recognition of conscientious objection is integral to the modern character of military service.

COALITION POLITICS

Pacifists affected peace coalitions in which they participated by their cultivation of a political base in specific publics and by the political techniques they employed. In the Cold War period they introduced new techniques of nonviolent protest. They also gave distinctive emphases to movements in which they were associated.

Pacifists were drawn together both by their opposition to World War I and by their isolation from the American public during the conflict. Increasingly, they became committed to a campaign against all future wars (and to campaigns for social and labor justice). They cooperated with those who had supported the war effort as a vehicle of internationalism and who, in the 1920s, supported membership in the League of Nations and the World Court, or ratification of a treaty outlawing war. In an era when leading peace advocates maneuvered to secure their own pet approaches at the expense of others, the more pacifist among them tended to be the most inclusive. Pacifists also systematically cultivated constituencies that had been largely neglected by other peace workers: religious bodies, college youth, Christian youth organizations, and labor. Although their primary appeal was to repudiate warfare altogether, pacifists also educated the public on international relations and recruited support for specific legislation, notably arms limitation. They lobbied through their own associations and also created a major coalition organization, the National Council for Prevention of War (1921).

By the mid-1930s a core of pacifist leaders had developed a network of support groups, a political base from which they tried to build a public consensus for strict neutrality. To this end they managed to align nonpacifist internationalists affiliated with the League of Nations Association in their $500,000 Emergency Peace Campaign. Occasionally they were able to translate public opinion into congressional positions, and they considerably reinforced popular resistance to overseas involvement. In the course of the neutrality controversy, however, the League of Nations Association gradually broke from its coalition with pacifists and organized a counter-campaign for collective security arrangements. In this respect, the activity of pacifists heightened the political organization of the interwar peace movement, which, however, it also helped to polarize.

During World War II pacifists were largely isolated from political influence except insofar as they cooperated with prowar internationalists to popularize the proposed United Nations. They remained isolated after the war, as the world became polarized between the United States and the Soviet Union, and collective security was reinterpreted in terms of Cold War containment, still ostensibly in the service of internationalism.

Then, in 1957 pacifists became instrumental in forming a new national coalition to challenge nuclear weapons testing. Disclosures about the threat of nuclear fallout engendered worldwide protest that was led in the United States by the National Committee for a Sane Nuclear Policy (SANE) and the Committee for Nonviolent Direct Action (CNDA). The former was a coalition with nonpacifist liberals like Norman Cousins, and it used traditional techniques of education, lobbying, and electoral action. CNDA represented an activist pacifist core, and it employed the tactics of nonviolent direct action, including civil disobedience like climbing or sailing into nuclear test zones and blockading nuclear submarines.

The bulk of the test-ban campaign was carried by SANE and the pacifist groups that had sponsored it—the American Friends Service Committee, the Fellowship of Reconciliation, and the Women's International League for Peace and Freedom. The cause also spawned new organizations, notably Women Strike for Peace and the Student Peace Union, and the whole U.S. effort was in limited measure coordinated with the international campaign. It contributed to a moratorium on atmospheric testing during the Eisenhower administration and had a direct role in the adoption of the 1963 partial nuclear test-ban treaty under President John F. Kennedy.

The test-ban coalition formed the initial base for the antiwar coalition that challenged the U.S. war in Vietnam, even before that conflict became formalized in the bombing campaign early in 1965. Again SANE negotiated the linkage between pacifists and nonpacifist liberals, although increasingly an independent left wing competed for recognition. In the first three years of the Vietnam War, antiwar constituencies multiplied: business and professional groups, cultural and entertainment notables, Peace Corps and social service groups, Old Left socialists and New Left students (notably Students for a Democratic Society), and religious leaders (notably Clergy and Laity Concerned). The latter was predominantly though not exclusively pacifist, while a core of radical pacifist Catholics led by the priests Daniel and Philip Berrigan developed a sharp civil disobedience witness in the Catholic Worker tradition.

In 1968 the antiwar coalition fully informed Democratic Party politics and conditioned even the Republican platform on the war. The following year the coalition severely constrained President Nixon's war policies. By then the large liberal wing of the antiwar movement was becoming thoroughly politicized, especially in Democratic Party politics, while its smaller radical wing spun apparently out of control (where it could not be disciplined by pacifists). Given its media-driven stereotype as radical and countercultural, the movement seemed to have died, whereas actually the coalition had become mainstreamed.

Throughout this period, activist pacifists in the Fellowship of Reconciliation, American Friends Service Committee, Clergy and Laity Concerned, and Catholic and other groups were intensely involved in coalition politics of the political left and center. By the same token, pacifist communities were sharply tested by the tension between the radical and liberal approaches their members espoused.

Two other large-scale peace coalitions made serious impacts on twentieth-century U.S. foreign relations: the nuclear freeze campaign against nuclear weapons of the 1980s and the concurrent campaign for solidarity with Latin American liberation movements. In the case of the 1991 Gulf War, by contrast, no serious coalition arose. At the outset it was widely conceded that the evenly divided country was ripe for protest, and pacifist groups were prepared even to wield nonviolent disobedience. However, the limited duration and tight control of military operations obviated the development of a broad public coalition in opposition to the Gulf War.

The nuclear freeze campaign in the first half of the 1980s was systematically organized against the background of massive European protest, dramatic revelations of the destructive scope of nuclear weapons, and fear of nuclear war that was intensified by the Ronald Reagan administration. Pacifists were among the organizing and motivating core of a broad, diverse public coalition that was fed by media coverage. Although it failed to secure an outright freeze on nuclear weapons building or deployment, the nuclear freeze campaign was substantially responsible for reinstating the policy and institutions of arms control that the administration had begun to scrap.

Out-publicized by the more visible and larger nuclear freeze campaign, another coalition successfully challenged the Reagan administration on Latin America. It consisted of innumerable grassroots groups with direct contacts in Central America, which were linked by a few national organizations. These groups disseminated information from sources abroad, mounted public pressure, and lobbied in Congress. Their main focus was on human rights abuses in El Salvador and Honduras and U.S. intervention in the civil war in Nicaragua through the contras. In the former two countries, transnational associations channeled economic help to revolutionary forces and peasant war victims, exposed human rights abuses, and challenged U.S. ties to military regimes. On Nicaragua, peace groups lobbied and

disseminated information. In all three cases they worked with the international community. Pacifists also brought organized nonviolent action to bear in the solidarity campaign.

NONVIOLENT DIRECT ACTION

From World War I on, a core of pacifists supported domestic reform programs as a concomitant of cultivating labor and reform constituencies for peace. Increasingly, they developed techniques of nonviolent direct action (often modeled on the example of Mohandas Gandhi) that they employed on behalf of labor and especially in the civil rights struggle. Thus, the Congress of Racial Equality (CORE, 1942) was nourished by the Fellowship of Reconciliation. By the time of the Reverend Martin Luther King's campaign to desegregate buses in Montgomery, Alabama (1955–1956), a few pacifists had considerable experience with these forms of protest. The Fellowship of Reconciliation, American Friends Service Committee, and War Resisters' League played an active role in the early civil rights movement about the same time that the core of radical pacifists in the Committee for Nonviolent Direct Action employed civil disobedience in the test-ban campaign. Accordingly, nonviolent direct action was a ready tool in the pacifist repertoire during the Vietnam War.

The technique took many forms: it involved returning or burning draft cards, trespassing, blocking arms shipments and troop trains, or otherwise challenging authority. On occasion it meant defiling or destroying draft records or providing sanctuary for draft resisters. It was street theater, designed to dramatize the tragedy and moral turpitude that pacifists attached to the war. Occasionally, direct action was applied violently by nonpacifists, and then it was counterproductive.

It was again applied in the 1980s campaign against nuclear weapons, notably in the actions of the Berrigans' Plowshares group, which aimed to defile or destroy missile components, or of Women's Pentagon Action. By that time the technique had become widely, even legally, accepted as a viable form of public protest. It found expression in the last decade of the twentieth century as a form of protest against economic globalism, where it appears to have inclined governments to be more discreet if not more responsive to protest.

TRANSNATIONAL LINKS

It has become conventional to regard transnational nongovernmental organizations (NGOs) as players in the foreign relations field. The peace movement, viewed as a transnational social movement, spans two centuries, and its pacifist core comprises a century of transnational experience.

The International Fellowship of Reconciliation (IFOR, 1919), the Women's International League for Peace and Freedom (WILPF, 1919), and the War Resisters' International (WRI, 1921) all were transnational associations with strong U.S. components. Except for the WRI, they were formed during World War I. (Indeed, the WILPF derived from a 1915 meeting in The Hague, where mainly pacifist women from the then belligerent countries delegated emissaries to heads of government in search of a mediated peace.) In wartime these groups linked isolated pacifists and conscripted war resisters. Thereafter they cooperated in relief and reconstruction projects, except that the WRI focused on providing a socialist matrix for war resistance.

In the interwar years the WILPF established an office in Geneva from which it sought to mobilize a transnational, citizen constituency for disarmament and other League of Nations initiatives. Pacifists in fascist countries were part of an international network. As the prospect of war grew again, U.S. pacifists strengthened their international ties, sponsoring colleagues from abroad to the United States on behalf of neutrality legislation.

The largely pacifist-initiated U.S. test-ban coalition of the 1950s was part of a world movement, as was its successor campaign against nuclear weapons in the 1980s. In both cases transnational coordination was secondary to national concerns, although the 1980s campaign was explicitly interfaced with the UN agenda. Similarly, pacifists extended their international links during the Vietnam War. The Fellowship of Reconciliation mounted an ambitious attempt to coordinate Vietnamese Buddhist and American antiwar efforts, publicized the existence and persecution of antiwar South Vietnamese, sent reconciliation and information teams to North Vietnam, and tried to relate public protest in Europe to that in the United States.

In Latin America the International Fellowship of Reconciliation and its U.S. national chapter worked from the 1960s to the 1980s to spread the concept and techniques of nonviolent resistance as a viable alternative to both violent revolution and apathy. U.S. civil rights and Fellowship of Reconciliation leaders reached both Protestants and Catholics in Latin America, while IFOR emissaries Jean Goss and Hildegard Goss-Mayr were particularly effective in Catholic circles. A period of social evangelism and preliminary organization led to the formation of SERPAJ (Servicio Paz y Justicia en América Latina, or Service for Peace and Justice) in 1974. Itself a regional organization, SERPAJ provided Latin American national and church leaders with nonviolent resistance techniques and with contacts in the international community, greatly empowering, for example, Nobel Peace Prize winner Adolfo Pérez Esquivel of Argentina.

Nonviolent direct action was brought to bear upon the region's human rights crises and civil wars. Beginning in 1983, for example, Witness for Peace stationed trained North Americans in teams along the Nicaraguan border. They helped with economic development, but their high visibility was designed also to deter contra attacks. After U.S. support for the contras was withdrawn in 1988, the Witness for Peace program of intercession was expanded to other areas. Pacifist nonviolent action thus became one of several instruments through which a coalition with transnational linkages effectively challenged U.S. Latin American policy in the 1980s. Meanwhile, within the United States there was a surge of refugees from political life-threats in Central America. The U.S. government's reluctance to grant them asylum led to a sanctuary movement to provide safety, most often in churches. By the time the refugee flow subsided late in the decade, hundreds of sites were networked to smuggle people across borders and provide safe havens and legal and humanitarian services. Sometimes this modern Underground Railroad moved refugees on into Canada. The operation was a case of large-scale civil disobedience so widely condoned that the U.S. Immigration and Naturalization Service was slow to challenge it.

FRAMING POLICY ISSUES WITH PACIFIST PERSPECTIVES

Pacifists have not evolved a vision of foreign policy as coherent as collective security or its counterpart, containment. Nonetheless, they have shared distinctive qualities with which they helped to frame foreign policy issues. These qualities include their transnational orientation, moral thrust, and skepticism about the efficacy of military force.

Transnational Orientation The orientation of nineteenth-century pacifists was largely religious and resulted from the dualism of Christian perfectionism, which assigned different roles to religious bodies and secular societies. To this was added the antistate individualism of philosophical anarchists and the class analysis of socialists. But none of these elements yielded specific implications for foreign policy.

In the twentieth century the perspective of pacifists was secularized, but it remained essentially ethical and humanistic rather than political. It was oriented to the quality of life and the equitable distribution of power rather than to the political relations of states. In this sense, leading pacifists found World War I, for all its magnitude, to be irrelevant to the solution of fundamental world problems. What they found truly basic was human need, creativity, and community. Progressive pacifists, and especially the articulate women among them, thus brought a strong sense of community to peace work (by contrast to the social, legal, and political structures emphasized by other peace advocates). They eventually supported the League of Nations, but they harbored the reservation that such international organizations were inadequate vehicles for change and human welfare.

But some pacifists were systems oriented. The outstanding pacifist analyst of international affairs in the 1930s was Kirby Page, who argued that traditional European rivalries had vitiated the League of Nations and would lead to another world war unless a new foundation could be built for international relations. Ironically, although pacifists viewed historical revisionism as the basis for a realistic assessment of traditional diplomacy and a justification for radically internationalizing world power, many Americans used it as their justification for a new isolationism.

Following World War II some pacifists followed pacifist leader Abraham J. Muste in seeking a new basis for a transnational foreign policy. By the 1950s, Muste viewed the Third World as the fulcrum for a global policy beyond the bipolar terms of the Cold War. This notion was taken up in the following decade by some New Left radicals; but as a basis for foreign policy analysis, it was eclipsed by the rhetoric against nuclear arms and then war in Vietnam. Nonetheless, the American Fellowship of Reconciliation and other pacifists actively promoted the "Third Force" concept of Vietnamese Buddhists as a standard against which to frame U.S. policy goals.

Moral Emphasis The moral emphasis of nineteenth-century pacifism was individualistic. Pacifists tended to assume that good people would make a good world. Twentieth-century pacifists, however, initially reflected the Progressive emphasis on social environmentalism. They included war among the social institutions in which good men and women become enmeshed with devastating consequences. Accordingly, they made pacifism an expression of social ethics; and their journal, *The World Tomorrow* (published 1918–1934), became the most forthright exponent of the social gospel. "If war is sin," wrote Kirby Page, then it must be abjured and overcome by every available stratagem. Their essentially moral outlook enabled several pacifist leaders to transcend the narrow allegiances to specific programs that set so many internationalists at odds with one another.

In the 1920s, for example, Page and his colleagues made futile attempts to devise a plan of unity between the advocates of a World Court and of a general treaty to outlaw war. Similarly, in the 1930s pacifists were able to write an umbrella platform that attracted nonpacifist internationalists to their Emergency Peace Campaign, with its neutralist bias. In 1957 a pacifist nucleus stimulated the formation of both the National Committee for a Sane Nuclear Policy and the Committee for Nonviolent Direct Action in order to enlist both liberal and pacifist constituencies in action against nuclear arms. And in the 1960s, a generalized sense of moral outrage accounted for whatever cohesion there was in the organized antiwar movement. It was the basis on which pacifists could associate with groups having nonpacifist political biases.

The very sense of moral commitment that led to comprehensiveness in some circumstances engendered division in others. Ideologies often have served as standards of factional loyalty within out-of-power groups, and the principled total repudiation of violence and warfare sometimes functioned in this way among pacifists in the coalitions they joined. A few examples illustrate this problem. Prior to the Civil War, the American Peace Society was impelled by a sense of moral obligation, but it was wracked by factional disputes over the question of whether to prohibit all wars or only aggressive ones. Again, in World War I absolute pacifism was both the cohesive element of pacifist organization and the reason that prowar liberals refused to work with pacifists even for liberal goals. Although the Women's International League for Peace and Freedom, formed just after the war, included pacifists Jane Addams and Emily Balch, the coalition was too broad for Fanny Garrison Villard and other absolutists, who created the separate Women's Peace Society. Early in the 1930s both the Fellowship of Reconciliation and the Socialist Party were sharply divided over how completely they should renounce violence in a potential class struggle. Socialists never recovered from the political effects of that controversy, and they also were faced with the theoretical issue of whether to support an antifascist war.

By 1938 pacifist groups were united against intervention, but they tended to withdraw from political action in order to prepare communities of believers for the coming crisis. During World War II the pacifist community was divided over the implications of its moral commitment to conscientious objection, and its support groups disagreed about the limits of cooperation with Civilian Public Service, the administrative agency for objectors.

The antiwar movement of the 1960s was no more immune to factionalism than its predecessors, and the division was often over conflicting principles. Divisive issues included whether to exclude communists from coalitions, whether to criticize North Vietnamese and communist policy in the context of analyses of American involvement, tactics for demonstrations, and organizational principles within the movement. Protest during the Vietnam conflict was united under an intense sense of moral outrage, but it also was divided by the question of allegiance to specific principles, of which the total repudiation of violence and authoritarianism was one.

In any case, pacifists have reinforced an essentially ethical interpretation of national interest: that world interest should be a criterion of national policy and that the concomitants of peace are change as well as order, justice as well as stability. This moral thrust is not unique to pacifists, but it has been sharpened by their participation in American peace movements.

Skepticism of War

No less than belief, skepticism has characterized pacifist propaganda and attitudes. Indeed, modern pacifism was formed in opposition to a popular war, the so-called Great War, and to the power assumed by government in it. That skepticism became a valuable credential when disillusionment followed the war. Pacifists themselves assiduously propagated skepticism about the justness of specific wars, the credibility of war aims, and the constructive potential of victory. For most of the twentieth century they challenged the general claim that preparedness deters warfare and the specific claims of military security needs. From Woodrow Wilson's 1916 preparedness campaign to legislation for arms spending in the 1920s and nuclear arms in the 1950s, from the inauguration of conscription in 1917 to its reinstatement in 1940 and the peacetime draft of 1948, the small body of pacifists constituted a core of political opposition. They challenged not only programs but also the rationale for them. Some pacifists also marshaled economic and antiimperialist interpretations of war to expose the economic linkages of warfare and to challenge official explanations of foreign policy. And they propagated skepticism about the efficacy of American intervention abroad, whether public or covert, whether in World War I or the Cold War, in Southeast Asia or Latin America.

Skepticism about the use of military power and the rationale for violence has been extended to systematic inquiries about the nature of power by building first on the experience of Mohandas Gandhi and then on American reform experience. Late-twentieth-century scholarship put nonviolent application of social force on a systematic and empirical basis and explored its implications for national security. In this sense the study of nonviolence is no longer confined to ethical pacifism.

Skepticism about foreign policy and governmental accountability is the legacy of the nonresistants and the experience of the peace sects. It was reinforced when pacifists were persecuted or were treated as irrelevant. It is the concomitant of the pacifist values of individual worth, harmony, and brotherhood, contrasted as they are with articles of foreign policy such as national interest, conflict, and sovereignty. Skepticism follows from the pacifist emphasis on a transnational orientation and moral commitment, as against foreign policy based on national interest and pragmatic choices. It is at the heart of the demand that foreign policy be tested publicly by the very values it purports to secure. Skepticism is not unique to pacifism, but it has been significantly sharpened in the American peace movement as a result of pacifist activity.

CONCLUSION

Foreign policymaking can be interpreted as the process of relating national interest to international situations. A crucial stage of the process is the definition of national interest, and it is at this point that ideals are related to concrete self-interests. A given principle of American institutions is that policy choices should be subject to public scrutiny and popular pressure. Accordingly, coalitions of peace advocates are essential in a democratic republic because they serve the twin functions of providing independent education about international affairs and of organizing public opinion and translating it into political pressure.

Pacifism has been significant for foreign policymaking insofar as pacifists have influenced peace coalitions. Pacifists have broadened the popular base of pressure, stimulated political organization, and developed techniques with which minorities may challenge majority consensus. They also have imbued the peace movements with such distinctive qualities as their transnational orientation, moral thrust, and skepticism about the efficacy of military force to bring about orderly change or an equitable distribution of world power.

Furthermore, organized pacifists have occasionally played historical roles in consensus formation, notably in the resistance to preparedness and intervention in World War I, in the neutrality controversy of 1935–1937, in constraining nuclear weapons, in the protest against the Vietnam War, and in solidarity with Latin Americans resisting repression. They have attempted to abolish conscription and have liberalized the treatment of conscientious objectors. At the opening of the twenty-first century, pacifists mobilized Nobel Peace Prize winners to challenge U.S. sanctions on Iraq and were working directly with the United Nations to promote a culture of peace.

Influenced by social-movement approaches, modern analysts have treated peace movements as transnational social change movements, often with liberal pacifists at their core. Pacifists in this sense can be understood as integral to foreign policymaking as they collectively interact with the general public, national government, other national and international nongovernmental organizations, and international agencies.

Most people who repudiate violence and war on the basis of pacifist beliefs are not politically active. But even their faith is significant for American foreign policy in two respects. First, in its conduct of foreign relations, including warfare, the nation has been obligated to protect principled dissent from persecution or repression. The fact that this rule has been abrogated does not minimize its constraint on the foreign policy process. Second, the definition of national interest and power is subject to openly advocated alternative conceptions. Whatever the merits of pacifist judgments on specific policies, the free existence of pacifism and its political expression constitute a significant index of the consistency of foreign policymaking with democratic institutions.

BIBLIOGRAPHY

Ackerman, Peter, and Jack DuVall. *A Force More Powerful: A Century of Nonviolent Conflict*. New York, 2000. A sweeping account of twentieth-century nonviolent campaigns that form the global context of U.S. activist pacifism.

Allen, Devere. *The Fight for Peace*. New York, 1930. Written by a journalist and editor who advocated war resistance and political activism, this substantial volume remains an important primary source of pacifist thought and history.

Alonso, Harriet Hyman. *Peace as a Women's Issue: A History of the U.S. Movement for World Peace and Women's Rights*. Effectively fills a gender gap in the history of twentieth-century peace activism.

Brock, Peter. *Pacifism in the United States from the Colonial Era to the First World War*. Princeton, N.J., 1968. The best history of the subject, thorough in its coverage of pacifism in sects, peace churches, and antebellum reform and includes a valuable bibliography.

Brock, Peter, and Nigel Young. *Pacifism in the Twentieth Century*. Syracuse, N.Y., 1999. A brief, balanced treatment of pacifism in an international context.

Chatfield, Charles. *For Peace and Justice: Pacifism in America, 1914–1941*. Knoxville, Tenn., 1971. Rev. ed., New York, 1973. Traces the development of modern, liberal pacifism through the interwar period in relation to peace coalitions and foreign policy issues, and also in relation to reform movements.

———. *The American Peace Movement: Ideals and Activism*. New York, 1992. The standard survey of the subject that includes a resource mobilization approach.

Curti, Merle Eugene. *Peace or War: The American Struggle, 1636–1936*. New York, 1936. Unsurpassed for its balanced, chronological narrative of the period and treats pacifism in relation to the broad peace coalition.

DeBenedetti, Charles, with Charles Chatfield. *An American Ordeal: The Antiwar Movement of the Vietnam Era*. Syracuse, N.Y., 1990. A thorough and comprehensive narrative.

Early, Frances H. *A World Without War: How U.S. Feminists and Pacifists Resisted World War I*. Syracuse, N.Y., 1997. A full treatment that fills a gender gap in the literature on the period.

Howlett, Charles F. *The American Peace Movement: References and Resources*. Boston, 1991. Indispensable resource that combines an annotated bibliography with a history of the field.

Josephson, Harold. *Biographical Dictionary of Modern Peace Leaders*. Westport, Conn., 1985. A massive reference work that includes biographies of major pacifists.

Kleidman, Robert. *Organizing for Peace: Neutrality, the Test Ban, and the Freeze*. Syracuse, N.Y., 1993. A well-researched comparative study.

Klejment, Anne, and Nancy L. Roberts, eds. *American Catholic Pacifism: The Influence of Dorothy Day and the Catholic Worker Movement*. Westport, Conn., 1996. Treats this modern dimension of Catholicism biographically.

Moskos, Charles C., and John Whiteclay Chambers, II, eds. *The New Conscientious Objection: From Sacred to Secular Resistance*. New York, 1993. The standard treatment.

Patterson, David S. *Toward a Warless World: The Travail of the American Peace Movement, 1887–1914*. Bloomington, Ind., 1976. A scholarly narrative of the rise of the modern peace and internationalist movement with particular attention to organizational roles, social origins, and attitudes.

Powers, Roger S., and William B. Vogele, eds. *Protest, Power, and Change: An Encyclopedia of Nonviolent Action from ACT-UP to Women's Suffrage*. New York, 1997. A basic reference work.

Wittner, Lawrence S. *Rebels Against War: The American Peace Movement, 1941–1983*. Revised ed. Philadelphia, 1984. A work in which pacifists provide the thread of continuity, although Wittner describes shifting and contending patterns within the broad peace coalition; contains an extensive bibliography.

———. *The Struggle Against the Bomb*. Stanford, Calif., 1993. A trilogy (of which two volumes have been published) narrating the history of transnational movement against nuclear weapons; the only comprehensive account of a transnational peace movement.

See also COLLECTIVE SECURITY; DISSENT IN WAR; IDEOLOGY; INTERNATIONALISM; INTERVENTION AND NONINTERVENTION; ISOLATIONISM; THE NATIONAL INTEREST; NEUTRALITY; PEACE MOVEMENTS; PUBLIC OPINION.

PAN-AMERICANISM

★ ★ ★ ★

Thomas M. Leonard and Thomas L. Karnes

According to Joseph B. Lockey, the closest student of Pan-Americanism's early days, the adjective "Pan-American" was first employed by the *New York Evening Post* in 1882, and the noun "Pan-Americanism" was coined by that same journal in 1888. The convening of the first inter-American conference in Washington the next year led to wider usage of the first term about 1890 and popularization of Pan-Americanism in the early years of the twentieth century. While the terms have since become familiar expressions to most of the reading public in the Western Hemisphere, their connotations remain vague. Broadly defined, Pan-Americanism is cooperation between the Western Hemisphere nations in a variety of activities including economic, social, and cultural programs; declarations; alliances; and treaties—though some authorities narrow the definition to include political action only. However, the specific definition must always be partly in error, and the broad one borders on the meaningless.

THE ROOTS OF PAN-AMERICANISM

Pan-Americanism is more easily traced than defined. In the middle of the nineteenth century, various "Pan" movements achieved popularity as adjuncts or exaggerations of the powerful nationalisms of the times, throwbacks to ancient Pan-Hellenism. Pan-Slavism was perhaps the first to acquire some measure of fame; Pan-Hellenism revived about 1860 and was followed by Pan-Germanism, Pan-Islamism, Pan-Celtism, Pan-Hispanism, and others. Probably all these "Pan" movements share certain predicates: their believers feel some unity, some uniqueness—perhaps superiority—and they share mutual interests, fears, history, and culture. In short, their similarities make them different from the rest of the world, and they combine for strength. Pan-Americanism, however, fails to meet most of those criteria and must fall back upon the weaker elements of a common geographical separation from the rest of the world and something of a common history.

From early colonial times, Western Hemisphere peoples believed that they were unique. Statesmen of the Americas, both North and South, were united in affirming that some force—nature, or perhaps God—had separated the Old World and the New World for a purpose; and this isolation in an unknown land had brought a common colonial experience that deserved the name of "system." Among leaders who saw and described this division was Thomas Jefferson; Henry Clay often argued before Congress for its preservation; Simón Bolívar acted upon it; and President James Monroe's doctrine most fundamentally assumes it.

What were the elements of this American system? First was independence, defined by Clay as freedom from despotism, either domestic or European. Peoples of the Americas believed in a common destiny, a body of political ideals, the rule of law, and cooperation among themselves (at least when threatened from the outside). In later years Secretary of State James G. Blaine saw these factors strengthened by commerce; the Brazilian statesmen Joaquim Nabuco and José Maria da Silva Paranhos, Baron Rio Branco, talked of a common past; Woodrow Wilson thought he saw a unique American spirit of justice.

Americans could not ignore geography. They had moved to, or been born in, an underpopulated continent, where the strife of Europe was put aside and mobility, vertical or horizontal, was easily achieved. Nature isolated the American, and that isolation would produce a different people. But the most apparent difference between Americans and their European cousins was in the form of government. The vastness of America enhanced the individual's worth, and the right of each person to have a share in government found fertile soil there. Thus, when the Spanish and Portuguese colonies struggled to gain their freedom in the half-century after 1789, most deliberately chose the unfamiliar republican form of government that would safeguard the rights of citizens to choose those who would govern them. Inevitably some constitutions were copied, but that was the plagiarizing of words; the ideas were pandemic. (That a few nonrepublican administrations arose was a matter singularly ignored and always easily explained away to anyone who pursued the puzzle.) From Philadelphia to Tucumán in the Argentine, new constitutions proclaimed that Americans had a new way of life and a new form of government to ensure its continuance.

Nowhere were these American ideas better expressed than in paragraphs of the presidential address that became known as the Monroe Doctrine. Monroe asserted a belief in the existence of two worlds, one monarchical and one republican; the New World was closed to further colonization by the Old, and neither should interfere with the other. Third parties were not to tamper even with regions in the Americas that were still colonies. Whether the U.S. will to protect this separation was based upon geography or, ironically, the British fleet, the doctrine expressed what Americans believed and would fight to preserve.

At times Americans have been carried away with the enthusiasm of their rhetoric and have found unifying interests where they did not exist. Proponents of Pan-Americanism have often spoken of the existence of a common heritage, a statement with limited application, for in the hemisphere there is no common language, culture, or religion. Contrary to most "Pan" movements, Pan-Americanism has little basis in race or ethnicity, and it scarcely seems necessary to belabor the cultural diversity of the persons who bear the name American. If heritage were the chief basis of community, Spanish Americans would have their strongest ties with Spain, Brazilians with Portugal, Anglo-Americans with Great Britain, and so on. Nor can Pan-Americanism ignore those millions of African heritage or those who are indigenous to the Americas. Language and religion are even more varied than race in the Americas and can offer no more means of unification.

Finally, consideration must be given to the geographical basis for Pan-Americanism. It is a fact that the Americas occupy their own hemisphere and that they had been comfortably separated from the disturbances of Europe by great seas until the mid-twentieth century. Clearly this isolation resulted in some community of interest. The danger lies in exaggeration, for the modern traveler soon learns that in terms of dollars, hours, or miles, much of the United States is far closer to Europe than it is to most of Latin America, and Buenos Aires is far closer to Africa than it is to New York or Washington, D.C. In short, it is a fallacy to contend that the Americas are united by their proximity. The Americas, North and South, occupy the same hemisphere, and that does present an important mythology and symbolism to the world. More than that cannot be demonstrated.

Who are the Pan-Americans? No one has ever established requirements for membership nor set forth the procedures by which a people can become part of the elect. Form of government played a more or less clear part; the American nations all seemed to understand that colonies could not participate in Pan-American movements, but that local empires (the only one bearing that title for any duration was Brazil) were welcome. Nations sent delegates to the various conferences called during the nineteenth century primarily because they were invited by the host, not because of any established rules. Thus, some meetings that are classified as Pan-American might have had delegates from only four or five states. After 1889 nearly all of the republics of the hemisphere took part. The proliferation of new states in the years following World War II is reflected in Pan-Americanism, and former British colonies, no matter how small (and perhaps unviable), seem to have been welcomed into the American family, as has Canada, though generally the Canadians have often pursued their own policies. A nation can also be excommunicated, as Cuba was in 1961. And despite sanctions imposed upon Cuba by the Organization of American States (OAS), it continued to have diplomatic and economic relations with several American states, particularly following the collapse of the Soviet Union in 1991.

PAN-AMERICANISM TO 1850

Pan-Americanism most often expresses itself through international conferences, very loosely joined in the early years, highly structured in more recent decades. In the nineteenth century, conferences were often called to seek combined action against some specific problem. In the twen-

84

tieth century, sessions have been scheduled long in advance and have had wide-ranging agendas. Attendance at the latter meetings has neared unanimity; in the early days it was irregular, made the worse by slow communications. The record is filled with accounts of delegations not formed in time or sent too late to take part in the proceedings. A final distinction is clear: while in recent times the impetus usually has come from the United States, during the nineteenth century almost all of the leadership came from Spanish America, often to the exclusion of the Anglo-Americans and Portuguese Americans. Some writers, in fact, seeking to divide Pan-Americanism chronologically, have classified the years 1826–1889 as the "old," or Spanish-American, period of the movement.

While many Latin Americans, including José de San Martín, Martínez de Rozas, Bernardo O'Higgins, and Bernardo Monteagudo, understood the necessity for Spanish-American cooperation, the "liberator" of Spanish-American independence, Simón Bolívar, is considered the father of the "old" Pan-Americanism. Long before any other leader, he dreamed of a strong league of American states leading to permanent military and political cooperation. Initially, at least, Bolívar thought of a confederation of only the Spanish-American states, if for no other reason than their common heritage and struggle for freedom from Spain. In 1815 he predicted the creation of three Spanish-American federations: Mexico and Central America, northern Spanish South America, and southern South America. But his ultimate goal, what became known as the "Bolivarian dream," was the unification of all Spanish America. In defeat and in victory his plan never disappeared, and in 1818 he (somewhat inaccurately) wrote to an Argentine friend, "We Americans should have but a single country since in every other way we are perfectly united."

By the 1820s the freedom of most of the Latin American colonies seemed assured, and the United States and some European nations began extending diplomatic recognition to the new governments. Bolívar saw this as an opportunity to implement his plan, and in 1822 he persuaded the government of Gran Colombia to send emissaries to the other South American nations, which resulted in general treaties with Chile, Peru, Buenos Aires, Mexico, and Central America. The signatories agreed to cooperate in sustaining their independence from foreign domination. Still, Bolívar sought much more.

The fear that Spain might attempt to reclaim its empire with the assistance of Europe's Holy Alliance provided Bolívar with the opportunity for his grand alliance. In December 1824 he called for an "assembly of plenipotentiaries" to meet at Panama to address the security issue. Bolívar's notice was addressed to "the American republics, formerly Spanish colonies," and therefore omitted several American states. The invitation included Great Britain, signaling Bolívar's understanding that British support was essential for the success of his confederation. He also permitted the Netherlands to send an observer, apparently without an invitation. Bolívar had ignored both the United States and Brazil, which of course, were not "formerly Spanish colonies"; but when their attendance was sought by other Latin Americans, he posed no objection.

Bolívar's classical training caused him to see Panama as the modern counterpart of the Isthmus of Corinth, and parallel to the Greek experience, he selected Panama as the site of the conference. That unsavory location had many defects as a host of an international conference. In fact, every delegate took ill during the sessions, but it did have the advantage of a central location. In June 1826 the representatives of Peru, Gran Colombia, Mexico, and the Central American Federation met and planned the first steps toward Pan-Americanism.

Technically speaking, attendance was much greater, for in time Gran Colombia was to be divested of Venezuela, Ecuador, and Panama, and in 1838 the Central American Federation was split into its original five parts, which became the republics of Guatemala, El Salvador, Honduras, Nicaragua, and Costa Rica. In that sense, the four nations accounted for eleven future Latin American republics. But what of the others? The United Provinces of La Plata already evidenced the isolationism and antipathy to alliances that were to mark the policy of its successor state, Argentina. Even more self-contained was Paraguay, which simply declined to be represented. Brazil, Chile, and Bolivia exhibited some interest but for various reasons failed to send delegates to Panama.

Bolívar not only mistrusted U.S. intentions in the hemisphere but thought its presence would preclude an honest discussion about the African slave trade. For its part, when the invitation did come, the United States, officially neutral in Latin America's wars for independence, could quite properly have declined the invitation. However, members of President John Quincy Adams's administration, led by Secretary of State Henry

Clay, were eager to join in any movement toward inter-American cooperation, if for no other reason than economic opportunity. Strong congressional opposition arose. Some of it could be attributed to the Democrats seeking to embarrass the Adams administration, but there were more serious concerns. The isolationists objected to participating in any conclave that might produce a permanent and entangling alliance. Many southerners feared a discussion of the slavery issue. In contrast, representatives from the Northeast saw the need to protect commercial interests against British competition. After four months of debate, Congress approved sending two delegates, but to no avail. One died en route to Panama; the other made no effort to reach Panama, but journeyed instead to Tacubaya, Mexico, where the Spanish-American statesmen planned further meetings.

Rivalries, both petty and large, soon appeared at Panama. Some states professed to fear Bolívar's ambitions; others wanted only a temporary league to complete the independence of Latin America from Europe. Even the role of the British at the sessions was debated. Owing to the local climate and unsanitary conditions, the Panama Congress lasted less than one month, but not before concluding a treaty of perpetual union, league, and confederation; a convention providing for future meetings; and a second convention outlining each participating state's financial support for maintenance of an armed force and the confederation's bureaucracy. The treaty contained thirty-one detailed articles designed to implement the treaty's objective: "to support in common defense . . . the sovereignty and independence" of each state against foreign domination.

After signing the agreements, some of the representatives departed for home; others traveled to Tacubaya, a small village near Mexico City, where they planned to reconvene if their governments deemed the effort worthwhile. Some informal talks were held at Tacubaya, but no formal sessions ever took place, and the Panama Congress had to stand upon its completed work. A dismal fate awaited the Panama Congress treaties across Latin America. Only Gran Colombia ratified them all, despite the surprising opposition of Bolívar.

In only one regard can the Panama Congress be looked upon as a success: the fact of its existence perhaps made the holding of future such conferences a bit easier. Little else was accomplished. Why did it fail so badly? The end of the threat from Spain and the beginnings of civil strife all over Latin America had coincided to make the congress a forum for expressing the new republics' distrust of each other. For the time being, the newly independent nations of Latin America set about the task of nation building. Panama was a noble experiment. Though its aims were obviously far ahead of its time, they were appropriate to any time.

The failure of the Panama Congress also demonstrated that its prime mover, Bolívar, had changed his mind about the vast confederation of states, and would concentrate instead upon establishing a tight federation of the Andes with himself as permanent dictator. This change left a leadership vacuum in Pan-Americanism that was briefly filled by Mexico. Despite rapid shifts from conservative to liberal administrations, the Mexican government for a decade followed a policy of urging the Latin American states to consummate some of the plans drafted at Panama and help protect the region against the possibility of European intervention. Armed with a proposal for a treaty of union, and calling for renewal of the Panama discussions, Mexican ministers were dispatched to several capitals. Mexico was willing that the meetings be convened in almost any convenient spot, but the suggestion received little support. This first bid of 1832 was repeated in 1838, 1839, and 1840, by which time Mexico faced an increasing North American presence in Texas. However, the other nations lacked Mexico's concern, and the proposals did not result in even one conference. Only when the South Americans feared for their own security did they decide to band together again.

The United States also distanced itself from Latin America. President James Monroe's 1823 announcement that the Western Hemisphere was off-limits to European encroachments because the hemispheric nations shared common democratic and republican ideals lost its luster as U.S. diplomats reported back from the region that the Latin American nations were anything but democratic or republican. Nor did the visions of commercial success ever materialize. These same diplomats found the British, who helped to finance Latin America's independence, well entrenched.

The second Latin American conference took place in Lima, Peru, from December 1847 to March 1848. The conference was in response to two threats: the fear of Spanish designs upon South America's west coast and the U.S. incursion into Mexico. General Juan José Flores, a Venezuelan-born conservative, became Ecuador's first president but was subsequently exiled. Flores went to Europe for help and appeared to be successful in raising private troops and a fleet to restore himself to the presidency. Anticipating an invasion by Spain or Great Britain, the government of Peru invited the American republics to meetings at Lima in December 1847. The sessions lasted until March 1848, even though it was known by that time that the British government would prohibit the sailing of the Spanish fleet.

The United States was invited to send a representative, ostensibly to demonstrate to Europe that all the hemispheric nations would unite against a foreign threat. The Latin Americans also intended to remind the North Americans, then engaged in a war with Mexico, that the conference's fundamental purpose was to demonstrate mutual respect for the territorial integrity of all nations. President James K. Polk refused the invitation to send a delegate and instead dispatched J. Randolph Clay as a nonparticipating observer.

Only ministers from Colombia, Chile, Bolivia, Ecuador, and Peru participated in the Lima conference, where they concluded four treaties, most of them concerning mutual assistance. Only Colombia ratified one of the agreements. Ironically, Clay, the U.S. observer, expressed great satisfaction with the conference resolutions regarding noncolonization and denying Europe the right to intervene in hemispheric affairs. The conference concluded just as the U.S. Congress was ratifying the Treaty of Guadalupe Hidalgo, which stripped Mexico of its vast northern territories for annexation to the United States.

PAN-AMERICANISM, 1850–1900

What appeared to be the insatiable U.S. appetite for territory prompted two Latin American meetings in 1856. Santiago, Chile, was the site of the third Pan-American conference under Spanish-American auspices. The conference was called because Ecuador proposed granting the United States the right to mine guano on the Galápagos Islands, an action that disturbed Ecuador's Pacific Coast neighbors. The republics of Peru, Ecuador, and Chile sent delegations to Santiago, where they drafted plans for another confederation and agreed upon joint measures for handling "piratical" expeditions. In September 1856 the delegates signed the Continental Treaty, dealing with many aspects of international law, filibustering, and acts of exiles, as well as the usual nod in the direction of a confederation. Significantly, while all of the nations of Latin America were urged to join, including Portuguese-speaking Brazil, the United States was not invited to attend the conference or to join the confederation. But once more failure ensued. The Continental Treaty was not ratified.

Meanwhile the United States, not a European nation, appeared as the chief threat to Latin America's territorial integrity. Its acquisition of more than one-third of Mexico was followed by the presence of filibusters in the circum-Caribbean region. William Walker's filibustering expedition into Nicaragua caused the ministers of Costa Rica, Guatemala, Mexico, New Granada, Peru, El Salvador, and Venezuela assigned to Washington, D.C., to sign a treaty of alliance and confederation on 9 November 1856. The signatories pledged themselves to prevent the organizing of expeditions by political exiles against an allied government and, if an attack occurred, to provide military assistance to the aggrieved nation. Hoping to convert this arrangement into a Hispanic-American Confederation, the delegates called for a conference to convene in Lima in December 1857. As in the past, nothing materialized. The Washington agreement was not ratified, and the conference was not convened.

The fourth and last of the "old" Spanish-American conferences took place at Lima, Peru, in 1864. The weakness of many of the Latin American states and the U.S. preoccupation with its Civil War had allowed a series of European flirtations in the American hemisphere. Spain claimed the reannexation of the Dominican Republic in 1861; Spain, Great Britain, and especially France threatened, and then invaded, Mexico; and Spain occupied Peru's Chincha Islands to collect debts, under the pretext that Peru was still a Spanish colony. In response, in 1864, the Colombian government encouraged the Peruvians to invite all former Spanish colonies to a conference at Lima to take up the matter of intervention by foreign powers. In addition to Peru, states attending included Argentina, Chile, Colombia, El Salvador, Guatemala, and Venezuela. The United States and Brazil were not invited, ostensibly because they were not former Spanish colonies. The Lima Congress failed to negotiate with Spain for the withdrawal of its troops from the Chincha Islands, and when the delegates turned their full attention to the usual grand treaty of confederation, the failure was just as complete. Once again no nation ratified any of the agreements. The end of the American Civil

War and the renewed preoccupation of Spain and France with domestic and foreign problems elsewhere account for the departure of those two nations from their Latin American adventures.

The War of the Triple Alliance (1865–1870), which pitted Paraguay against a loose league of Argentina, Brazil, and Uruguay, and the War of the Pacific (1879–1884), in which Chile easily mastered Bolivia and Peru, left bitter residues that in the short run meant the end of any program of Pan-Americanism led by Spanish-American republics. Although a few technical and nonpolitical conferences were held in the next few years, Pan-Americanism was discarded until the United States assumed the responsibility.

U.S. leadership marks the beginning of the "new" Pan-Americanism, dating from the 1880s until its demise in the 1930s. The "new" Pan-Americanism differed significantly from the "old." The four early conferences were dominated by the Spanish-American states and concerned themselves with problems that, while not exclusively Spanish American, seemed to threaten those states particularly. The meetings were usually provoked by the threat of outside aggression, and the solutions sought were political and military in nature. The "new" Pan-Americanism was more inclusive yet less ambitious in scope. It focused on low-profile issues, which contributed to increased conference participation and the building of Pan-Americanism into an institution of imposing size and machinery. Concomitantly, Latin Americans became increasingly vocal regarding U.S. dominance of hemispheric relations, culminating at the 1928 Havana conference.

Credit for inaugurating the series of "new" Pan-American conferences rests with James G. Blaine, who served as secretary of state in the brief (March to September 1881) administration of James A. Garfield. Blaine owed much of his genuine interest in Latin America to his admiration for Henry Clay. Both men envisioned a free-trade relationship among the countries of the Western Hemisphere. While U.S.–Latin American trade was nearly immeasurable during Monroe's presidency in the 1820s, by the 1880s the United States faced a healthy unfavorable trade balance caused by its large purchases of Latin America's raw materials and the small sales of manufactured goods to the area in return.

In addition to trade issues, Blaine confronted several ongoing disputes. The worst of these was the War of the Pacific, in which Bolivia had been decisively defeated by Chile, whose troops were occupying Lima, Peru. The Chileans gave every indication of making vast territorial acquisitions at Bolivia's and Peru's expense. In addition, several boundary disputes threatened the stability of Latin America and provoked Blaine into assuming the unpopular role of peacemaker. Blaine's intentions were better than either his methods or his agents, and he incurred significant displeasure from Latin Americans during his brief first term in office. Following Garfield's death, Blaine resigned the secretaryship. Before leaving the State Department, however, he promoted a call for the first International Conference of American States, to be held in Washington, D.C. Blaine's successors, Frederick T. Freylinghuysen and Thomas F. Bayard, had little interest in Latin American affairs. Freylinghuysen withdrew Blaine's invitation for an Inter-American conference in Washington.

The movement was renewed a few years later by the U.S. Congress, when it sponsored a survey of Latin America's economic conditions. With a more friendly atmosphere, the First International Conference convened in 1889, when the secretary of state was again James G. Blaine. All of the American states except the Dominican Republic (its absence was due to U.S. failure to ratify a trade treaty with its Caribbean neighbor) sent delegations of high caliber. With some opposition Blaine was chosen chairman of the sessions, a post in which he demonstrated considerable tact and skill.

In the midst of its industrial revolution, the United States anticipated that the conference would bring economic benefits through a customs union. Toward that end, the Latin American delegates were entertained lavishly and given an impressive and fatiguing six thousand mile railroad tour through the industrial heart of the nation. Understanding the U.S. intention, the Latin American delegates, led by the Argentines, failed to accept Blaine's proposed customs union. As producers of raw materials, the Latin Americans preferred open markets. Opposition also came from some U.S. congressmen, particularly those from the nation's agricultural sectors. Instead, a program of separate reciprocal trade treaties was recommended; a few were instituted, decades ahead of the Good Neighbor program of the 1930s. On the political front, an ambitious arbitration treaty was watered down in conference, nullified by a minority of delegations, and ratified by no one.

The most notable achievement of the Washington conference was the establishment of the International Union of American Republics for the collection and distribution of commercial information. The agency to execute this command was the Commercial Bureau of the American Republics, supervised by the U.S. secretary of state in Washington, D.C. This bureau met regularly and, expanding in both size and functions, became a useful agency to the American states, though a far cry from the Pan-Americanism of Bolívar's day. The date of the union's establishment, 14 April 1890, became known as Pan-American Day.

Although the delegates to the First International Conference had not scheduled any future meetings, they left Washington with the clear intention of so doing. Nothing happened until 1899, when President William McKinley suggested another conclave. Only then did the Commercial Bureau act. It selected Mexico City as the site for the second conference and handled the drafting of agenda and invitations.

PAN-AMERICANISM, 1900–1945

In this fashion the institutionalization of the International Conferences of American States developed. To reduce the appearance of U.S. domination, the conferences were held in the various Latin American capital cities, with the presumed hope of meeting in all of them. The record of attendance was very high, frequently unanimous, and only once were as many as three states absent (from Santiago, Chile, in 1923). The frequency of the sessions varied because of world wars, but four- or five-year intervals were the norm.

The second through sixth conferences (Mexico City, 1901–1902; Rio de Janeiro, 1906; Buenos Aires, 1910; Santiago, Chile, 1923; Havana, Cuba, 1928) experienced minimal success. The issues recurring most prominently at these meetings were arbitration, hemispheric peace, trade, the forcible collection of debts, U.S. dominance of the organization, and intervention by one state in the affairs of another (and, in the 1920s, arms control). Specific accomplishments of these many conferences were more modest. Resolutions, conventions, and treaties were often debated, but compromise was endless, and major solutions were rarely reached or ratified. One exception was the 1923 Gondra Treaty, designed to create machinery for the peaceful settlement of American disputes. This treaty served as the basis for similar machinery in the later Organization of American States. Major alterations included the substitution in 1910 of the name Pan-American

INTERNATIONAL CONFERENCES OF AMERICAN STATES

First	Washington, D.C.	1889–1890
Second	Mexico City	1901–1902
Third	Rio de Janeiro	1906
Fourth	Buenos Aires	1910
Fifth	Santiago	1923
Sixth	Havana	1928
Seventh	Montevideo	1933
Eighth	Lima	1938
Ninth	Bogota	1948
Tenth	Caracas	1954

Union for the Commercial Bureau, and in popular usage Pan-American Conference replaced International Conference of American States. From time to time some delegates expressed their dismay that Pan-Americanism was taking no steps toward the confederation so often praised, but the majority clearly preferred the use of the Pan-American Union as a sounding board for international public opinion and an agency that moved slowly in the settlement of specific problems.

The growing U.S. presence in the circum-Caribbean region after 1898 gave the Latin Americans cause for concern, and they used the Pan-American forums as the vehicle to chastise Washington's imperialistic policies. Before World War I, at Mexico City, Rio de Janeiro, and Buenos Aires, the Latin Americans insisted on recognition of national sovereignty as a means to thwart U.S. intervention. For the same reasons, they joined the League of Nations following the end of World War I, hoping to use that international forum to curtail U.S. ambitions south of the Rio Grande River. When the United States failed to join the league, the Latin Americans lost interest in the organization, and by the mid-1920s their attendance at annual meetings had dwindled greatly. At Santiago in 1923 and again at Havana in 1928, the Latin Americans vociferously protested the U.S. domination of the hemispheric agenda and its continued presence in several circum-Caribbean countries. Only the efforts of former Secretary of State Charles Evans Hughes prevented the passage of a resolution declaring that "no state has the right to intervene in the internal affairs of another." This was the last major U.S. stand on behalf of its interventionist policies.

In addition to the growing Latin American pressure, other factors influenced the United States to abandon its interventionist policy, and with it bring to an end the era of the "new" Pan-Americanism. The roots of the U.S. policy change can be traced to the end of World War I, which left Europe incapable of threatening the Western Hemisphere. Also, within the State Department since the early 1920s there was a growing frustration about the failure of the numerous interventions. The 1924 Democratic Party platform criticized the interventionist policy, a position repeated by Franklin D. Roosevelt, writing in *Foreign Affairs* in 1928. What did the United States have to show for its interventions in the circum-Caribbean region? the critics asked. As secretary of commerce, Herbert Hoover argued that the larger and more prosperous Latin American states refused to purchase U.S. goods as a protest against its Caribbean presence. And as president-elect in 1928, Hoover embarked on a goodwill tour of Central and South America, a harbinger of forthcoming change. Subsequently, State Department official Joshua Reuben Clark's *Memorandum on the Monroe Doctrine* renounced U.S. interventions in Latin America's domestic affairs under the terms of the Monroe Doctrine.

The policy shift climaxed on 4 March 1933, when President Franklin Roosevelt, in his inaugural address, promised to be a "good neighbor." Originally intended for all the world, in application it came to apply to Latin America. A further indicator of Roosevelt's intention not to interfere in Latin America's internal affairs was the selection of Sumner Welles as assistant secretary of state, a man who believed that hemispheric relations should be conducted on the basis of absolute equality. The policy shift was completed at the 1933 Montevideo conference, where the U.S. delegation approved the Convention on Rights and Duties of the States. It affirmed that "No state has the right to intervene in the internal or external affairs of another." The Latin American delegates at Montevideo were equally pleased when Secretary of State Cordell Hull announced that their countries need not fear intervention during the Roosevelt administration. Still, the Latin Americans needed to be reassured. Not sharing Washington's concerns about the rising European war clouds, they were not interested in discussing hemispheric defense at the 1936 Inter-American Conference for the Maintenance of Peace held in Buenos Aires, and in 1938 at the Lima Conference. Instead, they pressed for, and received, additional U.S. pledges of nonintervention. With these pledges, the "new Pan-Americanism" passed into history.

Roosevelt's words were followed by pragmatic actions. American troops were withdrawn from Haiti, the Dominican Republic, and Nicaragua. The United States did not interfere in either the Cuban or the Panamanian political turmoil of the 1930s. In fact, a new treaty with Panama provided additional advantages to the isthmian republic. Nor did the United States act when Central American dictators Tiburcio Carías, Maximiliano Hernández-Martínez, Anastasio Somoza, and Jorge Ubico illegally extended their presidential terms. A potentially explosive question raised by Mexico's expropriation of vast foreign oil holdings was treated by the Roosevelt administration as a matter of concern between the Mexican government and the oil companies.

Contrasted with the "old," the "new" Pan-Americanism was marked by more concern for nonpolitical objectives, both technical and social. The "old" had been geographically more restrictive and often purely Spanish; the "new" was deliberately hemispheric in scope, and the leadership clearly rested with the United States. Just as the "new" Pan-Americanism was passing into history, the trajectory of inter-American relations took yet another turn, and again the United States took the leadership role. Confronted with international crises—the Great Depression, World War II, and the cold war—the United States attempted to incorporate the Pan-American movement into its international policies.

The world was staggering under economic collapse when Franklin D. Roosevelt took the presidential oath in March 1933. World trade had declined by 25 percent in volume and by 66 percent in value since 1929. At the same time, U.S. trade with Latin America had declined more drastically: exports, by 78 percent in value and imports, by 68 percent. Convinced that economic nationalism exacerbated the depression, Secretary of State Hull sought the liberalization of trade polices. Congress consented in 1934 with the passage of the Reciprocal Trade Agreements Act, which enabled the U.S. government to strike beneficial tariff agreements with trading partners. Latin America fit neatly into the plan because it did not have a competitive industrial sector, nor did its major exports compete with U.S. commodities. In comparison, the United States was in a stronger position because it could serve as Latin America's chief supplier of manufactured goods, and given the fact that reciprocal trade agreements favored the principal supplier, tariff negotiations would focus only on products that constituted the chief source of supply. In sum, the act gave the U.S. a favorable negotiating position.

The Latin Americans understood the U.S. position, and that understanding contributed to the refusal of Argentina, Bolivia, Chile, Peru, Paraguay, and Uruguay to reach trade agreements with the United States. The United States managed to conclude agreements only with countries that were heavily dependent upon its markets for agriculture (usually monoculture) exports: Brazil, Colombia, Costa Rica, Cuba, El Salvador, Guatemala, Honduras, and Nicaragua. In the end, the reciprocal trade agreements with these countries had little economic impact, but for the Central American dictators the agreements provided an air of legitimacy for their illegal regimes.

Negotiations with Brazil illustrated the need to address another international issue: the threat of Nazi Germany to the Western Hemisphere. In addition to Brazil, influential German communities were located in Argentina, Chile, Colombia, Guatemala, Costa Rica, Mexico, Panama, and Paraguay. Over the course of the 1930s the United States viewed these communities as threats to hemispheric stability by spreading German propaganda, sending funds back to Berlin to be used for Nazi purposes, and engaging in espionage and, possibly, sabotage. The increased U.S. concern with Axis influence prompted Washington policymakers to commence western hemispheric defense plans in 1936. For the most part, Latin America's political leadership did not share Washington's concerns, and believed that Roosevelt was using the European troubles to circumvent the nonintervention pledge made in 1933 at Montevideo. Only after the German invasion of Poland in 1939 and the fall of France in June 1940 did the Latin American nations feel a sense of urgency about hemispheric defense. Until then, the United States obtained only an innocuous agreement at the 1936 Buenos Aires conference, reaffirmed at Lima in 1938, which called for consultation when an emergency threatened the hemisphere. The Lima conference was the last regular meeting of the American states until after World War II, but on three occasions the foreign ministers convened to confront wartime issues. Their work proved essential to the continuity of Pan-Americanism at a time when world-scale military agreements took precedence.

The first meeting of the foreign ministers took place in Panama City after the German invasion of Poland in September 1939. To protect hemispheric neutrality, the ministers agreed upon a safety zone south of Canada, extending an average of three hundred miles out to sea around the remainder of the hemisphere. Belligerent nations were warned not to commit hostile acts within this zone. Within a matter of weeks the zone was violated by both the British and the Germans, and frequent ship scuttlings in American waters in 1940 made the zone something of a nullity. More important, however, was the unanimity of the Americans in their resolve to keep the war away.

The second meeting of the Consultation of the Ministers of Foreign Affairs (the full title of these sessions) followed the fall of France to the Germans in June 1940. Again at the urging of the United States, the ministers met at Havana, Cuba, in July to discuss the question of European colonies in the Western Hemisphere and the danger of their falling into German hands. They agreed upon the Act of Havana, which provided that if a non-American state (Germany) should attempt to obtain from another non-American state (France, for example) any islands or other regions in the Americas, one or more American states would step in to administer such territory until it was able to govern itself freely or had been restored to its previous status. Fear that the Axis powers might attempt to occupy some of the many possessions in America was real enough; however, no such attempt was made. The ministers also affirmed the Declaration of Reciprocal Assistance and Cooperation for the Defense of the Nations of the Americas, the gist of which was that an attack upon the sovereignty of any American state was to be treated as an attack upon them all, a further broadening or multilateralizing of the Monroe Doctrine in process since 1933.

The third and last wartime meeting of the foreign ministers convened at the request of Chile and the United States as a consequence of the Japanese attack upon Pearl Harbor in December 1941. The statesmen met at Rio de Janeiro in January 1942, by which time ten American nations, including the United States, had declared war upon the Axis powers. The U.S. military services were not anxious for the participation of underequipped and poorly trained Latin American forces in a global struggle. U.S. military officials agreed with many of the ministers that the proper gesture would be the severing of diplomatic relations, which would eliminate the Axis influence in the Americas, and thereby help to reduce the flow of classified information to those governments. However, a strong declaration requiring the American states to break relations (favored by Secretary Hull) was so rigidly opposed by Argentina and Chile that the U.S. delegation, led by Sumner Welles, settled for a milder version that merely recommended such an action. The issue was deeper than one of semantics, for the Argentines were doing more than expressing their usual reluctance to appear to be following U.S. policy. The Argentine military was actually pro-German and gave considerable assistance to the Axis in the war.

The most important agreements at Rio dealt with the elimination of Axis influence in the Americas. With the exception of Argentina and Chile, the Latin American governments agreed to cooperate with the United States in deporting selected German nationals and their descendants back to Germany or to internment camps in the United States. Those who remained behind would be subject to tight supervision of their properties and greatly restricted freedoms. With a few exceptions, such as Brazil, Chile and Mexico, the war impacted adversely upon the Latin American economies, setting the stage for postwar political and social upheaval.

The United States also spread its ideals, values, and culture throughout Latin America via the wartime Office of Inter-American Affairs (OIAA), headed by Nelson A. Rockefeller. OIAA proselytized the war's democratic objectives through educational programs and dissemination of propaganda literature and Spanish-language Walt Disney films. It sponsored visits by U.S. artists, writers, and athletes to Latin America, and brought many Latin American students and professionals to U.S. institutions for advanced training. Of course, this was Pan-Americanism as seen by the United States, and it did not always achieve universal acceptance. Sometimes too glossy, and frequently expensive, it was reasonably sincere even when some cultural programs insulted the intelligence of the Latin Americans. But under the veneer was a solid construction of goodwill, and the U.S. policymakers—Sumner Welles, Cordell Hull, Nelson Rockefeller, and Franklin D. Roosevelt—understood the Latin American need for equality and dignity.

PAN-AMERICANISM SINCE 1945

Toward the close of the war, the American states met in the Inter-American Conference on the Problems of War and Peace at Mexico City in February 1945. Uninvited Argentina was conspicuously absent. The diplomats focused their attention upon the place that Pan-American regionalism would have in the plans for the proposed United Nations. Prodded by the United States, the Latin Americans insisted upon their right to protect themselves without having to seek the approval of the UN Security Council. Ultimately this demand was approved in the UN Charter. The conference also recommended that Argentina, after declaring war on the Axis, be permitted to participate in the San Francisco sessions that formalized the United Nations. The delegates drafted the Act of Chapultepec, which required the states to conclude a treaty of reciprocal assistance, a treaty on the settlement of disputes, and a new regional arrangement that would substitute a permanent treaty for the various informal agreements underlying the inter-American association in the past. These objectives were concluded in 1947 at a special conference in Rio de Janeiro and in 1948 at Bogota, Colombia, when the next regular International Conference of American States (the ninth) convened. Significantly, these meetings came at a time when the Truman administration was fashioning a Latin American policy that reflected its larger global strategy of containing Soviet aggression.

The Inter-American Treaty of Reciprocal Assistance, signed at Rio de Janeiro on 2 September 1947, committed the signatories to the solidarity sought against external aggression since Bolívar's days. An armed attack by a state against any American state was henceforth considered an attack against all, and each contracting party agreed to assist in meeting the attack. The assistance would be rendered collectively, following a consultation of the inter-American system and in accordance with the constitutional process of each nation, a recognition that not all countries were practicing democracies. The same obligations also applied should an armed attack occur within the region. In 1947, however, influenced by the World War II experience, policymakers focused upon potential external aggression.

The 1948 Bogota conference was nearly destroyed when the assassination of a popular Liberal Party leader was followed by citywide rioting. Nevertheless, the sessions were completed. The treaty for the pacific settlement of disputes was signed, but with so many additions and amendments that several states failed to ratify it. The major achievement was the reorganization of the entire inter-American system by the Charter of the Organization of American States (OAS), the first permanent treaty basis for the old structure. The charter declares the principles upon which the organization is based and the necessity for such machinery to be welded into the UN framework. Briefly, the OAS accomplishes its purposes by means of the following:

1. The Inter-American Conference, the supreme organ of the OAS, meeting every five years to decide general policy and action.
2. The Meeting of Consultation of Ministers of Foreign Affairs, called to discuss urgent matters and to serve as the organ of consultation.
3. The Council of the Organization of American States, meeting in permanent session and composed of one delegate from each member state. The council takes cognizance of matters referred to it by the agencies listed above and supervises the Pan-American Union.
4. The Pan-American Union is the general secretariat of the OAS, with a wide variety of functions. In addition there are several organs of the Council, specialized organizations, and special agencies and commissions.

In the 1960s several amendments were made to the OAS charter, the most fundamental being the replacement of the Inter-American Conference with an annual general assembly.

The final measure that incorporated Pan-Americanism into the U.S. global strategies came with U.S. congressional approval of the Military Assistance Program (MAP) in 1951. Since the end of World War II in 1945, the Truman administration had pushed Congress to approve MAP, designed to harmonize military equipment, training, and strategy throughout the hemisphere. Congress consistently resisted, on the grounds that the United States would be blamed for securing the positions of Latin American dictators. But with a global cold war, Congress relented. From 1951 through 1960, the U.S. materiel supplied to Latin America focused upon the need to resist external aggression in general, and to protect the Panama Canal and Venezuelan and Mexican oil supplies, in particular. In addition, Latin American military officers received training at U.S. military bases and institutions, most notably the School of the Americas in the Panama Canal Zone.

During the period 1945–1951, administration spokesmen continued to espouse traditional Pan-American ideals, such as the need for political stability, faith in democracy, and promises of nonintervention. While preaching these ideals, the United States ignored Latin American demands for an end to dictatorships and an improvement in the quality of life for the less fortunate. Until the mid-1950s, communism in Europe and Asia appeared more important.

In Latin America the tendency to indict social and political reformers as communists intensified as the cold war took root. Fearing the personal consequences of changes to the established order, Latin America's political leadership and socioeconomic elites came to accept the U.S. view that these reformers were Moscow-directed communists and that they were part of the Soviet scheme for world domination. The test case became Guatemala, where reformers Juan José Arévalo and Jacobo Arbenz introduced social programs that challenged the local elite's privileges. Arbenz's nationalization of United Fruit Company lands convinced Secretary of State John Foster Dulles of the need for action. In 1954 he took his case to the tenth inter-American conference at Caracas, where he sought a multinational blessing for a unilateral action. Dulles denied the existence of indigenous communist movements and asserted that every nation in the hemisphere had been penetrated by international communists under Moscow's direction. He called for decisive action, presumably under the terms of the Rio treaty, to eliminate subversive activities in the hemisphere. In effect, Dulles sought to Pan-Americanize the Monroe Doctrine in order to prevent what he alleged was Soviet penetration of the Western Hemisphere. Dulles did not single out Guatemala, but all present understood it was the target. Following the vote, Dulles left Caracas just as the conference began its discussion of Latin America's social and economic distress.

At Caracas, the U.S.-sponsored resolution was approved by a 17–1 vote, with Guatemala dissenting and Argentina and Mexico abstaining. A month later the Central Intelligence Agency sponsored an "invasion" of Guatemala by loyalist forces that ousted Arbenz and restored the traditional order. The United States manipulated events at the United Nations to prevent international scrutiny of its actions. Under Article 51 of the UN Charter, regional organizations were permitted to deal with regional problems before the United Nations intervened. In this case, the United States convinced the Security Council that the OAS had the Guatemalan situation under control.

The U.S. actions fueled anti-American sentiment across Latin America. Coupled with its failure to address the region's socioeconomic problems, the intervention in Guatemala reaffirmed Latin America's view that the United States did not intend to treat its southern neighbors as equals. Security from foreign intervention remained at the heart of Pan-Americanism, but since the late 1930s only the United States had determined the parameters of the threat.

The rise of communism as a threat in Latin America unquestionably provoked the feeling among many Americans, both North and South, that the Pan-American movement needed a long-range program to improve the economy and quality of life across South America. The first organized economic assistance to Latin America had been a part of the Good Neighbor program of the 1930s. Other precedents rested with the Point Four and mutual security programs during the Truman administration. Still, these programs did not address the disparities that characterized Latin America's socioeconomic landscape. In 1958, when Brazilian President Juscelino Kubitschek suggested some kind of "Economic Pan America," he unknowingly forewarned of Latin America's impending social revolutions. In response to Kubitschek's appeal, the OAS and the United Nations developed financial assistance programs for the hemisphere, and the Eisenhower administration initiated the Social Progress Trust Fund, but little was accomplished until the success of Fidel Castro's revolution in Cuba, which by 1961 destroyed Cuba's traditional political, social, and economic orders.

To meet the challenge, in 1961 President John F. Kennedy implemented the Alliance for Progress, which pledged a U.S. contribution of $1 billion per year over a ten-year period to modernize Latin America's economic and political systems. In effect the alliance was an admission that previous private and public investment and technical assistance programs alone were insufficient for the steady development of the region. The Latin Americans were to raise a total of $80 billion in investment capital over that ten-year period. Machinery for the alliance was established in 1961 at Punta del Este, Uruguay. The aim was to increase the per capita wealth of participating Latin American states by 2.5 percent each year for ten years. The revolutionary elements of the alliance, the vast amount of cooperative spending, and the strict requirements—such as tax reform, a commitment to land distribution, and broadening the democratic process—in order to qualify for alliance assistance raised the expectations of many Latin Americans.

For the most part, expectations were not realized. Despite advances in gross national products and progress in land tenure patterns, education, and health care, the same people who were in power in 1960 remained the most privileged in the 1970s, and the socioeconomic gap between them and the poor had not narrowed. There was sufficient blame to go around. Latin American elites refused to accept economic and political reforms. Latin Americans wanted a larger share in the decision making; the U.S. government wanted to give them less. As the fear of Castroism diminished by the late 1960s, owing to the bankruptcy of the Cuban economy and the emergence of military governments throughout Latin America, so did regional interest in socioeconomic reform. U.S. administrators and members of Congress became frustrated with Latin America's graft and corruption. Latin America's blip on the U.S. radar screen disappeared with the continuing crises in the Middle East and in Vietnam. Subsequently, the Watergate scandal preoccupied the Nixon administration until its downfall in 1973 and marred the brief presidency of Gerald Ford. Although aid to Latin America continued in reduced form after 1970, the U.S. Congress continually asked questions about the validity of any foreign aid program. In the vacuum created by the U.S. absence, the Latin American governments either turned inward or looked beyond the Western Hemisphere for economic assistance.

If the spirit of mutual respect projected in the early days of the alliance was jeopardized by the program's inadequacies, it was destroyed by unilateral U.S. political decisions: the Bay of Pigs invasion in 1961; the Cuban missile crisis in 1962; the landing of U.S. marines in the Dominican Republic in 1965; and the sale of U.S. arms to Latin America's military governments in the late 1960s and early 1970s. For all intents and purposes, a Pan-American consciousness did not exist by the mid-1970s.

President Jimmy Carter came to Washington in January 1977 determined to repair the damage done to Pan-Americanism during the previous fifteen years. He set the tone by negotiating treaties with Panama that returned the canal to that country in 2000. He made friendly gestures toward Cuba, which had been ousted from the inter-American system and had been experiencing a U.S. trade embargo since 1961. His human rights policy gave credence to the ideals of Pan-Americanism, but prompted the military governments in Argentina, Brazil, and Chile to produce their own armaments, and forced the besieged Central Americans to purchase their equipment on the world market.

If Carter had nudged toward closer cooperation with Latin America, President Ronald Reagan took several steps backward. His insistence that the Central American civil wars of the 1980s were yet another Soviet effort to extend communism in the Western Hemisphere fell on deaf ears in Latin America. Not only did Reagan fail to gain the support of the OAS, but his position was openly challenged by the Contadora Group—Colombia, Mexico, Panama, and Venezuela—which received encouragement from the "support group" of Argentina, Brazil, Peru, and Uruguay. The Latin Americans perceived the Central American crisis as a local one, caused by the socioeconomic and political disparities that characterized the region, not Soviet interventionism. These nations were determined to bring peace to the embattled region at the expense of the United States. Their efforts led eventually to the successful peace initiative by Costa Rican President Oscar Arias Sánchez, who received the 1987 Nobel Peace Prize for his efforts. Other U.S. unilateral actions that damaged inter-American relations included its invasions of Grenada (1983) and Panama (1989) and the threatened invasion of Haiti (1993). In tightening its embargo against Cuba in the early 1990s, the United States placed itself outside the hemispheric trend, which included the opening of trade relations between Cuba and several Latin American countries and Canada.

While U.S. Cold War policies gave credence to the charges of U.S. hegemonic influence over hemispheric affairs, they also severely damaged the spirit of Pan-Americanism. And the political purpose of Pan-Americanism, hemispheric security from a European threat that dated to the days of Simón Bolívar, disappeared with the collapse of the Soviet Union in 1991.

As the twentieth century came to a close, three issues dominated the hemispheric agenda: illegal drugs, migration, and commerce. Because these problems are multinational, each provides the opportunity for reviving the intention of Pan-Americanism: cooperation among the nations of the Western Hemisphere. While drugs have corrupted governments and terrified society in such places as Colombia, Mexico, Bolivia, and Peru, all hemispheric nations pay a heavy social and economic price for drug use. Rather than find a common ground for cooperation, the United States and Latin America place responsibility at one another's doorstep. Washington policymakers appear determined to eradicate drugs at the source—the remote areas of Colombia and the Andean countries—and to punish those nations that serve as transit points for the entry of drugs into the United States. In contrast, the Latin Americans charge that if U.S. residents cut their demand, there would be a concomitant decrease in the production of illegal drugs.

Migration, particularly of Latin Americans to the United States, is a most vexing problem. Given the fact that since the mid-1980s democratic governments have taken root across the region, save Cuba, immigrants can no longer claim to be escaping political persecution, the most valid reason for seeking asylum in the United States. Instead the new migrants are seen as economic refugees, and therefore are not admissible under current U.S. law. The United States also focuses its attention on the poor and unskilled immigrants, not the skilled or professional workers who are absorbed quickly into the North American economy and society. The unskilled workers are viewed as a threat to U.S. workers and a drain upon state and federal social programs that sustain them. On the other hand, Latin American nations fret at the loss of skilled and professional workers, but not the loss of the unskilled (because of limited economic opportunities for them at home). Furthermore, these workers remit badly needed U.S. currency to their relatives at home, and these monies become an important part of smaller nations' gross domestic product.

One way to address the drug and migration problems in Latin America is economic development, and since the 1980s these nations have become increasingly involved in the global economy. At first, regional cooperation appeared to be the best route. Toward that end several regional economic organizations were formed. The Central American Common Market (CACM) dates to 1959. Others include the Andean Pact (1969) and the Caribbean Community and Common Market (CARICOM) of 1972. Each took on new significance with the globalization process that began in the 1980s. The most promising organization appears to be the Southern Cone Common Market (MERCOSUR). Established in 1991, it brought together Argentina, Brazil, Paraguay, and Uruguay for the purpose of establishing a customs union similar to the European Union. By

2000 Chile and Bolivia had become associate members in anticipation of full membership at some point in the future. The United States joined the parade in 1993 when Congress finally approved the North American Free Trade Agreement (NAFTA), linking it with Mexico and Canada in what is to be a free market by 2005. But the United States would go no farther. Congress denied President Bill Clinton "fast track" negotiating privileges to reach an accord with Chile that would bring the latter into the NAFTA accord. The latter congressional action may be symptomatic of the basic problem that has plagued the Pan-American movement since its inception in the early nineteenth century: national interest.

In June 1990, President George H. W. Bush launched the Enterprise for the Americas Initiative, its ultimate goal being a free trade zone "stretching from the port of Anchorage to the Tierra del Fuego." Shortly thereafter the NAFTA agreement was concluded, prompting many analysts to predict that it would become the vehicle to expand free trade throughout the Western Hemisphere. President Bill Clinton kept the initiative alive when he convened a meeting of thirty-four heads of state (only Cuba's Fidel Castro was not invited) in Miami in December 1994. This was the first such gathering since 1967. In the end, the signatories designated 2005 as a deadline for the conclusion of negotiating a Free Trade Association of the Americas (FTAA), with implementation to follow in subsequent years. Advocates hailed the agreement for its high-minded principles and ambitious goals. Critics lamented its vagueness and its drawn-out timetable. The pledge of free trade was repeated when the heads of state gathered again in Santiago, Chile, in 1998 and Quebec City, Canada, in April 2001. In between, technical committees have been working on the details of a free trade pact. Still, national interests stand in the way. Given the history of inter-American relations, Latin Americans question the sincerity of the U.S. commitment to hemispheric free trade. Brazil has made clear its intention to unite all of South America into one trading bloc before dealing with the FTAA. Mexico has signed a trade agreement with the European Union, and the MERCOSUR partnership is seeking agreements with Europe and South Africa. Chile, the unabashed example of free market reforms, pursues its own global strategies.

The world has changed drastically since the Latin Americans sought security from European intervention in the nineteenth century. It also has changed from the early twentieth century through the end of the cold war, when the United States single-handedly worked to keep the Europeans out of the Western Hemisphere. With the end of the Cold War, the need for hemispheric political security disappeared, at least momentarily, and with it, the original reason for the Pan-American movement. But the realities of the new world—drugs, migration, and commerce—provide the opportunity to revive the Pan-American spirit. The challenge before the nations of the Western Hemisphere is great: Can they overcome the national interests that have plagued the relationship in the past?

BIBLIOGRAPHY

Aguilar, Alonzo. *Pan-Americanism from the Monroe Doctrine to the Present.* New York, 1968. A critical Latin American assessment of Pan-Americanism.

Burr, Robert N., and Roland D. Hussey, eds. *Documents on Inter-American Cooperation.* 2 vols. Philadelphia, 1955. Includes well-selected and well-edited documents from 1810 to 1948.

Gellman, Irwin F. *Good Neighbor Diplomacy: United States Policies in Latin America, 1933–1945.* Baltimore, 1979.

Gil, Federico G. *Latin American–United States Relations.* New York, 1971. A dated but popular survey of the subject, providing broad, not intensive, coverage.

Gilderhus, Mark T. *Pan-American Visions: Woodrow Wilson in the Western Hemisphere, 1913–1921.* Tucson, Ariz., 1986.

———. *The Second Century: U.S.–Latin American Relations Since 1889.* Wilmington, Del., 2000.

Harrison, Lawrence E. *The Pan-American Dream.* Boulder, Colo., 1991. A most critical assessment of U.S. aid policies to Latin America.

Inman, Samuel Guy. *Inter-American Conferences, 1826–1954.* Washington, D.C., 1965. Gives accounts, both personal and official, by perhaps the most zealous specialist on Latin America and includes intimate information available from no other source.

Johnson, John J. *A Hemisphere Apart: The Foundations of United States Policy Toward Latin America.* Baltimore, 1990.

LaRosa, Michael, and Frank O. Mora, eds. *Neighborly Adversaries: Readings in U.S.–Latin American Relations.* Lanham, Md., 1999. Updates the volume by Burr and Hussey.

Lockey, James B. *Pan-Americanism: Its Beginnings.* New York, 1920. A good starting point for understanding the concept of Pan-Americanism that provides a detailed, sympathetic study of the movement from independence through the end of the Panama congress of 1826.

Mecham, J. Lloyd. *The United States and Inter-American Security, 1889–1960.* Austin, Tex., 1961. One of the foremost studies of Pan-Americanism, providing a detailed, chronological approach to all the major conferences.

Merk, Frederick. *Manifest Destiny and Mission in American History: A Reinterpretation.* New York, 1963.

Pastor, Robert A. *Condemned to Repetition: The United States and Nicaragua.* Princeton, N.J., 1987.

Paterson, Thomas G. *Contesting Castro: The United States and the Triumph of the Cuban Revolution.* New York, 1994.

Perkins, Whitney T. *Constraint of Empire: The United States and Caribbean Interventions.* Westport, Conn., 1981. A crisp analysis of the circum-Caribbean region.

Rabe, Stephen G. *Eisenhower and Latin America: The Foreign Policy of Anticommunism.* Chapel Hill, N.C., 1988.

Scheman, L. Ronald. *The Inter-American Dilemma: The Search for Inter-American Cooperation at the Centennial of the Inter-American System.* New York, 1988.

Scheman, L. Ronald, ed. *The Alliance for Progress: A Retrospective.* New York, 1988.

Schoultz, Lars, ed. *Security, Democracy and Development in U.S.–Latin American Relations.* Miami, Fla., 1994.

Sheinin, David, ed. *Beyond the Ideal: Pan-Americanism in Inter-American Affairs.* Westport, Conn., 2000. An important collection of essays that demonstrates the utilization of Pan-Americanism beyond the security issue.

Smith, Peter H. *Talons of the Eagle: The Dynamics of U.S.–Latin American Relations.* New York, 1996. A broad survey that includes the Latin American response to U.S. hegemony.

Weintraub, Sidney, ed. *Integrating the Americas: Shaping Future Trade Policy.* New Brunswick, N.J., 1994.

Whitaker, Arthur P. *The Western Hemisphere Idea: Its Rise and Decline.* Ithaca, N.Y., 1954. A stimulating study of Pan-Americanism as an idea and of how time has destroyed much of the buttressing hemispheric relations.

See also DICTATORSHIPS; INTERVENTION AND NONINTERVENTION; NARCOTICS POLICY; RECOGNITION.

PARTY POLITICS

Fredrik Logevall

"A splendid little war," John Hay called the 1898 conflict between Spain and the United States. It was splendid, he told his fellow Republicans Theodore Roosevelt and Henry Cabot Lodge, because it had moved things "our way." In other words, military victory and overseas expansion were helping President William McKinley and his Republican administration against William Jennings Bryan's Democrats. "I do not see a ghost of a chance of Bryanism in the new few years," remarked Hay. At the time, the summer of 1898, John Hay was the U.S. ambassador to Great Britain. Before long he would be appointed secretary of state. Thus, his was no ivory tower statement pronounced far from the halls of power. Rather, his comments on the connection between party politics and foreign policy came from the highest level of American officialdom.

The ambassador was not claiming that McKinley had chosen war to help the Republican Party, although it was widely believed that the president would have suffered politically if he had not requested a declaration of hostilities against Spain. What Hay was saying was that the course of American foreign policy was inextricably tied to domestic politics in the United States, and that the party in power has partisan politics partly in mind when it acts on international developments. Hay saw nothing wrong with this. The developments in 1898 meshed with his own worldview; he had no objection to the use of force "when necessary," and he saw an imperial push into the Caribbean and Pacific as potentially helpful to his business friends. If the Republicans benefited as well, so much the better. Hay believed in the GOP, considering it the "party fit to govern," a bulwark against inflation, radicalism, and civil disorder. Bryan's Democratic-Populist rural alliance almost won the 1896 presidential election on free silver, a domestic issue. Hay now judged that the Republicans would pick up strength on foreign policy and could establish themselves in power for a decade or more.

This is by no means an unusual example in American history. If anything, John Hay represents less than the usual identification of domestic politics with U.S. foreign relations. He never ran for elective office, although other secretaries of state have, from Thomas Jefferson and John Quincy Adams to William H. Seward and James G. Blaine on down to William Jennings Bryan, Charles Evans Hughes, James F. Byrnes, and John Foster Dulles. Nor did Hay depend on politics for his living after his early thirties. Hence, he was not forced to think of the next election in terms of personal financial survival.

In contrast, most of those who have shaped American foreign policy have been professional politicians, accustomed to thinking of individual recognition, career progress, and personal income in connection with party favor and victory at the polls. So it has been with presidents of the United States, the most important makers of foreign policy. So also with secretaries of state and defense, at least until the last few decades, when these offices have usually been held by nonpoliticians (who, of course, are bound to the president's political positions). So with a number of those who have headed American diplomatic missions abroad; now, as always, many of these assignments are handled under political patronage. So also with congressmen who specialize in international matters and with other leaders in both major parties, in and out of office.

Could these individuals, being practical party politicians, be expected to forget domestic politics when they weigh foreign policy alternatives? Hardly. And, as a general rule, they do not. No doubt some have obsessed about it more than others, but all, or virtually all, have operated from the assumption that if they do stop thinking of the next election or ignore the reaction of the other professional politicians in Congress and in the field, they are not likely to be able to put across their programs. In the words of the historian Fred Harvey Harrington, "Success in American foreign policy, like success on domestic issues, requires continuing success in domestic politics."

Which is not to say it is only about winning elections. As the Hay example illustrates, politicians often have had particular and deeply felt ideas about international matters, ideas that their party (or a large segment of their party) have shared or endorsed. Often the candidates of the opposing party have had different ideas. Foreign policy, therefore, is about choosing among real policy choices as well as getting partisan advantage from those choices.

That said, the argument here is that elections are particularly important in determining why the United States has followed the international course it has. In America the jockeying for political advantage never stops. Viewed from a president's perspective the next election (whether midterm or presidential) will arrive all too soon, and presidents are well aware that voters are capable of giving incumbent parties the boot (as they have done with regularity since 1945: in 1952, 1960, 1968, 1976, 1980, 1992, and 2000). Moreover, the overall state of a president's relations with Congress and his standing in public opinion deeply impact his ability to get things done and, in general, to lead effectively. As Ralph Levering reminds us, political campaigns are significant because they indicate which foreign policy issues each candidate believes his opponent is vulnerable on, and which issues each candidate believes are likely to strike a response chord in the voting public. "The interplay between candidates and voters, culminating in the voting first in the primaries and then in the general election in November, thus establishes (a) the winners who will have primary responsibility for shaping U.S. foreign policy, and (b) the broad parameters of acceptable political discourse on foreign policy for the foreseeable future."

It seems obvious, then, that those who analyze U.S. foreign policy decisions should carefully consider the role of domestic politics in those decisions and in what happened afterward. Analysis must, of course, also take into account geostrategic, economic, cultural, moral, and other influences. Sometimes these influences, rather than practical politics, have been decisive. More often than not, however, the nonpolitical factors have been interwoven with political considerations, which need to be identified and explained. Although students of the interplay between domestic politics and foreign policy often include within their purview—and properly so—a wide range of potential influences, including public opinion, the media, and ethnic groups and other special interest groups, the focus here is on party politics, in particular on the impact of partisan imperatives and election-year concerns on presidential decision making in foreign affairs.

A CURIOUS NEGLECT

Over the years scholars have produced some excellent special studies of the interrelationship between politics and diplomacy. What is striking, though, is how often studies altogether omit mention of domestic politics. Some do so because they tell the story in the old-fashioned way, recording exchanges of diplomatic notes and making no attempt to get behind the formal documents. Others dig much deeper yet still treat the professional politicians involved in the making of foreign policy as though they were not politicians at all.

Historiographical trends among diplomatic historians, it is clear, have conspired against a prominent place for domestic politics. Most of the early giants in the field, among them Samuel Flagg Bemis, Dexter Perkins, and Arthur Whitaker (Thomas A. Bailey was a notable exception), focused on state-to-state interaction, on high U.S. officials and their counterparts in the countries with which Washington dealt. The research of these "orthodox" historians was often intelligent and exceptionally valuable, but they tended to frame their questions in a manner that allowed them to avoid inquiring into the domestic political calculations that helped shape policy, or the partisan disputes that often accompanied the implementation of that policy. Perkins's three-volume study of the Monroe Doctrine of 1823, for example, takes more or less as a given that national security concerns brought about the doctrine, while Bemis's book on Jay's Treaty concludes before the bitter debate in Congress in 1795–1796 on the treaty's implementation. Herbert Feis, an orthodox historian of the early Cold War, likewise focused exclusively on the White House, the State Department, and state-to-state relations in his effort to assign responsibility for the origins of the Soviet-American confrontation.

This emphasis among orthodox historians on high politics met with a spirited response from a group of "revisionist" scholars who came of age in the late 1950s and 1960s. But although revisionists distinguished themselves by emphasizing the importance of domestic forces in the conduct of U.S. foreign policy, they paid curiously little attention to party politics. No less than the traditionalists, they treated the U.S. government as a monolithic actor, albeit one shaped largely by the economic and ideological interests associated with the U.S. government's capitalist structure. The emphasis was on internal sources of foreign policy, but not on partisan wrangling, election-year maneuvering, or other political concerns. Thus, Walter LaFeber's *The New Empire* (1963), which dealt with Gilded Age foreign relations, gave little room to the congressional coalition that time and again thwarted the expansionist initiatives of the high officials that are a chief concern of the book. In William Appleman Williams's classic work *The Tragedy of American Diplomacy* (1959) one looks in vain for any sense that partisan concerns have on occasion played a key role in shaping American foreign policy. In this and other Williams works, congressional speeches and campaign pronouncements were generally cited only to show the supposed consensus behind American economic expansion. As the historian Robert David Johnson has rightly noted, revisionist interpretations of the Cold War by the likes of Gabriel Kolko and Noam Chomsky share little or nothing in common with Herbert Feis apart from a tendency to treat the U.S. government as a unitary actor unencumbered by internal dissension.

The emergence in the last two decades of the twentieth century of "postrevisionists"—a loose collection of scholars of the Cold War who did not fit easily into either the orthodox or revisionist camps—did not change the pattern. John Lewis Gaddis, a founder of postrevisionism, gave close scrutiny to domestic politics in his first book, *The United States and the Origins of the Cold War,* but gave steadily less attention to it in his subsequent works—to the point that in *We Now Know* (1997), Gaddis's major reinterpretation of the early Cold War, party politics figured hardly at all. Melvyn P. Leffler's *A Preponderance of Power* (1992), a highly important volume on the Truman administration's national security policy, likewise gave little space to the interplay between foreign policy and party politics, a characteristic shared as well by Marc Trachtenberg in his prize-winning book *A Constructed Peace* (1999). Trachtenberg's study, subtitled "The Making of the European Settlement, 1945–1963," says nary a word about domestic politics, and his American policymakers appear to operate in a rarefied geopolitical stratosphere that keeps them largely immune to domestic pressure.

What is striking about these and other postrevisionist studies is not that they have tended to place geopolitics at the top in their hierarchy of causality; given the neorealist or national security perspectives to which many postrevisionists adhere, that is to be expected. Rather, what is striking is that domestic politics appears so far down in that hierarchy, if it even makes it on the list at all.

To a remarkable degree, then, scholars of American diplomacy, whatever their other disagreements, have tended over the years to agree on one important point: partisan wrangling and electoral strategizing have generally not been significant determinants of the nation's foreign policy. It is a perspective that accords with the popular belief that political differences among Americans should, and in fact usually do, stop at the water's edge, that it would be improper and indecent to mix politics and foreign policy, and that American leaders generally have avoided doing so.

In 1974, when the Watergate scandal was catching up with President Richard M. Nixon, Secretary of State Henry A. Kissinger was asked if the resignation of the chief executive and the resulting damage to the Republican Party would change the course of American diplomacy. Certainly not, retorted Kissinger, everything would be the same. "The foreign policy of the United States," he maintained, "has always been, and continues to be conducted on a bipartisan basis in the national interest and in the interest of world peace." Others have voiced like sentiments, though usually without introducing quite so much historical error. Operating here is the traditional belief that national patriotism holds Americans together against the outside world. However much citizens may disagree on domestic questions, runs the argument, they must—and will—present a united front on foreign relations, in the national interest and to uphold the nation's honor. Discussions of this subject can become heated and bring forth Stephen Decatur's celebrated toast given at Norfolk in 1816: "Our Country! In her intercourse with foreign nations may she always be in the right; but our country, right or wrong."

It is a comforting notion, since it protects America's leaders from charges of "sordid political calculation" or "playing politics with the national honor." But it also separates diplomatic history from reality. It fails to consider the plain fact that there inevitably are differences of opinion on foreign policy, and that in a democracy these differences are put before the people, if at all, through the political process (that is, through politics)—facts that professional politicians are not likely to forget.

THE FIRST DECADES

These differences were much in evidence from the very beginning of the two-party system, in the 1790s. Few were the foreign policy decisions in that decade that were not affected by partisan concerns. Even George Washington's Farewell Address, to this day the major statement of the need for American freedom of action in foreign affairs (it warned against "permanent alliances"), must be seen in light of the 1796 election. The French minister to Philadelphia, Pierre Adet, upset over the pro-British Jay's Treaty and America's failure to honor the 1778 alliance with France, worked hard to have Thomas Jefferson win the 1796 presidential race over the Federalist candidate, John Adams. That interference influenced Washington (and his coauthor Alexander Hamilton, a bitter foe of Jefferson) to issue the Farewell Address that warned Americans against tying themselves to the fortunes of any "foreign influence." The historian Alexander DeConde put it succinctly: "Although cloaked in phrases of universal or timeless application, the objectives of the address were practical, immediate, and partisan."

Party politics and electoral strategizing also permeated the atmosphere in the lead-up to the War of 1812 and indeed helped bring on the hostilities. As many historians have demonstrated, the increasingly bitter partisan struggle over domestic and foreign policy in the early years of the century, exacerbated by the effects of the war between Britain and France, grew into corrosive mutual distrust. Federalists and Republicans were deeply split on the best policy vis-à-vis Great Britain, and the vote for war followed partisan lines—81 percent of Republicans in both houses voted for war (98 to 23), and all Federalists voted nay (39 to 0).

But President Madison's concerns went deeper than defending against Federalist attacks on his commercial warfare policy. He also had to worry about dissension among fellow Republicans and the possibility that these "malcontents"—who wanted a tougher line against the British—might move to create an anti-Madison

ticket in 1812. By the spring of 1811, sympathetic legislators were warning Madison that he had to do something to unify the party, and by July of that year the pressures of domestic politics were making it very hard for the administration to agree to anything short of Britain's total capitulation to American demands. According to the historian J. C. A. Stagg, for Madison "there seemed to be only one course of action that would be both honorable and effective. He could regain the initiative at home and abroad by moving toward the positions advocated for so long by his Republican opponents. If he did not do so, there was the possibility that they would coalesce into a formidable anti-administration party, make the issue of war and preparedness wholly their own, and turn them against him in the months to come." In Stagg's words, "the nation's honor, the president's political salvation, and the unity of the Republican Party required that American policy now be directed toward war." What's more, the strategy worked: by May 1812 the malcontents had faded and a sufficiently large Republican majority had emerged in both houses to renominate Madison. The declaration of war followed in June.

This is not to suggest that Madison's fears for his domestic political standing alone drove the decision making that led to war with Great Britain. Monocausal history is seldom satisfactory history. The violations of American maritime rights, the impressment of American seamen, British incitement of hostile Native Americans, American designs on Canada and Florida, the depressing effects of British policy on American farm prices—each of these mattered as well, as did the long-standing partisan squabbling between Federalists and Republicans. It is also clear, though, that the president's perceived political needs, specifically his concern about possibly losing his party's nomination in 1812, shaped American policy in crucial ways. In particular, understanding why the war happened when it did—in a presidential election year, and with the incumbent in a precarious position at home—requires understanding the high-stakes struggle within the Republican Party.

Consider again the Monroe Doctrine of 1823. In a provocative work bearing the prosaic title *The Making of the Monroe Doctrine* (1975), the historian Ernest R. May rejected the claim of Perkins and others that conceptions of national interest and foreign policy were supreme in the origins of the doctrine. Instead, May argued, party politics were decisive. ("The positions of the policymakers were determined less by conviction than by ambition.") In May's view the outcome of the foreign policy debates can only be understood in relation to the struggle for the presidency, because the Monroe Doctrine was "actually a by-product of an election campaign." The threat of intervention by the European powers into the Western Hemisphere was nonexistent, and American officials knew it. As a result, they could play politics with the British proposal for a joint policy statement; John Quincy Adams opposed joint action while his bitter presidential rival John C. Calhoun fervently supported it. Adams's candidacy would have been hurt by consummation of an alliance with Britain because the British were thoroughly unpopular among the U.S. electorate. As secretary of state, Adams would have been attacked for joining with the British even if he opposed the alliance in private cabinet discussions. Calhoun pushed for acceptance of the London government's offer, knowing Adams would be blamed for it, while President Monroe, anxious to leave the presidency with his reputation intact, gave in to Adams to avoid a fight that might tarnish his record. It is a compelling argument, made in part, as May noted, on the basis of "inference from circumstantial evidence." One does not have to embrace May's thesis in its entirety—Were officials really so certain that no foreign danger existed?—to see that party politics were instrumental in the making of the doctrine.

And party politics were instrumental in foreign policymaking at various other times as well in the decades before John Hay took such delight at the outcome of the war against Spain. Here one thinks, for example, of the debate over whether to recognize Greek independence in 1823 (which, like the Monroe Doctrine, was intimately bound up with the 1824 presidential race); of President Franklin Pierce's attempt to acquire Cuba in 1854 in order to placate proslavery leaders in the American South; and of Grover Cleveland's decision—made partly for partisan reasons—not to submit the 1884 Berlin agreement on Africa's partition (of which he basically approved) to the Senate for approval.

Nor did things change after the century turned. The Wilson administration's original decision to postpone recognition of Bolshevik Russia in 1918 was not primarily the product of political pressure within the United States, but the fact that this nonrecognition continued for fifteen years and was intimately connected with domestic politics. A few politicians seem to have felt that nonrecog-

nition would damage the Soviet Union or protect the United States against real dangers. Many more were convinced that taking a stand against the Soviet Union and domestic radicals was "good politics" or that those who openly favored diplomatic recognition of the Soviet Union would suffer political punishment. Consequently, practical politics in the United States served to prevent these two major powers from discussing their differences until the need for foreign trade enabled Franklin D. Roosevelt to reestablish diplomatic relations in 1933.

In 1936 and again in 1940, Roosevelt allowed reelection concerns to affect his approach to the Nazi menace. In the late summer of 1936, Roosevelt told journalists of his desire to convene a conference of world leaders to discuss ways to assure the peace of the world; at the same time, he ruled out taking any steps prior to the election that could open him to Republican charges that he was embroiling the United States in overseas commitments. Four years later, Roosevelt's hesitation in finalizing the destroyers-for-bases deal with Great Britain—he delayed for nearly four months after receiving Winston Churchill's desperate pleas for destroyers—owed much to his fear that Republican challenger Wendell Willkie might use the issue to rouse isolationist sentiment and thereby cost Roosevelt the election that fall. Only after Willkie agreed not to make the transaction a campaign issue was the deal struck. Overall during that critical year, Roosevelt moved cautiously on foreign policy, concerned that open diplomatic moves would evoke isolationist predictions of U.S. involvement in the fighting and undermine his chances for a third term.

THE EARLY COLD WAR

To be sure, Americans have on occasion set partisan and personal political concerns aside in foreign policy, in line with the sentiment of Stephen Decatur's toast. This has been the pattern in the early stages of the nation's wars. But such consensus on international matters has often been short-lived, more so than is generally acknowledged. It is often assumed, for example, that the period surrounding the onset of the Cold War—from the end of World War II to the start of 1950—was a bipartisan period in U.S. foreign policy. A close examination of these years suggests otherwise. There was a period of strong bipartisanship on foreign policy decisions in Washington from the passage of the aid to Greece and Turkey in 1947 through the middle of 1949, but it was not there before that time or after.

In late 1945, with the popular Franklin D. Roosevelt dead and World War II over, Republicans in Congress saw a chance to gain control on Capitol Hill in the 1946 elections and to take the presidency two years later. On domestic issues they could run against the federal government and against trade unions, especially the open influence of the American Communist Party in those unions. On foreign policy issues the GOP could denounce Truman's "weakness" in dealing with the Soviet Union—that is, unless the administration preempted this line of attack by standing up forcefully to Moscow.

Domestically, Truman could do relatively little to deflect the Republican challenge on policy issues. He could, however, be firmer with the Soviets—a shift urged on him in the fall of 1945 by his White House chief of staff, Admiral William Leahy, and by the two leading senators on the Foreign Relations Committee, Democrat Tom Connally of Texas and Republican Arthur Vandenberg of Michigan. Vandenberg, who represented a state with a large number of Polish Americans unhappy with developments in their native land, was especially adamant about standing up to the Kremlin on all fronts.

It is unclear just how much of an effect partisan politics had on Truman's decision to "stop babying" the Soviets in early 1946. But he was very much aware of the growing congressional criticism of Secretary of State James Byrnes's continuing efforts to make deals with Moscow, and also Congress's aim, now that World War II was over, to reassert legislative authority of some foreign policy issues. The evidence is not conclusive, but it appears Truman was significantly affected by strong pressures from Congress to take a harder line toward the Soviet Union in the early weeks of 1946. In the election campaign that autumn, political paranoia and exploitation was much in evidence. Republican campaigners delighted in asking voters: "Got enough inflation? . . . Got enough debt? . . . Got enough strikes? . . . Got enough communism?" Senator Robert Taft, one of the most distinguished figures on Capitol Hill, accused Truman of seeking a Congress "dominated by a policy of appeasing the Russians abroad and fostering communism at home," while in California, a young House candidate named Richard Nixon denounced his opponent as a "lip service American" who consistently voted the

Moscow line in Congress and who fronted for "un-American elements." And indeed, the GOP scored a resounding victory in the election, gaining control of both houses of Congress for the first time since 1928. The day after the election several of Truman's advisers met and concluded that the White House would have to take definite steps to put the Democratic coalition back together if Truman was to have any chance of winning the 1948 election. One such step: make clear to the American people that Harry Truman opposed Soviet domination of eastern Europe.

As the 1948 election approached, Truman missed few opportunities to talk up the Cold War, a strategy urged on him by numerous advisers. Such a stance, they pointed out, would insulate the president against Republican charges that he was too soft on Moscow and at the same time undercut Henry Wallace's bid for the presidency on the Progressive ticket. In November 1947, White House aide Clark Clifford and former FDR assistant James Rowe predicted that relations with Moscow would be the key foreign policy issue in the campaign, that those relations would get worse during the course of 1948, and that this would strengthen Truman's domestic political position. "There is considerable political advantage in the administration in its battle with the Kremlin," the two men told the president. "The worse matters get . . . the more is there a sense of crisis. In times of crisis, the American citizen tends to back up his president." In the months that followed, White House speechwriters talked tough on Soviet-American relations and mocked Wallace's call for improved relations with the Kremlin, portraying him as an unwitting dupe of communists at home and abroad.

It was a conscious blurring of domestic and foreign communism, and it would have important implications for politics in Cold War America. In the spring of 1947, Truman had created the Federal Employee Loyalty Program, which gave government security officials authorization to screen two million employees of the federal government for any hint of political deviance. It marked the inauguration of an anticommunist crusade within America's own borders that paralleled the Cold War abroad, a crusade that contained a large element of practical politics. Opposing radicals and the Soviet Union was a way of attracting votes and building a political reputation, or of avoiding being denounced as a fellow traveler. Meanwhile, any possibility for honest debate and criticism about policy toward the communist world disappeared, as those on the left who might have articulated an alternative vision lost cultural and political approval. For at least a quarter of a century thereafter, campaign attacks from the left on either Democratic or Republican foreign policies proved singularly unsuccessful.

Truman went on to win the 1948 election against the expectations of many. Stunned Republicans immediately began working overtime to exploit the communist victory in China, allegations of communists within the U.S. government, and Secretary of State Dean Acheson's support of the accused spy Alger Hiss as they maneuvered for revenge in the midterm election two years later. When the Korean War broke out in June 1950, Truman initially received strong bipartisan support for his decision to intervene. But he knew the Republican support could evaporate quickly. When Truman that summer considered a plan to expand the war into North Korea, he feared that what the historian Melvin Small called "the prudent but not anticommunist-enough decision" to halt at the Thirty-Eighth Parallel could hurt the Democrats at the polling booth in November. Truman authorized General Douglas MacArthur to try to liberate North Korea and announced his decision at a cabinet meeting where the major item on the agenda was the election.

MacArthur's gambit caused Chinese forces to intervene from the North in November 1950, and a military stalemate quickly developed. When the Truman administration commenced armistice talks in 1951, GOP leaders, still determined to make foreign policy a central part of their criticism of the Democrats, immediately went on the attack. Any truce at or near the Thirty-Eighth Parallel would be an "appeasement peace," they charged. When the presidential election campaign geared up the following year, Republican leaders, including nominee Dwight D. Eisenhower, asserted that Truman had been foolish to agree to negotiations and that he was compounding the error by continuing them in the face of clear evidence that the communists were using the time to build up their forces in Korea. Even the apparent economic health of the nation was turned against the White House: the prosperity, GOP spokesmen charged, "had at its foundation the coffins of the Korean war dead," slaughter that as yet appeared to have no end. The historian Rosemary Foot, in her study of the Korean armistice talks, showed that this partisan pressure contributed to the hardening of the administration's bargaining posture in 1952. "Sensitivity to public charges, to congressional

attacks, and to electoral charges that the Democratic administration had been led into a negotiating trap by its 'cunning' enemies, all reinforced the administration's preference for standing firm rather than compromising," Foot concluded. Pleas from the State Department for a flexible posture, especially on the nettlesome issue of repatriating prisoners of war, fell on deaf ears.

Attacking an incumbent's policies is a simpler matter than governing, as the Republicans would soon learn. Upon taking office in January 1953, Eisenhower faced not merely the task of bringing the Korean War to an end (a deal was reached in July 1953) but a myriad of other thorny issues as well. Party politics, it is clear, influenced his approach to many of them. And it was not just the Democrats Eisenhower had to think about; he also confronted differing impulses on foreign policy within his own party. Some so-called old guard Republicans such as Robert Taft were dubious about the Europe-centered internationalism to which Eisenhower and his soon-to-be secretary of state, John Foster Dulles, adhered in the 1952 campaign; many of them wanted a limited American role in world affairs, rooted in an airpower-oriented Fortress America strategy and weighted more toward Asia. Eisenhower immediately set upon placating this old guard on military, Asian, and domestic security matters to gain its acquiescence in a Europe-first internationalism. He undoubtedly had the old guard partly in mind when he wrote to his NATO commander, Alfred Gruenther, in the midst of the Quemoy-Matsu crisis of 1954–1955, that "at home, we have the truculent and the timid, the jingoists and the pacifists." On Taiwan, the president continued, he was considering "what solutions we can get that will best conform to the long term interests of the country and at the same time *can command a sufficient approval in this country so as to secure the necessary Congressional action*" (original emphasis).

VIETNAM

On Indochina, as well, domestic political imperatives affected Eisenhower's policymaking. During the intense administration discussions about whether to intervene militarily to help the beleaguered French forces at Dien Bien Phu in 1954, Eisenhower told his cabinet that he could not afford to let the Democrats ask who lost Vietnam. But he was not prepared to get involved without broad domestic and international backing. At a news conference Eisenhower invoked the domino theory to try to create support for intervention (probably less because he believed in the theory than because its dramatic imagery could rally support to the cause), and he consulted with Congress and key allied governments. The misgivings of the Senate leadership and the British government convinced the president to reject air strikes to save the French position, but there is no doubt that fear of the "who lost Vietnam" charge continued to weigh on his mind. One reason the administration worked hard to distance itself from the Geneva Accords on Indochina later that year was that it feared it might get a hostile reaction from vocal anticommunists on Capitol Hill.

It was not the first Vietnam decision by an American president in which domestic politics played a role, nor would it be the last. Indeed, a good argument could be made that for all six presidents who dealt with Vietnam from 1950 to 1975—from Truman to Ford—the Indochina conflict mattered in significant measure because of the potential damage it could do to their domestic political positions.

This was especially true of the three men who occupied the White House during the high tide of American involvement—John F. Kennedy, Lyndon B. Johnson, and Richard Nixon. From the start in 1961, and especially after Kennedy agreed to seek a negotiated settlement in Laos giving the communist Pathet Lao a share of the power, senior U.S. officials feared what would happen to the administration at home if South Vietnam were allowed to fall. Kennedy told his ambassador to India, John Kenneth Galbraith: "There are just so many concessions that one can make to communists in one year and survive politically. . . . We just can't have another defeat this year in Vietnam." In November 1961, Secretary of State Dean Rusk and Secretary of Defense Robert McNamara advised JFK that the loss of South Vietnam would not merely undermine American credibility elsewhere but would "stimulate bitter domestic controversies in the United States and would be seized upon to divide the country and harass the administration." U.S. assistance to South Vietnam increased steadily in 1962 and 1963, ultimately reaching the amount of $1.5 million per day. Still, success remained elusive. By mid-1963 the president had grown disillusioned about the prospects in the struggle, and he reportedly told several associates of his desire to get out of the conflict. But it could not happen, he added, until after the 1964 election.

Johnson's misgivings did not go quite so deep, but he too, after he succeeded JFK in office in November 1963, ruled out a major policy change before voting day. As McGeorge Bundy would later say, "Neither [Kennedy nor Johnson] wanted to go into the election as the one who either made war or lost Vietnam. If you could put if off you did." Bundy's comment carries great historical importance, and not merely because he was right in his assessment—Johnson, we now know, sought above all else that year to keep Vietnam from complicating his election-year strategy, judging all Vietnam options in terms of what they meant for November. No less important, the comment matters because 1964 proved so crucial in the making of America's war in Vietnam. It was a year of virtually unrelieved decline in the fortunes of the South Vietnamese government, a year in which the Vietcong made huge gains and the Saigon government lost steadily more support. It was a year when America became increasingly isolated on Vietnam among its Western allies, and when influential voices in Congress and the press—and indeed within the administration itself—began voicing deep misgivings about the prospect of a major war. And it was a year when the administration made the basic decisions that led to Americanization early in 1965. Already in the spring of 1964 the administration commenced secret contingency planning for an expansion of the war to North Vietnam, but with the tacit understanding that nothing substantive would happen until after Election Day. In November and December, with LBJ safely elected, the administration moved to adopt a two-phase escalation of the war involving sustained bombing of North Vietnam and the dispatch of U.S. ground troops (subsequently implemented in February–March 1965). The White House strategy of delay through the first ten months of 1964 had not eliminated Johnson's freedom of maneuver, but it had reduced it considerably.

Nixon, it is clear, had his eyes very much on the home front in making Vietnam policy, not merely in the lead-up to the 1972 election but from the start of his administration in 1969. In vowing to get a "peace with honor," he and his national security adviser Henry Kissinger thought as much about voters in Peoria as about leaders in Moscow and Beijing and Hanoi. Top-level conversations captured on the taping system Nixon had installed in the Oval Office early in 1971, for example, make clear just how deeply concerns about Nixon's domestic standing permeated Vietnam policy. In a phone conversation that took place late in the evening of 7 April 1971, shortly after a televised Nixon speech announcing further Vietnam troop withdrawals, Nixon and Kissinger concurred on the matter of the "breathing space" they would get domestically by ending the draft:

KISSINGER: I think, Mr. President, I'm gonna put the military to the torch [on the matter of the draft].

NIXON: Yeah. They're screwing around on this.

KISSINGER: They're screwing around. They're worried that it will make the volunteer army not work. But the hell with that if we can get ourselves breathing space for Vietnam.

NIXON: Listen. Ending the draft gives us breathing space on Vietnam. We'll restore the draft later, but goddamn it, the military, they're a bunch of greedy bastards that want more officers clubs and more men to shine their shoes. The sons of bitches are not interested in this country.

KISSINGER: I mean, ending, going to all-volunteer in Vietnam is what I mean, is what we ought to do.

NIXON: Mmm-hmm.

In the summer of 1972, as a negotiated settlement with Hanoi looked to be within reach, Nixon expressed ambivalence about whether the deal should come before or after the election that November. On 14 August Nixon told aides that Kissinger should be discouraged from expressing too much hopefulness regarding the negotiations, as that could raise expectations and be "harmful politically." On 30 August, Nixon chief of staff H. R. Haldeman recorded in his diary that Nixon did not want the settlement to come too soon. The president, according to Haldeman, "wants to be sure [Army Vice-Chief of Staff Alexander] Haig doesn't let Henry's desire for a settlement prevail; that's the one way we can lose the election. We have to stand firm on Vietnam and not get soft."

Even before he assumed the presidency, Nixon had sought to manipulate foreign policy for personal political advantage. In the final weeks of the 1968 campaign, rumors that Johnson was on the verge of announcing a bombing halt (to hasten a peace settlement and thereby help Democratic presidential candidate Hubert H. Humphrey), sent the Nixon campaign into a panic. Nixon secretly encouraged the South Vietnamese president Nguyen Van Thieu to refuse to participate in any talks with Hanoi before the election, with assurances that if elected he would

provide Thieu with more solid support than Humphrey would. It is possible that Thieu's subsequent refusal to take part in the negotiations in Paris, announced just days before Election Day, might have damaged Humphrey's campaign sufficiently to deliver what was a razor-thin victory to Nixon.

THE LATE COLD WAR AND BEYOND

The Vietnam War may be somewhat unusual in the degree to which it linked domestic political considerations and foreign policy, but it is by no means exceptional in the nation's recent history. Jimmy Carter's decision to launch a risky and ultimately disastrous mission to free American hostages in Iran in the spring of 1980, for example, owed something to his domestic political difficulties in an election year, including a tough challenge for the Democratic nomination from Senator Edward Kennedy. Carter's chief of staff, Hamilton Jordan, urged the action "to prove to the columnists and our political opponents that Carter was not an ineffective Chief Executive who was afraid to act." Carter himself explained that he had "to give expression to the anger of the American people. If they perceive me as firm and tough in voicing their rage, maybe we'll be able to control this thing."

A decade later another president confronted the perception that he was too timid. During the 1988 campaign George Bush had to endure a *Newsweek* story on him in which the words "Fighting the Wimp Factor" were emblazoned on the cover, and there were charges from conservative quarters in the months after the inauguration that he was not resolute enough in foreign policy. The "wimp" charges could be heard again in October 1989, when Bush failed to back a nearly successful coup d'état against the drug-running Panamanian strongman Manuel Noriega. "We'll be hit from the left for being involved at all," the president noted privately, "and we'll be hit harder from the right for being timid and weak." This right-wing reaction to his inaction—Republican Senator Jesse Helms referred to a "bunch of Keystone Kops" in the administration—almost certainly contributed to Bush's decision in December to order the invasion of Panama to arrest Noriega. In August 1990 various motives moved Bush to adopt an uncompromising position toward Saddam Hussein's invasion of Kuwait, but one of them was surely the domestic political benefits that he and his advisers believed could accrue from it. Locked in a budget battle with Congress, faced with a messy savings and loan scandal, and with approval ratings sagging, Bush saw a chance to demonstrate forceful presidential leadership and galvanize popular support. Tellingly, perhaps, he received encouragement to "draw a line in the sand" from British prime minister Margaret Thatcher—who herself had received a powerful boost to her domestic position from Britain's "splendid little war" in the Falkland Islands eight years earlier.

The war against Iraq was the first military conflict of the post–Cold War era. In the years thereafter various commentators complained that America's newfound status as the world's sole superpower, one without a compelling external threat to unify the populace, had allowed party politics to infuse foreign policymaking to an unprecedented degree. Many drew a contrast with the supposedly bipartisan and selfless days of the Cold War. It was a dubious claim; party politics and foreign policy have always enjoyed a close relationship in the United States. This was so in the most tense periods of the superpower confrontation—during the Cuban missile crisis, John Kennedy considered the domestic political implications of the various options before him—and it was true in less traumatic times.

Still, few would deny that the partisanship became more pronounced in the Clinton years than it had been in decades, the atmosphere in Washington more poisonous. The power of the presidency in foreign policy seemed diminished and that of Congress as well as ethnic and other special-interest lobbies enhanced. Republicans saw personal political advantage as motivating virtually every one of Bill Clinton's foreign policy decisions and, after capturing control of Congress in the 1994 midterm elections, worked diligently to thwart many of his initiatives. In April 1999, for example, during the war in Kosovo, the House of Representatives refused to vote to support the bombing; that October, the Senate voted down the Comprehensive Test Ban Treaty—an action the *New York Times* compared with the Senate defeat of the League of Nations after World War I—even though the president and sixty-two senators asked that it be withdrawn. Clinton and his advisers, meanwhile, insisted that their only concern in making policy was promoting the national interest. The early evidence about the policymaking process in the Clinton White House suggests strongly that he and his aides paid close attention

to how various policy options would be perceived at home and that their determinations in this regard helped inform their decisions. In other words, Clinton was much like his predecessors.

During the debate over the North Atlantic Treaty Organization's eastward enlargement in 1996–1997, Clinton administration officials insisted that bringing as much of Europe as possible under the NATO banner would serve the nation's strategic interests. They also said it was important to reassure the eastern and central European populations after Moscow became more nationalistic and assertive in 1994. No doubt they were being truthful in these claims, but Democratic Party leaders surely also saw enlargement as a surefire vote-getter among eastern European ethnic communities in battleground states in the Midwest, states Clinton had to win in the 1996 election. Foreign observers often perceived this domestic political element to be the root motivation behind the expansion. Said Canadian prime minister Jean Chrétien (who thought his microphone was turned off) to Belgium's prime minister about NATO enlargement in August 1997: "All this for short-term political reasons, to win elections. In fact [U.S. politicians] are selling their votes, they are selling their votes. . . . It's incredible. In your country or mine, all the politicians would be in prison."

EVERY VOTE COUNTS

The skeptical reader will wonder if the case here is not being made too strongly. After all, foreign policy issues seldom decide elections in the United States. Does it not follow that American diplomacy and party politics must have only minor influence on each other? Not necessarily. It is true that in the United States, as in other countries, voters tend to give their chief attention to domestic matters. But foreign policy questions, though of less importance, have in most years been significant enough to merit the attention of practicing politicians. The professionals in politics have always realized that when domestic issues are in the forefront, diplomatic questions can still shift a few votes in swing districts in critical states. This can mean the difference between victory and defeat for a national ticket or decide control of Congress. That, essentially, has always been the politician's interpretation of the politics of American foreign policy—both for those who are in and those who are out of office.

This is still true and can be seen in the care with which presidential aspirants take on Israeli questions and the related matter of the Jewish vote. Small in national totals, this vote is critically important in New York, California, and other states with major urban centers. Even in 1948, Clark Clifford and other Truman aides were thinking partly about electoral politics in urging the president to extend recognition to the new State of Israel. Since 1876, Clifford knew, every winner of a presidential election had carried New York State, where in the 1940s Jews constituted 14 percent of the population. Extending recognition to Israel would help deliver the state to Truman in November and could also help the president in other states with sizable Jewish populations. The Emergency Committee on Zionist Affairs, and later the American Zionist Council and the American Israel Public Affairs Committee—the latter self-described as "the most powerful, best-run, and effective foreign policy interest group in Washington"—proved effective in exploiting the potential power of the Jewish vote to gain continued material and diplomatic backing for Israel.

True, the close U.S.–Israel relationship after 1948 was the product of many things. Israel had the strongest military force in the Middle East, and there were good geostrategic reasons why Washington sought to maintain close ties with Israel and work together on matters of common interest. Moreover, the convictions of evangelical Christians, as well as the feelings of other Americans touched by the courage of Israel, meant that a broad cross-section of Americans could be counted on to back firm U.S. support for Israel's security. Nevertheless, it would be foolish to deny that electoral imperatives influenced American policy toward the Middle East at all points after the late 1940s.

Likewise, America's policy toward Cuba after 1959 was deeply affected by the influence of the Cuban-American community in South Florida and the desire of presidential contenders to win Florida's sizable chunk of electoral votes. In October 1976, for example, Cyrus Vance, then a foreign policy adviser to Jimmy Carter's presidential campaign, advised that "the time has come to move away from our past policy of isolation. Our boycott has proved ineffective, and there has been a decline of Cuba's export of revolution in the region." If the United States lifted the long-standing embargo on food and medicine, Vance speculated, the Castro government might reduce its level of support for the leftist Popular Movement for the Liberation of Angola (MPLA) in Angola. Carter was sympathetic, but he acted cautiously in the campaign. "There were no votes to be won, and many to be lost, by indicating friendliness toward Castro," the historian Gaddis Smith wrote of Carter's thinking. Subsequent presidents would encounter the same dilemma when they contemplated a change in Cuba policy: the need to weigh an alteration to a failed and indeed counterproductive embargo policy against the perceived power of the militantly anti-Castro Cuban American National Foundation (CANF) to sway the Florida vote.

These kinds of calculations were nothing new in American politics. From 1865 to 1895, for example, most Americans were too absorbed in goings-on at home to spare much time for overseas developments. Voter attention revolved around such domestic concerns as the reconstruction of the South, sagging prices, and recurrent depressions. Nevertheless, national politicians labored hard on the diplomatic sections of their party platforms, and candidates spent time outlining or camouflaging their opinions on foreign policy. The reason was plain. The Republicans and Democrats were evenly balanced, and presidential and congressional elections were decided by razor-thin margins. The least slip, even on diplomatic positions, might mean the loss of a handful of votes, which could spell calamity at the polls.

It is well to remember that, when domestic questions rule, they often relate closely to foreign policy. This has been the case with tariffs, immigration, witch hunts against radicals, and, in the early twenty-first century, with agricultural prices and production and trade deals such as the North American Free Trade Agreement of 1994. The relation of these problems to party politics—which is often very close—again draws diplomacy into the domestic political arena.

CONCLUSION

In an interview in the summer of 1965, McGeorge Bundy, a former Harvard dean who served John Kennedy and Lyndon Johnson as national security adviser and was an architect of the Americanization of the Vietnam War, was asked what was different in the actual conduct of American diplomatic affairs from how it had seemed to be "from the safety of Harvard Yard." According to the interviewer, Bundy replied that the first thing that stood out was "the powerful place of domestic politics in the formulation of foreign policies."

It was a revealing comment, but not a surprising one (except to the extent that officials seldom make this admission on the record). The relationship between domestic politics and foreign policy has been an intimate one throughout the nation's history. It may be debated whether the connection is a good thing or a bad thing—whether overall it has been beneficial to the nation's record on the world stage. For the moment, though, it is enough to say that the connection is there and is important. Just why so many students of American diplomacy seemingly have lost sight of this reality over the years is somewhat of a mystery. Partly, the inattention can be explained by the historiographical trends outlined early in this essay, which moved many diplomatic historians away from giving serious and sustained attention to domestic politics. Partly, too, it may reflect an overreliance by scholars on official U.S. government documents in their research; essential though these documents are, they can mislead. American statesmen have always been averse to admitting, even to themselves, that their foreign policy decisions could be affected by private political interest. As a result, a reader of the vast archival record, finding little or no evidence of partisan wrangling or election year strategizing, could (wrongly) conclude that these must have mattered little in shaping American policy.

Whatever the case, it is clear that the influence of party politics on the American approach to international affairs needs to be identified, measured, and explained. Foreign policy, it turns out, is always a political matter. It is not always a crass partisan matter. It is well to remember that the parties historically have tended to speak for different constellations of values and interests, different constituencies with genuine philosophical differences about America's place in the world, and that those differences have sometimes also been evident within parties. But it is always political.

BIBLIOGRAPHY

Blumenthal, Sidney. *Pledging Allegiance: The Last Campaign of the Cold War.* New York, 1990.

Chafe, William H. *The Unfinished Journey: America Since World War II.* 4th ed. New York, 1999. A first-rate textbook on the United States after 1945.

DeConde, Alexander. "Washington's Farewell, the French Alliance, and the Election of 1796." *Mississippi Valley Historical Review* 43, no. 4 (March 1957): 641–658. A provocative article on the shaping of the Farewell Address.

———. *Ethnicity, Race, and American Foreign Policy: A History.* Boston, 1992.

Divine, Robert A. *Foreign Policy and U.S. Presidential Elections, 1940–1948, 1952–1960.* 2 vols. New York, 1974.

Drew, Elizabeth. *On the Edge: The Clinton Presidency.* New York, 1994.

Foot, Rosemary. *A Substitute for Victory: The Politics of Peacemaking at the Korean Armistice Talks.* Ithaca, N.Y., 1990. The second of two important studies by the author on the Korean War.

Freeland, Richard M. *The Truman Doctrine and the Origins of McCarthyism: Foreign Policy, Domestic Politics, and Internal Security, 1946–1948.* New York, 1972.

Gaddis, John Lewis. *The United States and the Origins of the Cold War, 1941–1947.* New York, 1972. An essential study of U.S. decision making in World War II and the early Cold War.

Haldeman, H. R. *The Haldeman Diaries: Inside the Nixon White House.* New York, 1994. An indispensable source on the Nixon presidency.

Hughes, Barry B. *The Domestic Context of American Foreign Policy.* New York, 1978.

Johnson, Robert David. "Congress and the Cold War." *Journal of Cold War Studies* 3 (2001): 76–100.

Kegley, Charles W., and Eugene R. Wittkopf, eds. *The Domestic Sources of American Foreign Policy: Insights and Evidence.* New York, 1988.

Lebow, Richard Ned. "Domestic Politics and the Cuban Missile Crisis: The Traditional and the Revisionist Interpretations Reevaluated." *Diplomatic History* 14 (1990).

Levering, Ralph B. "Is Domestic Politics Being Slighted as an Interpretive Framework?" *Society for Historians of American Foreign Relations Newsletter* 25 (1994): 17–35. An accomplished historian calls for greater attention by foreign relations historians to domestic politics.

———. *The Cold War: A Post–Cold War History.* Arlington Heights, Ill., 1994.

Logevall, Fredrik. *Choosing War: The Lost Chance for Peace and the Escalation of War in Vietnam.* Berkeley, Calif., 1999.

May, Ernest R. *The Making of the Monroe Doctrine.* Cambridge, Mass., 1975.

Perkins, Bradford. *Castlereagh and Adams: England and the United States, 1812–1823.* New York, 1964.

Quandt, William. "The Electoral Cycle and the Conduct of Foreign Policy." *Political Science Quarterly* 101 (1986). A specialist on the Middle East expresses concern about the influence of elections on the conduct of foreign policy.

Rosati, Joel A. *The Politics of United States Foreign Policy.* New York, 1993.

Rosenau, James N., ed. *Domestic Sources of Foreign Policy.* New York, 1967.

Small, Melvin. *Democracy and Diplomacy: The Impact of Domestic Politics on U.S. Foreign Policy, 1789–1994.* Baltimore, 1996. A concise and penetrating history that defines "domestic politics" broadly.

Smith, Gaddis. *Morality, Reason, and Power: American Diplomacy in the Carter Years.* New York, 1986.

Smith, Tony. *Foreign Attachments: The Power of Ethnic Groups in the Making of American Foreign Policy.* Cambridge, Mass., 2000.

Snyder, Jack. *Myths of Empire: Domestic Politics and International Ambition.* Ithaca, N.Y., 1991. A leading political scientist tackles the subject with verve and insight.

Stagg, J. C. A. "James Madison and the Malcontents: The Politics Origins of the War of 1812." *William and Mary Quarterly* 33 (1976): 557–585.

————. *Mr. Madison's War: Politics, Diplomacy, and Warfare in the Early American Republic, 1783–1830.* Princeton, N.J., 1983.

Westerfield, H. Bradford. *Foreign Policy and Party Politics: Pearl Harbor to Korea.* New Haven, Conn., 1955.

Woods, Randall B., and Howard Jones. *Dawning of the Cold War: The United States' Quest for World Order.* Athens, Ga., 1991.

See also CONGRESSIONAL POWER; THE NATIONAL INTEREST; PRESIDENTIAL POWER; RECOGNITION; REVISIONISM; THE VIETNAM WAR AND ITS IMPACT.

PEACEMAKING

Berenice A. Carroll

"Peacemaking" appears to be a commonplace term, easily understood and frequently used in public discourse and in peace movements. The Internet reports more than 50,000 entries containing the term "peacemaking." On closer examination, it is much more elusive. Dictionaries define it tautologically as "the making of peace"; standard encyclopedias do not recognize it as a topic for separate entry (though it does appear in two encyclopedias of peace); and there is surprisingly little on "peacemaking" in academic texts on international politics.

Where it does appear, the term "peacemaking" is used primarily in four senses:

1. Settlement or termination of a war or dispute by explicit agreement among the belligerent parties or others ("peace settlements").
2. The process of transition from hostility to amity, or from war to peace ("ending hostilities and preferably also resolving the active issues of war"), with or without explicit agreement.
3. The development of procedures and institutions to facilitate conflict resolution, or termination or prevention of wars or conflicts ("pacific settlement of disputes").
4. Efforts to create the foundations or conditions for lasting peace ("peacebuilding").

THE STUDY OF PEACEMAKING

The number of scholarly works explicitly devoted to peacemaking has been relatively small as compared to studies of war and its causes, but there is now a substantial literature available to scholars and practitioners. Until about 1985, almost all of the scholarly studies devoted to peacemaking limited their concern to peace settlements, particularly settlements of interstate wars by explicit agreement. Since that time, the focus has shifted to related topics such as conflict resolution and prevention, preventive and multitrack diplomacy, humanitarian intervention, peacekeeping, and peacebuilding. In addition, a large body of work has emerged that examines or applies these concepts in regard to specific conflict areas in various parts of the world.

There have been many works on specific peace settlements, such as Richard B. Morris's *The Peacemakers* (1965), dealing with the negotiation of the settlement of the American Revolution, and Harold Nicolson's *Peacemaking 1919* (1965) as well as Arno J. Mayer's *Politics and Diplomacy of Peacemaking, 1918–1919* (1967), dealing with the settlement reached at the end of World War I. Robert Randle, in *The Origins of Peace: A Study of Peacemaking and the Structure of Peace Settlements* (1973), broadened the scope to a wider range of examples, but made clear in the preface: "Although I have dealt with a number of aspects of peacemaking, I have concentrated mainly upon the structure and content of *peace settlements.*" In a later work, while recognizing that peacemaking studies embrace "all matters relating to the transition from a state of war to a state of peace," including "an analysis of the conditions prompting the parties to move toward peace," Randle still placed central emphasis upon settlements by explicit agreement. Thus, in Randle's summation, peacemaking studies include, first, study of the peace negotiations; second, "an analysis of the form, content and meaning of the peace settlement"; and third, "a study of the impact of the war and its settlement, including consideration of any postwar negotiations aimed at completing, amending or improving the settlement, a history of the implementation of its terms, and its value as precedent for the management or resolution of future disputes."

This focus on agreed peace settlements was consistent with the position, then generally accepted in the field of international law, that "The most frequent mode of terminating a war . . .

is a treaty of peace, negotiated either while operations continue or after the conclusion of a general armistice." This was true of wars between recognized members of the international system in the period prior to World War II, but since 1945 fewer peace treaties have been concluded, and truce or cease-fire agreements have "tended in some respects to move forward to the place of the old treaty of peace."

For a general understanding of peacemaking, however, it must be recognized that a great many wars, or large-scale hostilities, ended without any agreed settlement—for example, by outright conquest, annexation, or military rule of foreign territory, by suppression of insurrectionary forces, or by overthrow of an existing regime and its replacement by a new government. The number of armed conflicts ending with any kind of agreement diminished significantly over the last half of the twentieth century, and many were transformed into long-term protracted conflicts. Of ninety post–Cold War conflicts in the years 1989–1993, only forty-one were terminated in that period, the rest remaining active years later. Of the forty-one, only six ended with a peace accord, the others ending either with a clear-cut victory by one side (seventeen), some form of cease-fire or truce without a peace settlement, or various patterns of decline in armed hostilities.

Study of the causes of war has engendered a vast literature since at least the monumental work of Quincy Wright, *A Study of War,* first published in 1942. Analysis of peacemaking, or "the causes of peace," is a more recent project that presents difficulties even greater than analysis of the causes of war. While the latter has received much more attention, there is no consensus among scholars on the solution of either problem. With respect to the causes of making peace, however, debate has centered upon the relative importance of selected events, conditions, or policies in inducing the parties to make peace. Battle victories, war costs, "unconditional surrender" policies, misperception, coalition diplomacy, secrecy, the role of mediators, and domestic politics are among the factors often treated as primary to the process of ending or prolonging hostilities. In reality, all these and other factors enter into the calculations of belligerents weighing the prospects for peace, and it is unlikely that any simple formula could lead us to predict which would be "decisive" in any given case.

As the decade of the 1960s drew to a close,

special issues of the *Journal of Peace Research* (December 1969) and of *The Annals of the American Academy of Political and Social Science* (November 1970) were devoted to the topic "How Wars End," providing illuminating early analyses of war termination. Robert F. Randle's *The Origins of Peace* (1973) was followed by David Smith's *From War to Peace: Essays in Peacemaking and War Termination* (1974). In subsequent years, the number of works addressing peacemaking grew rapidly and expanded the information base, the scope, and the analytical complexity of knowledge and theory on the subject. Nevertheless, peacemaking remains a relatively neglected area of study as compared with warmaking.

ATTITUDES TOWARD PEACEMAKING

Throughout its history, the United States has sought to project an image of dedication to peace and to peacemaking. George Washington, in his Farewell Address in 1796, exhorted Americans to avoid "overgrown military establishments which, under any form of government, are inauspicious to liberty," and urged Americans: "Observe good faith and justice toward all nations. Cultivate peace and harmony with all." Nearly two centuries later, President John F. Kennedy was obliged to acknowledge that, far from "cultivating peace and harmony," the United States found itself "caught up in a vicious and dangerous cycle in which suspicion on one side breeds suspicion on the other and new weapons beget counterweapons"; nevertheless, he too exhorted Americans to turn their attention to "the most important topic on earth, world peace":

> What kind of peace do I mean? What kind of peace do we seek? Not a Pax Americana enforced on the world by American weapons of war. Not the peace of the grave or the security of the slave. I am talking about genuine peace . . . not merely peace for Americans but peace for all men and women, not merely peace in our time but peace for all time.

But the record of the behavior of the United States in regard to both "peace in our time" and "peace for all time" has been ambiguous at best.

Certainly there have been strong traditions of antimilitarism, internationalism, and pacifism in American society. The history of peace movements in the United States, reaching back at least to the formation of the New York, Massachusetts, and Ohio Peace Societies in 1815, is long and rich, and can lay claim to having influenced the peace settlements in a number of wars or other conflicts, most prominently in World War I. On the level of governmental action, the long-term peacemaking efforts of the United States have focused on the development of international legal and institutional instruments for pacific settlement of disputes and peacekeeping by international organizations. The Rush-Bagot Convention (1817) established a lasting basis for disarmament on the long border between the United States and Canada, and the Treaty of Washington (1871) provided for the resolution of other outstanding issues (boundary and fisheries questions, and the Alabama Claims) by a court of arbitration.

The United States has also given strong support to the formulation of treaties of arbitration, both voluntary and compulsory, though the Senate has as strongly resisted acceptance of compulsory arbitration without significant reservations. The United States has also shown itself willing and even eager to extend its services as mediator, and has had some success in this role—for example, in mediating the Russo-Japanese peace settlement of 1905. In the protracted conflicts that troubled many parts of the world in the late twentieth century, the efforts of the United States to serve as mediator, as in the Middle East, Northern Ireland, and the former Yugoslavia, have had mixed success and have elicited charges of bias, hypocrisy, and even direct military aid to preferred parties in the conflicts.

Finally, the United States has sometimes adopted the role of peacemaker on a global scale, taking the initiative in the establishment of the Permanent Court of International Justice and the League of Nations. Although the United States never joined the league and even declined to become a party to the Statute of the Permanent Court, it later played a major role in the establishment and development of the United Nations, and has accepted (though with major reservations) the jurisdiction of the International Court of Justice as reconstituted under the United Nations Charter.

There has also been strong interest in the United States in the development of techniques of peacekeeping and other approaches to conflict resolution. On the governmental level, United States involvement in "peacekeeping" or "peace enforcement" operations has unfortunately been associated with the large-scale use of military force, especially in Korea, the Persian Gulf, and the former Yugoslavia.

Nevertheless, on the level of independent citizen action and professional research, there has been widespread interest in peacekeeping without the use of military force and in nonviolent modes of conflict resolution at international as well as domestic and interpersonal levels. The decades since World War II have witnessed the establishment of numerous peace studies programs, research institutes and centers, journals and professional associations devoted to peace and peacemaking, in the United States and around the world. In 1978 a citizen campaign in the United States led to the appointment by Congress of a commission to consider the establishment of a national academy of peace that would carry out and support research about international peace and peacemaking; educate and train persons from government, private enterprise, and voluntary associations about peace and peacemaking skills; and provide an information service in the field of peace learning. In 1984 legislation to create the United States Institute for Peace was passed by Congress, providing for an agency to support research but not to serve as a teaching and training academy. Since that time, Congress has increased funding and other forms of support for the institute's programs, including grants and fellowships, conferences, publications, library resources, and other activities, and has designated a tract of land for the institute's permanent headquarters, "in recognition of the Institute's accomplishments and the heightened relevance of its work in a dangerous and uncertain world."

FORMAL PEACE AGREEMENTS

In the period between 1775 and 1945, the United States entered into a great many treaties or other formal peace agreements, of which the overwhelming majority were treaties with the Indian nations or tribes. Five major wars between the United States and recognized foreign states were concluded by peace treaties: the American Revolution (Treaty of Paris, 3 September 1783), the War of 1812 (Treaty of Ghent, 24 December 1814), the Mexican War (Treaty of Guadalupe Hidalgo, 2 February 1848), the Spanish-American War (Treaty of Paris, 10 December 1898), and World War I. The U.S. Senate declined to ratify the Treaty of Versailles and associated treaties negotiated by President Woodrow Wilson at the conclusion of World War I, but the United States subsequently signed separate treaties of peace with Germany (Berlin, 25 August 1921), Austria (Vienna, 24 August 1921), and Hungary (Budapest, 29 August 1921). No treaties were signed and ratified by the United States with Bulgaria and Turkey, and the Soviet Union was absent from the entire peace settlement.

A number of lesser foreign wars or partial engagements of the United States were also concluded by treaties of peace: the Moroccan War (treaty of 28 June 1786), the Tripolitan War (Treaty of Tripoli, 3 June 1805), two Algerian wars (treaties of 1795 and 1815), the second Opium War (Treaty of Tientsin, 18 June 1858), and the Boxer Rebellion (Treaty of Peking, 7 September 1901). The undeclared naval war with France (Quasi-War) of 1798–1800 was also settled by a formal convention of 30 September 1800.

WAR ENDINGS WITHOUT FORMAL SETTLEMENTS

The United States has been involved in a considerable number of undeclared foreign wars or "interventions," particularly in the twentieth century. Such wars typically were not concluded by formal agreement but were ended rather by U.S. suppression of opposition, military rule, unilateral imposition of terms, or, in some cases, unilateral withdrawal of American forces. These undeclared wars included the suppression of the Philippine independence movement in 1899–1902, the Siberian interventions of 1918–1921, and numerous interventions in Cuba, Haiti, Mexico, Nicaragua, Panama, the Dominican Republic, and Grenada. They also included military interventions in civil wars in Greece, China, Korea, Lebanon, Vietnam, and others since World War II; covert actions and coups or attempted coups in Iran, Chile, and elsewhere; enforcement actions under "coalition" or North Atlantic Treaty Organization authority against Iraq and Serbia; and "antiterrorist" bombings in Libya and Afghanistan.

A study of American peacemaking must give some attention to the way the United States has handled the conclusion of civil wars and insurrections. The distinction between these and "foreign wars" becomes somewhat doubtful when we recall that the United States itself originated in an insurrectionary war. When an incumbent government is obliged to concede statehood and separate territorial sovereignty to rebel belligerents, the ending of the conflict takes on the character of a settlement between sovereign states. On the other hand, the treatment accorded to defeated belligerents in civil wars and insurrections often is not significantly different from the treatment accorded to defeated foreign nations in colonial wars of conquest or interventions.

The United States has experienced a substantial number of insurrections or rebellions, including at least thirty-five slave uprisings, at least five significant domestic insurrections or civil conflicts, the great Civil War of 1861–1865, and other types of conflicts such as large-scale riots, vigilante expeditions, and mass protests in labor, civil rights, and antiwar struggles. The United States government has consistently refused to give rebels, rioters, or protestors any recognized status as belligerents or negotiating partners, and these conflicts have been terminated by piecemeal suppression of the uprisings by military or police forces or by tacit concessions.

This was true even for the Civil War, in which the refusal of the U.S. government to negotiate with the rebel forces affected both the duration of hostilities and the character of the outcome. Efforts of the Confederate generals Robert E. Lee and Joseph E. Johnston to negotiate terms of general surrender with Union generals Ulysses S. Grant and William T. Sherman were expressly rejected by both President Abraham Lincoln and President Andrew Johnson. Far from welcoming the opportunity to put a rapid end to the fighting, on 3 March 1865 Lincoln instructed Grant "to have no conference with General Lee, unless it be for the capitulation of General Lee's army, or on some minor or purely military matter." Furthermore, Grant was "not to decide, discuss, or confer upon any political questions. Such questions the president holds in his own hands, and will submit them to no military conferences or conventions. Meantime you are to press to the utmost your military advantages."

Similarly, when Sherman, unaware of this directive to Grant, later met with Johnston and drafted terms for a general surrender of the Confederate forces remaining after Lee's surrender at Appomattox, the draft agreement was sharply rejected by President Johnson and his cabinet. Sherman was authorized to accept only the surrender of the army commanded by Johnston, and to engage in no negotiations. As Sherman observed, this policy meant that the war might continue indefinitely in sporadic engagements with dispersed "guerrilla bands." Indeed, while the Civil War formally terminated one year later with a proclamation by President Johnson (2 April 1866), some hostilities continued even after that date and a separate proclamation was required to end the fighting in Texas (20 August 1866).

While the position taken by Lincoln and Johnson appears at first sight to be based primarily on the principle of civilian control over vital political and civil questions, it must be observed that it was not particular political terms drafted by the generals that were rejected, but any conference or negotiation between the military leaders for terms of general surrender. Nor was the United States government itself willing to negotiate with the Confederate government or its generals. In contrast, in both World War I and World War II, general surrender or armistice agreements were received and signed by military leaders of the Allied armies. Marshal Ferdinand Foch, general-in-chief of the Allied armies in France, signed the armistice agreement for the Allies in World War I. In 1945, Lieutenant General Walter Bedell Smith, chief of staff to General Dwight D. Eisenhower, signed the German instrument of surrender, while General Douglas MacArthur signed the Japanese surrender agreement for the Allied powers in World War II. Although the terms of these documents were determined ultimately by the civilian authorities, the Allied governments did not hesitate to have the military leaders receive the surrenders and, indeed, accorded them considerable influence on the formulation of surrender terms and occupation policies.

It seems probable that the refusal of the presidents during the Civil War to approve the receipt by either Grant or Sherman of general surrender by Lee or Johnston was less a question of military versus civilian control of policy than it was a question of refusing to treat with any party claiming to represent or exercise general authority in or over the Confederate states or forces. Such a position is characteristic of incumbent governments faced with insurrectionary forces, not only at the cost of prolonging armed hostilities but even at the cost of making impossible a settlement based on mutual accord and amity.

PEACEMAKING WITHOUT PEACE: THE INDIAN WARS

In *Custer Died for Your Sins* (1969), Vine Deloria wrote that "Indian people laugh themselves sick" when they hear American whites charge Soviet Russia with breaking treaty agreements: "It would take Russia another century to make and break as many treaties as the United States has already violated" in its dealings with American Indians. In the century between 1778 and 1871, the United States government made some 370 treaties with Indian tribes and nations. About one-third of these were peace treaties, but it is open to question what relationship should be understood between these treaties and "peacemaking" as construed above.

Since 1871 the United States has declined to sign treaties with Indian tribes, though it has continued to sign "agreements" understood to have the same binding force as treaties. The difference lies in rejection of the notion that the Indian tribes should be recognized as independent nations. Prior to 1871 this had been a matter of dispute, subject to varying interpretation and practice. In 1828, President John Quincy Adams declared that at the establishment of the United States, "the principle was adopted of considering them as foreign and independent powers." But in 1831, in the case of *Cherokee Nation* v. *Georgia,* Chief Justice John Marshall gave the majority judgment of the Supreme Court that the Indians were "domestic dependent nations," not to be considered "a foreign state in the sense of the Constitution." However, the Supreme Court was closely divided on the issue. In their dissent, Justices Smith Thompson and Joseph Story argued that the history of past treatment of the Indians led irresistibly to the conclusion that "they have been regarded, by the executive and legislative branches of the government, not only as sovereign and independent, but as foreign nations or tribes, not within the jurisdiction nor under the government of the states within which they were located."

Moreover, while Chief Justice Marshall maintained that the Indians were not "foreign states in the sense of the Constitution" with respect to the jurisdiction of the Supreme Court, he acknowledged that for other purposes the Cherokee nation clearly did have the character of

a state, as a distinct political society, separated from others, capable of managing its own affairs and governing itself. . . . The numerous treaties made with them by the United States recognize them as a people capable of maintaining the relations of peace and war, of being responsible in their political character for any violation of their engagements, or for any aggression committed on the citizens of the United States by any individual of their community.

The following year, in the related case of *Worcester* v. *Georgia,* Marshall reaffirmed as the judgment of the Court that treaties with the Indians had the same standing as treaties with other nations:

> The constitution, by declaring treaties already made, as well as those to be made, to be the supreme law of the land, has adopted and sanctioned the previous treaties with the Indian nations, and consequently admits their rank among those powers who are capable of making treaties. The words "treaty" and "nation" are words of our own language, selected in our diplomatic and legislative proceedings, by ourselves, having each a definite and well understood meaning. We have applied them to Indians as we have applied them to the other nations of the earth. They are applied to all in the same sense.

The first treaty of peace ever made by the U.S. government was with the Delaware Indians in 1778, at Fort Pitt (Pittsburgh). This was in fact a treaty of alliance between the United States and some of the Delaware tribes, at a time when most of the Indians of Ohio and New York, including the Delaware, were fighting on the side of the British in the revolutionary war. The treaty repudiates the allegations of "enemies of the United States" who have

> endeavoured by every artifice to possess the Indians with an opinion that it is our design to extirpate them, and take possession of their country; to obviate such false suggestions, the United States guarantee to said nation of Delawares, and their heirs, all their territorial rights in the fullest and most ample manner as bounded by former treaties.

Similar guarantees were reiterated numerous times in succeeding years—for example, in 1790, when President George Washington assured the Iroquois Nations that the U.S. government would "protect you in all your just rights. . . . You possess the right to sell, and the right of refusing to sell your lands. . . . The United States will be true and faithful to their engagements." In reality, the United States repeatedly violated these engagements, systematically dispossessing the Indian tribes of their lands and depriving them of their traditional means of subsistence, utilizing every means at hand including force and fraud, trickery and bribery, and finally murder, arson, and massacre. Although no war was ever declared by Congress against an Indian nation, one may well name the entire period of white colonization of the territory now comprising the United States the "Four Hundred Years' War." This protracted war reduced the Indian population of some twelve million in the area of the continental United States before the

arrival of the colonists to about 300,000 in 1872. By that time the Delaware, who had been assured in 1778 that it was only the "false suggestions" of "enemies of the United States" that it was "our design to extirpate them, and take possession of their country," had been driven from their native territory and so reduced and dispersed that the report of the commissioner of Indian affairs for 1872 mentioned only eighty-one Delaware, living with the Wichita in Indian Territory.

In the present context, three main points are salient about the relations between the United States and the Indian nations: first, the consistent failure of the U.S. government to adhere to commitments made in numerous treaties of peace and amity; second, the outright resistance of many officers of the U.S. Army, and many state and federal government officials, to making peace with Indians on any terms other than unconditional surrender, removal to reservations, or, if necessary, extermination; and third, the use of peace treaties as weapons of war.

Although the full history of "broken peace pipes" has yet to be written, one may read parts of it in such works as Helen Hunt Jackson's *A Century of Dishonor* (1881), Dee Brown's *Bury My Heart at Wounded Knee* (1971), Vine Deloria's *Of Utmost Good Faith* (1971) and *Behind the Trail of Broken Treaties* (1985), and M. Annette Jaimes's collection *The State of Native America: Genocide, Colonization, and Resistance* (1992). With respect to peacemaking, the effect of the most glaring atrocities, such as the Sand Creek massacre, was to shut all doors to peace. On 29 November 1864, Colonel John M. Chivington and Major Scott Anthony led seven hundred men to mutilate and slaughter some two hundred Indians, encamped at Sand Creek under assurances from Anthony himself that they would be under the protection of Fort Lyon. As Dee Brown concludes: "In a few hours of madness at Sand Creek, Chivington and his soldiers destroyed the lives or the power of every Cheyenne and Arapaho chief who had held out for peace with the white men. After the flight of the survivors, the Indians rejected Black Kettle and Left Hand, and turned to their war leaders to save them from extermination."

Despite the hideousness of this and other massacres, far more Indians were killed and driven off their lands by the devices of dishonest, dictated, and disregarded peace treaties. Among the clearest examples of this was the case of the Cherokee. First persuaded by treaty commitments in 1785–1791 that the United States "solemnly guarantees to the

Cherokee nation all their lands" not expressly ceded in the treaties, the Cherokees refrained from making war despite many hostile encounters with whites and the illegal entry onto their lands of numerous white settlers. Pressured into ceding more territory by treaty in 1817, some of the Cherokee began to move west of the Mississippi; but many refused to sign the treaty and most of the Cherokee clung stubbornly to their traditional lands. In 1829, however, the state of Georgia adopted an act that annexed their whole territory to the state and deprived them of all legal and political rights, annulling "all laws made by the Cherokee nation, . . . either in council or in any other way," and providing that "no Indian . . . shall be deemed a competent witness in any Court of this State to which a white man may be a party." The Cherokee sought to challenge this in the Supreme Court, but were discouraged by the Indian Removal Act of 1830, the refusal of the Supreme Court to hear their case in 1831, and the refusal of President Andrew Jackson to implement the more favorable decision of the court in *Worcester* v. *Georgia* (1832).

Under these circumstances, some of the Cherokee were induced to sign the Treaty of New Echota (1835), relinquishing all the Cherokee lands east of the Mississippi (encompassing territory in four southern states exceeding in size the states of Massachusetts, Rhode Island, and Connecticut) in return for five million dollars and seven million acres west of the Mississippi. The treaty again assured the Cherokee that the new lands ceded to them "shall in no future time, without their consent, be included within the territorial limits or jurisdiction of any State or Territory." Whether they recognized that these assurances would be as worthless as earlier ones, or simply preferred their ancestral lands, most of the Cherokees refused to sign the Treaty of New Echota; in 1837, General John Ellis Wool reported that the Cherokee people "uniformly declare that they never made the treaty in question." Nevertheless, at the expiration of the stipulated time the U.S. Army appeared to carry out the removal, "in obedience to the treaty of 1835." Fifteen thousand Cherokee were forcibly evicted under conditions of such inadequate food, shelter, and sanitation that four thousand died on the long trek west. Thus, in retrospect, treaty-making takes on the appearance of the most deadly weapon employed by the whites in their war to wrest the continent from the Indians; to persuade, trick, or coerce them into giving up their lands;

and to reduce them to a remnant of their former numbers.

Nevertheless, with the emergence of Indian activism in the Americas and other indigenous movements around the world since the 1970s, there was a revival of interest in past treaties and contemporary treaty-making to clarify and reaffirm the rights of Indian tribes and other indigenous groups promised in earlier treaties and agreements, resolve the destructive conflicts over these rights that persist today, and restore the dignity and lands of indigenous peoples. In 1974 the International Indian Treaty Council (IITC) was established to press for the rights of indigenous peoples across the Americas and around the globe. The IITC has worked through the United Nations and through autonomous meetings and action to secure recognition and redress, with some degree of success.

For example, in 1995, Queen Elizabeth II signed an apology to the Maori people of New Zealand and announced the return to the Maori of 39,000 acres of land the British had confiscated from them illegally in 1863, and the provision of a $42 million fund for the repurchase of privately owned land. Although the amount restored was far less than had been taken, and hundreds of tribal claims remained in litigation, this was an unprecedented and important gesture of reconciliation. In the United States some lands and rights were restored to Native Americans through the Indian Claims Commission between 1946 and 1978, the Indian Civil Rights Act of 1968, and other legislative acts. However, the claims settlements have been very limited, and since 1978, Indian claims have been pressed mainly through the federal courts and acts of Congress. Some of these have been settled, notably the Seneca Nation Settlement Act of 1990, which provided a settlement award of $60 million to the Seneca, but in 2001 many claims were still pending, including the long-fought Black Hills land claim of the Lakota Nation, and there was little ground for optimism about early resolution of the major claims and issues.

In 1996 a subcommission of the United Nations Commission on Human Rights issued a Draft Declaration of the Rights of Indigenous Peoples. While the General Assembly did not vote to approve the draft, it recognized the adoption of such a declaration as one of the main goals of the International Decade of the World's Indigenous People (1995–2004). Article 36 of the Draft Declaration states: "Indigenous peoples have the right to the recognition, observance and enforcement of treaties, agreements and other constructive arrangements concluded with States or their successors, according to their original spirit and intent, and to have States honour and respect such treaties, agreements and other constructive arrangements."

TREATY MAKING VERSUS PEACEMAKING

The experience of the American Indians is the most glaring example, but by no means unique, illustrating the limitations of treaty-making as a model for peacemaking. It is widely recognized that so-called "peace settlements," explicit agreements for the termination of a particular war or dispute, may fail to resolve key issues in dispute, and may even plant the seeds for new hostilities.

In the case of World War I, for example, President Woodrow Wilson resisted strong pressures from political opponents at home to demand "unconditional surrender" as the only basis for a settlement of the war with Germany, but he was later obliged to make many concessions weakening or contradicting the principles of his Fourteen Points, and forcing Germany to accept dictated terms of peace. When the Senate declined to ratify the resulting Treaty of Versailles, it was in the setting of a national campaign portraying the treaty terms and even the Covenant of the League of Nations as a betrayal of hopes for a lasting peace. Senator Henry Cabot Lodge argued before the Senate on 12 August 1919:

> Whatever may be said, it [League of Nations] is not a league of peace; it is an alliance, dominated at the present moment by five great powers, really by three, and it has all the marks of an alliance. The development of international law is neglected. The court which is to decide disputes brought before it fills but a small place . . . it exhibits that most marked characteristic of an alliance—that its decisions are to be carried out by force. Those articles on which the whole structure rests are articles which provide for the use of force; that is, for war.

Nor did the opposition to the treaty as a provocation of future wars come only from the right. Indeed, the first organized group to condemn the Treaty of Versailles was the Women's International League for Peace and Freedom, whose international congress at Zurich, meeting 12–17 May 1919, declared:

> This International Congress of Women expresses its deep regret that the terms of peace proposed at Versailles should so seriously violate the principles upon which alone a just and lasting peace can be secured, and which the democracies of the world had come to accept.
>
> By guaranteeing the fruits of the secret treaties to conquerors, the terms of peace tacitly sanction secret diplomacy, deny the principles of self-determination, recognize the right of the victors to the spoils of war, and create all over Europe discords and animosities, which can only lead to future wars.
>
> By the demand for the disarmament of one set of belligerents only, the principle of justice is violated and the rule of force continued.

One may argue that the Treaty of Versailles was not so bad as its opponents portrayed it, that its terms were less harsh than they might have been, that the disarmament of Germany was a first step toward the general disarmament that the treaty envisaged for the future, and that the League of Nations, imperfect as it was, offered a framework for international cooperation and peace that would have been effective had it been given responsible support and leadership by the United States and other great powers. One may argue that the failure of the peace settlement of 1919 was less a consequence of its internal flaws than of its abandonment in the subsequent years, first by the withdrawal of the United States and then by successive retreats by other major signatories (especially Great Britain and France), particularly from the treaty's provisions for general disarmament and for collective action against breaches of the peace. These questions are still debated; nevertheless, it is probable that disillusionment with the settlement of 1919 contributed to the failure to arrive at any general peace settlement in World War II, and perhaps to the near abandonment of treaties of peace as a mode of terminating hostilities in the period since 1945.

Doubts concerning the necessity and advisability of concluding a treaty of peace at the end of World War II were expressed in the work on planning for peace during the last years of the war. In the report "Procedures of Peacemaking: With Special Reference to the Present War," the Legislative Reference Service of the Library of Congress pointed out in August 1943 that the Declaration of the United Nations bound the signatories not to conclude a separate peace. Nevertheless, the report noted:

> The worldwide scope of the present war and the multitude of problems which its settlement

entails constitute a strong temptation for the solution of certain questions independently of the overall settlement. . . . Even the major problems of boundaries, of federations, and of economic and political alliances among foreign States, insofar as the United States is not directly committed, might be thus decided without these decisions ever appearing in the text of a treaty which the United States would be called upon to ratify. . . . The cessation of hostilities in different parts of the world may be far from simultaneous. . . . And should a prolonged interval intervene between the end of the fighting in the main theatres of war and the definitive peace, the situation might become so deeply influenced by decisions made and regimes established in the meantime, that the peace conference might find its freedom of action considerably prejudiced. As a result of this development, the peace treaty or treaties may lose a great deal of their importance.

This analysis proved remarkably close to the actual course of events at the end of World War II. As one text summed it up, "peacemaking was a long drawn-out process which never quite ended but turned into the Cold War between the Soviet Union and its wartime allies." The wartime conferences at Casablanca, Teheran, Yalta, and Potsdam laid down some of the principles and specific terms of the postwar arrangements, including the demand for "unconditional surrender" of the Axis powers, the policy of "complete disarmament, demilitarization and dismemberment of Germany," the establishment of the United Nations, and various specific provisions relating to the Far East and Eastern Europe, particularly Poland. Nevertheless, many key issues were left imprecise or totally unresolved, and all the agreements were understood to be provisional pending a final peace treaty. By the time the peace conference convened in Paris, however, the situation had indeed become "so deeply influenced by decisions made and regimes established in the meantime" that the formulation of a general peace settlement acceptable to all the major participants had become impossible.

Thus, no general treaty settlement of World War II in Europe was concluded; the peace treaty with Japan was delayed until 1951, and was not signed by the Soviet Union. Nor were peace treaties concluded in other wars fought by the United States since then. No peace treaty followed the armistice in the Korean War, concluded at Panmunjom in July 1953. The withdrawal of U.S. forces from Vietnam was arranged by a cease-fire agreement of 28 January 1973. Although this was called "An Agreement Ending the War and Restoring Peace in Vietnam," it was actually, as Randle notes, "a military settlement without the concomitant political settlement that completes the peacemaking process." Moreover, the withdrawal of U.S. uniformed forces did not end the war or restore the peace; fighting continued among the Vietnamese and other Indochinese belligerents in subsequent years.

On the whole, the United States has held an image of peacemaking as "sitting down around the table to negotiate." But with the exception of the early period of its history in relations with European powers, especially Great Britain, the United States has not had a strong record of making peace on negotiated terms, such as to establish a lasting basis of concord. The terms of the treaties with Mexico in 1848, Spain in 1898, and Germany in 1919 were essentially dictated, as were the terms of surrender of the Axis countries in World War II. In the latter cases, the United States was obliged to negotiate at least with its own allies. In World War I, negotiation with allies may have cost the United States the freedom to negotiate with the opposing belligerents, but in World War II, it was the declared policy of the United States to achieve "unconditional surrender." This was also the policy most often adopted by the United States in dealing with insurgents, both domestic, as in the Civil War, and foreign, as in the Philippines. Moreover, in dealing with Native Americans, the United States has shown that negotiating treaties may be a device not to establish peace but to disarm, defeat, and gradually drive an opponent into a dependent condition.

The United States has sometimes sought to ameliorate the harshness of terms imposed on defeated opponents by financial awards (payments and annuities to Native Americans, $15 million to Mexico for 40 percent of its territory from Texas to California) or postwar programs of aid and rehabilitation (loans to Germany after World War I, the Marshall Plan after World War II). Even in this respect, however, the provision of aid has been more generous and given on less humiliating terms to powerful opponents, especially those of white race, than to those peoples of different race and culture who have found themselves in the path of "manifest destiny" and U.S. global expansion, whether Native Americans, Filipinos, or Vietnamese.

RACE AND PEACEMAKING

In the scholarly literature focusing on peacemaking in the international arena, surprisingly little attention has been given to issues of race. Although "ethnic" conflict is recognized as a cause of war or internal armed conflict and as sometimes especially intractable, the treatment of racial conflicts as such in works on "peacemaking" has been limited mainly to those concerned with conflict resolution in the schools, in the criminal justice system, or in community relations. Yet the salience of race as a factor in international relations and peacemaking has been called to our attention repeatedly, from W. E. B. Du Bois's declaration that "the problem of the twentieth century is the color line" to a number of contemporary works that emphasize the international and transnational importance of race. These include, in particular, George W. Shepherd, Jr., *Racial Influences on American Foreign Policy* (1970); Hugh Tinker, *Race, Conflict, and the International Order* (1977); and Paul Gordon Lauren, *Power and Prejudice: The Politics and Diplomacy of Racial Discrimination* (1988).

As Shepherd argued in 1970, "all great powers must face the reality of racial attitudes in their policies." This includes recognition of the dominant group interests as well as attitudes of racial superiority that may drive foreign policy choices and decisions and may shape support or disaffection from those choices at home. It has been suggested, for example, that the failure of the United States and other powers to support preventive action in Rwanda, while intervening at much higher levels of commitment in the Middle East and the Balkans, reflected a racially biased choice. Another aspect of the influence of race in international politics is that of transnational communication and interaction. As in the case of indigenous peoples, the transnational force of race identity and solidarity may have a powerful influence on policies relating to conflicts both at home and abroad. At the same time Shepherd called upon us to engage "a more perceptive study of the special contribution of nonwhite and non-Western peoples within and among nations."

Lauren later expanded on these themes, recognizing the problematic nature of the very concept of "race" but arguing that it has nonetheless profoundly influenced global politics and diplomacy. As he sums it up, race issues have affected relations between and among states and have posed serious threats to international peace and security. They have "motivated domestic groups concerned with racial discrimination to exert noticeable pressure upon the foreign policy of their own governments and to seek the active support of other nations for their protection." Despite the silence on these issues in most of the "peacemaking" literature, they have held a very high place on the international agenda of matters relating to a broad conception of peace. The first global attempt to speak for equality focused upon race. The first human rights provisions in the United Nations Charter were placed there because of race. The first international challenge to a country's claim of domestic jurisdiction and exclusive treatment of its own citizens centered upon race. The first binding treaty of human rights concentrated upon race. The international conventions with the greatest number of signatories is that on race. Within the United Nations, more resolutions deal with race than with any other subject. It may be hoped that as work continues and grows in the peacemaking field, more direct attention will be accorded to the issues of race at the international level.

GENDER AND PEACEMAKING

Given the widespread and persistent popular association between women and peace, and the worldwide presence of women's peace movements, it is not surprising that we now have several large bodies of literature on women, war, and peace. These include histories and biographies of women's peace activism, collections of women's poetry, fiction, and other writings on war and peace, sociological and political studies on women's peace movements, the gender gap on peace issues, and women's roles in peace and war, grueling accounts of women's losses, sufferings, displacement, and subjection to torture, rape, and sexual slavery in situations of war and armed conflict. Also portrayed are inspiring accounts of women's creativity, intellectual brilliance, courage, daring, and solidarity in the use of nonviolent direct action or other techniques of resistance, and a wide variety of theories to explain and comprehend women's struggles to overcome violence and subjection and build peace.

It may seem surprising, however, to find that in all this wealth of theory and knowledge there is relatively little about women and the processes of peacemaking as such. Less surprising, but more troubling, is that there is even less on women and gender in the mainstream studies on peacemaking, suggesting that women's peace work remains nearly as invisible to scholars and experts in the academy as the male political and military establishments would like it to be in the arenas of "real world" conflict. Of course the reason for this invisibility is above all the practical exclusion of women from most of the official and even unofficial avenues of peacemaking. At peace talks for Burundi in Arusha, a delegation of women was not welcomed to participate—male delegates declared: "The women are not parties to this conflict. This is not their concern. We cannot see why they have come, why they bother us. We are here and we represent them." While these sentiments may not be so readily expressed aloud in other contexts, they are in fact all too common in practice. On a positive note, women have gained high-level positions in U.S. foreign relations, including Madeleine Albright as secretary of state under President Bill Clinton and President George W. Bush's national security adviser Condoleezza Rice. However, the number of women admitted to the sacrosanct premises of peace or cease-fire negotiations is minuscule, and the adage, "out of sight, out of mind," is all too accurate here. The women themselves, their proposals for peace, and their concerns with regard to peace settlements, are steadfastly relegated to the sidelines. Nonetheless, the multiple roles women play relative to settling conflicts and restoring peace are in fact highly important, sometimes decisive, and the gendered character of all wars and armed conflicts is central to a clear comprehension of the context and path to resolution.

There are a number of works that are especially valuable in this regard, including: Gita Sen and Caren Grown, *Development, Crises, and Alternative Visions: Third World Women's Perspectives* (1987), Betty A. Reardon, *Women and Peace: Feminist Visions of Global Security* (1993), and Sanam Naraghi Anderlini, *Women at the Peace Table: Making a Difference* (2000). The latter, a publication of UNIFEM (United Nations Development Fund for Women), deals most directly with women's participation in peace movements during wars and conflicts and in the processes of negotiation and peacebuilding to end the conflicts and secure a sustainable peace with benefits not only for the "winners" but for women and people at the grassroots. Anderlini interviews women who have been engaged in the peace processes, including Hanan Ashrawi, and explores both the

obstacles the women have faced and the importance of their contributions to the peace processes. Further research and analysis in this area are urgently needed.

PEACEMAKING AND THE PERILS OF "VICTORY"

It was long held in the scholarly literature that wars for the most part end in victory for one side and defeat for the other. Stalemates and settlements with no discernible victor or defeated were regarded as relatively rare. This was not often stated as a general principle and was sometimes subjected to challenge. Nevertheless, it appeared repeatedly, sometimes as an empirical observation on selected groups of wars, sometimes as an underlying assumption in the theoretical analysis of war endings.

Thus, Melvin Small and J. David Singer in *The Wages of War: 1816–1965, A Statistical Handbook* (1972), assigned victor or defeated status to the belligerents in all but one of fifty interstate wars and forty-three "extra-systemic" wars that they included in their study. Similarly, George Modelski found that some four-fifths of one hundred internal wars since 1900 ended in an "outright win" or victory of one side or the other. The theoretical significance of assigning victory had been set forth earlier by H. A. Calahan, who held that the key to peacemaking lies simply in the recognition of defeat on the part of the vanquished: "war is pressed by the victor, but peace is made by the vanquished."

This view was echoed later by others, including Paul Kecskemeti and Lewis Coser, but its fullest theoretical statement appears in Nicholas S. Timasheff's *War and Revolution* (1965). Timasheff views war as "a means of solving an inter-state conflict by measuring the relative strength of the parties." Timasheff goes on to make clear that the return to peace must take place through the initiative of the defeated, concluding that in studying the "movement from war to peace" (that is, war endings), the determination of victory is central: "Therefore, the study of the causal background of the return of political systems from war to peace is tantamount to the study of the premises of victory and of the mechanism converting victory into peace."

This preoccupation with victory and defeat persists in some measure today despite the fact that, as James D. Smith and others have pointed out, there has been a significant trend away from the conclusion of wars and armed conflicts by clear-cut victory of one side. Negotiated settlements, stalemates, and withdrawals of all parties are increasingly prevalent as outcomes of war in the late twentieth century. "'Victory,' then, is becoming increasingly elusive in modern warfare." Yet in their text *How Nations Make Peace* (1999), Charles W. Kegley, Jr., and Gregory A. Raymond center their entire analysis on "situations in which there was a clear winner and loser," exploring the "policy problems and moral dilemmas victors face," the choices to be made by "victors" after a "decisive military victory," and particularly "the relative merits of compassionate versus punitive peace settlements." In posing these issues, Kegley and Raymond express the laudable hope that their work may help to "bring the ethical dimension of decision making into the study of international relations." However, by narrowing the focus to exclude the great diversity of contemporary armed conflicts and their different kinds of endings, Kegley and Raymond obscure the broader question of "how nations make peace" and direct disproportionate attention to the relatively few instances in which the winner/loser, victor/defeated model prevails. Meanwhile, the elusive goal of victory continues to command the imaginations of both military and civilian leaders, often standing as a significant obstacle to timely and effective peacemaking, as illustrated in a number of case studies examined by James D. Smith in *Stopping Wars* (1995).

ON THE ROAD TO PEACE: PEACE PROCESSES SINCE WORLD WAR II

With the decline of formal peace settlements as the prevailing mode of terminating wars in the period since World War II, studies of peacemaking have shifted to the analysis of peace processes: the factors influencing parties in a conflict to move toward peace, procedures to facilitate the process, methods and techniques to bring about cessation of hostilities and implement cease-fire terms, and approaches to peacebuilding for the longer term. In these processes, the United Nations has been called on with increasing frequency to play a central part, yet often sidestepped to suit great-power interests.

In his 1992 report *An Agenda for Peace,* Secretary-General Boutros Boutros-Ghali spelled out the multiple roles that the United Nations has taken in regard to peace, under the rubrics of preventive diplomacy, peacemaking, peace enforcement, and peacekeeping. It may be noted that "peacemaking" appears here in a specific sense as one of a series of stages in the peace process, though the term is still widely used to denote the entire process, and the designations cover actions and procedures that are overlapping and interrelated.

"Preventive diplomacy" refers to efforts to resolve disputes before violence occurs. Such efforts may be conducted by the secretary-general or other offices of the United Nations, or by diplomatic engagement of others such as neutral states or regional associations, or by multitrack diplomacy involving both public and private parties. These may lead to a variety of steps to encourage resolution of the disputes without armed force, such as confidence-building measures, fact finding, early-warning systems, preventive deployment, and demilitarized zones. As Gareth Evans notes, in some circumstances "the preventive diplomacy techniques—negotiation, enquiry, mediation and so on—which are aimed at averting armed hostilities, are also appropriate if fighting *does* break out."

"Peacemaking" in the specific sense used here refers to efforts to bring together parties already engaged in hostilities to seek agreement for peaceful resolution of their conflict. The United Nations role in this context is spelled out under chapter 6 of the UN Charter, which specifies the options of mediation, negotiation, conciliation, arbitration, judicial settlement, sanctions, and "other peaceful means." Mediation, negotiation, arbitration, and judicial settlement have been central to the theory and practice of peacemaking over the course of history and have been treated in numerous historical, legal, and political works. Two noteworthy contemporary examples are Paul R. Pillar, *Negotiating Peace: War Termination as a Bargaining Process* (1983), and I. William Zartman and J. Lewis Rasmussen, eds., *Peacemaking in International Conflict: Methods and Techniques* (1997). Peacemaking efforts in the last decades of the twentieth century sought less to arrive at any comprehensive peace agreement than to achieve a cessation or pause in hostilities in the form of a cease-fire, truce, or "suspension of arms." The processes of arriving at a cease-fire have been somewhat neglected in the existing literature, but have been addressed particularly by James D. Smith in *Stopping Wars: Defining the Obstacles to Cease-fire* (1995).

Sanctions, which are conceived in this context as an inducement to bring parties to the negotiating table, have also been invoked to bring international pressure on a state in favor of internal change, as in the case of sanctions imposed upon South Africa to end its apartheid policies. Here it can be argued that the combined impact of economic, strategic, social, and cultural sanctions imposed by the international community played an important peacemaking role in promoting an end to a violent system. On the other hand, sanctions used as a form of peace enforcement can become punitive action, amounting to a weapon of war. Sanctions imposed upon Iraq in conjunction with the Persian Gulf War of 1991 were maintained (though with some modifications) for over a decade at the insistence of the United States, with devastating consequences for the Iraqi people.

"Peace enforcement" under United Nations auspices is authorized under chapter 7 of the UN Charter. This provides for the use of any measures deemed necessary by the Security Council, including the use of armed force, to "maintain or restore international peace and security." In general, the United Nations has been somewhat reluctant to resort to this provision of the Charter, the main exceptions being the two major military enforcement actions spearheaded and directed by the United States in Korea and the Persian Gulf. In contrast, the efforts of Secretary-General Boutros-Ghali in 1994 to assemble a peace enforcement mission of five thousand troops to prevent the genocidal violence that eventually claimed over half a million lives in Rwanda were rebuffed by the United States and other powers. The United States also spearheaded the military enforcement action against Yugoslavia in 1999, under the aegis of NATO, declining to take the matter to the United Nations.

"Peacekeeping" refers to intervention by unarmed or lightly armed forces of the United Nations or other intergovernmental bodies, to monitor or supervise implementation of cease-fires, troop withdrawals, or other agreements reached through preventive diplomacy or peacemaking efforts. Peacekeeping bodies may include military personnel, police forces, or civilians and, as Evans points out, their presence usually presupposes "that the governments or parties involved in the conflict are willing to cooperate and are able to reach and maintain agreement." In the decades since the establishment of the United Nations Truce Supervision Organization for Palestine in 1948, the United Nations and other international bodies have accumulated extensive experience with scores of peacekeeping operations around the world. A large body of works reporting, analyzing and assessing these operations has appeared, ranging from individual case histories such as Connor Cruise O'Brien's *To Katanga and Back: A UN Case History* (1964) and overviews such as *The Blue Helmets: A Review of United Nations Peacekeeping* (United Nations, 1990, 1996), to collections of scholarly and interpretive studies such as Tom Woodhouse et al., eds., *Peacekeeping and Peacemaking: Towards Effective Intervention in Post-Cold War Conflicts* (1998), and Olara A. Otunnu and Michael W. Doyle, eds., *Peacemaking and Peacekeeping for the New Century* (1998).

"Peacebuilding" is a newer concept, emerging from a growing recognition that termination of armed conflict is no guarantee of "peace," which depends on underlying social, political, and economic conditions. Peace studies as a field has moved away from an exclusive focus on "negative peace," conceived simply as the *absence* of organized warfare and other forms of armed violence, to the study of "positive peace." In the context of peacemaking, this means going beyond cease-fire or even peace accords to address underlying issues of justice and the structural violence of exploitation, racism, patriarchy, and other forms of oppression and dominance relations. This is sometimes described as a process of "conflict transformation," designed to build "cooperative, peaceful relationships capable of fostering reconciliation, reconstruction, and long-term economic and social development." John Paul Lederach, in *Building Peace: Sustainable Reconciliation in Divided Societies* (1997), sets out to provide "a set of ideas and strategies that undergird sustainable peace." As summarized in the foreword by Richard H. Solomon, a president of the United States Institute for Peace: "Sustainable peace requires that long-time antagonists not merely lay down their arms but that they achieve profound reconciliation that will endure because it is sustained by a society-wide network of relationships and mechanisms that promote justice and address the root causes of enmity." Peacebuilding thus expands the field of vision in peacemaking to encompass a broad range of individual, group, and societal and international problems and action.

It may be that there is no better symbol of the paradoxes in the history of United States peacemaking than dubbing the Colt .45 gun "the Peacemaker." Yet it may be hoped that the voices will be heard of those other peacemakers who hold with Jane Addams that peace cannot be secured merely by the temporary conclusion of fighting, but "only as men abstained from the gains of oppression and responded to the cause of the poor; that swords would finally be beaten into plowshares and pruning hooks, not because men resolved to be peaceful, but because the metal of the earth would be turned to its proper use when the poor and their children should be abundantly fed," and when peace came to be conceived "no longer as an absence of war, but the unfolding of worldwide processes making for the nurture of human life."

BIBLIOGRAPHY

Bell, Christine. *Peace Agreements and Human Rights*. New York, 2000.

Boulding, Elise. *Building a Global Civic Culture: Education for an Interdependent World*. Syracuse, N.Y., 1990.

Brown, Dee. *Bury My Heart at Wounded Knee: An Indian History of the American West*. New York, 1971.

Caplow, Theodore. *Peace Games*. Middletown, Conn., 1989.

Carroll, Berenice A. "How Wars End: An Analysis of Some Current Hypotheses." *Journal of Peace Research* (December 1969): 295–320.

———. "War Termination and Conflict Theory: Value Premises, Theory, and Policies." *Annals of the American Academy of Political and Social Science* 392 (November 1970): 14–29.

Challinor, Joan R., and Robert L. Beisner, eds. *Arms at Rest: Peacemaking and Peacekeeping in American History*. New York, 1987.

Daffern, Thomas Clough. "Peacemaking and Peacebuilding." In Lester Kurtz and Jennifer Turpin, eds. *Encyclopedia of Violence, Peace, and Conflict*. Vol. 2. San Diego, 1999.

Deloria, Vine, Jr. *Behind the Trail of Broken Treaties: An Indian Declaration of Independence*. Austin, Tex., 1985.

Diamond, Louise, and John McDonald. *Multi-Track Diplomacy: A Systems Approach to Peace*. 3d ed. West Hartford, Conn., 1996.

Elias, Robert, and Jennifer Turpin, eds. *Rethinking Peace*. Boulder, Colo., 1994.

Fox, William T. R., ed. *How Wars End*. Special issue of *Annals of the American Academy of Political and Social Science* 392 (November 1970).

Goldstein, Erik. *Wars and Peace Treaties: 1816–1991*. London, 1992.

Hampson, Fen Osler. *Nurturing Peace: Why Peace Settlements Succeed or Fail*. Washington, D.C., 1996.

Ikenberry, G. John. *After Victory: Institutions, Strategic Restraint, and the Rebuilding of Order After Major Wars*. Princeton, N.J., 2001.

Ireton, Steven W. "Conflict Resolution and Indian Treaties on the American Indian Frontier, 1730–1768." Ph.D. dissertation. University of California at Santa Barbara, 1988.

Jackson, Helen Hunt. *A Century of Dishonor: A Sketch of the United States Government's Dealings with Some of the Indian Tribes*. 2d ed. Boston, 1885.

Jaimes, M. Annette, ed. *The State of Native America: Genocide, Colonization, and Resistance*. Boston, 1992.

Karsh, Efraim, and Gregory Mahler, eds. *Israel at the Crossroads: The Challenge of Peace*. New York, 1994.

Kegley, Charles W., Jr., and Gregory A. Raymond. *How Nations Make Peace*. New York, 1999.

Kurtz, Lester, and Jennifer Turpin, eds. *Encyclopedia of Violence, Peace, and Conflict*. Vol. 2. San Diego, 1999.

Lederach, John Paul. *Building Peace: Sustainable Reconciliation in Divided Societies*. Washington, D.C., 1997.

Mayer, Arno J. *Politics and Diplomacy of Peacemaking: Containment and Counter-revolution at Versailles 1918–1919*. New York, 1967.

Morris, Richard B. *The Peacemakers: The Great Powers and American Independence*. New York, 1965.

Nicolson, Harold. *Peacemaking, 1919*. New York, 1965.

Otunnu, Olara A., and Michael W. Doyle, eds. *Peacemaking and Peacekeeping for the New Century*. Lanham, Md., 1998.

Pauling, Linus, Ervin Laszlo, and Jong Youl Yoo, eds. *World Encyclopedia of Peace*. Vol. 2. Oxford, 1986.

Phillipson, Coleman. *Termination of War and Treaties of Peace*. London, 1916.

Pillar, Paul R. *Negotiating Peace: War Termination as a Bargaining Process*. Princeton, N.J., 1983.

Powers, Gerard F., Drew Christiansen, and Robert T. Hennemeyer, eds. *Peacemaking: Moral and Policy Challenges for a New World*. Washington, D.C., 1994.

Randle, Robert F. *The Origins of Peace: A Study of Peacemaking and the Structure of Peace Settlements*. New York, 1973.

Regan, Patrick M. *Organizing Societies for War: The Process and Consequences of Societal Militarization*. Westport, Conn., 1994.

Rupesinghe, Kumar, with Sanam Naraghi Anderlini. *Civil Wars, Civil Peace: An Introduction to Conflict Resolution*. London, 1998.

Smith, David S., ed. *From War to Peace: Essays in Peacemaking and War Termination*. New York, 1974.

Smith, James D. D. *Stopping Wars: Defining the Obstacles to Cease-fire*. Boulder, Colo., 1995.

Stiffarm, Lenore A., with Phil Lane, Jr. "The Demography of Native North America: A Question of American Indian Survival." In M. Annette Jaimes, ed. *The State of Native America: Genocide, Colonization, and Resistance*. Boston, 1992.

Stone, Julius. *Legal Controls of International Conflict: A Treatise on the Dynamics of Disputes and War-Law*. New York, 1959.

United Nations. *Handbook on the Peaceful Settlement of Disputes Between States*. New York, 1992.

Woodhouse, Tom, ed. *Peacemaking in a Troubled World*. New York, 1991.

Woodhouse, Tom, Robert Bruce, and Malcolm Dando, eds. *Peacekeeping and Peacemaking: Towards Effective Intervention in Post-Cold War Conflicts*. New York, 1998.

Wright, Quincy. *A Study of War*. 2d ed. Chicago, 1965.

Zartman, I. William, and J. Lewis Rasmussen, eds. *Peacemaking in International Conflict: Methods & Techniques*. Washington, D.C., 1997.

See also ALLIANCES, COALITIONS, AND ENTENTES; ARBITRATION, MEDIATION, AND CONCILIATION; DISSENT IN WARS; GENDER; INTERVENTION AND NONINTERVENTION; PACIFISM; PEACE MOVEMENTS; RACE AND ETHNICITY; TREATIES.

PEACE MOVEMENTS

Robert H. Ferrell

The idea of peace is ancient, reaching back to the beginnings of organized society and perhaps even earlier; but until the Renaissance it had not passed beyond the stage of individual thought. Society was rural, save for a few towns and cities. Nationalities, while recognized, were not well formed. International relations did not exist. The relations of the Greek city-states were casual and unorganized, moving from hostilities to lack of hostilities without much of a dividing line. The very basis of international organization—existence of different peoples, organized in states, usually speaking different languages, was not present in the Greek world. Nor was it present in the world of Rome, where a single city, through extension of citizenship, recognized no equals in the area of the Mediterranean. To the Romans the people with whom they came in touch were either to submit to the domination of the empire or forever remain barbarians. There was no such thing as interstate relations. The same lack of international relations marked medieval life, where princes and principalities might fight or not fight, for whatever reason, conducting warfare as if it were a natural state of affairs and halting it when convenient, without much or any formality. In such disorganized relations between the peoples of Europe there was, to be sure, little reason to try for a better order of affairs when all that people knew was chaos or domination. In any event, the generality of the citizens or subjects was not consulted in advance of fighting or its conclusion.

The appearance of peace movements awaited both the formal division of Europe into nation-states and a notable intellectual development often overlooked by analysts of modern European history—the division of international relations into times of peace and times of war. This latter change came during the Thirty Years' War in the seventeenth century, and did not occur so much in the statecraft of the time as in the thinking of jurists and students of law, who began to see not merely that the primitive international customs and traditions of the era must be ordered but also that the task of ordering involved division into laws for fighting and laws for peaceful existence. In this regard the Dutch jurist Hugo Grotius proved most influential. A citizen of one of the major maritime states of the era, and therefore interested in the freest possible trade on the high seas, he found the military forces of his countrymen outnumbered by the professional armies of the monarchs whose territories surrounded the States-General. The convenience of trading with many European states had fascinated the Dutch, and they wanted to continue this commerce. At the same time they needed guarantees of freedom of trade. Life during the Thirty Years' War was almost insufferable for so rich a group as the Dutch burghers. Grotius was imprisoned, and friends contrived his escape in a large chest. With reason he wished to try to order the international relations of his time, and the result was *De jure belli ac pacis* (1625). In it he drew a sharp line between what was war and what was peace. It was, incidentally, a line that was not recognized until the nineteenth century, when there were no major European wars except the Franco-Prussian War (1870–1871). Grotius's distinction between war and peace would be blurred by the statesmen of the twentieth century, who through cold wars and other such undeclared conflicts pushed international relations back toward the pre-Grotian chaos. In any event, the drawing of a war-peace line—however theoretical, and thereafter slowly accepted and eventually violated—set the stage for popular peace movements. In a real sense Grotius and his supporters among the legal theorists were the originators of peace movements.

The essentially theoretical nature of peace movements was observable from the outset, and it may well have been one of the reasons why the innumerable drawings of ideal international societies, the perfect renderings of international relations, have never been translated even approximately into reality.

The first designs of men of peace in modern times, which themselves were not characterizable as the programs of peace movements but received a good deal of attention during their periods of interest, were markedly theoretical. One of the leaders of France in the early seventeenth century, the duc de Sully, was the author of the "great design" of King Henry IV, which, though it stipulated an international force, asked for one so small that it amounted to disarmament. Much notice was taken of this hope for peace, and it was speculated upon for years thereafter. The supporters of later peace movements were also accustomed to cite the hopes of Benjamin Franklin, who was convinced that standing armies diminished not only the population of a country but also the breed and size of the human species, for the strongest men went off to war and were killed. He pointed out obvious waste in the maintenance of armies. His analysis made sense to many Americans who themselves, or whose ancestors, had come to the New World to escape the constant wars of the Old. The Farewell Address of President George Washington in 1796 was plain about the need for peace and the wastefulness of war: "Overgrown military establishments are, under any form of government, inauspicious to liberty, and are to be regarded as particularly hostile to republican liberty." Here was another rationale that would recur in the pronouncements of the nineteenth-century peace movements in both the United States and Europe.

The intellectual foundations of peace movements were laid in the years prior to 1815. Beginning in that year, with the wars of the French Revolution and Napoleon at an end, and the emperor of France on his way to St. Helena in a British frigate, it was possible to bring together the formalities of the international lawyers and the philosophical hopes of Sully, Franklin, and Washington, and to enlarge upon and systematize ideas about how American or European—or even world—peace might be achieved.

The years from 1815 to 1848 saw major developments in organization of peace groups in the United States. For a while it appeared as if they might carry everything before them. Peace seemed secure between the United States and Great Britain. In the Rush-Bagot Convention (1817) the two English-speaking nations undertook a virtual disarmament of their borders upon the Great Lakes, across New York State, and along the northern borders of the New England states. Why could not such an arrangement between erstwhile enemies spread to the entire world? This was the era of the founding of the American Peace Society in 1828 and of state peace societies. It was an ebullient time, often characterized by later historians as an age of reform: the antislavery movement, prison reform, insane asylum reform, experiments in communitarian living, and the rise of reformist religions such as the Church of Jesus Christ of Latter-Day Saints.

Members of the new peace organizations advanced their ideas with unwonted vigor and with a very considerable intellectual precision. The principal organizer of the American Peace Society, William Ladd, arranged for distribution of tracts and advocated a congress of nations, together with the riddance of war through treaties of arbitration. Elihu Burritt established the League of Universal Brotherhood in 1846, which soon was claiming an American membership of twenty thousand and a similar number of British members; Burritt's organization was largely responsible for a series of "universal peace congresses" held in European cities over the next years.

The peace groups of the first half of the nineteenth century took interest in international law, as Grotius had two centuries before, and the American Peace Society in the person of Ladd, as well as the reformer Alfred Love, founder of the Universal Peace Union (1866), looked to a stronger law of nations that, they were certain, would make war more difficult, perhaps even impossible.

As for precisely how influential the peace groups were, during the years from Waterloo to the revolutions of 1848 and the Crimean War (for Europe) and to the Mexican War and the passing of the slavery issue into national politics, and ultimately the coming of the Civil War (for the United States), it is impossible to say. The problem of analysis here is that during an age of reform there was goodwill in so many directions, often expressed by the same individuals, that its forcefulness or lack thereof cannot be easily determined. Moreover, the absence of even fairly small international conflicts was probably not a result of the peace movement, but of contemporary circumstances in the international relations of Europe—the unpopularity of war after the wars of the French Revolution and Napoleon, and the momentary sense of community among the great powers known as the Concert of Europe. To many people of the time, peace nonetheless seemed a logical outcome of the peace movement; and the workers for peace tended to pursue their plans and purposes—abolition of standing armies, development of international law on land and sea, organization of peace congresses—with a confidence that was unjustified by the international relations of the time.

In the latter half of the nineteenth century, peace workers began to have a new sense of urgency because of an armaments race that at first was not very noticeable but later became highly evident. By the 1860s and 1870s the stresses and strains incident to the rise of a Prussia-dominated German state in Europe began to send armament expenditures on an upward trend that continued into the twentieth century. The sharpening of nationalisms everywhere, and the increasing authority of national bureaucracies, impelled nations to increase their armaments. Weapons also began to increase in complexity and costliness. Muskets gave way to rifles. Smooth-bore cannon were replaced by rifled guns, and projectiles went farther and penetrated deeper. The navies of the world converted from sail to steam. They armored their ships. Transport—first the railroad and then, after the end of the century, motor transport over paved roads—made land armies mobile in ways unknown to generals during the age of Napoleon, Gebhard von Blucher, and the duke of Wellington.

The Industrial Revolution allowed nations with heavy industries to produce arms for themselves and sell arms to their agricultural neighbors in exchange for foodstuffs. Introduction of such weapons as the French 75, a new field gun, forced all the leading European states to purchase the new ordnance. By the 1890s men of goodwill everywhere were alarmed at the dreadfully costly battles and campaigns of any new war, given the new equipment. They were alarmed at the talk about military might by the leaders of Germany after Bismarck. The surge of imperialism in the 1890s momentarily took European and American energies into the Far East. Earlier the Europeans had devoted themselves to the imperial task of dividing Africa. Shortly after the turn of the century, there was no more territory to divide, and rivalries began to concentrate in Europe, as they had just before outbreak of the Napoleonic wars. It was a vastly troubled situation; and peace groups began to look for solutions, to try to do what statesmen seemed incapable of doing—to contrive some kind of international arrangement of ideas and interests so that war could be prevented.

Limitation of armaments was the task of the peace movements prior to 1914, and the result was disappointing. Calvin D. Davis has justly remarked that a strange dichotomy of thought existed in the United States and Europe. International rivalries never had burned so brightly, and never had there been so much talk about national interest; yet never had there been more popular interest in peace. Peace groups received broad public support, even from statesmen, who perhaps saw them as so important, so obviously influential, that it would be best to join them, at least in appearance. Universal Peace Congresses began to assemble, the first such meeting being held in 1889. The men and women who attended these meetings favored disarmament and the advance of arbitration through treaties. The Dissenting churches of Great Britain heartily supported disarmament during the 1890s, before the British army and navy were modernized on the eve of World War I. British members of these groups looked anxiously to their American cousins, hoping that from unity of language could come unity of national purposes. The English-Speaking Union was a reflection of this hope. During the years from the turn of the century until 1914, a rapprochement became apparent between the two countries and was much remarked upon. The two countries together could join their European friends in a peace movement that would overwhelm the forces for war. It was thought by people who were interested in peace that the two English-speaking nations might well be considered impartial in urging a disarmament conference because of their separation from Europe by water—not very much in the case of Britain but a vast expanse in the case of America.

The pre–World War I years seemed to promise a great peace reform. Baroness Bertha von Suttner in 1889 published a book titled *Die Waffen Nieder (Lay Down Your Arms)*. It was perhaps the greatest peace novel of all times and was translated into almost every known tongue. The British journalist W. T. Stead reprinted it in English in 1896, and sold the book at the nominal price of one penny. The Russians appeared to be interested in world peace, or at least it was clear that the great novelist Leo Tolstoy was fascinated by the idea. At the suggestion of Baroness von Suttner, the inventor of dynamite, Alfred Nobel, became devoted to the peace movement. Nobel, who believed that he could cooperate with the baroness through making dynamite, wrote to her on one occasion, "Perhaps my factories will put an end to war even sooner than your Congresses; on the day when two army corps may mutually annihilate each other in a second, probably all civilized nations will recoil with horror and disband their troops." Little did Nobel know that this day to which he looked mystically, albeit seriously, would arrive in the latter twentieth century, but civilized nations not only would fail to recoil with horror and disband their troops, but also would prove willing to allow the weapons of destruction to proliferate.

Nobel characterized the hopes of his generation by endowing a peace prize that was to go annually "to that man or woman who shall have worked most effectively for the fraternization of mankind, the diminution of armies, and the promotion of Peace Congresses." This was the spirit that produced the most notable product of the peace movement of the turn of the century, the Hague Peace Conferences of 1899 and 1907.

Unfortunately, the first conference did little for peace. The czar of Russia called it in the vain hope that it would limit adoption of French 75 rifles by the armies of Europe, so that the Russian government could put available funds into modernizing its navy. This purpose was well understood by representatives of the nations meeting at The Hague, and nothing came of it. Evidence of how little the administration of President William McKinley expected from the First Hague Peace Conference could be seen in the composition of the American delegation, which included Captain William Crozier of the U.S. Army and Captain Alfred Thayer Mahan, who had recently retired from the U.S. Navy. Crozier was coinventor of an ingenious disappearing gun carriage, and Mahan was the philosopher of a large American navy; neither was about to let the czar's government get away with anything. The first conference did, however, define the rules of civilized warfare. It arranged for an international tribunal that nations thereafter promised to use, albeit excepting so many of their national interests that such use was virtually a symbol of the court's uselessness.

The Second Hague Peace Conference was delayed until after the Russo-Japanese War, by which time the European armaments race was so far developed that the conference's prospects were almost zero. President Theodore Roosevelt knew that 1907 was not a good year for peace, yet felt that he had to do something, for many of his Republican friends in New England were members of peace societies and anxious for achievement. He sent the American fleet around the

world that year, and later wrote that the voyage was the best thing he had done for peace. He considered doing more, and urged the British government to limit the size of battleships to fifteen thousand tons displacement. Apparently he was seeking to halt the naval arms race begun by the British with the launching of the battleship *Dreadnought* the preceding year. But then Roosevelt's idea disappeared, as naval architects pointed out to him that fifteen thousand tons was too small a platform for the best combination of the essentials of fighting ships—guns, armor, and propulsive machinery. Neither the British nor the German government wished to do anything serious about disarmament at the Second Hague Peace Conference, and so the idea languished and the conferees contented themselves with tidying up the projects for judicial settlement and international law advanced at the initial conference. The Third Hague Peace Conference was scheduled just about the time World War I broke out; and the Hague idea, as it was called, then blended into the larger notion of a League of Nations.

The American peace groups in these years concentrated not merely on congresses and conferences but also on a national program of bilateral treaties of arbitration and conciliation. Secretaries of State Richard Olney, John Hay, Elihu Root, Philander C. Knox, and William Jennings Bryan sought to negotiate such treaties, and Hay, Root, and Bryan concluded several dozen. The only way that this program of the American peace groups could have ensured world peace was for the United States to have signed up every nation—and the other nations would have had to arrange their own treaty networks. Because of the outbreak of World War I there was not enough time for so many instruments to be signed and ratified. Although the American network remains on the statute books, nothing came of the hope for peace through treaties of arbitration and conciliation.

THE INTERWAR YEARS

World War I marked the end of the program of the peace movement of preceding years. The war was a chilling experience. Although statesmen had anticipated the war, they and people everywhere were shocked when it did not end quickly, like the Franco-Prussian War, and lasted more than four years. The United States intervened. It became necessary, so it seemed, for the New World to redress the balance of the Old. It was necessary,

Americans believed, to get the Europeans off dead center, to move them toward peace.

The principal accomplishment of peace-minded Americans during the war and in the months of negotiations afterward in Paris was to draw up the constitution, or Covenant, of the League of Nations. Participation in the war convinced many Americans that they had not merely repaid their debt to the marquis de Lafayette but that their country, as President Woodrow Wilson said, comprised all nations and therefore understood all nations, and American organization of the peace would ensure a decent future for mankind.

But then came another shock for the millions of Americans who looked forward to world peace—rejection of the Treaty of Versailles and thereby of the Covenant, which constituted the first twenty-six articles of the treaty, by the Senate in 1919–1920. President Wilson had told everyone who would listen that Article X, which promised international action to prevent war, was the "heart" of the Covenant. To the millions of League of Nations supporters in the United States, it seemed that the Senate had broken the heart of the world.

The American peace groups of the interwar era divided over the wisdom of establishing a League of Nations, and perhaps the best way to understand the division is to characterize it as pro-league and anti-league—or conservative and radical—because of differing outlooks on the organization of peace. Most conservative peace groups—including the Carnegie Endowment for International Peace, the World Peace Foundation, the League of Nations Association, and the Woodrow Wilson Foundation—had originated in the eastern portion of the country. They possessed financial strength—at its foundation in 1910 the Carnegie Endowment received $10 million in bonds of the United States Steel Corporation. Those bonds had been insured by the profits of World War I, a situation presenting the odd picture of a peace organization operating on the profits of war. The World Peace Foundation had also begun its work in the same year, with $1 million. The Woodrow Wilson Foundation, created in 1923, received initial contributions of nearly $1 million.

The work of the conservative wing of American peace organizations varied, for their members realized that all sorts of activity could come under the general heading of peace. The Carnegie Endowment annually spent $500,000 sponsoring such projects as a monthly bulletin, *International Conciliation,* and "international mind alcoves" in small libraries throughout the United States. Its publishing program included the monumental *Economic and Social History of the World War* in one hundred volumes. It financed smaller peace organizations in the United States and abroad, maintained the Paris Center for European Peace, rebuilt the library of the University of Louvain in Belgium, endowed university chairs in international relations, and advanced codification of international law. The World Peace Foundation worked in favor of the World Court and distributed League of Nations publications in the United States. The Woodrow Wilson Foundation worked to perpetuate Wilsonian ideals.

Radical peace organizations of the interwar era were far less staid and restrained. Almost all had come into existence as a result of World War I. Names of these groups changed as finances and memberships waxed and waned, but altogether there were perhaps forty operating at the national level, with many more local organizations. These were groups of believers in world peace, filled with hope for their programs. Often their purposes were revealed in their names: the American Committee for the Outlawry of War, the American Committee for the Cause and Cure of War, the Women's International League for Peace and Freedom, the National Council for the Prevention of War, the Committee on Militarism in Education, the Fellowship of Reconciliation, the Parliament of Peace and Universal Brotherhood, the Peace Heroes Memorial Society, the War Resisters' League, the Women's Peace Society, the World Peace Association.

Operating procedures of the radical peace organizations, the evangelists among the peace workers, varied markedly. Some were virtually one-man operations, such as the American Committee for the Outlawry of War, financed by the Chicago lawyer Salmon O. Levinson, who spent $15,000 a year to spread the idea that war should not be permitted under international law—it should be outlawed. The Women's International League for Peace and Freedom had as many as six thousand members and thousands of dollars each year for expenses, much of the money provided by friends of the Chicago social worker Jane Addams. The National Council for the Prevention of War was the creation of the Congregational minister Frederick J. Libby to work against arms manufacturers during the Washington Naval Conference of 1921–1922, and after the success of that meeting Libby continued his group in support of other causes. It acted as a Washington lobby for peace groups, but always reflected the pacifism of its founder. It spent $100,000 a year; in 1928 its office roster included twelve secretaries and eighteen office assistants. Among other radical groups the Women's Peace Society had two thousand members; the Fellowship of Reconciliation, forty-five hundred; and the War Resisters' League, four hundred. Their financial situations were relatively modest.

How, one might ask, could even substantial groups (in terms of finances) like the conservative organizations, or small groups such as the radical peace organizations, hope to influence the millions of American citizens in the years after World War I? How can one speak of the peace movement in America when the organizations for peace, affluent or otherwise, were composed of such disparate groups and often of committees dominated by a few persons or even one individual?

An important reason for their influence was their ability to act through a maze of supporting peace groups and interlocking committees. Membership of the radical peace organizations was astonishingly small, and within it the core of full-time peace workers was less than one hundred individuals in Washington and New York. But individuals could join more than one group or otherwise obtain cooperation between peace organizations. And the ardent peace worker Carrie Chapman Catt federated organizations not primarily interested in peace; she brought together as many as a dozen of these national organizations—such as the American Association of University Women and the Young Women's Christian Association—into the American Committee for the Cause and Cure of War.

Peace organizations were influential because of their frequent claim to represent the female voters of the United States. After World War I the franchise had been extended to all American women. Their voting preferences were highly uncertain, and Catt was able to threaten the nation's political leaders with a unified female vote in support of whatever she was advocating.

Still another reason for the extraordinary influence of American peace groups during the 1920s and 1930s perhaps needs to be explained. Elected officials of the time were sensitive to pressure from voters advocating a program. Of course there has always been pressure upon officials. But to leaders of the postwar period a new force, an aroused public opinion, seemed to be at work. Participation in the war had brought interest in

propaganda, and in turn produced much learned and unlearned speculation about public opinion. Walter Lippmann published a book on the subject during the early 1920s. The science of persuasion, as applied to mass consumption, came into vogue, with advertising taking on the proportions of a national industry. Political leaders felt that they were being watched, their actions scrutinized, as never before. Any individuals or small groups who could claim to represent larger groups or great organizations received instantaneous attention. It was a nervous, rather unsophisticated era in which claims to importance, carefully advanced, could propel their bearers toward success in whatever they were advocating.

American peace organizations indulged in a pressure politics that for years proved far more successful than it should have been—because of the hypersensitive political climate. They did everything possible to give the impression that their programs represented the thoughts of the American people. In their letter-writing campaigns to members of Congress, workers for peace learned early on that it was advisable to make each letter appear different, even if it was for the same purpose and said the same thing; the technique was to have separately written appeals, individually signed—never should there be forms that, apparently, had been signed without much thought or purpose. They also engaged in the tactic of presenting petitions, and in the time-honored activity of interviewing members of Congress. In the latter work Catt was an expert; she warned one of her workers that she never believed a senator's attitude was sincere unless he had been interviewed by several people and said the same thing to each one.

As for the ideas of American peace workers during the period from the Armistice in 1918 to the Japanese attack on Pearl Harbor, Hawaii, in December 1941, ideas about world peace, or peace for the United States, proliferated but most Americans interested in peace found a reason for advocacy of one of several major plans or purposes. The League of Nations was the greatest source of hope for peace, and many Americans looked to the future, if not immediate, membership of their country in that organization. The force of the league idea owed a great deal to its novelty. The United Nations has never captured the imagination of Americans in the way that the League of Nations did. The idea of a league had not been a part of earlier American peace programs, which had looked either to the codification of international law, including treaties of arbitration and conciliation, or to a working out of more diplomatic arrangements through periodic congresses like the Hague Peace Conferences.

Only during World War I did the idea of a more political League of Nations find favor in the United States. Interest had risen to a considerable height by the summer of 1919—so far, indeed, that Senator Henry Cabot Lodge found himself forced to temporize during hearings of the Foreign Relations Committee until popular sentiment lessened. During passage of the Treaty of Versailles through the tortuosities of Senate maneuver, Lodge always avoided criticism of the league idea; if he criticized, it was because the League of Nations was Wilson's league, not because of the idea itself. As the years passed, it became evident that American membership in the league was, practically speaking, impossible, because the league seemed too concerned about the smaller points of European politics. But many Americans—Wilsonians, they frequently called themselves—continued to feel that the Senate amendments of the League Covenant had broken the heart of the world and that the turning of the world toward war during the 1930s was a direct result of failure of the United States to join the League of Nations.

A second program for American peace workers during the 1920s and 1930s was membership in the World Court. Advocates of the League of Nations often were advocates of the court, which, though technically separate from the league, was actually one of its organs. The World Court reflected the traditional American concern for codification of international law. Its protocol stated, in classic form, that among the sources of this law (in addition to treaties, decisions of international conferences, and writings of publicists) were decisions of jurists. It seemed sensible to assist in codification in this way, just as municipal law was organized through daily work of the courts. Yet connection of the league with the World Court, the proviso that the court could give advisory opinions to the league's council, encouraged the league's enemies in the Senate to affix so many onerous conditions to membership in the World Court as to make it impossible. Peace organizations did their best to secure membership, but failed to anticipate the importance of the league connection.

Disarmament was a popular program, and at least in the realm of naval disarmament (a better term would be "limitation" of armaments) there was some progress. As is now fairly evident, limitation of American, British, Japanese, Italian, and French naval arms was a useful activity during the 1920s. In the next decade it made less sense. It was not a major support of peace, for the peace of Europe was conditioned upon the size of armies, not navies. Germany and the Soviet Union were unaffected by the naval conferences sponsored by the allies of World War I. Germany and the Soviet Union attended the World Disarmament Conference held at Geneva in the early 1930s, and the Soviet spokesman, Maxim Litvinov, was eloquent in support of proposals for peace. But these two powers placed little trust in disarmament. Peace workers in the United States never really understood the peripheral importance of disarmament. It seems safe to say that they attached far too much meaning to it, spending too much time and energy working for it. Like the World Court, disarmament acted as a magnet, drawing their attention away from German and Japanese aggression that in the 1930s brought the collapse of world peace.

Another fascination of Americans interested in peace after World War I was the Kellogg-Briand Pact (1928), in which almost all nations of the world promised to renounce and outlaw war. The pact was the crowning achievement of American peace groups in the interwar period. Despite Secretary of State Frank B. Kellogg's initial and private feeling that peace workers were "a set of God-damned fools" and "God-damned pacifists," the groups managed to coerce and then convert Kellogg to support the Pact of Paris. The secretary received the Nobel Peace Prize in 1929. Unfortunately, the Kellogg-Briand Pact was too ethereal a creation, too impossible in terms of practical world politics, to assist world peace. It was an illustration of the traditional American liking for pronouncement, for doctrine and dogma. Peace movements, by their nature doctrinaire, were much attracted to formulas officially announced. Insofar as American groups occupied themselves with Kellogg's pronouncement, they failed, as in other programs, to work realistically for peace.

In the interwar years Americans continued to adhere to their traditional faith in freedom of world trade—in a trade largely unrestricted by tariffs, quotas, and other regulations. The American peace groups frequently championed this path to peace, although the idea of freedom of world trade failed to attract them in the manner of such programs as the League of Nations, the World Court, naval disarmament, and the Kellogg-Briand Pact, for it seemed to be a less direct

★ ★ ★ ★

FROM THE KELLOGG-BRIAND PACT (1928)

"The president of the German Reich, the president of the United States of America, his majesty the king of the Belgians, the president of the French Republic, his majesty the king of Great Britain, Ireland and the British Dominions beyond the seas, emperor of India, his majesty the king of Italy, his majesty the emperor of Japan, the president of the Republic of Poland, the president of the Czechoslovak Republic,

"Deeply sensible of their solemn duty to promote the welfare of mankind;

"Persuaded that the time has come when a frank renunciation of war as an instrument of national policy should be made to the end that the peaceful and friendly relations now existing between their peoples may be perpetuated;

"Convinced that all changes in their relations with one another should be sought only by pacific means and be the result of a peaceful and orderly process, and that any signatory Power which shall hereafter seek to promote its national interests by resort to war should be denied the benefits furnished by this Treaty;

"Hopeful that, encouraged by their example, all the other nations of the world will join in this humane endeavor and by adhering to the present Treaty as soon as it comes into force bring their peoples within the scope of its beneficent provisions, thus uniting the civilized nations of the world in a common renunciation of war as an instrument of their national policy;

"Have decided to conclude a Treaty. . . . and for that purpose have appointed as their respective Plenipotentiaries . . . who, having communicated to one another their full powers found in good and due form have agreed upon the following articles:

Article I The High Contracting Parties solemnly declare in the names of their respective peoples that they condemn recourse to war for the solution of international controversies, and renounce it as an instrument of national policy in their relations with one another.

Article II The High Contracting Parties agree that the settlement or solution of all disputes or conflicts of whatever nature or of whatever origin they may be, which may arise among them, shall never be sought except by pacific means."

attack on war. Secretary of State Cordell Hull was fascinated by the problem of lowering tariff barriers. An old Wilsonian, he received much favorable public comment by promoting what to his mind was almost a substitute for American membership in the League of Nations, the Reciprocal Trade Agreements Act (1934).

In the late 1930s, with war beginning to be talked about in Europe and then becoming a reality, many Americans interested in peace restricted their concerns to their own country's neutrality. The idea of neutrality flourished, an ancient American hope embodied in belief in a New World and an Old. There was a desire to restrict the merchants of death, the dealers in the international arms trade. Another belief of the time was that President Wilson's interpretation of neutral rights to include the right of Americans to travel aboard belligerent ships had taken the country into World War I; and if this interpretation and other latitudinarian views of neutrality were avoided, with the nation seeking only the most narrow of rights upon the sea, then the forthcoming European war would not touch the United States. The series of neutrality enactments beginning in 1935 attracted immense attention from American workers for peace. Congress eventually changed this legislation to permit American trade with the democratic nations of Europe, but the changes were made in gingerly fashion so as to avoid offending the predominantly isolationist peace organizations.

AFTER 1939

To speak of an American peace movement in the years after 1939 is to look to a far more complicated effort to preserve the peace of Europe and the world than had been made in the years before. Americans interested in peace realized the need for much more organization and much more money.

The number of peace groups proliferated beyond the imagination of workers during the 1920s and 1930s. A survey of peace groups in 1988 found that there were 500 with budgets of more than $30,000 annually, and 7,200 groups with budgets of less.

The programs to which the new and old peace groups turned were remarkably diverse. Most groups took interest in the United Nations, notably the surviving conservative groups of the interwar era, which easily changed their support from the League of Nations to the United Nations. During World War II the country concentrated on victory, but there was much interest in the Department of State's plans for a United Nations, which were well advanced by 1944, when the Dumbarton Oaks Conference met to draw up a draft of the United Nations Charter. Undersecretary of State Edward R. Stettinius, Jr., carefully encouraged the formation of a network of committees and organizations across the country that was to give advice on the structure of the new world organization. He provided for public representation at the San Francisco Conference (1945). The resultant charter and the constitutions of its many supporting organs showed that the people of the United States this time considered the maintenance of peace to be more than a political task, and that it comprised social, economic, and intellectual concerns.

In the immediate years after World War II, peace groups found an almost dizzying group of issues to focus upon, but principally their concern was the developing Cold War with the Soviet Union. This turned attention to the American and Soviet buildup in armaments, both conventional and nuclear.

After such foreign policy developments as the Truman Doctrine and support of Greece and Turkey against the Soviet Union; Soviet explosion of a nuclear test device in 1949; the Korean War; the Suez crisis of 1956, involving intervention in Egypt by Britain, France, and Israel; and continuing troubles in the Middle East, notably American occupation of Lebanon in 1958, there came the intervention in Vietnam, which for a dozen years in the 1960s and early 1970s, until withdrawal in 1975, brought a coalition of American peace groups in strident opposition.

When the issue of the Vietnam War arose, could it be said that the many youthful dissenters represented a revival of the older peace movements, which were generally against war rather than advocating special causes? Some of the antiwar protesters generalized their feelings about Vietnam to include all wars. In the 1960s young people everywhere, not merely in the United States, found war distasteful. It might have appeared that they were reconstituting the world peace movement of the interwar years. Or perhaps they were harking back to the views of Tolstoy and other philosophical pacifists at the end of the nineteenth century. Yet in the United States the antiwar protesters focused on involvement of the country in Vietnam. Their special cause set them apart from older peace movements. Their tactics also were markedly different; they took inspiration from the Indian protest movement of Mohandas K. Gandhi, a generation and more earlier, against British imperialism. Gandhi's movement had been a means of registering dissent and forcing change. In the United States the civil rights protesters in the South were employing civil disobedience, with marked success. The Vietnam protesters similarly employed it to persuade the American public to stop supporting the Vietnam War.

Americans interested in peace after World War II were necessarily attracted to the problems of nuclear disarmament, but here the technicalities proved so complex that no single assemblage, such as another Washington Naval Conference, and certainly no campaign by private individuals, could hope to resolve them. The contentions of the 1920s over gun calibers and tonnage and the thickness of armor plate now appeared to represent an antediluvian age. In the years after 1945 much initiative passed to the federal government, which sponsored nuclear disarmament programs and organized the Arms Control and Disarmament Agency. Private organizations assisted in its work. The atomic physicists organized themselves through the *Bulletin of the Atomic Scientists* and through the Federation of Atomic Scientists.

Such efforts tended to attach to aspects of nuclear disarmament, and in the early years after World War II peace groups in America concentrated on an end to nuclear testing, once the dangers of tests became evident. The limited test ban of 1963 appeared to be the initial result—although it might be argued that for the nuclear powers testing by that time no longer was of advantage. Another factor, seldom mentioned, in passage of the test ban treaty through the U.S. Senate was an arrangement for Republican support in exchange for a promise by President Lyndon B. Johnson not to undertake an investigation of the income tax returns of President Dwight Eisenhower's chief of staff, Sherman Adams—a deal negotiated by former president Eisenhower.

In the early 1980s the groups in the United

States concentrated on limitation of intermediate-range ballistic missiles in Europe, and the success of this endeavor raised a question as to what tactics—those of the movement in America and Europe, or the competitive rearmament sponsored by the Ronald Reagan administration vis-à-vis the Soviet Union—were successful. The administration sponsored the B-1 bomber, the MX missile system, and the Strategic Defense Initiative ("Star Wars"). The last sought a defense against Soviet missiles by an antiballistic missile system. The movement cited the enormous cost of competition over many years, and it was easy to show all the alternatives, peaceful alternatives, available for the same price: construction of schools, of roads and dams, of rail lines between cities, of new or improved airports; better health care; housing for the poor. Groups cited the risk of destruction of cities and national infrastructures, not to mention the millions of people who would die in a nuclear war.

The attack against the nuclear programs of the Reagan era led to the nuclear freeze campaign, an issue that appeared on ballots in many states during the November 1982 elections, and 11.5 million people, 60 percent of those voting on the freeze issue, voted in favor. State legislatures, city councils, and national labor unions declared themselves in favor of a freeze on testing, production, and deployment of nuclear weapons. All this resulted in the Intermediate-Range Nuclear Forces (INF) Treaty with the Soviet Union in 1987. Not long afterward the Soviet Union collapsed, and with it a considerable part of the world's nuclear competition, although the remaining nuclear powers constituted a considerable threat to peace and a very real complexity in negotiating further arms cuts.

Continuing concerns meanwhile were arising over threats to peace of a conventional sort, including American actions in scattered places around the world. Each threat or action gathered its groups in opposition. Here one speaks of interventions in Grenada (1983), Panama (1989), and Somalia (1992), the last two occurring during the George H. W. Bush administration. The Reagan administration's support of the contras in Nicaragua led to clashes with peace groups opposing sponsorship of right-wing partisans against a left-wing government.

In 1990 another opportunity arose for protesting intervention, again in the Middle East, where the U.S. government and the United Nations sought to press the regime of the dictator of Iraq, Saddam Hussein, whose troops had invaded and occupied the neighboring country of Kuwait and threatened Saudi Arabia. The immediate concern of the movement during the time of negotiation, prior to the UN military attack, Desert Storm, was to give sanctions time to work rather than rushing to war. Some American groups supporting the need for time believed that it was also an opportunity to spread their message and recruit new members. Most groups simply desired more time than President Bush and his increasingly supportive UN allies were willing to offer.

The older generation of peace movement supporters, one should remark, was not altogether pleased with the diffuse concerns of the younger generation, and beheld weakness rather than strength in the much larger numbers of American groups and their far larger finances. Their criticisms perhaps had a point, and are worth mentioning. The historian Arthur Ekirch, who had been a conscientious objector during World War II, was disgusted with the postwar peace workers. He wrote of the factionalism, self-examination, and debate over alternatives after 1945. He thought that the only purpose of a peace movement was opposition to militarism and war.

And what to say of this criticism? Of the factionalism there could be no question, for each of the bewildering number of American groups, numbering into the thousands, had its purpose. A Canadian group in the 1970s began publication of a periodical—a digest of peace books, articles, and conference papers—on the principle that chemists and other scientists possessed such digests, and so should the peace movement. The span of the books, articles, and papers was almost unlimited, displaying the way in which the post–World War II groups had edged into subjects never hitherto deemed of much, if any, interest to a peace movement. One conference participant advocated tourism, because seeing other cultures would produce tolerance, and therefore understanding, and maybe peace. The confusion of purposes, the welter of what Ekirch described as factionalism, was evident in the categories of the digest's editors, who changed their categories every few years, to the confusion of readers.

In the factionalism of the post-1945 movement it was evident that only two general distinctions, which might be described as organizing principles, marked the new movement. The authors of the survey of peace groups in 1988 wrote that pacifist groups tended to lead the entire movement; in times of slumps of interest in peace, they tended to stay together and offer new ideas. Pacifist groups served as "halfway houses" to ensure the movement's survival during the doldrums. They were especially persistent during troubling experiences, as when in Iran they sought to "do peace" but found the task difficult in the midst of violence. Their task of testimony was also difficult. How could they be heard when the United Nations engaged in peacekeeping, and its proposals and programs dominated public attention?

According to the analysts of the movement, the nonpacifist groups sought to change foreign policy by working within the political system. In the United States this entailed proposing legislation to halt development of particular weapons or generally cut spending for programs, creating support for such efforts through lobbying, and making positions known during elections.

Another point made in the survey, somewhat countering the accusation of factionalism, was that constituents of groups were not themselves divided into a few factions: women, students, and professionals. Constituents were more diverse than expected, among both pacifist and nonpacifist groups. With the exception of religious persons, the often cited constituent groupings were small proportions of any of the peace groups. Students were found in small-budget groups and professionals in nonpacifist groups, but differences otherwise were not large.

Self-examination also was a characteristic of the post–World War II American groups. Interviewers of "persistent peace activists" developed a theory of sustained commitment that included creating an activist identity, integrating peace work into everyday life, building beliefs that sustain activism, bonding with a peace group, and managing burnout. Ekirch's third criticism, that the American peace advocates were fond of debate, was undeniable, as all readers of the *Peace Research Abstracts* could see.

But in retrospect one might conclude—despite present-day factionalism and self-examination and debate over issues, and the failure of peace movements of the past—that groups everywhere have done much good. In the United States they have had public support based on the nation's history. The resort to colonies in the New World was in part to escape the incessant wars of Europe, including enforced military service. Through experience involving the exploitation of a great new continent, Americans became hopeful people, and the age-old hope of peace naturally appealed to them. The very success of the American experiment in democracy raised the possibility of changing the ways of other peoples. *E pluribus unum* has succeeded beyond all expectation in the United States, and Americans have expected this motto to have meaning for Europe and the world.

Another factor has entered into support for the peace movement in the United States that was not present in earlier years. The American people have come to realize that the bounties of geography and the rivalries of other nations have given their country protection for many decades longer than they could have expected, and it is time now for them to take part in the organization of world order. Jules Jusserand, France's ambassador to the United States (1902–1920), was fond of saying that America was bordered on north and south by weak nations, and on east and west by nothing but fish. During the American Revolution, and throughout the nineteenth century, the United States benefited from what President Washington described as the ordinary combinations and collisions of the European powers. The noted twentieth-century historian of American foreign relations, Samuel Flagg Bemis, was accustomed to write regarding this era that "Europe's distress was America's advantage." C. Vann Woodward aptly labeled it a time of "free security." Beginning with World War I, this remarkable period was no more. After World War II most Americans realized that fact. When the nuclear age opened, the problems of world peace became so omnipresent, so persistent, that they no longer were possible to ignore.

BIBLIOGRAPHY

Alonso, Harriet H. *The Women's Peace Union and the Outlawry of War: 1923–1942.* Knoxville, Tenn., 1989.

———. *Peace as a Women's Issue: A U.S. Movement for World Peace and Women's Rights.* Syracuse, N.Y., 1993.

Brock, Peter, and Thomas P. Socknat, eds. *Challenges to Mars: Essays on Pacifism from 1918 to 1945.* Toronto, 1994. Half of the twenty-eight essays are on the interwar period.

Buckley, Thomas H. *The United States and the Washington Conference: 1921–1922.* Knoxville, Tenn., 1970.

Chatfield, Charles. *For Peace and Justice: Pacifism in America, 1914–1941.* Knoxville, Tenn., 1971.

———. *The American Peace Movement: Ideals and Activism.* New York, 1992.

Cooper, Sandi E. *Patriotic Pacifism: Waging War on War in Europe, 1815–1914.* New York, 1991. Emphasis on the peace movement between 1889 and 1914.

Curti, Merle. *Peace or War: The American Struggle, 1636–1936.* New York, 1936.

Davis, Calvin D. *The United States and the First Hague Peace Conference.* Ithaca, N.Y., 1962.

———. *The United States and the Second Hague Peace Conference: American Diplomacy and International Organization, 1899–1914.* Durham, N.C., 1976. Relates the history of "the Hague idea" until World War I.

DeBenedetti, Charles. *The Peace Reform in American History.* Bloomington, Ind., 1980.

Doenecke, Justus. *Discerning the Signs: American Anti-Interventionism and the World Crisis of 1939–1941.* Lanham, Md., 2000.

Early, Frances H. *A World Without War: How Feminists and Pacifists Resisted World War I.* Syracuse, N.Y., 1997.

Ferrell, Robert H. *Peace in Their Time.* New Haven, Conn., 1952.

Foster, Carrie A. *The Women and the Warriors: The U.S. Section of the Women's International League for Peace and Freedom, 1913–1946.* Syracuse, N.Y., 1995.

Howlett, Charles F. *The American Peace Movement: Reformers and Resources.* New York, 1991. Annotated, 1,600 entries.

Joseph, Paul. *Peace Politics.* Philadelphia, 1993. Peace movement of the 1980s.

Kleidman, Robert. *Organizing for Peace: Neutrality, the Test Ban, and the Freeze.* Syracuse, N.Y., 1993. Covers the years 1936–1937, 1957–1963, 1979–1986.

Marullo, Sam, Alexandra Chute, and Mary Anna Colwell. "Pacifism and Nonpacifist Groups in the U.S. Peace Movement of the 1980s." *Peace and Change* 16, no. 3 (July 1991): 235–259.

Patterson, David S. *Toward a Warless World: The Travail of the American Peace Movement, 1887–1914.* Bloomington, Ind., 1976.

Peace and Change. Vols. 1–16 (1975–2001).

Peace Research Abstracts Journal. Vols. 1–38 (1964–2001).

Schott, Linda K. *Reconstructing Women's Thoughts: The Women's International League for Peace and Freedom Before World War II.* Stanford, Calif., 1997.

Small, Melvin, and William Hoover, eds. *Give Peace a Chance: Exploring the Vietnam Antiwar Movement.* Syracuse, N.Y., 1992.

Tracy, James. *Direct Action: From the Union Eight to the Chicago Seven.* Chicago, 1996. Half the book addresses racial conflict.

Wells, Tom. *The War Within America: America's Battle over Vietnam.* Berkeley, Calif., 1994.

Wittner, Lawrence S. *Rebels Against War: The American Peace Movement, 1933–1984.* Philadelphia, 1984.

———. *One World or None: A History of the World Nuclear Disarmament Movement Through 1953.* Stanford, Calif., 1993.

———. *Revisiting the Bomb: A History of the World Nuclear Disarmament Movement, 1954–1970.* Stanford, Calif., 1997.

Ziegler, Valarie H. *The Advocates of Peace in Antebellum America.* Bloomington, Ind., 1992.

See also ARBITRATION, MEDIATION, AND CONCILIATION; DISSENT IN WARS; GENDER; IDEOLOGY; INTERNATIONALISM; INTERNATIONAL LAW; INTERNATIONAL ORGANIZATION; ISOLATIONISM; NEUTRALITY; PACIFISM; PEACEMAKING; PUBLIC OPINION; THE VIETNAM WAR AND ITS IMPACT; WILSONIANISM.

PHILANTHROPY

* * * *

James A. Field, Jr., and Tim Matthewson

The idea of philanthropy, of concern for the welfare of the human race, has from the beginning been so tightly interwoven with other aspects of the American experience that the strand is difficult to disentangle. To many, the survival of the colonies and the success of the new nation were works of philanthropy: John Winthrop, colonial governor of Massachusetts, spoke of the "city on a hill"; aspiring revolutionaries felt themselves to be forwarding "humanity's extended cause"; to the young Herman Melville "national selfishness [was] unbounded philanthropy"; to Abraham Lincoln the nation was the last best hope of earth. In the active sense, as well, the philanthropic purpose appeared with the first attempts at colonization. The Virginia Company and Massachusetts Bay Company charters included the propagation of the Christian religion among the principal ends of these enterprises; this aim was reflected in the work of John Eliot, the apostle to the Indians, and in the concern of Cotton Mather and Samuel Sewall for the evangelization of Mexico.

Despite this background, accomplishments during the colonial period were small: the requirements of survival governed; missionary work among the Indians proved unrewarding and among black slaves was precluded as an interference with local self-government. The development of active American philanthropy dates from the first half-century of independence, which in this area, as in so many others, imposed an abiding structure upon American attitudes and institutions. Success in the Revolution produced a confidence in an American worldview in which philanthropy and self-interest happily appeared to coincide, and which led, in the external sphere, to a beginning export of American answers to the problems of the human race. In politics this brought forth a bias in favor of liberal revolution, self-determination, and economic freedom that would inform the conduct of foreign affairs through the period of Woodrow Wilson's missionary diplomacy, and beyond.

Faith in applied science and in the educability of mankind encouraged Americans to take service with foreign rulers in order to teach a generalized modernity, which focused in the early years on military skills, agriculture, and the mechanic arts. While proffering the gift of salvation, the greatest gift of all, an expanding foreign missionary movement took with it powerful cultural influences: literacy, educational systems, new techniques, civil servants, and advisers. With the growing wealth of America there developed a notable philanthropy in the narrower sense of the giving of money or goods or skills, first for the relief of disaster and subsequently for measures of constructive social policy and cultural preservation. Originally manifested in extemporized individual or group activity, these endeavors in time became institutionalized in such organizations as the American Red Cross and the major foundations, while their political and modernizing aspects attracted increased government participation.

The efforts to transfer American ideas, skills, and institutions to those "dwelling in darkness" had, prior to the development of American funding agencies, an inevitable admixture of careerism; nevertheless, the early work of individuals established precedents on which organized philanthropy, with its inherited assumption of the malleability of mankind, could subsequently build. The latter years of the eighteenth century saw the work of the American Tory, Benjamin Thompson, Count Rumford, in Bavarian administrative reform, and John Paul Jones's brief command of the Russian Black Sea fleet. The French Revolution attracted the helpful efforts of Joel Barlow, Thomas Paine, and Robert Fulton. New waves of revolution, first in the New World and then in the Old World, emphasized the relation between military skills and the universal benefits of freedom and self-determination: Americans held important posts in the revolutionary navies of Argentina and Mexico; the Greek War of Independence drew American philhellenes across the Atlantic; American naval constructors rebuilt the Ottoman navy after Navarino.

LIMITED GOVERNMENT

Over its course, American philanthropy has often reflected constitutional scruples about separation of powers. As secretary of state, Thomas Jefferson urged that, if government were to engage in philanthropy, it should be state governments—not the federal government—that should take up the cause. In 1793–1794 refugees from the black revolution in Saint Domingue (present-day Haiti) received assistance from a mixture of private, state, and federal funds. In 1812, Congress appropriated $50,000 for earthquake victims in Venezuela. Generally, however, reservations as to the constitutional propriety of federal government action prevailed, the work remained voluntary, and help from the United States was limited to the occasional loan of a public ship to transport and distribute relief supplies.

Outside the area of federal funding, however, the situation was less clear-cut and constitutional scruples have not been so engaged. Rather than charge the federal government, Jefferson paid out of his own pocket for the transport of different types of plants to further agriculture while he tried via personal correspondence and private groups such as the American Philosophical Society to advance knowledge to those who would benefit, domestic and international. President Andrew Jackson, "acting in his private capacity," recommended a naval constructor to the Turks, and the Turkish request for agricultural experts brought favorable response from the Department of State. In various far places, missionaries, as citizens residing abroad, by mid-century became the occasional beneficiaries of diplomatic interposition or show of naval force, while their local knowledge at times made them helpful in diplomacy, as in the missions of Caleb Cushing to China and of Matthew C. Perry to Japan.

As contact with non-European societies increased, Americans served as generals in the Afghan and Chinese armies and as diplomatic representatives of the Hawaiian kingdom and the Chinese empire. The early nineteenth century also saw the first efforts to encourage economic modernization: the attempts of William Maclure to improve Spanish agriculture (1819) and the condition of the Mexican Indians (1828) proved abortive, but the 1840s witnessed the railroad building of G. W. Whistler in Russia and the response of American agronomists to a Turkish request for assistance in the introduction of cotton culture.

In contrast to the sporadic work of individuals in the antebellum years was the organized and continuing effort of the foreign missionary movement. The Reverend Samuel Hopkins's ideas of "disinterested benevolence," the sense of urgency deriving from the felt imminence of the millennium, new knowledge of far places, and the example of Great Britain stimulated interest in overseas evangelism: the founding of the American Board of Commissioners for Foreign Missions in 1810 was followed by that of denominational boards. From the small beginnings of the mission to India the work grew rapidly: by 1860 the American Board alone had deployed 844 men and women overseas, and the country's expenditures on foreign missions, concentrated on the Indian subcontinent and the Near East, exceeded $500,000 a year.

The effort to evangelize the world had significant secondary consequences. The emphasis on a Bible religion called for the translation of Scripture into the vernacular and stimulated the founding of schools. The imperative to do good and the need for access to closed societies encouraged the dispatch of medical missionaries: Peter Parker's dispensary at Canton in China, founded in the 1830s, was the first of many missionary-supported health care centers. The stress on the importance of the individual, whether in the conversion experience, in education, or in medical care, was emphasized, in a manner startling to the traditional societies, by the prominent role of women in mission work and by the early establishment of schools for girls; from this attitude also stemmed the attacks on caste, polygamy, suttee, prostitution, foot binding, opium, and rum.

But of all these by-products of the missionary enterprise, work in education proved the most important. The success of lower schools created a demand for more advanced instruction, a prospect so congenial to American preconceptions that the 1860s brought the founding of overseas colleges at Constantinople and Beirut. And whether in the area of conversion, medicine, education, or the status of women, the missionary enterprise emphasized not only the American view of the importance of the individual but also the idea of change, and of the possibility of breaking through layers of custom into a more open and modern world.

The emergence of a free black population in the United States following the Revolution had led an unstable coalition of antislavery advocates and slaveholders to found the American Colonization Society (ACS) in 1817, which sought to establish a refuge for free black men and women on the African coast and to further the evangelization of Africa. Even many genuine evangelicals believed that blacks and whites could not live together peaceably on the basis of equality, so strong was the racism prevalent in the North and South. Expecting black immigrants to serve as missionaries to Africa, the ACS helped purchase the land for Liberia in 1821 and the settlement of Monrovia was established in 1822. By the eve of the Civil War, some 15,000 free black men and women lived in Liberia, about 12,000 of them having voluntarily immigrated with the assistance of the ACS. The ACS had joined with state and federal governments to form the freedman's colony on the African coast, modeling their plan on the British colony for free blacks at Sierra Leone.

The period before the Civil War also saw the development of a tradition of relief of disaster, whether natural or human-made. In 1816 and 1825 the citizens of Boston and New York assisted Canadian victims of great conflagrations. Support of the Greek War of Independence in the years after 1823 led not only to the departure of volunteers but also to contributions totaling perhaps $250,000 and to the relief work of Samuel Gridley Howe. In the 1830s and again two decades later, famine relief was sent to the Cape Verde Islands. Despite the distractions of the Mexican War, the years 1847–1848 saw the greatest effort thus far, as more than $1 million worth of supplies was sent to the victims of the great Irish famine in more than a score of ships, two of which were on loan from the U.S. Navy. In 1860, when civil war and massacres in Lebanon led to a major refugee problem, missionary influence brought about the creation of an Anglo-American relief committee and the dispatch of supplies by naval store ship. In 1862–1863, at the height of the American Civil War, further funds were raised in response to another failure of the Irish potato crop, while humanitarianism and policy combined to provide $250,000 to assist Lancashire mill operatives suffering from the cotton famine.

Like much else in post–Civil War America, the philanthropic effort grew larger, richer, and more highly organized, while the transfer of skills to countries striving to modernize themselves continued on an expanded scale. American military men served the governments of Egypt, China, Japan, and Korea; and Americans advised the Japanese Foreign Office, the king of Korea, the Dalai Lama, and the Chinese viceroy Li Hung-chang. In economic development, mining engineers like Raphael Pumpelly and agronomists like Horace Capron provided their expertise. In Japan, American teachers contributed notably to the new educational structure; in China, W. A. P. Martin became the first president of the Imperial University in Peking; in Siam, S. G. McFarland served as head of the royal school in Bangkok and superintendent of public instruction.

Although many of the teachers were laymen, some of the most distinguished—Martin and McFarland, for example—were products of the foreign missionary movement, which in these years increasingly concentrated its efforts on East Asia. Assisted by their new allies from the Student Volunteer Movement for Foreign Missions and the Young Men's Christian Association, and supported by large gifts from the new fortunes of William E. Dodge, John F. Goucher, H. J. Heinz, John D. Rockefeller, and Louis H. Severance, the missionaries continued to export, together with their sectarian versions of God's word, their American bias in favor of modernization, resource development, health care, and education.

By the end of the century the effort overseas had created a network of Christian colleges reaching from the Balkans to Japan and had opened wide, for those who wished to enter, the doors to Western knowledge and to informed participation in the activities of an increasingly westernized world. So valued, indeed, had the educational enterprise become, that governments came to embrace the cause, as in proposals within the administration of Abraham Lincoln for the establishment of a Sino-American college, in the Chinese employment of the remitted excess of the Boxer Rebellion indemnity, and much later (and most notably) in the Fulbright Act of 1946, which transmuted overseas war surplus into an extensive program of educational exchanges.

If the missionary movement and its associated enterprises provided the chief vehicle for late nineteenth-century philanthropy in Asia, the new wealth deriving from finance and industry also found outlets in the Old World. In this area in the 1860s the pioneer modern philanthropist George Peabody led with gifts, in part intended to diminish Civil War tensions, of $2.5 million for English working-class housing. A concern for the preservation of other countries' valued pasts was evidenced in the founding of the American School of Classical Studies in Athens (1881) and the American Academy in Rome (1894). These years also saw the beginning of gifts by immigrants who had prospered in the United States to churches, libraries, orphanages, and the like in their countries of origin. With the new century the social concern evidenced in the Peabody gift reappeared in the contribution of Edward and Julia Tuck, retired in France, of a hospital, school, and park to the environs of Paris, and in the work of Joseph Fels, who, abandoning the manufacture of soap, spent largely to promote the single-tax doctrine abroad.

A similar solicitude for the social and cultural improvement of the advanced countries of western Europe informed the philanthropies of a most successful immigrant, Andrew Carnegie. Beginning in 1873 with a gift of baths to his Scottish birthplace, Carnegie subsequently gave Dunfermline a library, a park, and an endowment. His contribution of public libraries to American towns and colleges was repeated abroad; 660 in Great Britain and Ireland, 156 in Canada, and others in other dominions and colonies. In 1901 Carnegie gave $10 million to revive the Scottish universities, and in 1913 a like sum for the Carnegie United Kingdom Trust for "the improvement of the well-being of the masses." His gifts to the British Empire totaled $62 million.

For many philanthropists, Carnegie's philosophy regarding philanthropy remains the essence of the philanthropic ideal, as spelled out in *The Gospel of Wealth* (1900):

> This, then, is held to be the duty of the man of wealth: first, to set an example of modest unostentatious living, shunning display; to provide moderately for the legitimate wants of those dependent upon him; and, after doing so, to consider all surplus revenues which come to him simply as trust funds which he is strictly bound as a matter of duty to administer in the manner which, in his judgment, is best calculated to produce the most beneficial results for the community.

Carnegie spent his later years implementing this ideal and in the process gave new shape to American philanthropy. His grants to Marie Curie and Robert Koch inaugurated American support of foreign scientific research. Transcending all national boundaries and reflecting the aspirations of the Progressive Era, he supported the peace and arbitration movements, as evidenced in his 1907 gift of the Hague Peace Palace and (following Edwin Ginn's establishment in 1910 of the World Peace Foundation) in the $10 million Carnegie Endowment for International Peace for "the speedy abolition of international war between the so-called civilized nations."

In contrast with the evangelical effort in the non-European world and the projects of individual donors in Europe and Canada, the relief of disaster long depended on the efforts of individuals on the spot and ad hoc appeals to the public at large. Such traditional methods provided relief for victims of revolution in Crete (1866) and for France during the Franco-Prussian War. On various occasions in the 1870s and 1880s missionary groups worked to mitigate hunger in Persia, China, and Turkey. But by this time new agencies were assuming an important role. A vigorous campaign by the *New York Herald* spurred relief of the Irish famine of 1880. Some $1 million in goods and services contributed to help victims of the Russian famine of 1892 owed much to the support of Western flour interests, concerned both for humanity and for the agricultural price level, and to the energy of Louis Klopsch, editor of the *Christian Herald,* whose subsequent campaigns—for example, in the Indian famines of 1897 and 1900—raised in the course of fifteen years more than $3 million in gifts averaging less than $3. Under the leadership of Clara Barton and with presidential support, the American National Red Cross (1881) provided both funds and an increasing continuity of administration for the relief of disaster abroad as well as at home.

Generally speaking, American relief efforts in the years before 1914 were unaffected by political developments. Famines in Japan and China drew generous response, but sympathy for Russia was seriously diminished by end-of-the-century violence against Russian Jews. In 1895–1896 concern for Armenian victims of Turkish atrocities led to congressional agitation for American intervention; and in 1897–1898 the collection of funds for Cuban relief was encouraged by President William McKinley, among others, in the hope of dampening pressures to intervene.

GROWING INFLUENCE

During the twentieth century, American philanthropy was increasingly influenced by American foreign policy while the philanthropic ideal exerted a powerful influence on the formulation of foreign policy. Before World War I, as European colonial powers sought to acquire territory in the Americas, federal policymakers sought to prevent

European interventions in the Caribbean and Philippines, which led them to fund public works projects and schools in the region. The Messina earthquake of 1908 resulted in an unprecedented congressional appropriation of $800,000 and a reconstruction program supervised by American naval personnel. And a public-private partnership resulted in a proactive agenda to prevent flooding in China. The agenda aimed to extend cooperation between the American Red Cross, the federal government, and private bankers.

World War I produced a vast outpouring of philanthropic activity abroad, and resulted in remarkable federal-state-private cooperation and cooperation of philanthropic and foreign policy agencies. Early in the war, the American Red Cross attempted to provide hospitals for both sides, but an upsurge of sympathy for Belgium and France produced a pro-Allied tilt to American philanthropy. In the United States there sprang up numerous pro-Allied relief groups, for care of the wounded, and for aid to widows and orphans. Most important was the feeding of nine million Belgians, as Americans contributed some $34.5 million, and established the worldwide reputation of its director, Herbert Hoover.

Following the American declaration of war, military and philanthropic mobilization marched together. A significant development was expansion of the Red Cross, which, with new leadership from finance and industry and vastly expanded membership and contributions, deployed some 6,000 workers to France and provided hospitals, relief supplies, and an antituberculosis campaign, as well as refugee resettlement. At the same time the newly founded American Friends Service Committee (1917) sent volunteers to help with reconstruction.

Far from demobilizing after the war, American relief efforts expanded, owing to a large infusion of federal government funds. In 1919, with Europe suffering from destruction, starvation, and disease, Congress established the American Relief Administration (ARA) under Herbert Hoover with an appropriation of $100 million; within a year, public appeals yielded an additional $29 million for assistance. The ARA emphasized feeding undernourished children and delivered large quantities of food. The aid was intended, moreover, to bolster feeble East European parliamentary regimes against the Bolshevik threat.

Despite opposition to Bolshevism, famine in Russia brought forth a vigorous response. Congress raised $20 million, and by 1922 the ARA, under the direction of Colonel William N. Haskell, operated 18,000 feeding stations in Russia, as public and private contributions grew to a total of $80 million. The American Jewish Joint Distribution Committee contributed to the peoples of Poland and the Ukraine. Some liberal groups, suspicious of the ARA's presumed aims, contributed several million dollars more.

In the Near East, the Ottoman Empire was beset by revolutionary activity, ethnic conflict, and Greco-Turkish warfare. Some urged the United States to accept a philanthropic mandate for the former empire, but when Congress failed to respond, they turned to private initiative, and between 1918 and 1924, they raised almost $90 million for Near East relief. Moreover, chaotic conditions in Turkey, Persia, and Armenia stirred missionary interests to raise almost $7 million by 1917, while concern for coreligionists in central Europe and Palestine yielded contributions of $15 million from Jewish groups in America. Coincident with these initiatives, Chinese famine relief produced gifts from both churches and government, and gave rise to an extensive program of work relief.

Despite the Senate's rejection of the League of Nations, American philanthropists were not isolationist; indeed, between 1919 and 1939 the philanthropic expenditures of American voluntary agencies averaged $63.5 million annually. As at earlier times, the pattern of giving reflected cultural and ethnic affinities: Europe and Asia received the lion's share and Latin America lagged far behind, as did Africa. Protestants contributed 47 percent of the total, which focused on Europe, India, China, and Japan; nonsectarian donors contributed 34 percent of the total and focused on Europe, the Near East, and China; Jewish contributors gave 12 percent and it went mainly to Europe and Palestine; and the Catholic portion, 7 percent, went mainly to Europe and China.

During the interwar period, philanthropy's attention focused on problem areas of the world involving large population groups. Civil strife in Ireland drew forth from the Irish-American community generous contributions for relief, as well as for support of independence. American Jewish donors provided more than one-third of the outside support for the Jewish community in Palestine, while it also aided the resettlement of some 200,000 Jews in the Ukraine, Crimea, Poland, and Germany. In the case of China, the American public responded to the disastrous famine of 1927 and the Yangtze flood of 1931.

Natural disasters also called forth American responses, the most dramatic being for the great Tokyo earthquake of 1923, which left some 200,000 dead and 2 million homeless. The U.S. Asiatic Fleet and the Philippine Department of the Army sent supplies costing $6 million for immediate help; private donations totaled more than $12 million, including $1.5 million donated by Rockefeller foundations to help rebuild the University of Tokyo. American contributions amounted to almost three-quarters of total relief, but such generosity was vitiated by the ban on Japanese immigration, which was imposed by the same Congress that had funded emergency relief.

Between the wars, American foundations assumed an increasingly prominent role in the totality of American philanthropy, especially in cultural activities and health care. The Carnegie Endowment rebuilt libraries and supported large-scale academic studies of war. John D. Rockefeller, Jr., built the League of Nations Library at Geneva, while the Rockefeller Foundation financed foreign policy studies and international scholar exchanges. The Harkness family founded the Commonwealth Fund (1918), which dedicated itself to the welfare of mankind; and in 1930 the Pilgrim Trust gave $10 million to Great Britain for its "future well-being." The Rockefeller Foundation helped rebuild the University of Louvain and the cathedral at Rheims, and it underwrote maintenance costs of Versailles and Fontainebleau, as it expanded the American schools at Athens and Rome.

Moreover, the Rockefeller Foundation, the Carnegie Corporation, and private individuals made sizable gifts to British, European, Canadian, and Mexican universities. Outside the Atlantic world, educational efforts were concentrated on the Near Eastern colleges, Hebrew University of Palestine, Chinese colleges, and surveys of educational programs in Africa and East Asia. James Loeb supported a psychiatric institute in Munich and George Eastman provided dental clinics in a number of European capitals. The Rockefeller Foundation funded work on parasitic and infectious diseases when it established Peking Union Medical College.

As world peace gave way in the late 1930s, American philanthropists watched with foreboding and, despite the U.S. Neutrality Acts, philanthropists engaged from the outset of the growing world crisis. In 1939 there developed a coordinated effort marked by cooperation between sectarian relief agencies, organized labor, and government. The Spanish Civil War drew American volunteers to the Loyalist side in opposition to fascism, but the Neutrality Acts dampened the spirit of giving and led to only $3 million raised for humanitarian assistance.

Relief funds followed the chronology of disaster and were sent to the Czechs after the Munich agreement, as well as the conquered Poles, Finns, Dutch, French, Greeks, and Russians as their countries were overrun. Especially notable was the rapid organization of a Russian relief effort and its impressive backing from professional and financial groups. In 1941 assistance provided to China by missionary organizations and the Chinese-American community gained new support when growing concern for Asia led to the organization of the United China Relief Agency with Eleanor Roosevelt as honorary chairperson.

By far the greatest assistance went to Britain, as the mother of parliaments stood alone against the Nazi threat. The Bundles for Britain campaign was followed by a dispatch of ambulances and medical personnel, and by the summer of 1941, British War Relief achieved backing from business and labor and raised more than $10 million and $90 million had been raised for overseas war relief by the time of the Japanese attack on Pearl Harbor. The U.S. Department of State coordinated these efforts and by 1945 the number of relief agencies had been reduced from 300 to 90.

The Axis occupation of Europe posed the difficult ethical question of whether the subject populations should be helped, for fear of assisting the occupying Axis powers. Although Herbert Hoover strongly urged feeding the victims of Nazi aggression, the opposite view prevailed. Only about $2 million went to relief in Nazi Germany. Congress appropriated $50 million for relief, which was administered by the Red Cross, and more than half went to Britain and none to occupied areas.

By 1945 organized labor emerged as a major donor and together with religious and ethnic groups, it raised the annual total of private giving for overseas assistance to $234 million. By this time, government coordination had coalesced voluntary agencies, and total contributions, between 1939 and 1945, included $54 million for Russia, $38 million for Great Britain, $36 million for Palestine, $35 million for China, and $30 million for Greece.

However impressive, this private assistance was not nearly enough. As increasing needs called for increased response, and as relief supplies followed the armies into liberated areas, stop-gap governmental efforts were succeeded first by interallied coordination and then by the United Nations Relief and Rehabilitation Administration (UNRRA), headed by Herbert H. Lehman. The work of UNRRA, on a wholly new scale, was of necessity largely American-supported: of almost $4 billion dispensed between 1943 and 1947, 70 percent was provided by the United States. Again with victory the demands increased. In the theaters of conflict the destruction vastly exceeded that of World War I, an enormous refugee problem existed, and dislocations between city and countryside threatened a dangerously deteriorating food situation.

Although some Americans, relieved of the strains of war, evinced a willingness to let the world be, most still saw a compelling need to help, both on ethical and humanitarian grounds and for reasons of policy, as they sought to further democracy, stability, peace, and prosperity, reminiscent of the period after World War I. Given the tensions that later developed, it is worth noting that the appeal of Russian relief, so strong during the fighting, survived the moment of victory: $32 million in cash and kind was provided in 1945 and assistance continued into 1946. But soon the Soviets declared their independence of outside aid, while the coming of the Cold War brought the containment of communism into the forefront of motives for reconstruction.

The response of the voluntary agencies in the immediate postwar period was impressive: expenditures between 1945 and 1948 totaled $1.1 billion. For the government, withdrawal from UNRRA on grounds of bad administration and ideological conflict was followed by support of the International Refugee Organization; by implementation of the Marshall Plan, a mixture of policy and humanitarian objectives between 1948 and 1952; contribution of some $13 billion to the rebuilding of postwar Europe; and by the Food for Peace program inaugurated in 1954 under the Agricultural Trade Development and Assistance Act.

The postwar years were also marked by a "remarkable partnership" of public and private efforts founded on the extemporized successes of private agencies in postwar Germany and Japan; by the contributions of American Jews, who taxed themselves more heavily than any other sectarian group; and by the innovative Cooperative for American Relief Everywhere (CARE), which advanced from early shipment of surplus army rations to the large-scale movement of surplus

agricultural products and whose deliveries grew in value from $500,000 in 1946 to $54 million in 1955. Whether all this generosity, if such it can be considered, was adequate to the need may be argued. Perhaps the best assessment comes through comparison of this treatment of liberated and conquered peoples with that provided by other nations in other campaigns.

In the 1950s, as European reconstruction progressed, the focus of overseas philanthropy shifted back to the less developed world: after 1958 more than half of disposable resources went to non-European areas. This shift also emphasized the surprising vigor of the missionary movement, now more than ever equated with social welfare, to which in 1956 American Protestants contributed some $130 million and American Catholics some $50 million. In the early 1950s, indeed, Protestant groups spent more for overseas technical assistance than the United States and the United Nations combined, and their accomplishments provided precedents for governmental action: the Point Four program, launched in 1950, early modeled itself on the Near East Foundation; a decade later the Peace Corps drew on the experience of the interdenominational International Voluntary Services (1953).

These private and public efforts were accompanied by expanded activity on the part of the larger foundations, which greatly increased their contributions to projects concerned with international affairs. Of these institutions, two were preeminent. Shifting its focus from its prewar concern with the eradication of disease, and following in the steps of such nineteenth-century pioneers as Horace Capron, Charles J. Murphy, and David Lubin, the Rockefeller Foundation took as its major goal the modernization of agriculture in the developing countries. Among the striking results were a doubling of Mexican food production between 1943 and 1963 and that of India between 1951 and 1971, and the establishment in 1960 of the International Rice Research Institute in the Philippines.

Important assistance in establishing the Rice Institute came from the Ford Foundation, a new giant of philanthropy, whose resources of $3.6 billion (1968) enabled it to provide more than a quarter of all foundation grants devoted to international affairs. In pursuit of its ambitious aims, reminiscent of Andrew Carnegie, of the "establishment of peace," the Ford Foundation undertook extensive efforts to attack poverty, hunger, and disease, and to further social science and planning. And as birth rates steadily threatened to outstrip production, notwithstanding the successes of plant geneticists in producing high-yield varieties ("Green Revolution"), foundations and government agencies alike edged delicately into stabilizing population growth.

Except for Liberia, American philanthropy had stayed away from Africa, but neglect shifted somewhat in the 1970s, partly owing to the emergence of an African-American lobby. During the 1920s and 1930s, African Americans had protested against U.S. occupation of Haiti and Italian aggression in Ethiopia via traditional channels like the National Association for the Advancement of Colored People, but it was in the 1970s that African Americans organized groups devoted solely to the purpose of influencing American foreign policy and leveraging private and government aid for Haiti and Africa. Following the congressional elections of 1970, African Americans in the House of Representatives organized the Black Caucus.

In March 1971 the Black Caucus urged President Richard Nixon to enact economic sanctions against minority white rule in South Africa. In Washington in May 1978, U.S. Congress Representatives Charles C. Diggs, Jr., and Andrew Young, among others, organized TransAfrica, Inc., a mass-based African-American foreign policy lobby. As leader of TransAfrica, Randall Robinson helped orchestrate an economic blockade against South African apartheid and TransAfrica established itself as the foremost voice for expressing African-American opinion on foreign policy issues. In 1986, when President Ronald Reagan vetoed a ban of loans and investments in South Africa, African Americans regarded it as hostile to their interests. In October, Congress overrode the presidential veto, as it responded to the lobbying of TransAfrica and white liberal opinion. South Africa is now free from apartheid partly because of the U.S. economic sanctions enacted following 1986. And once apartheid was eliminated, TransAfrica and other groups shifted their focus from imposing an embargo to leveraging increases in private and government grants to South Africans and to fighting the scourge of AIDS in Africa.

Meanwhile, as head of TransAfrica, Robinson's highly publicized twenty-seven-day hunger strike, which called upon President William Jefferson Clinton to restore democratic rule in Haiti, led the president to initiate new policies toward the repressive military dictatorship in Haiti. President Clinton intervened there with a force of 20,000 U.S. troops, which resulted in the restoration of the democratically elected leader, Jean-Bertrand Aristide, to the presidency of the former French West Indian colony. Robinson has helped leverage private and government assistance for Haiti while the George Soros Foundations provided private assistance to island republics and southern Africa.

GEORGE SOROS AND THE CAPITALIST THREAT

A leading global philanthropist, the Hungarian-born George Soros was attacked as a corporate raider, a speculator who achieved billionaire status via fluctuations in stocks, commodities, and currencies, but he has also been recognized as a billionaire who, like others before him, seemed determined to give away much of his money. He also received substantial attention because of the books he wrote that sought to explain his ambitious agenda for strengthening democracy and the rule of law on a global scale. Born in Budapest, he moved to England in 1947 and graduated from the London School of Economics; he moved to the United States in 1956 and founded the Open Society Fund (1979) and Soros Foundation–Soviet Union (1987). Soros's goals were "to help open up closed societies, to help make open societies more viable, and to foster a critical mode of thinking." He established some thirty semiautonomous foundations, principally in central and eastern Europe and the former Soviet Union but also in Guatemala, Haiti, and southern Africa. Established in 1993 in New York City, his Open Society Institute provided administrative, financial, and technical support, as well as establishing network programs to address certain issues on a regional or network-wide basis. In 1997, the various Soros foundations spent a total of $428.4 million on philanthropic activities. Along with the Austrian philosopher Karl Popper and others, Soros juxtaposed totalitarian ideologies with recognition that nobody has a monopoly on truth. Different people have different views and different interests, and he notes a need for institutions that encourage people to live together in peace and respect democracy and the rule of law. His goal was to protect individual rights and ensure freedom of choice and freedom of speech, and as an ardent supporter of toleration, he sees questions of choice and freedom as keys to the open society. By 2001, Soros had donated $1 billion: $350 million in 1997, including $50 million to a fund to help legal immigrants, and $100 million to set up Internet centers at universities in Russia. Soros's donations strengthened U.S. commitments in Eastern Europe and helped compel the realization that the region was vital to American foreign policy.

TED TURNER AND PHILANTHROPIC COMPETITION

Robert Edward "Ted" Turner, CNN founder and Time Warner vice chairman, announced on 18 September 1997 that he would donate $1 billion ($100 million per year in Time Warner stock) over the next decade to United Nations programs. Speaking of his gift, Turner said, "This is only going to go for programs, programs like refugees, cleaning up land mines, peacekeeping, UNICEF for the children, for diseases, and we're going to have a committee that will work with a committee of the UN so that the money can only go to UN causes." He announced that his goal was to stimulate philanthropic competition, and his grant of $1 billion was intended to raise the bar to a new level.

Starting in 1970 with a single UHF television station in Atlanta, Turner's business grew into a global colossus that included cable channels, movie studios, and professional sports teams. He started his TBS satellite superstation in 1976 and CNN in 1980. In 1996, Turner gave away $28 million, mainly to environmental causes, so the donation of $1 billion to the UN was a departure for him. Because the UN could not legally accept money from individuals, Turner created a foundation to spend the money and administer the programs, which he expected to focus on job creation, eradication of land mines, expansion of education, and research on global warming. He also became a fundraiser for the United Nations and actively sought publicity both for himself and for a number of causes, such as the environmental movement and world peace. His gift of $1 billion to support the United Nations was considered at the time the largest single donation by a private individual. By comparison, all charitable giving by Americans in 1996 was approximately $120 billion. "Few Americans," noted *Newsweek,* "have cut such a swath through life." Turner's donations strengthened the United Nations as a platform for the resolution of world conflicts and a commitment to international peace.

BILL GATES

Bill Gates, in 2001 the world's richest person, had a personal philosophy of philanthropy that seemed to reflect the views of Andrew Carnegie: "If they want to put in the consent decree that I'm going to give away 95 percent of my wealth, I'd be glad to sign that." A Harvard dropout, Gates had seemed an unlikely successor to his overachieving parents. His father was a prominent Seattle attorney, and his gregarious mother served on charitable boards and ran the United Way. At age thirteen Gates wrote his first computer program, at a time when computers were still room-sized machines run by scientists in white coats. In December 1974, his friend Paul Allen showed Gates a *Popular Mechanics* cover featuring the Altair 8800, a $397 computer that any hobbyist could build. The only thing the computer lacked, besides a keyboard and monitor, was software. Following complex developments, the company Gates and Allen formed, Microsoft, introduced the Windows operating system, and by 1993 Microsoft was selling a million copies of Windows a month. In 1986, when Microsoft went public, Gates became a paper billionaire at the age of thirty-one. Meanwhile, he increased his charitable giving: He earmarked $750 million over five years to the Global Alliance for Vaccines and Immunization, which involved an alliance with the World Health Organization, the Rockefeller Foundation, UNICEF, pharmaceutical companies, and the World Bank.

In 1999 the Gates Foundations awarded more than $2 billion in grants, including what is believed to be the largest single private grant in U.S. history—$750 million to the global vaccine program over a five-year period. His vaccine project specifically targeted HIV and AIDS, which he identified in a speech in Redmond, Washington, on 18 October 2000 as having potentially dramatic consequences for the infrastructure of many countries, including Botswana. He also joined with Ted Turner on the vaccine program to give $78 million to eradicate polio from the world by the end of 2000. Gates's donations helped alert the world to the problems of disease as problems of international relations and of American foreign policy.

CONCLUSION: THE CRITICS

At the beginning of the twenty-first century, American philanthropists could point with pride to two centuries of giving and voluntary association for the good of humanity abroad. But as some critics have suggested, the American philanthropic tradition reached a crossroads arising from the broader context of American diplomacy and from unprecedented criticism from abroad and at home.

The advent of America's hyperpower status since the collapse of the Soviet Union led many to turn a critical eye toward the United States and its philanthropy. As the hegemonic power in the world, even American allies and friends sought to portray the United States as part of the problem, not the solution. American missionaries were criticized as self-righteous meddlers and cultural imperialists and U.S. foreign aid as philanthropic imperialism. Foundations came under attack, as when missionaries were criticized for accepting tainted Rockefeller oil money. Critics suggested that American philanthropy was corrupted by excessively close connections to U.S. foreign policy. Some foreign critics interpreted American philanthropy as the last refuge of Western colonialism.

Some accusations were true enough, but the goals of salvation, survival, or modernization, were always among American philanthropy's goals, and the foundations, like the missionaries, emphasized the unity of mankind and tried to downgrade the importance of nationalism, political frontiers, and political differences. Such attitudes were reflected in practice, for not all private charities cooperated with the U.S. government, and most had reservations. Fidel Castro's victory in Cuba in 1959 moved the Ford Foundation to direct a major effort toward Latin America. Still, the philanthropic ideal remained deeply rooted in the American people.

Far more significant than any politicizing of philanthropy has been the continued influence of the philanthropic ideal on the conduct of American foreign relations. Persistent hope for liberal causes were exemplified in the nineteenth century by James Monroe and Richard Rush during the French and Latin American revolutions, in the reception accorded the Hungarian revolutionary Lajos Kossuth in the United States in 1851, and in Daniel Webster's attacks upon the Habsburg Empire. Moreover, the U.S. view that expanding trade has advanced civilization informed early American commercial treaties with the Islamic world and the Far East and U.S. relations with the Soviet Union and the People's Republic of China. Although open to charges of racism, an important domestic philanthropic concern underlay the founding of Liberia in 1847, as did a genuine desire to enhance the welfare of African Americans. Persistent American belief in self-determination gave American policy an anticolonial bias and led to diplomatic support for weak regimes against their more powerful oppressors.

President Jimmy Carter's emphasis on human rights during the second half of the 1970s was well received around the world and seemed to be an extension or reflection of earlier pronouncements of his predecessors. Early in the twentieth century, Woodrow Wilson had noted that it was "a very perilous thing to determine the foreign policy of a nation in terms of material interest"; as Wilson had led the American nation into World War I, he had defined American war aims as seeking "no material compensation for the sacrifices we shall freely make." In later periods of crisis, Franklin D. Roosevelt offered the Four Freedoms to the world, and his successor, Harry S. Truman, noted that "it must be the policy of the United States to support free peoples who are resisting attempted subjugation," while John F. Kennedy in the 1960s promised that America would "pay any price . . . to assure the survival and the success of liberty." At times, however, philanthropy has been ill advised; at times change has proved destabilizing, as expectations rose faster than performance. Often results did not materialize, as custom proved resistant and ruling groups were averse to the American plan. Some recipients were resentful of gifts and donations, feeling that being unable to reciprocate to a gift from the United States has brought dishonor upon them. Indeed, it would be possible to write about U.S. philanthropy from the perspective of recipients rather than donors and arrive at much different conclusions.

As critics have noted, a danger of both foreign aid and philanthropy has been entanglement in the local politics and power struggles occasioned by wars, famines, and natural disasters. In Africa, CARE unwittingly assisted a Somali dictator in building a political and economic power base; and the United Nations, Save the Children, and many other groups provided raw materials for ethnic rivalries. A case of frustrated ambitions has been that of India, where an assistance program measured in billions of dollars turned out to be a holding operation, ending in mutual disillusionment, even before population explosion, limited resources, and an energy crisis suggested a very different future.

Some critics have rejected American foreign aid and private philanthropy abroad, but they have failed to acknowledge the good that has been achieved, as in education and health care. Faced by such critics, some have suggested that, if America perfected its own ideals at home, perhaps America's greatest gift to the twenty-first century would be its example rather than its philanthropic aid packages and coercive powers. So, perhaps it is now possible, given current skepticism, to achieve a new balance, one that recognizes the virtue of limiting American political intervention abroad and yet acknowledges the genuine achievements of America's philanthropic tradition. And while seeking a new balance, it may be useful to keep in mind Bill Gates's insight that it is at least as difficult to give money away as it is to make money.

BIBLIOGRAPHY

Anheier, Helmut K., and Stefan Toepler, eds. *Private Funds, Public Purpose: Philanthropic Foundations in International Perspective.* New York, 1999.

Arnove, Robert F., ed. *Philanthropy and Cultural Imperialism: The Foundations at Home and Abroad.* Bloomington, Ind., 1980.

Chambers, Clarke A., and Beverly Stadum. *An Exploration of New Themes in the Study of American Philanthropy Arising from Archival Research.* Bloomington, Ind., 1998.

Curti, Merle Eugene. *American Philanthropy Abroad: A History.* New Brunswick, N.J., 1963. Though dated regarding its context and inclusiveness, still the best survey.

Curti, Merle Eugene, and Kendall Birr. *Prelude to Point Four: American Technical Missions Overseas, 1838–1938.* Madison, Wis., 1954.

Daniel, Robert L. *American Philanthropy in the Near East, 1820–1960.* Athens, Ohio, 1970.

Davis, David Brion. *The Problem of Slavery in Western Culture.* Ithaca, N.Y., 1966.

———. *The Problem of Slavery in the Age of Revolution, 1770–1823.* New York, 1999. This work and the preceding book discuss the antislavery movement as a form of philanthropy.

DeConde, Alexander. *Ethnicity, Race and American Foreign Policy: A History.* Boston, 1992. Provides fresh insight on politics of foreign policy.

Dennis, James S. *Christian Missions and Social Progress: A Sociological Study of Foreign Missions.* 3 vols. New York, 1898–1906. Discusses nineteenth-century philanthropy.

Field, James A., Jr. *America and the Mediterranean World, 1776–1882.* Princeton, N.J., 1969. Information on early American philanthropy.

Ilchman, Warren F., Stanley N. Katz, and Edward L. Queen II, eds. *Philanthropy in the World's Traditions.* Philanthropic Studies Series. Bloomington, Ind., 1998. Information on philanthropy in Western and non-Western societies.

Jordan, Winthrop D. *White Over Black: American Attitudes Toward the Negro, 1550–1812.* New York, 1977.

King, Kenneth. *Pan-Africanism and Education: A Study of Race Philanthropy and Education in the Southern States of America and East Africa.* Oxford, 1971.

Lewis, Robert Ellsworth. *The Educational Conquest of the Far East.* New York, 1903.

Maren, Michael. *The Road to Hell: The Ravaging Effects of Foreign Aid and International Charity.* Glencoe, Ill., 1996. Twentieth-century philanthropy.

Miller, Christopher L. *Prophetic Worlds: Indians and Whites on the Columbia Plateau.* New Brunswick, N.J., 1985.

Morris, David. *Gift from America: The First Fifty Years of CARE.* Atlanta, 1996.

Nichols, Bruce, and Gil Loescher, eds. *The Moral Nation: Humanitarianism and U.S. Foreign Policy Today.* South Bend, Ind., 1989.

Osgood, Robert Endicott. *Ideals and Self-Interest in America's Foreign Relations: The Great Transformation of the Twentieth Century.* Chicago, 1953.

Saillant, John. *Black, White and "The Charitable Blessed": Race and Philanthropy in the American Early Republic.* Bloomington, Ind., 1998.

Schneewind, Jerome B., ed. *Giving: Western Ideas of Philanthropy.* Bloomington, Ind., 1996.

Schrift, Alan D., ed. *The Logic of the Gift: Toward an Ethic of Generosity.* New York, 1997. Provides anthropological perspectives on gift giving.

Schwantes, Robert S. *Japanese and Americans: A Century of Cultural Relations.* New York, 1955.

Wall, Joseph Frazier. *Andrew Carnegie.* 2d ed. Pittsburgh, 1989.

See also CULTURAL RELATIONS AND POLICIES; FOREIGN AID; HUMANITARIAN INTERVENTION AND RELIEF; RELIGION; WILSONIAN MISSIONARY DIPLOMACY.

POST–COLD WAR POLICY

Richard A. Melanson

While the precise dates that marked the beginning and the end of the Cold War remain the subjects of scholarly debate, the era's major foreign policy focus was unambiguous: containing the spread of Soviet power and international communism by supporting friendly governments with aid, arms, and, occasionally, troops; deterring nuclear attacks on the United States and its allies; and supporting economic institutions like the World Bank and the International Monetary Fund created at the Bretton Woods Conference in 1944. Deprived of a global enemy, American foreign policy since the Cold War seemingly became more diffuse, perhaps even incoherent. But, though political elites awaited the arrival of a reincarnated "X" (the pseudonym senior State Department official George F. Kennan used in his famous article on the strategy of containment in 1947) to articulate a crystalline, new strategy, several discernible and related themes and concepts have, nevertheless, characterized post–Cold War American foreign policy.

At least six themes and concepts have steered U.S. foreign policy since the Cold War:

1. the preservation of American global hegemony
2. the fostering of globalization through the continued development of liberal international economic institutions
3. the promotion of an ever-growing "zone of democratic peace"
4. the repeated employment of military power to ease humanitarian disasters
5. the isolation and punishment of a handful of "rogue" states that allegedly threatened regional stability and American security;
6. growing concerns about the vulnerability of the United States to attacks from these regimes as well as from transnational terrorist groups.

Efforts to formulate concrete policies from these themes and concepts have provoked both domestic and international dissent about their appropriateness and feasibility.

PRESERVING AMERICAN GLOBAL HEGEMONY

American foreign policy officials almost never use the word "hegemony" in their public discourse. When Henry Kissinger did so at his first press conference after being named President Richard Nixon's special assistant for national security affairs in 1968, puzzled reporters scurried to their dictionaries for help. Presidents and their advisers prefer more positive terms such as "global leadership" or "indispensable nation" to describe America's role in the world, yet "hegemony," because it is less loaded, better captures the essence of recent U.S. strategy. The ancient Greeks understood "hegemony" to mean preponderant international influence or authority, and preserving such preponderance has been a fundamental goal of all post–Cold War administrations.

At century's end the American economy had experienced the longest peacetime expansion in its history. Low inflation, sustained growth, and rising worker productivity had made it the engine of global prosperity and technological change. Americans owned more than half of the world's computers and received more than half of the world's royalties and licensing fees. The eight largest high-tech companies were headquartered in the United States. American pop culture was virtually ubiquitous, with Michael Jordan posters, McDonald's golden arches, and Hollywood movies its most familiar symbols.

The United States retained the globe's most powerful and expensive military establishment with expenditures larger than all of the other nations combined. Its forward presence in Europe, East Asia, and the Persian Gulf was secured by a host of garrisons, air bases, and aircraft carrier task forces. U.S. regional commanders often acted like Roman tribunes, not only leading American forces but also initiating direct diplomatic contacts with foreign governments. The technological gap

153

between American weapons systems and those of other nations, already evident in the Gulf War of 1991, had become enormous by the 1999 Kosovo air campaign against the Yugoslav strongman Slobodan Milosevic.

At the same time, American global commitments expanded. U.S. ground troops landed in Somalia in 1992 to help end a famine (only to be withdrawn the next year as a result of casualties that were incurred after the mission had grown); returned Haiti to its ousted democratically elected president in 1994; and entered Bosnia in 1995 and Kosovo in 1999 as "peacekeepers." American aircraft carriers protected Taiwan from the People's Republic of China, patrolled the Persian Gulf, and sailed the Indian Ocean. Its warplanes routinely bombed Iraq for more than a decade, helped end the war in Bosnia in 1995, and brought Yugoslavia to its knees in 1999.

Far from disappearing after the collapse of the Soviet Union in 1989, the North Atlantic Treaty Organization, at Washington's insistence, expanded into central and eastern Europe. In Asia, American planners anticipated maintaining troop levels at around 100,000 for at least twenty more years. And at the United Nations, the United States, under congressional pressure, prevented Boutros Boutros-Ghali from being reelected secretary-general, primarily because he had criticized the United States for failing to play a more active role in UN peacekeeping efforts in Somalia and Rwanda.

Surely such power and influence constituted "global hegemony," and American leaders, as well as those of a surprisingly large number of foreign nations, wished to preserve it. But domestic divisions surfaced about whether it could best be accomplished unilaterally or by working closely with allies and international organizations. This debate began in the immediate aftermath of the Gulf War and by the millennium remained unresolved. President George H. W. Bush, envisioned America's role as that of benevolent hegemon, protecting the growing "zone of democratic peace" against regional outlaws, terrorists, nuclear proliferators, and other threats to world order. It would do so in concert with others, if possible, as in the Gulf War, or unilaterally, if necessary.

Work soon began in the Department of Defense to make this concept operational, and in March 1992 the results were leaked to the press. The main Pentagon planning group outlined a strategy of "global leadership" that presumed America's continuing international preeminence and argued that the United States should actively prevent the emergence of states that could challenge it. By using existing security arrangements to ensure the safety of its allies, Washington would view as potentially hostile any state with sufficient human and technological resources to dominate Europe, East Asia, or the Middle East. This strategy acknowledged that within a decade Germany or Russia might threaten Europe; Japan, Russia, and eventually China might do likewise in East Asia; and that the domination of either region would consequently imperil the Middle East. But this group suggested that the United States could create incentives for Germany and Japan to refrain from challenging American preeminence. No mention was made of the United Nations or any other international organization, and because the strategy smacked of unilateralism, a number of allies, led by France, condemned it. And, although its untimely release embarrassed the George H. W. Bush administration, these recommendations nevertheless reflected the thinking of an important segment of the foreign policy community.

Upon entering office in 1993, President Bill Clinton adopted—initially, at last—"muscular" or "assertive" mulilateralism to preserve America's position in the post–Cold War world, while he concentrated on reviving the domestic economy. But the poor performance of the United Nations in Somalia and the European Union's failure to halt the war in Bosnia gradually persuaded the administration that American leadership was, indeed, "indispensable." Nevertheless, many Republicans in Congress, fresh from their historic 1994 triumph at the polls, remained deeply suspicious of international organizations because they allegedly threatened American sovereignty and freedom of action. During the 1996 presidential campaign, Robert Dole, the Republican nominee, promised that when he was in the White House, "no American fighting men and women will take any orders from Field Marshal Boutros Boutrous-Ghali." Republican unilateralists opposed aiding Mexico during its peso crisis in 1994 and 1995, repeatedly criticized the International Monetary Fund and the World Bank, refused to pay American dues owed to the United Nations, and tried to abolish the Agency for International Development (AID). Jesse Helms, chairman of the Senate Foreign Relations Committee, called for AID's replacement with a new international development foundation with a mandate "to deliver block grants to support the work of private relief agencies and faith-based institutions." The Senate defeated the Comprehensive Test Ban Treaty in

2000 with many members convinced that it represented "unilateral disarmament," and a majority in Congress opposed U.S. membership in the new International Criminal Court, fearing that U.S. military personnel stationed overseas could be hauled before it.

Although the Clinton administration attempted to discredit these critics by calling them isolationists, they were, in fact, determined to preserve American global hegemony by protecting it against the encroachments of international organizations. In effect, Republican unilateralists echoed many of the arguments made by Senator Henry Cabot Lodge against U.S. membership in the League of Nations after World War I.

While certain nations clearly resented America's preeminent position in the post–Cold War world, none was able to mobilize an international coalition against the United States. China grumbled about American "hegemonism," France complained about the U.S. exertion of "hyperpower," Russia deeply resented the expansion of NATO, and states like Iraq and Iran tested Washington's patience. Yet the stability and protection afforded by America's global predominance were welcomed, or at least tolerated, by the vast majority of foreign nations. East European states clamored for admission to NATO, Israel and the Palestinian Liberation Organization participated in a U.S.-led "peace process," and countries from South America to Africa invited the United States to serve as an honest broker to help settle regional disputes.

Global preeminence, of course, has never been permanent. Previous hegemons were eventually humbled by overextension, a weakening domestic social fabric, or by rising competitor states. No doubt the "American century" would not endure forever, but in the absence of some unanticipated catastrophe like a nuclear war or a massive biological attack, it remained difficult to imagine an imminent end to American primacy.

FOSTERING GLOBALIZATION

The makers of post–Cold War American foreign policy believed that by fostering globalization, the growth of both the U.S. and the world economy would be increased. Globalization was not a wholly new phenomenon, but it did attain unprecedented prominence in the public discourse during the 1990s. Indeed, one of its chief articulators, the journalist Thomas L. Friedman,

suggested that the post–Cold War world be dubbed "the age of globalization." Although difficult to define precisely, scholars and policymakers appeared to understand globalization as the integration of markets, finance, and technologies in a way that shrunk space and time. Some observers even predicted that the ultimate consequence of this process would be the elimination of all national borders and, thus, the nation-state.

That was clearly not the aim of U.S. foreign policy officials. Rather, they saw globalization as an economic tool that could be managed to open foreign markets, stimulate American exports in goods and services, and bring economic growth and prosperity to large portions of the world. The Clinton administration had a strategy for accomplishing these goals—the "big, emerging markets" (BEM) strategy—though its origins can be traced to Robert Zoellick, a senior policymaker in both Bush administrations. From Zoellick's perspective, the United States could best serve its economic interests by acting as the primary catalyst for a series of integrative economic structures that would substantially increase global prosperity. First, it would deepen the institutionalized economic and security relations with western Europe and Japan. Second, the United States would reach out to a second tier of potential partners in Latin America, East Asia, and Eastern Europe to develop dense institutional linkages such as the North American Free Trade Association (NAFTA) and the Asia-Pacific Economic Cooperation Forum (APEC). And third, even farther on the periphery loomed Russia, China, and the Middle East, areas that in the more distant future might be brought into this global economic system too. This foreign economic strategy asserted the indispensability of American global leadership, for it strongly supported the creation of a host of regional economic institutions in which the United States would function as the common linchpin.

By elaborating and refining Zoellick's ideas, the Clinton administration developed the BEM strategy that lay at the core of its foreign policy. The strategy identified ten regional economic drivers supposedly committed to trade-led economic growth and reasonably cordial relations with the United States. The "Big Ten," as they were called, included China (plus Taiwan and Hong Kong), India, Indonesia, South Korea, Mexico, Brazil, Argentina, Poland, Turkey, and South Africa—states whose expansion could benefit neighboring markets as well. Clinton officials projected that by 2010 American trade with these countries would be greater than combined trade with the European Union and Japan. Jeffrey E. Garten, undersecretary of commerce for international trade and a chief architect of this strategy, argued that the BEMs possessed enormous potential for the expansion of U.S. trade in goods and services, because they purchased heavily in economic sectors dominated by the United States: information technology, health and medical equipment, telecommunications, financial services, environmental technology, transportation, and power generation.

To achieve these goals the Clinton administration launched a global effort to persuade the BEMs to open their markets to both trade and investment. The push for financial liberalization was directed at East Asia and Southeast Asia, in particular, largely because it was seen as especially fertile ground for American banks, brokerage houses, and insurance companies. To further this strategy, Secretary of the Treasury Robert Rubin persuaded the G-7 nations (the world's leading industrial democracies) in April 1997 to issue a statement "promoting freedom of capital flows" and urging the International Monetary Fund to amend its charter so it could press countries for capital account liberalization. But other Clinton economic officials like Laura D'Andrea Tyson and Joseph Stieglitz, successive chairs of the president's Council of Economic Advisers, warned of the dangers of opening these capital markets too rapidly, and soon Rubin and Deputy Secretary of the Treasury Lawrence H. Summers began to publicly caution that financial liberalization in the BEMs must be accompanied by banking and other fundamental economic reforms. Yet, convinced that the International Monetary Fund would bail them out of any trouble (as the United States had done in Mexico in 1994), the leaders of many of these states ignored this advice.

In 1997 and 1998 the dark side of globalization appeared in the form of a series of currency collapses in Thailand, Indonesia, South Korea, Malaysia, the Philippines, and Taiwan. Social unrest in Indonesia claimed one thousand lives and led to the forced resignation of its long-serving president. The so-called Asian dynamos fell like dominoes as currency speculators undermined their financial systems. Deeply shaken by these events and fearful that the crisis would spread to the United States, the Federal Reserve Bank cut short-term interest rates three times within six weeks, and President Clinton called on

Rubin to devise ways to reform the global financial system in order to avert future disasters. The secretary responded with a series of speeches in which he called for the creation of a new global financial "architecture" that involved improving transparency and disclosure in emerging markets, giving the International Monetary Fund additional power, encouraging the private sector to share some of the economic burden in times of crisis, and strengthening the regulation of financial institutions in emerging economies. Rubin implicitly acknowledged what many economists had argued for years: any attempt to liberalize capital markets lacking the structures to support the subsequent inflow in foreign investment was dangerous.

In fact, the seemingly inexorable growth of globalization produced both academic debates and public protests. Globalization enthusiasts celebrated the unprecedented extent to which poorer economies had been incorporated into the international system of trade, finance, and production as partners and participants rather than colonial dependencies and believed that this condition had produced greater economic growth. But skeptics worried that since substantial numbers of nations were landlocked and isolated, they would find it extremely difficult to attract trade and investment. Furthermore, other countries, such as the Persian Gulf oil states, in possession of huge natural resource bases, found it impossible to establish competitive, and more sustainable, manufacturing sectors. Hence, the process of globalization was far from global. Second, while proponents of increased capital flows across borders argued that they gave to developing nations an enhanced ability to borrow and lend (and thus better control patterns of investment and consumption), others pointed to the destabilization and financial panics that these unfettered capital flows had allegedly caused in Latin America and Asia during the 1990s as worried investors hurriedly withdrew their assets at the first sign of weakening currencies. Third, economists disagreed about the impact that globalization had on domestic and international income distribution. Some suggested that since the United States exported high technology products to Asia in return for less expensive labor-intensive goods, American workers in certain industries had suffered a loss of income in the face of low-wage foreign competition, while, at the same time, skilled workers in Asia incurred similar dislocations. On the other hand, the number of U.S. workers directly competing with unskilled workers in emerging markets appeared to be too small to explain widening income disparities among Americans.

The age of globalization also produced contradictory political impulses. On the one hand, it fostered a host of new international organizations, including, most prominently, the World Trade Organization (WTO). Some observers feared that the proliferation of such institutions, accompanied by rules regulating the behavior of its members, posed a threat to national sovereignty. On the other hand, defenders of the nation-state also worried about the growing tendency of local governments, regions, and ethnic communities to pursue greater political and cultural autonomy as a way to ward off the demands of globalization. In his Farewell Address, President Clinton, while noting that the global economy was giving "more of our own people and billions around the world the chance to work and live and raise their families with dignity," acknowledged that integration processes "make us more subject to global forces of destruction—to terrorism, organized crime and narco-trafficking, the spread of deadly weapons and disease, the degradation of the global environment."

Indeed, concerns such as these and others triggered a series of public, sometimes violent demonstrations against the World Trade Organization, the International Monetary Fund, and the World Bank in Seattle (November 1999), Washington, D.C. (April 2000), Prague (September 2000), and several other locations. Loose coalitions of protesters made up of union members, animal rights advocates, environmentalists, anarchists, and senior citizens claimed that wealthy countries and their institutional tools—the International Monetary Fund and the World Bank— had incurred an "ecological debt" to the Third World by draining its natural resources, destroying the environment, and causing human rights violations. They believed that this ecological debt should wipe out the monetary debt that poor countries owed to these organizations. They wanted the World Bank to order a moratorium on foreign investments in oil, mining, and natural gas projects because of their environmental threats. Others argued that fledgling democracies should be forgiven the debts incurred by previous, repressive regimes. All were convinced that multinational corporations—most of them based in the United States—behaved more like robber barons than responsible global citizens.

In sum, the nature and consequences of globalization remained deeply contested in the post–Cold War world. The Clinton administration's initial desire to foster its spread had been tempered by foreign financial crises and public dissent. Yet it was not even clear whether globalization should be viewed as a conscious national policy or as an unstoppable force ultimately immune to either governmental management or control.

PROMOTING DEMOCRACY

By the late 1980s, as Mikhail Gorbachev allowed anticommunist revolutions to sweep through Moscow's satellites, President Bush called for a Europe "whole and free." Soon he began to speak more broadly of a growing "zone of the democratic peace," tacitly accepting the academic thesis that democracies did not fight wars against one another. According to this view, the roots of which can be traced back at least as far as Immanuel Kant in the late eighteenth century, democracies (or "republics" as he called them), shared certain characteristics that precluded conflict among them. His claims were expanded by several American political scientists, including, most prominently, Michael Doyle and Bruce Russett. They and others advanced several arguments to account for the "democratic peace." Some emphasized that because of the internal structures of democratic states, leaders could not mobilize their publics to support any wars except those against authoritarian and totalitarian regimes. Others stressed the norms of peaceful resolution of conflicts within democracies because of the habit of compromise and the rule of law. Still others argued that the transparency of democratic institutions and the easy flow of information between democracies made violence extremely unlikely. Another group of scholars was impressed by the shared social purposes of democratic states and an underlying identity of interests that sharply limited the rise of disputes worthy of war.

Indeed, virtually every president since Woodrow Wilson accepted the basic tenets of this "liberal" argument about how democracies behave. He believed that militarized, autocratic regimes had caused World War I and that American security depended on the successful transition of these states to democracy. Franklin Roosevelt and Harry Truman shared similar sentiments about the origins of World War II and the requirements of U.S. security in the postwar world. In the 1980s, the Reagan Doctrine, which reserved to the United States the right to assist groups attempting to overthrow Marxist dictatorships, sprang from the same set of assumptions. All of these presidents were convinced, as the political scientist G. John Ikenberry put it, that democracies were "more capable of developing peaceful, continuous, rule-based, institutionalized relations among each other than [was] possible with or between non-democracies."

Nevertheless, a lively scholarly debate arose after the Cold War about the merits of these arguments and assumptions. Christopher Layne examined four instances when democracies nearly went to war against one another and found that conflict was averted not because of shared values but because of national self-interest. Further, he argued that the War of 1812 and the American Civil War should be seen as wars between democratic states. David Spiro claimed that because the chance that any given pair of states will be at war at any given time was low, and because before 1945 few democracies existed, the absence of conflict between them might be the result of random chance. He also complained that proponents of the democratic peace thesis often failed to offer clear definitions of "democracy." Finally, Henry Farber and Joanne Gowa concluded that only after 1945 were democracies significantly less likely to be involved with disputes with one another, and that was because most democracies were aligned against the Soviet threat. With the ending of the Cold War, the chief impediment to intrademocratic conflict had been removed.

These counterclaims notwithstanding, democracy promotion represented a fundamental theme in post–Cold War American foreign policy and was closely tied to the preservation of U.S. hegemony and the fostering of globalization. In its efforts to create a successor to the strategy of containment and to rally domestic support for the Gulf War, the George H. W. Bush administration offered a "new world order," which, among other things, included the notion that the United States should help to widen the "zone of the democratic peace." Although Bush quickly dropped this phrase from his public rhetoric in the face of heavy media criticism and the need to focus on domestic issues in advance of the 1992 presidential campaign, the administration, nevertheless, acted to promote democracy in Eastern Europe, Russia, Latin America, and Africa through a variety of diplomatic and economic initiatives. Bush officials could not help but be impressed by the democratization process then occurring in many parts of the world.

The Clinton administration, also groping for a post-containment strategy and similarly taken by the sweep of democratization, soon unveiled "engagement and enlargement" as its lodestar. In a September 1993 speech tellingly entitled "From Containment to Enlargement," Anthony Lake, Clinton's first special assistant for national security affairs, attempted to explain this strategy. After noting that its geography and history had continually tempted the United States to be wary of foreign entanglements, Lake argued that the Clinton administration intended "to engage actively in the world in order to increase our prosperity, update our security arrangements, and promote democracy abroad." Beyond engagement, then, lay enlargement, and Lake identified four components of such a strategy. First, the United States would "strengthen the community of major market democracies . . . which constitutes the core from which enlargement is proceeding." Second, the Clinton administration would "help foster and consolidate new democracies and market economies, where possible, especially in states of special significance and opportunity." Third, America "must counter the aggression—and support the liberalization—of states hostile to democracy and markets." And fourth, "we need to pursue our humanitarian agenda not only by providing aid, but also by working to help democracies and market economies take root in regions of greatest humanitarian concern." At the same time, Lake hedged "engagement" with several caveats. He warned that the tide of democratic advance could slow and even reverse; he stressed that this strategy had to be tempered by pragmatism, for other national interests would doubtless require the United States to befriend and defend nondemocratic states for mutually beneficial reasons; and he noted that this strategy must view democracy broadly and not insist that all adhere rigidly to the American example.

In the short term, this strategy was seemingly discredited by the bloody battle in Mogadishu, Somalia, the following month as well as the embarrassment suffered when a U.S. ship carrying training personnel to Haiti was turned back by a protesting mob in Port-au-Prince. Furthermore, opinion polls repeatedly indicated that only one in five Americans thought it important to promote democracy abroad. Nevertheless, to a remarkable degree, Lake's speech anticipated much of the Clinton administration's democratization efforts, which, in turn, adhered closely to those of the first Bush presidency.

Both gave primacy to Eastern Europe and Latin America—those regions that were already the most democratized—to initiate a policy of "democratic differentiation" in order to urge further movement toward democracy and open markets. A variety of carrots and sticks were employed to nudge these nations along. In the case of Haiti, the Clinton administration threatened force to reinstall the democratically elected president, but this action was taken more for domestic political reasons than from any confidence that genuine democracy would take root in that troubled country.

Initially, Clinton tried to link the continuance of most-favored-nation trading status to improvements in China's human rights record, but by 1994 he was forced to abandon that approach in light of Beijing's intransigence. Indeed, neither administration wanted to allow democracy promotion to undermine the opening of markets throughout Asia. And in the Middle East the need for energy security and fears about Iraq and Iran dissuaded both George H. W. Bush and Bill Clinton from evincing any interest in democratization. Post–Cold War American foreign policy was frequently frustrated in its attempts to foster democracy in Russia because of a combination of rampant corruption, the physical decline of Boris Yeltsin, and Moscow's resentment of NATO enlargement. Yeltsin's replacement by the enigmatic former KGB agent Vladimir Putin triggered a debate in Washington about his devotion to democracy. By the time of George W. Bush's election in 2000, more Americans viewed Russia with hostility than at any time since the mid-1980s.

But in Africa, where there was palpable evidence of a democratization trend, American actions appeared inconsistent. On the one hand, economic assistance programs were restructured to reward those governments undertaking democratic reforms, and every embassy in Africa was ordered to formulate a strategy for democracy promotion. Yet when the dictatorship of Mobutu Sese Seko in the Congo collapsed in 1997, the United States encouraged Uganda and Rwanda to offer armed support to Laurent Kabila's efforts to seize power. Kabila's democratic credentials were questionable at best, yet the Clinton administration chose him over Etienne Tshisekedi, the popular prime minister who possessed the clearest

claim on democratic legitimacy. Washington's decision to endorse the strongman approach proved disastrous, as Kabila proceeded to wreck what was left of this long-suffering nation before being assassinated in a palace coup in 2001. Critics charged that despite official rhetoric about the importance of bringing democracy to Africa, the United States continued to patronize African nations and to tacitly believe that they remained unprepared for democratic governance.

On balance, however, post–Cold War American foreign policy generally promoted democracy where economic and security interests and discernible democratization trends existed. In those regions where U.S. interests required working with authoritarian regimes and where prospects for democratization were bleak, no effort was made to promote democracy. Indeed, a rough consensus emerged among American political elites in support of this pragmatic approach to democracy promotion.

UNDERTAKING HUMANITARIAN INTERVENTIONS

Humanitarian interventions—the use of military force to save civilian lives in the absence of vital national interests—emerged as a major theme in post–Cold War American foreign policy and generated heated political and scholarly debates about their advisability, efficacy, and legitimacy. During the Cold War humanitarian interventions were rare, unilateral, and generally condemned by the international community. For example, in 1971 India invaded East Pakistan (Bangladesh) during a Pakistani civil war allegedly to save civilian lives, but the consequence was to split India's traditional enemy in two. Comparable international skepticism greeted the 1978 Vietnam invasion of Kampuchea (Cambodia)—supposedly to end the "killing fields" of the Khmer Rouge—and the 1979 Tanzanian intervention in Uganda was not only designed to oust the abhorrent Idi Amin but also to retaliate against a Ugandan invasion the previous year.

But after the Cold War a commitment among democratic states to respond to humanitarian disasters became the norm, if not always the rule. The United States assumed a global humanitarian role, intervening both unilaterally and multilaterally in an unprecedented number of situations. In 1991, U.S. forces provided aid and protection to the Iraqi Kurds shortly after the conclusion of the Gulf War. Many commentators and members of Congress criticized President Bush for not intervening sooner.

In December 1992, U.S. troops were ordered to Somalia in an effort to end a disastrous famine and then to turn over responsibility to the United Nations. But when eighteen U.S. Rangers were killed in a firefight with hostile Somali clan members in October 1993, an outraged Congress pressured a panicked Clinton administration to withdraw all U.S. forces. Misery soon returned to southern Somalia. No doubt in reaction to this experience, the United States did virtually nothing to halt a full-scale genocide the following year in Rwanda that claimed the lives of hundreds of thousands of ethnic Tutsis. Europeans, in particular, criticized this inaction, and several years later Clinton apologized for his failure to provide more assistance.

In September 1994, in the face of an imminent U.S. invasion, Haiti's junta left the country and the democratically elected president, Jean-Bertrand Aristide, was reinstalled. At the time, former President Bush and former Secretary of State James Baker publicly opposed this action on the grounds that no vital national interests were at stake. But confronted with a humanitarian disaster in the form of thousands of Haitian refugees attempting to reach the U.S. mainland, and pressured by the Black Congressional Caucus to return President Aristide to power, the Clinton administration—armed with a UN resolution—prepared to use military force.

A decade earlier, in 1984, Ronald Reagan's secretary of defense, Caspar Weinberger, suggested that six tests ought to be passed before dispatching U.S. troops: (1) "The United States should not commit forces to combat overseas unless the particular engagement or occasion is deemed vital to our national interest"; (2) the commitment should only be made "with the clear intention of winning"; (3) it should be carried out with clearly defined political and military objectives"; (4) it "must be continually reassessed and adjusted if necessary"; (5) it should "have the support of the American people and their elected representatives in Congress"; and (6) it should "be a last resort." Believing that the outcome of the Vietnam War would have been vastly different if these stringent tests had been applied, the Weinberger Doctrine was quickly embraced by many senior military officers, including Colin Powell, who would serve as chairman of the Joint Chiefs of Staff from 1989 to 1993. And it was the

fear of creating a "Balkan quagmire" that steered American policy toward Yugoslavia for much of the 1990s.

Prompted by the inspiring example of democratic revolutions sweeping Central and Eastern Europe in 1989, several republics in the Yugoslav confederation sought to break away from Belgrade's rule. In June 1991, Slovenia and Croatia declared their independence. While Yugoslav President Slobodan Milosevic did little to oppose the Slovenian action, he directly supported an uprising of ethnic Serbs in Croatia, and a ghastly civil war ensued. In December, Germany recognized both new governments, and the European Union and the United States soon followed, even though Secretary of State James Baker had declared previously that "we don't have a dog in this fight."

Macedonia was allowed to secede from the federation, but after Muslims held an independence referendum in multiethnic Bosnia-Herzegovina that was boycotted by its Serbian residents, a horrific war broke out among Croats, Serbs, and Muslims. The Bosnian Serbs, who were enthusiastically supported by Milosevic, undertook a systematic "ethnic cleansing campaign" designed to rid the republic of its Muslim population. The Bush administration, while recognizing the independence of a Muslim-led Bosnia, maintained that the Balkans constituted a European problem and refused to send U.S. forces there as part of a UN "peacekeeping" operation, even though several members of NATO did so. Some senior Clinton officials, led by Anthony Lake and UN Ambassador Madeleine Albright, argued that the United States should lift the arms embargo that the United Nations had imposed on all the warring parties and initiate air strikes against Bosnian Serb positions. But the Joint Chiefs chairman Powell repeatedly rejected the feasibility of this "lift and strike" option, while nations such as Britain and France, with peacekeepers on the ground, argued that their troops would be the first targets of Serb retaliation.

Despite the worst fighting in Europe since World War II, the Clinton administration did little until August 1995, when, after an exceptionally heinous slaughter of Muslim civilians in the town of Srebrenica, NATO carried out five days of bombing that had the ultimate effect of bringing all of the factions to the negotiating table in Dayton, Ohio. Soon, NATO peacekeepers with American participation entered Bosnia, but Clinton, under congressional pressure, announced quite unrealistically that U.S. forces would remain there for only one year. Indeed, their continued presence became a major campaign theme in 2000 when George W. Bush and several of his advisers suggested that the Balkans should be policed exclusively by Europeans. On the other hand, in 1999, when reporting on the Srebrenica massacre, UN Secretary-General Kofi Annan warned that "the tragedy will haunt our history forever. A deliberate and systematic attempt to terrorize, expel, or murder an entire people must be met decisively with all necessary means and with the political will to carry the policy through to its logical conclusion." He implied that the United States bore a major responsibility for providing that political will.

In early 1999, Milosevic indicated his intention to purge Kosovo—a province of Yugoslavia whose semiautonomous status he had revoked ten years earlier—of its ethnic Albanian (Muslim) majority. After rejecting a demand that NATO forces be allowed to enter Kosovo to prevent "ethnic cleansing," Milosevic was subjected to an unprecedented seventy-seven-day bombing campaign. During Operation Allied Force, which ultimately threatened the cohesion of NATO, Yugoslav troops forced hundreds of thousands of Muslim Kosovars into neighboring Albania and Macedonia and thus created the very humanitarian catastrophe that the air strikes had been designed to avoid. From the outset, Clinton, fearing public and congressional criticism over possible casualties, ruled out the use of ground troops. American officials, remembering how quickly NATO bombing had ended the fighting in Bosnia four years before, expected a similar outcome in Kosovo. But it was not until Russia withdrew its support from Belgrade that Milosevic finally capitulated. Then he allowed peacekeepers under UN—not NATO—authority to enter Kosovo, where they encountered sustained hostility from both Muslims and Serbs.

All of these humanitarian interventions—as well as the decision to ignore Rwanda—provoked intense debate within the United States about the essential purposes of American foreign policy. Michael Mandelbaum, a leading scholar of American foreign relations, captured one side of the issue quite colorfully in a 1996 *Foreign Affairs* article entitled "Foreign Policy as Social Work," in which he likened Anthony Lake to Mother Teresa for telling a newspaper reporter that "when I wake up every morning and look at the headlines and the stories and the images on television, I

want to work to end every conflict, I want to save every child out there." In rejoinder, Stanley Hoffmann, another renowned student of American foreign policy, predicted that the twenty-first century would be full of ethnic conflict and disintegrating states. While not all of them would be preventable or resolvable, instances of extreme violence should be considered as inherently dangerous for international peace and security and morally and prudentially unacceptable.

The national debate about humanitarian interventions involved at least four issues. First, under what circumstances would military power be used as opposed to other, less coercive tools of statecraft? Some observers, like Henry Kissinger, argued that unless a clear, vital interest could be found, military force should never be used. A substantial number of congressional Republicans shared his view. This position obviously reflected that of the Weinberger Doctrine. Yet no U.S. official or influential commentator suggested that the United States should intervene in all humanitarian crises, for the obvious reason that because resources were limited, priorities had to be set. Most political elites reached the conclusion that these situations should be decided on a case-by-case basis. Yet they disagreed about which ones warranted American action. Positions often were taken on the basis of ethnic identity. For example, the Congressional Black Caucus was especially eager to intervene in Haiti and Rwanda. Similarly, Cuban Americans, Armenian Americans, and American Muslims expressed other, predictable preferences.

Second, how much and what kind of force would be needed? Because there was a widely shared perception by civilian and military leaders that, after the Somalia "debacle," the American public would not tolerate casualties suffered during humanitarian operations, the Clinton administration refused to deploy ground combat troops in the Balkans. Rather, it relied exclusively on airpower. In fact, the administration may have misread the "lessons" of Somalia, for polling data indicated that the public was considerably more tolerant of casualties as long as the intervention resulted in success.

Third, what kind of training should be given to U.S. troops who might become peacemakers or peacekeepers? This facet of the debate was primarily conducted within the Defense Department between those who believed that special peacekeeping units should be created and those who argued that all forces should be taught to be potential peacekeepers. But some observers outside the Pentagon questioned the whole concept of training forces for what they compared to police duties rather than traditional military roles.

And, fourth, how central a role should humanitarian missions play in U.S. foreign policy? In general, liberals like Anthony Lewis of the *New York Times* contended that their role should be central. Moreover, the interventions should do more than simply restore order and feed and clothe civilians; they should also aim to rebuild failed states, arrest war criminals, and integrate ethnic groups. Conservatives, who remained skeptical that such operations should be undertaken at all, believed that they should occur infrequently and seek to achieve modest objectives. These disagreements became prominent during the 2000 presidential campaign when Condoleeza Rice, a top adviser to George W. Bush and his future special assistant for national security, called for the rapid return of U.S. peacekeepers from Bosnia and Kosovo at the same time that Vice President Albert Gore indicated that, if elected, he would devote even more resources to humanitarian missions.

ISOLATING AND PUNISHING "ROGUE" STATES

American foreign policymakers used the terms "rogue," "outlaw," and "backlash" states virtually interchangeably after the Cold War. As early as July 1985, President Reagan had asserted that "we are not going to tolerate . . . attacks from outlaw states by the strangest collection of misfits, loony tunes, and squalid criminals since the advent of the Third Reich," but it fell to the Clinton administration to elaborate this concept.

Writing in the March–April 1994 issue of *Foreign Affairs,* Anthony Lake cited "the reality of recalcitrant and outlaw states that not only choose to remain outside the family [of democratic nations] but also assault its basic values." He applied this label to five regimes: Cuba, North Korea, Iran, Iraq, and Libya and claimed that their behavior was frequently aggressive and defiant; that ties among them were growing; that they were ruled by coercive cliques that suppressed human rights and promoted radical ideologies; that they "exhibited a chronic inability to engage constructively with the outside world"; and that their siege mentality had led them to attempt to develop weapons of mass destruction and missile delivery systems. For Lake, "as the sole super-

power, the United States [had] a special responsibility . . . to neutralize, contain and, through selective pressure, perhaps eventually transform" these miscreants into good global citizens.

The first Bush administration had agreed with Lake's analysis and in 1991 adopted a "two-war" strategy designed to enable U.S. forces to fight and win two regional wars simultaneously against "renegade" nations. The second Bush administration emphasized the urgent need to develop a national missile defense to protect the United States from weapons launched by rogue states. In short, the "outlaw" nation theme pervaded U.S. foreign policy throughout the post–Cold War era.

Critics seized on these terms as inherently fuzzy, subjective, and difficult to translate into consistent policy. Although Lake had defined rogues as nations that challenged the system of international norms and international order, disagreement existed about the very nature of this system. For example, whereas the Organization for European Security and Cooperation (OSCE) and UN Secretary-General Annan advocated international norms that would expose regimes that mistreated their populations to condemnation and even armed intervention, others argued that such norms would trample on the traditional notion of state sovereignty. Nevertheless, the State Department sometimes included Serbia on its outlaw list solely because President Milosevic had violated the rights of some of his nation's citizens, and NATO undertook an air war against him in 1999 because of his repression of an internal ethnic group.

In theory, at least, to be classified as a rogue, a state had to commit four transgressions: pursue weapons of mass destruction, support terrorism, severely abuse its own citizens, and stridently criticize the United States. Iran, Iraq, North Korea, and Libya all behaved in this manner during at least some of the post–Cold War era. Yet the inclusion of Cuba, which certainly violated human rights and castigated the United States, was put on the list solely because of the political influence of the American Cuban community and specifically that of the Cuban American National Foundation. Moreover, in 1992 Congress approved the Cuban Democracy Act, which mandated secondary sanctions against foreign companies who used property seized from Americans by the Castro government in the 1960s. Attempts to implement this law outraged some of Washington's closest allies, and President Clinton, while

★ ★ ★ ★

ROGUE STATES AND STATES OF CONCERN

In a long and vigorous round of questioning at a 21 June 2000 State Department press briefing, spokesman Richard Boucher tried to explain the implications of the change in terminology from "rogue" to "state of concern":

Question: Is "rogue state" then out of the lexicon as of today?

Boucher: I haven't used it for a while.

Question: Is it possible that some states will still be referred to as "rogue states" if they—

Boucher: If they want to be rogues, they can be rogues, but generally we have not been using the term for a while, I think.

Question: So it's not a matter of some countries continue to be "rogue states" and others have progressed to "states of concern"; all of them henceforth are "states of concern"?

Boucher: Yes.

Question: But does this lower the bar for what a "state of concern" is, now that there's no "rogue state"?

Boucher: Does this lower the bar? No, because, as I said, it's more a description than a change in policy, because

the issue is: Are various countries whose activities around the world have been troubling to us, are they actually dealing with the issues that we have been concerned about? And if we are able to encourage them or pressure them or otherwise produce changes in their behavior, and therefore a change in our relationship, we're willing to do that. If they're not, then we're going to keep our sanctions on and we're going to keep our restrictions on and we're not going to change our policies.

Question: Can you tell us how many there are?

Boucher: No.

Question: Has anyone actually done a rough list?

Boucher: We have found the opportunity to express our concerns about different states at different times in different ways. We try to deal with each one on its behavior, on its actions, on its merits.

Question: I just want to ask a question on the former rogue state of North Korea. (Laughter)

Boucher: The state previously known as rogue; is that it? (Laughter)

---

backing this legislation as a presidential candidate, tried hard to avoid enforcing it. On the other hand, states like Syria and Pakistan, hardly paragons of rectitude, avoided being added to the list because the United States hoped that Damascus could play a constructive role in the Arab-Israeli "peace process," and because Washington had long maintained close relations with Islamabad—a vestige of the Cold War.

The United States employed several tools to isolate and punish rogue states. Tough unilateral economic sanctions, often at congressional behest, were imposed on or tightened against Iran, Libya, Cuba, Sudan, and Afghanistan. Airpower was used massively against Serbia in 1999 and selectively against Iraq for years after the conclusion of the Gulf War in 1991. Cruise missiles were fired at Afghanistan and Sudan in retaliation for terrorist attacks against U.S. embassies in Kenya and Tanzania in September 1998. The Central Intelligence Agency supported a variety of

covert actions designed to depose Saddam Hussein, while Congress approved the Iraq Liberation Act in 1998 aimed at providing Iraqi opposition groups with increased financial assistance. Several leading Republicans who would occupy high positions in the George W. Bush administration publicly urged President Clinton in February 1998 to recognize the Iraqi National Congress (INC) as the provisional government of Iraq. Some of these critics, including Paul Wolfowitz and Robert Zoellick, hinted that U.S. ground forces might ultimately be required to help the INC oust Saddam. In all of these anti-rogue efforts, however, Washington found it exceedingly difficult to persuade other nations (with the partial exception of Britain) to support its policies of ostracism and punishment.

In light of these difficulties, some observers suggested that the United States drop its "one size fits all" containment strategy that allegedly limited diplomatic flexibility in favor of a more differentiated approach that addressed the particular conditions in each targeted nation. Indeed, the Clinton administration adopted this policy alternative with North Korea and, to a lesser degree, with Iran. Faced with the dangers posed by Pyongyang's ongoing efforts to develop nuclear weapons and missile delivery systems, the United States briefly considered air strikes against suspected nuclear facilities or stringent economic sanctions. Yet both options were rejected out of fear of triggering a North Korean invasion of the South. Consequently, the Clinton administration reluctantly entered into negotiations designed to compel Pyongyang's nuclear disarmament. In October 1994 the U.S.–North Korea Agreed Framework was signed, committing North Korea to a freeze on nuclear weapons development and the eventual destruction of its nuclear reactors. In exchange, the United States, South Korea, and Japan promised to provide two light-water nuclear reactors that would be virtually impossible to use to produce nuclear weapons, along with petroleum to fuel North Korea's conventional power plants and food assistance to alleviate near-famine conditions. During the last years of the Clinton administration, relations with Pyongyang warmed considerably. North Korea claimed that it had suspended its missile development program pending a permanent agreement, and Madeleine Albright, now secretary of state, made the first official American visit to North Korea in 2000. Nevertheless, because this conditional engagement with North Korea involved reaching agreements with a regime widely perceived as extremely repressive and untrustworthy, many in Congress attacked this approach as tantamount to appeasement and called on George W. Bush to cease negotiations with Pyongyang. He obliged, announcing that he had no intention of quickly resuming efforts to reach an agreement on North Korean missile development.

Interestingly, despite the budding rapprochement between these two states in the late 1990s, officials in the Clinton administration repeatedly argued that a national missile defense system needed to be constructed to protect the United States against nuclear missile attacks from rogue states such as North Korea. George W. Bush's decision to end talks with Pyongyang suggested to many observers that he preferred to pursue national missile defense. To critics of the rogue state concept, these actions merely reinforced their view that while the concept had proven to be very successful in garnering domes-

tic support for punitive measures, the derogatory nature of the term necessarily complicated efforts to improve relations with states like North Korea.

Similarly, Iran represented another case in which altered circumstances challenged the rogue-state strategy. The surprise election of Mohammed Khatemi to the presidency in May 1997 and his subsequent invitation for a "dialogue between civilizations" led Secretary Albright to propose a "road map" for normalizing relations. Conservative Shiite clerics warned Khatemi against engaging the "Great Satan," but the continued designation of Iran as a rogue state also contributed to the Clinton administration's difficulty in responding constructively to positive developments in Tehran.

The gradual realization that calling states "rogues" might in some cases have proven counterproductive induced the United States in June 2000 to drop this term in favor of the less fevered "states of concern." Secretary Albright emphasized that the change in name did not imply that the United States now approved of the behavior of these regimes: "We are now calling these states 'states of concern' because we are concerned about their support for terrorist activities, their development of missiles, their desire to disrupt the international system." Yet State Department officials acknowledged that the "rogue" term had been eliminated because some of these states—such as North Korea, Libya, and Iran—had taken steps to meet American demands and had complained that they were still being branded with the old label.

Regardless of the terms employed, however, on another level this post–Cold War strategy of regional containment reflected an effort by the United States to define acceptable international (and even domestic) behavior. As a hegemonic state it was, perhaps, appropriate that Washington attempted to write these rules. Yet it inevitably risked exposing the United States to charges of arrogance and imperiousness.

DEFENDING THE AMERICAN HOMELAND

The Cold War had barely ended before American policymakers began to worry about the possibility that hostile states and transnational terrorist organizations would soon be able to undertake nuclear, chemical, biological, and informational attacks against the continental United States. Recognizing that the United States, because of its overwhelming military superiority, would not be threatened in the foreseeable future with traditional adversaries, national security planners pointed to the dangers posed by "asymmetrical" assaults on the American homeland. These might include nuclear missiles launched by rogue states, national plagues caused by the clandestine introduction of biological agents, and the destruction of the American financial system through the use of computer viruses by unknown enemies.

Such fears intensified in 1997 when the blue-ribbon National Defense Panel warned that the United States remained utterly unprepared for dealing with these threats. Three years later, the U.S. Commission on National Security, cochaired by former senators Warren Rudman and Gary Hart, concluded that "a direct attack against American citizens on American soil is likely over the next quarter century." Consequently, the commission proposed that the Coast Guard, Customs Service, Federal Emergency Management Agency, and Border Patrol be unified as a new homeland security body, whose director would have cabinet status. The new agency would coordinate defense against attacks as well as relief efforts if deterrence proved unsuccessful. According to Rudman, "the threat is asymmetric, and we're not prepared for it."

American foreign policymakers responded to these alleged vulnerabilities in several ways. First, as we have seen, diplomatic and military instruments were used to prevent rogue states from developing weapons of mass destruction. These efforts proved to be only partially successful, and in 1998, Pakistan, formerly a close ally, enraged Washington by testing a nuclear device. Second, counterterrorism programs were intensified after the 1998 embassy bombings. But they could not prevent the attack on the USS *Cole* in Yemen in October 2000. Moreover, the bombing of a federal building in Oklahoma City in April 1995 by two Americans with homemade explosives, and the attempted destruction of the World Trade Center in New York City in February 1993 by foreign nationals, had demonstrated the extreme difficulty in defending the nation against asymmetrical assaults. And while a consensus about the need to make the U.S. homeland less vulnerable to these sorts of occurrences certainly emerged in the post–Cold War era, designing a strategy for doing so proved to be extremely difficult.

In March 1983, President Ronald Reagan had proposed that the United States build weapons capable of defending the nation against Soviet nuclear attack. His Strategic Defense Initia-

tive proved to be very controversial and expensive, yet the program managed to survive the Cold War. In 1992 the Bush administration opened negotiations with Russia seeking to amend the Anti-Ballistic Missile (ABM) Treaty of 1972 that prohibited the deployment of sea-based or space-based missile defenses and placed strict limits on land-based defenses. President Bush wished to permit the construction of several hundred land-based ABM systems to protect the United States and its allies against between 200 and 250 ballistic missiles from any source. But these talks produced no agreement, and in late 1993 the Clinton administration withdrew Bush's proposed amendments to the ABM Treaty and further reduced the scale of national missile defense (NMD) research and development.

The Republican Party, however, remained deeply committed to NMD, and upon capturing both houses of Congress in 1994 quickly increased appropriations for research and development. Moreover, Congress created a commission to assess the ballistic missile threat to the United States. Chaired by former (and future) Secretary of Defense Donald Rumsfeld, the commission issued its final report in July 1998. Directly contradicting a 1995 National Intelligence Estimate that concluded that the United States need not fear missile attacks until at least 2010, the Rumsfeld Commission claimed that such nations as Iran and North Korea could threaten the United States within five years of a decision to acquire this capability—and that Washington might not be aware of the point at which such a decision had been made.

Just six weeks later, on 31 August 1998, North Korea test launched a Taepo Dong-1 missile, which, to the surprise of the U.S. intelligence community, possessed a third stage, which meant that in theory, at least, this missile had intercontinental capability. Congressional Republicans seized on the Rumsfeld report, as well as the North Korean test launch, to pressure Clinton to sign the Missile Defense Act of 1999, which made it official policy to "deploy as soon as technologically possible an effective NMD system." Strongly encouraged by Ted Stevens, chairman of the Senate Appropriations Committee, planning began on the construction of a radar system on an Alaskan island, but after a series of embarrassing failures by the Defense Department to intercept missiles from ground-based sites, in September 2000 Clinton decided to delay deployment.

President George W. Bush's determination to

construct a national missile defense system as soon as possible unleashed a fractious and complex public debate. Opponents offered six main arguments against NMD. First, the deployment of even the limited system envisioned by Bush, which would be designed to intercept no more than twenty-five warheads, would be expensive. The Congressional Budget Office estimated that a ground-based NMD would cost at least $60 billion. Critics recalled that ambitious Defense Department programs had in the past frequently encountered significant cost overruns and warned that NMD could contribute to future budget deficits if pursued in tandem with President Bush's proposed tax cuts. Second, opponents strongly doubted the technological feasibility of any NMD. They emphasized the difficulties of intercepting incoming warheads, likening it to hitting a bullet with a bullet, and suggested that the task would be made even more daunting if enemy ICBMs were equipped with decoys and other countermeasures.

Third, even if these enormous odds were somehow overcome and a reliable NMD system was deployed, critics worried that the creation of a Fortress America mentality among the public could be a major result. They warned that some congressional Republicans might seize on NMD and the consequent public retreat into isolationism as a pretext to reduce dramatically America's international role. Fourth, even if Russia could be persuaded that a limited NMD posed no threat to its massive nuclear arsenal, China, in possession of only about two dozen ICBMs, would be likely to build more missiles in order to deter a U.S. nuclear attack. Beijing's actions would trigger an Indian response to increase its nuclear capabilities, and that, in turn, would spur Pakistan to do likewise. Hence, an unintended consequence of NMD would be to heighten the likelihood of a South Asian nuclear war.

Fifth, critics contended that NMD constituted a quick technological "fix" that would serve as a poor substitute for patient diplomacy and nonproliferation efforts. Thus, instead of negotiating further agreements with North Korea, for example, armed with an NMD, the United States would have no incentive to try and help Seoul improve North-South relations or to attempt to alter peacefully the nature of the Pyongyang regime. Finally, opponents claimed that NMD represented a "Maginot Line" approach to nuclear defense. Recalling that the Nazis had invaded France in 1940 by simply circumventing the elaborate defensive fortifications known as the Ma-

ginot Line, critics predicted that NMD would, at best, defend the United States against an extremely remote sort of attack with ICBMs. Much more plausible was the so-called "man in a van" scenario, whereby a single terrorist could kill millions of Americans with a suitcase bomb or through the release of deadly biological agents into the water supplies of major cities.

While some NMD advocates, especially House Republicans, harbored isolationist sentiments, most in the Bush administration believed, at least privately, that a limited national missile defense system would enhance American global hegemony. Robert Joseph, Bush's counterproliferation expert at the National Security Council, dismissed the likelihood of a rogue state launching a preemptive missile attack on the United States as a false issue created by NMD opponents. He argued that such regimes viewed weapons of mass destruction as their best means of overcoming the American technological advantages that would lead to their certain defeat in conventional wars. Rather, ICBMs would enable these states to hold American and allied cities hostage, thereby deterring the United States from intervention in regional crises. In other words, their missiles could reduce the likelihood of massive retaliation by the United States if they employed chemical and biological weapons regionally, even against American forces. Implicit in Joseph's hypothesis was the assertion that a limited national missile defense system would cement the ability of the United States to intervene anywhere it deemed necessary. Russian and Chinese appreciation of this consequence doubtless explained much of their hostility to such a program.

Proponents furthermore claimed that only China had the ability to defeat an NMD system with decoys and that any effort to substantially increase its inventory of ICBMs would be extremely expensive and threaten future economic development. They also rejected the arguments of those who doubted the technological feasibility of such a system, noting that the United States only succeeded in placing a satellite in orbit after thirty failed attempts. Moreover, unlike Reagan's "Star Wars" plans, this system would only be aimed at intercepting a small number of missiles.

Yet NMD advocates disagreed about what sort of national missile defense system to build. In order to adhere to the provisions of the ABM Treaty, the Clinton administration decided to pursue a land-based system, and three trials were conducted. As a result, a consensus within the

Pentagon developed that the Alaskan system could be finished more rapidly. Some in the Bush administration, however, preferred a sea-based NMD that would use and upgrade the navy's Aegis air defense system. They suggested that in addition to being less costly, it would also have the ability to defend U.S. allies against rogue attacks by simply moving ships close to Europe and Japan. Moreover, it would have the advantage of firing at ICBMs in their "boost" phase (that is, immediately after launch), when their speed is much lower than during the reentry phase. But others argued that such a system would take many more years to construct, because it could not, in fact, rely on existing Aegis technology. Some observers predicted that the Bush administration would attempt to pursue both land- and sea-based systems simultaneously despite the enormous costs involved. In any event, homeland defense and the closely related issue of national missile defense appeared ready to assume prominent roles in early twenty-first century American foreign policy.

For the Bush administration the post–Cold War era ended on the morning of 11 September 2001, when international terrorists used hijacked U.S. commercial airliners to destroy the World Trade Center in New York City and to damage the Pentagon. American foreign policymakers announced that the nation was at war with terrorism and girded it for a long and potentially frustrating struggle. Putting aside its early unilateralist inclinations, the administration immediately began to organize a broad international coalition to assist it in "draining the swamps" where terrorism thrives. For the first time since the fall of the Soviet Union, the United States apparently confronted a direct threat to its physical and moral well-being, albeit one that seemed extraordinarily elusive, ruthless, and hydra-headed. Some commentators suggested that the period between the breaching of the Berlin Wall in October 1989 and the attacks of 11 September 2001 be renamed "the interwar era."

CONCLUSION

Inasmuch as the United States emerged from the Cold War as the world's sole superpower, it should not be surprising that American policymakers worked hard to sustain this hegemonic situation. Eventually another state or coalition might attempt to challenge America's preemi-

nence. Many conservatives became convinced that China had geopolitical goals that directly clashed with U.S. interests and predicted the onset of a Sino-American cold war. Others believed that the continuing integration of China into the international capitalist economy would discourage it from trying to undermine American primacy. As the post–Cold War era entered its second decade, it had become obvious that relations with the People's Republic of China would occupy a central place in U.S. foreign relations. The future nature of that relationship, however, remained unclear.

In seeking to keep America the world's "indispensable nation," post–Cold War American foreign policymakers fostered globalization, promoted democracy, undertook humanitarian interventions, isolated and punished rogue states, and worried about homeland defense. Each of these initiatives proved controversial both domestically and internationally. None was pursued with perfect consistency, but all were designed to preserve America's enviable position in the post–Cold War world.

The views expressed here are those of the author exclusively and do not represent the views of the National Defense University, the Department of Defense, or the United States Government.

BIBLIOGRAPHY

Berger, Samuel. "American Power: Hegemony, Isolationism, or Engagement." Remarks delivered at the Council on Foreign Relations, 21 October 1999.

Bowden, Mark. *Black Hawk Down: A Study of Modern War.* New York, 1999. Graphically describes the fire-fight that erupted in the streets of Mogadishu, Somalia, between U.S. forces and Somali clans on 3 October 1993.

Brilmayer, Lea. *American Hegemony: Political Morality in a One-Superpower World.* New Haven, Conn., 1994.

Brinkley, Douglas. "Democratic Enlargement: The Clinton Doctrine." *Foreign Policy* 106 (spring 1997): 111–127.

Brown, Michael E., Sean M. Lynn-Jones, and Steven E. Miller, eds. *Debating the Democratic Peace: An International Security Reader.* Cambridge, 1996.

Carothers, Thomas. "Democracy Promotion Under Clinton." *Washington Quarterly* 18 (summer 1995): 13–25.

Cox, Michael, G. John Ikenberry, and Takashi Inoguchi, eds. *American Democracy Promotion: Impulses, Strategies, and Impacts.* New York, 2000. An exceptionally valuable volume as an introduction to this issue.

Daalder, Ivo H., and Michael E. O'Hanlon. *Winning Ugly: NATO's War to Save Kosovo.* Washington, D.C., 2000.

Friedman, Thomas L. *The Lexus and the Olive Tree.* New York, 1999. A spirited defense of globalization that is engagingly written.

Garten, Jeffrey E. *The Big Ten: The Big Emerging Markets and How They Will Change Our Lives.* New York, 1997.

Goodman, Melvin A. "The Case Against National Missile Defense." *Journal of Homeland Defense* (20 October 2000).

Hirsch, John L., and Robert B. Oakley. *Somalia and Operation Restore Hope: Reflections on Peacemaking and Peacekeeping.* Washington, D.C., 1995.

Holbrooke, Richard C. *To End a War.* New York, 1999. Holbrooke's valuable memoir on his efforts to end the war in Bosnia.

Joseph, Robert. "The Case for National Missile Defense." *Journal of Homeland Defense* (20 October 2000).

Kaplan, Lawrence F. "Offensive Line: Why the Best Offense Is a Good Missile Defense." *New Republic* (12 March 2001).

Klare, Michael. *Rogue States and Nuclear Outlaws: America's Search for a New Foreign Policy.* New York, 1995.

Lake, Anthony. "From Containment to Enlargement." Remarks delivered at the Nitze School of Advanced International Studies, 21 September 1993.

———. "Confronting Backlash States." *Foreign Affairs* 73 (March–April 1994): 45–55.

Layne, Christopher. "Rethinking American Grand Strategy: Hegemony or Balance of Power in the Twenty-First Century?" *World Policy Journal* 15 (summer 1998): 8–28.

Litwak, Robert. *Rogue States and U.S. Foreign Policy: Containment After the Cold War.* Baltimore, 2000.

Mandelbaum, Michael. "Foreign Policy as Social Work." *Foreign Affairs* 75 (January–February 1996): 16–32. A highly critical article about the Clinton administration's humanitarian interventions in Somalia, Haiti, and Bosnia that fully reflects the "realist" critique of these operations.

Melanson, Richard A. *American Foreign Policy Since the Vietnam War: The Search for Consensus from Nixon to Clinton.* Armonk, N.Y., 2000.

O'Sullivan, Meghan L. "Sanctioning 'Rogue' States: A Strategy in Decline?" *Harvard International Review* 22 (summer 2000): 56–61.

Rubin, Barry. "U.S. Foreign Policy and Rogue States." *Middle East Review of International Affairs* 3 (September 1999): 49–57.

Sachs, Jeffrey. "Unlocking the Mysteries of Globalization." *Foreign Policy* 110 (spring 1998): 97–111.

Stiglitz, Joseph. "The Insider." *New Republic* (17–24 April 2000). An article by a former senior official at the IMF criticizes that organization for its imperious policies toward developing countries.

Walker, Martin. "The New American Hegemony." *World Policy Journal* 13 (summer 1996): 13–21.

Waltz, Kenneth N. "Globalization and American Power." *The National Interest* 59 (spring 2000): 46–56. An article by a leading "realist" scholar that debunks globalization as a wildly exaggerated phenomenon that has done little to alter the ways states conduct their foreign policies.

See also ARMS CONTROL AND DISARMAMENT; COLD WAR EVOLUTION AND INTERPRETATIONS; COLD WAR ORIGINS; COLD WAR TERMINATION; COLD WARRIORS; CONTAINMENT; ENVIRONMENTAL DIPLOMACY; GLOBALIZATION; HUMANITARIAN INTERVENTION AND RELIEF; INTERNATIONALISM; INTERNATIONAL MONETARY FUND AND WORLD BANK; INTERNATIONAL ORGANIZATION; NUCLEAR STRATEGY AND DIPLOMACY; POWER POLITICS; SCIENCE AND TECHNOLOGY; SUPERPOWER DIPLOMACY; TERRORISM AND COUNTERTERRORISM.

POWER POLITICS

★ ★ ★ ★

Thomas H. Etzold and Robert L. Messer

On the level of international politics, power can take many forms, from moral suasion to the carrot of economic benefits to the stick of sanctions or military force. "Power politics" is one of the more equivocal terms in the lexicon of international affairs. In common usage, including that of politicians, it often is value-laden, usually in a negative sense. It implies using coercion—force or threats of force—to impose one's will upon others. However, in academic usage, especially among scholars specializing in the history and theory of international relations, it is more often treated as a neutral phenomenon, descriptive of special or general characteristics of international politics. Further semantic or linguistic confusion results from the divergent shades of meaning that attach to the words in languages of Western scholarship such as German, English, and French. Among these three languages there is no precise equivalent for the phrase "power politics."

Thus one can define power politics both as a term commonly used in political rhetoric and a theoretical description of how states interact in pursuit of their interests in the international arena. In American English it usually means politics based primarily on coercion rather than on cooperation, whether that coercion be military or economic. More often than not it also implies pursuit of national self-interest rather than broader ideals, principles, or ethics. Such a definition shows clearly the value judgment usually implied by use of the term. Those who are accused of practicing power politics are condemned for having abused power in pursuit of a self-serving political agenda.

As a description of political behavior rather than a condemnation of it, scholars use the term in a variety of ways. Some theorists of the "realist" school believe that states inherently seek power for its own sake, so that competition and struggle naturally characterize international relations. Others argue that power is not an end but a means. They propose that states seek security above all, that they try to attain or maintain security by identifying and working toward national interests, and that they require power to achieve such national interests and security. The fact that no state has complete power and that all states have some power creates what one political scientist has called the "power problem," for each state must reckon with the potential hostility of other members of the international community. Relative security for one state all too often seems to mean relative insecurity for others, and so in this schema one must expect conflict and competition.

Another important theory about the nature of power and its effects in international affairs is set forth in the writings of the French political theorist Raymond Aron. By comparing the variant languages, philosophies, and practices of European and American states in regard to power politics, he has elaborated the important distinction between the politics of force and the politics of power. Power, he argues, is the ability to influence or control others. At times that may require the threat or use of force; at other times it will be possible to influence or control the behavior of other states with much less drastic methods. The latter two ideas are particularly useful in examining the history of American foreign affairs.

AMERICA'S POWER PROBLEM

Over the last two centuries, U.S. diplomatic history has been marked by varying attempts to solve the "power problem" in the form of debates, decisions, and divisions over the politics of force and of power. Some of these attempts and decisions shaped foreign policy for decades, so that, from 1775 to 1945, American diplomacy assumed distinctive and what might be termed traditional forms. After 1945 the changing position of the United States in international affairs altered, but did not destroy, such traditions.

Any discussion of early American foreign relations is complicated by Americans' contradictory sense of themselves in two very different roles. One role was that of victims of Old Word power politics—colonists vulnerable to imperial machinations and abuse of power from abroad. But these same Americans also saw themselves as an aggressive, powerful people destined to expand into "the West" as a new "rising American empire." Both these self-images had foreign policy implications.

How Americans reconciled their sense of mission or "manifest destiny" in expanding over the continent with the dispossession, and in the case of Indian tribes virtual extermination, of foreign competitors is discussed later. The American colonists' sense of victimization by Old World power politics was ultimately dominated by the issue of independence from Britain. It is probably an error to assume that most Americans in 1776 sanctified liberty by force in revolution, notwithstanding Thomas Jefferson's later glorification of bloodshed in the French Revolution, of which he remarked that the tree of liberty needed to be refreshed from time to time with the blood of patriots and tyrants. American colonists were, on the whole, reluctant to resort to force even to win independence. For many years they were more ready to negotiate than to fight.

The clearest indications of the ways in which Americans first hoped to resolve the problems of power, influence, and force in foreign affairs appear in explicit plans for the organization and conduct of foreign relations, the treaty plans of 1776 and 1784. In those documents American leaders recognized, and at the same time abhorred, the predominant features of international politics in their time: war, deception, and ruthlessness. In their view, international relations could be, and should be, harmonious. Americans devised plans for a diplomacy antithetical to that of Europe. Their treaty plans called for freer trade in an era of mercantilism and assumed national independence in the heyday of colonial empire. Americans proposed to influence nations great and small and to establish foreign ties by granting or withholding access to the riches of the nation's commerce.

In sum, Americans hoped both to solve their initial power problem—the way in which they would deal with the threat posed by the power of France, Spain, Britain, and other great states—and to avoid the strenuous and immoral politics of force by basing foreign policy on neutral economics. In demoting the power of force and promoting the power and mutual benefits of commerce, they looked forward to a new nation freed from the immorality and violence of European-style power politics by the principle of mutual advantage. Finally, Americans of the founding generation hoped to guard themselves from baneful Old World powers by studious noninvolvement in the affairs of Europe. The warnings of President George Washington and President Thomas Jefferson against foreign alliances and entanglements, as well as the additional principles enunciated by John Quincy Adams and James Monroe in 1823, shaped and limited American foreign affairs well into the twentieth century.

POWER IN PRACTICE

Despite their best hopes and intentions, Americans soon encountered difficulties in conducting foreign affairs peacefully and without entanglements. As set out in the treaty plans of 1776 and 1784, their program contained contradictions and weaknesses that would lead to conflict. The three great themes of America's first century of foreign affairs—peace, commerce, and growth or expansion—proved incompatible in practice rather than mutually supportive, as they had seemed in theory. As for weaknesses in design, it was soon clear that those three themes would bring the new United States into contention with the powers of the time rather than solve America's power problem or obviate the difficult politics of force.

The bright hopes of the revolutionary years dimmed almost before the nation had well begun its independent course in world affairs, for the French Revolution and Napoleonic wars revived the American power problem. Although in private and public life Americans vigorously contested the questions of political theory and governmental policy raised by the Revolution and the moribund Franco-American alliance dating from 1778, President Washington's attempt to preserve the first solution to the American problem was clear. The principal of noninvolvement in European affairs during peacetime became the principle of neutrality in war as of 1794.

Greater difficulties attended American attempts to carry on business as usual—that is, to trade in and transport commodities and merchandise with and among belligerents, and yet remain at peace. The warring nations of Europe lost little time in denying the broadening interpretations of neutral rights that Americans propounded, with the result that by the latter 1790s the United States faced the uncomfortable necessity of negotiating with the French for an end to the now-entangling Treaty of Alliance of 1778 and to the French practice of interfering with and seizing American merchant ships trading with France's enemies. The diplomatic mission sent from America in 1797 ended in the infamous XYZ affair, named for three French secret agents, who shocked their American counterparts by proposing that negotiations regarding American aid to the French in its war against Britain be facilitated by a substantial bribe. The American response was summed up in the slogan "millions for defense, not one cent for tribute" and the ensuing undeclared war between French and American naval forces in the Atlantic. Ironically, one may suspect that Americans fought the French at sea not so much over the larger questions of the day—the matter of the alliance and neutral rights at sea—as because of the almost insignificant issues of honor and propriety raised by the venality of the French court.

Later, during the Napoleonic wars, the contradictions between the goals of peace and commerce became more acute. In the years following the turn of the nineteenth century, American ideals and plans for foreign affairs based on economics failed the test. Attempts to maintain neutrality and neutral rights in trade amid the wars of the time led President Jefferson to close access to, or embargo, American trade. The results were catastrophic. Americans themselves were not willing to accept the interruption of foreign trade, for whatever reasons, and smuggled the Jeffersonian embargo of 1807–1809 into uselessness. When the Jefferson and Madison administrations attempted to play off the British and French against each other in the years of the Nonintercourse Act, wily European diplomats, especially Napoleon's foreign minister, the duc de Cadore, Jean Baptiste de Champagny, outsmarted the Americans and emphasized the weakness and consequent ineffectiveness of American economic diplomacy.

Finally, American economic coercions and maneuvers led to the almost disastrous War of 1812, an unnecessary conflict, since within weeks of its outbreak the British government rescinded the most offensive orders in council affecting American commerce with the Continent. But the people of the time, caught up in political and sectional quarrels and interests, apparently overlooked the flaws of design in foreign affairs. The War of 1812, which ended in 1814, did not prevent American statesmen from continuing to believe that peace rather than war was mankind's natural condition, and that the surest way to unnatural behavior (to war) was the politics of force.

EXPANSION AND POWER

Throughout the nineteenth century one notable American activity—continental expansion—regularly threatened to revive the power problem and to exacerbate disagreements over the relative merits of force and suasion in foreign affairs. Time and again Americans took advantage of opportunities for territorial expansion, but few such opportunities were without opposition from the established powers of the day. The United States had to face British opposition in the Old Northwest until the signing of Jay's Treaty in 1794. Within a generation there were the further complications of the Oregon dispute. Despite the jingoist cry of "Fifty-four forty or fight," the Oregon question was settled peacefully, but there remained contentions over the Canadian-American boundary, including Alaska, until 1903. French resistance to American expansion seemed to disappear with the Louisiana Purchase of 1803, but it reappeared in the diplomacy and maneuvering surrounding the annexation of Texas, the war with Mexico, and during the Civil War in the ill-fated imperium of Maximilian in Mexico. Spanish-American antagonism over expansion marked the era of the 1790s and of separatism in the early American Southwest, flared in connection with the disputed boundaries and the American annexations of East Florida and West Florida as well as over use of the Mississippi River, and culminated in contests for predominance in Cuba and the Philippines in the Spanish-American War (1898). The United States even managed to come into conflict with Russia in the matter of the Oregon boundary, which provided occasion for some of John Quincy Adams's most pointed démarches.

Expansionism also affected those without sufficient power to resist or negotiate its progress across the continent. For four centuries expansion was the central theme of European-Indian relations. Much of the devastation of the Indian peoples in colonial America can be attributed to disease. But their fate was also the result of how white Americans used their power in dealing with Indians. A succession of treaties attempted to reconcile the traditional cultural norms of hunting-gathering, often nomadic, communal peoples with the demands of an expanding agrarian, capitalist culture driven by an unprecedented immigration and population explosion. Twenty-five years before the American Revolution, Benjamin Franklin used demographic projections to prove the need for new lands in the west to support a population that doubled every twenty years. He also pointed out that such expansion would mean war with the Indians and their French allies—a price Franklin and others before and after him were willing to pay.

Other Americans wrestled with the "Indian problem." Thomas Jefferson considered these "noble savages" possible candidates for assimilation. Andrew Jackson rationalized removal of the so-called Civilized Tribes of the Southeast to Indian Territory beyond the Mississippi as a version of protective custody. The reservation system continued this "Great White Father" paternalism. On both sides of the debate over Indian policy, what were termed humanitarians and exterminationists shared social Darwinism ideas of white racial and cultural superiority and faith in the inevitaly of progress in the form of the economic development of the American frontier. The West, or frontier, was both a powerful myth in the American mind and in reality a colonial area to be exploited for its resources by the more developed East and investors from abroad. Indians, buffalo, the environment itself had to give way to this economic imperative wrapped in the myth of progress, prosperity, and "manifest destiny."

Often Americans regarded continental expansion as a matter of destiny and strength, the strength of righteousness. Because the United States was a progressive, moral, humane country, its extension to the Pacific Ocean was foreordained, proper, and inexorable. In contrast to the repressive Old World empires, theirs was an "empire of liberty." The end justified the means in this case, and most Americans believed that in the grand process of expansion, force was allowable and probably necessary. It was likewise necessary to counter the attempts of Old World governments to subdue other territories in the New World and reintroduce autocratic government and Machiavellian diplomacy into the hemisphere.

To a certain extent the enthusiastic expansion and protection of American interests by John Quincy Adams, James Monroe, James Polk, and the signers of the Ostend Manifesto (1854), which set forth American designs on the annexation of Cuba, were counterbalanced by the hesitations and objections of other prominent Americans. Some people doubted the wisdom and propriety of each expansion of national domain, especially beginning with the Louisiana Purchase. There were dissenters in each instance of armed conflict—for example, Henry David Thoreau's civil disobedience and jailing during the Mexican War. Expansionist secretaries of state such as William Seward were succeeded by more restrained and prudent men such as Hamilton Fish, who rejected some of the grand imperial designs toward the Caribbean and Mexico that his predecessor had elaborated. Despite internal disagreements and external power problems, by the end of the nineteenth century the process of continental expansion had resulted in an American "imperial democracy" that stretched from Atlantic to Pacific and included Puerto Rico, Hawaii, Guam, and the Philippines. That continental expanse and newly acquired overseas empire was bolstered by an economic power that rivaled and in many cases surpassed that of the Old World colonial empires. By virtually any measurement the United States had become a world power.

AMERICA AS A WORLD POWER

The era of American prominence in world politics, which began with the twentieth century, occasioned reconsideration of traditional attitudes regarding foreign entanglements and the use of force. From a foreign perspective, the United States was too powerful to ignore but too unpredictable to deal with satisfactorily. From the American viewpoint, global interests and capabilities made for uneasiness and confusion. The new circumstances of American foreign affairs seemed to require reevaluation of traditional American policies and portended new military necessities.

Americans found themselves caught up in new difficulties rather suddenly; they had not fully appreciated the problems that policies and developments of the last decades of the nineteenth century had brought. They had traded as they always had, vigorously and aggressively. They had expanded their boundaries, sought naval strength (beginning in the 1880s), and acquired a position unchallengeable in the hemisphere—but they had not anticipated the effects of such changes on their position beyond the hemisphere. They had hoped to exert a considerable influence on the nations of the world, but by example rather than by forcible instruction. American strength was meant to make the nation impervious to the caprice or malice of European governments and to enable it to vindicate rights and protect interests, but not to require U.S. participation in European political affairs.

Citizens of the United States took pride in the energy, growth, and strength of their nation. Only after they had acquired great power did they begin to consider the problems that national strength created. One idea was appealing: Could not the issue be resolved if the United States were to use force only in just causes, and thus make it the servant of morality? In such terms, Americans preferred to explain their "splendid little war" with Spain—a war, they said, to end Spanish tyranny and repression in Cuba, where the situation of the people had become intolerable. But the liberation of Cuba coincided with the "benevolent assimilation" of the Philippines. The brutal suppression of an insurrection by Filipinos who sought independence rather than assimilation was neither splendid nor little, and it sparked an anti-imperialist protest against what was termed an immoral, un-American abuse of power. The American anti-imperialists failed to alter U.S. counterinsurgency policy in the Philippines. But some of the issues they raised about the legitimacy of the use of force in pursuit of foreign relations objectives would arise again later in the century.

At the turn of the twentieth century, Theodore Roosevelt could confidently add his corollary to the Monroe Doctrine's assertion of the separation of the New World from the Old by proclaiming the right of the United States to wield "police power" in the hemisphere to correct either incompetence or wrongdoing. For Roosevelt and those who shared his vision of America's role in the world, righting wrongs in Latin America and elsewhere ultimately would be determined by American power.

Participation in World War I even more clearly demonstrated the determination to make power and force serve good ends. After two and half years of neutrality, during which he attempted to negotiate a "peace without victors," President Woodrow Wilson called upon Americans to embark on a crusade to make the world safe for democracy. In that war to end all wars, the United States was not content to defeat enemies but fought for principles embodying the liberal features of American diplomacy. So, at least, Wilson explained his conversion from opposing force in 1914–1916 to calling for force without stint in 1917.

★ ★ ★ ★
POLITICS AND POWER

Harry Truman, who as president presided over the creation of modern American foreign relations, once wryly observed that a statesman was merely a dead politician. He in turn defined a successful politician as someone who got other people to do what they should have done all along. From this perspective, politics is simply the process of getting people to do the right thing. But even under this seemingly benign formulation, politics involves power—the power to move people in a particular direction, toward a particular end. It begs the questions of who decides what direction, to what end, and what the right thing to do might be. In domestic politics the answers to such questions are often contested. The range of political discourse and debate is still broader in international relations. What to one party is obviously the proper or right course can be to another not only wrong but a threat to well-being or perhaps even survival. At the international level, politics and power, so obviously interrelated, are not so easily reconciled.

Statesmen and politicians have long wrestled with the problems of power—its acquisition, use, and sometimes abuse. Increasingly in world affairs, power emanates not only from states but also from nongovernmental organizations such as multinational corporations, economic communities, or cartels. By the end of the twentieth century, the process of globalization had become the focus of scholarship and public debate. Power, a constant in politics at all levels at all times, had taken on new forms and new meaning as the world and the United States, the preeminent superpower, entered the third millennium.

By the end of World War I, many Americans were no longer convinced that the United States could ensure that good intentions in the use of force would bring right results. Except for the defeat of the Central Powers, none of the things for which Americans had fought seemed to have been achieved. The keystone of Wilson's fourteen-point peace plan, the League of Nations, was rejected by the U.S. Senate as a result of a combination of partisan politics and Wilson's physical incapacity following a massive stroke. Lacking participation by the most important world power, what has been called the Versailles system of world politics was, in the view of some historians, fatally flawed from its beginning. Others have argued that the peace Wilson sought might have endured but for the actions of revisionist powers such as Germany, Italy, and Japan. The lessons of Versailles and the failure of the League of Nations were even less clear to those who guided American foreign relations between the world wars.

POWER AND RESPONSIBILITY

After World War I, debate in the United States over the use of force in pursuit of national goals continued. What has been misleadingly called a period of isolation did not witness an American withdrawal from world power, only from an active leadership role in world politics. Americans in the 1920s pointed to the perversity of war and the perversion of the peace to prove that power—power politics, the old politics of Europe—was still corrupt and corrupting. They did not refuse to recognize that their country was powerful, but they proposed a narrower definition of the national interest than that proposed by Wilson. They also advocated restraint in the use of force and a partial withdrawal, at least at the political and diplomatic level, from the complicated and uncontrollable world arena. In opposition, other Americans, imbued with what was described as Wilsonian or liberal idealism, held out the prospect of harmonious, just, lawful international relations, dependent on the determination of upright men and a policing of the international community by moral nations—forcibly, if necessary.

For the ensuing interwar period the polarization of opinion on the proper uses of American power defined the limits of the nation's diplomacy. Chastened by the experience of the world war, Americans were uncomfortable with the use of force and determined not to employ it except within the Western Hemisphere. Even there, American policy was noticeably uncertain; the days of repeated and prolonged military intervention slowly but surely came to an end. What emerged came to be known under Franklin Roosevelt as the Good Neighbor Policy, a shift from the use of military force to reliance on economic hegemony to lead hemispheric affairs in a direction consistent with U.S. national interests. But even earlier, in the 1920s, American foreign policy had turned once more to economics as an alternative to the politics of force; not to coercive economic diplomacy but to defensive diplomacy, the conservative economics of protection, sound money, and relatively equal treatment for all comers to the American marketplace. This was policy until the Great Depression overturned the conventional wisdom of economics and diplomacy and forced politicians to use untried and previously unimaginable expedients.

In one sense the limits on power imposed by divisions of opinion in the 1920s and 1930s proved a liability for policy and leadership, or so it seemed in retrospect. The same doubts about the uses of power and force that caused Americans to terminate interventions in Latin America later caused them to hesitate, equivocate, and delay too long in dealing with the aggressive European and Asian autocracies of the 1930s.

At the same time Adolf Hitler came to power in Germany, President Franklin D. Roosevelt, having learned the lesson of Woodrow Wilson's failure in forging too far ahead of public and congressional opinion, focused on anti-Depression New Deal policies as the international system forged at Versailles began to come apart in Asia and Europe. Having tacitly endorsed the popular policy of appeasement as late as the 1938 Munich Conference, Roosevelt aligned U.S. economic power with the anti-Axis Allies after the outbreak of war in 1939, declaring that America would act as the "arsenal of democracy." That policy of supplying both the British and later the Soviet Union with American-made arms and other matériel led by late 1941 to an undeclared naval war in the North Atlantic. In Asia and the Pacific, Roosevelt's increasingly determined opposition to Japanese expansion included a show of force in the form of forward basing of American naval and air power and ever-tightening economic sanctions aimed at forcing Japan into abandoning its imperial aims. In what was perhaps the first test of the lessons of Munich, Japan responded by attacking the U.S. Pacific fleet at Pearl Harbor. In the end, the American dilemma of whether and how to use its power finally was settled not by Americans but by the course of events—that is, by the power and politics of Europe and Asia.

AMERICA'S RISE TO GLOBALISM

In World War II, Americans realized they could not wish or will away the implications and complications of power. As one leader of Senate Republicans and a former critic of international commitments put it, after Pearl Harbor "isolationism was dead for any realist." Autocrats in Europe and Asia threatened U.S. security in a drastic revival of the power problem. Americans had to face both the necessity and the consequences of force and violence in international affairs. Even such an idealist as Secretary of State Cordell Hull was led to believe that only total victory based on unconditional surrender would bring total peace. The greatest debates in the United States in the late months of the war focused less on the iniquity of force than on the question of who was a friend and who an enemy.

At war's end some Americans tried to grasp a second chance to internationalize their power problem and the specter of force. They believed or hoped that international organization might provide a solution to the power problem and a way to avoid perpetually violent international politics through collective security and peacekeeping. At the same time, other Americans, less confident in the future of international politics, favored unilateralism and national security based on America's unparalleled economic and military power. They relied especially on the newfound power of the atomic bomb as the ultimate or absolute weapon. What Harry Truman called America's "sacred trust" would not be shared with the world or with the new international peacekeeping body until such time that Americans could be sure that there could be no abuse of this awesome power.

After the demonstrated weakness of the United Nations, which proved incapable of subordinating great-power conflicts of interest or of assuming responsibility for control of atomic technology and weapons, international idealism was supplanted in 1947 by a determined application of American power and force in every form and in virtually every forum. What was dubbed the Truman Doctrine committed American might to the containment of communism in whatever form, be it internal subversion or external aggression. However, in a larger sense, American leaders in the years following World War II redefined the idea of national security. The goal of this new postwar or Cold War policy was to establish and maintain a preponderance of American power throughout the world. This globalist approach to world affairs involved both military alliances such as the North Atlantic Treaty Organization (NATO) and massive economic programs such as the Marshall Plan. Although sometimes collective, these commitments were predicated on U.S. military and economic power. Looking back on this period, Truman's secretary of state, Dean Acheson, aptly described it as the "creation" of modern American foreign relations.

After World War II, Americans accommodated themselves to the possession and exercise of economic power and military force on an unprecedented scale and sought new answers to the perennial problems of power. The various forms of traditional unilateralism—nonentanglement, neutrality, isolationism—gave way to a new structure of American globalism. Most important, Americans became reconciled to the use of force to such an extent that they entered a new era of interventionism that, with the Cold War, resulted in a huge standing military establishment.

THE BURDENS AND LIMITS OF POWER

Unfortunately but predictably, new solutions to the old problems brought new problems that in some ways were more complicated than the old ones. The societies of the United States and most other nations prominent in world affairs had to shoulder the enormous costs of standing military forces and modernization of rapidly changing technology. In the inflationary 1970s those costs would mean unpleasant choices of priorities in both internal and external affairs.

In some cases, as in Korea, the use of military force, despite critics on both ends of the political spectrum, was supported by most Americans as justified and, if not conclusive, at least an effective application of American power in pursuit of the Cold War goal of containment of communism. In other cases, such as the war in Vietnam, the prolonged and seemingly ineffective use of force destroyed the Cold War consensus, divided the nation, and contributed to moral and political uncertainty. For many Americans the protracted and ultimately unsuccessful involvement in Vietnam destroyed the Cold War consensus that containment of communist influence justified paying any price and bearing any burden anywhere in the world. In the face of the uncensored image of war, many in the United States rejected the idea of using force to destroy what one was trying to save.

In the years following the Vietnam War, American public attitudes regarding the use of force in foreign relations reflected what was termed, usually by its detractors, the Vietnam syndrome, or neo-isolationism—a reluctance to commit American power and prestige abroad. In the face of public and congressional resistance, American foreign policymakers felt obliged to pursue power politics in a more circumspect and sometimes secret manner. A policy of covert or deniable applications of power, dating back at least to Dwight D. Eisenhower's "hidden hand" presidency of the 1950s, was revived in the 1980s under President Ronald Reagan. Through circuitous and even questionable routes, American support went to anti-Sandinista contras in Nicaragua and anti-Soviet rebels in Afghanistan.

The danger of direct military intervention was dramatically brought home in 1983 by the deaths at the hands of a terrorist bomber of 241 U.S. marines who had been dispatched to Lebanon to protect an airfield in the midst of renewed Arab-Israeli fighting. The U.S. invasion of the Caribbean island of Grenada a few days later was an easy military victory, but it had little foreign policy significance. Perceived threats by anti-American regimes such as the one in Grenada might be dealt with effectively by decisive and "surgical," or specifically targeted, military intervention. But terrorist violence frustrated attempts at retaliation at an elusive, often unknown enemy.

By the 1990s Americans had discovered that in some ways the resort to force was achieving less and less. The Cold War, which had cost trillions in military spending on both sides, ended not by military victory but as a result of the Soviet Union's political and economic collapse. The breakup of the Soviet empire appeared to have left the United States the victor by default. But the world's only remaining superpower still found that its power did not necessarily guarantee hegemony or control over world politics.

In the Gulf War of 1991, the single most massive application of U.S. military force in the post–Cold War era, the United States, in partnership with Arab and European allies, successfully expelled Iraqi forces from Kuwait. But that tactical military success did not translate into significant changes in the geopolitical power relationships in the region. At the time, President George H. W. Bush pointed to the stunning military victory and the successful coalition diplomacy as evidence that America had "kicked the Vietnam syndrome." Yet that same victorious commander in chief was voted out of the presidency the following year. Short-term military success—the effective use of force—did not necessarily mean political success either abroad or at home.

THE DIFFUSION OF POWER

At the close of the twentieth century the United States continued to commit its military power for humanitarian purposes, such as famine relief in Somalia, or as part of multilateral peacekeeping efforts, such as in the Balkans. Nonetheless, it seemed that the subtleties of power—influence, suasion, nonmilitary coercion—often played more important roles in the post–Cold War environment.

Ironically, as the utility of force seemed to decline, the significance of economic diplomacy seemed to be growing more important, although its role differed from what it had been in early American foreign affairs. In many cases this meant that the game of power politics would be played by relatively small countries that hitherto had not participated in what the great powers had always considered their private pastime. The members of the Organization of Petroleum Exporting Countries (OPEC)—not all of which were Arab countries—had by the 1970s begun to play a substantial role in world affairs. Despite remarks by Secretary of State Henry A. Kissinger in response to OPEC's 1973 oil embargo that force might be necessary to break the cartel's stranglehold over so much of the world's oil, the politics of force was not an effective course in the novel international circumstances.

This was particularly true in the case of economic competition by America's allies, such as Japan and the European Economic Community, or in relation to multinational corporations' growing power over national economies, particularly those of developing countries. In a post–Cold War atmosphere characterized by the diffusion of power, growing concerns about global environmental and health issues did not fit the established norms of international power politics. In this increasingly complex and challenging world order, there was the concurrently developing possibility that many small nations, and perhaps criminals and terrorist groups, might develop or acquire nuclear weapons.

In the face of such challenges, neither the hopes of a young nation nor the confidence of a strong one were sufficient to provide answers to the perennial problems of power. The only certainty was that the problems would endure, change form from time to time, and require new solutions. As it entered the new millennium, the United States would have to deal with the aspirations of newer and smaller nations from the position of an established power adjusting to the diffusion of power and the profusion of conflicting rights characteristic of the new world order. In such an environment American leadership and statesmanship would be tested. It was not inconceivable that one principle of early American diplomacy—mutual benefit, as proposed by Benjamin Franklin—might revive in importance along with the traditional virtues of caution, prudence, and modesty.

BIBLIOGRAPHY

Acheson, Dean. *Power and Diplomacy*. Cambridge, Mass., 1958. Truman's secretary of state treats the relation between sources of power and the problems of postwar American foreign affairs.

Aron, Raymond. *Peace and War: A Theory of International Relations*. New York, 1967. One of the most thoughtful examinations of the differences between politics of influence and politics of force.

———. *Imperial Republic: The United States and the World, 1945–1973*. Translated by Frank Jellinek. Englewood Cliffs, N.J., 1974.

Burns, Arthur Lee. *Of Powers and Their Politics: A Critique of Theoretical Approaches*. Englewood Cliffs, N.J., 1968. A survey of the contemporary status of ideas on the logic and nature of power relationships.

Cohen, Warren I., ed. *The Cambridge History of American Foreign Relations*. 4 vols. New York, 1993. The authors of each volume in this history provide a thorough and expert treatment of the development of American power in the world since 1776.

Craig, Gordon A., and Alexander L. George. *Force and States Craft: Diplomatic Problems of Our Time*. 3d ed. New York, 1995. This collection of essays and case studies includes a discussion of America's dilemma of power.

Kennan, George F. *American Diplomacy, 1900–1950*. Chicago, 1951. In this series of early Cold War lectures the "father" of the containment doctrine popularized the realist critique of Wilsonian idealism.

Kennedy, Paul M. *The Rise and Fall of the Great Powers: Economic Change and Military Conflict from 1500 to 2000*. New York, 1987. This sweeping overview gives global and comparative perspective on the acquisition and complications of world power.

Kissinger, Henry. *Diplomacy*. New York, 1994. A student and practitioner of balance-of-power politics surveys America's changing role in the new world order.

Leffler, Melvyn P. *A Preponderance of Power: National Security, the Truman Administration, and the Cold War*. Stanford, Calif., 1992. A detailed account of how U.S. leaders developed a global framework for national security after 1945.

Morgenthau, Hans Joachim. *In Defense of the National Interest: A Critical Examination of American Foreign Policy*. New York, 1951. Presents the views of the best known of the "realist" political scientists who suggest that states seek power for its own sake.

Morgenthau, Hans Joachim, and Kenneth W. Thompson. *Politics Among Nations: The Struggle for Power and Peace*. 6th ed. New York, 1985. Morgenthau develops his theoretical approach at length.

Nye, Joseph S., Jr. *Bound to Lead: The Changing Nature of American Power*. New York, 1990. Describes the challenges and limits of American power after World War II and the diffusion of power at the end of the Cold War.

Osgood, Robert Endicott. *Ideals and Self Interest in America's Foreign Relations: The Great Transformation of the Twentieth Century*. Chicago, 1953. Focuses on the realist versus idealist approaches to peace, internationalism, and the responsibilities of world power.

Prucha, Francis Paul. *The Great Father: The United States Government and the American Indian*. Abridged edition. Lincoln, Nebr., 1986. A thorough but very readable history of American Indian policy from 1776 to 1980.

Stannard, David E. *American Holocaust: The Conquest of the New World*. New York, 1992. An impassioned account of the destruction of the native peoples of the New World.

Van Alstyne, Richard Warner. *The Rising American Empire*. Chicago, 1960. An interpretive history that emphasizes uses of force and the theme of expansion in American foreign relations from Washington to Wilson.

See also COLLECTIVE SECURITY; CONTINENTAL EXPANSION; EMBARGOES AND SANCTIONS; GLOBALIZATION; INTERNATIONAL ORGANIZATION; POST–COLD WAR POLICY; RACE AND ETHNICITY.

PRESIDENTIAL ADVISERS

★ ★ ★ ★

Albert Bowman and Robert A. Divine

In his foreword to *Decision-Making in the White House* by Theodore C. Sorensen, President John F. Kennedy wrote:

> The American presidency is a formidable, exposed, and somewhat mysterious institution. It is formidable because it represents the point of ultimate decision in the American political system. It is exposed because decision cannot take place in a vacuum: the presidency is the center of the play of pressure, interest, and idea in the nation; and the presidential office is the vortex into which all the elements of national decision are irresistibly drawn. And it is mysterious because the essence of ultimate decision remains impenetrable to the observer—often, indeed, to the decider himself.

After more than two centuries of experience, there is no longer any doubt concerning the formidability of the presidency. The spare and general presidential powers conferred by the Constitution have evolved and developed in proportion to the phenomenal growth of the nation, although until recently at a much slower rate. A list of the powers included in Article II of the Constitution contains the barest hint of presidential power and authority today: the vesting in the president of the executive power of government, his designation as commander in chief of the military forces of the United States, the power to make treaties and to appoint ambassadors and other public officers—powers exercised in both cases in partnership with the Senate of the United States, and the authority to receive ambassadors and other public ministers. Perhaps the most interesting of the president's constitutional powers, since it touches on the mysterious process of decision making, is this: "he may require the Opinion, in writing, of the principal Officer in each of the executive Departments."

The Constitution created no executive departments. That was left to the Congress, which on 27 July 1789 created the Department of Foreign Affairs (later changed to Department of State). It was headed by a secretary who was to conduct its business "in such manner as the president of the United States shall, from time to time, order or instruct."

It was hardly to be expected, however, that so formal a line of authority would be restrictive; and every president has to some degree relied on the counsel of advisers outside of and in addition to the Department of State. Indeed, in view of "the play of pressure, interest, and idea in the nation," an important element in arriving at wise presidential decisions may well lie in the diversity and quantity of opinions or, as they are now referred to, options among which to select. Limits are indispensable, of course, and the quality of the opinions, as well as the president's capacity to discriminate, are of the highest importance.

Mystery is inherent in the presidency, and it may seem paradoxical that the office is at the same time the most exposed one in the land. From George Washington, reluctant first president and probably the only one who did not aspire to the office with some degree of cupidity, to Richard Nixon, perhaps at the opposite extreme, the presidency of the United States has usually been described as a lonely eminence. Even those presidents who relished the power and majesty of the office managed to convey a sense of the solitary nature of the presidential decision-making process.

But the ultimate solitude of the presidency is not mysterious; the singular and final responsibility of the president is generally visible. The mystery, the impenetrability, lies in the sources of presidential decision, which, as Kennedy noted, may be unfathomable even by the president himself. If the president cannot always know how he decides, how can even the closest observer know? After declining a request to rate the performance of previous presidents, Kennedy exclaimed to Arthur M. Schlesinger, Jr., then serving as a White House special assistant: "How the hell can you tell? Only the president himself can know what his real pressures and his real alternatives are. If you don't know that, how can you judge performance?"

Presidents have the further advantage of making their decisions in private. Unlike Congress and the judiciary who conduct their business, for the most part, in public, the president cannot only keep the decision-making process secret, but he can keep the records sealed even after leaving office. A president may publicly state one thing while secretly planning another, he may say one thing in public and another in private, and he may inexplicably—even to his advisers—change his mind. But even more difficult for the student of presidential decision making is the deliberate obscuring of presidential intentions from everyone. Intimates of Franklin D. Roosevelt have been unanimous in attesting to his delight in mystifying even his closest lieutenants and in setting them at cross-purposes. Schlesinger, a Roosevelt biographer, assessed the Rooseveltian technique thus: "Once the opportunity for decision came safely into his orbit, the actual process of deciding was involved and inscrutable."

However mysterious and inscrutable the processes of presidential decision, there can be no doubt that every president has recognized the need of advice and counsel, if not consent. Nor can there be any doubt concerning at least two aspects of the presidential use of advisers: in addition to the formal, almost cryptic constitutional provision relating to "principal Officers of executive Departments," presidents have always solicited or received counsel from both public and private sources, and there has been an evolutionary growth in the number and variety of presidential advisers.

THE FOUNDERS

Understandably and characteristically, George Washington began his presidency by following the letter of the Constitution as closely as he could. Not only had he presided over the debates in the Constitutional Convention in 1787, but he was keenly aware that his every act as the first president of the United States would tend to set a precedent.

The first potential foreign crisis of Washington's administration arose in 1790, when war between Great Britain and Spain appeared to be imminent over remote Nootka Sound on the northwest coast of America. Anticipating a British request to move troops through American territory to attack Spanish Louisiana, Washington requested written opinions on a possible answer from the three heads of departments—Thomas Jefferson, secretary of state; Alexander Hamilton, secretary of the Treasury; and Henry Knox, secretary of war—and of Attorney General Edmund Randolph and Vice President John Adams. Although the matter related most directly to the duties of the secretary of state, it obviously had implications much broader than simply diplomatic, and Washington evidently wanted to widen his range of advice as much as was constitutionally possible. On later questions of significant national or constitutional import, he adhered to much the same procedure.

On matters of direct personal concern, however, Washington turned to old and trusted friends for advice. He had decided by the spring of 1792 that he would retire from public life. As he had so often done, he wrote to a fellow Virginian, James Madison, for help: "namely, to think of the proper time, and the best mode of announcing the intention; and that you would prepare the latter." Despite his long collaboration with Madison, his affectionate regard for Randolph, and his esteem for Jefferson, Washington's foreign policy was nevertheless increasingly directed by Hamilton. Looking upon himself as a kind of prime minister in addition to being finance minister, after the British tradition that frequently combined the two roles, Hamilton secretly conducted his own foreign policy and consistently opposed the secretary of state in meetings of Washington's official advisers. When Washington made his firm decision to retire at the end of his second term as president, he turned to Hamilton for advice on both the method and the substance of his farewell to public service.

Washington was, according to James David Barber's model, a "passive-negative" type, a president who sought stability as the precondition to establishing the legitimacy of the American experiment in self-government, so it was natural that he should resist innovation and generally choose the path of least resistance. In a period of intense foreign and domestic turmoil, such a president would naturally be drawn to the adviser whose counsel seemed most likely to promise tranquillity at home and safety abroad. That meant validating the power of the central government over its citizens while bowing to superior force in the conduct of foreign relations. Specifically, it meant a succession of centralizing fiscal and economic measures and a persistent tilting toward Britain in its war against revolutionary France. Hamilton's pro-British foreign policy, culminating in Jay's Treaty of 1794, could easily have been fashioned in London. In fact, Hamilton has been described as the effective minister of the British government to the American, although Washington never knew how intimate and cooperative were Hamilton's relations with the nominal representatives of George III.

By the end of Washington's second term, all dissenters to Hamiltonian policy had been purged and Hamilton himself had left office. But President John Adams, to his later undoing, kept the department heads he had inherited from Washington, most of them unswervingly loyal to Hamilton. The latter, who once wrote that he had not "lost my taste for a little politics," continued to run the government from his New York law office. Adams only later, in the midst of an undeclared war with France, realized that the advice he received from his subordinate officers originated with his arch rival. Perhaps Hamilton had this extension of his influence over the Adams administration in mind when, after Washington's death, he described their relationship: "he was an *Aegis very essential to me*" (Hamilton's emphasis).

After he had removed the Hamiltonian influence over his administration, Adams was able to end the Quasi-War with France. His son John Quincy Adams had recently been sent as minister to Berlin and, with the treachery of Secretary of State Timothy Pickering in mind, the president told his son to "write freely" to him but "cautiously to the office of State." It was the advice of John Quincy Adams that convinced the president that France sincerely wanted peace and led him to extricate the United States from a war only the Hamiltonian extremists wanted.

John Adams yielded to no one when it came to knowledge of foreign affairs, although until his break with the war faction in his Federalist Party, he had allowed himself to be influenced by the Hamiltonians in his cabinet and in the Senate. Jefferson, however, after the "revolution of 1800," was able to make a fresh start, with a cabinet of his own choosing and Democratic-Republican majorities in both houses of Congress. No American, save perhaps Benjamin Franklin, had had a richer diplomatic experience than the new president, and probably no president ever had a secretary of state who was closer, both personally and intellectually, than James Madison was to Jeffer-

son. The advice of his brilliant secretary of the Treasury, Albert Gallatin, was valuable to Jefferson, but the efficiency and subtlety with which Jefferson and Madison synchronized their efforts in pursuit of American foreign policy objectives probably have never been matched.

THE NINETEENTH-CENTURY EXPERIENCE

Two periods of intense involvement in foreign affairs have marked the history of the United States: the nation-forming period, when the new Republic sought to register its independence while the world was being shaken by the mortal conflict of the great powers of the time, France and Great Britain; and the period beginning with World War II, when the United States itself became the world's greatest power. A more striking contrast between two eras could scarcely be imagined, though the simple substitution of the roles of all the powers involved is a start.

In addition to the irrelevance of affairs outside of North America to the growth of the United States during the nineteenth century, those who would probe the sources of national action are faced with another problem: how to detect and analyze possible connections between domestic influences and foreign policy actions. It is probably safe to say of this period, however, that presidents generally felt little need of advice on foreign affairs except from their secretaries of state, and sometimes not even from them.

Some presidents, such as James Madison, acted as their own foreign ministers. Deprived by Senate hostility of his first choice for secretary of state, the able Albert Gallatin, Madison was forced to appoint the incompetent Robert Smith and for a time even found it necessary to rewrite Smith's dispatches. Historians still debate the influence on Madison in 1812 of such war hawks as Henry Clay, John C. Calhoun, and Felix Grundy; but Madison's most perceptive and thorough biographer, Irving Brant, believes that the president reached his own decisions.

President James Monroe, who had been secretary of state under Madison, relied almost exclusively on Secretary of State John Quincy Adams, except for the president's questions to his Virginia friends and predecessors, Jefferson and Madison, during the formulation of what became the Monroe Doctrine. Indeed, Adams, generally recognized as the greatest of all American secretaries of state, was responsible for the two major foreign policy achievements of the Monroe administration. It was Adams who negotiated the Transcontinental Treaty of 1819 (Adams-Onís Treaty) by which the United States not only acquired Florida but also laid claim to the Oregon territory. And it was Adams who persuaded the president and the cabinet to reject a British offer and instead have the United States alone declare itself the protector of the New World against European interference, and thus was responsible for the doctrine that bore Monroe's name.

President James K. Polk evidently had imbibed the elixir of "manifest destiny" long before John O'Sullivan coined the phrase in an editorial in the *Democratic Review* (1845). The idea of westward expansion was at least as American as the Declaration of Independence—it had been a fact since 1607—but the war with Mexico to advance it was mostly the president's idea. The accusation "Mr. Polk's war" was undoubtedly accurate.

The Civil War marked an end and a beginning to many things in America, but neither an end nor a beginning to expansionism. William H. Seward, secretary of state under Abraham Lincoln and Andrew Johnson, had in the 1840s believed that "our population is destined to roll its resistless waves to the icy barriers of the north, and to encounter oriental civilization on the shores of the Pacific." Thus he welcomed the suggestion that Russia might be willing to sell Alaska. Presented with an opportunity to expand to "the icy barriers of the north," ostensibly to guarantee Alaskan fishing rights and to repay Russian Unionist sympathy during the war, Seward rushed through a treaty to purchase Alaska in 1867.

THE RISE TO WORLD POWER

In the American rise to world power, which began in the 1890s, one man who was neither president nor secretary of state played a crucial role. Captain Alfred Thayer Mahan, naval strategist and historian, provided the theoretical framework for the extension of American power into the Pacific as the key to national security and world peace. If Seward can be called the precursor of American imperialism, then Mahan was its prophet. Mahan's influence upon American foreign policy is easy to demonstrate because he was so visible. His first book, *The Influence of Sea Power Upon History, 1660–1783,* achieved an instant success when it was published in 1890, and it had an

effect on the Anglo-American world comparable with Charles Darwin's *Origin of Species* a generation earlier. A rising group of dynamic, nationalistic American leaders pondered Mahan and became his fervent disciples.

Theodore Roosevelt brought to the presidency a coherent program for the expansion of American power. The ideas of Mahan formed Roosevelt's frame of reference in almost all his discussions of foreign policy: a large navy that could control the sea-lanes; the acquisition of naval bases and coaling stations, and possibly colonies; the construction of an isthmian canal to connect the Atlantic and Pacific oceans by water, with bases to guard the approaches on either side; and the development of a large merchant marine to expand American foreign trade. By tireless propaganda (Roosevelt described the presidency as "a bully pulpit"), cajolery of Congress, and often by breathtaking expansion of presidential powers, Roosevelt was able to realize Mahan's program. Although it was not as large as he wished, he built the "Great White Fleet" and sent it around the world. He acquired naval bases in Cuba and the Philippines, and he carried out what Secretary of State Elihu Root described as the rape of Colombia in order to build the Panama Canal.

Personally much closer to Roosevelt was Senator Henry Cabot Lodge of Massachusetts who was also a disciple of Mahan. Lodge thought as Roosevelt did and consistently supported him in his imperialistic initiatives. Other notable members of Roosevelt's circle of intimates were the brothers Brooks and Henry Adams, grandsons and great-grandsons of the Massachusetts presidents. They were historians, as was the president himself, and they shared his expansionist views without, however, possessing his ebullient optimism.

If foreign policy had always been an unpleasant distraction to American government officials, it was so no longer. The administrations of Theodore Roosevelt were the turning point, and the hopes of Mahan, Lodge, the Adamses, and Roosevelt himself for the growth of American power and influence were realized. The War with Spain, which Roosevelt and his friends had promoted so ardently, and World War I, even more so, thrust the United States into a commanding world position.

WILSON AND COLONEL HOUSE

Ironically, it was not Theodore Roosevelt but rather Woodrow Wilson who presided over this breakthrough. Wilson brought to the White House not only a total lack of experience in foreign affairs but also a disinterest of similar proportion. He had been untouched by the muscular doctrines of Mahan, and he might have been content to establish his "New Freedom" only in America if it had not been for World War I. Wilson's response to that challenge contrasted sharply with the aggressive Rooseveltian style, giving point to John F. Kennedy's remark, "to govern . . . is to choose."

Presidents choose their advisers and weigh the advice they receive. Probably more than any president before him, Wilson focused his confidence on one adviser, "Colonel" Edward M. House, a Texan whose only title was friend of the president. House and Wilson first met late in 1911, when the former was shopping for a Democratic presidential candidate he could support. They hit it off instantly, and House managed Wilson's 1912 campaign. Thenceforth, he was Wilson's alter ego. His New York City apartment and his summer home in Magnolia, Massachusetts, were both connected by direct telephone lines to the president's study in the White House. Once, when asked whether House accurately reflected his thinking, Wilson replied: "Mr. House is my second personality. He is my independent self. His thoughts and mine are one." House was the outstanding example of the species of presidential advisers whom Patrick Anderson called "distinguished outsiders."

Wilson and House had extraordinarily complementary personalities. Both were extremely ambitious, but Wilson reveled in the limelight while House preferred the shadows. Wilson's style was rhetorical, and he was at his best in public exhortation. House, on the other hand, liked to work behind the scenes; he once told an interviewer: "I do not like to make speeches. I abhor routine. I prefer the vicarious thrill which comes to me through others. . . . I want to be a myth." Wilson saw this as selflessness: "What I like about House," he told Secretary of the Navy Josephus Daniels, "is that he is the most self-effacing man that ever lived. All he wants to do is serve the common cause and to help me and others."

It was House who, at the outbreak of war in Europe, tried to turn Wilson's attention to foreign affairs, arguing that the president's leadership would offer a unique opportunity to effect a revolution in international morals. House wanted Wilson to assume the mediator's role in the war: "the world expects you to play the big part in this tragedy—and so indeed you will, for God has given you the power to see things as they are."

Wilson sent House to Europe early in 1915 to sound out the leaders of the warring powers on the possibilities of a negotiated peace. That mission was unproductive but, with the end of the war in sight, in October 1918, House returned to Europe to obtain Allied acceptance of Wilson's peace program. He wrote in his diary: "I am going on one of the most important missions anyone ever undertook, and yet there is no word of direction, advice or discussion between us." Wilson had simply said: "I have not given you any instructions because I feel you will know what to do." It was Wilson and House who, on the morning of 5 January 1918, hammered out the Fourteen Points. They had the work of the Inquiry to assist them, a mountain of maps and special studies drawn up by the 150-man team of experts House had established to do the research for Wilson's reordering of Europe.

Franklin D. Roosevelt's rule that "an adviser should have a passion for anonymity" has special relevance to the break that eventually ended the Wilson-House collaboration. Wilson wanted agreement, support, and of course loyalty from his confidants; and House supplied all of these, even while sometimes recording criticism of the president in his diary. When asked for advice, House wrote early in 1918, "I nearly always praise at first in order to strengthen the president's confidence in himself which, strangely enough, is often lacking." Between the president's triumphal visit to Europe late in 1918 and his return in early 1919, most of the bloom had faded from Wilson's peace plans as nationalistic interests of the Allies asserted themselves.

As Wilson's "second personality," House fought for the Fourteen Points but realized that compromise was inevitable; he got along better with the Allied statesmen than had Wilson, and he increasingly deplored Wilson's mistakes and believed he himself could have avoided them. The attention showered on him during the president's absence produced a new and overpowering desire to "come into his own." This was probably the crucial factor in the president's withdrawal of affection from House and the end to consulting him. In the final stages of the peacemaking, Wilson consulted no one.

Colonel House had beguiled Wilson and encouraged him in the intense moral commitment that became an obsession. Wilson had depended too much on House, and then not enough; ultimately he was isolated in the destructive rigidity that defeated, and then destroyed, him.

FDR AND HARRY HOPKINS

No other foreign policy adviser would exercise House's almost exclusive influence over presidential decision making until Henry Kissinger, save perhaps Franklin D. Roosevelt's Harry Hopkins. In some ways, Hopkins's relationship to Roosevelt resembled that of House to Wilson, whom Roosevelt had served as a rather free-floating assistant secretary of the navy. By 1941, as Hopkins's biographer Robert E. Sherwood explained it: "The extraordinary fact was that the second most important individual in the United States government . . . had no legitimate official position nor even any desk of his own except a card table in his bedroom. However, the bedroom was in the White House." To the recently defeated Republican candidate, Wendell Willkie, who had asked why the president kept so close to him a man widely distrusted and resented, Roosevelt replied: "I can understand that you wonder why I need that half man around me. But someday you may well be sitting here where I am now as president of the United States. And when you are, you'll be looking through that door over there and knowing that practically everybody who walks through it wants something out of you. You'll learn what a lonely job this is, and you'll discover the need for somebody like Harry Hopkins who asks for nothing except to serve you."

During his unprecedented three-plus terms as president, of course, Roosevelt had hundreds of advisers. But none wielded more than a transitory and peripheral influence on foreign policy, while Hopkins's brilliant talent for getting things done was exercised with authority throughout the government and the coalition against Germany and Japan. Sherwood described Hopkins's service thus: "Hopkins made it his job, he made it his religion, to find out just what it was that Roosevelt really wanted and then to see to it that neither hell nor high water, nor even possible vacillations by Roosevelt himself, blocked its achievement."

But Hopkins was not without convictions of his own, although they usually coincided with those of the president. Eleanor Roosevelt once wrote that Hopkins "gave his opinions honestly, but because Franklin did not like opposition too well—as who does—he frequently agreed with him regardless of his own opinion, or tried to per-

suade him in indirect ways." But Hopkins could intervene directly. Once, when Roosevelt was unable to join Winston Churchill and Joseph Stalin at a conference because of the 1944 election, he was about to send Churchill a cable implying that the prime minister could speak for him. Hopkins ordered the cable to be held and rushed to get Roosevelt to cancel it, which Roosevelt did. Hopkins had the respect of Stalin, who spoke to him with "a frankness unparalleled in my knowledge in recent Soviet history," according to the American ambassador to Moscow, Averell Harriman, and the respect and deep affection of Churchill, who dubbed him "Lord Root of the Matter" and talked feelingly to Sherwood of "the great heart that is within that frail frame." Hopkins successfully supported Churchill in persuading Roosevelt that France had to share in the postwar occupation of Germany, and he often toned down the president's communications with the haughty General Charles de Gaulle.

Roosevelt and Hopkins last saw each other after the Yalta Conference, when Hopkins, too ill to return home by ship with the president, flew back to enter the Mayo Clinic, where he was still hospitalized when Roosevelt died. He returned to Washington to brief the new president, Harry Truman, who later recalled that "I hoped that he would continue with me in the same role he had played with my predecessor." Hopkins undertook one more mission to Moscow and succeeded in obtaining Russian concessions that opened the way to the United Nations founding conference at San Francisco, but he was too sick to continue. Six months later he was dead, leaving behind another fascinating historical "if": How differently would subsequent Soviet-American relations have developed if Hopkins could have fulfilled the wish of President Truman?

CREATION OF THE NATIONAL SECURITY COUNCIL

Notwithstanding the preeminence of Harry Hopkins during the last years of the Roosevelt administration, far-reaching changes were in the making. During World War II, Roosevelt accelerated one developing pattern, the bypassing of the secretary of state and his department, and established another, what the veteran diplomat Charles Yost considered "an even more unfortunate precedent . . . the persistent and intimate involvement of the military in foreign-policy decision making."

Another development of the Roosevelt years was the beginning of the growth of a large bureaucracy. However, since Roosevelt had an improvised and very personal administrative style, and there was no rationalization by statute, his personal assistants were scattered throughout the government. Truman introduced a significant degree of order, albeit with a large increase in the size of the White House staff. Moreover, under Truman the policymaking process was institutionalized through the creation of agencies responsible to the president. The National Security Act of 1947 created the Department of Defense and established the National Security Council (NSC) to serve as a top-level forum for thrashing out policy alternatives for the president's decision. An important corollary of the NSC was that it was provided with a staff, thus potentially giving the president his own mini Department of State.

Truman's belief in orderly administrative methods included a belief in a strong cabinet. He once said: "I propose to get Cabinet officers I can depend on and have them run their affairs," and as a result his White House staff was singularly weak. Secretaries of State George Marshall and Dean Acheson were the principal architects of Truman's foreign policy, with Defense Secretary James Forrestal at times playing a significant role. But the star of the Truman White House, Clark Clifford, made a mark because of the confidence Truman placed in him. Clifford generally reinforced with the president the views of such activist department officers as Acheson, Forrestal, and Undersecretary of State Robert Lovett, with one notable exception. In May 1948, Truman followed Clifford's advice to recognize the new State of Israel over the objections of George Marshall and the Department of State.

As principal speechwriter, Clifford drafted the address enunciating the Truman Doctrine. George F. Kennan, then counselor of the United States embassy in Moscow, is usually credited with originating the doctrine of containment in his famous "long telegram" from Moscow, later published in *Foreign Affairs* under the title "The Sources of Soviet Conduct." Truman read the message and was impressed, but then he asked Clifford to prepare a memorandum on United States–Soviet relations. After talks with Marshall, Acheson, Forrestal, Lovett, and others, Clifford presented to Truman in September 1946 a memorandum differing from Kennan's chiefly in its military emphasis. "The language of military power

is the only language which disciples of power politics understand," Clifford wrote. "The United States must use that language in order that Soviet leaders will realize that our government is determined to uphold the interests of its citizens and the rights of small nations." Kennan had stressed political and economic measures to contain Soviet expansionism and in later years, notably in his *Memoirs,* repeatedly deplored the military interpretation placed on his thesis.

Clifford resigned at the beginning of 1950 and later became a "distinguished outsider," advising Presidents John F. Kennedy and Lyndon B. Johnson, who in the last months of his presidency drafted him to be secretary of defense. Ironically, it was the man who had helped to militarize the American posture vis-à-vis the Soviet Union in 1946 who helped persuade President Johnson to end the bombing and seek a negotiated peace in Vietnam in 1968.

THE EISENHOWER AND KENNEDY YEARS

President Dwight D. Eisenhower brought to the White House an unprecedented experience with the military staff system and a settled conviction that it was the only sensible and efficient way to run the government. The White House was therefore reorganized to resemble a military table of organization: the assistant to the president became the chief of staff, and other positions were established under him to systematize the flow of paperwork to and from the White House. Like Truman, Eisenhower believed that cabinet officers should run their departments, and he discouraged them from bringing their problems to the White House.

Like his successors Kennedy and Nixon, Eisenhower was most interested in foreign affairs. Eisenhower's passion for organization was exercised most closely in an attempt to perfect foreign policy decision making through formalizing and expanding the National Security Council. He converted the NSC staff into a planning board under a special assistant for national security affairs, with responsibility for preparing policy papers and coordinating them among interested government departments and agencies for NSC consideration. The Operations Coordinating Board was established to see that NSC decisions were carried out.

Despite this formal machinery, Eisenhower relied heavily on key advisers in deciding what policies to implement. While Secretary of State

John Foster Dulles played an important role as the chief spokesman and negotiator for Eisenhower, the president gathered advice and counsel from such individuals as disarmament adviser Harold Stassen, psychological warfare advocate C. D. Jackson, Atomic Energy Commission Chairman Lewis Strauss, UN Ambassador Henry Cabot Lodge, and, after the launch of *Sputnik,* presidential science advisers James Killian and George Kistiakowsky. As a result, Eisenhower's foreign policy was never as rigid as the organizational charts suggested but instead included such innovations as Atoms for Peace, "open skies," and an expanded and generous foreign aid program.

Under John F. Kennedy, the elaborate national security structure of the Eisenhower years gave way to a more modest and informal foreign policy apparatus. Distrusting bureaucracy, and disappointed in Dean Rusk, his choice as secretary of state, the president preferred to deal directly with desk officers in the Department of State who had operational responsibility for specific foreign policy issues. Kennedy did away with the cumbersome Operations Coordinating Board and relied instead on his special assistant for national security affairs, McGeorge Bundy, a former Harvard dean. Bundy assembled a small group of academic experts to staff the scaled-down NSC in the basement of the White House, where they attempted to reconcile the conflicting foreign policy recommendations of the Pentagon and the Department of State.

Several others on the White House staff had regular access to the president, among them Theodore Sorensen, special counsel, chief speech writer, and long Kennedy's closest aide; scientific adviser Jerome Weisner; and special military representative General Maxwell Taylor, former army chief of staff, whose advocacy of a "flexible response" defense strategy in opposition to the Eisenhower-Dulles "massive retaliation" doctrine suited the activist approach of the New Frontier. Kennedy also placed great reliance on Secretary of Defense Robert McNamara, who became a sort of "supersecretary." But as the Cuban missile crisis of 1962 proved, Kennedy's most trusted and valued adviser was always his brother Robert, the attorney general.

JOHNSON AND THE TUESDAY LUNCH

Suddenly thrust into the presidency by the assassination of John Kennedy, Lyndon Johnson did what other "accidental" presidents had done under similar circumstances: he promised to continue unchanged the policies of his predecessor. Johnson also retained the Kennedy staff and, in general, the loose Kennedy system. As a formerly close aide, Bill Moyers, noted after he had left the White House, Johnson had regarded the National Security Council as "not a live institution, not suited to precise debate for the sake of decision." Johnson much preferred to "call in a handful of top advisers, confidants, close friends." Johnson also tried to emphasize the foreign policy leadership of the secretary of state and was persuaded to create a system of interdepartmental committees to promote this. Johnson leaned heavily on Secretary of State Rusk, but the system was less than successful. Rusk made little use of it and Johnson came to rely, as Kennedy had, on Bundy and his NSC staff as well as on Secretary of Defense McNamara.

When Bundy left the White House staff for the presidency of the Ford Foundation in 1966, he was succeeded by Walt W. Rostow, formerly his deputy and then chief of the Policy Planning Staff in the Department of State, who had been a professor of economic history at the Massachusetts Institute of Technology. The change was significant. Rostow had written extensively on American foreign policy, notably a book entitled *The United States in the World Arena*. As that title suggested, Rostow thought in terms of broad historical frameworks; he was a theoretician who from beginning to end saw American involvement in Vietnam as essential to the nation's world preeminence. Along with General Maxwell D. Taylor, who later changed his mind, Rostow had urged Kennedy in 1961 to bomb the Vietnamese insurgents and Rostow's advice to Johnson was always slanted toward escalation.

Like Wilson after 1914 and Roosevelt after the fall of France in 1940, Johnson became totally absorbed in a foreign war after the decision to escalate in 1965. Increasingly, his circle of advisers contracted, as the president immersed himself in the details of the Vietnam conflict and tolerated dissent less and less. Johnson continued to rely, however, on a small group of friends outside the White House, often speaking to them at length on the telephone or meeting with them individually and off the record. His intimates included Senator Richard Russell of Georgia, Supreme Court Justice Abe Fortas, and Clark Clifford, who replaced McNamara as secretary of defense in early 1968. On Vietnam, Johnson also relied on the advice of a group of distinguished former government officials known as the Wise Men, who included Dean Acheson, Henry Cabot Lodge, and, by 1968, McGeorge Bundy. Initially strong supporters of the Vietnam War, the Wise Men had a change of heart after the Tet offensive and helped persuade Johnson to seek peace with Hanoi in March 1968.

Early in 1965, Johnson instituted the "Tuesday lunch," which for the next four years represented the focal point of foreign policymaking. While Vietnam came to dominate the agenda, topics ranged across the globe, from the Dominican intervention in 1965 to the Six Day War in 1967. The initial grouping of Dean Rusk, Robert McNamara, and McGeorge Bundy gradually expanded to include the chairman of the Joint Chiefs of Staff, Earle Wheeler, CIA Director Richard Helms, and Johnson's press secretary, first Bill Moyers, later George Christian. Johnson kept the proceedings informal to encourage give-and-take, but eventually Deputy Press Secretary Tom Johnson was added to keep a record of major points.

The Tuesday lunch helped the president hear a variety of views on important foreign policy issues. "They were invaluable sessions," Rusk claimed, "because we all could be confident that everyone around the table would keep his mouth shut and wouldn't be running off to Georgetown cocktail parties and talking about it." Others, however, contended that the sessions were too disorganized and rambling, rarely leading to thoughtful decisions. The Tuesday lunch, however, was never intended to be a decision-making body. As H. W. Brands points out in *The Wages of Globalism,* Johnson used it as "a forum for receiving information and opinions. Sometimes he announced decisions at the Tuesday lunch. More often he took the information and opinions back to his private quarters, where he compared them with intelligence obtained from his night reading and from his telephoning to Fortas, Clifford, and who knew who else, and only then gave his verdict."

THE KISSINGER YEARS

In April 1975 President Gerald Ford was asked whether he received advice on foreign policy from anyone besides Secretary of State Henry Kissinger. He replied that he was advised by the National Security Council, where decisions were made, but added that he met with Kissinger for an hour each day "on day-to-day problems." Ford's invocation of the NSC was ritualistic—there was presumed

to be something reassuring to the public mind about it—and his comment was also circular, for to a hitherto unimaginable degree Kissinger was the NSC. The former Harvard professor had been chosen by president-elect Richard Nixon in 1968 to be his assistant for national security affairs. By September 1973, Kissinger so dominated foreign policy, which he had made his own, that he had won a Nobel Peace Prize (for negotiating an end to American involvement in Vietnam) and senatorial confirmation as secretary of state by an overwhelming vote. Significantly, Kissinger retained the title of assistant to the president; that was still the source of a power greater than that wielded by most other presidential advisers or even secretaries of state in American history.

During the Nixon years, it was almost always impossible to determine whether Nixon or Kissinger made foreign policy decisions, and commentators became accustomed to writing of "Nixon-Kissinger" policies. The judgment that that reflects is probably correct. The president's unlimited personal confidence in Kissinger apparently was grounded in an identity and a congeniality of their respective views of the world and of the role of the United States in it. The two men favored similar operating styles: a driving, essentially amoral stance in which the end justified the means and results were what counted, and a secretive, almost conspiratorial approach that delighted in dramatic surprises. Neither Nixon, who had built a political career on hard-line anticommunism, nor Kissinger, whose writings of a decade and a half had accepted the Cold War stereotypes, was inhibited from engineering new approaches—détente—to the Soviet Union and the People's Republic of China. The secrecy and then the carefully staged theatrics of the Nixon visit to China represented the epitome of Nixon-Kissinger collaboration.

Kissinger was Nixon's resident philosopher, master planner, and personal executor of foreign policy. He provided Nixon with a coherent theory of international relations that postulated the maintenance of a balance-of-power equilibrium constantly adjusted to minimize friction. The principal problem was that it was initially impossible for "revolutionary" and status quo powers to negotiate: hence the necessity for painstaking planning to reduce international insecurity and create a "legitimate" world order. A supremely self-confident perfectionist, Kissinger believed that only he had the necessary conceptual expertise and skill to manage the slow process of accommodation.

Kissinger's power depended not only on his unique relationship with the president but also on the bureaucratic machinery he created and controlled. The staff Bundy assembled in 1961 had grown steadily in size, but by 1971 Kissinger's NSC staff was three times the size of Rostow's, with more than fifty professionals and one hundred clerical employees. In addition, under Kissinger's chairmanship there was a proliferation of new groups at the undersecretary and director levels, groups that exercised operational control over every aspect of national security policy, including the most comprehensive one of all, the Defense Program Review Committee, created to review "major defense, fiscal, policy and program issues in terms of their strategic, diplomatic, political, and economic implications." When Kissinger became secretary of state, therefore, he merely acquired the added prestige of the title and direct authority over the vast Department of State bureaucracy. Little else changed, except that with the Watergate scandal Kissinger seemed to personify whatever legitimacy the sinking Nixon administration could claim.

In the post-Vietnam era much of the Kissinger structure of international relationships appeared to be coming unstuck. A coalition of liberal Democrats and conservative Republicans in Congress passed the Jackson-Vanik Amendment in 1973, which stymied the policy of détente by making the legal emigration of Jews a precondition for liberalizing American trade with the Soviet Union. In late 1975, growing opposition to détente from conservative Republicans led President Ford to strip Kissinger of the position of national security adviser to the president, but he remained as secretary of state. During the 1976 presidential campaign against challenger James Earl Carter, Ford felt compelled to stop using the term "détente." Although Carter's narrow victory turned primarily on domestic issues, especially energy and inflation, the outcome clearly was a rejection of the secretive and power-oriented diplomacy practiced by Kissinger under Nixon and Ford.

DISSENSION UNDER CARTER

As president, Jimmy Carter proved unable to stamp American foreign policy with his own imprint. Rhetorically, he did succeed in stressing human rights in contrast to Kissinger's obsession with power politics. But his own lack of experience with world affairs and a serious rift between his principal foreign policy advisers left him ill-prepared to deal with a series of crises overseas that eventually overwhelmed his presidency.

Carter relied on two very different men, representing conflicting foreign policy positions, to help him deal with world affairs. The first, Secretary of State Cyrus Vance, was an establishment figure who hoped to continue the policy of détente with the Soviet Union, stressing cooperation rather than confrontation between the superpowers, while at the same time expanding American aid and assistance to emerging nations. Carter's appointment of civil rights leader Andrew Young as UN ambassador was a further attempt to appeal to Third World sensibilities. In contrast, the president's choice of Zbigniew Brzezinski as national security adviser invited conflict within the administration. The Polish-born Brzezinski opposed Kissinger's policy of détente and instead favored a hard line against the Soviet Union. Carter's two primary foreign policy advisers could not have been more different. "While Mr. Vance played by the Marquis of Queensbury rules," remarked one observer, "Mr. Brzezinski was more of a street fighter." The president, however, believed that he could draw upon each man's ideas in framing his foreign policy.

In the first two years, Carter sided with Vance and Young in seeking to improve relations with the Soviet Union and assist Third World countries. Policies such as the return of the Panama Canal to Panamanian sovereignty by the end of the century and support for black majority rule in southern Africa, especially in Rhodesia (Zimbabwe), together with the Camp David Accords between Egypt and Israel, marked early victories for the softer approach. But by 1978, as the result of aggressive Soviet moves in the horn of Africa and difficulty in negotiating a SALT II disarmament agreement with Leonid Brezhnev, Carter began to turn to Brzezinski more than to Vance for advice. The climax came when the administration extended full diplomatic recognition to China in 1979, a move advocated by Brzezinski as a way to bring pressure on the Soviet Union. The result was a return to Cold War tensions, especially after the Soviet invasion of Afghanistan in late 1979. At the same time, the growing conflict between the Department of State and the National Security Council had a paralyzing effect on the American response to the Iranian revolution. With Brzezinski backing the shah of Iran and Vance favoring change in

Iran, the Carter administration lost control of the situation and finally ended up in the hopeless hostage crisis.

Carter's foreign policy failures were not entirely self-inflicted. The legacy of the Vietnam War, the rising tide of nationalism among emerging nations, and the reactionary leadership of the Soviet Union all worked against effective American diplomacy. But Carter's belief that he could transform the conflicting views of such antagonistic foreign policy advisers as Vance and Brzezinski proved unfounded. By 1980, the American people had lost confidence in Carter's ability to use American power effectively in the world and were responding instead to the promise of his Republican challenger, Ronald Reagan, to "make America great again."

SUCCESS AND FAILURE UNDER REAGAN

Presidential advisers played an important, if sometimes unfortunate, role in the administration of Ronald Reagan. The president set forth the goals he sought to achieve—challenge the "evil empire" of the Soviet Union, assist those around the globe fighting against communist subversion, and do everything possible to spare the world a nuclear catastrophe. But Reagan had little interest in the details of foreign policy and delegated broad authority to his subordinates in the day-by-day conduct of diplomacy. As a result, his presidency helped pave the way for the end of the Cold War, but also was badly shaken by the Iran-Contra scandal.

At the outset, Reagan tried to avoid the internal tension that had hampered the Carter administration by relying on a strong secretary of state and downplaying the status of the national security adviser. Alexander Haig, his first secretary of state, proved too imperious and domineering and the White House staff finally forced him to resign in 1982. His successor, George Shultz, was much more successful. A conservative economist skilled at bureaucratic maneuvering, he ran the Department of State smoothly and became an effective advocate of negotiation with the Soviet Union. The first five national security advisers, on the other hand, lacked stature and yet were allowed a surprisingly large amount of discretion in carrying out their duties. Only the final two, Frank Carlucci and Colin Powell, had the high professional qualifications that the post required.

Within the Reagan administration, the primary tension was between Shultz, who favored a more cooperative policy toward the Soviet Union, and Secretary of Defense Caspar Weinberger, who championed Cold War confrontation. As president, Reagan tried to avoid siding with either antagonist, often seeking a middle course or avoiding a clear-cut policy decision. At the same time, Reagan turned to others in his administration for advice, notably two hard-liners. Jeane Kirkpatrick, the American ambassador to the UN, challenged Carter's stance against aid to friendly dictators like the shah of Iran, arguing instead that the United States should support "authoritarian" leaders who believed in the free market and were cooperative. William Casey, the Central Intelligence Agency director, a wealthy lawyer and veteran of the wartime Office of Strategic Services, favored an active American role in challenging what he and Reagan saw as Soviet surrogates, notably Cuba.

Reagan's reliance on Kirkpatrick and Casey proved most dangerous in Central America. The administration's efforts to use the CIA to back the contras in Nicaragua, as well as to defeat the rebels in El Salvador, led Congress to use its power of the purse to cut off funding for the contras. The president, moved by the plight of American hostages in Lebanon, approved a plan to sell arms to Iran in exchange for the release of Americans held by groups friendly to Iran; the NSC staff, led by National Security Adviser Robert McFarlane and his successor Admiral John Poindexter, assisted by Colonel Oliver North, went much further. Following the advice of CIA Director Casey, they channeled the money generated by the arms sales to Iran into the hands of the contras, in defiance of Congress. When the resulting Iran-Contra scandal became public in late 1986, McFarlane, Poindexter, and North all insisted that the president knew nothing of the illegal diversion of funds (Casey died of a brain tumor in early 1987). While Reagan took responsibility for the unwise decision to sell arms to Iran, he went along with his aides' assertion that he was ignorant of the financial transaction.

Reagan finally was able to offset the damage done by the Iran-Contra affair by his success in a series of summit conferences with the new Soviet leader, Mikhail Gorbachev. Encouraged by the quiet diplomacy of George Shultz, the president abandoned his stinging rhetoric and instead embraced the new polices of *glasnost* and *perestroika* begun by

Gorbachev in an effort to reform the Soviet system. Although the end of the Cold War, symbolized by the tearing down of the Berlin Wall and the breakup of the Soviet Union, would take place after Reagan left office, he could claim credit for laying the foundation with his highly publicized meetings with Gorbachev and his negotiation of the Intermediate Nuclear Forces Treaty, a first step toward meaningful arms control by the superpowers. Reagan could also claim that the massive buildup of the American military carried out under Weinberger had played a crucial role in bringing the Soviet Union to the bargaining table. His presidency, however, would remain tarnished by the Iran-Contra affair, the result of granting excessive discretion to his national security advisers.

BUSH IN COMMAND

George H. W. Bush was deeply involved in foreign policy throughout his presidency. Unlike Ronald Reagan, he brought a depth of experience in international affairs to the oval office—ambassador to the UN, envoy to China, director of the CIA, and frequent travels abroad as vice president. Bush's hands-on approach meant that in his administration American foreign policy would emanate from the White House, not the Department of State.

President Bush appointed James Baker, a close personal friend and successful campaign manager, to be secretary of state. Baker had shrewd political judgment, but little experience with foreign affairs. For advice, the president leaned more on two others within his administration. Brent Scowcroft, his national security adviser, was a retired air force general who had served in the same position under Ford as Kissinger's successor. Prudent and cautious, Scowcroft had been critical of Reagan's policy toward the Soviet Union, viewing the early denunciation as too confrontational and the later meetings with Gorbachev too accommodating. When the Berlin Wall was torn down in 1989 and the Soviet regime gradually collapsed, Scowcroft reinforced Bush's careful policy of letting events take their course without active American participation. The other man Bush relied on heavily was Secretary of Defense Richard Cheney. Experienced both as a member of Congress and as Ford's White House chief of staff, Cheney would play a key role in defining the dominant foreign policy event of the Bush administration—the Persian Gulf War.

When Saddam Hussein caught the United States by surprise with the Iraqi invasion of Kuwait on 2 August 1990, Bush reacted strongly, sending American troops to Saudi Arabia to protect the vital flow of oil from the Persian Gulf region. Once Saudi Arabia was secure, the critical issue was whether the United States should use force to liberate Kuwait or rely instead on economic pressure. Secretary of State Baker, along with the chairman of the Joint Chiefs of Staff, General Colin Powell, warned against getting involved in a ground war with Iraq. Scowcroft and Cheney, however, argued that sanctions would take too long to work, and the president sided with them. Cheney played an especially important role, criticizing the initial army plan to liberate Kuwait with a frontal assault and suggesting a flanking maneuver instead.

Bush's advisers also had considerable influence on the controversial decision to end the fighting short of full success. After five weeks of intense aerial bombardment, General Norman Schwarzkopf launched the ground offensive on 24 February 1991. When American armored units swept into southern Iraq in a daring flanking movement and coalition forces liberated Kuwait in just three days, Bush heeded the advice of Scowcroft and Powell to halt the attack after only a hundred hours of fighting. Powell was concerned that the United States not be seen as a heartless bully, commenting, "You don't do unnecessary killing if you can avoid it." Scowcroft had strategic concerns, primarily a fear that a prolonged invasion of Iraq would alienate Arab allies and shatter the international coalition. He also saw the need for a postwar Iraq strong enough to balance off the power of Iran in the vital Persian Gulf region. After insisting on securing Schwarzkopf's consent, Bush followed the advice of Powell and Scowcroft, thus ending the war with Saddam, still in power in Baghdad. Later, when Schwarzkopf suggested he could have destroyed the Republican Guard on which Saddam relied so heavily with just a day or two more of fighting, Powell intervened to remind the theater commander that he had agreed to the early cease-fire.

Despite the regrets over the failure to depose Saddam, the Bush foreign policy team proved effective in action. The cautious policy toward the downfall of the Soviet Union prevented the United States from providing an excuse for a final effort by hard-liners in Russia to revive the Cold War. In the Middle East, the Bush administration had succeeded in forging a remarkably broad international coalition to liberate Kuwait and thus uphold the principle of collective security. Bush's foreign policy advisers had accomplished these goals by displaying a high degree of teamwork. In contrast to the infighting that had characterized the Carter and Reagan presidencies, Bush, in the words of Baker, had "made the national security apparatus work the way it was supposed to work."

CLINTON: LEARNING ON THE JOB

In contrast to George H. W. Bush, William Jefferson Clinton relegated foreign policy to a secondary concern when he took office in 1993. As he put it, he focused "like a razor beam" on domestic issues—reviving the sluggish American economy, balancing the budget, and proposing a sweeping reform of the health care system. He delegated foreign policy to two veterans—Warren Christopher, the secretary of state, who favored a cautious, lawyerly approach to world affairs, working harmoniously with National Security Adviser Anthony Lake, a former aide to Henry Kissinger who had resigned in protest during the Vietnam War.

Two other foreign policy advisers came to play an important part in the Clinton administration. The first was Strobe Talbott, a journalist and expert on the Soviet Union, who had close personal ties with Clinton, his Rhodes Scholar roommate at Oxford. After brief service as ambassador-at-large to the countries of the former Soviet Union, Talbott became deputy secretary of state and oversaw the administration's efforts to support Boris Yeltsin's leadership of Russia. Talbott supervised the granting of $2.5 billion in economic aid as well as the Clinton administration's efforts to promote free market reforms and democracy in Russia.

Richard Holbrooke, another veteran of the Carter administration, emerged as a key player in the most critical foreign policy problem confronting the Clinton presidency—the civil war in Bosnia. Although Clinton had criticized Bush for failing to halt the bloodshed in this former Yugoslavian territory, the new president proved equally reluctant to intervene militarily to stop the fighting. In 1995, however, Clinton finally approved U.S. participation in North Atlantic Treaty Organization air strikes designed to halt Bosnian Serb shelling of the Muslim city of Sarajevo. Holbrooke, assistant secretary of state for European affairs, carried out the difficult task of

negotiating a cease-fire among the ethnic rivals in Bosnia—Croats, Serbs, and Muslims. The accords that he succeeded in getting representatives of the three groups to sign in Dayton, Ohio, in November 1995 ended the fighting in Bosnia and led to a fragile but viable political settlement.

The ethnic tensions in the Balkans continued to create difficulty for Christopher's successor, Madeleine Albright, who became secretary of state at the start of Clinton's second term in 1997. The first woman to hold the office, Albright, the daughter of a Czech diplomat, had taught international affairs at Georgetown University and served as ambassador to the UN from 1993 to 1996. More activist than Christopher, she was a firm believer in democracy and was willing to use force to achieve American goals abroad. When Serbian leader Slobodan Milosevic began terrorizing the majority Albanian population in Kosovo, Albright was determined to halt his ethnic cleansing. After Holbrooke's efforts to negotiate a peaceful settlement had failed by early 1999, Albright helped persuade Clinton to intervene militarily to protect the Kosovars. For nearly three months, from March to June 1999, NATO aircraft bombed Serbia in an effort to halt Milosevic's attempt to drive all the Albanians out of Kosovo. The secretary of state defended this policy against fierce criticism and she and Clinton were vindicated when the air offensive began to target the infrastructure of Serbia (bridges, power plants, TV stations), finally forcing Milosevic to withdraw from Kosovo. Remarkably, not a single American life was lost in this military campaign. The outcome in Kosovo, however, was ambiguous—the territory was still nominally Serbian but only the presence of NATO troops kept an uneasy peace between the returning Kosovars and the minority Serbs.

Inevitably, foreign policy came to occupy more of Clinton's attention during his second term in office. The failure of his health care reform and the Republican control of Congress after 1994 limited his freedom of action on domestic matters. He became personally involved in two difficult efforts at mediation—trying to broker peace between the Protestant and Catholic factions in Northern Ireland and attempting to achieve a peaceful settlement of the Israeli-Palestinian rivalry in the Middle East. Although he relied on advisers in both cases (former Senator George Mitchell in Northern Ireland and troubleshooter Dennis Ross in Israel), Clinton took an active personal role, most notably in negotiating the Wye River Accord between Benjamin Netanyahu and Yasir Arafat in Maryland in 1998. By the time he left office, Clinton had traveled to nearly every part of the world and felt much more confident, and less dependent on his advisers, than when he had entered the White House.

CONCLUSION

Modern presidents have learned that foreign policy is a major responsibility for the office they hold and that they must rely on talented and experienced advisers in handling the diverse problems they encounter in the world. The dual system of national security advisers and secretaries of state, while sometimes leading to great friction as under Carter, helps a president choose between two different sets of advisers, while still leaving him free to seek the counsel of others outside the government. But the days when one individual, such as Colonel House or Harry Hopkins, would act as the president's surrogate in foreign policy, are long past. Future presidents are likely to draw on a wide variety of experts, both within and outside their administrations, in seeking ways to fulfill their responsibilities as world leaders.

BIBLIOGRAPHY

Acheson, Dean. *Present at the Creation: My Years in the State Department.* New York, 1969.

Anderson, Patrick. *The President's Men: The White House Assistants of Franklin D. Roosevelt, Harry S. Truman, Dwight D. Eisenhower, John F. Kennedy, and Lyndon B. Johnson.* Garden City, N.Y., 1968.

Baker, James A., III. *The Politics of Diplomacy: Revolution, War, and Peace, 1989–1992.* New York, 1995.

Barber, James David. *The Presidential Character: Predicting Performance in the White House.* 4th ed. Englewood Cliffs, N.J., 1992.

Brands, H. W. *The Wages of Globalism: Lyndon Johnson and the Limits of American Power.* New York, 1995.

Brzezinski, Zbigniew. *Power and Principle: The Memoirs of the National Security Adviser, 1977–1981.* New York, 1983.

Bush, George, and Brent Scowcroft. *A World Transformed.* New York, 1998.

Cannon, Lou. *President Reagan: The Role of a Lifetime.* New York, 1991.

Christopher, Warren. *Chances of a Lifetime.* New York, 2001.

Clifford, Clark, with Richard Holbrooke. *Counsel to the President: A Memoir.* New York, 1991.

Destler, I. M. *Presidents, Bureaucrats, and Foreign Policy: The Politics of Organizational Reform.* Princeton, N.J., 1974.

Greene, John Robert. *The Presidency of George Bush.* Lawrence, Kans., 2000.

Greenstein, Fred I. *The Presidential Difference: Leadership Style from FDR to Clinton with a New Afterword on George W. Bush.* Princeton, N.J., 2001.

Hess, Gary R. *Presidential Decisions for War: Korea, Vietnam, and the Persian Gulf.* Baltimore, Md., 2001.

Holbrooke, Richard. *To End a War.* New York, 1998.

Immerman, Richard H. *John Foster Dulles: Piety, Pragmatism, and Power in U.S. Foreign Policy.* Wilmington, Del., 1999.

Kaufman, Burton I. *The Presidency of James Earl Carter, Jr.* Lawrence, Kans., 1993.

Kennan, George F. *Memoirs, 1925–1950.* Boston, 1967.

Kissinger, Henry. *White House Years.* Boston, 1979.

———. *Years of Upheaval.* Boston, 1982.

———. *Years of Renewal.* New York, 1999.

McJimsey, George T. *Harry Hopkins: Ally of the Poor and Defender of Democracy.* Cambridge, Mass., 1987.

Neustadt, Richard E. *The Politics of Leadership from FDR to Carter.* New York, 1980.

Paterson, Thomas G., J. Garry Clifford, and Kenneth J. Hagan. *American Foreign Policy: A History.* 3d ed. 2 vols. Lexington, Mass., 1991.

Reedy, George E. *The Twilight of the Presidency: From Johnson to Reagan.* Rev. ed. New York, 1987.

Schlesinger, Arthur M., Jr. *The Imperial Presidency.* New ed. Boston, 1989.

Schulzinger, Robert D. *Henry Kissinger: Doctor of Diplomacy.* New York, 1989.

Sherwood, Robert E. *Roosevelt and Hopkins: An Intimate History.* New York, 1948.

Shultz, George Pratt. *Turmoil and Triumph: My Years as Secretary of State.* New York, 1993.

Small, Melvin. *The Presidency of Richard Nixon.* Lawrence, Kans., 1999.

Sorensen, Theodore C. *Decision-Making in the White House: The Olive Branch or the Arrows.* New York, 1963.

Vance, Cyrus R. *Hard Choices: Critical Years in America's Foreign Policy.* New York, 1983.

Walker, Martin. *The President We Deserve: Bill Clinton, His Rise, Falls, and Comebacks.* New York, 1996.

See also AMBASSADORS, EXECUTIVE AGENTS, AND SPECIAL REPRESENTATIVES; DECISION MAKING; DEPARTMENT OF STATE; ELITISM; NATIONAL SECURITY COUNCIL; PRESIDENTIAL POWER.

PRESIDENTIAL POWER

★ ★ ★ ★ ★

Alexander DeConde

From the founding of the United States to the present, concerned citizens have debated the breadth of presidential power in foreign affairs. The Founders, from their reading of European history and their experience with the English Crown, feared extensive executive authority. Believing that broad control over the military over the shaping of relations with foreign nations and over the making of war paved the way to tyranny, in these matters they placed explicit constitutional curbs on the executive. As the nation grew, these restraints led often to tension between the president and Congress. Regardless, except in a few instances, the authority of the executive expanded along with the growth of the nation's wealth and influence in the world.

The reasons why the executive prevailed and in the twentieth century presidential wars became virtually standard procedure are complex. Some scholars maintain the presidents could use massive force on their own because Congress abdicated its constitutional authority. Others saw as a cause the rise of the United States to the status of a world power, an imperial power, and a superpower. Many perceived the executive's dominance in war as a logical consequence of the corrupting influence of vast power. Still others saw that power as politically and personally based. They maintained that presidents catered to popular sentiment because, often in the guise of patriotism, strong, violent muscle-flexing against foreign foes was rewarded at the ballot box.

CONSTITUTIONAL SOURCES

Writing in the 1830s, the French political theorist Alexis de Toqueville described the American president as possessing, especially in foreign relations, "almost royal prerogatives." More than a century later, Harry S. Truman claimed the presidency had "become the greatest and most important office in the history of the world." Into the twenty-first century, the media and scholarly treatises repeated this concept so often it became commonplace.

Ironically, leaders of the generation that fought the revolutionary war had a deep distrust of wide-ranging executive power. When they drafted the nation's first constitution, the Articles of Confederation and Perpetual Union, they omitted a permanent executive office. They feared concentrating immense power in any one person because they regarded executive authority the natural enemy of liberty and a potential repository for military tyranny. So they established a single legislature that chose a member as president. He could not serve more than one year in any three-year congressional term and had no special authority in the conduct of foreign affairs.

After the United States won independence, political leaders such as John Jay, George Washington, Alexander Hamilton, and James Madison perceived the Articles as inadequate, particularly in the making of foreign policy. They desired a permanent president with sufficient authority to carry out a unified policy toward the rest of the world. With this objective, they sought to amend the Articles in a manner that would provide for a stronger central government. They persuaded Congress to authorize a convention for that purpose. After delegates from seven states met on 25 May 1787 in Philadelphia, they decided to get rid of the Articles of Confederation and frame a new constitution.

The debate over the nature of the presidency consumed more time than did any other major problem before the convention. Framers supposedly influenced by an eighteenth-century doctrine of an inherent executive prerogative—advanced by political thinkers such as John Locke—desired "a vigorous Executive." Others pointed out that the people opposed anything resembling an elective monarchy. After much discussion, the Founders created a presidential office with specific constraints as well as considerable power. They separated it from the legislative and judicial branches with a system of checks and balances designed to prevent the president from becoming a tyrant.

In keeping with this objective, the framers placed more curbs on the president's power in domestic affairs than in foreign relations. They also denied him the most vital of monarchical powers, that of initiating war. Envisaging him as the agent of Congress, they vested the war power in the legislature. They conferred on the president the authority, with the approval of the Senate, to appoint ambassadors and other emissaries and to receive similar diplomats from other countries. With the advice and consent of the Senate, given in a two-thirds vote, only he could make and negotiate treaties.

The new constitution also stated that the "President shall be Commander in Chief of the Army and Navy . . . and of the Militia of the several States when called into the actual Service of the United States." This title did not give him authority to declare or instigate war. In *The Federalist* No. 69, Hamilton assumed, therefore, that the president's role as commander in chief would amount to nothing more than the supreme command and direction of the military and naval forces. The real power, as he perceived it, belonged to Congress. In the long run, Hamilton's assumptions proved wrong. Increasingly, presidents would use the commander in chief clause to expand their authority over foreign policy in its most vital aspect, the power to make war. For this reason, presidents, their political supporters, and others would come often to refer, incorrectly, to the clause as the president's war power.

Other powers, such as the president's choosing heads of executive departments or cabinet members, his pardoning and veto authority as in budget matters, his right to inform and request legislation from Congress, and his duty to execute laws faithfully, all touched on foreign affairs. Regardless of the safeguards built into these various powers, the Founders created what they had tried to prevent, an office that in foreign affairs had the potential of becoming a kind of elective monarchy.

George Washington had an acute awareness that as the first president his behavior would set precedents for future occupants of the office, and it did. For instance, frustration in August 1789 in dealing with legislators over treaties with Indian tribes led him to abandon the constitutional requirement of obtaining the advice and consent of the Senate before or during negotiation of treaties. Instead, he concluded treaties and then asked for Senate approval, a procedure that since his time other presidents have followed. With a broad view of his authority, he viewed the president as having the power to enforce aspects of relations with foreign peoples even if his actions could lead to armed conflict. He first seized the initiative in using force in dealing with security on the western frontier, where he regarded the Native Americans as a foreign people who menaced white inhabitants. Beginning in October 1790, he sent three armies against Native Americans in the Northwest. In August 1794, the third expedition, headed by General "Mad" Anthony Wayne, crushed the Indian resistance.

Washington also acted with considerable independence in dealing with Europeans. After revolutionaries in France in September 1792 abolished the monarchy and established a republic, he used his power to receive foreign representatives to establish formal relations with the new regime. This decision established precedent for prompt de facto recognition of a government when it demonstrated effective control of a nation. The first significant controversy over the president's power in foreign affairs erupted after January 1793, when England and France went to war. France expected help from Washington because of its alliance with the United States during the American Revolution. Instead, on 22 April, he proclaimed neutrality. Critics regarded this policy as pro-British with the potential of provoking France to hostilities. Hence, they denounced it as usurping Congress's war power. Supporters of the policy, such as Hamilton, defended it as flowing logically from the executive's conduct of foreign affairs.

Writing under the pseudonym "Helvidius," Madison denied the president possessed the power on his own to take actions that would precipitate war. "Those who are to conduct a war," Madison wrote, "cannot in the nature of things, be proper or safe judges, whether a war ought to be commenced, continued, or concluded." Regardless of the validity of this perspective, Washington had indeed taken a bold step in setting a precedent for presidents to claim the right to determine foreign policy unilaterally.

Meanwhile, despite the neutrality policy, friction with England over trade practices, over the frontier with Canada, and especially over the royal navy's seizure of American shipping and impressment of American seamen roiled relations with the mother country. Fearing possible hostilities, members of the newly formed Federalist Party pressed the president to send a special mission to London to resolve the differences. He chose John Jay, then chief justice, for the task and abandoned his usual practice of sharing an envoy's instructions with the Senate. Washington's action angered Democratic-Republicans, members of the opposition party, but the Federalist majority in the Senate approved the mission, and on 19 November 1794, Jay concluded a treaty that aroused harsh public criticism. Despite bitter controversy, the Senate approved the treaty and on 14 August 1795, the president ratified it. From this time on, Washington increasingly became a target of political abuse—"the head of British faction," one critic characterized him. French leaders called the treaty a negation of their alliance. Opponents in the House of Representatives tried to kill it by withholding appropriations for carrying it out. They also demanded to see the documents of the negotiation, thus raising the question, To what extent did the constitutional right of control over funding give the House power to participate in the treaty-approving process?

Democratic-Republicans argued that the House, as the immediate representative body of the people, had a right, even a duty, to consider whether or not a treaty should go into effect. Federalists countered that the Constitution restricted the treaty power to the president and Senate. On this premise, Washington refused to release the Jay papers. Finally, on 29 April 1796, by the margin of one vote, the House agreed to appropriate funds to implement the treaty. Thus, on the basis of party-line considerations, Washington set another precedent that extended presidential power in foreign affairs, one that exempted the executive in this process from close legislative oversight.

Washington reacted defensively to the criticism that he had wrongly inflated presidential authority. During the controversies over that issue, he maintained that the powers of the American president "are more definite and better understood perhaps than those of almost any other Country," and that he had aimed "neither to stretch, nor relax from them in any instance whatever, unless imperious circumstances shd. render the measure indispensable." Later, in discussing the content of his Farewell Address, in which he set the principles for an isolationist policy, he wanted to make clear to all that "he could have no view in extending the Powers of the Executive beyond the limits prescribed by the Constitution." Regardless, when he left office and foreign policy became an issue in the presidential election of 1796, critics still believed he had aggrandized executive authority in a manner that placed the nation on the verge of war with France. Later generations of historians who characterized presidents as weak or strong would rank him as a strong executive.

THE QUASI-WAR AND AFTER

John Adams thought carefully about the powers of the evolving presidency. He believed in a strong executive because "the unity, the secrecy, the dispatch of one man has no equal." To prevent abuses in the office, he felt that "the executive power should be watched by all men." He described the president as the leader of "a monarchical republic" who exercised greater power than heads of government in various European countries. He perceived the American president's prerogatives as "so transcendent that they must naturally and necessarily excite in the nation all the jealousy, envy, fears, apprehensions, and opposition that are so constantly observed in England against the crown." While deploring limitations on the president's authority, as "in cases of war," he still acknowledged that "the legislative power in our constitution is greater than the executive."

In July 1797, after the French stepped up attacks on American commerce, Adams moved to resolve the crisis, much of which he had inherited. When French officials humiliated his emissaries, he asked his cabinet if he should recommend to Congress an immediate declaration of war. When the cabinet split, he decided against seeking a formalized war, sent copies of the envoys' dispatches to Congress substituting the letters W, X, Y, and Z for the French officials involved, and asked the legislators to authorize preparations for war. He also took steps to protect the lives of American citizens from French attacks and to convey publicly the image of a vigorous executive. When Congress, under Federalist pressure, published the XYZ documents, much of the public reacted with a demand for war that brought Adams a popularity he had always lacked. He gloried in the role of a warrior-leader, delivering numerous combative speeches while sporting a military uniform and a sword. He told approving crowds, "Let us have war." This bellicosity alarmed opposition Republicans. One of them, George Logan of Pennsylvania, warned that ambitious executives launched wars more for their own aggrandizement than for the protection of their country.

Despite such sentiment, Federalists in Congress voted for warlike measures. For the first time under the Constitution, in recognition of undeclared hostilities at sea, Congress empowered the president to deploy naval forces on a scale larger than a short-term police action. When extreme Federalists pressured Adams to expand this Quasi-War, as it later became known, Adams wavered. He did so not because of an unwillingness to use more force but because he questioned his power to do so without the consent of Congress. He believed, furthermore, that minority Republicans, with some moderate Federalists, would vote against a declaration of war.

Extreme Federalists then characterized Adams as lacking the virile qualities they presumed necessary in the strong executive. Feeling betrayed by many of his own party on this issue, Adams changed his perspective toward a full-scale war. Consequently, when the French offered a second round of peace negotiations, Adams welcomed the overture. He then a sent a second mission to France, and expansion of the Quasi-War became an issue in the presidential campaign of 1800. Republicans portrayed themselves as friends of peace and Federalists as partisans of war. On 1 October the American negotiators in France signed the Convention of Mortefontaine that ended the war. News of the peace arrived in the United States too late to benefit Adams in the election. Thomas Jefferson won. Nonetheless, Adams later regarded his decision for peace as the "most disinterested and meritorious action of my life." It set a noble example for posterity but his use of naval force set a less admirable precedent. Future presidents would invoke it, under the concept of an implied constitutional power, when they employed the military unilaterally in limited hostilities against weak foes.

Even though Jefferson took office as a believer in strict construction, meaning a narrow interpretation of the Constitution, he acted on the assumption of a magnified construction of presidential power in foreign policy in the pattern set by Washington. He claimed that only the president could carry on transactions with foreign governments. Within two weeks of his inauguration, Jefferson decided to send four warships to North Africa to protect American shipping against attack by alleged pirates along the Barbary Coast.

Shortly thereafter he asked his cabinet if he should seek a declaration of war from Congress. Treasury Secretary Albert Gallatin responded that the president "cannot put us in a state of war," but if other nations put us in that state the executive could on his own use military force. Without consulting Congress or receiving its sanction, he waged war, or what later would be called a police action, against the Barbary States. Later, Congress did authorize the president to employ the navy at his discretion.

Meanwhile, after Jefferson learned in May 1801 that France had reacquired Louisiana from Spain, his strict constructionist views clashed with his concept of a strong executive power in foreign affairs. He considered the possibility of war to block consummation of the transfer and to safeguard the American right of deposit at New Orleans. First, in January 1801, he sent a special emissary to France with a proposal to purchase New Orleans and territory at the mouth of the Mississippi River. When Napoleon Bonaparte offered to sell all of the Louisiana Territory, Jefferson hesitated to act on his own. Soon, though, he decided to act "beyond the Constitution" and not let "metaphysical subtleties" stand in the way of a great bargain that would benefit the nation. He thus added to the precedents for extending presidential authority in international matters beyond its original constitutional limits. Under the concept of enlarged authority, Jefferson claimed, on questionable ground, Spain's West Florida as part of the Louisiana Purchase. He threatened force if Spain did not acquiesce. Although most cognizant Americans approved of his bellicosity as proper presidential vigor, he backed off from hostilities mainly because of deteriorating relations with England and France. In a crisis with Britain in June 1807, when a British warship attacked the American naval frigate *Chesapeake,* Jefferson at first appeared eager for war, but when public sentiment for it dwindled he retreated. When he left office, he retained faith in the strong executive willing to use military force with the support of Congress and in some circumstances on his own.

When James Madison took over the White House, he had the experience of having helped create the presidency and, as Jefferson's secretary of state, of having administered foreign affairs for eight years. Still, he had less confidence in executive authority than did Jefferson. He had frequently expressed the view that the president, "being a single individual, with nothing to balance his faults and deficiencies, was as likely to go wrong as the average citizen." His views fluctuated over time, leading him later to believe "in the large construction of Executive authority," notably in the conduct of foreign affairs.

As president, Madison secretly backed American settlers who in July 1810 seized West Florida from its Spanish authorities. For a time he hesitated in annexing it to the United States, fearing such openly unilateral action would raise "serious questions as to the authority of the Executive." Within four months he overcame his qualms and took over the territory. Many Americans applauded what they saw as proper presidential power. One senator said that if the president had not taken West Florida, he would have been charged with imbecility.

For almost three years, Madison resisted pressure from hawks in his own party to take bold measures against Britain, action that would most likely precipitate war. Federalists, however, opposed hostilities. When on 1 June 1812 he requested a declaration of war, he used his power to persuade wavering legislators to support him. During the hostilities he could not, however, capitalize on that power without encountering considerable public defiance. The war went badly and became unpopular. Critics denounced him for lacking effective leadership. Some scholars would later characterize him as a failed executive and a weak war leader. Yet in annexing West Florida he had been high-handed and as tough as his predecessors.

James Monroe, too, acquired a reputation as a passive leader, but he contributed to the enlarging of presidential power in international affairs through the use of an executive agreement. In the Rush-Bagot Agreement in April 1817 with Britain that limited naval armaments on the Great Lakes, he bypassed the Senate's veto power over treaties. He thus set the precedent for unilateral action that technically operated only during the term of a president who negotiated an agreement. Nonetheless, executive agreements became an effective means for presidents to exercise power in foreign affairs without congressional consent.

Monroe faced the possibility of war with England and Spain when Andrew Jackson, at the head of a small army, in April 1818 raided East Florida and executed two English subjects. Although Monroe had not authorized the incursion, Secretary of State John Quincy Adams defended Jackson, stating that his actions involved "the Executive power to authorize war without a declaration of war by Congress." He believed that

if the president disclaimed such power he would set "a dangerous example; and of evil consequences." Monroe quickly embraced this argument, calling Jackson's invasion of a neighbor's territory self-defense. Critics denounced the invasion as an act of war without the consent of Congress. "If it be not war . . . ," one of them stated, "let it be called a man-killing expedition which the President has a right to direct whenever he pleases."

Several years later, when militants wanted Monroe to defend Spain's rebelling colonies against reconquest, he decided to act on his own but not with force. On 2 December 1823, he warned European powers not to intervene in the New World struggles. This concept, in what became known as the Monroe Doctrine and accepted by future presidents, demonstrated another aspect of executive power in foreign matters, the ability to influence with words.

Through deed as well as word, Andrew Jackson acquired the reputation of a vigorous no-nonsense president in both foreign and domestic affairs. His concept of an expansive authority surfaced in an incident in 1831 with Argentine authorities in the Falkland Islands (Islas Malvinas). On the basis of slim evidence, he accused them of endangering the lives of American seal hunters. He threatened force that critics said brought the nation to the brink of war, but he did not go much beyond words.

In another dispute, when marauders from the town of Kuala Batu, Sumatra, killed three American pepper traders, Jackson used force. On his orders, on 6 February 1832, an assault force of 262 heavily armed marines attacked the town, torched it, and slaughtered more than a hundred Sumatrans, some of them women. Political opponents wondered, "If the President can direct expeditions with fire and sword against the Malays . . . why may he not have the power to do the same in reference to any other people." In this manner, "a very important provision of the Constitution may in time become a mere nullity." Defenders, though, praised Jackson for his executive energy.

Jackson also secretly aided American rebels in Texas in their fight in 1836 to secede from Mexico. In addition, he occupied militarily Mexican territory, ostensibly to protect Louisiana from cross-border raiders. John Quincy Adams, who had now abandoned his earlier advocacy of a presidential war authority, condemned this "most extraordinary power" as illegal. When Congress approved Jackson's action, Adams commented, the startling "idea that the Executive Chief Magistrate has the power of involving the nation in war even without consulting Congress" had taken root. It had grown, he maintained, out of fifty years of presidents' de facto exercise of such power.

Contemporaries characterized John Tyler as a man with talents not above mediocrity while historians rate him a weak president. Yet, he came up with a tactic for placing more power in the hands of the executive at the expense of Congress that later presidents would adopt. He wanted to acquire Texas but could not obtain a two-thirds majority in the Senate for a treaty of annexation. So, he asked the whole Congress to approve annexation with joint resolution that required only a mere majority. It agreed. Opponents, who called this action an abuse of power that evaded constitutional restraint, urged impeachment. Tyler prevailed, he explained later, because in handling foreign affairs he had been "freer of the furies of factional politics than he had been in domestic affairs."

THE MEXICAN AND CIVIL WARS

James K. Polk came to the presidency belittled as another mediocrity. He vowed to reverse this popular perception by asserting vigorous leadership. He defended the annexation of Texas, with its potential for war with Mexico, and quickly stoked a quarrel with Britain over title to the Oregon territory. Despite some saber rattling, in the spring of 1846 he resolved the Oregon dispute peacefully. All the while he took a tougher stance against Mexico, which refused to recognize its loss of Texas.

Polk ordered troops to occupy disputed territory between Texas and Mexico implicitly, if not explicitly, with the intent to provoke hostilities. This tactic led a critic to ask, "Why should we not compromise our difficulties with Mexico as well as with Great Britain?" The answer could be found in the classic policy of aggressive leaders—compromise with the strong but bash the weak. So, when Mexican forces killed several of the American soldiers occupying the no-man's land north of the Rio Grande, the president claimed the Mexicans had shed American blood on American soil, an assertion disputed by Abraham Lincoln and other Whigs. Nonetheless, on 13 May 1846, a majority in Congress ratified the president's action by resolving that a state of war existed.

Dissenters charged that "a secretive, evasive, and high-handed president himself had provoked Mexico into firing the first shots." John C. Calhoun of South Carolina denounced Polk's procedure as "monstrous" because "it stripped Congress of the power of making war." The war bill "sets the example," he warned, "which will enable all future presidents to bring about a state of things, in which Congress shall be forced, without deliberation, or reflection, to declare war, however opposed to its convictions of justice or expediency." John Quincy Adams stated, "It is now established as an irreversible precedent" that the president "has but to declare that War exists, with any Nation upon Earth . . . and the War is essentially declared." Critics called the Mexican War an "Executive War" or "Mr. Polk's War." The House of Representatives voted to censure Polk for "unnecessarily and unconstitutionally" bringing on war. Lincoln stated that by accepting Polk's rationale, Congress allowed the president "to make war at pleasure." Polk mustered support for his policies with a quasi-official newspaper he established in Washington, D.C., but garnered most of his popularity by winning the war at low cost and bringing vast territory into the Union. In subsequent years, his aggressive style earned him the enduring admiration of the strong-presidency cult. In all, Polk stretched the president's power as commander in chief more than had his predecessors.

Polk's immediate successors readily accepted a narrow constitutional interpretation of their powers, sometimes called the Whig conception, and faced no foreign crises that tested that view. Although as a Whig congressman Abraham Lincoln had condemned Polk's amplification of executive power, as president he exercised that power boldly in both domestic and foreign affairs. In waging war against the Confederacy, Lincoln enlarged the army and navy by decree, paid out funds from the Treasury without congressional appropriation, suspended the writ of habeas corpus, and closed the mails to reasonable correspondence. He proclaimed, with questionable legality, a naval blockade of Confederate ports that embroiled the Union in unnecessary foreign quarrels. In the *Trent* affair, his government claimed exaggerated powers but backed down when confronted with the possibility of hostilities with Britain.

In September 1864, when Western powers organized an international naval force to retaliate against the Japanese for assaults on their shipping in the Strait of Shimonoseki, Lincoln cooperated with Britain and other nations. Thus, for the first time a president authorized a U.S. vessel to join a foreign armada in a police action to punish a foreign people for harming American nationals and others. American sailors remained engaged in this kind of policing, solely on presidential initiative, for a decade.

More importantly, during the Civil War critics denounced Lincoln's exercise of presidential authority as despotic. He justified his use of military force as within the executive's power to suppress rebellion, as within the scope of his authority as commander in chief, and as necessary for enabling him to take any necessary measure to subdue the enemy. His tough measures, he told Congress, "whether strictly legal or not," were forced upon him. He prevailed because he won both popular and legislative support. Numerous contemporaries and scores of scholars since his time have defended his arbitrary rule as necessary to preserve the Union and to emancipate four million slaves. These were noble causes and hence validate his actions as proper. Lincoln gave substance to the concept that, in a crisis, the president, in the name of the people, should dominate the government. Congress and the courts should defer to him. He enhanced the power of commander in chief beyond what the framers of the Constitution had envisioned or what previous executives had done. Aggressive successors would exploit this precedent, primarily in the conduct of foreign affairs.

Unlike most presidents, Benjamin Harrison came to office reputedly without the drive to amass power. Biographers indicate that this attitude changed after a dispute principally with Germany over Samoa. After tasting executive power in a foreign confrontation, it entranced him. He used this authority harshly in a dispute in 1891 with Italy over a lynching of Italian subjects in New Orleans and in humiliating Chile in the same year in a quarrel that grew out of a barroom brawl in Valparaiso, where a mob killed two American sailors. He demanded an apology and reparations. When the Chilean government hesitated, he threatened force. Analysts maintain he trumped Congress's war power as decisively as if he had unilaterally committed troops to battle. The constitutional niceties involved did not concern most Americans, who in large numbers applauded his toughness. Harrison intervened also in a revolution in Hawaii. He denied personal involvement but backed the revolutionaries and sought to annex the islands. In later years, he again shifted his perspective on foreign policy. He told a journalist, "We have no commission from God to police the world."

Grover Cleveland also had an ambivalent attitude toward presidential power. He came to office believing in a cautious interpretation of the Constitution's clauses on executive functions. He also regarded the presidency as superior to any executive position in the world, implying it had divine sanction. In office, he bridled at legislative restraints. During his first term, Cleveland intervened with surprising toughness in a domestic uprising in Nueva Granada (later Colombia), when he exaggerated a threat to America's right of transit across the Isthmus of Panama. Unilaterally, he dispatched more than twelve hundred marines backed with artillery to help crush rebels defying the central government. Jingoes applauded his vigor but people in the region regarded him as an imperialist bully. When Germany threatened to take over Samoa, in a kind of police action, he sent three warships to the islands to preserve their independence. No hostilities ensued but the big-power confrontation continued.

In his second term, Cleveland acted with unnecessary bellicosity toward Britain in a dispute over the boundary separating British Guiana and Venezuela. Through an inflation of the Monroe Doctrine, he claimed unwarranted authority over the Western Hemisphere. Members of Congress and much of the public cheered the president's stance as a proper defense of national honor. Historians and others perceived his saber rattling, with its risk of war over a quarrel posing no threat to the United States, as a dangerous exploitation of presidential power.

In a rebellion in Cuba, Cleveland resisted pressure from Congress, journalists, and much of the concerned public to lead the country into war to force Spain to relinquish its colony. He told legislators, "There will be no war with Spain over Cuba while I am president." When one of them reminded him that Congress could on its own declare war, he responded that the Constitution also made him commander in chief. As such, he said, "I will not mobilize the army." Cleveland's perception of presidential power produced a standoff with Congress that lasted until he left office. Views vary on William McKinley's exercise of power in foreign affairs. Historians depict him as both dominant and passive. He entered the presidency with respect for congressional authority and with a circumscribed view of its powers.

Instead of asking Congress for a declaration of war against Spain, he requested discretionary authority to use the armed forces. It led a senator to ask why legislators should "give the President power to intervene and make war, if he sees fit, without declaring war at all?" Congress granted McKinley the power he desired. He served an ultimatum on Spain, blockaded Cuban ports, and thus initiated hostilities. On 24 April 1898, Spain declared war, and the following day Congress voted that a state of war had existed since the date of the blockade. After that, the story goes, McKinley shed his passivity and became an aggressive, virile leader. He willingly took on the responsibility of war and, after victory, of policing another country's possession. Also at this time, when he could not round up enough votes in the Senate to annex Hawaii by treaty, he did so with a joint resolution of Congress, following the precedent set by Tyler. McKinley then governed the islands with a presidential commission.

When Filipinos demanded the right to rule themselves, McKinley refused, and they fought the American occupiers. He then deployed large forces in an undeclared war he justified as a police action. Critics asked, "How can a president of the great republic be blind to the truth that freedom is the same, that liberty is as dear and that self-government is as much a right in the Philippines as in the United States?"

McKinley exerted his will in another military venture. As commander in chief, he sent five thousand troops to China to join an international expeditionary force to suppress Boxer rebels. Analysts point out that he intervened for political purposes, or to demonstrate hard-hitting leadership in foreign affairs in an election year. Publicly, though, he justified his "international police duty" with the now established principle of protecting American lives and property. The *Philadelphia Times,* however, termed the intervention "an absolute declaration of war by the executive without the authority or knowledge of Congress, and it is without excuse because it is not necessary." Neither constitutional restraints nor the critics mattered much because both Congress and the public approved of McKinley's conduct. Partisan biographers and analysts have viewed him as a courageous executive who maneuvered both Congress and the public into accepting presidential primacy in foreign relations. They praise him also for asserting executive power in external affairs in an era of purported congressional ascendancy.

THE STEWARDSHIP THEORY

Unlike his immediate predecessors, Theodore Roosevelt came to the presidency with an expansive view of its power and an appetite to use it. Immediately, he decided to continue the war in the Philippines, cloaking his reliance on force there with irrelevant rhetoric. For example, he justified it as part of a mission to keep "barbarous and semi-barbarous peoples" in line, or as "a necessary international police duty which must be performed for the sake of the welfare of mankind." The casualties in this presidential policing, which he called the most glorious war in the nation's history, were lopsided. Some 4,200 Americans died while they killed 18,000 Filipino military, and through war-induced hunger and disease well over 100,000 Filipino civilians died.

Roosevelt also claimed success for presidential power in thwarting Germany in a crisis involving debts owed by Venezuela and for extorting a favorable boundary for Alaska at Canada's expense. In the Russo-Japanese War in 1904 and the Algeciras Conference in 1906 over the fate of Morocco, he meddled in foreign quarrels that only remotely touched American national interests. In haste to build a canal at the Isthmus of Panama, he used executive power to order warships and marines to wrench a province from Colombia, a weak country unable to counter with either effective diplomacy or force. Critics denounced his contention that he had a right to take Colombia's land as the robber's claim of might makes right. Admirers, though, perceived his Panama diplomacy as a symbol of presidential strength and a new American internationalism.

The president used similar big-stick tactics to coerce other small Latin American countries, rationalizing his actions with what became known as the Roosevelt Corollary to the Monroe Doctrine. Their "chronic wrong doing, or an impotence which results in a general loosening of the ties of civilized society," he explained, required him on behalf of a civilized nation, to exercise "an international police power." When he sent marines to occupy Cuba in September 1906, he defended his sidestepping of Congress with the argument "that it is for the enormous interest of this Government to strengthen and give independence to the Executive in dealing with foreign powers."

This conduct reflected Roosevelt's personal conception of executive authority. He believed "there inheres in the Presidency more power than in any office in any great republic or constitutional monarchy in modern times." He perceived no harm "from the concentration of powers in one man's hands," boasting he had "been President most emphatically" and had "used every ounce of power there was in the office." At another time he stated, "I believe in a strong executive; I believe in power." This attitude stemmed from Lincoln's exercise of executive power that Roosevelt adopted as his own and came to be known as the stewardship theory of the presidency. It claimed that "the executive power was limited only by specific restrictions appearing in the Constitution or imposed by Congress under its constitutional powers." Historians, popular writers, and others credit Roosevelt with transforming the presidency by bringing to it a popularity, an aggressiveness, a dynamic leadership, and an empowerment greater than in the past. Roosevelt's conduct marked a significant incremental change rather than a new transition from passiveness to strength.

Historians paint William Howard Taft as a passive executive who governed in the Whig tradition. Still, in foreign affairs he exercised his power aggressively in interventionist polices in Asia and Latin America, derided often as dollar diplomacy. Less flamboyantly than Roosevelt, he took upon himself the role of policeman. He ordered marines into Nicaragua and Honduras, ostensibly to protect American lives and property but basically to advance American economic interests. As in the past, Congress acquiesced in these uses of force. Some legislative skeptics, though, wanted to deny appropriations for these interventions without the consent of Congress, except in emergencies. When out of office, Taft defended his presidential style and attacked the stewardship theory. He maintained "that the President can exercise no power" unless granted by the Constitution or by an act of Congress. He had "no residuum of power which he can exercise because it seems to him to be in the public interest." Even so, Taft did not regard himself a passive leader.

Well before reaching the White House, Woodrow Wilson held clear-cut views on presidential power. As a young academic, he regarded Congress as possessing the dominant federal power and the chief executive as feeble. Four years before running for president, he reversed his outlook on how much power a president could command in competition with Congress. Once a president assumed control with popular backing, he maintained, no single force could

withstand him. He "is at liberty, both in law and conscience, to be as big a man as he can. His capacity will set the limit." Wilson believed the president could exercise his greatest power in foreign affairs, primarily because of his ability to initiate policy. In sum, Wilson maintained that the executive "office will be as big and as influential as the man who occupies it."

In 1914, in a minor incident involving American sailors and a Mexican revolutionary leader Wilson detested, he decided to use military force. He claimed constitutional authority to act as he wished "without recourse to the Congress" but said he preferred to have its consent. The House approved his request. Before the Senate acted on the measure, however, a German ship with arms for revolutionaries headed for Veracruz, and Wilson, on his assumed authority as commander in chief, ordered warships to bombard the city and troops to occupy it. The legislators then consented to a fait accompli. Outside Washington, most observers found no satisfying justification for this violence. Many perceived it as a capricious use of executive power against a feeble opponent.

Wilson relied on the same personal conviction of being compelled to act in support of a righteous cause in policing Haitians. When he wanted to extend the occupation of Haiti, his secretary of state told him international law could not justify it but humane reasons might. The president said he too feared "we have not the legal authority to do what we apparently ought to do." Nonetheless, he proceeded with the occupation. He reported his action to Congress only after he had taken control. As usual, by now in such unilateral intervention, Congress acquiesced. With similar reasoning, Wilson policed the Dominican Republic with U.S. troops commanded by a naval officer.

In 1916, when Mexican rebels command by Francisco "Pancho" Villa raided American border towns, raising demands in Congress and elsewhere for retaliation and even war, Wilson resisted. Then, for a number reasons, including an assumed need to appear tough to an electorate that would soon vote on his bid for a second term, he ordered an invasion of Mexico to capture and punish Villa. It brought the nation to the brink of war before the president pulled back to face a crisis with Germany.

When World War I erupted, Wilson proclaimed neutrality and, despite his feelings of kinship with England, tried to maintain a balanced policy toward the belligerents. When he took a hard position against Germany because of its submarine warfare against Allied and neutral shipping, his secretary of state, William Jennings Bryan, resigned in protest. He said the country opposed the intervention in Mexico and to being drawn into the war in Europe. Nonetheless, on his own authority in defiance of Congress and "without special warrant of law," the president armed merchant ships and took other measures against Germany.

Finally, Wilson declared German submarine attacks "a warfare against mankind" but did not ask Congress to declare war. Instead, he requested it to declare Germany's actions "nothing less than a war against the . . . United States," asserting that "the status of a belligerent" had been "thrust upon" the nation. People from all walks of life begged the legislators to vote against war, but Congress did as the president desired. As some biographers and others point out, Wilson's will and his exercise of presidential power stand out as decisive in taking the nation from neutrality to armed neutrality and then to war. Immediately, as commander in chief he requested, and Congress granted, vast authority to mobilize the nation's resources, a power he used dictatorially because he believed it necessary to win the war. He curbed civil liberties and squelched dissenters at home more fiercely than had Lincoln.

At his own discretion, the president also thrust 14,000 troops into Russia to fight Bolshevism, or what skeptics dubbed "Mr. Wilson's little war with Russia." On his own authority, he also dispatched troops to Manchuria. Critics attacked these interventions as usurping congressional authority. In 1919, Wilson broke the tradition of having the secretary of state and others negotiate with foreign leaders by himself leading the American delegation to the Paris Peace Conference. He thus set the precedent for presidents to participate in summit conferences. At Paris he exploited the prestige of his office and the force of his personality to achieve personal goals he identified with those of the nation. In this instance, his use of power backfired. When, as a semiparalyzed invalid, he insisted that the Senate approve the Treaty of Versailles with the League of Nations embedded in it, his exploitation of presidential power came to an end that he refused to recognize. He had lost the confidence of both Congress and the public.

In subsequent years, evaluators differed sharply, and sometimes emotionally, over Wilson's wielding of power in foreign relations. Friendly biographers and historians viewed his extension of presidential power, mostly in foreign affairs, as virtuous. They contend he performed extraordinarily well and praise him as a splendid example of the strong, decisive executive. Critics argue that he abused his powers, pointing out he had resorted to force more often than any previous president. Regardless of the varying perspectives on his handling of power, Wilson set new precedents for expanding the president's role in foreign affairs and domestically in matters related to war.

In part as a backlash against Wilson's perceived arrogance in wielding power, the electorate chose Warren G. Harding and then Calvin Coolidge to lead the nation. Both men usually left management of foreign affairs to their secretaries of state and diplomats in the field. Coolidge, though, drew on presidential authority according to precedent in what he termed police actions to protect American lives and property abroad. When he intervened in China with warships and marines, he said that the civil turmoil there had compelled him to employ force. When he deployed some 5,500 marines in Nicaragua, ostensibly to protect Americans and their investments but especially to battle revolutionaries he called bandits, Democrats called the clash his private war. Coolidge shot back that his actions no more constituted making war than those of a policeman carrying out his job. He demonstrated again that even a weak president could unilaterally use his power abroad on the basis of ideology or a personal agenda.

Herbert Hoover believed "the increasing ascendancy of the Executive over the Legislative arm . . . has run to great excesses" and that the legislature's authority "must be respected and strengthened." In his memoirs he stated that the "constitutional division of powers . . . was not designed as a battleground to display the prowess of Presidents." Yet as president, he wanted to shape foreign policy in his own way. He repudiated dollar diplomacy and promised not to use his foreign relations power to intervene in small states, as in Latin America. When Japan in 1931 seized Manchuria, he withheld recognition of the conquest but resisted pressure to impose economic sanctions on Japan because he believed they would trigger war. He opposed employing force because "it would be a recommendation that Congress should declare war." Contemporaries and numerous historians mark him as a failed president because he embraced what they called isolationism and refused to exercise his power expansively to combat the Great Depression or to police Japanese, Cubans, and others. Yet he did not act as a weakling. Unlike some other presidents, he used his power in foreign affairs to keep the nation at peace when some advisers wanted to court war.

THE WAR POWER AS PREROGATIVE

Franklin D. Roosevelt believed a president should exude strength and use his power boldly to achieve what he perceived as desirable goals. In his inaugural address in 1933, alluding to the nation's economic crisis he said, "I shall ask Congress for . . . broad Executive power to wage a war against the emergency, as great as the power that would be given me if we were in fact invaded by a foreign foe."

From the start, Roosevelt had to contend with the isolationist and revisionist theory that America's intervention in World War I had stemmed from a malign presidential discretion in foreign affairs. In 1936 his perspective on executive authority received a boost from the Supreme Court case *United States* v. *Curtiss-Wright Export Corporation*. This case involved the right of the president to ban the sale of arms to a belligerent, in this instance to Bolivia during the Chaco War with Paraguay. The Court's ruling, in the words of Justice George Sutherland, described the president incorrectly as "the sole organ of the federal government in the field of international relations." This decision would confer an erroneous legitimacy beyond the Constitution on the unilateral actions of executives in matters of war and peace. In contrast, the legislative branch wanted to prevent the president from manipulating the nation into war.

So, in legislation known as the neutrality acts, Congress placed restraints on the president's power in foreign affairs. Roosevelt disliked the laws but accepted them because they might quiet the public fear of "excessive fear of presidential control." In a speech in Chicago on 5 October 1937, he spoke out against the neutrality laws as favoring aggressors, whom he wanted to quarantine. He also expressed alarm over a referendum movement headed by Louis Ludlow, a Democratic representative from Indiana, that proposed a constitutional amendment requiring voter approval before a declaration of war could go into effect. Roosevelt contended it "would cripple any President in his conduct of our foreign relations." His opposition proved critical in defeating it.

As war loomed in Europe, Roosevelt became increasingly assertive about his foreign policy prerogatives, announcing in January 1939 he would as commander in chief provide arms to Britain and France for defense against Nazi Germany. In September, when Adolf Hitler triggered World War II by invading Poland, the president's standing in opinion polls shot up. Increasingly, he acted in foreign matters independently of Congress, as when Britain requested old warships in exchange for some of its bases in the Western Hemisphere. Even though legislation prohibited such a transaction, Roosevelt made use of Sutherland's opinion, circumvented the Senate, and made the deal. Critics condemned the swap as a breach of the Constitution and violation of international law, but it stood.

Proclaiming the United States the arsenal of democracy, Roosevelt in March 1941 persuaded Congress to pass the Lend-Lease Act, which permitted him to give arms to beleaguered Britain. Critics called it a qualified declaration of war and the most sweeping delegation of legislative power ever made to a president. When German submarines sank vessels carrying American munitions, he ordered the navy to patrol the North Atlantic sea lanes to protect the shipping. Patrol in this case functioned as a euphemism for convoy, an act of war under international law. By unilateral executive action he ordered troops to occupy Greenland, imposed increasingly stiff economic sanctions against Japan, and took over Iceland. By November, clashes with Axis submarines brought the United States into an undeclared naval war with Nazi Germany, a belligerent status he did not make clear to the American people. On his own authority, he also promised armed support to the British, Dutch, and Thais in Asia if Japan struck at them.

When Japan on 7 December 1941 attacked the United States, with Germany and Italy then declaring war, the president asked Congress to recognize that a state of war already existed. Political opponents and others charged him with leading the nation into war through deception via the back door of Asia rather than Europe and by maneuvering the Japanese into firing the first shot because he could not obtain enough support for a congressional declaration of war. No one had proof for these theories, but the president's supporters as well as his critics acknowledge that step by step he exploited his foreign relations power to move the nation toward active belligerency.

Roosevelt also utilized his augmented power to conduct the war with virtually dictatorial authority. He seldom referred to Congress, violated civil liberties by incarcerating with an executive order thousands of Japanese Americans, inaugurated secret security files on government employees, and instituted price controls. "This total war . . . ," he told Congress, "makes the use of executive power far more essential than in any previous war." He added, "I shall not hesitate to use every power vested in me" to win the war. With Winston Churchill and Joseph Stalin at Yalta, he slipped around Congress with personal promises on territorial questions and international organization. He assumed full responsibility for developing the atomic bomb. Viewing himself as the nation's steward and his leadership role as personal and institutional, he rarely allowed anything to stand in the way of his exercise of power. The courts supported that role, upholding as constitutional every wartime measure he took. Nonetheless, his hoarding of power alarmed the enemies of executive aggrandizement.

In thirteen years, Roosevelt raised presidential power in foreign affairs to a level higher than that reached by any of his predecessors. As had Lincoln and Wilson, he upset the constitutional balance of checks and balances using the same justification of the need to rescue the nation from a great peril. Various scholars maintain he transformed the presidency, or, at least in the area of foreign policy, brought changes to it that have endured and influenced successors.

The public, together with academics who admired the strong president regardless of how he stretched his constitutional powers, welcomed the changes and praised Roosevelt and his leadership style. This admiration, along with the cumulative effect of the previous presidents who had swelled executive authority in dealing with foreign affairs, laid the basis for a kind of cult that exalted the presidency at the expense of Congress. The flowering of this cult could be seen during the presidency of Harry S. Truman and the start of the Cold War.

Roosevelt had kept Truman in the dark on the intricacies of foreign policy. For instance, Truman did not learn the details of the atomic arms project until several weeks into office, but he soon made one of his most controversial foreign policy decisions. He ordered the atomic bombing of Hiroshima and then of Nagasaki. Skeptics denounced this action as ethically wrong and unnecessary, but he took full responsibility for it

as necessary to save lives. Thereafter, he became accustomed to wielding power and was determined to prove himself a take-charge executive.

Truman asked Congress to extend the executive's wartime power as Roosevelt had possessed it. In December 1945 the legislators agreed and Truman carried that authority into the Cold War. Largely at his insistence, in the Atomic Energy Act of August 1946, Congress placed control over nuclear weapons in the president's hands. Proponents of the strong-executive concept then began to argue that atomic weapons and the need for quick response to foreign dangers increased the need for presidents to have more power as commander in chief.

In January 1946, with an executive directive, Truman created a central intelligence agency group directly responsible to the president. In July 1947, in the National Security Act, Congress converted the group into the Central Intelligence Agency, later freed it from budgetary controls imposed on other agencies, and with it amplified presidential power abroad. In addition to analyzing intelligence, the CIA quickly engaged in covert activities. It thus came to serve as a shield for secret executive decisions on the use of military force. The legislation also established the National Security Council, a body designed to advise the president on all matters affecting military power and national security as well as foreign policy. Since the law, amended in 1949, required neither the council nor the national security adviser to be approved by Congress or to report to it, the act had the effect of enhancing the president's power in deploying the military on his own and on embarking unilaterally on foreign policy ventures that could lead to war.

As an avid anticommunist, Truman used his power to embark on a program, usually called the Truman Doctrine, of containing Soviet expansion, at first in Turkey and Greece and then in Western Europe with the Marshall Plan. This program, approved by Congress, became the vehicle for another expansion of executive authority in foreign affairs. It had precedents, as in Theodore Roosevelt's policing in the Caribbean, but since Truman viewed communism as a global threat, he asserted a right to intervene militarily anywhere in the world when he deemed the action proper. He converted the nation's military machine into the world's foremost anticommunist police force with himself as its commander in chief.

During a crisis that began when the Soviets in June 1948 blockaded Berlin, 110 miles into East

> ✦ ✦ ✦ ✦ ✦
>
> ## THREE VIEWS ON PRESIDENTIAL POWER
>
> "In no part of the Constitution is more wisdom to be found than in the clause which confides the question of war or peace to the legislature and not to the executive department. . . . War is in fact the true nurse of executive aggrandizement. In war, a physical force is to be created; and it is the executive will which is to direct it. . . . In war the honors and emoluments of office are to be multiplied; and it is executive patronage under which they are to be enjoyed. It is in war, finally, that laurels are to be gathered, and it is the executive brow they are to encircle. . . . Hence it is the practice of all states, in proportion as they are free, to disarm this propensity of its influence: hence it has grown into an axiom that the executive is the department of power most distinguished by its propensity to war."
>
> *—James Madison, "Helvidius" no. 4,*
> *14 September 1793 —*
>
> "Allow the President to invade a neighboring nation, whenever *he* shall deem it necessary to repel an invasion, and you allow him to do so, *whenever he may choose to say* he deems it necessary for such purpose—and you allow him to make war at pleasure. Study to see if you can fix *any limit* to his power in this respect. . . . Kings had always been involving and impoverishing their people in wars, pretending generally, if not always, that the good of the people was the object. . . . [The Constitution maintains] that *no one man* should hold the power of bringing this oppression upon us."
>
> *—Abraham Lincoln,*
> *15 February 1848 —*
>
> "When the push of a button may mean obliteration of countless humans, the President of the United States must be forever on guard against any inclination on his part to impetuosity; to arrogance; to headlong action; to expediency; to facile maneuvers; even to the popularity of an action as opposed to the rightness of an action. He cannot worry about headlines; how the next opinion poll will rate him; how his political future will be affected."
>
> *—Dwight D. Eisenhower,*
> *4 November 1960 —*

Germany, the question of presidential power came up in the courts. As usual, they upheld executive activism, ruling that "the war power does not necessarily end with the cessation of hostilities." Justice Robert H. Jackson, who had justified the stretching of executive authority in the destroyer-bases deal, objected to "this vague, undefined and undefinable 'war power'" that presidents "invoked in haste" to deal with crises, often of their own making. "No one will question," he wrote, "that this power is the most dangerous one to free government in the whole catalogue of powers."

Truman nonetheless pressed ahead with his Cold War policy. He negotiated and persuaded Congress to approve a series of multilateral treaties that ended the nation's traditional policy of avoiding formal alliances in time of peace. Consequently, the Inter-American Treaty of Reciprocal Assistance (1947, known also as the Rio Pact), the charter of the Organization of American States (1948), and the North Atlantic Treaty (1949) placed more of the war-making power in the executive branch.

In January 1950, as part of his anticommunist crusade, Truman on his own authorized the building of a hydrogen bomb. Five months later, he made another swift decision of worldwide significance. When communist forces from the north invaded the Republic of Korea to the south, he intervened militarily. In rushing into hostilities, he circumvented both Congress and the United Nations Security Council. When opponents in Congress wondered if Truman had arrogated to himself the authority of declaring war, he denied being at war. Using a traditional euphemism, he called the conflict a police action. Later, though, he contended that "when a nation is at war, its leader . . . ought to have all the tools available for that purpose." When pressed to seek a congressional declaration, he dismissed the idea because public opinion polls indicated broad support for his stance. When the war went badly, with mounting costs and casualties, the polls reported a sharp decline in his popularity and support for what many called "Truman's War."

As the discontent grew, so did distrust of presidential authority as wielded by Roosevelt and Truman. In consequence, in February 1951 a movement for a two-term cap for any president succeeded in making the limitation part of the Constitution as the Twenty-second Amendment. As time would reveal, it did not curb presidential power in foreign matters. In April 1952, when Truman seized steel mills under the guise of his war power, his elastic use of executive authority received another setback. In one of its rare decisions against a president in time of war, the Supreme Court ruled the takeover unconstitutional because it considered neither the Korean War nor the Cold War full-scale emergencies that justified such an arrogation of executive power.

Again, a president had amplified the foreign policy powers of his office beyond his predecessors. Where others had employed the military on their own in small ventures abroad or had maneuvered Congress and the public into supporting major wars, Truman, without congressional assent, initiated a large-scale war against a sovereign nation backed by two great powers. He and his advisers cited earlier small commitments of troops as precedents for his actions, but legal scholars pointed out that reliance on previous executive breaches of the constitutional war power did not legitimate subsequent violations. He and his advisers, such as Secretary of State Dean Acheson, also claimed that as commander in chief he possessed a prerogative to initiate war. Other presidents had also theorized about inherent power, but he became the first to exploit that concept as though it were fact. Regardless of the questioned legitimacy of Truman's use of the foreign policy power, other presidents would follow his lead.

COLD WAR INTERVENTIONISM

Dwight D. Eisenhower sought the presidency because he disliked the assaults on what he perceived, in his words, as "the President's constitutional rights, in peacetime, to deploy and dispose American forces according to his best judgment and without the specific approval of Congress." He regarded those rights as "unassailable" and wanted to thwart politicians in his own party, the Republicans, eager to diminish executive authority. He also had a Whiglike conception of the office based on his conviction that Franklin Roosevelt and Truman had upset the proper balance between the branches of government at the expense of Congress. So, despite his determination to protect executive authority, contemporaries viewed him as opposed to aggrandizing the presidency.

In practice, Eisenhower, like Jefferson, did not allow abstract considerations to stand in the way of actions he perceived appropriate. To end the Korean War, for example, he informed the North Koreans through several channels that he would employ atomic weapons against them if they refused an armistice. He acted with similar determination when conservatives in his own party, led by Senator John W. Bricker of Ohio, tried, with a proposed constitutional amendment, to eliminate the president's power to make executive agreements. Eisenhower contended the measure would cripple executive authority in world affairs. "The President," he insisted, "must not be deprived of his historic position as spokesman for the nation in its relations with other countries." His opposition proved critical in the amendment's narrow defeat.

When the French, involved in an anticolonial war in Southeast Asia, begged the president to intervene to save troops beleaguered in a fortress in northern Vietnam, despite his deep anticommunist convictions, Eisenhower refused. "Part of my fundamental concept of the Presidency," he explained, "is that we have a constitutional government and only when there is a sudden, unforeseen emergency should the President put us into war without congressional sanction." Despite this perspective and contrary to what many assumed, Eisenhower was not a dove. He was willing to use armed force in Vietnam but only on his own terms.

At the same time, Eisenhower expanded use of the CIA as a weapon in covert Cold War armed ventures. With secret anticommunist operations he put aside the constitutional restraints on the presidency he professed to value. He ordered the CIA to topple Mohammed Mossadegh, Iran's nationalist prime minister, which with local help it did. Eisenhower also employed covert violence to overthrow the legally elected president of Guatemala, Jacobo Arbenz Guzmán, a populist he viewed as a communist. These episodes reveal that despite what contemporary pundits perceived as passive qualities in Eisenhower's leadership, when determined to attain his own foreign policy objectives, he would use a heavy hand.

Eisenhower exercised his power as commander in chief more openly when the People's Republic of China threatened to attack Chiang

Kai-shek's Nationalist government on Taiwan (Formosa). When the mainland communists bombed Quemoy and Matsu, two offshore islands held by the Nationalists, his military advisers urged retaliatory strikes. Ike said no, indicating that against a major foe he would not use the war power lightly. Although Eisenhower assumed that in this situation as commander in chief he had authority to act on his own, he asked Congress for consent to deal with any emergency that might subsequently arise in the Taiwan Strait. He wanted to avoid the divisive debate that had followed Truman's intervention in Korea. Congress responded with a joint resolution authorizing him to use the armed forces "as he deemed necessary" to protect Taiwan and other islands in friendly hands. In voting this blank check, Congress diminished its own war power, enhanced that of the president, and opened a door for later presidents to seek similar authority.

Meanwhile, with a secret CIA operation the president had launched a program to foment rebellion in Eastern European countries that would liberate them from Soviet domination. Then, in October 1956, as he campaigned for reelection, students in Budapest, Hungary, revolted. When Soviet troops crushed the uprising, Eisenhower admitted he could do nothing tangible to aid them without risking a major war, thus recognizing the limitations on executive power. His decision also reflected what he had stated many times, that he would "never be guilty of any kind of action that can be interpreted as war until Congress, which has the constitutional authority, says so."

The foreign relations power also became an issue in a concurrent crisis. It began when Egyptian strongman Gamal Abdel Nasser seized the Suez Canal from its European owners. On 29 October 1956, Israeli troops, followed by British and French forces, invaded Egypt without informing their American ally. An angry Eisenhower condemned the attack, but when the Soviets threatened intervention, he ordered a partial mobilization of the armed forces. In addition, with economic and diplomatic pressure, he compelled the British, French, and Israelis to withdraw from Egypt. In this situation, he exercised his foreign policy power unilaterally, swiftly, and decisively.

Next, fearing that the Russians might still resort to force in the Middle East, Eisenhower moved to deter them. As during the Taiwan Strait crisis, he asked Congress to authorize him to employ the armed forces to defend the "independence and integrity" of Middle Eastern countries menaced by "communist armed aggression." After two months of debate, the legislators voted him another blank check, this one termed the Eisenhower Doctrine, that endorsed his role as a global, anti-Marxist policeman. A year later, the president applied the doctrine indirectly to a civil war in Lebanon. In his only overt intervention, in July 1958, on his authority as commander in chief, he ordered troops to invade Lebanon. Insisting he had not committed an act of war, Eisenhower argued he had acted within his constitutional authority and in keeping with executive precedents. Critics, though, maintained he had initiated a presidential war. At the same time, he used the CIA in a secret intervention in Indonesia designed to crumble the regime of Achmad Sukarno, considered too cozy with communists. Popular sentiment could speak less clearly on Eisenhower's overt and covert policy toward a left-wing revolutionary government in Cuba headed by Fidel Castro. At his discretion, the CIA clandestinely launched commando strikes against Castro, hatched schemes to assassinate him, and planned, with Cuban exiles in Florida, an invasion of the island. Before Eisenhower could unleash this operation, his presidency ended.

Analysts differ in their assessments of Eisenhower as president and his use of power in foreign affairs. Some say he delegated too much of his authority while others portray him as a strong executive who exercised his power with a hidden hand. He claimed to have had the final word in every major foreign policy issue and hence had served as an activist president. He also believed that he had curbed executive aggrandizement. Yet, through his aggressive anticommunist ventures, his covert operations, and the global reach of American power, under him the power of the president in foreign affairs as commander in chief continued to rise.

During the presidential election campaign of 1960, John F. Kennedy announced he would "be the Chief Executive in every sense of the word" and that the president should "exercise the fullest powers of his office—all that are specified and some that are not." He also carried into office a preference for dealing with foreign over domestic affairs. For instance, he devoted most of his inaugural address to the Cold War. "Domestic policy," he later repeated, "can only defeat us, foreign policy can kill us."

Into his official family Kennedy brought intellectual young zealots "full of belligerence," as one of them later remarked, who admired the concept of the tough, activist executive. With them he quickly immersed himself in the details of foreign policy, deciding at the outset to continue Eisenhower's covert plan to crush Cuba's Castro. Most of Kennedy's intimate advisers backed the venture. Among the few who knew of it, Senator J. William Fulbright, chairman of the Senate Committee on Foreign Relations, objected. He pointed out that "the Castro regime is a thorn in the flesh, but it is not a dagger in the heart." Dismissing this advice, Kennedy continued the practice of using the CIA to harass Cubans and prepare for an invasion, which, without the consent of Congress, he launched on 17 April 1961, on Cuba's south shore at the Bay of Pigs. It turned into a fiasco, for which the president publicly accepted blame. Despite the bloody blunder, polls showed that his popularity shot up. In a private discussion of the disaster, he asked, "It really is true that foreign affairs is the only important issue for a President to handle, isn't it? . . . Who gives a shit if the minimum wage is $1.15 or $1.25 in comparison to something like this?" As confidants noted, Castro then became a personal affront, an obsession that Kennedy transmuted into a threat to American security. He persevered, therefore, in covert efforts to overthrow the dictator.

At the same time, Kennedy had to deal with the Berlin question. Soviet premier Nikita Khrushchev renewed demands that Allied occupiers depart the city and set a deadline with an implied threat of war if not met. With a determination to show toughness, Kennedy prepared for possible hostilities. He expanded the armed forces, ordered reservists to active duty, and asked Congress for an additional $3 billion in military spending, which it granted. When this crisis passed, he again focused on Castro.

State Department officials and others reported the presence of Soviet troops and missiles in Cuba. Kennedy warned that if the communist buildup menaced American security, he would take forceful action. He said that "as President and Commander in Chief" he had full authority to act on his own. But he did request Congress to endorse the use of arms. It agreed overwhelmingly with a joint resolution. On 14 October 1962, when a U-2 surveillance plane reported Soviet launching pads in Cuba with medium-range missiles targeted on American cities, the crisis deepened. Initially, as his closest

advisers urged, the president wanted to respond with air strikes on Cuba and even possibly on the Soviet Union. After six days of discussion, he chose to ring Cuba with a naval blockade he called a quarantine. If the Soviets challenged it, the world would face its first nuclear war. Except for a few friendly members whom the president had informed of his decisions, Congress had no role in this war scare. Fortunately, Khrushchev backed down and the crisis passed. With toughness, the president appeared to have won a great diplomatic victory.

Kennedy's admirers praised his behavior as brilliant, as an example of "genuine statesmanship" that in thirteen critical days "dazzled the world," and as the greatest achievement of his presidency. They cited his conduct as validation for supreme presidential control over foreign policy and war-making in the nuclear age. Skeptics, and even several close advisers, thought differently. They perceived his rattling of nuclear arms as irresponsible and reckless. One critic commented that he risked "blowing the world to hell in order to sweep a few Democrats into office" in forthcoming congressional elections. Others questioned the wisdom of placing so much power in the hands of one man. As for the public, that power did not bother it much. Polls showed that after the crisis, Kennedy's approval rating climbed from 61 to 84 percent. Later, when Soviet sources revealed the presence of nuclear weapons in Cuba, Kennedy's conduct proved more prudent than either the public or detractors had realized.

Elsewhere, Kennedy continued his armed interventionism, as in the Dominican Republic to get rid of an aging dictator and to aid Joaquín Belaguer, a leader he thought would edge the republic toward democracy. When elections brought to power a left-wing intellectual, Kennedy refused to help him because he saw him as tainted with communism. As in other instances, the personal perception of a president, as much as policy considerations, governed use of the foreign policy power.

This happened also in Southeast Asia, where Kennedy accepted Eisenhower's domino theory that if communism prevailed in one country, as in Laos or Vietnam, it would spread over the entire region. Kennedy believed that if he tolerated communism there, he could not win reelection. So, he poured economic and military assistance into the anticommunist Republic of Vietnam. In addition, he sent in military advisers, who ferried troops into battle against local communists called Vietcong and against northern communists. Ultimately, he committed more than 16,000 troops to the anticommunist side in the civil wars in Laos and Vietnam.

Kennedy left a mixed legacy. Strong-presidency believers praise him as a vigorous, charismatic leader who understood the true art of statecraft. Other appraisers charge him with crisis mongering, escalating the arms race, and being enamored with military power. His unilateral use of power abroad, his conviction that he must make his mark primarily in foreign affairs, and his belief in an exceptional authority in those affairs, reflected the prevailing public approval of an expansive presidential power.

PRESIDENTIAL WAR IN VIETNAM

As an experienced politician, Lyndon B. Johnson moved swiftly to exploit this sentiment. Johnson told an aide, "Just you remember this: There's only two kinds at the White House. There's elephants and there's pissants. And I'm the only elephant." This attitude encapsulated Johnson's conception of the presidency. He saw the president as the initiator of major legislation, the creator of the national agenda, and the dominant force in foreign affairs. "The congressional role in national security," he maintained, "is not to act but to respond to the executive." He proceeded with this perspective in dealing with the warfare in Southeast Asia. "I am not going to lose Vietnam," he told an ambassador. Accordingly he sent more troops to South Vietnam and instituted secret incursions along North Vietnam's coast and naval patrols in the Gulf of Tonkin. This activity led to escalating clashes with North Vietnamese forces. After an alleged second torpedo boat attack on U.S. naval vessels, without verifying the reality of the assault and determined to give the communists "a real dose," Johnson ordered massive bombing of North Vietnamese coastal bases. Then he asked Congress for a resolution, modeled on that handed to Eisenhower in the Taiwan crises. With it, Congress promised to support all measures he would take against armed attacks or to prevent aggression. Only two senators objected to this open-ended grant of power. One of them pointed out that "the Constitution does not permit the President to wage war at his discretion."

Johnson argued he possessed that power but wanted it reinforced by the resolution, which he compared to Grandma's nightshirt because "it covered everything." He also made clear the decision to use force "was mine—and mine alone." On this basis, initially with high public approval as measured by polls, he steadily enlarged the American war in Vietnam. Slowly, though, an antiwar movement gained support and spread over the country. Some of its leaders accused him of seeking support for a war that involved no vital national interest by lying to the public.

Briefly, Johnson's intervention in a civil conflict in the Dominican Republic in April 1965 shifted attention from the Vietnam debate. He gave a variety of reasons for deploying 23,000 troops on the island. Most often, he said he acted to avert a communist takeover and to protect endangered American lives. The occupiers found no evidence of a communist plot or peril to American lives. At home and abroad, jurists and others denounced the intervention as a violation of international law. Domestic critics pointed out that he had invaded without seeking congressional consent. He responded that he merely exercised what had become traditional executive power in foreign affairs.

Johnson offered similar rationalization for making war in Vietnam. He cited the Tonkin Gulf resolution as evidence of congressional support for his policy but asserted that he did not need its approval because the "Commander in Chief has all the authority that I am exercising." In the summer of 1966, as the public's approval rating of his presidency plummeted, he said defiantly, "I'm not going down in history as the first American President who lost a war." He persisted in viewing conflict largely in terms of his own stake in it, which he stretched to identify with the national interest. He spoke of "my troops" and of his war that he would run his way.

In an effort to refute critics, Johnson ordered the State Department to prepare a tract justifying the war. Dutifully, a subordinate argued that the president had ample authority to use force on his own, to decide what constituted an attack on the United States, and thus to commit troops anywhere in the world for such defense. He cited the Quasi-War and the Korean War as precedents, thus in the latter case using an example of dubious constitutionality to sanction another case of questionable validity. All the while, antiwar activists denounced Johnson as a "slob" and "murderer." This personal disdain stained the presidency. Reverence for it declined. Polls indicated that about half the public considered the war a mistake. Johnson took criticism personally, dismissing it usually as unpatriotic. He placed antiwar leaders under surveillance and violated their civil rights. At one point he blurted, "This is not Johnson's war. This is America's war."

Finally, much of the public and various legislators, even in the president's own party, could stand no more. They said he had come to exercise "virtually plenary power to determine foreign policy" and "it is time for us to end the continual erosion of legislative authority." Gallup polls showed that the public view of the war as wrong had risen to 79 percent. Then, when a primary in New Hampshire indicated that Johnson could not win reelection, he withdrew his candidacy. The pubic did not turn against Johnson for using power illegitimately, for lying, or for waging war unilaterally. They wanted him out because of a failed use of the foreign affairs power in a war with high casualties and no benefits. Americans had tolerated, and even praised, comparable use of the war power by other presidents. None, though, had exploited that power as outrageously as he did. With that power he ran amok but did not, as some analysts claim, weaken the presidency. Although Richard M. Nixon, in his second bid for the presidency in 1968, benefited from the backlash against Johnson's Vietnam policy, he too believed in the concept of executive supremacy in foreign affairs. Like Johnson, Nixon was a man of vaulting ambition well known for his hawkish views on the war. In his election campaign he stressed that "the next President must take an activist view of his office" and have a strong will. Nixon maintained that bold initiatives abroad always had come from strong presidents. In office, he acted on that premise.

From the start, Vietnam clouded Nixon's administration. Even though he had promised to terminate the entanglement there, at his inaugural, antiwar demonstrators—shouting "Four more years of death!"—pelted his limousine with debris. Undeterred, he reshaped Johnson's Vietnam policy while retaining its substance. He continued an air war in Laos and peace negotiations in Paris, began sustained bombing of North Vietnam, and launched secret air strikes in neutral Cambodia. We must, he explained, negotiate from strength and not withdraw unilaterally from the conflict in Southeast Asia.

Alarmed senators then passed a resolution that deplored past executive excesses and recognized no presidential commitment to continue the war. Claiming that as commander in chief he possessed sole authority over the armed forces and could order them abroad without specific congressional approval, Nixon ignored the resolution. He thereby charted a collision course with Congress. He did pull some troops out of Vietnam, but peace advocates complained about the slow pace. As antiwar demonstrations escalated, Nixon bristled. As had Johnson, he declared he would not be the "first American President to lose a war." Polls taken at this time, October 1969, indicated majority support for his position.

In April of the next year, without consulting Congress, the president launched an invasion of Cambodia, justifying it with various explanations such as routing North Vietnamese ensconced there. "Bold decisions," he said, "make history." A substantial segment of the public viewed the action differently, as an unwarranted widening of the war. Peace demonstrations escalated across the nation. To counter the furor, Nixon asked the State Department to make a case for his decision. Accordingly, an assistant attorney general, William H. Rehnquist, argued that as commanders in chief, presidents had the authority to order troops "into conflict with foreign powers on their own initiative" and even to deploy them "in a way that invited hostile retaliation." Hence, Nixon had acted properly. Historian Arthur M. Schlesinger Jr. dismissed Rehnquist's contention as "persiflage"—compromising historical and legal scholarship for service to his client. Congress then revived an endeavor to restrain the president's assumed power to make war unilaterally. The Senate passed a bill forbidding involvement in Cambodia without its consent and repealed the Tonkin Gulf Resolution. Nixon dismissed these measures, avowing that as commander in chief he could maintain the warfare on his own. At this juncture, for seemingly personal reasons, Nixon unilaterally made another controversial foreign relations decision. In a war between India and Pakistan that broke out in December 1971, despite considerable sentiment for at least neutrality, he sided with Pakistan. He ordered a naval task force into the Bay of Bengal to intimidate India. Critics pointed out that the United States had no vital stake in the conflict, yet he alienated India and risked possible war with the Soviets, who sided with India. In February he did enhance his image as a maker of foreign policy with a trip to the People's Republic of China that initiated a détente with that old foe.

In December 1972, Nixon ordered twelve days of around-the-clock bombing of Hanoi and Haiphong. Critics denounced it as war by tantrum, as violence beyond all reason, and called him a maddened tyrant. He responded that if the Russians and Chinese thought "they were dealing with a madman," they might then "force North Vietnam into a settlement before the world was consumed by larger war." Finally, public pressure drove him in January to conclude cease-fire accords with North Vietnam, but he continued secret bombing raids in Cambodia and Laos as well as aid to anticommunist regimes in the region. When these actions became known, Congress decided to enact "definite, unmistakable procedures to prevent future undeclared wars." It compelled Nixon to end hostile actions in Indochina.

Meanwhile, the Cold War presidential practice of covertly aiding conservative candidates for high office in foreign countries backfired. Nixon had directed the CIA to block Salvador Allende Gossens, a socialist legally elected president in Chile, from taking office. When that effort failed, Nixon ordered the CIA to organize a military coup against Allende that on 12 September 1973 led to his murder and to a right-wing dictatorship in Chile.

In October, as Nixon's involvement in the Watergate scandal came to light, the Yom Kippur War between Israel and Egypt and Syria erupted. He airlifted supplies to Israel. To counter an alleged Soviet plan to intervene, he ordered a worldwide alert of U.S. forces, including nuclear strike forces. Critics regarded this order as unnecessarily drastic. They suspected he issued it to divert public attention from his troubles with Congress, or as an example of using the foreign policy power to deal with domestic political exigencies. Then, on 7 November, after decades of debate over the war-making capacity in the president's foreign-affairs power, Congress overrode Nixon's veto to adopt the War Powers Resolution. It required the president, in the absence of a declaration of war, to report to Congress within forty-eight hours after ordering troops into a foreign conflict. Unless the legislators approved a longer deployment, he had to withdraw the force within sixty days. The law allowed an extension of thirty days if the president deemed that time necessary for a safe withdrawal. It also placed curbs on his ability to circumvent Congress, to deploy armed forces in hostile situations, and to engage in covert military ventures. But by permitting the president to deploy forces for a limited time without congressional consent, it subverted the aim of collective decision making in foreign policy. As skeptics pointed out, the resolution delegated to the president more power in foreign affairs than the Constitution allowed. It granted him freedom to wage war for several months anywhere in the world as he chose.

Despite his critics and facing impeachment, Nixon contended he had acted much like other strong executives who had taken for granted an inherent right to employ their foreign policy power to intervene unilaterally in other nations, especially weak ones. They, too, had lied, acted covertly, and had skirted Congress. Only he suffered punishment, and only because of evidence uncovered in secret tapes he made of White House conversations about his involvement in the Watergate scandal. This was true, but he did abuse the foreign policy power more than his predecessors.

While out of office, Nixon continued to defend his extravagant conception of the strong executive. He contended that in wartime the president has "certain extraordinary powers" that make otherwise illegal acts lawful when taken to preserve the nation. In this perspective, the president alone decided what served the best interest of the nation. Critics maintained that with such views and his behavior, primarily in foreign affairs, he demonstrated that unrestrained power in the hands of a paranoid president could endanger democratic government.

REVIVAL OF THE STRONG PRESIDENCY CULT

On taking over the presidency in 1974 after Nixon's resignation, Gerald R. Ford made clear he would continue his predecessor's war policy and that he had no intention of reducing what he perceived as the executive's power in foreign affairs. In his first speech before Congress, he expressed briefly his view of that authority: "Throughout my public service, I have upheld all our Presidents when they spoke for my country to the world. I believe the Constitution commands this." For example, he continued covert operations. So, in the Foreign Assistance Act of 1974, Congress placed minor restraints on this practice. With this law, for the first time it openly recognized the president's assumed power to engage in covert ventures in the name of national security. Congress thus augmented the executive's power to initiate warfare unilaterally.

Ford tried to salvage what remained of Nixon's policy by asking Congress for $972 million in military and other aid for South Vietnam. Congress refused. In April 1975 the government of South Vietnam collapsed and the northern communists took over, uniting Vietnam. Several weeks later, when a Khmer Rouge, or communist, gunboat seized an American merchant ship, the SS *Mayaguez,* sixty miles off the Cambodian coast, Ford called the capture piracy and demanded release of the vessel and crew. Tardily, the Cambodian communists said they would free the men and ship. Determined to demonstrate that the commander in chief could still flex muscle, Ford resorted to force. Furthermore, instead of consulting Congress as the War Powers Resolution required, Ford "informed" it of his decision to use force. He ordered air strikes on Cambodian bases and marine commandos to rescue forty crew members already out of danger at the cost of eighteen marines and twenty-three Air Force personnel dead. Ford's popularity zoomed upward because, as Senator Barry Goldwater commented, he had not allowed "some half-assed country" to kick him around. Admirers of the strong presidency called the venture Ford's finest moment. Critics denounced this "indulgence in machismo diplomacy" as "another example of military overkill and trigger happiness." Once more, a supposedly weak president, without significant restraint by law or Congress, for personal benefit used his foreign affairs power to magnify a minor incident into an unnecessary crisis.

In his bid for the presidency, Jimmy Carter promised a foreign policy that would distinguish the United States as "a beacon light for human rights throughout the world." He also denounced covert military operations and intervention in the internal affairs of other countries. The foreign policy crisis that most bedeviled Carter's administration began with the overthrow of Shah Mohammad Reza Pahlavi of Iran. In November 1979 the trouble escalated when a mob in Teheran invaded the American embassy and seized a hundred people as hostages. When Carter failed to obtain their release through diplomacy and the crisis threatened to torpedo his chances for reelection, he decided on force in his capacity as commander in chief. He did not consult Congress, because, he contended, in this instance the War Powers Resolution did not apply. As had other presidents involved in questionable military strikes, he claimed an "inherent constitutional right" to act unilaterally. So, on his orders, on 24 April 1980, a commando group attempted by air to rescue the hostages. The oper-

ation failed, and much of the public viewed it as fiasco. Carter did not, as some advisers urged, try to smother his failure with a massive show of force and possibly war.

A civil war in Afghanistan followed by a massive invasion of Soviet troops also led Carter to shift his attitude toward the use of his power in foreign affairs. He imposed sanctions on the Soviet Union and, when they did not work as desired, exaggerated the Soviet threat to American security. He warned the Soviets that if they seized the Persian Gulf, war would follow. When European allies opposed this bellicosity, Carter pulled back. He then embarked on a program of supposedly covert aid to the Afghans. Carter exhibited less reluctance to use force in perceived low-risk, undercover interventions in Central America and Africa. Despite his tough moments, Carter did use foreign policy power effectively but for human rights and peace rather than for war.

In campaigning for the presidency, Ronald Reagan disparaged Carter for bungling the Iranian crisis, described the Vietnam War as a noble cause, promised to deal harshly with terrorists, and declared he would regenerate American pride. He pictured communism as a monolithic enemy and the Soviet Union as an "evil empire." He said little about theories of executive power, even when in office. In foreign affairs matters that interested him, however, he was an activist, hands-on executive. Reagan began using his power promptly by directing the CIA to engage in domestic spying, clandestine foreign ventures, and surveillance of Americans abroad. Within three years, he launched more than fifty covert operations, more than half of them in Central and South America. He claimed, in a form of intervention that became known as the Reagan Doctrine, the right to support with arms and other means "people fighting for their freedom against Communism wherever they were." Most international jurists regarded this globalism untenable in law.

Reagan applied his doctrine most tenaciously in Nicaragua, where, starting in March 1981, he ordered the CIA to conduct military operations against a Marxist government. The agency created an army of military adventurers and anticommunists in Honduras, called contras, from the abbreviation in Spanish for counterrevolutionaries, to carry out this mission. When the intervention became known in the United States, several legislators charged Reagan with violating the War Powers Act, but he persisted with impunity. Finally, in three pieces of legislation known as the Boland Acts, Congress cut off direct executive aid to the contras.

At the same time, in a quarrel with Libyan dictator Muammar al-Qaddafi, Reagan, as commander in chief, ordered the Sixth Fleet to Libyan waters. In a violent confrontation, it destroyed two Libyan warplanes. Reagan again defied the War Powers Resolution by twice deploying hundreds of troops in Lebanon to aid a conservative government fighting a civil war. After the fact, Congress approved this commitment. Rebels in Beirut attacked the troops, and U.S. warships shelled rebel positions. In October 1983 a rebel suicide bomber in a truck crashed through the American compound, slaughtering 241 marines. In December, after a minor confrontation, U.S. forces struck at Syria. Fearing that the casualties would become a damaging issue in the forthcoming presidential election, Reagan reluctantly removed the troops from the area.

Earlier the president had manufactured another crisis, this one on the island of Grenada in the Caribbean, reputedly to divert attention from the Beirut losses. He intervened there with some 2,000 troops to oust a far-left regime that, he said, without substantiation, threatened the lives of American students living there. He again violated the War Powers Act but defended his unilateral violence as within his power as commander in chief. Some Democrats demanded enforcement of the law and seven asked for impeachment, but Congress stood by the president. He called the events in Lebanon and Grenada "closely linked," because "Moscow assisted and encouraged the violence in both countries." Polls showed that Americans, by a margin of 90 percent, approved his bashing of Grenada.

Later, again on meager evidence, Reagan blamed Qaddafi for the bombing of a disco in Berlin frequented by American servicemen. In retaliation, he ordered the bombing of Benghazi, killing scores of civilians but not the dictator. Jurists maintained Reagan had unilaterally carried out an act of war, and again violated the War Powers Act. Similarly, in his proxy war in Nicaragua, he breached international law by having the CIA lay magnetic mines in three of that nation's harbors. Later, the International Court of Justice at The Hague found the United States guilty of an unlawful use of force. Reagan dismissed the condemnation without qualm.

Finally, the president's illegal use of his foreign policy power led to negative repercussions. Congress had banned the export of arms to Iran,

but Reagan's subordinates secretly sold it weapons to finance the undercover contras, contrary to the Boland laws. They also used some of the money for ransom for release of American hostages in Lebanon. When details of this Iran-Contra affair leaked to the public, the president's popularity plummeted. Some legislators again talked of impeachment. Initially, Reagan denied knowledge of the affair. Later, he admitted that the decision to trade arms for hostages was his. Senate and House investigating committees concluded he had been responsible, but neither Congress nor the courts held him accountable for his illicit actions.

Reagan continued to use force in the Persian Gulf, in Nicaragua, and indirectly in covert aid in Afghanistan against the Russians. When the Russians withdrew in 1988, he and his aides touted their retreat as a victory for the Reagan Doctrine. When he left office, harsh critics stood by their characterization of him as an amiable dunce, but most of the public thought differently. It overlooked or forgave his illicit behavior to view him as a decisive leader who had regained for the presidency much of the foreign relations power it presumably had lost in the Watergate scandal.

In contrast to Reagan, George H. W. Bush initially seemed bland, but he sought to demonstrate qualities as a strong, activist leader in a clash with the small-time Panamanian dictator Manuel Antonio Noriega, who had been on the payroll of Washington intelligence agencies but lost favor because of criminal activity. The Reagan administration had imposed economic sanctions against Panama, and Bush quickly assigned high priority to Noriega's removal, through various means including a coup. This strategy fizzled, leading hard-liners to speak of executive weakness.

When questioned about ousting the dictator, Bush answered, "Well, I want as broad a power as possible, and I think under the Constitution the President has it." He "has broad powers, broader than some in the Senate or the House might think." On this assumption, Bush exploited a clash between Panamanian soldiers and two American servicemen as a reason to resort openly to force. On 15 December 1989, on his own as commander in chief, he ordered the invasion of Panama. Six weeks later, U.S. troops captured Noriega. Ultimately a U.S. court tried, convicted, and jailed him.

Many Americans asked why this massive force over a minor quarrel? The president came up with a variety of answers, including self-defense, upholding democracy, and protecting

American lives. Skeptics dismissed the arguments as flimsy, pointing out that virtually every day in some part of the world somebody harassed Americans. To safeguard them or uphold nascent democracy everywhere with bayonets would commit the nation to endless hostilities. They accused Bush of using violence politically to dispel the wimp factor. The General Assembly of the United Nations condemned the invasion as a "flagrant violation" of international law, but Americans overwhelmingly approved the muscle-flexing. Hence, only a few legislators challenged the president's defiance of the War Powers Act. The House even passed a resolution praising him for his decisive action.

Seemingly intoxicated by such commendation, the president turned on another international villain, Iraq's Saddam Hussein. On 2 August 1990, some 80,000 Iraqi troops invaded and quickly overran Kuwait. Properly condemning the invasion as "naked aggression," Bush took the lead in a movement to reverse it. The American public and the United Nations supported him in a policy of sanctions against Hussein. Impatiently, Bush decided sanctions took too long to work, prepared for war, and claimed he did not need congressional assent before taking military action. Many legislators disagreed. Senator Daniel P. Moynihan of New York pointed out that "the great armed force" created to fight the Cold War was now "at the president's own disposal for any diversion he may wish, no matter what it costs." Undeterred, Bush insisted that "I have the right, as commander in chief, to fulfill my responsibilities, and I'm going to safeguard those executive powers." Fifty-four legislators filed suit in a federal court to prohibit the president from using force without congressional authorization. The court ruled the suit premature but reiterated that only Congress could declare war. Still, Bush announced that no matter what Congress or the people had to say, he would decide for or against war. As had various predecessors, he cited flawed precedents for presidential war-making. Most of the media sided with him.

Finally, the president gave in to pressure from advisers not to defy Congress but to persuade it to go along with him. He asked for a resolution approving force but not for a declaration of war. Congress agreed and on a partisan vote narrowly passed such a measure, thus sanctioning a presidential war. On 16 January 1991 he led the nation into war. Two days later, he informed Congress of his action, in a manner, he said, "consis-tent with the War Powers Resolution." In the Gulf War of 1991, the U.S. military juggernaut blasted the Iraqis into a lopsided defeat, Bush's popularity rating zoomed to an unprecedented height, and he bathed in the glory of a Caesar.

During Bush's term, the Soviet Union broke up, the Cold War ended, and ethnic strife tore apart Yugoslavia. He campaigned for reelection as a successful war leader and the master of an aggressive foreign policy, who, along with Reagan, had finalized the winning of the Cold War. But he lost. Nonetheless, as a lame duck president, he once more exercised his power as commander in chief. For humanitarian reasons, or what he called "God's work," he intervened in Somalia, torn apart by civil war and famine. He ordered more than 30,000 troops to take "whatever action is necessary" to carry out their mission. As various analysts noted, Bush with his war-making pushed the presidential power in foreign affairs to its outer limits.

THE INDISPENSABLE NATION AND PRESIDENT?

During his run for the presidency, William Jefferson Clinton campaigned on a domestic program. When he did refer to foreign affairs, he tried to sound tougher than Bush. For instance, Clinton favored forcible intervention in the Bosnian civil war to punish aggressive Serbs. As president, his first major foreign policy decision was on the peacekeeping mission in Somalia. Initially, Clinton anticipated no difficulties because he planned gradually to withdraw U.S. troops and turn over the operation to the United Nations. When clan warriors killed Pakistani peacekeepers and wounded American soldiers, that goal changed. The president authorized U.S. troops to use force against what he called "two-bit" terrorists. When Somalis killed eighteen Americans and wounded seventy-four, Clinton ordered 5,000 more troops, heavy armor, and additional warships to Somalia. What had started as a humanitarian mission took on the coloring of a military occupation. This change alarmed many in Congress. Some talked of placing restrictions on how the president could deploy the armed forces. As had predecessors in comparable circumstances, Clinton contended questionably that the executive possessed the ultimate authority on the use of troops. Finally, without relinquishing this claim but in reaction to the criticism, he withdrew the forces from Somalia.

During this episode, the president also flexed muscle in the Middle East. He learned of an alleged plot to assassinate George Bush while the former president was visiting Kuwait in April 1993. The CIA attributed this conspiracy to Saddam Hussein. Denouncing it as "an attack against our country and against all Americans," Clinton on 26 June ordered a missile attack on battered Baghdad. Constitutional lawyers commented that "calling the U.S. bombing of Iraq an act of self-defense for an assassination plot that had been averted two months previously is quite a stretch." Other skeptics viewed this exercise in force as personal, or as countering a reputation for indecisiveness with an image of a strong, assertive leader. The tactic worked. According to polls, the public approved of the president's rash resort to force by a large margin.

Concurrently, Clinton plunged into another sticky minor foreign problem, this one involving corruption in Haiti and special-interest group politics in the United States. In a coup, militarists ejected Jean-Bertrand Aristide, Haiti's first elected president, from office. Various liberal groups, media pundits, and especially the congressional black caucus demanded that Clinton restore Aristide to power. The president agreed. He tightened sanctions against the island republic, ordered warships to patrol its waters, and placed troops on alert for a possible invasion. He justified his actions with what he designated as important national interests in Haiti, a need to protect American lives there, and an obligation to promote democracy. In Congress, dissenters came up with legislation to prevent Clinton from committing troops. He denounced the proposal as encroaching "on the President's foreign policy powers." Congress avoided a direct clash with a nonbinding resolution that opposed the executive actions. Involved legislators asked should a president act as a global gendarme with authority to intervene with force whenever dictators seize or hold power anywhere. Others perceived personal or domestic political considerations as motivating the president's determination to move on his own. Advisers admitted that in this manner Clinton would demonstrate "the president's decision making capability" and his firmness in using his foreign affairs power.

Clinton remained defiant, announcing that, like predecessors, he did not regard himself "constitutionally mandated" to obtain congressional approval before invading. He also repeated muddled justifications, such as a duty to secure the nation's borders and safeguard national security,

though neither was threatened. At the last minute, in September 1994, he avoided another clash with Congress by accepting an arrangement that permitted the Haitian militarists to retreat peacefully and made a hostile invasion unnecessary. American troops then occupied the country and returned Aristide to power. Clinton boasted, "We celebrate the return of democracy," even though democracy had never flowered in Haiti. Two years later, the occupation officially ended without violent mishap. The administration touted it as a foreign policy triumph but others viewed it as a revival of big-stick paternalism. The intervention and $2.2 billion in aid produced neither democracy nor well-being. In Haiti viable politics and the economy crumbled.

Clinton also embroiled himself in controversy over brutal ethnic warfare in former Yugoslavia, expressing a desire to intervene for the laudable purpose of protecting human rights. "We have an interest," he said, "in standing up against the principle of ethnic cleansing." He intruded in a number of instances with food and medicine air drops for beleaguered Muslims in Bosnia, with deployment of a few hundred troops in Macedonia, and with bombings and other attacks on Serb forces. Finally, in a conference in Dayton, Ohio, in November 1995, Clinton brokered an end to the civil war in Bosnia. He considered the peace agreement a diplomatic triumph, but it had problems. The settlement called for deployment of 23,000 U.S. ground troops as part of a NATO peacekeeping mission. A majority in Congress and most Americans opposed the policing commitment. Regardless, Clinton deployed the troops, counting on the usual rally-round-the-flag attitude of the public when soldiers were placed in harm's way. As aides admitted, the decision in an election year also had a political dimension. It could increase his stature as a bold leader. He had learned, a staffer asserted, "that foreign policy can help your image. It makes him look like a president." Ultimately, the Senate backed the troop commitment and, as anticipated, the public rallied behind the president.

Clinton also flexed muscle over an incident with Castro's Cuba and another with China over Taiwan, and continued to blast Iraq with missile attacks. In these crises the president portrayed himself as a global crusader committed to combating evil. At the start of his second term, he explained this concept as part of doing "what it takes to remain the indispensable nation . . . for another fifty years."

Two years later, on 7 August 1998, while Clinton was entangled in scandal over a relationship with Monica Lewinsky, a young White House intern, terrorists bombed American embassies in Kenya and Tanzania. Ten days later, he publicly admitted the sexual liaison and three days after that ordered missile attacks on suspected terrorists in Sudan and Afghanistan. Opponents accused him of using violence abroad to divert attention from a domestic problem. On 19 December, the House of Representatives voted to impeach Clinton on charges of perjury and abuse of power related to the Lewinsky affair. On 12 February 1999, after a five-week trial, the Senate acquitted Clinton. A month later, when asked if he had damaged the Office of the President, Clinton responded, "I hope the presidency has not been harmed. I don't believe it has been."

Clinton continued to exercise his foreign relations power boldly, primarily against another international villain, Slobodan Milosevic, the hard-line president of what remained of Yugoslavia. Clinton accused him of brutal ethnic cleansing of Albanian residents in the Serb province of Kosovo and decided to employ force against him. Clinton explained this decision, as a skeptic pointed out, with an "orgy of analogy" that included an obligation to humanity to halt what he termed genocide, defend American interests, stop Serb aggression, and enforce democratic values. Critics asked, why the selective humanitarianism? Did not genocide in Rwanda, Chinese brutalities against Tibetans, Russian repression in Chechnya, ethnic horrors in the Sudan, and Taliban atrocities in Afghanistan call for comparable military intervention?

Regardless, on 24 March the United States, supported by eighteen other NATO countries that Clinton had persuaded to join him, launched an air war against Milosevic's Yugoslavia. Clinton and his aides avoided the word "war," describing the vast violence they unleashed with an impersonal euphemism, a campaign to "degrade" the enemy. In eleven weeks of war, or degrading, the NATO forces flew 37,000 sorties and dropped 23,614 bombs on Kosovo and other parts of Yugoslavia, most of them by American planes. The United Nations did not support the war, nor did many people even in NATO countries. Congress and the American public, though, as usual in the initial stages of hostilities, backed the executive but with less enthusiasm than in previous presidential wars.

With the rise of domestic opposition to the war, with its destruction of much of Serbia, Clinton resorted to the dubious contention that the executive as commander in chief needed no congressional declaration to fight a war. The House, mainly along party lines, voted against supporting him with a declaration of war, but it did not try to stop the hostilities. In addition, a bipartisan group of legislators filed suit seeking a ruling that the bombing violated the Constitution and laws such as the War Powers Resolution. Across the country a new antiwar movement began taking shape. Elsewhere, as in Japan, people viewed Clinton as an international bully.

On 10 June, before opposition to the war became full blown, it ended. The Serbs agreed to withdraw from Kosovo and to accept a NATO occupation of the province. Clinton then claimed another triumph for a presidential war. The victory proved tarnished when postwar investigators could produce no evidence of grand-scale genocidal Serb activities. Clinton had claimed that under Milosevic's orders, Serbs had slaughtered tens of thousand of Albanians. In addition, when Albanians returned to Kosovo, they carried out ethnic cleansing of Serbs and Gypsies.

In other instances, Clinton used his foreign affairs power constructively, notably through diplomacy to help control ethnic violence in Northern Ireland and in the Middle East and to save Mexico from bankruptcy with some $25 billion in loans. To the end of his presidency, he liked the taste of power that enabled him to influence events the world over and stuck to his self-assumed role, which he often denied, of global policeman. He left office, according to polls, with most Americans approving of his handling of foreign affairs.

In the 2000 election, foreign policy played a minor role, though the Republican candidate, George W. Bush, criticized morally based armed interventions. He preferred using force only where tangible, perceivable American interests were at stake. He won the presidency even though his Democratic opponent received more of the popular vote, despite ballot snafus in Florida, and by surviving various court challenges. In the crucial challenge, the Supreme Court awarded him the office on the basis of shared ideology. In the aftermath, academics and others contended that this outcome tarnished the presidency. As critics pointed out, Bush's awkward handling of foreign affairs during his first months in office indicated that this assessment had merit.

On 11 September 2001 this view of the presidency changed. Unknown Islamic terrorists hijacked four commercial airplanes, smashed two of them into the twin towers of the World Trade Center in New York City and one into the Pentagon, outside Washington, D.C., and crashed the fourth in a field in Pennsylvania. They killed an estimated seven thousand people. The disaster galvanized the nation, rallying the citizenry, as usual in foreign affairs crises, around the flag and behind the president.

Bush responded with incendiary rhetoric laced with references to war and by asking Congress for expanded power to combat terrorism "with all necessary and appropriate force." As had his predecessors, he claimed he already had the authority to initiate military action on his own but wanted a resolution of approval from the legislators to cement national unity. Polls indicated that more than 70 percent of the public supported his stance. Congress rushed to go along with the president's request. On 14 September, unanimously in the Senate and with only one dissenter in the House of Representatives, Congress voted approval for the president to strike at "nations, organizations, or persons he determines planned, authorized, committed, or aided the terrorist attacks."

A few in Congress maintained that this resolution, unlike the Tonkin Gulf Resolution, did not give the president blanket authority to make war. In substance, though, it amounted to that, and Bush interpreted it that way. Five days later, speaking to Congress and to the nation via television, he announced "a war on terror," issuing an ultimatum to Afghanistan: deliver to the United States the prime suspects behind the attacks, especially Osama bin Laden, a shadowy anti-Western terrorist who had sanctuary in that country, or expect the consequences. Again, Bush's standing in the polls soared. Afghanistan's Taliban rulers, refused surrender of bin Laden without, they said, seeing convincing evidence of his guilt.

Once more, despite the War Powers Act and post-Vietnam War concerns over untrammeled presidential war power, the public, Congress, and most media pundits eager for retaliation backed the use of military force virtually as the executive saw fit. Moreover, for the first time in the role of a warrior who spoke of involvement in "the first war of the twenty-first century," even to those who previously had belittled him, Bush appeared presidential.

This crisis reinforced what has been, virtually from the first presidency, a steady expansion of the executive power in foreign affairs at the expense of Congress. This happened often because of the force of strong executives' personalities and their thirst for power. It happened also because the American public and its elected representatives, initially at least, in times of foreign crises willingly put aside original intent in the warmaking power as the framers had embodied it in the Constitution. Again, in the September 2001 crisis, without hesitation, they shifted this ultimate power to one person—the president.

BIBLIOGRAPHY

Abbott, Philip. *Strong Presidents: A Theory of Leadership.* Knoxville, Tenn., 1996.

Adler, David Gray. "The President's War-Making Power." In Thomas E. Cronin, ed. *Inventing the American Presidency.* Lawrence, Kans., 1969.

———. "The Constitution and Presidential Warmaking: The Enduring Debate." *Political Science Quarterly* 103 (spring 1988): 1–36.

Ambrose, Stephen E. "The Presidency and Foreign Policy." *Foreign Affairs* 70 (winter 1992): 120–137.

Bailey, Thomas A. *Presidential Greatness: The Image and the Man from George Washington to the Present.* New York 1966. Readable and provocative.

———. *The Pugnacious Presidents: White House Warriors on Parade.* New York, 1980.

Berger, Raoul. "The Presidential Monopoly of Foreign Affairs." *Michigan Law Review* 71 (November 1972): 1–58.

Bledsoe, W. Craig, et al. *Powers of the Presidency.* 2d ed. Washington, D.C., 1997.

Cheever, Daniel S., and H. Field Haviland, Jr. *American Foreign Policy and the Separation of Powers.* Cambridge, Mass., 1952.

Corwin, Edward S. *The President's Control of Foreign Relations.* Princeton, N.J., 1917.

Corwin, Edward S., et al. *The President: Office and Powers, 1787–1984, History and Analysis of Practice and Opinion.* 5th rev. ed. New York, 1984. Corwin's books are the pioneering works on the subject. They are still valuable for their scholarship and analyses.

DeConde, Alexander. *Presidential Machismo: Executive Authority, Military Intervention, and Foreign Relations.* Boston, 2000. Covers in greater detail, with documentation and an extensive bibliography, much of the subject and interpretations in this essay.

Eagleton, Thomas F. *War and Presidential Power: A Chronicle of Congressional Surrender.* New York, 1974.

Fisher, Louis. *Presidential War Power.* Lawrence, Kans., 1995. Both of Fisher's books are scholarly, authoritative, and important sources.

———. *Constitutional Conflicts Between Congress and the President.* 4th ed. Lawrence, Kans., 1997.

Franck, Thomas M., ed. *The Tethered Presidency: Congressional Restraints on Executive Power.* New York, 1981.

Friedman, David S. "Waging War Against Checks and Balances: The Claim of an Unlimited Presidential War Power." *St. John's Law Review* 57 (winter 1983): 213–273.

Glennon, Michael J. "Can the President Do No Wrong?" *American Journal of International Law* 80 (October 1986): 923–930.

Goldsmith, William M. *The Growth of Presidential Power: A Documented History.* 3 vols. New York, 1974. A collection of documents with commentary.

Graber, Doris A. *Public Opinion, the President, and Foreign Policy: Four Case Studies from the Formative Years.* New York, 1968. Covers the early national era.

Henkin, Louis. *Foreign Affairs and the United States Constitution.* 2d ed. New York, 1996. A scholarly and perceptive mainstay in the field.

Lehman, John F. *Making War: The 200-Year-Old Battle Between the President and Congress over How America Goes to War.* New York, 1991. A readable popular account.

Levy, Leonard W., and Louis Fisher, eds. *Encyclopedia of the American Presidency.* 4 vols. New York, 1994.

McDonald, Forrest. *The American Presidency: An Intellectual History.* Lawrence, Kans., 1994.

Marks, Frederick W., III. *Independence on Trial: Foreign Affairs and the Making of the Constitution.* Baton Rouge, La., 1973.

May, Ernest R., ed. *The Ultimate Decision: The President as Commander in Chief.* New York, 1960. Essays on selected presidents and their influence.

Mullen, William F. *Presidential Power and Politics.* New York, 1976.

Murray, Robert K., and Tim H. Blessing. *Greatness in the White House: Rating the Presidents.* 2d ed. University Park, Pa., 1994.

Neustadt, Richard E. *Presidential Power and the Modern Presidents: Politics and Leadership from Roosevelt to Reagan.* Rev. ed. New York, 1990. An influential study that stresses the power of persuasion.

Rakove, Jack N. *Original Meanings: Politics and Ideas in the Making of the Constitution.* New York, 1996. The chapter "Creating the Presidency" is particularly rewarding.

Riccards, Michael P. *The Ferocious Engine of Democracy: A History of the American Presidency.* 2 vols. Lanham, Md., 1995.

Robinson, Edgar Eugene, Alexander DeConde, Raymond G. O'Connor, and Martin B. Travis, Jr. *Powers of the President in Foreign Affairs, 1945–1965.* San Francisco, 1966.

Rose, Gary L. *The American Presidency Under Siege.* Albany, N.Y., 1997.

Rourke, John T. *Presidential Wars and American Democracy: Rally 'Round the Chief.* New York, 1993.

Schlesinger, Arthur M., Jr. *The Imperial Presidency.* Boston, 1973. Scholarly, insightful, and gracefully written, this book is a fundamental read.

Shenkman, Richard. *Presidential Ambition: How the Presidents Gained Power, Kept Power, and Got Things Done.* New York, 1999. A readable popular account.

Skowronek, Stephen. *The Politics Presidents Make: Leadership from John Adams to George Bush.* Cambridge, Mass., 1993.

Smith, J. Malcolm, and Stephen Jurika, Jr. *The President and National Security: His Role as Commander-in-Chief.* Dubuque, Iowa, 1972.

Thomas, Ann Van Wynen, and A. J. Thomas, Jr. *The War-Making Powers of the President: Constitutional and International Law Aspects.* Dallas, Tex., 1982.

Warburg, Gerald F. *Conflict and Consensus: The Struggle Between Congress and the President over Foreign Policymaking.* New York, 1989.

Wildavsky, Aaron. *The Beleaguered Presidency.* New Brunswick, N.J., 1991.

See also CONGRESSIONAL POWER; THE CONSTITUTION; DEPARTMENT OF DEFENSE; DEPARTMENT OF STATE; MILITARISM; NUCLEAR STRATEGY AND DIPLOMACY; PARTY POLITICS; POWER POLITICS; PRESIDENTIAL ADVISERS; SUMMIT CONFERENCES.

THE PRESS

★ ★ ★ ★

Ralph B. Levering and Louis W. Liebovich

Officially, American foreign policy is made by the executive branch of the federal government, led by the president, and by Congress, with rare involvement by the Supreme Court. Unofficially, other institutions—notably interest groups and the press (including electronic media as well as the print media)—typically play a large role in the often lengthy and politically charged policymaking process in Washington. Most voters also learn of impending and completed U.S. foreign policy initiatives through the news media. Roughly three-fourths of adult Americans read daily newspapers and many read magazines that discuss foreign policy issues. The press thus occupies a central place in the communication of ideas that lies at the heart of the ongoing political process both in Washington and in the two-way flow of information between officials and the voting public.

Because of its importance, journalist Douglass Cater and other writers have called the press the "fourth branch of government." But neither the news media as institutions nor journalists as individuals have any formal power to shape U.S. foreign relations. The communication of ideas is different from making or implementing policy. Unlike specific presidential decisions or votes in Congress, moreover, the press's influence on an issue normally cannot be measured precisely. And because the day-to-day influence of journalists on the thinking of policymakers and the public varies from individual to individual and from issue to issue, it is important not to overestimate the press's impact. Yet Cater's metaphor has considerable validity because the role of the press in foreign policy decisions—and in the reactions to those decisions that influence future actions—often has been substantial. Since the 1950s this fascinating, intellectually challenging topic has attracted the interest of numerous journalists, officials, and political activists. It also has lured scholars from several disciplines, notably communications, history, political science, and sociology.

DIVERSITY AND ETHNOCENTRISM

There is a diversity of views that exists within multifaceted institutions—"the government" and "the press"—that often are written about as if each were unitary and hence susceptible to broad generalizations and concise theories. The reality is much more complex. In establishing the federal government, the Founders set up an inherent competition between the prerogatives and powers of the executive branch and Congress. On both the proper goals of U.S. foreign policy and the best means to achieve them, moreover, there repeatedly have been strong differences of opinion within the executive branch, within Congress, and between the two branches. Thus, when scholars discover that as many as 70 or even 80 percent of sources used in news stories on some foreign policy issues are "government" sources (either executive branch alone or executive plus congressional), one normally need not be concerned that only one or two viewpoints are being presented. Such statistics do point to a lack of aggressiveness by journalists in gathering information outside official circles, however.

On any major foreign policy issue, the few thousand journalists who work in Washington are almost certain to present varied perspectives based on public statements, interviews, and "leaks" (information whose source or sources cannot be named) from the president and members of Congress and from the many thousands of officials who work for the White House, for the other executive agencies, and for Congress. Especially since the mid-1970s, journalists also have used as sources spokespersons for affected interest groups, academics, diplomats stationed in Washington, and experts from public interest groups and from the capital's numerous liberal and conservative think tanks. As several scholars have shown, foreign policy stories in the 1990s generally were based less heavily on "government sources" (themselves often diverse) than they had been thirty years earlier.

The diversity of views from sources is paralleled by the diversity of views on foreign policy presented in the press. It is true that both the number of daily newspapers (about 1,600 by the 1990s) and the number of cities with more than one daily newspaper declined steadily throughout the twentieth century. But these declines have been at least partly offset by other developments: the widespread availability in recent decades of three national newspapers (the liberal *New York Times,* the moderate *USA Today,* and the conservative *Wall Street Journal*); the growing use by many dailies of foreign policy coverage and foreign stories from the news services of such papers as the *New York Times, Washington Post,* and *Los Angeles Times;* and the practice by many local-monopoly dailies of featuring both liberal and conservative columnists. Also, the widespread publication of weekly or biweekly alternative papers, many of which are distributed free of charge and feature liberal or mildly radical perspectives, and the availability of liberal and conservative viewpoints on the growing number of television and radio news programs and talk shows, as well as at numerous Internet sites, have all increasingly complemented the daily newspapers.

For Americans interested in foreign affairs, the greatest diversity of views and depth of analysis during the twentieth century typically were found in magazines. Mass-circulation weekly news magazines—*Time, Newsweek,* and *U.S. News and World Report*—generally were strong supporters of America's anticommunist policies from the mid-1940s through the mid-1960s. Their coverage of foreign affairs generally has become more varied since then, though it sometimes comes across (like some newspaper stories) as simplistic or overblown. It must be remembered, however, that news magazines are intended to appeal to the general public, which normally is less interested in foreign affairs than the much smaller number of Americans who regularly read journals of opinion.

Among journals of opinion, such long-established liberal periodicals as the *New Republic* and *Nation* have flourished, as have conservative periodicals, including *National Review* and *Commentary.* In the center, with much in-depth analysis of foreign affairs, are journals like *Foreign Affairs* and *Foreign Policy.* Many religious and environmental periodicals also discuss foreign affairs regularly. Therefore, diversity thrives in foreign policy coverage in magazines.

As in most other nations, ethnocentrism—the belief that one's own nation and its values are superior to all others—has long been a standard feature of the American press's reporting and commentary on U.S. foreign policy and on other nations. Throughout modern American history, most liberal, moderate, and conservative journalists have praised other nations that practiced political democracy and freedom for individuals (for example, Great Britain, Norway, and Costa Rica), and have criticized governments that quashed democracy and freedom (such as Adolf Hitler's Germany, Joseph Stalin's Soviet Union, and Fidel Castro's Cuba). As the sociologist Herbert Gans has noted, the press's "ethnocentrism comes through most clearly in foreign news, which judges other countries by the extent to which they live up to or imitate American practices and values."

During the Cold War, many newspapers and magazines—often including the prestigious *New York Times*—applied the nation's core values unevenly by being much more critical of the communist dictatorships that gave at least verbal support to the overthrow of noncommunist governments in other countries than they were of pro-Western dictatorships. Yet even during the long struggle against communism, many newspapers and magazines sharply criticized right-wing dictatorships in such allied nations as South Korea, South Vietnam, Chile, and the Philippines.

The largest policy failure to which ethnocentrism in the press (and among officials) contributed was the common assumption in news stories and editorials from the mid-1950s through the mid-1960s that most of the people living in South Vietnam deeply desired to continue to have a pro-Western, noncommunist government—even if that meant having a dictatorial and corrupt one. This dubious assumption, based on wishful thinking much more than on facts, contributed greatly to America's ill-fated war in Vietnam. Although the particular double standards and blind spots of the Cold War era are history, the sharp criticisms of mainland China's and Iraq's repressive dictatorships by contemporary journalists of all political persuasions suggest that ethnocentrism continues to influence America's news and commentary.

THE PRESS'S MANY ROLES

Among the press's roles are what are called the "three I's"—information, interpretation, and interest. Roger Hilsman, a political scientist and State Department official in the John F. Kennedy administration, identified "the gathering and dissemination of information" as a major function of the press. The flow of information through the press—among all the people seeking to influence policy in Washington, from the capital to the public, and from the public back to officials partly through press coverage and reporters' questions—is the lifeblood of America's democratic system.

Information in press coverage of foreign affairs is almost always accompanied by interpretation. Journalists provide contexts (often called "frames") in which information is conveyed. "By suggesting the cause and relationships of various events," the political scientist Doris A. Graber observes, "the media may shape opinions even without telling their audiences what to believe or think. For example, linking civil strife in El Salvador [in the 1980s] to the activities of Soviet and Cuban agents ensured that the American public would view the situation with considerable alarm." Among policymakers in Washington, Hilsman notes,

> the press is not the sole source of interpretation. The president, the secretary of state, the assistant secretaries, American ambassadors, senators, congressmen, academic experts—all are sources of interpretation. But the fact that the press is there every day, day after day, with its interpretations makes it the principal competitor of all the others in interpreting events.

The press also can play an important role in stirring interest in an issue both in Washington and among the public. During the Ronald Reagan years media reporting awakened public interest on starvation in Ethiopia, a topic that Americans had shown little interest in prior to the appearance of illustrated stories about dying children in the press and on television. An example from the James Earl Carter years was the debate over whether to deploy enhanced radiation nuclear bombs (also called neutron bombs) in western Europe. The debate began with a story by Walter Pincus in the *Washington Post* on 6 June 1977. A quotation in the story noted that the bombs would "kill people" while "leaving buildings and tanks standing." Once the story was framed in this negative way—on television and radio as well as in newspapers and magazines—the administration was not able to gain public and congressional support for deploying the new weapon. The unfolding of this story illustrates a frequent pattern in foreign policy: print journal-

ists often bring stories to public attention, after which they are covered by other print and electronic reporters.

Stirring interest through extensive news and editorial coverage is often called the agenda-setting function of the media. The political scientist Bernard C. Cohen explained this concept cogently: "The press is significantly more than a purveyor of information and opinion. It may not be successful much of the time in telling people what to think, but it is stunningly successful in telling its readers what to think *about*."

Building on Cohen's path-breaking research, other scholars have refined the concept of agenda setting. While agreeing that the news media often play an important role in the agenda-setting process, most analysts now believe that agenda setting is a complex process in which unexpected events or administration officials or (less frequently) members of Congress or interest groups often play at least as significant roles as journalists. Because officials and other participants in the policymaking process in Washington frequently work hard to get their viewpoints into the press, the communications professor J. David Kennamer notes, "[t]he news media are as much the target of agenda-setting as they are the source." Moreover, the relative importance of journalists to other actors in agenda setting varies from issue to issue. Thus, although the press plays a significant role in deciding which foreign policy issues to cover and which ones to make into "big stories," it shares the agenda-setting function with other actors in the political process.

In another important role, that of "watchdog," the press ferrets out and publicizes questionable policies or abuses of authority. As a reporter for a Midwestern newspaper told Cohen: "We are the fourth estate, and it is our duty to monitor—to watch and interpret—what our government does." Because officials often control the flow of information to the press in regard to secret operations, the press's performance as a watchdog has been mixed. During the Iran-Contra scandal of the mid-1980s, for example, American journalists were slow to learn about the operation—indeed, the story was broken by a publication in Lebanon well after the administration had engaged in illicit activity in the Middle East and in Central America. After the story broke, however, leading newspapers and magazines did an excellent job of bringing details to the attention of policymakers in Washington (including members of Congress) and the American people.

Journalists also can play an important role as critics of particular foreign policies. Although far fewer people read editorials and columns (opinion pieces) than read front-page news stories (or, for that matter, the comics and the sports pages!), the people most interested and involved in foreign affairs—officials, journalists, other leaders in society, and the "attentive public" (the roughly 10 to 20 percent of the public with the greatest interest in public issues)—not only read editorials and columns regularly, but they often discuss them with other people, thus enhancing their impact. In influencing the thinking of elites, editorial writers and columnists affect the public discussion of foreign affairs that gradually works its way down to many average voters. While the exact influence of editorials and columns cannot be determined, it seems clear that the serious questions that were being raised about the U.S. involvement in Vietnam on the editorial pages of numerous newspapers beginning in the mid-1960s helped to create the climate of opinion in which the continuation of the war by the Lyndon B. Johnson and Richard M. Nixon administrations became increasingly difficult.

Finally, the press contributes greatly to the policymaking process in Washington, both in the executive branch and in Congress. Administration officials read leading papers and magazines to learn what other officials and members of Congress are thinking and doing, and to try to figure out which other officials are "leaking" information to the press and what policy goals they are seeking to advance by doing so. Officials also are interested in reading stories by journalists stationed in other countries in order to get opinions other than the ones being sent from the U.S. embassies there.

Members of Congress and their staffs are eager to learn what is going on in the administration, so that they can support or oppose the current direction of policy. Especially since the late 1960s, many members of Congress—particularly ones who are not members of the president's party—have been eager to limit the executive branch's power in foreign affairs and increase their own influence on particular foreign policy issues. To achieve these goals, they frequently have worked closely with reporters.

Robert J. Kurz, a former legislative assistant, wrote in 1991 that members of Congress "form alliances with the press because they share a common interest, often a rivalry, against the executive." Kurz continued:

These alliances solidify during times of controversy and tension with a president. It is not unusual for the Congress and the press to work together to discover what the executive is up to, uncover wrongdoing, or expose inherent contradictions in policies or their implementation. They share the desire for the notoriety and attention that comes with this conflict.

An important role for the press, therefore, has been to help to maintain the tenuous balance of power between the executive branch and Congress in foreign affairs. Cohen has written that, because "the media are themselves one of the most articulate and informed outside participants in the foreign policymaking process," they "unavoidably affect the environment in which foreign policy decisions are made by 'insiders.'"

The "alliances" between reporters and members of Congress that Kurz writes about provide an apt illustration of Cohen's point.

REPORTERS AND OFFICIALS: CONFLICTING GOALS, FREQUENT TENSIONS

In Washington, the officials responsible for foreign policy and the reporters who cover them have such fundamentally different jobs that conflicts frequently erupt between them. Officials—especially presidents, much of whose power stems from perceived competence and popularity—understandably want to look good as they make and implement policies. Officials generally want an orderly, rational decision-making process in which decisions are reached—and then announced—after discussions both within the executive branch and, if needed, with leaders in Congress and in other nations. In other words, officials want to control the content and timing of statements and other initiatives relating to particular foreign policies. Based on several case studies, including the Iran hostage crisis of 1979–1981, journalism professor Philip Seib describes what can happen when media coverage of a crisis undermines the president's control of the timing of decision making:

News coverage can accelerate the tempo by heightening public interest. Depending on which aspects of the story the press emphasizes, coverage can also influence public opinion in ways that increase political pressure on the president to act in a specific fashion, such as more aggressively or more compassionately. The chief executive may soon realize that the ideal of nicely insulated policy formulation has evaporated. Instead, his every move is anticipated and then critiqued almost instantly.

High officials also want to leak secret information when it suits their purposes to do so, but not before and not by a lower-level official unauthorized to do the leaking. A wry joke that made the rounds during the Kennedy years—a time when the president himself was a frequent source—sums up their view of appropriate leaks: "The ship of state leaks from the top." Viewing favorable press coverage as necessary for high levels of public and congressional support, presidents and other top officials prefer to manage the news as much as possible.

Except during an obvious national emergency such as World War II, reporters reject this vision of favorable, managed news as incompatible with their jobs as journalists and with what they call "the public's right to know." In competition with reporters for other media organizations, journalists seek to "get the story" and move it quickly into print. And because disagreement, conflict, and failure are key components of the definition of "news," the more these components are part of the story, the more likely it is to be featured on the front page in newspapers or as the cover story in magazines. As the Associated Press international editor Tom Kent rightly noted at a 1996 conference at Ohio University, "There's something in the human condition that finds a greater fascination in bad news than in good news."

As long as stories are factually accurate and deal with legitimate public issues, reporters and editors believe that America's freedom of the press gives them the right—even the duty—to publish them, regardless of whether they portray an administration favorably. From the press's viewpoint, moreover, very few stories should be kept out of print for the reason that officials often cite—national security. To reporters, invoking national security is often an attempt to ward off embarrassment or bad news.

Frequently, therefore, officials and reporters come into conflict when the press publishes stories that officials believe should have remained secret or when stories contain information that might upset delicate negotiations within the government or with other nations. Officials often have been scathing in their criticisms of journalists. "The competitive press finds it almost impossible to exercise discretion and a sense of public responsibility," Secretary of State Dean Rusk wrote. "If a man digs a secret out of an official or a department and takes it around to the Soviet Embassy, he is a spy; if he digs out the same secret and gives it to the Soviet Union and the rest of the world at the same time, he is a smart newspaperman." Complaining to journalists about some coverage his administration was getting, President Lyndon Johnson commented, "I know you don't like your cornpone president." Criticisms of the press by administration officials have been bipartisan. Republican George Shultz, who served as secretary of state under President Reagan, commented that "these days . . . it seems as though the reporters are always against us."

Scholars often have used metaphors like "rocky marriage" or "bad marriage" to characterize the relationship between reporters and officials. At least the "marriage" part fits: like married couples, the press and government are tied to each other as each carries out its activities in the same home, Washington, D.C. And, despite some journalists' claim that they occupy an inferior role relative to officials, officials (in making policy) and journalists (in deciding what is news) are equal in the same ways that married couples are: neither partner has inherent power over the other, and both have ways to get back at the other if they feel mistreated or disrespected.

The marriage metaphor is useful, moreover, because officials and journalists have needs that only members of the other group can satisfy. Officials (including members of Congress) need publicity for their ideas to win support for them in the administration, in Congress, and among the American people. In order to meet their editors' and readers' demand for stories, reporters need officials who are willing to talk with them about what is going on in the administration and Congress. Because of these complementary needs, overall relations between officials and reporters are inherently cooperative as well as adversarial. Like spouses who wish to stay married, individual officials who desire to remain effective have to keep talking to reporters even if some stories have angered them, and individual journalists have to attempt to be fair in writing their stories lest they lose access to the officials who have been talking to them. Officials who repeatedly lie to reporters lose their credibility and hence their value as sources; reporters who repeatedly misrepresent officials' views lose their sources and hence their ability to write news-breaking stories. These informal rules help to maintain both the flow of information and the balance of power between reporters and officials in Washington.

The difficulty with the "rocky marriage" metaphor, at least as applied to dealings on foreign policy, is that it overgeneralizes. It was much more persuasive for some presidencies (Lyndon Johnson and Richard Nixon) than it is for others (John Kennedy and George H. W. Bush). Kennedy, a former reporter, understood how to deal with journalists on foreign policy issues far better than Johnson and Nixon did. Like most presidents, Kennedy often became upset after reading press coverage that, in his view, was inaccurate or portrayed his administration unfavorably. But at a press conference on 9 May 1962, Kennedy made it clear that he understood and accepted the press's role in disseminating information, interpretation, and criticism: "I think that they are doing their task, as a critical branch, the fourth estate. I am attempting to do mine. And we are going to live together for a period, and then go our separate ways." Unlike Johnson and Nixon, Kennedy also had friendships with several journalists; he generally was forthright and respectful during frequent interviews, and he tried to be as forthcoming as possible at press conferences. Overall, despite occasional deserved criticisms of "news management," Kennedy's (and his administration's) relationships with the press were fair to good, especially considering the inherent conflicts between government and press.

In contrast, Johnson and Nixon's press relations on foreign policy issues typically were poor. In 1965, during the first year of the large U.S. troop buildup in Vietnam, journalists began writing about the "credibility gap," one definition of which was the gap between the administration's statements about what the U.S. military was doing in Vietnam and what reporters learned from lower-level officials in Vietnam about what was actually occurring. David Broder of the *Washington Post* offered a definition more narrowly focused on Johnson's efforts to stifle the flow of information that helps to explain why many reporters and members of Congress had become highly suspicious of the president well before the Tet Offensive in Vietnam in early 1968 effectively ended his political effectiveness:

> I do not believe that the press . . . ever made it clear to the readers and viewers what the essential issue was in the "credibility gap" controversy. It was not that President Johnson tried to manage the news: all politicians and all presidents try to do that. It was that in a systematic way he attempted to close down the channels of information from his office and his administration, so that decisions could be made without public debate and controversy. Ultimately he paid a high price, politically, for his policy.

During the Nixon years, some officials and conservative commentators claimed that press coverage unflattering to the administration's foreign policies (especially its Vietnam policy) resulted from "liberal bias" in the "eastern establishment press." That argument would have been much more persuasive if, first, newspapers like the *New York Times* and the *Washington Post,* magazines like *Time* and *Newsweek,* and the major television networks had been overwhelmingly supportive of Johnson's Vietnam policies until he left office and then had become highly critical of Nixon's approach, and, second, clear majorities of the public and Congress had been strongly supportive of Nixon's continuation of America's military involvement in Vietnam. In fact, given the media's penchant for disagreement, conflict, and violence, it seems certain that the "liberal press" would have included large amounts of negative coverage on Vietnam and on domestic dissent if Nixon's liberal Democratic opponent in 1968, Hubert Humphrey, had been elected and had continued the war.

The fact that Nixon's relations with most journalists were, if anything, more strained and adversarial than Johnson's also did not help him get favorable coverage on Vietnam. The columnist James Reston of the *New York Times* believed that Johnson and Nixon's difficulties with the press stemmed from the same roots:

> Mr. Nixon has had more than the normal share of trouble with reporters because, like Lyndon Johnson, he has never really understood the function of a free press or the meaning of the First Amendment. . . . He still suffers from [the] old illusion that the press is a kind of inanimate transmission belt which should pass along anything he chooses to dump on it.
>
> Both presidents, in other words, neither understood nor accepted the inherent equality of officials and reporters. Unlike the Netherlands and some other democratic nations where officials normally do not treat journalists as equals, this equality—and the tensions that partly result from it—is a hallmark of America's political system.

THE PRESS AND FOREIGN POLICY TO 1941: SOME HIGHLIGHTS

During the first century of America's independence, the most notable feature of the discussion of foreign affairs in America's steadily growing number of newspapers and magazines was partisanship. The sharp divisions of opinion between patriot and loyalist newspapers during the American Revolution arose in new contexts in the 1790s as Federalists and Republicans debated many of President George Washington's policies, including relations with Great Britain and France. Federalist editors strongly supported Washington's emphasis on good relations with Great Britain and neutrality in the Franco-British war, whereas Republican editors believed that America should side with France, its ally during the American Revolution.

From the 1790s through the Civil War, most newspapers that discussed political issues were founded to support a particular party or candidate. Their coverage of public issues, including foreign affairs, tended to be highly partisan. An example was coverage during the Mexican War (1846–1848). In general, Democratic newspapers supported their party's president, James K. Polk, whose actions had contributed greatly to the outbreak of the war. Most Whig newspapers, in contrast, sharply criticized "Mr. Polk's war." They raised doubts about the public's support for it and repeatedly questioned Polk's motives and goals.

Between the Civil War and World War II, the editorial pages of most newspapers remained partisan, especially during election years. But there were important changes during these seventy-five years that affected coverage of foreign affairs. First, there were advances in technology that permitted much more timely coverage. Whereas news of military developments in Mexico in the 1840s typically took two weeks or more to reach the East Coast, telegraph and radio transmissions permitted news of the fighting in Europe during World War I to reach American cities within hours or even, in some cases, almost instantaneously. Second, many papers' rapidly growing paid subscriptions and advertising revenues gave them money to spend on foreign and Washington correspondents, on memberships in such news services as the Associated Press, and on nationally syndicated columnists who often wrote on foreign affairs. Third, in their competition for readers and advertising dollars, newspapers and magazines could emphasize illustrated stories with broad public appeal (for example, lurid crimes and Spanish "atrocities" in Cuba), they could stress in-depth, "objective" reporting of major public issues, or, like most newspapers and magazines by the early 1900s, they could try to strike a balance between these two approaches. Fourth, English-language newspapers and maga-zines faced significant competition by 1900 from foreign-language publications that appealed to the millions of recent immigrants from Europe (and, to a lesser extent, from Latin America and East Asia) who retained ties to their former homelands and native languages. These publications often championed causes associated with governments or opposition movements in the former homelands and urged readers to contact U.S. political leaders on behalf of these causes. And fifth, the rapid growth of radio, newsreels, and news magazines after 1920 meant that newspapers and magazines of opinion had novel competitors not only in coverage of news and information, but also for the public's attention.

Newspapers' involvement in the events leading up to the Spanish-American War of 1898 especially illustrates two of these changes: the fierce competition for readers and the issue of sensationalism versus relative objectivity in coverage. In New York City, where the competition for readers was intense, the two papers with the largest circulations—Joseph Pulitzer's *New York World* and William Randolph Hearst's *New York Journal*—used Cuba's war for independence from Spain that began in 1895 as a source of sensational stories about Cuban heroism and Spanish atrocities that helped to sell newspapers. Unfortunately, many of these stories were partly or entirely false, thus leading to the epithet "yellow journalism." An example of "yellow journalism" was a headline in the *Journal* after the U.S. battleship *Maine* blew up—probably from an accidental explosion in a boiler—in Havana's harbor on 15 February 1898: "The Warship Maine Was Split in Two by an Enemy's Infernal Machine." Meanwhile, the *New York Times* and other newspapers tried to increase their circulations by contrasting their "responsible" coverage with the unsubstantiated claims that often appeared as news in the *World* and the *Journal*.

Whether sensational or responsible, the extensive press coverage of the war in Cuba—and the overwhelming sympathy in newspapers and magazines for Cuba's independence movement—helped to prepare the American public for possible war with Spain. In other words, the coverage helped to give President William McKinley the public and congressional support he would need if he decided to ask Congress for a declaration of war against Spain. By the time McKinley did so in April 1898, he shrewdly had waited until enough tensions had built up in U.S.–Spanish relations to make it appear that war had become inevitable.

As the United States gradually moved between August 1914 and April 1917 toward another war, this time with Germany, the overwhelming majority of English-language newspapers and magazines were more sympathetic toward Great Britain and its allies than they were toward Germany and its allies. Most editors blamed Germany for starting the war and for invading France through neutral Belgium; most agreed with President Woodrow Wilson that German submarine attacks without warning on British and U.S. ships were immoral and unacceptable violations of international law; and most found Britain's anti-German propaganda more persuasive than Germany's often clumsy anti-British propaganda. British-inspired stories about German "atrocities" in Belgium and elsewhere were especially effective in the contest for American sympathies. The fact that England cut the telegraph cable from Germany to America early in the war, thus limiting Germans' ability to communicate with Americans, also helped the Allied cause.

Nevertheless, a significant minority of editors opposed U.S. arms sales to England and France, and a larger number opposed efforts by Allied governments and some of their American supporters to draw the United States into the war against Germany. The best known journalistic opponent of America's pro-Allied approach was William Randolph Hearst, who owned newspapers in several major cities. The journalism historian Frank Luther Mott explained Hearst's opposition:

> Hearst had long shown an anti-British feeling; and now he supported the Irish insurrectionists, savagely attacked the English censorship, and featured the extremely pro-German wireless dispatches sent from Berlin by his special correspondent William Bayard Hale. In retaliation, both the British and French governments in October, 1916, denied further use of their mails and cables to Hearst's International News Service.

In addition to the Hearst papers, the anti-British *Chicago Tribune,* leading newspapers in such heavily German-American cities as Cleveland and Cincinnati, socialist and pacifist publications, and many German-American and Irish-American journals all challenged pro-Allied attitudes and policies. The criticisms were so intense, especially from German- and Irish-Americans, that President Wilson scolded "hyphenates" for being more loyal to their former homelands than to America.

★ ★ ★ ★

"THE LAW OF THE LUSITANIA CASE"

On 7 May 1915 the Cunard passenger liner was sunk in the Atlantic without warning by a German submarine; close to two thousand civilians and crew perished, including 128 Americans. The following are excerpts from a *New York Times* editorial that appeared on 9 May.

"The rule of maritime warfare which imposes upon the commander of a ship of war the duty of providing for the safety of the passengers and crew of any vessel he may elect to destroy is plain, unmistakable in its application to every case, and . . . everywhere and by all civilized nations accepted as a binding obligation. . . .

"The man in the street may have some possible excuse for ignorance of this humane usage of war, but it is . . . surprising to hear from the lips of Senator William J. Stone of Missouri, Chairman of the Senate Committee on Foreign Relations, . . . insinuated excuses or palliations of the dastardly crime committed by Germany. . . .

"Now that we are warned that Germany has resolved to make war in disregard of the laws of God and man, like a Malay running amuck, we know what to do. The time for protests has passed. It becomes now our duty as a nation to demand that Germany shall find means to carry on her war without putting our citizens to death.

If the dispatch without warning of torpedoes against the great Lusitania with 2,000 human beings on board is to be accepted as a true manifestation of the German spirit, . . . if she has deliberately determined that all the world shall know that this is the way in which she proposes to make war, that this is her attitude toward law, . . . then all neutral nations are on notice that the complete defeat of Germany and eradication of the military spirit of Germany are essential to their peace and safety.

After Congress approved Wilson's request for war against Germany in April 1917, the president and Congress made it a crime to criticize America's involvement in the war or to encourage young men to refuse to cooperate with the military draft. During the war, the postmaster general denied mailing privileges to publications that continued to criticize America's involvement. Three editors of a German-language newspaper in Philadelphia were sent to jail for publishing disloyal articles. Partly due to a widespread perception by the early 1920s that suppression of dissenters had been excessive, the courts generally gave better protections to America's basic freedoms—including freedom of the press—during future wars than they had during World War I.

After briefly disappearing during World ßWar I, the rich diversity of press opinion on foreign affairs returned during the debate over the Treaty of Versailles and the League of Nations in 1919–1920. Ethnic and socialist publications offered a wide range of views, many critical of specific provisions of the Treaty of Versailles. Liberal editors who had supported Wilson during the war were dismayed that the peace treaty was harsh in its treatment of Germany. Most Republican editors favored the provisions in regard to Germany and U.S. participation in the League of Nations, but they also supported the efforts of Republican leaders in the Senate to add reservations that would clarify U.S. obligations as a member of the league. When the Senate rejected the Treaty of Versailles (including U.S. membership in the league) after Wilson refused to accept the Republicans' reservations, most Republican and Democratic editors were disappointed that a compromise that would have permitted passage had not been found.

Press coverage of the wars in East Asia, Africa, and Europe in the 1930s that eventually led to the U.S. involvement in World War II also was highly diverse. Generally not having to fear alienating Japanese-American readers, editors and columnists sharply criticized Japan for occupying Manchuria in 1931 and then invading China in 1933. Italy's invasion of Ethiopia in 1935 especially angered African-American editors. Communist and liberal publications tended to support the leftist government in the Spanish Civil War, whereas Catholic and conservative journals generally sympathized with the rebel movement led by General Francisco Franco. Even when the overwhelming majority of newspapers and magazines denounced Germany's invasion of Poland on 1 September 1939, which began World War II in Europe, a scattering of communist and pro-Nazi publications disagreed.

Like the American public as a whole, journalists often disagreed about which policies to pursue toward the wars in Europe and Asia between September 1939 and the Japanese attack on Pearl Harbor in December 1941. In Chicago, for example, the leading newspaper, the *Chicago Tribune,* opposed President Franklin D. Roosevelt's proposal to revise the neutrality acts in the fall of 1939 to permit England and France to buy supplies in the United States, whereas the other major paper, the *Chicago Daily News,* supported the president's proposal. Although antifascist, the *Chicago Defender,* a leading African-American newspaper, urged its readers to continue to focus on fighting racism in America.

The great debate on foreign policy in the press between 1939 and 1941 generally took place at a more sophisticated level than the debate between 1914 and 1917 over involvement in World War I. For one thing, syndicated columnists like Walter Lippmann and Dorothy Thompson gave newspaper readers a deeper understanding of the issues involved than did the reading of news stories and editorials alone. For another, the issue this time was the nature and extent of U.S. involvement, not the relative merits of the Allied versus the Axis side. Most important, journalists and readers alike understood the stakes: if America became a belligerent in this war, it almost certainly would give up its selectively interventionist heritage and be transformed into a world power with unprecedented global responsibilities.

THE PRESS AND GLOBAL AMERICA SINCE 1941: AN OVERVIEW

The year 1941—when the United States went to war against Germany, Japan, and the other Axis powers in World War II—marked a watershed in America's participation in world affairs. Before then, the U.S. government's involvement outside the northern half of the Western Hemisphere had been limited and episodic. Since then, America has been so internationalist that it has had interests and troop deployments on every continent and ocean. Among many other things, America's perceived interests have included military security, international institutions, opposition to communism, trade and investment, foreign aid, health issues, and freedom of information. The press as a whole has supported this, the most expansive definition of national interests in human history. At the same time, the press has been the major locus of an often heated debate about precisely how America's internationalism should be defined and applied in many of the thousands of specific issues that have faced policymakers during the years since 1941.

In retrospect, the history of the relationship between the press and U.S. foreign policy since 1941 divides at the time of the large-scale U.S. involvement in Vietnam (1965–1973). If one were forced to pick one event that formed the watershed between the two eras in the press-government relations on foreign policy, it might well be the heavily publicized hearings on the Vietnam War held by Senator J. William Fulbright's Senate Foreign Relations Committee in the winter of 1966. These hearings exposed the sharp differences of opinion between witnesses like Secretary of State Dean Rusk who strongly supported the U.S. involvement in Vietnam and the continued validity of a firm stance against communism, and witnesses like former State Department official George Kennan who argued that the containment policy should not be applied in Southeast Asia and that major changes were underway in communist nations that made earlier anticommunist approaches obsolete.

As part of a continuum of developments beginning with the well-publicized improvement in U.S.–Soviet relations during 1963, the hearings helped to make it intellectually respectable for some newspapers and magazines (for example, the *New York Times* and *Newsweek*) to abandon their strong traditional support for containment, whereas others (the *Wall Street Journal* and *National Review*) largely continued their Cold War approach. Thus the hearings—and, much more, the Vietnam War that prompted them and continued long after the hearings ended—divided press coverage of U.S. foreign policy from a pattern of largely supportive coverage of major administration policies—from the Japanese attack on Pearl Harbor in 1941 roughly through 1965—to a new pattern from 1966 forward in which coverage was much more divided and typically was contested—at least until the end of the Cold War—along liberal/conservative ideological lines.

The Vietnam War coincided with a marked shift in news coverage away from the ideal of "objectivity" toward the acceptance of more analysis and interpretation in news stories in newspapers (news magazines like *Time* and *Newsweek* had never hesitated to mix news and interpretation). In part this shift by newspapers was a response to the fact that, by the 1960s, television had become the major source of breaking news for growing numbers of Americans. Thus print journalists moved toward a new focus: interpretation in greater depth than network television news could accomplish.

The shift toward larger numbers of interpretive stories also resulted from (1) a growing recognition that the norm of objectivity, however desirable in theory, was an unattainable ideal; and (2) the belief that this ideal had given government officials (including the notorious Senator Joseph McCarthy) too much power to get their often questionable views into print in such a way that they appeared to be facts. In practice, interpretation meant that most newspapers carried more stories that raised questions about particular foreign policies, notably on the front pages that previously had been reserved for "news."

Although it is accurate to emphasize the greater diversity and more critical tone of press coverage of U.S. foreign policy after the mid-1960s, one should not draw too sharp a contrast between pre-Vietnam and post-Vietnam coverage. It is true that most journalists (and most newspapers and magazines) supported the major goals of U.S. policy from Pearl Harbor through the early 1960s: defeating Germany and Japan, helping to establish a peace favorable to American interests and ideals, and then providing leadership in containing communist and other challenges to America's preferred postwar world order. It is also true that the press generally accepted government censorship of news relating to military activities during World War II and the Korean War.

Yet anyone who reads large numbers of newspapers and periodicals on foreign affairs between the early 1940s and the early 1960s will find a tremendous diversity of views. That was true on many subjects during World War II, and it was even more evident thereafter. During the late 1940s, for example, the leading syndicated columnists—Walter Lippmann and Joseph Alsop—disagreed sharply about the approach America should take in containing the Soviet Union. And the nation's leading magazine publisher, Henry Luce of Time Incorporated, vehemently disagreed with the government and with the editors of the nation's leading newspaper, the *New York Times,* about U.S. policy toward China. Despite their differences of opinion, leading journalists like Lippmann, Alsop, and Luce were befriended and courted by presidents and other high officials after World War II to an extent that was unprecedented in American history.

Diversity of coverage was found in both of the studies of the press and foreign policy during this era in which the authors of this essay were involved. Both studies used content analysis of coverage during several periods. In *The Press and the Origins of the Cold War, 1944–1947,* Louis W. Liebovich did content analysis of coverage between 1944 and 1947 in *Time* magazine, the *New York Herald Tribune,* the *Chicago Tribune,* and the *San Francisco Chronicle.* He repeatedly found varied coverage in the four publications, with coverage in the highly idiosyncratic *Chicago Tribune* (the newspaper with the largest circulation in the Midwest) diverging the most sharply. In a time of considerable uncertainty in relations between America and Russia in which President Harry S. Truman did not spell out his own views on U.S.–Soviet relations for more than eighteen months after the end of World War II, Liebovich concluded that "[o]nly the *Chicago Tribune* could claim steady opposition to any Soviet-U.S. accord."

In a book on the press and four foreign policy crises during the Kennedy years, Montague Kern, Patricia W. Levering, and Ralph B. Levering found substantial differences in coverage in all five newspapers studied—the *New York Times, Washington Post, Chicago Tribune, St. Louis Post-Dispatch,* and *San Francisco Examiner.* Not surprisingly, given its location in Washington, the *Post* gave the most weight to administration sources, the *Times* had the most foreign sources, the *Post-Dispatch* offered the most criticisms from a liberal perspective, the *Tribune's* news stories and editorials frequently were imbued with the paper's unique blend of isolationism and militant anticommunism, and the *Examiner* emphasized a Republican internationalism that viewed President Kennedy as too weak in dealing with communist nations.

In light of the relative liberalism and internationalism of northeastern elites and government employees, the fairly liberal, internationalist views of the *Post* and *Times* are easily understood. But could even most residents of Chicago and St. Louis explain why the leading papers in their cities were, respectively, militantly isolationist and liberally internationalist? And who would expect a conservative Republican paper to be one of the two leading newspapers (along with the *San Francisco Chronicle*) in traditionally liberal San Francisco? Diversity indeed.

A broad range of opinion on foreign policy between Pearl Harbor and the mid-1960s was even more pronounced in magazines. During World War II, for example, several prominent conservative magazines published articles warning that it would be impossible for America to continue to cooperate after the war with the dicta-

torial, expansionist Russian government. During the mid-1950s, writers for the liberal *Nation* and *New Republic* argued that America should pursue policies designed to end the Cold War; meanwhile, contributors to the conservative *National Review* were insisting that World War III already was underway and that the communist side was winning. In the late 1950s and early 1960s, some conservative journals prematurely denounced Fidel Castro's "communist" revolution in Cuba, whereas some liberal magazines featured articles praising Castro even after he acknowledged his allegiance to communism.

Despite this diversity of coverage even at the height of the Cold War, there were significant differences beginning about 1966. The changes resulted primarily from the Vietnam War and the breakdown of the Cold War consensus among the "responsible" mainstream journalists who worked for leading newspapers and magazines. Because the *New York Times* was the most respected newspaper among officials and journalists in Washington, and because its news and editorial judgments influenced coverage at the major magazines and television networks located in New York, the shift at the *Times* away from the Cold War consensus was especially significant.

During the 1950s and early 1960s, the *Times* effectively had supported Central Intelligence Agency interventions designed to overthrow existing governments, either by accepting official denials of U.S. involvement (for example, Iran in 1953 and Guatemala in 1954) or by playing down coverage of planned interventions (such as Cuba in 1961). The *Times* also helped the government maintain numerous official secrets, including the fact that some U.S. journalists stationed abroad were part-time CIA employees who assisted the government in waging the Cold War. In contrast, when the *Times* learned from disgruntled officials that the Nixon administration had secretly been bombing North Vietnamese forces inside Cambodia, it printed the information and thus demonstrated the falsity of the administration's public statements on the subject.

In subsequent years the *Times* repeatedly exposed and denounced the CIA's (that is, Nixon's) efforts to oust Chile's Marxist president and the CIA's (Reagan's) efforts to defeat Nicaragua's Marxist leaders. The *Washington Post,* which had given at least as fervent support as the *Times* to most anticommunist policies, also challenged the government's continuing Cold War approach by the late 1960s and early 1970s. The publication of large sections of the Pentagon Papers (a classified official study of the evolution of U.S. policy in Vietnam) by the *Times, Post,* and *Boston Globe* in June 1971 was a clear sign from leading news organizations that the era of unquestioning cooperation with officials on national security issues was over.

In addition to growing differences of opinion over U.S. foreign policy, the 1960s ethos of questioning authority—an ethos reinforced by Nixon's dishonesty during the Watergate affair that cost him his presidency—also affected relations between reporters and officials for many years thereafter. During and after Watergate, Energy Secretary James Schlesinger recalled, "the press took great delight in demonstrating that the government was wrong." In comparing Dean Rusk's relations with reporters in the early 1960s with the experience of another Democratic secretary of state, Cyrus Vance, in the late 1970s, Martin Linsky found "no sense from Vance of personal intimacy with reporters, and no sense that from his perspective they were waiting for his wisdom." Vance told Linsky that he saw the press as "playing a critically important role. The press can either make or break a policy initiative."

Many high officials in the Reagan administration believed that the government, by giving the news media a relatively free hand in covering the conflict in Vietnam, had contributed to America's failure there. Accordingly, when Reagan in October 1983 ordered U.S. troops to invade the small Caribbean nation of Grenada and overthrow its pro-Cuban government, the administration did not permit any reporters to accompany the troops. Two immediate results were the press's dependence on administration sources for information about the invasion and criticism of official news management in many news stories and editorials. The invasion revealed that conservative concerns about a monolithic "eastern liberal press" were overblown: after U.S. troops had defeated Cuban forces and installed a noncommunist government, editorials in the liberal *New York Times* criticized the invasion, but the moderate *Washington Post* concluded that "President Reagan made the right decision in Grenada."

Press coverage of the Grenada invasion and its consequences largely occurred within a couple weeks in late October and early November 1983. A relatively big story that spanned the entire decade—U.S. policy toward the civil wars in Central America—illustrated the sharp divisions within Congress and American society that found

their way into press coverage of many foreign policy issues after the mid-1960s. To the Reagan administration and its conservative supporters, the Marxist left, aided by the Soviet Union and Cuba, had gained power in Nicaragua in the late 1970s and was threatening to establish pro-Soviet communist regimes in El Salvador and Guatemala as well. Deeply concerned that communist ideology and Soviet power were expanding in "America's backyard," conservatives believed that the Marxist left needed to be defeated decisively. Liberals, who viewed the existing governments in El Salvador and Guatemala as highly repressive and feared "another Vietnam," thought that America should send neither military aid nor troops to assist anticommunist governments in those two nations or rebel "contra" forces in Nicaragua. Because of the sharp ideological divisions on this issue and most Americans' lack of knowledge about the region, U.S. policy toward Central America in the 1980s was a subject on which many reporters, editorial writers, and columnists had almost as much difficulty in obtaining accurate information and presenting balanced perspectives as did administration officials, members of Congress, academics, religious leaders, and political activists.

With the ending by early 1990 of both the Cold War and the U.S.–Soviet–Cuban contest in Central America, journalists and officials turned their attention to new issues that thankfully could no longer be placed in Cold War frames. America still had alliances and a strong general interest in peace and stability, but vital interests in specific situations were harder to define in the absence of an international communist movement. When foreign policy issues involving possible military interventions arose in the 1990s, therefore, the debate in Washington and in the press focused on whether the nation had sufficient national interests to send troops to nations like Kuwait, Somalia, Bosnia, and Haiti.

Even within the affluent news organizations, the issue of priorities became more difficult to resolve in the absence of a communist threat. "We have chosen to invest major resources in covering the former Yugoslavia, but is this the correct move?" Bernard Gwertzman of the *Times* wrote. "Should we care what happens to Serbs, Croats, and Bosnians?" Except in a few papers like the *Times* with a strong tradition of international reporting, the volume of foreign news coverage dropped sharply in both newspapers and news magazines in the 1990s.

There were positive trends as well. Reporting and commenting on the lengthy deliberations over the North American Free Trade Agreement (NAFTA) treaty in the early 1990s and over most-favored-nation trading status for China several years later, the press played important roles in the largest public discussions of America's international economic policies since the debates over tariff policy in the 1920s and early 1930s. Because the print media are indispensable for detailed analysis, and television excels in presenting vivid images, newspapers and magazines may well have had relatively greater influence than television in the debates over economic policy than in the discussions of possible military interventions.

The press also has played an important role in bringing environmental issues—including proposed international actions to deal with them—to public attention. An example is the debate over the 1997 Kyoto Protocol to address global warming. An analysis by Brigitte Nacos, Robert Shapiro, and Pierangelo Isernia of press coverage in two national newspapers during a six-month period from September 1997 through February 1998 found that the *New York Times* published sixty-five articles on the subject and the *Wall Street Journal* published twenty-three. The authors also found that

> contrary to the American media's more common coverage of foreign policy issues, government officials did not dominate that press coverage. Taken together, policy and scientific experts, a variety of organized interests (business, labor unions, environmentalists), as well as the public, were more frequently covered than officials at Washington's major news beats. . . . As a result, the media—especially newspapers—reflected the kind of robust debate that is especially essential in the American system of government, where decision makers pay considerable attention to public opinion.

This and other studies suggest that, with the Cold War over, the press is less likely to rely as heavily on administration and congressional sources for its news stories as it did earlier. To be sure, the views of governmental leaders in a democracy need to be publicized and evaluated, so that voters can have information on which to base judgments in future elections. But the views of others—including the representatives of the groups listed in the above quotation—also need to be included so that voters have a broad base of information and perspectives upon which to form their opinions. By giving detailed coverage to relatively neglected issues like international economics and the environment, and by providing greater balance between governmental and nongovernmental sources for news stories about these issues, the press may well be doing a better job in covering foreign policy issues today than it did during the Cold War.

THE PRESS AND FOREIGN POLICY CRISES

Much of the most systematic scholarship on the press and foreign policy has focused on coverage during the many crises that occurred from the early 1960s through the early 1990s. Two studies that include systematic analysis of the Cuban missile crisis, *The Kennedy Crises* (1983) by Montague Kern and colleagues and *The Press, Presidents, and Crises* (1990) by Brigitte Nacos, agree that the Kennedy administration faced difficulties from negative press coverage of issues relating to Cuba, especially in Republican-leaning newspapers, in the months leading up to the discovery of the missiles in mid-October 1962. Conservative newspapers highlighted the charges of Republican politicians and anticommunist Cuban exiles that the administration was too weak in dealing with Castro and with a large-scale Soviet military buildup in Cuba that, contrary to administration denials, might well include nuclear weapons.

The two studies also agree that, after Kennedy went on national television and radio on 22 October to reveal the missiles' presence in Cuba and to insist upon their removal, coverage in all studied newspapers swung decisively in his favor, thus building up his reputation as a strong and sensible leader who was "in control." After Soviet leader Nikita Khrushchev publicly agreed on 28 October to remove the missiles and thus handed Kennedy a widely perceived victory, coverage gradually returned to the more normal pattern of liberal support for the administration on Cuba and conservative questioning of its resolve to "stand up to" Khrushchev and Castro.

Based on their study of the missile crisis and three other crises of the Kennedy years, Montague Kern and her colleagues concluded that "the president dominates press coverage primarily in situations [such as the climatic week of the Cuban missile crisis] where competing interpretations of events are not being espoused by others whom journalists consider important." Brigitte Nacos agreed with this conclusion and added another: "The extent to which the president's domestic proponents or opponents were highlighted or downplayed in the news depended on the editorial stance of each newspaper. During all phases of the Cuban crisis there was a relationship between so-called straight news reporting and editorial positions of each news organization." This finding, confirmed in her study of other crises, suggests that editorial perspectives—especially general support for or opposition to the administration in power—correlated with news coverage of crises in the pro-Democratic *New York Times* and *Washington Post* and in the pro-Republican *Chicago Tribune*.

On the Sunday before Kennedy planned to take to the airwaves to confront Khrushchev and state the administration's policy, he learned that James Reston of the *New York Times* and other reporters had pieced together large parts of the story about the missiles in Cuba and about Kennedy's plan to blockade the island and demand that the missiles be removed. Fearing that premature publication of this information might derail his efforts to resolve the crisis peacefully, Kennedy phoned Reston and high-level officials of the *Times* and the *Post* and *Time* magazine and pleaded that details of the administration's plans not be published before Tuesday. Reston recalled that Kennedy "didn't deny what was afoot, but said that if I printed what we knew, he might get an ultimatum from Khrushchev even before he could go on the air to explain the seriousness of the crisis." Reston and the "eastern establishment" executives agreed to cooperate with Kennedy.

Kennedy's phone calls stand as striking high-level testimony about the perceived importance of the press in the policymaking process during international crisis. They also raise an intriguing question, prompted by Nacos's conclusion: if one of the reporters for the *Chicago Tribune* had gotten the story, would that anti-administration paper have responded as positively as the *Times* and the *Post* did to Kennedy's request not to reveal his plans?

During the Cuban missile crisis, Kennedy received highly positive, "rally 'round the flag" coverage at the time he needed it most. During the Vietnamese communists' Tet Offensive a little more than five years later, in contrast, the Johnson administration generally failed to get the positive press coverage that might have strengthened public and congressional support for America's war in Vietnam. At a time when U.S. and allied troops were being killed and wounded in unprecedented numbers, why was most of the coverage in the mainstream media unsupportive of the administration?

A major reason is that most journalists viewed the large-scale communist offensive beginning at the end of January 1968 as yet another example of the gap between U.S. officials' optimistic public assessments of America's and South Vietnam's "progress" in the war, and the reality that North Vietnam and its Vietcong allies were determined enemies who were far from being beaten. In other words, many journalists were skeptical about U.S. leaders' depictions of the war before Tet, a skepticism that the communist offensive appeared to confirm. Writing later, Don Oberdorfer of the *Washington Post* mentioned another factor: "One reason the press was not 'on the [government's] team' was because the country was not 'on the team.' To a substantial degree, the newsmen represented and reflected American society, and like the rest [of the public], they had no deep commitment to or enthusiasm for the war."

Several developments during the offensive also contributed to the largely unfavorable press coverage. The fact that Vietcong troops attacked targets in Saigon—including the U.S. embassy—frightened the hundreds of American journalists stationed there and suggested that U.S. military leaders had been wrong to describe parts of South Vietnam as "secure." Another example: the widely published photo (and widely played television footage) of the shooting of a captured Vietcong suspect by a South Vietnamese brigadier general on a Saigon street raised new questions about that government's standards of behavior. And an American major's comment to a reporter about the battle to remove the enemy from Bentre—"It became necessary to destroy the town to save it"—increased doubts at home about whether some of America's own military practices in the war were moral.

In a detailed study of press coverage during the offensive, journalist Peter Braestrup argued that the media mistakenly portrayed Tet as a "defeat for the allies" and hence by implication a victory for the communist forces. In fact, after early reverses, America and its allies won a major victory over enemy forces throughout most of South Vietnam—a victory that received little coverage compared with the heavy dose of negative news early in the crisis. "Rarely has contemporary crisis-journalism turned out, in retrospect, to have veered so widely from reality," Braestrup concluded.

Although Braestrup rightly pointed out failings in press coverage, his thesis is only partly persuasive. One can agree that, from a military viewpoint, allied forces by mid-March generally had dealt communist troops at least a temporary defeat. But the Vietnam War also had large psychological and political components. From those viewpoints, the communists were strikingly successful: they convinced most Americans (including most journalists and many members of Congress) that, after three years of heavy fighting with superior equipment, America still faced capable, courageous opponents who could not be defeated in the foreseeable future, if ever. Braestrup's criticisms notwithstanding, journalists were right to portray the Tet Offensive as an impressive military attack and, more importantly, as a severe blow to Johnson's belief that America could "prevail" in Vietnam while continuing to fight a limited war there.

The third crisis, sparked by Iraq's conquest of neighboring Kuwait in August 1990, was so different from the first two situations—themselves very different from each other—as to demonstrate that the concept "foreign policy crisis" is itself multifaceted. Unlike the situation in Cuba or South Vietnam, a sovereign nation was conquered before U.S. leaders had time to take effective action. Moreover, the public (including the press) debate about what moves, if any, America should make in response took place with memories still strong about America's painful departure from Vietnam only fifteen years before.

Scholars rightly point out that, during the first few weeks after Iraq's invasion of Kuwait on 2 August, the George H. W. Bush administration largely framed the issue in terms of the immorality of the conquest, the Hitler-like expansionism of Iraqi leader Saddam Hussein that threatened such important U.S. allies as Saudi Arabia and Israel, and the necessity of restoring Kuwait's independence through either diplomacy or force. What some scholars opposed to President Bush's policy are less likely to acknowledge, however, is that the overwhelming majority of mass-circulation newspapers and magazines (and major television and radio news operations) basically agreed with the administration's arguments and willingly assisted in building public support for an active U.S. role in ending the Iraqi occupation. In newsrooms across the nation as well as in Congress, the only large-scale debates centered on whether America and its allies could achieve this objective through economic sanctions, or whether the nations opposed

to the occupation also needed to be prepared to use military force in the relatively near future. A broadly based study of newspaper editorials on the Gulf crisis found them overall to be "respectful toward the president and generally supportive. When there was dissent, it was usually over tactics and timing, rather than goals and principles."

Especially helpful to the administration was support from respected news organizations that frequently had disagreed with recent presidents—especially with Republicans like Nixon and Reagan—on major foreign policies. An example was the *New York Times*. From the start of the crisis, political scientist Benjamin I. Page noted, editorials in the *Times* "condemned the Iraqi invasion and insisted upon a complete and unconditional withdrawal from Kuwait." Page also lamented the limited range of opinions expressed in the *Times* columns as well as editorials: "There was certainly no talk of U.S. imperialism or hegemony, or of our historical policy of trying to control Middle Eastern oil reserves." Compared with the *Times*, however, *Newsweek* was blatantly supportive of the administration. In late November it even published a column by President Bush entitled "Why We Must Break Saddam's 'Stranglehold.'"

Building upon solid but far from unanimous backing at home, during the fall of 1990 Bush gained strong support from allied nations in western Europe and the Middle East and from the United Nations Security Council. The administration and its allies (notably Great Britain) also built up a large, well-equipped military force in Saudi Arabia and threatened to go to war with Iraq if Hussein did not withdraw from Kuwait. Assuming that Iraq did not end its occupation quickly, only two important questions remained. First, would the Democratic-controlled Congress, many of whose members still had vivid memories of the Vietnam debacle, pass a resolution supporting a war with Iraq to liberate Kuwait? And second, would the mainstream media accept the unprecedented degree of control over journalists and their stories that the administration, with its own fresh memories of press coverage of Vietnam and other interventions, insisted upon imposing? When Congress and the mainstream media effectively answered "yes" to both questions, the administration's victory over potentially powerful domestic opponents was complete.

Now all that the United States and its allies had to do was liberate Kuwait, which occurred more quickly and with fewer casualties—at least on America's side—than most observers had anticipated. Begun with allied bombing attacks on Iraqi targets on 16 January 1991, the war ended with a cease-fire agreement six weeks later. Although systematic studies remain to be done, it appears that, given the almost total absence of congressional criticism while the nation was at war, news and editorial coverage was even more favorable to the administration during the war than it had been earlier. In this and other ways, both press coverage and the press-government relationship during the Gulf War were strikingly different from what they had been during the Tet Offensive twenty-three years earlier.

If past experience holds, one would expect continued diversity in press coverage and in press-government relations during foreign policy crises in the future. One also would expect continued diversity in noncrisis situations and in coverage of the many different kinds of foreign policy issues that draw journalists' attention.

BIBLIOGRAPHY

Berry, Nicholas O. *Foreign Policy and the Press: An Analysis of the New York Times' Coverage of U.S. Foreign Policy.* New York, 1990. Although limited to analysis of the *Times,* this is a superb study of how journalists cover foreign policy issues during various stages of crises.

Braestrup, Peter. *Big Story: How the American Press and Television Reported and Interpreted the Crisis of Tet 1968 in Vietnam and Washington.* 2 vols. Boulder, Colo., 1977.

Broder, David S. *Behind the Front Page: A Candid Look at How the News is Made.* New York, 1987. A leading journalist's account of relations between the press and government, and especially valuable for the presidencies of Lyndon Johnson and Richard Nixon.

Cater, Douglass. *The Fourth Branch of Government.* Boston, 1959. Especially useful for the presidencies of Truman and Eisenhower.

Cohen, Bernard C. *The Press and Foreign Policy.* Princeton, N.J., 1963. An important scholarly study of the press and U.S. foreign policy at the height of the Cold War.

———. *Democracies and Foreign Policy: Public Participation in the United States and the Netherlands.* Madison, Wisc., 1995.

Gans, Herbert J. *Deciding What's News: A Study of CBS Evening News, NBC Nightly News, Newsweek, and Time.* New York, 1979. A study by a well-known sociologist known for effective use of interviews and for comparisons of journalistic practices at leading news magazines and television networks.

Graber, Doris A. *Mass Media and American Politics.* 4th ed. Washington, D.C., 1993. A standard work that includes an excellent section on the press and foreign policy; especially helpful for the 1970s and 1980s.

Hallin, Daniel C. *The "Uncensored War": The Media and Vietnam.* New York, 1986. A detailed study that argues that the executive branch of the U.S. government greatly influenced press coverage of the Vietnam War.

Hilsman, Roger. *The Politics of Policy Making in Defense and Foreign Affairs.* 3d ed. Englewood Cliffs, N.J., 1993. An insightful study by a political scientist who also was a high-level official in the Kennedy administration.

Kennamer, J. David, ed. *Public Opinion, the Press, and Public Policy.* Westport, Conn., 1992. Useful partly because it is more theoretical and conceptual than most other works that analyze the subject.

Kern, Montague, Patricia W. Levering, and Ralph B. Levering. *The Kennedy Crises: The Press, the Presidency, and Foreign Policy.* Chapel Hill, N.C., 1983.

Liebovich, Louis W. *The Press and the Origins of the Cold War, 1944–1947.* New York, 1988.

———. *The Press and the Modern Presidency: Myths and Mindsets from Kennedy to Election 2000.* 2d ed. Westport, Conn., 2001.

Linsky, Martin. *Impact: How the Press Affects Federal Policymaking.* New York, 1986. Based partly on interviews, this book contains in-depth analysis of press coverage of several foreign policy issues in the late 1970s and early 1980s.

Mott, Frank Luther. *American Journalism; A History: 1690–1960.* 3d ed. New York, 1962. A standard history of American journalism, it pays more attention to the press and foreign policy than most other surveys.

Nacos, Brigitte Lebens. *The Press, Presidents, and Crises.* New York, 1990. An excellent study that includes quantitative analysis of both news and editorial coverage in leading newspapers.

Nacos, Brigitte Lebens, Robert Y. Shapiro, and Pierangelo Isernia, eds. *Decisionmaking in a Glass House: Mass Media, Public Opinion, and American and European Foreign Policy in the 21st Century.* Lanham, Md., 2000. Several chapters contain excellent analyses of press coverage of selected issues in U.S. foreign policy in the 1990s.

Newsom, David D. *The Public Dimension of Foreign Policy.* Bloomington, Ind., 1996. A former U.S. diplomat offers insights into the press and foreign policy and other subjects; especially useful for the 1980s and early 1990s.

Page, Benjamin I. *Who Deliberates?: Mass Media in Modern Democracy.* Chicago, 1996. Especially useful for press coverage of the events leading up to the war in the Persian Gulf in 1991.

Rivers, William L. *The Adversaries: Politics and the Press.* Boston, 1970. An analysis of the frequent conflicts between officials and journalists during the 1960s.

Rosati, Jerel A. *The Politics of United States Foreign Policy.* 2d ed. Fort Worth, Tex., 1999. Includes a well-argued chapter on the news media and foreign policy; especially useful for the 1980s and early 1990s.

Schneider, James C. *Should America Go to War?: The Debate over Foreign Policy in Chicago, 1939–1941.* Chapel Hill, N.C., 1989. An excellent study of the role of the press and other actors in shaping public discussion in one city.

Seib, Philip. *Headline Diplomacy: How News Coverage Affects Foreign Policy.* Westport, Conn., 1997. An outstanding nonquantitative study of the press and foreign policy over the past several decades.

Serfaty, Simon, ed. *The Media and Foreign Policy.* New York, 1991. Excellent analyses, primarily by journalists and officials, of press coverage and relationships between journalists and officials on foreign policy issues; especially insightful on the 1980s.

Thompson, Kenneth W., ed. *The White House Press on the Presidency: News Management and Co-Option.* Lanham, Md., 1983. Journalists and former officials discuss press coverage, including coverage of foreign policy during the 1960s and 1970s.

See also PUBLIC OPINION; TELEVISION.

PROPAGANDA

★ ★ ★ ★

Kenneth A. Osgood

The United States has utilized propaganda techniques repeatedly through its history, particularly during periods of war and international crisis. As early as the revolutionary period, Americans evinced a shrewd grasp of the utility of propaganda as an instrument of foreign policy. The total wars of the early twentieth century led the U.S. government to employ propaganda on a massive scale as an accessory to military operations, but the Cold War institutionalized propaganda as a central component of American foreign policy. The governmental use of propaganda continued to expand in the twenty-first century, largely due to the harnessing of the revolution in communications. But for most Americans, propaganda has a negative connotation as a treacherous, deceitful, and manipulative practice. Americans have generally thought of propaganda as something "other" people and nations do, while they themselves merely persuade, inform, or educate. Americans have employed numerous euphemisms for their propaganda in order to distinguish it from its totalitarian applications and wicked connotations. The most common of these has been "information," a designation that has adorned all of the official propaganda agencies of the government—from the Committee on Public Information (1917–1919) and the Office of War Information (1942–1945) to the U.S. Information Agency (1953–1999) and its successor, the Office of International Information Programs in the Department of State.

For a brief period during the 1940s and early 1950s, the terms "psychological warfare" and "political warfare" were openly espoused by propaganda specialists and politicians alike. Increasingly, they turned to euphemisms like "international communication" and "public communication" to make the idea of propaganda more palatable to domestic audiences. During the Cold War, common phrases also included "the war of ideas," "battle for hearts and minds," "struggle for the minds and wills of men," "thought war," "ide-

ological warfare," "nerve warfare," "campaign of truth," "war of words," and others. Even the term "Cold War" was used to refer to propaganda techniques and strategy (as in "Cold War tactics"). Later, the terms "communication," "public diplomacy," "psychological operations" (or "psyops"), "special operations," and "information warfare" became fashionable. Political propaganda and measures to influence media coverage were likewise labeled "spin," and political propagandists were "spin doctors" or, more imaginatively, "media consultants" and "image advisers."

The term "propaganda" has spawned as many definitions as it has euphemisms. Harold Lasswell, a pioneer of propaganda studies in the United States, defined it as "the management of collective attitudes by the manipulation of significant symbols." Like other social scientists in the 1930s, he emphasized its psychological elements: propaganda was a subconscious manipulation of psychological symbols to accomplish secret objectives. Subsequent analysts stressed that propaganda was a planned and deliberate act of opinion management. A 1958 study prepared for the U.S. Army, for example, defined propaganda as "the planned dissemination of news, information, special arguments, and appeals designed to influence the beliefs, thoughts, and actions of a specific group." In the 1990s the historian Oliver Thomson defined propaganda broadly to include both deliberate and unintentional means of behavior modification, describing it as "the use of communication skills of all kinds to achieve attitudinal or behavioural changes among one group by another." Numerous communication specialists have stressed that propaganda is a neutral activity concerned only with persuasion, in order to free propagandists (and their profession) from pejorative associations. Some social scientists have abandoned the term altogether because it cannot be defined with any degree of precision; and others, like the influential French philosopher Jacques Ellul, have used the term but refused to define it because any definition would inevitably leave something out.

As these examples indicate, propaganda is notoriously difficult to define. Does one identify propaganda by the intentions of the sponsor, by the effect on the recipients, or by the techniques used? Is something propaganda because it is deliberate and planned? How does propaganda differ from advertising, public relations, education, information, or, for that matter, politics? At its core, propaganda refers to any technique or action that attempts to influence the emotions, attitudes, or behavior of a group, in order to benefit the sponsor. Propaganda is usually, but not exclusively, concerned with public opinion and mass attitudes. The purpose of propaganda is to persuade—either to change or reinforce existing attitudes and opinions. Yet propaganda is also a manipulative activity. It often disguises the secret intentions and goals of the sponsor; it seeks to inculcate ideas rather than to explain them; and it aspires to modify or control opinions and actions primarily to benefit the sponsor rather than the recipient.

Although manipulative, propaganda is not necessarily untruthful, as is commonly believed. In fact, many specialists believe that the most effective propaganda operates with different layers of truth—from half-truths and the truth torn out of context to the just plain truth. Propagandists have on many occasions employed lies, misrepresentations, or deceptions, but propaganda that is based on fact and that rings true to the intended audience is bound to be more persuasive than bald-faced lies.

Another common misconception identifies propaganda narrowly by its most obvious manifestations—radio broadcasts, posters, leaflets, and so on. But propaganda experts employ a range of symbols, ideas, and activities to influence the thoughts, attitudes, opinions, and actions of various audiences—including such disparate modes of communication and human interaction as educational and cultural exchanges, books and scholarly publications, the adoption of slogans and buzzwords, monuments and museums, spectacles and media events, press releases, speeches, policy initiatives, and person-to-person contacts. Diplomacy, too, has been connected to the practice of propaganda. Communication techniques have been employed by government agents to cultivate public opinion so as to put pressure on governments to pursue certain policies, while traditional diplomatic activities—negotiations, treaties—have been planned, implemented, and presented in whole or in part for the effects they would have on public opinion, both international and domestic.

TYPES OF PROPAGANDA

Modern practitioners of propaganda utilize various schema to classify different types of propaganda activities. One such categorization classifies propaganda as white, gray, or black according to the degree to which the sponsor conceals or acknowledges its involvement. White propaganda is correctly attributed to the sponsor and the source is truthfully identified. (The U.S. government's international broadcast service Voice of America, for example, broadcasts white propaganda.) Gray propaganda, on the other hand, is unattributed to the sponsor and conceals the real source of the propaganda. The objective of gray propaganda is to advance viewpoints that are in the interest of the originator but that would be more acceptable to target audiences than official statements. The reasoning is that avowedly propagandistic materials from a foreign government or identified propaganda agency might convince few, but the same ideas presented by seemingly neutral outlets would be more persuasive. Unattributed publications, such as articles in newspapers written by a disguised source, are staples of gray propaganda. Other tactics involve wide dissemination of ideas put forth by others—by foreign governments, by national and international media outlets, or by private groups, individuals, and institutions. Gray propaganda also includes material assistance provided to groups that put forth views deemed useful to the propagandist.

Like its gray cousin, black propaganda also camouflages the sponsor's participation. But while gray propaganda is unattributed, black propaganda is falsely attributed. Black propaganda is subversive and provocative; it is usually designed to appear to have originated from a hostile source, in order to cause that source embarrassment, to damage its prestige, to undermine its credibility, or to get it to take actions that it might not otherwise. Black propaganda is usually prepared by secret agents or an intelligence service because it would be damaging to the originating government if it were discovered. It routinely employs underground newspapers, forged documents, planted gossip or rumors, jokes, slogans, and visual symbols.

Another categorization distinguishes between "fast" and "slow" propaganda operations, based on the type of media employed and the immediacy of the effect desired. Fast media are designed to exert a short-term impact on public opinion, while the use of slow media cultivates public opinion over the long haul. Fast media typically include radio, newspapers, speeches, television, moving pictures, and, since the 1990s, e-mail and the Internet. These forms of communication are able to exert an almost instantaneous effect on select audiences. Books, cultural exhibitions, and educational exchanges and activities, on the other hand, are slow media that seek to inculcate ideas and attitudes over time.

An additional category of propaganda might be termed "propaganda of the deed," or actions taken for the psychological effects they would have on various publics. The famous Doolittle Raid of April 1942 is a classic example. After months of negative news from the Pacific during World War II, Lieutenant Colonel James Doolittle of the U.S. Army Air Corps led a force of sixteen planes on a bombing raid of Japan. The mission was pointless from a military point of view, but psychologically it was significant. For Americans, it provided a morale boost and evidence that the United States was "doing something" to strike at the enemy directly; for the Japanese, it was a warning that the United States possessed the capability to reach their homeland with strategic bombers and a reminder that the attack at Pearl Harbor had not completely destroyed the U.S. fleet. "Propaganda of the deed" can also include such disparate actions as educational or cultural exchanges, economic aid, disaster relief, disarmament initiatives, international agreements, the appointment of investigating commissions, legislation, and other policy initiatives when employed primarily for the effects they would have on public opinion.

REVOLUTION, WAR, AND PROPAGANDA TO 1917

By whatever name we call it, propaganda has a long history. War propaganda is as ancient as war itself. Anthropologists have unearthed evidence that primitive peoples used pictures and symbols to impress others with their hunting and fighting capabilities. The Assyrian, Greek, and Roman empires employed storytelling, poems, religious symbols, monuments, speeches, documents, and other means of communication to mobilize their armed forces or demoralize those of their enemies. As early as the fifth century B.C., the Chinese military philosopher Sun Tzu advocated various techniques to maintain fighting morale and to destroy the enemy's will to fight. The nineteenth-century German military strategist Carl von Clausewitz identified psychological forces as decisive elements of modern war.

Thus, propaganda is not, as it is sometimes believed, a twentieth-century phenomenon born of the electronic communications revolution. Throughout history the governors have attempted to influence the ways the governed see the world, just as critics and revolutionaries have aspired to change that view. The word itself originated during the Reformation, when the Roman Catholic Church created a commission of cardinals to "propagate" the faith in non-Catholic lands. The principle differences between modern and ancient propaganda are the use of new techniques and technologies, greater awareness of the utility of propaganda, and perhaps also the sheer pervasiveness and volume of modern propaganda.

Although the concept is often associated with dictatorship, propaganda has figured prominently in American life and history. Political propaganda has been an essential ingredient of the democratic process, as politicians and political parties have employed a range of communication techniques to win public support for their ideas and policies. Similarly, countless private groups—from early antislavery societies to modern political action committees—have turned to propaganda techniques to push their agendas. Advertising and public relations, fields that came into fruition during the early twentieth century, have made commercial propaganda a permanent feature of the cultural landscape. War propaganda has been utilized by both government agencies and private groups to win the support of neutrals, demoralize enemies, and energize domestic populations. The pluralistic nature of American life and the existence of a free press has prevented the emergence of a monolithic propaganda apparatus, but it could be argued that these factors have in fact made American democracy better equipped than totalitarian societies for effective propaganda, if only because the free marketplace of ideas has required would-be propagandists to develop ever more sophisticated means of persuasion.

As far back as the colonial period, influential Americans exhibited a remarkable grasp of propaganda techniques. Propaganda and agitation were essential components of the American Revolution. Prior to the outbreak of hostilities, propaganda played a pivotal role in creating the intellectual and psychological climate of the Revolution itself.

Philip Davidson, in his history of the propaganda of the American Revolution, documented a remarkably sophisticated grasp of propaganda techniques among the leading organizers of the Revolution. Although the Founders are rarely recognized as propagandists—probably because of propaganda's pejorative associations—the evidence of a conscious, systematic effort by colonial leaders to gain public support for their ideas is unmistakable. Benjamin Franklin admitted to exposing "in as striking a light as I could, to the nation, the absurdity of the [British] measures towards America"; Thomas Jefferson spoke of "arousing our people from . . . lethargy"; and George Washington advocated the release of information "in a manner calculated to attract the attention and impress the minds of the people." Thomas Paine was the Revolution's most famous (and radical) propagandist. He wrote numerous pamphlets articulating with rhetorical flourish the ideological justification for the Revolution, including the influential *Common Sense* and the poetic *Crisis,* which began with the memorable words, "These are the times that try men's souls."

These men were keenly sensitive to the importance of public opinion, and they employed a wide variety of techniques to arouse public sentiment against the British. Through town meetings, assemblies, churches, legal documents, resolutions, demonstrations, songs, plays, oratory, pamphlets, newspaper articles, and letters they agitated relentlessly against the policies of the British government. Newspapers such as the *Providence Gazette* and the *Boston Gazette* were crucial in organizing opposition to the Stamp Act and in exploiting such incidents as the Boston Massacre. Powerful slogans such as "No Taxation Without Representation" and "Liberty or Death" were utilized to mobilize colonists for revolution, as were such rituals as effigy burning and the planting of "liberty trees."

Several revolutionaries employed the tactics that would later be known as gray propaganda. They wrote articles, letters, and pamphlets under pseudonyms to disguise their identities and to create the impression that opposition to British policies was much greater than it was. Samuel Adams, for example, wrote under twenty-five different pseudonyms in numerous publications.

Benjamin Franklin articulated a shrewd understanding of the techniques of propaganda, including the use of gray and black materials. He remarked: "The facility with which the same truths may be repeatedly enforced by placing them daily in different lights in newspapers . . . gives a great chance of establishing them. And we now find that it is not only right to strike while the iron is hot but that it may be very practicable to heat it by continually striking." The tactics Franklin was referring to—incessant repetition of propaganda themes and the transmitting of ideas through local media outlets in the form of news—described core techniques of modern propaganda and are an indication of the sophistication of revolutionary war propaganda.

The Revolution also saw the utilization of these and other propaganda techniques as instruments of diplomacy. Franklin worked assiduously to mold European views of the conflict and he especially cultivated French opinion to secure France's assistance in the war. To isolate the British diplomatically and to encourage domestic opposition to the war in Britain, Franklin widely publicized British war atrocities, even resorting to black propaganda to exaggerate and fabricate crimes. In 1777 he distributed a phony letter, purportedly written by a German commander of Hessian mercenaries, indicating that the British government advised him to let wounded soldiers die. The letter caused a sensation in France and also induced numerous desertions by the Hessian mercenaries. Franklin also forged an entire issue of the *Boston Independent,* which contained a fabricated account of British scalp hunting. The story touched off a public uproar in Britain and was used by opposition politicians to attack the conduct of the war. The historian Oliver Thomson described these efforts as "one of the most thorough campaigns of diplomatic isolation by propaganda ever mounted."

The revolutionary war itself promoted themes common to most war propaganda: the righteousness of the cause, the savageness of the enemy, and the necessity and certainty of victory. Although no theme received greater treatment than the depravity of the enemy, it was the Revolution's appeal to high moral purpose that had the most lasting impact on American life. The Declaration of Independence was a brilliant document on the rights of man, but, at the same time, it was a brilliant document that employed emotive rhetoric to justify the Revolution and to rally public opinion to the cause. The war itself was portrayed as a struggle for liberty against tyranny, freedom against slavery. In this, the Revolution provided the model for the themes and ideas that would animate many subsequent propaganda campaigns (and much of the political rhetoric) of the United States. From the planting of liberty trees during the Revolution, to the cultivation of liberty gardens during World War II, symbolic appeals to freedom and liberty were staples of wartime mobilization efforts.

During the American Civil War both the Union and Confederate governments utilized propaganda abroad to influence foreign sentiment. The Union sent propaganda commissions to Europe to influence the governments and people of England and France. President Abraham Lincoln personally appealed to British opinion by writing directly to labor unions and textile industrialists to press the Union case. Lincoln, who had a strong appreciation of public relations techniques, was perhaps the Union's best propagandist. His "house divided" metaphor was one of the most powerful images of the 1860s, and his public addresses—most notably the Gettysburg Address—were calculated to unite Northerners behind the cause. The Emancipation Proclamation was deliberately timed to encourage defections from the Confederacy by border states and was skillfully exploited by Union representatives abroad to win European sentiment.

The Confederate government sponsored a meagerly funded, but relatively sophisticated, propaganda operation in Britain under the direction of Henry Hotze. Hotze successfully placed numerous articles in British newspapers by giving them gratis to journalists, who in turn sold them to newspapers in their own names for personal profit. In this manner he both courted the goodwill of a select company of journalists and concealed his own sponsorship of the articles—a classic tactic of gray propaganda. He also developed a scheme whereby he paid several journalists to work for a weekly paper he produced, *The Index*. While earning their salaries as Hotze's editors, they also continued writing for influential London dailies. *The Index* thus provided Hotze with a mechanism for articulating pro-Confederate viewpoints and for subtle bribery of the press.

The Confederacy also sent a representative to France, Edwin De Leon, who openly bribed French newspapers to print favorable editorials on the Confederate cause. De Leon also penned a fervid defense of slavery that probably did more harm than good; few hated the "peculiar institu-

tion" as much as the French, and his arguments merely reinforced French hostility to Southern slavery. Despite some successful operations, Confederate propagandists in Europe failed in their ultimate objective of securing recognition by foreign governments. Above all else, this was due to the existence of slavery in the South, which isolated the Confederacy from British and French public opinion.

Propaganda accompanied other pre–twentieth century conflicts in which the United States participated, but it was conducted primarily by private groups and news organizations. Propaganda during the War of 1812 reiterated many of the themes of the revolutionary period by portraying the British as tyrannical opponents of American liberty. American westward expansion in the nineteenth century was justified by appealing to the "manifest destiny" of the United States to colonize North America, while the Indian wars and the Mexican-American War were bolstered by racist and bigoted portrayals of Native Americans and Mexicans. At the end of the nineteenth century, the infamous "yellow press" incited U.S. participation in the Spanish-American War by portraying the Spaniards as monsters, by sensationally reporting and fabricating Spanish atrocities, and by emphasizing the noble and enlightened intentions of the United States. Similarly, during the American-Filipino Wars, U.S. advocates of imperialism portrayed the Filipinos as uncivilized monkeys and as children in need of American tutelage. Much of this propaganda was private, but it reflected popular sentiment and official attitudes, if not direct policy.

TOTAL WAR, 1917–1945

Notwithstanding this early experience with propaganda, it was primarily the age of total war that inducted the U.S. government into the business of propaganda. During World War I, national governments employed propaganda on an unprecedented scale. The arrival of the modern mass media together with the requirements of total war made propaganda an indispensable element of wartime mobilization. All of the major belligerents turned to propaganda to woo neutrals, demoralize enemies, boost the morale of their troops, and mobilize the support of civilians.

One of the most vital of all World War I propaganda battles was the struggle between Germany and Britain for the sympathy of the American people. The German government organized a program of propaganda in the United States that was so heavy-handed it did more to alienate American public opinion than to win it. The British government, on the other hand, conducted most of its propaganda in the United States covertly, through a secret propaganda bureau directed by the Foreign Office. The British adopted a low-key approach that selectively released news and information to win American sympathies. The publication of the Zimmerman telegram in 1917 (in which Germany sought to enlist Mexico in a war with the United States) was undoubtedly the most important propaganda achievement of the British, and it helped to bring the Americans into the war on the Allied side.

A week after declaring war, President Woodrow Wilson established the first official propaganda agency of the U.S. government to manage public opinion at home and abroad—the Committee on Public Information. Headed by the muckraking journalist George Creel, the committee was responsible for censorship, propaganda, and general information about the war effort. The Creel committee focused on mobilizing support on the home front, but it also conducted an extensive campaign of propaganda abroad, overseeing operations in more than thirty overseas countries.

The committee bombarded foreign media outlets with news, official statements, and features on the war effort and on American life, using leaflets, motion pictures, photographs, cartoons, posters, and signboards to promote its messages. The committee established reading rooms abroad, brought foreign journalists to the United States, crafted special appeals for teachers and labor groups, and sponsored lectures and seminars. In its international propaganda, the committee advertised American strength and commitment to victory in order to curb defeatism among Allied troops and to demoralize enemy soldiers. Stressing the unselfish, anti-imperialistic war aims of the United States, it put forth an idealistic message that reflected the idealism of the Progressive Era, the tone of the Wilson presidency, and long-standing traditions in American ideology. Creel himself spoke excitedly about using the committee to spread the "gospel of democracy" around the world, and staff members pursued that objective with religious fervor. Taking its cue from the president (and British propaganda), the Creel committee stressed that the war was fought for freedom, self-determination, and democracy.

Despite the many successes Creel attributed to the Committee on Public Information, Congress swiftly abolished it in June 1919—a decision that reflected both the natural American distrust of propaganda and Congress's fear that the president would utilize the committee for domestic political purposes. The Creel committee had a short life but a lasting impact. It established the principle that government-sponsored propaganda was a necessity in times of war or national emergency. It also demonstrated the utility of propaganda as a tool of national policy and became the basic model for subsequent U.S. propaganda agencies.

The years that followed nurtured a popular fascination with, and revulsion toward, the practice of propaganda. A series of investigations in the 1920s exposed the nature and scope of Britain's propaganda campaign in the United States, including revelations that the British had fabricated numerous stories about German atrocities. Many Americans came to blame British propaganda for bringing the United States into a wasteful and ruinous war, and the practice of propaganda became associated with deceit and trickery. It was thus in the aftermath of World War I that propaganda acquired its negative connotations—a development that stemmed from the employment of propaganda by a democracy, not, as is generally supposed, from that of a dictatorship. Although British propaganda was probably more effective than Germany's because of military and political blunders by the Germans—such as unrestricted submarine warfare—many observers took from the war a legendary belief in the power of propaganda.

These propaganda campaigns affected the United States in other ways as well. The belief that Americans had been tricked into participating in the first world war delayed U.S. intervention in the second. Moreover, news of Nazi atrocities connected to the Holocaust were greeted incredulously by the American public in part because of the exaggerated and fabricated atrocity propaganda released by the British two decades earlier.

At the same time, the social science revolution and Freudian psychology brought about a public fascination with ideas about subconscious psychological manipulation and mind control. The science of persuasion, in the form of advertising and public relations, came into vogue in the 1920s, and advertising became a large-scale national industry. These developments created a skilled group of professionals with expertise in the employment of symbols, images, and techniques to interpret and to manipulate perceptions.

The development of radio revolutionized the practice of propaganda by making it possible to reach audiences of unprecedented size instantaneously. A short-wave propaganda battle began in the mid-1920s as the Soviet Union, Germany, Japan, and Britain developed international broadcasting capabilities. American suspicion of foreign propaganda was sufficiently aroused that in 1938 Congress passed the Foreign Agents Registration Act, which required foreign propagandists to register with the U.S. government. The same year, Nazi propaganda in Central and South America led the Roosevelt administration to create the first peacetime propaganda agency of the U.S. government, the Office of the Coordinator of Inter-American Affairs (CIAA), headed by Nelson Rockefeller.

Initially, the CIAA focused on cultural and educational activities designed to improve relations between the United States and Latin America. The CIAA inaugurated a new tradition in U.S. foreign policy: government sponsorship of educational and cultural exchanges. It sponsored tours by ballet, theater, and music groups, archaeological expeditions, art exhibits, comic books, and academic conferences. Publicly, the CIAA's cultural programs were defended for their reciprocal benefits in promoting "international understanding." Behind closed doors, however, the agency frankly emphasized propaganda motives. It attached far greater importance to interpreting the United States to Latin America than vice versa. The principle theme promoted by the coordinator's office was "Pan-Americanism," stressing that the key to defense of the region lay in hemispheric solidarity. After the United States entered World War II, Rockefeller's CIAA became a full-blown propaganda agency, utilizing film, publications, and radio to "combat the Nazi lie." By 1943, the CIAA had become a large federal agency with a generous budget and nearly 1,500 employees.

In the early part of 1941, as war appeared imminent, Roosevelt created several additional agencies to disseminate propaganda at home and abroad. In 1942 these various information programs were combined into the Office of War Information (OWI) under the direction of the well-known journalist and broadcaster Elmer Davis. Roosevelt also established the Office of Strategic Services (OSS), the forerunner of the Central Intelligence Agency, and authorized it to engage in black and gray propaganda abroad, mostly in connection with military operations.

The OWI was a sprawling organization that conducted domestic and international propaganda on a truly massive scale. In addition to millions of leaflets, it produced entire newspapers, which were dropped by airplane to France, Norway, Spain, Ireland, and Germany. One newspaper distributed by the OWI in France achieved a circulation of 7 million per week, compared to a grand total of 3 million leaflets distributed in Europe through all of World War I. The OWI established posts attached to U.S. diplomatic missions overseas, known as the U.S. Information Service, and it operated reading rooms and libraries in more than twenty countries. Radio was the most crucial medium in the overseas propaganda war, and in 1942 the Voice of America was established under OWI jurisdiction. By the end of the war, the Voice of America was broadcasting around the world in forty different languages.

Combat propaganda, or what began to be called "psychological warfare," was utilized by all the belligerents, including the United States. These operations focused on breaking enemy morale, encouraging enemy troops to surrender, publicizing U.S. military victories, positively projecting U.S. war aims, providing aid and encouragement to partisans in occupied territories, and stiffening the resolve of American and Allied troops. Initially, these operations were conducted by OWI personnel, but the idealistic outlook of many of the agency's propagandists clashed with the more conservative mindset of many U.S. military officers who believed it was more interested in advertising Franklin D. Roosevelt and the New Deal than in promoting military objectives. In December 1942, General Dwight D. Eisenhower created a separate psychological warfare branch of the army to participate in the Allied invasion of North Africa. In 1944 he created an even larger organization, the Psychological Warfare Division of the Supreme Headquarters, Allied Expeditionary Force, to prepare propaganda for the D-Day invasion. Psychological warfare was especially important in the Pacific theater, where U.S. propaganda sought to convince Japanese soldiers—who had been taught by their army that to surrender meant relinquishing their place as members of Japanese society—to cease resistance.

COLD WAR

Despite the importance of propaganda and psychological warfare to the war effort, the United States moved quickly to dismantle the propa-

★ ★ ★ ★

THE POLITICS OF PROPAGANDA

One of the most difficult tasks facing all U.S. propaganda agencies has been simply convincing the American people and members of Congress of their right to exist. This was dramatically revealed in the debate over the 1948 Smith-Mundt Act—the first peacetime legislative charter for government propaganda—which was one of the most controversial pieces of legislation ever enacted. By the time it was passed, it had been rewritten twice and had acquired more than one hundred amendments. It also earned more days of debate and filled more pages of the *Congressional Record* than the controversial Taft-Hartley labor disputes legislation—at that time arguably the most controversial bill in U.S. history.

Controversy surrounding government-sponsored propaganda has also been a recurring theme in modern American political history. U.S. information programs have been subjected to incessant harassment from journalists, American citizens, and from both conservative and liberal members of Congress. These critics often charged that the information programs were ineffective, unnecessary, and wasteful. Critics also held that these programs were infiltrated by spies and saboteurs, or that they were promulgating undesirable and un-American ideas. During World War I and World War II, when the Committee on Public Information and the Office of War Information were openly conducting propaganda in the United States, critics also charged that these agencies were being used for partisan political advantage.

The best-known (and most strident) criticism of the U.S. information program came at the beginning of the 1950s, when Senator Joseph McCarthy launched a prolonged attack on the Voice of America in concert with his broader assault on suspected communists in the State Department. In 1953, two of McCarthy's aides toured the U.S. Information Service libraries in Europe and announced that they had found 30,000 books by authors with communist sympathies in the stacks. Although these charges were wildly exaggerated, hundreds of books were purged from the libraries and in some cases burned. As a result of the investigations, the U.S. information program lost dozens of employees who resigned or were pushed from their jobs (one prominent official committed suicide), while those that remained were thoroughly demoralized. Perhaps the most serious effects were felt abroad, where the highly publicized investigations devastated American prestige.

Although McCarthy's investigation was the most famous case of domestic political controversy generated by the information program, it was by no means the only one. From the 1917 decision to create the Committee on Public Information to the 1999 decision to dissolve the U.S. Information Agency, American propaganda agencies have been a favorite target of congressional critics. This incessant criticism has in part stemmed from a general American apprehension about any government program that influences, sponsors, or promulgates ideas and values. It has also reflected a powerful belief that democracies have no business engaging in cynical propaganda either at home or abroad. The belief that information activities are wasteful and unnecessary except in times of war or national emergency underlined the decision by Congress to dissolve the U.S. Information Agency.

---

ganda apparatus it had constructed during World War II. Within weeks of Japan's surrender, President Harry Truman liquidated the Office of War Information, transferring only the bare bones of an information service to the Department of State. Although the OWI was abolished and the budget of its successor was slashed, Truman insisted that the United States maintain at least a modest information program to support U.S. foreign policy. This was a remarkable step, since prior to the 1940s no one seriously considered an organized, government-sponsored effort to influence foreign peoples except during a national emergency.

While Truman acknowledged the importance of propaganda as a peacetime instrument of foreign policy, it was primarily the Cold War that institutionalized propaganda as a permanent instrument of U.S. foreign policy. A widespread belief developed that the United States was losing the "war of ideas" to the Soviet Union's supposedly superior propaganda apparatus. As Cold War tensions intensified, the United States gradually expanded its propaganda capabilities.

In 1948, the information program received permanent legislative sanction with the passage of the Smith-Mundt Act—the first legislative charter for a peacetime propaganda program. The act gave the State Department jurisdiction over both international information operations and cultural and educational exchange programs. Additional propaganda activities were conducted by the newly created Central Intelligence Agency, the economic assistance agencies (forerunners to the Agency for International Development), and the armed forces, especially the army.

In 1950, Truman called for an intensified program of propaganda known as the Campaign of Truth. In a speech delivered to the American Society of Newspaper Editors, Truman articulated the perennial domestic justification for official U.S. propaganda: in order to combat enemy lies, the U.S. needed to promote the truth. Under the Campaign of Truth, the State Department's budget for information activities jumped from around $20 million in 1948 to $115 million in 1952—a development aided by the outbreak of the Korean War a few weeks after Truman's speech. The Campaign of Truth also brought a change in the style and content of U.S. propaganda output, which shifted from objective-sounding news and information to hard-hitting propaganda in its most obvious form—cartoons depicting bloodthirsty communists, vituperative anticommunist polemics, and sensational commentary.

In April 1951, Truman created the Psychological Strategy Board to coordinate the American psychological warfare effort. The board acted as a coordinating body for all nonmilitary Cold War activities, including covert operations. It supervised programs for aggressive clandestine warfare and propaganda measures against the Soviet bloc and it developed "psychological strategy" plans for dozens of countries in western Europe, Asia, and the Middle East. By the time Truman left office, the U.S. government had established a far-reaching apparatus for influencing public opinion in both friendly and hostile countries.

During these years, the practice of propaganda became inextricably tied to the practices of psychological warfare and covert action. During World War II, psychological warfare was largely seen as an accessory to military operations, but with the onset of the Cold War, psychological warfare specialists defined the concept broadly to include any nonmilitary actions taken to influence public opinion or to advance foreign policy interests. Psychological warfare was transformed into a catchall formula that went beyond mere propaganda to embrace covert operations, trade and economic aid, diplomacy, the threat of force,

cultural and educational exchange programs, and a wide range of clandestine activities. Psychological warfare became, in essence, a synonym for Cold War. It reflected the belief of many politicians and foreign policy analysts that the Cold War was an ideological, psychological, and cultural contest for hearts and minds that would be won or lost on the plain of public opinion rather than by blood shed on the battlefield.

Psychological warfare in the Cold War context was also associated with the policy of "rollback," or the employment of nonmilitary means to force the retraction of Soviet power and the "liberation" of Eastern Europe. Rollback was openly espoused by the Republican administration of Dwight D. Eisenhower, which campaigned in 1952 against the "immoral" and "futile" policy of containment. Contrary to conventional wisdom, however, the policies of liberation and rollback did not originate with the Eisenhower administration. Scholarship in the late 1990s by Gregory Mitrovich, Scott Lucas, and others reveals that Truman's Democratic administration inaugurated a muscular form of rollback years earlier. To these scholars, U.S. efforts to liberate areas under Moscow's control indicate that American foreign policy in the early Cold War was not as defensive and fundamentally nonaggressive as the term "containment" implies or as earlier historiography suggested.

Indeed, the "father of containment," George F. Kennan, was also the driving force behind an aggressive program of psychological warfare and covert action against the Soviet bloc. In early 1948, Kennan, who was then serving as head of the State Department's Policy Planning Staff, developed a plan for "organized political warfare" against communism. The plan was set forth in National Security Council Document 10/2. The document, approved by President Truman in June 1948, authorized a comprehensive program of clandestine warfare, including black propaganda, psychological warfare, subversion, assistance to underground resistance movements, paramilitary operations, and economic warfare. NSC 10/2, although not generally recognized as a landmark policy paper like the future NSC 68, was especially significant in that it established psychological warfare and covert action as vital instruments of U.S. foreign policy in the Cold War.

Under the authorization provided by NSC 10/2, the Central Intelligence Agency made a botched attempt to detach Albania from the Kremlin's grip, launched leaflet-dropping operations via enormous unmanned hot-air balloons, encouraged defections from behind the Iron Curtain, and sponsored provocative (and generally unsuccessful) paramilitary operations involving U.S.-trained émigrés from Russia and Eastern Europe. The agency's most famous form of anti-Soviet propaganda came in the form of Radio Free Europe and Radio Liberty, which broadcast to Eastern Europe and Russia, respectively. The radios were staffed by émigrés and exiled political leaders from the Soviet bloc, but the CIA maintained a fairly loose control over their broadcasts through the National Committee for a Free Europe (also known as the Free Europe Committee), an ostensibly private organization created to camouflage U.S. government involvement.

The CIA also conducted clandestine propaganda operations in allied and neutral areas. The agency subsidized noncommunist labor unions, journalists, political parties, politicians, and student groups. In western Europe the CIA conducted a secret program of cultural and ideological propaganda through the Congress for Cultural Freedom, a purportedly private, but CIA-funded, organization that supported the work of anticommunist liberals. Through the Congress for Cultural Freedom, the agency published more than twenty prestigious magazines, held art exhibitions, operated a news and feature service, organized high-profile international conferences, published numerous books, and sponsored public performances by musicians and artists.

For much of the Cold War, the CIA also organized both successful and unsuccessful "political action" programs to influence democratic elections, sponsor revolutions or counterrevolutions, and, on a few occasions, topple governments. It conducted numerous operations to influence political developments around the world, most notably in Italy, the Philippines, Iran, Guatemala, Indonesia, Cuba, Vietnam, Thailand, Chile, Iraq, and Angola. Although details surrounding these operations are murky, the available evidence indicates that propaganda and psychological warfare were the principle instruments of the agency's political action programs. These activities became a means for the United States to influence and manipulate developments in foreign countries so that they served the perceived interests of American national security policies. The extensive employment of covert action signaled an unacknowledged revolution in the way the government conducted its foreign policy: it was now actively intervening in the internal affairs of sovereign nations to encourage the development of ideas, actions, and policies to benefit the United States.

During the Korean War, sensationalized charges that the United States had been waging bacteriological warfare, accounts of Soviet brainwashing techniques, and communist-inspired "peace" campaigns, focused American attention on psychological warfare as a mysterious Cold War weapon. During the 1952 presidential campaign, Eisenhower repeatedly called for an expansive and coordinated psychological warfare effort on a national scale. In San Francisco he delivered a major speech on the subject, arguing that every significant act of government should reflect psychological warfare calculations. He emphasized that the Cold War was a struggle of ideas and argued that the United States must develop every psychological weapon available to win the hearts and minds of the world's peoples. Defining psychological warfare in truly expansive terms, Eisenhower included among the means of psychological warfare diplomacy, mutual economic assistance, trade, friendly contacts, and even sporting events.

These campaign speeches were not mere rhetoric; they reflected Eisenhower's unparalleled faith in psychological warfare. This faith grew in part from his experience with it during World War II and in part from his strong conviction that the Cold War was a long-haul struggle that would be won by nonmilitary means. Whereas Truman was relatively uninvolved in the information activities of his administration, Eisenhower was personally involved in several major propaganda campaigns and played an active role in establishing propaganda themes and tactics.

One of his very first acts as president was to appoint a personal adviser to serve as special assistant for psychological warfare planning, a position filled first by Time-Life executive C. D. Jackson and later by Nelson Rockefeller. He also established a high-level committee, chaired by William H. Jackson, to make recommendations on how to strengthen the U.S. psychological warfare effort. The Jackson committee investigation was arguably the most influential study of U.S. information policy ever conducted. The investigation led to numerous innovations including the establishment of a high-level coordinating body attached to the National Security Council devoted to psychological warfare and strategy. Euphemistically designated the Operations Coordinating Board (OCB), it replaced the Psychological Strategy Board in the fall of 1953.

Under Eisenhower, the United States abandoned the aggressive anti-Soviet psychological warfare tactics initiated by his predecessor. The Voice of America, Radio Free Europe, and Radio Liberty continued to broadcast propaganda to the Soviet bloc, but gradually they abandoned the strident, polemical tone that characterized the Campaign of Truth. This trend was accelerated by controversy surrounding the involvement of Radio Free Europe in provoking the 1956 Hungarian Revolution. The brutal suppression of the revolt by Soviet armed forces demonstrated that Moscow would fight to maintain its influence over Eastern Europe and revealed that the policy of liberation carried with it unacceptable psychological, political, and human costs. By the end of 1956, as the historian Walter Hixson has shown, "liberation" had been replaced by an evolutionary strategy that stressed cultural infiltration and straight news and information over aggressive psychological warfare.

Eisenhower also oversaw the creation of an independent propaganda agency, the United States Information Agency (USIA). (Information posts abroad were called the U.S. Information Service, or USIS, because "information agency" had an intelligence connotation in many languages, but both names referred to the same organization.) The agency was modeled after the Office of War Information and Creel's Committee on Public Information, but, unlike its predecessors, the USIA was authorized to conduct only foreign propaganda; domestic operations were explicitly forbidden. The USIA assembled under one roof all the various information programs scattered throughout the government, except those administered by the CIA and the military. It operated a press and publication service and a motion picture and television service. The USIA also assumed responsibility for the Voice of America and for U.S. libraries and information centers abroad.

Despite the many attempts by the United States to "pierce the Iron Curtain" with American propaganda, most of the USIA's resources were directed on the other side of that curtain, in the so-called free world. The agency was primarily concerned with winning the support of neutrals and strengthening the resolve of allies. As a USIA policy document stated: "We are in competition with Soviet Communism primarily for the opinion of the free world. We are (especially) concerned with the uncommitted, the wavering, the confused, the apathetic, or the doubtful within the free world." The agency oversaw more than 208 USIS posts in ninety-one countries, all of them in allied or neutral countries. For much of the Cold War, the USIA's largest programs were in Germany, Austria, Japan, India, Indochina (Vietnam), Thailand, France, and Italy. The USIS also maintained sizable operations in Spain, Yugoslavia, Egypt, Greece, Iran, Mexico, Brazil, and Pakistan. Beginning in the mid-1950s, an increasing amount of attention was spent "targeting" countries in Africa, Asia, and Latin America with U.S. propaganda—a development that reflected the growing importance of the developing world to the Cold War competition.

When the USIA was created in 1953, Congress insisted that the Department of State retain jurisdiction over cultural programs in order to distinguish cultural relations from propaganda. In practice, the distinction proved mostly symbolic, since public affairs officers abroad, under orders from the USIA, managed both cultural and information policy and pursued both with an eye to improving the "climate of opinion." Increasingly, foreign policy experts recognized that such activities could be more effective in promoting pro-American attitudes than conventional types of propaganda. During the Cold War, such activities as the Fulbright exchange program, the People-to-People program, and the Peace Corps were utilized to promote goodwill between the United States and other countries through person-to-person contacts. Although many Americans who participated in these programs did not see themselves as propagandists, government administrators saw them as positive, long-range programs to create a favorable atmosphere abroad for U.S. political, economic, and military policies.

In broad form, the USIA's principal propaganda themes remained fairly constant throughout the Cold War. The obvious theme was anticommunism, and the agency exploited the ideological contradictions, forced labor camps, restrictions on freedom, and absence of consumer goods in communist countries. The agency devoted a greater percentage of its programming, however, to positive themes about the United States. The USIA publicized U.S. economic and technical assistance programs, scientific and technological advances, and other policies, programs, and developments that reflected positively on the United States. It promoted free trade unionism, explained the workings of American democracy, and extolled the benefits of consumer capitalism. The agency also developed cultural propaganda depicting the lives of ordinary Americans in a favorable light and celebrating American achievements in the arts. Many USIA films, radio broadcasts, publications, and other programs were devoted to educational purposes, covering topics ranging from agriculture to English-language instruction. Most of these activities were slow media operations that aspired to cultivate favorable attitudes over the long haul. They also reflected the belief that, in addition to military defense and economic prosperity, U.S. security required the active promulgation of American ideas, values, and beliefs.

One of the most important activities of the USIA was simply to present U.S. policies favorably to international audiences on a daily basis. The USIA explained and promoted policy decisions through all its media, transmitted complete texts of important speeches to news organizations around the world, and distributed, authored, and secretly subsidized books and publications that defended controversial aspects of U.S. policies.

The USIA professed to adhere to a "strategy of truth" in its operations, in the belief that to be effective its propaganda had to be credible, and to be credible, it had to be truthful. The agency thus repudiated the sensationally propagandistic tone that had characterized the Campaign of Truth, instead adopting as its model the neutral tone and style of the British Broadcasting Corporation (BBC). That does not mean, however, that the USIA merely dished out objective information; there was undoubtedly an element of protesting too much in the agency's claim to truth. While the agency generally avoided deliberate distortions, wild exaggerations, and broad generalizations, it remained in the business of shaping, influencing, and manipulating popular opinion. As the first director of the USIA, Theodore C. Streibert, noted: "We are no less engaged in propaganda because we are to minimize the propagandistic."

The USIA operated on the assumption that it could best influence international opinion in the free world by influencing opinion makers. Its most important target was the world press. The bulk of USIA operations fell under the category of "media control projects" designed to influence the news and information that reached the public through indigenous media outlets. Rather than address audiences directly—through radio and overtly propagandistic materials—the USIA preferred to plant news, place programs on local television, and utilize personal contacts to influence the views of foreign journalists and other influential persons.

U.S. propagandists also worked to enhance the potential persuasiveness of American propaganda by obscuring the source. A large percentage of USIA propaganda was of the unattributed gray variety, even though the agency was not explicitly authorized to engage in covert propaganda. USIA operatives maintained a network of contacts with journalists and media outlets in countries around the world, many of whom knowingly cooperated with the agency in placing unattributed materials prepared by the U.S. government. Another strategy involved the participation of private groups and nongovernmental organizations, or what the USIA termed "private cooperation." The agency maintained an Office of Private Cooperation, which worked to involve nongovernmental organizations, businesses, and ordinary Americans in campaigns to promote a positive image of the United States abroad.

When John F. Kennedy won the presidency in 1960, he attached a high priority to the USIA. Kennedy was acutely sensitive to the importance of images and ideas to international relations, and he made the apparent decline in American prestige abroad a major theme of his campaign. Upon his election, Kennedy appointed the respected journalist Edward R. Murrow as the agency's new director. Murrow's appointment raised the stature and visibility of the agency both at home and abroad. Murrow's prominence also helped the USIA in Congress: agency funding increased dramatically from around $100 million in 1960 to more than $160 million in 1963. Despite Murrow's journalistic background, the USIA under his tenure became more, rather than less, focused on hard-hitting propaganda. It also became increasingly focused on propaganda in the developing world. In just under three years, it opened more than two dozen new posts in newly independent countries in Africa.

Kennedy also assigned the USIA a new advisory function. The agency was now explicitly charged with contributing to the formulation of U.S. foreign policies by advising the president on issues pertaining to international opinion. Nevertheless, it was primarily an operational agency rather than a policymaking one. (In fact, on several notable occasions, such as the Bay of Pigs invasion, the agency was not informed of what the U.S. government was doing.) Its most important advisory function began in the 1950s, when it administered international public opinion surveys to collect "psychological" intelligence. This information was used in part to gauge and improve the effectiveness of USIA propaganda, but it was also sent to the president and the National Security Council for consideration in the policymaking process. Successive U.S. presidents, especially Eisenhower and Kennedy, monitored these public opinion surveys very closely, an indication of the seriousness with which they took international public opinion.

As the United States became involved in Vietnam, the information program, like the rest of the country, became focused on the war. Both overt and covert propaganda programs had been going on in Southeast Asia since the 1940s and continued through the Vietnam War. In 1964, President Lyndon B. Johnson appointed Carl T. Rowan as director of the USIA—at the time the highest post held by any African American in the U.S. government. Rowan oversaw the creation of the Joint United States Public Affairs Office, which managed all the U.S. psychological warfare programs in Vietnam and accounted for some 10 percent of the agency's overseas manpower. In May 1965, Johnson assigned the USIA responsibility for all U.S. propaganda in Vietnam, the largest role ever undertaken by the agency.

Perhaps the greatest challenge facing U.S. propagandists during this period lay outside the combat zone, where the USIA tried to sell an unpopular war to international public opinion. The agency presented the war as a noble defense of a free country under attack by communist insurgents. It stressed American peaceful intentions and argued that the United States had turned to military force only as a last resort. The Johnson and Nixon administrations attached a high priority to propaganda in support of the war effort, but their information policies ultimately devastated the credibility of the USIA as it became widely known that the United States was painting an excessively rosy, and at times patently false, picture of the events in Vietnam.

These distortions were less the fault of the agency's propaganda than of the policies and public relations strategies employed by the White House. For example, in April 1965 the USIA widely publicized a speech by Johnson indicating U.S. willingness to enter into "unconditional" negotiations with the government of North Vietnam. When it was later revealed that the Johnson administration maneuvered and delayed to avoid such negotiations, the United States was criticized abroad (and at home) for manipulating the peace issue for propaganda purposes. International public opinion was further alienated by the USIA's portrayal of the government of South Vietnam as a functioning democracy and by its unceasing publicity of U.S. military progress when evidence presented by the independent news media contradicted such claims. Cases of deliberate deception, such as President Richard Nixon's secret bombing campaign, worsened the "credibility gap" that plagued all official U.S. pronouncements.

All in all, the Vietnam War served as a reminder of a principle U.S. propagandists knew but neglected: obvious falsehoods, when exposed, could exact irreparable harm on the credibility, and hence the believability, of the propaganda and of the sponsor. The war also demonstrated how a crusading and skeptical press could counterbalance the effects of propaganda. No amount of clever spin-doctoring could counteract the powerful images that appeared on television screens around the world.

During the presidency of Jimmy Carter, the USIA adopted a remarkable change of mission. Carter argued that the agency should not simply communicate to the world about America; it should also communicate to America about the world. He renamed the agency the United States International Communication Agency (ICA), curtailed its anticommunist programming, and ordered it to cease its covert propaganda programs. Carter also assigned the ICA a "second mandate" to educate Americans about foreign countries. It was an idealistic task that the agency, which had spent twenty-five years selling the United States to foreigners, was ill-equipped to perform.

When Ronald Reagan took control of the White House, he promptly shelved Carter's "second mandate" and restored the USIA's name. During Reagan's tenure the agency adopted the crusading zeal of the cold warrior in the White House. The president who presided over the massive arms buildup of the 1980s also presided over psychological rearmament through the USIA. In a speech in 1982 he called for a new war of ideas and values against communism. He repackaged the Campaign of Truth as Project Truth to rally the country behind an expanded psychological offensive to spread democracy and combat Soviet propaganda. Under Reagan, the USIA was funded more lavishly than ever before. The new director, Charles Z. Wick, embarked on a number of reforms to modernize the agency, including the creation of the Worldnet satellite television broadcasting system and Radio Marti, which broadcast U.S. propaganda to Cuba. Reagan himself, the "great communicator," set the tone for the new ideological offensive by branding the Soviet Union the "evil empire."

With the end of the Cold War, the USIA turned its attention from the communist threat to promoting economic expansion. National security and anticommunist justifications for propaganda and exchange activities gave way to economic justifications: these programs were now evaluated in terms of their contributions to American commerce. In October 1999, largely as the result of Senator Jesse Helms, the USIA was abolished and its functions transferred to the Office of International Information Programs in the Department of State.

PROPAGANDA, DIPLOMACY, AND INTERNATIONAL PUBLIC OPINION

The Cold War inaugurated a paradigm shift in the U.S. practice of diplomacy that reflected changes in the nature of diplomatic activity worldwide. Through propaganda, policy initiatives, and covert action, agents of the U.S. government acted directly to influence the ideas, values, beliefs, opinions, actions, politics, and culture of other countries. Foreign affairs personnel not only observed and reported, they also participated in events or tried to influence the way that they happened. The old maxim that one government does not interfere in the internal affairs of another had been swept aside.

The pattern of international relations was further transformed by the electronic communications revolution and the emergence of popular opinion as a significant force in foreign affairs. Foreign policy could no longer be pursued as it had during the nineteenth century, when diplomacy was the exclusive province of professional diplomats who used (often secret) negotiations to reach accords based on power and interest. Developments in mass communication and the increased attentiveness to domestic audiences abroad to foreign affairs meant that the target of diplomacy had now widened to include popular opinion as much, if not more so, than traditional diplomatic activities.

A report published by the House Foreign Relations Committee in 1964, entitled "Winning the Cold War: The U.S. Ideological Offensive," captured this sentiment well:

> For many years military and economic power, used separately, or in conjunction, have served as the pillars of diplomacy. They still serve that function but the recent increase in influence of the masses of the people over government, together with greater awareness on the part of the leaders of the aspirations of people . . . has created a new dimension of foreign policy operations. Certain foreign policy objectives can be pursued by dealing directly with the people of foreign countries, rather than with their governments. Through the use of modern instruments and techniques of communications it is possible today to reach large or influential segments of national populations—to inform them, to influence their attitudes, and at times perhaps even to motivate them to a particular course of action. These groups, in turn, are capable of exerting noticeable, even decisive, pressures on their government.

In other words, by appealing over the heads of governments directly to public opinion, effective propaganda and other measures would encourage popular opinion to support U.S. policies, which would in turn exert pressure on government policymakers.

Throughout the Cold War, propaganda and diplomacy operated on multiple levels. At the most obvious level, propaganda as it is conventionally understood (the utilization of communication techniques to influence beliefs and actions) was employed as a distinct instrument of U.S. foreign policy. Through the United States Information Agency, Central Intelligence Agency, and other mechanisms, the United States waged a war of words and of ideas that attacked communism, promoted capitalism and democracy, defended U.S. foreign policies, and advertised the American way of life in order to win the Cold War.

On another level, the awareness that international public opinion had become a major factor in the conduct of diplomacy meant that propaganda considerations intruded on the policymaking process itself. American policymakers were increasingly aware that international public opinion had to be an ingredient in policy formulation at all levels: in the planning and policy formulation stage, in the coordination and timing of operations, and finally in the last phase of explanation and interpretation by government officials and information programs.

This attitude played itself out most visibly in the United Nations, which became one of the most important arenas for Cold War propaganda. It also was reflected in the marked increase in the foreign travel of U.S. presidents and vice presidents, an important device for generating news coverage and for reaching international audiences directly. On a more routine basis, consideration of international public opinion simply involved the careful selection of words and phrases to describe the objectives of American foreign policy—including the process of creating what came to be known as a "sound bite."

Even within the State Department—an institution wedded to traditional diplomacy and wary of popular opinion—the Policy Planning Staff began to argue in the mid-1950s that convincing foreign officials was often less important than carrying issues over their heads to public opinion, reasoning that popular opinion would exert more of an impact on government officials than vice versa. The extensive and instantaneous media coverage that accompanied diplomatic conferences meant that negotiations needed to be conducted on two levels: on the diplomatic level between governments, and on the popular level to win international public support for policies. Diplomatic conferences were no longer merely opportunities for resolving international disputes; they were sounding boards for public opinion and forums for propaganda. Arms control proposals in particular were not infrequently tabled predominantly to satisfy the demands of public opinion for progress in disarmament. President Eisenhower's Atoms for Peace and Open Skies initiatives, for example, were sophisticated propaganda exercises designed to put the Soviet Union on the defensive and establish the U.S. commitment to peace and disarmament without making costly concessions or entering into protracted negotiations.

The psychological dimension of postwar American diplomacy also included a preoccupation with American prestige and credibility—concepts that connoted the reliability of American commitments and served as code words for America's image and reputation. As Robert McMahon has argued, throughout the postwar period American leaders invoked the principle of credibility to explain and justify a wide range of diplomatic and military decisions. American actions in such disparate crises as Korea (1950–1953), Taiwan Strait (Quemoy-Matsu) (1954–1955), Lebanon (1958), and Vietnam (1954–1973) were driven by a perceived need to demonstrate the resolve, will, and determination—in a word, credibility—of the United States. In these and other cases, American actions were driven as much if not more by calculations of how the U.S. would be perceived abroad than by narrowly focused calculations of national interest.

Concerns about the maintenance of American prestige and credibility were undoubtedly magnified by the presence of nuclear weapons. The high stakes of all-out war in an age of nuclear devastation meant that the United States and Soviet Union channeled the competition into symbolic modes of combat. Nothing better illustrates this than the space race, which became the preeminent propaganda contest of the Cold War. Spectacular feats in outer-space exploration were at once symbolic of the scientific, technological, economic, educational, and military achievements of the superpowers. The space race also allowed the United States and the Soviet Union to demonstrate their military prowess—and thus reinforce the credibility of their deterrent capabilities—without appearing warlike. The successful Soviet launch of *Sputnik I* in 1957 and the American moon landing in 1969 were two of the most significant events of the Cold War, largely because of what they symbolized to people around the world.

The infusion of psychological considerations and propaganda tactics into the practice of diplomacy is one of the Cold War's most important legacies, but given the revolution in communication technologies of the late twentieth century it was perhaps inevitable that the ancient art of diplomacy would become affected by the techniques of propaganda and public persuasion. Despite the collapse of the Soviet Union and the end of the Cold War's propaganda battles, foreign policy continued to be swayed by images transmitted instantly around the globe.

The days of brazenly propagandistic posters and radio broadcasts may have faded into history, but the science of propaganda has simply evolved into less overt forms of image making and media manipulation. Paralleling a broader development in international politics, where symbols and images loom large as critical components of political power, the phenomenon of posturing for public opinion has become increasingly sophisticated, involving such techniques as staged media events, generated news, orchestrated public appearances, and carefully scripted sound bites. The communication techniques that camouflage modern propaganda have obscured the basic fact that the end of the Cold War has brought about more propaganda, not less.

BIBLIOGRAPHY

Daugherty, William E., and Morris Janowitz, eds. *A Psychological Warfare Casebook*. Baltimore, 1958. Compiled for U.S. Army psychological warfare experts, the work covers a wide range of subjects from both theoretical and historical perspectives.

Davidson, Philip. *Propaganda and the American Revolution, 1763–1783*. Chapel Hill, N.C., 1941.

Ellul, Jacques. *Propaganda: The Formation of Men's Attitudes*. Translated by Konrad Kellen and Jean Lerner. New York, 1973. Influential philosophic treatise on modern propaganda.

Haefele, Mark. "John F. Kennedy, USIA, and World Public Opinion." *Diplomatic History* 25, no. 1 (winter 2001): 63–84. Useful on the importance of international public opinion to U.S. foreign policy, especially during the Kennedy administration.

Henderson, John W. *The United States Information Agency*. New York, 1969.

Hixson, Walter L. *Parting the Curtain: Propaganda, Culture, and the Cold War, 1945–1961*. New York, 1998.

Jackall, Robert, ed. *Propaganda*. New York, 1995. Focuses on the twentieth century.

Krugler, David F. *The Voice of America and the Domestic Propaganda Battles, 1945–1953*. Columbia, Mo., and London, 2000. Explores the domestic political controversies surrounding the Voice of America.

Lasswell, Harold Dwight. *Propaganda Technique in the World War*. New York, 1927. Classic work that influenced a generation of propaganda specialists.

Laurie, Clayton D. *The Propaganda Warriors: America's Crusade Against Nazi Germany*. Lawrence, Kans., 1996. Focuses on combat propaganda.

Lucas, Scott. *Freedom's War: The American Crusade Against the Soviet Union*. New York, 1999. Focuses on state-private collaboration in Cold War propaganda campaigns.

McMahon, Robert J. "Credibility and World Power: Exploring the Psychological Dimension in Postwar American Diplomacy." *Diplomatic History* 15, no. 4 (fall 1991): 455–471.

Mitrovich, Gregory. *Undermining the Kremlin: America's Strategy to Subvert the Soviet Bloc, 1947–1956*. Ithaca, N.Y., 2000. Explores the relationships among psychological warfare, covert action, and national security strategy in the early Cold War.

Ninkovich, Frank A. *The Diplomacy of Ideas: U.S. Foreign Policy and Cultural Relations, 1938–1950*. Cambridge, 1981.

———. *U.S. Information Policy and Cultural Diplomacy*. New York, 1996. A brief but thorough and insightful overview of postwar information and cultural policies.

Osgood, Kenneth A. "Form Before Substance: Eisenhower's Commitment to Psychological Warfare and Negotiations with the Enemy." *Diplomatic History* 24, no. 3 (summer 2000): 405–433. On the relationship between propaganda and diplomacy during the Eisenhower administration.

———. "Total Cold War: U.S. Propaganda in the 'Free World,' 1953–1960." Ph.D. dissertation. University of California, Santa Barbara, Calif., 2001. Many of this essay's conclusions are drawn from the original research in the dissertation.

Page, Caroline. *U.S. Official Propaganda During the Vietnam War, 1965–1973: The Limits of Persuasion*. London and New York, 1996.

Puddington, Arch. *Broadcasting Freedom: The Cold War Triumph of Radio Free Europe and Radio Liberty*. Lexington, Ky., 2000. Celebrates the purported successes of Cold War propaganda.

Saunders, Frances Stonor. *The Cultural Cold War: The CIA and the World of Arts and Letters*. New York, 1999.

Snow, Nancy. *Propaganda Inc.: Selling America's Culture to the World*. New York, 1998.

Sorensen, Thomas C. *The Word War: The Story of American Propaganda*. New York, 1968.

Taylor, Philip M. *Munitions of the Mind: War Propaganda from the Ancient World to the Nuclear Age*. Glasgow, 1990. A good overview of the wartime use of propaganda in world history.

Thomson, Oliver. *Easily Led: A History of Propaganda*. Gloucestershire, Eng., 1999. Comprehensive investigation of propaganda in world history.

Winkler, Allan M. *The Politics of Propaganda: The Office of War Information, 1942–1945*. New Haven, Conn., 1978. Focuses on domestic politics.

See also COLD WAR EVOLUTION AND INTERPRETATIONS; COLD WARRIORS; CONTAINMENT; COVERT OPERATIONS; DISSENT IN WAR; PUBLIC OPINION.

PROTECTION OF AMERICAN CITIZENS ABROAD

Burton F. Beers

In December 1995 Peruvian police arrested and jailed twenty-one members of a terrorist group, the Tupac Amaru Revolutionary Movement (MRTA). Among those jailed was Lori Berenson, an American woman, then twenty-seven years old, accused of having conspired with leaders of the MRTA to seize and hold members of Peru's Congress as hostages who would be exchanged for imprisoned members of the MRTA. Berenson and the Peruvians arrested with her were promptly tried in secret sessions of a military court, one of several tribunals established outside the civil court system to expedite the trials of prisoners swept up in police raids. The judges—military officers untrained in law—excelled at conducting swift trials, and almost everyone coming before the courts went to jail. In January 1996 the court found Berenson guilty and sentenced her to life in prison.

In August 2000 the highest military tribunal threw out the 1996 verdict, finding that the prosecution had failed to establish that Berenson had been a leader of the terrorists as they shaped their plot. The evidence at best demonstrated only a close association between the American and leaders of the MRTA. The prosecution ordered a second trial, on the new charge of "collaboration with terrorists," a crime carrying a maximum twenty-year sentence. The case was transferred to a civil court where the sessions were open and transmitted to the public in live telecasts. In June 2001 Berenson was convicted for the second time and given the maximum penalty, reduced by the five years she had already served. Her release was scheduled for 2015. As of the summer of 2001, the defense has filed an appeal with Peru's Supreme Court, and if that fails, Berenson's parents say that they will seek a hearing before one or more international bodies.

At this point, even as unfinished business, the Berenson case is worth examining as an introduction to one of the most serious challenges that the United States faces in its efforts to protect American citizens abroad. In some respects the case is much like those of other Americans imprisoned abroad. Berenson, like other Americans on foreign soil, is subject to overlapping jurisdictions of two nations. The United States has defended her because she is one of its citizens, but she is also subject to the laws of Peru. Under international law, Peruvian authorities may arrest her, put her on trial, and imprison her for any violation of law. Thus far the circumstances of the case seem much like those of other Americans imprisoned abroad but, unlike others, Berenson has suffered the misfortune of becoming involved in international politics. This latter entanglement has made a solution elusive. The continuing disagreement has been deeply disturbing for the Berenson family, and it has imposed strains on American-Peruvian relations.

THE PROSECUTION'S CASE

The explanation for the impasse can be found partly in an ongoing disagreement between the United States and Peru over whether or not Berenson was accorded justice in either of her trials. The Department of State had criticized Peru's courts in each annual *Country Human Rights Report* in the 1990s. It noted in 1999, for example, that "Proceedings in the military courts—and those for terrorism in civilian courts—do not meet internationally accepted standards for openness, fairness, and due process." Indeed, reports of the initial trials, which Peru has not refuted, portray a panel of judges, hooded to conceal their identity; prosecutors who were allowed virtually unlimited opportunities to present their case; and a defense that had few opportunities to speak. After the trial, Berenson reported that she had been allowed to spend very little time with her attorney to prepare her defense.

Also, reports that are unconfirmed but not refuted indicate that the prosecution's cases in both trials were very similar. Berenson was portrayed as a key figure drawing plans to invade the Congress and kidnap its members. She was not, as she claimed, a freelance journalist writing about impoverished women. Rather, she was a professional revolutionary who had come to Peru after an agent of the MRTA had discussed with her how she might aid his organization and had paid in advance for her assistance. In Lima, the agent had helped her rent a large house in which a cadre of terrorists took over the top floor. Here she formulated plans while the terrorists built an arsenal of guns, ammunition, and explosives. She had also used her credentials as a journalist to take the wife of a terrorist leader, who posed as her photographer, to Congress, where the two gathered information on the layout of the building and identified the seats occupied by every member of Congress. To corroborate these latter activities, police displayed a chart filled with this information and produced evidence that presumably proved the handwriting was the defendant's. Finally, Berenson was said to have purchased a computer and other electronic equipment for the MRTA.

BERENSON'S DEFENSE

In the second trial, the defense was afforded more opportunities to plan and present its rebuttal to these allegations. Berenson spoke frequently in fluent Spanish. American reporters noted her cool self-possession and were struck by her quick, articulate responses to questions. Peruvian prosecutors, however, described her as an unrepentant, calculating, and dangerous terrorist.

Berenson described her political views as "slightly to the left" and affirmed her deep sympathy for Peru's impoverished people. Peru, she said, must undergo a revolution before the status of the poor could be improved. She said repeatedly that the revolution she envisioned would not—indeed, could not—emerge from terrorism. It followed, therefore, that she was not a terrorist and had no sympathy for those employing terrorism. When asked how these views squared with her association with the MRTA, Berenson refused to condemn the organization. She knew its members only as people who were working peacefully to bring about the kind of revolution that she had in mind.

The defense denied any deal with the MRTA. Berenson had indeed met the man whom the prosecution claimed was an agent of the organization, but she knew nothing of his alleged links to terrorists and she had not taken any payments to become their leader. Moreover, she was completely unaware of any links between the MRTA and tenants in her house or her photographer. The men on the top floor of her house had used assumed names and concealed their store of arms and explosives. She had hired the photographer solely because she was skilled with a camera.

Berenson, the defense continued, was a journalist who had been drawn to Peru by the country's rich history as well as the plight of its poor. Prior to her arrest, she knew nothing of any plans to seize members of Congress, and she had not knowingly provided her acquaintances with any assistance that might serve this purpose. Finally, the defense charged the prosecution with using tainted evidence to make its case. A man convicted of terrorism had served as the government's witness, testifying that Berenson had been paid to come to Peru to assist the MRTA. Other potentially damaging evidence, such as the detailed drawing of the Congress building, had been forged. In summation, the defense dismissed the government's case as flimsy and irrelevant. The government had not brought charges against Berenson because it had uncovered incriminating evidence of terrorist activity. She was on trial as a symbol of the government's determination to wipe out terrorism.

AMERICAN PRESSURE: OFFICIAL AND UNOFFICIAL

Americans who are arrested in almost any foreign country should expect that their host government will promptly notify the United States and that officials—usually from the American consulate—will be present as observers at their trials. Such steps have become standard procedures, the particulars of which have usually been defined in bilateral treaties.

Peru evidently notified the United States when Berenson was arrested, but since her initial trial was secret, an American official may not have been present. In any event, the Department of State was not surprised by her conviction and sentencing on 11 January 1996. On that day the State Department issued a sharply worded note to the Peruvian government. The United States, the note said, deeply regretted that "Ms. Berenson was not tried in an open civilian court with full rights of legal defense, in accordance with international juridical norms." The note went on: "The United States remains concerned that Ms. Berenson receive due process. . . . We call upon the Peruvian Government to take the necessary steps in the appeals process to accord Ms. Berenson an open judicial proceeding in a civilian court."

When President Alberto Fujimori visited the White House in May 1996, demonstrators outside chanted, "Fujimori, free Lori." Inside, President Bill Clinton urged that Peru grant Berenson a fair trial in a civilian court. In August, Representative Bill Richardson, a Democrat from New Mexico and the Clinton administration's informal diplomatic troubleshooter, went to Peru. He and Fujimori discussed several possible solutions, including the exchange of Berenson for a Peruvian jailed in the United States.

Meanwhile, the congresswoman representing the Berenson family's district was collecting letters in both the House and the Senate calling for the young woman's release. Former President Jimmy Carter joined the cause. Human rights groups on a number of college campuses sent letters to the World Bank asking that body to block loans to Peru, and to American corporations urging them not to invest in that country. Operating out of their apartment in New York City, Berenson's parents set up a web site encouraging such protests and drawing media attention to their daughter's imprisonment. By the autumn of 1996, an unidentified Peruvian official described the case as "a stone under everybody's foot." The government wanted to rid itself of this source of tension with the United States, but officials also had to satisfy a public that believed Berenson was guilty.

THE BERENSON CASE IN PERUVIAN POLITICS

There was considerable substance to Berenson's allegation, made during her second trial in 2001, that the Peruvian government had profited politically from her conviction and imprisonment. In the months following her first trial, the Fujimori administration spoke repeatedly of its success in thwarting the MRTA plot against the Congress, and it seldom missed an opportunity to boast of its courage in jailing the terrorists' "American leader." The case touched deep-seated public sensitivities. Almost everyone had felt the deep-seated economic problems of the 1980s and the compounding of them by the emergence of left-wing guerrilla groups, especially the Sendero Luminoso (Shining

Path) and MRTA, both of which employed terror. In ten years, guerrilla attacks and government counterattacks took some thirty thousand lives.

Fujimori, a controversial figure at the outset of his presidency in 1990, gained popularity when his administration began to bring inflation under control and the government launched a determined effort to wipe out terrorism. His initial triumph against terrorism came in 1992, when police seized the leaders of the Shining Path and military courts sentenced them to life in prison. Late in 1996, the MRTA handed Fujimori a means for countering the increasing American pressures to grant Berenson a new trial. In December, armed members of the MRTA stormed the Japanese ambassador's residence in Lima during a party and took hundreds of hostages. In return for their release the MRTA demanded release of imprisoned members of their group. By April 1997 only seventy-two hostages remained. Government troops then attacked, killing all of the guerrillas and freeing all but one of the hostages.

If Berenson had any Peruvian sympathizers, they were gone by the time the hostage episode was over. As Berenson's second trial approached in 2001, American reporters heard Peruvians repeatedly condemn her as a "gringa terrorist," deserving harsh punishment. The MRTA's operation against the Japanese embassy echoed the plan that Berenson had allegedly helped to draft against the Peruvian Congress. Moreover, the guerilla leading the charge on the embassy was Nestor Cerpa Cartolini, the man the Peruvian prosecutors claimed had asked Berenson to establish a safe house in Lima.

Despite Department of State pressure after April 1997 for a new trial for Berenson in a civil court, Peru would not back away from the life sentence handed down by its military court and Berenson's incarceration in a bleak, unheated prison high in the Andes.

THE ROAD TO A NEW TRIAL

The United States may not have had any advance notice of Peru's decision in August 2000 to concede to demands for a new trial in a civil court, yet the State Department was certainly aware that the Fujimori government had become vulnerable to American pressure. Fujimori's political fortunes had plunged at home, and he had come under sharp criticism in the U.S. Congress. In the Senate, bipartisan support had emerged for linking foreign aid payments to Peru to "substantial progress" toward holding fair elections and respecting human rights, free speech, and the rule of law, as had a threat to cut by half the $125 million allocated to Peru in foreign aid.

Fujimori could not offer much resistance. He had come under fire at home for forcing revision of the constitution so that he could seek an unprecedented third term as president. Then his opposition found two serious charges to bring against him: widespread fraud in the balloting for president and a key aide's corruption. Given these circumstances, Peru's judicial system did what it could to placate the United States. The country's supreme military tribunal, presumably the same body that had earlier described Berenson as a "dangerous leader" of the MRTA, cleared the way for a new trial by announcing that she had not been proven guilty of treason.

However, Fujimori quickly found that these and other steps were not enough to save him. He fled to his parents' home country, Japan, from which he sent word of his resignation to Lima. An interim president took office, and a new presidential election in the spring of 2001 brought Alejandro Toledo, the most prominent of Fujimori's opponents, to office in midsummer. Shortly thereafter Berenson's parents appealed for a pardon for their daughter from president-elect Toledo, but he turned down the request. He explained to reporters that presidential intervention would be a poor way of initiating his administration's efforts to build an independent judiciary. The trial had been open, and he intended to respect the independence of the courts. Toledo added that he had visited with Berenson's family in New York City during the latter part of June but refused to reveal the substance of their conversation.

State Department officials in Washington told reporters soon after the second trial that the embassy in Lima had reviewed with Berenson options she might pursue. The department thought that a request for clemency or a pardon offered the best chance, especially if she first requested—as she was entitled to do under a United States–Peruvian treaty—transfer to a prison in the United States. Berenson had rejected each of these possibilities. Her position appears to have been that since she was innocent of the charges against her, she refused to request a pardon for something she had not done. Moreover, she refused to ask for any special consideration. To do so would separate her from people who had been unjustly arrested and convicted with her.

THE BERENSON CASE AND BROADER AMERICAN CONCERNS

The Berenson family's web site regularly posted material that called attention to the disparity between the Department of State's annual reports on Peru's violations of human rights and its reliance on quiet diplomacy in dealing with their daughter's plight. Supporters were asked to write letters to the president or secretary of state that cited 22 U.S. Code 1732, which directs the president to take all necessary steps—short of going to war—to secure the release of an incarcerated American citizen, "if it [the incarceration] appears to be wrongful."

About half of the members of the House of Representatives signed a letter, addressed to President Clinton, in April 2000 (three months before Peru agreed to a second trial in civil court) citing this statute. The letter advised, "A failure to intervene on Ms. Berenson's behalf would send the message that the United States will not act when its citizens are wrongfully imprisoned in foreign countries." Those signing the letter did not specify what they meant by "intervene."

LIMITS OF POWER

It had been difficult to find solid grounds for requesting that Berenson be given special treatment because she has steadfastly denied wanting any favors and is determined to stand with the Peruvians who had been arrested with her. In addition, the United States has been peculiarly handicapped in requesting special treatment for a citizen found guilty of crimes growing out of her association with the MRTA. The United States had welcomed Peru's efforts to wipe out terrorism, and the Clinton administration had joined Peru in designating the MRTA as a terrorist organization.

LEGAL FOUNDATIONS

The overlapping jurisdiction of the United States and Peru in the Berenson case is a fundamental characteristic of modern international relations. In part it is the product of a legal principle related to the concept of a nation's sovereignty. As nations took shape, individuals and property (today that means—among other things—companies or corporations, ships, and aircraft) came to be identified for legal purposes with some sovereign, and

★ ★ ★ ★ ★

EXTRATERRITORIALITY

Chinese authorities in 1821 charged a seaman, Francis Terranova, a crewman aboard an American merchant vessel trading in Canton, with having killed a woman. Her death was accidental. An earthen pot had been knocked overboard, striking the victim, who was in a boat below. Neither the ship's captain nor crew believed Terranova was guilty, but the woman's family was offered a cash settlement. Chinese authorities, however, stepped in to insist on a trial that was held on the deck of the American vessel. The proceedings were brief. The magistrate heard the charges and promptly sentenced Terranova to death by strangulation. No testimony on behalf of the defendant was allowed. The outraged Americans initially refused to surrender Terranova, but they relented when authorities embargoed any further trade. After Terranova died, trade resumed.

Incidents such as this prompted the United States to go along with European nations in negotiating treaties that granted extraterritorial rights to Americans in China. Reduced to essentials, extraterritorial rights exempted Americans from the operation of Chinese law and courts. If an American in China committed either a criminal or a civil offense, he could theoretically be charged and tried in an American court. As a practical matter, this proved virtually impossible.

China was not alone in granting extraterritorial rights. Other countries in the Middle East and Asia signed similar treaties. None of them, of course, did so willingly. They capitulated in the face of the superior power of British or French forces. Americans shared these rights, largely because their government proved adept at negotiating treaties that embodied the advantages Europe had won.

Extraterritoriality was not destined to survive very long (except as a special privilege known today as diplomatic immunity). The system was doomed by the resurgent power of the "Third World" states. It was gone everywhere by the end of World War II. An American in Saudi Arabia, for example, may not seek refuge in his own nation's laws if he violates his host's dress codes or prohibitions against consumption of alcohol. He will be subject to the full weight of the host nation's system of justice.

---

this identification followed them wherever they went. This principle was then joined with an affirmation that the honor of a nation was injured when one of its citizens abroad or his or her property was subjected to an injustice. These two principles were interpreted to mean that each state would decide for itself when its citizens abroad had suffered mistreatment, how seriously the offenses had damaged the national honor, and what had to be done in order to make amends.

But these asserted rights had to be accommodated to the claim that nations exercised jurisdiction over everyone and everything within their boundaries. In effect, the individual or property abroad was placed in a legal relationship with two governments: one that claimed the individual as a citizen and one that insisted on the individual's compliance with its laws.

The awkwardness (or potential for trouble) of these overlapping claims was scarcely noted in the formative years of nation-states. Even in the relatively limited confines of the place of their birth (western Europe), nations tended to be isolated. Few people crossed their sovereign's borders. That being so, the father of international law, Hugo Grotius, the seventeenth-century statesman and jurist, made no explicit reference to how governments should ensure the protection of nationals traveling or residing abroad. Before the end of the eighteenth century, however, the Western world's commercial and industrial revolutions were opening a new era in international intercourse. By 1758, the year in which Emerich von Vattel's classic *The Law of Nations* was published, the treatment—or mistreatment—of foreign nationals had become a problem. From that point on, governmental agencies and law aimed at their protection developed rapidly.

THE PRINCIPLES OF PROTECTION

Early law and practices for protecting nationals abroad reflect the fact that the first nation-states were few in number and shared in some degree heritages derived from civilizations rooted in Judeo-Christian and Greco-Roman traditions—and thus some commonalties in law. This encouraged European nations—and the United States after independence—to agree that their nationals should submit to the full operation of local law whenever their nationals traveled in one another's domains. Generally speaking, these nations acted on the presumption that their nationals would be accorded justice. However, if their nationals suffered wrongs and found no relief in local remedies, these nations reserved rights to intervene on their nationals' behalf.

However, the system was scarcely trouble-free. The United States, for example, quarreled with European states when the latter imprisoned immigrants who had returned from America to visit family. The returned immigrants were often charged with having failed to meet their military obligations. At issue in such cases was whether the immigrants, while in the United States, had established indisputable claims to American citizenship and whether the United States could legitimately spring to their defense.

Sometimes disagreements generated serious tensions. In 1891, for example, American sailors on shore leave in one of the seamier sections of Valparaiso, Chile, were set upon by a mob that killed two of the sailors and injured others. Chile dismissed the incident as an unfortunate drunken brawl, but the United States charged the Chilean government with complicity in the clash. The assault had been a premeditated way of expressing Chilean resentment of the United States. The exchange of recriminatory charges escalated and led the United States to threaten war. At that point Chile met American demands for "prompt and full reparations" by issuing a formal apology and paying $75,000 in damages.

RESPONSIBILITIES OF THE EXECUTIVE BRANCH

The president, the secretary of state, and the American ambassador in Lima worked on the Berenson case, but the involvement of such high officials occurs in only a small percentage of problems relating to protection. However, Berenson's second trial in 2001 proved to be only one of a number of cases drawing the attention of the president and secretary of state. China arrested half a dozen Americans of Chinese descent and convicted them of spying for Taiwan. Russia jailed two Americans. One was charged with espionage, and the other was convicted on minor drug charges, following more serious allegations that

he was an American spy-in-training. In each instance, these convictions occurred at times when the Chinese and Russian leaderships looked toward serious discussions with the United States on a number of vital concerns. The Chinese defused the problem by releasing the prisoners and expelling them from the country. Russian President Vladimir Putin pardoned the man convicted of espionage after discussions with President George W. Bush. The second American was paroled after six months in prison and allowed to return to the United States.

SANCTIONS AND MILITARY FORCE

When the United States has resorted to measures extending beyond negotiation—such as the rupture of diplomatic relations or use of military force for the protection of citizens—the president and secretary of state have inevitably been involved. In Brazil (1826) and Mexico (1858), for example, American diplomats demanded their passports and prepared to return to Washington when those governments refused to indemnify Americans for the seizure of property and mistreatment. Both governments promptly capitulated by making the required payments.

In the nineteenth and early twentieth centuries, the United States used, or sometimes just displayed, military force when American lives and property were threatened. For example, the secretary of state warned Turkey's minister in Washington in 1895 that the United States had dispatched a warship to stand guard off his nation's coast as long as disorder in that country threatened American lives and property.

Not infrequently the United States has moved beyond showing its flag. In 1927, for example, warring factions in China trapped Americans and British nationals in Nanking. Both Western nations had warships anchored in the Yangtze River, positioned so that they could aid their beleaguered countrymen. The ships laid down protective curtains of shellfire that proved crucial in saving foreign lives. And in 1962, during a congressional debate on the potential use of force in Cuba, Secretary of State Dean Rusk had the State Department compile a list of about 150 instances, dated 1798 to 1945, in which American forces had acted without congressional approval. On most of these occasions, the military had been employed to protect American lives and property abroad.

POLITICS OF PROTECTING PROPERTY ABROAD

Among the duties of the U.S. Consular Service, the facilitation of American trade and investment abroad has figured prominently. Since the 1920s and 1930s, however, the United States has increasingly found it difficult to safeguard American property abroad against the rise of intense nationalist feelings in Latin America, Africa, the Middle East, and Asia. Attempts to use military power in their defense, especially if the use of force assumes the character of "gunboat diplomacy," has often proven counterproductive. In these circumstances, the United States has increasingly come to depend on diplomacy.

By the 1920s, for example, Presidents Calvin Coolidge and Herbert Hoover, recognizing that military intervention was arousing the ire of Latin American nations, began a shift toward cooperation. This new line, which President Franklin D. Roosevelt publicized as the policy of the "Good Neighbor," was welcomed in the Western Hemisphere, but private interests in the United States were notably less enthusiastic.

Confirmation of the private interests' apprehensions came in the late 1930s, when Mexico ordered the nationalization of American, British, and Dutch oil companies. The American firms valued their expropriated property at $100 million and demanded that their government force Mexico to make restitution. The Roosevelt administration instead embarked on extended and difficult negotiations that ultimately produced a comprehensive settlement. It provided Mexico with economic assistance, an advantageous trade agreement, and a mechanism for settling a variety of claims. The Roosevelt administration regarded such a sweeping settlement as a major success, especially since it promised the United States increased security along its southwestern frontier at a time when the world was going to war. Administration officials also thought that American negotiators had won a substantial victory in gaining $24 million for American interests in Mexican oil. Mexico's initial intent had been to expropriate those interests, making no payment. American oilmen saw much less to praise, but they had no alternative to taking the sum offered.

After World War II, U.S. corporations faced wholesale nationalization of their overseas property in eastern Europe, Asia, the Middle East, and Latin America. The United States attempted to counter what amounted in most cases to uncompensated seizures with two steps: the negotiation of commercial treaties with guidelines for compensation for nationalized property, and passage of the Economic Cooperation Act of 1948, a measure that provided government-financed insurance for a limited range of investments. Neither the treaties nor the legislation helped much because they covered relatively few of the businesses that were taken over. In consequence, the United States sought, wherever it could, lump-sum settlements on property that had been seized. These settlements were reached in the early years of the Cold War, a time when bitter U.S.–Soviet rivalries prompted competitive bidding for the friendship of "Third World" nations. Again, American investors claimed that the negotiated sums were much less than what they had lost. Moreover, the payments came in so slowly that investors suffered additional losses.

THE CONSULAR SERVICE

Nothing has been said yet about the work of the Bureau of Consular Affairs, an agency that operates within the Department of State, in the Berenson case. Throughout the years of Berenson's imprisonment, American consular officials have visited her regularly, checking on the conditions of her jail, her needs, and her well-being. Soon after her initial conviction, Berenson was shipped to a prison that had been constructed to house terrorists. It was in a remote location, some twelve thousand feet high in the Andes. No heat warmed the frigid mountain air. Rats were everywhere, and medical services were not provided.

What the consuls saw touched off sustained American efforts to have Berenson moved to another prison. American consuls argued that, given the prison environment, her health would suffer. Peruvian authorities initially refused, but they eventually conceded when Berenson's physical condition did begin to deteriorate. Beyond these efforts, the consular office facilitated her family's shipments of warm clothing, blankets, medicine, and food. Except for the disagreement over where Berenson was to be imprisoned, Peru did not interfere with the services of the consular office. The United States, Peru, and almost all other nations signed the Vienna Convention on Consular Relations of 1963. In addition, the United States had concluded with Peru, as it has with most other nations, bilateral agreements that refined the Vienna Convention's understandings so that they more precisely fit the circumstances of the two countries' relationships. This means that what the consular officers may do on behalf of American citizens varies from country to country, but, generally speaking, they provide an impressive array of services for citizens almost everywhere in the world.

America's Founders, as former British subjects, knew how much Great Britain valued its consular officers as facilitators of that nation's trade. It is scarcely surprising, therefore, that the Constitution links presidential appointment of consuls with other officials representing the United States abroad. However, the consular service of the infant Republic did not resemble the one operating today. American consuls were initially assigned to posts—often foreign ports—where American merchants traded.

Not infrequently, these early consuls were themselves merchants willing to perform official duties on the side. When an American ship sailed into port, the consul received and held the ship's papers until the captain had met his obligations to the crew and local authorities. He certified invoices on merchandise bound for the United States. He might also send to the State Department information that helped American merchants identify local marketing trends. In lieu of salaries, consuls retained a portion of the fees that they collected for handling documents related to trade. In only a very few places could substantial incomes be realized from these fees. Nineteenth-century consuls in Amoy, China, reputedly collected upward of $40,000 annually, and those at Liverpool, England, earned about $60,000 a year.

American seamen were the most likely recipients of any protective services offered by these early consuls. Sometimes consuls found themselves mediating controversies between officers and crews of American vessels, investigating charges of mutiny, or representing American seamen in trouble with local authorities. A stranded and destitute seaman could sometimes look to the consul for a loan that funded his return to the United States. If an American died abroad, the nearest consul might ship his body home and help with settling his estate.

By the latter half of the nineteenth century, the number of Americans traveling or residing abroad escalated rapidly. The U.S. government, however, apparently gave little thought to the impact of these developments on the Consular Service. The impact, however, immediately became apparent when some fifty thousand Americans were trapped in Europe at the outbreak of World War I. Most of those in Europe had gone abroad without passports. Only as war closed in did they discover an urgent need to establish their national identity. The disruption of banking facilities left thousands without funds, and pressures on shipping stranded thousands of those anxious to return home. American consuls throughout Europe attempted to locate and report to families in the United States on Americans scattered over the continent. Their offices issued emergency passports, arranged loans, and pressured steamship lines into providing immediate passage for thousands of Americans. This emergency proved to be one of the experiences that prompted efforts to modernize and expand the Consular Service. The Rogers Act of 1924, for example, authorized important steps toward staffing the Consular Service with trained professionals and integrating consuls into the nation's corps of career foreign service officers.

The modern Bureau of Consular Affairs' efforts to protect Americans abroad have become much broader than those of the agency in its earlier years. Americans preparing to leave the United States to travel or live may consult the bureau's voluminous, and continually updated, files on the Internet. Those who do, will find much more than detailed descriptions of how consular officers may assist those who are arrested and jailed or those caught in emergencies.

THE RANGE OF CONTEMPORARY CONSULAR SERVICES

Much on the bureau's web site addresses the potential concerns of travelers, some routine and some dealing with emergencies:

Passports and visas; travel publications; country background notes; key officers at U.S. Foreign Service posts and how to contact them.

Travelers' health concerns; U.S. customs information; cruise ship sanitation inspection scores; foreign airline safety data and related performance information.

Emergency services available through consular offices and aid available in international parental child abduction.

Detailed travel warning for each of the world's countries, covering all manner of things that might catch Americans by surprise (everything from slight differences in U.S. and Canadian traffic laws to rigidly enforced dress codes in Muslim countries).

Those going abroad to work for an American corporation may attend seminars (the Bureau of Consular Affairs does not release agendas for these gatherings) that in all likelihood deal with business law in one or more targeted countries, policies of host governments relating to foreign corporations, labor relations, and—in countries where terrorism has been a threat—security for executives and their families. Both those in business and others planning to live abroad are offered information for most countries on a number of domestic issues: marriage and divorce, dual citizenship and births overseas, and schools for American children.

BIBLIOGRAPHY

Borchard, Edwin M. *The Diplomatic Protection of Citizens Abroad.* New York, 1928. Remains basic, despite its age.

Crane, Katherine. *Mr. Carr of State.* New York, 1960. Biography of the man who helped transform the Department of State into a twentieth-century institution.

Dunn, Frederick S. *The Protection of Nationals.* Baltimore, 1932. An older but still indispensable study.

Frey, Linda S., and Marsha L. Frey. *The History of Diplomatic Immunity.* Columbus, Ohio, 1999. A splendid study of the origins of modern immunity bestowed on diplomatic personnel and the roots of extraterritoriality.

Gordon, Wendell C. *The Expropriation of Foreign-Owned Property in Mexico.* Washington, D.C., 1941.

Hackworth, Green H. *Digest of International Law.* 8 vols. Washington, D.C., 1940–1944. Updates and supplements John B. Moore's older multiple-volume work (1906).

Law, Castor H. P. *The Local Remedies Rule in International Law.* Geneva, 1961. Deals with the complex interplay between municipal and international laws.

Lee, Luke T. *Consular Law and Practice.* New York, 1961.

———. *The Vienna Convention on Consular Relations.* Leiden, 1966. Complements Lee's 1961 study.

Lillich, Richard B. *The Protection of Foreign Investment: Six Procedural Studies.* Syracuse, N.Y., 1965.

———. "The Diplomatic Protection of Nationals Abroad: An Elementary Principle of International Law Under Attack." *American Journal of International Law* 69 (1975). Criticizes the tendency of nations to subordinate the protection of nationals to political considerations.

McDougal, Myres S., Harold Laswell, and Lung-chu Chen. "The Protection of Aliens from Discrimination: Responsibility of States Conjoined with Human Rights." *American Journal of International Law* 70 (1976). Another criticism of the subordination of human rights to politics.

Plischke, Elmer. *Conduct of American Diplomacy.* 3d ed. Princeton, N.J., 1967. Offers insights into the impacts of Cold War politics on the protection offered by the United States to its citizens.

Stuart, Graham H. *The Department of State: A History of Its Organization, Procedure, and Personnel.* New York, 1949. A classic.

———. *American Diplomatic and Consular Practice.* 3d ed. New York, 1976. Especially useful for the early work of the consular service.

Von Glahn, Gerhard. *Law Among Nations: An Introduction to Public International Law.* 3d ed. New York, 1976. Contains four chapters summarizing the nature of law pertaining to the protection of foreign nationals abroad.

White, Gillian. *Nationalization of Foreign Property.* New York, 1962.

See also DEPARTMENT OF STATE; EXTRATERRITORIALITY; HUMAN RIGHTS; INTERNATIONAL LAW; TERRORISM AND COUNTERTERRORISM.

PROTECTORATES AND SPHERES OF INFLUENCE

★ ★ ★ ★

Raymond A. Esthus

The word "protectorate" usually describes the relation between a protecting state and a protected state, though it sometimes may describe the country under protection. In a protectorate relationship, the protecting state normally assumes control of the foreign relations of the protected state in addition to providing for its defense. Often the protecting state has some control over the internal affairs of the protected state. As to the status of a protecting state in international law, the Permanent Court of International Justice in 1923 rendered an advisory opinion stating that the extent of the powers of a protecting state depended upon the treaties between it and the protected state that established the protectorate, and upon the conditions under which the protectorate was recognized by third powers whose interests were affected by the protectorate treaty. The court went on to observe that despite common features possessed by protectorates under international law, they had individual legal characteristics resulting from the special conditions under which they were created. United States protectorates, as traditionally defined, have been limited to the Caribbean area, except for a brief protectorate over Hawaii in 1893.

The term "sphere of influence" signifies a claim by a state to some degree of control or preferential status in a foreign territory or in some region of the world. It may refer to a military, political, or economic claim to exclusive control or influence that other nations may or may not recognize. As in the case of protectorates, the legal status of a sphere depends upon the treaties establishing it and the extent to which other affected nations recognize it. American policy regarding spheres of influence has not adhered to a definite pattern. On many of the treaties creating spheres, the United States has not had occasion or necessity to take a stand. In cases where a position has been taken, policy has varied greatly. Generally, advocacy of an Open Door policy for

trade and investment has placed the United States in opposition to spheres of influence, but on occasion it has not only acquiesced but actually looked with favor upon spheres.

U.S. PROTECTORATES PRIOR TO WORLD WAR II

When the white sugar barons in Hawaii overthrew the native dynasty in 1893, the United States minister to Hawaii, John L. Stevens, proclaimed a protectorate. Stevens acted without instructions from Washington, and the incoming administration of Grover Cleveland soon repudiated the arrangement. In addition to this short-lived protectorate over Hawaii, the relationship between the United States and Samoa in 1889–1899 has sometimes been characterized as a protectorate, specifically a tripartite protectorate of the United States, Great Britain, and Germany over Samoa. It is doubtful, however, that the United States possessed sufficient rights or obligations in Samoa to justify the use of the word "protectorate" in this case.

The first United States protectorate in the Caribbean was established when the Platt Amendment was incorporated in a treaty with Cuba in 1903. Having helped Cuba win its freedom from Spain, the United States endeavored to assure the political and financial stability of the island republic by limiting its freedom. The Platt Amendment, initially written by Secretary of War Elihu Root, had been attached to the Army Appropriations Bill in 1901 by Senator Orville H. Platt. By one of its many provisions, the United States could intervene in Cuba for the preservation of Cuban independence and for the maintenance of a government adequate for the protection of life, property, and individual liberty. This right of intervention was exercised in 1906–1909, and in subsequent years various American missions were sent to the island to untangle electoral difficulties and financial problems. This protectorate lasted until the administrations of Herbert Hoover and Franklin D. Roosevelt fashioned the Good Neighbor Policy in the early 1930s. In a new treaty signed in 1934, the United States relinquished all its Platt Amendment rights except the right to retain a naval base at Guantánamo Bay.

The acquisition of the Cuban protectorate in 1903 was followed in the same year by the establishment of a protectorate over Panama. Having aided a Panamanian rebellion against Colombia, the administration of Theodore Roosevelt proceeded to secure valuable Canal Zone rights from the newly created nation. Simultaneously, the United States sought to protect these rights by making Panama a protectorate. In the canal treaty signed by Secretary of State John Hay and the Panamanian minister to the United States, Philippe Bunau-Varilla, the United States agreed to guarantee and maintain the independence of Panama. Outside the Canal Zone, which it administered, the United States could use lands necessary and convenient for the operation and protection of the canal. It also could intervene to maintain public order in the cities of Panama and Colón. These extensive powers were reduced in 1936, when a new treaty was negotiated. The United States gave up most of its rights outside the Canal Zone. Also, the obligation to guarantee and maintain the independence of Panama was replaced by a provision stating that in the event of an international "conflagration" or the existence of a threat of aggression that endangered Panama or the security of the canal, the two governments would take such measures as they deemed necessary for the protection of their common interests. Measures taken by one government that might affect the territory of the other would be the subject of consultation. When the United States Senate approved the treaty in 1939, Panama agreed by an exchange of notes that in an emergency, consultation might follow rather than precede action. The United States thus retained at least a limited right of intervention to protect both Panama and the Canal Zone.

In 1977 the United States concluded two treaties with Panama that completely changed their relationship. The Canal Zone was abolished, and the canal was to be administered until 2000 by a joint commission. At the end of the interim period, the canal would be turned over to Panama. United States armed forces would be withdrawn by the end of 1999. The United States retained only the right to defend the neutrality of the canal.

Despite the restricted wording of the new treaty provision limiting the United States to defending the canal's neutrality, a U.S. intervention occurred in 1989 that could have been more easily justified under the old protectorate treaty rights. In the 1980s, politics in Panama became unstable, with demonstrations and attempted coups. There emerged from the chaos a military dictator, Manuel Noriega. From his position as commander of the National Defense Forces, he intimidated civilian political leaders and undermined the democratic processes. A pivotal turning point came in 1988 when two U.S. grand juries indicted Noriega on drug smuggling charges. When in December 1989 a rump political body named Noriega head of state, President George H. W. Bush sent in 24,000 U.S. troops to capture Noriega and restore civilian rule. Bush's administration based its legal position on the right to defend the neutrality of the canal. Noriega was captured and taken to the United States for trial. He was subsequently convicted of conspiracy to manufacture and distribute cocaine and sentenced to forty years in prison. Meanwhile, civilian government was reestablished and U.S. forces withdrew to the Canal Zone. In the years following the American intervention, Panama's politics remained somewhat chaotic, but the treaties of 1977 were nevertheless effectively carried out. In December 1999, the withdrawal of U.S. forces from the Canal Zone was completed.

In addition to the protectorates of Cuba and Panama, the administration of Theodore Roosevelt sought to establish a protectorate over the Dominican Republic. Roosevelt feared that European creditor nations might intervene there to collect debts, and he feared particularly that Germany might thereby gain some lodgment in the Caribbean. This was one of the considerations that led to the enunciation in 1904 of the Roosevelt Corollary to the Monroe Doctrine, affirming that when debt default or other wrongdoing or impotence made intervention necessary in the Western Hemisphere, the adherence of the United States to the Monroe Doctrine required U.S. intervention.

Having announced this policy, Roosevelt proceeded to conclude a treaty with the Dominican government (1905) placing the collection of customs revenues under U.S. control and making the country a protectorate. The treaty provided that the United States would, at the request of the Dominican government, render assistance to preserve order. When the U.S. Senate delayed approval of the treaty, Roosevelt set up the customs receivership and applied the protectorate principle. With a characteristic flourish, the president told his secretary of the navy: "As to the Santo Domingo matter, tell Admiral [Royal B.] Bradford to stop any revolution. . . . That this is ethically right, I am dead sure, even though there may be some technical or red tape difficulty." When Elihu Root became secretary of state later in 1905, he limited the protectorate role to protection of the customs administration. It was this policy that prevailed. When it became evident that the Senate would not approve the general protectorate provision, a new treaty, obligating the United States to protect only the customs administration, was concluded and approved (1907).

The administration of William Howard Taft made Nicaragua a protectorate in practice, though the relationship was never regularized by treaty. In 1911 a customs receivership was set up, even though the Senate failed to act on the treaty, concluded in that year, that provided for it. In 1912 marines were landed to aid the regime of President Adolfo Díaz against rebel forces. When the rebels were defeated, most of the troops were withdrawn, but a legation guard remained behind to police elections, train a Nicaraguan constabulary, and serve as a reminder that more troops could be landed. In 1913 the outgoing Taft administration signed a canal treaty with the Díaz government; it provided for the purchase by the United States, for $3 million, of an option on a canal route and leases on naval base sites.

The Senate did not take action on the treaty before Woodrow Wilson entered the White House, but the new administration did not repudiate the protectorate policy. On the contrary, at the request of the Nicaraguan government, it agreed to include in the treaty a new article giving the United States the right to intervene for the preservation of Nicaraguan independence and for the maintenance of a government adequate for the protection of life, property, and individual liberty. The Senate Foreign Relations Committee refused to approve this article, and Secretary of State William Jennings Bryan finally signed a new treaty in 1914 that omitted the protectorate provision and essentially reiterated the terms of the 1913 canal treaty. Even this treaty was held up in the Senate for two years before being approved. Meanwhile, U.S. troops remained in Nicaragua. They were withdrawn in 1925 but landed again in 1926 as a result of renewed revolutionary unrest. The protectorate-in-practice was

not ended until January 1933, when the troops were withdrawn again. The control over the customs was not ended until 1944.

The failure of the Wilson administration to gain Senate approval for the Nicaraguan protectorate in 1913–1914 did not dissuade it from pursuing the protectorate policy in the Caribbean. Indeed, Wilson pushed the policy with far more vigor than his predecessors had. Theodore Roosevelt's policy toward the Dominican Republic had been motivated primarily by strategic considerations, especially the desire to protect the approaches to the Panama Canal. Taft had been motivated by this consideration, but he had also pursued a complementary interest, that of having U.S. capital force European bondholders out of the Caribbean area. The Wilson administration added to the strategic and financial motivations a missionary zeal to spread U.S. political institutions and practices to the nations of the Caribbean. As Wilson remarked on one occasion, he wished to teach the South Americans how to elect good men.

The protectorate policy was carried out most vigorously in Haiti and the Dominican Republic. In 1915, when Haiti's chronic revolutionary disturbances reached a high point, Wilson wrote to Secretary of State Robert Lansing: "I fear we have not the legal authority to do what we apparently ought to do. . . . I suppose there is nothing for it but to take the bull by the horns and restore order." Wilson proceeded to land troops and force a protectorate treaty upon the Haitian government. Restating the Platt Amendment formula, the treaty provided that the United States would "lend an efficient aid" for the preservation of Haitian independence and the maintenance of a government adequate for the protection of life, property, and individual liberty. Along with this went a U.S. customs administration and a constabulary with officers from the United States. In 1916 the U.S. Senate approved the treaty without public debate. The outbreak of World War I and the developing submarine controversy with Germany had brought the Senate to share at least Wilson's strategic concerns, if not his politico-missionary zeal. The protectorate was to last until 1934, at which time the troops were withdrawn and the constabulary was "Haitianized." The treaty of 1916 actually expired in 1936, and until then the United States still had the right to intervene. The customs control lasted until 1941.

The intervention in the Dominican Republic came in 1916, the year after the neighboring

Haitian protectorate was set up. The outbreak of a revolution in the Dominican Republic in that year brought the landing of U.S. troops. When Dominican authorities refused to cooperate in setting up a Haitian-style protectorate, U.S. military rule was imposed. Six years later this military regime allowed a provisional Dominican government to take office, and two years after that the military overlordship was ended and the troops were withdrawn. The protectorate thus came to an end without having been regularized by treaty. The agreement concluded in 1924, at the time of the withdrawal, did provide, like the 1907 treaty, that the United States could protect the customs administration, which was to continue under its administration. This financial control, as in the case of Haiti, ended in 1941.

In the era preceding World War II, the policy of the United States toward the protectorates of other powers was generally to accept the establishment of protectorates and attempt to preserve as many of its rights in the protected state as was consistent with its overall interests. An example of this is the case of Morocco. By treaty between France and Morocco in 1912, France was given the right to occupy Morocco militarily, control Moroccan foreign relations, and station a French resident commissioner general in Morocco. Later in the same year, by agreement between France and Spain, the latter was allowed to assume a protectorate over small segments of Morocco. In recognizing the French protectorate in 1917, Secretary of State Lansing informed the French government that the question of U.S. extraterritorial rights, as well as other rights, would remain for later negotiation. In subsequent talks the United States refused to relinquish its extraterritorial rights. American recognition of the Spanish protectorate in Morocco was blocked by Spain's demand that the United States give up its extraterritorial rights with the act of recognition.

The United States has not always attempted to preserve its existing rights in recognizing another power's protectorate. When, as a consequence of victory in the Russo-Japanese War, Japan established a protectorate over Korea in 1905, President Theodore Roosevelt enthusiastically approved the development because he believed it would help secure a balance of power in East Asia. Subsequent U.S. policy continued to be shaped by this consideration as well as by the expectation that Japan would in time annex the area outright. The Roosevelt administration was not even greatly concerned about preserving com-

mercial rights in Korea. When in 1907 some Japanese leaders considered the advisability of establishing a Japan-Korea customs union—a step that would enable Japan to dominate the Korean market—Roosevelt was willing to approve such a scheme if in return he could get some concession on the Japanese immigration question. In this case and in many other instances, U.S. policy toward the protectorates of other powers has varied and has been determined primarily by the overall national interests as interpreted by succeeding administrations.

SPHERES OF INFLUENCE PRIOR TO WORLD WAR II

The first agreement to use the term "spheres of influence" was one concluded between Britain and Germany (1885) that separated and defined their respective spheres in the territories on the Gulf of Guinea. By its provisions, Britain agreed not to acquire territory, accept protectorates, or interfere with the extension of German influence in that part of Guinea lying east of a specified line. Germany undertook a like commitment regarding Britain and the territory west of the line. As the terms of this treaty indicate, it is possible for a nation to have a protectorate within a sphere of influence when the sphere concept is applied in a broad regional sense.

In the last decade of the nineteenth century and the first decade of the twentieth century, many agreements were concluded recognizing spheres of influence in Africa, the Middle East, and China. By the Anglo-French agreement of 8 April 1904, Britain recognized that Morocco was within France's sphere of influence and France recognized that Egypt was within Britain's sphere. Britain and Russia signed a treaty on 31 August 1907, specifying that Afghanistan was outside of Russia's sphere—meaning, of course, that it was within Britain's. Persia was divided into three zones: a Russian sphere in the north, a British sphere in the south, and a neutral area in between.

In China, the spheres of influence were initially marked out in 1896–1898. At the beginning of that period, Russia secured from China the right to construct a railway line across Manchuria that would provide a short route for the Trans-Siberian Railway to reach Vladivostok on the Pacific coast. The Russian-owned Chinese Eastern Railway Company, which was to construct and operate the line, was given exclusive administrative control of the railway zone stretching across Manchuria. Two years later, in 1898, Russia secured from China a twenty-five-year lease on Port Arthur, a naval base site in southern Manchuria. By this agreement, Russia was also permitted to construct a north-south railway line between Port Arthur (Lüshun) and Harbin, thus connecting the naval base with the main line of the Chinese Eastern Railway running across Manchuria. Russia also secured some mining concessions in Manchuria.

The treaties between Russia and China did not specifically recognize Manchuria as a Russian sphere of influence, but by the end of 1898, Russia's rights in Manchuria were so extensive that it was apparent that the czarist regime would seek to dominate capital investment and to make its political influence preeminent in that area of China. An Anglo-Russian agreement in 1899 greatly strengthened Russia's claim to a Manchurian sphere of influence. Britain agreed not to seek any railway concessions north of China's Great Wall, which separated China proper from Manchuria and Inner Mongolia. Russia reciprocated with a pledge not to seek railway concessions in the Yangtze (Chang) Valley.

While Russia was seeking rights in Manchuria, Germany was gaining a sphere in China's Shantung (Shandong) province. Using the murder of two German missionaries as an excuse, Germany landed troops in Shantung in 1897 and proceeded to extract from China (1898) a treaty granting extensive rights in Shantung. By its terms, Germany obtained a ninety-nine-year lease of a naval base site at Kiaochow (Jiaoxian) on the southern coast of Shantung and the exclusive right to furnish all foreign capital and materials for projects in Shantung. Added to these sweeping rights were specific railway concessions and mining rights in the province. The monopoly on capital investment in Shantung province gave Germany a claim to a sphere of influence in China stronger than that of any other power.

The British and French spheres in China that were delineated in 1898 were not granted in such definitive terms. Britain's sphere in the Yangtze Valley rested primarily upon an Anglo-Chinese treaty concluded in February 1898, whereby China committed itself not to alienate any of the Yangtze area—meaning that China could not cede or lease territory in that area to another power. Britain secured a lease on a naval base site on the China coast in the same year but not in the Yangtze area. It was, rather, on the northern coast of Shantung, across the Gulf of Chihli (Bo Hai) from the Russian base at Port Arthur. France's claim to a sphere in southern China rested partly upon specific concessions and partly upon a nonalienation agreement. In 1885, France began securing railway concessions in southern China, and in 1895, China agreed to call exclusively upon French capital for the exploitation of mines in the three southernmost provinces. In 1898, China concluded a treaty with France in which it agreed not to alienate any Chinese territories bordering French Indochina. Later in the same year, France obtained a ninety-nine-year lease on a naval base site at Kuangchow (Guangzhou) Bay, on China's southern coast.

As stated, although advocacy of an open door for trade and investment has generally led the United States to oppose spheres of influence, it has occasionally looked upon them with favor. During the Moroccan crisis of 1905–1906, for instance, the United States vigorously opposed any compromise that might lead to a German sphere in a portion of Morocco. At the same time, after receiving assurances that the open door would remain in effect for thirty years, the administration of Theodore Roosevelt voiced no opposition to terms of a settlement that obviously recognized Morocco as being in France's sphere. In fact, Roosevelt gave every indication that he favored a virtually complete takeover of Morocco by France.

It is with regard to spheres in China that American policy has been most thoroughly delineated. When in 1899 the United States enunciated the Open Door policy for China, it sought only the preservation of equal opportunity for ordinary trade within the spheres, not the destruction of the spheres themselves. Equal investment opportunity was not demanded. Although the Open Door Notes did not formally recognize the spheres, Secretary of State John Hay accepted the spheres as existing facts. When Russia militarily occupied Manchuria in 1900 during the Boxer Rebellion and then proceeded to demand extensive rights there, the United States was willing to recognize the exceptional position of Russia in Manchuria if Russia would permit equality of opportunity for trade. When in 1905, at the conclusion of the Russo-Japanese War, Japan secured all the Russian rights and concessions in southern Manchuria, it did so with the full blessing of the U.S. government. President Theodore Roosevelt even indicated to China that it could not question the transfer to Japan of either the Port Arthur leasehold or the part of the Chinese Eastern Railway that was in southern Manchuria.

There were, however, limits to the accepting attitude of the Roosevelt administration. When in 1908 Russia attempted to take over the administration of Harbin on the ground that it was part of the railway zone, Secretary of State Elihu Root resisted vigorously. His opposition was motivated by the desire not only to restrain Russia in its northern Manchurian sphere but also to forestall Japan from making a similar interpretation of its railway zone rights in southern Manchuria. U.S. policy in the Harbin dispute indicates clearly that the Roosevelt administration did not give either Russia or Japan a free hand in their respective spheres.

The administration of William Howard Taft, redefining the Open Door policy to include the demand for equal investment opportunity, launched a full-scale attack on the spheres of influence in Manchuria. Secretary of State Philander Knox came forward with a plan to have the major powers loan China money to purchase the Russian railway line (the Chinese Eastern Railway) and the Japanese railway (later known as the South Manchurian Railway). He also proposed, as an alternate plan, the construction of a new line from Chinchow (Jinzhou) to Aigun that would parallel and compete with the Japanese line. Neither of these schemes was implemented because of lack of support from the other interested powers, including Britain. The principal result of the Knox program was to drive Russia and Japan closer together. In 1907 they had signed a secret treaty recognizing each other's spheres in Manchuria; and in 1910 they signed another accord, this time agreeing to support each other in the further development of their spheres. Meanwhile, the spheres were softening in China south of the Great Wall. In 1909, Germany, Britain, and France agreed to share in a project for a railway line stretching from Canton to Hankow and then westward to Chungking (Chongqing). The following year the United States was admitted to the project and the Four-Power Consortium was formed by the United States, Britain, France, and Germany for the purpose of sharing Chinese railway concessions.

The outbreak of World War I significantly changed the power relationships in the Far East. Whereas the Taft administration had waged an offensive campaign against the spheres in Manchuria, the administration of Woodrow Wilson was forced into a defensive position. In the first months of the war, Japan seized the German sphere in Shantung. This was followed in January 1915 by the presentation to China of the Twenty-one Demands, which included assent to the transfer of German rights in Shantung and a great increase in Japan's rights in southern Manchuria. Japan also demanded rights in eastern Inner Mongolia that would make that area a Japanese sphere. Wilson, Secretary of State William Jennings Bryan, and Robert Lansing attempted, by making concessions to Japan, to influence it to observe restraint. In doing so they made some remarkable statements relating to the Japanese spheres. In a note to Japan drafted by Lansing and sent over Bryan's signature, the United States recognized that territorial contiguity created "special relations" between Japan and the districts of southern Manchuria, eastern Mongolia, and Shantung.

The attempt to restrain Japan was only partly successful. The Japanese settled for considerably less than they had sought in the Twenty-one Demands, but this was probably due more to British than to U.S. influence. In 1917, Lansing, now secretary of state, made another attempt to restrain the Japanese. In doing so, he concluded an exchange of notes with a special Japanese envoy, Kikujiro Ishii, that contained an even more sweeping recognition of Japan's special interests than had been given in 1915. It stated that territorial propinquity gave Japan "special interests" in China, particularly in that part of China contiguous to Japanese possessions. In return for this extraordinary statement, Lansing obtained a secret protocol in which the United States and Japan agreed not to take advantage of conditions in China to seek special rights that would abridge the rights of other friendly states. Again, the endeavor to bridle the Japanese met with only limited success. At the Paris Peace Conference in 1919, Japan won approval for the transfer of the German rights in Shantung, a gain that was softened only by Japan's informal agreement to give up the navy base at Kiaochow.

Many of the goals that the Wilson administration sought in East Asia were finally achieved by the administration of Warren G. Harding at the Washington Conference of 1921–1922. By the Nine-Power Treaty of 6 February 1922, Japan and the other signatories pledged to refrain from seeking new rights in China that would create new spheres of influence or enhance rights in existing spheres. Furthermore, in bilateral negotiations with China during the Washington Conference, Japan gave up all the former German rights in Shantung, retaining only a mortgage on the Tsingtao-to-Tsinan railway line that was sold to China. Later in 1922, Japan agreed to the abrogation of the Lansing-Ishii exchange of notes. Existing historical accounts do not fully explain why Japan pursued such a moderate policy at the Washington Conference. It was in any case a moderation that ended with the seizure of Manchuria in 1931–1933. In 1937 came full-scale war with China, and by the end of 1938, Japan was claiming all of East Asia as its sphere.

Japan's application of the sphere of influence concept to an entire region of the world was not wholly new. The Western Hemisphere had often been referred to as being in the United States sphere as a result of the Monroe Doctrine. In 1940 the sphere concept received another regional application. The Tripartite Pact among Germany, Italy, and Japan in that year, though not specifically using the term "sphere of influence," in essence recognized East Asia as a Japanese sphere and Europe as a German and Italian sphere.

SPHERES OF INFLUENCE SINCE WORLD WAR II

Following World War II, Eastern Europe became a Russian sphere. This was foreshadowed by wartime agreements on spheres that resembled the traditional type. In May 1944, Britain sought U.S. approval for a trade-off giving the Soviet Union a controlling influence in Romania and giving Britain a controlling influence in Greece. Secretary of State Cordell Hull flatly opposed the scheme, fearing that it would lead to a division of Europe into spheres of influence. As he later wrote: "I was not, and am not, a believer in the idea of balance of power or spheres of influence as a means of keeping the peace." Despite Hull's opposition, when the secretary of state went out of town for a few days in June 1944, Roosevelt gave his assent to the arrangement on a three-month trial basis, with the understanding that it was only a wartime agreement. Later, Hull felt that his apprehensions were justified when Churchill and Stalin reached an informal accord in October 1944 giving the Soviets 90 percent predominance in Romania and 75 percent predominance in Bulgaria, Britain a 90 percent predominance in Greece, and specifying an equal sharing of influence in Yugoslavia and Hungary.

Actually, it was Russian power, not wartime agreements, that made Eastern Europe a Russian sphere of influence consisting of satellite states.

Hull's concept of a world without spheres of influence—a world with a broad and effective system of general security—was not to be. The realities of power continued to operate.

U.S. PROTECTORATES SINCE WORLD WAR II

Following World War II, the United States undertook by treaty responsibility for the defense of a number of countries in the Pacific: the Philippines in 1946 (revised in 1951), Japan in 1951, South Korea in 1953, and Taiwan in 1954. The relationships between the United States and these entities were so different in character from the prewar concept of protectorates that it would probably produce more confusion than clarity to use the term "protectorate" in these cases. With the exception of Japan, all have substantial armed forces of their own, and U.S. influence on their domestic affairs and even on their foreign relations is limited. The treaties, again with the exception of Japan, have some measure of mutuality in that they provide for assistance in the western Pacific if the forces of either signatory are attacked. The 1951 treaty between the United States and Japan came closest to the old protectorate concept. By its terms the United States could maintain troops in Japan not only to protect that country but also to defend East Asia. United States troops could, at Japanese request, even be used to quash internal disturbances in Japan. When the treaty was revised in 1960, largely one-sided defense provisions were agreed upon. The United States undertook to protect Japan, while Japan undertook to aid the United States only in case of an attack on U.S. forces on Japanese territory. Under this treaty Japan is certainly a protectorate of the United States in a military sense, but to use that word without qualification to describe the relationship between the first- and third-ranking industrial nations of the world is obviously to give a new definition to the term.

A closer parallel to the traditional concept of protectorates can be seen in the case of the islands of the North Pacific. These islands had been acquired by Germany during the heady years of nineteenth-century imperialism. During World War I, in agreement with its ally Britain, Japan seized the German Islands in the Pacific north of the equator: the Marshall Islands, the Caroline Islands, and the Marianas. At the close of the war, the island groups became a League of Nations mandated territory under the administration of Japan. More than two decades later, during World War II, the islands were the scene of some of the bloodiest battles of the Pacific War, including Saipan and Peleliu. Following Japan's surrender in 1945, the islands were made a United Nations trusteeship territory under U.S. administration. Subsequently, in a process spread over several decades, the UN trusteeship status was ended, replaced in three cases by compacts of free association with the United States and in one case a commonwealth covenant with the United States. In all cases, the United States undertook the responsibility for armed defense and retained a role in the foreign relations of the new entities, at least as related to defense.

It was the relationship between the United States and the Marshall Islands that was the most controversial case. During the trusteeship period, these islands, situated more than two thousand miles southwest of Hawaii, became a testing site for U.S. nuclear weapons. A total of sixty-six nuclear tests were carried out on Bikini (1946–1958) and Enewetak (1948–1958). The operations were conducted with scant consideration for the health and welfare of the islanders. It was not until 1986 that the United States agreed to set up a fund of $150 million to settle claims for compensation. The first payments did not begin until 1992, by which time many suffering from radiation sickness had died.

A compact of free association for the Marshall Islands was drafted in 1982. By that time the United States had overseen the setting up of a locally elected government. The compact provided that the Marshall Islands would constitute a new international entity capable of conducting foreign relations and entering into treaties. The United States, however, was given full authority and responsibility for security and defense, and in recognition of that, the government of the Marshall Islands was obligated to consult with the United States in the conduct of its foreign affairs. The United States agreed to a number of funding arrangements, the largest of which was an annual rent of $170 million for the use of Kwajalein as a missile-testing range. The compact was approved by the islanders in a referendum in 1983. It went into effect in 1986.

It was not until 1990 that the United Nations formally ended the trusteeship status of the Marshall Islands and the other island groups. In 1986, when the Marshall Islands gained free association status, the United States secured a majority vote in the UN Trusteeship Council to end the Pacific islands trusteeships, but the council lacked the authority to make such a change. From the outset of those trusteeships, they had been designated "strategic," and under Articles 82 and 83 of the United Nations Charter, decisions concerning such trusteeship were to be exercised by the United Nations Security Council. In the Security Council, the Soviet representatives threatened a veto. It was only after the collapse of the Soviet Union that the Russians relented. In December 1990, Russia and all other members of the Security Council except Cuba voted to formally end the trusteeship status of the Marshall Islands, the Federated States of Micronesia, Palau, and the Northern Marianas.

The Federated States of Micronesia (formerly the eastern Caroline Islands) took the same path to free association as the Marshall Islands. The federation was made up of four states: Kosrae, Pohnpei, Chuuk, and Yap. Situated to the west of the Marshall Islands, the Federated States stretched eighteen hundred miles from east to west. Chuuk (formerly Truk) had been the Japanese Imperial Fleet's most important central Pacific base during the Pacific War. Today, some sixty Japanese warships lie at the bottom of Chuuk Lagoon. Despite this heritage of war, in the postwar years the United States showed little interest in maintaining a military or naval presence in the Federated States.

The compact of free association that was concluded between the Federated States and the United States was identical with that which applied to the Marshall Islands. In fact, the two compacts were included in a single document. As with the Marshall Islands, it obligated the United States to protect the Federated States of Micronesia, and it gave the United States a consultative role in the foreign affairs of the federated government. The compact went into effect in 1986, although, as noted, the UN did not formally approve the termination of the trusteeship until 1990.

Palau (formerly the Western Caroline Islands), which are directly to the west of the Federated States, agreed to a compact of free association with the United States in 1982, but its coming into force was long delayed. In setting up an elected Palau government in the 1970s, a provision was included in the constitution outlawing the transit and storage of nuclear materials. The United States had no plans to make Palau a nuclear base, but it did not wish to agree to such a restriction when it was accepting the responsibility to protect

Palau. A change in the constitution required passage by a 75 percent vote of the electorate, so it was assumed that the compact (which invalidated the restriction) would require a like majority. Over the period of a decade (1983–1992), seven referenda on the compact were conducted; each time the favorable vote was substantially more than a simple majority but short of the 75 percent mark. Finally, in 1992, a referendum approved a process for adoption of the compact that required only a simple majority vote. The following year the compact was approved by a 68 percent vote of the electorate, and it went into effect in 1994.

The Palauan compact of free association gave the United States exclusive military access to Palau's waters and the right to operate two military bases. As in the case of the other compacts, various financial payments agreed to by the United States meant the continuing financial dependence of Palau upon its former trusteeship overlord.

The people of the Northern Marianas did not opt for a compact of free association, choosing instead a closer relationship with the United States. The Northern Marianas included all the Marianas except Guam, a U.S. territory at the southern end of the island chain. In 1975 the people of the northern area, by a majority of more than 78 percent, approved what was called commonwealth status. Similar to the protectorates of the later nineteenth and early twentieth centuries, the commonwealth covenant gave the United States "complete responsibility for and authority with respect to matters relating to foreign affairs and defense affecting the Northern Mariana Islands." The covenant gave the United States fifty-year leases on three military bases, the largest base being on the island of Tinian.

Implementation of the commonwealth status was long delayed due to apprehension that the Soviet Union would block the termination of the UN trusteeship status. Finally, in 1986, without waiting for UN approval, the commonwealth covenant was instituted. When the Russians ended their resistance to the termination of the Pacific trusteeships in 1991, the Commonwealth of the Northern Marianas was formally freed from UN control along with the island groups that chose free association.

BIBLIOGRAPHY

Beers, Burton Floyd. *Vain Endeavor: Robert Lansing's Attempts to End the American-Japanese Rivalry*. Durham, N.C., 1962. The best treatment of Lansing's policy regarding the Japanese spheres in China.

Bemis, Samuel Flagg. *The Latin American Policy of the United States*. New York, 1943. A good general survey.

Buckley, Thomas H. *The United States and the Washington Conference, 1921–1922*. Knoxville, Tenn., 1970. Contains an excellent chapter on the Nine-Power Treaty relating to spheres of influence in China.

Calder, Bruce J. *The Impact of Intervention: The Dominican Republic During the U.S. Occupation of 1916–1924*. Austin, Tex., 1984. Asserts that U.S. intervention did not emanate from largely economic motives but from strategic considerations.

Challener, Richard D. *Admirals, Generals, and American Foreign Policy, 1898–1914*. Princeton, N.J., 1973. Gives extensive coverage of the military aspects of the protectorate policy.

Esthus, Raymond A. *Theodore Roosevelt and Japan*. Seattle, 1966. Includes an analysis of the Roosevelt administration's policy toward Japan's sphere in southern Manchuria.

Europa Publications. *The Europa World Year Book*. London, annual publication.

Fifield, Russell H. *Woodrow Wilson and the Far East: The Diplomacy of the Shantung Question*. New York, 1952. The standard monograph on the topic.

Griswold, Alfred Whitney. *The Far Eastern Policy of the United States*. New York, 1938. Old but still useful, particularly for McKinley and Wilson administrations.

Healy, David F. *The United States in Cuba, 1898–1902: Generals, Politicians, and the Search for Policy*. Madison, Wis., 1963. Analyzes the development of policy leading to the Platt Amendment.

———. *Gunboat Diplomacy in the Wilson Era: The U.S. Navy in Haiti, 1915–1916*. Madison, Wis., 1976. A detailed and colorful narrative.

———. *Drive to Hegemony: The United States in the Caribbean, 1898–1917*. Madison, Wis., 1988. An indictment of many aspects of U.S. policy.

Hunt, Michael H. *Frontier Defense and the Open Door: Manchuria in Chinese-American Relations, 1895–1911*. New Haven, Conn., 1973. Based on both Chinese and Western sources.

Kamman, William. *A Search for Stability: United States Diplomacy Toward Nicaragua, 1925–1933*. Notre Dame, Ind., 1968. An excellent monograph.

LaFeber, Walter. *The Panama Canal: The Crisis in Historical Perspective.* New York, 1989. An updated edition of the author's study published in 1978; a comprehensive history.

Langer, William Leonard. *The Diplomacy of Imperialism, 1890–1902.* 2d ed. New York, 1951. The most exhaustive treatment of the acquisition of spheres of influence in China.

Langley, Lester D. *The United States and the Caribbean, 1900–1970.* Athens, Ga., 1980. Contains much information on the Caribbean protectorates of the United States.

——. *The Banana Wars: An Inner History of American Empire, 1900–1934.* Lexington, Ky., 1983. Covers U.S. military and financial interventions in Cuba, Mexico, Haiti, the Dominican Republic, and Nicaragua.

Major, John. *Prize Possession: The United States and the Panama Canal, 1903–1979.* Cambridge and New York, 1993. Critical of U.S. paternalism toward Panama.

Miner, Dwight Carroll. *The Fight for the Panama Route: The Story of the Spooner Act and the Hay-Herrán Treaty.* New York, 1940. An excellent account of the acquisition of the Canal Zone and the Panama protectorate.

Monger, George W. *The End of Isolation: British Foreign Policy, 1900–1907.* London, 1963. Excellent study from the British records that includes analyses of the treaties of 1904 and 1907 relating to spheres in Egypt, Morocco, Afghanistan, and Persia.

Munro, Dana G. *Intervention and Dollar Diplomacy in the Caribbean, 1900–1921.* Princeton, N.J., 1964. The most detailed study of the diplomatic aspects of U.S. protectorates policy.

Plummer, Brenda Gayle. *Haiti and the Great Powers, 1902–1915.* Baton Rouge, 1988. Recounts Haiti's relations with the Germans, French, British, and North Americans.

Price, Ernest B. *The Russo-Japanese Treaties of 1907–1916 Concerning Manchuria and Mongolia.* Baltimore, 1933. The standard work.

Schmidt, Hans. *The United States Occupation with Haiti, 1915–1934.* New Brunswick, N.J., 1971. Stresses the cultural impact of American influence.

Scholes, Walter V., and Marie V. Scholes. *The Foreign Policies of the Taft Administration.* Columbia, Mo., 1970. The best account of the beginnings of intervention in Nicaragua.

See also CONSORTIA; DOLLAR DIPLOMACY; EXTRATERRITORIALITY; IMPERIALISM; INTERVENTION AND NONINTERVENTION; MANDATES AND TRUSTEESHIPS; OPEN DOOR POLICY.

PUBLIC OPINION

★ ★ ★ ★ ★

Melvin Small

The public's role in the American foreign policy process is a controversial subject. Generations of diplomats, political theorists, and historians have argued about the nature of the elusive opinion-policy relationship. They have been concerned about the abilities of American leaders to operate according to democratic precepts in a pluralistic international system often dominated by autocratic powers.

In arguing for greater authority in foreign affairs for the proposed new Senate in the *Federalist Papers,* Alexander Hamilton saw the senior house of the U.S. Congress as serving as a defense to the people against their own temporary errors and delusions. Striking a similar theme almost a half-century later, that perceptive observer of the American scene Alexis de Tocqueville was not very sanguine about the prospects for a democratic foreign policy. Writing during a period when the diplomatic activities of the United States were relatively unimportant, he explained:

> Foreign politics demand scarcely any of those qualities which a democracy possesses; and they require, on the contrary, the perfect use of almost all of those faculties in which it is deficient. . . . [A] democracy is unable to regulate the details of an important undertaking, to persevere in a design, and to work out its execution in the presence of serious obstacles. It cannot combine measures with secrecy, and it will not await their consequences with patience. . . . [D]emocracies . . . obey the impulse of passion rather than the suggestions of prudence and . . . abandon a mature design for the gratification of a momentary caprice.

According to Tocqueville and other so-called realists, diplomacy should be the province of a small group of cosmopolitan professionals who perform their duties in secret and with dispatch. Leaders must not encourage their constituents to mix in heady matters of state because the uninformed and unsophisticated mass public is unable to comprehend the subtle rules of the game of nations. Democratic leaders are severely handicapped in diplomatic jousts with authoritarian rulers who are able to contain the foreign policy process within chancellery walls.

Defenders of popular participation in international politics maintain that despite the clumsiness and inefficiency inherent in open diplomacy, the alternative is worse. Leaders who employ devious means to defend a democratic system will, in the long run, pervert or transform that system. At the least, the public and its representatives must have as much influence in the making and execution of foreign policy as they have in domestic policy. A foreign policy constructed and controlled by the people is stronger than one that rests upon a narrow popular base. The victory of the United States in the Cold War can be offered to support that contention.

Historians are just as contentious as political theorists. Despite an enormous amount of rhetoric, speculation, and research, very little is known about the actual relationship between public opinion and foreign policy. Since the late 1940s, survey researchers have explored the dimensions of public opinion while political scientists have considered the ways in which decision makers perceive opinion. Nevertheless, a broad consensus about the nature of the opinion-policy nexus has yet to emerge.

Many studies describe the power of the public and how it has forced presidents into wars and crises against their better judgments. The journalist Walter Lippmann, among others, felt that Tocqueville's prophecies have been fulfilled:

> The people have imposed a veto upon the judgements of informed and responsible officials. They have compelled the governments, which usually knew what would have been wiser, or was necessary, or was more expedient, to be too late with too little, or too long with too much, too pacifist in peace and too bellicose in war, too neutralist or appeasing in negotiation or too

intransigent. Mass opinion has acquired mounting power in this century. It has shown itself to be a dangerous master of decisions when the stakes are life and death.

Lippmann's position is supported by a host of historical legends: that congressional war hawks, responding to popular jingoism, compelled James Madison to ask for war in 1812, during a period of improving British-American relations; that a spirit of manifest destiny swept James K. Polk along in its wake into the Mexican War of 1846; that expansionist fervor and humanitarian impulses created by an irresponsible yellow press propelled William McKinley into war against hapless Spain in 1898; that myopic popular isolationism restrained Franklin D. Roosevelt's realistic anti-Axis program in the late 1930s; that antiwar protesters humbled the once-omnipotent Lyndon Johnson in 1968 and forced both his withdrawal from public life and his de-escalation of the war in Southeast Asia; and that the bitter memories of that war made it difficult for presidents to intervene militarily in the Third World during the last quarter of the twentieth century. All of these examples lend credence to the principle that the public is sovereign in the United States, even when it comes to matters of *weltpolitik.*

But all of those historical cases have been interpreted in a very different fashion. Many reputable historians contend that war hawks were not elected in 1810 and that an unimaginative Madison merely lost control and mindlessly drifted into war in 1812; that Polk was the prime instigator of jingoism in 1845 and 1846 with his blunt messages to Great Britain about the Oregon dispute and his provocative movement of troops into an area claimed by Mexico; that McKinley, who exercised weak leadership in 1897 and early 1898, created a serious political problem for the Republicans—a problem whose solution depended upon a declaration of war against Spain; that Roosevelt underestimated his ability to move the nation and, in any event, was more of an isolationist than an internationalist; that Johnson backtracked in Vietnam because the military policies he had pursued for four years had failed on the battlefield; and that when necessary, as in Grenada in 1983 and the Persian Gulf in 1991, presidents had little trouble convincing their constituents to accept their interventions.

To be sure, there is a certain degree of truth in both sorts of interpretations; but, in the last analysis, a careful reading of American history reveals few clear-cut situations in which public opinion has forced presidents to adopt important foreign policies that they themselves opposed. Furthermore, in most diplomatic confrontations, American decision makers were able to act in secrecy and with dispatch to meet challenges from rivals representing authoritarian systems. Indeed, during his administration, the secretive Richard Nixon may have exercised more personal control over his nation's foreign policy than did his counterpart, Leonid Brezhnev, the ruler of the totalitarian Soviet Union. At the least, there was more genuine debate in his Politburo than in Nixon's National Security Council.

Historians, political scientists, and even the participants themselves report that American decision makers pay little direct attention to public preferences, especially in a crisis. Presidents have maintained that it would be unseemly to worry about the public's often uninformed views, and thus their own political futures, when the nation's security is threatened. All the same, fear of outraged public opinion undoubtedly serves as an implicit veto against such extreme options as the preemptive bombing of North Korean nuclear facilities or unilateral disarmament. Moreover, popularly elected statesmen are loath to adopt policies that could lead to a loss of personal prestige. Thus, with their votes U.S. citizens allegedly hold the ultimate club over the heads of their representatives.

Nevertheless, despite the occasional case of a Robert Kennedy who worried openly about popular reactions to a sneak attack on Cuba in the fall of 1962, most decision makers do not consciously consider public opinion when they discuss responses to external threats. As for that ultimate club, foreign policy has rarely figured prominently in national or local elections. The personalities of the candidates, party loyalties, and domestic politics have obscured such major electoral issues as imperialism in 1900, the League of Nations in 1920, the escalation of the war in Vietnam in 1964, and the apparent renewal of the Cold War in 1984.

It is true, however, that although elections may not frequently turn on foreign policy issues, foreign policy sometimes turns on electoral politics. Beginning in October 1968, Americans became aware of the "October Surprise," a dramatic diplomatic or military démarche in the weeks before an election that appeared to have been orchestrated to affect that election. That year, Lyndon Johnson announced a breakthrough in peace talks with the communists in Vietnam a week before what was going to be a very close election. Four years later, the shoe was on the other foot when Richard Nixon's national security adviser, Henry Kissinger, announced a breakthrough in his peace talks with the North Vietnamese in late October.

Other nations may also "participate" in U.S. elections. The Russian leader Nikita S. Khrushchev claimed he helped elect John F. Kennedy by refusing to release U.S. flyers who had been shot down and captured by the Soviets until Kennedy, and not his opponent Nixon, was elected. In 1988, as Vice President George H. W. Bush genuflected toward the anticommunists in his party during his run for the president, he sent a message to the Soviet premier Mikhail Gorbachev to not pay much attention to his campaign rhetoric about U.S.–Soviet relations.

THE PUBLIC AS GOAL SETTER

The lack of compelling evidence for direct popular influence in diplomatic interaction does not necessarily make American foreign policy undemocratic. On the contrary, theorists see the public as sovereign, because it establishes parameters for action and sets goals for presidents and their agents. Broad national policy is said to originate with the people. For example, during the Cold War, the public's foreign policy mandate was clear. It included the desires to defend U.S. interests around the world against the onslaughts of communism and anti-Americanism, to refrain from direct involvement in unnecessary wars, and to engage in diplomatic conduct becoming to a great democratic power. Theoretically, such a mandate was implemented by policymakers who developed shorter-term tactical programs. This widely accepted view is not without its logical and evidential flaws.

In the first place, because of their preeminent roles in the opinion-making process, presidents generally define the relationship of the United States to international events. Consequently, they can make almost any of their actions appear to defend the national interest and to be within the bounds of decorous democratic foreign policy. Further, the limits that the public ostensibly sets for them are remarkably flexible. They can be expanded because of the exigencies of a changing international climate that, according to the policymaker, demand new approaches. In

early 1946, for example, Americans looked forward to a long period of normalcy and nonentanglement. Apparently, joining the United Nations was all the internationalism they desired. At the time, few would have approved of the permanent stationing of military units in Europe, nor would they have accepted giving away millions of dollars to foreign friends. By 1948, however, the impact of events—events interpreted by the foreign policy establishment—convinced a majority of citizens that unprecedented interventionist activities were needed to maintain national security. The limits that restrained American diplomats in 1946 were expanded by 1948 through a combination of events and propaganda.

The view is also inadequate when analyzed from the bottom up. The abstract differentiation between the public's task of defining strategic interests and the government's task of developing tactical policies is difficult to make operational. During the early 1960s most Americans supported their government's general attempt to stop "communism" in Southeast Asia. Yet, the bombing of North Vietnam, putatively a tactical policy decision implemented to achieve that goal, became a matter for widespread public debate. Both hawks and doves refused to leave the bombing issue to the planners in the Pentagon. And rightly so, for most major military policies are fraught with serious political implications.

In sum, despite widespread scholarly agreement about its basic outlines, the dominant paradigm delineating the public's role is faulty. The suggestion that the public sets goals and limits while the president executes policy does not adequately describe the opinion-policy relationship in American diplomatic history.

The public and the policymaker do interact in a more fundamental way. Historic periods are marked by unique climates of opinion. From time to time, Americans have been more isolationist than expansionist, more tolerant than intolerant, or more pessimistic than optimistic. Such general moods, which develop as a result of a concatenation of social, economic, and, to some degree, psychological factors, cannot be rapidly changed through elite manipulation.

Those who challenge the notion that national mood is impervious to sudden transformation point to the Spanish-American War and the manner in which the yellow press supposedly created mass interventionist hysteria. Interestingly, many of the explosive elements present during the crisis of 1895–1898 were also present during the Cuban Revolution of 1868–1878. However, the earlier stories of atrocities, gun running, assaults on American honor, and the struggle for Cuban freedom did not arouse a population recovering from its tragic and bloody Civil War. During the 1890s, a different generation of Americans was receptive to the inflammatory accounts in the newspapers of William Randolph Hearst and Joseph Pulitzer. The "psychic crisis" of the Gilded Age produced an audience primed for jingoist journalists and politicians.

Similarly, Richard Nixon, the architect of détente with the People's Republic of China in 1972, could not have proposed such a démarche in 1956. According to most indicators of public opinion, American citizens then would not have been willing to consider such a drastic reorientation of national policy. No one could have been elected to a position of power in 1956 who talked openly about sitting down with Mao Zedong, the "aggressor" in the Korean War. Five years later, President John F. Kennedy, a Democrat from the party that "lost" China in 1949, believed it impossible to alter U.S. policy in Asia. A majority of Americans would first have to unlearn the propaganda lessons of the early 1950s before such a dramatic program could be safely broached by a national leader.

In the years after the Vietnam War, the American public was in no mood to intervene in other distant struggles in the Third World. It is possible that had the public not felt so strongly about this issue, Ronald Reagan would have intervened with U.S. troops in El Salvador in 1981. And while Americans had apparently licked their so-called Vietnam syndrome by 1991, when George H. W. Bush led the nation into war in the Persian Gulf, Bush was convinced he had to terminate the war before marching on Baghdad because he feared his constituents would not support a longer war or more GI casualties. Bush's chair of the Joint Chiefs of Staff, General Colin Powell, supported that decision with what came to be called the Powell Doctrine. The United States could not again participate in a lengthy, Vietnam-style war unless the public expressed enthusiasm about such a venture at the outset.

PRESIDENTIAL POWERS

Aside from participating in the development of a climate of opinion and possessing a latent electoral veto over major foreign policy decisions—two not insignificant functions—the public's direct influence in the making of foreign policy is minimal. Here, more than in domestic affairs, presidents are dominant over both Congress and the mass public. Their ability to create opinion and dominate the opposition assures them a relatively free hand in planning and executing foreign policies.

Because of the vast information-gathering and information-disseminating facilities at their disposal and because they are the only truly national spokespersons, presidents are the most important source of information on foreign affairs. Through their public attention to specific international problems, they can go a long way toward determining the agenda of the national foreign policy debate. Although congressional committees and the mass media have developed their own informational and promotional capabilities, until recently they have not commanded the resources available to the president. It was only during the last decade of the twentieth century that round-the-clock cable television news and Internet sources, available everywhere around the world, began to level the information and propaganda playing fields.

The president's ability to conduct day-to-day diplomacy, free from public pressures, rests on the fact that most Americans are not very interested in esoteric international issues. Naturally, some obscure policies that the public does not care to monitor eventually become major issues. One such example was the unpublicized U.S. assistance to forces opposing Salvador Allende's socialist regime in Chile during the early 1970s.

If presidents' freedom of action in the development of foreign policy depends in good measure upon public inattention, their power in a crisis depends upon public helplessness. During sudden crises citizens must accept their accounts of fast-breaking events or risk further loss of American lives. In May 1846, Americans had no option but to accept President Polk's misleading account of the way American blood had been shed on American soil by Mexican soldiers. Given the apparent need for immediate retaliation and Polk's relative credibility, the public rallied behind his policies and asked questions later. In similar situations Americans supported their leaders during the Korean crisis in the summer of 1950 and the Gulf of Tonkin incident in August 1964. Surprisingly, the public does not always withdraw its support when crisis diplomacy or military intervention fails. After the Bay of Pigs fiasco in April 1961, John F. Kennedy's popularity rose in the polls, as did Jimmy Carter's after the failed rescue mission in Iran in April 1980.

In noncrisis periods the president can develop support for a program by selectively suppressing or releasing secret information. Madison published letters from a turncoat British spy in an attempt to demonstrate that Federalists who challenged his British policies had been conspiring with the enemy. More than a century later, Woodrow Wilson's release of the purloined Zimmermann telegram contributed to the onrushing torrent of anti-German sentiment on the eve of American entry into World War I.

As for the suppression of important information, Harry S. Truman decided to withhold General Albert C. Wedemeyer's 1947 report on China because it was potentially offensive to Jiang Jie-shī (Chiang Kai-shek). More important, its conclusions ran counter to official policies. From 1970 to 1973, Richard Nixon suppressed information on the bombing of Cambodia while some of his aides participated in a cover-up that involved falsification of military records. In one of the most celebrated cases of all, Franklin D. Roosevelt concealed the extent of his involvement as a silent partner in the Allied effort in World War II for fear that such revelations might lead to his electoral defeat and a change in the direction of national policy. His defenders contend that the president and his advisers had a better grasp of what constituted national security than did the well-meaning but untutored public. Like the doctor who tells his patient that the bitter but vitally important medicine tastes good, Roosevelt obscured the issues and misled the people for their own alleged best interests.

Such a position might seem tenable in the light of the times, but its acceptance as a legitimate procedure for all presidents is unlikely. Many of those sympathizing with Roosevelt's position were displeased when Lyndon Johnson was not entirely forthcoming with the electorate about his plans for the war in Vietnam during the 1964 election campaign. Yet both presidents later cited national security in defense of their tactics.

Conceivably, an alert, crusading press can counterbalance the awesome power of the president to mold foreign policy opinions. However, editors move with caution when it comes to printing material potentially detrimental to national security. The New York Times learned of the 1961 Bay of Pigs operation on the eve of the attack. After conferring with the White House, its editors decided not to run the story because they were convinced that the success of that covert operation was a matter of the highest national interest. In a related vein, when columnist Jack Anderson published excerpts from the minutes of the National Security Council during the Bangladesh war of 1971, many reporters joined with the government to criticize his "impropriety." Nixon's aides went beyond mere criticism as they contemplated ways to do away with the columnist who told Americans that contrary to what the White House was saying, the administration was supporting the rapists of West Pakistan against the freedom fighters in East Pakistan.

In general, the press has been far more circumspect in printing diplomatic than domestic exclusives. For journalists, it is one thing to uncover scandals and quite another to publish material that could render aid and comfort to a foreign enemy. Since the 1990s, however, unaffiliated investigative reporters on the Internet have not been so circumspect.

Despite their general mastery of the opinion problem, American leaders have traditionally claimed that the people are important to them as a source of support and inspiration. Since the Jacksonian period, most have probably believed that they were duty-bound to heed the people. Thus, they have constantly attempted to assess public opinion, or at least the opinions of relevant publics. Of course, the opinion evaluated and used by decision makers does not always meet the social scientists' definition of public opinion.

Public officials have traditionally relied heavily upon newspapers and other mass media to discover what people are thinking about. The media, however, are better indicators of the topics in the current foreign policy debate than of the range of opinions on those topics. Despite charges about the biases of the "liberal press," most U.S. newspapers have been owned by Republicans who fill their editorial pages with materials that do not always represent majority opinion in their communities.

Many leaders consider newspaper and magazine columnists to be peers whose approval they covet. Occasionally, they use friendly journalists to float trial balloons for them, so that they can test the political waters before committing themselves to a new course. In some cases columnists may become directly enmeshed in the policy process. In the fall of 1962, Walter Lippmann proposed the dismantling of U.S. missile bases in Turkey as a quid pro quo for the dismantling of Russian bases in Cuba. Nikita Khrushchev mistakenly interpreted the trade-off presented by

America's most distinguished columnist as a cue from the White House. This misunderstanding about the nature of Lippmann's relationship to the inner circles of the Kennedy administration contributed to the tension during the Cuban missile crisis. Moscow may have been confused by the fact that the Americans were using John Scali, a television journalist, as an unofficial go-between with one of their diplomats during the affair.

Congress has been the policymakers' second most important source for public opinion. Primarily, they are concerned about the activities of committees with interests in foreign affairs, but they also view senators and representatives as reflecting constituents' interests. From time to time such an interpretation of opinion on Capitol Hill has affected policy outcomes. During the late 1930s, President Roosevelt may have underestimated the public's interventionist sentiment when he treated congressional isolationism as an accurate reflection of the national mood. Today, social scientists suggest that though legislators may reflect the majority opinion in their respective districts on domestic issues, they frequently support foreign policies that run counter to their constituents' preferences. In part, they tend to vote their consciences or party lines on international issues because foreign policy is not important to their constituents. In most cases, members of Congress will be neither rewarded nor punished for their endeavors in the international sphere.

Even when they attempt to reflect faithfully their districts' foreign policy attitudes, the aggregation of their views is not always an accurate reflection of national public opinion. After all, there is no guarantee that national opinion leaders, to whom the president looks for guidance, will share the opinions of local leaders to whom legislators may listen.

During the first twenty years of the Cold War, the handful of congressional critics of presidential foreign policy on both sides of the aisle was not influential. The concept of bipartisanship meant that the opposition was expected to approve executive programs while the president went through the motions of prior consultation. As a product in part of the Vietnam War, in the late 1960s, Congress began to flex its long-atrophied muscles and offer programs and ideas independent of the president and, to some degree, more representative of the range of opinions in the country.

Since the 1930s, policymakers have employed polls as a third indicator of opinion. Even the best of them, however, are not always reliable, especially when they attempt to elicit opinions on foreign affairs. Survey instruments do not lend themselves to sophisticated treatment of such questions and, moreover, rarely cover enough contingencies to be of immediate use to decision makers. During the months before the attack on Pearl Harbor, a majority of those polled thought that the United States would go to war in the near future and recommended such a course if it appeared that England was about to go under. But up to December 1941, only a very small minority told interviewers that they favored an immediate declaration of war. It is impossible to determine on the basis of these data how Americans would have responded to a presidential request for war in the absence of a direct attack on U.S. territory. In addition, some polls are worded so ambiguously that antagonists derive support from the same poll. So it was during the 1960s, when hawks and doves often utilized the same poll to prove that they spoke for the majority concerning the Vietnam involvement. During the last decade of the twentieth century, particularly during the administration of Bill Clinton, policymakers used their own sophisticated polling techniques and focus groups to see how various foreign initiatives might be received by the public. This reliance on first trying out foreign policies on focus groups drew a good deal of criticism during the presidential campaign in 2000 from those who argued that presidents must do what they think is right without checking the nation's pulse and then lead the public to accept their policies.

Phone calls, mail and e-mail, telegrams, and faxes received by the White House and other executive branches represent a fourth source of information about public opinion for the president. Modern administrations keep careful count of the weekly "scores" on specific issues, paying attention to communication that does not appear to be mass-produced by a lobby or political organization. Presidents view significant changes in the direction of opinion or in the number of complaints or commendations on an issue as possibly representing shifts in national public opinion, even though they understand that their sample is very small and hardly a random one. When the mail flow is going their way, presidents often trumpet the news, hoping to affect those who did not write in to climb aboard the bandwagon. Richard Nixon took this part of the activity so seriously that he organized secret Republican operatives around the country to send in supportive letters and telegrams on demand after a speech or a foreign policy initiative.

⭑ ⭑ ⭑ ⭑ ⭑

NIXON AND THE VIETNAM WAR

When Richard Nixon became president in 1969, he vowed not to make the mistakes his predecessor, Lyndon Johnson, had made in conducting foreign policy. In particular, he was most concerned with the way some elements in the public had affected Johnson's policies in Southeast Asia through telegenic mass demonstrations and other dissenting actions of their anti–Vietnam War movement. Foreign policy should not be made in the street, he and his national security adviser, Henry Kissinger, insisted. They wanted to demonstrate that they could operate just as their foes did in the communist bloc, unencumbered by domestic opinion.

On 15 July 1969, Nixon sent the North Vietnamese leader Ho Chi Minh a secret ultimatum that demanded, in effect: Soften your negotiating position for ending the war in Vietnam by 1 November or face a new and potentially devastating military escalation in the war. Soon after, White House security aides began considering a variety of options that would mete out punishment if Ho failed to meet the president halfway. At the time that Nixon sent his ultimatum, the antiwar movement was relatively dormant, giving the new president a brief honeymoon while he fulfilled his campaign promise to bring the war in Vietnam to a speedy conclusion. When this did not happen by that summer, activists began to plan for a new series of demonstrations against the war. On 15 October 1969, protesters held their largest and most successful antiwar action of the entire war, the Moratorium. In a decentralized series of mostly quite dignified and decorous demonstrations, marches, and prayer vigils, more than two million Americans in some 200 cities took time off from work or school to send the message to Washington that they were displeased with the pace of withdrawal from Vietnam. More important for Nixon, the tone was liberal, not radical, the participants more middle-class adults than hippies. Even Lyndon Johnson's chief negotiator at the Paris peace talks, the distinguished diplomat W. Averell Harriman, took part in the ceremonies. And Moratorium leaders promised another such demonstration every month until the war in Vietnam ended.

Nixon was astonished by the breadth and depth of antiwar sentiment. When the North Vietnamese called his bluff and failed to respond to his ultimatum on 1 November, he decided not to go through with any of the retaliatory "savage blows" planned by his aides. Although the vast support for the Moratorium was not the only reason why he chose not to escalate, it weighed heavily with him. Indeed, it compelled him to go on the offensive against the antiwar movement, beginning with his celebrated Silent Majority speech of 3 November and with a concurrent campaign against the allegedly antiwar liberal media, spearheaded by Vice President Spiro T. Agnew. When the time came again to escalate, Nixon hoped to neutralize if not destroy those who disagreed in public with his policies in Vietnam.

Last, and most important, politicians claim they have developed finely tuned antennae that enable them to "sense" public opinion. Through an unscientific sampling of opinion from newspapers, Congress, and the polls, and from talking to family members, friends, advisers, and influential leaders, they contend that they can accurately read public opinion on any major issue. Harry Truman told his friends that the polls were wrong in 1948. As he traveled across the nation, he sensed a swing to the Democrats that did not show up in the polls.

To some degree Truman's faith in his political intuition was warranted. Social scientists report that leaders of small groups are better able to assess the range of opinion in their groups than other members are, and, in fact, their rise to leadership status may relate to their superior ability to assess group opinion.

Nevertheless, the politicians' antennae sometimes pick up only opinions that conform to their preconceived notions. Thus, when William McKinley toured the country in 1898 to determine what Americans thought of expansion, he apparently saw and heard only those who favored acquisition of the Philippines. In a slightly different case in the fall of 1937, Franklin D. Roosevelt publicly proposed that the United States begin to take a more active role in curbing expansionists in Asia and Europe. According to most opinion indicators available today, a majority of Americans supported his bold quarantine speech. However, before the fact, the president had convinced himself that his remarks would launch a storm of isolationist protest. Consequently, after scanning the newspapers, telegrams, and letters, he found more opposition than was merited by the empirical data. It is irrelevant to students of the foreign policy process that presidents and their advisers often assess public opinion in an unscientific manner and confuse opinions stated publicly with public opinion. When officials act on the basis of an inaccurate reading of opinion, the opinions they hear represent effective public opinion. Naturally, this might indicate that they use public opinion to rationalize or justify a course already decided upon.

The public is usually most important to the decision maker after a major policy has been implemented. At that point, dissenters who challenge both the legitimacy of the policy and presidential authority may be heard. In most cases, presidents have been able to cope with those who oppose their foreign programs. When they are confronted with some negative and little positive reaction to a policy, they can argue that the absence of widespread dissent is the same as tacit support—the silent majority assents by remaining silent. When the ranks of the dissenters swell in Congress and in the media, presidents can dismiss them as partisans who sacrifice national security for political gain. When, as in the 1960s, hundreds of thousands of dissenters march on Washington and support moratoriums, presidents can call attention to the 250 million who stay home. Most citizens would never think of protesting publicly or marching in open opposition to an official foreign policy. Such behavior appears unpatriotic, especially when it is confounded by officials and the media, sometimes purposely, with the scattered violence and revolutionary rhetoric present on the fringes of contemporary mass protests.

In general, presidents can secure their positions by assailing critics for their irresponsibility—they do not know what the presidents know, nor do they have access to the intelligence reports that flow across a president's desk. Furthermore, critics lack knowledge of the intricate linkages between all diplomatic activities from Asia to Latin America. However, this line of argumentation lost some of its power after the 1970s. Many of the more sensational revelations contained in the *Pentagon Papers* merely documented rumors and leaks that perceptive citizens gleaned from fragmentary accounts in the media during the 1960s. The spirited public debates over the wisdom of intervention in Vietnam demonstrated that critics in the opposition often have as accu-rate intelligence and knowledge about the issues as those in the White House.

In the last analysis, presidents can usually contain their critics because they hold the office of president, the most visible symbol of the American nation. Many who may privately express skepticism about certain foreign policies are reluctant to speak up for fear of insulting the dignity of the presidency and, perhaps, the prestige of the United States in the international arena.

The power of the president to mold opinion has been enhanced in the twentieth century by electronic media. During much of American history, national leaders encountered difficulties when they tried to appeal to the mass public. In the 1840s, James K. Polk threatened to "go to the people" whenever Congress challenged him. His threat, however, lacked credibility because he did not possess the physical means to reach them. Almost seventy-five years later, Woodrow Wilson might have succeeded in developing irresistible public pressure for his League of Nations had national radio hookups been available.

In the 1920s radio began to play an important role in the political life of the nation. Franklin D. Roosevelt, a consummate master of the new medium, increased his popular support through frequent direct contact with the public. Television, in the right hands, is an even more powerful tool than radio. During the period following World War II, Americans began to suffer from information overload, a condition brought on by constant bombardment with all sorts of material on complex problems. This condition can produce both frustration and confusion. It is only natural, therefore, that Americans turn to the president for relief; he appears on television as a reassuring father figure to simplify reality and ease anxiety. During most of the post–World War II era, contemporary presidents enjoyed easy access to the airwaves. Even when network executives were skeptical about the importance of a presidential speech or a press conference, they could not resist White House demands for free airtime. According to the journalist Tom Wicker, writing in October 1974:

> This is a Presidential "power" that no one wrote into the Constitution, or even "implied" in that document. . . . It is the power to command a vast audience almost at will, and to appear before that audience in all the impressive roles a President can play—from manager of the economy to Commander in Chief. . . . This "power" . . . gives a President an enormous advantage over his political opposition, as well as over the other branches of govern-

ment, in molding opinion. It magnifies a thousandfold what Theodore Roosevelt, long before television, called the "bully pulpit" of the Presidency.

Naturally, after presidents lose credibility, even the cleverest television and media experts are unable to help them regain their audiences. And with the advent of cable television, which meant that Americans could view scores of stations, the major networks began to refuse to carry many presidential appearances, arguing that interested viewers could always find the president on a public-service channel.

Presidents have been assisted by agencies and departments of the executive branch in their dealings with the public. The Department of State has assumed the major responsibility in foreign affairs. Through the years it has been more interested in information and lobbying functions than in survey research. In 1909, Secretary of State Philander C. Knox established the Division of Information, which was responsible for placing news releases into newspapers and other information channels. In 1934 the department became especially active when it launched a lobbying campaign to assist passage of Secretary of State Cordell Hull's Reciprocal Trade Agreements Act. During World War II, the department began systematically to survey the press and to provide opinion studies to foreign service officers. In 1944 all of its information functions were placed under an assistant secretary for public affairs. During the Cold War, the promotional aspects of the department's work with the public were expanded through liaison with such influential private foreign policy groups as the Council on Foreign Relations and the Foreign Policy Association.

The government has had one unfortunate experience with a formal propaganda agency. The Committee on Public Information (also known as the Creel Committee), operating during World War I, angered legislators and other influential leaders because of the methods it used to sell the war effort to Americans. When the Office of War Information was established during World War II, Congress explicitly prohibited domestic propaganda work. The United States Information Agency and the Voice of America are similarly banned from operating in the United States.

WHO IS THE PUBLIC?

No matter how we assess the public's role in the foreign policymaking process, Americans do have opinions on international affairs. The range of their attitudes, knowledge, and interest is wide. As there are many opinions, so are there many publics.

At the apex of the pyramidal structure often used to depict the American polity is a small group of opinion makers: business leaders, politicians, statesmen, publishers, journalists, intellectuals, and organizational spokespersons. There are four basic types of opinion makers. In descending order of importance, they are national multi-issue opinion makers, such as senators; national single-issue opinion makers, such as presidents of corporations with defense contracts; local multi-issue opinion makers, such as the president of a large bank; and local single-issue opinion makers, such as a professor of Islamic studies at a local university.

This elite, which is involved with international affairs in its daily professional capacities, constitutes the policymakers' primary constituency. Many members of this foreign policy establishment periodically serve in either official or advisory government positions. As opinion makers they transmit their ideas through the media to the rest of the population. In their ancillary role as opinion submitters, they present their policy preferences to those in power. These opinion makers influence, articulate, and represent mass opinion. In such relatively low-profile areas as tariff and trade policies (except for such issues as the North American Free Trade Agreement and the World Trade Organization), they may be the only interested public. Consequently, they can exercise a good deal of influence in the policymaking process. Through their lobbies, pressure groups, and informal contacts with decision makers, they are often able to ensure that national policy serves their needs.

Through most of American history a disproportionate number of opinion makers lived along the eastern seaboard. By the mid-twentieth century, however, they were more widely dispersed throughout the country. Although New York City still maintained its hegemony as the national media and financial capital, new opinion makers in regional power centers like Atlanta and Los Angeles began to play leading roles in the foreign policymaking process.

Below this rarefied group of powerful individuals is a segment of the population, perhaps as large as 10 percent, that has been labeled "the attentive public." This well-educated group, whose composition can shift from issue to issue, is informed about foreign affairs and may be mobilized for some form of political activism. These members of the middle and upper-middle class read intellectual magazines and books, belong to organizations and pressure groups with continuing interests in problems in the international sphere, and are likely to be among those who sign petitions and write letters to politicians. The attentive public helps to transmit ideas and information from opinion makers to the rest of the population through interpersonal communications. Much of the foreign policy debate takes place within the ranks of the attentive public, the primary audience for the opinion makers on most issues.

The remainder of the population, a vast and generally silent majority, is basically disinterested in most diplomatic events and uninformed about the nature of the international system. Wars and crises that result in banner headlines or preemption of popular television shows will arouse them, but they ignore the day-to-day operation of the foreign policy machine. Furthermore, they rarely contemplate the broad strategic concerns that define the American national interest.

The mass public is latently powerful. On occasion it can be persuaded to exert pressure upon the directors of the nation's foreign policy, or even to counterbalance more articulate critics among opinion makers and the attentive public. When Lyndon Johnson and Richard Nixon began to lose the backing of the foreign policy establishment, they appealed to the silent majority for support of their Vietnam policies.

The static pyramidal structure masks some of the behavioral interaction among the three groups. One of the leading students of the issue, James N. Rosenau, proposes the analogy of a gigantic theater featuring daily dramas of international intrigue on its stage. Seated in a disproportionately large and distant balcony, the mass public is unable to see and hear much of the action and, consequently, becomes involved only when the actors reach dramatic peaks. The attentive public, in the much smaller orchestra section, follows the performance closely and even helps those from the balcony whom it meets during intermissions. The players or opinion makers on stage variously direct their attentions to other actors, to specific groups in the orchestra, and, occasionally, to those in the balcony. From time to time, almost everyone within the theater is engaged in activities simultaneously, although the majority in the balcony only rarely applauds or boos.

The American public's ignorance of and disinterest in international affairs is not unique. Sur-

veys tell us that most people in most countries are little concerned with diplomacy. Nevertheless, when compared with their peers in western Europe, Americans tend to score lower on questions demanding knowledge of the outside world.

This situation appalls many observers. Americans are better-educated and more literate today than they have ever been. Print and electronic mass media provide their audiences with more essential information than was available to the decision makers themselves in the nineteenth and early twentieth centuries. Nonetheless, the public is still woefully uninformed about foreign affairs. As late as 1964, more than one-quarter of those polled in a national survey did not know that a communist regime, which had been in power since 1949, ruled on the mainland of China. During the same period, only a handful of Americans could distinguish among Prince Souvanna Phouma, General Phoumi Nosavan, and Prince Souphanouvong, the three rival leaders contending for power in Laos, a country to which millions of dollars and some U.S. military personnel had been committed. In 1997, only 5 percent of the population could name one European nation that was a candidate for membership in NATO. Paradoxically, in earlier days, despite primitive means of communication, the average American probably was better-informed about foreign affairs than he or she is now. Then, boundary disputes and tariff imbroglios not only were diplomatic problems but also dominated the domestic political debate and determined the health of the economy. Of course, the U.S. role in the international system was not very complicated during the first century and a half of American history.

According to several influential scholars, the widespread disinterest in many political issues is not necessarily an undesirable feature of contemporary American democracy. As long as the majority of the uninformed and noncosmopolitan mass public is disinterested, leaders do not have to worry about irrational inputs into the foreign policy process. Indeed, some theorists contend that democracy in a large polity depends upon mass apathy in order to function effectively. If all Americans were to become interested, informed, and active in the political process, decision makers would be subject to constant crosscutting pressures that would render them incapable of performing their duties. Such a model of the civic culture in the United States disturbs some commentators. They call attention, among other things, to a period in the early 1960s when, insulated from public opinion, the government made decisions about political and military commitments to South Vietnam that had tragic consequences for Americans and Vietnamese alike. Had more Americans been aware of the covert and, at the time, relatively obscure programs, the ensuing ventilation of the issues might have led to the development of alternate policies for South Vietnam. The mass public is not always correct in its assessment of prudent foreign policies, but it can monitor and challenge decision makers who may be moving along dangerous pathways.

THE MEDIA AND THE PUBLIC

The American public's lack of interest in and information about foreign affairs is intimately related to the relative lack of interest displayed in such topics by their news and informational organs. Except for a handful of cosmopolitan dailies, few newspapers maintain a staff of foreign correspondents or offer many column inches of international news. Most rely upon one of the major wire services for whatever foreign news they see fit to print. By 2000, the Associated Press, which had come to dominate the wire services in the United States, was used by 1,700 U.S. newspapers and 5,000 U.S. radio and television outlets. The most influential shapers of media presentations of international problems may be the handful of journalists who produce the daily news budgets for the wire services. The *New York Times* plays a comparable role, particularly for the editors of the television networks' nightly newscasts, who, like most journalists and politicians, consider its judgment about what is important foreign news preeminent among all newspapers.

Electronic media bring foreign news to Americans over regularly scheduled news broadcasts and special programs. For the most part, however, their treatments lack the continuity and background material that would enable their audience to make sense out of a one-minute report on a riot in Nigeria or a thirty-second reference to the fall of the Euro. Television time is so expensive, and the time allocated to news so limited, that viewers are afforded only fleeting, disjointed glimpses of complex international events. News of body counts, bombings, and inflammatory rhetoric are treated without concern for the historical processes in which they are embedded. Only when there is a major crisis do some networks, particularly the cable news networks, offer

sustained treatment of an international problem that goes beyond the brief snapshot of the sensational happening. And even then, most viewers, except "news junkies," quickly begin to surf other channels to find lighter programming.

Publishers and editors are convinced that, except in times of crisis, foreign news does not attract large enough audiences to satisfy the demands of their cost accountants. Although they probably are correct in their judgment, a feedback process is at work here. The directors of the mass media perceive their audience as uninterested in most stories with international datelines. Consequently, they offer a skimpy diet of such materials. Presented with such fare, the audience will never become either informed about or interested in international affairs. Whatever the explanation for public and media disinterest in such news, the situation is unlikely to change radically in the foreseeable future. The increasingly complicated diplomatic arena, with its numerous international organizations and nations no longer operating in a simpler bipolar world, makes the task of understanding foreign policy more difficult than it has ever been and, perhaps, not worth the effort for most Americans. After all, to become competent in international affairs in the 1990s, one had to know something about the history of the Balkans, the nature of Islamic fundamentalism, and the social structure of the Peruvian peasantry. In the 2000 election campaign, many Americans sympathized with the Republican presidential candidate George W. Bush, who not only had a difficult time pronouncing "foreign" names but often could not remember them at all. This lack of interest in learning about the world intensified after the Cold War ended and the international system became a less dangerous but also far more complicated place for most citizens.

SOURCES OF THE PUBLIC'S OPINIONS

Although the vast majority of Americans do not closely follow foreign affairs, they do express opinions about foreign countries and problems of peace and war. These opinions, as well as their underlying attitudinal and value structures, are developed in various ways from a variety of sources. Quite often people form attitudes about public affairs because of factors that may have nothing to do with the merits of a case.

An individual's attitude toward foreign policy is determined in part by his or her educational experiences, religious affiliation, age, place of residence, and even sex. Citizens belonging to the same cohorts tend to share similar foreign policy attitudes. College graduates are more likely to be internationalists than people with a high-school education; Catholics are more likely to be hostile to socialist nations than non-Catholics; young people in the 1990s were more friendly to the Japanese than those who remembered Pearl Harbor; midwesterners are usually more isolationist than easterners and westerners; and women tend to be less militaristic than men. All of these rather simplistic dichotomous generalizations are more complicated than they appear at first glance. For example, midwesterners may be isolationist because they live hundreds of miles from the coasts, or because farmers are more isolationist than city dwellers, or for several other reasons. Young people may be relatively friendly to Japanese because they are more tolerant of Asians in general, or because they have learned to understand the Japanese point of view in 1941, or because they harbor guilt feelings about the atomic bombings of Hiroshima and Nagasaki in 1945.

The groups to which an individual belongs are not the only predictors of foreign policy attitudes. Psychological and personality factors also influence, and may even determine, political attitudes. In one of the most famous explorations in this area, researchers discovered that those who score high on the "F" or authoritarian scale are often xenophobic and militaristic, while those with low scores are more tolerant of foreigners and more pacific. The authoritarian and other specific personality types are affected by the pattern of the individuals' relationship to their parents, their sexual experiences, and their career development. In one study of the impact of personality on foreign policy attitudes, psychologists theorized that a subject was pro-Russian during the 1950s because his mother had been an oppressively dominant factor during his childhood. At the other end of the political spectrum, a subject's violent Russophobia was attributed to his need to display the courage and toughness that he lacked as a youth. Interestingly, it is likely that the more important a public issue is for an individual, the more his or her attitudes will be determined by such psychological factors.

Regardless of the social or personality group to which one belongs, people the world over are generally suspicious of outsiders, whether those outsiders represent a different church, commu-

nity, or country. Such suspicions increase in inverse proportion to knowledge. Since many Americans lack knowledge of other nations, they often view foreigners both in negative and in stereotypical terms. Stereotypes that simplify a complicated world are most comforting when the individual who relies upon them is not exposed to dissonant information.

For many Americans, and a good many Europeans, Latins are lazy, Jews are shrewd, and Arabs are terrorists. Not all stereotypes are negative. The smaller and less threatening the country, the more likely Americans are to admire its people. Charming and peaceful countries like the Denmark of Hans Christian Andersen and the Switzerland of hardy democrats have long had pleasant images in the United States. Stereotypes for larger and more powerful states are usually more ambiguous. Depending upon the specific historical situation, the positive or negative components of those stereotypes may be dominant. Although at times Americans have been attracted to the polite and clever Chinese seen in the Charlie Chan character, they have at other times been fearful of the fiendish Mandarin Fu Manchu. Germans have been esteemed for their efficiency and cleanliness but also despised for their arrogance and brutality. During the 1940s, Russians went from godless communist conspirators to partisan freedom fighters and then back to godless communist conspirators in a matter of eight years.

In some cases, Americans have confused a country's foreign policy with its nationals. However, when asked about this distinction, they respond that they have nothing against ordinary folk in a rival state, only the ruling class. Indeed, they express sympathy for those who live under dictatorial regimes. All too often Americans have assumed that such benighted people must be hostile to their overlords. This sort of analysis led some to conclude, during the early years of the war in Vietnam, that the North Vietnamese and Vietcong performed so well in the field because they were either drugged or chained to their weapons. Similarly, in the 1990s many Americans believed that the people of Iraq could not wait to overthrow their evil dictator, Saddam Hussein.

The Soviet-American relationship during the Cold War produced the intriguing hypothesis that the antagonists tended to view each other in terms of a mirror image. That is, each side saw its rival as its polar opposite. Russians viewed themselves as defensive and conciliatory and Americans as offensive and refractory, while Americans reversed these images. Such an interpretation is supported by the general psychological principle of projection, in which individuals project their own character flaws onto those whom they dislike. As they emerged from the crushing Vietnam experience in the 1970s, Americans became more self-critical and began to see themselves as others saw them. The mirror-image phenomenon of the 1950s was replaced by a more realistic view of America's role and actions in the international system, at least for a while. Such realistic introspection did not sit well with many citizens who rallied to their old vision of national superiority under the administration of Ronald Reagan.

Although American images of foreign countries may shift from generation to generation, groups organized around their ethnic origins often constitute permanent lobbies for their homelands. Such Americans have been active throughout American diplomatic history. The mythical melting pot has failed to create a new American; even to the fourth and fifth generations, many citizens cling to their original nationality. In diplomatic and military disputes that do not directly involve the United States, German Americans, Polish Americans, and Arab Americans, among others, tend to support their homelands. Often this support is given without regard to the national interest of their adopted country. Fenians of Irish origin tried to bring England and the United States to war in the 1860s. During World War I, German Americans vigorously contested Woodrow Wilson's drift toward the British and ultimately his decision for war. Throughout much of the post–World War II era, Jewish Americans exercised a powerful influence, if not a veto, over U.S. Middle East policy. Cuban Americans played a similar role in affecting the nature of U.S. policy toward Cuba under Fidel Castro.

The ethnically based lobby is only one type of mass pressure group. Other segments of the public can be mobilized because of shared economic interests. In the months before the outbreak of the War of 1812, midwestern farmers agitated for war against England because they blamed their depressed condition on the British Navigation Acts. In the late twentieth century, New England fishermen pressured the State Department to support measures that would keep Russian and other competitors away from their traditional fishing grounds, while most corporate leaders pressured Washington to break down tariff barriers through free-trade and other international organizations.

Ideology can also arouse citizens to action. During the 1930s, many American Catholics worked to prevent the administration of Franklin D. Roosevelt from permitting arms sales to the Republican government of Spain. Conversely, many college students who saw the Spanish Republicans as heroic antifascists attempted to force Roosevelt to relax the arms embargo. During the 1950s, the conservative Committee of One Million was a powerful voice in the debate over America's China policy. Two decades later, a comparable anticommunist group, the Committee on the Present Danger, exercised great influence within the Republican Party in destroying support for Nixon and Ford's policy of détente with the Soviet Union.

Although, from time to time, special interest groups have been able to play powerful roles in American diplomatic history, they have not been as influential in the shaping of foreign policy as they have been in domestic policy. For the most part, American diplomats have been able either to ignore them or to play them off against one another.

CONCLUSION

Wherever we probe in our study of public opinion and foreign policy, we encounter frustrating complexities and ambiguities. Political theorists and historians disagree about the ways the public ought to influence foreign policy and the dimensions of the actual nature of the relationship in American history. Most contend that presidents are somehow constrained by a public that defines broad national goals and sets parameters for action. Yet the presidents' preeminence in the opinion-making process guarantees them almost as much freedom in the international arena as leaders from less democratic systems. The public itself is not monolithic. Several publics possess varying degrees of knowledge of, interest in, and influence on foreign policy. Individuals develop foreign policy attitudes because of exposure to events and as a result of socioeconomic status and personality development.

The wealth of sophisticated research produced by social scientists since World War II underscores the gaps in knowledge about the opinion-policy relationship. Although we know much more about the origins of foreign policy attitudes, as well as the world of the decision maker, the precise nature of the opinion-policy nexus still eludes us. Because of the questions raised about the meaning of the Vietnam experience for the American democratic system, scholars and statesmen began reexamining the public's impact on foreign policy. As might have been expected, considering the earlier debates over this complicated and contentious issue during the life of the republic, they have failed to reach a clear consensus on this most important and often troubling aspect of their unique political system.

BIBLIOGRAPHY

Almond, Gabriel A. *The American People and Foreign Policy.* New York, 1950. A pathbreaking effort by a social scientist, now rather dated.

Bailey, Thomas A. *The Man in the Street: The Impact of American Public Opinion on Foreign Policy.* New York, 1948. The classic impressionistic and wonderfully anecdotal treatment by a dean of diplomatic historians.

Barnet, Richard J. *The Rocket's Red Glare: When America Goes to War—The Presidents and the People.* New York, 1990.

Benson, Lee. "An Approach to the Scientific Study of Past Public Opinion." *Public Opinion Quarterly* 30, no 4. (1967–1968): 522–567.

Cohen, Bernard C. *The Public's Impact on Foreign Policy.* Boston, 1973. One of the soundest treatments of the subject, especially the introductory chapter on the state of the art.

Foster, H. Schuyler. *Activism Replaces Isolationism: U.S. Public Attitudes, 1940–1975.* Washington, D.C., 1983.

Foyle, Douglas C. *Counting the Public In: Presidents, Public Opinion, and Foreign Policy.* New York, 1999. An interesting attempt by a political scientist to categorize the approaches of recent presidents.

Graber, Doris A. *Public Opinion, the President, and Foreign Policy: Four Case Studies from the Formative Years.* New York, 1968.

Hilderbrand, Robert C. *Power and the People: Executive Management of Public Opinion in Foreign Affairs, 1897–1921.* Chapel Hill, N.C., 1981.

Holsti, Ole R. *Public Opinion and American Foreign Policy.* Ann Arbor, Mich., 1996.

Kegley, Charles W., Jr., and Eugene R. Wittkopf, eds. *The Domestic Sources of American Foreign Policy: Insights and Evidence.* New York, 1988. Several useful contemporary studies in this political science volume.

Levering, Ralph B. *The Public and American Foreign Policy, 1918–1978.* New York, 1978. A valuable brief survey by a leading specialist in the field.

Lippmann, Walter. *Public Opinion.* New York, 1922. Still a thought-provoking treatise.

———. *Essays in the Public Philosophy.* Boston, 1955. A critique of democratic leaders' pandering to the emotional masses.

May, Ernest R. "An American Tradition in Foreign Policy: The Role of Public Opinion." In William H. Nelson, ed. *Theory and Practice in American Politics.* Chicago, 1964, pp. 101–222.

Mueller, John E. *War, Presidents, and Public Opinion.* New York, 1973. An influential work by a political scientist concentrating on the Korean and Vietnam wars.

Newsom, David D. *The Public Dimension of Foreign Policy.* Bloomington, Ind., 1996. A practitioner takes a look at the problem.

Rosenau, James N. *Public Opinion and Foreign Policy: An Operational Formulation.* New York, 1961. A still-important study of the various publics and their relationships to the policymakers.

Shapiro, Robert Y., and Benjamin I. Page. "Foreign Policy and Public Opinion." In David A. Deese, ed. *The New Politics of American Foreign Policy.* New York, 1994.

Small, Melvin. "Historians Look at Public Opinion." In Melvin Small, ed. *Public Opinion and Historians: Interdisciplinary Perspectives.* Detroit, Mich., 1970. An analysis of the shortcomings of traditional historical approaches to the subject.

———. *Johnson, Nixon, and the Doves.* New Brunswick, N.J., 1988. An attempt by a historian to evaluate the influence of the antiwar movement on presidential decision making.

———. *Democracy and Diplomacy: The Impact of Domestic Politics on U.S. Foreign Policy, 1789–1994.* Baltimore, 1996.

See also DEPARTMENT OF STATE; DISSENT IN WAR; THE NATIONAL INTEREST; PRESIDENTIAL POWER; THE PRESS; RACE AND ETHNICITY; REALISM AND IDEALISM; TELEVISION; THE VIETNAM WAR.

RACE AND ETHNICITY

★ ★ ★ ★

John Snetsinger

To many observers one of the surprises of the 2000 census was that fully 10 percent of Americans reported that they had been born in a foreign country. Thirty years earlier the figure had been just 4.7 percent, the smallest in the Republic's history. The significance for the future formulation of U.S. foreign policy is not to be lost in the current number of foreign-born within the population. The political reality of the American system is that the greater the number of foreign-born, as well as of others within the population who retain ties with ancestral associations, the more likely it is that ethnic group politics can influence foreign policy. Demographic trends in twenty-first century America hold the promise that ethnicity may well play an even greater role in the making of foreign policy than has generally been the case.

A defining element of the American experience has been the degree to which ethnic affiliations, and to a lesser degree racial identity, have influenced foreign policy. Since the first census in 1790, the federal government has gathered information on ethnicity and race, although the type of data collected has changed over time as interests have shifted. With public awareness heightened by the impact of surging immigration by 1850, census respondents were asked not just their place of birth but also that of their parents. The influence of ethnic groups on the making of foreign policy has fluctuated with the ebb and flow of immigration.

Because there has never been a time in which a higher percentage of Americans had themselves been born in a foreign country, or had at least one parent born overseas, historians commonly focus on the influence of ethnic constituencies on President Woodrow Wilson's diplomacy of war and peace. There is merit in identifying the winners and losers among those engaging in ethnic politics in this era, as will be discussed later. The 1920 census reported that approximately one-third of the national popula-

tion either had been born overseas or had at least one parent who had been. This remarkably high figure is worthy of attention, but it is also significant that ever since the founding of the Republic, foreign policy issues have been viewed by millions of Americans through the prism of their ancestral ties of culture, nation, language, religion, or race.

ORIGIN OF ETHNIC POLITICS IN DIPLOMACY

Reasons for the link between American diplomacy and ethnicity are found in the manner in which the country was settled. In Europe it was common to have a single national or religious identification shared by the public. In the emerging American republic, however, the composition of the population reflected a high degree of national, religious, and racial diversity. One wave of immigrants after another swelled the American population with persons of vastly dissimilar backgrounds.

White English settlers made up the clear majority in the American colonies, but only through the second half of the eighteenth century. During that period three-quarters of the new settlers were Scotch-Irish, Scottish, German, French, and Swiss. Thirty percent of New Englanders came from places other than England in the years immediately preceding the War for Independence. Settlers of English ancestry were only 30 percent of the population in German-dominated Pennsylvania. In the southern colonies African slaves comprised the single largest ethnic or racial group.

These immigrants, and in many instances their descendants, have retained ancestral loyalties. Over centuries, waves of immigration have brought to America innumerable groups and tens of millions of immigrants whose ancestral identity has been handed down to present generations. It has been, and remains, common for ethnic minorities—such as Italian Americans, Jewish Americans, and Polish Americans—to embrace their new American loyalties while clinging to their kinship ties. Groups with millions of immigrants, such as those noted above, have the advantage of their large numbers in lobbying for a particular foreign policy. A fascinating element of ethnic politics that will be explained is that even a relatively small ethnic group representing only a fraction of 1 percent of the national population, such as Armenian Americans, can exert significant influence on the conduct of foreign policy.

The process through which American foreign policy is formulated works to the advantage of ethnic groups interested in assisting some cause of their homeland. All forms of government, including dictatorships, ultimately rely upon the support of public opinion to sustain their activities abroad. In a democracy, however, the link between the nation's diplomacy and the desires of the citizenry is more direct than in nondemocratic states.

The extent to which ethnic minorities are able to shape foreign policy is a uniquely American phenomenon. No other nation has absorbed such extensive waves of immigration as the United States. Sixty percent of the world's international migration between the early nineteenth century and 1930 came to the United States.

IMMIGRATION ACT OF 1965 AND ETHNIC POLITICS

Until the 1960s many historians believed that ethnic group influence on foreign policy would gradually diminish as the population became an American population with fewer immediate ethnic ties. Beginning in the 1920s, the flow of immigration slowed dramatically with laws reflecting anti-immigration public sentiment. Depression and war continued the trend to the point where under 5 percent of the population had been born in a foreign country. The political and cultural trends that lasted through the 1950s stressed the need for assimilation and conformity to the mainstream norms. The Cold War, with its emphasis on the righteousness of the American position and its constant invocation of national patriotism, further inhibited criticism of mainstream American values and institutions. School textbooks extolled the virtues of the "melting pot" to which

other cultures contributed, but nonetheless stressed the importance of unity and adaptation to the national norm.

As with so much else in national life, these concepts and the national ethnic and racial makeup changed dramatically in the 1960s. An event that unmistakably precipitated the changes, and one whose legacy might well include significantly altering the policies of American diplomacy in the decades ahead, is the Immigration Act of 1965. Sponsored by liberal Democrats in Congress and Presidents John Kennedy and Lyndon Johnson, this law changed the rules of entering, and thereby opened the doors to the greatest influx of immigrants in history. The Hart-Celler Act, as it was then known, received little attention when it was passed, and continues to be relatively ignored in histories recounting Johnson's reform program, the Great Society. Nonetheless, it may be the single most significant legislation of that era as far as its impact on the nation's future.

Rejecting national origin quotas as the basis for admittance, as had previously been the case, in the 1965 law family reunification became the basis for admittance for nearly two-thirds of those who would immigrate. Three subsequent laws increased the impact of the 1965 law: the Refugee Act of 1980, which recognized a separate category of those fleeing political oppression; the Immigration and Control Act of 1986, which provided amnesty for three million immigrants who had entered the United States illegally before 1982; and a 1990 amendment to the 1965 law that substantially raised the number who could enter as legal immigrants.

The flow of immigrants has risen steadily, particularly after 1990, when the annual totals for legal immigration peaked for several years at approximately 1.5 million. Between 1965 and 2000, approximately 23 million immigrants legally entered the United States. Adding estimates that there are also from 8 to 12 million illegal immigrants, the total attests to a massive foreign-born influence. Twenty-five percent of California's population is foreign born, and New York state is not far behind, with about 20 percent.

As important as the sheer number of immigrants is, it is also significant that 85 percent of the legal immigrants are from non-European backgrounds without the traditional foreign policy interests of most Americans. Europeans comprise approximately 15 percent of legal immigrants, Asian Americans about one-third, and Latin Americans most of the rest. The foreign policy issues that concern these new Americans have already begun to shape the direction of diplomacy, notably on trade and on immigration issues, such as amnesty for undocumented workers already in the country. Future diplomacy is likely to concern such issues more directly. One reason is that demographers project that, because of higher Hispanic birthrates and the origins of future immigrants, the United States will see a decline in its population of European background and a substantial rise in its Hispanic and Asian population.

POLITICAL REALITIES

Astute politicians not only must be aware of broad-based national sentiment concerning a diplomatic issue, but also must give a hearing to ethnic minorities who have a particular interest in certain areas of the nation's foreign policy. Organized ethnic minorities can bring pressure on the government for specific policies that are peculiarly their own and that may favor their original homeland in relation to another nation or a particular political movement within the homeland, or simply reflect an attitude that is common to similar American immigrant groups.

So apparent and consistent are the desired diplomatic policies of some ethnic minorities that politicians can frequently anticipate what actions will solidify their support among these groups. Even though the resulting positions may flout foreign policy objectives outlined by the federal government, politicians have made attempts to please the large ethnic blocs within their constituency. Mayor William H. ("Big Bill") Thompson, for example, placated citizens of Irish extraction when in the late 1920s he threatened that he would "punch the snout" of the king of England should the monarch dare to enter Chicago.

New York City mayors Robert F. Wagner, John V. Lindsay, and Abraham D. Beame pursued a policy designed to meet with the approval of the city's three million Jews by refusing to welcome Arab rulers on goodwill tours of the United States. Politicians across the political spectrum share their contempt for Cuba's Communist dictator, Fidel Castro, in seemingly endless verbal assaults when the goal is to win the support of Cuban Americans.

Mayors and other local officials may irritate foreign leaders, but the extent to which such actions affect American diplomacy is relatively slight. More serious consequences can arise when ethnic minorities place sufficient pressures on the national government to alter the direction of foreign policy. During the first half of the twentieth century, for example, the development of a close understanding between the United States and Great Britain was blocked on several occasions by persistent Anglophobia that centered among citizens of Irish and German ancestry. These two minorities opposed early American intervention to aid Britain in both world wars. Partly on account of such opposition, the United States not only postponed early wartime alliances with Britain, but also handled peacetime rapprochement with extreme caution.

ETHNIC GROUP INFLUENCE PRIOR TO THE TWENTIETH CENTURY

Concern about ethnic groups and efforts they might make to pressure policy decisions dates from before the founding of the Republic. James Madison and others who collaborated in writing the *Federalist Papers* (1787–1788) translated their concerns over what they saw as the inevitable impact of ethnic factions into a representative government in which popular passions and individual pressure groups could be countered by calmer and wiser leaders. President George Washington expressed misgivings over what the impact of ethnic factions might be on the young nation's diplomacy. One of the earliest examples of ethnic group pressure came from Irish Americans, who by 1800 made up a majority of the newly naturalized immigrants to America. Favoring the cause of an independent Ireland, and the revolutionary activities already under way to accomplish that goal on the home island, Irish Americans broke with the pro-British stance of Washington and the Federalists and backed the political fortunes of Jeffersonian Republicans.

During John Adams's presidency the passage of the restrictive Alien and Sedition Laws (1798) were in part an effort to silence the criticisms voiced by Irish Americans. Although never seriously competing in effectiveness with the greater influences that moved national foreign policy toward association with Great Britain throughout the nineteenth century, Irish Americans were a consistent and significant force in diplomatic deliberations. The large-scale immigration of Irish to America during the famine of the 1840s, the political activism with which the Irish became associated, and the constant turmoil that seemed to define the struggle in Ireland itself demanded the attention and concern of those who had left. These factors combined to heighten interest in attempting to shape their new nation's diplomacy toward Irish independence and relations with the British.

A domestic affinity group, the Fenian Brotherhood—which was associated with the revolutionary Irish Revolutionary Brotherhood in Ireland—had substantial support among Irish Americans in attempting to achieve twin goals. First, the Fenians were committed to assist their revolutionary brothers abroad and, second, to try to foment a war between the United States and Britain as a way to somehow secure Irish independence. Both the Republican and the Democratic Parties looked the other way when the Fenians engaged in activities as radical as launching abortive armed raids on Canada. These raids (1866–1870) were intended to bring the United States into a war over Canada, but they were dropped after Canadian forces easily repelled them.

As the United States moved inexorably toward closer association with the British around the turn of the twentieth century, Irish Americans' hatred toward their avowed enemy, and any diplomatic understanding between them and America, were translated into political campaigns. Irish-American organizations, lobbyists, and voters unsuccessfully opposed U.S. support for the British in the Boer War, the Hay-Pauncefote treaties (1900 and 1901) that ensured an accommodation on the building of a U.S. canal in Central America, and, most significantly, the U.S. entry into the Great War in 1917.

Racial minorities, including African Americans and Chinese Americans, found themselves excluded from the democratic system as it existed in the nineteenth century, and therefore without leverage to influence policy. Some Caucasian immigrant groups found that they had limited influence because of their precarious economic status and widespread prejudice directed against them. A diplomatic episode involving Italian Americans demonstrates this situation. In 1891 a mob of white nativists in New Orleans converged on the jail in which eleven Italians and Italian Americans were being held following their acquittal on murder charges. Stirred by ethnic animosities, the mob lynched the eleven and subsequently received what must be considered general plaudits from "respectable" Americans,

some public figures, and the press. Future president Theodore Roosevelt declared the lynching "a rather good thing."

Italian Americans were justifiably outraged, and demanded prosecution of those involved in the lynching and compensation to the victims' families. The perfunctory rejection of their demands by the American government led to a campaign, spearheaded by Italian Americans, to engage the help of the Italian government. Italy severed diplomatic relations with the United States, and rumors of war between the two nations were widely circulated. President Benjamin Harrison defused the situation by issuing an apology and agreeing to pay compensation to the families of those who had been lynched.

It was less than a satisfying resolution for Italian Americans, who unsuccessfully sought to have justice served through the arrest and conviction of those who had participated in the lynching, and who also wanted some efforts to be made to dampen anti-Italian prejudice. Although Italian Americans lacked any real political influence and were commonly subjected to vicious discrimination that isolated them, they were white and they had sufficient numbers to gain them at least some role in electoral politics.

Tempering any dynamic role that ethnic groups might play in the shaping of policy in the nineteenth century was the reality that for all but the final few years of the century, the United States was not much of an influential player in world affairs. That would change abruptly in the new century.

WILSONIAN DIPLOMACY

President Woodrow Wilson projected the United States into the center of postwar European political issues, and his call for self-determination to become an underlying principle in drawing the new map of Europe excited many domestic ethnic constituencies with the possibilities of national independence for their ancestral homes. After having stirred the aspirations and raised hopes of ethnic groups as never before, Wilson the peacemaker could not match expectations. He had not counted on either the multiple conflicting aims among the hopeful nations or his inability to win the approval of the other allied powers. Ethnic groups that had once supported him now fought the approval of the Treaty of Versailles (1919). His inability to press for Irish independence as part of the World War I peace settlement resulted in bitter Irish-American attacks against the president and the treaty, and played a key role in blocking its passage in the Senate.

Whether to ratify the treaty was, in fact, an issue that resulted in several other emotionally charged campaigns. Various ethnic minorities, each specially motivated to seek a negative Senate vote on ratification, assailed Wilson's handiwork. German Americans could not accept the relatively harsh punishment meted out to Germany. Since the Versailles agreement failed to provide for the expanded Italy hoped for by Italian nationals, initial Italian-American enthusiasm for Wilson soon turned to denunciation. Exclusion of the Adriatic city of Fiume from Italy's control was considered to be one of the treaty's most objectionable points.

Not only the larger and more influential ethnic minorities resisted Wilson's endeavors to secure U.S. acceptance of the treaty; Armenian Americans, Syrian Americans, Greek Americans, and Lithuanian Americans, as well as several other groups, joined forces with the foes of ratification for a variety of reasons. Millions of Americans viewed Wilson as the man who had betrayed dreams of nationalistic glory for their land of origin.

New nations did come into existence as a result of Wilson's insistence that the treaty recognize self-determination, and Americans with ties to those fortunate nations were delighted. Few ethnic groups have been as successful in influencing foreign policy as were Polish Americans during the peacemaking following the world war. The re-creation of Poland following the war has been linked to the Wilson administration's interest in securing the Polish-American vote.

Scholars have clashed over the issue of whether Anglo Americans, whose contributions of language, law, and culture have been synonymous with the launching of the Republic, can legitimately be considered another of the nation's ethnic groups. There is no doubt, however, that Americans of English ancestry have had a significant impact on formulating diplomatic relationships with Great Britain. Since the earliest days of the Republic, Anglo Americans have influenced American foreign policy. For instance, by placing pressure upon President Wilson, who was of English ancestry, the Anglo Americans exerted a powerful influence in stimulating American intervention in World War I.

JEWISH AMERICANS AND THE CAMPAIGN FOR ISRAEL

Examining individual ethnic groups and their particular campaigns on behalf of shaping policy in a region or toward a particular nation provides clues as to how and why ethnic politics can work in America's pluralistic democracy. It is likely that the most extraordinary case of an ethnic group successfully shaping the direction of foreign policy is the campaign of American Jews to win U.S. support for both the creation of Israel and the close partnership between the two nations that has followed.

Many factors need to be in place for ethnic politics to succeed; what is interesting about the campaign initiated by American Jews following World War II is that the community did so many things so well. Although small in numbers, there was near unanimity among American Jews in support of the Zionist goal of creating a viable Jewish state. Furthermore, it was understood that although direct support to those creating Israel in Palestine was important, what was essential politically would be to bring the United States in on the side of the new state.

American Jews represented only 3 percent of the population, but in the presidential election year of 1948, when Zionists declared the existence of Israel, American Jews were concentrated in those states that constituted the biggest electoral prizes. Half of the nation's Jews lived in New York State, which had by far the most electoral votes.

Winning American support for Israel became the community's most important political objective, ensuring that politicians would pay attention to the issue. Firmly established within the political structure, almost all Jews voted, many were activists involved in campaigns, and as a high-income group they had already established a record of financial support for candidates and organizations that backed their causes. President Harry Truman, and most members of Congress, responded favorably to the call to assist the newly established state when Zionists proclaimed the creation of Israel on 14–15 May 1948.

It was Truman's support in extending de facto American recognition of Israel just eleven minutes after it was declared to exist that proved crucial. It not only gave Israel, which was immediately plunged into defense of itself in the first Arab-Israeli war, great moral legitimacy by being acknowledged as a state by the most powerful nation in the world, but it also proved to be the first step in a continuing stream of support from the United States. It is always difficult to attribute motivation, but a case can be made that Truman recognized Israel and continued American support for the new nation out of a concern for the political consequences in a presidential election year.

Thanks in large measure to American Jews' fostering the "special relationship" that grew between Israel and the United States, by the 1970s the political, economic, and military ties were so firm that they became a foundation of American foreign policy. American Jews identified with and felt pride when Israel achieved its goals in the face of constant adversity. When Israel stunned the world with its unexpected military victories in the 1967 Arab-Israeli War, perhaps no citizens of one nation have ever been as committed to another nation's fate as Jews in America were to Israel. More than any other event, the outcome of the war forged unanimity toward Israel on the part of Jewry in the United States.

An American lobbying group, the American Israel Political Action Committee (AIPAC), has met with so much success that it has become a symbol of foreign policy lobbying effectiveness. Some political observers have said that AIPAC has become the most powerful foreign policy lobbying group in Washington. Focused exclusively on lobbying the U.S. government for Israel's needs, AIPAC avoids identification with the liberal causes with which Jewish groups usually associate. This has allowed AIPAC to remain ideologically comfortable with anticommunist conservatives such as Ronald Reagan and the territorial expansionists on the political right in Israel. AIPAC developed the capacity to mobilize thousands of activists across the United States when needed, and into the 1980s they were able to stifle dissent among Jews who questioned the direction Israel was taking.

DIVISION AMONG JEWISH AMERICANS

Israel's policies first stirred signs of unease among American Jews when Israeli bombers destroyed an Iraqi nuclear reactor in 1981 and, in a separate event, the Palestine Liberation Organization (PLO) headquarters in Beirut, Lebanon, was the target of Israeli bombers. It was, however, the 1982 Israeli invasion of Lebanon and the subsequent massacre of at least six hundred Palestinian

civilians by Christian Phalangist (Lebanese) troops allied with Israel that began a new era for American Jews. Prior to the invasion of Lebanon, Israel's wars had been struggles for survival. The invasion tested the resolve of many Jews who had followed the unwritten prohibition against Jews publicly criticizing Israel.

In their dash north, the sixty to ninety thousand Israeli troops, supplemented by naval and air support, left mass destruction of property and substantial numbers of civilian casualties. World public opinion, including most Americans, opposed the invasion. American Jews rallied to Israel's cause at the time, but an erosion of support had begun. One poll found that 93 percent of American Jews still supported Israel, and 83 percent reported that if Israel were destroyed, it would "be one of the great personal tragedies in my life."

Yet as time passed, individual mainstream Jewish leaders and major organizations spoke out in anger and dismay at the actions taken in Lebanon by Prime Minister Menachem Begin's right-wing government. The massacres were particularly troubling because the Israeli army had taken responsibility for the civilians' safety and had been nearby during the two days in which the killings occurred. How could a nation of Jews, with a 5,000-year heritage of respecting human life and a history of suffering nearly as long, be in any way involved in massacres of civilians? As the debate heated up, criticism of Israel reached a new level within Jewish circles in America and elsewhere.

Three years later, Jonathan Jay Pollard, an American Jew employed by the navy as a civilian analyst, was arrested and charged with being the most prolific spy in American history. Over a two-year period he had stolen and turned over to Israel 360 cubic feet of top-secret files. The U.S. government argued that Pollard had compromised the entire American intelligence-gathering apparatus. Many American Jews found it incomprehensible that Israel would engage in such spying. Israel's use of an American Jew seemed to play into the hands of anti-Semites who would surely charge American Jews with dual loyalty. Why, it was written, would Israel steal secrets from the one ally whose goodwill was essential and upon which the country was almost absolutely dependent?

One more event undercut the breadth of support that Israel had had from American Jews. Beginning in 1987, Palestinians in the occupied West Bank, Gaza, and Israel itself, engaged in a mass revolt against Israeli authority. Led mainly by the young, the Intifada has transformed relations between Palestinians and Israelis, and among many American Jews has led to greater calls for a peace process that will end the fighting and provide Palestinians with some degree of self-governance.

Israel still has the support of American Jews, and the "special relationship" that underpins U.S.–Israeli relations continues. Israel receives more foreign aid from America than any country in the world, and is likely to continue to do so. However, Jewish-American unity has fragmented, with significant criticism of Israel being expressed openly as never before. AIPAC remains a model of how a successful lobbying group can represent the policy goals of an ethnic pressure group, but even its supporters acknowledge that it may have lost its edge because there no longer is community consensus on some issues. These changes have created an opportunity for an opposition group to emerge and challenge pro-Israeli policies of the American government. Still relatively in the shadows, an Arab-American group has taken on the direction of U.S. policy in the Middle East.

PUBLIC OPINION AND ISRAEL

Proponents of pro-Israel policies might well be sobered by changing public attitudes toward Israel and Middle Eastern issues, and what such changes might mean for future U.S. policy. In the fifteen surveys since 1989 in which the Gallup Poll has asked Americans to describe their attitude toward Israel, there is still a 59–30 percent advantage of favorable to unfavorable. However, these results indicate declining public support from earlier times. For comparison, the three countries with the highest rankings in the Gallup survey are Canada (17 May 1999), Australia (12 February 2001), and Great Britain (16 February 2001), with, respectively, 90–7, 85–8, and 85–9 percent favorable to unfavorable ratings.

Events in the Middle East occasionally signal the very real possibilities of regional war, a world energy crisis, the use of nuclear weapons, or an unleashing of worldwide terrorist activities. As a result the American public has heard, read, and seen more about this region than most others, and increasingly has arrived at conclusions not shared by the government of Israel or its American proponents. Successful lobbying groups would often prefer to have their issues exist "under the radar" of public attention.

A Gallup Poll survey in May 1999 indicated that the American public, by a margin of 53–26 percent, favored the establishment of an independent Palestinian state on the West Bank and the Gaza Strip. Creating such a state has long been the goal of the Palestinian Authority, the internationally sanctioned agency that legally represents the interests of Palestinians currently living within the boundaries of Israel.

Israel remains one of the firmest allies of the United States, and it continues to draw support from the majority of Americans. Arabs are generally viewed unfavorably by the public. The Palestinian Authority received a 22–63 percent unfavorable rating when Gallup surveyed public opinion in February 2001. What is likely to change in the future is that the efforts of Jewish Americans, and other supporters of Israel, will no longer go unchallenged by other ethnic groups or larger elements of the general public who have views contrary to those of Israel and Israel's American supporters.

AN ARAB-AMERICAN CHALLENGE

The emergence of a significant Arab-American population, along with its inclination to be more engaged in politics, may already have begun to change the dynamic of how the United States deals with Middle Eastern issues. Until the 1970s Arab Americans were few in number and seemingly invisible on issues involving their ancestral lands. James Abourezk, an articulate senator of Arab-American descent from South Dakota, became one of the first outspoken proponents of the Arab position in national life.

Enumerated at one million in the 1990 census, Arab Americans were estimated to have increased to 3.5 million in preliminary figures of the 2000 Census Report. A source of emerging strength rests in the clustering of Arab Americans in four states crucial in presidential elections. Arab voters are a factor in southern California, New York City, northern New Jersey, and, most critically, Detroit and southern Michigan. The largest concentration in the country is in metropolitan Detroit, with 350,000 Arab Americans. Only African Americans represent a larger minority group in Detroit.

There is now recognition that Arab Americans are a factor in political strategy, particularly in Michigan, where they represent 4 percent of the vote. Spencer Abraham, an Arab American, was elected to the U.S. Senate in 1994. Arab Americans vote in high percentages (62 percent in the 1996 election), they have high incomes, and they are increasingly involved in national elections. In 1996 neither Democratic President Bill Clinton nor the Republican challenger, Bob Dole, attended events, but in 2000 all the serious presidential contenders addressed Arab-American groups.

CUBAN AMERICANS AND FIDEL CASTRO

Another contemporary case of an ethnic group dominating regional policy is provided by Cuban Americans. As with Jewish Americans, the record of Cuban Americans in shaping policy toward Cuba proves that groups do not need to be large in number to succeed. Only in the 1960s did significant numbers of Cuban exiles arrive in the United States, fleeing Castro's revolution. Driven by an often all-consuming singleness of purpose concerning one overriding foreign policy issue, Cuban Americans gradually became the driving force behind Washington's unyielding hard-line policy toward the Cuban regime. Most exiles left behind their property in Cuba and settled in Florida, and a significant number among them devoted their time and resources to pressuring the U.S. government to bring down the Castro regime and restore an anticommunist government. Since this result has never occurred, the movement has continued to thrive among Cuban Americans.

Cuban exiles were close to their homeland, only ninety miles away, and expected that the Castro regime might collapse at any time, which in turn would allow them to return. Thus in their first decade in the United States, Cuban Americans were said to have a "visitor mentality," which acted against engagement in local civic activities. Cuban Americans instead promoted an intense interest in how Washington dealt with Cuba and Castro.

Other factors have also been responsible for Cuban Americans' rapidly becoming a force in shaping foreign policy. Many of the early exiles, from the upper classes, were well educated and provided leadership for the group. Continued emigration from Cuba has provided a reasonably significant population base; the 2000 census reported 1.24 million Cuban Americans. A population of over a million is enough for politicians to pay attention. Yet that number dramatizes how even a relatively small ethnic group can be effective. Cuban Americans represent less than 0.50 percent of the national population and less than 10 percent of Hispanics in the United States.

An important factor enhancing the influence of Cuban Americans as a group is their shared political ideology, and the fact that the conservative Republicans with whom they identify have controlled the presidency, and hence the levers of foreign policy implementation, during recent decades. In 1984, for example, Ronald Reagan received 90 percent of the Cuban-American vote in Dade County (which includes Miami). Since it has been estimated that 63 percent of Cuban Americans live in the Miami area, the political significance of winning the support of this group is not lost on presidential candidates. Florida is a crucial swing state in presidential elections, as the presidential race in 2000 amply demonstrated. It is simply political reality that those seeking the presidency must consider the implications of their policy toward Cuba if they wish to win Florida's electoral votes.

Another advantage Cuban Americans have had in driving policy is that there is no significant group challenging their anti-Castro agenda. In fact, the anticommunism expounded by Cuban exiles fit in easily with the Cold War rhetoric that dominated the campaigns of presidential contenders. A series of chief executives, who have been humbled by Castro's resilience, have found it politically advantageous to align with the hard-line policies proposed by the exiles.

The result has been a U.S. diplomatic assault on Cuba so virulent and excessive that it has been condemned by many nations, including some that are considered staunch American allies. No other regime anywhere in the world can currently be said to suffer from as clearly prejudicial diplomatic measures on the part of the United States as the Castro regime. Since the early 1960s an embargo has denied trade and investment from the United States. Travel by U.S. citizens has been denied, although since the 1990s exceptions have been made for travelers who can justify their trips as having an educational purpose. Alone among all nations the United States denies the right of its citizens to send medicine or food to Cuba.

In 1992 passage of the "Cuban Democracy Act" prohibited U.S.-owned or -controlled subsidiaries overseas from engaging in any business with Cuba. The harshest measure of all has been the 1996 Helms-Burton Act, a tightening of the embargo that allowed U.S. citizens to sue foreign corporations that had purchased U.S. property confiscated by the Castro regime.

Almost alone in the world, the island nation of Cuba struggles with a total embargo, including medical and food products, imposed by the United States. With a gross domestic product that is less than 6 percent of what the United States spends on its military, the island hardly poses a security threat to its northern adversary. The degree of the isolation and hostility aimed at the Cuban regime is in large measure the result of a successful campaign of a relatively small but dedicated and powerful advocacy group, the 1.24 million Cuban Americans.

SIZE OFTEN NOT A BARRIER

American Jews and Cuban Americans, respectively 3 percent and 0.50 percent of the national population, are two groups with enormous influence in shaping foreign policy even though they are relatively small in number. Other similarly marginal groups in terms of population have demonstrated that size alone is not always an impenetrable barrier. One such group, Armenian Americans, were at first unsuccessful when they sought American support against Turkey during World War I. From 1915 to 1923 Turkey engaged in a policy of genocide that cost approximately one million Armenian lives. Yet when Armenia declared itself a republic independent of Turkey in 1918, Armenian Americans waged a campaign that resulted in Wilson extending de facto recognition of the new state. Similar efforts to prevent the United States from recognizing Turkey during this period proved futile.

More recently, Armenian Americans, who number over one million, have demonstrated that they wield a certain degree of influence in their particular area of interest. A California-centered group whose politics leans to the Republican, Armenian Americans lobbied Congress in 1990 to commemorate the aforementioned genocide. Even though Turkey's long-standing record as a crucial NATO military ally of the United States might have suggested different treatment, Congress nearly passed the resolution. Even though the administration of George H. W. Bush opposed it, it took a Senate filibuster to defeat the resolution and prevent a likely break with Turkey. If Congress had approved the measure, which used the term "genocide," Turkey made it clear that a grave crisis would result. Even though they lost, the political acumen of the Armenian-American lobbyists in nearly securing passage of a measure that had significant implications for diplomacy had to be acknowledged.

Although Turkey was firmly integrated within American defense policies during the Cold War, Greek Americans were able to lobby successfully in favor of punitive diplomatic measures against that nation in the wake of bitter Greek-Turkish disputes over Cyprus in 1974. Even though Greece was governed by militarists who had overthrown elected democratic leaders, and had instigated the troubles on Cyprus, the fact remained that there were one million Greek Americans whose lobbyists knew how to use political leverage to affect foreign policy. Washington responded to the pressure by placing a three-year embargo on military sales to Turkey and agreeing to provide Greece with 70 percent of the military aid that would be given to Turkey in future years. Ethnic politics prevailed over what was accepted to be the national security interest in maintaining good relations with a crucial geopolitical partner on the Soviet border.

Finally, the intervention of the United States in the Balkans in the 1990s revealed not only that the Balkan nationalities themselves were broken into competing factions, but also that the conflicts among the various nationalities within America presented policymakers with another kind of Balkanization. U.S. troops entered Bosnia, and then Kosovo, in an effort to block Serbian territorial expansion and genocide ("ethnic cleansing"). As a strategy to stop Serbian genocide in Kosovo, and at the same time limit American armed forces personnel in the campaign, President Bill Clinton in 1999 began a massive bombing campaign within Serbia.

Constituencies in the United States associated with those nationalities that benefited from American intervention supported Clinton's action. Orthodox Christian ethnic groups, including Serbian Americans, Greek Americans, and Russian Americans, all protested. Although there are Serbian enclaves on the east coast, the most politically sensitive Serbian population is made up of the 250,000 who live in Chicago and comprise the largest community of Serbs outside Serbia. Orthodox Christians in America charged Washington with being insensitive to the suffering of their coreligionists in the Balkans while overlooking the excesses and favoring the cause of western Christians and Muslims.

MEXICAN AMERICANS: TOMORROW'S LEVIATHAN?

Because the results to date have been so marginal for Mexican American efforts to influence diplomatic issues that affect them, there is some temptation to conclude that this is a group destined to fall short in the future. Yet with the 2000 census reporting what might well be described as an explosion in Hispanic and Mexican populations, cautious observers will likely reserve judgment before suggesting that the future will resemble the past for Mexican Americans. Demographics, the current attention being paid by both political parties, and group activism seem likely to combine to make this ethnic group one with enormous future influence on foreign policy.

From the time of the Mexican cession in 1848, Mexicans were targets of prejudice, violence, and economic exploitation in the land that was once theirs. Whether established residents or itinerant agricultural workers, they were an underclass striving to avoid poverty and discrimination in the United States. The Mexican government was indifferent toward them, and public attitudes in the United States ensured that they remained politically inactive.

Civil war in their homeland and severe economic problems drove one-tenth of Mexico's population into the United States in the two decades prior to the Great Depression. However, a search for scapegoats in the 1930s led to mass deportation of Mexicans back to Mexico. Distinctively dressed Mexican-American youths were frequently attacked by white servicemen in Los Angeles during World War II. These "zoot suit riots" led the Mexican government to protest, and request that measures be taken to end the violence. After the war the Mexican population in the United States rapidly increased with the addition of millions of contract laborers (braceros) and undocumented workers. These groups did not participate in politics, and even those immigrants who could have participated did not move quickly toward naturalization and a role in the political system.

Political activism at the national level began in the 1960s with Mexican-American organizations lobbying for immigration legislation, congressmen of Mexican ancestry playing the major role in forming the Hispanic Caucus, and the Mexican government finally cooperating with the community's leaders and associations. The first real success Mexican Americans demonstrated as a pressure group on foreign policy issues was in shaping the Immigration Reform and Control Act of 1986. The inclusion of an amnesty program for millions of the undocumented who could prove they had been in the United States prior to 1982 was a striking victory.

Because of demographic changes and their emerging political activism, Mexican-American leaders have suggested that in the future their record of influencing foreign policy in areas of interest could match that of any other ethnic group. The increase in Hispanic population, to 35,305,818 (13 percent of the national total), was the phenomenon of the 2000 census. Mexican Americans comprised 59 percent of that Hispanic total and 7 percent of the national total. The 20,640,711 Mexican Americans represented a 53 percent increase in just ten years. Eighty-seven percent of Mexican Americans live in the West and the South, giving them a regional importance in both sections that could well be translated into even greater political advantage. In two crucial states in presidential elections, Mexican Americans make up 24 percent of the population of Texas and 21 percent in California.

Barriers still exist that militate against Mexican Americans' reaching their potential political strength. Even those Mexican Americans who have been in a position to exercise their citizenship rights by participating in electoral politics have failed to take advantage of the opportunity. Proximity to Mexico has made it possible for some immigrants to travel back and forth and not identify themselves with the cause of working for their rights as residents of the United States. As an ethnic group in the lower economic strata, the route to political influence through financing candidates and causes is not as likely as it might be for high-income groups. The median age of Mexican Americans is twenty-four, compared with a national median age of thirty-five, so a substantial percentage of Mexican Americans are not yet of an age that allows them to participate in the electoral system. Yet with all these qualifications, the overriding conclusion is that someday Mexican Americans will play an influential role in American foreign policy.

The major foreign policy initiatives that most interest Mexican Americans involve immigration and trade issues between Mexico and the United States. These include amnesty for undocumented Mexicans working in the United States, consideration of a new guest-worker program, controls over drug trafficking, liberalizing trade and investment ties, regulation of the border, and fighting discrimination and violence against immigrants. The attention that has recently been given to these issues by the political parties and politicians testifies to an awareness of the political potential of Mexican Americans.

When he ran for governor of Texas, George W. Bush made a concerted and successful effort to win the Mexican-American vote. Both as a candidate and as an elected president, Bush has stressed his understanding of Mexican-American concerns, his interest in immigration liberalization, the promotion of Hispanics to high government positions, implementation of policies to improve the economic status of the group, and his ties with Mexico and its new president, Vicente Fox. Most dramatically, in 2001 Bush promised to work to legalize the status of millions of undocumented workers, mostly Mexicans, living in the United States.

Republicans consider Mexican Americans an ethnic minority that can be won over from its tradition of being Democrats. In 1996 Bill Clinton received 72 percent of the Hispanic vote, so there is no reason why Democrats will concede Hispanics and Mexican Americans to the Republicans. However, since Bush won one-third of the Hispanic vote in 2000, Republicans are confident that a shift is under way. Throughout the presidential and congressional elections from 1990 to 2000, the two major political parties have been as evenly divided in electoral strength as has ever been the case. Perhaps whichever is more successful with Mexican-American voters will prevail early in the twenty-first century as the majority party. Given the history of ethnic politics in making foreign policy, it seems likely that politicians and parties will endorse much of the agenda in foreign policy that Hispanic and Mexican-American groups will put forward in the future.

RACE AND FOREIGN POLICY

Since the time of the Constitution, racism frequently has been a part of the mix of factors that shaped diplomacy. Although there were other forces involved, such as the unbridled national enthusiasm for "pole to pole" territorial expansion, race became an articulated element of the expansionist policies associated with "manifest destiny." The term first appeared in 1845, and suggested that the Almighty in his ultimate wisdom had "manifestly destined" the procreative and vigorous Americans to extend their ennobling institutions of republican governance. The result was seen by some as way to spread superior democratic ways of life, but to others, focused on race, it provided a way to replace uncivilized and backward populations with those of purer blood.

President James K. Polk (1845–1849) translated "manifest destiny" into a plan of action, and the result was the annexation of Texas, purchase of the Oregon Territory, and a war with Mexico that resulted in the northern one-third of that nation being ceded to the victorious United States. Settling the western land acquired during the Polk administration, and the intervening Civil War, dampened further interest in foreign policy initiatives until the 1890s. By the turn of the century there were new ideas that had gained currency and influenced incorporating race into the making of foreign policy.

The British biologist Charles Darwin had introduced his theory of evolution in *On the Origin of Species* (1859), and by the turn of the century his views had been widely popularized in America. Evolutionary theory suggested that in the biological world, higher life-forms evolved through a process of "natural selection," popularized as "survival of the fittest" in the struggle for existence. Such a hypothesis was easily applied by some to sociological theorizing, even in the realm of international affairs. Since there was a ruthless struggle for existence within the biological sphere that resulted in survival of the fittest, or "best," some concluded that a similar struggle among nations or races might produce similar results. Ruthless international competition might well be justified in the name of "progress." Popular writers and clergymen believed that in the future, Anglo-Saxons, particularly Americans, would dominate in the world.

America's foreign policy initiatives were the result of a variety of forces, and one such force was racism. Before, during, and after his presidency (1901–1909), Theodore Roosevelt expounded upon the Social Darwinist interpretations of "natural selection," "survival of the fittest," the supremacy of Anglo-Saxons, and the "whiteman's burden" to uplift and civilize backward peoples. It is sometimes difficult to separate the racism from other factors that motivated conduct. Yet as America began to move into the world at large around the turn of the twentieth century, attitudes of racial superiority were observable. One example is provided by the American presence in the Philippines following the settlement of the war with Spain in 1898.

When it became clear to the Filipino nationalists that the United States was intent on occupying the islands rather than providing for their independence, a four-year war ensued. The historian Brian McAllister Linn, in *The Philippine War,*

1899–1902, warns that it is incorrect to ascribe racism to all the vicious behavior of American troops against the Filipinos. However, even with Linn's cautionary note that such behavior has been typical of combat soldiers for hundreds of years, the evidence demonstrates that part of the reason for the poor treatment of Filipinos was racial hostility.

The pacification and occupation of Central America and the islands of the Caribbean during the early decades of the twentieth century also reflect America's attitude of racial superiority. The occupation of Haiti from 1915 to 1934, for instance, resulted from a mixture of morality and strategic concerns, along with racism. Reflecting the racial attitudes of American policy and the occupation troops, Haitians were involuntarily placed in labor gangs, beaten and terrorized, and treated as prisoners. Marines killed two thousand "workers" in 1919, following an insurrection. Enforced segregation was imposed, and Americans favored the mulattos over the darker-skinned Haitians. Secretary of State Robert Lansing, who had deployed marines in Haiti, wrote that the "African race" had an "inherent tendency to revert to savagery and to cast aside the shackles of civilization which are irksome to their physical nature. Of course there are many exceptions to this racial weakness, but it is true of the mass as we know from experience in [Haiti]."

RACE AND THE NEW WORLD ORDER

Racism continued as a sometimes expressed element in American foreign policy through the 1920s and 1930s. World War II, however, set in motion events that resulted in a change in attitude on race both domestically and in foreign policy. Ambivalence on racial issues marked the U.S. record during the war. On the one hand, the tradition of white supremacy and racial prejudice, enforced through segregation, in many ways remained the standard of race relations in American society. Following the Japanese attack on Pearl Harbor, Hawaii, on 7 December 1941, some 112,000 Japanese Americans living in the western states were arrested and removed to a series of "relocation centers" in isolated interior locations. Two-thirds of this group were U.S. citizens, and most of the rest had been denied the right of citizenship because they were not born in the country. The sole criterion for removal was their Japanese ancestry.

Military service was rigidly segregated by race and defined the nonwhite soldier as inferior in every way. Decorated war heroes returned to a society in which they could not get a haircut from a white barber if their skin was not white. However, World War II also proved to be the cauldron from which dramatic changes in race relations would come forth. The beginning of the modern civil rights movement can be traced to the national wartime experience, and these domestic events, as well as the imperative of dealing with a different world, would influence changes in how U.S. foreign policy would deal with racial issues in international affairs.

The world order that emerged from the war was one in which a handful of western European nations no longer were supreme over the majority of the world's populations. The United States, emerging as the single most powerful economic and military nation, found it was in its own interest to distance itself from the racism with which Western nations had been identified. It was essential to Washington that a distinction be drawn between current American policies and association with the European legacy of colonialism, antinationalism, and racism. Interacting with a world no longer predominantly white or European, American policy distanced itself as much as it could from the influence of racism in its past.

Although this new emphasis was pragmatic in nature, it also was shaped by undeniable changes in attitude toward race that were occurring in American society. By the end of the 1960s, the colonies once held by European nations had largely disappeared. Nonwhite populations were assuming control of their own fate around the world, and proponents of white supremacy were increasingly on the defensive. During the war the United States had condemned the racism inherent in Nazi German society. Postwar policies increasingly reflected a condemnation of racial prejudice.

In planning for a continued global American presence, the reality was that the governments and populations with which the United States would deal were inevitably going to be nonwhite. In the presidencies of Harry Truman (1945–1953) and Dwight D. Eisenhower (1953–1961), nationalism among the nonwhite populations of the world was publicly acknowledged to be a force that the United States supported. Although the administrations did not always back up their rhetoric on nationalism with action, there were important examples of the United States supporting nationalistic aspirations of nonwhite populations at the expense of traditional European allies. One such example was Eisenhower's decision during the 1956 Suez crisis to side with the cause of Arab nationalism at the expense of British and French interests.

HUMAN RIGHTS, RACISM, AND THE UN CHARTER

U.S. commitment to the ideals incorporated in the principles of the United Nations symbolized the change in attitude toward race that marked postwar foreign policy. A legacy of Wilsonian diplomacy, the impetus for a United Nations developed during the presidency of Franklin Roosevelt. The charter of the world organization was written by Roosevelt's aides, and it came into existence in October 1945 largely because Roosevelt made it a centerpiece of his postwar diplomacy.

The charter provides evidence of how postwar U.S. diplomacy identified with policies of fundamental human rights, and had taken a step back from policies that were influenced by racist attitudes. The UN Charter "reaffirm[s] faith in fundamental human rights, in the dignity and worth of the human person, in the equal rights of men and women and of nations large and small." Pledging its member nations to "practice tolerance and live together in peace," the charter promotes the development of "friendly relations among nations based on respect for the principle of equal rights and self-determination of peoples" and "respect for human rights and fundamental freedoms for all."

Although this ideal was not necessarily always adhered to, the concepts noted above became major elements in the message that America presented to leaders, governments, and populations throughout the world. Policies of the United States were to be based on fundamental human rights and an acceptance of the nationalistic strivings of underdeveloped, largely nonwhite populations. It was never an option in diplomacy to revert to the ideological racism that for so long had been one of the factors shaping the making of policy.

The continued overt existence of racism within American society, and the increasing attention that was drawn to it by the civil rights movement, posed problems for Washington. It made it more difficult to assure others that the racism that had marked American diplomacy for so long was gone for good. News reports of racial discrimination, violence against peaceful civil rights activists, and growing white resistance to integration undercut the message of equal rights and tolerance abroad. When violent protest blocked the integration of Central High School in Little Rock, Arkansas, in 1957, President Eisenhower commented that it was "a tremendous disservice . . . to the nation in the eyes of the world." When dark-skinned diplomats were refused service in segregated restaurants, it was reported around the world.

The passage of time brought success for much of the civil rights agenda at home, which was reported the world over. The United States has identified with many of the third world nationalist movements, and it has opposed its European allies when they moved toward policies that could be interpreted as a reassertion of colonial-style conduct. A good example of the latter was the blunt warning given in 1956 by President Eisenhower to Britain and France during the Suez crisis. In effect the American president said that if these two European allies did not end their military campaign in the Suez region, swift economic and political retaliation from the United States would result.

EMERGING POLITICAL IDENTITY OF ASIAN AMERICANS

Racial attitudes in the United States ensured that prior to World War II, Asian populations would have little political leverage and would play only a marginal role in determining foreign policy in Asia and the Pacific region. With dramatically increased population and economic affluence, since the 1970s Asian Americans have built the political structure that has allowed them to participate in the process of influencing American foreign policy. It is still more the promise of what the future holds in this arena for Asian Americans than their current ability to shape policy that should be noted.

Chinese were the first Asians to immigrate to the United States in significant numbers: by 1880, with their community numbering seventy-five thousand, they comprised 10 percent of California's population. Fear that Chinese Americans might use the vote was one reason behind congressional passage of the Chinese Exclusion Act in 1882. Among the provisions was one that made Chinese "aliens ineligible to citizenship." With this legislation Chinese Americans were banished to the political margins, and a significant precedent was set for the political and social marginalization of all Asian groups who would follow. Only in 1952 were the last of the legal restrictions against Asian citizenship removed.

During World War II the United States lifted the ban on Chinese immigration; in the first year of implementation (1943) the change was as much symbolic as substantive as only 105 persons were allowed to enter the United States. Chinese immigrants were allowed to become naturalized citizens. Since China was an ally of the United States during World War II, these moves were made in large measure to win favor with Chiang Kai-shek's regime. Chinese Americans were too few in number and too politically inexperienced to be of much influence in promoting such changes. After the war Asian Americans remained politically marginalized in foreign policy decisions. No Asian-American group or individual, for instance, proved influential in shaping the events and policies that brought America into the Korean War.

Koreans in America were too few in number, and they had little experience with American politics. The condescension shown by many U.S. government officials toward both the Korean and the Chinese Communist combatants in the war smacks of racist mentality; these leaders were unlikely to have taken seriously those Asian Americans who would have tried to influence policy. White American soldiers commonly disparaged both the Chinese and the Koreans (including their South Korean allies) with racial barbs. The same pattern prevailed in the growing involvement of the United States in Southeast Asia that began in the 1950s. No Asian-American ethnic groups, nor individual Asian Americans, had any meaningful role in the policies that led to the war in Vietnam.

Several factors changed for Asian Americans beginning in the 1970s. Driven by a surge of immigration from Asia as the result of the 1965 immigration law, Asian Americans command attention by their sheer numbers—10,242,998 (3.6 percent of the nation's population, according to the 2000 census). They are well situated politically because in California, the greatest electoral prize by far, between 11 and 12 percent of the population is Asian American. These ethnic groups collectively can boast exceptionally high levels of educational attainment. Education is a primary reason for another political strength shared by Asian Americans, their affluence. Median family income for Asian Americans is 138 percent of the national average.

Obstacles continue to block the path of these groups as they attempt to achieve a level of political sophistication and develop the capability to influence foreign policy toward their ancestral homes in Asia. The population numbers themselves may be misleading when the level of political participation is considered. Because so many of the immigrants allowed in by the 1965 law are part of reunited families, the rate of immigrants who become naturalized is low. The percentage of Asian Americans who register to vote is low, as is the percentage of those who actually vote. If some other ethnic groups have attracted political attention because of their community solidarity and bloc voting tradition, it remains a liability for Asian Americans that they evenly split their votes between Republicans and Democrats. Split votes inevitably remove political leverage. Certain groups also split on the issues involving their land of ancestry. Chinese Americans, for instance, divide over the central issue of what policy should be promoted by the United States toward the communist regime in Beijing.

An "80–20 initiative" was begun in the 1990s with the goal of delivering 80 percent of the Asian-American vote to one presidential candidate. However, there are six significant Asian groups represented, and the ideological differences among them make the kind of political solidarity that the "80–20 initiative" promotes unlikely. Chinese Americans are the largest ethnic group, with nearly 2.5 million, followed in order by Filipinos, Indians, Vietnamese, Koreans, and Japanese. Each has its own particular foreign policy issues that relate to the homeland, so collaboration among the groups has proved to be difficult.

The Vietnamese, politically the most conservative group, have focused on U.S. policy toward the government in Hanoi. As opponents of the regime, Vietnamese Americans have acted as somewhat of a brake on the inexorable American move toward normalizing relations. With a huge influx of immigrants within their community, Chinese Americans have focused on both immigration issues and the U.S. relationship with China. Dubious charges of espionage against Lee Wen Ho, a Chinese-American nuclear scientist at Los Alamos, New Mexico, in 2000 mobilized Chinese Americans to protest that the American government perpetuated the stereotype that Chinese Americans were somehow doing the bidding of the government of China. Because China is seen as the enemy by many Americans, Chinese Americans believe they are tainted by association because they are ethnic Chinese. In a fund-raising scandal in the 1996 election, millions of dollars were illegally collected from Chinese sources outside the United States; Chinese Americans protested that press coverage did not adequately explain that it was not Chinese Americans engaged in raising illegal contributions, but foreign Chinese who may well have been associated with the communist Chinese government. Chinese Americans believe that their ability to influence policy has been compromised by these episodes in which they have been unfairly accused of wrongdoing and of being in the service of a foreign nation disliked by the American public.

Each of the Asian groups wants to bring more Asian Americans into the foreign policy decision-making process involving Asia and the Pacific region. With so many different cultures involved, finding a consensus has not been easy for the Asian-American groups.

THREE BALANCING FACTORS

There are countervailing pressures that can neutralize or even eliminate the opportunity an ethnic group has to affect foreign affairs. If public sentiment is clearly defined as opposed to the policy being sought, or if nonethnic special-interest lobbies in the United States wage a campaign against an ethnic minority's goals, or if other ethnic groups commit themselves to work on behalf of a different policy, the influence that an ethnic minority can command is mitigated.

The first of these balancing factors has frequently proved to be critical to ethnic minorities desiring to convince a president and Congress that specific policies should be accepted. Ethnic groups can exert disproportionate pressure in a specific area if their demands arouse no broad opposition from the public at large. Part of the Jewish-American success in winning American support for the creation of a Jewish state following World War II resulted from the existence of this condition.

It was fortunate for the Zionists that throughout the struggle to obtain official U.S. backing for a Jewish state, the American public was either mildly sympathetic or at least apathetic. The basic Zionist aim of establishing a Jewish state was consistently favored by those in the polling samples who had an opinion, although at times the margin of support was as narrow as a few percentage points.

Perhaps as significant as the opinions expressed was the fact that so large a percentage of the public did not follow the Palestine controversies. Only 45 percent of those questioned in one poll (National Opinion Research Center poll, May 1946) could identify Britain as the country that had the mandate for Palestine. As late as the fall of 1946, 49 percent admitted that they had not followed the discussion about establishing a Jewish national homeland (American Institute of Public Opinion poll, September 1946). Outside the Jewish community the Zionist program did not raise very intense political issues.

Generally, the public tunes in to foreign policy issues only at times of international crisis or when a policy debate is infused with overwhelming significance—for example, when a war may be on the horizon, or when policies fail (as with the continuing commitment to fighting in Vietnam). Most international issues do not interest the public at large; such apathy translates into public ignorance. In 1964 only 58 percent of those surveyed knew that the United States was a member of NATO. Nearly two-fifths replied that the Soviet Union was a member,

Only half of Americans polled in 1978 knew that the United States imported any oil, at a time when approximately half of the nation's oil came from overseas. It is a tremendous advantage to members of a unified, organized ethnic group when they have the field to themselves to promote an issue that does not interest the public at large.

When an ethnic group does recommend a policy position that is clearly opposed by the general public, they are unlikely to receive it. Significantly, the one aspect of the Zionist program in 1948 that ran into clear-cut public disapproval was never accepted by the American government. Following Israel's birth in May 1948, the new nation asked for positive action by the American president on three specific issues. One was for President Harry S. Truman to extend de jure recognition to Israel. Great urgency was also attached to the request for a $100 million American loan to Israel. Truman responded favorably to both requests. Truman was also asked to lift the American arms embargo on the Middle East, thereby allowing Israel to purchase weapons. On 5 December 1947 the American arms embargo had been imposed at the request of the UN Security Council.

Truman was persuaded by the State Department that any unilateral revocation of the embargo would be regarded as exhibiting a striking disregard for UN efforts to pacify the Middle East. Another compelling reason for presidential inaction derived from the public response to the embargo. Although the Zionist program generally met with either mild public approval or indifference, one nationwide poll (National Opinion Research Center, 1 July 1948) indicated that 82 percent of the electorate opposed any change in the status of the embargo.

A second balancing factor that can challenge the influence of an ethnic minority's ability to influence policy is nonethnic special-interest lobbies that are determined to have foreign policy conducted along the lines they desire. For example, economic interests within the United States might seek policies that are diametrically opposed to the programs sought by ethnic groups. In a democracy, ethnic minorities make up just a small percentage of pressure groups hoping to influence foreign policy.

A third factor that works against the policy-making influence of a particular ethnic minority consists of other ethnic groups taking on the role of the adversary. President Wilson was faced with a variety of ethnic groups, each of which insisted that he fully endorse the claims of their homeland. America's ethnic populations collided over how the map of the world should be redrawn. Wilson's attempts at compromise left most of the groups dissatisfied, and led in part to his inability to have the Treaty of Versailles ratified.

The situation of having one ethnic group lined up against another occurred in 1935 when the Italian dictator Benito Mussolini sent his troops into Ethiopia in an effort to expand his colonial empire. Supporting their ancestral home, most Italian Americans defended the action, and many lobbied against any American plan to establish a discriminatory embargo against Italy. Since President Franklin D. Roosevelt opposed Mussolini's actions during the Ethiopian campaign, large numbers of Italian Americans turned against the president and the Democrats.

On the other side, African Americans rallied to Ethiopia's support on the basis of their ethnic identification with the black African nation. They called for the United States to stand up firmly against Italy. Lester Taylor, the chairman of the New African International League, wired the State Department: "Black citizens are surprised and filled with misgivings at the lukewarm attitude of this government." In the Ethiopian crisis of 1935, there was a tendency for the two ethnic groups, Italian Americans and black Americans, to cancel

out whatever political influence the other hoped to wield on this issue.

In summary, the three countervailing factors that can diminish an ethnic group's ability to shape particular policies are the existence of widespread public sentiment in opposition, the presence of nonethnic special-interest lobbies on the other side, and the existence of other ethnic groups who take a contrary position. Where none of the three countervailing pressures exist, even a relatively small ethnic minority can dominate a policy area.

Placing foreign policy in the context of electoral politics, the candidate or officeholder has everything to gain and nothing to lose by endorsing the goals of a particular ethnic group. Politicians can obtain the political support of the members of the group who consider the issue in question to be of significance; at the same time no voters are alienated.

Truman's political advisers made just this argument in obtaining the president's support for the new state of Israel during the 1948 presidential election. White House staff members Clark Clifford and David Niles suggested to the president that he could obtain the support of Jewish voters by taking a pro-Israel stand; at the same time he would not lose any significant number of votes.

MULTICULTURALISM AND FOREIGN POLICY

For nearly two centuries following the establishment of the American republic, it was generally accepted that a common identity and purpose bound the nation together even though the population itself had various ethnic origins, languages, and religions. Although there was an acknowledgment that immigrants added to the culture through their unique contributions, unmistakably the American standard was white, Anglo-Saxon, Protestant, and European.

Often referred to as the "melting pot," American society was constantly in transition as new ideas changed it. It remained clear that the dominant values and traditions were still those of the generation of the Founders and their Anglo-Saxon heritage. This tradition provided a standard to which immigrants must strive. Early in the twentieth century the largest influx of immigration in world history brought millions of eastern and southern European immigrants into the

★ ★ ★ ★

ELECTORAL POLITICS AND THE BIRTH OF ISRAEL

At age thirty-eight Clark McAdams Clifford arrived in Washington, D.C., in 1945 to serve in a relatively minor position as an assistant to the president's naval aide. By 1946 Harry Truman was so delighted with Clifford's performance that he chose the lawyer from St. Louis to be special counsel to the president. Clifford was immediately responsible for preparing many of Truman's state papers, speeches, and memoranda.

Once at the center of power, Clifford displayed an intelligence and an instinct for power that made him Truman's most influential adviser and one of the handful of most important White House aides in history. Labeled a "golden boy," the elegant, handsome, and charming aide seemed an unlikely political and personal partner of the president. With the enthusiastic backing of Truman, Clifford prepared a memorandum that in general terms outlined a strategy for Truman to win the 1948 election. In November 1947 the forty-three-page document, "The Politics of 1948," was presented to the president. This bold report demonstrated that Clifford was a tough political pragmatist.

Recommending a "course of political conduct" for Truman, his aide emphasized that the approach was based "solely on an appraisal of the politically advantageous course to follow." Truman read the memorandum carefully, and agreed with Clifford's analysis and proposed victory strategy. The report became the blueprint for the 1948 campaign waged by the president. One section dealt with the various special interest groups that the Democrats hoped to attract, including Jewish voters.

The memorandum, "The Politics of 1948," from Clifford to Truman on 19 November 1947, stated:

> The Jewish vote . . . is important only in New York. But (except for Wilson in 1916) no candidate since 1876 has lost New York and won the Presidency, and its forty-seven [electoral] votes are naturally the first prize in any election. Centered in New York City, that vote is normally Democratic and, if large enough, is sufficient to counteract the upstate vote and deliver the state to President Truman. Today the Jewish bloc is interested primarily in Palestine and will continue to be an uncertain quantity right up to the time of election.

Throughout the election year of 1948 Clifford recommended policies on the Palestine issue (involving the Zionist effort to establish a Jewish state in Palestine) that were intended to improve the president's standing with the American Jewish community. In the final six months of the campaign the president's decisions on Palestine bore the mark of Clifford's influence. Truman was increasingly willing to follow recommendations based upon domestic political considerations.

United States. Since these newcomers were less familiar with the accepted American values (such as democracy) than previous immigrant groups had been, "Americanization" programs were initiated to ensure that new Americans came to accept the values of the old. Education, politics, and popular culture promoted the bedrock message that America was a single nation, one people, with a common culture regardless of the mixture of backgrounds.

Until the collapse of the Soviet Union there had been a perceived common threat to national security that further emphasized to Americans the importance of consensus and approaching problems with a singleness of purpose. The Cold War created a mood that encouraged solidarity and reinforced the argument that Americans should remain a unified people with shared values. The failure to replace that Cold War consensus with any coherent foreign policy agenda that might have brought the public together has become a factor in the disintegration of consensus for at least a segment of the public.

In recent years a contrary vision concerning how much Americans hold in common has received wide currency and has in turn opened up a serious dialogue concerning what the rights and obligations of individuals and groups should be in a democracy. The question of what it is that holds a nation together is at the heart of the issue. Implications regarding how foreign policy should be determined, as well as the appropriate influence of ethnic and racial groups in the making of policy, are involved.

World War I destroyed the European order and empowered Wilson's doctrine of self-determination, and World War II ended western colonial empires and opened the way for greater racial and ethnic militancy everywhere, including the United States. Changes in immigration law in the 1960s ensured that most immigrants would no longer come from Europe, but rather from Central and South America and Asia. Along with a new militancy on the part of African Americans, millions of non-European immigrants were equally unwilling to accept the old rules of assimilation because their backgrounds were so different from that of the mainstream American ideal.

Among African Americans, other racial minorities such as Native Americans, and new immigrants there has been a growing acceptance of what has been labeled the multiculturalist interpretation of what holds America together. Rejecting assimilation and promoting the concept of America not as one nation but rather a nation of groups, the multiculturalists aim for an acceptance of pluralism without any cultural hegemony. In a nation of groups, race and ethnicity, rather than a national identity, can be the defining experience for individuals. The basic meaning of American history, say the multiculturalists, is as much the divisions into racial and ethnic groups as the traditional explanation of there being one nation and one people.

Is there one national interest that should be protected in the making of foreign policy? In the past, ethnic groups hoping to influence policy had to justify their specific goals as being consistent with basic policy guidelines. Blaming the change on the influence of multiculturalism, Samuel Huntington has written: "They [multiculturalists] deny the existence of a common culture in the United States, denounce assimilation, and promote the primacy of racial, ethnic, and other sub-national cultural identities and groupings."

Critics of multiculturalism decry what they see as a higher priority being placed on ethnic identity than on identifying with the greater American community. By pursuing a diplomatic agenda that is of interest only to itself, an ethnic group is expecting the entire nation to serve its interests. The political scientist Tony Smith, in *Foreign Attachments,* comes down hard on multiculturalists, who, he charges, have given a higher priority to one's sense of ethnic identity than to the greater American community. Smith believes that American influence in the world, which should be used for goals related to the common national good, is at risk of being squandered by a process in which ethnic minorities split up the resources and use them for individualized group interests.

With the end of the Cold War leaving America without a defined policy that sets boundaries on what ethnic constituencies can request, and with influencing policy so easy today because of the scramble for money and votes in a political system so evenly balanced between the two major parties, Smith fears that the balance has tipped in favor of pressure groups that include ethnic minorities. While ethnic groups certainly have the right to lobby the government, Smith believes that they also have an obligation to reconcile their ethnic agenda in foreign policy with a broader national interest.

Smith argues that as difficult as it sometimes is to define, America needs a sense of national purpose in world affairs. Individual ethnic groups cannot define that purpose, and they should not have exclusive rights to determine policy, as they sometimes claim they do. Who speaks for America in international affairs? Smith says that the answer should be that it is those who think of themselves first as Americans. Too many multiculturalists are unable to give that answer.

ETHNIC POLITICS AND SOUND POLICYMAKING

As American diplomacy enters a new century, it is indisputable that ethnic politics plays an important role in shaping policy. A substantive question is whether such influences upon the conduct of foreign affairs are an obstruction to sound policymaking or make a legitimate contribution. The traditional approach has been for students of American diplomacy to condemn the interrelationship between ethnic pressure and the direction of foreign policy. Diplomatic decision making, it is often said, should be determined solely on the basis of what is best for the national interest of the United States. This sentiment was presented clearly by the political scientist G. Lowell Field, who in 1964 wrote that he was interested in discovering remedies "for the curse of ethnicity in American politics."

According to Field, ethnicity poses a "danger to prudent national decision-making." Besides suggesting the abolition of the nationalities divisions of the Republican and Democratic parties, Field favors the "ostracism . . . [of] any political leader who obviously directs special appeals for the support of particular foreign policies to ethnic groupings with an undue emotional involvement."

Field argues that in the "proper moral climate" an ethnic group should be embarrassed when politicians make "this kind of appeal, just as a judge would be embarrassed by efforts to get him to participate in the decision of a case involving a close relative." It is simply illegitimate, Field says, to promote or even "tolerate situations—like those in which foreign policy hearings are conducted by the major parties before their national conventions—in which it appears that the feelings of ethnic minorities are legitimate grounds for deciding whether or not such intervention by American power is possible or desirable."

Taking decision making in foreign policy out of domestic politics and consigning it to the experts is a suggestion not limited to academe. In 1961 Senator J. William Fulbright insisted that foreign policy should not be determined in a deliberative forum in which parochial domestic interests would have influence. "The question I put," wrote Fulbright, "is whether in the face of the harsh necessities of the 1960s we can afford the luxury of 18th century procedures of measured deliberation."

Fulbright doubted that a successful foreign policy could originate "by continuing to leave vast and vital decision-making powers in the hands of a decentralized, independent-minded, and largely parochial-minded body of legislators. . . . I submit that the price of democratic survival in a world of aggressive totalitarianism is to give up some of the democratic luxuries of the past." Foreign policy, Fulbright argued, should be determined by the experts in the executive branch of government and should not be a political football in Congress. Implementation of Fulbright's thesis that Congress should play less of a role in foreign policy formulation would clearly hinder the ability of ethnic groups to lobby for their particular interests.

At the beginning of the twenty-first century, those who approve of the link between ethnic minorities and foreign policy no longer argue from a defensive position. They instead point out that policymakers are themselves often highly partisan and political on specific foreign policy issues. For example, Jewish Americans have long contended that the Middle East desk at the State Department has traditionally been staffed by personnel who are pro-Arab. Since some persons in the State Department contend that the national interest lies in protecting American commercial interests in the Middle East, ethnic bias is not the only possible explanation of the State Department

position. Similarly, supporters of America's pro-Israel stance are not necessarily Zionists but can instead insist that the national interest is best served by supporting democracies, such as Israel, wherever they exist. Why, the critics of official Washington ask, should it be assumed that the State Department's interpretation of the national interest is any more creditable than the views of State Department critics?

Ethnic leaders have suggested that nothing could be more appropriate in a democracy than to bring interest groups into the decision-making process. Following an era in Washington marked by governmental disdain for the public, the concept of broadening the public's role in decision making has substantial appeal.

Promoting good relations with foreign nations is basic to American diplomacy. One way to foster such friendly ties would be to make conspicuous a link between specific ethnic minorities and U.S. foreign policy toward their homeland. Ethnic leaders have argued that the goodwill that can be won by emphasizing the interrelationship between the ethnic group and policy toward the land of origin provides a compelling argument for encouraging such a relationship.

Among world powers, only the United States, with its diversity of ethnic populations, has had such obvious opportunities. Individual representatives, as well as an entire ethnic community, can be effectively used for diplomatic purposes. When President John F. Kennedy visited his ancestral home in Ireland and when he frequently referred to his Irish background, the resulting benefit to Irish-American relations was enormous. Similar goodwill is gained when a prominent member of an ethnic group is given a diplomatic assignment.

One example of using an entire ethnic group to obtain a foreign policy goal was presented in Italian-American relations during the late 1940s. Washington became concerned that the Italian electorate might vote the Communist Party into control of the national government. Encouraged by U.S. officials, Italian Americans mounted a mail campaign in which relatives in Italy would be persuaded to vote against the Communists. Italian Americans responded enthusiastically.

The legitimacy of ethnic groups' lobbying for policies they desire no longer seems as questionable as it was once considered to be. American elections and the political process have moved in the direction of multiple interests seeking to have their ideas heard and the policies they support accepted. Why is the attempt by ethnic minorities to influence the direction of foreign policy any less legitimate than the lobbying efforts of any number of economic interest groups? Why should it be any less legitimate to vote from ethnic considerations than for economic or social reasons? These are questions asked by spokesmen for ethnic minorities involved in foreign affairs issues.

ETHNIC GROUP INFLUENCE IN FOREIGN POLICY: PRO AND CON

An argument made against ethnic influence on foreign policy is that such influence is likely to spring from emotional loyalties rather than rational objectives. The goals of U.S. foreign policy can be summarized as military security, protection of economic interests, and minimization and peaceful settlement of international disputes. Ethnicity certainly has no obvious relation to any of these goals, and to the extent that it might be in conflict with them, it is an improper influence.

What this argument ignores is that the rational objectives articulated by professional policymakers generally omit such "emotional" factors as fairness to downtrodden or impoverished peoples. This has usually been the case with respect to colonial or dictatorial governments friendly to the United States. Such governments, especially in strategically located or mineral-rich countries, have consistently been supported by the United States for the reasons previously suggested.

Thus, the articulation of arguments for a contrary policy—based on justice, commitment to democracy, and other ideals—is typically left to the affected ethnic groups. An example in the recent past is the dictatorship in Greece, in the creation of which the United States played a considerable and unsavory role. American support was drastically curtailed, in large measure, on account of the persistent efforts of Greek Americans. Similarly, the ethical commitment to displaced Jewry after World War II was argued mainly by Jewish Americans, while the State Department and the public at large took little interest. Any ethical commitment to Palestinian Arabs, who had been consistently under foreign domination, was overlooked. There was not a significant Arab-American lobby to promote the cause of the victimized Palestinian Arabs.

It is argued that to insist that the formulation of foreign policy should remain separate from the right of ethnic groups to exert influence would be to abandon a central attribute of a vital democratic state. Ethnic participation in foreign policy is defended as being consistent with the American political ideals of democracy and freedom.

Those opposed to ethnic participation counter by saying that the result of openly sanctioning such political bartering would be a foreign policy in which a president or Congress would risk national survival simply to uphold a political pledge. The safeguard against such a disaster would likely be the general public. The political reality would seem to be that the public would not tolerate a president or a Congress embroiling the United States in some ill-conceived adventure designed to placate a particular group.

Although it would have been popular with a variety of ethnic voters, the Republican Party did not "liberate" eastern Europe from communism following the 1952 election. Republican campaign pledges proved to be insincere, since there was little likelihood that the new administration was actually going to war in order to terminate communist control of eastern Europe. Presented with the opportunity to intervene in the 1956 Hungarian revolt against the Soviet Union, the administration quickly indicated that it would stay uninvolved in that effort to throw off Soviet domination.

The political scientist Lawrence Fuchs, arguing in favor of a close interrelationship between minority group pressure and American diplomacy, has suggested "that foreign policy is too important to be left to the experts." Opponents of the enhanced role that ethnic constituencies have in contemporary foreign policy decision making remain unimpressed. They instead forecast grave danger ahead for any coherent national diplomatic agenda if foreign policy continues to be even more of a political football than it has in the past. The question of the appropriateness of mixing ethnicity with foreign policy will no doubt continue to be debated, but even diehard opponents of the phenomenon now concede that ethnicity is probably an inevitable concomitant of the American political process.

BIBLIOGRAPHY

Ahrari, Mohammed E., ed. *Ethnic Groups and U.S. Foreign Policy.* New York, 1987. Articles on selected ethnic constituencies and their efforts to shape American diplomacy.

Baldassare, Mark. *California in the New Millennium: The Changing Social and Political Landscape*. Berkeley, Calif., 2000. A treasury of quantified data and political analysis of California's current political scene that includes much on the state's multiple ethnic constituencies.

Chang, Gordon, ed. *Asian Americans and Politics: Perspectives, Experiences, and Prospects*. Washington, D.C., 2000. Rich collection of articles on both the collective Asian-American political experience and individual studies of particular ethnic groups. Section on voting behavior contains useful quantified data on the political behavior of Asian Americans.

Cohen, Michael J. *Truman and Israel*. Berkeley, Calif., 1990. Account of both the Jewish-American campaign to influence the Truman administration before and after the creation of the Jewish state, and the administration's response to the pressure, always with its own political interests in mind.

DeConde, Alexander. *Ethnicity, Race, and American Foreign Policy: A History*. Boston, 1992. By far the best and most thorough contemporary history of ethnic groups and the influence they have in shaping American foreign policy.

Druks, Herbert. *The Uncertain Friendship: The U. S. and Israel from Roosevelt to Kennedy*. Westport, Conn., 2001. Political history of the diplomacy of four presidential administrations and how they responded to the campaign to establish a Jewish state, and the alliance that developed between Israel and America.

Free, Lloyd, and Hadley Cantril. *The Political Beliefs of Americans: A Study of Public Opinion*. New York, 1968. Public opinion study with useful material on attitudes on foreign policy issues.

Fuchs, Lawrence. "Minority Groups and Foreign Policy." *Political Science Quarterly* 76 (1959). An early exception to the view that ethnic pressure on foreign policy goals was undesirable.

Gerson, Louis. *Woodrow Wilson and the Rebirth of Poland, 1914–1920*. New Haven, Conn., 1953. Specialized study of how one ethnic group affected a particular aspect of foreign policy. Gerson identifies the role played by Polish Americans in helping to create an independent Poland in the aftermath of World War I.

———. *The Hyphenate in Recent American Politics and Diplomacy*. Lawrence, Kans., 1964. One of the first thorough studies of ethnicity and American foreign policy, Gerson's perspective was the inappropriateness of ethnic group pressure being an important factor in shaping diplomacy.

Gomez Quinones, Juan. *Chicano Politics: Reality and Promise, 1940–1990*. Albuquerque, N.M., 1990. Examines the barriers Hispanics encountered in efforts to establish a position of legitimacy within the American political system, and the initial successes they experienced within the Democratic Party structure beginning in the 1970s.

Gutierrez, David G. *Walls and Mirrors: Mexican Americans, Mexican Immigrants, and the Politics of Ethnicity*. Berkeley, Calif., 1995. Of particular value for the material on the relationship between Mexican Americans and the Mexican government.

Huntington, Samuel P. "The Erosion of American National Interests." *Foreign Affairs* 76, no. 5 (1997): 28–49.

Levering, Ralph B. *The Public and American Foreign Policy, 1918–1978*. New York, 1978. Valuable work on the link between public opinion and foreign policy from the end of World War I through the late 1970s.

Levy, Mark, and Michael Kramer. *The Ethnic Factor: How America's Minorities Decide Elections*. New York, 1972. Contains some valuable statistical data on ethnic group voting patterns.

Linn, Brian McAllister. *The Philippine War, 1899–1902*. Lawrence, Kans., 2000. History of the war waged in the Pacific that includes material on U.S. troops' racial attitudes and antagonisms toward the native population.

Moynihan, Daniel P., and Nathan Glazer, eds. *Ethnicity*. Cambridge, Mass., 1975. Moynihan and Glazer sympathize with the goals of ethnic political campaigns and emphasize the significant impact ethnicity has had on American diplomacy; they state "that immigration is the single most important determinant of American foreign policy."

Nathan, James A., and James K. Oliver. *Foreign Policy Making and the American Political System*. 3d ed. Baltimore, 1994. Survey of what Americans know of world affairs.

O'Grady, Joseph P. *The Immigrants' Influence on Wilson's Peace Policies*. Lexington, Ky., 1967. Account of the efforts by several groups to influence Wilson's peacemaking.

Rosenthal, Steven T. *Irreconcilable Differences? The Waning of the American Jewish Love Affair with Israel.* Hanover, N.H., 2001. Well-argued study to the effect that what was once unquestioned American Jewish support for Israel has been replaced by a number of sharp disagreements over Israel's conduct that have divided American Jews.

Schlesinger, Arthur M., Jr. *The Disuniting of America: Reflections on a Multicultural Society.* New York, 1998. A highly influential rejoinder to multiculturalism by a noted historian identified with the establishment. Although there is no real attempt to examine multiculturalism and its relationship to the issue of who should speak for the United States in foreign policy, the arguments nonetheless relate to the central issue of identity and policy.

Smith, Tony. *Foreign Attachments: The Power of Ethnic Groups in the Making of American Foreign Policy.* Cambridge, Mass., 2000. Persuasive argument that ethnic groups play a larger role in making foreign policy than is widely understood, and that the negative consequences of this phenomenon far outweigh any benefits.

Snetsinger, John. *Truman, the Jewish Vote, and the Creation of Israel.* Stanford, Calif., 1974. An effort to explain the critical role that Jewish Americans played in bringing the state of Israel into existence.

Torres, Maria de los Angeles. *In the Land of Mirrors: Cuban Exile Politics in the United States.* Ann Arbor, Mich., 1999.

United States Census 2000. Washington, D.C.: Department of Statistics and Administration, United States Census Bureau, Department of Commerce, 2001.

See also ASYLUM; CULTURAL IMPERIALISM; CULTURAL RELATIONS AND POLICIES; IMMIGRATION; PUBLIC OPINION; REFUGEE POLICIES; WILSONIAN MISSIONARY DIPLOMACY.

REALISM AND IDEALISM

★ ★ ★ ★ ★

Norman A. Graebner

Philosophically, realism and idealism comprise opposing approaches to the definition and pursuit of national objectives abroad. Realists tend to accept conditions as they are and to define the ends and means of policy by the measures of anticipated gains, costs, necessities, and chances of success. Idealists tend to define goals in ideal, often visionary, forms, and presume that the means for their achievement lie less in measured policies, relying on diplomacy or force, than in the attractiveness of the goals themselves.

CONFLICTING PERCEPTIONS

These two modes of perceiving world politics were never uniquely American in precept or experience. Western political thought always recognized the tension between realist and idealist views toward the actions of governments in both domestic and international transactions. The stark realism of Niccolò Machiavelli stood in profound opposition to the dominant Christian teachings that favored ethical constraints upon rulers. In the eighteenth century, doctrines of *raison d'état* contended with Enlightenment doctrines propounded by philosophers who objected to such practices of monarchical statecraft as mercantilism, balance-of-power politics, and the pursuit of dynastic goals at the expense of peace and human welfare.

While the American clash between realism and idealism owes an intellectual debt to antecedent European thought, it was in the United States that both doctrines were fully established, in theory and in practice. Whereas in continental Europe, utopian idealism remained excluded from the realm of practice, in the United States it became a recurrent, contrapuntal theme of statesmen and politicians, commentators and theorists. What underlay the conflicting presumptions regarding the requirements and possibilities of external

action was the anarchical nature of the international environment. Whereas governmental structures within established countries assured some degree of order and security, the absence of international authority compelled individual countries to fend for themselves, relying on their own capacities to coexist in what social contract theorists termed a state of nature. Realists and idealists disagreed totally over the capacity of human society, and especially international politics, to eliminate the vagaries of existence in an anarchic state system.

Realists, recognizing no genuine alternative to coexistence in an anarchical world of individual sovereign nations, accepted the modern state system as a necessity. They would defend the country's interests by following the rules of diplomacy and war as propounded by a host of seventeenth- and eighteenth-century writers and statesmen. These rules of conduct were not designed to prevent conflict and war, but rather to mitigate their effects and thereby assure the survival of states. For realists, moreover, war was not an aberration, but a condition sometimes unavoidable, a contingency for which to prepare, but also, when possible, to deter by force or accommodation. Wars, they knew, were generally the only means available for changing unwanted political or territorial conditions. Realists thus accepted power politics as a natural phenomenon of international life, with the concomitant reliance on armies and navies, secret diplomacy, and alliances. Asserting the primacy of national over individual interests, they viewed the universal norms governing human rights as conditional when they threatened the national welfare. Realists observed the essential truth that nations existed successfully amid the world's anarchy. The evidence lay in the precedence of peace over war, as well as the continued material advancement in human affairs.

Idealists viewed the international system, with its accoutrements of conflict and war, as not only deeply flawed but also capable of melioration, if not total cure. For them, international strife was the unnecessary and reprehensible product of outmoded forms of human organization, both in the internal structuring of states and in their international practices. Idealists saw in the trappings of power politics little but ambition, opportunism, deception, and impositions. Whereas realist doctrine focused on national interests and security, idealist concerns looked to individual welfare and the general interests of humanity. Idealists presumed that the objective validity and authority of universal norms, laws, and principles could and should apply to international as well as domestic affairs.

Realists and idealists disagreed fundamentally on the primary determinants of state behavior in international politics. For realists, external factors defined the options available to policymakers. Those options were uncertain and elusive, requiring preparedness as well as caution. Secretary of State Dean Acheson once remarked: "The future is unpredictable. Only one thing— the unexpected—can be reasonably anticipated. . . . The part of wisdom is to be prepared for what may happen, rather than to base our course upon faith in what should happen." The German historian Leopold von Ranke formulated this view in terms congenial to American realists. The dangers and uncertainties of international life, he wrote, not only established the primacy of foreign affairs but also dictated the precedence of security interests over domestic concerns. While cognizant of the historical vicissitudes in national fortunes, realists nevertheless saw constancy in the essential traits and behavior of nations. Policies might vary with regimes, but fundamental interests, once established, tended to remain consistent.

Idealists, on the contrary, tended to view the sources of external state action as residing in internal political processes, based largely on political structures, the distribution of political power, and the ambitions of ruling elites. Involvements abroad reflected not external necessity, but internal choice. To idealists, different forms of government led to different modes of foreign policy. Autocratic states, some idealists presumed, too readily threatened the cause of humanity by placing demands on individuals that were sharply at odds with private conscience. By ordering men into mortal combat with other members of the human race, they shattered the peace and defied the civilized norms of human conduct. Authentic republics did not wage aggressive wars, nor did free peoples impose imperial control over others.

However apparent the wellsprings of aggressive national behavior, realists accepted limits on both their intentions and their power to interfere. They recognized the barriers that national sovereignty placed on meliorist efforts to alter the political structures and domestic decisions of other countries. Idealists, as children of the Enlightenment, expected more of themselves and society. For them, the world was not hopelessly corrupt, but could, through proper leadership and motivation, advance morally and politically. This optimistic view of the world became endemic to the idealists' presumptions of human progress and the concomitant conviction that the United States, because of the superiority of its institutions, was ideally constituted to lead the world toward an improving future. The belief that institutional and moral superiority distinguished the United States from other countries found its central expression in the concept of "exceptionalism." This assigned to American suppositions of exceptional virtue the imperative of exceptional obligation to serve the peace and improve the human condition.

THE REVOLUTIONARY ERA

America's idealist crusade to minimize the country's role in power politics was heavily influenced by the debates of eighteenth-century British politicians, journalists, and pamphleteers. Despite the quarrel between Britain and its American colonies after the Seven Years' War (1756-1763), largely over Parliament's jurisdiction in imperial, commercial, and political matters, the contestants were closely linked intellectually. What troubled English critics of Britain's role in European politics was the heavy burden of taxation, alliances, and perennial wars demanded of Britain because of its continental connections. By steering clear of such attachments, Britain could concentrate on the pacific activities of trade and commerce, assigning the saved resources to benign uses. Such arguments for reducing Britain's role in European politics applied as well to America's ties with Britain.

Thomas Paine, above all other American writers, created the link between English reformist thought and that of the colonies. Bankrupt and a failure at everything he attempted, Paine immigrated to America in 1774. There he quickly emerged as the chief pamphleteer for American independence. In his famed essay *Com-*

mon Sense (1776), Paine argued that America's attachment to Britain alone endangered its security. It was the British connection that tended "to involve this Continent in European wars and quarrels, and set us at variance with nations who would otherwise seek our friendship, and against whom we have neither anger nor complaint." More specifically, Paine predicted that France and Spain, both New World powers, would never be "our enemies as *Americans,* but as our being *subjects of Great Britain.*" An independent United States would have no cause to defy other countries with demanding foreign policies. He assured his readers that "our plan is commerce, and that, well attended to, will secure us the peace and friendship of Europe; because it is the interest of all Europe to have America a free port." American independence would symbolize the rejection of Europe and the entire system of power politics. During the ratification debates regarding the U.S. Constitution a decade later, the Antifederalists employed these isolationist arguments against ratification, convinced that the oceans assured the country's security without the Constitution's war-making powers.

Paine's writings contained the fundamental assumptions of idealist thought on foreign policy. For him the young republic, freed from the contamination and constraints of power politics, appeared ideally constituted to create a new order in world affairs. The American Revolution, as a triumphant avowal of the principle of free government, seemed an auspicious event in the eternal quest for peace and human rights. "The cause of America," proclaimed Paine, "is in great measure the cause of mankind." He regarded the institution of monarchy the chief cause of human misery and war. "Man is not the enemy of man," he wrote, "but through the medium of a false system of government." How, he wondered, could the monarchies of Europe, unable to satisfy the needs of their citizens, survive the revolutionary pressures being unleashed by events in America? Those moral principles, which allegedly maintained peaceful and just relations among individuals, would, in time, rule the behavior of nations.

Other American contemporaries found Paine's views highly congenial. Benjamin Franklin proclaimed such sentiments when, in April 1782, he said: "Establishing the liberties of America will not only make that people happy, but will have some effect in diminishing the misery of those, who in other parts of the world groan under despotism, by rendering it more cir-

cumspect, and inducing it to govern with a lighter hand." Thomas Jefferson elaborated virtually identical views in both his public and private observations. "I have sworn upon the altar of God," he wrote, "eternal hostility against every form of tyranny over the mind of man." For Jefferson, force was evil unless informed by some moral purpose. But whereas Paine harbored visions of an activist, messianic role for the United States in world politics, Jefferson generally held to more modest aspirations. America would best serve the interests of mankind by setting an example of purity and perfection, and by offering an asylum for the wretched and oppressed. "A single good government," he once wrote, "becomes a blessing to the whole earth." James Madison, a contemporary idealist, echoed the sentiment: "Our Country, if it does justice to itself, will be the workshop of liberty to the Civilized World, and do more than any other for the uncivilized."

Contemporary conservatives attacked as utopian Paine's idealist notions regarding the world's future and America's role in its creation. They knew that the United States could not project a successful international crusade beyond the reach of American law. What determined the external behavior of republics, they believed, was not the uniqueness of their political structures or the outlook of their people, but the international environment beyond their control, the demands imposed by their own ambitions, and the countering requirements of other states. James Madison, no less than others, denied that the foreign policies of republics differed essentially from those of monarchies. Hard experience had taught the revolutionary generation that nations dealt with others solely on the bases of interests and the capacity to render them effective.

Alexander Hamilton, in *The Federalist* (1788), questioned the assumption that commerce softened the manners of men and extinguished "those inflammable humors which have so often kindled into wars." He observed that nations responded more readily to immediate interests than to general or humane considerations of policy. He asked: "Have republics in practice been less addicted to war than monarchies? . . . Are not popular assemblies frequently subject to the impulses of rage, resentment, jealousy, avarice, and of other irregular and violent propensities? . . . Has commerce hitherto done any thing more than change the objects of war?" Hamilton suggested that Americans look to experience for answers to such questions. Carthage, a commercial republic, was the aggressor in the very war that terminated its existence. Holland, another trading republic, played a conspicuous role in the wars of modern Europe—as did Britain, markedly addicted to commerce. Hamilton concluded: "The cries of the nation and the importunities of their representatives have, upon various occasions, dragged their monarchs into war, or continued them in it, contrary to their inclinations, and sometimes contrary to the real interests of the state."

Hamilton dwelled on the dangers that the real world of power politics posed for the United States. Some Americans, he warned, had been amused too long by theories that promised them "an exemption from the imperfections, weaknesses, and evils incident to society in every shape." It would be better for the country to assume, as did all other nations, that the happy empire of wisdom and virtue did not exist. "To look for a continuation of harmony between a number of independent, unconnected sovereignties . . . ," he wrote in *The Federalist* No. 6, "would be to disregard the uniform course of human events, and to set at defiance the accumulated experience of [the] ages." Because constant disputes could lead to war, he concluded that national safety required a strong central government, with a capacity to wage war and advance common interests in a potentially hostile world. For him, defense against the nation's external challenges lay in the powers granted by the new U.S. Constitution.

THE EARLY NATIONAL PERIOD

Not surprisingly, the French Revolution, and the subsequent war between revolutionary France and England after 1792, kindled the burgeoning rivalry between Jefferson and Hamilton, members of President George Washington's cabinet as, respectively, secretary of state and secretary of the Treasury. Earlier, such idealists as Paine and Jefferson had abhorred power politics and war; Hamilton, the realist, had preached preparedness with its warlike implications. The idealism generated by the French Revolution compelled a reversal of positions. Paine, supported by Jefferson, roused public clamors for support of the French Revolution and its principles. Idealists demanded that the United States support France's war effort. Hamilton, with Washington, inclined to peaceful neutrality, with the effect, if not the intention, of serving the British cause. The idealists argued from principle, the real-

ists from prudence and experience. Hamilton's view prevailed when Washington issued his Neutrality Proclamation of 1793.

In Jefferson's subsequent debate with Hamilton over the wisdom and morality of Washington's proclamation, he based his advocacy of U.S. support for revolutionary France on the grounds that the United States must be faithful to its obligations under the Franco-American alliance of 1778, demonstrate gratitude for French assistance during the war against Britain, and reveal its affinity for republican institutions in a monarchical world. Jefferson's three arguments rested on sentiment, not interests. Hamilton attacked these propositions head-on in a series of long public letters. In "Pacificus" of 6 July 1793, he argued that a country's first obligation was to itself. The United States, he noted, had no power to aid France in its European war. No country, he concluded, could be obligated to do what it could not do. Next, Hamilton attacked Jefferson's notion of gratitude to France for past favors, noting simply that France had aided the United States to serve its own interests in England's defeat, not those of the United States. Governments, he argued, could not operate as individuals. Individuals could engage in actions of generosity or benevolence at the expense of their own interests, but a government, he said, could rarely be justified in pursuing such a course. It was responsible for the welfare of all of its citizens and for all time. In his "Americanus" papers of 1794, Hamilton denied, thirdly, that the cause of revolutionary France, with all of its excesses, was the cause of liberty, or that the failure of French revolutionary principles would undermine the security of the United States.

Hamilton read the nation another series of lectures on the fundamentals of a realist foreign policy in his "Camillus" essays of 1795. He published these papers in defense of Jay's Treaty, negotiated with Britain and signed in November 1794. Hamilton made little effort to defend the treaty's specific provisions or omissions, but lauded the settlement's role in preventing war. In no way, he declared, were the negotiations dishonorable, the terms disgraceful. He counseled moderation: "Nations ought to calculate as well as individuals, to compare evils, and to prefer the lesser to the greater; to act otherwise, is to act unreasonably; those who advocate it are imposters and madmen." Hamilton admonished Americans to recall that the United States, no less than the powers of Europe, were bound by the established modes of international behavior. "In national controversies," Hamilton averred, "it is of real importance to conciliate the good opinion of mankind, and it is even useful to preserve or gain that of our enemy. The latter facilitates accommodation and peace—the former attracts good offices, friendly interventions, sometimes direct support, from others." Against such appeals to tradition and common sense, Jefferson stood helpless. He confessed to Madison that Hamilton was "really a colossus. . . . In truth, when he comes forward, there is no one but yourself who can meet him." "For God's sake," he pleaded, "take up your pen, and give a fundamental reply to . . . Camillus." Madison declined the challenge.

Washington's Farewell Address of 17 September 1796 was the culminating statement of Federalist thought on matters of external policy. It reflected the views of Madison, Hamilton, and John Jay, the three authors of *The Federalist.* Hamilton, in revising it, made it largely his own. Washington's valedictory was a message for the times, but it was far more. He admonished the country to behave in accordance with established eighteenth-century principles as they applied to international affairs. Throughout his second term, Washington had been troubled by the dangerous attachments of too many Americans to the European belligerents. In October 1795 he had stressed the necessity of greater independence in a letter to Patrick Henry: "My ardent desire is . . . to see that [the United States] *may be* independent of *all,* and under the influence of *none.* In a word, I want an *American* character, that the powers of Europe may be convinced we act for *ourselves* and not for *others.*" In his Farewell Address, Washington explained why foreign attachments endangered the country's well-being: "The Nation, which indulges toward another an habitual hatred, or an habitual fondness, is in some degree a slave. It is a slave to its animosity or its affection, either of which is sufficient to lead it astray from its duty and its interest." Sympathy for favored countries or governments, he warned, assumed common interests that seldom existed and enmeshed a people in the enmities of others without justification. For Washington, there was no room in the country's external relations for crusades against evil.

Hamilton's voluminous writings during Washington's two administrations comprised a single, massive plea that the United States weigh its interests carefully before venturing abroad. Still, the persistent upheavals on the European continent, and their extension onto the Atlantic, touched American interests and sentiments sufficiently to keep alive the tensions between realists and idealists as they sought to influence national reactions to events abroad. The Napoleonic wars, especially as they ventured onto the Atlantic in one gigantic commercial conflict between the British navy and Napoleon's continental system, challenged the profits of America's neutral trade with Europe's belligerents. President Jefferson demanded both British and French recognition of American neutral rights and responded to his failure to obtain either with his embargo on American trade in late 1807. Under President Madison, after 1809 the country's frustration and animosity began to center on Britain because its infringements on the principle of freedom of the seas were more apparent than those of France.

As anti-British sentiment pushed the country toward war, it separated idealist sentiment, which focused on British immorality and the need to defend the principle of neutral trade, from realist arguments that war with Britain would be needless and futile. What those known as the War Hawks in Congress required was a rationale that would justify a declaration of war; the Republican Party, generally cohesive, would readily fall into line. That rationale lay in the supposition that Britain sought less the defense of belligerent rights than the ruination of the United States itself. Henry Clay of Kentucky claimed proof that Britain "will do everything to destroy us." Peter B. Porter of New York added that if the United States continued to submit to British indignities, it "might safely calculate to be kicked and cuffed for the whole of the remainder of [its] life." For some War Hawks, Britain desired no less than the recolonization of America. John A. Harper of New Hampshire charged that British conduct "bespeaks a determination to rule us, and can only be answered by the appeal to the God of Battles." Similarly, John C. Calhoun of South Carolina warned Congress that Britain was determined to reduce the United States to a colonial status.

Realists in Congress contested the march toward war. John Randolph, Virginia's noted conservative, questioned the assumption that American honor and security required a British-American conflict. In December 1811, he reminded Congress that the United States had no interest in contributing to Napoleon's success. Why, he wondered, should the country regard Britain as its special enemy? Every consideration of blood, language, religion, and interest, he observed, should incline the American people toward England. Randolph reminded Congress that the United States had no power to defeat England in war. Similarly, John Quincy Adams, U.S. minister in St. Petersburg, recalled from the Gospel of Saint Luke (14:31): "Or what king, going to make war against another king, sitteth not down first, and consulteth whether he be able with ten thousand to meet him that cometh against him with twenty thousand." The conditions confronting the United States, Adams reminded his wife, Abigail, on 1 January 1812, were even less favorable than that. When Congress, without preparation, declared war on 19 June 1812, Obadiah German of New York condemned the action. "After the war is once commenced . . . ," he warned, "I presume gentlemen will find something more forcible than empty war speeches will be necessary." It was his purpose, said German, "to check the precipitate step of plunging [the] country prematurely into a war, without any of the means of making the war terrible to the enemy; and with the certainty that it will be terrible to ourselves." Having declared war, the country would have peace only with the enemy's consent.

LATIN AMERICA AND GREECE

In 1815 the United States emerged from the War of 1812 amid a burst of nationalism and a sense of deep satisfaction from having faced England. On the one hand, the war experience encouraged a pervading interest in the future of the North American continent and a pride of distinctness and separation from Europe's international politics. On the other hand, it perpetuated a popular sensitivity to events abroad that repeatedly reopened the realist-idealist debate in the United States. The immediate postwar challenge to U.S. sentiment was Latin America's struggle for independence from Spain. Determined to sever Europe's ties to the New World in what they believed would be a triumph for humanity, editors led by William Duane of Philadelphia's *Aurora* demanded U.S. guardianship of Latin American independence. In Congress, the powerful Henry Clay denounced the administration of James Monroe, with John Quincy Adams as secretary of state, for neglecting U.S. interests and the cause of liberty in Latin America. Adams was appalled at the widespread defiance of the official U.S. policy of neutrality. "There seems to me," he complained in June 1816, "too much of the warlike humor in the debates of Congress—propositions even to take up the cause of the South Americans . . . , as

if they were talking of the expense of building a light house."

As the public pressure for involvement continued, Adams, in December 1817, reminded his father, John Adams, that Latin America had replaced the French Revolution as the great source of discord in the United States. "The republican spirit of our country . . . sympathizes with people struggling in a cause. . . . And now, as at the early stage of the French Revolution, we have ardent spirits who are for rushing into the conflict, without looking to the consequences." Monroe and Adams, against mounting public and congressional pressures, sustained the country's official neutrality until, in 1821, the striking victories of the revolutionary forces all but destroyed Spain's remaining authority in South America. In a special message to Congress on 8 March 1822, Monroe recognized the independence of Argentina, Peru, Chile, Colombia, and Mexico.

Already, a similar debate over the future of Greece had divided the Monroe administration as well as much of the country. The Greek revolution had gathered momentum until, by 1821, it posed an immediate threat to Turkey's Ottoman rule. Turkish sultan Mahmud II retaliated against the Greek revolutionaries with such violence that he aroused anti-Turkish sentiment throughout western Europe and the United States. American idealists took up the cause of the repressed Greeks even as Adams expressed his total disapproval of foreign crusades. In his famed speech of 4 July 1821, Adams declared that the United States "goes not abroad, in search of monsters to destroy. She is the well-wisher to the freedom and independence of all. She is the champion and vindicator only of her own." Monroe expressed regret over Turkey's despotic rule in his annual message of December 1822. Then, in 1823, Edward Everett, professor of Greek at Harvard, championed Greece's independence in a long essay that appeared in the *North American Review,* a journal that he edited. Adams was not impressed and argued strongly against any U.S. meddling in the affairs of Greece and Turkey, especially since the country was not prepared financially or militarily to intervene.

In January 1824, Adams's allies in Congress disposed of the Greek issue. Among Everett's converts was Daniel Webster, then a U.S. representative from Massachusetts. In December 1823, Webster introduced a resolution into the House that provided for defraying the expense of an agent or commissioner to Greece, whenever the president might deem such an appointment expedient. On 19 January 1824, while discussing this apparently noncommittal text, Webster launched into an eloquent appeal to American humanitarian sentiment. The Greeks, he said, look to "the great Republic of the earth—and they ask us by our common faith, whether we can forget that they are struggling, as we once struggled, for what we now so happily enjoy?" He asked nothing of Congress. Previously, he acknowledged, "there was no making an impression on a nation but by bayonets, and subsidies, by fleets and armies; but . . . there is a force in public opinion which, in the long run, will outweigh all the physical force that can be brought to oppose it. . . . Let us direct the force, the vast moral force of this engine, to the aid of others."

In his reply on 24 January, Randolph challenged Webster's effort to commit the country abroad to what it could not accomplish, except at enormous cost to its own interests. How, Randolph wondered, would the United States operate effectively in a country as distant as Greece? "Do gentlemen seriously reflect," he asked, "on the work they have cut out for us? Why, sir, these projects of ambition surpass those of Bonaparte himself." Finally, Randolph attacked the resolution itself:

> We are absolutely combatting shadows. The gentleman would have us to believe his resolution is all but nothing; yet again it is to prove omnipotent, and fills the whole globe with its influence. Either it is nothing, or it is something. If it is nothing, let us lay it on the table, and have done with it at once; but, if it is that something which it has been on the other hand represented to be, let us beware how we touch it. For my part, I would sooner put the shirt of Nessus on my back, than sanction these doctrines.

Such argumentation, much to Adams's delight, eliminated the issue of Greek independence from the nation's consideration.

THE MONROE DOCTRINE

Although scarcely a subject of controversy, the Monroe Doctrine, after its promulgation in 1823, remained vulnerable to disagreement over its meaning. For realists, the Monroe Doctrine represented a fundamental interest in preserving the nation's unique position as the predominant force in the hemisphere. As such, it was a policy rendered effective by the realities of power and interest in the Atlantic world. So realistic, indeed, was American purpose in preventing the establishment of rival power in the Western Hemisphere that the United States required neither war nor the threat of war to protect this essential interest. British leaders tended to accept the Monroe Doctrine as a statement of policy and nothing more.

Idealists viewed the Monroe Doctrine as a broad declaration of liberal principles. For them, the United States, in defying the Holy Alliance, had promoted less the nation's interests than the liberty of Latin America. Because the doctrine appeared to attach American purpose to a universal democratic ideal, many European masters of Realpolitik viewed it as purely utopian. They condemned it because, as a body of abstract principle, it would overreach actual U.S. economic and security interests, as well as seek to diminish European influence in Latin American affairs, solely on claims to superior political virtue. For Prince Metternich of Austria, such suppositions were nothing less than sheer arrogance. "The United States of America," he complained, "have cast blame and scorn on the institutions of Europe most worthy of respect. . . . In permitting themselves these unprovoked attacks, in fostering revolutions wherever they show themselves, in regretting those which have failed, in extending a helping hand to those which seem to prosper, they lend new strength to the apostles of sedition and reanimate the courage of every conspirator." In practice, every administration from Monroe to John Tyler recognized the Monroe Doctrine as policy, not principle. They accepted changes in the region, such as the British seizure of the Falkland Islands in 1833, because they did not endanger U.S. economic or security interests.

In 1845, President James K. Polk provided John C. Calhoun, at the time one of the nation's stellar realists, an opportunity to read the country a lesson on the Monroe Doctrine. During the summer of 1845, the president received reports of British designs on California. In June, François Guizot, in a speech before the French Chamber of Deputies, claimed a European interest in preserving "the balance of the Great Powers among which America is divided." In his December message to Congress, Polk, under pressure from American expansionists, repeated Monroe's declaration on noncolonization. On 14 January 1846, Senator William Allen of Ohio, chairman of the Senate Committee on Foreign Relations, introduced a resolution designed to commit Congress to the principles of the Monroe Doctrine as

★ ★ ★ ★

WAR AND DOCTRINES

The economist and social scientist William Graham Sumner (1874–1910) was a prolific publicist of social Darwinism. Through public addresses and periodical essays, he carried on a warfare against economic and political evils, treating practically every social question of his day in an unsentimental and critical fashion. In 1903 he published his observations on the role of doctrines as a guide to foreign policy:

"If you want war, nourish a doctrine. Doctrines are the most frightful tyrants to which men ever are subject, because doctrines get inside a man's own reason and betray him against himself. Civilized men have done their fiercest fighting for doctrines. . . . What are they all? Nothing but rhetoric and phantasms. Doctrines are always vague; it would ruin a doctrine to define it, because then it could be analyzed, tested, criticised, and verified; but nothing ought to be tolerated which cannot be so tested. Somebody asks you with astonishment and horror whether you do not believe in the Monroe Doctrine. You do not know whether you do or not, because you do not know what it is; but you do not dare to say that you do not, because you understand that it is one of the things which every good American is bound to believe in. Now when any doctrine arrives at that degree of authority, the name of it is a club which any demagogue may wing over you at any time and apropos of anything. . . . A doctrine is an abstract principle; it is necessarily absolute in its scope and abstruse in its terms; it is a metaphysical assertion. It is never true, because it is absolute, and the affairs of men are all conditioned and relative. . . .

"The process by which such catchwords grow is the old popular mythologizing. Your Monroe Doctrine becomes an entity, a being, a lesser kind of divinity, entitled to reverence and possessed of prestige, so that it allows of no discussion or deliberation. The President of the United States talks about the Monroe Doctrine and he tells us solemnly that it is true and sacred, whatever it is. He even undertakes to give some definition of what he means by it; but the definition which he gives binds nobody, either now or in the future, any more than what Monroe and Adams meant by it binds anybody now not to mean anything else. He says that, on account of the doctrine, whatever it may be, we must have a big navy. In this, at least, he is plainly in the right; if we have the doctrine, we shall need a big navy. . . .

"What has just been said suggests a consideration of the popular saying, 'In time of peace prepare for war.' If you prepare a big army and navy and are all ready for war, it will be easy to go to war; the military and naval men will have a lot of new machines and they will be eager to see what they can do with them. There is no such thing nowadays as a state of readiness for war. It is a chimera, and the nations which pursue it are falling into an abyss of wasted energy and wealth. When the army is supplied with the latest and best rifles, someone invents a new field gun; then the artillery must be provided with that before we are ready. . . . A wiser rule would be to make up your mind soberly what you want, peace or war, and then to get ready for what you want; for what we prepare for is what we shall get."

— From "War." In Albert Galloway Keller and Maurice R. Davie, eds. Essays of William Graham Sumner (1934) —

repeated by the president. Senator Lewis Cass of Michigan led the enthusiastic response of Democratic expansionists.

Calhoun challenged the resolution as a dangerous commitment; it seemed to invoke U.S. guardianship for all New World states against foreign aggression. If this be settled policy that was intended to have meaning, Calhoun warned, the country must concentrate its energies to carry out the policy. For Calhoun, policy required that the ends of policy be determined not by rhetoric, but by the means that the country intended to use.

For him, the country had no intention of acting. Thus, Calhoun advised the Senate that it was

the part of wisdom to select wise ends in a wise manner. No wise man, with a full understanding of the subject, would pledge himself, by declaration, to do that which was beyond the power of execution, and without mature reflection as to the consequences. There would be no dignity in it. True dignity consists in making no declaration which we are not prepared to maintain. If we make the declaration, we ought to be prepared to carry it into effect against all opposition.

Cass, in another exchange with Calhoun, argued that the United States could enunciate principles without assuming any obligation to act on them. "Will mere vaporing bravado," Calhoun replied, "have any practical effect?" Effective policy, if resistance seemed proper, Calhoun asserted, required armies, navies, powerful revenues, and a determination to act. Declarations of principle would achieve nothing except to needlessly antagonize countries normally well disposed to the United States. The Senate returned the Allen resolution to committee—from which it never reemerged.

In April 1848, President Polk inaugurated the most searching examination of the Monroe Doctrine and its relevance to U.S. foreign policy in the nation's history. That month an agent of the Yucatán government, Don Justo Sierra, appealed to Polk for military aid against the rebellious Indians of the Mexican interior who threatened to drive the whites into the sea. He offered the United States, in return for its support, "dominion and sovereignty" over the state of Yucatán, adding that the same appeal had been extended to England and Spain. On 19 April, Polk, in his message to Congress, repeated his earlier sweeping assertion that it was the settled policy of the United States "that no future European colony or dominion shall . . . be planted or established on any part of the American continent." Polk anchored his appeal for U.S. involvement in Yucatán on both the moral obligation to rescue its white inhabitants and to prevent the possible reduction of the region to the status of a European colony. The Senate Committee on Foreign Relations quickly reported a bill to provide for an American military occupation of Yucatán. Democratic nationalists rushed to the defense of the president's request.

Again it was left for Calhoun, in a major speech of his long career, to dispose of the president's appeal to the Monroe Doctrine by demonstrating historically that the doctrine had no relevance to the Yucatán question. As a member of Monroe's cabinet in 1823, Calhoun reminded the Senate that Monroe's message was directed at one specific threat to Latin American independence—the Holy Alliance. That alliance's disintegration rendered the doctrine meaningless. Then Calhoun turned to the Monroe Doctrine as policy. In response to the president's insistence that Monroe's declarations were the settled policy of the United States, Calhoun retorted: "Declarations are not policy and cannot become settled policy." Then he asked, "Has there been one instance in

which these declarations have been carried into effect? If there be, let it be pointed out." Control of Yucatán, declared Calhoun, would add nothing to the protection of Cuba or U.S. commerce in the Gulf of Mexico. For Mexico, U.S. intervention in Yucatán would be a breach of faith. Mere occupancy would resolve nothing, and without some resolution, would either collapse or become permanent. Fortunately, a sudden, unanticipated agreement between the Yucatán contestants terminated the question of U.S. intervention.

KOSSUTH AND HUNGARY

America's seldom expressed but widely shared antagonism toward Europe's monarchical governments broke loose at the first news of the revolutions that, beginning in France during February 1848, swept rapidly across Germany and the whole continent. The U.S. minister in Paris recognized France's provisional government. Senator Edward Hannegan of Indiana reported a joint resolution from the Committee on Foreign Relations that offered the country's congratulations to the people of France. The absence of any obligations to France assured the resolution's overwhelming approval.

By 1849, the spontaneous uprising of one European people after another diverted attention from France to Hungary, where the Magyar patriots were engaged in a heroic struggle against Austrian rule. That summer, while the American people applauded the successive Hungarian triumphs, Secretary of State John M. Clayton dispatched Ambrose Dudley Mann as a special agent to report on the progress of the revolution and offer the nation's encouragement. After winning momentary success under their eloquent leader, Lajos Kossuth, the Hungarians suffered disaster at the hands of Russian troops brought to the aid of the Austrian emperor. Early in 1850 Cass proposed a resolution demanding that the administration sever diplomatic relations with Austria. Clay, a realist since his stint as secretary of state under John Quincy Adams, turned his ridicule on Cass's proposal. There was, he told the Senate on 7 January, no relationship between the Michigan senator's premises and his conclusions. His resolution offered nothing to the Hungarians. Why, Clay asked, single out Austria? Hungary lost its independence struggle to Russian, not Austrian, forces. The country's very greatness, Clay cautioned, "draws after it great responsibilities . . . to avoid unnecessary wars, maintaining our own rights with firmness, but invading the rights of no others." The Senate tabled Cass's resolution.

Meanwhile, the exiled Kossuth languished under detention in Turkey. But in September 1851, Webster, now secretary of state, with the cooperation of U.S. minister George Perkins Marsh, secured the release of Kossuth and fifty of his Magyar associates. Congress passed a resolution inviting Kossuth to visit the United States, while the president dispatched the USS *Mississippi,* already in the Mediterranean, to carry him to England. After a triumphal stop in England, he proceeded to the United States. Upon his arrival in New York City on 5 December, announced by the booming of cannon, Kossuth received the city's greatest ovation since the visit of Lafayette a quarter century earlier. New York experienced a Magyar-mania epidemic. Soon the Kossuth craze spread from the Atlantic to the Great Lakes. American orators used the occasion of his presence to express sympathy for the oppressed of Europe. Whigs—largely realists—were not amused; they resented both the cleverness of Kossuth's appeal to the country's idealist sentiment, as well as the approval his words apparently received. What troubled Kossuth's realist critics especially was his open quest for diplomatic, economic, and even military assistance to rekindle the Hungarian independence movement. For them, such appeals exceeded the bounds of acceptable international behavior.

Congress voted to invite Kossuth to Washington, D.C. The Hungarian accepted with alacrity; the success of his mission in America hinged on his acceptance by an administration that was determined to offer him nothing. On 23 December, Webster acknowledged privately the need for caution in dealing with Kossuth: "We shall treat him with respect, but shall give him no encouragement that the established policy of the country will be in any degree departed from." Two days later, Webster admitted that Kossuth's presence in Washington would be embarrassing. Upon Kossuth's arrival, Webster privately outlined his course of action: "I shall treat him with all personal and individual respect, but if he should speak to me of the policy of 'intervention,' I shall 'have ears more deaf than adders.'" At the White House on 31 December, Kossuth, despite Webster's request, could not resist the temptation to make a lengthy plea for American aid. President Millard Fillmore reminded the Hungarian leader that U.S. policy on intervention had been

uniform since the Republic's founding. At subsequent dinners hosted by the Websters and the president, Kossuth's scarcely concealed anger embarrassed all who attended.

At a congressional banquet in Kossuth's honor, Webster expressed his hope to see the American model established upon the Lower Danube. He toasted Hungarian independence but refused to offer what Kossuth needed: something tangible for the Hungarian cause. On 9 January 1852 ,Clay received Kossuth in his chamber. Clay assured the Hungarian leader that the United States could not transport men and arms to eastern Europe in sufficient quantity to be effective against Russia and Austria. Such an attempt, he added, would depart from the country's historic policy of nonintervention. "Far better is it for ourselves, for Hungary, and for the cause of liberty," Clay concluded, "that, adhering to our wise, pacific system . . . , we should keep our lamp burning brightly on this western shore as a light to all nations, than to hazard its utter extinction amid the ruins of fallen and falling republics in Europe." Kossuth soon returned to Europe, suffering the disillusionment of those who expect too much of sentiment.

WAR WITH SPAIN

During the generations of general peace between 1815 and 1898, American idealism and realism remained compartmentalized, the former residing in the realm of opinion, ideas, and moral posturing, the latter existing in the realm of policy and action. On occasion, the levers of policy were put at the disposal of moral purposes, but not in a manner that would deflect the basic guidelines of American external policy. But in 1898 the compartments began to break down; the surge of popular passion on behalf of other peoples, against which realists such as Hamilton had warned, erupted on behalf of moral crusades in defense of Cuba, the Philippines, and China.

Following the outbreak of the Cuban revolt in February 1895, the Cuban junta, with headquarters in New York, supported by the Cuban League, its American counterpart with branches in all large cities, launched a campaign to involve the United States in this renewal of the Cuban struggle for independence. Cuban rebels understood the peculiar appeal of humanitarian causes to nineteenth-century Americans. The Spanish government, by employing measures of extreme repression, played into their hands. The Madrid government damaged its image almost beyond recall when, in 1896, it dispatched General Valeriano Weyler to Cuba, where he proceeded to herd civilians suspected of rebel leanings into concentration camps. President Grover Cleveland resented the Cuban assault on American emotions and held to a policy of neutrality against the rising tide of pro-Cuban sentiment. The Spanish government offered Cuba autonomy, but President William McKinley's decision of 1897 to oppose any arrangement unacceptable to the revolutionaries, whose minimum goal was indepen-dence, eliminated every possibility of a peaceful Cuban settlement. Washington gave Spain the choice of capitulation or war. The sinking of the battleship *Maine* on 15 February 1898, along with other unfortunate incidents, aroused a congressional demand for war, a responsibility that McKinley accepted to protect the principle of executive leadership in external affairs. On 21 April the United States broke diplomatic relations with Spain and embarked on a war for Cuban independence.

Few Americans attempted to justify the war except in humanitarian terms. Such motives were not strange to American liberal thought, but before 1898 they had never governed action. Whether it was a people's war, forced on a reluctant administration, or one reflecting a slow, steady evolution of presidential policy, it did not result from any deliberate weighing of interests and responsibilities. The president asked for war in the name of humanity and civilization as well as endangered American interests. "Our own direct interests [in Cuba] were great," observed Theodore Roosevelt in his *An Autobiography* (1913), "but even greater were our interests from the standpoint of humanity. Cuba was at our very doors. It was dreadful things for us to sit supinely and watch her death agony." Similarly, Senator George F. Hoar acknowledged that the American people could not "look idly on while hundreds of thousands of innocent human beings, women and children and old men, die of hunger close to our doors." Had Cuba not lain off the coast of the United States, there would have been no war of liberation in 1898. Previous generations of Americans had sought new deals for Greeks and Hungarians in vain. In 1898 sentiment mattered because it was directed at oppression by a weak power in an adjacent region where the United States held the clear strategic advantage.

Commodore George Dewey's destruction of the Spanish fleet in Manila harbor on 1 May did not presage an annexationist movement in the Pacific. But almost immediately a number of expansionists, both inside and outside the administration, clamored for the occupation and annexation of the Philippines—islands in the western Pacific where other nations possessed greater naval power than did the United States. Succumbing to expansionist pressure, the administration, in its instructions to the peace commission dated 16 September, announced its intention to acquire the Philippines. McKinley rationalized the decision by citing the country's obligation to humanity. This theme dominated his speeches during his midwestern tour in October 1898. Always he dwelt on the accidental nature of the country's de facto possession of the Philippines and its special responsibility to the Filipinos that, he insisted, flowed from that possession. He declared at Cedar Rapids, Iowa, that "we accepted war for humanity. We can accept no terms of peace which shall not be in the interests of humanity." He repeated that appeal in Omaha: "The war was no more invited by us than were the questions which are laid at our door by its results. Now as then we will do our duty." Later, in Boston, he declared that "our concern was not for territory or trade or empire, but for the people whose interests and destiny, without our willing, had been put into our hands." Thucydides, the Greek historian, wrote many centuries earlier: "You cannot decline the burdens of empire and still expect to share its honours." McKinley, however, failed to dwell on the burdens of empire at all. It was not strange that the American people, given the simple choice between humanity and irresponsibility, assured him of their overwhelming support.

Realists charged that the acquisition of the Philippines was a serious departure from the country's traditional conservatism in foreign affairs. They noted that the annexation of distant territories would entail financial and military burdens with few rewards. The United States, wrote Andrew Carnegie, lacked not only the naval power to protect the Philippines but also the will to create it. The former U.S. Senator Carl Schurz feared that Philippine annexation would so completely overcommit the nation that it would reduce the United States to complete reliance on the British fleet. Such reliance would demand a heavy price. "If we do take the Philippines," he predicted, "and thus entangle ourselves in the rivalries of Asiatic affairs, the future will be . . . one of wars and rumors of wars, and the time will be forever past when we could look down with condescending pity on the nations of the old world groaning under militarism and is burdens." Senator Augustus O. Bacon of Georgia foresaw "peace at evening, perhaps, with no certainty but that the morrow will find us participants in a world's war." Against such arguments Senate approval of the annexation treaty came hard. The final vote was fifty-seven to twenty-seven, one more than necessary to gain the required two-thirds.

CHINA AND THE OPEN DOOR

Events in China drew the United States ever deeper into the politics of the western Pacific, largely as the consequence of another moral crusade. After 1897, China's political and military weakness exposed it to foreign encroachments that threatened to reduce it to colonial status. The McKinley administration, through Secretary of State John Hay's Open Door Notes of 1899 and 1900, saved China from further disintegration. In the process, however, the United States assumed an immense, if informal, obligation to defend the commercial and administrative integrity of China. For its adherents, these apparently cost-free obligations comprised not a burden, but a remarkable triumph for American humanitarian principles. Some observers hailed Hay's achievement equal to those of the country's greatest nineteenth-century diplomats. Senator Shelby M. Cullom of Illinois offered a characteristic eulogy: "The magnitude of the man [Hay] will only appear in the magnitude of his work when it reaches its colossal proportions in the proper perspective of the past." Much of the press lauded the secretary for his momentous success. The *New York Journal of Commerce* called the Open Door episode "one of the most important diplomatic negotiations of our time." The *Nation* praised the Open Door policy as a great national triumph. "Our intervention in China," ran its conclusion, "has given the world a transcendent exhibition of American leadership in the world of ideas and the world of action. We have proved that we are guided by a diplomacy unsurpassed . . . in its patient moderation, its firmness, its moral impulse."

Others explained why Hay's apparent achievements on behalf of China carried the seeds of disaster. Like the acquisition of the Philippines, Hay's easy successes confirmed the illusion that the United States could have its way in Asia at little or no cost to itself. Realistic observers noted, however, that Hay's diplomacy either had committed the United States to the use of force in a distant, disorganized region of the Far East, or it had achieved nothing; no nation would have compromised its essential interests in China merely at Hay's request. "Diplomacy has done nothing to change the situation," warned the *Springfield Republican*, "while the Government has gone far toward placing itself in a position where, to be consistent, it must guarantee by military force the territorial integrity of China, or share in its possible partition." Similarly, Alfred Thayer Mahan observed in November 1900 that the United States could not "count on respect for the territory of China unless we are ready to throw not only our moral influence but, if necessity arise, our physical weight into the conflict." Mahan noted that both Russia and Japan, the two dominant powers in the Far East, had far greater interests in China than did the United States. The Open Door policy, by establishing a powerful and exaggerated American concern for the commercial and territorial integrity of China, rendered any country that might interfere in Chinese affairs the potential enemy of the United States.

WILSONIAN DIPLOMACY

This repeated willingness of the United States to permit its burgeoning obligations, especially in the Pacific, to be driven by moral considerations culminated in Woodrow Wilson's crusade in Europe. The outbreak of war in the summer of 1914 thoroughly conjoined the realist and idealist elements in U.S. foreign policy. While realists and idealists differed in their judgments of the causes and meaning of the war, they agreed on the necessity of the struggle. Theodore Roosevelt, like other realists, feared that a German victory would endanger U.S. interests by undermining the historic European balance of power—a balance that had provided the United States almost perfect security through much of its history. Wilson, however, quickly turned the war into another moral crusade. For him, the breakdown of the peace revealed serious flaws in the international system that required correction. Determined to exert a powerful voice in world affairs at the war's end, he favored a policy of strict neutrality to hold America above the fray. When German submarine warfare brought the United States into the war, Wilson would seek to reform the world through his dominant voice in erecting the postwar peace structure.

Wilson's program for avoiding another catastrophic crisis, such as that of 1914, required both changes in the quality of national behavior and an international mechanism for settling international disputes peacefully. To that end, he believed it essential that the world relieve itself of the traditional accoutrements of power politics: the balance of power and the pursuit of national interests. His solution lay in the principle of collective security, in which all peace-loving nations would pledge themselves to joint action in behalf of peace. The necessary multilateral institutions, through which the protectors of the peace would function, took the form of the League of Nations and the World Court, both enforcing the rule of law. Wilson found additional hope for a peaceful future in the expansion of world commerce, operating under a body of most-favored-nation treaties that would assure equal access to world markets. The result would be both a more prosperous and a more peaceful international system. For Wilson, finally, the new world order would require the active leadership of the United States.

Wilson's vision of enduring peace required, as well, a democratic foundation that would assure the necessary fusion of policy and moral purpose. In his war message to Congress in April 1917, Wilson declared:

> A steadfast concert for peace can never be maintained except by a partnership of democratic nations. No autocratic government could be trusted to keep faith within it or observe its covenants. It must be a league of honor, a partnership of opinion. . . . Only free peoples can hold their purpose and their honor steady to a common end and prefer the interests of mankind to any narrow interest of their own.

Wilson's faith in a concert of democracies to maintain the peace presumed a common interest that would eliminate conflict and war. In his advocacy of a world of law and order, Wilson identified the interests of humanity with the interests of the United States and other democratic, status quo powers. This vision of universal peace acquired its special appeal from Wilson's insistence that peace required not the wielding of superior power by advocates of the status quo, but the limitation of change to general agreement and the rule of law. In a world governed by law, based on a common interest in peace, neither the United States nor any other country had the right to bargain with aggressors over changes in established treaties. Peaceful change alone was a morally acceptable burden of diplomacy.

Unfortunately, the essential assumption of a common interest in peace ignored the reality that, while all nations favored peace, some favored the status quo and some did not. E. H. Carr addressed this dilemma in *The Twenty Years' Crisis* (1939): "The utopian assumption that there is a world interest in peace which is identifiable with the interest of each individual nation helped politicians and political writers everywhere to evade the unpalatable fact of a fundamental divergence of interest between nations desirous of maintaining the status quo and nations desiring to change it." Nowhere in the Wilsonian approach to international affairs was there any recognition of the persistence of conflict that defied easy solution or the need to define the interests of the United States in a still troubled world and prepare a strategy for their defense. It was not strange that wishful thinking and generalization soon prevailed over analysis of the ongoing realities of international life. The end of lasting and universal peace overwhelmed the problem of means. Wilson once quieted the doubts of his adversaries who questioned the effectiveness of the League of Nations by assuring them that "if it won't work, it must be made to work." Schemes for rendering the league effective did not require explanations of how they would work; the consequences of failure were too disastrous to contemplate.

ISOLATIONISM, INTERNATIONALISM, AND WORLD WAR II

In proclaiming goals whose achievements always eluded the possibilities of his prescriptions, Wilson laid the foundation for a pervading postwar isolationism. For countless Americans, nothing in the country's recent experience dictated the necessity of a permanent, continuous American involvement in European politics.

For other Americans, often intellectuals and academicians, Wilson's vision of a new world order, free of all reliance on force, was too essential for the world's welfare to be discarded in deference to isolationism. Inasmuch as both groups were antagonistic to the conservative tradition of American diplomacy, there was little to separate idealists from realists in the national debate. Isolationism insisted that the nation had no external interests that merited the use of force, that events outside the hemisphere were inconsequential.

In apparent contrast, internationalism declared that U.S. interests existed wherever governments challenged peace or human rights. It insisted not only that they mattered but also that the universal acceptance of democratically inspired principles of peaceful change would control them. Every program fostered by American internationalists during the two postwar decades—membership in the League of Nations and the World Court, the employment of arbitration conventions, the resort to consultation in the event of crises, collective security, naval disarmament, or the outlawry of war—denied the need of any precise definition of ends and means in American foreign policy. The burgeoning fields of diplomatic history and international law rested on Wilsonian principles. Under the presumptions of a controlling public opinion and a common interest in peace, international lawyers joined national leaders in rationalizing inaction in the face of growing threats. Notions of collective security served as a device of the status quo powers to prevent change in the international system. The Western preference for the status quo, in the absence of any program to change it peacefully, never recommended the means for preserving it beyond the acceptance of war.

Whatever remained of the realist-idealist cleavage in American thought and action was again clouded by the almost universal national acceptance of U.S. involvement in World War II. Realists presumed that the war, like the Great War of 1914, would, with the defeat of the Axis, reaffirm Europe's traditional balance of power and reestablish the essential elements of the Versailles settlement of 1919. To that end, Winston Churchill and Franklin D. Roosevelt, in the Atlantic Charter of August 1941, advocated the return of East-Central Europe to its prewar status. American idealism, however, assigned the war a deeper, largely humanitarian purpose. In his lend-lease proposal of January 1941, Roosevelt adopted the goal of the Four Freedoms—freedom of speech, freedom of worship, freedom from want, and freedom from fear—in his crusade against the Axis powers. In his book *Price of a Free World* (1942), Secretary of Agriculture Henry Wallace proposed, as the war's true purpose, not only the elimination of fascism from the world, but also the establishment of freedom for all peoples, the final triumph of democracy, and the elimination of poverty and hunger everywhere. At the Casablanca Conference of January 1943, Roosevelt announced his goal of unconditional surrender to eliminate any German, Italian, or Japanese influence from the postwar treaty-making

process—essential for the construction of the perfect peace. Unfortunately, such idealist presumptions failed to anticipate the Soviet Union's overwhelming contribution to the allied victory and the demands that the Kremlin would make on any postwar settlement.

THE COLD WAR

It required no more than the postwar Soviet occupation of Eastern Europe, in defiance of the Western principle of self-determination, to create doubts regarding the Kremlin's ultimate intentions. As early as 1946, anti-Soviet officials and members of Congress predicted further Soviet expansion into war torn Europe and elsewhere. Clark Clifford's September 1946 report to President Truman, reflecting the views of top U.S. officials, described a deeply threatened world. When suspected Soviet ambitions, in early 1947, seemed to focus on Greece and Turkey, the Truman administration framed the Truman Doctrine, with its corresponding rhetorical predictions of falling dominoes across Europe, Africa, or Asia, should Greece fall to the country's communist-led guerrillas. Senator Arthur Vandenberg of Michigan accepted the administration's dire predictions uncritically. "Greece," he wrote on 12 March, "must be helped or Greece sinks permanently into the communist order. Turkey inevitably follows. Then comes the chain reaction which might sweep from the Dardanelles to the China Seas." Never before, critics noted, had U.S. leaders described external dangers in such limitless, imprecise terms. Secretary of State George C. Marshall, Soviet expert George Kennan, and columnist Walter Lippmann objected to the language. Lippmann accused the administration of launching a crusade, not defining a policy.

Even as the West triumphed in all of its anti-Soviet policies during the next two years, including the creation of West Germany and the formation of NATO, U.S. fears of the Soviet Union continued to mount. The National Security Council's study NCS 7, dated 30 March 1948, defined the Kremlin's challenge in global terms. "The ultimate objective of Soviet-directed world communism," the document averred, "is the domination of the world." NCS 68, of April 1950, comprised the final and most elaborate attempt of the Truman Cold War elite to arrive at a definition of the burgeoning Soviet threat. It concluded that the Soviet Union, "unlike previous aspirants to hegemony, is animated by a new fanatic faith, antithetical to our own, and seeks to impose its absolute authority over the rest of the world." What underwrote such fears was not the prospect of Soviet military expansionism; Soviet armed forces were not prepared to march anywhere. Rather, it was the fear that the Kremlin, with its alleged control of international communism, could expand endlessly, without force, merely by inciting communist revolutions. Actually, by mid-century, Europe was stabilized with a vengeance. The United States and its allies would not risk war to change the status quo on the European continent; the Soviets had no power to do so. Europe was divided, but incredibly stable.

Events in East Asia, where the United States faced two unwanted, powerfully led communist revolutions in China and Indochina, seemed to confirm the fears of Soviet expansionism. The reason is clear. Washington officials presumed, logically, that both revolutions were under Soviet control. The State Department's China experts, in a memorandum of October 1948, concluded that the Soviets had established control of China as firmly "as in the satellite countries behind the Iron Curtain." The Soviet Union, apparently, had taken over China without one conquering or occupying soldier. Dean Acheson claimed no less. "The communist leaders," he declared, "have foresworn their Chinese heritage and have publicly announced their subservience to a foreign power, Russia." Following the Chinese communist victory in late 1949, NSC 48/1 declared: "The USSR is now an Asiatic power of the first magnitude with expanding influence and interests extending throughout continental Asia and into the Pacific."

By the 1960s, much of America's predominant realism had become soft, emphasizing less the requirements of security and defense than the need of accommodation with the realities of coexistence. Convinced that previous administrations had exaggerated the Soviet threat, President Jimmy Carter set out in 1977 to establish a more relaxed, flexible, nonideological relationship with the Soviet Union and China. With the U.S. failure in Vietnam, the country could no longer maintain the illusion of global power. Carter recognized that reality by lessening the strategic importance of Asia, Africa, and Latin America. Nationalism, he believed, limited Soviet as well as American influence in the Third World. In dismissing the Cold War commitment to global containment, the Carter administration accepted Soviet activity in the Afro-Asian world with profound indifference. It expected the Soviets to respond by showing strategic restraint in exploiting opportunities for adventurism created by the new burst of revolutionary turmoil across the Third World. By the mid-1970s, former Democratic liberals launched, as neoconservatives, an anticommunist crusade to reassert America's role as defender of the free world against the renewed Soviet danger. The neoconservatives found themselves aligned with the traditional Right, characterized by Republican columnists William Buckley, George Will, William Safire, and Patrick Buchanan.

Already facing open challenges to its alleged loss of will, the Carter administration reacted to the Soviet invasion of Afghanistan, in late December 1979, with bewilderment and rage. National security adviser Zbigniew Brzezinski warned the country that the Soviet Union now threatened American interests from the Mediterranean to the Sea of Japan. On 4 January, the president revealed his fears to the nation. "A Soviet-occupied Afghanistan," he declared, "threatens both Iran and Pakistan and is a stepping stone to possible control over much of the world's oil supplies. . . . If the Soviets . . . maintain their dominance over Afghanistan and then extend their control to adjacent countries, the stable, strategic and peaceful balance of the entire world will be changed."

The widespread assumptions that the Soviet invasion of Afghanistan exposed south and Southwest Asia to further Soviet encroachment pushed American hawkishness to a new high. For many journalists and public officials, the Soviet invasion sounded the inauguration of another cold war. Polls as well as the reports of newspaper correspondents around the country revealed the return of an assertive, Cold War mentality.

Ronald Reagan caught the country's post-Afghan alarms at full tide, embellished them, and rode them to victory in the presidential campaign of 1980. He and the Republican Party pilloried the Carter administration for leading the country into the posture of "weakness, inconsistency, vacillation, and bluff" that enabled the Soviet Union to surpass the United States in military power. Under Reagan, the Committee on the Present Danger gained the influence that Carter had denied it; fifty-one of its members secured positions in the Reagan administration. The Reagan team determined to counter the global Soviet threat by aiding Nicaragua and El Salvador, thereby preventing the rhetorical dominoes from falling across both South America and North America.

Despite the new administration's tough rhetoric and massive expansion of the military budget, it maintained the same defense posture of previous administrations, much to the disgust of those who took the Reagan rhetoric of rollback seriously. The Reagan administration made no effort to recover the alleged losses of the Carter years in Africa and the Middle East. It accepted the Soviet presence in Afghanistan, but held the established containment lines. Indeed, what perpetuated the decades of laudable superpower coexistence was the decision of successive administrations to abjure the dictates of ideology and pursue the limited goals of containment.

The process of Soviet disintegration culminated in the collapse of the Soviet satellite empire in Eastern Europe in 1989 and the demise of the Cold War during the following year. Reagan supporters attributed the Soviet collapse to the rhetorical toughness and military buildup of the Reagan years. For Soviet experts, the communist regime's crash flowed naturally from its internal flaws, its political erosion, and its ideological rejection.

THE POST–COLD WAR ERA

With the termination of the Cold War and collapse of the USSR in 1990–1991, the United States quickly emerged as the world's lone superpower. Under the leadership of President Bill Clinton, the realization of the country's superpower status inaugurated another massive disagreement over the country's proper role in world affairs. Not since classic Rome had a single state towered so completely over its potential rivals. Behind the debate over American global responsibility was President George H. W. Bush's refusal, in 1992, to confront the well-publicized genocide in Bosnia and his tardy, reluctant involvement in feeding the starving people of Somalia. For his critics, the end of the Cold War presented the United States, with all its power, an unprecedented opportunity to embrace the country's historic mission to humanity. The risk-avoiding approaches of the Bush years seemed to assure only the loss of national self-respect and the denial of America's proper role in world affairs. The country, some argued, had the obligation to exercise its exceptional power aggressively in its own and the world's deepest interests.

Undaunted by the doubtful relevance of America's self-assigned obligations to humanity,

President Clinton promised that, after January 1993, U.S. foreign policy would focus on the goal of expanding democracy and humane values. In his inaugural address, he pledged U.S. action whenever "the will and conscience of the international community is defied." There would be interventions, he promised, not only to defend national interests, but also to satisfy the national conscience. On becoming U.S. ambassador to the United Nations in February 1993, Madeleine Albright acknowledged: "If there is one overriding principle that will guide me in this job, it will be the inescapable responsibility . . . to build a peaceful world and to terminate the abominable injustices and conditions that still plague civilization." Clinton elucidated his agenda before the UN General Assembly on 27 September 1993. "During the Cold War," he said, "we sought to contain a threat to [the] survival of free institutions. Now we seek to enlarge the circle of nations that live under those free institutions." For the first time in history, he added, "we have the chance to expand the reach of democracy and economic progress across the whole of Europe and to the far reaches of the world." From the outset, Clinton faced a powerful realist critique of the necessity and feasibility of his burgeoning campaign, much of it based on the admonitions of Hamilton, Washington, and John Quincy Adams against foreign crusading.

For the Clinton administration, three countries seemed to require immediate attention—Somalia, Haiti, and Bosnia. It launched immediate interventions in all three, with doubtful results. In none of the three did Washington achieve its stated objectives. Haiti remained a basket case, economically and politically; the death of American soldiers in Somalia late in 1993 prompted Clinton to withdrew those that remained. In Bosnia, the three goals of U.S. involvement—the return of the refugees, the creation of a multiethnic state, and the arrest and trial of Serb war criminals—remained unfulfilled. In 1999, Kosovo emerged as the defining issue in Clinton's crusade for human rights by scolding and chastising foreign transgressors. On 24 March he unleashed a NATO-backed air war against Serbia, both to protect the Kosovars and to bring Slobodan Milosevic, the Serbian president, to justice. Clinton's Kosovo intervention was the first resort to force for purely humanitarian objectives in the nation's history. The seventy-eight days of bombing brought a Serb capitulation without creating the desired peaceful, multi-ethnic regime in Kosovo.

NATO leaders, meeting in Washington during April 1999, accepted membership in Clinton's global crusade for human rights. They proclaimed human rights, not national sovereignty, as the guiding principle in international affairs. It mattered little. U.S. critics of both the ends and the means of the Kosovo war predicted that the experiment would not be repeated.

Clinton's idealist crusade to improve the human condition turned out to be Eurocentric; in the Atlantic world, at least, massive repression had become unacceptable, especially if it occurred in a small, defenseless region. The Serbian experience was no measure of the West's response to ubiquitous challenges to Western values elsewhere. Neither Washington nor the European capitals responded to the pervading horrors of Africa and Asia, beginning in Rwanda in 1994 and continuing through central Africa to Sierra Leone and elsewhere. Continued global suffering illustrated the magnitude and tenacity of the world's political and societal disabilities, as well as the absence of external power and will to confront them.

Through two centuries of its history, the United States experienced a persistent debate over approaches to foreign policy. It was a controversy absent in nations whose political philosophy derived from different assumptions about humanity and the state. In general, the American debate embraced a realist-idealist contest, although at times the issues produced shifting positions and clouded the fundamental clash between realist and idealist goals and assumptions. But the continued debate, with neither side acknowledging defeat, attested to the abiding fundamentals of both positions. Realists argued that the country's external policies be guided by national interests and the simple desire to maximize stability and minimize harm. They asked that the United States exert its leverage in pursuit of humane objectives only where assured successes were commensurate with costs and effort. For them, no policy choice would achieve utopia. Idealist proposals comprised largely sentimental and rhetorical responses to meliorist visions of a malleable world, supposedly subject to the reforming influences of American political and economic institutions. It was an approach dominated by seductive ends, with little concern for means.

America's vibrant civilization enhanced the attractiveness of the American model, while the uniqueness of the country's traditions and environment limited the expansive power of its example. The country's long pursuit of meliorist dreams demonstrated its limited knowledge and authority to institute democracy and a humane order in other lands. Still, the meliorist vision never faltered and always remained subject to arousal by the trials of other lands. In practice, however, realism defined the fundamental formulations of all U.S. foreign policy, except the moral crusading in Cuba and East Asia at the turn of the nineteenth century, as well as the Wilson-dominated responses to the challenges of the interwar decades. The country's long experience in foreign affairs demonstrated that objectives that ignored or transcended the nation's interests could not long endure.

BIBLIOGRAPHY

Acheson, Dean. *Power and Diplomacy.* New York, 1958. Provides a former secretary of state's reflections on morality and power.

Beard, Charles Austin. *The Republic: Conversations on Fundamentals.* New York, 1943. Seeks to test the validity of current conceptions of foreign policy against the wisdom of the Founders.

Boorstin, Daniel J. *The Genius of American Politics.* Chicago, 1953. Argues that the uniqueness of America's experiences as a nation makes its political principles inapplicable to the problems of other nations.

Gilbert, Felix. *To the Farewell Address: Ideas of Early American Foreign Policy.* Princeton, N.J., 1961. Traces the intellectual origins of Washington's departing advice to his countrymen, finding his ideas about the nature of international politics in the views of early eighteenth-century English thinkers.

Graebner, Norman A., ed. *Ideas and Diplomacy: Readings in the Intellectual Tradition of American Foreign Policy.* New York, 1964. Presents countering arguments in all the major realist-idealist debates in American history.

Hamilton, Alexander, John Jay, and James Madison. *The Federalist Papers.* New York, 1961. Written originally as tracts supporting the proposed U.S. Constitution, includes coherent realist arguments in favor of strong centralized control of foreign affairs and national defense.

Kennan, George F. *American Diplomacy, 1900–1950.* Chicago, 1951. An ex-American diplomat's denunciation of utopianism in foreign affairs and advocacy of an elitist conduct of statecraft.

Kristol, Irving. *On the Democratic Idea in America.* New York, 1972. The chapter "American Intellectuals and Foreign Policy" attacks the validity of the notion that concrete foreign policy decisions can be judged according to abstract principles.

Morgenthau, Hans Joachim. *In Defense of the National Interest: A Critical Examination of American Foreign Policy.* New York, 1951. A leading American realist's arguments in favor of judging international events according to the realities of interest and power.

Niebuhr, Reinhold. *The Irony of American History.* New York, 1952. Argues that America's pre-1941 experiences as a nation provide poor groundwork for purposeful existence in a world of competing rival nations.

Osgood, Robert Endicott. *Ideals and Self-Interest in America's Foreign Relations: The Great Transformation of the Twentieth Century.* Chicago, 1953. Offers a historical account of the enduring dispute among America's realists and idealists, particularly useful for its treatment of concrete episodes of controversy.

Perkins, Dexter *The American Approach to Foreign Policy.* Rev. ed. Cambridge, Mass., 1962. A forceful defense of the vitality of democratic principles in the conduct of foreign relations.

See also DOCTRINES; EXCEPTIONALISM; INTERNATIONALISM; THE NATIONAL INTEREST; OPEN DOOR POLICY; POWER POLITICS; SELF-DETERMINATION; WILSONIANISM.

RECIPROCITY

★ ★ ★ ★

Robert Freeman Smith

Reciprocity in diplomatic negotiations is a process of exchange between nations, a negotiating tool whereby nations bargain with each other for equivalent treatment. It can be either restrictive or open in nature. The restrictive form usually is embodied in a bilateral agreement between two countries and can involve privileges (or different types of treatment) that are denied to other parties, or that must be specifically bargained for by third parties. For the United States, the latter type of quasi-restrictive reciprocity was embodied in the conditional most-favored-nation principle, which was part of almost every commercial treaty negotiated between 1778 and 1922. This was not necessarily an exclusion policy, but it did require continued bargaining after an agreement was ratified, and it could lead to discriminatory practices. The term "restrictive reciprocity" also can be applied to agreements that affect only a limited number of items and leave various prohibitive discriminations intact.

Open reciprocity can be embodied either in bilateral treaties or in multilateral agreements. In general, it means that concessions granted to one nation are automatically extended to all others that have signed most-favored-nation agreements with the granting nation. Since the 1840s (and especially since the British shift to free trade), the unconditional version of the most-favored-nation principle has contributed to open reciprocity. Prior to the development of liberal trade policies, it only tended to generalize discrimination (or guarantee equality of discrimination), and in practice was as restrictive as the conditional version.

Open reciprocity is closely connected to a liberal trading system, with the emphasis on lowering barriers to international intercourse in as broad a manner as possible. Open reciprocity also applies to agreements that tend generally to abolish or modify discriminatory practices rather than provide for the privileged treatment of certain items.

The reciprocity concept has been applied to negotiations over tonnage dues on ships and goods, access to ports and rivers, access to markets, and various types of port fees and internal taxes. Starting in the eighteenth century, reciprocity negotiations also dealt with the equivalent treatment of foreign nationals, especially in matters of religious practice. Since the latter part of the nineteenth century, the meaning of reciprocity has been enlarged to include equal access to raw materials, the protection of foreign investments, aviation overflight and landing rights, treatment of tourists, and a host of financial matters involving such items as exchange controls and debt payments.

If the American concept of reciprocity only involved reciprocity as a bargaining tool, then the historical record would be one of treaty negotiations and little else. But in the historical experience of the United States, reciprocity has been more. It also has been a concept of international relations involving the breaking down of barriers to international intercourse and opposing closed or highly restrictive economic systems. Intimately related to this has been the idea of a peaceful world based upon complete reciprocity, with nations freely exchanging goods, services, and ideas. This conceptual and ideological aspect of reciprocity can be characterized as the open world schema. Bargaining reciprocity can take place, and has done so, on a matter-of-fact basis. But in the experience of the United States, it has been viewed generally as part of the larger world schema, as an instrument to help secure the broader objectives of an open world. There have been periods in American history when this relationship has been obscured or modified, as between 1860 and 1922, but overall the history of reciprocity has been a combination of diplomacy and of concept and ideal. The historical experiences and the cultural heritage of the United States have combined to give a peculiar and unique shape to the history of reciprocity in American foreign policy.

In its original format the concept of an open world of unlimited reciprocity was basically nonimperial. Many prominent leaders in the late eighteenth century broadly viewed reciprocity as rather the polar opposite of power politics, European-style mercantilism, and traditional imperialism. But in the years after American independence, the harsh realities of international politics produced modifications and compromises in the practice of reciprocity. Mercantilistic elements were introduced into American policy as part of the interplay between conflicting sectional and group ambitions and ideas of national interest. Similarly, the open world concept developed a peculiar duality during the nineteenth century. Such elements as the mercantilist idea of the need for economic and social "safety valves," perceptions of external threats, and the messianic thrust of the Redeemer Nation idea (that the United States was chosen by God to remake the world in both a religious and a secular sense) combined in the development of a restrictive and imperial version of the open world. This variant can be labeled the open-door view, and these dual versions of world order have competed and coexisted in American policy-making since the late nineteenth century. Like many historical developments, the reciprocity policies and concepts of the United States have been afflicted by ambiguity and paradox.

1776–1830

The first treaty signed by the infant republic was the Treaty of Amity and Commerce with France in 1778. The preamble to the document stated that equitable and permanent commercial relations between the two countries

> could not be better obtained than by taking for the basis of their agreement the most perfect equality and reciprocity, and by carefully avoiding all those burdensome preferences which are usually sources of debate, embarrassment, and discontent; . . . and by founding the advantage of commerce solely upon reciprocal utility and the just rules of free intercourse, reserving withal to each party the liberty of admitting at its pleasure other nations to a participation of the same advantages.

Writing in 1823, John Quincy Adams declared that this preamble "was to the foundation of our commercial intercourse with the rest of mankind, what the Declaration of Independence was to that of our internal government. The two instruments were parts of one and the same system matured by long and anxious deliberation of the founders of this Union in the ever memorable Congress of 1776." To the younger Adams, "the most perfect equality and reciprocity" constituted the "cornerstone" for the commercial foreign policy of the United States. And, he argued, it was the United States that first proclaimed not only the political ideals of equality and independence but also the "true principles of all fair commercial negotiations between independent states."

Adams may have been indulging in a bit of nationalistic enthusiasm, but he was generally accurate concerning the origins of the American policy of reciprocity and the pioneering role of the United States in promoting a liberal international commercial system. The American concept of reciprocity was shaped by a mixture of the colonial experience and eighteenth-century economic liberalism. During the first three-quarters of the century, the British North American colonies made substantial gains in international shipping. By 1776 they were already a major power engaged in carrying not only domestic goods but also the goods of other nations. In fact, shipping provided a major source of colonial income.

Yankee merchants were not noted for their adherence to mercantilist restrictions on trade. They pushed into the Caribbean and the Mediterranean and to the coasts of Africa, often violating the imperial restrictions of France, Spain, and even Britain. Of course, they enjoyed the privileges of the British Empire even though they did not obey the extracolonial restrictions of the Navigation Acts. In short, the Yankee merchants were breaking down trade barriers by various means prior to 1776, and before Adam Smith put the thoughts on paper, they were firm believers in the liberty to "truck, barter, and exchange." In his *Summary View of the Rights of British America* (1774), Thomas Jefferson argued that the colonists had a "natural right" to trade freely with all parts of the world. Many of the Founders saw the new nation as a preeminent commercial republic where prosperity and independence would be ensured by the free flow of goods and ships.

The ideas of English liberals and French philosophes reinforced the commercial experience of American colonials and added new dimensions to their concept of international commercial relations. Adam Smith summarized many of these ideas in his book, *The Wealth of Nations* (1776), but the themes of distribution of labor among nations, comparative advantage, and unrestricted commerce had already been developed by various English and French thinkers. The French Physiocrats argued that the unrestricted flow of goods among the nations would replace power politics and war, since merchants were "citizens of the whole world." Many of the policymakers of the new American republic were quite familiar with these ideas. Economic liberalism in international commerce not only coincided with their concept of the interests of the United States, but also justified the mission of the nation to promote a new system of international relations. Thus, the Founders viewed reciprocity as a bargaining tool and as an integral part of a peaceful, open world order based on equality of treatment and the free flow of goods and ships.

These ideas were first spelled out in the Model Treaty that the Continental Congress adopted in 1776 for purposes of negotiating with France. John Adams drafted the treaty with the assistance of John Dickinson, Benjamin Harrison, Robert Morris, and Benjamin Franklin. He probably was influenced by the writings of Thomas Paine. The latter's *Common Sense* (1776) had expressed the idea that America's "plan is commerce, and that, well attended to, will secure us the peace and friendship of all Europe, because it is the interest of all Europe to have America as a free port." Adams and the other committee members generally agreed with this proposition and believed that the principles of the Model Treaty would ensure the independent existence of the United States. They hoped that the offer of "perfect" commercial reciprocity would repeal the British Navigation Acts as they affected America, and secure French assistance without involving the nation in the European alliance system. Adams's Model Treaty clearly defined "perfect" reciprocity as complete equality of treatment; France and the United States were to make no distinctions between natives and the citizens of the other country (the doctrine of reciprocal national treatment). This was freedom of trade in the eighteenth-century context, which meant equality of treatment rather than elimination of all duties and dues (the definition that developed in the nineteenth century).

The Model Treaty was a fine declaration of American hopes and aspirations, but it was grounded on an exaggerated idea of the value of American trade to France and other nations. The American principles were stated in the preamble to the commercial treaty of 1778. The French, however, were not willing to grant national treatment; the Americans had to settle for most-

favored-nation treatment in the "King's European dominions" and admission to established free ports in the French colonies. French Foreign Minister Charles Gravier, Comte de Vergennes, did add a special proviso that created the conditional version of the most-favored-nation clause. Accordingly, if either party to the treaty granted a special commercial favor to a third party, this favor would not be granted automatically to the other signatory; an equivalent compensation would be required if the third party had paid a price. The historian Vernon Setser has argued that Vergennes added the proviso to demonstrate to the world that France was not demanding special privileges from the United States. This interpretation of reciprocity was added to the treaty without much discussion or analysis.

The negotiations of the French commercial treaty clearly revealed the impact of external circumstances on the American concept of "perfect reciprocity." In addition, they also indicated the role of internal political and economic factors in modifying the use of reciprocity. The original draft contained a reciprocal prohibition on certain export duties; the French would drop export duties on molasses shipped from the West Indies to the United States, and the latter would drop such duties on all domestic products sent to the French islands. A majority of Congress opposed this article, and it was suppressed. This incident was a mild foretaste of future domestic battles over the nature and use of reciprocity.

An independent United States faced an international system in which all the major participants followed restrictive, monopolistic policies. The anticipated trade bonanza did not materialize, and the nation was now cut off from almost all of the formerly lucrative West Indian trade. The closing of the British islands was especially painful. In 1782, John Adams negotiated a commercial treaty with the Netherlands, but the Dutch would agree only to a most-favored-nation clause and not to reciprocal national treatment. The conditional clause was omitted, because its utility had not yet been recognized.

The policymakers of the Confederation government began to realize that their nation's economic and political position allowed it almost no bargaining power. As minister to France, Jefferson realized that the most-favored-nation principle worked to the disadvantage of the nation with the most liberal system. In practice, French traders had almost the same rights in the United States as natives, since the United States had very few restrictions on trade. In contrast, the French controlled the entry of goods, even into free ports, by subjecting trade to the monopolistic control of the Farmers General. This group fixed the quantity and price of goods admitted. The most-favored-nation principle only granted the United States equal discrimination. In 1785, Jefferson launched an attack on the French monopolies with the assistance of the Marquis de Lafayette, but the results were very limited. Indeed, as Representative Elbridge Gerry of Massachusetts noted, under existing circumstances the most-favored-nation principle was a system of "cobwebs to catch flies."

Jefferson realized that in a world of monopolies, the United States had few favors to grant because it had a relatively open economic system. In such a world, commercial restrictions obviously meant bargaining power. During the 1780s, Congress devoted considerable attention to this dilemma, and to the lack of congressional power to enact navigation laws and regulate trade. A special committee reported in 1784: "It will certainly be admitted that unless the United States can act as a nation and be regarded as such by foreign powers, and unless Congress for this purpose shall be vested with powers competent to the protection of commerce, they can never command reciprocal advantages in trade; and without such reciprocity, our foreign commerce must decline and eventually be annihilated."

In the spring of 1785 another committee studied these problems, and its recommendations marked a distinct modification in the concept of perfect reciprocity. The committee noted that without authority to impose restrictions, "reciprocity means nothing and foreign powers may follow what policy they please." It also recommended that treaties were not needed with nations that had no colonies, since the United States must consider giving special advantages in return for some trading rights in the West Indies (and the most-favored-nation principle would prohibit such special advantages).

Various proposals were made during the 1780s to amend the Articles of Confederation or to request the states to provide Congress with more power. The states could not agree, however, and nothing happened. Some states did impose commercial restrictions on their own; but the effect was limited because several states, including Connecticut, took advantage of the restrictions of others by acting as a free entrepôt.

During negotiations with the British in October 1782, Congress formally recognized the use of the conditional most-favored-nation principle as a bargaining device. The draft commercial treaty provided for the reciprocal free navigation of all rivers, lakes, and harbors. Congress insisted that a conditional most-favored-nation clause be added so that other nations would have to "purchase them [navigation privileges] by a reciprocal grant." The negotiations for a commercial treaty were dropped, however, when the British issued an order in council closing the West Indies to American ships.

By 1787 a number of American leaders generally agreed that the United States could not obtain any effective degree of reciprocity without a national government possessing the power to regulate commerce both externally and internally. This sentiment was part of the movement for a constitutional convention, and the document produced at Philadelphia reflected the congressional debates of the Confederation government. The new Constitution provided much of the power that the advocates of commercial diplomacy had demanded; the international scene had not changed, however, and, internally, sectional and group interests provided a continuing debate over the exact use of the power.

Generally, the debate took place between two groups. One was led by Alexander Hamilton (secretary of the Treasury) and George Washington, the other by James Madison (a U.S. representative) and Thomas Jefferson (secretary of state until 1793). All of these men agreed that perfect reciprocity was not possible in the world of the late eighteenth century, and that as a result some important modifications would have to be made in the practical uses of reciprocity. They also had retreated from the dreams of a world thirsting for American trade. Most of them still retained some hope that eventually the policies of the United States might lead to an open world of unrestricted trade, but in the interim their main concern was what immediate steps could be taken to ensure the prosperity and independence of the nation. The two groups disagreed significantly not over basic principles, but over tactics and the interpretation of primary interests.

Madison and Jefferson believed that a considerable degree of economic independence could be obtained immediately through a modified system of exclusive reciprocity. They wanted to break the British monopoly on American trade by enacting a navigation law that would favor continental nations and encourage bargaining through discriminatory duties and dues that would affect nations discriminating against the United States. Jefferson explained the need for discrimination in his final report as secretary of state in December 1793. He began by extolling the physiocratic ideals of open trade as the best course for human happiness, then added:

> But should any nation contrary to our wishes suppose it may better find its advantage by continuing its system of prohibitions, duties, and regulations, it behooves us to protect our citizens, their commerce, and navigation, by counter prohibitions, duties, and regulations, also. Free commerce and navigation are not to be given in exchange for restrictions and vexations, nor are they likely to produce a relaxation of them.

Jefferson hoped that an initial policy of exclusive reciprocity would eventually produce a system of open trade.

Hamilton considered such a retaliation policy to be a declaration of commercial war against Britain. He was convinced that in the short run the United States should accept economic subordination and British restrictions because import duties, largely derived from trade with Britain, were vital to the economic development of the country. His goal was economic independence through the development of domestic industry. Hamilton and Washington opposed any measures designed to force reciprocity and proclaimed a simple policy of equal treatment for all nations. Thus, they hoped to buy time and not be drawn into European controversies.

The first congressional battle over commercial policy continued from 1789 to 1795. In July and August 1789, Congress passed four acts that laid the foundation for a new commercial system. These were the Tariff of 1789, the Tonnage Act, the act to regulate the collection of duties, and the act for registering and clearing vessels. They provided protection for American industry and shipping but did not discriminate against any foreign country in particular. All foreign vessels were required to pay fifty cents per ton, in comparison with six cents for American ships. A 10 percent discount on customs duties was provided on dutiable goods imported in American ships, a provision changed in 1790, after which merchandise imported in American ships paid the normal duty and a 10 percent surcharge was added to all goods imported in foreign ships. Madison had attempted to add further discriminatory tonnage dues for nations that had not negotiated commercial agreements with the United States. He was not successful then, or in his subsequent efforts to enact retaliatory measures, such as closing American ports to vessels that came from ports closed to American ships.

Jay's Treaty (1794) settled several outstanding questions between the United States and Britain and provided for some reciprocity. Trade with the British Isles was opened on a most-favored-nation basis, and provisions were made for reciprocal trade across the Canadian border. The West Indies remained closed, however, because the Senate rejected the clause providing for a very limited access and a prohibition on exports of certain agricultural products from the United States. Opponents of the treaty claimed that a policy of exclusive reciprocity would have done more to break down the restrictive systems. In his Farewell Address, however, Washington defended the noncoercive method of obtaining reciprocity, which he characterized as "consulting the natural course of things; diffusing and diversifying by gentle means the streams of commerce, but forcing nothing."

Between 1796 and 1815, American leaders did very little about reciprocity. The wars in Europe generally stimulated exports and led to the relaxation of restrictions (especially in the West Indies). Questions of neutral rights and impressment took precedence over matters that appeared less urgent. In fact, Congress refused to act on a reciprocity bill, proposed in 1802, that would have allowed, for any nation that would reciprocate by repealing its similar legislation, the abolition of the discriminatory tonnage dues on ships and the customs surcharges on the produce of the country owning the vessel. Rufus King had negotiated such an arrangement with Britain, and a bill providing for repeal had even been rushed through Parliament.

In 1815 the United States government, in a burst of nationalistic vigor, launched an attack on the restrictive systems of the European states. American leaders were determined to open the world to U.S. shipping and to make reciprocity an effective tool in breaking down the "excluding and exclusive" policy of the old colonial order. The first step was the passage of the Reciprocity Act of 1815. This was the proposal that had been rejected in 1802, and it affected only the direct trade between countries. Several months later, the United States and Great Britain signed a convention that reciprocally abolished all discriminatory duties and dues levied on ships and goods in the direct trade. (This convention was still in force in 2001.) In April 1818, Congress passed a special reciprocity act providing that discriminating duties on goods shipped from the Netherlands would be dropped, not only for goods produced by the Dutch but also for "such produce and manufactures as can only be or most usually are first shipped from a port or place" in the Netherlands. According to this broader principle, national treatment would be accorded all goods that a country normally exported even if they were not produced within that country. In January 1824, Congress extended this principle to Prussia, the Hanseatic cities of Bremen and Hamburg, Sardinia, the dukedom of Oldenburg, and Russia.

In his annual message in December 1825, President John Quincy Adams recommended that the rule of complete reciprocity be adopted, and that all discriminatory duties and dues be dropped for those countries that would do the same for the United States. The origin of goods no longer would be a factor. In the same month Secretary of State Henry Clay negotiated a treaty of complete reciprocity with the Central American Federation. He considered this to be a model treaty and later wrote, "All the shackles which the selfishness or contracted policy of nations had contrived, are broken and destroyed by this broad principle of universal liberality."

By the Marine Reciprocity Act of 1828, Congress gave the president power to proclaim complete reciprocity with all reciprocating nations. In the next few years, this principle was embodied in more than thirty commercial treaties negotiated by the United States. In 1830, Congress repealed the tonnage dues on American ships and offered the same concession to the vessels of any nation that would extend such treatment to American ships.

The attempt to apply reciprocity to the West Indian trade proved to be more difficult. Congress utilized retaliation against the British in the Navigation Acts of 1818 and 1820. The first closed all American ports to British ships that came from ports closed to the United States. The second applied the closing to British ships coming from any colonial port in America, and prohibited the importation of goods from British colonial ports, even in American ships, unless the goods came directly from the producing colony. The latter provision was designed to block the circuitous trade through Bermuda, Nova Scotia, and New Brunswick. The British Parliament offered a liberalization of the West Indies trade in 1822, and the United States relaxed its restrictions by presidential proclamation and by an act of Congress in March 1823. President Adams did not respond to subsequent British offers of relaxation, but President

Andrew Jackson accepted these in 1830. As a result, reciprocal trade relations between the United States and the British West Indies (with some exceptions) were established. Negotiations with France and Sweden concerning their West Indian colonies led to reciprocal agreements in 1828 and 1837. The Spanish colonies of Cuba and Puerto Rico had been closed officially, but the regulations were not enforced. In 1830, Spain accepted a United States consul for Cuba, and trade between the United States and Cuba increased.

Official U.S. attitudes and policies toward the newly independent nations of Latin America were part of the same ideological structure that produced the reciprocity system. John Quincy Adams stressed this in 1822 when he informed Stratford Canning, the British minister to Washington, that the "liberation of the Spanish colonies would mean the end of exclusive commercial policies everywhere." The Latin American policy of the Monroe and Adams administrations was aimed at establishing reciprocity as a key element in inter-American relations, and preventing the reestablishment of the old colonial order of economic mercantilism and political authoritarianism. In May 1823, Secretary of State Adams stressed the U.S. policy "to counteract the efforts which it cannot be doubted European negotiations will continue to make in the furtherance of their monarchical and monopolizing contemplations." In regard to Latin America he noted, "The only object which we shall have much at heart in the negotiation [on commercial relations] will be the sanction by solemn compact of the broad and liberal principle of independence, equal favors, and reciprocity." In addition, Adams hoped that the principle of complete national treatment of foreigners would be established in the hemisphere, and that all discriminating duties would be abolished.

To Adams and Monroe, the open world was to be established first in the Western Hemisphere. And the Monroe Doctrine was, in part, a general declaration of these aspirations. Commercial freedom was an important part of the American rivalry with the European system, but the authors of the Monroe Doctrine envisioned the "American system" in a broader sense. As Adams pointed out in his policy statement of May 1823: "Civil, political, commercial, and religious liberty, are but the various modifications of one great principle, founded in the unalienable rights of human nature, and before the universal application of which the colonial domination of Europe over the American hemisphere has fallen."

During the 1820s and subsequently, the gap between power and aspirations would limit the efforts of the United States. During the 1820s, treaties embodying commercial reciprocity were negotiated with Colombia and Brazil, but economic liberalism in the hemisphere would not become a widespread reality for more than a century. Adams and Monroe did, however, proclaim the integral nature of reciprocity, the open world, and a Western Hemisphere independent of the European colonial system.

1830–1860

By 1830 the American push for commercial reciprocity was bringing results, and discriminatory barriers to trade were falling rapidly. In fact, the Western world was entering a period of widespread commercial liberalism. Leading British statesmen were pushing for reciprocity and for the general elimination of customs duties. The British Corn Laws were repealed in 1846, the Navigation Acts were abolished three years later, and the Cobden-Chevalier Treaty of 1860 with France greatly stimulated free trade in Europe. During this period the meaning of free trade was expanded to encompass the elimination or reduction of all tariffs on goods.

With a few exceptions, the United States participated in the trend that it had helped to promote. Tariff rates generally dropped after 1832. The "Black Tariff" of 1842 was highly protective, but the Walker Tariff of 1846 dropped the rates, and the Tariff of 1857 pushed them even lower. In his 1845 report, Secretary of the Treasury Robert Walker identified "reciprocal free trade" with low duties and argued that such a policy "would feed the hungry and clothe the poor of our fellow-men throughout all the densely peopled nations of the world." The Democratic Party pushed for lower duties, and the platform of 1856 pledged the party to a policy "in favor of free seas, and progressive free trade throughout the world." One of the Democratic Party's main areas of strength was the agricultural South, and farmers opposed protective tariffs because they raised prices on the manufactured goods they purchased. During this period, many large industries wanted protection from foreign competition and the Republican Party favored industry over agriculture.

The United States–Canadian Reciprocity Treaty of 1854 constituted a milestone in this expanded definition of reciprocity, establishing almost complete free trade in natural products between the two countries. It also provided for the joint use of the Atlantic coast fisheries and for reciprocal transit rights in canal systems, the St. Lawrence River, and Lake Michigan.

During this period another version of reciprocity and the open world began to emerge. This was the right and duty of the "Christian nations" to force closed states to trade and to accept the Western system of commercial rights. John Quincy Adams praised the British during the Opium War with China for forcibly upholding the natural right of free commerce among nations. According to Adams, the "righteous cause" of Britain was not opium but the principle of "equal reciprocity." He also hoped that the peace treaty would establish future trade with China "upon terms of equality and reciprocity." Perhaps Adams and others did not necessarily envisage the system of rather unequal treaty relations that developed after the 1840s, but he had completely accepted the idea that the Western nations had the right and duty to force the "backward," or non-Christian, nations to accept the Western presence and systems. During these years, however, the open-door version of reciprocity was still in its infancy, and very limited in its application.

The United States followed Britain in the opening of China and took the lead in opening Japan. In the process, Americans altered the interpretation of reciprocity. As in commercial treaties with Morocco (1836) and Zanzibar (1837), the treaties with Japan (1854) and China (1858) provided unconditional most-favored-nation treatment for the United States in those countries. However, the United States did not give most-favored-nation treatment in return. In addition, China and Japan accorded the United States the privilege of extraterritoriality, which meant that in many cases Chinese and Japanese laws did not apply to Americans. The United States did not grant reciprocal privileges because American officials did not regard reciprocity in "backward" nations as a two-way street. The United States did continue to stress the principle of equality of treatment for all foreign interests.

1860–1922

After 1860 the United States moved into a period of increasingly high tariffs. At the same time, the American economy became much more diversified, encompassing both commercial agriculture and industry. Various groups within these sectors disagreed on market priorities and the need for a protective tariff. This conflict carried over into political debates and made the tariff one of the primary political issues of the period. For the most part, the Republican Party supported high tariffs and the Democratic Party campaigned for reduction. Both, however, reflected the diverse nature of the economy and the concomitant effect on tariff views. As a result, most tariff acts were complicated bundles of regional, group, and political demands. Some free trade sentiment continued. In *Free Land and Free Trade* (1880), Samuel S. Cox argued that "under its benignant influence, the enmities, wars and brutalities of men will yield to concordant reciprocity." The physiocratic ideal had slipped on the American value scale, however, and the dominant protectionist group stressed national independence based on the home market. They agreed that world peace and internationalism were fine aspirations, but decidedly unrealistic in a world of nation-states. The reductionists wanted low tariffs but not free trade. Another group emerging in the 1870s stressed a limited form of reciprocity as a compromise between absolute protectionism and reduction, thus reflecting a combined interest in some home market protection and a vigorous push for foreign markets.

Internationally, protectionism surged during the late 1870s and 1880s. Ironically, American economic strength contributed to this reversal. The Bismarck tariff of 1879 reflected the desertion of free trade by the German agrarian conservatives in the face of American competition. The protective push was renewed after 1902, except for Britain.

Reciprocity underwent changes after 1860 in response to new priorities and interests. A rigidly exclusive version of reciprocity was utilized. American officials sought preferential agreements and special privileges, especially concerning customs duties. As a symbol of this trend, the nonexclusive Canadian Reciprocity Treaty was abrogated in 1866.

Reciprocity was also used to secure political advantages for the United States as part of exclusive economic arrangements. The first political use of reciprocity came in 1875 with the Hawaiian Reciprocity Treaty. The Hawaiians gave the United States special economic privileges that were denied to other nations, and in return Hawaiian sugar was given preferential treatment in the United States market. In addition, the Hawaiian government agreed not to make any territorial grants or to lease ports to other powers. The British protested that this treaty violated their most-favored-nation agreement with Hawaii, but the United States replied that this was a "special and extraordinary" case arising from "geographical and political reasons." This was the beginning of a limited United States imperial preference system that after 1900 was extended to Cuba, Puerto Rico, and the Philippine islands (the latter two by act of Congress). When the renewed treaty was ratified in 1887, the United States received exclusive rights to the use of Pearl Harbor. The Cuban Reciprocity Treaty of 1902 had been promised by Secretary of War Elihu Root to the members of the Cuban Constitutional Convention in order to secure their acceptance of the Platt Amendment. The treaty provided more privileges for Cuba in the American market than the United States received in Cuba. However, American officials believed the treaty would ensure Cuban prosperity and the strengthening of American influence by peaceful means.

During the 1870s the administration of Rutherford B. Hayes considered other reciprocity treaties, but only the Hawaiian treaty reached completion. In the early 1880s, Secretary of State James G. Blaine became a vigorous proponent of reciprocity as a means of opening markets, especially in Latin America, and broadening the domestic support of the Republican Party. Blaine initiated talks with Mexico, which were completed in 1882 by his successor, Frederick T. Frelinghuysen. The latter, with the support of President Chester A. Arthur, also started negotiations with the Dominican Republic, Spain (for Cuba and Puerto Rico), El Salvador, Colombia, and Great Britain (for the West Indies). Treaties were negotiated with the first two in 1884, and both emphasized tariff reductions or eliminations for American manufactured goods. The Mexican treaty also gave the United States a privileged concession by eliminating Mexican interstate taxes on American goods.

Rigid protectionists stalled consideration on these treaties. The Senate approved the Mexican treaty but added a proviso calling for enabling legislation by the House. This was not given, and the treaty lapsed. President Grover Cleveland withdrew the Spanish and Dominican treaties, and ended the other negotiations.

Blaine returned to the State Department and the reciprocity struggle in 1889. One of his first efforts was to push for a customs union at the

Conference of American States (1889–1890). The Latin American states did not approve such a bold and exclusionary move, but they did recommend the negotiation of individual reciprocity treaties.

Blaine then began a campaign to have reciprocity bargaining powers included in the tariff bill being drafted by Congress. After much maneuvering, Congress finally included in the McKinley Tariff of 1890 a provision for a very restricted penalty method of bargaining. Sugar, molasses, coffee, tea, and hides (the "tropical list") were placed on the free list. The president was given the power to restore these items to the dutiable list for any country that had duties on American products that "he may deem to be reciprocally unjust or unreasonable." In addition, the president was given the power to negotiate reciprocity treaties with countries to bind the specified items on the free list. These did not require Senate approval. In 1891 and 1892 the United States concluded such agreements with ten countries. Eight treaties concerned the Western Hemisphere, and seven of these involved nations or possessions in the Caribbean and Central America. Penalty duties were imposed on three Western Hemisphere nations when they refused to make concessions.

The Wilson-Gorman Tariff of 1894 did not include bargaining provisions and undermined the agreements by reimposing the duty on sugar. Subsequently, the Republican Party, with some internal dissent, adopted reciprocity as a compromise position designed to secure the principle of protective tariffs yet give some consideration to groups arguing that the country had to build up foreign trade. "Protection and Reciprocity are twin measures of Republican policy and go hand in hand," the platform of 1896 declared. William McKinley became president in 1897 and immediately pressed Congress for a new tariff act that would ease the protective system and modify the policy of exclusive reciprocity.

The Dingley Tariff of 1897 increased duties but provided for three types of reciprocity treaties. The first was a limited version of the 1890 penalty-bargaining section. The new tropical list of free items consisted of coffee, tea, tonka beans, and vanilla beans. The only treaty of any consequence negotiated under this section was a reciprocity agreement with Brazil in 1904. Brazilian coffee remained on the free list (more than 50 percent of the crop), and the Brazilian government gave a 20 percent reduction on many American products.

The second and third types of reciprocity bargaining reflected the administration's growing concern over trade with Europe and the retaliatory measures enacted by countries such as France. These sections of the tariff act provided for concessionary bargaining. The second type authorized the president to negotiate agreements with countries exporting argol (crude tartar used in winemaking), brandy, champagne, all other sparkling wines, vermouth, paintings, and statuary. If "reciprocal and equivalent concessions" were given to American goods, the president was empowered to grant specified lower duties. The McKinley administration concluded four of these "argol agreements," and the administration of Theodore Roosevelt signed nine more. None of these had any significant effect.

The third type of bargaining provision marked an important modification in the system of exclusive reciprocity and had some potential for trade liberalization. It authorized the president to negotiate reciprocity treaties that could lower duties up to 20 percent on all goods. He also could negotiate the transfer to the free list of goods not produced in the United States. However, such treaties would have to be approved by both houses of Congress and would have five-year limitations.

President McKinley had appointed a reciprocity commission in 1897, under the leadership of John Kasson. This commission negotiated the treaties authorized by the tariff act, and thirteen of these (called the Kasson treaties) were under the provisions of the third section of the act. The treaty with France was the most significant, since it shifted most American products to the minimum schedule. However, the protectionists in Congress would not accept the Kasson treaties, realizing that the executive branch was proposing an important step toward open reciprocity concerning customs duties. In 1901, McKinley took the reciprocity fight to the public. In his last speech, at Buffalo, New York, a few hours before his assassination, he declared: "The period of exclusiveness is past. The expansion of our trade and commerce is the pressing problem. . . . Reciprocity treaties are in harmony with the spirit of the times; measures of retaliation are not."

McKinley's death took much of the drive out of the reciprocity movement. The National Reciprocity Convention was held in November 1901, under the auspices of the National Association of Manufactures, and the National Reciprocity League was organized in 1902. Neither had any effect on congressional protectionists, and the executive branch under Theodore Roosevelt did not press the issue. As a result, the treaties failed, but a pattern had developed that still characterizes the reciprocity struggle. Leadership for trade liberalization through reciprocity would come from the executive branch and would encounter resistance from a Congress representing diverse interests.

The Payne-Aldrich Tariff of 1908 repealed all of the reciprocity agreements made by the Kasson commission. It did, however, mark a slight shift in bargaining objectives from special concessions to equality of treatment. The act set minimum rates and provided for penalty rates in cases of undue discrimination.

The reciprocity movement revived during the administration of William Howard Taft because of various political and economic factors. Taft, under considerable pressure to revise the tariff, believed that some limited reciprocity was needed to save the protective system. Canada seemed to offer several advantages for such a move, and a reciprocity treaty was negotiated in 1911. Newspapers rushed to support the treaty because of the provision for free admission of paper and wood pulp. The U.S. Congress approved the treaty, but it was rejected by the Canadian Parliament.

The Democratic-sponsored Underwood-Simmons Act of 1913 provided for a significant lowering of the tariff and the elimination of penalty bargaining. One section authorized trade agreements containing reciprocal concessions, but none were negotiated. The act also contained a peculiar reversion to the 1790s: lower duties for goods imported in American ships, unless existing treaties prohibited the discrimination. World War I soon obliterated all questions of reciprocity and bargaining, and the negotiating potential of the act was never tested. Protectionist pressures mounted after the war, leading to the Emergency Tariff Act of 1921.

Reciprocity as part of a concept of world order was a limited and inconsistent part of the open-door concept that reached maturity in the 1890s. Equality of opportunity and nondiscrimination tended to be applied to competition with other industrial powers in Asia and Africa, areas where American power was limited. In its new colonial empire the United States enforced a discriminatory commercial system and, despite the open-door rhetoric, the government made some efforts to achieve a privileged position in various Latin American countries. The effects were limited to the Caribbean and Central America. The administra-

tion of Woodrow Wilson tried to expand the Monroe Doctrine to include the restriction of European economic activity in these areas.

American officials also used the arguments of equality of opportunity and nondiscrimination to justify the "right" of Americans to invest in underdeveloped countries and have access to their raw materials. In some cases they defended this position by citing reciprocity. When the Mexican government attempted some regulation of foreign oil companies after the adoption of the constitution of 1917, State Department officials argued that such action violated the principle of reciprocity, since Mexican capital in the United States was not subject to discriminatory treatment. For Mexico and other underdeveloped countries, this was a hypothetical argument, since there was little if any Mexican capital invested in the United States.

Revolutionary nationalism, with its concomitant policy of control or elimination of foreign investments and properties, first emerged during this period. The United States and other industrial-creditor nations attempted to meet the challenge with a special definition of openness that implied a limitation on the sovereignty of the expropriating or regulating nations. How far would the United States go, and what means would it use, to enforce the open door? This question dogged American policymakers throughout the twentieth century. The results were mixed, and even ambivalent, as a result of changing circumstances and interpretations of national interest.

Part of the ambiguity was caused by the revival of the noncoercive, open world view. The peace movement prior to 1914 sought some type of world order beyond the open door. And, paradoxically, Woodrow Wilson in his Fourteen Points described a partial vision of an open world with the "removal, so far as possible, of all economic barriers, and the establishment of an equality of trade conditions among all the nations consenting to the peace and associating themselves for its maintenance." To some Americans, the League of Nations seemed to promise the establishment of an open world order. Although a mixed opposition prevented United States entry, various Americans continued to try to implement peace and reciprocity by other means.

1922–1975

After World War I the nations of Europe began to assert a greater degree of economic nationalism.

The unconditional most-favored-nation clause that had generalized bilateral tariff negotiations before the war was not effectively rehabilitated. After 1930 the Great Depression accelerated these trends, and a wide variety of new discriminatory economic tactics emerged. These included exchange controls, quotas, internal taxes on foreign goods, and the creation of vast preferential trading systems. The British created the imperial preference system in 1932, and Germany developed a similar structure using barter and a special currency that could be exchanged only for German goods.

Subject to the same pressures, the United States also exhibited some protective reactions. In the Fordney-McCumber Tariff Act of 1922 and the Smoot-Hawley Tariff Act of 1930, Congress pushed the tariff to the highest levels in American history. In 1920, Congress attempted to restrict the entire commercial treaty system by "authorizing and directing" the president to scrap the existing treaties and thereby reimpose discriminatory tonnage duties on foreign ships. During the 1930s, Congress authorized import quotas on agricultural products, and imposed these in some cases. It also levied excise taxes on imports.

Paradoxically, the executive branch began gradually and sporadically to move against the prevailing trends and toward a revitalization of equality of treatment and reciprocity. By the latter half of the 1930s, the United States had emerged as the leading (and perhaps only) exponent of an open world commercial system.

All of the Republican administrations of the 1920s refused to implement the act providing for merchant marine discrimination. The Tariff Commission under William S. Culbertson launched a campaign to revitalize reciprocity by shifting the United States to the unconditional most-favored-nation principle. President Warren Harding and Secretary of State Charles Evans Hughes accepted the argument that the conditional principle had produced "discriminatory reciprocity" and implemented the change. The tariff acts of 1922 and 1930 contained elastic clauses, advocated by the Tariff Commission, that authorized the president to raise or lower duties by 50 percent on a nondiscriminatory basis (that is, if the duty was reduced on an item, the reduction would apply to all nations, regardless of treaty status). This was not implemented because of the political conflicts involved.

The administration of Franklin D. Roosevelt divided into two factions over the issue of economic nationalism, and followed a vacillating and even contradictory policy for several years. The home market group, led by George Peek of the Agricultural Adjustment Administration, wanted import quotas and bilateral barter deals. In 1933 this group seemed to be winning the internal power struggle, especially when Roosevelt undermined Secretary of State Cordell Hull's liberalization efforts at the London Economic Conference.

Hull was the leader of the trade liberalization group. In many respects, he and other officials of the period were intellectual descendants of the philosophes, who believed that an open world based upon reciprocity in all areas was the only prescription for a peaceful world. The international scene of the 1930s provided a powerful argument for this position. Hull believed that economic nationalism had produced the collapse of the world economy and was continuing to provoke a vicious cycle of economic retaliation, militarization, and a struggle for privileged positions that could end only in war. In the last analysis, it was a struggle between open and closed economic systems, and between freedom and tyranny. The two were indivisible.

Hull's position gradually, and with some difficulty, gained ground after 1933. The victories were limited and mixed with contradictory elements. The first breakthrough came with the passage of the Reciprocal Trade Agreements Act in 1934. This amendment to the tariff act of 1930 was a tactic that avoided a congressional battle over consideration of the entire tariff schedule. The president was empowered to conclude bilateral trade agreements that reduced duties as much as 50 percent. All such treaties were to incorporate the most-favored-nation principle, which was broadened to include negotiations over internal taxes, import prohibitions and quotas, and exchange controls. All treaties, however, were to contain the "Cuban exception" clause (allowing preferential treatment) and an "escape" clause.

Between 1934 and 1945 the United States concluded twenty-seven treaties, and tariff rates were reduced on average by 44 percent of their base rate. Hull's efforts to eliminate other forms of discrimination produced mixed results, and his attack on the British imperial preference system was shelved during World War II. Hull also used the reciprocity argument in demanding "equitable" treatment for U.S. interests in Latin America, arguing that the Good Neighbor Policy of the United States required reciprocal behavior. However, the administration did relax the insistence on extraterritorial rights, as evidenced by U.S. policy toward Mexico's expropriation of the oil industry in 1938.

Planning for the postwar world by American officials cannot be comprehended adequately without an understanding of their intense belief, even to the point of obsession, that the United States must lead the way to an open world or face another cycle of depression and war. At times the intensity of this belief blinded them to other factors and produced a self-righteous image of the purity of American policies. The fears and ideological fervor engendered by the Cold War complicated and confused the push for an open world. In the years after 1945 many of the ideas and impulses associated with the imperial, open-door concept were reasserted, to coexist and compete with the open world view.

American officials wanted to make reciprocity an integral part of the postwar world order. Many hoped that the United Nations would lead the way in eliminating spheres of interest. In addition, the United States helped to create the International Monetary Fund and the International Bank for Reconstruction and Development as means to restore multilateralism and nondiscrimination in international economic relations.

In 1947, twenty-three nations took another important step toward a liberal trading system by concluding the General Agreement on Tariffs and Trade (GATT). This agreement provided for multilateral reciprocity and included a code for fair trading in international commerce. In 1948, the U.S. Congress refused to ratify a charter that would have institutionalized GATT in the International Trade Organization, because Congress opposed the creation of an international body that would exercise control over U.S. trade policies. But GATT has survived through periodic conferences. By the 1970s, eighty nations accounting for more than 80 percent of total world trade had joined. In 1963 the national representatives of GATT relieved the underdeveloped nations within the system of the necessity to reciprocate fully for concessions granted by the more developed countries.

Since 1945 Congress has periodically extended the president's bargaining power and authorized additional reductions in the tariff. However, protectionist sentiment has moderated reciprocity and preserved some areas of discrimination. A "United States exception" clause was added to the GATT charter, in deference to American desires to retain import quotas on some agricultural products. In the 1950s, Congress also directed the president to place import quotas and embargoes on various products in the interest of national security. Oil import quotas were imposed in 1959, and during the 1950s similar restrictions were applied to such goods as Gouda cheese, safety pins, and dental burs.

Cold War antagonisms also produced some retreat from complete reciprocity. In 1950 the United States placed an embargo on all trade with the People's Republic of China and North Korea, and most-favored-nation status for the Soviet Union and other communist nations was withdrawn in 1951. In 1960–1961 the government proclaimed an embargo on all trade with Cuba and tried to obtain European and Latin American cooperation; even to the point of blacklisting ships going to Cuba and forbidding them entry into United States ports. In August 1975 the Organization of American States abolished the "paper" embargo against Cuba. Subsequently, the United States eliminated the blacklist and other sanctions imposed on nations trading with Cuba. In May 1977, President James E. Carter began the process of restoring trade relations by authorizing Cuban purchases of food and medicine.

In August 1971, under mounting economic pressures, President Richard M. Nixon took several steps that seemed to imply a retreat from reciprocity and a shift to a decidedly nationalistic policy. The president suspended the convertibility of the dollar into gold, imposed a surcharge on imports and export quotas on soybeans, and threatened quotas on textile imports from Asia. Paradoxically, in June he had lifted the embargo on trade with China and removed some restrictions on wheat, flour, and grain shipments to the Soviet Union and Eastern Europe.

Subsequently, President Nixon removed or modified the restrictions imposed in 1971 and requested authority from Congress to enter a new round of GATT negotiations. In December 1974, Congress finally passed the Trade Act of 1974, an extensive bill that clearly revealed the duality of American policy. The Japanese described it as a "two-edged sword." The act gave the president broad new powers to bargain away various tariff and nontariff trade barriers, but it also provided for several retaliatory actions against "unfair trade practices." In the area of nontariff barriers, the president could negotiate pacts guaranteeing access to the products of other nations (with congressional approval required). This would allow the United States to enter a world food reserve program.

However, the president for the first time was given explicit authority to raise tariffs and tighten import quotas to deal with balance-of-payments deficits and import competition problems. The act also provided duty-free treatment (with some items excluded) for about one hundred underdeveloped nations, but the preferences were denied to nations enforcing export embargoes against the United States (aimed especially at those belonging to the Organization of Petroleum Exporting Countries) and not cooperating on expropriation and drug matters. Most-favored-nation treatment was authorized for communist nations that permitted free emigration (earlier acts had extended the principle to Poland and Yugoslavia). In 1975 most-favored-nation treatment was extended to Romania. The Soviet Union objected to the emigration provisions and withdrew the trade agreement (with most-favored-nation status) that had been negotiated earlier.

1974–2001

After eight rounds of GATT negotiations, this regime was finally transformed into the World Trade Organization in 1995. During its lifetime, average tariff rates on industrial products had been lowered from 40 percent in 1947 to 4 percent by the early 1990s. Although every U.S. administration supported liberalized trade, in fact, Cold War diplomacy took precedence over reciprocity until the 1990s. U.S. leaders tended to take a soft line when its allies or trade partners were less than faithful in this area.

Congress in 1974 renewed for five years the president's trade negotiating authority and established the fast track authority for considering trade legislation. The president promised regular consultation, and Congress gave up the right to amend any trade agreement and agreed to consider any agreement within ninety days. In this act Congress emphasized reciprocity with developed nations ("the harmonization, reduction, or elimination of devices which distort trade or commerce"). Congress, however, stated that it would not insist on full reciprocity for developing countries.

The seventh GATT (Tokyo) round of negotiations began in 1973 and lasted until November 1979. These negotiations stressed nontariff barriers for the first time. In many cases these had become more important than actual tariffs. Among other factors, health and safety regulations were quietly used to limit imports. The

members approved a series of specialized, nontariff codes pertaining to countervailing duties, antidumping duties, subsidies, product standards, import licensing, and government procurement. Relatively few countries signed these codes, and a decade later the six nontariff codes had little effect outside of the European Community, the United States, and Japan.

After 1975 the U.S. trade deficit began to grow rapidly. In 1975 the United States had nearly a $1 billion surplus in trade with Asia, but by 1987 this had changed to a $101 billion deficit. During the 1980s, U.S. attempts to promote free trade and reciprocity faced difficult times. The administration of Ronald Reagan imposed some import restraints for steel, motorcycles, semiconductors, and automobiles. In the latter case, strong hints that Japan needed to head off congressional action led to voluntary limitations. Although Japan lowered its tariffs significantly after the Tokyo Round, foreign manufactured imports were impeded by restrictive marketing customs and through a combination of cultural loyalties and administrative guidance.

The Reagan administration also began a two-track approach to liberalizing trade. It urged GATT members to begin negotiations to expand the Tokyo Round Codes and it developed a bilateral approach to free trade agreements (FTAs). Such an agreement was signed with Israel in 1984 and Canada in 1987. The latter provided for some integration of the two economies. All tariffs and nontariff barriers were to be eliminated by 1998, and in the agricultural area all tariffs were to be eliminated during a ten-year period and nontariff barriers would be reduced. Several major controversies and legal challenges have developed in the agricultural area. To complicate matters, each nation continued to enforce its own antidumping and countervailing duty laws to imported goods. Publishing and communications were excluded from the nontariff provisions because of the Canadian policy of "protecting" its cultural heritage. Financial services were not included in this agreement.

President George H. W. Bush pushed for a trilateral free trade agreement with Canada and Mexico. This North American Free Trade Agreement (NAFTA) was signed in October 1992. Two of the most important elements were the investment provisions and the mandatory dispute settlement. Foreign investors, for the most part, received national treatment and various other safeguards. President Bill Clinton supported

NAFTA despite heated opposition from labor unions and his own party. He negotiated limited side agreements concerning labor and environmental issues but a majority of House Democrats voted against NAFTA. Businessman and 1992 presidential candidate Ross Perot predicted a "great sucking sound" of jobs moving south of the border.

Economic historian Alfred E. Eckes, Jr. has written an overall summary of the FTAs. He notes:

> Interestingly, the FTA's with Israel, Canada and Mexico (NAFTA) represented significant departures from U.S. commitment to the multilateral GATT process. FTA provisions digressed somewhat from the principle of nondiscrimination, but arguably they complemented the overall objective of liberalizing trade in that bilateral FTA's sought to address specific issues not handled successfully in the GATT forum—agriculture, services, investments, intellectual property, and other non-tariff issues.

One of the most controversial aspects of NAFTA has been the binational panel process to revise the application of antidumping and countervailing duties. One of the three-member panel's first decisions was to reverse the U.S. Commerce Department's subsidy determination. It was later revealed that two of the Canadians on the panel had business and government connections that compromised their neutrality. A U.S. judge ruled that the process was flawed under U.S. law and ordered Canada to negotiate restraints on its softwood lumber exports to the United States. Some authorities believe, however, that the binational panels have been effective in "relatively routine" cases.

In early 2001 the United States and Mexico clashed over a Clinton administration refusal to allow Mexican trucks full access to U.S. highways—they were limited to a twenty-mile zone north of the border where they had to transfer their loads to U.S. trucks. A NAFTA arbitration ruled that the United States had violated the treaty. In May 2001 the U.S. government issued revised rules to meet the arbitration panel's ruling. Under the new rules, all Mexican trucks that operate in the United States must apply for permission and their companies must provide detailed information about their safety practices and show that they are in compliance with U.S. trucking regulations.

The United States and Canada were at odds over a U.S. ban on the import of potatoes from Prince Edward Island, on the grounds that potato wart fungus had been found in a field on the island. Canada referred the issue to NAFTA negotiations.

In April 2001 newly elected President George W. Bush provided the leadership for a Free Trade of the Americas initiative called Super NAFTA. A three-day summit meeting of hemisphere leaders in Quebec, Canada, hoped to outline a free trade zone that would wipe out most trade restrictions by 2005. If it comes to fruition it will be the greatest advance for reciprocity in the history of the world. The leaders ratified a plan barring undemocratic nations from the free trade zone. The so-called democracy clause would suspend the benefits of the free trade zone from any country that ceases to be a democracy. Cuba was the only nation excluded from the summit because of its totalitarian regime. An odd amalgamation of anarchists, communists, labor activists, environmentalists, New Agers, and others took to the streets in violent protests against free trade and capitalism in general. President Bush noted that he was willing to discuss their grievances, and in his address to the meeting, he stated that the proposed agreement had to be accompanied by a "strong commitment" to protecting the environment and improving labor standards. Brazilian President Fernando Henrique Cardoso pledged to push for "trade openings that are reciprocal and [to] help close rather than widen the disparities in our region."

The eighth round of GATT talks (the Uruguay Round) began in 1986. In 1984, 109 nations signed a new agreement to create a World Trade Organization to replace GATT and implement the last GATT accord. This final accord, in December 1993, cut overall import duties by about 40 percent, phased out import limits that made clothing and textiles more expensive, scaled back (but did not end) state support to farmers, boosted protection for copyrights and patents, and set new rules to help liberalize trade in services such as tourism. Separate accords also covered government contracts, dairy products, and beef. The World Trade Organization was given enforcement authority. In January 1995 the new accords became official.

For the next two years the WTO did very little and negotiations to extend free trade failed. In December 1996 a conference of ministers from 128 nations finally agreed to sweep away customs duties on computers, software, semiconductors, and hundreds of other information technology products by 2000. Significant progress in telephone services negotiations was also made.

The mandatory dispute settlement provision has created a problem for the United States. In the WTO it has one vote, while the European Union, which negotiates as a bloc, has fifteen separate votes. And developing nations have 83 percent of the votes. But this disparity does not seem to have had serious consequences for the United States to date. In late 2000 the General Accounting Office testified that out of forty-two cases involving the United States as a plaintiff or defendant, America had won fourteen and lost eight; the remaining cases were decided through negotiation.

But in some areas reciprocity continues to take a beating. The European Union has set up trade barriers to U.S. beef produced with growth hormones and to bananas grown on American-run plantations in the Caribbean and Central America. In turn, the United States retaliated with $116.8 million in trade sanctions on a range of European goods. Negotiations in late 2000 failed. The EU did relax its ban on genetically modified organisms. This prepared the way for an end to Europe's moratorium on bioengineered seeds and food. But debates continued over the role of government subsidies in protecting industries. The United States pointed to British, French, and German low-interest loans to Airbus Industries in its efforts to build a rival to Boeing's jumbo jet. The French demanded the right to protect their film industry from U.S. competition and to extensive agricultural subsidies. In turn, the Europeans complained that the United States also provided massive support to farmers and used restrictive quotas and high tariffs to protect sectors such as sugar, peanuts, and tobacco.

Another complicating factor in reciprocity negotiations is the demand by labor unions, environmentalists, and leading Democrats that any agreements must include worker protection and environmental concerns. Robert Zoellick, the Bush administration's trade representative, argued that free trade should be about free trade and nothing else. According to Zoellick, "the WTO should not be seen as a global government with power to order new environmental or labor laws—or, for that matter, better tax regimes, pension plans, health programs, civilian control of militaries, or a host of other meritorious outcomes."

Trade with the People's Republic of China was an ongoing problem. For years the U.S. Congress annually reviewed China's trade status before voting on renewing most-favored-nation status. In 2000 the Clinton administration pushed to make this status permanent and even changed its name to "permanent normal trade relations." Under the terms of the new agreement, China consented to cut tariffs and restrictions on American agriculture, industrial products, banking, insurance, telecommunications, and movies. The United States agreed to accept Chinese membership in the WTO and give up its annual review of China's trade status. The opponents argued that with this deal the United States gave up its efforts to influence China's human rights policies. But in past annual reviews, the United States had never done anything except lecture the Chinese government. A new antidumping law took effect in 2001. Under its provisions, any company that proves it was harmed by "unfair competition" will be given protection by a special antidumping duty. The proceeds from this duty will be paid to the companies involved. For example, on behalf of the Diamond Sparkler Company, the U.S. government imposed a 93.4 percent import tax on Chinese sparklers. It is estimated that $100 million will be collected in 2001 as a result of all such special duties. The steel industry dominates the list of companies in line for the payments, with 46 percent of the 360 cases preliminarily qualified for payment.

According to the law, the funds received by each company can be used only for training, new technology, health benefits, pensions, and other specific items. That leaves the Customs Service with the problem of determining whether the funds are spent legally. Thus, the problem of "unfair competition" continues to plague reciprocity.

As of 2000, the European Union, Japan, Australia and several other countries had filed complaints with the WTO. The government of Canada warned that if duties levied against Canadian or Mexican products were turned over to competing U.S. companies, Canada will charge this to be a violation of NAFTA.

President George W. Bush in 2001 requested that Congress restore "fast track" negotiating authority to the president. The authority was first granted in 1974 and expired in 1994. Congress refused to renew it in 1997, because of congressional demands that environmental and labor rights protection be included in all trade negotiations. Under fast-track authority, Congress cannot amend a treaty—it can only approve or disapprove.

As in 1789, reciprocity in 2001 was buffeted and shaped by internal pressures and external circumstances. In the twentieth century the United

States emerged as the leader in the struggle for an open world based on reciprocity. Contradictions, limitations, and modifications are still present, but the world is more open and reciprocity is more widespread than in 1789. The ideas proclaimed in that earlier period are still a vital part of American foreign relations.

BIBLIOGRAPHY

Bovard, James. *The Fair Trade Fraud.* New York, 1991. A very harsh denunciation of U.S. trade policies.

Culbertson, William Smith. *Reciprocity: A National Policy for Foreign Trade.* New York: London, 1937. A valuable source of information about reciprocity policy from the 1890s to the 1930s, especially good for the 1920s.

Eckes, Alfred E., Jr. *Opening America's Market: U.S. Foreign Trade Policy Since 1776.* Chapel Hill, N.C., 1995.

Ellis, L. Ethan. *Reciprocity 1911: A Study in Canadian-American Relations.* New Haven, Conn., and Toronto, 1939. An intensive study of political and economic factors in both countries.

Evans, John W. *The Kennedy Round in American Trade Policy: The Twilight of the GATT?* Cambridge, Mass., 1971. One of the best treatments of American commercial policy since the 1930s, although the focus is on the 1960s.

Gilbert, Felix. *To The Farewell Address: Ideas of Early American Foreign Policy.* Princeton, N.J., 1961. A valuable analysis of the conflicting ideas that influenced the foreign policy concepts of the Founders; the main theme is the interaction and conflict between realism and idealism.

Hornbeck, Stanley K. "The Most-Favored-Nation Clause in Commercial Treaties: Its Function in Theory and in Practice and Its Relation to Tariff Policies." *Bulletin of the University of Wisconsin.* 343: Economics and Political Science series, 6, no. 2 (1910). Remains the most complete treatment of a generally ignored subject.

Kottman, Richard Norman. *Reciprocity and the North Atlantic Triangle, 1932–1938.* Ithaca, N.Y., 1968. One of the most detailed and well-researched discussions of the negotiations of reciprocal trade agreements with Canada and Britain.

Lovett, William A., Alfred E. Eckes, Jr., and Richard L. Brinkman. *U.S. Trade Policy: History, Theory and the WTO.* Armonk, N.Y., 1999. A highly critical work on recent trade policy; argues that the U.S. must be much more aggressive in pushing for true reciprocity.

Low, Patrick. *Trading Free: The GATT and U.S. Trade Policy.* New York, 1993. An in-depth examination of the way GATT has worked.

Ratner, Sidney. *The Tariff in American History.* New York, 1972. A succinct history but needs supplementing for fine points and technicalities.

Setser, Vernon G. *The Commercial Reciprocity Policy of the United States, 1774–1829.* Philadelphia and London, 1937. Absolutely essential to any understanding of economic foreign policy for the period; an intensive study based on multiarchival research.

Terrill, Tom E. *The Tariff, Politics, and American Foreign Policy 1874–1901.* Westport, Conn., 1973. A valuable analysis of economic policies and their relationship to domestic politics and economic factors.

Williams, Benjamin H. *Economic Foreign Policy of the United States.* New York, 1929. Still one of the best reference works for all aspects of the subject; organized topically with many details.

Zeiler, Thomas W. *Free Trade, Free World: The Advent of GATT.* Chapel Hill, N.C., 1999.

See also ECONOMIC POLICY AND THEORY; MOST-FAVORED-NATION PRINCIPLE; OPEN DOOR POLICY; TARIFF POLICY; TREATIES.

RECOGNITION

★ ★ ★ ★ ★

Paolo E. Coletta

Until a global organization competent to extend recognitions binding upon the world can be created, each state handles the question of recognition on the basis of national policy rather than international law. The principle of recognition can be traced back to the Dutch jurist Hugo Grotius, who asserted that the obligation of a state remains unmodified despite changes made by constitutional, revolutionary, and other means. Given the large number of states and the peaceful or forcible changes often made in them (regular elections or successor states in the first instance; accretion, prescription, conquest, occupation, and cession in the second), and the application of recognition to belligerency as well as to statehood, the question of recognition remains a constant in the conduct of international relations.

DEFINITIONS OF "RECOGNITION"

All "new" states seek recognition from other states because recognition admits that a state has an international personality. All states have the legal duty to decide whether a "new" state meets certain conditions and therefore warrants being recognized. Does it have complete independence from parent and other states, exercise authority over a defined geographic area, enjoy the obedience of the great majority of its population, reveal willingness and ability to assume international obligations and duties?

Express recognition may be extended unilaterally in an explicit executive statement by one state or collectively following the agreement of several states. Recognition is implied if a state undertakes some sort of intercourse with another, as in concluding treaties with it or sending diplomatic representatives to it, without, however, having recognized it, thereby revealing at least intent to recognize it explicitly at a later time. A state's imposition of demands upon a community seeking recognition is a conditional type of recognition. Contingent recognition is generally reserved for acknowledgment by a parent state that a revolution against it has succeeded—indeed, it endorses the rupture. Recognition is granted by some states if a state is admitted to an international conference (for example, China, Persia, and Siam at the Hague Conference of 1907), or to an international organization (Ethiopia admitted to membership of the League of Nations in 1923, Syria and Lebanon admitted to the United Nations in 1945), or if a mother country grants independence to a former colony, mandate, or trusteeship.

Despite much argument over precise meanings, de facto recognition seems to mean a "qualified" or "provisional" recognition that subsequently may be withdrawn, whereas de jure recognition is final and irrevocable, indicates the legitimacy of title, and signifies closer political ties than de facto recognition. The phrase "de facto" has caused confusion because it has been applied indiscriminately in constitutional and international law and also with respect to recognition. De jure or de facto describes the character of the act of recognition, whereas recognition of a de facto or de jure government or state characterizes the status of the entity recognized. The courts or other agencies of the recognizing power, however, treat the validity of the acts of recognized powers in identical fashion, regardless of how they were recognized.

The determination of the government to be recognized, even of the "policy" governing such determination, is an executive function in the United States. In 1897, when congressional resolutions sought recognition of Cuban independence and United States mediation between Cuba and Spain, the Senate Foreign Relations Committee objected, saying, "Resolutions of their [nation's] legislative departments upon diplomatic matters have no status in international law."

President Grover Cleveland agreed—indeed, he said privately that he would not mobilize the army even if Congress declared war.

Controversies involving certain aspects of foreign affairs occasionally provoke conflict between the president and the courts, the latter of which may or may not agree to recognize a new state in legal proceedings and to enforce that state's laws in American territory. It is nevertheless possible to have *officieuses* ("officious") intercourse, as the French put it, with states that are denied recognition—for instance, by carrying on private undertakings in such fields as the recovery of property and exchange of persons.

A distinction is often made between "constitutive" (or "creative" or "positivist") and "declaratory" (or "de facto") recognition. According to the constitutive theory, prior to recognition a community possesses neither the rights nor the obligations associated with statehood. Moreover, recognition is a political rather than a legal action. The declaratory theory, denying the legal necessity for a community to be recognized as a state, holds that a community seeking recognition possesses many of the characteristics inherent in statehood but has no right to claim recognition as such. The constitutive doctrine remains the preferred one.

The precise timing of the acceptance of a new state into the community of nations thus may vary. The British colonists in America, for example, proclaimed their independence on 4 July 1776. Although Britain never formally recognized their belligerency, they were recognized as independent by France on 6 February 1778, when Benjamin Franklin, Silas Deane, and Arthur Lee signed the Treaty of Amity and Commerce. Britain recognized the United States as independent in the Peace of Paris of 3 September 1783. Not until the Nootka Sound controversy of 1789–1790 did it realize that the United States existed as a viable community. In consequence, in 1791 Britain sent a minister plenipotentiary and then began diplomatic relations with its former colony. A commercial treaty was not written, however, until Jay's Treaty of 1794. In accordance with the declaratory theory, the United States became a state when it declared its independence, 4 July 1776; in accordance with the preferred constitutive view, toward which Britain leans, the date is 6 February 1778, when it was recognized by France. In more recent years the question of timing arose in October 2000, after North Korean officials contacted British and German officials and requested recognition—already granted by Canada, Italy, and Australia. While on his way to a summit meeting in Seoul, British Prime Minister Tony Blair was asked by a reporter when he would grant recognition. Blair replied, "Diplomatic moves of that kind move at a leisurely pace. But we intend to give a positive response to the letter we received last month." German Chancellor Gerhard Schroeder revealed a similar attitude.

U.S. POLICY IN THE RECOGNITION OF STATES

The distinction between a state and its government is made primarily for the purpose of recognition, since a state as a corporate person may continue after change has occurred in its government. Indeed, a state remains a state until it has been abolished. That recognition extends to a government rather than to a person was decided upon early in the American government and set a pattern followed by most states. When Louis XVI of France was deposed and beheaded in 1793, Alexander Hamilton argued that the supplanting of an admittedly tyrannous government by an equally tyrannous mob should go unrecognized and that the Treaty of Amity and Commerce with France should be considered suspended until a French government was formed. Secretary of State Thomas Jefferson instead held that the French people had the inherent right to form their own government, and that the treaty should remain in full force regardless of change in the French government, because treaties, not governments, bind nations. President George Washington agreed with Jefferson and recognized the new French republic and subsequent governments, as did the British, although they were at war with France.

For its first century, the policy of the United States was to recognize de facto governments. (Despite many military coups and dictatorial governments established in Mexico between 1823 and 1860, for example, the United States withdrew its diplomatic representatives from Mexico City only three times, and that for only short periods.) In the early twentieth century this changed somewhat as a large element of moralism motivated the administration of Woodrow Wilson. Subsequent administrations reverted to the policy of "de factoism" during the 1920s and 1930s, but the United States refused to recognize forcible changes made in the territory or governments of victims of aggression, be the offender Japan, as in the case of Manchuria, the Soviet Union with respect to the Baltic states, or Germany with respect to its conquest of western Europe during World War II. A policy of nonrecognition was followed toward the Baltic states until these were freed of Russian control at the end of the Cold War. The United States also obtained collective support for the policy from democratic European nations and the Latin American states.

Until Wilson's presidency, United States practice prior to extending recognition was to eschew the question of legitimacy and to demand effectiveness and evidence of popular consent, with the element of democratic legality proved by means of free elections. Although monarchic heads of state took as an open declaration of war by the French National Convention in 1792 that it would aid those seeking to recover their liberties, Secretary of State Thomas Jefferson stated, "It accords with our principles to acknowledge any government to be rightful which is formed by the will of the people, substantially declared." By adding, however, that he would deal in certain instances with a "government de facto," he has been declared a pioneer of "de factoism."

Rather than insisting rigidly that a new government have the consent of its people, the United States, recalling its own revolutionary origin, adopted the principle of the people's subsequent legitimation of a government deemed to be de facto. The result was that the United States almost automatically extended recognition to de facto governments even though it took into account the use of democratic processes by a new government and the latter's disposition to fulfill international obligations. Sometimes, however, Jefferson's dictum with respect to "the will of the nation" was "interpreted" so as to take on a tinge of legitimism and to equate legitimism with legality or constitutionalism, as under Secretary of State William H. Seward in the 1860s and under Wilson early in the twentieth century.

Legally, the quality of a state's civilization, municipal law, legitimacy, politics, and religion should not be weighed, but states sometimes pay attention, for reasons of national advantage, to constitutional, political, legal, commercial, and even partisan, moral, and humanitarian considerations before extending recognition. Excellent examples are available in President Wilson's relations with China, Mexico, and Bolshevik Russia. With respect to China, Wilson and his first secretary of state, William Jennings Bryan, wished to see it become a constitutional republic freed from imperialistic powers and the clutches of American

dollar diplomacy. They were also moved by humanitarian and moral considerations, for they spoke of love, brotherhood, and friendship. They therefore rejected a proposal of collective recognition made by Great Britain, Germany, Japan, and other powers and unilaterally recognized the government of Yüan Shih-k'ai on 2 May 1913, after which the European powers and Japan accorded formal recognition.

Abuse of the weapon of recognition appeared in especially aggravated form with respect to Mexico. Early in 1913, the government of Victoriano Huerta controlled about 80 percent of Mexico and had been recognized by twenty-eight states. Assistant Secretary of State Alvey A. Adee, counselor of the Department of State John Bassett Moore, and most American businessmen demanded its recognition. Wilson, however, demanded an orderly government that would not only protect Americans in Mexico and their large investments there—and perhaps keep out competing foreign investors, such as the British—but also fulfill the social aspirations of its people. The administration clearly meant to exercise a moral judgment upon Mexico's internal affairs and so apply the test of constitutionality before granting recognition.

Over a two-year period, Wilson obtained a recision of recognition from the important European and Latin American powers; violated U.S. neutrality laws by letting arms reach Huerta's constitutionalist opponents, even though he refused to recognize them as belligerents; probably made a "deal" over Panama Canal tolls in which Great Britain let the situation in Mexico become strictly an American affair; intervened militarily at Veracruz, and then grasped eagerly at mediation offered by Argentina, Brazil, and Chile. Huerta fled into exile in July 1914, but Wilson's relations with the government of Venustiano Carranza remained unhappy even though de facto recognition was granted to it in 1915. In 1918, Carranza's threat to make retroactive Article 27 of the Mexican constitution of 1917, which nationalized Mexico's subsoil properties, increased acerbities. It was not until 1923, after being clubbed again with a threat of nonrecognition, that President Alvaro Obregón pledged that the article would not be applied retroactively. His government was then recognized.

As Louis L. Jaffe has put it, "The whole world went off the de facto standard in its policy toward Soviet Russia." Giuseppe Mazzini and other Italians had followed the "principle of nationality," or self-determination, in creating the Italian state between 1861 and 1870. Wilson had used the principle to obtain independence for the subject nationalities of central Europe between 1918 and 1920. He considered some extremely subjective, as well as objective, factors in declining to recognize the Soviet Union, however. Russia had "defected" to Germany in World War I. Its Bolshevik leaders, not the people, had made the accommodations reached in the Treaty of Brest-Litovsk. The new government, which did not reflect popular political desires, faced such turmoil and revolution that it lacked definite geographical boundaries and a recognizable bureaucracy. And the minority in control of the government killed or imprisoned certain groups in the interest of progress for others.

In 1920, Bainbridge Colby, Wilson's third and last secretary of state, said that the United States refused to recognize the Soviet Union because it had subverted popular government and denied Russians the democratic right of self-determination, had taken American property without paying for it, had sent agents abroad to foment communist revolutions, and had negated the conventions of international law.

In 1922 Secretary of State Charles Evans Hughes asserted: "We recognize the right of revolution and we do not attempt to determine the internal concerns of other states." He added, however, "There still remain other questions to be considered." Since the acquiescence of the people was the most important question, Hughes seemed to be abandoning the Wilsonian concept of moral intervention. In 1930, Secretary of State Henry L. Stimson agreed that subsequent legitimation by constitutional methods would warrant the recognition of a new government. In that year, when the United States recognized new governments in Argentina, Bolivia, and Peru on a de facto basis, and in 1932, when it recognized a new government in Chile, all Stimson required was that a new government furnish evidence "that it is in control of the country and that there is no active resistance to it." He suggested, however, that each government "hold in due course elections to regularize its status." Stimson had thus retreated to the principle of recognition based simply upon the effectiveness of a government, thereby repudiating the Wilson policy of moralism.

Even though it had apparently reverted to a policy of "de factoism," the United States refused to recognize a number of states other than the Soviet Union in the 1920s and 1930s. Although not a signatory, it sometimes acted in accordance with the so-called Tobar Doctrine that grew out of the treaties written among the Central American republics in 1907 and renewed in 1923. Designed to discourage revolutions, these provided that the parties "shall not recognize any other Government which may come into power in any of the five Republics as a consequence of a coup d'etat, or of a revolution against the recognized Government, so long as the freely elected representatives of the people thereof have not constitutionally reorganized the country." They also disqualified the leaders of a coup d'état from assuming the presidency or vice presidency. The United States applied the doctrine to the revolutionary leader Federico Tinoco in Costa Rica in 1917, to Honduras in 1924, and to the government of Emiliano Chamorro of Nicaragua in 1925, thereby giving extreme expression to Jefferson's "will of the nation substantially declared," perhaps out of fear that dictatorships and revolutionary governments posed a danger for international peace.

States may withhold recognition or withdraw it in order to punish regimes they regard as illegitimate and those guilty of illegal conduct. In either case the executive, legislative, and judicial acts of an offender are treated as nonexistent. Treaties with the offender can be suspended, and foreign forces may be admitted to aid rebels against it. It may be rejected as a plaintiff in foreign courts and denied property situated abroad. Secretary of State Seward refused to recognize a revolutionary government in Peru in 1868; at the request of the Wilson administration a number of states rescinded their recognition of the Mexican government of Victoriano Huerta in 1918; still others refused to recognize the state of Manchukuo that Japan created in Manchuria on 18 February 1932. The major reason for recognizing the Soviet Union in 1933 was the (vain) hope that trade with it would help the United States climb out of the Great Depression.

When Nazi Germany overran a number of western European states in 1940, the United Kingdom and the United States, without declarations of recognition, regarded the governments in exile of these countries as de jure, even though they could not exercise effective control over their national territory. The United States took a similar hard line toward the victims of Soviet aggression in Latvia, Estonia, and Lithuania, which were quickly recognized as independent after the downfall of the Soviet Union and end of the Cold War, but it refused to recognize North Korea and

North Vietnam. Conversely, Austria, which lost its international personality in 1938, when forced into an *Anschluss* with Germany, had it restored by treaty with the United States, Great Britain, France, and the Soviet Union in 1955. The United States has also followed the principle that recognition would not be granted to territorial changes made by force in violation of treaty rights. The principle was first enunciated in the Continental Treaty resulting from the Inter-American Conference held at Santiago, Chile, in 1847–1848, and was restated in the recommendations of the International Conference of American States held at Washington in 1890. In 1915, Bryan used it in dealing with Japan's Twenty-one Demands on China. If agreed to, the demands would have made China a Japanese protectorate, in violation of the treaty rights of Americans and others, and of the Open Door policy. Bryan told Japan, "The United States frankly recognizes that territorial contiguity creates special relations between Japan and these districts"(Shantung, Manchuria, and eastern Mongolia). Japan's demands, however, "while not infringing the territorial integrity of the Republic, are clearly derogatory to the political independence and administrative entity of that country." On 11 May 1915, Bryan issued the blunt caveat that the United States would not honor "any agreement or undertaking which has been entered into or which may be entered into between the Governments of Japan and China, impairing the treaty rights of the United States and its citizens in China, the political or territorial integrity of the Republic of China, or the international policy relative to China commonly known as the open door policy."

As viewed by the United States, Japan's seizure of southern Manchuria in 1931 countered its adherence to the Open Door as expressed in the Nine-Power Treaty of 1922, to the renunciation of war as an instrument of national policy written into the Kellogg-Briand Peace Pact of 1928, and to the comportment of nations as required by the Covenant of the League of Nations. Herbert Hoover would have no part of war. Although Secretary of State Stimson strongly supported collective security, he realized that there was a popular American and official British and French opposition both to strong unilateral action and to joint action with the League, of which the United States was not a member. Admittedly building on Bryan's note of 11 May 1915, Stimson told China and Japan that the United States would not recognize arrangements in Manchuria detrimental to American rights and that it "does not intend to recognize any situation, treaty, or agreement which may be brought about by means contrary to the covenants and obligations of the Kellogg-Briand Pact." But he could not persuade Hoover, such powers as Britain and France, or the League of Nations to impose even economic sanctions against Japan, or convince Britain to invoke the Nine-Power Treaty. When Manchukuo, as Japan renamed its stolen territory, proclaimed itself a new state, the United States denied it recognition. The Assembly of the League of Nations followed suit, with no observable results; and it was not until the end of World War II that Manchuria was restored to China.

Similarly, when Italy forcibly annexed Ethiopia, most league members handled the situation "in the light of their own situation and their own obligations." By denying Ethiopia de facto existence, they vitiated the league covenant. The United States stood by the Stimson Doctrine but refused to intervene. After World War II began, the European Allied powers rescinded their action, thereby admitting previous error, and "restored" Ethiopia's independence. These actions notwithstanding, the U.S. demand for an expression of popular will was slackening, as it was also in Great Britain, particularly toward states like Italy, the Soviet Union, and Japan, in which free popular expression was not provided for or tolerated. Britain recognized the Soviet Union de facto in 1921 and de jure in 1924. The United States extended recognition in 1933 even though to some persons it appeared that the unchallenged exercise of governmental authority had been substituted for the principle of subsequent legitimation through popular consent as a test for recognition. However, because the choice of self-determination extends to constitutions, the legal source of validity of a state's actions, and must not restrict the opportunity for change, international law permits the recognition of nondemocratic states that give evidence of effective government.

MULTINATIONAL RECOGNITION

A multinational approach to recognition has been observable since the mid-1930s. The Declaration of the Principles of Inter-American Solidarity and Confederation (1936) proscribed both the recognition of territorial conquest through violence and the intervention by one state in the internal or external affairs of another. When it appeared that the Axis powers might seek to acquire the

American possessions of European nations they had overrun, the Act of Havana (1940) stated that those possessions would be placed under the provisional administration of the American republics. In 1943 it was suggested that the countries of the Western Hemisphere that had declared war or broken relations with the Axis powers should not, for the duration of the war, recognize governments created by force in Latin America without prior consultation among themselves.

In the Atlantic Charter (August 1941) the United States and the United Kingdom declared their desire "to see no territorial changes that would not accord with the freely expressed wishes of the people concerned," and sought respect for "the right of all peoples to choose the form of government under which they will live." The Crimean Charter of the Yalta Conference suggested the admission of democratic procedures in the determination of governments in countries liberated from Axis control; those governments should then be recognized collectively following consultations by the Allied powers. The Charter of the United Nations states: "All Members shall refrain in their international relations from the threat or use of force against the territorial integrity or political independence of any state" and bars from membership any state unwilling to carry out its international obligations. For example, Francisco Franco's Spain was barred. The United Nations has thus sought to substitute for unilateral recognition a collective decision whether a state seeking membership is a "peace-loving state" able and willing to carry out the obligations of the charter, hence deserving of recognition. The question of whether the nationhood of a people is better determined by the United Nations or by the several states nevertheless remains moot.

In a rare case, an international organization has practiced nonrecognition. Despite sympathy for Fidel Castro among left-wing Latin American groups, the Organization of American States condemned Castro's denial of popular liberty in Cuba, his attempts to make his island a launching pad for Soviet missiles, and his exporting of communism to neighboring nations. In 1964 it voted economic sanctions against him and barred official relations with Havana to all its members, thereby technically rescinding recognition. Since 1974, however, six major and several minor Latin American states have violated the ban, and in 1975 the United States relaxed its trade restrictions. Presidents Richard Nixon and Gerald Ford and their secretary of state, Henry Kissinger,

declined to recognize Castro on terms he proposed, but President Jimmy Carter sought a rapprochement. The United States in 2000 did not recognize Castro but permitted the sale to him of foods and medicines and a limited amount of American tourism to Cuba.

West Germany, strongly supported by the North Atlantic Treaty Organization, tried for many years to avoid a "two-Germany" concept by threatening economic sanctions and breaking diplomatic relations with third states that recognized East Germany, which was fully recognized by the communist world but denied representation in most international organizations. It was not until September 1974 that the United States sent an ambassador, John Sherman Cooper, to East Germany. Both Taiwan and Beijing (capital of the People's Republic of China), under the Mao Doctrine of 1949, refuse to deal with any third power that has recognized the other as the government of all of China. Taiwan maintains that the communist government of Beijing does not enjoy the support of its people, while Beijing insists that Taiwan is an inseparable part of Chinese territory. The issue is confused because some states that recognize Beijing also recognize Taiwan as de facto. Although some states, like France, broke relations with Taiwan after recognizing Beijing, the long-held idea that both Chinas could not be represented in the same international organizations gave way when Beijing was admitted to the United Nations in 1972, and Taiwan was ejected as a member of its Security Council.

From 1 October 1949, when the People's Republic of China was formed, until 1972, the United States refused to recognize it and also tried to keep it out of the United Nations because it lacked the character of a "peace-loving" nation, proved unwilling to abide by international regulations, and might replace Taiwan on the UN Security Council. Other considerations included U.S. unwillingness to dishonor its commitments to Taiwan by rescinding recognition; fear that the "domino theory," starting with Taiwan, would work its way through Southeast Asia; Chinese intervention in Korea and support for North Vietnam; the bombing of the islands of Matsu and Quemoy (1958); Beijing's brutal takeover of Tibet (1959) and attack on India (1962); the seizure of American property without compensation, mistreatment of American citizens, and implementation of a "Hate America" campaign; and the repression of democratic reforms at home and denial of liberty to its people. Moreover, the dictatorship threatened to spread communist doctrine by war rather than follow methods of peaceful coexistence, and its recognition would increase its power and prestige.

Among the reasons for a change of decision were President Nixon's desire to achieve a historic diplomatic victory; the conclusion that Taiwan could never recover mainland China; the effective de facto character of a government controlling some 800 million people; its military, including atomic power; its serving as a buffer against the Soviets; the absence in its government of the bribery, graft, and corruption that had characterized the prerevolutionary Chiang Kai-shek regime; and its recognition not only by Britain, France, and West Germany but also by most of the nations of the Third World. With a large number of "developing" nations in the United Nations that favored Beijing over Taipei (Taiwan's capital) and were critical of America's role as the "world's policeman," it was clear that Beijing would be admitted to the United Nations. By a vote of 76 to 65 it was admitted on 25 October 1971.

The United States had begun to thaw the frigid Sino-American relations in 1969 by relaxing some trade and travel restrictions. In April 1971, Beijing invited American Ping-Pong players to visit China. Nixon then began to gradually abolish all trade restrictions and let it be known that Beijing would receive him. To this end, he secretly sent his adviser on national security affairs, Henry Kissinger, to speak with Premier Chou En-lai and others and arrange for an eight-day presidential visit in late February 1972. The joint communiqué issued stressed the national interests of the parties, but Nixon said he would remove his troops from Taiwan. Chou En-lai predicted that normalization of relations would follow enlarged contacts. With Sino-American diplomatic relations reestablished, other nations had to adjust to the new situation. Australia, New Zealand, Malaysia, and eventually other Southeast Asia states jumped on the bandwagon. While liaison offices were opened in Beijing and Washington, it was not until 15 December 1978 that, after several months of secret meetings, President Jimmy Carter announced that the United States and China had agreed to establish diplomatic relations on 1 January 1979 and that they would exchange ambassadors and establish embassies on 1 March. Further, the United States would maintain commercial and unofficial relations with Taiwan and sell it materials needed to keep its defenses operating but would terminate the mutual defense treaty of 1954. While some in Congress regarded the agreement as "selling Tai-

wan down the river" and others as a "historical inevitability," China said that returning Taiwan to mainland control would be an "internal" problem.

BELLIGERENT RECOGNITION

Because recognition applies to belligerency as well as to state governments, precise discrimination and timing must be paid to the facts in a civil war. Premature recognition of political parties seeking to establish a state separate from a parent state may be deemed tortious or delictual, if not actual intervention, and may even lead to war with the parent state, which is vested with the presumption of right until the rebels triumph. The writing of the Treaty of Amity and Commerce (1778) between France and the rebellious British subjects in America resulted in a war between France and Great Britain, as France intended. The United States threatened war because of what it believed to be too prompt a recognition of belligerency of the Confederate States of America by Great Britain, and Colombia assumed a very aggrieved stance after what appeared to it as the precipitous—six hour—recognition by the United States of the Panama Republic in 1903. In contrast, belated recognition of eventually victorious rebels may result in unpleasant relations, such as those attending the unwillingness of the United States to recognize for a dozen years the Latin American republics that seceded from Spain, Texas throughout 1836, Mexico at times between 1913 and 1923, the Soviet Union from 1917 to 1933, Manchukuo from 1932, the People's Republic of China from 1949 to 1972, and East Germany from 1945 to 1974.

The test applied to belligerents, unless the parent state has stopped trying to impose its authority or has assented to its loss of sovereignty, is whether they have created a separate political existence capable of maintaining order at home and worthy of respect from abroad. Applicable to rebellions or secessions seeking independence is the formula stated by Secretary of State John Quincy Adams when writing to the American minister to Colombia on 27 May 1823: "So long as a contest of arms with a rational or even a remote prospect of eventual success, was maintained by Spain, the United States could not recognize the independence of the colonies as existing de facto without trespassing on their duties to Spain by assuming as decided that which was precisely the question of the war." By prematurely recognizing the independence of the Latin American republics, Adams might give Spain justification for declaring war and for not negotiating with the United States for the release of the Floridas. On the other hand, if he recognized the Latin Americans too late, he would arouse resentment in their governments and also lose trade to active British rivals. Consequently, he devised the "utterly desperate" formula. "It is the stage," he wrote President James Monroe on 24 August 1818, "when independence is established as a matter of fact so as to leave the chances of the opposite party to recover their dominion utterly desperate." After Spain protested the intention of the United States to recognize the revolted provinces as independent, Adams replied that American policy was to recognize as independent states "nations which, after deliberately asserting their right to that character, have maintained and established it against all the resistance which had been or could be brought to oppose it."

Timing is important, as the Texas revolution against Mexico and the American Civil War reveal. Friction between U.S. settlers and the Mexican government provoked a revolution in 1835. President Andrew Jackson remained neutral until 3 March 1837, the last day of his administration, when he recognized the independence of Texas, announced in 1836. When Mexico protested that recognition, Secretary of State John Forsyth replied that it was the policy of the United States to recognize de facto governments. For seven years an independent Texas had been recognized by at least the United States, Great Britain, and France but not by Mexico, which had repeatedly stated that its annexation by the United States would mean war. The question of recognition became academic when the United States annexed Texas in 1845 and, in the treaty ending the Mexican War, won confirmation of its title to the former republic.

Until the Civil War, the United States looked upon secessionist activity, such as that of the Latin American states, as following its own revolutionary model. Moreover, it frowned upon the monarchical principle and objected especially to the forcible maintenance of monarchical legitimacy in the New World. In brief, rebellion against monarchy was not illegal; it was the assertion of natural right. During the American Civil War, although the shoe appeared to be on the other foot, the Union refused to change its historic policy with respect to the recognition of belligerency or, for that matter, the duty of neutrals.

On 19 April 1861, President Abraham Lincoln proclaimed a maritime blockade of seven seceded southern states. By thus granting the Confederacy the status of belligerent, he elevated a domestic disturbance to a full-fledged war and recognized the Confederacy as an "apparent" international entity, or "embryonic state," or "local de facto government" possessed of all the rights of a state with respect to the conduct of war. Although the Union never recognized the belligerency of the Confederacy, the U.S. Supreme Court decided, in the prize cases (1863), that the Confederacy was engaged in a civil war.

With two parts of the United States at war, third states could agree that the as yet ineffective blockade was legal and thereby uphold the Union; could recognize the Confederacy as a belligerent by proclaiming neutrality; could recognize the Confederacy as an independent state and invite war with the Union; or could do nothing and leave their international relations to the vicissitudes of an ill-defined international law.

Particularly involved was Great Britain, whose ubiquitous ships could be captured by Union ships enforcing the blockade. Its decision to remain neutral—based upon the announced Union blockade, President Jefferson Davis's proclamation of the intent of the Confederacy to exercise the rights of a belligerent, and upon its own Foreign Enlistment Act of 1819—was followed by all the major powers. Such neutrality gave the Confederacy both a morale boost and hope for eventual recognition as being independent, because both belligerents were placed on a legal par; the Confederacy could license privateers, send ships to the ports of recognizing powers, exercise the right of visit and search at sea, seek foreign loans, conduct a blockade, and seize contraband. The British proclamation was issued on 6 May 1861. Had the British waited until after the Union defeat at the second Battle of Bull Run, they might have opted for recognition of independence instead of merely belligerency.

Instead, in July 1862, when a representative asked Britain to recognize the Confederacy as a separate and independent power, the prime minister, Henry John Temple, Lord Palmerston, advised Earl John Russell, the foreign minister, that recent military reverses indicated that the time for recognition had not yet come. Russell therefore replied that "In order to be entitled to a place among the independent nations of the earth, a State ought to have not only strength and resources for a time, but afford promise of stability and permanence." On the other hand, when the Union protested Britain's having any relations with the Confederacy, Russell stated that the protection of British interests there might cause him to deal with the Confederate capital and even with southern state capitals, "but such communications will not imply any acknowledgment of the Confederacy as a separate state." The French took the same attitude, so that both Britain and France acknowledged that belligerents obtain their rights from the fact of war rather than from recognition.

Following the crushing Union defeat at the second Battle of Bull Run, Palmerston suggested to the French a joint mediation proposal that Washington accept as an "arrangement on the basis of a separation." The ability of the Union to hold southern forces at Antietam Creek, Maryland, blunted British and French ardor for this proposal. Resolution of the question of recognition had thus depended upon a military victory over the North that attested to the viability of the South as a community warranting membership in the international sphere. Then, as an example of how moral and humanitarian elements may alter a situation, Lincoln's Emancipation Proclamation drove all thought of the recognition of the Confederacy from the minds of the leaders of the major European powers.

The law of belligerent recognition attained maturity during the Civil War. Because the historical policy of the United States was to remain neutral in case of civil war, the Union secretary of state, William H. Seward, took umbrage at the attempts by the European powers to recognize the Confederacy. He denied that the southern rebellion amounted to a state of war, and saw no need for foreign action even if a state of war existed. On 28 February 1861, he instructed U.S. ministers abroad to counter any suggestion of recognition and to ask foreign powers to "take no steps which may tend to encourage the revolutionary movement of the seceding states; or increase danger of disaffection in those which still remain loyal." In April he told the U.S. minister to Great Britain, Charles Francis Adams, that European states customarily used the collective method of granting recognition, a method not used in the Americas.

Furthermore, Seward was inclined to treat recognition of even belligerency as an unfriendly act, to the point that he pondered seeking compensation for damages done by a premature grant of belligerent rights, which he viewed, he told

Adams, as interference with the sovereign rights of the United States. Indeed, Seward asserted that a proclamation of neutrality by Great Britain would challenge the right of the Union to protect its government and territory, and that he would declare war on any nation that recognized the independence of the Confederacy. Throughout the Civil War, then, the policy of the United States with respect to the recognition of belligerency remained consistent with earlier practice.

Consistency continued with respect to both Cuban revolutions. In 1875, during the Ten Years' War, President Ulysses S. Grant told Congress that the policy of the United States was to recognize de facto governments. Cuba was not at the time "a fact" because it lacked an effective and stable government. Therefore, it could not be recognized. Similarly, President William McKinley told Congress on 11 April 1898 that "recognition of independent statehood is not due to a revolted dependency until the danger of its being again subjugated by the parent state has entirely passed away"—a rewording of John Quincy Adams's "utterly desperate" formula.

The Spanish Civil War (1936–1939), "the most disputed case of belligerent recognition since the American Civil War," presents a special case illustrative of the abuse of power of recognition. Few will deny that war existed and that a recognition of belligerency was in order. Germany and Italy championed the rebel, pro-Catholic General Francisco Franco, against the anticlerical Republican (Loyalist) regime supported by the Russians and enjoying the sympathy of a goodly number of Americans. By recognizing Franco two and a half years before the end of the war, much too early to tell how the struggle would end, Adolf Hitler and Benito Mussolini reversed the situation so that the lawful government became the rebellious party. Most other countries simply stood by. Twenty-seven European states banned the export of war materials and departure of volunteers to Spain, and Britain announced its neutrality.

Although several thousand Americans volunteered to fight with the Loyalists, such was the popular support for noninvolvement that the administration of Franklin D. Roosevelt amended its neutrality laws to cover civil wars and thus denied support customarily given to the legitimate government, as in embargoing the export of munitions. When Franco won in 1939, the United States recognized him de facto and took steps to resume diplomatic relations suspended during the civil war. Instead of the test of effectiveness being the free expression of popular approval or of democracy, it was made to read effectiveness of authoritarian control, or of dictatorship.

If the character of a civil war will be admitted to the Arab-Jewish conflict in Palestine, that will serve as a fine example. The British shifted responsibility for their League of Nations mandate over Palestine on 3 December 1947, effective 15 May 1948, to the United Nations, which late in 1947 adopted a partition plan vehemently opposed by the Arabs but upheld by President Harry S. Truman. At midnight local time, 14 May 1948, the provisional government of Israel proclaimed the existence of the Republic of Israel that it had carved out of Palestine. Overriding objections from the Department of State, disregarding the wishes of Britain, France, and the Soviet Union, overlooking the nonrecognition of Israel by strategically located and oil-rich Arab states, the general fighting between Arabs and Jews throughout Palestine, and stating that he did so in keeping with the principle of self-determination and for humanitarian reasons, Truman extended de facto recognition when Israel was but eleven minutes old. Perhaps his need to win the Jewish vote in the fall elections stimulated his prompt action. After Israel held its first elections, on 25 January 1949, Truman extended it de jure recognition six days later. War between Israel and its Arab neighbors has been intermittent since the Republic of Israel first saw light. At the beginning of the twenty-first century the Palestinian leader Yasser Arafat was demanding a Palestine state with the capital in Jerusalem and sovereignty over shrines sacred to both Jews and Muslims—which Israel would not let him have.

A most unexpected and exciting transfer of sovereignty occurred in Yugoslavia beginning in September 2000. Elections held on 24 September chose a fifty-six-year-old attorney, Vojislav Kostunica, rather than Slobodan Milosevic, who had enjoyed thirteen years of autocratic and corrupt rule. The latter asked for a runoff election and sent an aide to summon Kostunica. When Milosevic said he had won the election, Kostunica informed him that a constitutional court had ruled in his own favor—information Milosevic lacked. In any event, a crowd of some 200,000 persons paraded in Belgrade and burned the parliament building, with the army and police doing little to hinder them. On 6 October, Milosevic admitted defeat. Following Kostunica's formal investiture as president, the United States and western Europe quickly recognized him. After holding out for several days, Russia and China extended recognition as well.

CONCLUSION

It is the prerogative of each state to extend recognition to a new community. Recognition admits to a state's having an international personality, yet the tests applied to statehood have often been violated by the use of constitutional, moral, humanitarian, and other subjective judgments. The practice of democratic states generally has been to recognize effective, or de facto, governments; the practice of undemocratic states, to recognize states espousing the objectives of their own national policies. Even if popular legitimation by free elections does not follow their extension of de facto recognition, democracies manage to live with undemocratic governments that are stable and permanent. States may withhold or withdraw recognition to punish illegitimate state or illegal conduct—by the latter, for example, for undertaking territorial changes by force in violation of the sovereignty of the victim and of the treaty rights of third parties. It is, of course, possible to have intercourse on a limited basis with states that are not recognized. Recognition is an executive act that extends to governments rather than to persons. Although regional and world organizations have used collective recognition to admit states to their membership, and thereby recognize them, unilateral recognition is still practiced.

Belligerent parties seeking freedom from a parent state may be recognized whenever they have created a new government capable of maintaining order within its boundaries and worthy of respect from abroad. If the parent state has stopped trying to impose its authority or has assented to its loss of sovereignty, recognition may be granted freely. Otherwise questions of timing and of degree must be weighed carefully by third parties, lest premature recognition lead to war with the parent state and belated recognition leads to loss of the friendship and trade of the victorious belligerents. In this connection it is difficult to improve upon John Adams's "utterly desperate" formula. Nevertheless, because insurgency has largely replaced civil wars, the recognition of belligerency by the United States was rarely accorded between World War I and World War II and has not been granted since 1945.

BIBLIOGRAPHY

Chen, Ti-chiang. *The International Law of Recognition, with Special Reference to Practice in Great Britain and the United States*. London, 1951. Pays particular attention to the many similarities of international law with respect to recognition policy as adopted by the United States and the United Kingdom.

Goebel, Julius. *The Recognition Policy of the United States*. New York, 1915. Although dated, provides an excellent account of the recognition policy of the United States for its first century, when it largely followed the de facto principle.

Hackworth, Green Hayward. *Digest of International Law*. 8 vols. Washington, D.C., 1940–1944. A very careful and learned synthesis of international law subjects by an expert in the U. S. Department of State.

Harcourt, Sir William Vernon. *Letters by Historicus on Some Questions of International Law*. London-Cambridge, 1863. Explains why war was averted between the United States and United Kingdom despite Lincoln's proclamation of blockade, the Trent affair, and British recognition of Confederate belligerency.

Jaffe, Louis Leventhal. *Judicial Aspects of Foreign Relations, in Particular of the Recognition of Foreign Powers*. Cambridge, Mass., 1933. Deals mostly with the theory and practice of recognition and nonrecognition and with legal questions involved in recognition.

Kissinger, Henry. *White House Years*. Boston, 1979. Fully details how Richard Nixon granted recognition to Red China.

Lampe, John R. *Yugoslavia as History: Twice There Was a Country*. 2d ed. Cambridge, 2000. Holds that Yugoslavia failed to develop a sense of common citizenship that could override competing national loyalties.

Lauterpacht, Sir Hersch. *Recognition in International Law*. Cambridge, U.K., 1947. Written by perhaps the greatest authority on modern international law; includes a close examination of British and American practices in the field.

Moore, John Bassett. *A Digest of International Law*. 8 vols. Washington, D.C., 1906. Indispensable reference on international law matters.

Oppenheim, L. (Lassa). *International Law, A Treatise*. 2 vols. 8th ed. Toronto, 1955. Edited by Hersch Lauterpach, London and New York, 1948. Not as extensive as Moore, Hackworth, or Whiteman but deals separately and clearly with the myriad subjects included in international law.

Silber, Laura, and Allan Little. *Yugoslavia: Death of a Nation*. Rev. ed. Santa Monica, Calif., 1997. Discovery Channel video that covers the history of the Balkans and explains why ethnic conflicts continue to exist.

Tarulis, Albert N. *American-Baltic Relations, 1918–1922*. Washington, D.C., 1965. Explains why it took the United States four years to recognize the Baltic states after they obtained their independence from Russia in 1918.

Tyler, Patrick. "The (Ab)normalization of U.S.–Chinese Relations." *Foreign Affairs* 78 (Sept.–Oct. 1999): 122. Concerns the battle between Secretary of State Cyrus Vance and National Security Adviser Zbignew Brzezinski over the matter of fully recognizing Red China.

Whiteman, Marjorie M. *Digest of International Law*. 15 vols. Washington, D.C., 1963–1973. Brings Hackworth and Moore up to date in a learned and meticulous manner, using copious references to the literature of international relations and law.

See also INTERNATIONAL LAW; INTERVENTION AND NONINTERVENTION; NEUTRALITY; REVOLUTION; SELF-DETERMINATION; WILSONIANISM.

REFUGEE POLICIES

★ ★ ★ ★

David M. Reimers

According to the 1951 Geneva Convention, a refugee is someone with "a well-founded fear of being persecuted in his country of origin for reasons of race, religion, nationality, membership of a particular social group or political opinion." The U.S. Senate accepted this definition sixteen years later, but it was not officially made part of immigration law until the enactment of the Refugee Act of 1980. From 1789 to 1875 the states controlled immigration policy and admitted refugees, but they did not label them as such. From 1875 to the 1940s the federal government continued this policy. During the early years of the Cold War, refugees were generally defined as persons fleeing communism.

In admitting refugees, foreign policy has often played a key role, but it has not been the only factor. Economic conditions in the United States have helped determine how generous the nation would be in accepting refugees. Lobbying by particular ethnic, nationality, and religious groups also has influenced refugee flows. Finally, Americans liked to think of the nation as, in George Washington's words, an "asylum for mankind." This humanitarian impulse often dovetailed with foreign policy as the United States wanted to appear generous to other nations. It is also important to realize that many refugees also have economic motives for wanting to escape their home countries and seek their fortunes in the United States. Indeed, the line between "a well-founded fear" and the desire for an improved lifestyle is often blurred.

THE NEW REPUBLIC

The American colonies had little control over the admission of newcomers; they could not even halt the English practice of sending convicts to the New World. Americans began to shape their own destinies after 1789 when the nation's Constitu-

tion went into effect. That document said nothing about refugees, or immigrants for that matter. Moreover, the federal government did not begin to regulate the flow of newcomers until 1875. Three events and subsequent flows of migrants to the United States emerged in the 1790s. First was the French Revolution (1789), second, the Haitian Revolution (1791), and third, the failure of the United Irishmen to win independence for Ireland in the 1790s.

The first test of the nation's policy occurred when French émigrés, fleeing the increasing violence of the French Revolution, began to come to America. Those arriving in the fall of 1789 were mostly of the elite classes who witnessed the collapse of the old regime and who feared that their wealth, status, and privileged positions were under siege. Their numbers were small by comparison to those who followed. The second wave consisted of patriotic and intellectual nobles and the middle classes who had supported them. These refugees, who had backed liberal reform, watched with dismay as the French Revolution turned radical and violent. A few priests who opposed the confiscation of their lands and secularization of the revolution joined them, as did some members of the military who did not favor the ideals of the French Revolution. Numbers are not precise, but between ten and fifteen thousand crossed the Atlantic. They settled in Atlantic coastal towns and cities, with Philadelphia receiving the largest number.

Americans, including George Washington and the ruling Federalist Party, were supportive of the revolution in its first days. The Marquis de Lafayette sent the key to the Bastille to Washington, but as bloodshed increased, many Americans turned against the revolution. The Federalists especially were shocked by the growing violence. When war broke out between England and France, the Jeffersonian Republicans supported France and the Federalists England. Yet neither party wished to go to war, and the government's policy of neutrality was widely accepted. The cities and states where the refugees settled raised money to aid them, many of whom had brought little money and few possessions with them. In other cases, individuals and voluntary groups assisted in finding employment. The refugees themselves raised funds and even published several newspapers. The French minister Edmond-Charles Genet was not sympathetic to the refugees, especially those who seemed to favor England over revolutionary France. When he tried to influence American politics, he won little favor and was recalled to France. Yet the intrigues of a French minister and the radicalization of the revolution in France did not change the official neutrality of the United States, and émigrés were still permitted to enter even though the two political parties differed over aspects of exile culture and politics. However, as conditions changed in France some of the refugees returned.

Closely allied to the events in France was the slave uprising in St. Domingue (Haiti) in the 1790s. The revolt erupted in 1791, three years before revolutionary France outlawed slavery. After thirteen years of civil war, Haiti achieved independence in 1804 and became the first independent black state in the Western Hemisphere. Initially, the United States supported white planters' efforts to put down the revolt, but the French were ultimately unsuccessful. After 1791, as the white planters witnessed losses of their estates and power and increasing violence, they fled—a few to France, some to Cuba and Jamaica, and others to the United States. These refugees differed from those from France proper. To be sure, the elite planters held political views similar to the elite of France, but the refugees were not limited to the white elite; only a minority of the newcomers were white. Some planters carried their slaves with them. These slaves remained slaves whether they were brought to slaveholding states or even if they were brought to northern cities such as Philadelphia and New York, for the northern states were just beginning to end slavery in the 1790s. In addition, "free people of color"—a mixed-race group in Haiti who were not equal to whites in law but who were free and often skilled workers—believed that they would not prosper in a successful slave rebellion and fled too.

The slave revolt posed the question of whether Americans should receive another influx of refugees and how the United States should respond diplomatically if the uprising succeeded.

The white Haitians were welcomed especially by American slaveholders who sympathized with the principle and reality of slavery. Some others believed the nation should receive the refugees because it would maintain the principle of America as an "asylum for mankind." The refugees settled in coastal cities, with New Orleans the center of their community. That city did not become part of the United States until after the Louisiana Purchase, but even then it continued to receive refugees when many of the St. Domingue exiles who at first went to Cuba were forced by the Spanish to settle elsewhere in 1809.

Like those fleeing France, many of these exiles brought few possessions and little money with them. Funds were raised by cities, states, and community groups to assist them. An official position was taken by the U.S. Congress when it appropriated $15,000 to assist the refugees and suspended duties on French ships arriving in American ports if they were carrying exiles.

While welcoming St. Domingue's planters, slaveholders grew alarmed that so many slaves and free people of color entered. They feared that persons from these two groups were too familiar with events in Haiti and might attempt to stir up opposition to slavery in the United States. To white southerners a black-ruled Haiti was a symbol of decadence and ruin. Moreover, they were alarmed by the rise of antislavery sentiment and groups in the North. Faced with these perceived threats, the southern states tightened restrictions on slavery. Several banned the importing of slaves from the Caribbean, but the federal government did not outlaw the international slave trade until 1808 as it was required to do by the Constitution. In 1861 the United States finally recognized the black republic and established diplomatic relations.

The third revolution of the 1790s was a failed one, but it sent refugees to the United States and prompted a debate about foreign policy and immigration. The Society of United Irishmen, composed of both Catholics and Protestants, sought to end English control of Ireland. However, Ireland did not win its freedom; England crushed the rebels, tried and sentenced some leaders to jail, and encouraged others to leave. England also passed the Act of Union in 1800, which merged the mother country with Ireland and divided the Protestant-Catholic alliance. The failure to win Irish independence led thousands of Irish refugees to immigrate to America in the next one hundred years.

The Jeffersonian Republicans generally sympathized with the rebels, but the Federalists wanted to align American foreign policy with that of Great Britain against France. Many Federalists also believed the Irish were a "wild horde" and were none too eager to see them settling in American coastal towns and cities. The Irish refugees in turn sided with the Jefferson party. As a result, the Federalists succeeded in raising the number of resident years needed for naturalization from two to fourteen. Some Republicans joined the Federalists in raising the time required for naturalization because they believed the Naturalization Act of 1790, which set two years as the required period, did not provide enough time for newcomers to be indoctrinated in the principles of republicanism. Congress also passed the Alien and Sedition Acts, one of which gave the president power to deport immigrants even in peacetime if they were considered dangerous. President John Adams did not exercise this provision, but the Sedition Act did lead to several newspaper editors being arrested and sent to jail, including the Irish-born Representative Matthew Lyon of Vermont.

One wing of the Federalist Party favored war against France and alliance with England. But while fighting an undeclared war against France in the last few years of the 1790s, President Adams blocked efforts for a declaration of war, and the crisis passed. With the election of Thomas Jefferson as president in 1800, the naturalization period dropped from fourteen to five years, where it has remained ever since. The Alien and Sedition Acts were also allowed to lapse.

THE NINETEENTH AND EARLY TWENTIETH CENTURIES

The crisis of the 1790s set the tone for the next century. The United States would proclaim neutrality but permit refugees from foreign lands undergoing war or revolution to settle in the United States. In the 1820s, when the Greeks revolted against Turkish rule over Greece, most Americans sympathized with the Greek cause, and they willingly received a few Greek refugees in the United States. However, the official position of the United States was the new Monroe Doctrine (1823). President James Monroe declared that he expected European powers to refrain from ventures in the Western Hemisphere and not attempt to halt the revolutionary process there, and in return the United States would stay out of European affairs.

★ ★ ★ ★
CARL SCHURZ (1829–1906)

Carl Schurz participated in the German revolutionary activities of 1848. He joined a failed attempt to seize the arsenal at Siegburg and was forced to flee to the Palatine, also in Germany, where he joined the revolutionary forces there. He quickly became a wanted man by German authorities; rather than face charges of treason, he fled to France. He did return long enough to liberate one of the leaders but was forced to take refuge again in France and also England. Schurz came to the United States in 1852 and began a long career in American politics and government. He eventually became a U.S. senator, fought in the Civil War on the side of the Union, and served as secretary of the interior. He also worked with German groups, encouraging them to fight in the Civil War and become active in politics. Most scholars believe that Schurz was the most prominent German American in the nineteenth century.

In 1831, Poles sought to overthrow Russian domination of their land. After exchanges of notes between the United States and Russia, the former remained neutral in the dispute and both powers agreed to a commercial treaty in 1833. However, important American citizens expressed their sympathy with the Poles and warmly welcomed several hundred Polish exiles who fled when the rebellion failed and raised money to assist in their settlement. Some Poles wanted Congress to grant them a tract of land in the West that was to become a new Poland in America. The legislators, while willing to permit the refugees to obtain land on the same terms as all others, rejected the scheme.

Revolutions broke out once more in Europe in 1848, and when they failed, thousands of refugees, chiefly Germans, fled to the United States. Once again, many Americans hailed the principles of the "forty-eighters" in their quest for constitutional government in their homelands, but officially the United States government elected to pursue a policy of neutrality. No case represents this position more than that of Hungarian Lajos Kossuth. While American officials proclaimed to the Austrians that they favored the principles of liberty anywhere, and sympathized with those Hungarians seeking independence from Austria, the United States did not intervene in the affairs of Hungary and Austria. When the Hungarian leader Kossuth arrived in the United States in 1852, he drew large crowds, but there was no chance that America would intervene in European affairs.

When the Irish Revolutionary Brotherhood, called the Fenian Brotherhood in the United States, launched two attacks on Canada from the United States in 1866 and 1870, America was faced with a diplomatic crisis or embarrassment. As much as many Americans opposed English rule in Ireland, the government moved to halt these assaults, which seemed to many to have the flavor of a comic opera. Moreover, the United States was at peace with Great Britain, and American officials said that the Irish question was Britain's affair, not that of the United States.

In Latin America the United States pursued a different policy. Americans sympathized with the Cuban revolt against Spain that began in 1868 and lasted until the Spanish-American War (1898) ended Spanish rule. In the early years of the rebellion, when conditions deteriorated for the rebels, many sought asylum in the United States, where they settled in New York and Florida and began to organize again to overthrow Spanish control. American politicians demanded that Spain grant Cubans their independence. Relations between the United States and Spain deteriorated in the 1890s, and when the battleship *Maine* exploded in Havana's harbor, the cries for action led to a congressional declaration of war in 1898. As a result of the ensuing Spanish-American War, Cuba received independence but found itself closely tied to America.

A MODIFIED REFUGEE POLICY

The federal government finally took control of immigration in 1875 when it banned prostitutes from entering the United States, as well as convicted felons and Asians said to be "coolies." Coolies were defined as Asians brought into the United States without their consent. Seven years later, Congress barred Chinese immigrants, but not dissenters of one kind or another from Europe. After President William McKinley was assassinated by an American-born anarchist in 1901, Congress passed the first law barring immigrants because of their political beliefs when it restricted anarchists from coming to the United States.

Various ethnic groups put pressure on the federal government to take an active role in aiding their people in their homelands, either by admitting refugees or by condemning the oppression faced by their countrymen. Armenian groups periodically attacked the government of Turkey for fostering massacres of Armenians under Turkish rule, especially the particularly violent one in 1915. In a similar manner, American Jews attacked Russia for permitting and even fostering pogroms. German Jews organized the American Jewish Committee in 1906 in order to influence the U.S. government to put pressure on Russia to end such violence and to assist Jewish immigrants. These efforts by various groups had only limited success until 1945, but they did foster aid to fellow ethnics in their homelands.

During and after World War I, which witnessed the communist seizure of power in Russia, some European refugees considered too radical and sympathetic to communism found themselves unwanted. Raids carried out by the federal government, peaking in 1920, led to thousands of arrests and deportation of foreign-born immigrants. In addition to shipping some radicals to Russia, the federal government refused to recognize the Soviet Union until 1933.

With the rise of fascism in Italy in the 1920s and Adolf Hitler's winning power in Germany in 1933, a new crisis of refugees loomed. As nazism spread, thousands of Jews and political dissenters searched for a haven outside Germany. Many fled to neighboring countries, but as the German army overran those nations, to emigrate was understandable, but getting into the United States was difficult. High unemployment tempered the desire to immigrate to America, and if they did want to come, the "likely to be a public charge" provision of the immigration laws was strictly enforced during the early days of the Great Depression. Moreover, the national origins quotas established during the 1920s limited the number of Europeans who would come.

Groups working to aid immigrants did suggest that the nation open its doors, but Congress was in no mood to change laws, and public opinion polls indicated strong opposition to admit many immigrants. In the depression years and during World War II, advocates of a tight immigration policy, such as the Daughters of the American Revolution and the American Legion, even suggested that all immigration be halted. The Roosevelt administration did ease its restrictions in 1938 but then tightly enforced the rules again

ALBERT EINSTEIN (1879–1955)

Albert Einstein was the most prominent man to take refuge in the United States during the twentieth century. He won the Nobel Prize in Physics in 1921 for his work on the photoelectric effect, but is best known for his theories of relativity. When Adolf Hitler and the Nazi Party seized power in Germany in 1933, he was in Princeton, New Jersey, at the Institute for Advanced Study. He elected to remain in the United States, becoming a U.S. citizen in 1940. He never returned to Germany. Alarmed by the rising power of Hitler's Germany, he wrote his most famous letter, a plea to President Franklin D. Roosevelt urging that the United States fund research into the possibility of the making of an atomic bomb.

in 1939. With nearly a quarter of the labor force unemployed during the worst years of the Great Depression, the Roosevelt administration was reluctant to embark upon a liberal policy for refugees. Because many of those trying to leave were Jews, anti-Semitism also played an important role. President Franklin Roosevelt denounced the atrocities in Germany, but the plight of refugees did not prompt the administration to change immigration policy. Several hundred thousand refugees did manage to come to the United States during the 1930s, but overall only one half million immigrants were admitted, a figure considerably less than admitted during a single year between 1900 and 1914.

Fewer people arrived during World War II when shipping was disrupted. Roosevelt and his cabinet and other government officials were informed about the Holocaust by reports from Europe relayed to Washington by Jewish organizations, but the administration insisted that defeating Germany quickly was the best way to bring the Holocaust to an end. As more news about the Holocaust reached Washington, the president expressed concern and other officials hinted that refugees be allowed to come to America. In June 1944, President Roosevelt admitted 1,000 persons who were living in North African internment camps to a temporary refuge shelter at Fort Ontario in Oswego, New York. The president's action was meant to provide an emergency home for these refugees, but they were eventually allowed to stay.

REFUGEES AND THE COLD WAR

It was after World War II that the United States finally recognized refugees in law, with foreign policy playing a key role in the emerging legislation and executive action, especially the Cold War between the United States and Russia. It is also important to note that American refugee policy was not limited to the admission of immigrants. During the 1930s a number of organizations, operating in an international arena, were formed to deal with the European crisis, but they had little impact. These groups continued to function in the postwar decades. Moreover, the newly formed United Nations also played a growing role in settling refugees. Building upon the work of the League of Nations, the United Nations emerged as the most important international agency coping with refugees when it created the United Nations High Commissioner for Refugees (UNHCR) and adopted the Convention on Refugees in 1951. The United States supported the UNHCR financially and eventually accepted the convention's statement as its own. While more than three million refugees settled in the United States from 1945 to 2000, American support of the UNHCR was based on the belief that most refugees wanted to return home when conditions permitted and not necessarily immigrate to the United States.

The sweep of the Allies across Europe in 1944 and 1945 made possible a huge population movement as persons enslaved in Germany attempted to go home, as ethnic Germans were forcibly removed from nations where they had lived, and as millions who had seen their villages and cities destroyed sought refuge. The liberation of Jews from the concentration camps also left these survivors homeless, and most were in poor health. Other persons fled the approaching Russian army and ended up in the Western powers' territory. Many of these unfortunate people found themselves housed in displaced persons camps.

On 22 December 1945, President Harry S. Truman directed that 40,000 refugees be admitted and charged against national origins quotas, in the future if necessary. Truman's action was only a first step in dealing with the postwar refugees, and it hardly scratched the surface. American authorities and their European allies realized that the refugee situation had to be resolved if the economies and societies of western Europe were to be rebuilt. And as relations between the United States and the Soviet Union deteriorated, American leaders also developed other programs to bolster their allies. These included the Truman Doctrine of aid to Turkey and Greece in combating communism (1946), the Marshall Plan for stimulating the economies of western Europe (1948), and the North Atlantic Treaty Organization (1949) for its collective security. Congress barred communist immigrants from coming to America and voted to admit others by passing the Displaced Persons Act of 1948. As amended in 1950, the measure eventually permitted roughly 400,000 persons to immigrate to the United States, which relieved the western Europeans of some of their financial and population burdens.

While the immediate crisis in western Europe eased, there still remained people without homes. President Dwight D. Eisenhower asked Congress for a law to admit additional refugees, and the legislators responded with the Refugee Relief Act of 1953 that admitted another 189,000 persons. The measure also included a few thousand Palestinians from the Middle East and 5,000 Asians. This marked the first time that the term "refugee" appeared in U.S. law. Subsequent legislation in the 1950s admitted other persons fleeing communist nations and the Middle East. Most Middle Easterners came under regular immigration laws, even though many were stateless or fleeing from violence. It is not known how many were Palestinians because many entered as immigrants from Jordan or other nations.

The emerging Cold War refugee policy faced another test when the Hungarian Revolution of 1956 failed. Some 180,000 Hungarian "freedom fighters," as they were called, fled to Austria before the Austrians closed the border. The Austrian government was willing to temporarily aid them but wanted the Western powers to provide for their permanent settlement. The Hungarian quota allowed for only 865 immigrants, but President Eisenhower established a precedent that evoked the "parole" power of the McCarran-Walter Act of 1952 to admit nearly 40,000 refugees. Being classified as "parolees" left them in limbo because parolees could remain in the United States but were not permanent resident aliens (immigrants) or refugees. Congress had to pass legislation to permit them to change their status. Because this provision had been intended for individual cases, some in Congress protested. In the Cold War climate of the 1950s, however, the

desire to strike a blow against communism and aid these anticommunists overcame congressional qualms, and the lawmakers passed the Hungarian Escape Act of 1958 to grant the Hungarians refugee status.

The ad hoc nature of refugee admissions bothered some legislators, and when Congress revamped the national origins system in 1965 they provided for a more organized policy. The Immigration and Nationality Act Amendments of 1965 created seven preferences for the Eastern Hemisphere, mostly based on family unification. However, the seventh preference set aside 10,200 places for refugees, defined as persons fleeing communist or communist-dominated nations or the Middle East. Under this provision several thousand Czechoslovakian refugees came to the United States when the Soviet Union and its allies crushed the "Prague Spring" rebellion in 1968. Thousands of Soviet Jews also entered under the new laws. The president was also given the power to admit refugees from a "natural calamity." The last part of the definition was meant to be humanitarian. For example, some refugees had come in the 1950s following an earthquake in the Azores. Originally, the new system covered only the Eastern Hemisphere, but when a uniform worldwide system was created in 1978, the seventh preference increased to 17,400.

Thousands of Soviet Union Jews also entered under the new laws, but Jewish immigration became a foreign policy matter when Congress put in place trade restrictions against the Soviets. A bill sponsored by Senator Henry Jackson and Representative Charles Vanik passed in late 1974 and was signed by President Gerald Ford in early 1975. The Jackson-Vanik Amendment to a trade bill made future trade and credit policies tied to Jewish immigration. The Soviets responded by severely curtailing Jewish emigration and thereby cutting trade with the United States. Jewish immigration from the Soviet Union had to wait until the end of the 1980s for a major increase.

The Cold War was by no means limited to Europe. In Asia the United States intervened in the Korean War (1950–1953) and again in the Vietnam War in the 1960s and 1970s. In the Western Hemisphere, Fidel Castro seized power in Cuba in 1959 and embarked upon a policy making it a communist country. These wars, along with Castro's victory, led to another wave of refugees. Shortly after Castro won control, some elite Cubans fled to Miami. As the flow grew, Presidents Eisenhower, John F. Kennedy, and Lyndon Johnson used the parole power to admit them. From 1959 to the Cuban missile crisis of 1962, more than 200,000 arrived. Flights were suspended after the missile crisis, although some escaped by boat to Florida. In early 1965 Castro indicated that he was interested in renewing the exodus, and when President Johnson signed the new immigration act at the foot of the Statue of Liberty in October, he said that the United States was willing to accept all who desired to leave Castro's communist state. American policymakers believed that accepting refugees would demonstrate the failure of communism in Cuba and also be a humanitarian gesture. Once again the president paroled them. In 1966, Congress passed the Cuban Adjustment Act that assumed that any Cuban to reach American soil was a refugee from communism and was welcome in the United States. Several hundred thousand Cubans took advantage of the new law, but the flow slowed to a trickle in the early 1970s. In addition, the federal government provided aid for these newcomers, which marked the first time after World War II that the government gave monetary assistance for refugee resettlement.

Another wave from Cuba entered in the spring of 1980. They sailed from the Cuban port of Mariel and were thus called "Marielitos." The Marielitos were picked up by boats operated by Cubans already in the United States, and by the time the U.S. government halted the exodus, about 130,000 had arrived. President Jimmy Carter did not use immigration laws to admit them; he created a new classification called "conditional entrants," a limbo status. Eventually, they were permitted to change their status under the Cuban Adjustment Act. The entire episode made it seem that immigration policy was out of control, especially in view of the fact that Castro dumped criminals and mental patients into the boats heading for America.

As Cuban emigration slackened, that of Southeast Asia began. The Vietnam War uprooted tens of thousands of Vietnamese, many of whom left rural areas for cities. The U.S. government aided these persons in settling in their new homes in Vietnam, but officials had no thought of bringing them to America. Then came the 1975 collapse of the American-backed regime in Vietnam. As Saigon was besieged and conquered by communist forces, tens of thousands of Vietnamese were rescued by helicopters and thousands more fled by boat. Roughly 130,000 came in this first wave of 1975. They were brought to the United States for resettlement. In view of the American military role in Vietnam, U.S. officials believed that the United States had to accept them. In 1978 and 1979 Vietnam's ethnic Chinese also fled, largely by boat, which earned them the name "boat people." Moreover, conditions in Cambodia and Laos deteriorated, which prompted many to cross the Thailand border for the safety of refugee camps supported by the United States and the United Nations. The total from 1975 to 1980 vastly exceeded the 17,400 slots provided annually for refugees. Presidents Gerald Ford and Jimmy Carter paroled them into the United States, and Congress provided funds for their settlement and allowed them to become refugees.

It seemed to many that refugee policy, other than aiding those fleeing from communism, still lacked coherence. In 1980, Congress passed a new law, the Refugee Act of 1980. It increased the annual "normal flow" of refugees to 50,000 and established and funded programs to assist them. In addition, it dropped the anticommunist definition of "refugee" and substituted for it the United Nations statement. While the law said 50,000 refugees were the "normal flow" to be admitted annually, the president retained the power to permit more to arrive, and in no year after 1980 did the number drop as low as 50,000; it usually averaged twice that figure. More than one million Vietnamese, Cambodians, and Laotians alone came to the United States from 1975 to the 1990s.

Cubans and Southeast Asians were the main beneficiaries of American foreign and refugee polices, but others also managed to become refugees. When the anticommunist Polish Solidarity movement sputtered in the early 1980s, Poles in the United States were permitted to remain temporarily and eventually to become refugees. It was a common practice to permit citizens of another nation visiting or studying here to win a temporary reprieve from returning home when their visas expired if their country suddenly experienced violence. Eventually, like the Poles, many were able to stay permanently in the United States.

The Cold War mentality was clearly evident when citizens of countries who were not fleeing communist regimes tried to win refugee status. After the successful 1973 revolt against the socialist government of Chile led to the execution and internment of thousands of Chileans, the United States took in fewer than 1,700 Chilean refugees. Since the United States had opposed the socialists and had been involved with the revolt, the American acceptance of so few refugees is understandable.

The government's position on communism and the admission of refugees also explain why so few refugees were admitted from Haiti. The dictatorial regime there run by the Duvalier family from 1957 to 1986 supported American positions taken on Western Hemisphere affairs and the Cold War, which pleased the State Department. There is no doubt that Haitians lived under oppressive rule, but there is also no doubt that Haiti was one of the poorest nations in the world. Immigration officials stressed the poverty of potential immigrants, not their lack of political rights and the violence conducted by authorities. Consequently, few immigrants were granted refugee status from Haiti. During the Mariel Cuban crisis, thousands of Haitians also made it by boat to Florida. They were included in President Carter's "entrant" category, but their status remained in limbo until the Immigration and Reform Control Act of 1986 (IRCA) granted amnesty to those in the United States before 1982.

The IRCA did not mean a new policy for Haitians coming after 1982. The immigration authorities and the State Department continued to call them economic migrants. Federal officials insisted that if Haitians were considered refugees, a tide of boat people would head for America. After the end of Duvalier rule, a democratically elected president, Jean-Bertrand Aristide, took power. When the Haitian military overthrew the regime of Aristide in 1991, the boat exodus picked up again. Under presidents Ronald Reagan and George H. W. Bush, the U.S. Navy and Coast Guard seized boats trying to escape from Haiti to Florida and sent them back to Haiti or temporarily housed them at the Guantánamo naval base in Cuba, where their claims could be processed. Bill Clinton had criticized the policy of President Bush, but he continued it when he became president in 1993. Moreover, the fear of Haitians fleeing the military regime and flocking to America, without proper documents and claiming asylum, motivated President Clinton to order an invasion of Haiti in the fall of 1994 to restore democracy. Among other reasons, the president repeated the belief that if democracy were not restored to Haiti, tens of thousands would try to come to America.

A similar situation prevailed in Guatemala and El Salvador and to a lesser extent in Honduras. These nations lived under right-wing and dictatorial governments recognized and supported by the United States and were plagued by civil wars. Many Salvadorans, Guatemalans, and Hondurans claimed that they should be considered refugees, but the Immigration and Naturalization Service (INS) insisted that, like Haitians, they were economic migrants and not legitimate refugees fearing persecution. Nor did the INS believe that the fear of being killed in a civil war was sufficient for winning refugee status; hence, few managed to emigrate as refugees.

In Nicaragua a different situation prevailed. There, the left-wing movement, the Sandinistas, overthrew the dictatorial rule of the Somoza family. The Carter administration attempted to work with the new government, but under Ronald Reagan the Central Intelligence Agency armed so-called contra forces that crossed Nicaragua's border in guerrilla raids attempting to overthrow the Sandinistas. Yet Nicaraguans fleeing to the United States also had difficulty emigrating as refugees.

There was another way to become a refugee, an immigrant, and eventually a U.S. citizen. According to immigration law, if a migrant was on American soil, even if one had entered illegally, one could claim asylum, arguing that the applicant had a "well founded fear" of persecution if returned home. Only two thousand or so persons won asylum annually in the 1970s. For example, the government denied asylum to most of the Haitian boat people during the 1970s and deported them. After the 1980 refugee act incorporated the new UN definition of refugee status in place of the anticommunist one, and when the civil wars in Central America escalated, the number applying for asylum skyrocketed. More than 140,000 applied in 1995, for example, and by the end of the 1990s the backlog reached several hundred thousand. Haitians came by boat, but tens of thousands of Central Americans illegally crossed the border separating the United States and Mexico. The State Department and the INS insisted they were mostly illegal immigrants who should be deported. INS officials in Florida did modify policy slightly toward Nicaraguans. An official said that he could not deny asylum to Nicaraguans when the United States insisted that the government of that country was undemocratic and that the CIA-backed contras were trying to overthrow it. Nicaraguans still had difficulty in winning asylum status, but their approval rate was more than double that of their neighbors. In 1989, for example, 5,092 Nicaraguans won asylum, compared with 102 Guatemalans and 443 Salvadorans.

Friends of these contestants for asylum insisted that a double standard was being applied:

Cubans merely had to get to the United States, but Central Americans had to win their claims on an individual basis. Many undocumented immigrant Salvadorans, Guatemalans, Hondurans, Haitians, and Nicaraguans did adjust their status due to an amnesty for undocumented immigrants passed in 1986. As noted, the law covered those in the United States before 1982, but for others fleeing violence in Central America after that date individual asylum was required, which was even more difficult to demonstrate when the civil wars in Central America ended in the early 1990s. Fewer than 10 percent of Salvadorans, Guatemalans, and Hondurans were granted asylum in 1999—up slightly from the rate of the 1980s but less than half of the general approval rate. Those who came after the IRCA amnesty were left in limbo, although minor modifications in immigration policy did permit some to remain. Moreover, once these Central Americans won asylum, they were eligible to adjust their status to that of regular immigrants and could then use the family preference system to sponsor their relatives. For example, in 1996 Haitian immigrants numbered 18,386, with 8,952 of these under the family preference system and another 4,815 coming as immediate family members of U.S. citizens who were exempt from the quotas. Comparable figures for Salvadorans were 17,903; 8,959; and 5,519. Data for Hondurans and Guatemalans were similar. The United States did permit Salvadorans and Hondurans the right to stay temporarily in the United States when earthquakes and hurricanes struck in the 1990s. These temporary stays, called temporary protected status (TPS), were not asylum; when TPS ended, the undocumented aliens were expected to go home.

Although during the Cold War the United States clearly favored persons fleeing communism, it also accepted those seeking refuge from other oppressive regimes. The United States accepted more than 20,000 refugees from Afghanistan when the Soviets invaded in 1979, but after the Soviets left and the Islamic fundamentalist Taliban took control of the nation in the 1990s, the United States still accepted some Afghan refugees, numbering about 2,000 annually.

American relations with Iran changed dramatically when another Islamic movement overthrew the American-backed shah of Iran in 1979. U.S. policy was aimed at keeping Iran's oil flowing to the West and at using the shah's government as a buffer against Soviet expansion. Anti-shah Iranians stormed the U.S. embassy in Tehran and imprisoned fifty-three Americans for more than a year. They were released at the same time that Ronald Reagan replaced Carter as president. Clearly, the United States could not oppose this new government holding American employees and at the same time deny refugee status or asylum to those Iranians already in the United States who did not want to return to Iran. In the 1980s, 46,773 persons from Iran arrived as refugees or recipients of asylum. Over 60 percent of those applying for asylum won it, which was among the highest rates of acceptance of any group.

POST–COLD WAR REFUGEES AND POLICY

The end of the Cold War in Europe in 1989 changed the nature of refugee policy, but it was still closely tied to foreign affairs, if not to the Cold War's anticommunism. The United States gave asylum to Chinese dissidents, the largest single group being Chinese students in the United States when the pro-democracy demonstrators were violently repressed in China in 1989. When the movement collapsed in bloodshed at Tiananmen Square in Beijing, President George H. W. Bush granted the students the right to remain in the United States on a temporary basis. The students' allies pointed out that because some of the students had been outspoken in their opposition to the Chinese government, they faced persecution at home. Congress later made them refugees; they did not have to prove on an individual basis that they qualified under the principles of the 1980 immigration act.

In 1996 Congress also provided 1,000 asylum places for Chinese who opposed the one-child-per-family policy of the Chinese government. There had been precedent for this political decision. When the *Golden Venture,* a ship loaded with 282 Chinese immigrants without legal documents, ran aground off the coast of Long Island in 1992, the INS took the passengers into custody and heard their claims for asylum. About one-third of the passengers' claims were denied and they were deported; another third were settled in Latin America, and the rest were eventually allowed to stay in the United States. Some had claimed that they were refugees because they opposed the one-child-per-family policy and forced abortions in China.

Refugees also continued to arrive from Russia and other nations of the former Soviet Union. Senator Frank Lautenburg of New Jersey convinced Congress in 1989 to amend the Foreign

Aid Appropriations Act to permit Jews and evangelical Christians to be considered religious refugees provided that they could demonstrate a "credible basis for concern about the possibility" of persecution rather than the more difficult to prove "well founded fear." This shift was motivated by political factors rather than anti-Russian fears or fears of communism. Congress extended it until 1994 and eventually 300,000 persons came to America under the Lautenburg amendment.

Immigrants still came from Indochina. Most were Vietnamese; only a few thousand Cambodians and Laotians arrived. Even the Vietnamese numbers were drastically cut by the 1990s, and most simply arrived under the family unification preferences of the immigration system. Indeed, relations improved between the United States and Vietnam in the 1990s, and the U.S. government no longer perceived communism to be a threat in Asia.

Armed conflict against Iraq during the Gulf War of 1991 was hardly a Cold War affair. The United States marshaled military support from several Arab and European nations after Iraq occupied Kuwait. While the struggle was unfolding, persons from Kuwait and Iraq were granted temporary protected status. The U.S.-led forces quickly drove the Iraqis out of Kuwait, so a large stream of refugees did not develop. Nonetheless, Iraqis who managed to leave before the war began or after were given refuge in the United States. The INS could hardly do otherwise. More than a thousand per year were admitted as refugees in the last years of the twentieth century.

A sign of the shifting priorities of the post–Cold War era was the treatment of Cubans trying to reach the United States by boat in 1994. Because the Mariel exodus included mentally ill and criminal passengers, the U.S. and Cuban governments argued about Cuba taking back these persons considered undesirable. Negotiations partly resolved the crisis, with Cuba receiving some Marielitos and the United States agreeing to process Cubans who wanted to emigrate. Roughly 11,000 Cubans managed to come through regular channels between 1985 and 1994. A few also reached Florida by boat after the Mariel exodus ended, but their numbers were not large from 1980 to 1994.

As social and economic conditions deteriorated in Cuba, many more Cubans, using what boats they could find, headed for Florida in the summer of 1994. These "rafters" posed a diplomatic problem for the Clinton administration. Not wishing to see a repeat of the Mariel crisis,

when more than 130,000 entered the United States without inspection, the president announced that the "rafters" would not be allowed to reach the United States. Rather, the Coast Guard returned them to Cuba or detained them at the Guantánamo naval base in Cuba. The administration knew that if the Cubans reached Florida, they would be covered by the 1966 Cuban Adjustment Act. Eventually, Cuba and the United States worked out an agreement for an orderly process to admit eligible Cubans, up to 20,000 annually, and in return Cuba would try to halt the exodus. Those at the Guantánamo base were to be processed through careful screening. Cuban Americans and their friends in the United States claimed that under this arrangement the Cuban Adjustment Act was effectively repealed, but the Clinton administration did succeed in preventing another Mariel exodus. With no support from the Soviet Union, Cuba seemed much less threatening—hardly a danger to the noncommunist nations of the Western Hemisphere.

American interest in Africa was considerably less than its interest in Latin America, Europe, and Asia during the Cold War years. As a result, few African refugees entered, and most of them originated in Ethiopia. That country had been an American ally in the Cold War until 1974, when a military and left-wing revolution succeeded in overthrowing the existing government. Washington gave Ethiopians who were in the United States at that time the right to remain temporarily. When it did not appear that the left-wing government would be replaced, the State Department and INS agreed to the admission of a few thousand Ethiopians annually and granted asylum to many who were already in the United States. By the end of the Cold War confrontation with the Soviet Union, about 20,000 Ethiopians had won asylum cases or had been permitted to enter as refugees. These numbers are not large compared to Asian, European, and Cuban refugees, but until the early 1990s, Ethiopians constituted the vast majority of African refugees.

Ethiopians continued to arrive as refugees after 1989, but American policy toward Africa looked to other issues than Marxism or communism. Stability and humanitarian concerns were at the center of the new policy. In 1992 the United States entered a civil war in Somalia. The effort to stabilize Somalia failed, and U.S. troops were ordered home. However, as an aftermath to aid those caught in the war, the door was opened to Somali refugees, numbering nearly 30,000 during the 1990s. In 1997, Somalis accounted for half of all African refugees.

Somalia was by no means the only nation divided by civil war and violence. Other African nations experienced such upheavals, and although U.S. forces were not engaged in a major way, the Clinton administration admitted African refugees from some of these conflicts. When Liberia, a nation that the United States had helped establish in the nineteenth century, experienced violence, Liberians in the United States received temporary protected status and others became refugees. The State Department and INS also admitted several hundred ethnic Nuer from the Sudan. Included were the "Lost Boys of Sudan," part of a group of 10,000 boys who had fled the Sudan's violence in 1992 and had lived in various African refugee camps. The United Nations High Commissioner for Refugees and the State Department recommended that 3,600 of these young men be admitted, and the first group of 500 arrived in the United States in 2001. Sudanese, Ethiopians, Liberians, and Somalis arrived from Africa in the largest numbers, but a few hundred others also found a safe haven in the United States during the 1990s. Among these were the sensational cases of several African women who received asylum on the grounds that if they returned to their homeland they would be subject to genital mutilation. The INS announced that it would consider mutilation as a factor in determining what a "well-founded fear" meant for asylum cases. While the United States avoided military intervention in the ethnic bloodshed in Rwanda, it announced that more refugees from that nation would be admitted. However, the numbers were only a few hundred.

While the decisions rested in part on humanitarian considerations, President Clinton was also responding to the pressures of the Black Caucus in Congress and various lobbying groups that wanted to increase the number of refugees arriving from Africa. The Black Caucus also attacked the INS and the State Department for sending Haitian refugees back to Haiti or interning them at the Guantánamo naval base for careful screening. Clinton signaled a shift in foreign policy to give more attention to Africa during two visits he made there toward the end of his second term. After his first trip in 1998, the president announced that the refugee quota from all of Africa would be increased. African quotas were upped to 7,000 in 1997 and 12,000 the next year. After Clinton's second visit in 2000, the State Department said that the African quota would be increased to 20,000. The figure was still only 25 percent of the total, but it marked a major increase in African refugees.

The last area of foreign policy considerations with implications for refugee policy was the Balkans and the bloodshed there in the 1990s. When Yugoslavia began to disintegrate in the 1990s, ethnic violence erupted. The Bosnian parliament declared independence from Yugoslavia in 1991, but Bosnian ethnic Serbs violently opposed it. Soon a three-way war broke out between Bosnia's Serbs, Muslims, and Croats. Serbs massacred thousands of Muslims and engaged in "ethnic cleansing" to drive Muslims out of Bosnia. The western European powers and the United States condemned Serbs for their killing and raping in Bosnia and finally negotiated a peace in 1995 and put in place an international peacekeeping force. The truce was an uneasy one, and before it and after, tens of thousands of Bosnians fled to western Europe and the United States for refuge. The flow continued even after the peacekeepers arrived. From 1986 to 1999 more than 100,000 Bosnians entered as refugees, with 30,906 recorded in 1998 and 22,697 the next year. In 1991, 1,660 refugees from Croatia were also received as refugees. The INS does not keep religious data, but most Bosnian refugees were Muslims.

When Yugoslavian Serbs expanded the ethnic conflict to Kosovo and killed many ethnic Albanians or sent them across the border to Albania, the West once again witnessed more "ethnic cleansing." This time NATO powers carried out their threat of military force and used airpower to drive the Serbs out of Kosovo and attacked Yugoslavia as well. After a successful air war in 1999, NATO troops occupied Kosovo to try to maintain a truce between those Serbs and ethnic Albanians remaining there. While the "ethnic cleansing" of Albanians was under way and during the war itself, as in so many other cases, the number of refugees increased: 14,280 refugees, who were mainly Kosovars, were received in the United States from Yugoslavia. A few hundred others in the United States won their asylum pleas.

CONCLUSION

In sum, the United States has always accepted refugees, even though such immigrants were not necessarily defined in the immigration laws. Government officials in Washington, including members of Congress and the president, often responded to overseas crises by linking refugees to foreign policy. A variety of nationality, religious, and ethnic private groups also pressured the government to admit refugees. Most of the admissions, from the arrival of exiles from the French Revolution in the 1790s to World War II, were permitted because the nation wished to inform the world that the United States was an "asylum for mankind."

After World War II, refugee policy underwent change. America's new role in the world prompted political leaders to admit thousands of refugees and displaced persons in Europe. As the Cold War came to dominate American foreign affairs, most refugees were perceived as fleeing communism. With the collapse of the Soviet Union and communism in eastern Europe, America changed the type of refugee it was willing to receive, but that new policy was still heavily influenced by foreign affairs and domestic politics.

From 1789 to the present, refugee policy was often made on an ad hoc basis. Even following the 1965 immigration act's provisions and the Refugee Act of 1980, government officials often responded to political pressure groups in determining which persons were accepted. Cubans were refugees but Haitians were not. Refugee policy differs little from immigration policy in that it is often confused, ad hoc, and constantly changing. For the immediate future it appears that these policies will continue to be the result of foreign affairs and internal pressures.

BIBLIOGRAPHY

Catanese, Anthony V. *Haitians: Migration and Diaspora.* Boulder, Colo., 1999.

Childs, Frances Sergeant. *French Refugee Life in the United States, 1790–1800: An American Chapter of the French Revolution.* Baltimore, 1940. Short work on the French refugees to the United States during the 1790s.

Coutin, Susan Bibler. *Legalizing Moves: Salvadoran Immigrants' Struggle for U.S. Residency.* Ann Arbor, Mich., 2000. Careful study of Salvadoran attempts to win refugee status and asylum in the United States.

DeConde, Alexander. *Ethnicity, Race and American Foreign Policy: A History.* Boston, 1992. An important book on the connection between American ethnic groups and foreign policy.

Dinnerstein, Leonard. *America and the Survivors of the Holocaust.* New York, 1982. The defin-

itive work on passage of the Displaced Persons Act after World War II.

Gimpel, James G., and James Edwards, Jr. *The Congressional Politics of Immigration Reform.* Boston, 1999. Detailed study of congressional immigration policy, with a discussion of refugee policy.

Hein, Jeremy. *From Vietnam, Laos, and Cambodia: A Refugee Experience in the United States.* New York, 1995.

Hunt, Alfred N. *Haiti's Influence on Antebellum America: Slumbering Volcano in the Caribbean.* Baton Rouge, La., 1988. Solid book on how America responded to Haitian attempts to win asylum.

Keely, Charles B., Robert W. Tucker, and Linda Wrigley, eds. *Immigration and U.S. Foreign Policy.* Boulder, Colo., 1990.

Koehn, Peter H. *Refugees from Revolution: U.S. Policy and Third World Migration.* Boulder, Colo., 1991. Good summary of post–World War II immigration policy as it relates to developing nations.

Lerski, Jerzy Jan. *A Polish Chapter in Jacksonian America: The United States and the Polish Exiles of 1831.* Madison, Wis., 1958.

Loescher, Gil. *Beyond Charity: International Cooperation and the Global Refugee Crisis.* New York, 1993.

Loescher, Gil, and John A. Scanlan. *Calculated Kindness: Refugees and America's Half-Open Door, 1945 to the Present.* New York and London, 1986. Excellent account of anticommunism and American refugee policies after 1945.

Masud-Piloto, Felix Roberto. *From Welcomed Exiles to Illegal Immigrants: Cuban Migration to the U.S., 1959–1995.* Lanham, Md., 1996. Useful summary of American policy toward Cuba, noting the shifts beginning in 1994.

Miller, Kerby A. *Emigrants and Exiles: Ireland and the Irish Exodus to North America.* New York, 1985.

Poyo, Gerald Eugene. *With All, and for the Good of All: The Emergence of Popular Nationalism in the Cuban Communities of the United States, 1848–1898.* Durham, N.C., 1989.

Reimers, David M. *Still the Golden Door: The Third World Comes to America.* 2d ed. New York, 1992.

Robinson, W. Courtland. *Terms of Refuge: The Indochinese Exodus and the International Response.* London and New York, 1998. Good summary not only of American but world response to the Indochinese refugees.

Schrag, Philip G. *A Well-Founded Fear: The Congressional Battle to Save Political Asylum in America.* New York, 2000. Detailed summary of congressional politics and recent refugee policy.

Smith, Tony. *Foreign Attachments: The Power of Ethnic Groups in the Making of American Foreign Policy.* Cambridge, Mass., and London, 2000. Important study of ethnic groups and their role in shaping American foreign policy, with useful material on refugees.

Stepick, Alex. *Pride Against Prejudice: Haitians in the United States.* Boston, 1998.

Wilson, David A. *United Irishmen, United States: Immigrant Radicals in the Early Republic.* Ithaca, N.Y., 1998.

Wyman, David S. *The Abandonment of the Jews: America and the Holocaust, 1941–1945.* New York, 1984. Major study of American policy toward the Holocaust during World War II, critical of U.S. policy.

Zucker, Norman L., and Naomi Flink Zucker. *The Guarded Gate: The Reality of American Refugee Policy.* San Diego, 1987.

See also ASYLUM; HUMAN RIGHTS; HUMANITARIAN INTERVENTION AND RELIEF; IMMIGRATION; NEUTRALITY; RACE AND ETHNICITY.

RELIGION

Leo P. Ribuffo

For national leaders and specialists in the study of diplomacy alike, the notion that religion has affected United States foreign policy is familiar—too familiar. Whereas the Massachusetts Puritan John Winthrop's charge in 1630 to build an inspiring "city upon the hill" came to be quoted almost routinely by presidents as different as John F. Kennedy, James Earl Carter, and Ronald Reagan to sanctify one version or another of American mission, students of diplomacy rarely go beyond citing such rhetorical conventions to explore the complicated influence of religious ideas or denominational interests.

Thus, any discussion of religion and foreign relations must begin with an appreciation of the diversity of American faiths, their development over the centuries, and the problematical nature of their connection to international affairs. Contemporary liberals who celebrate a "Judeo-Christian tradition" and contemporary conservatives who conflate all "people of faith" both homogenize American religion, past and present. Not only have people of faith differed among themselves about domestic and foreign policy issues, but they have also often done so precisely because they took their respective faiths seriously. Nonetheless, even the most devout among them were also affected, usually without any sense of contradiction, by political, economic, strategic, racial, and ethnic considerations, as well as by personal feelings about worldly success, power, and glory. Furthermore, American foreign policy decisions, especially those relating to expansion, war, and peace, have affected religious life as well as the other way around.

Nor has a high level of religious commitment been constant throughout American history. Both the intensity of belief in the aggregate and the strength of particular religious groups have waxed and waned. So have interdenominational tolerance, competition, and cooperation. Religious groups have proliferated for reasons ranging from constitutional disestablishment to theological disagreement to mass immigration. In this context—and much to the consternation of clergy committed to one orthodoxy or another—individual Americans have always tended to create their own syncretic belief systems.

FROM EUROPEAN SETTLEMENT TO MANIFEST DESTINY

Few of the Europeans who settled North America in the sixteenth, seventeenth, and early eighteenth centuries held the contemporary liberal view that all faiths were essentially equal before God. On the contrary, divergent religious doctrines bolstered imperial rivalries. For the British subjects in North America, almost all of whom were heirs in some respect to Reformation-era Protestantism, Spain and France represented not only economic rivals and strategic threats, but also tyrannical "popery." During the French and Indian War, anti-Catholic sentiment rose and some of the colonies forbade "papists" to bear arms.

Although residents of the thirteen colonies that formed the United States in 1776 were overwhelmingly Protestant, the religious situation already showed signs of the complexity that would become an American perennial. Roughly half of the colonists were at least pro forma Anglicans, Congregationalists, and Presbyterians, but there were also large numbers of Baptists, Lutherans, Dutch Reformed Calvinists, Quakers, and German pietists. Differences among these Protestants may look insignificant to the contemporary secular eye, but they bulked large at a time when taxes were levied to support established churches in most of the states. In addition, the Great Awakening of the 1740s had left a legacy of division in several denominations between evangelical "new lights" and more stolid "old lights." There were also roughly 25,000 Catholics and 2,000 Jews.

Equally important, by several criteria the era in which the United States was formed qualifies as the least religious period in the country's history. Fewer than 20 percent of Americans were church adherents. Many of the foremost Founders, including the first four presidents, were influenced to some extent by deism and viewed God as a distant force in human affairs.

Recent religious developments influenced the first and foremost event of American foreign policy: the decision to separate from Great Britain. These also affected the shape of the revolutionary coalition, the size of the country, and the form of the new government. While dividing denominations, the Great Awakening had fostered colonial unity as men and women saved by the same itinerant evangelists hundred of miles apart felt a common bond. To the British government, the Awakening provided further evidence that the colonists needed a resident Anglican bishop to limit their religious autonomy. None was named, but even colonial deists viewed such an appointment as part of the comprehensive British "conspiracy" to strangle American freedom, religious as well as political and economic. The Quebec Act of 1774, which granted civil rights to French Catholics and all but established the Roman Catholic Church in that province, underscored the threat of "ecclesiastical slavery." Now, many American Protestants concluded, British tyranny had allied with papal absolutism. On balance, religious forces and issues speeded the momentum toward independence.

Religious factors also influenced decisions to support the Revolution, remain loyal to King George III, or try to avoid the conflict altogether. Adherents to the Church of England frequently sided with the Crown but there were many notable exceptions, including George Washington. Evangelical heirs to the Great Awakening disproportionately joined the patriot cause; Scots-Irish Presbyterians were particularly zealous. New England Congregationalists, the clearest spiritual heirs of John Winthrop, frequently framed the cause as part of a divine mission. On the other hand, the Declaration of Independence reflected Enlightenment republicanism rather than evangelical Protestantism. Jews usually favored independence. In general, however, religious minorities feared the loss of royal protection. Catholics were wary of living in an overwhelmingly Protestant republic. Yet Charles Carroll, the only Catholic signer of the Declaration of Independence, expected—correctly, as

matters turned out—that independence would foster disestablishment. Neither Carroll's diplomacy nor military force convinced Quebec Catholics to join the United States. French Canadian bishop Jean-Olivier Briand denounced the invading "Bostonians" and threatened to withhold sacraments from Catholics who aided them.

Decisions about the war were particularly difficult for adherents to what are usually called the historic peace churches. The Society of Friends (Quakers) and the predominantly German pietists—notably, the Mennonites, Moravians, and Dunkers—are best known for their repudiation of violence. But also, instead of building ever larger cities, states, or imperial republics "upon a hill," they hoped to change the world, if at all, through a separatist moral example. During the Revolution, as in all future wars, they struggled to determine the right mix of cooperation and resistance.

Members of all of the peace churches faced some degree of ostracism, seizure of property, loss of employment, and imprisonment when they refused to pay taxes or swear allegiance to the new government. The German pietists—predominantly rural, further from the political mainstream, and generally willing to pay fines in place of military service—suffered less than the Quakers. The Society of Friends contained some strong loyalists and was suspected of shielding many more. Other members were expelled for fighting in the Revolution; a prowar contingent seceded to form the Free Quakers. Quakers also began their practice of providing humanitarian assistance to all victims of the war

Just as religious affiliations influenced the Revolution, both the war and the ultimate victory decisively affected the religious scene. The departure of loyalist Anglican clergy left the successor Episcopal Church weakened. The alliance with France dampened fears of "popery," much to the benefit of American Catholics. The Constitution precluded religious tests for federal office and the First Amendment banned an "establishment of religion." Religious minorities, sometimes in alliance with Enlightenment deists, began a long but ultimately successful campaign for disestablishment in the states. Thus, although religious denominations would continue to influence foreign policy, they enjoyed no constitutional advantage over secular lobbies. A treaty with Tripoli in 1796 assured the Muslim ruler of that country that the government was "not in any sense founded on the Christian religion." The absence of a federal establishment prompted competition, which in turn encouraged both religious commitments and a proliferation of faiths as clergy from rival denominations competed to win adherents. Also, the grassroots egalitarianism nurtured by the Revolution provided a hospitable environment for the theologically and institutionally democratic Baptists and Methodists.

The victorious revolutionary coalition began to fall apart almost immediately. Disagreements about faith and foreign affairs shaped the development of acrimonious party politics starting in the 1790s. The Jeffersonian Republicans were religiously more diverse and tolerant than the Federalists. Looking abroad, the Republicans tilted toward revolutionary France, while the Federalists typically admired Great Britain—which they viewed as a bastion of Christianity rather than French infidelity. During the War of 1812, Federalist Congregationalists and Presbyterians reiterated their admiration of British Protestantism and characterized impressed seamen as runaway Irish Catholics unworthy of sympathy. Baptists and Methodists denounced the autocratic Church of England and hailed the Republican President James Madison as a friend of religious liberty.

Above and beyond these controversies was the broad consensus that the United States must expand its territory, trade, and power. Expansion often received but did not require a religious rationale. Thomas Jefferson, who held the least conventional religious beliefs of any president, arranged the Louisiana Purchase, the largest single land acquisition in American history. Even Protestant clergy who viewed expansion as part of a divine plan often supplemented Scripture with economic and geopolitical arguments.

John L. O'Sullivan, editor of the *Democratic Review,* captured the dominant expansionist theme of republican mission when he famously proclaimed the "manifest destiny" of the United States in 1845. The continent was destined to be American by a nonsectarian Providence for a great experiment in freedom and self-government.

Even so, religious controversies relating to foreign policy proliferated between the 1810s and the 1850s—partly because the United States was expanding its territory and international interests. Equally important, this era of manifest destiny coincided with another revival among Protestants that lasted at least through the 1830s and the first mass immigration of non-Protestants. By the 1850s the three largest religious groups were the Methodists, Baptists, and Catholics; the population also included 150,000 Jews, most of them recent immigrants from German states.

The second Great Awakening energized virtually every reform campaign of the first half of the nineteenth century. Two in particular intersected with the history of foreign policy: the creation of an organized peace movement and a systematic Protestant missionary effort.

Northern Congregationalists, Presbyterians, and Unitarians provided most of the leadership and rank-and-file strength of the peace movement. In 1815, David Low Dodge, a devout Presbyterian, founded the New York Peace Society, perhaps the first such organization in the world. There were many other local stirrings in the wake of the War of 1812. In 1828 the most important among them coalesced into the American Peace Society.

Historical accounts of Protestant missionaries typically begin with the creation of the first "foreign" mission board in 1810 and then trace evangelical activities in Asia, Africa, and the Middle East. This perspective has a certain plausibility, not least because many missionaries viewed the story that way. Yet it obscures the essential fact that for several generations U.S. foreign policy also occurred on the North American continent. The Africans and Asians encountered overseas were no more alien to bourgeois Protestant missionaries than were the Native Americans whom their precursors had been trying to convert since the 1600s. Moreover, mission boards sent evangelists to American Indian "nations" well into the nineteenth century. As the historian Kenneth Scott Latourette observed in *The Great Century in the United States of America* (1941), the conquest of the American West was a "vast colonial expansion, nonetheless significant because it was not usually regarded as such."

Missionaries played three major roles in this continental colonialism. First, their glowing descriptions of the land drew settlers westward—sometimes to disputed territory. Oregon was such a case, where the U.S. advantage in population helped secure a peaceful division with Great Britain in 1846. Second, along with Methodist circuit riders and countless local revivalists, missionaries instilled bourgeois traits useful for developing and holding the frontier. Third, they worked to christianize the Indians as part of an effort to assimilate them. In 1819 the federal government began funding churches to inculcate the "habits and arts of civilization" among Native Americans. Missionary successes in this area did not save the Native Americans from the inexorable forces of expansion. The Cherokees in the southeastern United States accepted Christianity and their leader adopted the name Elias Boudinot, after the first president of the American Bible Society. Even so, they were forcibly removed beyond the Mississippi River in the 1830s.

Overseas missions ultimately became, as the historian John K. Fairbank wrote in *The Missionary Enterprise in China and America* (1974), the nation's "first large-scale transnational corporations." The institutional beginnings were modest. Spurred by the awakening at Williams College and Andover Seminary, Congregationalists took the lead in 1810 in founding the (temporarily) interdenominational American Board of Commissioners for Foreign Missions (ABCFM). Within a decade, missionaries were sent to India, Hawaii, and the Middle East. Although diverse denominations soon created their own boards, the ABCFM remained the leading sponsor of overseas missions for the next fifty years.

The fields of activity were determined by opportunity as well as theology. The ABCFM established missions in India and Ceylon because Great Britain barred their establishment in Burma. Not only did the Holy Land have an obvious appeal, but also the Ottoman Empire permitted missionaries to work with its Christian communities (although they were quite willing to offer Protestantism to Muslims and Jews as well as Coptics, Catholics, and Eastern Orthodox believers when those opportunities arose).

While rarely advocating racial equality, white religious leaders were nonetheless eager to send black missionaries to sub-Saharan Africa. According to prevailing medical theory, blacks were less susceptible than whites to tropical diseases. Whatever the motives of their (usually) white sponsors, black missionaries often felt a special calling to save Africa from paganism and Islam. In addition, thriving African Christian communities might serve as a refuge from persecution and show the world that blacks could build civilized societies.

The first missionaries concentrated on bringing individual men and women to Christ, perhaps as a prelude to his imminent Second Coming. Always few in number, they hoped to establish indigenous congregations to carry on the work. At first, too, they paid close attention to the quality of faith among aspiring converts. Missionaries and their sponsoring agencies frequently agonized over the question of how much they should modify indigenous cultures. Some

evangelical Protestants thought a large measure of "civilization" necessary for Christianity to take hold. In theory, most wanted to change local ways of life as little as possible consistent with the demands of the gospel. In practice, both the prevailing definition of civilized morality and their own personal traits undermined missionary restraint. Inevitably, they fostered values esteemed by middle-class Protestants: hard work, efficiency, technological innovation, sexual propriety, and respect for "true womanhood." The missionaries were usually ignored, often opposed, and sometimes physically attacked. Even converts mixed Protestant precepts with aspects of their previous religious faiths. Missionaries learned to simplify Christianity and relax their requirements for spiritual rebirth.

Pre–Civil War missionaries did not see themselves as agents of American economic expansion. Frequently they set out for places where trade was negligible and unlikely to develop. They often assailed merchants for their chicanery, sale of alcohol, and promotion of prostitution. Yet Charles Denby, Jr., U.S. minister to China later in the nineteenth century, was correct to see missionaries as "pioneers of trade." Businessmen who contributed to missionary societies and provided free passage on ships agreed. In many cases missionaries were the only translators available to entrepreneurs trying to open foreign markets.

Government officials saw the missionary enterprise as a means to extend American political influence. Writing on behalf of the ABCFM to King Kamehameha of Hawaii, President John Quincy Adams declared that "a knowledge of letters and of the True Religion—the Religion of the Christian's Bible" were the only means to advance any people's happiness. Despite such endorsements, the U.S. government offered less direct help than overseas missionaries wanted.

The Middle East, which attracted the largest number of missionaries before the Civil War, provides a case in point. Commodore David Porter, the American chargé d'affaires in the Ottoman Empire from 1831 until 1843, urged Turkish officials at all levels to safeguard the missionaries, worked to establish consulates in places where they operated, and occasionally arranged visits by the navy as quiet demonstrations of American strength. At the same time, Porter repeatedly warned against offending Muslims. From the perspective of the Turkish government, missionaries were welcome as long as their activities were not disruptive. But their proselytizing inevitably offended not only Muslims, but also Greek and Armenian Orthodox Christians. Disruptive responses included riots, destruction of property, and occasional murders.

The missionaries in the Middle East and their patrons at home worked diligently to influence government policy and enjoyed mixed success. Missionaries themselves received consular or diplomatic appointments in Athens, Beirut, and Constantinople. Encouraged by an ABCFM lobbyist, Secretary of State Daniel Webster wrote Porter in 1842 that missionaries should be assisted "in the same manner" as merchants. Indeed, in the Middle East they seem to have received slightly more direct assistance than businessmen. Still, government action fell short of their hopes. Warships were dispatched only to "show the flag," not to fire their cannon in retribution for attacks on missionaries, and the Turkish-American treaty of 1862 contained no provision guaranteeing the right to evangelize.

The worldwide Christian missionary campaign was confined neither to Protestants nor to Americans. From the perspective of the Vatican, the United States itself remained a mission field under the supervision of the Sacred Congregation for the Propagation of the Faith until 1908. While this subordinate status should not obscure the American hierarchy's quest for influence and autonomy, Catholic bishops, priests, and nuns necessarily concentrated on preserving—or creating—faith among millions of immigrants and their children. Thus, few Americans participated in the Vatican's far-flung missionary efforts. Among Protestants, the largest number of overseas missionaries came from Great Britain until roughly 1900. Friendly contacts between Protestant and Catholic missionaries were rare in the early nineteenth century. More typical was the complaint by ABCFM representatives in the Middle East that agents of popery allied with Islamic infidels to thwart their efforts. On the other hand, American Protestant missionaries not only cooperated with their British counterparts, whose efforts predated their own by at least two decades, but also sought protection from British diplomats and warships. This cooperation was both a sign of and modest contribution to the rapprochement that proceeded fitfully between the two countries.

Although no more than two thousand American missionaries had been sent abroad by 1870, their impact on indigenous cultures was occasionally extraordinary. Nowhere was their influence more apparent than in the Hawaiian Islands.

When the first missionaries, from the ABCFM, arrived in 1820, Hawaii was already enduring rapid—and usually destructive—change through contact with the outside world The missionaries were appalled by many Hawaiian practices, including polygamy, incest, and the "licentious" hula dance. To some Hawaiians, however, these evangelical Protestants seemed preferable to the merchants and sailors who had introduced alcohol, prostitution, and deadly diseases. The missionaries' shrewdest tactic was to cultivate Hawaiian royalty. By 1840 they had transformed the islands into a limited monarchy with a legislature, judiciary, and constitution barring laws "at variance with the Word of Lord Jehovah."

Although the ABCFM initially cited Hawaii as an example to emulate, success there was neither problem-free nor permanent. Many pro forma converts lapsed into what the missionaries considered sin. Despite zealous efforts to exclude religious rivals, advocates of Catholic and Mormon "idolatry" established footholds. Even Hawaiian Christians prayed for relief from white "mission rule." The ABCFM reprimanded its representatives for going beyond their charge to bring the gospel. Yet the political and social changes were irreversible. By the 1850s former missionaries, their children, and protégés had established themselves as Hawaii's elite.

No field offered less promise than China in the early nineteenth century. The population was indifferent. The Manchu dynasty barely tolerated missionaries (often disguised as businessmen) along with other foreign "barbarians" in an enclave near Canton. In 1858 the Reverend Samuel Wells Williams judged the Chinese "among the most craven of people, cruel and selfish as heathenism can make men." Thus, the gospel must be "backed by force if we wish them to listen to reason."

Force came primarily in the shape of the British navy. American missionaries enthusiastically backed Britain's frequent assaults and regretted only that U.S. warships rarely joined the fray. The Opium War that began in 1839 was a turning point for China and the missionaries there. With few exceptions they cheered the British victory, even though it meant continuation of an illegal narcotics trade the Chinese were trying to suppress. Perhaps, they reflected, God was using naval bombardments to open China to the gospel.

The Sino-British agreement that ended the Opium War in 1842 and established five treaty ports was the first of many "unequal treaties" that provoked Chinese resentment. In 1844 the Treaty of Wanghia granted the United States access to these ports and most-favored-nation status. The pact was largely the work of three missionaries, one of whom, Dr. Peter Parker, became U.S. commissioner in China a decade later.

The Taiping Rebellion, led by Hung Hsiuchuan, again showed that evangelism could be a catalyst for extraordinary and wholly unanticipated consequences. After living briefly in the house of a missionary, Hung baptized himself and created a religious movement combining elements of Christianity, Confucianism, his own mystical visions, and a reformist social program. In 1851 he led an uprising against the Manchu dynasty; by the time he was defeated, at least twenty million Chinese had been killed.

Although missionary influence certainly did not cause the Taiping Rebellion, and both Protestants and Catholics repudiated Hung's syncretic faith after an initial show of interest, the revolt made the Manchu court more wary than ever of Western religion. At the same time, the revolt rendered China less able to resist Western power. After further British bombardment, in a few instances aided by the U.S. Navy, China agreed in the late 1850s to new and increasingly unequal treaties with the West. Thus, unlike their colleagues in the Middle East, missionaries in China were guaranteed the right to spread the gospel.

A second Great Awakening at a time of mass non-Protestant immigration energized prejudice as well as domestic reform and missionary activity. Slurs against Jews routinely included the charge that their ancestors had crucified Christ. Nonetheless, Jews seemed less threatening than the more numerous and raucous Catholic immigrants. Neither the nativists who burned convents nor the Catholics who fought back with equal vigor were moved by the fine points of theology. Even so, well-publicized attacks on "popery" by prominent clergy hardly served the cause of tolerance. No clergyman was more prominent than Congregationalist Lyman Beecher. In *A Plea for the West* (1835), Beecher accused the Vatican of flooding the frontier with ignorant immigrants who were easily manipulated by priests. Unlike anti-Semitism, hostility to Catholics affected national politics. In the mid-1850s the nativist American Party, popularly called the Know-Nothings, became a powerful force in Congress.

As the population grew more diverse during the first half of the nineteenth century, so too did diplomatic personnel and political controversies involving religion and foreign policy. Starting with the Jeffersonian Republicans, Jews served as diplomatic and commercial representatives abroad, notably in Scotland and the Caribbean. The first major post went to Mordecai Noah, appointed consul at Tunis in 1813. Removing Noah two years later, Secretary of State James Monroe claimed that his Judaism had been an "obstacle" to performance of his duties. It seems doubtful that the Muslim ruler of Tunis was discomfited by Noah's religion. Indeed, Noah's appointment continued a diplomatic tradition in which Jews often served as mediators between Christians and Muslims. Responding to inquiries by Noah's political backers of various faiths, Secretary Monroe backtracked to say that his religion, "so far as related to this government," played no part in the recall. Many Jews remained unconvinced.

In 1840 the persecution of Jews in parts of the Ottoman Empire attracted widespread attention. Officials in Damascus charged Syrian Jews with killing a Catholic monk and his servant in order to use their blood in Passover services, arrested dozens of Jews, and tortured some of them to secure spurious confessions. Both the "blood libel" charge and attacks upon Jews quickly spread to other parts of the empire. French diplomats apparently encouraged the persecution in order to maximize their own country's influence. Great Britain led the international protests and the United States joined in. American diplomats were instructed to use their good offices "with discretion" to aid Jewish victims of persecution. According to Secretary of State John Forsyth's instructions, the United States was acting as a friendly power, whose institutions placed "upon the same footing, the worshipers of God of every faith."

Public meetings by Christians and Jews alike encouraged government action. Some Jewish leaders hesitated to rally behind their Eastern coreligionists; others doubted the prudence or propriety of seeking government action. Ultimately, however, the Damascus affair brought American Jews closer together and legitimated demonstrations against anti-Semitism abroad. Six years later they organized protests against the persecution of Russian Jews. During the 1850s, along with such Christian allies as Senators Henry Clay and Lewis Cass, they denounced a treaty that recognized the right of Swiss cantons to discriminate against Jews. The administration of President Millard Fillmore negotiated cosmetic changes in the agreement.

Foreign policy issues prompted animosity as well as cooperation among religious faiths. Many Protestants supported Jewish protests not only because they valued the republican principle of equal treatment of all white citizens, but also because they wanted to set a precedent for receiving equal treatment in Catholic countries. John England, the Catholic archbishop of Charleston, attended a mass meeting condemning the Ottoman persecution of Jews in 1840. Conversely, Jews and Catholics were bitterly divided over the Mortara affair in the 1850s. Edgardo Mortara, a Jewish child in Bologna, Italy, was secretly baptized by a servant and then removed from his family by the church. Caught between Catholic and Jewish constituencies, President James Buchanan claimed that he could not intervene in the affairs of another state.

The Mexican War was the most controversial foreign policy event between the War of 1812 and World War I. Although sectarian religious arguments were not absent, rival interpretations of the nation's nonsectarian republican mission predominated among proponents and opponents alike. According to opponents, President James K. Polk had provoked an illegitimate war with a fellow Christian republic. According to proponents, not only did the United States need to defend itself in an undemocratic world, but also the corrupt Mexican state resembled European autocracies rather than a true republic. Therefore, an American triumph would help to purify Mexico and inspire the forces of liberty everywhere. Instead of fostering freedom, opponents countered, such a victory would increase the territory open to slavery.

In this complicated ideological context, the major denominations took no official stand on the war. The Disciples of Christ, which had just begun to emerge during the awakening, called it a crime. Presbyterian leaders showed the most enthusiasm, especially about the prospect of saving Mexico from Catholic "idolatry." Congregationalists, Unitarians, and Quakers, the strongest foes of slavery, were also the most ardent opponents of the war.

The issue of Catholic loyalty to the United States engaged American nativists, Mexican military strategists, and the Polk administration. Circulating lurid tales of seductions by Mexican nuns, nativists feared that the Catholic troops, roughly 1,100 in number, would spy for or defect to the enemy. The Mexicans hoped so. Despite their propaganda efforts, only a few Irish-American soldiers switched sides to join the Battalion of Saint Patrick.

As president and leader of the Democratic Party, which received a disproportionate share of the Catholic vote, Polk declined to make the war an anti-Catholic crusade. Emissaries to the Mexican Catholic hierarchy emphasized that their church was not endangered by the U.S. invasion. Polk asked the American bishops to recommend Catholic chaplains for the army. In addition, Moses Beach, Catholic editor of the *New York Sun*, served as one of Polk's numerous agents seeking to secure a peace treaty. Many American soldiers accepted the ready-made stereotype that Catholicism had corrupted the Mexican government and rendered the population docile, yet some found the priests surprisingly amiable and enjoyed the romance of billeting in monasteries.

FROM THE CIVIL WAR TO WORLD WAR I

The Civil War era affected the American religious life in important ways. What some scholars consider a third Great Awakening began in the 1850s and continued during the war itself. Indeed, the conflict looked much more like an evangelical Protestant war than had the Revolution, the War of 1812, or the Mexican War. Union and Confederate clergy called upon God to aid their respective causes, military camps hosted revival meetings, and soldiers sometimes marched into battle singing hymns. Thoughtful supporters of the Union from President Abraham Lincoln on down framed the war as a time of testing. For many northerners, victory in 1865 proved that the test had been passed and that God truly blessed America and its mission in the world.

The consequences for Catholics were mixed. On the one hand, service for the North and South brought new legitimacy; on the other hand, erstwhile Know-Nothings found a home in the Republican Party. Although Jews served disproportionately in both the Union and Confederate armies, rising evangelical fervor combined with venerable stereotypes about Jewish profiteering to provoke notable anti-Semitic incidents and accusations. Finally, except for the historic peace churches, the war decimated the organized antiwar movement as even fervent pacifists were tempted to acquiesce in violence to end slavery.

Important as these developments were, the Civil War affected the religious scene much less than the powerful trends of the following four decades. Starting in the 1880s, millions of poor Catholic and Jewish immigrants began to arrive from eastern and southern Europe. Although the population remained predominantly Protestant and the elite institutions overwhelmingly so, politics and popular culture were soon affected. For the Catholic and Jewish minorities, the problem of defining and defending their Americanness acquired fresh urgency. Moreover, the "new immigration" coincided with a rapid industrialization rivaled only by that of Germany. Both the benefits and liabilities were obvious. On the one hand, unprecedented wealth was available to a few Americans and upward mobility possible for many. On the other hand, the gap widened between the rich and poor, frequent economic busts interrupted the long-term boom, and violent social conflict escalated. Perhaps God was once again testing rather than blessing America.

Worse yet, perhaps God did not exist at all—or at least His mode of governing the universe may have differed from what Christians had taken for granted since the ebbing of the Enlightenment. Amid the social turmoil, Protestants in particular faced serious intellectual challenges. The Darwinian theory of evolution undermined the Genesis account of creation. Modern science raised doubts about all biblical miracles. Less known to the praying public but especially distressing to educated clergy, archaeological discoveries and "higher criticism" of the Bible suggested that Scripture was in no simple sense the word of God.

The religious responses to this social and intellectual turmoil included insular bigotry and cosmopolitan reflection, apocalyptic foreboding and millennial optimism, intellectual adaptation and retrenchment, withdrawal from the world and expanded efforts to perfect it. The choices made by individual men and women involved anguish, ambivalence, and inconsistency. In the aggregate, their decisions transformed American religious life.

By the 1890s Protestantism was entering a fourth Great Awakening, which, like its predecessors, was marked by heightened emotions, stresses and splits within existing denominations, and the founding of new faiths. Among believers in new faiths were the followers of former Congregationalist Charles Taze Russell (known since 1931 as Jehovah's Witnesses), whose teachings required separation from a world ruled by Satan. Other spiritual searchers, convinced that God's grace brought a second blessing with such signs

as the gift of speaking in tongues, formed their own Pentecostal churches. Doctrinal differences strained relations within the major denominations. Theological liberals, who often called themselves modernists, viewed the Bible as a valuable but not necessarily infallible book, emphasized Jesus's humanity and moral example, and aspired to build God's kingdom on earth. Theological conservatives, most of whom called themselves fundamentalists after World War I, championed the "inerrancy" of the Bible, the divinity of Jesus, and the expectation that God's kingdom would be established only after His miraculous return. While staunch modernists and conservatives occasionally confronted each other in heresy trials, moderates from both camps usually continued to work together until World War I.

Although theological conservatives were not necessarily politically conservative, they emphasized that the church as an institution must above all else save souls. While modernists stressed the church's role in improving this world, their earthly version of God's kingdom fell far short of twenty-first-century political liberalism. Indeed, sophisticated religious ideas coexisted in the typical theological liberal's worldview with routine affirmations of laissez-faire economics. A few theological liberals preached an explicitly "social gospel" in support of workers' rights, a regulatory state, and (occasionally) moderate socialism. Yet even social gospelers were susceptible to anti-Semitism, anti-Catholic nativism, and ostensibly scientific theories of "Anglo-Saxon" superiority.

By the 1880s affluent and assimilated American Jews experienced growing social discrimination. By that point, too, anti-Catholic activism was again on the rise. The American Protective Association (APA), founded in 1887, attracted 100,000 members who pledged not to hire or join strikes with Catholics. In countless tracts, efficient, fair, and democratic Anglo-Saxon Protestants were celebrated at the expense of tricky Jews, drunken Irish, sullen Poles, and impulsive Italians. Despite this emphasis on racial or cultural superiority, religious motifs were not absent from this latest form of nativism. Jewish chicanery came naturally, many Christians believed, because Jews had crucified Jesus. Ignorant Catholic peasants from eastern or southern Europe, like the Mexicans defeated in the 1840s, looked dangerously susceptible to clerical manipulation. The affirmation of papal infallibility at the First Vatican Council in 1869 and 1870, the increasingly insular papacy of Pope Leo XIII, and the Holy See's suspicion of the American

Catholic Church suggested that Protestant fears were not entirely fanciful.

The behavior of Jews and Catholics was much more complicated than even tolerant Protestants supposed. On the one hand, many immigrants were rapidly acculturated and their native-born children considered themselves Americans. On the other hand, rivalry among "nationalities" within the same religious community was commonplace. Sephardic and German Reform Jews viewed Judaism as a religion akin to liberal Protestantism; for the Orthodox eastern European Jews who outnumbered them by the early twentieth century, Judaism was central to cultural identity. Catholic bishops disagreed among themselves about their religion's place in a democracy devoid of a state church but nonetheless dominated by an informal Protestant establishment. Nationalists like Cardinal James Gibbons and Archbishop John Ireland expected Catholicism to thrive in such circumstances. They warned, however, that strict Vatican control would only fuel Protestant animosity.

All of these developments not only affected the immediate relationship between faith and foreign policy, but also left a long legacy of beliefs and institutions. Most obviously, sermons, articles, and books by mainstream clergy put a religious imprimatur on post–Civil War expansion. In 1885 the Reverend Josiah Strong's *Our Country,* the most widely read of these tracts, was published. The book itself was a mixture of nativist themes, popularized Darwinism, apocalyptic foreboding, and millennial hope. *Our Country* also reflected Strong's participation in both the home and overseas mission movements. Strong believed that authoritarian religions threatened the political freedom and "pure spiritual Christianity" that Anglo-Saxons had nurtured in the United States. Echoing Lyman Beecher's earlier "plea for the West," he considered the heartland particularly vulnerable. Not only were ignorant European Catholics settling there, but the Mormon heresy was also firmly established.

If the peril was great, so were the opportunities. Despite his ethnocentrism, Strong did not consider eastern and southern European Catholics inherently inferior. If converted to Protestantism and Americanized in the public schools, these ersatz Anglo-Saxons would make the country stronger than ever. "Our country" could then fulfill its destiny. As the fittest nation in the international struggle, the United States would easily impress its institutions on the world.

Beyond tracts and sermons, the fourth Great Awakening sparked a resurgence of overseas missions, which had been suffering from a lack of recruits. In 1886 the cause struck a nerve among hundreds of young people attending a conference under the auspices of Dwight L. Moody, the foremost evangelist of the day. The next year some of those present took the lead in founding the Student Volunteer Movement for Foreign Missions (SVM). The Reverend Arthur Pierson, a theological conservative who expected an imminent Second Coming, gave the group a millenarian motto: "The evangelization of the world in this generation." John R. Mott, a Methodist layman, became SVM executive secretary and master organizer. Mott recruited educated missionaries, built a network of supporters on college campuses, and fostered interdenominational and international cooperation. Ties to Canadian Protestants were particularly strong.

The SVM was only the most striking manifestation of growing interest. Once again, diverse religious groups founded mission boards, auxiliary societies, and umbrella organizations. Between 1890 and 1915 the number of overseas missionaries rose from roughly one thousand to nine thousand. This was the largest group of Americans living abroad on a long-term basis. By 1920 Americans and Canadians together made up half of the Protestant missionary force worldwide. Equally important, the campaign to "evangelize the world" became a vivid presence in thousands of congregations. Many Americans first learned something about life in Asia, Africa, or the Middle East, however ethnocentric the perspective, from a returned missionary's Sunday sermon.

The expanding movement reflected general social and cultural trends. Appropriating the military analogies that abounded for two generations after the Civil War, missionaries framed their task as a religious "war of conquest." In an era of scientific racial theories, legal segregation, and disfranchisement of African Americans, denominations led by whites ceased sending black missionaries to Africa. As middle-class women sought to bring the benefits of "social housekeeping" to a corrupt and sinful world, some found careers—as well as adventure and fulfillment—in missionary work. By 1890, 60 percent of overseas missionaries were women. Confined to working within their own gender, they focused on such "female" issues as seeking to end the crippling binding of women's feet in China.

The expanding movement also reflected prevailing religious animosities. Isolated Westerners in alien lands, American Protestant and European Catholic missionaries now occasionally fell into ad hoc cooperation during medical or military emergencies, but suspicion continued to characterize their relations in calmer times. The international missionary war of conquest led to increased cooperation among Protestants in other areas. At the same time, the doctrinal differences spreading within most major denominations produced disputes about what exactly overseas missionaries were supposed to do. Theological liberals, especially those with a social gospel bent, emphasized the improvement of living standards both as an ethical imperative and an effective evangelical strategy. According to theological conservatives, preaching of the unadorned gospel was both a Christian duty and a better way to attract sincere converts. Ironically, the cosmopolitan modernists usually sanctioned greater intrusion on indigenous ways of life. A few of them, however, edged toward the position long held by Quakers and Unitarians that no people should be evangelized into surrendering their historic religion.

Indigenous peoples were not passive recipients of the missionary message. In many cases, missionary activity responded to local demands for medical care and education. As early as 1885, eight colleges had been founded in the Ottoman Empire; by the 1910s a majority of missionaries in China were no longer involved in directly spreading the gospel. Moreover, Western learning was sometimes seen as a way to resist further Western encroachments.

As was the case before the Civil War, missionaries sometimes significantly influenced the countries in which they served. A few did so by switching from religious to diplomatic careers. No one followed this path with greater success than Horace N. Allen, who arrived in Korea as a Presbyterian medical missionary in 1884. After tending to a wounded prince, Allen became the royal family's favorite physician and began giving a wide range of advice to the king and queen. After representing Korean interests in the United States, Allen served as secretary to the American legation and then as minister to Seoul from 1897 until 1905. Often evading State Department instructions against meddling in Korean affairs, he secured mining and lumbering concessions for American investors as well as contracts to install trolley, electric, and telephone lines. And while warning missionaries against offending Koreans' sensibilities, Allen used his influence at court to protect them.

Allen's career underscores a major development in late-nineteenth-century foreign policy: an intensified interest in Asia by merchants and missionaries alike. Indeed, religious leaders now frequently stressed the confluence of conversion and capitalism. Lecturing on the "Christian Conquest of Asia" at Union Theological Seminary in 1898, the Reverend J. H. Barrows, president of Oberlin College, envisioned the Pacific Ocean as the "chief highway of the world's commerce." By the 1890s missionaries in the Far East outnumbered those sent to the Middle East for the first time.

The convergence of evangelism, commerce, and politics should be no surprise. Much as merchants sought foreign markets to relieve economic stagnation, and as political leaders thought expansionism an antidote to real class conflict or alleged cultural decline, Protestants looked overseas to solve their particular domestic problems. Indeed, well-publicized missionary campaigns did reinvigorate the churches at home.

Symbolic of an era marked by strong religious hopes, fears, and tensions, the two major political parties in 1896 nominated the most devout pair of presidential candidates in American history: Methodist Republican William McKinley and Presbyterian Democrat William Jennings Bryan. Two years later, McKinley, the winning nominee, ushered in a new phase of "manifest destiny" (a term then still in common use) when he reluctantly led the United States to war against Spain.

As the United States moved toward war, religious leaders followed the general trajectory of opinion with two notable variations. They worried less than businessmen about the domestic side effects and kept a watchful eye on the interests of their respective creeds. Even after the USS *Maine* exploded in Havana harbor, most urged caution, though some Protestant editors could not resist openly coveting Spanish colonies as mission fields. Catholics felt special misgivings because Pope Leo XIII was actively seeking a peaceful settlement. The church hierarchy and press found Protestants altogether too bloodthirsty. Despite his devout Methodism and opportunistic flirtation with the American Protective Association, McKinley was no more eager than Polk had been to start an anti-Catholic crusade. He made at least a show of pursuing papal mediation. Archbishop Ireland, McKinley's emissary to the Vatican, believed that patient diplomacy could have preserved the peace. Pressed by Republican hawks, however, the president decided on war in April 1898 and told Congress that intervention in Cuba was the duty of a "Christian, peace loving people."

Clergy and laymen outside of the peace churches joined in the patriotic surge. As had been the case with Mexico five decades earlier, Protestants frequently framed the war as a symbolic battle against the Spanish Inquisition and a few warned of treacherous Catholic soldiers. Catholics once again rallied to the flag, urged on by bishops who kept doubts to themselves. In the end, many citizens joined McKinley in viewing the quick victory with few casualties as a gift from God.

Nationalists in the Catholic hierarchy thought they saw a silver lining in the war clouds: now that the United States had clearly emerged as a world power, the American church would have to be respected by the Vatican and allowed to adapt to its special situation. The reaction in Rome was just the opposite. The U.S. military victory provided an additional reason, if any were necessary, for the Vatican to curb these bishops before their tolerance of democracy and religious pluralism spread to Europe. In 1899 Pope Leo XIII condemned an incipient "Americanist" heresy that challenged Vatican authority. Although the Pope did not explicitly accuse any churchmen of "Americanism," his encyclical signaled a turn toward tighter control over Catholic institutions and intellectual life in the United States.

With varying degrees of enthusiasm, the major Protestant denominations supported the wartime annexation of Hawaii and acquisition of Cuba, Puerto Rico, and the Philippines via the peace treaty. Except among white southerners, qualms about ruling nonwhites deemed unfit for citizenship were generally overshadowed by a sense of missionary duty. Congregationalists and Presbyterians expressed the fewest reservations; Methodists tended to trust their coreligionist in the White House on this issue.

Religious adversaries quickly exported their conflicts to the Philippines, the most Christian land in Asia. While Protestants viewed the overwhelmingly Catholic population as potential converts, Catholic editors asked with sarcasm if they planned to replicate the Hawaiian pattern of bringing disease and disruption. Catholics credited priests with protecting the indigenous population; Protestants portrayed "greedy friars" clinging to their estates. This controversy subsided after the McKinley administration negotiated with the Vatican to purchase the land. Another followed when the superintendent of the new public school system hesitated to hire

Catholics. On other fronts, Protestants assailed the army for distributing liquor, sanctioning prostitution, and acquiescing in polygamy among the Muslim minority.

These struggles for religious influence paled beside the squalid little war to defeat the Filipinos seeking independence. Yet only a handful of prominent clergy joined the antiwar movement. The Reverend Leighton Parks, a noted Episcopalian, repeatedly denounced atrocities committed by the American military. Although the Catholic hierarchy sought primarily to evade this controversy lest its church appear unpatriotic, Bishop John Spalding broke ranks to address an antiwar meeting. Protestant expansionists considered suppression of the insurrection a necessary evil on the way to spreading Christian civilization to Asia. The Philippines looked like an ideal base for capturing the great China market in souls.

During the late nineteenth century Christian missionaries, including the substantial American contingent, became the largest group of foreigners in China. Increasingly, too, they were subject to attack as flesh-and-blood symbols of Western intrusion. In 1900 the secret society of Boxers rose up to kill hundreds of missionaries and thousands of Chinese converts. An attack on the legation compound in Peking followed. A combined Western and Japanese military expedition marched to the rescue, engaging in murder, rape, and looting en route. A few missionaries joined in the looting; most at a minimum justified the brutality with the familiar contention that the Chinese only understood force.

The use or threat of force became commonplace during the administrations of Theodore Roosevelt and William Howard Taft. Indeed, both presidents illustrate that the American pursuit of world power required no evangelical Protestant motivation. Roosevelt was a pro forma member of the Dutch Reformed Church who may have doubted the existence of God and an afterlife. Yet no president sounded more fervent calls to enforce "righteousness." His endorsement of overseas missionaries was grounded in what he considered practicality. For example, he believed, mistakenly, that missionaries brought stability to China. Taft's Unitarian rejection of the Trinity elicited criticism from grassroots theological conservatives, but he felt none of his denomination's doubts about forcing American ways on others.

Taft's administration was marked by one of the most successful instances of religious activism in the history of American foreign relations: the campaign by Jews and their gentile allies to abrogate a Russian-American trade agreement that had been on the books since 1832. The State Department often investigated and sometimes politely complained about the anti-Semitic acts that increased abroad in the late nineteenth century. The motives behind these diplomatic initiatives were mixed: humanitarian concern; protection of American citizens; responsiveness to Jewish voters; and fears that victims of persecution would immigrate to the United States. The results were mixed, too. Benjamin Peixotto, a Jewish consul appointed to Bucharest in the 1870s, negotiated a temporary remission in Romanian anti-Semitism. The Russian situation grew steadily worse. In 1903 a pogrom in Kishinev left dozens of Jews dead while police stood aside. Similar outbreaks followed elsewhere. Still, the Russian government blandly rebuffed Roosevelt administration inquiries and refused to receive a petition of protest forwarded by Secretary of State John Hay. Nor would Russia guarantee the safety of visiting American Jews.

After discrete lobbying failed to secure action by Taft to revise or abrogate the commercial treaty, the American Jewish Committee (AJC) led an effective public mobilization. As had been the case with the Damascus blood libel persecution in 1840, anti-Semitism abroad inspired cooperation among American Jews, who were now more diverse in national background than ever before. The AJC stressed the "sacred American principle of freedom of religion." Amid widespread hostility to czarist autocracy, thousands of gentiles in civic organizations, state legislatures, and Congress joined the call for abrogation. In December 1912 the Taft administration informed the Russians that the treaty would be allowed to expire the next year.

During the two decades before World War I, religious leaders helped to build a new peace movement—a peace movement adapted to an era in which the United States assumed the right to enforce righteousness. Almost all participants in the proliferating peace groups shunned pacifism, a term just coming into general use, often as a slur; many celebrated American and Christian expansion as the best ways to assure global amity in the long run. They typically emphasized prevention of war between "civilized" countries through arbitration and international law. Although a handful of noted Catholics and Jews joined secular peace societies, the religious wing of the movement was overwhelmingly Protestant

and disproportionately modernist. For instance, the Federal Council of Churches of Christ in America (FCCCA), formed in 1908 by thirty-three liberal-leaning denominations, sponsored both the Commission on Peace and Arbitration and the Church Peace Union.

The notion that religion influenced the actions of President Woodrow Wilson and his first secretary of state, fellow Presbyterian William Jennings Bryan, is familiar to students of American diplomacy—too familiar. Standard accounts stress their respective religious styles, often in caricature, at the expense of substance. In fact, their lives illustrate the divergent responses to the Protestant intellectual crisis of their time. Equally important, their disagreement about World War I underscores the peril of tracing an unambiguous American conception of mission from John Winthrop's "city upon a hill" to the early twentieth century and beyond.

Both Wilson and Bryan felt some religious skepticism during their college years. Wilson's father, a modernist Presbyterian minister, urged him to cease worrying about doctrine and simply love Jesus. Thereafter, Wilson lived comfortably as a religious liberal, sometimes poking fun at orthodox assaults on Darwinism and at visions of hellfire. Along with other liberal Protestants, he saw the world improving under the amorphous guidance of "Divine Providence." With few exceptions—notably, his own election as president—he rarely credited God with direct intervention. As the "people's book of revelation," the Bible inspired human action to achieve high personal and social standards but contained little practical advice. Among the actors Wilson lauded were "my missionaries." Unlike Roosevelt, he sensed their role as agents of change rather than stability. China, a republic after the revolution of 1911, had been "cried awake by the voice of Christ," Wilson said.

Although Bryan followed the theologically conservative path, he was initially undogmatic on many doctrinal issues. For example, he corresponded with Leo Tolstoy, whose heterodox Christianity he thought compatible with his own conception of Jesus as the Prince of Peace. Like many of his fellow citizens, Bryan was torn between peace and world power. As secretary of state he both negotiated "cooling-off" treaties with two dozen countries and supported military intervention in the Mexican Revolution. Bryan resigned in 1915 because he considered Wilson's strictures on German submarine warfare a lapse from neutrality. Yet Bryan went beyond the secular crisis at hand to affirm a restrained sense of American mission at least as old as the president's internationalist activism. Rather than descending into European-style power politics, the United States should "implant hope in the breast of humanity and substitute higher ideals for the ideals which have led nations into armed conflict."

After Congress declared war in 1917, religious leaders supported the cause at least as strongly as did other elites. With customary flamboyance, conservative evangelist Billy Sunday declared that Christian pacifists should be left to the lynch mob and the coroner. Although usually less blunt, liberal Protestants maintained that German militarism must be destroyed as a prerequisite for international peace. With customary prudence the Catholic hierarchy stepped carefully from neutrality to "preparedness" to patriotic cooperation. Cardinal Gibbons dutifully forwarded Pope Benedict XV's peace proposals to the White House, fended off plausible allegations of a papal tilt toward the Central Powers, and headed an interfaith League for National Unity. All of the major denominations mobilized to offer religious and social services to their men in uniform. Churches and synagogues conducted war bond drives and disseminated propaganda for the Committee on Public Information. Few discouraged the zealous rhetoric that sometimes did lead to the lynch mob and the coroner.

Grassroots skepticism was greater than might be inferred from the behavior of mainstream clergy and congregations. Pentecostals, still on the fringe of theologically conservative Protestantism, were especially unenthusiastic. Roughly 65,000 draftees claimed conscientious objector status; overwhelmingly, these men came from the peace churches. In the Selective Service System and in the courts, Jehovah's Witnesses fared worse than the less strident and more familiar Quakers and Mennonites.

FROM VERSAILLES TO PEARL HARBOR

Missionaries, representatives of the Federal Council of Churches, and delegates from the newly formed American Jewish Congress converged on the Versailles peace conference in 1919. Like their secular counterparts, religious interest groups discovered that a humane international order was more easily promised than attained. The fate of Armenians in the disintegrating

---

★ ★ ★ ★

"THE PRINCE OF PEACE"

"Christ deserves to be called the Prince of Peace because He has given us a measure of greatness which promotes peace. . . .

"Christ has also led the way to peace by giving us a formula for the propagation of good. Not all of those who have really desired to do good have employed the Christian method—not all Christians even. In all the history of the human race but two methods have been employed. The first is the forcible method. . . .

"The other is the Bible plan—be not overcome of evil but overcome evil with good. And there is no other way to overcome evil. . . .

"In order that there might be no mistake about His plan of propagating good, Christ went into detail and laid emphasis on the value of example—'so live that others seeing your good works may be constrained to glorify your Father which is in Heaven.'
. . .

"It may be a slow process—this conversion of the world by the silent influence of a noble example, but it is the only sure one, and the doctrine applies to nations as well as to individuals. The Gospel of the Prince of Peace gives us the only hope that the world has—and it is an increasing hope—of the substitution of reason for the arbitrament of force in the settling of international disputes."

— *William Jennings Bryan,*
"The Prince of Peace" (1908) —

Ottoman Empire provided a brutal case in point. Protestant missionaries had tried unsuccessfully in 1894 and 1895 to secure Western military action to halt Turkish pogroms. They pressed their case again after the Ottoman government orchestrated the killing of hundreds of thousands of Armenians during World War I. Wilson rejected armed intervention but would accept Armenia as a U.S. mandate under the League of Nations mandate. Congress quickly dismissed this proposal.

No event associated with religion during World War I proved more consequential for U.S. foreign policy than the British promise in the Balfour Declaration to establish a Jewish homeland in

Palestine. The question divided Zionists and non-Zionists within Judaism. Reform Jews in particular thought a full-fledged state might prejudice their status as U.S. citizens. Protestant missionaries were adamantly opposed because they expected a hostile Arab reaction that would, in turn, disrupt their own efforts. According to Secretary of State Robert Lansing, Christians would resent control of the Holy Land by the "race credited with the death of Christ." Nonetheless, Wilson gave early and repeated support to the Zionist cause.

Ultimately, World War I changed American religion much more than religious beliefs or activities affected the conduct of the war or the shape of the peace. There were noteworthy organizational consequences. The Federal Council of Churches asserted itself as the premier voice of the de facto Protestant establishment. More convinced than ever of human sinfulness and Jesus's imminent return, theological conservatives founded the World's Christian Fundamentals Association (WCFA) in 1917. The National Catholic War Council, renamed the National Catholic Welfare Council (NCWC), remained in operation after the armistice. So did the American Friends Service Committee (AFSC) and the Fellowship of Reconciliation (FOR), which had been a haven for conscientious objectors and pacifist social gospelers.

Even more important, the emotional charge of the war and its offspring, the Red Scare of 1919 and 1920, fueled religious anxieties and animosities. The main clashes involved domestic issues, especially Prohibition, looser sexual mores, and the possibility of a Catholic president. Yet several domestic developments intersected with foreign policy. In 1924 the prevailing nativist zeitgeist eased passage of the Johnson-Reed Act, which sharply curtailed immigration. Amid a nationwide surge of anti-Semitism, the Foreign Service joined other elite institutions in rejecting Jewish applicants on the basis of their religion.

Except for strongly separatist sects, clergy and churchgoers still paid attention at least to some portion of the outside world. Although bitterly disappointed by the defeat of the Treaty of Versailles, liberal Protestants persisted in urging American affiliation with the League of Nations. A handful of social gospelers expressed cautious interest in the "Soviet experiment." Catholic clergy used their pulpits to denounce Mexican anticlericalism as well as atheistic communism. Influenced by a form of Bible prophecy called premillennial dispensationalism, fundamentalists became avid if unconventional students of foreign affairs. They found in Zionism fulfillment of the prophecy that the Jews would regather in the Holy Land shortly before Jesus's return and speculated that the Antichrist might be on earth already in the person of Benito Mussolini.

The evident decline of the Protestant missionary movement during the 1920s looks in retrospect like a pause and an adaptation to domestic and international trends. Few now thought that the world could be converted within a generation and some doubted the right to convert anybody. A Chinese student movement directed specifically against Christianity left many missionaries disheartened; others responded to rising Chinese nationalism by urging renegotiation of the "unequal treaties" granting special privileges to westerners. The modernist philosopher William Ernest Hocking, head of a layman's inquiry into missions that was completed in 1932, recommended against attacking "non-Christian systems" of thought. Theological conservatives in the major Protestant denominations felt no such qualms. Nor did Mormons, Seventh Day Adventists, and Jehovah's Witnesses, all of whom hoped to save at least some portion of humanity. Moreover, in 1912 the American Catholic Church finally authorized an overseas mission society, popularly known as the Maryknolls.

Thus, in religion as in commerce, the United States was not isolated from the rest of the world during the interwar era. What is usually misconstrued as isolationism is the pervasive belief that the United States must keep out of any future European war. This sentiment needed little encouragement to flourish, but no group encouraged it more actively than the Protestant clergy. Of 19,372 ministers polled by a pacifist magazine in 1931, 12,076 said they would never sanction a war. Few of these ministers were absolute pacifists themselves. Rather, most were making symbolic amends for their martial ardor in 1917 and 1918.

The coalition Franklin D. Roosevelt created during his presidency was as complex in its religious dimensions as in its explicitly political aspects—and foreign policy was central to the complications. Roosevelt himself was an Episcopalian with an uncomplicated faith in God and a genuine commitment to religious tolerance. His supporters included a large majority of Catholics and Jews, southern theological conservatives still loyal to the Democrats as the party of segregation, and a small but vocal minority of Protestant modernists attracted to the Soviet Union and the Popular Front. Opponents included a distinctive religious right. These Protestant and Catholic theological conservatives viewed the Roosevelt administration as a subversive conspiracy and some of them considered it the American arm of an international Jewish plot.

Roosevelt's strongly anticommunist Catholic constituency required constant attention. The hierarchy and press in particular opposed the president's recognition of the Soviet Union in 1933. The Good Neighbor Policy appealed as an entrée for the American church in Latin America, but complications soon arose. The administration seemed too neighborly to the Mexican revolutionary government, whose anticlericalism sometimes turned into outright persecution. Moved by ten thousand letters, a probable congressional investigation, and the approaching 1936 election, Roosevelt quietly urged Mexico to curb its anti-Catholicism.

When the Spanish Civil War broke out in 1936, Americans overwhelmingly favored neutrality and legislation banning arms sales to either side. The Catholic clergy pointedly preferred a victory by the insurgent general, Francisco Franco, despite his alliance with Nazi Germany and fascist Italy. Lay opinion was less monolithic. According to a Gallup poll in 1938, 42 percent of Catholics sided with the Spanish republic. Nonetheless, wariness of Catholic political power reinforced Roosevelt's decision in 1938 not to seek an end to the arms embargo, an action that would have benefited the loyalists. Meanwhile, liberal Protestants criticized Catholic priests for tilting toward Franco and far right fundamentalists discerned hitherto unobserved merit in the Roman church. Similarly, religious appeals, loyalties, and animosities affected the tone of the debate about American participation in World War II. In urging aid to the Allies in the 1939–1941 period, Roosevelt said—and perhaps half believed—that Germany planned to abolish all religions and create an international Nazi church. Even clergy, however, typically framed the argument in terms of geopolitics and general morality rather than religious ideas or interests. Protestant ministers who had recently vowed to stay aloof from any European war now endorsed administration policies that undermined neutrality. Nor was there a clear correlation between theology and foreign policy positions. For instance, the anti-Semitic radio priest Charles Coughlin, numerous far right fundamentalists, and the social gospelers at *Christian Century* magazine all chastised Roosevelt as he moved from efforts to repeal neutrality legislation in 1939 to undeclared naval warfare against German submarines in late 1941. After Pearl Harbor, the major denominations rallied to the flag. They did so with fewer rhetorical excesses than during 1917 and 1918, however, and some prominent mainstream Protestants remained pacifists.

As had been the case with the Spanish-American War and World War I, Catholics trod a distinctive path to the same patriotic destination. They feared from the outset that the European war would promote communist expansion; most also initially rejected aid to the Soviets after Germany invaded in June 1941. Here, too, clergy were less flexible than their parishioners. Responding with varying degrees of finesse, Roosevelt urged Joseph Stalin to ease restrictions on religion, professed to see signs of religious freedom in the Soviet Union, and tried to convince Pope Pius XII to soften his strictures against communism. Some bishops came around to the position that the Soviet people, as opposed to the regime, deserved help in their resistance to nazism. In striking contrast to the prudence of the World War I years, the hierarchy displayed its divisions in public. One bishop spoke under the auspices of the noninterventionist America First Committee, another joined the interventionist Committee to Defend America by Aiding the Allies, and several sniped incessantly at the president.

In December 1939, Roosevelt named Myron Taylor, an Episcopalian, as his personal representative to the Vatican. Roosevelt hoped simultaneously to court Catholic voters, establish a listening post in Rome, and influence papal pronouncements on the war. Taylor's mission had no significant impact on the pope but did reveal—and probably exacerbated—domestic religious tensions. Only a few Protestant leaders managed to express grudging acquiescence. On the whole, Roosevelt was accused of religious favoritism and chided for violating the First Amendment; theological conservatives discerned a capitulation to satanic popery.

No foreign policy question associated with religion has elicited greater controversy than whether or not more European Jews could have been saved from the Holocaust. American Jews denounced Adolf Hitler's regime from 1933 onward. Once again they found gentile allies—but not enough of them. The level of American anti-Semitism reached a peak during the interwar years. Limits on immigration were strictly enforced, often at the behest of anti-Semites in the State Department and the foreign service. Reports that the Nazis had begun to exterminate European Jewry were readily available by late 1942. The president was urged to bomb the death camps, announce plans to punish genocide, and extricate Jews from such inconstant Axis satellites as Romania and Bulgaria. The latter two tactics showed the most promise. Nonetheless, Roosevelt took no effective action until he created the War Refugee Board in January 1944. In short, even after the United States entered the war, greater effort could have saved hundreds of thousands of lives.

THE COLD WAR AND THE FIFTH GREAT AWAKENING

World War II catalyzed the revival evangelical Christians had been praying for since the 1920s. Like its four predecessors, this fifth Great Awakening reshaped religious life in unanticipated ways and influenced the relationship between faith and foreign affairs. Three aspects of the revival stand out. First, while modernist churches stagnated, theologically conservative Protestantism flourished, with Billy Graham leading one branch of the movement from fundamentalism toward a less separatist and less strident "evangelicalism." Second, Catholics grew more assertive and (especially after the Second Vatican Council from 1962 to 1965) more cosmopolitan. Third, the bulk of the awakening coincided with the Cold War, which officials from the White House on down described as a spiritual battle against "godless communism."

The relationship between Cold War faith and foreign policy is often misconstrued in ways comparable to clichés about the Wilson era. Once again, standard accounts render the religious beliefs of policymakers in caricature and postulate an unambiguous sense of mission from John Winthrop to John Foster Dulles. Despite his image as a Puritan avenger, Dulles himself was a theologically liberal Presbyterian who began in the 1930s to use the Federal Council of Churches as a convenient forum for publicizing his foreign policy prescriptions. Insofar as he became a dogmatic cold warrior by the time he was named secretary of state in 1953, Dulles was moved by Republican partisanship rather than religious doctrine.

Unlike Dulles, Reinhold Niebuhr applied serious religious ideas to foreign policy. Yet Niebuhr's image as the premier theologian of the Cold War needs refinement. In Niebuhr's view, because human beings are fallible and sinful (at least in a metaphorical sense), even their best actions fall short of altruism and yield ironic results. This "neo-orthodox" worldview is consistent with any number of conflicting positions on foreign policy. Indeed, without changing his theology, Niebuhr had moved from the pacifist Fellowship of Reconciliation to the interventionist Committee to Defend America by Aiding the Allies. In *The Irony of American History* (1952), he sounded more reflective than the typical Cold War ideologist. Applying neo-orthodox premises, he warned the United States against international arrogance and described communism and American capitalism as arising from the same "ethos" of egotism. Niebuhr was less dispassionate in day-to-day polemics against those whose skepticism about the Cold War exceeded his own. Moreover, valued for his intellectual reputation rather than his ideas, Niebuhr had no discernible impact while serving as a State Department consultant.

Religious interest groups, rather than serious religious ideas, did affect foreign policy. Yet here, too, we must beware of exaggerating their influence or their uniformity. For instance, while many in the missionary movement lobbied on behalf of Chiang Kai-shek during the Chinese civil war, others initially hoped to arrange a modus vivendi with the communists. Although a remarkable mobilization by American Jews nudged President Harry S. Truman toward quick recognition of Israel in 1948, prominent Reform Jews organized the American Council for Judaism to lobby against a full-fledged Jewish state.

The Catholic role in the Cold War especially needs to be extricated from folklore. Certainly priests, nuns, and lay leaders mobilized against international communism, particularly after Soviet satellites suppressed Catholicism in Eastern Europe. Yet, following a long tradition, non-Catholics overstated the church's power and understated the autonomy of its adherents. When Catholics joined in urging Italians to vote against communism in 1948, they were advancing Truman administration policy rather than vice versa. And contrary to legend, Cardinal Francis Spellman was not responsible for Ngo Dinh Diem's appointment as prime minister of the Republic of Vietnam.

On balance, international events between Pearl Harbor and the mid-1960s fostered increased tolerance as well as surface religious consensus. Partly as a reaction against Nazi genocide, anti-Semitism began a steady decline in the late 1940s. Ubiquitous invocations of the "Judeo-Christian tradition" not only legitimated Judaism, but also minimized differences within Christianity. Nonetheless, division and animosity persisted beneath the rhetorical conventions. The National Council of Churches, which superseded the Federal Council in 1950, appeared to be the authoritative voice of Protestantism, yet its leaders barely noticed the extraordinary revival among theological conservatives.

The tension between Catholics and Protestants was harder to ignore. Most clashes concerned such domestic questions as birth control and federal aid to education, but foreign policy was involved too. Yielding to Protestant complaints, Truman in 1951 abandoned his attempt to establish formal diplomatic relations with the Vatican. Senator Joseph McCarthy, the country's best-known Catholic politician during the early 1950s, provoked even greater controversy. Although their attitudes ranged from pride to disgust, Catholics disproportionately considered McCarthy an admirable anticommunist. His zeal furthered the rapprochement between the Catholic and Protestant political right begun during the 1930s. Conversely, prominent liberal Protestants considered McCarthy the latest personification of Catholic authoritarianism; some chided the church for failing to condemn him. Ironically, such attacks reinforced defensiveness among Catholics struggling to break out of their insularity. In 1960, John F. Kennedy proved that a cosmopolitan Catholic could be elected president. Equally important to his victory, however, Kennedy combined secular urbanity with wartime heroism and public commitment to winning the Cold War.

The next two decades revealed both the fragility of Cold War orthodoxy and the superficiality of the domestic religious consensus. Indeed, the collapse of the former during the Vietnam War hastened the deterioration of the latter. American escalation in 1965 not only reinvigorated the pacifist remnant that had survived World War II; in addition, between 1965 and 1970 roughly 170,000 draft registrants applied for conscientious objector status. In contrast to the Korean "police action," mainstream religious figures opposed the war. In 1966 prominent liberal Protestants and Jews took the lead in founding Clergy and Layman Concerned About Vietnam (CALCAV), a nondenominational coalition whose arguments against escalation usually echoed those of secular doves. Members ranged from

chastened cold warrior Reinhold Niebuhr to African-American social gospeler Martin Luther King, Jr. Ultimately, the Vietnam conflict widened the split between Protestant theological liberals and conservatives. Most evangelicals and fundamentalists either stood aloof from this worldly issue or supported American policy.

For the first time, numerous Catholics remained part of a peace movement after the United States entered a war. Indeed, the radical priests Daniel and Philip Berrigan became vivid symbols of nonviolent resistance for doves and hawks of all faiths. In 1968, when Eugene McCarthy and Robert Kennedy sought the Democratic presidential nomination as antiwar candidates, only strict fundamentalists worried about their Catholicism. In 1971 the bishops reversed their earlier endorsement of the war to advocate a "speedy" peace.

The Catholic left remained active following the war. By 1970 roughly half of all American Catholic missionaries served in Latin America, where many joined local clergy in opposing brutal dictatorships. Some of these priests and nuns—along with a few bishops—became proponents of "liberation theology," whose advocates adapted Marxist analysis and urged the church to champion the Third World poor.

Clearly, many Catholic liberals now felt sufficiently secure to risk accusations of disloyalty. Yet ironies abounded. These allegations often came from within their own church. Reversing the historical pattern, working-class Catholics pushed rightward by the turmoil of the 1960s often thought their priests too liberal. Liberals themselves came face to face with questions that had perplexed Protestants earlier in the century—for example, whether anyone should be converted from an ancestral religion. Finally, Catholics looked increasingly American to the rest of the country because they, too, were obviously divided among themselves.

In 1976 the two major political parties nominated the most devout pair of presidential candidates since McKinley and Bryan. Both Episcopalian Gerald Ford and Baptist Jimmy Carter considered themselves "born again" Christians. A competent lay theologian, Carter stands out as the only modern president whose foreign policy was affected by serious religious ideas. Simply put, he took to heart Niebuhr's warning against national egotism. Thus, within limits set by prevailing Cold War assumptions, Carter was distinctive in his calls for national humility, wariness of military intervention, and respect for poor and nonwhite countries. For a growing number of his constituents, stunned by the lost Vietnam War and wary of Soviet exploitation of détente, humility seemed a source of the country's diplomatic problems.

Many of Carter's harshest critics were moved by religious concerns. After helping him defeat Ford, evangelical voters discovered that Carter was theologically, culturally, and politically more liberal than they had thought. By 1979 clergy were organizing a militant minority of theological conservatives into a "new Christian right." Interested primarily in domestic issues, they routinely adopted the foreign policy prescriptions of staunch Republican cold warriors, with one important twist: the strong belief that Israel deserved special protection because it fulfilled the Biblical prophecy that Jews would regather in the Holy Land on the eve of Jesus's return. This philo-Semitic interpretation of Scripture was one aspect of the new Christian right that actually was new.

A Jewish political right began to form at roughly the same time, with deep concerns about foreign policy. As early as 1967, some Jews had begun to reconsider their political alliances when Protestant and Catholic liberals sharply criticized Israel's attack on Egypt. Then, Soviet limits on the emigration of Jews seemed to illustrate the failure of détente. Despite initial misgivings, Jewish groups rallied behind the Jackson-Vanik Amendment, which in 1974 denied most-favored-nation trade status to communist countries restricting emigration. Carter not only continued détente, but also pushed Israel harder than Egypt during the peace negotiations of 1978 and 1979. By that point, prominent Jewish intellectuals were helping to formulate an influential "neoconservative" critique of détente in general and Carter's diplomacy in particular. Losing to Ronald Reagan in 1980, Carter received only 45 percent of the Jewish vote.

Reagan never wavered in his conviction that God blessed America. Nor did he doubt the nation's mission—or his own—to end the Cold War by bringing down the Soviet "evil empire." A Protestant with a Catholic father and eclectic religious interests, he was well suited to manage a religious coalition as complex as Franklin Roosevelt's. In addition to moderate Protestants, the Republican base since the 1850s, his backers included Jewish neoconservatives as well as evangelicals and fundamentalists on the right. Furthermore, Reagan was the first Republican to win the Catholic vote twice.

Despite Reagan's frequent denunciations of communist evil before evangelical audiences, Catholics played a larger role in his Cold War diplomacy. No Catholic was more important in this respect than Pope John Paul II. The pope and the president coordinated efforts to weaken communism in Eastern Europe; their tactics ranged from public denunciations to covert Central Intelligence Agency funding of the anticommunist underground via the Vatican. When Reagan established full diplomatic relations with the papacy in 1984, Protestant theological conservatives in his coalition barely complained.

Cooperation across denominational lines also marked the opposition to Reagan's foreign policy. The grassroots movement to hold nuclear arsenals at their current levels—the "nuclear freeze"—became a powerful symbolic challenge to the administration's military buildup during the early 1980s. Advocates of the freeze included veteran pacifists in FOR and AFSC, theological liberals in Clergy and Laity Concerned (as CALCAV was renamed after the Vietnam War), and half of the Catholic bishops. Catholics were particularly active in providing humanitarian aid and opposing military intervention in Central America. Victims of rightist "death squads" in the El Salvador civil war included missionary nuns. While the U.S. Catholic Conference urged peace talks between the Salvadoran government and leftist rebels, numerous parishes assisted refugees who reached the United States. These actions were particularly impressive because Pope John Paul II gave de facto support to Reagan's anticommunist intervention in Central America.

By the 1990s the Cold War had ended but the effects of the fifth Great Awakening continued to be felt. In numbers, evangelicals, fundamentalists, and charismatics (as Pentecostals increasingly called themselves) constituted the religious mainstream. To an unprecedented degree, theological liberalism and conservatism correlated respectively with political liberalism and conservatism. Conservatives especially sponsored a resurgence of overseas missions; fifty thousand Americans lived abroad as missionaries or representatives of faith-based humanitarian organizations, often working closely with strong indigenous churches. To some extent the dream of the earliest missionaries had come true. At the end of the 1990s, there were 258 million Christians in Africa and 317 million in Asia.

Although references to the Judeo-Christian tradition lingered, use of this phrase to describe

American religious life was even more problematic than during the 1950s. Significant numbers of Muslims, Hindus, and Buddhists came to the United States after immigration law was liberalized in 1965. Astute political leaders took notice. President Carter denied any animosity toward Islam during the Iran hostage crisis of 1979 and 1980; President George H. W. Bush stressed the same point during the war against Iraq in 1991. Moreover, the appearance of yet another "new immigration" reinforced the American identity of those Catholics and Jews descended from earlier immigrants.

As Israel became both more secure and less central to their own identity, American Jews no longer felt obliged to defend all Israeli foreign policy. From the time President Carter negotiated the Camp David Accords of 1978 and the Egyptian-Israeli peace treaty of 1979, the United States served as primary mediator in what was called (with undue optimism) the Middle East "peace process." The Oslo Accords signed at the White House in 1993 established a quasi-independent Palestinian National Authority in territory contested by Israel and the Palestine Liberation Organization. As with Protestants and Catholics, Jewish approaches to foreign policy increasingly correlated with their religious beliefs. While Conservative and Reform Jews overwhelmingly endorsed negotiations in general and the Oslo agreements in particular, Orthodox Jews were skeptical or hostile. In 1998, President William Jefferson Clinton prodded the Israelis at the Wye River negotiations to surrender more disputed territory to the Palestine Authority. Once again, Conservative and Reform Jews responded favorably while Orthodox Jews joined Israeli hawks in opposition. Like Protestants and Catholics, Jews were now openly divided on a foreign policy issue.

The expansion of missionary activity overseas may have stirred increased persecution of Christian minorities around the world. Religious conservatives had no doubts about it and sought legislation mandating a diplomatic response. Humanitarian motives aside, these activists hoped to keep evangelicals and fundamentalists politically involved in the post–Cold War era. Furthermore, recalling the impact of the Jackson-Vanik Amendment, they thought religious freedom could be used to undermine Chinese communism. Still wary of imposing Christianity on non-Christian cultures, liberals hesitated to join the campaign. Even so, in 1997 and 1998, 100,000

Protestant and Catholic congregations sponsored annual days of prayer to "shatter the silence" about persecution. Ultimately, a broad coalition extending beyond the ranks of Christians and Jews supported the International Religious Freedom Act (IRFA), which passed Congress unanimously in 1998. The IRFA established an Office of International Religious Freedom in the State Department, a comparable position in the National Security Council, and an independent commission to monitor persecution.

Both the breadth of the coalition and the constitutional ban on preferential treatment of any religion required officials to concern themselves with small sects as well as large denominations, and with minor harassment as well as with serious violations of human rights. For instance, the commission's reports criticized European democracies for treating Seventh Day Adventists, Jehovah's Witnesses, and Scientologists (products respectively of the second, fourth, and fifth Great Awakenings) as second-class faiths. The chief concern, however, was the arrest, torture, or killing of believers, usually Christians but sometimes Muslims, too, in communist states and Islamic republics. American government responses ranged from public denunciations to behind-the-scenes diplomacy. No country attracted greater attention than the People's Republic of China, which persecuted both the Falun Gong, an indigenous mystical religion, and Christian churches unwilling to register with the government. Religious activists, including some Protestant liberals and the Catholic bishops, joined the unsuccessful campaign to deny China permanent normal trade relations status. Indeed, despite the passage of the IRFA, American policy toward religious persecution abroad in the early twenty-first century resembled that of the early nineteenth century: a mixture of popular protest and diplomatic inquiries without direct economic or military intervention.

CONCLUSION

Five generalizations can be made about the history of religion and foreign policy. First, notwithstanding the frequent, formulaic references to John Winthrop's "city upon a hill," the impact of Reformation era Protestantism is typically oversimplified and exaggerated. Appeals to an amorphous Providence and Enlightenment republicanism rather than invocations of a Puritan mission were the main motifs of nineteenth-century manifest destiny. Similarly, Presidents Thomas Jefferson and Theodore Roosevelt needed no Christian doctrine to bless their efforts to extend American power. Even those devout Protestants who tried to apply religious beliefs to foreign affairs not only disagreed about specifics, but also disputed the overall nature of the national mission. Although less often acknowledged than international Wilsonian activism, a visceral Bryanism—the sense that the United States should lead the world by separatist moral example—has been and remains a powerful force.

Second, religious beliefs and interests did not change the outcome of any first-rank foreign policy decision—for example, whether or not to declare independence, expand westward, develop an "informal empire" abroad, or fight a war. These factors, however, have affected the ways in which Americans framed and debated such major questions.

Third, religious concerns have influenced the outcome of some second-level foreign policy decisions. Abrogation of the Russian-American commercial treaty in 1912 and passage of the Jackson-Vanik Amendment in 1974 serve as cases in point. Awakenings and immigration have rendered "people of faith" increasingly diverse. In this pluralist context, religious interest groups have been most effective when they found allies outside of their own communities and invoked widely held American values.

Fourth, the role of missionaries merits special attention. As has been the case with businessmen and soldiers, a relatively small number of Americans were able to exert great influence—for good or ill—in a few distant lands. Missionaries not only facilitated political and economic expansion, either deliberately or inadvertently, but also inspired, educated, and infuriated foreign elites.

Fifth, major foreign policy decisions have affected domestic religious life more than the other way around. Often the effects were unanticipated. For instance, the revolutionary war with France undermined fears of "popery"; World War I exacerbated the multisided conflict among Catholics, Jews, Protestant modernists, and theological conservatives; and World War II sparked a religious revival that defied cosmopolitan predictions of secularization. These five general trends will probably persist for the foreseeable future, though with no diminution of ironic results.

BIBLIOGRAPHY

Abrams, Elliott, ed. *The Influence of Faith: Religious Groups and U. S. Foreign Policy.* Lanham, Md., 2001. Essays on the contemporary situation by authors from diverse ideological perspectives.

Ahlstrom, Sydney E. *A Religious History of the American People.* New Haven, Conn., 1972. Still the best one-volume survey.

Chatfield, Charles. *The American Peace Movement: Ideals and Activism.* New York, 1992. Historical survey from a sociological perspective.

Ehrman, John. *The Rise of Neoconservatism: Intellectuals and Foreign Affairs, 1945–1994.* New Haven, Conn., 1995. The best study of the neoconservatives and foreign policy.

Fairbank, John K., ed. *The Missionary Enterprise in China and America.* Cambridge, Mass., 1974. Excellent collection of essays with implications beyond China.

Feingold, Henry L. *The Politics of Rescue: The Roosevelt Administration and the Holocaust, 1938–1945.* New Brunswick, N.J., 1970. Still the most insightful study of Roosevelt's policy.

Field, James A., Jr. *America and the Mediterranean World, 1776–1882.* Princeton, N.J., 1969. Much material on missionaries.

Flynn, George Q. *Roosevelt and Romanism: Catholics and American Diplomacy, 1937–1945.* Westport, Conn., 1976. The standard work on the subject.

Fogarty, Gerald P. *The Vatican and the American Hierarchy from 1870 to 1965.* Stuttgart, Germany, 1982. Good coverage of the hierarchy's role in American politics and foreign policy.

Gribbin, William. *The Churches Militant: The War of 1812 and American Religion.* New Haven, Conn., 1973. The standard work on the subject.

Hall, Mitchell K. *Because of Their Faith: CALCAV and Religious Opposition to the Vietnam War.* New York, 1990. Standard account of the main religious group opposing the war.

Harrington, Fred Harvey. *God, Mammon, and the Japanese: Dr. Horace N. Allen and Korean American Relations, 1884–1908.* Madison, Wis., 1994. Biography of an important missionary and diplomat.

Hennesey, James. *American Catholics: A History of the Roman Catholic Community in the United States.* New York, 1981. Still the best one-volume synthesis.

Hero, Alfred O., Jr. *American Religious Groups View Foreign Policy: Trends in Rank-and-File Opinion, 1937–1969.* Durham, N.C., 1973. Good use of survey data.

Hunter, Jane. *The Gospel of Gentility: American Women Missionaries in Turn of the Century China.* New Haven, Conn., 1984. Fine social history with implications beyond China.

Jacobs, Sylvia M., ed. *Black Americans and the Missionary Movement in Africa.* Westport, Conn., 1982. An anthology that approaches the subject from varied angles.

Johannsen, Robert W. *To the Halls of the Montezumas: The Mexican War in the American Imagination.* New York, 1985. Places the religious response in broad cultural context.

Latourette, Kenneth Scott. *The Great Century in the United States of America A.D. 1800–A.D. 1914.* Volume 4 of *The Expansion of Christianity.* New York, 1941. Insightful pioneering work.

Marchand, C. Roland. *The American Peace Movement and Social Reform, 1898–1918.* Princeton, N.J., 1972. The best treatment of the Progressive-era religious peace movement is in chapter 9.

May, Ernest R. *Imperial Democracy: The Emergence of America As a Great Power.* New York, 1961. New edition, Chicago, 1991. Good on religious aspects of 1898 diplomacy.

Merk, Frederick. *Manifest Destiny and Mission in American History: A Reinterpretation.* New York, 1963. An astute essay on the varied conceptions of American mission in the nineteenth century.

Pierard, Richard V., and Robert D. Linder. *Civil Religion and the Presidency.* Grand Rapids, Mich., 1988. The best single account of the subject.

Piper, John F., Jr. *The American Churches and World War I.* Athens, Ohio, 1985. The standard work on the subject.

Pratt, Julius W. *Expansionists of 1898: The Acquisition of Hawaii and the Spanish Islands.* Baltimore, 1936. Chapter 8 is still a valuable analysis of religious opinion.

Ribuffo, Leo P. "God and Jimmy Carter." In his *Right Center Left: Essays in American History.* New Brunswick, N.J., 1992. The connection between Carter's Niebuhrian beliefs and his foreign policy.

Rosenthal, Steven T. *Irreconcilable Differences: The Waning of the American Jewish Love Affair with Israel.* Hanover, N.H., 2001. Thorough treatment of American Jewish attitudes toward Israel.

Sachar, Howard M. *A History of the Jews in America.* New York, 1992. Comprehensive survey.

Sarna, Jonathan. *Jacksonian Jew: The Two Worlds of Mordecai Noah.* New York, 1981. Biography of an important early diplomat and politician.

Silk, Mark. *Spiritual Politics: Religion and America Since World War II.* New York, 1988. Insightful essay on religion and politics.

Toulouse, Mark G. *The Transformation of John Foster Dulles: From Prophet of Realism to Prophet of Nationalism.* Macon, Ga., 1985. The fullest examination of Dulles and religion.

Welch, Richard E., Jr. *Response to Imperialism: The United States and the Philippine-American War, 1899–1902.* Chapel Hill, N.C., 1979. Good account of religious opinion and conflicts in chapter 6.

Wyman, David S. *The Abandonment of the Jews: America and the Holocaust, 1941–1945.* New York, 1984. A broad look at American attitudes.

See also COLONIALISM AND NEOCOLONIALISM; CONTINENTAL EXPANSION; CULTURAL IMPERIALISM; DISSENT IN WARS; IMMIGRATION; NATIVISM; PACIFISM; RACE AND ETHNICITY; WILSONIAN MISSIONARY DIPLOMACY.

REPARATIONS

★ ★ ★ ★

Carl P. Parrini and James I. Matray

If popular wisdom holds that prostitution is the oldest profession, and spying only a slightly younger occupation, then surely reparations—a country demanding payment or indemnity from another in land, goods, or money for damage inflicted as a result of war—also dates from a very early point in human history. Modern practice on indemnities or reparations has its origins in the late nineteenth century, when statesmen at Hague conferences in the Netherlands began to rewrite the rules for warfare, to limit armaments, to encourage peaceful settlement of international disputes, and, by such indirect means, to fashion a definition of what constituted "a just cause" for war. Indemnities or reparations as a concept developed from the idea that there were clear "laws of war" arising from treaties, conventions, and other international agreements. When in the course of warfare a nation, including all institutions legally subordinate to it, violated these legal norms and brought about "wrongful injury to life, body, health, liberty, property, and rights," that nation must make pecuniary indemnification to the injured persons. It is important to emphasize that in its origins, reparations was conceived of as indemnification for violations of existing international law, rather than for actions contrary to the current "moral" precepts of society.

Germany's Second Reich under Otto von Bismarck established a modern benchmark for indemnities when it collected nearly $1 billion from France in 1871, at the conclusion of the Franco-Prussian War. That same year, the Treaty of Washington provided for arbitration to settle U.S. claims against Britain for the destruction that Confederate privateers built in British shipyards had inflicted on Union merchant ships during the American Civil War. The United States at first requested not only indemnification for direct damages but also $8 million in "war prolongation claims" for all Union costs after the Battle of Get-

tysburg in 1863. The settlement provided for British payment of $15.5 million in *Alabama* claims, while the United States would pay $1.9 million for illegal wartime acts against Britain, such as property seizures and imprisonments. In 1885, France wanted an indemnity from the Qing dynasty to end its war against China, but later dropped the demand. Japan was not so lenient after its victory in the Sino-Japanese War of 1894–1895, extracting 200 million taels of silver from China in the peace treaty.

During 1900, the Boxer Uprising resulted in Chinese rebels killing the German minister and trapping the diplomatic legations of Japan and other Western nations, including the United States; foreign business people; and thousands of their Chinese servants and Christian converts in prolonged sieges at Tianjin and Beijing. After a multinational military force liberated the captives, China signed the Boxer Protocol, which required payment of an indemnity of $333 million to eleven nations. The American share was $25 million, but in 1908 Washington remitted all but $7 million to cover private damages. The U.S. government used the remainder to fund a program that sent Chinese students to schools in the United States. Meanwhile, Japan had won the Russo-Japanese War of 1904–1905 and wanted Russia to pay an indemnity. However, bowing to pressure from President Theodore Roosevelt, Japan dropped its monetary demand and accepted the southern half of Sakhalin Island. In 1907, when another conference convened at The Hague, the statesmen had not contemplated a long war that would result in the partial crippling of the economic life of nations. They had envisaged wars of short duration, in which the civilian economies of the belligerents would hardly be touched. But World War I would cause enormous destruction, shaking the foundations on which the "legal" conception of reparations was based.

THE VERSAILLES SETTLEMENT

The Great War was a total conflict of nation against nation, resulting in differential destruction of national social systems. It therefore changed the reparations question into an issue of apportioning the relative gains or losses from participation in the war. Because of the unexpectedly long duration of World War I, none of the belligerents could impose sufficiently large taxes to pay for their economic needs. Internal tax income proved too small to pay for necessary imports. Consequently, the Allies largely had financed the war in the United States through selling international investments and through first-year borrowing. Until April 1917, the British, and to a lesser extent the French, Russian, Italian, and Belgian governments, had borrowed by floating their bond issues through American bankers. The British loans were secured by the international investments of its citizens that the government had sequestered. As the war dragged on, it became clear to British leaders that the longer the conflict continued, the greater the probability that Britain would emerge from the war minus its international investment empire, the protection of which was one of the reasons it was fighting the war. In the view of Prime Minister David Lloyd George, the burden of war costs had somehow to be shifted to the Central Powers, so that Britain would be able to keep its international investments.

U.S. entry into the war in April 1917 presented the possibility to Allied leaders that the United States somehow could be made to bear some of the burden of the war costs. They accordingly began to shape reparations plans that would redistribute Allied war costs not only to Germany but also to American taxpayers and investors. With this ultimate intention in mind, the Allied efforts to impose war costs on Germany began on 5 April 1919, when Lloyd George asserted that Germany should stipulate in the peace treaty "her obligation for all the costs of the war." The United States opposed, on legal grounds, the inclusion of war costs in the reparations total, although, paradoxically and illogically, President Woodrow Wilson did agree that pensions for Allied soldiers, despite not being part of existing international legal definitions of reparations, and thus in no way "civilian damages," ought to be part of the total. In order to limit the amount that Germany would be required to pay, the United States made two broad proposals concerning the parameters within which reparations totals ought to be determined. First, no matter what the amount, Germany would be required to make payments for no more than thirty-five years. Second, a reparations commission would be set up to fix the amount that Germany would be able to pay.

American leaders assumed that these parameters would limit reparations demands to the surplus the German economy could produce, over and above what was necessary for a restoration of a level approximating the nation's living standards in 1914. On the other hand, the provision that thirty-five years be the longest period of payment allowable would roughly fix the total of reparations to be paid. These limits were intended to encourage Allied interest in restoring German economic life. At the Paris Peace Conference early in 1919, the chief American experts, Norman H. Davis and Thomas W. Lamont, suggested a maximum figure of roughly $28.5 billion, half in gold and the remainder in German marks. But Lloyd George and French Premier Georges Clemenceau pressed for a much higher amount. To prevent this disagreement from dividing the Allies, negotiators agreed to a compromise providing for creation of a reparations commission with responsibility to determine Germany's exact liability by May 1921. Veterans' pensions would be included, as Wilson had agreed, but in fact this would have an impact only on distribution, not on the final reparations amount. This decision to postpone determination of an exact amount and the terms of repayment resulted in the United States failing to gain either of its main objectives.

Superficially, the establishment of a reparations commission would seem to have been a victory for the American position. However, France insisted that the commission have no independent power to modify the length and amount of payment in accord with ability to pay. The French position, which prevailed, allowed the postwar commission simply to total up the claims and required at least fifty years of payment from Germany. Meeting its deadline, the commission in 1921 fixed Germany's total liability at about $33 billion. Of this total, approximately $11 billion was assessed to pay for all damaged Allied property. The rest represented war costs imposed by the victors as punishment for Germany's "war guilt" under article 231 of the Versailles Treaty. Under this provision, Germany accepted responsibility for "all the loss and damage to which the Allied and Associated governments and their nationals have been subjected as a consequence of the war imposed upon them by the aggression of Germany and her allies." By then, the U.S. Senate had rejected the League of Nations Covenant and the Treaty of Versailles to which it was attached. The United States therefore had withdrawn from the reparations commission and only had "observers" at its deliberations.

Close examination of the $33 billion in reparations reveals, however, that the amount was less than it appeared to be. The commission specified that about $11 billion of A and B bonds would be payable at 5 percent interest over thirty-seven years. The remainder, in C bonds, would bear no interest and would come due only when the commission determined that Germany's new Weimar Republic was able to pay. The Allies in fact planned not to collect on these C bonds if Washington canceled the war debts to the United States. The U.S. government resented this attempted coercion and refused to cancel all Allied war debts. Administration officials under Wilson and his successor, Warren G. Harding, also were appalled by both the totals fixed and the procedures designed to collect them. Starting with President Wilson, American leaders tried to use the war debts owed to the United States to coerce the European leaders into easing the German reparations burden, not least because the Allies presumably now would collect on the C bonds. Washington's scheme was essentially the same as the one Wilson proposed at Versailles. German reparations had to be based upon Germany's capacity to pay and the period of payment had to be shortened, so that eventually German economic health could be restored.

During negotiations at Versailles, Wilson, as an inducement to the Allies to change their position, offered to cancel that part of the war debts to the United States that the Allies actually had incurred in fighting the war, in exchange for a reduction in the amount of German payments and in the length of time Germany was expected to pay. From 1921 to 1924, Presidents Warren G. Harding and Calvin Coolidge honored Wilson's offer. But the Allies refused. Instead, they demanded that Washington cancel all the war debts, including that portion of what they had borrowed from the United States after the fighting ceased ($3.3 billion of the total of $10.3 billion) that had been used for reconstruction and for civilian commercial trading. Wilson's Treasury secretaries, Carter Glass and David Houston, refused general cancellation on the ground that the Allies already had distributed among themselves spoils of war, including special concession trading advantages, greater than the postwar commercial debts they had contracted with the United States. At first, their successor, Republican secretary of the Treasury Andrew W. Mellon, followed the same policy.

With hindsight, it became fashionable among west European and U.S. intellectuals to accuse American leaders of ignorance and even selfishness in connection with their stubborn refusal to acknowledge any link between the reparations and the war debts. The majority seemed to accept the French argument that the war against Germany was a common effort, in which the United States had belatedly done its small part by contributing its money. "Some gave their ships, some munitions, some the lives of their sons, some money," a member of the French Chamber of Deputies told his colleagues, "and today those who gave money come saying to us: 'Give back what we loaned.'" If the United States indeed had been in "alliance" by treaty or moral commitment with the west European allies, this would have been a telling argument. But Wilson genuinely had tried to stay out of World War I—as long as he could do so—without facing some sort of settlement changing the balance of power against the Allies. To avoid a German military victory of this sort, he had joined the war, but he did not do so on behalf of Allied war aims. He opposed the division of spoils outlined in the "secret treaties" and rejected every Allied effort to induce the United States to share in the booty of war. Wilson in this specific sense sought a "peace without victory," which would allow the vanquished to reenter the community of industrial-capitalist states without disabling prohibitions.

From Wilson's standpoint, World War I was a civil war within the social system of industrial capitalism. Its basic causes were political and economic rivalries over issues such as access to raw materials, foreign markets, and investment outlets, with the allies attempting to defend the existing apportionment of world market opportunities and the Central Powers challenging it. But in Wilson's view neither side had gained as much as it had lost, because the war aroused forces that challenged the very legitimacy of industrial capitalism as a system. In general terms, the Arabian, Chinese, and Bolshevik revolutions were outgrowths of the war; specifically, they reflected the fact that the people in the Third World were dissatisfied with the pace at which they were achieving self-determination and industrial development under the management of the advanced industrial nations. To Wilson, the political destabilization inherent in national revolution appeared to exacerbate the original problem of economic rivalries among industrial states by effectively withdrawing more resources and people from the world market. He believed that to protect, stabilize, and allow for the expansion of industrial capitalism as a social system in the future, leaders formulating the peace after World War I had to establish a peace that would avoid another world war and possible future national revolutions.

FROM DAWES TO DEFAULT

After World War I, the United States struggled to persuade European leaders to accept its definition of just amounts and terms for reparations payments. Presidents Harding and Coolidge, like their predecessor Wilson, applied a criterion in evaluating the different reparations payment proposals that reflected their view of its potential impact against war among industrial states and revolution in the Third World. They were certain that the high reparations required of Germany would militate against the rapid recovery of its economic and political life. Because they knew Germany was the industrial "power plant" of Europe, its slow recovery would retard that of eastern Europe. Narrowed world markets would reignite the kind of trade wars that had in great part caused World War I. At the same time, a failure to return Germany to equality among nations rather quickly would tend to inflame nationalist tendencies in that country. Far more frightening was the prospect of Bolshevik ideology gaining popularity among the German people, especially after the Soviet Union had established the Comintern in 1919 to promote a global communist revolution.

From the standpoint of the United States, the closed trade doors and special privileges arranged among the Allies would set in motion trends toward stagnation, if not contraction, of world markets. While it was true that closed doors and special-concession organization of world markets would tend to diminish both the share and the volume of world trade enjoyed by the United States, and so were against the immediate as well as the long-run interests of the United States, such policies were also against the long-run interests of industrial capitalism as a social system. It was true that Britain, France, Italy, and Belgium would achieve a larger share of world trade in a slowly growing global market under a regime of closed doors and special concessions, but the total volume of growth would be much smaller than under an open door regime—where each nation had equal opportunities to use its capital, technicians, and technology. However, it was also true that the total volume of goods and services available to satisfy the demands of competing domestic interests in the industrial states and of economic developers in the Third World would be greater in an open door world.

American leaders refused to cancel the war debts entirely in order to try to obtain an "expansionist" direction for the postwar world economy. This meant that the United States rejected a program for priority reconstruction of the victors, and instead pushed for priorities that would give the most economic growth for the whole system. It utilized war debts to press the victors to accept a "business-based" set of criteria providing for maximum efficiency of resource utilization. At any time that Britain and France were willing to accept such a businesslike "composition," the United States was willing to negotiate and make concessions in which it would give equivalent for equivalent. This was shown in 1922, when the U.S. Congress created the World War Foreign Debt Commission to set terms for the Allies to fund their borrowing, requiring an interest rate of at least 4.25 percent and repayment over twenty-five years with no reduction in principal. Britain, in the Balfour Note, stated that it would collect from its debtors only what was necessary to pay Washington. After prolonged haggling, the United States was forced to moderate its stand; the Coolidge administration canceled up to 80 percent of some nations' war debts. Thirteen countries agreed in 1926 to repay the lower amounts over sixty-two years at an average of 3.3 percent interest.

After 1926, U.S. and European leaders continued to disagree about the justice of these payments and the propriety of linking reparations to war debts. Meanwhile, the Allies expected the Weimar Republic to comply with the terms for payment of reparations, thereby financing reconstruction of their economies. But Germany refused to raise the taxes necessary to pay, allowing spiraling inflation to destroy the value of the mark. After a series of partial postponements, the Germans defaulted in January 1923. France and Belgium responded with joint occupation of the Ruhr Valley in an attempt to force Germany to devote its total surplus to reparations payments.

German workers organized passive resistance, and the Weimar Republic suspended all payments. These events provided an early indication of how in Germany political problems surrounding payment of reparations dominated economic ones. German refusal to comply with Allied demands, combined with the U.S. government's veto of projected reconstruction loans by the House of Morgan to France, on the ground that the French government had not yet settled its war debts to the United States, forced France and the other European powers to agree to convene a conference of business experts, with the Chicago banker Charles G. Dawes serving as chairman and with the task of settling the reparations according to U.S. standards.

Beginning in January 1924 and ending in September of that year, the conference worked out a system that U.S. delegates believed was based on Germany's ability to pay. In addition to measures for currency stabilization, the Dawes Plan provided for reductions in payments and, under very special circumstances, actual suspension of payments. Certain German revenues, to include taxes on alcohol and tobacco and railroad and budget revenues, were earmarked specifically for reparations payments. Furthermore, Weimar was not made responsible for obtaining the foreign exchange necessary to make the annual payments. Most significant, American and British bankers made a $200 million loan to enable German production to expand and reparations payments to begin. From 1924 to 1929, additional loans to Germany meant that net capital flow ran toward Germany. Foreign lending was responsible for a major transfer of wealth toward Germany that exceeded the amount of reparations and war debts. The total amount of reparations that the Dawes Plan imposed on Germany was not excessive, consuming between 5 and 6 percent of annual national income. Germany in fact maintained a higher standard of living than its production justified for the rest of the decade.

Subsequent to the Dawes agreements, German reparations payments to the Allies rose gradually. Germany's production also expanded. But what troubled the U.S. agent general for reparations payment, Seymour Parker Gilbert, was that most loans initially went for public works, unemployment relief, and investment in sectors with excess capacity, such as agriculture, textiles, and steel. Thus, the loans made no commensurate increase in Germany's ability to earn foreign exchange. While American officials objected to how Weimar was using the money, U.S. private bankers continued to extend loans to Germany, expecting profitable returns. German politicians hoped that increasing loans would work as a lever on the U.S. government, because, they believed, the more money Germany owed to U.S. banks, the more pressure Washington would place on the Allies to reduce reparations. This system could be sustained until German industry was essentially reconstructed, which came late in 1927. But then Germany's needs changed. Its heavy industry required new markets if it was to continue to expand. Germany's inability to find these markets revealed the major flaw in the Dawes Plan conception, which had envisioned a far more rapid development of world markets than actually occurred. Pointing to the necessity to deal with its inability to continue to balance foreign payments, the Weimar Republic requested a revision of the Dawes Plan. But Germany in fact resented paying even its already reduced reparations levy, viewing this as an act of national humiliation.

In recognition of the fact that the world market had not expanded as rapidly as the "Dawes planners" had expected, a new committee of experts on German reparations was formed to meet in Paris on 11 February 1929 to revise the Dawes Plan. General Electric Company executive Owen D. Young, one of the major architects of the Dawes Plan, was designated chair. Out of this meeting emerged the Young Plan, which scaled down the final amount of German payments again, reducing the amount by roughly 20 percent to $8,032,500,000 and making it payable over 58.5 years at an interest rate of 5.5 percent. An additional agreement placed limits on the length of German payments at 36.5 years, but this was dependent upon the organization of the Bank for International Settlements. In addition to functioning as a "trustee" for reparations payments, the new bank was supposed to provide financial facilities for making development loans, which planners thought would contribute to world market expansion. For the last twenty-two years of reparations payments, the profits of the new bank were used to make reparations payments. No nation was fully satisfied with the Young Plan. Reflecting the unhappiness in the United States, Secretary of the Treasury Ogden Mills complained that it "tied debts and reparations together," and thus ratified "the principles of the Balfour Note."

For various reasons, the Bank for International Settlements never functioned as a worldwide development bank. The new investment

---

★ ★ ★ ★

THE TREATY OF VERSAILLES, 28 JUNE 1919

Article 231 of the 400-article Treaty of Versailles placed responsibility for World War I on Germany. Articles 232 and 235 addressed the issue of German reparations.

Article 231   The Allied and Associated Governments affirm and Germany accepts the responsibility of Germany and her Allies for causing all the loss and damage to which the Allied and Associated Governments and their nationals have been subjected as a consequence of the war imposed upon them by the aggression of Germany and her allies.

Article 232   The Allied and Associated Governments recognize that the resources of Germany are not adequate, after taking into account . . . other provisions of the present Treaty, to make complete reparation for all such loss and damage.

The Allied and Associated Governments, however, require, and Germany undertakes, that she will make compensation for all damage done to the civilian population of the Allied and Associated Powers and to their property during the period of the belligerency of each. . . .

Germany undertakes . . . as a consequence of the violation of Treaty of 1839, to make reimbursement of all sums which Belgium has borrowed from the Allied and Associated Governments up to November 11, 1918, together with interest at a rate of five percent. . . . This amount shall be determined by the Reparation Commission. . . .

Article 233   The amount of the above damage for which compensations to be made by Germany shall be determined by an Inter-Allied Commission, to be called the *Reparation Commission. . . .*

This Commission shall consider the claims and give to the Germany Government a just opportunity to be heard.

The findings of the Commission as to the amount of damage defined as above shall be concluded and notified to the German Government on or before May 1, 1921, as representing the extent of that Government's obligations.

The Commission shall concurrently draw up a schedule of payments prescribing the time and manner for securing and discharging the entire obligations within a period of thirty years from May 1, 1921. If, however, within the period mentioned Germany fails to discharge her obligations, any balance remaining unpaid may, within the discretion of the Commission, be postponed for settlement in subsequent years, or may be handled otherwise in such manner as the Allied and Associated Governments . . . shall determine.

Article 234   The Reparation Commission shall after May 1, 1921, from time to time, consider the resources and capacity of Germany, and, after giving her representatives a just opportunity to be heard, shall have discretion to extend the date, and to modify the form of payments . . . in accordance with Article 233; but not to cancel any part, except with the specific authority of the several Governments represented upon the Commission.

Article 235   In order to enable the Allied and Associated Powers to proceed at once with the restoration of their industrial and economic life, pending the full determination of their claims, Germany shall pay in such instalments . . . as the Reparation Commission may fix . . . the equivalent of 20,000,000,000 gold marks. Out of this sum the expenses of the armies of occupation subsequent to the Armistice of November 11, 1918, shall first be met. . . . The balance shall be reckoned towards liquidation of the amounts due for reparation.

---

markets it was to create did not appear. Markets for capital goods and the growing capital surpluses they represented never came into existence. The amount of capital investments going into default became too great for the system to sustain. As world trade contracted, the means of settling payments globally disintegrated. On 16 June 1931, President Herbert Hoover proposed a one-year moratorium on payment of both reparations and

war debts. He was still hopeful that some way could be found to reexpand the world economy in order to prevent the development of nationalist autarky. But after 1931, each industrial nation began to erect trade barriers to its domestic markets by means of tariffs and discriminatory administrative procedures, and combined these with export offensives based on government subsidies and currency depreciation. As a result, reparations payments never resumed after Hoover's moratorium ended. At Lausanne, Switzerland, in 1932, the Allies canceled them altogether, subject to a final token payment that the Germans never made. Except for Finland, European nations also defaulted on their war debts to the United States.

Franklin D. Roosevelt, who became president after defeating Hoover's bid for reelection, rejected an international solution to world economic problems then being considered at the London Economic Conference of June–July 1933. The movement toward nationalist autarky that he thereby accelerated prevented any reconsideration of a settlement on war debts or reparations. It later became fashionable to lay responsibility for the world depression, economic nationalism, the rise of Adolf Hitler, and World War II not only on high tariff rates in the United States, but also on the American refusal to equate war debts with reparations, and hence agree to the cancellation of war debts in exchange for a reduction of German reparations payments. These criticisms are without much merit. The key point that such critics make is that the burden of war debts caused the world economic crisis and the rise of "Hitlerism." Their argument ignores the reality that German financial policies and eventual defaults were mainly the product not of U.S. actions but of the political weakness that was a structural component of the political economy of the time. Weimar's fragmented polity, combined with the emotionally charged symbolic issues of war guilt, reparations, and nationalism, meant that following significantly different policies to prevent insolvency would have been highly unlikely, if not impossible.

Nor were Germany's reparations and loans solely responsible for creating the economic crisis that led to the international instability of the 1930s and the eventual outbreak of World War II. There were deeper causes. From 1924 to 1927, when the underlying condition for the economic crisis took shape, Germany had three possible avenues for stabilizing its foreign trade and payments. First, it could export directly to reparations receivers such as France and Belgium. Second, it could export its capital goods to the Third World for development purposes. And third, it could export to the Soviet Union. As a practical matter, all three of these alternatives were not open by 1927. Direct exports to reparations receivers would tend to interfere with employment in those countries, and so were not welcome. Export of capital goods to the Third World was not really possible—except for Latin America, where German industry could not compete very successfully with the United States, and China, where prolonged civil war by and large blocked economic development—because most of the Third World was under the control of the Allied victors, who discouraged the export of German capital goods to their colonies and semicolonies to preserve them as monopoly markets for their home industries. Extensive exports of German heavy industrial goods to the Soviet Union were blocked by the unofficial but effective U.S. government embargo on long-term American financing for developing Soviet socialized industry.

Since new outlets for German heavy industry did not appear in the world market, Germany began to invest American banking loans in an economically wasteful fashion. Bankers lent to German states and municipalities, which used these funds for projects designed to bring about more social consumption, such as municipal beautification, parks, sports stadia, hotels, public bathhouses, and roads of little or no productive utility. Investments of this sort did not provide goods or marketable services that could be used to defray the costs of the borrowed foreign capital. But the irony was that the United States, with the Dawes loans, spent an amount in excess of what the Germans paid in reparations. Germany transferred a total of 16.8 billion marks to the Allies while receiving 44.7 billion in speculative mark purchases and loans that it never repaid after the Great Depression brought down the international monetary system in 1931. President Hoover was not entirely wrong when he claimed that economic forces originating in Europe had shattered the U.S. economy, although his critics at that time ridiculed him for attempting to avoid blame for the economic collapse. While Hoover shares responsibility for the Great Depression, President Roosevelt failed to make any effort to protect the equity of American bondholders. His embrace of the anticreditor mood of the era meant that Germany was able to default on its war debts, resulting in U.S. investors paying "reverse reparations."

COMPLICATIONS OF COLD WAR COMPENSATION

When American, British, and Soviet leaders began to grapple with the problem of war debts and reparations resulting from World War II, they had the benefit of the World War I experience. Instead of granting simple war loans, the U.S. Congress authorized the president in March 1941 to enable any country whose defense he defined as vital to the United States to receive arms, other equipment, and matériel "by sale, transfer, exchange or lease." Lend-lease aid to Britain, China, and the Soviet Union made possible a clear separation of wartime economic aid, reparations, and reconstruction credits. The Allies created a reparations commission at the Yalta Conference of 4–11 February 1945. Under Soviet pressure, the United States and Britain agreed that a figure of $20 billion would be the starting point for discussions about Germany's new reparations obligation. The Soviet Union would receive half of that amount. But at the Potsdam Conference in July 1945, President Harry S. Truman opposed Soviet efforts to collect reparations from current output until Germany exported enough to pay for imports to feed its labor force and fuel its industry. He was following the advice of Secretary of State James F. Byrnes, who was acting in accordance with his understanding of the negative impact of the reparations dispute on European reconstruction and world economic and social stabilization in the 1920s, but was unaware that only U.S. loans had made possible German reparations payments.

By the time of the Potsdam Conference, Germany's unconditional surrender in May 1945 had left the United States, Britain, France, and the Soviet Union with separate zones of occupation in the defeated nation. Even before Potsdam, Soviet occupation forces had begun to dismantle and transport whole German industrial plants to Soviet territory. The Soviets also designated special factories to produce exclusively for them. Moreover, Moscow kept the services of four million German prisoners of war and demanded forced labor from those living in its occupation zone. In general terms, the Soviet Union acted after World War II much as France had after World War I. It wished to reconstruct its own economy and to retard the reconstruction of Germany, both to stabilize itself and to prevent the stabilization of Germany. A destabilized Germany would remain militarily weak and the Soviet Union would become militarily strong. Moscow saw that large reparations taken quickly would facilitate both these objectives. U.S. leaders already had decided that imposition of large-scale reparations on Germany would retard postwar European economic recovery. During 1946, they concluded that without surplus production, the western zones of Germany would become a vast relief camp dependent on U.S. aid.

Concerns about German postwar economic recovery had not stopped the United States from developing plans and organizations late in World War II for conducting industrial espionage and seizing useful patents in chemicals, machine tools, and other technologically advanced industries in Germany. Operation Petticoat and Operation Paperclip sought to acquire German equipment, scientific research, and technical information of both military and industrial value, not only in hopes of shortening the war against Japan, but also for postwar economic advantage. Britain and France conducted similar operations, no doubt justifying exploitation of German industry, science, and technology as legitimate reparations. Subsequently, in the Harmssen Report of 1947–1951, the city of Bremen's economic minister calculated the total value of the information that the Western Allies secured at $5 billion. Citing this report, Soviet Foreign Minister Vyacheslav Molotov set the final amount of German intellectual reparations, including the Soviet portion, at $10 billion. British, French, and U.S. officials disputed these numbers then and thereafter. Also, defenders of the seizures later would point out that Germany looted French companies, practiced slave labor, expropriated possessions of concentration camp victims, and extracted tribute from the countries it occupied.

Discord between the Allies over reparations contributed to starting the postwar Soviet-American Cold War. Devastated by World War II, the Soviet Union insisted upon major reparations payments from Germany to hasten economic recovery. Consequently, Soviet Premier Joseph Stalin proposed that the Ruhr Valley industries be administered jointly by the Soviet Union and the three Western powers to secure reparations from the Western-controlled portions of Germany. The United States and Britain rejected this proposal, revealing the growing differences on matters of priorities to be observed in European reconstruction. Washington increasingly suspected that the Soviet Union's wish to strip Germany, and to slow European reconstruction, meant it wanted to dominate the balance of power in Europe. This negative view of Soviet intentions seemed to be confirmed by Moscow's refusal to accept the U.S. invitation to participate in the Marshall Plan, which was designed to solve the problem of European reconstruction on a joint Europe-wide basis. After considering the matter, Stalin decided to reject the offer, largely because this would have required the Soviet Union to reveal the secrets of its economic capacity. Furthermore, the Marshall Plan would have meant priority for west European reconstruction over that of the Soviet Union, as well as that the east European countries would be linked economically to western Europe, functioning largely as raw material suppliers.

Once the Soviet Union rejected participation in the Marshall Plan, the logic of its situation was to organize East Germany and other areas of Eastern Europe along lines allowing it to seize resources for its own reconstruction. Between 1947 and 1956, Moscow took large reparations from East Germany and much of Eastern Europe, probably far more than the $10 billion it had demanded at Yalta. Based on its experience with France in the controversy over German reparations following World War I, the United States must have expected that the Soviet Union would fail in its effort to achieve unilateral reconstruction based on reparations forcibly taken. Since France had no choice but to withdraw from the Ruhr in 1923 and accept U.S. conditions for European reconstruction, American leaders believed the Soviet Union would ultimately have to give up its domination of Eastern Europe. But what had worked against France in 1922–1923 did not work against the Soviet Union in the Cold War period. The Soviet Union and France were two dissimilar political economies. Because it engaged in state trading and had long been denied supplies for its industry by the Western industrial states, the Soviet Union was in effect isolated from the major impact of the world market. Unlike France after World War I, it had made its unilateral system of reparations collection in East Germany and much of Eastern Europe a sufficient base for its own reconstruction and for its strategic, political, and economic control of Eastern Europe to the Elbe River.

Acting on the same assumptions that guided its policy toward Germany, the United States did not collect reparations from Japan. But the nations victimized by Japanese aggression in World War II demanded compensation immediately after the conflict ended. In Tokyo, the Far Eastern Commission began discussions on how to meet these demands in the fall of 1945. Early in 1946, President Truman named Edwin W. Pauley as special ambassador, with instructions to conduct a fact-finding mission for recommendations on Japanese payment of reparations. Made public in April 1946, Pauley's plan provided for transferring to the devastated nations of Asia all Japanese industrial equipment beyond that needed to maintain Japan's prewar living standard. Japanese leaders criticized the plan as both unduly harsh and impractical. General Douglas MacArthur, the supreme commander of Allied powers and head of the U.S. occupation, agreed that the imposition of reparations would delay, if not prevent, Japan's economic recovery. Many American officials in Tokyo and Washington shared his concern. By the fall of 1946, as Soviet-American relations deteriorated in Europe, serious doubts about Pauley's plan arose in the War and State departments.

Early in 1947, the United States adopted the containment policy. This would lead to implementation of the "reverse course" in U.S. occupation policy toward Japan. Its objective was to create an economically powerful and friendly Japan that would be the cornerstone of a postwar U.S. policy in Asia to block Soviet-inspired communist expansion. While the United States abandoned Pauley's plan, the nations serving on the Far Eastern Commission were deadlocked over the complex question of how best to distribute the required reparations equipment. The War Department first commissioned several reevaluations of the reparations and economic policy that resulted in a two-thirds reduction of the demands. During May 1949, the United States broke the stalemate by unilaterally terminating all demands for reparations payments. The Philippines strenuously objected, compelling Washington to include in the 1951 Japanese Peace Treaty an article providing that Japan negotiate and pay reparations in goods and services to any former victim of its aggression that demanded compensation. Japan's government and its business community would make a virtue of necessity after U.S. occupation ended in May 1952. They pursued a successful strategy for establishing friendly and productive relations with its former imperial conquests that utilized reparations payments to help reopen East Asian markets and regain access to raw material sources in Southeast Asia.

After regaining its sovereignty, Japan negotiated a series of agreements providing consumer goods and industrial equipment, often tied to economic assistance and loan programs, with the Philippines, Burma, Indonesia, and South Vietnam (after the division of Vietnam in 1954). Controversy in Japan surrounding alleged government-business collusion in awarding reparations contracts prolonged the talks, but separate agreements finally were reached with all four countries. In November 1954, Burma gained $200 million over a term of ten years, and in March

1963 supplementary payment of $140 million paid over twelve years. In May 1956, the Philippines accepted $550 million in reparations over a term of twenty years, and the agreement with Indonesia in January 1958 provided for payment of reparations of $223 million over twelve years. South Vietnam in May 1959 accepted $39 million over a term of five years. These four nations received an additional $707.5 million in the form of loans. Cambodia and Laos accepted "free technical aid" rather than formal reparations. Under these agreements, recipient nations agreed to provide Japan with necessary raw materials. In addition, receipt of economic aid often required purchase of Japanese manufactured goods, contributing significantly to Japan's economic recovery and later expansion, especially in its steel, shipbuilding, and electronics industries.

Japan did not pay reparations to China after World War II because of the outcome of the civil war in that country. Under pressure from the United States, the Japanese did not recognize the People's Republic of China. This precluded negotiations regarding reparations with the Chinese communist government, and the Republic of China, in exile on Taiwan, could not make claims because that island had been part of the Japanese empire. South Korea demanded that Japan pay $8 billion in reparations for gold and art objects taken from Korea, forced labor, and lost Korean investments during forty years of Japanese imperial rule and brutal colonial exploitation of the Korean peninsula after 1905. After protracted negotiations beginning in 1952, Tokyo and Seoul finally signed in June 1965 the Treaty of Basic Relations Between Japan and the Republic of Korea, which provided for Japan's commitment to extend to South Korea's government $200 million in long-term, low interest loans, $300 million in goods and services over ten years, and $300 million in commercial loans to promote the development of South Korea's economy. Meanwhile, Japan had established and developed quasi-official contacts with North Korea, resulting in expanded trade that in 1964 reached $30 million. By that year, Japan had paid over $1 billion in reparations and $490 million in economic assistance to Burma, Indonesia, South Korea, Malaysia, Laos, Cambodia, and South Vietnam.

In August 1990, Saddam Hussein launched an invasion of Kuwait. The United Nations then authorized the United States to organize military action to liberate Kuwait if Iraqi forces refused to withdraw. The Gulf War during January and Feb-ruary 1991 resulted in Iraq inflicting tremendous destruction on Kuwait, including its oil wells. After Saddam's surrender, the UN Security Council in April passed Resolution 687 to impose punishment on Iraq. One of its provisions stated that Iraq was liable under international law for all direct loss, damage (including environmental damage), and the depletion of natural resources, or injury to foreign governments, nationals, and corporations, as a result of Iraq's unlawful invasion and occupation of Kuwait. No concrete plan for collection emerged, because the resolution also called for measures to restrict Saddam's ability to produce weapons of mass destruction. Accordingly, Iraq was prohibited from selling oil until it met the cease-fire conditions. But Saddam increasingly engaged in defiance and deceit to avoid full compliance with the resolution. The UN inspectors ultimately left Iraq in protest and new U.S. air strikes failed to alter Iraq's behavior, let alone revive any expectation of reparations payments. The Gulf War showed the supremacy of international power over international law.

REPARATIONS AND GROUP REMEDIATION

There were occasions in the twentieth century when the United States paid reparations or considered doing so. In 1903, President Theodore Roosevelt provided indirect assistance to a group of conspirators who staged a rebellion in Panama that resulted in the secession of this province from Colombia. His motivation was to help create an independent nation in Panama that would then sign a treaty authorizing the United States to build a canal across the Isthmus of Panama. Roosevelt succeeded, but embarrassment over the incident and hopes for oil concessions caused Congress in 1921 to approve payment of a $25 million indemnity to Colombia, satisfying a demand it first had made in 1914. A similar situation existed in Hawaii, where many natives believed that the United States played an unethical role in conspiring with white American businessmen to stage a rebellion during 1893. Although the United States did not annex Hawaii at that time, its actions eventually led to the overthrow of Hawaii's last monarchy. In August 1988, the U.S. House of Representatives held hearings on a proposal for payment of reparations to native Hawaiians. But in the end, native Hawaiians had to be satisfied with only an official apology that

Congress extended in November 1993 for U.S. actions in helping end Hawaiian home rule.

Much more controversial was the issue of whether the United States should pay reparations for the destruction that military operations inflicted on Vietnam during the Second Indochina War. In January 1973, as part of the Paris Peace Agreement, the Nixon administration agreed to provide North Vietnam with $4.75 billion in aid for economic reconstruction. This was intended as an inducement to respect the terms of the accord, but Hanoi was determined to reunite the country and achieved success in April 1975. Two years later, when President Jimmy Carter sought the establishment of diplomatic relations, the Socialist Republic of Vietnam made the payment of reparations at least equivalent to the amount of the promised reconstruction aid a condition for normalization. The House of Representatives, in a quick and angry response to perceived blackmail, voted to forbid aid, reparations, or payments of any kind to Vietnam. By contrast, a decade later, the United States paid compensation when it accidentally shot down an Iranian civilian airliner over the Persian Gulf. These differing outcomes revealed how the principle of reparation for damages had not been firmly set in international law. In 2000, the United States chose not to pay reparations to the families of South Korean civilians that U.S. soldiers had killed at No Gun Ri during the first weeks of the Korean War.

During the years after World War II, specific groups of people have made claims to reparations for a variety of transgressions. The Federal Republic of Germany, for example, voluntarily paid reparations to Israel for the policies and actions of the Nazi government that inflicted unspeakable suffering upon individual Jews. During the 1990s, U.S. World War II veterans who had been prisoners of war in Germany filed suit against Daimler-Benz and other firms to gain damages for German industry's ruthless exploitation of them as slave laborers. These demands gained legitimacy from a definition of reparations as an "act or process of making amends," usually by "giving compensation to satisfy one who has suffered injury, loss, or wrong at the hands of another." Consistent with this broader definition, in 1983 the U.S. Congress passed a remediation (remedy) law for Japanese Americans whom the U.S. government had put into internment camps during World War II. It provided for Congress first to pass a joint resolution, signed by the president, "which recognizes that a grave injustice was done and offers the apologies of the nation for the acts of exclusion, removal, and detention." Second, it granted official pardons to Japanese Americans convicted for violating orders to evacuate. Third, it created a foundation for educational and humanitarian purposes. Last, and most important, Congress established a $1.5 billion fund for the payment of reparations to survivors of the internment camps.

Remediation for Japanese Americans revived African-American demands to receive reparations for enslavement. Despite various legislative and legal attempts to redress the legacy of American slavery after 1865, large-scale payment of reparations never had gained widespread support in the United States as a viable option for indemnification. In 1989, Representative John Conyers, an African-American Democrat from Michigan, introduced in the House of Representatives legislation to allow African Americans to achieve remediation. It failed to pass then and again in 1991. But in February 1993, the first National Reparations Awareness Day program in Detroit presented strategies for accomplishing indemnification. Legal action, while not expected to succeed, was endorsed as a powerful symbol of white group responsibility for slavery that would set the stage for passage of remediation legislation once a favorable political context emerged. In 2001, at the National Reparations Conference in Chicago, activists argued that an honest reckoning of American history showed "the difficulty of transcending race without some attempt to repair the damage done by racial slavery and the structures of racism erected to justify it." That demands to indemnify the descendants of American slaves extended into the twenty-first century demonstrated that the principle of reparations for damages had not been firmly established either in U.S. domestic or international law.

BIBLIOGRAPHY

Bower, Tom. *The Paperclip Conspiracy: The Hunt for the Nazi Scientists.* Boston, 1987. Discusses Operation Paperclip, which brought German scientists to the United States, despite the involvement of many in Nazi war crimes.

DeConde, Alexander. *A History of American Foreign Policy.* 3d ed. New York, 1978. Provides succinct summaries of the terms of U.S. agreements that involve reparations prior to the Versailles Peace Treaty.

Falkus, M. E. "The German Business Cycle in the 1920's." *Economic History Review* 27 (1975). Argues that net declines in foreign investment in Germany in 1928 and 1929 contributed to the onset of the Great Depression.

Finn, Richard B. *Winners in Peace: MacArthur, Yoshida, and Postwar Japan.* Berkeley, Calif., 1992. Provides a well-researched and reflective study of the occupation that covers the deliberations of the Far Eastern Commission and reparations.

Gimbel, John. *Science, Technology, and Reparations: Exploitation and Plunder in Postwar Germany.* Stanford, Calif., 1990. Documents how after World War II the United States supervised a comprehensive and systematic intellectual reparations program to exploit German scientific and technical know-how.

Kent, Bruce. *The Spoils of War: The Politics, Economics, and Diplomacy of Reparations, 1918–1932.* Oxford and New York, 1989. Contends that the Allies were fully aware from the start that Germany could not pay the large reparations they demanded, but followed this policy as a way to silence calls for increased taxes to reduce government debt or finance expanded social programs.

Keynes, John Maynard. *The Economic Consequences of the Peace.* New York and London, 1919. Contains an excellent analysis of why the reparations settlement worked out at Versailles was bound to fail.

Leffler, Melvin C. "The Origins of Republican War Debt Policy, 1921–1923: A Case Study in the Applicability of the Open Door Interpretation." *Journal of American History* 59 (1972). Explains how domestic public opinion and administration, as well as congressional, views of American fiscal problems, complemented efforts of U.S. leaders to manipulate reparations to create an expansionist world market structure.

Link, Werner. *Die Amerikanische Stabilisierungspolitik in Deutschland, 1921–1932.* Düsseldorf, 1970. Demonstrates that American, and to a lesser extent British, bankers insisted on reversal of French reparations policy as the major key to U.S. investment in Germany.

Magee, Rhonda V. "The Master's Tools, from the Bottom Up: Responses to African-American Reparations Theory in Mainstream and Outsider Remedies Discourse." *Virginia Law Review* 79 (1993). Traces failed efforts after 1865 to gain compensation for African Americans, in land or money, for damages resulting from American slavery.

McNeil, William C. *American Money and the Weimar Republic: Economics and Politics on the Eve of the Great Depression.* New York, 1986. Explains how attracting and allocating foreign loans following the approval of the Dawes Plan became the center of conflict between German political factions and between the Allies and Germany.

Moulton, Harold G., and Leo Pasvolsky. *War Debts and World Prosperity.* New York, 1932. Although covering events only up to 1932, this is still the most useful account of the complex interrelationships among reparations, war debts, tariff structures, and the requisites of an expanding world economy.

Parrini, Carl P. *Heir to Empire: United States Economic Diplomacy, 1916–1923.* Pittsburgh, 1969. Shows that reparations were linked to war debts, and that the United States used war debts to force the European powers to modify the reparations settlement, and tried to find a place for Germany in an expanding world market without displacing other industrial states.

Rhodes, B. D. "Reassessing Uncle Shylock: The United States and the French War Debt, 1917–1929." *Journal of American History* 55 (1969). Asserts that the U.S. government maintained a moderate approach to war debts.

Rix, Alan. *Japan's Economic Aid: Policy-Making and Politics.* New York, 1980. Examines Japan's postwar foreign aid decision-making process.

Schaller, Michael. *The American Occupation of Japan: The Origins of the Cold War in Asia.* New York, 1985. Places the occupation within the context of overall postwar U.S. security strategy in East Asia from 1945 to 1950.

Schuker, Stephen A. *American "Reparations" to Germany, 1919–33: Implications for the Third-World Debt Crisis.* Princeton, N.J., 1988. Asserts, in a revisionist argument reflecting the new international history of the 1920s, that, contrary to the view of John Maynard Keynes, the reparations bill assigned Germany in 1921 was not unreasonable, but in fact reflected a measure of rough political justice.

Temin, Peter. "The Beginning of the Depression in Germany." *Economic History Review* 24

(1971). Contends that the impact of the reparation payments on investment in Germany had no relationship to the onset of the Great Depression there.

Trachtenberg, Marc. *Reparation in World Politics: France and European Economic Diplomacy, 1916-1923.* New York, 1980. Examines the reparations dispute after World War I from the French perspective.

U.S. Senate Committee on the Judiciary. *Loans to Foreign Governments.* Senate Document no. 86. Washington, D.C., 1921. A collection of correspondence on war loans, war debts, and reparations.

U.S. World War Foreign Debts Commission. *Combined Annual Reports of the World War Foreign Debt Commission with Additional Information Regarding Foreign Debts Due the United States.* Washington, D.C., 1927. Contains much of the correspondence between the U.S. Treasury Department and the British and French governments.

See also ALLIANCES, COALITIONS, AND ENTENTES; COLD WAR ORIGINS; FOREIGN AID; INTERNATIONAL LAW; LOANS AND DEBT RESOLUTION; SUMMIT CONFERENCES.

REVISIONISM

★ ★ ★ ★ ★

Athan G. Theoharis

The term "revise" is defined by the *Oxford English Dictionary* as "to re-examine or reconsider and amend faults in." This definition describes the process by which historians have consistently reconsidered and improved upon what had once been standard, often unquestioned interpretations of past events, movements, and personalities. A number of factors ensure this process: new information acquired through research into recently accessioned documents; the posing of new questions; the utilization of new and at times more sophisticated methods derived from disciplines such as psychology, anthropology, or sociology; the exploitation of new research tools such as the computer; the relative detachment provided by chronological distance from the particular event under study; or new insights gained from the impact of seminal thinkers.

Interpretations of American foreign relations have not escaped this process of revision. Virtually every major American diplomatic problem—for example, Jay's Treaty, the War of 1812, the Monroe Doctrine, the Mexican War, the Spanish-American War, World War I, isolationism, World War II, the Cold War, and the Vietnam War—has been subject to such reconsideration and reexamination. During the 1950s and 1960s, for example, the study of American foreign relations underwent a far-reaching change in focus with the emergence of the "realist" school. Robert Osgood, in *Ideals and Self-Interest in American Foreign Relations,* interprets Wilsonian diplomacy from a perspective based on considerations of national self-interest and international power relations; Paul Schroeder, in *The Axis Alliance and Japanese-American Relations,* applies "realist" principles to the study of the Roosevelt administration's diplomacy on the eve of World War II; and John Gaddis, in *The United States and the Origins of the Cold War,* similarly assesses the Roosevelt and Truman administrations' conduct of foreign relations during the 1940s. More recently, some historians of American foreign relations have applied the insights of multiculturalism and postmodernism to argue for a distinctly different approach to the study of war and diplomacy. The cumulative impact of these differing approaches has compelled students of American foreign relations to examine policy decisions from these perspectives. Since the 1950s, consequently, diplomatic historians have no longer been interested solely in questions involving state-to-state relations and international law, and have emphasized as well questions of power, rationalism, gender, race and ethnicity, bureaucracy, and the role of organized interest groups. The term "revise" clearly describes this historiography.

Yet, to adopt so literal a definition of revisionism does not clarify. As Warren Cohen points out in *The American Revisionist,* historians of American foreign relations have employed this term to describe "a number of men who, after one or both world wars, took upon themselves the task of persuading the American people to change their view of the origins of those wars and of the reasons for American intervention in them." Cohen's study, published in 1967, failed to account for three other groups of historians, the vast majority of whom began to publish after 1967 and who wrote instead about the origins of the Cold War, the reasons for the U.S. defeat in the Vietnam War, and the growth of the "national security state." Broadened to include these groups, Cohen's definition classifies a diverse group of writers, all of whom have discussed the processes leading to, and the consequences of, U.S. involvement in international conflict but who nonetheless differ in their emphases and conclusions.

Cohen's definition, however, while distinguishing these writers from others who have revised other historiographical issues (the coming of the Civil War, the Progressive Era), does not identify the particularity of "revisionist" historiography. Using Cohen's definition, historians like Osgood, Schroeder, and Gaddis could be classified as "revisionists." They challenged what were once standard interpretations of U.S. involvement in wars and were no less interested in "persuading the American people to change their views." Osgood, Schroeder, and Gaddis, however, have not been classified as "revisionists," not because their conclusions were widely accepted but because they share perspectives with the majority of those writing about the American diplomatic past.

Revisionist historiography can be distinguished from other works of revision because its practitioners go beyond a reexamination of specific events and decisions. Instead, the revisionists challenge the assumptions held by more conventional historians about how policy is formulated and justified, about whether the executive branch is responsive to public opinion, and about the ideas and sources of official foreign policy. The common themes of revisionist historiography are those of executive independence, the mendaciousness or secretiveness by which policymakers develop public support for particular decisions, the betrayal of the nation's democratic ideals, and an implicit (in certain cases, explicit) criticism of the principal ideas and priorities that determine official policy. The revisionists do not accept the rhetoric of policymakers at face value, and tend to perceive proclaimed idealism as masking less noble, if not sinister, purposes. More basically, the revisionists share a set of assumptions that the foreign policy decisions that led to both world wars and the Cold War or opposition to the Vietnam War were not the result of public demand, and were shaped by the priorities and (for some) the disloyalty of policymakers. To accept the assumptions of the revisionists is to locate American involvement in international conflict not in the narrowing of available options by international developments but in internal factors and in conscious (or, for some, unthinking) choice.

In portraying policymakers as manipulators of public opinion and U.S. involvement in international conflict as the consequence of presidential decisions or of the insidious influence of special interest groups, the revisionists have challenged the conclusions of traditional historians (for example, Gaddis and Schroeder) who view public opinion as unduly constraining the development of a realistic foreign policy. These conclusions, however, are assumptions more than descriptions of reality. We know little about how

or whether public opinion has shaped foreign policy. When referring to public opinion, most historians have frequently focused on elite opinion. From his interviews with State Department personnel during the 1960s, the political scientist Bernard Cohen, for example, established that when it was formulating policy, the foreign policy bureaucracy was not motivated to ascertain public opinion and viewed the public as an object to be manipulated or cajoled. There remains a need to ascertain even what constitutes evidence of public opinion. Recent studies suggest the need for greater caution when commenting on the public's influence on foreign policy.

The revisionist focus on elites and questioning whether official policy responds to the public's interests does not mean that the revisionists constitute a monolithic school. A further qualification is required. The revisionists' basic critique of the nature and sources of U.S. diplomacy and the methods by which government officials have conducted policy constitutes their principal commonality. Revisionists otherwise differ in their emphases and conclusions.

The revisionists can be classified into five broad schools: World War I, Right revisionism, Left revisionism, Vietnam revisionism, and national security revisionism, divisions reflecting both philosophical differences and the events commanding their attention. The subject matter of the World War I revisionists is obvious; the Right revisionists focus on the origins and consequences of World War II; the Left, Vietnam, and national security revisionists focus on different aspects of the Cold War. In an important sense, however, World War I revisionism created the intellectual climate and perspectives from which Right revisionism emerged. Some of the themes of World War I revisionism also appear in Left and national security revisionism. Right revisionists, moreover, can be classified as World War II revisionists, and their main themes underlie Vietnam revisionism. In contrast, although Left and national security revisionists focus on the Cold War, they differ in emphases and focus—the former on the origins and the latter on the consequences of the Cold War. In addition, the Right revisionists' conclusions about U.S. involvement in World War II indirectly shaped their analyses of the Cold War, while Vietnam revisionists endorse orthodox interpretations of the Cold War and the Right revisionist conspiratorial perspective on the reasons for harmful foreign and military decisions.

Revisionist historiography has also been influenced by three seminal thinkers writing about U.S. foreign policy—Harry Elmer Barnes on World War I and Right revisionists, William Appleman Williams on Left revisionists, and Charles Austin Beard on both Left and Right revisionists. These writers have not influenced either Vietnam or national security revisionists. The time of their writing and the degree to which their work was shaped by contemporary politics or research into recently accessible primary sources are factors underpinning the differences among the revisionists. The Right revisionists' conclusions about the origins of World War II derived in part from archival research documenting U.S. involvement in World War I and in part from their reaction to President Franklin D. Roosevelt's conduct of domestic and foreign policy during the 1930s and 1940s. For the Left revisionists, U.S. policy during the 1960s, particularly the Vietnam War, combined with research into recently accessible primary sources, shaped their conclusions about the origins of the Cold War. In contrast, Vietnam revisionists responded to the anticommunist analyses underpinning the debate over the Vietnam War and to Left revisionist interpretations of the Cold War, while national security revisionist interpretations were shaped by the unprecedented release of formerly classified Soviet and U.S. records and new public concerns about the consequences of secrecy and centralization on privacy rights and constitutional safeguards.

WORLD WAR I REVISIONISM

Harry Elmer Barnes   To a generation accustomed to a globalist foreign policy, large defense budgets, and foreign military-assistance pacts and involvement, the postwar reaction to World War I might seem perplexing. Almost immediately after the end of that conflict, after having accepted this as a "war to end all wars" and "to make the world safe for democracy," and the portrayal of the Germans as "barbarous Huns," many Americans became disillusioned with the war's consequences and began to reappraise what had been unquestioned beliefs about the nation's proper international role. Harry Elmer Barnes was one such American. He had written propaganda tracts for the American Defense Society and the National Security League during the war that extolled the morality and necessity of U.S. participation to defeat Germany.

Influenced by Sidney Fay's article "New Light on the Origins of the World War, I. Berlin and Vienna, to July 29," published in the *American Historical Review* (1920), which demonstrated the inequity of the Versailles Treaty's war guilt clause, Barnes reassessed those judgments he had helped to popularize during the war years. In a series of book reviews and articles published during the 1920s, he questioned whether Germany was solely responsible for the war and called for a multicausal conception of responsibility. These themes were summarized in his important study *Genesis of the World War* (1926), a book that the publisher Alfred Knopf solicited on the basis of a series of articles Barnes had published in *Christian Century*.

In *Genesis of the World War*, Barnes argues that the revisionist interpretation was the "correct one" and that his book demonstrates the "dishonesty and unreliability of diplomats and statesmen." Conceding Germany's partial responsibility for the outbreak of World War I, Barnes also chronicles French, Russian, and Serbian culpability. The errors of men, the irrational consequences of nationalism, the influence of propaganda, and the economic interests of munitions makers combined to provide the catalyst for war. Barnes reiterated these themes in the foreword he wrote for H. C. Engelbrecht and F. C. Hanighen's influential *Merchants of Death* (1934), contending that the authors had not singled out the armaments industry but the "broader forces, such as patriotism, imperialism, nationalistic education, and capitalist competition, [which] play a larger part than the armament industry in keeping alive the war system."

Focusing on the outbreak of the war in Europe, Barnes discusses only peripherally the factors leading to U.S. involvement in 1917. Just as he challenged the conventional view of German war guilt, representing the German invasion of Belgium as the precipitating event, but not the real cause, of a general European war, so Barnes debunks the then conventional wisdom that German submarine warfare was the basis for U.S. involvement. He argues instead that "unneutrality, lack of courage, or maladroitness of the Washington authorities in regard to English violations of international law . . . produced German submarine warfare that actually led us into war."

Mistakes in judgment, emotionalism, and unthinking patriotism, and not any threat to the national interest (whether defined in economic or strategic terms), were the bases for war. Believing that war was the consequence of myopia, and thus was avoidable, Barnes particularly emphasizes World War I's harmful legacy. It had not extended democracy or ensured against future wars, but had undermined world order and stability. Detailing but one of these revolutionary consequences, Barnes describes the war's "most unfortunate reaction upon the British Empire by stimulating nationalistic and independence movements everywhere."

Barnes's writings impelled other historians to consider these conclusions. His polemical tone, based on a conviction that this was no mere academic exercise, but involved the vital issue of war and peace, shaped his general approach to the study of war and his optimism that this research and writing could prevent the recurrence of war.

By the end of the 1930s, the dominant interpretation of World War I was that of the revisionists. In part, their writings provided a rationale for congressional enactment of the Neutrality Acts of 1935–1937. Yet despite this success, the United States would once again become involved in a major world war. This factor, as much as his conclusions about the causes and consequences of World War I, shaped Barnes's response to the debate precipitated by President Franklin D. Roosevelt's successful efforts of 1937–1941 to alter the nation's foreign policy course, first from one of neutrality to one of aid to Great Britain and the Soviet Union, and then to involvement as a cobelligerent.

World War II had a searing effect on Barnes. He was far less confident that he was speaking from a majority position, and the tone of his works after 1944 was more defensive and alienated. During the post–World War II period, Barnes also abandoned the multicausal approach characteristic of his writings on World War I. Instead, he attributed U.S. involvement in that later conflict to President Roosevelt's duplicitous conduct of the nation's foreign relations.

Central to Barnes's analysis was the conviction that the national interest did not require that the United States go to war. Quite the opposite; involvement in war would undermine national security and create continuous tensions that would inevitably ensure a militarized society. Minimizing German responsibility for World War II, as he had for World War I, in the introduction he wrote for *Perpetual War for Perpetual Peace,* Barnes bluntly claimed: "Sane internationalism is one thing; it is something quite different to support our entry into a war likely to ruin civiliza-

tion merely to promote the prospects of a domestic leader, however colorful or popular, to satisfy the neurotic compulsions of special interests and pressure groups, and to pull the chestnuts of foreign nations out of the fire." Presidential duplicity had been only one of the themes (and not a central one) in his earlier writing—witness his critical comment on the dishonesty and unreliability of statesmen and diplomats. Minimized in, if not totally absent from, Barnes's post–World War II writing, were his earlier emphases on competitive nationalism, emotionalism, and economic interest.

Resurrecting the correctness of the revisionist interpretation of World War I, Barnes attributed U.S. involvement in World War II partly to the decisions leading to that earlier conflict. World War I and U.S. involvement in that conflict, he argued, constituted "an ominous turning point" in American and world history. Barnes then returned to the principal theme of his writings about World War I: the war's disastrous consequences. He emphasized that both wars had inevitably resulted in "the rise and influence of Communism, military state capitalism, the police state, and the impending doom of civilization."

Barnes continued these themes in a later, more detailed study of how the nation became involved in World War II: "Pearl Harbor After a Quarter of a Century," published in 1968 in the right-wing libertarian journal *Left and Right.* He then emphasized still another theme: the truth about U.S. involvement in World War II was not more widely known owing to the "blackout" and "blurring" resorted to by "court historians," publishers, and book reviewers.

By the 1950s, Barnes had abandoned the qualifications underpinning his dogmatic analyses of the 1920s for the posture of an aggrieved proponent and seeker of the truth. In his earlier writing, he was convinced that research, thoughtful analysis by experts, and publication could avert war's recurrence. This confidence and these themes were virtually absent from Barnes's more conspiratorial and defensive analysis of World War II. There was a simpler explanation: the power and principles of President Roosevelt. This shift in tone coincided with and contributed to the emergence of a more restrictive revisionism that could properly be labeled Right revisionism.

Charles Austin Beard Unlike Barnes, Charles Beard had not been greatly concerned during the 1920s about German war guilt or the process by which the United States became involved in World War I. He first focused on foreign policy matters during the 1930s and 1940s and concentrated thereafter on U.S. involvement in World War II. Beard's published works on American foreign policy of the 1930s, however, differed markedly in tone and emphasis from his writings of the 1940s.

Although sharing Barnes's critical views on the uses of propaganda and the role of special interest groups in shaping U.S. foreign policy, Beard's analyses of the 1930s were broader and less conspiratorial. What particularly distinguished Beard from Barnes were his interests in the evolution of a more interventionist foreign policy and in the conceptions of national interest held by important political leaders. Unlike Barnes's more narrowly political and personalist approach, Beard's was more broadly cultural and economic. In this sense, Beard did not view certain men as culprits, war as irrational, and education as sufficient to avert undesirable developments. The principal themes of his writing on American internationalism were that an interventionist foreign policy was an outgrowth of domestic affairs more than of foreign developments, and that foreign policy decisions were the product of particular values that reflected the interests of powerful special economic interest groups. This was not, however, simply an economic interpretation of foreign policy decisions. Beard was interested in understanding the relationship between social and economic change and politics, and he denied that particular responses were foreordained. There were alternative policy options, but the specific direction that a nation pursued was based on its established national priorities.

In addition, Beard emphasized that "official foreign policy is always conducted by a few persons. . . . In this respect, democracies may differ little from dictatorships." Not representing policymakers as manipulators or as acting contrary to the national interest in his writings of the 1930s, Beard explored how the national interest (and hence foreign policy) was conceived and formulated. Foreign policy, moreover, could not be understood as a separate process; international involvement had far-reaching consequences both for republican principles and for reform. In *Open Door at Home*, Beard stressed the "control" that governments could exercise over domestic policies and national priorities. From these findings he offered a specific recommendation: "The argument thus far advanced is directed to the proposi-

tion that an efficiently operated commonwealth offers the best escape from the crisis in economy and thought in which the American nation now flounders."

In a different sense than Barnes, Beard advocated a restrictionist foreign policy. His recommendations, like those of Barnes, were rejected. Between 1937 and 1941, the Roosevelt administration successfully altered the noninterventionist stance of the American public and Congress. Beard became an active participant in the resultant debate over the wisdom of a course that risked involvement in an ongoing foreign war. After 1939 his writings became increasingly polemical. No longer directly assessing the intellectual framework within which the national interest came to be formulated, whether in *Giddy Minds and Foreign Quarrels* or *President Roosevelt and the Coming of the War,* Beard moved closer to Barnes's focus on the actions of particular individuals and to the duplicity of policymakers. His discussion increasingly centered on the rhetoric and policy decisions of President Franklin D. Roosevelt.

Beard's post–World War II books contrasted the disparity between President Roosevelt's rhetoric and reality. In a highly moralistic tone, Beard argues in *President Roosevelt and the Coming of the War:* "President Roosevelt entered the year 1941 carrying moral responsibility for his covenants with the American people to keep this nation out of war—so to conduct foreign affairs as to avoid war." Roosevelt had not followed that course while, at the same time, publicly minimizing the risks of his policies. In conclusion, Beard pointedly questions the consequences of this abuse of power: "Was it within the legal and moral competence of President Roosevelt in 1941 so to conduct foreign affairs as to maneuver a foreign country into firing a shot that brought on war—indeed to make war on his own authority?"

In his later years Beard no longer emphasized the domestic sources of foreign policy decisions, whether economic interest or value choices. By then he had become concerned principally with process issues: how the conduct of foreign policy affected a system of checks and balances and constitutional liberties. This, and not simply moral fervor or partisanship, shaped his historical writing. In combination, Beard's later writings and those of Barnes gave rise to the decidedly more intemperate Right revisionism of the post–World War II period. Yet, while the essays in *Perpetual War for Perpetual Peace* (1953) were dedicated to Beard, their intellectual debt was to the Beard of the 1940s. His earlier, more sophisticated emphases on intellectual attitudes and economic influence, through the writings of William Appleman Williams, during the 1960s gave rise to Left revisionism, which focused less on U.S. involvement in World War II than on the origins of the Cold War.

1930s Revisionism   Articulating themes suggested or emphasized by Barnes and Beard, other independent scholars during the 1930s examined the process leading to U.S. involvement in World War I. In contrast to the revisionist accounts published during the 1920s, the revisionism of the 1930s focused on the question of how the United States abandoned a neutrality policy to become involved in war in 1917. Revisionist writers of the 1930s concurred that U.S. involvement was neither necessary nor realistic, and thus that war could have been avoided. They also believed that those who had made policy (except former Secretary of State William Jennings Bryan and, with certain qualifications, President Woodrow Wilson) were shortsighted. Most policymakers (U.S. ambassador to London Walter Hines Page; President Wilson's influential adviser Edward House; Bryan's successor as secretary of state, Robert Lansing), they concluded, were Anglophiles and acted in ways contrary to the national interest. A further theme, popularized in C. Hartley Grattan's study *Why We Fought* (1929), was the important influence of propaganda (a thesis that derived from the pioneering work of Harold Laswell, *Propaganda Technique in the World War*).

The combination of traditional anti-German attitudes, pro-British sympathies, and the impact of the preparedness campaign of 1915–1916 had led to U.S. involvement in war. Yet, Grattan believed that the determining factor was domestic (and not Allied) propaganda, and principally President Wilson's unilateral and irresponsible conduct of foreign policy. By 1936, Grattan had considerably refined this emphasis on propaganda and presidential irresponsibility. In *Preface to Chaos,* he represented the system and needs of capitalism as creating the conditions leading to World War I.

These themes of propaganda and economic influences were either extended or refined by a larger group of revisionists. Thus, in *Merchants of Death,* H. C. Engelbrecht and F. C. Hanighen argue that arms merchants, in their efforts to sell military weapons, had contributed to international crises and influenced press reporting. Fur-

ther archival research was needed to uncover the full story, they conceded, while stressing the influence of arms merchants on governmental policy and the close relationship between the military and the armaments industry. They further conclude that "American commitments with the Allies were so enormous that only our entry into the war saved the country from a major economic collapse."

This conviction that U.S. involvement in the war was not inevitable and that the public was influenced by the insidious machinations of special interests was further developed, although without Grattan's and Engelbrecht and Hanighen's narrow economic focus, in the propaganda studies of H. C. Peterson, Walter Millis, and Edwin Borchard and William Lage. In *Propaganda for War,* Peterson explores how American opinion was influenced by British propaganda during the period 1914–1917, concluding that many American politicians "were actively engaged in fighting Britain's battles on the American political front." The combination of British propaganda efforts, the sympathies of policymakers, and the degree to which important economic interests profited from trade with the Entente powers and undermined American neutrality—and not the national interest—had ensured U.S. involvement in war with the Central Powers.

An implicit theme in Peterson's analysis is that un-American sympathies determined official Washington's actions during the crucial period 1914–1917; the only exception was former Secretary of State Bryan, who "thought primarily of his own country." The policymakers' defective vision, their "utterly fallacious conclusion, as to what could be achieved" (there was no suggestion here of disloyalty but simply of misguided sympathies), and their failure to act in terms of the national interest had led the nation into an unnecessary and harmful war. Sharing Barnes's sense of the lessons of history, in an almost preacherlike tone Peterson concludes that American leaders had "failed to see that the war was merely one in a long series of wars which the European set-up makes inevitable—that it was the natural concomitant of the political transition caused by Germany's rise to power." U.S. involvement in the war was both tragic and contrary to the public will, for "To Americans a vote for Wilson [in 1916] had meant a vote for peace. Through the only medium available to them they had expressed their unmistakable desire to keep out of the European conflict."

Peterson's definition of realism was shared by Borchard and Lage in *Neutrality for the United States*. The national interest required not intervention in "the wars of other peoples" but respect for international law and constitutional government. This was "rational" and had traditionally provided "the path of progress." Emphasizing the limits to American power and influence, Borchard and Lage condemned the unneutrality of the Wilson administration's policies and denied that these policies advanced the interests of the United States so much as those of other states. The authors, however, do not represent this as sinister or mendacious: "The surrender was not made through malevolence but through short-sighted emotionalism, a confusion of ideas as to where America's interest lay."

Another underlying theme in their (and Peterson's) analysis was the undesirability of exclusive presidential conduct of foreign policy. Borchard and Lage stress how the Congress had attempted to remain neutral, an effort that was frustrated by the Wilson administration. Emphasizing President Wilson's role in undermining U.S. neutrality, they attribute this to a messianic conception of the nation's responsibilities, a conception they find unrealistic and counterproductive. In *Road to War*, Millis develops this theme: "It was only natural that the New Freedom which appealed to nationalism to enforce peace, justice and liberty in the domestic sphere, should have thought of the American nation as an active force for peace and justice in the international world as well."

In combination, these writers characterized U.S. policy during World War I as based on a defective vision of reality, and their writings reflect a strong suspicion of globalism and of the exercise of power by the executive branch. Not impressed by the wisdom of high-level governmental personnel, they also feared that centralizing decision making within the executive branch invited abuses of this power. In their use of the term "propaganda," they distinguished between how policy was publicly justified and how it actually was and should be made. Convinced of the limits to American power, they deplored the war's adverse consequences for the postwar world.

In *America Goes to War*, Charles Tansill expands upon these themes: a multiplicity of factors had resulted in U.S. involvement in World War I. The more important were pro-British sympathy, anti-German suspicions, and the interests of bankers and exporters. Tansill's thesis was mul-

ticausal and ambivalent. There was no conscious purpose behind a policy that sacrificed U.S. neutrality to aid the Entente powers, he argued:

> The real reason why America went to war cannot be found in any single set of circumstances. There was no clear-cut road to war that the President followed with certain steps that knew no hesitation. There were many dim trails of doubtful promise, and one along which he traveled with early misgivings and reluctant tread was that which led to American economic solidarity with the Allies.

Tansill condemned the incompetence of House, Page, and Lansing and their failure to recognize and act upon American interests. Developing more sharply what had been only an implicit theme of other World War I revisionists, Tansill stressed how the ineptness and pro-Entente (hence un-American) loyalties of these policymakers had led to the nation's unfortunate involvement in a European war. And, unlike other World War I revisionists, except Barnes, Tansill did not attribute this failure to the limits to American power and influence.

RIGHT REVISIONISM

Having contended that U.S. involvement in World War I had been the consequence of a series of blundering decisions, Tansill concluded that war could have been avoided if statesmen had been more realistic and nationalistic. This emphasis on error and this multicausal analysis did not, however, constitute Tansill's interpretation of U.S. involvement in World War II. A far more doctrinaire, self-righteous, and conspiratorial tone pervaded his analysis of that subject and that of other Right revisionists.

Right revisionism emerged only in the 1940s. This assessment did not repudiate the themes of World War I revisionism so much as it put forth a sharpened, narrower focus on the role and power of the executive branch. Right revisionism sharply questioned the wisdom of the policies of the Roosevelt administration during 1937–1941 and when seeking accommodation with the Soviet Union during the war. The Soviet Union, the Right revisionists affirmed, was the main beneficiary of World War II. This was not happenstance, but the result of a policy that, by seeking the total defeat of Germany and Japan, had removed these powerful counterweights to the spread of communism. The Right revisionists

413

also adapted an implicit theme of World War I revisionism: the un-Americanism of policymakers. Making this theme more explicit, they added the charge of subversive influence. Right revisionists might have had little impact on the scholarly community: their writings reflected the conclusions advanced by many conservatives about the Truman administration's policy during the early Cold War years, and provided legitimacy and justification for what became known as McCarthyism.

Whether Tansill's *Back Door to War,* the various contributors to the collection of essays that Barnes edited, *Perpetual War for Perpetual Peace* (with the exception of William Neumann), Frederick Sanborn's *Design for War,* George Crocker's *Roosevelt's Road to Russia,* George Morgenstern's *Pearl Harbor,* John Flynn's *While You Slept,* James Martin's *Revisionist Viewpoints,* Freda Utley's *The China Story,* or Anthony Kubek's *How the Far East Was Lost,* the Right revisionists denied that war with Germany or Japan had been necessary. Emphasizing the flexibility and restraint of Japanese and German diplomats, these authors questioned whether U.S. interests had been compromised by German or Japanese expansion in Europe or the Far East. The Right revisionists further emphasized, and drew sinister conclusions about, how President Roosevelt brought the nation into war. Kubek and Utley extended this indictment to the Truman administration, stressing the McCarthyite themes of "communist influence" and "softness toward communism."

Unlike World War I revisionism, however, Right revisionism reflected no sense of ambiguity or multiple causality. There was one major culprit: Franklin Delano Roosevelt (for some, Harry Truman as well). And when not accusing Roosevelt of opportunism or affinity for leftist views, most Right revisionists emphasized the excessive influence of communist supporters within the Roosevelt administration in formulating policies that led tragically to war and then inevitably to Soviet expansion.

This sharpened criticism runs throughout Right revisionism. The contrast with World War I revisionism is pointedly demonstrated in Tansill's writings. In his description of romantic pro-British sympathies, in *Back Door to War,* Tansill affirms that "The main objective of American foreign policy since 1900 has been the preservation of the British Empire." This theme, however, was dropped from Tansill's later analysis. Condemning U.S. involvement in war with the Axis powers,

Tansill extolled the correctness of Japanese and German fears of communism. This realism, Tansill lamented, was not shared by President Roosevelt and his advisers: "It was apparent to Japan that Russia had long-range plans to communize China and thus eventually to control a large portion of eastern Asia. The very nature of international communism made it impossible to have stable relations with Russia, so Japan again turned to the United States in May 1934 in the hope of erecting a common front against the foes of capitalism." Opposed to the concentration of power in the executive branch and to the social reform policies of the Roosevelt New Deal, Tansill saw in the foreign policy of that administration the logical extension of its domestic principles to the international arena.

Tansill's analysis centered on two themes. First, he emphasized the sinister character of the president's deceitful conduct of diplomacy, whether during the prewar period of 1939–1941 or during the war years. No longer content to characterize presidential diplomacy as duplicitous, the Right revisionists denied that policies were based on popular support and emphasized the intentionally secret and unilateral process by which decisions were made.

The second theme of Right revisionism was that U.S. involvement in World War II and the secretive, unilateral conduct of foreign policy were so inimical to the national interest (having made possible Soviet expansion and the Cold War) that this could not have been the result either of mistaken judgment or of emotionalism. Rather, the Right revisionists maintained, this policy could best be understood as the result of subversion and treason. Anthony Kubek extended this theme to an extreme form: "The utter consistency of our policy in serving Soviet ends leaves no conclusion other than that pro-Communist elements in our government and press 'planned it that way.' But top American officials who sought to buy Soviet cooperation at any price must bear the final responsibility." Condemning the continued respectability of this "internationalist" and "accommodationist" thinking, Kubek concludes in *How the Far East Was Lost*: "We face . . . a criminal conspiracy and it must be dealt with as such. . . . The Communist conspiracy has been succeeding largely on the basis of our mistakes and of the ability of their agents to procure such mistakes on our part. . . . It should be clearly evident that the Communists cannot gain the world unless our government helps them to do it."

LEFT REVISIONISM

Convinced of the correctness of their interpretation of the two world wars and their lessons for current policy, the Right revisionists' analysis was based on a belief in American omnipotence. This led them to question why particular men pursued policies that undermined the national interest. Right revisionism, then, questioned why American power and interests did not dominate the postwar world. Left revisionists rejected this perspective. To them the central failings of U.S. diplomacy derived from the attempt to impose American interests and values on the world, and the inability to recognize that this quest was impossible and counterproductive. In striking contrast to the focus of Right revisionism on policymakers and criticism of their policies, eventually moving from emphasizing error to emphasizing treason, Left revisionists adopted a less personalist perspective.

William Appleman Williams   Influenced by the pre-1940s writings of Charles Beard, William Appleman Williams concentrated on the domestic sources of U.S. foreign policy. For him an understanding of policymaking required research not solely into diplomatic correspondence and international crises but also into the perceptions and priorities of policymakers. Far more sophisticated than Beard, Williams located the answer to why policymakers led the nation to war not in a conflict between Jeffersonianism and Hamiltonianism, and surely not in the emotionalism and duplicity of policymakers or their divided loyalties. Rather, he explained U.S. foreign policy in terms of the worldview of policymakers. For Williams the central question was not why the United States became involved in foreign wars but why it pursued a policy of overseas expansionism.

There are two central themes to Williams's analysis. Assuming an elite model of American decision making, Williams stressed how elites (based on the structure of the economy and the political system) made policy independent of popular support or involvement. Thus, in *Tragedy of American Diplomacy* he writes:

> One of the most unnerving features was the extensive elitism that had become ingrained in the policy-making process. The assault on Cuba was conceived, planned, and implemented by a small group of men in the executive department [who] opened no general dialogue with members of Congress (even in private conversation),

and expended great effort and exerted great pressure to avoid any public disclosure or debate.

In describing the process of U.S. involvement in the Vietnam War, Williams emphasizes "the elite's self-isolation . . . arrogance and self-righteousness, and . . . messianic distortion of a sincere humanitarian desire to help other peoples. Even the American public came more and more to be considered as simply another factor to be manipulated and controlled in the effort to establish and maintain the American Way as the global status quo."

More central to Williams's analysis than this description of elite manipulation and determination of policy are his conclusions about the ideological basis for U.S. policy. Williams depicted policymakers as at times naive and at times misguided, questioned whether the United States need have entered the two world wars and the Cold War, and stressed elite manipulation of public opinion. His basic premise, however, was not that different men or more open procedures could have averted war. The sources of policymaking instead were established values and priorities, and not, as Barnes and the Right revisionists argued, the insidious influence of propaganda and manipulative leaders. Williams did not portray Wilson, Page, House, Roosevelt, or Alger Hiss as evil and shortsighted, traitors to the public in whose interests they acted. Williams conceded that the decisions of policy elites commanded popular acceptance or acquiescence. While critical of the consequences of their decisions, he offered not moralistic condemnation but reasoned analysis in explaining the "tragedy of American diplomacy." The exploitative results of U.S. foreign policy were not, Williams argued, the "result of malice, indifference, or ruthless and predatory exploitation. American leaders were not evil men. . . . Nor were they treacherous hypocrites. They believed deeply in the ideals they proclaimed."

Williams also denied that abstract idealism determined specific policy responses so much as did the changing character of the American economy and the beliefs thus engendered. Since the 1820s, he wrote, "Americans steadily deepened their commitment to the idea that democracy was inextricably connected with individualism, private property, and a capitalist marketplace economy. Even the great majority of critics sought to reform existing society precisely in order to realize that conception of the good system." This particular view of the national interest, and the rejection of alternative models for organizing society, constituted the tragedy of American diplomacy. For Williams, there were no identifiable devils or correctable errors. History was too complex for such explanations. The dilemma was deeper, and stemmed partially from the American rejection of Marxism.

Commenting in *The Great Evasion*, Williams writes:

> We have never confronted his [Marx's] central thesis about the assumptions, the costs, and the nature of capitalist society. We have never confronted his central insight that capitalism is predicated upon an over emphasis and exaltation of the individualistic, egoistic half of man functioning in a marketplace system that overrides and crushes the social, humanitarian half of man. . . . And we have never confronted his argument that capitalism cannot create a community in which how men produce and own is less important than their relationships as they produce and distribute those products, less important than what they are as men, and less important than how they treat each other.

American foreign policy was the product of the definition of the national interest and the unquestioned beliefs held by policymakers, and not the actions of particular men. The combination of economic interest and the conviction of American omnipotence and omniscience led inevitably, and tragically, to a policy of overseas expansionism. Williams defined this policy as the Open Door. By the twentieth century, Williams argues in *Tragedy of American Diplomacy,* American foreign policy had come to be based on the "firm conviction, even dogmatic belief, that America's *domestic* well-being depends upon such sustained, ever-increasing overseas economic expansion. Here is a convergence of economic practice with intellectual analysis and emotional involvement that creates a very powerful and dangerous propensity to define the essentials of American welfare in terms of activities outside the United States."

Williams's radical analyses profoundly influenced a number of young historians, some of whom studied under him at the University of Wisconsin and others who were stimulated by his books, articles, and essays—notably *Tragedy of American Diplomacy, The Great Evasion,* and *Contours of American History.* Independent scholars, these Left revisionists have at times adopted part of Williams's complex analysis, at times have refined it, and at times have extended it to the point of fundamental departure from his conclusions. And, whereas Williams was synthetic, his scope broad, and the form of his writing essayist, these young scholars have written heavily documented monographs on narrowly defined subjects.

The principal focus of Left revisionism has been the Cold War, although Williams's influence is reflected in the studies of Walter LaFeber on U.S. expansionism during the 1890s, *The New Empire*; of Thomas McCormick on U.S. China policy, *China Market*; of David Green on U.S. policy toward Latin America, *The Containment of Latin America*; and of N. Gordon Levin on Wilson's wartime diplomacy, *Woodrow Wilson and World Politics.* (Since the basic analysis of these volumes does not differ from that of Cold War revisionism, this essay will concentrate exclusively on these studies.)

Not all Cold War revisionists have written within Williams's framework or were influenced by him; those who did so differed widely in their emphases and conclusions. While all dissented from the orthodox interpretation of the origins of the Cold War, some Left revisionists emphasized only the elitist nature of U.S. policy formation; others, the ideology of policymakers; others, the economic basis of particular policy decisions; and still others combined these themes. These differences are fundamental and range from rather limited critiques of particular men to a more radical characterization of U.S. policy as imperialistic and counterrevolutionary.

The most important Left revisionist writings include Lloyd Gardner's *Architects of Illusion,* Barton Bernstein's "American Foreign Policy and the Origins of the Cold War," Walter LaFeber's *America, Russia, and the Cold War,* Gabriel Kolko's *Politics of War,* Richard Barnet's *Roots of War,* Thomas Paterson's *Soviet-American Confrontation,* David Horowitz's *Empire and Revolution,* Bruce Kuklick's *American Policy and the Division of Germany,* Gar Alperovitz's *Atomic Diplomacy,* Harry Magdoff's *Age of Imperialism,* Ronald Steel's *Pax Americana,* Stephen Ambrose's *Rise to Globalism,* Richard Freeland's *Truman Doctrine and the Origins of McCarthyism,* Athan Theoharis's *Seeds of Repression,* Diane Shaver Clemens's *Yalta,* Lawrence Wittner's *Cold War America,* and D. F. Fleming's *The Cold War and Its Origins.*

Left revisionists have extended this analysis beyond the issue of the origins of the U.S.–Soviet conflict in Europe and have begun to examine the international dimensions of the Cold War. These historians—most notably Thomas Paterson in *On Every Front*, Thomas McCormick in *America's Half Century*, and Robert McMahon in *Colonialism and Cold War*—have shifted from exploring the origins of the containment policy in Europe and have instead placed the U.S.–Soviet conflict in the context of the international economic system and the rise of anticolonial movements in the post–World War II era.

In their dissent from orthodox historiography, the Left revisionists deny that the Cold War resulted simply from Soviet territorial expansionism or the objectives of international communism to which the United States responded defensively in order to preserve freedom and democracy. Stressing the caution and conservatism of Soviet policy, the Left revisionists locate the origins of the Cold War in U.S. foreign policies. As Barton Bernstein writes in "American Foreign Policy and the Origins of the Cold War," *Politics and Policies of the Truman Administration*:

> American policy was neither so innocent nor so nonideological. . . . American leaders sought to promote their conceptions of national interest and their values even at the conscious risk of provoking Russia's fears about her security. . . . By overextending policy and power and refusing to accept Soviet interests, American policy-makers contributed to the Cold War. . . . There is evidence that Russian policies were reasonably cautious and conservative, and that there was at least a basis for accommodation.

Left revisionist conceptions of the origins of the Cold War, however, mask important fundamental differences. The Left revisionists can be divided into two groups: radicals and Left liberals, the principal dividing line being that the radicals analyze American policy within a framework of imperialism and elite or class domination, while the Left liberals minimize power and ideology, and emphasize domestic politics, personality, and bureaucracy. According to this division, Fleming, Clemens, Steel, Theoharis, and Ambrose can be classified as Left liberals, and Kolko, Gardner, Bernstein, Paterson, Horowitz, LaFeber, Magdoff, Alperovitz, Freeland, Barnet, Wittner, and Kuklick as radicals. As with all definitions, this one sharpens differences, particularly in the distinction between elite domination and bureaucracy.

In addition to these broad divisions, the Left revisionists differ in their conclusions about two important questions. First, was the Cold War inevitable because the requirements of capitalism forced American leaders to pursue a consciously imperialistic foreign policy? This theme is developed by Gabriel Kolko in *Roots of American Foreign Policy*:

> The dominant interest of the United States is in world economic stability, and anything that undermines that condition presents a danger to its present hegemony. . . . From a purely economic viewpoint, the United States cannot maintain its existing vital dominating relationship to much of the Third World unless it can keep the poor nations from moving too far toward the Left. . . . A widespread leftward movement would critically affect its supply of raw materials and have profound long-term repercussions.

Only Kolko, Magdoff, and Horowitz among the radical revisionists hold to such a mechanistic view of U.S. foreign policy. In contrast, other radicals emphasize tactics and perception (the quote from Bernstein cited above portrays this view).

Left revisionists also differ over whether U.S. policy toward the Soviet Union shifted fundamentally with Harry S. Truman's accession to the presidency in April 1945, a thesis advanced by Alperovitz, Clemens, Fleming, Wittner, Theoharis, and Ambrose, and accepted with major qualifications by Bernstein, Paterson, Kuklick, and Gardner (the latter group stressing that the change was more one of tactics than of objectives or priorities).

In addition, radical and Left liberal revisionists (LaFeber, Gardner, Bernstein, Paterson, Wittner, Kuklick, Steel, Theoharis, and Ambrose) concur that American policymakers brought on the Cold War, not because they were innocent or seeking to reach accommodation with the Soviet Union but because they believed in American omnipotence and omniscience. In *Soviet-American Confrontation,* Paterson concludes: "Convinced that their interpretations of international agreements were alone the correct ones, . . . United States officials attempted to fulfill their goals through the unilateral application of the power they knew they possessed." Gardner and Bernstein slightly modify this thesis of omnipotence, averring that policymakers fell victim to mythical and illusory views of U.S. power and principle in the pursuit of what was a counterrevolutionary foreign policy. In *Architects of Illusion,* Gardner develops this theme: "Only the United States had the power [at the conclusion of World War II] to enforce its decisions world-wide, . . . American policy-makers [subsequently] developed a series of rationales, expedients, and explanations which grew into the myths and illusions of the Cold War. And men were later beguiled by their own creations."

Like Williams, the Left revisionists question whether public opinion constrained policymakers. To the contrary, they contend, officials of the Truman administration consciously sought to alter public opinion in order to ensure popular support for costly and controversial policy initiatives. Moving beyond Williams, they argue that this effort to alter public opinion created the climate that resulted in McCarthyism. This theme is developed by Theoharis and Freeland, though these historians' conclusions differ. Freeland contends that the Truman administration consciously pursued McCarthyite politics in an effort to develop support for a multilateral foreign policy, while Theoharis depicts the administration as reacting to partisan pressures and exigencies, as lacking a conscious and coherent strategy, and as sincerely if obsessively anticommunist.

Left revisionists have raised important questions about the nature of the decision-making process, the relationship between wealth and policy, the class and interest backgrounds of policymakers, and the process by which values and official policy are formed. Unlike Right revisionists, who simply chronicled executive branch manipulation of the public and suggested that certain policy decisions were harmful in their consequences, Left revisionists have moved beyond mere description of error and propaganda. Left and Right revisionism are distinctive, then, not simply because of differences in political philosophy and conclusions. The basic difference stems from the character of Left revisionism as intellectual and radical history (in the literal sense of seeking root causes).

VIETNAM AND NATIONAL SECURITY REVISIONISM

The emergence of Left revisionism during the 1960s coincided with a contentious public debate over U.S. involvement in the Vietnam War. The Left revisionist challenge to the core assumptions of the containment policy raised the question of whether the United States should continue a policy of supporting any and all anticommunist governments. As dissent over the Johnson and Nixon administrations' policies expanded beyond radical activists to the mainstream media and the halls of Congress, both administrations found it difficult to sustain support for the war. A further by-product of the resultant unraveling of the Cold War consensus was a heightened skepticism about the role of the presidency and the secretive conduct of national security policy. Tapping into this skepticism, Daniel Ellsberg, a former Defense Department and National Security Council aide, in 1971 leaked the classified Defense Department history of U.S. involvement in Vietnam, the so-called Pentagon Papers. Then, in 1973–1975, congressional investigations first of the Watergate scandal and then of the covert practices of federal intelligence agencies breached the wall of secrecy that had previously shrouded how national security policy was conducted, with the attendant result of the release of highly classified records of the White House and the intelligence agencies. One legacy of these companion developments was Vietnam and national security revisionism.

Vietnam Revisionism   Historians would have researched the history of U.S. involvement in Vietnam—the nation's longest war and only military defeat—if the earlier availability of relevant primary sources had expedited such research. A consensus quickly emerged, captured first in Stephen Ambroses's synthetic history of the Cold War era, *Rise to Globalism,* and later in the more thorough syntheses of George Herring, *America's Longest War,* James Olson and Randy Roberts, *Where the Domino Fell,* and George Moss, *Vietnam: An American Ordeal.*

The Herring, Olson and Roberts, and Moss surveys convey the consensus interpretations of the Vietnam War, placing that conflict in a broader context of anticolonial guerrilla movements and emphasizing the limits to American power and the containment policy. This critical assessment of the U.S. military role precipitated a Vietnam revisionism that reaffirmed the major tenets of Cold War orthodoxy while incorporating some of the core assumptions of Right revisionism (of mendacity, irresolution, erroneous judgment, and conspiratorial influence).

Two such revisionists, Harry Summers and Philip van Slyck, dissent from the consensus on the Vietnam War. Both deny that U.S. involvement was unwise and unnecessary, or the misapplication of military power to a guerrilla war. The U.S. defeat, they argue, was the product of a failure of will by the nation's presidents and the general public. Eschewing a conspiratorial analysis, they attribute this failure to achieve an attainable victory to skewed national priorities (a focus on domestic issues to the neglect of national security interests), to a failure to respond rationally to an underlying Soviet threat, and to profound changes in the popular culture (the so-called counterculture) and the rise in influence of narrow special interest groups. Summers wrote in *On Strategy: A Critical Analysis of the Vietnam War*, the Vietnam defeat was the by-product of President Lyndon Johnson's "conscious decisions" not "to mobilize the American people—to invoke the National will"—and to the "social upheaval in America where the old rules and regulations were dismissed as irrelevant and history no longer had anything to offer . . . the 'Age of Aquarius.'"

Van Slyck echoes this analysis, condemning the "errors of judgment" of five presidents (from Dwight Eisenhower to Jimmy Carter) to lobby for needed increases in military spending and the commitments essential to checking the Soviet threat and averting the "ill-starred, mismanaged, and ultimately humiliating national ordeal in Vietnam." Lamenting the rise of "single-issue political causes" (the civil rights and youth movements of the 1960s), which he claims "displayed uncertainties of purpose and conflicting social and economic priorities," he concludes that "in this increasingly antiwar climate, the preoccupation with domestic affairs insured that expenditures for national security would be assigned a declining priority through the decade of the 1970s" (*Strategies for the 1980s: Lessons of Cuba, Vietnam, and Afghanistan*). Michael Lind extends this analysis of the wisdom of U.S. involvement in the Vietnam War in *Vietnam, the Necessary War* (1999). In contrast, Martin Herz in *The Prestige Press and the Christmas Bombing, 1972* criticizes the reporting and commentary of the "prestige press" (mainstream newspapers such as the *New York Times* and *Washington Post*) as contributing to the "weakening and demoralization of the United States and South Vietnam" that led ultimately to the North Vietnamese victory in 1975.

Norman Podhoretz and Guenter Lewy expand upon this indictment, in language more vituperative and condescending. In *Why We Were in Vietnam*, Podhoretz defends the purpose and morality of U.S. efforts to ensure a noncommunist government in South Vietnam. Like Summers, Lind, and Van Slyck, he attributes the ultimate military defeat to a failure of will, to the limited uses of U.S. military power by presidents Kennedy and Johnson, and to misguided military tactics and strategies. Adopting the conspiratorial framework of Right revisionism, Podhoretz condemns the insidious role of antiwar activists within the academic, journalist, and liberal communities whom he derides as "apologists for the Communist side in the Vietnam War." Because Susan Sontag, Mary McCarthy, and Frances Fitzgerald were "very good writers," Podhoretz laments, "they were able to state the Communist case in a style acceptable to an audience that would normally be put off . . . by the crude propagandistic rhetoric of the hard-core inveterate pro-Communist elements." In his concluding assessment of the consequences of the North Vietnamese victory of 1975, Podhoretz argues:

> The truth is that the antiwar movement bears a certain measure of responsibility for the horrors that have overtaken the people of Vietnam; and so long as those who participated in that movement are unwilling to acknowledge this, they will go on trying to discredit the idea that there is not distinction between authoritarianism and totalitarianism. For to recognize the distinction is to recognize that in making a contribution to the conquest of South Vietnam by the Communists of the North they were siding with an evil system against something better from every political and moral point of view.

Guenter Lewy echoes Podhoretz. Writing with Harry Barnes's dogmatism, in the preface to his *America in Vietnam* (1978), Lewy describes his purpose as to "clear away the cobwebs of mythology that inhibit the correct understanding of what went on—and what went wrong in Vietnam" and to critique the "ideological fervor which has characterized much writing on the Vietnam War." Like Podhoretz, Lewy defends the purpose and morality of U.S. involvement, emphasizes the wisdom and necessity of a policy to contain the spread of communism, and condemns the bias of the media and the "growing permissiveness in American society . . . and widespread attitudes of disrespect toward authority and law enforcement." Lewy extends this indictment in *The Cause That Failed: Communism in American Political Life*, impugning the loyalty of anti–Vietnam War critics in the peace movement, the civil liberties community, and in the universities, and the "Leftward drift of the American political spectrum." He charges that

> Today a host of organizations, not formally linked to the Communist Party and in many cases defying the categories of Old and New Left, carry on an energetic agitation for a radical transformation of American society, push for drastic cuts in the American defense budget, if not for unilateral disarmament, and lobby for Communist guerrillas and regimes. The political outlook

of these groups provides Communists with a perfect cover and allows them to ply their trade with little need to seize actual control. . . . Such alliances provide the Communist Party with valuable political legitimacy and respectability.

National Security Revisionism   The public debate over the Vietnam War and the Watergate affair (and the resultant opening of formerly classified records of the federal intelligence agencies) also spawned a more critical assessment of the role of the presidency and federal intelligence agencies, and how bureaucracy and secrecy adversely influenced national security policy. This new historiography was previewed in Arthur Schlesinger's quasi-critical history of the U.S. presidency, *The Imperial Presidency.* Reassessing his own earlier endorsement of the "presidential mystique," Schlesinger chronicled how "Especially in the twentieth century, the circumstances of an increasingly perilous world as well as of an increasingly dependent economy and society served to compel a larger concentration of authority in the Presidency." Surveying how presidential power expanded (including by relying on secrecy and bypassing the Congress), Schlesinger nonetheless concludes that the abuses of power of the "imperial presidency" were peculiar to the Nixon presidency.

Published in 1973, at the time of the special Senate investigation of the Watergate scandal, Schlesinger's history of the Nixon administration's uses of the federal intelligence agencies (Central Intelligence Agency, National Security Agency, Federal Bureau of Investigation) for political purposes was soon challenged as the result of subsequent revelations that presidents since Franklin D. Roosevelt had similarly exploited these agencies—publicized in the hearings and reports of the Church and Pike Committees of 1975–1976 and in federal intelligence agency records released in response to Freedom of Information Act requests. These revelations confirmed how "national security" priorities and secrecy claims had altered executive-legislative relations, and how presidents and intelligence agency officials had exploited secrecy to violate the law, privacy rights, and First Amendment rights. These themes were developed in a number of studies, notably Frank Donner, *The Age of Surveillance;* Morton Halperin et al., *The Lawless State;* Edward Pessen, *Losing Our Souls;* Jessica Wang, *American Science in an Age of Anxiety;* John Prados, *Presidents' Secret Wars;* and Athan Theoharis, *Spying on Americans.*

Although differing in their interpretations, these authors share a common framework—emphasizing that the more centralized and secretive decision-making process by which national security policy was conducted, undermined civil liberties and democratic principles. In *Spying on Americans: Political Surveillance from Hoover to the Huston Plan,* Theoharis summarizes these themes in his conclusion:

> [The] Cold War encouraged a strong elite-dominated government with authority to make decisions and the gradual acceptance of the need for secrecy and uncritical deference to so-called national security claims. . . . The steady rise in influence of the FBI, NSC, the CIA and the White House staff to dominant policy-making roles and the displacement of the State and Justice departments and the Cabinet—served to reduce the congressional oversight role. By the 1970s, therefore, the intelligence bureaucrats . . . had become independent powers, effectively establishing national policy, even at times independent of the occupant of the Oval Office.

These themes of the undermining of congressional oversight and of privacy and First Amendment rights were central to the new historiography that focused on the impact of the Cold War on American institutions and decision making. Reflecting the differing assessments of presidential power that distinguished Schlesinger from these other historians, in *Secrecy: The American Experience,* Daniel Patrick Moynihan surveys the history of the "institutions of the administrative state that developed during the great conflicts of the twentieth century." Moynihan criticizes overclassification as undermining democracy and immunizing decisions from needed scrutiny, and calls for the replacement of this new "culture of secrecy" by a "culture of openness," but at the same time recognizes that secrecy "is at times legitimate and necessary." In contrast, the various contributors to Athan Theoharis's *A Culture of Secrecy* deny that the legacy of international conflict was simply unnecessary overclassification and emphasize the purposefulness of secrecy in ensuring controversial, at times illegal, programs and procedures.

These differences over the purpose and consequences of secrecy are replicated in the writings of other historians on the evolution of the "national security state." In a study that transcends the debate among revisionist and orthodox historians on the origins of the Cold War, Melvyn Leffler in *A Preponderance of Power* emphasizes how the "Cold War shaped our political culture, our institutions, and our national priorities; and how American officials, commanding a "preponderance of power," were emboldened to "refashion the world in America's image and create the American century." Leffler nonetheless concludes that the resultant exclusively executive decisions were neither aggressive nor mistaken, but "quite prescient," were reflective of a "sophisticated strategy," and "manifested sagacity, security, and wisdom" of "prudent officials" willing to take "calculated risks." Leffler had, however, introduced a distinctive theme—that executive decisions reflected the increased influence of bureaucrats whose expertise in formulating policy in secret ushered in the "national security state."

Michael Hogan in *A Cross of Iron* and Benjamin Fordham in *Building the Cold War Consensus* explicitly develop this theme of the "national security state." Surveying the congressional debate over Cold War policies, Hogan focuses on how during this era a "new class of national security managers" eventually triumphed over progressives and conservatives who feared that "bad policies could put the United States on the slippery slope to a garrison state dominated by military leaders and devoted to military purposes"—a debate between those who cast Cold War containment policies "in a new ideology of national security and those who adhered to values rooted in an older political culture." The national security ideology, Hogan argues, was shaped by the experiences of national security managers during World War II and the Cold War who came to see "the world and America's place within it. It laid the groundwork for a more international foreign policy and for a supportive program of state making, both of which challenged such traditions as isolationism and antistatism." Hogan concludes by emphasizing the "role of war and Cold War as agents of state formation" that in the process enabled bureaucrats "toward independent action and autonomy."

In contrast, Benjamin Fordham in *Building the Cold War Consensus* focuses on the intersection of domestic policy (and politics) and national security policy. Exploring the debate between "internationalists" and "nationalists" over the nature and costs of the nation's foreign policy role, Fordham locates national security decisions not as based on abstract conceptions of the national interest nor as responses to international crises, but as shaped by the "structure of the domestic political economy" and the ability of bureaucrats to "influence policy to the extent they can draw political support from interested groups in society."

CONCLUSION

The revisionists have had varying impacts on how historians understand the conduct of American foreign relations in the twentieth century and on the contemporary debate over the nation's role in the world. The World War I revisionists, for example, helped create a climate that moved many in Congress and the public to support the Neutrality Acts of 1935–1937 and that impelled President Roosevelt to move cautiously during the period 1939–1941 when seeking to reorient U.S. foreign policy. The Right revisionists provided the intellectual foundation for the McCarthyite charges of the early 1950s: the need to purge subversives from the federal bureaucracy, to repudiate the Yalta Conference agreements, and to restrict presidential foreign policy authority. Sharing this framework, Vietnam revisionists provided the intellectual rationale for the Committee on the Present Danger and the Reagan administration's military and foreign policy decisions of the 1980s—whether missile defense or aid to the contras in Nicaragua. In contrast, Left revisionists influenced the debate over the Vietnam War and the containment policy during the 1960s and 1970s. Finally, the national security revisionists have both tapped into and influenced the post-1975 debate over presidential power, the role of the intelligence agencies, and secrecy policy.

The long-term impact of revisionism on the public's understanding of American foreign relations, nonetheless, has been transitory, determined by the public's changing mood and priorities. The impact of revisionists on the scholarly community has been equally transitory, depending more on the quality of their scholarship than on the questions they have posed and the insights they have offered. Their most significant contribution has been to introduce new research issues and to lend support for the release of classified reports.

BIBLIOGRAPHY

Barnes, Harry Elmer. *The Genesis of the World War: An Introduction to the Problem of War Guilt*. New York, 1926. The most influential revisionist book written during the 1920s; most of the themes of later revisionism are suggested here.

Barnes, Harry Elmer, ed. *Perpetual War for Perpetual Peace: A Critical Examination of the Foreign Policy of Franklin Delano Roosevelt and Its Aftermath.* Caldwell, Idaho, 1953. A collection of essays reflecting the various themes of Right revisionists, this is based on minimal research into primary sources; most of the essays were written by nonhistorians.

Beard, Charles A. *The Open Door at Home: A Trial Philosophy of National Interest.* New York, 1934. An extremely heavy review of American diplomacy since the founding of the Republic and an important influence on Left revisionism, notably William A. Williams.

———. *President Roosevelt and the Coming of the War, 1941: A Study in Appearances and Realities.* Hamden, Conn., 1948. Beard's controversial study of the background to Pearl Harbor, based principally on the hearings and reports of the congressional committee investigating Pearl Harbor in 1945.

Bernstein, Barton J. "American Foreign Policy and the Origins of the Cold War." In Barton J. Bernstein, ed. *Politics and Policies of the Truman Administration.* Chicago, 1970. An important, subtle, and sophisticated radical Left revisionist analysis of the origins of the Cold War.

Borchard, Edwin, and William Potter Lage. *Neutrality for the United States.* New Haven, Conn., 1937. The most sophisticated and balanced of the revisionist studies published during the 1930s.

Brune, Lester, and Richard Dean Burns. *America and the Indochina Wars, 1945–1990.* Claremont, Calif., 1992.

Cohen, Warren I. *The American Revisionist: The Lessons of Intervention in World War I.* Chicago, 1967. A thoughtful, often insightful study of the more important revisionist writing about U.S. involvement in both world wars.

Doenecke, Justus D. *The Literature of Isolationism: A Guide to Non-Interventionist Scholarship, 1930–1972.* Colorado Springs, 1972. A useful annotated bibliography of the various articles, essays, books, and dissertations on the general theme of revisionism.

Engelbrecht, H. C., and F. C. Hanighen. *Merchants of Death: A Study of the International Armament Industry.* New York, 1934. A popular book that provides impetus and a rationale for the so-called Nye Committee investigation of the munitions industry.

Fordham, Benjamin. *Building the Cold War Consensus: The Political Economy of U.S. National Security Policy, 1949–1951.* Ann Arbor, Mich., 1998.

Gardner, Lloyd C. *Architects of Illusion: Men and Ideas in American Foreign Policy, 1941–1949.* Chicago, 1970. A series of portraits of the important foreign policymakers of the Roosevelt and Truman administrations, written from a radical Left revisionist perspective.

Herz, Martin. *The Prestige Press and the Christmas Bombing, 1972.* Washington, D.C., 1980.

Hogan, Michael. *A Cross of Iron: Harry S. Truman and the Origins of the National Security State, 1945–1954.* Cambridge and New York, 1998.

Hogan, Michael, ed. *America in the World: The Historiography of American Foreign Relations Since 1941.* Cambridge and New York, 1995.

Kirkendall, Richard S., ed. *The Truman Period as a Research Field: A Reappraisal, 1972.* Columbia, Mo., 1974. A balanced study of the literature on the Truman period that contains counterbalancing essays on domestic and foreign policy written by revisionists and nonrevisionists; an excellent source on the more important studies and on research collections.

Kolko, Gabriel. *The Politics of War: The World and United States Foreign Policy.* New York, 1968.

Kolko, Gabriel, and Joyce Kolko. *The Limits of Power: The World and the United States Foreign Policy, 1945–1954.* New York, 1972. An ambitious, heavily written and researched radical Left revisionist study of the diplomacy of the Roosevelt and Truman administrations that depicts American policy as counterrevolutionary and imperialistic.

Kubek, Anthony. *How the Far East Was Lost.* Chicago, 1963.

Leffler, Melvyn. *A Preponderance of Power.* Stanford, Calif., 1992.

Lewy, Guenter. *America in Vietnam.* New York, 1978.

———. *The Cause That Failed: Communism in American Political Life.* New York, 1990.

Lind, Michael. *Vietnam, the Necessary War: A Reinterpretation of America's Most Disastrous Military Conflict.* New York, 1999.

Millis, Walter. *Road to War: America, 1914–1917.* Boston, 1935.

Moynihan, Daniel Patrick. *Secrecy: The American Experience.* New Haven, Conn., 1998.

Olson, James S., ed. *The Vietnam War: Handbook of the Literature and Research.* Westport, Conn., 1993.

Paterson, Thomas G. *Soviet-American Confrontation: Postwar Reconstruction and the Origins of the Cold War.* Baltimore, 1973. An important Left revisionist study of the Cold War that reflects the evolution of Cold War revisionism away from the earlier, more exclusively economic analyses of Kolko and Williams.

Paterson, Thomas G., and Robert J. McMahon, eds. *The Origins of the Cold War.* 4th ed. Boston, 1999. Reprints excerpts and offers insightful commentary on the historiographical debate over the origins of the Cold War and the changes in Left revisionism; there is, however, no critical assessment to date on national security revisionism.

Peterson, H. C. *Propaganda for War.* Norman, Okla., 1939.

Podhoretz, Norman. *Why We Were in Vietnam.* New York, 1978.

Schlesinger, Arthur. *The Imperial Presidency.* Boston, 1973.

Siracusa, Joseph. *The Unexamined Victories and Final Tragedy of America's Last Years in Vietnam.* New York, 1999.

Sorley, Lewis. *A Better War: The Unexamined Victories and Final Tragedy of America's Last Years in Vietnam.* New York, 1999.

Summers, Harry. *On Strategy: A Critical Analysis of the Vietnam War.* Novato, Calif., 1982.

Tansill, Charles Callan. *America Goes to War.* Boston, 1938.

——. *Back Door to War: The Roosevelt Foreign Policy, 1933–1941.* Chicago, 1952. Relatively distinctive studies of the origins of the world wars, valuable principally because they reflect the changed focus and themes of Right revisionism.

Theoharis, Athan. *Spying on Americans: Political Surveillance from Hoover to the Huston Plan.* Philadelphia, 1978.

Theoharis, Athan, ed. *A Culture of Secrecy.* Lawrence, Kans., 1998.

Tucker, Robert W. *The Radical Left and American Foreign Policy.* Baltimore, 1971. A thoughtful critique of Left revisionist writings on the Cold War, principally focusing on the theories, not the research, of the revisionists.

Van Slyck, Philip. *Strategies for the 1980s: Lessons of Cuba, Vietnam, and Afghanistan.* Westport, Conn., 1981.

Wang, Jessica. *American Science in an Age of Anxiety: Scientists, Anticommunism, and the Cold War.* Chapel Hill, N.C., 1999.

Williams, William Appleman. *The Great Evasion.* Chicago, 1964.

——. *The Tragedy of American Diplomacy.* Rev. ed. New York, 1972. One of the most important books written about American diplomacy, this covers the period since the founding of the Republic and has shaped the thinking and research of the Left revisionist historians.

See also COLD WAR ORIGINS; ELITISM; THE NATIONAL INTEREST; OPEN DOOR INTERPRETATION; PRESIDENTIAL POWER; PUBLIC OPINION; REALISM AND IDEALISM; THE VIETNAM WAR.

REVOLUTION

★ ★ ★ ★ ★

Jeremi Suri

Many observers have noted the surprising resilience of certain ideas in American history. "Liberty," the belief that individuals should live free from most external restraints, is one particularly powerful American touchstone. "Enterprise," the virtue of hard work, business acumen, and wealth accumulation, is another. The belief that all people should share these ideas has prohibited Americans from ever accepting the world as it is. The assumption that individuals will, when capable, choose these "self-evident" propositions has made the nation a force for revolution. America's foreign policy has consistently sought to remake the external landscape in its own image.

As early as the eighteenth century, New World influences helped inspire revolutionary upheavals throughout the old empires of Europe. This pattern continued in the nineteenth century as thinkers from diverse cultures studied the American Declaration of Independence and the U.S. Constitution to guide modern state building. During the first half of the twentieth century, American soldiers fought to undermine authoritarian regimes and revolutionize the workings of the international system. By the end of the twentieth century, American cinema, music, and fashion challenged traditional values in all corners of the globe.

Self-confidence and ignorance of the wider world fed the nation's revolutionary aspirations. These qualities also made Americans intolerant of the diversity of revolutionary experience. The imagery of the thirteen colonies' fight for independence from British rule in the late eighteenth century provided a template for acceptable foreign revolutions that became more rigid over time. The whole world had to follow the American revolutionary path. Heretical movements required repression because they offered destructive deviations from the highway of historical change.

Enthusiasm for revolution, in this sense, produced many counterrevolutionary policies. These were directed against alternative models, especially communism, that violated American definitions of "liberty" and "enterprise." In the second half of the twentieth century this paradox became most evident as the United States employed revolutionary concepts like "development" and "democratization" to restrain radical change in Asia, Africa, and Latin America. "Globalization" came to reflect the dominance of the American revolutionary model, and the repression of different approaches. Paraphrasing French philosopher Jean-Jacques Rousseau, America has forced much of the world to be free, but only on American terms.

A DIPLOMATIC REVOLUTION BEFORE THE BREAK WITH BRITAIN

Decades before Americans contemplated a break with the British Empire, influential figures planned to promote a revolution beyond the boundaries of the original thirteen colonies. French, Spanish, Russian, British, and Indian groups uneasily interacted with one another in what eighteenth-century observers called the "western territories," then comprising more than two-thirds of what would later be the U.S. mainland. French and Indian encroachments on British settlements, in particular, threatened to encircle the residents of the colonies, imperiling their security and economy. Assembling in Albany, New York, between 19 June and 10 July 1754, representatives from seven of the colonies (Massachusetts, New Hampshire, Connecticut, Rhode Island, Pennsylvania, Maryland, and New York) responded to these circumstances. They outlined an agenda for the future political unity and diplomatic expansion of American society. Although never officially implemented, the so-called Albany Plan created the foundation for a future revolution on the North American continent and abroad.

Benjamin Franklin, the charismatic Pennsylvania entrepreneur and politician, drafted much of the Albany Plan. He began with a call for unity among the colonies, under the leadership of a president general. This figure would work with a grand council of colonial representatives to "make peace or declare war with the Indian Nations." Beyond issues of territorial defense, the president general would also purchase lands for new settlements outside of the original colonies. On the expanding American frontier, the president general would "make laws" regulating commerce and society. Franklin and the other contributors to the Albany Plan devoted little attention to the interests of the Indians or the French. This was a scheme designed to make the residents of the "western territories" live by American (and British) laws. Trade would be organized according to American customs of contract. Settled farming and industry would replace the migratory livelihoods of many indigenous communities. Most significantly, land would be apportioned as personal property, demarcated, and defended with government force.

The historian Richard White has shown that before the second half of the eighteenth century, the various groups encountering one another in the western territories engaged in a series of careful compromises. European traders negotiated with Indian communities as mutual dependents. They exchanged gifts, accommodated their different interests, and intermixed culturally. White has called this the "middle ground" that naturally existed where diverse peoples, each with expansionist aims, came together.

The Albany Plan was one of the first instances when Americans acted self-consciously to convert the middle ground into clearly American ground. Benjamin Franklin and his successors would not tolerate the uncertainty that came through constant compromise with diverse interests. They rejected a strategy of balance among various groups. The Albany Plan sought to remake the frontier in America's image. It marked a revolutionary application of liberty and enterprise beyond America's then-limited boundaries.

Franklin's 1754 proposals set a precedent for the Northwest Ordinance of 1787 and subsequent policies that unified the territories later comprising the United States as a single economic market, under a single set of "civilized" laws. Liberty and enterprise became the touchstones for legitimate authority in lands previously occupied by peoples with different traditions of political organization.

Americans had clear economic and security interests in the West, but they also felt a sense of racial and cultural superiority that was exemplified in Franklin's references to "savages" on the frontier. In the next century these assumptions would find expression in an asserted American manifest destiny to revolutionize the "backward" hinterlands.

American policy after 1754 emphasized westward expansion and the export of revolution. This translated into explicit territorial occupation, forced population removals, and the extension of a single nation. Before independence these ideas were recognizable. They became most evident, in North America and across the Atlantic Ocean, at the dawn of the nineteenth century. American support for revolutionary activities would soon extend far beyond the nation's western frontier.

INDEPENDENCE AND REVOLUTION ABROAD

In the months following the first clashes between American and British forces at Lexington and Concord, the nascent United States made two surprising efforts to convert its struggle into a broader international movement. On 28 July 1775 the Continental Congress, representing the colonies in rebellion, addressed "the people of Ireland," similarly subjects of British imperial rule. According to the Americans, King George III's ministers had converted the citizens of colonial lands "from freemen into slaves, from subjects into vassals, and from friends into enemies." Members of the Continental Congress asserted that they shared a "common enemy" with the Irish population. They expected a "friendly disposition" between the two peoples, and a similar struggle for freedom: "God grant that the iniquitous schemes of extirpating liberty from the British Empire may soon be defeated."

This call for international revolution was much more than idle rhetoric. As they struggled to raise the forces necessary to challenge the British military on the eastern seaboard, American soldiers attempted to carry their revolution beyond their borders. On 4 September 1775 an army of two thousand men invaded British-controlled Canada. In the middle of November, they occupied Montreal. The Americans did not rape and pillage the Canadian population but instead created a "virtuous" government that would allow the people to elect their leaders ("liberty") and protect their commerce ("enterprise"). Many residents of Montreal and other surrounding areas welcomed this imposed revolution.

American expansionism in 1775 reflected naive but serious enthusiasm for radical international change. Despite their relative weakness in relation to the British Empire, the former colonists felt that their revolution marked a turning point in world history. They believed that their cause would inspire men and women in Canada, Ireland, and other areas. Encouraging radical change abroad was not altruistic, but necessary for what the Continental Congress called the "golden period, when liberty, with all the gentle arts of peace and humanity, shall establish her mild dominion in this western world." The historian Joyce Appleby has demonstrated that even skeptics of political idealism like John Adams were "profoundly influenced by their belief in the unity of human experience and the general application of universal truths."

REVOLUTIONARY REALISM

The failure of the Irish population to rise in response to foreign overtures, and the rapid British success in recapturing the invaded areas of Canada, forced American leaders to rethink their tactics for securing independence. Men like Benjamin Franklin, John Adams, and Thomas Jefferson continued to believe that their cause was international in scope. They also understood that revolutionary ends called for pragmatic means. This required revolutionary realism: a willingness to make compromises and exhibit patience without corrupting ideals.

In February 1778, American leaders concluded a treaty of amity and commerce with the kingdom of France. This alliance brought the revolutionary colonists together with the conservative ancien régime of Louis XVI for the purpose of defeating British power. The French monarchy surely had no interest in seeing the cause of revolution spread beyond the British dominions. Nonetheless, most historians agree that without French aid the American Revolution might not have reached a successful conclusion. Paris supported American independence to promote its self-interest in the larger European balance of power.

Franklin, Adams, and Jefferson recognized the necessity of maintaining friendly but distant relations with unsavory regimes like that of France. Americans traded and procured aid from monar-

chical states. They generally avoided close political collaboration with these governments for fear of corrupting America's revolutionary principles. This explains, in part, the tradition of U.S. diplomatic aloofness, often termed "neutrality," that carried from the late eighteenth century up to World War II. While Americans sought to conduct profitable commerce with societies of all varieties—including France and Britain in the late eighteenth century—they attempted to remain separate from the politics of the conservative Old World.

President George Washington articulated this point of view in his Farewell Address, published on 19 September 1796. He called upon citizens to spread the virtues of commerce while avoiding "permanent alliances" that might threaten the new nation's security. American leaders like Washington were realistic enough to understand that they could never afford to isolate themselves from the international system. Through commerce and calculated political detachment from the powerful European monarchies, they hoped to protect their revolution, patiently spreading their principles abroad as opportunities opened.

The outbreak of revolution in France during the summer of 1789 offered Americans one of their first and most extraordinary opportunities. Louis XVI's attempt to increase his international power by supporting the American revolutionaries had the paradoxical effect of bankrupting his monarchy and opening the door to upheaval in his society. Franklin, Washington, and Jefferson came to symbolize for many French thinkers the enlightened possibilities of liberty and enterprise, unfettered from the chains of despotism. As violence spread and the monarchy crumbled, revolutionary leaders and propagandists in France looked to the American government for support.

Jefferson, then serving as America's minister to France, encouraged the initial spread of unrest against the ancien régime. Thomas Paine, whose pamphlet *Common Sense* (1776) had inspired many Americans to join their independence struggle, also traveled (in an unofficial capacity) to Paris to support the cause of revolution. Jefferson and Paine were the most eloquent American exponents of the ideals embodied in popular French attacks on monarchy, aristocracy, and political tradition. The two advocates of revolution were not, however, unique in their sympathies. French revolutionary figures— particularly Edmond Charles Genêt, a diplomat from the new regime—received the adulation of American crowds throughout the United States. Even early skeptics of the events in France, notably John Adams and Alexander Hamilton, sympathized with those who wished to throw off the repression of the Bourbon regime and replace it with a society of liberty and enterprise.

Adams, Hamilton, and other members of the Federalist Party in America differed from Jefferson and Paine in their fear that the French Revolution would careen out of control. They perceived the violence in Paris and other cities as a threat to the very ideals the revolution wished to serve. They also understood that revolutionary chaos during the Jacobin period after the execution of the king would open the door for dictatorship, which is what occurred, first in the hands of the Directory and later under the leadership of Napoleon Bonaparte.

Jefferson, Paine, and the early Republicans were slower than their Federalist counterparts to see these dangers. When they did, in the mid-1790s, they also separated themselves from the extremism of the French Revolution. Both the Federalists and the Republicans supported a revolution against the ancien régime, but the two parties came to despair the violence, anarchy, and seeming irrationality of events in comparison to America's less disruptive experience.

Federalists and Republicans exaggerated their differences over the French Revolution to gain support from different domestic groups. Northern merchants generally felt threatened by French revolutionary attacks on their commerce. Southern planters, in contrast, expected new opportunities for export to France under a revolutionary regime that denounced mercantilism. These sectional differences contributed to partisan acrimony in the late eighteenth century.

The breakdown in the American political consensus during this period reflected little change in attitudes toward revolution. Americans supported the overthrow of monarchy in France. They applauded appeals to liberty. They exhibited suspicion of excessive violence and social disruption. Most importantly, they denounced revolutions that appeared more radical than their own.

LAND ACQUISITION AND HEGEMONY IN THE WESTERN HEMISPHERE

During the first decades of the nineteenth century, the United States established itself as a dominant power in the Western Hemisphere. This was no small accomplishment for a young nation with fragile unity and a minuscule military. Presidents Thomas Jefferson, James Madison, and James Monroe exploited Europe's preoccupation with the Napoleonic wars and the relative weakness of potential rivals in North America. They constructed what Jefferson called an "empire of liberty" that combined force and commerce with a sincere commitment to enlightened government in "savage" lands.

America's self-confidence in the righteousness of its revolutionary model motivated many of the bloodiest massacres and dispossessions of native communities during this period. For Jefferson in particular, those who resisted democratic government and economic penetration threatened the American cause. Resistance justified temporary repression and, when necessary, brutalization. Nonwhite races received the most violent treatment. They appeared "immature" and "unprepared" for the blessings of liberty. Americans defined themselves as paternalists, caring for blacks and Indians until these groups were ready (if ever) for democratic self-governance. In this curious way, American sincerity about revolutionary change inspired more complete domination over nonwhite communities than that frequently practiced by other, less ideologically imbued imperial powers.

The American acquisition of the Louisiana Territory from France in 1803 doubled the size of the country. It allowed Jefferson to make his "empire of liberty" a reality. With full control of the Mississippi River, the United States could conduct commerce along the north-south axis of the continent free from European interference. Exploring, apportioning, and eventually settling the vast western territories, the United States would now "civilize" its surroundings, as envisioned in Franklin's Albany Plan of 1754. Foreign powers and Indian communities had, in American eyes, prohibited the spread of liberty and enterprise. By sponsoring a famous cross-continental "journey of discovery" directed from 1804 to 1806 by Meriwether Lewis and William Clark, Jefferson provided a foundation for altering the West with the creation of national markets, state governments, and, very soon, railroads. The transformation of the territories acquired with the Louisiana Purchase involved the rapid and forceful extension of America's Revolution.

During this same period, residents of French, Spanish, and Portuguese colonies in the Western Hemisphere revolted against European authority. While Americans remained wary of revolutions directed by nonwhite peoples, the U.S. government supported independence in Haiti, Mexico, Colombia, Brazil, and other former imperial possessions. Nonwhite revolutionaries, like Toussaint Louverture in Haiti, received aid, goodwill, and, most importantly, inspiration from Americans.

Fearful that the European powers, including Russia, would attempt to repress the Latin American revolutions, President James Monroe and his secretary of state, John Quincy Adams, worked to exclude this possibility. On 2 December 1823 the president announced what later became known as the Monroe Doctrine in his annual message to Congress. It explicitly prohibited "future colonization by any European powers" in the Western Hemisphere. The doctrine asserted the predominance of U.S. interests. The president and his secretary of state believed that the security of American borders, trading lanes, and revolutionary principles required freedom from Old World intervention.

Throughout the rest of the nineteenth century, the British navy enforced the Monroe Doctrine in order to weaken London's European rivals; American words and British seapower sheltered revolutionaries from their previous imperial oppressors. At the same time, the United States stepped into the place of the colonial empires, assuring that political and economic change followed its model. Americans intervened south of their border to support revolutions that promised democratic governance and free trade. They repressed revolutions that entailed extreme violence, limitations on commerce, and challenges to U.S. regional domination. As in their policies toward France during the late eighteenth century, Americans welcomed rapid change throughout the Western Hemisphere, but only on their own terms.

1848 AND "YOUNG AMERICA"

The year 1848 witnessed a string of upheavals throughout most of the major cities in Europe, including Paris, Naples, Berlin, Budapest, and Vienna. In a matter of weeks, urban revolutionaries forced the French king Louis-Philippe and Austrian prince Klemens von Metternich to flee from power. Inspired in part by the example of the American Revolution, many citizens of Europe were poised for a bright new democratic future.

Americans rejoiced at this prospect, as illustrated by the frequent parades and proclamations on behalf of popular liberty in Europe. Foreign revolutionaries, particularly the Hungarian nationalist Lajos Kossuth, emerged as national celebrities. Their names replaced the previous names for many towns throughout Indiana, Wisconsin, Mississippi, Ohio, Arkansas, and Pennsylvania, areas with large recent immigrant populations from the European continent. Small groups of Americans organized themselves for possible military action overseas on behalf of their revolutionary heroes. While most of this private militia activity came to very little, a small contingent of U.S. citizens joined the failed rebellion in Ireland. As in 1775, Americans believed that the long-term success of their Revolution was connected with events in Europe, and Ireland in particular.

At the highest levels of government, the United States supported the European uprisings with diplomatic means short of force. In May 1848, John C. Calhoun, the former secretary of state and prominent U.S. senator from South Carolina, used his connections with the Prussian minister-resident in America to encourage the formulation of "constitutional governments" upon the "true principles" embodied in the American federal system. The construction of new political institutions on this model, according to Calhoun, was necessary for "the successful consummation of what the recent revolutions aimed at in Germany" and "the rest of Europe." The White House also indulged in revolutionary enthusiasm. On 18 June 1849, President Zachary Taylor sent a special envoy, Dudley Mann, to support and advise Kossuth. When the ruling Habsburg government learned of the Mann mission, it protested to Washington. Secretary of State Daniel Webster publicly defended American action on behalf of the European revolutionaries. In response, Vienna severed its connections with the United States. Americans accepted this temporary break in their foreign relations for the purpose of articulating their sympathies with the brave men and women who hoped to overturn the old European political order.

These revolutionary hopes, however, failed to reach fruition. By the end of 1849 the established monarchies of Europe had reasserted their control over the continent. When necessary, they used military force to crush the reformers who had taken to the streets. Dismayed by this course of events, but conscious of its inability to affect a different outcome, the U.S. government reaffirmed its commercial relations with the conservative regimes. Americans condemned the brutality in Europe, but they took advantage of postrevolutionary stability to increase cotton and other exports across the Atlantic. This was another case of America's revolutionary realism: sympathy and support for political change overseas, but a recognition that compromise and patience were necessary. The United States took advantage of opportunities to push its ideals, and it also exploited existing markets to sell its products. This was an unavoidable balance.

After 1848 many Americans worried about the implications of their nation's failure to support the cause of revolution more concretely. A faction of dissatisfied Democrats came together at this time to form a group identified as Young America. In using this name they meant to differentiate their interventionist program from the caution of their party's so-called Old Fogies. Young America argued that the nation could only secure its ideals through more forceful "expansion and progress." Stephen A. Douglas, the U.S. senator from Illinois who would run against Abraham Lincoln in the 1860 presidential election, became the leading political figure for citizens who wished to make America a more effective beacon of revolution overseas. Douglas, however, failed to win the Democratic Party nomination for the presidency in 1852. Another Democrat, Franklin Pierce, was elected to the White House that year after making numerous appeals to Young America sentiment. Pierce advocated U.S. expansion for the purpose of opening markets and spreading American principles. The Democratic Party platform explained that "in view of the condition of popular institutions in the Old World, a high and sacred duty is devolved with increased responsibility upon the Democracy in this country." Americans believed that the vitality of their ideals required more effective support for political and economic change overseas. The spread of liberty and enterprise across the globe became more important as the United States suffered a profound crisis of identity in the years before the Civil War.

For American advocates of what the historian Eric Foner has identified as the ideology of "free soil, free labor, and free men," the post-1848 repressions in Europe threatened to reinforce unenlightened policies at home. This appeared most evident in the case of southern slavery. Transforming monarchies into democracies and liberating human beings from bondage became part of a single project. At home and abroad, free labor promised increased productivity, higher wages for workers of all races, and more democratic politics. Support for monarchy overseas and slavery in the American South constrained markets, depressed wages, and empowered conservative families.

Agitation around Young America in the 1850s, and broader attempts to foster the spread of liberty and enterprise, contributed to the American Civil War. The bloodshed between 1861 and 1865 resulted, at least in part, from a Northern attempt to enforce radical socioeconomic change in the South. Slavery and the South's "peculiar" precapitalist structure, according to Eugene Genovese, hindered the development of industry and democracy. The period of Reconstruction after the defeat of the Confederacy is, not surprisingly, called by many historians America's second revolution, when southern institutions—including slavery, voting restrictions, and property concentration in a landed aristocracy—were all radically dislocated by an interventionist Union government.

This second revolution went hand in hand with a more assertive U.S. foreign policy in Europe and Asia. Like Reconstruction at home, American activities abroad sought to eradicate "peculiar" obstacles to liberty and enterprise. "Free soil, free labor, and free men" was a global worldview that required U.S.-supported revolutions in the most tradition-bound empires, especially in Asia.

Between 1840 and 1870, American envoys forced China and Japan to open official contacts with Washington. In 1844, Caleb Cushing, U.S. representative from Massachusetts and longtime advocate of U.S. expansion, negotiated the Treaty of Wanghia with the Chinese emperor. This agreement guaranteed American trade access to key ports in Asia. Equally important, the treaty protected the legal rights of missionaries proselytizing on the mainland. For Cushing and his contemporaries, relations with China promised both wealth and the spread of America's "Christian" ideas of liberty. Commodore Matthew Perry's mission to the then-closed kingdom of Japan in 1853 served similar purposes. In 1858, Perry's successor, Townsend Harris, negotiated a treaty to open Japan for U.S. trade and ideas.

The upheavals in China and Japan during the second half of the nineteenth century were influenced significantly by these inroads. In both societies, Americans sought to undermine traditional political and economic institutions. Missionaries argued for new restrictions on monarchical authority. Merchants emphasized personal profit and private property. Intellectuals extolled the virtues of a learned and participatory citizenry. In all of these ways, the expansionist ideology of Young America encouraged U.S.-style liberty and enterprise to take root in some of the world's oldest civilizations. American ideas undermined conservative worldviews.

THE "NEW EMPIRE"

The historian Walter LaFeber wrote that the decades after the Civil War marked the beginning of modern American diplomacy. The dominance of northern and western economic interests, America's expansionist ideology, and the nation's growing industrial might made the United States a truly global power during this period. In the Philippines, Midway Islands, Hawaii, and Alaska the nation formed in a struggle for independence became, despite significant domestic opposition, a colonial overseer. The United States built an imperium that soon rivaled the empires of old.

The American empire was not only "new" in its chronology, according to LaFeber. It was also "new" in its structure and governing ideology. This was an empire predicated on the assumption that all of the world could become like the United States. William Henry Seward, secretary of state from 1861 to 1869, envisioned an almost unlimited expanse of liberty and enterprise. Railroads, ships, and other government-sponsored projects would allow for the free movement of people and products. Education and the rule of law would protect the freedom of the individual and the property of the merchant. Most importantly, Seward believed that America's model of a democratic society would improve the lives of citizens across the globe, even if it required violence and repression in the short run. This was a revolutionary vision that, like others, required sacrifice (usually most burdensome for non-Americans) on behalf of a higher cause. Democracy and markets were the perceived wave of the future, uprooting traditional hierarchies in Europe, Asia, Latin America, and other continents.

Seward's revolutionary vision served America's material and strategic interests, but it also had sincere racial and religious roots. Belief in an Anglo-Saxon mission to "Christianize" the world came through in one of the most widely read books of the post–Civil War years: the Reverend Josiah Strong's *Our Country*. Published in 1886 on behalf of the American Home Missionary Society, the first edition sold more than 130,000 copies (an astronomical figure for the time) and was serialized in countless newspapers. Like Seward, Strong affirmed the importance of expanded American influence throughout the world. Industrialization had brought the world closer together, Strong argued. Nations had to prepare for more intense international competition. Strong affirmed Seward's vision of a democratic and market-driven empire. He also elaborated on the importance of this imperial turn for America's "Anglo-Saxon Christian mission." In language that appealed to the prejudices of many readers, Strong asserted: "There is no doubt that the Anglo-Saxon is to exercise the commanding influence in the world's future."

Struggling as he saw it against "heathen" influences in Asia and other parts of the globe, Strong assured readers that "I cannot think our civilization will perish. . . . I believe it is fully in the hands of the Christians of the United States, during the next ten or fifteen years, to hasten or retard the coming of Christ's kingdom in the world by hundreds, and perhaps thousands, of years." For Strong and his many thousands of followers, the Anglo-Saxon "race" was uniquely suited to bring civilization to the rest of the world. *Our Country* contained extended "scientific" discussion about the superiority of Anglo-Saxon physiques, the adaptability of settlers from this stock, and, most importantly, the positive influence of Protestantism. Free from the oppression of a Roman Catholic Church, an emperor, or any superstitious deities, Anglo-Saxons developed unique qualities of liberty and enterprise. They were self-governing and capable of creative production, according to Strong. *Our Country* tapped into popular anxieties that the growth of competing empires, the migration of "inferior races," and the spread of industrialization in the second half of the nineteenth century threatened Anglo-Saxon virtues. In this context Strong wrote that "the destinies of mankind, for centuries to come, can be seriously affected, much less determined, by the men of this generation in the United States." A global American empire would protect the essential qualities of Anglo-Saxon civilization by remaking the rest of the world in the U.S. image. Racial characteristics were inherited, according to Strong, but they could be overcome by the socializing qualities of Christian doctrine.

Converted believers in far-off lands could receive grace from God. American expansion and colonization in places like Hawaii and the Philippines promised, in Strong's words, to "mold the destinies of unborn millions."

This was God's revolution on an international scale. Strong's words reflected a popular American disposition to dislodge "heathen" elites overseas. Businessmen claimed they were doing God's work when they seized local resources and established trading posts in formerly closed societies. Missionaries asserted divine sanction when they disregarded local traditions and proselytized their beliefs to native citizens. Most significantly, U.S. military forces in Asia, Latin America, and other areas argued that violence was a necessary means of building God's kingdom. Citing Charles Darwin on the "survival of the fittest," Strong claimed that resisting populations would be routed in a contest "of vitality and of civilization." As on the western frontier in earlier years, after the Civil War Americans built an extensive new empire, employing brutality for the sake of revolutionary ends.

THE EARLY TWENTIETH CENTURY

The Spanish-American War of 1898 was, according to Walter LaFeber, a natural outgrowth of America's revolutionary expansion in prior decades. When Cuban residents revolted in early 1895 against Spanish rule, the government of President Grover Cleveland offered support for the aspirations of the island's citizens. Cleveland did not advocate immediate Cuban independence—he condescendingly believed that the dark-skinned inhabitants of the island were unprepared for self-rule. However, the president pushed the Spanish government to initiate political and economic reforms that would make Cuba more like America. Cuban exiles residing in the United States and labor union leaders—especially Samuel Gompers of the American Federation of Labor—went beyond Cleveland's caution, advocating an immediate revolution against Spanish authority. By 1897 newspaper publishers picked up on these sentiments. They demanded a U.S. war aimed at destroying the Spanish empire.

Simultaneously, an uprising against Madrid's rule in the Philippines attracted American attention. In this case, American interest did not derive from geographical proximity to the United States but instead from the Philippines' location near China. As Britain, France, Germany, and Japan divided up the economic markets of China, businessmen and policymakers in the United States worried that they would be excluded. The United States lacked the imperial springboard that Hong Kong, for example, provided to the British. A revolution in the Philippines promised, in many American eyes, to create a regime both friendly and compatible with the nation's economic interests in China. Secretary of State John Hay expected that a Philippine revolution against Spanish rule would ensure the continued spread of liberty and enterprise in Asia. This was the basic assumption of Hay's famous Open Door Notes (1899–1900), which connected American interests with assured access to the people and markets of foreign societies.

Drawn into the Cuban and Philippine uprisings, the United States went to war with Spain in April 1898 to expand its "new empire" and assure that revolutions overseas followed the American model. This meant the destruction of monarchy and other inherited authorities. U.S. occupation armies replaced traditional institutions with free markets, personal property protections, and promises of democratic self-rule. Racist American fears that nonwhite populations would not properly govern themselves if left to their own devices meant that, in practice, democratic reforms were virtually nonexistent in Cuba and the Philippines after 1898. While the Caribbean island attained nominal independence, the Platt Amendment of 1901 (named for Connecticut senator Orville Platt) guaranteed American military and economic dominance. In the Philippines, the United States did not rely upon informal mechanisms of control. The archipelago became an American colony, where U.S. soldiers fought a bloody four-year war against Filipino rebels. America supported revolution in Cuba and the Philippines, but it also suppressed revolution when it challenged core assumptions about liberty and enterprise.

Washington would not tolerate radicalism that jeopardized markets and assumptions about just government. Americans remained revolutionary thinkers, as they had been since before 1776. Their nation continued to inspire unprecedented social transformations across the globe. By the end of the nineteenth century, however, Americans encountered numerous competing revolutionary models. These included the nationalism of many independence fighters (especially the Chinese Boxer rebels of 1900), the anti-industrialism of peasant activists, and the socialism of international-minded thinkers.

None of these forces was new. All three, particularly socialism, gained momentum from the disruption that accompanied heightened rivalries among the European imperial powers and the emergence of the United States as an important international player. Americans could begin to build a truly global empire of liberty and enterprise after 1898, but they quickly became aware of contrary, more radical tendencies throughout the world. For the United States the twentieth century was a struggle to spread the American Revolution and repress alternatives. Cuba and the Philippines were preludes to what lay ahead.

WILSONIANISM

On 15 March 1917, Czar Nicholas II, fearing the spread of domestic revolution, abdicated from the throne of imperial Russia. A provisional government, led by a recently formed party known as the Constitutional Democrats, asserted authority over the country. Inspired by British and other European liberals, the Constitutional Democrats promised to replace centuries of near absolute monarchy in Russia with a democratic society. They hoped to copy the social-market economies of western Europe that mixed industrial enterprise and private property with guarantees of basic public welfare.

The United States was far removed from events in Russia, but the nation and its leaders immediately expressed sympathy with the liberal revolution against the czar. Many immigrants in cities like New York, Pittsburgh, and Chicago had come to America as a refuge from czarist tyranny and the frequent ethnic violence encouraged by the old regime. In earlier years these groups had pressured President Theodore Roosevelt to protest against Russian pogroms. In 1917 they applauded the overthrow of the czar and supported friendly American gestures toward the revolutionaries now in power.

President Woodrow Wilson and his closest advisers shared much of this sentiment. On 22 March 1917, only seven days after the czar had abdicated, the United States officially recognized the legitimacy of the new government. Wilson was one of the first leaders to make this move because he hoped to encourage the spread of American-style liberty and enterprise in Russia and other areas emerging from long histories of autocratic rule. He followed the counsel of his confidant, Colonel Edward M. House, who

explained that by supporting "the advancement of democracy in Russia," Wilson would accelerate "democracy throughout the world." Secretary of the Navy Josephus Daniels recorded in his diary that the president spoke of the Russian Revolution as a "glorious act."

Wilson's vision of American-supported "democracy throughout the world" permeated his declaration of war against Germany on 2 April 1917, less than a month after the "glorious" Russian Revolution. After more than two years of bloody conflict on the European continent, accompanied by increasing attacks on American shipping, the president announced to Congress that "autocratic government," like that in Germany, was more than just distasteful to U.S. sensibilities. Autocratic militarism, repression, and economic nationalism had become profound threats to the life of democracy. Without the spread of American-style liberty and enterprise, the historian Frank A. Ninkovich has explained, Wilson feared the degradation and destruction of his society. World revolution on the American model was necessary for U.S. survival. This is what Wilson meant when he proclaimed that the "world must be made safe for democracy." The future of "civilization" had reached an apparent turning point. The president's Fourteen Points, announced on 8 January 1918 in a speech to Congress, outlined a program that sought to revolutionize the basic structure of international relations for the purpose of spreading democracy. Emphasizing the liberated "voice of the Russian people," Wilson called for political openness, free trade, disarmament, "independent determination" for oppressed peoples, and a "general association" of peace-loving nations. Liberty and enterprise, not balance of power or divine right, would govern the international system. Affairs between nations would evolve to look more like the relations among citizens in the United States.

In late 1917, just as the first American soldiers began to arrive on the European continent, a small group of communist, or Bolshevik, revolutionaries overthrew the new government in Russia. Under the leadership of Vladimir Lenin and Leon Trotsky, the Bolsheviks pledged to destroy capitalism and American-style democracy. Liberty and enterprise, according to Lenin, allowed for the strong and the wealthy to repress the weak and the poor. A global proletarian revolution, starting in Russia, would create a new international structure guaranteeing equality and individual welfare, not

★ ★ ★ ★

AMERICA, RUSSIA, AND REVOLUTION IN 1917

In early 1917 Russia's revolution against centuries of despotism excited Americans. President Woodrow Wilson hoped that the abdication of the czar on 15 March would elicit a period of worldwide democracy. He became one of the first foreign leaders to recognize the new regime, which was led by a party of Constitutional Democrats. Wilson imbibed the same faith in liberal revolution that had animated American thinkers like Benjamin Franklin, Thomas Jefferson, and William Seward.

The appearance of Vladimir Lenin and Leon Trotsky in Russia defied Wilson's hopes. In late 1917 these men took control of the Russian government. They pledged to pursue an international revolution that would undermine the liberal individualism and free market capitalism at the core of American foreign policy. Communism in Russia was a revolutionary challenge to America's own ideas of revolution.

Like his predecessors in the White House, Wilson had little tolerance for dissent. He believed that both communist ideas on the political Left and conservative traditions on the Right undermined his hopes for global democracy. To save the American revolutionary model overseas from its detractors, Wilson dispatched a small expeditionary force to assist anti-Bolshevik groups fighting in Russia's Siberian region during 1918 and 1919.

Thus began a long century of American hostilities with the communist regime in Russia. Sincere revolutionary enthusiasm in the United States often produced counterrevolutionary policies. Events in 1917 followed an American pattern set in the eighteenth century.

the empty promises of bourgeois democracy. In order to establish their regime, the Bolsheviks made many short-term compromises, particularly the signing of the Treaty of Brest-Litovsk with Germany on 3 March 1918, but they were as serious as Wilson in their aspiration to revolutionize the international system.

This second, Soviet phase of the Russian Revolution elicited reactions similar to those inspired by the Jacobin period of the French Revolution more than a century earlier. Americans sympathized with Russian citizens who sought to overthrow the czar, but they recoiled from the sight of violence, property confiscation, and civil war. Wilson believed that his program for a democratic peace after World War I was the only one worth pursuing. Lenin's contrary vision challenged basic assumptions about liberty and enterprise. The Bolsheviks promised to make the world profoundly unsafe for democracy on American terms. Russia's communist revolution endangered the American revolution.

On 6 July 1918, Wilson authorized a small American expeditionary force to join British, French, and Japanese soldiers supporting the anti-Bolshevik White armies in Russian Siberia. This intervention followed a model that the president had applied, more than any of his predecessors, throughout the Western Hemisphere during his two terms in office. Small groups of U.S. soldiers entered a foreign country to assist favored revolutionary elements against their opponents. In Siberia—as in Mexico, Haiti, the Dominican Republic, and Central American states—Wilson hoped to ensure the kind of political order that would allow liberty and enterprise to take shape. N. Gordon Levin, Jr., has explained that the president and his advisers convinced themselves that they were not threatening Russia's self-determination because the U.S. force was so small. Wilson viewed limited American intervention as the action required to nurture legitimate revolutionary impulses threatened by domestic competitors and foreign predators.

In this context historians have noted the conservative implications of the president's revolutionary rhetoric, especially at the Paris Peace Conference of 1919. The Versailles settlement negotiated by the victors in World War I broke apart the Austro-Hungarian and Ottoman Empires, as well as the German imperium outside of Europe. It established self-determination for the Poles, Hungarians, Greeks, and other long-repressed peoples. It also created a League of Nations that the United States, despite Wilson's efforts, refused to join. These constituted significant changes in the international system, but they paled in comparison to what the Versailles settlement left intact. Fearful that Bolshevism and other nonliberal revolutionary movements in places like Germany, Hungary, and China would create anarchy, Wilson and his counterparts allowed the major world empires—Britain, France, and Japan—to grow. American influence—formal and informal—also expanded, especially in Asia. Local elites in China, Korea, and Indochina found their expectations for national independence under the terms of Wilson's Fourteen Points disappointed. Through military and economic means, the great powers worked to constrain political change that challenged basic liberal-capitalist assumptions.

Wilson carried the paradox of Jeffersonian politics into the twentieth century. American leaders and citizens naturally applauded the overthrow of old regimes, particularly those of King Louis XVI and Czar Nicholas II. They expected that governments ensuring liberty and enterprise on the American model would replace centuries of despotism and autocracy. Because of his young nation's relative weakness, Jefferson had to rely largely on rhetoric to support overseas revolution. Wilson, in contrast, matched emotional words with extended military commitments.

When the revolutionary visions of Jefferson and Wilson encountered more radical ideas, especially Jacobinism and Bolshevism—these two men proved intolerant of diversity. They worked to repress rivals and eliminate the conditions that produced uncertainty instead of orderly change. Away from the American continent, this involved mostly rhetoric for Jefferson. Wilson, however, took advantage of his influence at the Paris Peace Conference to bolster efforts aimed at repressing challengers to American-style liberty and enterprise. In the early twentieth century, the United States had the power to enforce its worldview throughout Latin America and the Caribbean, as well as in parts of Europe and Asia. Wilsonianism revolutionized these areas by making them more like America and less like other revolutionary alternatives. U.S. policy followed this Wilsonian pattern in succeeding decades, albeit with important variations.

LIBERAL DEVELOPMENTALISM

The 1920s are traditionally identified with alleged American "isolationism." Recent scholarship has shown that this picture is far too simple.

Wilson's successors in the White House avoided foreign military commitments, but they pursued a consistent policy that the historian Emily S. Rosenberg has called "liberal developmentalism." This ideology, shared by U.S. leaders and citizens, assumed that "other nations could and should replicate America's own developmental experience." Businesses, philanthropic groups, labor unions, and government figures worked together after World War I to spread the "American dream" in Europe, Asia, and Latin America. This included encouraging the development of free markets, democratic institutions, and popular culture on the American model.

The last element of this triad proved most revolutionary. Manufacturers and advertisers—often working with government subsidies—contributed to a global diffusion of American-style automobiles, radios, and movie technologies, among other products. Rising criticisms of Americanization during this period attested to the ways in which U.S. cultural influence revolutionized foreign societies. The new popular culture made the nation of Jefferson and Wilson a focus of global attention. It disrupted social hierarchies by appealing to the desires of the average individual. Most significantly, it undermined traditional values by glorifying liberty and enterprise.

Contrary to the "isolationism" often associated with the White House during this period, American presidents shared public enthusiasm for the cultural spread of the American revolution abroad. As secretary of commerce and later as president, Herbert Hoover encouraged investment overseas, creating the foreign infrastructure and dependence that would guarantee access for American products and ideas. Instead of assuring fair competition among a variety of firms, the U.S. government supported the foreign expansion of near monopolies like J. P. Morgan, Standard Oil, and General Electric. These companies exerted strong influence over Republican presidential administrations. They also acted as "chosen instruments" for America's policy of supporting overseas revolution through economic and cultural means. Spreading the American dream in the 1920s promised massive profits and radical changes in the ways foreign societies functioned. Historians have generally avoided the temptation to glorify Americanization, but they have recognized that the nation's liberal developmentalism revolutionized international society.

FASCISM AND THE "AMERICAN WAY OF WAR"

During the Great Depression of the 1930s American culture lost some of its glow. In addition to Soviet communism, fascism emerged as a powerful challenger to America's revolutionary model. Scholars have long debated whether fascism constituted an alternative revolutionary paradigm or an antimodern regressive influence. Regardless of their position on this issue, historians agree that it sought to smother the influence of American-style liberty and enterprise in countries like Italy, Germany, Spain, and Japan. In all of these nations, fascists condemned the decadence of imported cars, radio programs, and movies. Fascist leaders sought to create more nationalist—and often racial—cultural forms.

Unlike the citizens of many European and Asian countries, Americans never showed much sympathy for fascism. As early as 1933, prominent figures, including President Franklin D. Roosevelt, expressed strong distaste for the "uncivilized" behavior of the Nazis in Germany. Mired in an economic depression, the United States offered little material support to antifascist fighters, but the leaders of the nation consistently criticized the violent infringements on individual liberty and free enterprise that accompanied the policies of dictators like Adolf Hitler and Benito Mussolini. Americans hoped for a string of antifascist revolutions.

When these upheavals failed to materialize and the regimes in Germany, Italy, and Japan began to undermine neighboring democracies, President Roosevelt initiated a policy of antifascist intervention overseas. He used a mix of foreign assistance, trade embargoes, and military expansion to bolster American influence. This included close cooperation with Britain, and after Germany invaded the Soviet Union in June 1941, the USSR. Like the revolutionary realists of the eighteenth century, Roosevelt recognized that alliance with unsavory regimes—in this case a communist state—was necessary to defeat a more pressing danger to American ideals.

On 14 August 1941 the president issued a public statement announcing what became known as the Atlantic Charter to guide the great powers during World War II and the postwar settlement. Negotiated during a three-and-one-half day meeting with British Prime Minister Winston Churchill off the coast of Newfoundland, this document pledged Washington and London (as well as Moscow, they hoped) to the Wilsonian principles of self-determination, free trade, disarmament, and a "permanent system of general security." In addition, the Atlantic Charter included promises of "improved labor standards, economic advancement, and social security" inspired by Roosevelt's domestic New Deal policies. The president sought to assure "that all the men in all the lands may live out their lives in freedom from fear and want." This was an extraordinary moment in the history of great power diplomacy. Roosevelt had pledged to support Britain against Nazi Germany, but in return he had extracted concessions that would revolutionize what was then the world's largest empire. Self-determination, as outlined in the Atlantic Charter, justified independence movements in Britain's Indian, Southeast Asian, and East African colonies. Free trade undermined the imperial preference system that had formerly allowed London to dominate the economies of its empire. A "permanent system of general security," soon to be named the United Nations, diminished the global predominance of the European capitals. Most significantly, New Deal guarantees of economic security and social welfare included in the Atlantic Charter helped to legitimize human rights, only a nascent concept before 1941.

Like Wilson, Roosevelt brought the United States into World War II with the purpose of making the world safe for democracy. This involved bloody battlefields on two fronts, in Europe and Asia, with frequent compromises concerning strategy and principle. The war was "total" for Americans because they saw no alternative but to eliminate their fascist enemies completely. All alliances and compromises served this purpose. Under American tutelage, political life in Europe and Asia had to start anew, infused with the principles of liberty and enterprise that foreign elites had resisted for too long.

Total annihilation of enemies and a revolutionary reconstruction of society on American terms was, according to historian Russell F. Weigley, "the American way of war." Acting to destroy threats to their way of life, U.S. leaders conquered much of Europe and Asia. They followed the same pattern pursued when men like Jefferson and Lincoln annexed the western territories during the nineteenth century and defeated the South during the Civil War. Operating under the guidance of the Atlantic Charter, U.S. soldiers forced foreign societies to accept American ideas of liberty and enterprise. They followed the vision of figures like Josiah Strong, who had proclaimed a global mission to make the Old World new. World War II was, in this sense, a conflict fought by the United States for worldwide revolution on American terms.

RECONSTRUCTION AND CONTAINMENT

If the Civil War was America's second revolution, the years after World War II marked a third revolution. Having created a new form of government and expanded it across much of North America, the United States now rebuilt western Europe, Japan, and South Korea from the ground up. Historians have devoted extensive attention to the vital role that local citizens and leaders played in charting new directions for these societies. This is undeniable, but the revolutionary impact of American policy deserves serious consideration as well. Men like George Marshall, Dean Acheson, John McCloy, Lucius Clay, and Douglas MacArthur forced the defeated societies to reconstruct themselves on America's model. In West Germany and Japan this meant the formulation of new constitutions that enshrined free speech, democratic elections, and capitalist markets. In western Europe as a whole, Washington pushed for regional integration along lines that resembled American federalism. Most importantly, through the European Recovery Program, better known as the Marshall Plan, the United States provided societies devastated by war with the material resources to finance private enterprise and citizen welfare. Life for those vanquished by war in western Europe and Japan changed radically after 1945, largely along lines compatible with American sensibilities.

Americanization of this kind was revolutionary, but it also had conservative consequences. Washington chose to work with local elites that had strong anticommunist credentials. In many cases, this resulted in the repression of radical ideas. The Communist Party in Italy, for example, suffered electoral defeat in April 1948 after the U.S. Central Intelligence Agency provided the Christian Democratic Party and the Catholic Church with a large infusion of covert campaign funding. Western Europe, Japan, and South Korea were ripe for revolution after World War II, and the United States worked to make certain that these areas followed America's model. Democratic liberties and capitalist enterprise provided the foundation for U.S.-directed reconstruction.

Soviet efforts to consolidate revolutionary change along communist lines in Eastern Europe, North Korea, and China inspired fears—some legitimate, some exaggerated—that Moscow would subvert the states in America's sphere of influence. The clash between American and Soviet revolutionary models gave rise to what contemporaries called the Cold War. In this prolonged ideological struggle, the lands devastated during World War II became the battlegrounds where the superpowers competed to influence the course of future developments. Both Washington and Moscow believed that they could only make the world safe for their respective ideals if key strategic areas in Europe and Asia followed their particular model of political organization. Americans expected that a Europe of liberal democracies would ensure long-term peace and prosperity. Soviet leaders hoped that a Europe of communist states would provide the resources needed to build something approximating Karl Marx's vision of a workers' paradise.

The incompatibility of these visions made the Cold War a prolonged period of Soviet-American hostility. Following the often-quoted advice of George Kennan—the chairman of the State Department's Policy Planning Staff between 1947 and 1949—Americans sought to protect their revolutionary ideals by containing the spread of communist influence. This meant increasing support for allies who appeared to share American sensibilities, while limiting the influence of dissidents. From a geopolitical point of view, it also required a permanent mobilization of force to deter Soviet incursions. The policy of containment, in this sense, militarized America's revolutionary influence overseas, adding to the nation's already evident distrust of diversity. It also created a short-term bias to the status quo. Social experimentation and cooperation with a devious enemy appeared too risky.

By the 1950s the Cold War had spread to what contemporaries called the Third World. These were former colonial possessions in Asia, Africa, and Latin America that began to attain their independence in the aftermath of World War II. In general, the superpowers had limited strategic and economic interests in these areas. They drew extensive American and Soviet intervention, however, because they served as natural showcases for each government's revolutionary model.

The economist and policy adviser Walt Rostow was only one of many to argue for extensive U.S. sponsorship of Third World development in America's image. Prosperous markets and free societies, he explained, would increase the worldwide attraction of American-style liberty and enterprise. Otherwise, Rostow warned, newly independent states would fall prey to the "disease" of communist influence. On a strategic level, Rostow and others warned that Soviet advances in peripheral areas like Indochina would eventually jeopardize the survival of American-inspired values in critical strategic areas like Japan. This was the alleged threat of "falling dominoes."

Both Washington and Moscow used violence to reconstruct the Third World. In the American case, the Vietnam War was the clearest example of this phenomenon. Throughout the 1960s policymakers generally believed that they were bringing a positive revolution to the impoverished villagers of Indochina. Containment of communism and industrial development promised to create peace and prosperity, according to American assumptions. In pursuit of this vision, Washington deployed extensive military force to bludgeon local resistance.

Installing the American version of revolution in Vietnam involved the repression of all other varieties of revolution, nationalist and communist. The United States found itself destroying traditional villages and killing innocent civilians as it attempted, in vain, to build a new society in its own image. This was the perversity of American-sponsored revolution in the Third World. Many of the earliest and most consistent opponents of these policies were people who, like George Kennan, criticized the revolutionary and idealistic strains in U.S. foreign policy.

Throughout Asia, Africa, and Latin America the United States frequently hindered the process of decolonization because nationalists—like Ho Chi Minh—refused to accept the American model of liberal capitalism. Ideological dogmatism, economic interest, and cultural condescension combined when Washington lent its support to imperial powers and local "strong men." There were the counterrevolutionary consequences of America's inherited revolutionary narrow-mindedness, magnified by Cold War competition with the Soviet Union. U.S. conceptions of liberty and enterprise tragically set the most democratic nation against the cause of national independence.

DÉTENTE AND ITS CRITICS

The difficulties of supporting overseas revolution during the Cold War contributed to a crisis of American confidence in the late 1960s. Citizens and leaders doubted whether they could make a world with nuclear weapons, ubiquitous protest movements, and profound economic inequalities safe for democracy. Many individuals—including President Richard M. Nixon and his national security adviser (and later secretary of state), Henry Kissinger—believed that inherited American sensibilities were out of touch with international realities. Radical critics condemned the nation's long-standing ideals for producing destruction and devastation instead of helping those most in need.

Nixon and Kissinger sought to curtail America's revolutionary ambitions. They emphasized an international balance of power rather than promises for positive change. Through a series of agreements with former adversaries—especially the Soviet Union and the People's Republic of China—they created a framework for great power cooperation that limited conflict between different revolutionary models. At home they discredited critics who called for a more idealistic foreign policy. This period, called the era of détente by contemporaries, was one of unprecedented American pessimism and retrenchment. Nixon and Kissinger's foreign policy cut against the grain of basic American assumptions regarding the virtues of liberty and enterprise. After the turmoil of the 1960s, citizens grew skeptical about the application of these values overseas. Americans, however, were also uncomfortable with the empty realpolitik of détente. A foreign policy guided by balance of power considerations, rather than principles, promised only permanent struggle. Americans could not escape their inherited belief in progress. The stability promised by Nixon and Kissinger was not enough. The period of détente ended in the late 1970s as the nation began, yet again, to pursue revolutionary aspirations abroad.

Despite their significant differences, Presidents James Earl Carter and Ronald Reagan embodied this return to revolution in the wake of détente. They promised a more open and democratic foreign policy, one that embraced human rights and condemned communist infringements on liberty and enterprise. They pledged to fight when necessary to make the world safe for democracy. Most importantly, these two presidents spoke of remaking foreign societies in America's image. This is what Reagan meant when he repeatedly claimed that it was "morning in America."

Reagan's popularity at home and abroad speaks to the power of this idealistic message. When the Soviet government began to loosen its grip on Eastern Europe and its own society after 1985, his affirmations of American-style liberty and enterprise contributed to a new period of international optimism. In contrast to the 1960s, the United States now appeared poised to bring democracy and wealth to long-repressed and impoverished lands. The world had reached, in the frequently repeated words of Francis Fukuyama, the "end of history." According to this argument, America's liberal capitalism embodied a system of values that would finally revolutionize the entire world.

Most observers understood that they had not reached anything like the end of history. American ideals remained highly contested. Their applicability in various environments awaited demonstration. Nonetheless, American citizens found themselves drawn to Reagan's rhetoric because it promised international revolution on U.S. terms. It affirmed the messianic quality of America's political model. All of Reagan's successors in the late twentieth century, especially President William Jefferson Clinton, repeated his rhetoric.

THE AMERICAN REVOLUTION ENTERS THE TWENTY-FIRST CENTURY

The twenty-first century offered a host of new opportunities and challenges for American foreign policy. The collapse of the Soviet Union and the end of the Cold War made the United States an unmatched international power. Its technology, economy, and culture exerted influence in virtually all corners of the globe. American dynamism produced a startling trend toward the Americanization of food, fashion, music, law, and even language. American notions of liberty and enterprise revolutionized education, work, and entertainment in many societies, replacing traditional assumptions about hierarchy and status. U.S. influence provided many people with new hopes of freedom and wealth, but also new difficulties in protecting cultural particularity.

The latter consequence of America's revolutionary impact overseas—international homogenization—has inspired determined and sometimes violent resistance among groups who find their values under siege. The long list of Americanization's opponents includes farmers, environmentalists, labor union activists, religious believers, nationalists, and social democrats—as well as terrorists like Osama bin Laden. For these groups, American-inspired liberty and enterprise have the effect of repressing contrary ways of life. American movies and other forms of popular culture, for example, undermine assumptions about religious piety and social roles in countries as diverse as Italy and Iran. The same can be said for many of Washington's claims about human rights. America's revolutionary presumptions may seem self-evident and universally beneficial to some, but they also appear self-serving and shallow to others.

Throughout their history, Americans have consistently emphasized the global virtues of their ideals. They have generally ignored the shortcomings and narrow-mindedness embedded in their political values. This duality has made the United States a far-reaching revolutionary force. Time and again, the nation has rejected ideological diversity. Instead, it has used persuasion, coercion, and force to impose its vision on others. Traditional points of view have appeared to Americans as fodder for radical change. Alternative revolutionary programs, especially communism, have suffered from extreme repression at the hands of freedom's advocates. Americans are revolutionaries because they wish to change the world in their own image, with very little compromise or variation. They are frequently dogmatic and self-righteous. There is little reason to expect these qualities to change in the twenty-first century.

Rousseau anticipated the paradox of America as a revolutionary power. Forcing freedom on the world, the United States has supported radical change while also repressing diversity. This paradox became more evident during the course of the twentieth century, but it surely dates back as far as Benjamin Franklin's Albany Plan of 1754. Even before they attained independence, Americans conceived of their revolution as an ongoing, global process of democratization. On the continent of North America, in the Western Hemisphere, and across the Atlantic and Pacific Oceans, this has meant the spread of individual freedoms and free markets. Americans have scoffed at foreign traditions and assumed that all human beings will attain happiness and wealth when their societies are governed by politically aware citizens and energetic business owners.

The steady growth of U.S. diplomatic power since the end of British rule allowed Americans remarkable success in remaking the world. The international system at the dawn of the twenty-first century was disproportionately an American system. It produced many benefits for citizens of the United States and other nations, but it also undermined the diversity upon which liberty, enterprise, and most other values must ultimately depend. Global American influence seriously limited the range of human experience. Like other revolutionaries in the past, Americans confronted the possibility that their achievements had become self-defeating.

BIBLIOGRAPHY

Appleby, Joyce Oldham. *Liberalism and Republicanism in the Historical Imagination.* Cambridge, Mass., 1992. A provocative discussion of how Americans have thought about revolution.

Brinkley, Douglas, and David R. Facey-Crowther, eds. *The Atlantic Charter.* New York, 1994. A series of thoughtful analyses of the Atlantic Charter and its legacy.

Cooper, John Milton, Jr. *The Warrior and the Priest: Woodrow Wilson and Theodore Roosevelt.* Cambridge, Mass., 1983. A superb comparative study that analyzes the politics of early twentieth-century America.

Curti, Merle E. "Young America." *American Historical Review* 32 (1926): 34–55. Still a penetrating account of American thought regarding overseas revolution in the mid-nineteenth century.

———. "John C. Calhoun and the Unification of Germany." *American Historical Review* 40 (1935): 476–478. An insightful document on Calhoun's views of European revolution.

Davis, David Brion. *Revolutions: Reflections on American Equality and Foreign Liberations.* Cambridge, Mass., 1900. A probing series of lectures on American views of revolution.

DeConde, Alexander. *This Affair of Louisiana.* New York, 1976. A thoughtful account of the politics surrounding the Louisiana Purchase and American imperialism.

Dull, Jonathan R. *A Diplomatic History of the American Revolution.* New Haven, Conn., 1985. A concise account of the American Revolution in a broad international context.

Engerman, David C. "Modernization from the Other Shore: American Observers and the Costs of Soviet Economic Development." *American Historical Review* 105 (2000): 383–416. An excellent study of how ideas about economic development influenced American views of the Soviet Union.

Foner, Eric. *Free Soil, Free Labor, Free Men: The Ideology of the Republican Party Before the Civil War.* New York, 1970. A penetrating account of American political ideology around the time of the Civil War.

Ford, Worthington Chauncey, et al., eds. *Journals of the Continental Congress, 1774–1789.* 34 vols. Washington D.C., 1904–1937. An indispensable source on early American revolutionary aspirations and foreign policy.

Fukuyama, Francis. "The End of History?" *The National Interest* 16 (Summer 1989). An extremely influential and controversial argument about the triumph of America's revolutionary vision around the world.

Gaddis, John Lewis. *Strategies of Containment: A Critical Appraisal of Postwar American National Security Policy.* New York and Oxford, 1982. The best analysis of the sources and implications of America's containment policy during the Cold War.

Gardner, Lloyd C. *Safe for Democracy: Anglo-American Response to Revolution, 1913–1923.* New York, 1984. A broad account of Wilson's opposition to radical revolution.

———. *Pay Any Price: Lyndon Johnson and the Wars for Vietnam.* Chicago, 1995. A provocative analysis of how American liberal ideas contributed to the Vietnam War.

Genovese, Eugene D. *The Southern Tradition: The Achievement and Limitations of an American Conservatism.* Cambridge, Mass., 1994. A provocative account of southern society before the Civil War, and its implications for American politics.

Gilbert, Felix. *To the Farewell Address: Ideas of Early American Foreign Policy.* Princeton, N.J., 1961. An eloquent and thoughtful essay on the meaning of Washington's address for American foreign policy.

Hahn, Peter L., and Mary Ann Heiss, eds. *Empire and Revolution: The United States and the Third World Since 1945.* Columbus, Ohio, 2001. A useful survey of American foreign policy in the Third World during the Cold War.

Hartz, Louis. *The Liberal Tradition in America: An Interpretation of American Political Thought Since the Revolution.* 2d ed. San Diego, Calif., 1991. A classic account of how ideas about liberty and enterprise have dominated American politics.

Hogan, Michael J. *The Marshall Plan: America, Britain, and the Reconstruction of Western Europe, 1947–1952.* New York and Cambridge, 1987. A penetrating account of how the Marshall Plan reconstructed Western Europe on America's model.

Hunt, Michael H. *Ideology and U.S. Foreign Policy.* New Haven, Conn., 1987. A stimulating account of how American ideas about liberty, race, and revolution have affected foreign policy.

Iriye, Akira. *The Globalizing of America, 1913–1945.* New York, 1993. A compelling discussion of Americanization in the first half of the twentieth century.

Kaplan, Lawrence S. *Jefferson and France: An Essay on Politics and Political Ideas.* New Haven, Conn., 1967. A classic account of how America's preeminent revolutionary theorist grappled with the French Revolution.

Knock, Thomas J. *To End All Wars: Woodrow Wilson and the Quest for a New World Order.* New York, 1992. The best late-twentieth-century account of Wilson's revolutionary foreign policy.

Labaree, Leonard W., et al., eds. *The Papers of Benjamin Franklin.* 35 vols. New Haven, Conn., 1959–2001. An indispensable source on early American revolutionary aspirations and foreign policy.

LaFeber, Walter. *The New Empire: An Interpretation of American Expansion, 1860–1898.* Ithaca, N.Y., 1963. A classic account of American ideas and expansion in the late nineteenth century.

———. *The American Age: United States Foreign Policy at Home and Abroad Since 1750.* New York, 1989. The best survey for the history of American expansionism.

Latham, Michael E. *Modernization as Ideology: American Social Science and "Nation Building" in the Kennedy Era.* Chapel Hill, N.C., 2000. A stimulating discussion of how American ideas about development influenced foreign policy.

Leffler, Melvyn P. *A Preponderance of Power: National Security, the Truman Administration, and the Cold War.* Stanford, Calif., 1992. A rich account of how American values and fears of Soviet power drove foreign policy in the early Cold War.

Levin, Norman Gordon, Jr. *Woodrow Wilson and World Politics: America's Response to War and Revolution.* New York, 1968. A classic criticism of Wilson's opposition to radical revolution.

Link, Arthur S., ed. *The Papers of Woodrow Wilson.* 69 vols. Princeton, N.J., 1966–1994. An indispensable source on Wilsonian ideas and foreign policy.

Maier, Pauline. *From Resistance to Revolution: Colonial Radicals and the Development of American Opposition to Britain, 1765–1776.* New York, 1972. An excellent discussion of the international context for the American Revolution.

McCormick, Thomas J. *China Market: America's Quest for Informal Empire, 1893–1901.* Chicago, 1967. A provocative account of America's expanding influence in Asia at the end of the nineteenth century.

Ninkovich, Frank A. *The Wilsonian Century: U.S. Foreign Policy Since 1900.* Chicago, 1999. A compelling account of Wilson's revolutionary influence on American foreign policy in the twentieth century.

Roberts, Timothy M., and Daniel W. Howe. "The United States and the Revolutions of 1848." In R. J. W. Evans and Hartmut Pogge von Strandmann, eds. *The Revolutions in Europe, 1848–1849: From Reform to Reaction.* Oxford, 2000. An excellent survey of how Americans perceived the European revolutions of 1848.

Rosenberg, Emily S. *Spreading the American Dream: American Economic and Cultural Expansion, 1890–1945.* New York, 1982. A thoughtful account of America's cultural and economic expansion between the two world wars.

Rostow, Walt W. *The Stages of Economic Growth: A Non-Communist Manifesto.* 3d ed. New York, 1990. One of the most influential books on the role of liberal capitalist ideas in Third World development.

Smith, Tony. *America's Mission: The United States and the Worldwide Struggle for Democracy in the Twentieth Century.* Princeton, N.J., 1994. A provocative analysis of America's support for democratic revolution abroad.

Strong, Josiah. *Our Country.* 1886. Reprint, Cambridge, Mass., 1963. One of the most influential polemics about America's revolutionary "mission" overseas.

Weigley, Russell F. *The American Way of War: A History of United States Military Strategy and Policy.* New York, 1973. A compelling analysis of America's revolutionary approach to war.

White, Richard. *The Middle Ground: Indians, Empires, and Republics in the Great Lakes Region, 1650–1815.* Cambridge and New York, 1991. The best account of relations between Americans, Europeans, and Indians in the eighteenth century.

Williams, William Appleman. *The Tragedy of American Diplomacy.* 2d and enlarged ed. New York, 1972. One of the most important works on the history of American foreign relations, a penetrating discussion of economics, ideas, and expansion.

See also CULTURAL IMPERIALISM; IMPERIALISM; ISOLATIONISM; REALISM AND IDEALISM; WILSONIANISM.

SCIENCE AND TECHNOLOGY

★ ★ ★ ★

Ronald E. Doel and Zuoyue Wang

Science did not become a major concern of U.S. foreign policy until the twentieth century. This is not to say that science was unimportant to the young republic. U.S. leaders recognized that, in the Age of Reason, the prestige of science was part of the rivalry between nations. Yet through the nineteenth century science was primarily linked to foreign policy as an adjunct of trade relations or military exploration. By contrast, mechanical ability was central to the identity of Americans, and debates about the proper role of technology in American relations to Britain and Europe raged through the late nineteenth century, as the United States gained worldwide recognition for creating the modern technological nation.

Technology—and enthusiasm for technical solutions to social problems—remained important in American foreign relations through the twentieth century. But its position relative to science changed markedly after 1900. By the start of World War II, science became a new and urgent topic for policymakers, inspiring an uneasy relationship that profoundly challenged both diplomats and scientists. As the Cold War began, the U.S. government funded new institutions and programs that linked science with diplomatic efforts and national security aims. Some were cloaked in secrecy; others were incorporated into major foreign aid efforts such as the Marshall Plan. By the late twentieth century, policymakers viewed science and technology as synergistic twins, significant yet often unpredictable agents of economic, political, and social change on both national and global scales.

THE EARLY REPUBLIC

In the earliest years of the American Republic, the ideas of natural philosophy informed the worldview of the framers of the American Constitution. The most educated of them, including Thomas Jefferson, James Madison, and Benjamin Franklin, were familiar with the ordered clockwork universe that the greatest of Enlightenment scientists, Isaac Newton, had created, and metaphors and analogies drawn from the sciences permeated their political discourse. But the pursuit and practice of science was seen as part of a transnational "Republic of Letters," above the petty politics of nations. When a group of Harvard scientists sought to observe an eclipse in Maine's Penobscot Bay at the height of the revolutionary war in 1780, British forces not only tolerated them but provided safe passage. Similarly, while Franklin was a singularly well-known scientist, widely revered in France as the founder of the science of electricity, he served as the new nation's emissary to Paris on account of his similarly impressive skills in diplomacy and familiarity with French centers of power. While a number of institutions responsible for scientific research emerged within several decades after the nation's founding, including the Coast and Geodetic Survey and the Naval Observatory, none dealt directly with areas of national policy. Alexis de Tocqueville overlooked significant pockets of learning when he declared in *Democracy in America* (1835) that "hardly anyone in the United States devotes himself to the essentially theoretical and abstract portion of human knowledge," but he was astute in observing that the "purely practical part of science"—applied technology—was what stirred the American imagination.

Still, adroit statesmen recognized that the apolitical "republic of science" could be a helpful tool in aiding foreign policy ambitions, a value connected with scientific research that would grow dramatically in later years. Exploration and geographic knowledge were important elements in contests for empire, and the nascent United States did support several successful exploring expeditions prior to the mid-nineteenth century. When President Thomas Jefferson sought to send

Meriwether Lewis and William Clark on an expedition to the Pacific northwest, but lacked funds to provide military escort, he asked whether the Spanish minister would object to travelers exploring the Missouri River with "no other view than the advancement of geography." But in his secret message to Congress in January 1803, Jefferson emphasized the value the Lewis and Clark expedition would have in aiding United States control over this vast territory. By insisting that Lewis and Clark make careful astronomical and meteorological observations, study natural history, and record Indian contacts, Jefferson underscored an important relationship between science and imperialism. A similar set of concerns motivated the U.S. Exploring Expedition (Wilkes Expedition), which between 1838 and 1842 visited Brazil, Tierra del Fuego, Chile, Australia, and the East Indies and skirted 1,500 miles of the Antarctic ice pack (providing the first sighting of the Antarctic continent). Pressure to fund the expedition had come from concerned commercial and military groups, including whalers, who saw the Pacific as important for American interests. They did not sail empty waters, for this U.S. expedition overlapped with the voyages of the *Beagle,* the Antarctic expedition of Sir James Clark Ross of England, and the southern survey by Dumont d'Urville of France, and thus owed to nationalistic as well as scientific rivalries. Yet government-sponsored expeditions in this era remained infrequent.

By contrast, technological concerns were very much on the minds of American leaders. The industrial revolution was well underway in Britain at the time of the American Revolution. Stimulated by the depletion of forests by the early eighteenth century as wood was consumed for fuel, Britain had developed coal as an alternative energy source, accelerating technological development through the steam engine (the crucial invention of the first industrial revolution) and the construction of water- and steam-powered mills. By the time of the American Revolution, British industries were supplying the American colonies with manufactured goods, spun cloth, textiles, and iron implements employed in farming. The former colonists' victory created a dilemma for the newly independent states, as Britain sought to forbid the export of machines or even descriptions of them to maintain its trading advantage. While the war in fact only temporarily cut off the United States from the output of the burgeoning industrial mills in Birmingham, Manchester, and London, and resumed migration after the war allowed mechanics to transfer technical knowl-

edge across the Atlantic, government leaders still faced the question of what kind of material society the United States would attempt to create.

Americans at the turn of the nineteenth century agreed on one matter: they did not wish the United States to acquire the "dark satanic mills" that had made Manchester and Birmingham grimy, filthy cities, with overflowing sewers, wretched working conditions, widespread disease, and choking smoke. But American leaders also realized that a rejection of mill technology raised fundamental questions about what standards of material comfort the United States would aspire to reach, and the means, domestic and foreign, it would need to adopt to achieve those ends. Since sources of power were needed to increase living standards, how and what ways the former colonies would develop means of production or acquire finished products would help to shape the future economic, political, and social structure of the nation.

The question of whether to import the factory system to America or to encourage the growth of the United States as an agrarian nation emerged as the initial critical struggle over the role of technology in American foreign policy. It fanned intense political passions in the nascent nation, and helped shape its first political parties. Thomas Jefferson favored limiting the import of technological systems and manufactured goods. Jefferson wanted a republic primarily composed of small farmers, who as independent landowners would enhance "genuine and substantial virtue." The growth of large cities, he feared, would lead to a privileged, capitalistic aristocracy and a deprived proletariat. Jefferson's vision of an agrarian republic represented an ideal in early American political thought, popularized by such works as Hector St. John de Crevecouer's *Letters from an American Farmer* in 1782. While Jefferson was not adverse to all forms of manufacturing and would later soften his opposition to it even more, he initially envisioned a republic in which American families produced needed textiles at home and traded America's natural resources and agricultural output to secure plows and other essential artifacts. His foreign policy thus sought autonomy at the cost of more limited energy production and a lower standard of living.

Opposition to Jefferson's vision came from Alexander Hamilton, the New York lawyer and protégé of President George Washington who served as the young nation's first secretary of the treasury. Hamilton favored a diversified capitalistic economy, backed by a strong central government and import tariffs designed to nurture fledgling American industries. In his influential *Report on Manufactures* in 1791, Hamilton argued that "The Employment of Machinery forms an item of great importance in the general mass of national industry." Fearing a lack of social order from overreliance on an agricultural economy, Hamilton declared that the development of industry would encourage immigration, make better use of the diverse talents of individuals, promote more entrepreneurial activity, and create more robust markets for agricultural products. Hamilton's prescription for nationalism and his support for technology gained favor from Franklin, Washington, and John Adams, although fears of Jeffersonian Republicans that virtue followed the plow still held sway among many Americans.

By the 1830s and 1840s, Hamilton's ideas had gained the upper hand, and the federal government became a firm supporter of technological development as a promising means to promote national prosperity. Jefferson's embargo of 1807 and the War of 1812, which illuminated the vulnerability of relying on Britain for manufactured goods, helped spur this development, but another critical factor was American success in developing technologies that increased agricultural output, including the invention of the cotton gin and the mechanical harvester. The abundance of powerful rivers in New England allowed manufacturers to develop textile mills that relied on water power, initially allowing new manufacturing centers like Lowell, Massachusetts, to avoid the industrial grime of Manchester. No less important, the rapid advance of canals, river boat transportation, and especially railroads provided a model for the integration of hinter regions and seat of the nation, a means for insuring economic development and the sale of manufactured goods and products to foreign markets. For many, like the influential legislator William Seward, technology was the key to securing American domination over the continent and advancing trade. After Seward helped reinterpret patent law to insure that U.S. inventors would profit from their creations, patent numbers swelled. Patents granted rose from an average of 646 per year in the 1840s to 2,525 in the 1850s. Dreams of a global commercial empire were similarly behind American efforts to open Japan to U.S. trading after 1852, as Japan possessed the coal needed by steamships bound to ports in China. These arguments became an enduring component of American perceptions about its global role,

finding expression in Alfred T. Mahan's influential late nineteenth-century work on the influence of sea power on history.

Events in the middle decades of the nineteenth century reinforced American acceptance of technology as central to national progress. U.S. manufacturing advantages became even more evident after the invention of the sewing machine and Charles Goodyear's patenting of a process to vulcanize rubber in 1844. The invention of the telegraph encouraged additional trade and opened new markets, and citizens heralded the completion of the first transcontinental telegraph cables in 1861 as a new chapter in establishing an American identity. Already ten years earlier, Americans had delighted at the positive reception British and European observers gave to U.S.-built technological artifacts exhibited at the Crystal Palace exhibition in London. The Civil War forcefully focused national attention on the production of guns and steel, but even before the war American citizens had become convinced of the value of embracing new technological systems. National desires to develop a transcontinental railroad were sufficient to overcome nativist American attitudes toward foreign labor and open the doors to the over 12,000 Chinese laborers who completed laying Central Pacific track to create the first transcontinental railroad. By the time the Centennial International Exhibit opened in Philadelphia in 1876, visitors flocking to Machinery Hall were already convinced, as Seward had argued in 1844, that technology aided nationalism, centralization, and dreams of imperialistic expansion.

THE SECOND INDUSTRIAL REVOLUTION AND THE PROGRESSIVE ERA

Three closely related factors—industrialism, nationalism, and imperialism—soon combined to reinforce American enthusiasm for technology as a key element of national policy. By the end of the nineteenth century, the first industrial revolution (begun in England and concerned with adding steam power to manufacturing) yielded to a larger, globally oriented second industrial revolution, linked to broader systems of technological production and to imperialistic practice. In contrast to the first industrial revolution, which was regional and primarily affected manufacturers and urban dwellers, the second industrial revolution

★ ★ ★ ★ ★

ON THE NEED TO SUSTAIN INTERNATIONAL SCIENCE AND TECHNOLOGY

"In the world of science America has come of age in the decade immediately preceding the second world war. Before this time, basic science was largely a European monopoly and Americans trained either in this country or abroad had large stores of accumulated ideas and facts on which to draw when building new industries or promoting new processes. The automobile, for example, was engineered from basic ideas many of which went back to Newton and the radio industry has developed from the late nineteenth century theories and experiments of Maxwell and Hertz. Unfortunately the technological advancements of the last war, extended as they were by every means possible, appear to have largely exhausted developments latent in the present store of basic knowledge. This means that, unless steps are taken, the technological development of really new industries will gradually become more difficult and that in time a general leveling off in progress will take place. The implication of this for America and particularly for American foreign policy could be quite serious for, if such a plateau is reached, other countries, such as Russia, could presumably catch up with or even surpass us in production and hence in military potential. The consequences of such an altered balance are not difficult to foresee. Competent American scientists have recognized this dilemma for some time and have consequently come to believe that efforts must be made to stimulate basic science throughout the world in order that subsequent development either in America or elsewhere will have something on which to feed."

— R. Gordon Arneson,
U.S. Department of State,
Secret Memorandum, 2 February 1950
(declassified 22 July 1998) —

introduced mass-produced goods into an increasingly technologically dependent and international market. The rise of mass-produced sewing machines, automobiles, electrical lighting systems, and communications marked a profound transformation of methods of production and economics, becoming a major contributor to national economies in America and its European competitors. Manufacturing in the United States steadily climbed while the percentage of Americans working in agriculture declined from 84 percent in 1800 to less than 40 percent in 1900.

The second industrial revolution caused three important changes in the way Americans thought about the world and the best ways they could achieve national goals. First, the process of rapid industrialism brought about a heightened standard of living for many Americans, creating for the first time a distinct middle class. By the turn of the twentieth century, the architects of the interlocked technological systems that had made the United States an economic powerhouse—from the steel magnate Andrew Carnegie to the oil baron John D. Rockefeller and the inventor and electrical systems creator Thomas Alva Edison—were increasingly represented in Washington, and their concerns helped shape foreign policy discussions. Second, and closely related, industrialization heightened an emerging sense of national identity and professionalization among citizens in the leading industrialized nations. The rise of nationalism was fueled not only by the technologies that these system builders created, but by other technologies and systems that rose with them, including low-cost mass-circulation newspapers, recordings of popular songs and national anthems, and public schools designed to instill in pupils the work ethic and social structure of the modern factory. The late nineteenth century was also the time that national and international scientific societies were created. American science was growing through the increasing numbers of young scientists who flocked to European universities to earn their Ph.D.s, carrying home a wealth of international contacts and commitments to higher standards. It was no coincidence that the rise of professional scientific communities paralleled the expanding middle class, as both groups found common support in the expansion of land-grant and private universities and in the industrial opportunities that awaited graduates of those universities. These new networks crystallized swiftly: they included the American Chemical Society (1876), the International Congress of Physiological Sciences (1889), the American Astronomical Society (1899), and the International Association of Academies (1899). The American Physical Society (1899) was founded two years before the federal government created the National Bureau of Standards, reflecting growing concerns from industrialists about creating international standards for manufacture.

Finally, the rise of advanced capitalist economies came to split the globe into "advanced" and "backward" regions, creating a distinct group of industrial nations linked to myriad colonial dependencies. Between 1880 and 1914 most of the Earth's surface was partitioned into territories ruled by the imperial powers, an arrangement precipitated by strategic, economic, and trade needs of these modern states, including the securing of raw materials such as rubber, timber, and petroleum. By the early 1900s, Africa was split entirely between Britain, France, Germany, Belgium, Portugal, and Spain, while Britain acquired significant parts of the East Asian subcontinent, including India. The demands of modern technological systems both promoted and reinforced these changes. The British navy launched the HMS *Dreadnought* in 1906, a super-battleship with greater speed and firing range than any other vessel, to help maintain its national edge and competitive standing among its trade routes and partners, while imperialistic relations were maintained by technological disparities in small-bore weapons. One was a rapid-fire machine gun invented by Sir Hiram Maxim, adapted by British and European armies after the late 1880s. Its role in the emerging arms race of the late nineteenth century was summed in an oft-repeated line of doggerel: "Whatever happens we have got / The Maxim gun and they have not."

The American experience in imperialism was less extensive than that of the leading European industrial nations, but nonetheless marked a striking shift from its earlier foreign policy. Until the early 1890s American diplomatic policy favored keeping the nation out of entangling alliances, and the United States had no overseas possessions. But by 1894 the United States came to administer the islands of Hawaii, and after the Spanish-American War of 1898 gained possession of (and later annexed) the Philippines. The story of America's beginnings as an imperial power has often been told, but the significance of technology and technological systems as a central factor in

this development is not well appreciated. It is perhaps easier to see in the U.S. acquisition of the Panama Canal Zone in 1903. President Theodore Roosevelt and other American leaders recognized how an American-controlled canal would enhance its trade and strategic standing within the Pacific; they also had little doubt that U.S. industrialists and systems builders could construct it. A widely published photograph from that time reveals Roosevelt seated behind the controls of a massive earthmover in the Canal Zone. This single technological artifact served as an apt metaphor for the far larger technological system that turn-of-the-century Americans took great pride in creating.

World War I—a global conflict sparked by the clashing nationalistic aims of leading imperialist nations—pulled scientists and engineers further into the realm of diplomacy. While scientists continued to insist on the apolitical character of science, publication of a highly nationalistic defense of the German invasion of Serbia by leading German scientists in 1914 had left that ideal in tatters. More important, perhaps, was how the war educated Americans about its emerging role as a premier technological nation, and the importance of maintaining adequate sources of petroleum. After 1918, U.S. firms gained Germany's treasured chemical patents as war reparations, expanding American domination of textiles and the petrochemical industries. Americans also found that the leaders of the Russian revolution of 1917, Vladimir Lenin and Leon Trotsky, coveted American machinery and the American system of production to build the Soviet republic. By 1929 the Ford Motor Company had signed agreements with Moscow to build thousands of Ford autos and trucks, and Soviet authorities sought to adapt the management principles of Frederick Winslow Taylor in a Russian version of Taylorism.

The widening intersection between science, technology, and foreign relations was not limited entirely to contests between the United States and other imperialist powers. In the Progressive Era, biologists began to urge diplomats to aid efforts to preserve threatened species whose migrations took them across international boundaries. While efforts to ameliorate overfishing in the boundary waters separating the United States and Canada and seal hunting in the Bering Sea in the early 1890s amounted to little, a strong campaign to aid songbird populations resulted in the Migratory Bird Act of 1918 between the United States and Great Britain (on behalf of Canada), one of the most important early instances of a bilateral science-based treaty negotiated by the federal government. The significance of this treaty was not just what it accomplished (even though it served as an exemplar for other environmental treaties between the United States and its neighbors, including the Colorado River water treaty signed with Mexico in 1944). It also underscored the growing appeal of conservation values among middle- and upper-class American citizens, who joined with scientists to create nature preserves in unspoiled wilderness areas outside the United States, particularly in Africa. In such places, "nature appreciation" emerged as a commodity for tourism, its value determined by declining opportunities to experience wilderness in the North American continent. Private investments of this kind became a potent area of U.S. influence in the world's less developed areas, and took place alongside more traditional interactions including trade relations and missionary work.

WORLD WAR II AND THE EARLY COLD WAR

Science and technology entered a new phase in American foreign relations at the end of the 1930s. Gathering war clouds in western Europe convinced scientists and military leaders that greater attention had to be paid to scientific and technological developments that might aid the United States and its allies. World War II and the ensuing Cold War marked a fundamental watershed in the role that science and scientists would play in American diplomatic efforts. By the late 1940s, new institutions for international science arose within an unprecedented variety of settings (including the Department of State and the Central Intelligence Agency). Secrecy concerns influenced the practice of science and international communications, and new career opportunities arose as science and technology became significant in U.S. foreign policy as never before.

The integration of science into U.S. foreign policy during World War II initially came from the urging of scientists. In August 1939, just months after the German chemist Otto Hahn and Austrian physicist Lise Meitner, working with others, discovered that heavy atomic nuclei could be split to release energy, three scientists including Albert Einstein urged President Franklin D. Roosevelt to fund a crash program to see if an atomic bomb could be constructed. The Manhat-

tan Project that ultimately resulted became the largest research project in the United States to date, one that involved intense and active cooperation with scientists from Great Britain and Canada. Advanced research in the United States also benefited from the emigration of outstanding Jewish scientists from Germany and Italy after the rise of Adolf Hitler and Benito Mussolini. But the atomic bomb project was only one area of international scientific cooperation: in 1940 the eminent British scientific leader Sir Henry Tizard flew to Washington on a secret mission to persuade the U.S. government to cooperate in building a system of radar and radar countermeasures. The Tizard mission laid the groundwork for effective Allied cooperation in building a wide range of science-based technological systems, including radar, the proximity fuze, and the atomic bomb. Scientists who served within the U.S. Office of Scientific Research and Development, with access to greater manufacturing capacity than Britain, also put into production the new drug penicillin.

Concern with devising new wartime weapon systems was equaled by strenuous Allied efforts to discover what science-based weapon systems Germany and Japan had constructed. Through such bilateral efforts, World War II thus nurtured two critical developments that would shape science and technology in the postwar world: the imposition of secrecy systems to protect national security concerns, and the creation of scientific intelligence programs to discover foreign progress in science and technology (particularly but not limited to advances in weaponry). Like penicillin, scientific intelligence was largely a British invention: British scientific intelligence was more advanced than U.S. efforts at the start of the war, owing to its need to buttress its island defenses. But by 1944 U.S. leaders joined Allied efforts to send scientific intelligence teams behind the front lines of advancing Allied troops in western Europe, known as the ALSOS intelligence mission. While the most famous and best-remembered goal of the ALSOS teams was to discover whether Germany had built its own atomic bomb, this was only part of its larger mission to determine German advances in biological and chemical weapons, aeronautical and guided-missile research, and related scientific and technological systems. Broad fields of science were now for the first time relevant to foreign policy concerns.

Allied scientific intelligence missions also served another function: to catalog and inventory German and Japanese research and technological facilities as assets in determining wartime reparations and postwar science policy in these defeated nations. Both Soviet and Allied occupational armies sent back scientific instruments and research results as war booty. In Germany, where the U.S. and Soviet armies converged in April 1945, U.S. science advisers sought to locate and capture German rocket experts who had built the V-2 guided missiles, including Wernher von Braun. Von Braun's team was soon brought to the United States under Project Paperclip, an army program that processed hundreds of Axis researchers without standard immigration screening for evidence of Nazi war crimes. Operation Paperclip was the most visible symbol of a concerted campaign to secure astronomers, mathematicians, biologists, chemists, and other highly trained individuals to aid American research critical for national security. In Japan, U.S. scientists focused primarily on wartime Japanese advances in biological warfare. While members of the Japanese Scientific Intelligence Mission that accompanied General Douglas MacArthur's occupation forces were unable to stop the senseless destruction of a research reactor by U.S. soldiers, science advisers successfully insisted that applied science and technology were critical components of Japan's economic recovery.

Above all it was the use of atomic weapons against Japan in the closing days of World War II that brought science and technology into the realm of U.S. foreign policy as never before. The roughly 140,000 who died immediately at Nagasaki and Hiroshima, combined with the awesome destructive power of a device that relied on the fundamental forces of nature, made the atomic bomb the enduring symbol of the marriage of science and the state. In subsequent decades the U.S. decision to employ atomic weapons has become one of the most fiercely debated events in American foreign policy. Even before the bomb decision was made, a number of American atomic scientists protested plans to use nuclear weapons against Japan since it, unlike Nazi Germany, lacked the capacity to construct atomic weapons of its own. How the decision to use the bomb was made has split historians. Some have argued that U.S. leaders sought to end the war before the Soviet Union could officially declare war on Japan and thus participate in its postwar government, but many have concluded that other motivations were at least as important, including fears that Japanese leaders might have fought far longer without a show of overwhelm-

ing force and domestic expectations that all available weapons be used to conclude the war. Others have pointed out that U.S. policymakers had long seemed especially attracted to the use of technology in its dealings with Asian countries.

The largest conflict over nuclear weapons in the immediate postwar period involved the American monopoly over them, and how the United States could best safeguard the postwar peace. Bernard Baruch, the financier and statesman, proposed that atomic power be placed under international control through the newly established United Nations. The Soviet Union vetoed the Baruch Plan, believing that the proposal was designed to prevent it from acquiring nuclear weapons. Meanwhile, conservatives promoted a congressional bill that placed atomic energy under military control. Liberal scientists opposed the bill and advocated civilian control instead. In 1946, with the support of President Harry S. Truman, a Senate committee under Brien McMahon drafted a new bill that eventually resulted in a civilian-led (but militarily responsive) Atomic Energy Commission (AEC), one of the first postwar agencies designed to address science in foreign policy.

As the Cold War began, debate over science and technology in American foreign policy split along familiar lines. The most well-known of these involved efforts to maintain the deeply eroded traditions of scientific internationalism. Atomic scientists who supported international control of atomic energy created new national organizations, including the Federation of American Scientists. Participating scientists, including Albert Einstein, argued that physicists could aid the development of world government that would avoid the political perils of atomic warfare. In July 1957 nuclear scientists convened the first Pugwash meeting, drawing nuclear scientists from Western and communist nations to discuss approaches to nuclear disarmament. But promoters of scientific internationalism were not solely interested in atomic issues. The liberal internationalist and Harvard astronomer Harlow Shapley backed prominent British scientists Julian Huxley and Joseph Needham in their efforts to highlight science within the United Nations Educational, Scientific, and Cultural Organization (UNESCO). Leaders of the Rockefeller Foundation launched major new science initiatives in Latin America, while the National Academy of Sciences urged policymakers not to restrict American access to the world community of science. While public support for these positions remained high during the early years of the Cold War, they faded after Soviet Premier Joseph Stalin resumed a well-publicized crackdown on "bourgeois" research in genetics in favor of Trofin Lysenko's promotion of Lamarckian inheritance. This repression convinced many Americans that objective Soviet science had succumbed to state control. By the McCarthy era unrepentant internationalists were targets of a growing conservative backlash. The biochemist and Nobel Laureate Linus Pauling—who won a second Nobel Prize in 1962 for his campaign to end nuclear testing—was one of several outspoken American scientists whose passport was temporarily revoked in the 1950s.

At the same time, other scientists began working with government officials in Washington, sometimes clandestinely, to investigate ways that scientists could aid U.S. national security by addressing major issues in American foreign policy. These activities took many forms. One of the more visible steps came in 1949, when President Truman announced, as the fourth point of his inaugural speech, that the United States was willing to "embark on a bold new program for making the benefit of our scientific advances and industrial progress available for the improvement and growth of under-developed areas." After Congress approved the so-called Point Four program a year later, tens of millions of dollars supported bilateral projects in science education, public health, agriculture, and civil engineering, adding to mainstream Marshall Plan funds used to restore technological and scientific capacity in the war-ravaged nations of western Europe. At the same time, U.S. scientists and technical experts worked to thwart Soviet efforts to obtain advanced Western computers, electronic devices, and other technologies and resources critical to weapons development. These included efforts to limit export of weapons-grade uranium to the Soviet Union and to deny Soviet access to Scandinavian heavy water as well as prominent Swedish scientists in the event of a Soviet invasion.

For U.S. policymakers, a principal challenge was to secure reliable overt and covert information on the scientific and technological capacity of other nations, since such intelligence was necessary to match enemy advances in weaponry—particularly in biological, chemical, and radiological warfare. A major point of intersection between physicists and U.S. policymakers came in efforts to discern Soviet advances in atomic bomb work and in developing methods to detect and analyze Soviet atomic tests, a task that gained greater urgency after the Soviet Union exploded its first nuclear device in August 1949. Hindered by a paltry flow of overt information from communist countries, U.S. scientists sought alternative means to secure such data. In 1947 several scientists who had managed the wartime U.S. science effort, including Vannevar Bush, James Conant, and Lloyd V. Berkner, helped create a set of new institutions devoted to the role of international science in national security. The first was the Office of Scientific Intelligence within the newly formed Central Intelligence Agency. Three years later, scientists working with the Department of State created a scientific attaché program, patterned on the U.K. Science Mission. A 1950 Berkner report to Secretary of State Dean Acheson, justifying this effort, declared that the program would strengthen Western science while providing American scientists and businesses helpful information; a secret supplement optimistically spelled out ways that attachés could covertly secure needed intelligence. Yet by 1952, national security experts concluded that foreign science and technology intelligence-gathering from the CIA and the Department of State remained woefully inadequate. The United States then created the top-secret National Security Agency to foster signals intelligence, employing the clandestine code-breaking strategies that had aided Allied victory during World War II.

Scientists and policymakers both found the abrupt integration of science into U.S. foreign policy unnerving. Many American scientists recognized that post-1945 national security concerns required pragmatic compromise of the unfettered exchange of information that had long been the ideal of science. The close relations that developed between scientists and the government during World War II also helped certain scientists undertake clandestine research programs. But most American scientists resented increasingly tight security restrictions, demands for secrecy, loyalty oaths, and mandatory debriefings by federal agents following overseas professional trips. Scientists who accepted posts in the State Department felt the snubs of colleagues who regarded such service less prestigious than lab-bench research. For their part, traditional foreign relations experts, trained in economics or history, were largely unfamiliar with the concepts or practices of science, disdained the capacity of scientists in war-ravaged western Europe and the Soviet Union to produce quality science, and perceived the inherent internationalism of scientists suspicious if not unpatriotic. Such views were widespread within the national security bureaucracy. Federal Bureau of Investigation director J. Edgar Hoover, familiar with top-secret Venona intercepts of encrypted Soviet communications used to discover atomic spies in the United States, regarded the internationalism of scientists as a threat to democracy and the proper aims of U.S. foreign policy.

Despite these mutual tensions, American leaders in the 1950s nonetheless sought to use science to influence foreign policy debates. Officials used scientific intelligence to refute highly publicized (and still unresolved) Chinese claims that American forces in Korea had violated international accords by employing bacteriological weapons in the winter of 1952. Even greater use of science as an ideological weapon was made by President Dwight Eisenhower, who in a major speech to the United Nations General Assembly in December 1953 offered his "Atoms for Peace" proposal calling for the peaceful uses of atomic power. Regarded at the time as a Marshall Plan for atomic energy, Atoms for Peace promoted the development of nuclear cooperation, trade, and nonproliferation efforts in noncommunist nations; it also provided nuclear research reactors to countries in South America and Asia. Eisenhower's advisers felt certain that the Soviet Union could not match the Atoms for Peace offer, and hence would suffer a political setback as a result. They also believed it would reduce the threat of nuclear warfare, an anxiety shared by western European leaders after the United States explicitly made massive retaliation the cornerstone of its national security policy.

Historians have debated the significance and meaning of the Atoms for Peace proposal. On the one hand, some maintain that Eisenhower correctly perceived that the most effective means of halting nuclear proliferation would come from promoting and regulating nuclear power through the auspices of the United Nations, while ensuring that the European western democracies would gain direct access to what at the time seemed a safe and low-cost source of energy. The program helped the United States secure 90 percent of the reactor export market by the 1960s. On the other hand, critics charge that Atoms for Peace actually served to increase the danger of nuclear proliferation. Yet other historians regard Atoms for Peace as part of a grander strategy to mute criticism of the accelerated buildup of U.S. nuclear weapons stockpiles and their secret dispersal to locations

---

★ ★ ★ ★

ON SCIENTIFIC INTELLIGENCE

"Historically, the major responsibility for intelligence in the United States, both during war and peace, has rested upon the military agencies of the government. Since World War II, intelligence has assumed a far greater peacetime role than heretofore and has had an increasing influence upon foreign policy decisions.

"In the overall utilization of intelligence in the policy making areas of the Department [of State], there appears to be too little recognition of the enormous present and future importance of scientific intelligence. In the past, military and political factors, and more recently economic considerations, have been the controlling elements in estimating the capabilities and intentions of foreign powers. Now, however, an increasingly important consideration in any such assessment is the scientific progress of the country concerned. For example, the determining factor in a decision by the U.S.S.R. either to make war or to resort to international political blackmail may well be the state of its scientific and technological development in weapons of mass destruction. It is therefore imperative that, in the Department, the scientific potential and technical achievements of the Soviet Union and their implications be integrated with the other elements of a balanced intelligence estimate for foreign policy determination."

— *Lloyd Berkner, Report of the International Science Policy Survey Group (Secret), 18 April 1950 (declassified 22 July 1998)* —

---

around the world, including West Germany, Greenland, Iceland, South Korea, and Taiwan. It is also clear that Eisenhower sought to exploit the apolitical reputation of science to wage psychological warfare and to gather strategic intelligence. In the mid-1950s the Eisenhower administration approved funds for the International Geophysical Year (IGY) of 1957–1958, an enormous effort to study the terrestrial environment involving tens of thousands of scientists from sixty-seven nations (a plan conceived, among others, by science adviser Lloyd Berkner). In one sense, Eisenhower's support for the IGY was overdetermined: policymakers saw an advantage in limiting rival nations' territorial claims to Antarctica by making the frozen realm a "continent for science" under IGY auspices, and Eisenhower recognized that a planned "scientific" satellite launch would enhance international claims for overflight of other nations' airspace, a concern because of U.S. reliance on high-altitude U-2 aircraft fights to gain intelligence on the Soviet Union. It was a strategy that his predecessor, Thomas Jefferson, had also understood.

Despite their greater involvement in foreign policymaking, scientists largely remained outsiders from diplomatic circles. This was due to several factors. Throughout his first term, Eisenhower maintained his small staff of science advisers in the Office of Defense Management, a marginal agency remote from the machinery of the White House. More importantly, the White House failed to defend scientists against charges from Senator Joseph McCarthy and the House Un-American Activities Committee that cast dispersions against the loyalty of atomic scientists, particularly after the Soviet atomic bomb test of 1949. With the declassification of the Venona intercepts, historians now understand that American espionage did provide Soviet agents with details of the "Fat Man" plutonium implosion bomb used at Nagasaki, giving Soviet physicists perhaps a year's advantage in constructing their own initial atomic weapon. This level of spying was greater than many on the left then believed, but far less than what Republican critics of scientific internationalism charged. These highly publicized accusations, and the loyalty investigation of atomic bomb project leader J. Robert Oppenheimer, nevertheless aided ideological conservatives convinced that scientists represented a threat to national security and that international science needed to be controlled along with foreign cultural and intellectual exchange. After the conservative-leaning *U.S. News and World Report* in 1953 reported a claim that the State Department's science office was "a stink hole of out-and-out Communists," Secretary of State John Foster Dulles, ignoring the protests of scientists, allowed the science attaché program to wither away.

These clashes pointed to fundamental tensions in efforts to employ science in American foreign policy. Moderates in the executive branch sought to use scientific internationalism to embarrass Soviet bloc countries by advertising links between Western democracy and achievements in science and technology (a theme heavily promoted in the Brussels World Exposition of 1958). Many believed that scientists in communist nations were the most likely agents for democratization and thus potential allies. Opposing them were ideological conservatives determined to limit international science contacts to strengthen national security and to restore clarity to U.S. foreign policy. These tensions came to a head in the mid-1950s when State Department officials refused to pay U.S. dues to parent international scientific unions in part because unrecognized regimes, including Communist China, were also members. American dues were instead quietly paid by the Ford Foundation, whose directors understood that the CIA's scientific intelligence branch greatly benefited from informal information and insights passed on by traveling American scientists. While the CIA's clandestine support for scientific internationalism helped sustain U.S. participation in major international bodies in the nadir of the Cold War, this conflict would not be resolved before the *Sputnik* crisis interceded.

SPUTNIK, THE ANTICOLONIAL REVOLUTION, AND SCIENCE AS AN IDEOLOGICAL WEAPON

By the late 1950s a second fundamental shift occurred in the role of science and technology in U.S. foreign policy. The shift had several causes. One was the launch of *Sputnik,* which established the Soviets as a potent technological force in the eyes of observers throughout the world, including western Europe. Another was that the Soviet Union's space spectacular occurred in the midst of the independence movement among former colonies in Africa and Asia. This worried U.S. officials who believed that Soviet triumphs in applied science and technology would tempt these emerging nations to develop socialist governments and build alliances with the Eastern bloc. Yet another factor was the heightened role of science in new multilateral treaty negotiations, including the Antarctic Treaty and the Limited Nuclear Test Ban Treaty, which brought scientists and policymakers into ever tighter orbits. Finally, increasing concern from American citizens about an environment at risk from radioactive fallout—a view shared by leaders of western European governments—helped make a wide range of environmental concerns from declining fish populations to improving agricultural productivity and addressing air and water pollution a greater focus of American foreign policy. Together, these led to a considerable transformation of U.S. foreign policy, increasing the influence of United Nations and nongovernmental organizations, and heightening diplomatic links between the northern and southern hemispheres. While efforts to coordinate U.S. science policy remained ineffective, and relations between scientists and policymakers were sometimes strained, this realignment would persist through the end of the twentieth century.

The launch of *Sputnik* was a major foreign relations setback to the United States, in no small part because of American faith in its technology and a widespread conviction in the West that scientific and technological development within a democracy would triumph over that within a totalitarian state. But on 4 October 1957, the 184-pound *Sputnik I,* emitting a pulsed electronic beep, became the Earth's first artificial satellite. The launch produced banner headlines around the world and convinced many Allies that Eastern bloc science and technology was equal to that of the United States. Secret U.S. Information Agency polling in Britain and in western Europe indicated that a quarter of their populations believed the Soviet Union was ahead in science and technology. In response, the United States accelerated programs designed to symbolize the nation's scientific and material progress, above all the space program. For the next quarter century science and technology would take on a new role in foreign policy—as a surrogate for national prosperity and stability.

Elevating science and technology as symbols of national potency, and hence as tools of foreign policy, took several forms. One was by investing in highly visible technological projects. The space program developed by the National Aeronautics and Space Administration (NASA) was a prime example. Technology as a symbol of national prestige was embodied in the bold (and ultimately successful) proposal to land humans on the moon by 1969, which President John F. Kennedy announced in a speech to Congress in May 1961 after his most embarrassing foreign policy failure, the Bay of Pigs disaster. But this was only one expression of many. The Kennedy administration also stepped up international programs in such fields as agriculture, medicine, and oceanography. As with the Wilkes Expedition a century before, the motivations behind such efforts were mixed. New research programs in oceanography were intended to help increase fish harvests by less developed countries, and American oceanographic vessels could show the flag at distant points of call. But oceanography was also a particularly strategic field because of growing concerns with antisubmarine warfare and efforts by less developed countries, working through United Nations bureaus, to extend their sovereignty to two hundred nautical miles beyond their coasts. Knowing the sizes of Soviet fish harvests was also of strategic value. Undertakings such as the multinational Indian Ocean Expedition of 1964–1965, which American scientists helped plan, seamlessly embodied all of these aims.

Science constituencies both within and outside the federal government responded to the Soviet achievement in various ways. Worried air force officials, anxious to demonstrate U.S. technological competence in the months following the launch of *Sputnik,* proposed detonating a Hiroshima-sized bomb on the moon in 1959 that would be instantaneously visible to watchers from Earth. Cooler heads at the Department of State and the White House did not consider this idea because of its militaristic connotations. The National Science Foundation advocated increasing the number of exchanges between U.S. and Soviet scientists, while White House staff members supported the AEC's Plowshare program to make peaceful uses of atomic bombs, among them creating new canals and harbors. Members of Congress echoed private science groups in arguing that the *Sputnik* crisis showed that the United States had fallen behind in training future scientists. The massive rise in federal spending for math and science education after 1958 was another direct consequence of this foreign relations crisis.

The *Sputnik* shock forced administration officials to recognize that existing mechanisms for coordinating science and technology within foreign policy were inadequate. In 1957, President Eisenhower announced the creation of the position of special assistant to the president for science and technology (commonly known as the presidential science adviser) and the President's Science Advisory Committee (PSAC) to provide the White House with advice on scientific and technical matters domestic and foreign. While members of PSAC, which was always chaired by the science adviser, were initially drawn from the physical sciences, reflecting continued preoccupation with space, nuclear weapons, and guided-missile delivery systems, PSAC's mandate soon expanded to include a wide range of scientific disciplines. The State Department's Science Office and attaché program, nearly eviscerated before

Sputnik, was revived and handed new responsibilities for coordinating bilateral and multilateral programs. Not all government officials saw the increased focus on science and technology as positive. A Latin American ambassador complained that the U.S. embassy in Rio de Janeiro "needs a science attaché the way a cigar-store Indian needs a brassiere." Despite such criticisms, Washington exported these conceptions into its regional security alliances, creating a new science directorate within the North Atlantic Treaty Organization (NATO). While Democrats worried that this plan would militarize western European science and limit contacts with Soviet colleagues, NATO's science directorate steered new research contracts to its closest allies.

Another response to the *Sputnik* crisis was a dramatic expansion of foreign aid programs to support science and technology. In 1961 President Kennedy announced the creation of the Agency for International Development (AID), with an explicit mandate to fund research, education, and technology-based programs around the world. Advocates of old-style scientific internationalism supported AID programs as a way to extend UN programs that nurtured emerging research centers and sustainable development in less developed countries. In certain respects they were not disappointed: AID science programs provided significantly greater support to Latin-American countries in the 1960s and 1970s than their feeble counterparts in the early Cold War period. Grants funded desalination projects, teacher training, and scientific equipment; in cooperation with science attachés, officials also protested the mistreatment of academics in Argentina and Brazil in the 1960s. But as with the Marshall Plan, foreign aid programs in science and technology were adjuncts in the greater struggle to extend U.S. influence to Latin America, the Asian subcontinent, and sub-Saharan Africa, and to win the hearts and minds of leaders in less developed countries deciding between Western and Soviet models of economic development. In practice, however, it was often difficult to separate humanitarian motives from calculation of Realpolitik. U.S. support for costly rain experiments in India's Bihar-Uttar Pradesh area in the mid-1960s was justified by noting that these programs aided American policy aims by mitigating Indian embarrassment at lagging behind Chinese efforts to create an atomic bomb. But this secret research, however fanciful, did attempt to mitigate a life-threatening drought.

The best-known science and technology foreign-assistance program from this period was the Green Revolution. Based on hybrid forms of rice and wheat that had been developed in the United States in the 1930s, the Green Revolution promised to allow poorer nations to avoid the Malthusian dilemma by increasing the efficiency of planted fields to satisfy the demands of growing populations. In India, where severe drought crippled crops between 1965 and 1967, the planting of high-yield grains nearly doubled wheat and rice yields by the late 1970s. Stimulated and financed by the Rockefeller and the Ford Foundations, the Green Revolution was one of the most well-known private foreign aid programs during the Cold War.

Historians have reached differing conclusions about the impact and effectiveness of U.S. scientific and technological aid programs to Latin America and to sub-Saharan Africa in the 1960s and 1970s. Some argue that American aid programs in science and technology represent long-nurtured humanitarian impulses similar to those that informed the Marshall Plan and in general no less successful. Few scholars doubt that the American scientists and policy officials who designed these programs genuinely believed their efforts would achieve positive social ends. However, other historians have pointed out that scientists who sought grandiose results such as weather modification and greatly enlarged fish catches were overconfident about their ability to master nature without harming natural processes, and recent assessments of the Green Revolution have made clear that production gains were less than earlier claimed. A more significant problem was that planners often failed to realize that technical systems developed in advanced capitalistic countries could not be transported wholesale into other regions without concurrent local innovations and adaptive technologies. American enthusiasm about exporting the fruits of U.S. technologies was often accompanied by hubris in assessing the environments of less developed countries.

Beginning in the 1960s, American policymakers also faced new demands to negotiate international agreements governing applications of science and technology. A convergence of factors brought this about. The economic costs of maintaining the U.S. nuclear arsenal, concerns about proliferation, and a desire to moderate the arms race led the Eisenhower administration to begin discussions with the Soviet Union about what became the 1963 Limited Nuclear Test Ban

Treaty. The close call narrowly avoided in the Cuban missile crisis of 1962 inspired President Kennedy and Premier Nikita Khrushchev to sign it. But another reason was the growing realization among scientists and policymakers that even the testing of nuclear, biological, and chemical weapons represented a genuine threat to the health of American citizens and populations worldwide, and that such tests could have unintended consequences for diplomatic relations and regional stability. From secret monitoring of man-made radioactivity levels in the 1950s, scientists understood that measurable amounts had already spread worldwide. Policymakers were also unnerved by the "Bravo" nuclear test on Bikini Island in March 1954, a fifteen-megaton blast more than a thousand times the size of the Hiroshima bomb. Radioactive ash from the test spread across a broader area of the Pacific than expected, contaminating the Japanese tuna ship *Lucky Dragon* and in turn causing a panic in the Japanese fishing market and outrage in Japan and elsewhere. National Security Council members worried that a disruption of Japan's primary food resource might destabilize government and allow Soviet encroachment. Amplifying these worries was growing popular concern with an environment at risk, accentuated by anxiety concerning nuclear and chemical fallout and the contaminants issue exemplified by Rachel Carson's 1962 *Silent Spring*. International treaties served policymakers' ends by reassuring citizens of limitations on uses of science-based weapon systems that many Americans found unsafe and threatening.

To be sure, policymakers often found it difficult to steer science to aid foreign policy goals, in part resulting from the elite nature of science, in part because the goals of scientists were often tangential to those of the state. But part of the problem was that by the 1960s policymakers could no longer count on a compliant media to keep covert activities involving international scientific activities secret. In 1962, the *New York Times* reported a highly secret test of a U.S. atomic bomb exploded in outer space eight hundred miles from Hawaii, code-named Starfish. The resulting controversy intensified suspicions of citizen groups on the left that science had become an extension of state power and morally suspect. Though U.S. officials successfully concealed many related projects from view, demands for greater openness led the 1975 Church Committee to examine unauthorized medical experiments within the CIA, and subsequent revelations about U.S. efforts to employ

radiological warfare and to steer hurricanes toward enemy lands raised ethical dilemmas for many citizens. Yet at times the government successfully mobilized public support behind using science as a moral weapon. In 1982 the U.S. government canceled its bilateral science agreements with the Soviet Union to protest its treatment of atomic physicist and dissident Andrei Sakharov and its persecution of Jewish scientists. But at least as often relations between policymakers and their scientific advisers fractured. President Richard Nixon abolished PSAC in 1973 for its opposition to his antiballistic missile, supersonic transport, and Vietnam policies. In 1983 President Ronald Reagan announced his decision to proceed with his "Star Wars" Strategic Defense Initiative after consulting a small circle of scientists, bypassing standard review circles in an attempt to use science for strategic advantage.

By the 1970s and 1980s, policymakers also found that the critical defining relations for international science were no longer exclusively East-West but also North-South, between the developed and developing nations. U.S. scientists and diplomats were slower to react to this change than to the upheavals of anticolonialism in the late 1950s, misperceiving the significance of the change. When the Pakistani physicist and Nobel Laureate Abdus Salam created the International Center for Theoretical Physics in Trieste, Italy, in 1964, a center devoted to researchers from less developed nations, leading U.S. scientists and policymakers criticized Salam's plan as simply duplicating existing Western research facilities. But Salam's institute (backed by the United Nations and private foundations) was soon followed by parallel efforts in other fields, whose leaders sought to set research agendas reflecting the peculiar needs of these developing lands. Although often wary of these new centers (which reflected the growing influence of the UN, UNESCO, and other multilateral agencies such as the International Atomic Energy Agency remote from American influence), U.S. officials sought to remain appraised of their activities.

Even if science sometimes seemed an uncertain asset in American foreign policy, U.S. policymakers continued to regard technology as a key indicator of the superiority of American capitalism, illuminating the nation's core values of productivity and resourcefulness. Most Americans still believed that technological solutions existed for a large range of social and political problems. Early in the Cold War, many Americans suggested that Soviet citizens would revolt if sent Sears catalogs showing a cornucopia of American products, and their faith in technological fixes persisted after the launch of *Sputnik*. Perhaps technology, as embodied in military power, could cut through cultural differences to get the American message across. There was a sense of technological superiority on the part of American policymakers with a penchant for technological solutions to complex social and political problems in U.S. interactions with Asian countries. This was especially the case during the Vietnam War, when American scientists, engineers, military, and civilian leaders worked together to create and implement carpet bombing, defoliants, and electronic battlefields.

American policymakers also sought to capitalize on Asian countries' desire to catch up with the West in science and technology. This interest was not new: the U.S. government, when returning part of the Boxer indemnities to China in the early 1900s, had stipulated that the Chinese government had to use the returned funds for sending students to the United States to study science and technology-related subjects. As a result, the Boxer fellowships helped train several generations of Chinese scientists and engineers. In the 1970s and 1980s, American policymakers again hoped that American science and technology would play a role in the reopening and the normalization of U.S.–China relations. The Shanghai Communique signed by Henry Kissinger and Zhou Enlai during Richard Nixon's famous trip to China in 1972 highlighted science and technology, along with culture, sports, and journalism, as areas for people-to-people contacts and exchanges. Indeed, the ensuing exchange of students and scholars, including large numbers of scientists and engineers, shaped U.S.–China relations in many ways during this period. In this connection, the disproportionately large number of Chinese Americans who work in science and technology-related fields often played an important role in facilitating such exchanges and in mitigating U.S.–China tensions.

Faith in technological solutions to problems of U.S. foreign policy remained evident in the waning days of the Cold War, even as significant manufacturing sectors were shifted from the United States to lower-cost labor markets throughout the globe. This same faith was applied to relations with the Soviet Union. As historian Walter LaFeber has noted, Secretary of State George P. Shultz learned about the rapid advances of information technology and communications in the early 1980s, at the start of the Reagan presidency. He decided that communications technology could be used to make the Soviet Union face a potentially undermining choice: to yield control over information, at the cost of weakening the system, or maintaining communist controls at the cost of dramatically weakening its science and technology (and hence its economy and military). Against the advice of intelligence and State Department officials who saw few inherent technological weaknesses to exploit within the Soviet system, and convinced that the information revolution would lead to decentralized rather than central controls, Shultz pressed to bring this hard choice to the fore of American Soviet policy. While the decline and ultimate collapse of the Soviet Union resulted from a complex set of social, political, and technological factors, modern information technology had become an important tool in U.S. foreign policy.

THE END OF THE TWENTIETH CENTURY

The fall of the Berlin Wall in 1989, and the collapse of the Soviet Union two years later, accelerated two significant and already evident trends. The first was the decreased ability of the federal government to regulate the involvement of Americans in international science and technological ventures. This decline owed to further advances in communications technology, the continued globalization of manufacture and research, and an unprecedented expansion of nonprofit organizations involved in myriad aspects of foreign science policy. The second was greater international support for global treaties designed to limit technologies that threatened the natural environment.

Reduced state control over the conduct and practice of science and technology as aspects of foreign policy had several causes. One was the general relaxation of state restrictions that followed the end of the Cold War, including a reduced level of concern about the threat of nuclear annihilation (though, as the abortive spy trial of the Los Alamos physicist Wen Ho Lee in the late 1990s would attest, the federal government remained vigilant, or even overzealous, as critics charged, about prosecuting alleged violations of nuclear secrets trade). By 1990, international scientific exchanges had become so commonplace that the Department of State, which thirty years before had scrutinized each case, gave up trying to count them. Yet another was the rising influence of the biological and environmental sciences, challenging the dominance of the physical sciences as the key determinant of foreign policy in the sciences and providing nongovernmental organizations greater influence on policy decisions. In 1995 some 110,000 biological and life scientists were employed by the federal government, double the number from twelve years before. Well-funded conservation groups such as the World Wildlife Federation continued to export wilderness values and sustainable development concerns around the globe, including that for the Amazon rainforests, while more militant organizations, including Greenpeace, succeeded in stimulating public pressure to address problems with international whaling practices and the regulation of drilling platforms in international waters. No less influential were private foundations—notably the Bill and Melinda Gates Foundation, which announced a $100 million commitment to international AIDS research in 2001—their undertaking reminiscent of the early twentieth century foreign health campaigns of the Rockefeller Foundation. But commercial concerns from powerful business interests also shaped State Department policies toward international science and technology, particularly as the growing commercial value of products derived from molecular biology and genetics inspired Eli Lilly, Hoffman-LaRoche, Genentech, and other large multinational firms to organize research and production facilities on a global scale.

Another factor that undermined the ability of the state to regulate international science and technological projects was the increasingly transnational character of fundamental scientific research. While the institutional structure of science remained largely national in character—since the state remained the dominant patron of scientific research—scientists found fewer barriers to participating in international collaborations than at any prior time in history. Transnational coauthorships in leading scientific nations reached 19 percent by the mid-1980s, and scientists found it easier to cross borders to conduct experiments at major foreign research facilities and to attend conferences in once off-limit cities such as Havana and Beijing. Financial exhaustion caused by the Cold War also inspired new transnational technological collaborations, including the U.S.–Russian space station, the Cassini Mission to Saturn, and the multinational Human Genome Project, the first big-science undertaking in the biological sciences. While

Washington policymakers generally saw these developments as advantageous to U.S. interests, the reduction of centralized controls over technical systems occasionally disturbed security-conscious officials. During the administration of President William Jefferson Clinton, law enforcement agencies attempted to restrict the importation of foreign encryption programs, seeking to retain access to information transmitted via computers for criminal investigations and national security purposes, but technological firms successfully resisted this effort.

But the ending of the Cold War, which left the United States as the sole surviving superpower, also caused policymakers to scale back on efforts to convince other world leaders of the merits of capitalist-based science and technology. Despite calls for a new Marshall Plan to aid the democratic transformation of the former Soviet Union (which included providing ways to keep unemployed Russian nuclear technicians and bioweapons specialists from taking their skills to Iran, Libya, and other sponsors of international terrorism), the United States provided little support. Private efforts to provide such support did not succeed, despite a $100 million investment provided by the financier George Soros from 1992 to 1995. Soros argued (as American national security advisers had done throughout the Cold War) that Russian scientists were bulwarks of liberal democracy and antidotes to religious fundamentalism and mystical cults, but terminated his support when Western democracies failed to match his contributions. While citizens generally backed such measures, budget constraints did not permit policymakers to offer more than patchy responses to these problems.

The United States and other Western governments have proven more inclined to address the impact of scientific and technological developments on the global environment, seeing these threats as more immediate and more amenable to international negotiation. By the 1980s and 1990s, American leaders began playing active roles in negotiating treaties that sought to mitigate the effects of industrial and military byproducts in the environment, including efforts to maintain biodiversity, to reduce the destruction of ultraviolet-shielding stratospheric ozone, and to limit the emission of carbon dioxide and other greenhouse gases that heightened global warming. In certain respects these treaties resembled the 1963 Limited Nuclear Test Ban Treaty, which limited the global spread of radioactive fallout. Like the much earlier Migratory Bird Treaty Act of

1918, these also sought to employ the best scientific knowledge available to address an evident problem, and they were controversial in their day. But these late twentieth-century treaties were profoundly different from their predecessors in several ways: they posed major economic and national security questions at the highest levels of government, they involved the full-time work of large numbers of scientists and policymakers, and they addressed issues intensely familiar to citizens (by 1989, 80 percent of Americans had heard of global warming). They were also multilateral treaties rather than bilateral—as most earlier international environmental treaties had been—thus reflecting the growing influence of the United Nations as a force in international science policy. In the mid-1990s the Clinton administration, aware that a majority of Americans backed these efforts (and believing, as historian Samuel P. Hays has argued, that they reflected deep-rooted American values about the environment), explicitly declared its support for environmental diplomacy. The Clinton administration also suggested that environmental degradation could lead to political and social stress, even major instability, and thus became the first to publicly argue that water rights disputes and overfishing were as significant in foreign policy as traditional issues of ideology, commerce, and immigration.

By the beginning of the twenty-first century, U.S. willingness to take part in the post–Cold War framework of international science-based treaties appeared to wane. During his first six months in office, President George W. Bush signaled his intention to take a more unilateral stance, refusing to sign the Kyoto Accord on global warming while backing away from the 1996 Nuclear Test Ban Treaty and a pact designed to enforce an international ban on biological weapons (which powerful U.S. biotech groups had opposed, fearing the loss of trade secrets). In the early summer of 2001 Secretary of Defense Donald H. Rumsfeld voiced willingness to "cast away" the 1972 antiballistic missile treaty, the bedrock of mutually assured destruction that had guided U.S. nuclear weapons policy throughout the Cold War era. These actions are a reminder that conservative concerns about limiting American power and the political unreliability of scientists have not faded. Yet these efforts ought not be taken as a sign of a major reorientation of the role of science and technology within U.S. foreign policy. The growth of an international framework for science and technology was largely determined by events beyond the control of the American people, who remain part of an international science and technological community more extensive than many realize. Constituencies for this system, within scientific community and within Congress and bureaucracy, are large. As with environmental values within the United States, global approaches to environmental regulation have gained favor with a significant portion of the U.S. population, and will remain a driving force in setting U.S. foreign policy.

BIBLIOGRAPHY

Badash, Lawrence. *Scientists and the Development of Nuclear Weapons: From Fission to the Limited Test Ban Treaty, 1939–1963.* Atlantic Highlands, N.J., 1995.

Bamford, James. *Body of Secrets: Anatomy of the Ultra-Secret National Security Agency: From the Cold War Through the Dawn of a New Century.* New York, 2001.

Barth, Kai-Henrik. "Science and Politics in Early Nuclear Test Ban Negotiations." *Physics Today* 51 (1998): 34–39.

Cohen, I. Bernard. *Science and the Founding Fathers: Science in the Political Thought of Thomas Jefferson, Benjamin Franklin, John Adams and James Madison.* New York, 1995.

Cueto, Marcos, ed. *Missionaries of Science: The Rockefeller Foundation and Latin America.* Bloomington, Ind., 1994.

DeGreiff, Alexis. "A History of the International Centre for Theoretical Physics, 1960–1980. Ideology and Practice in a United Nations Institution for Scientific Co-operation for the Third World Development." Ph.D. dissertation. Imperial College London, 2001.

Divine, Robert A. *The Sputnik Challenge.* New York, 1993.

Doel, Ronald E., and Allan A. Needell. "Science, Scientists, and the CIA: Balancing International Ideals, National Needs, and Professional Opportunities." In Rhodri Jeffreys-Jones and Christopher Andrew, eds. *Eternal Vigilance: Fifty Years of the CIA.* London, 1997.

Dorsey, Kurk. *The Dawn of Conservation Diplomacy: U.S.–Canadian Wildlife Protection Treaties in the Progressive Era.* Seattle, 1998.

Dupree, A. Hunter. *Science in the Federal Government: A History of Policies and Activities.* Baltimore, 1986.

Graham, Loren R. *What Have We Learned About Science and Technology from the Russian Experience?* Stanford, Calif., 1998.

Hays, Samuel P. *Beauty, Health, and Permanence: Environmental Politics in the United States, 1955–1985.* Cambridge, Mass., 1987.

Hindle, Brooke, and Steven Lubar. *Engines of Change: The American Industrial Revolution, 1790–1860.* Washington, D.C., 1986.

Holloway, David. *Stalin and the Bomb: The Soviet Union and Atomic Energy, 1939–1956.* New Haven, Conn., 1994.

Hughes, Thomas P. *American Genesis: A Century of Invention and Technological Enthusiasm, 1870–1970.* New York, 1989.

Kevles, Daniel J. "'Into Hostile Political Camps': The Reorganization of International Science in World War I." *Isis* 62 (1970): 47–60.

LaFeber, Walter. "Technology and U.S. Foreign Relations." *Diplomatic History* 24 (2000): 1–19.

Manzione, Joseph. "'Amusing and Amazing and Practical and Military': The Legacy of Scientific Internationalism in American Foreign Policy, 1945–1963." *Diplomatic History* 24 (2000): 21–56.

Needell, Allan A. *Science, the Cold War, and the American State: Lloyd V. Berkner and the Balance of Professional Ideals.* London, 2000.

Rydell, Robert W., John E. Findling, and Kimberly D. Pelle. *Fair America: World's Fairs in the United States.* Washington, D.C., 2000.

Schröder-Gudehus, Brigitte. "Nationalism and Internationalism." In R. C. Olby et al., eds. *Companion to the History of Modern Science.* London, 1990.

Skolnikoff, Eugene B. *The Elusive Transformation: Science, Technology, and the Evolution of International Politics.* Princeton, N.J., 1993.

Wang, Jessica. *American Science in an Age of Anxiety: Scientists, Anticommunism, and the Cold War.* Chapel Hill, N.C., 1999.

Wang, Zuoyue. "U.S.–Chinese Scientific Exchange: A Case Study of State-Sponsored Scientific Internationalism During the Cold War and Beyond." *Historical Studies in the Physical and Biological Sciences* 30, no. 1 (1999): 249–277.

Weiner, Charles. "A New Site for the Seminar: The Refugees and American Physics in the Thirties." *Perspectives in American History* 2 (1968): 190–234.

Wright, Susan. "Evolution of Biological Warfare Policy." In Susan Wright, ed. *Preventing a Biological Arms Race.* Cambridge, Mass., 1990.

See also ENVIRONMENTAL DIPLOMACY; NUCLEAR STRATEGY AND DIPLOMACY; OUTER SPACE; PHILANTHROPY.

SELF-DETERMINATION

★ ★ ★ ★

Betty Miller Unterberger

The principle of self-determination refers to the right of a people to determine its own political destiny. Beyond this broad definition, however, no legal criteria determine which groups may legitimately claim this right in particular cases. The right to self-determination has become one of the most complex issues facing policymakers in the United States and the international community at large. At the close of the twentieth century, it could mean the right of people to choose their form of government within existing borders or by achieving independence from a colonial power. It could mean the right of an ethnic, linguistic, or religious group to redefine existing national borders to achieve a separate national sovereignty or simply to achieve a greater degree of autonomy and linguistic or religious identity within a sovereign state. It could even mean the right of a political unit within a federal system such as Canada, Czechoslovakia, the former Soviet Union, or the former Yugoslavia to secede from the federation and become an independent sovereign state.

Self-determination is a concept that can be traced back to the beginning of government. The right has always been cherished by all peoples, although history has a long record of its denial to the weak by the strong. Both the Greek city-states and the earlier Mesopotamian ones were jealous of their right to self-determination. Yet to the Greeks, non-Greeks were barbarians, born to serve them and the object of conquest if they refused to submit. The development of modern states in Europe and the rise of popular national consciousness enhanced the status of self-determination as a political principle, but it was not until the period of World War I that the right of national independence came to be known as the principle of national self-determination. In general terms, it was simply the belief that each nation had a right to constitute an independent state and to determine its own government.

The historian Alfred Cobban has said that not every kind of national revolt can be included under the description of self-determination. The movement for national independence, or self-determination, falls into the same category as utilitarianism, communism, or Jeffersonian democracy. It is a theory, a principle, or an idea, and no simple, unconscious national movement can be identified with it. Struggles like the rising of the French under the inspiration of Joan of Arc or the Hussite Wars are fundamentally different from the national movements of the last two hundred years because of the absence of a theory of national self-determination, which could appear only in the presence of a democratic ideology.

THE AMERICAN REVOLUTION

In this context, then, the revolt of the British colonies in North America has been defined as the first assertion of the right of national and democratic self-determination in the history of the world. Resenting domination from across the seas, and especially the imposition of taxes without representation, the American colonists invoked natural law and the natural rights of man, drawing inspiration from the writings of John Locke to support their view. Locke taught that political societies are based upon the consent of the people who compose them, each of whom agrees to submit to the majority. Man has a natural right to life, liberty, and property. Sovereignty belongs to the people and is therefore limited by the necessity to protect the individual members.

Thomas Jefferson emphasized Locke's theories as American ideals and epitomized the republican spirit of the century. In drafting the Declaration of Independence in June 1776, Jefferson stated his fundamental philosophy of government, upon which the modern concept of self-determination rests. He asserted that "all Men

461

are created equal, that they are endowed by their Creator with inherent and unalienable Rights ["certain unalienable Rights" in the Continental Congress's final draft], that among these are Life, Liberty and the Pursuit of Happiness"; that the "just Powers" of government are established "by the Consent of the governed" to protect these rights; and that when government does not, "it is the Right of the People to alter or abolish it, and to institute new Government."

In considering the American Revolution as the seminal example of the modern principle of self-determination, it is important to focus attention on both elements of Jefferson's view. He was concerned not only with throwing off the foreign yoke but also with ensuring that the government was that of the people and that their will was supreme.

Since the formation of the United States, American statesmen have continually expressed sympathy for the basic principle of self-determination. In 1796, President George Washington stated that he was stirred "whenever, in any country, he saw an oppressed nation unfurl the banner of freedom." Three years earlier, Thomas Jefferson, then the American secretary of state, had said: "We surely cannot deny to any nation that right whereon our own is founded—that every one may govern itself according to whatever form it pleases and change those forms at its own will."

Jefferson's view, supported by his fellow Virginians James Madison and James Monroe, was widely accepted by the American public during the ensuing years although never actually implemented as official policy. Nevertheless, regardless of its original intent, throughout the nineteenth and twentieth centuries the Declaration of Independence provided a beacon of hope both to European peoples struggling for independence against autocratic governments and to colonial peoples seeking to advance toward independence. Frequently, American idealists threatened to drag the nation into European affairs by demanding that the government underwrite a policy of liberation abroad. For example, when the Greeks staged an abortive independence movement against the Turks in the 1820s, the Monroe administration was assailed by Daniel Webster in Congress and by many others for its apparent indifference to the cause of liberty in other parts of the world. Although realists like John Quincy Adams opposed the expression of sentiments unsupported by action, President James Monroe nonetheless placed on record his public support of the Greek struggle for self-determination in his famous message of December 1823.

NONINTERVENTION VERSUS SELF-DETERMINATION

But it must be noted that while Adams recognized that American history fostered a sympathy for self-determination, that same tradition also had established as a cardinal priority the doctrine of nonintervention so forcefully enunciated by Washington in his Farewell Address. For Adams, concerned with the limits of American power in this period, the doctrine of nonintervention took precedence over the principle of self-determination.

Yet throughout the nineteenth century the American public frequently expressed sympathy for the struggles of oppressed peoples in Europe. This feeling was most vigorously demonstrated in relation to the Hungarians upon the failure of their revolution of 1848–1849. After the revolution had been crushed by Russian troops, Lajos Kossuth, the eloquent Hungarian leader, arrived in New York City in 1851 to the greatest ovation given anyone since the visit of the Marquis de Lafayette twenty-five years earlier.

When the Austrian chargé d'affaires protested to the State Department against the overt public sympathy expressed in favor of Hungary's liberation, Daniel Webster, then secretary of state, responded in a note explaining America's sympathy for Hungary as a natural expression of the national character, and assuring the Austrian government that such popular outbursts constituted no desertion of the established American doctrine of noninterference in the internal affairs of other countries. Nevertheless, many persons in official positions demanded that the United States use its moral and physical power to support the freedom of Hungary. Furthermore, the government did not suppress the right of Congress to pass resolutions expressing the sympathy of the nation for struggling peoples, like the Hungarians, seeking freedom.

CIVIL WAR AND IMPERIALISM

The attitude of the federal government changed at the outset of the Civil War, when the United States found itself in the embarrassing position of using force to suppress the will of a minority of the nation seeking to establish its own independence.

Among the interested European observers of the American Civil War, there were perhaps as many partisans of the South as of the North. To some it seemed that the Southern states, by fighting for their self-determination as a nation, were striking a blow for political freedom and independence in the spirit of similar revolutionaries and national movements in the Old World. Southerners themselves contended that they were following the example of the American patriots of 1776, a view that appeared reasonable to many Englishmen. To the latter, Secretary of State William H. Seward made it clear that the United States could not regard as friends those who favored or gave aid to the insurrection under any pretext. In taking this position the United States pointed out that it was claiming only what it conceded to all other nations. Thus, the Civil War clearly determined the official policy of the United States toward self-determination. The United States in effect denied the right of communities within a constituted federal union to determine their allegiance, and that denial had been enforced by military power. Clearly, the doctrine of national sovereignty, supported by the principle of nonintervention, had officially and unequivocally taken precedence over the concept of self-determination.

This official view also influenced the policy of the United States in regard to the use of the plebiscite as a means of settling questions of sovereignty and self-determination. For example, Secretary Seward adamantly opposed a plebiscite on the abortive cession of the West Indian islands of St. Thomas and St. John in 1868. Again, in August 1897, in response to the Japanese minister's suggestion that a plebiscite be taken regarding the annexation of the Hawaiian Islands, Secretary of State John Sherman drew upon the history of international relations to confirm the impropriety of "appealing from the action of the Government to 'the population.'" "In international comity and practice," said Sherman, "the will of a nation is ascertained through the established and recognized government," and "it is only through it that the nation can speak." The same principle in regard to annexed territories was asserted in the memorandum of the American Peace Commission at the conclusion of the Spanish-American War. Thus, by 1899 the United States had emphatically asserted its adherence to the principle and practice of annexation without the consent of the peoples annexed.

On the fall of the Spanish empire in the Western Hemisphere in 1898, the United States gained colonial control of Guam, Puerto Rico, and the Philippines, and enjoyed quasi-suzerainty over Cuba, from which it withdrew its military presence in 1902 while reserving certain rights for itself. This put the United States in the anomalous position of having fought a war against Spain at least officially for Cuban self-determination, only to deny that principle to the colonies acquired in the peace settlement. Those who opposed annexation constituted a powerful anti-imperialist movement, headed by many political and intellectual leaders. Deeply concerned over the concept of self-determination, although they did not specifically mention it, they clearly opposed annexation on the ground that it involved the suppression of a conquered people. Although the anti-imperialists could not defeat the peace treaty, they were able to bring the issue of imperialism into the open and to raise considerable national doubt as to whether the treaty was in accord with the direct traditions of self-determination as revealed by the establishment of the nation.

The nation's ambivalence concerning the proper interpretation and appropriate application of the concept of self-determination was exposed again when the American people were called upon to decide the novel questions of whether the Constitution followed the flag across the Pacific and whether democracy could be preserved at home in its new imperial setting. Anti-imperialists argued against the abandonment of American principles for the ways of the Old World. Imperialists, also calling upon American traditions, maintained that democracy could be extended only to a people fit to receive it. Self-government depended upon a nation's capacity for political action, and if a people was not ready for independence, it must undergo a period of political tutelage and protection. Thus, the imperialists joined the American conception of manifest destiny with Rudyard Kipling's call for the Anglo-Saxon nations to take up the white man's burden. In the curious reasoning of an official U.S. commission to the Philippines, "American sovereignty is only another name for the liberty of the Filipinos." And yet it must be noted that every president after William McKinley extended the prospect of freedom and independence to the Philippines until it was actually granted in 1946.

By 1899, then, the American conflict of principle in regard to self-determination might clearly be seen by examining two great heroes in American history. The popular reputation of George Washington rested less on his great work as the nation's first president than on his successful conduct of a struggle for self-determination, while Abraham Lincoln's rested on his success in suppressing such a struggle. Although pursuing diametrically opposite principles, both were judged right by posterity—even, in the main, by the descendants of the defeated sides. Later events have caused the Civil War to be regarded as waged on the issue of slavery, but at the outset Lincoln asserted that it was fought not to abolish slavery but to maintain the Union—that is, to resist the claim of the Southern states to independence. Such a claim or right has its limits, and—to state the matter from the cold standpoint of political philosophy—the national government believed that in this case the claim was not within the limits where the principle properly applied.

Considerations like these induce one to reflect upon the limited nature of principles commonly accepted as universal; upon the conflicts that arise when two inconsistent universal principles come into collision; and how far such conflict may be avoided by recognizing that there are limits, with a debatable region in which neither can be rigorously applied.

Wilsonianism   World War I and the leadership of President Woodrow Wilson provided the nation an opportunity for a supreme effort to reconcile the principles of self-determination and national sovereignty in a way that might provide a lasting peace. In a May 1916 address before the League to Enforce Peace, he announced as a fundamental principle "that every people has a right to choose the sovereignty under which they shall live. . . . " During the following two years, Wilson continued to proclaim vigorously and with passionate conviction his version of the right of national self-determination. He stated that "No peace can last or ought to last which does not accept the principle that governments derive all their just powers from the consent of the governed," and that "no right anywhere exists to hand peoples about from sovereignty to sovereignty as if they were property." The president's repeated affirmation of an abstract principle of justice that should be universally applied had a profound influence on the subsequent statements of both the Allies and the Central Powers. In a dramatic appearance before Congress in January 1918, Wilson crystallized his war aims in the famous Fourteen Points address. Although the phrase "self-determination" was not specifically used, at least six of the Fourteen Points dealt with some interpretation or application of the principle.

The Bolsheviks in Russia played a decisive role in the specific clarification and implementation of the American concept of self-determination. When the Bolshevik leaders Vladimir Lenin and Leon Trotsky came to power in November 1917, they demanded an immediate, general, and democratic peace with the Central Powers, based on no "annexations and contributions [reparations] with the right of all nations to self-determination." On 3 December the Russians suspended hostilities with Germany and its allies, a state that lasted until 17 December. During this period the Bolsheviks used the concept of self-determination heavily on behalf of peace. After a powerful propaganda campaign, they were finally able to convince their opponents to allow more time for the negotiations, so as to permit the Allies to define their war aims and decide whether they wished to participate. During this period the Bolsheviks published the six points for world peace that they had laid down for the guidance of the peace conference. Five dealt with self-determination. Although the United States and the Allies failed to perceive it until Trotsky pointed it out to them, the points were directed at them as much as at the Central Powers. Indeed, the Russians had proposed five points that in essence were the same as five of the Fourteen Points of President Wilson, published only a few weeks later.

On 29 December, with six days remaining during which the Entente Powers could exercise their option to participate in the negotiations, Trotsky sent them an appeal, pointing out that the Allies could no longer insist on fighting for the liberation of Belgium, northern France, Serbia, and other areas since Germany and its allies had indicated a willingness to evacuate those areas following a universal peace. Some response appeared to be necessary, for not only did Trotsky call for violent proletarian revolution against the Allied governments, but he had also shrewdly based his primary argument on Wilson's principle of self-determination. Although probably not realizing it, Wilson was in an ideological corner; either he must accept the Bolshevik conclusion that all peoples in all states, including all colonies, had the right to immediate self-determination, or he must reject it but in its place offer some standard of what constituted an acceptable unit for the application of that principle.

While Wilson had been sympathetic to the principle of self-determination as enunciated by Lenin, he had no illusions concerning the German response to it. By the end of December 1917 it appeared clear that self-determination, as understood by the Germans, justified the severance from Russia of the territories occupied by the German army: Russian Poland, most of the Baltic provinces, and parts of Belarus. Indeed, by the middle of December the State Department was aware that the Ukraine, Finland, and Transcaucasia were in the process of declaring themselves independent under the auspices of Lenin's program of self-determination. Finally, it was apparent that if Russia was to have peace according to the German interpretation of self-determination, it would entail heavy territorial sacrifices. Wilson was opposed to such an interpretation of self-determination, and on several occasions declared his opposition to the dismemberment of empires. But in that case, what did Wilson's concept of self-determination really mean? Trotsky had made it clear that to demand self-determination for the peoples of enemy states but not for the peoples within the Allied states or their own colonies would "mean the defense of the most naked, the most cynical imperialism."

Since Trotsky's invitation presented an ideological challenge, an analysis of the American response becomes crucial. Secretary of State Robert Lansing totally opposed it. His attack was based on his social conservatism, his animosity toward Bolshevik ideology, and, most important, his insight into the logical and political requirements for a meaningful application of the principle of self-determination in foreign policy. His advice to the president betrayed the contradictions that still existed in his thinking. On the one hand, he argued that the president should refuse to make any response whatsoever to their appeals. On the other, he admitted that Trotsky's logic demanded some answer and that a more detailed restatement of American war aims might well be expedient.

In his analysis of the Bolsheviks' reasoning, Lansing apparently also sought to convince the president of the undesirability of settling territorial problems by means of self-determination. He pointed out that the existing concept of the sovereignty of states in international relations would be destroyed if the "mere expression of popular will" were to become the governing principle in territorial settlements. He reminded Wilson of the nation's decision in regard to popular sovereignty in its own civil war and stated: "We, as a nation, are therefore committed to the principle that a national state may by force if necessary prevent a portion of its territory from seceding without its

consent especially if it has long exercised sovereignty over it or if its national safety or vital interests would be endangered." The Bolshevik proposal, Lansing warned, would be "utterly destructive of the political fabric of society and would result in constant turmoil and change."

One of the strongest points in Lansing's analysis was his discovery that the discussion regarding self-determination up to that point had a major ideological flaw. There was no definition of the "distinguishing characteristic" of the unit to which the principle was to be applied. Trotsky had discussed the right of nationalities without defining what a nationality was. Was it based on blood, habitation of a particular territory, language, or political affinity? Clearly, accurate definition of the word was necessary if the terms proposed were to be properly interpreted; otherwise, they were far too vague to be considered intelligently. Lansing added that if the Bolsheviks intended to suggest that every community could determine its own allegiance to a particular state, or to become independent, the political organization of the world would be shattered. The result, he said, would be international anarchy. Lansing did not provide a definition of "nationalities." He surely must have perceived that his criticism of the Bolsheviks applied equally to Wilson's position.

THE WILSONIAN RESPONSE: PRINCIPLES AND PRACTICE

President Wilson was now in possession of two totally divergent views on self-determination. Whereas Trotsky had pushed the principle to its limits, advocating that all peoples, not just a selected list, be liberated from foreign rule, Secretary Lansing had drawn his sword against Trotsky and negated the usefulness of self-determination in settling world issues. He insisted that if the present political and social order was to be preserved, then the principle of the legal sovereignty of constituted states must take precedence over any consideration of the popular will of minorities.

The president was at odds with both points of view. At the core of his belief, self-determination meant the moral necessity of government by consent of the governed. Self-determination was to Wilson almost another word for popular sovereignty; *vox populi* was *vox dei*. Rousseau's "general will" was for him not merely ideal will, but the actual will of the people, which had only to be freed from the ill will of autocratic governments for its innate goodness to be manifested. The idealization of democracy was an essential part of Wilsonian ideology. Firmly convinced of the goodness of the people's will, he believed in the possibility of building a new and better international order on the basis of national sovereignty, in which he assumed the democratic will of the people to be embodied.

To put it in another way, Wilson's belief in the goodness and power of world opinion, which might be termed the general will of humanity, and its identity with the general will of every democratic nation, enabled him to hold the view that the self-determination of nations and national sovereignty was a possible basis—indeed, the only basis—of world peace. The president never conceived of these principles as divided or as being applied separately. He had concluded that the primary cause of aggression by one state against another was a desire for territorial and economic security in the absence of international political security. The hallmark of this lack of international security was the bipolar alliance system that operated in an atmosphere of struggle for the elusive balance of power. This being the case, the president reasoned, if national security could be restored to the various states, then the motive for political and economic aggression would be removed from international politics. Wilson believed that an international organization of states, through the common resources of a community of power, would provide the required security. Once states adjusted to operating for the common welfare of humankind, without resorting to the exploitation of one state by another, then the existing inequities regarding points of sovereignty could be resolved by an international organization based on the principle that government must be with the consent of the governed. This was Wilson's long-range view of the application of self-determination. Even before the United States entered the war, he had come to regard the League of Nations as central to his thought.

Nevertheless, the day after receiving Lansing's letter opposing the Bolsheviks, President Wilson revealed, in a conversation with the retiring British ambassador, that while he sympathized with the Bolshevik desire to settle the war on the basis of self-determination, he was also deeply influenced by the views of his secretary of state: "In point of logic, of pure logic, this principle which was good in itself would lead to the complete independence of various small nationalities now forming part of various empires. Pushed

to its extreme, the principle would mean the disruption of existing governments, to an indefinable degree." Wilson's introduction to his Fourteen Points speech appeared to be a direct answer to the challenge presented by the German-Russian negotiations then being conducted at Brest-Litovsk. His deep concern with Russia's plight seems apparent from a reading of his eloquent passages concerning that nation. Apparently seeking to impress both the ruler and the ruled, he did not call for the overthrow of Bolshevik power as a condition for renewed cooperation. Moreover, fully resolved to continue the crusade regardless of all suggestions for a negotiated peace, Wilson refused to abandon Russia's borderland to the tortured interpretation of self-determination put forth by the Central Powers. Thus, the sixth of the Fourteen Points called for an evacuation of all Russian territory and the adoption of diplomacy by all other nations of the world, of actions that would permit an unhampered and unembarrassed opportunity for Russia's independent self-determination under institutions of its free choosing.

Even though the United States later, under tremendous pressure from the Allies, participated in expeditions to Siberia and northern Russia, Wilson justified these departures from his clearly enunciated principles on the ground that he was seeking to preserve the territorial integrity of Russia and the ultimate right of self-determination for its people, while at the same time "rescuing" the Czech legion presumably trapped in Russia and preserving the Open Door policy in the Russian Far East and northern Manchuria against suspected Japanese imperialism. But perhaps even more important, he was seeking to retain the goodwill of the Allies, whose support was vital to the success of a League of Nations, the capstone of his Fourteen Points. Thus, to block Japan and further the league, Wilson followed a policy that appeared to be totally at variance not only with the principle of self-determination, but also with the principles of his proposed league. Wilson, above all the man of principle, found himself caught, as had the nation itself many times since its inception, in a debatable situation where, despite deep convictions, none of his principles could be rigorously applied.

Wilson was in a somewhat similar quandary in relation to the tenth point, concerning Austria-Hungary. From the U.S. entry into the war, he had disapproved of the dismemberment of the Dual Monarchy. In doing so he hoped to divide Vienna and Berlin by strengthening those elements in Austria-Hungary that favored an early negotiated peace. Although sympathetic to the desires for self-determination of the oppressed nationalities within the empire, he could not accept "the extreme logic of this discontent which would be the dismemberment of Austria Hungary." Thus, in the tenth point Wilson stopped short of a clear-cut endorsement of independence by placing his emphasis on providing the peoples of Austria-Hungary with the free opportunity for "autonomous development" within a Danubian Confederation of States.

In January 1918, Wilson had reason to believe that such a policy might still keep open the door to a negotiated peace with Austria-Hungary. However, subsequent events, especially Czech belligerency against the Germans in Russia and the failure of his efforts to negotiate a separate peace with Austria-Hungary, led Wilson to give up his dream for a Danubian Confederation and support an independent Czechoslovakia. Nevertheless, it should be noted that although Lansing and the State Department had presented strong arguments for the recognition of Czech independence on the basis of ethnicity, language, and shared historical experience, Wilson would accept none of these. It was only Czech belligerency in Russia against Germany that provided the rationale for his recognition of the de facto independence of Czechoslovakia.

Curiously, the first of Wilson's territorial points dealt with the colonial problem. Here the president very cautiously advocated "a free, open-minded, and absolutely impartial adjustment of all colonial claims." Regardless of how broad or narrow the interpretation of "colonial claims," Wilson insisted that their settlement be based upon the principle that in determining all such questions of sovereignty, the interests of the populations concerned must have equal weight with the equitable claims of the governments whose title was to be determined. Lansing's caution surely had an effect. Once again, the president appeared, perhaps without realizing it, to be seeking some reconciliation of the historic conflict of principles.

An examination of the remainder of Wilson's points on self-determination reveals that only in the case of Poland did the president offer an outright and unqualified commitment to independence. The thirteenth point, then, contrasted sharply with Wilson's application of the self-determination principle in the preceding seven points. It must have been evident to Wilson that the

national and language conflicts destined to emerge with the rebirth of Poland were likely to be intense. It is therefore noteworthy that Poland was given specific political and economic guarantees. First, Wilson publicly proclaimed Poland to be in need of a "free and secure access to the seas." Second, this economic and strategic safeguard was further supplemented by Wilson's proposal that Poland's "political and economic independence and territorial integrity should be guaranteed by international covenant." His thirteenth point, which gave an international guarantee for the independence of Poland, might be looked upon as the link to the fourteenth point, which called for the establishment of the League of Nations.

Although millions rallied to the idea of a League of Nations as the essential guarantee for a perpetual peace, Wilson—without even mentioning peace—chartered an association of nations in order to secure "mutual guarantees of political independence and territorial integrity." Peace was the ultimate objective, but the immediate function of the league was the preservation of the territorial arrangements that would emerge from the peace conference. The association of nations was meant to be a sort of midwife to nations about to be born; it would help them pass from the precarious stage of infancy through adolescence, to full maturity in a new "community of power."

Even the president himself possibly did not realize the full significance of the explosive principle that he had done so much to set in motion. Certainly a fundamental weakness of Wilson's ideas was his failure to realize how indeterminate a criterion nationality might be, and how little assistance it might sometimes give in deciding actual frontiers. Moreover, although he had spoken of self-determination as though it were an absolute principle of international right, from the very beginning he perforce allowed competing principles to influence his decisions and derogate from its claims. Yet by and large the peace conference of 1918 proceeded on the theory that, insofar as possible, boundaries should be readjusted by balancing the principle of national self-determination against other factors. The new boundaries would then be guaranteed against forcible change.

THE INTERWAR YEARS AND WORLD WAR II

Despite Wilson's efforts, the principle of self-determination was not explicitly written into the

League of Nations Covenant. Therefore, many predicted that it would soon be forgotten. Moreover, after the war U.S. officials tended to regard the Slavic states of Europe as politically corrupt, economically unstable, and strategically insignificant. During the interwar years, U.S. concern for the region was limited to occasional statements on behalf of religious freedom and self-determination of peoples. U.S. officials never formulated any specific policies to achieve such aims for the simple reason that Eastern Europe lay outside the region of historic American interest. It was obvious, therefore, that America would not oppose any serious German or Russian challenge to the newly created states. Thus, when Nazi power destroyed Czechoslovakia and Poland in 1939 and overran all of Eastern Europe in 1940, the American people were reluctant to offer anything more than deep sympathy. Nevertheless, nationalists in Asia such as Mahatma Gandhi in India and Ho Chi Minh in Indochina continued to seek national liberation, inspired in part by Wilson's ideal of self-determination.

However, as events were to demonstrate, the view that self-determination was merely an anomaly of World War I proved to be false. Amid the confusion of World War II, the outline of the future world settlement began to appear and take shape. Franklin D. Roosevelt was as challenged and as baffled by the idea of self-determination as Wilson had been. Just as Wilson believed that an international organization was needed to transform the doctrine of self-determination into political reality, so Roosevelt saw the United Nations, Wilson's grandchild, as hopefully playing the role in which Wilson had cast it. The United Nations was to accept "the fact of nationalism and the need for internationalism." Just as Wilson had experienced difficulties in interpreting and applying the doctrine of self-determination in the face of Allied objections, the secret treaties, and Bolshevik competition, Franklin Roosevelt had similar problems. In the Atlantic Charter of August 1941, he and Prime Minister Winston Churchill of Great Britain joined to make known certain common principles and national policies on which they based their hopes for a better future. Once again the principle of self-determination of peoples was affirmed and the desire expressed "to see no territorial changes that do not accord with the freely expressed wishes of the peoples concerned." Respect was also reaffirmed for "the right of all peoples to choose the form of government under which they will live" and "to see sovereign rights and self gov-

ernment restored to those who have been forcibly deprived of them."

As in World War I, both the meaning and the scope of these abstract principles were open to conflicting interpretations. For example, the Atlantic Charter ignored the burgeoning interests of the Soviet Union in European politics. For Joseph Stalin the charter's repudiation of any alteration in the prewar political and territorial status of Eastern Europe—the only region that offered the Soviets any tangible and lasting fruits of victory—rendered it totally unacceptable as a basis of action. That the Soviet Union, unlike both the United States and Britain, suffered incalculable physical destruction and twenty million deaths at the hands of the invading Nazis made inevitable vast disagreements over the applicability of the Atlantic Charter to the territories of Germany and Eastern Europe. While both Britain and the United States recognized that without the continued and unlimited military efforts of the Soviet Union the West could hardly hope to defeat Germany, the Atlantic Charter assumed that the two Western democracies, even before the United States had formally entered the war, could dominate the postwar settlements in a region that comprised not only the historic territorial objectives of the Russian nation but also the area the Soviet armies might actually occupy.

Fighting for their existence, the Russians were in no position to antagonize their Western allies. At the meeting of the Allies in London in September 1941, they accepted the principle of self-determination; clearly, though, the Soviet Union would follow the precepts of the Atlantic Charter only to the extent that they served its security interests. That the immediate military requirements far outweighed ultimate political intention was illustrated in January 1942, when the Soviet Union and twenty-five other nations signed the United Nations Declaration, the opening paragraph of which accepted the purpose and principles of the Atlantic Charter.

In 1944, as the Allies began to free vast areas of Europe from Nazi control, their political differences could no longer be submerged. As the Russian armies rolled across Eastern Europe, what the United States had denied Stalin by refusing to accede to a spheres-of-influence agreement, now fell to the Soviet Union through rapid military advancement. But as late as April 1944, Secretary of State Cordell Hull, committed to the Wilsonian vision of self-determination, not only opposed any negotiation of spheres of influence with the

Soviet Union but also promised the American people a postwar world based on the principles of the Atlantic Charter. Whatever security Stalin required along his western boundaries, said Hull, he could obtain through a strong postwar peace organization. When it became clear to Stalin that free governments in such nations as Poland and Romania would not do his bidding, he employed his military advantage to impose governments friendly to the Soviet Union through the agency of communist puppet regimes. This eliminated the possibility of any serious negotiation on the postwar Soviet frontiers of Eastern Europe. By 1945 the Western powers could no longer assure even limited self-determination for the Slavic peoples of Europe. What remained for the United States was the cruel choice of compromising the principles of the Atlantic Charter or sacrificing the alliance itself.

DECOLONIZATION AND SELF-DETERMINATION

The principle of self-determination fared considerably better in other areas of the world. In effect, what World War I did for Eastern Europe, World War II accomplished in Asia and Africa. Between 1946 and 1960, thirty-seven new nations emerged from colonial status in Asia, Africa, and the Middle East. Roosevelt's efforts to implement the concept of self-determination were augmented enormously—indeed, decisively—by the rising tide of nationalism on these continents. Nevertheless, the United States was again beset with the problem of balancing its conflicting interests and its conflicting principles. As Cordell Hull wrote in his memoirs, the prime difficulty generally with regard to Asian colonial possessions was to induce the colonial powers—principally Britain, France, and the Netherlands—to adopt American ideas with regard to dependent peoples. Yet they could not be pressed too far without jeopardizing the very close cooperation the United States sought with them in Europe. Fortunately for Roosevelt's objectives, the movement for national self-determination in Asia and Africa was greatly accelerated by the quick, total collapse of French resistance to German aggression and the Japanese conquest and "liberation" of European colonial possessions in the Far East.

These events profoundly changed the attitudes of the Asian and African masses. Moreover, Roosevelt himself sought to exert a beneficial influence on his allies. For instance, despite suggestions that the date for granting full independence in the Philippines be postponed as a consequence of the ravages of war and the cooperation of prominent Filipinos with the Japanese, the United States kept its promise and the islands became independent on 4 July 1946. Nor did Britain, in its old liberality and realistic wisdom, attempt to restore its Asian empire. From 1947 it brought to fulfillment the work of true liberation that had started throughout the empire even before World War I. France, resenting its humiliation in World War II and seeking to restore old imperial glory, deeply resented Anglo-American accommodation to changing reality. Britain was held responsible for France's loss of Syria and Lebanon, and American greed or innocence—or perhaps a combination of both—was suspected of being behind the national liberation movements in Indochina and North Africa. Yet the American conflict of principles was revealed by the fact that France fought wars in Indochina and Algeria with the help of American arms and money.

On the other hand, the United Nations Charter reflected both the triumph of Wilson's concept of self-determination and the change in international relations that had occurred during the intervening years. Whereas the Covenant of the League of Nations ultimately had no references to the concept of national self-determination, the charter of the United Nations mentioned it three times. However, the charter did not insist on independence, but spoke only of self-government. The principle of federation was more promising than that of national independence. What was essential in the democratic tradition—and here the charter drew largely from Wilsonian thought—was not national independence but self-government, government based upon the consent of the governed, and respect for the equality of the peoples involved. After 1960 the right of colonial peoples to self-determination and independence was reaffirmed almost annually by the General Assembly of the United Nations.

THE COLD WAR

Yet throughout these years the United States continued to face the dilemma of which it became aware during and immediately following World War II. On the one hand, it hesitated to antagonize western European countries whose cooperation was needed in the postwar world. On the other

★ ★ ★ ★ ★

PERSPECTIVES ON SELF-DETERMINATION

"Wherever the standard of freedom and independence has been or shall be unfurled, there will her heart, her benedictions, and her prayers be. But she goes not abroad in search of monsters to destroy. She is the well-wisher to the freedom and independence of all. She is the champion and vindicator only of her own."

— *John Quincy Adams,*
4 July 1821 —

"We are glad . . . to fight thus for the ultimate peace of the world and for the liberation of the people . . . for the rights of nations great and small and the privilege of men everywhere to choose their way of life and of obedience. . . . We shall be satisfied when those rights have been made as secure as the faith and freedom of the nations can make them."

— *Woodrow Wilson,*
2 April 1917 —

"This is a principle of the Atlantic Charter—the right of all peoples to choose the form of government under which they will live—the restoration of sovereign rights and self-government to those peoples who have been forcibly deprived of them by the aggressor nations."

— *Franklin D. Roosevelt, 1945* —

"A despotism of the present Soviet type cannot indefinitely perpetuate its rule over hundreds of millions of people who love God, who love their country, and who have a sense of personal dignity. The Soviet system, which seeks to expunge the distinctive characteristics of nations, creed, and individuality must itself change or be doomed ultimately to collapse."

— *John Foster Dulles, 1952* —

"The United States doesn't now and never has advocated open rebellion by an undefended populace against force over which they could not possibly prevail."

— *Dwight D. Eisenhower, 1956* —

"We must be staunch in our conviction that freedom is not the sole prerogative of a lucky few, but the inalienable and universal right of all human beings. . . . This is not cultural imperialism, it is providing the means for genuine self-determination and protection for diversity. . . . It would be cultural condescension, or worse, to say that any people prefer dictatorship to democracy."

— *Ronald Reagan,*
8 June 1982 —

"No society, no continent should be disqualified from sharing the ideals of human liberty. . . . Abandonment of the worldwide democratic revolution could be disastrous for American security."

— *George H. W. Bush,*
15 December 1992 —

"Our dream is that of a day when the opinions and energies of every person in the world will be given full expression in a world of thriving democracies that cooperate with each other and live in peace."

— *Bill Clinton,*
27 September 1993 —

hand, American idealists continued to express their deep-rooted sympathy with any people aspiring to freedom. The problem, however, was exacerbated by the onset of the Cold War and the American adoption of a policy of containment. Actually, the rationale for the policy developed in the Truman Doctrine drew heavily upon American ideological support of the principle of self-determination. However, the new interpretation changed America's early historic role of merely expressing sympathy to one of active and official economic and military support of the self-determination of "free peoples" who were "resisting attempted subjugation by armed minorities or by outside pressures." For the first time, President Harry S. Truman officially endorsed the necessity of actually assisting "free peoples to work out their own destinies in their own way." From this point on, official American policy held that international communism violated the principle of self-determination and was irreconcilable with the right of each state to develop its own political, economic, and cultural life. Nevertheless, Washington supported the efforts of Marshal Josip Broz Tito to hold together a unified federal Yugoslavia as an effective counterweight to the influence of the Soviet Union.

On the other hand, while the United States paid homage to independence for the Baltic republics of the Soviet Union and provided token support for Tibetan nationalism in its claims against the People's Republic of China, because of the need to minimize the possibility of war or political crisis with the Soviet Union or the Sino-Soviet bloc, the United States did nothing to buttress these causes. The United States also sought to preserve existing states. It feared that the breakup of a state into its ethnic components would increase the risk of armed conflict and destabilize other multi-ethnic states. The United States not only favored the preservation of existing states, it also favored the integration of a number of states into multilateral groupings, such as the European community. Thus, the United States encouraged states of some ethnic diversity to join together and support one another in larger integrated communities.

The official pursuit of anticommunism raised pertinent questions concerning the nature and use of America's commitment to self-determination. For example, in the Western Hemisphere the Monroe Doctrine had been used by the United States to bar undesirable outside influence while securing the dominance of its own influence. Within ten years after World War II, the Monroe Doctrine—extended, supplemented, and reinterpreted by the Inter-American Treaty of Reciprocal Assistance (Rio Treaty) in 1947 and the Declaration of Caracas in 1954—gave the United States a claim to keep communism, now clearly accepted as incompatible with the concept of self-determination, out of the American states. In furtherance of this policy the United States intervened in Guatemala in 1954 to unseat the incumbent government. The invasion of Cuba at the Bay of Pigs in 1961 was an abortive attempt to unseat the socialist and populist government of Fidel Castro. When disturbances broke out in the Dominican Republic in 1965, the United States occupied the capital, Santo Domingo. President Lyndon Johnson justified this action in May 1965 by asserting that what had begun as a popular revolution committed to democracy and social justice had fallen into "the hands of a band of communist conspirators."

In Asia, Africa, and the Middle East, the United States adopted a somewhat similar stance. The triumph of communism in China, the Korean War, McCarthyism at home, and the moral principles enunciated by John Foster Dulles, Dwight D. Eisenhower's secretary of state, enormously enhanced this position. Thus, the recognition that communism itself was a basic threat to the self-determination of virtually any nation, as well as a threat to the American way of life, led the United States to support almost any anticommunist regime or to associate itself with traditional authoritarian regimes whose days were numbered because they had alienated mass support: Bao Dai and Ngo Dinh Diem in Indochina and King Faisal II in Iraq were only three such examples. The fact that their governments were pro-American and anticommunist qualified them in American eyes as democratic, or at least potentially so; by the same token, the United States opposed internal movements to overthrow them and condemned these as communist or procommunist. Moreover, such policies were implemented and elaborated by the formation of pacts like the Southeast Asia Treaty Organization (SEATO) in 1954 and proposals like the Eisenhower Doctrine in 1957. Such a response was typical of the apparent inability of the United States to understand the unique social and political nature of the struggles for self-determination of Asia and the Middle East. In the attempt to contain communism and thus maintain its new concept of self-determination, the United States became committed to the domestic, social, and political status quo throughout the world.

VIETNAM

Nowhere did such a policy ultimately come to be regarded by the American public as more bankrupt than in Vietnam. When France was driven from Indochina by the communist forces of Ho Chi Minh in 1954, the United States established a noncommunist regime in South Vietnam in the hope of confining communism to the northern half of Vietnam. The objective was not only to help "free people" maintain their independence but also, the rationale went, to save neighboring Southeast Asian regimes that, it was believed, would fall like dominoes should South Vietnam fall. Then, communism would be in a position to threaten the Indian subcontinent. By 1968 the weakness of the Saigon government and the military success of the Vietcong had led the U.S. government to commit a military force of 550,000 soldiers and a budget of roughly $24 billion. But as President Johnson escalated the war and the costs and casualties mounted, public criticism reached a level that made the Vietnam conflict the most unpopular war in American history.

Such criticisms ultimately led to President Johnson's decision to announce a halt in bombing north of the seventeenth parallel and to stay out of the 1968 presidential election. Among the arguments used to oppose the war was the charge that not only had the United States betrayed its own revolutionary traditions by becoming the aggressor in a civil war between peoples of the same linguistic background who resented foreign interference, but that it was also violating the Wilsonian principle of self-determination by conniving at the flouting of the Geneva Agreement of 1954, which had stipulated that general elections to unify the country be held in Vietnam in 1956. In the early 1970s, as criticism of the war continued to mount, and particularly after President Richard Nixon authorized ill-starred incursions into Cambodia and Laos, serious peace negotiations were begun by Secretary of State Henry Kissinger. But the Paris accords, which Kissinger negotiated in early 1973 with North Vietnam and South Vietnam, never worked. The pact promised discussions leading to reunification "without coercion or annexation by either party." By late 1973, however, full-scale war had emerged. In 1974 an economically troubled United States cut aid by 30 percent. By early 1975, South Vietnamese president Nguyen Van Thieu, forced to surrender two-thirds of the country, prepared to defend Saigon and called for President Gerald Ford to provide the American "full force" promised by President Nixon in 1973. In late 1973, however, Congress had prohibited the reintroduction of any U.S. forces in Vietnam. Furthermore, Nixon's 1973 promise was of no effect, for he and Kissinger did not make the promise public, while Congress never acted to make it a national commitment. In April 1975, South Vietnam fell into communist hands. After the failure of the United States to impose self-determination by military means in Southeast Asia, foreign liberation movements and separatist groups rarely attracted any sizable American constituency.

The military collapse of South Vietnam in 1975, combined with the serious pursuit of détente with both the Soviet Union and the People's Republic of China beginning in the late 1960s, appeared to offer the possibility not only of a redefinition of the American concept of self-determination but also of a modified implementation of the doctrine of intervention as a means of supporting it. The Nixon Doctrine offered to provide money, arms, and training, but no American troops. Nations seeking self-determination must now provide their own armies.

Yet it must be noted that throughout this period, Washington continued to oppose self-determination movements that appeared to favor any communist cause. This could be clearly seen even in the most cursory review of American policies in South Asia, Chile, and southern Africa.

SELF-DETERMINATION IN SOUTH ASIA AND CHILE

On 9 August 1971, some three weeks after President Nixon had announced his visit to Peking in an effort to normalize relations, the Soviets signed a twenty-year treaty of friendship (and quasi-alliance) with India. The Indians feared another crushing onslaught from the bordering Chinese (as in 1962), while the Soviets were evidently eager to clasp hands with India against an increasingly menacing China. Although India and Pakistan had been enemies since the partition of British India in 1947, the United States had been supplying arms to Pakistan, an American ally. This unpromising Asiatic pot came to a furious boil in March 1971, when populous East Pakistan, separated by more than a thousand miles from West Pakistan, formally rebelled against alleged mistreatment by its West Pakistan overlords. The secessionists officially proclaimed the independent state of Bangladesh. The West Pakistan army, with alleged genocidal intent, undertook to crush the uprising with full-scale butchery, rape, and pillage. An estimated nine million destitute refugees began to pour across borders into already overpopulated and underfed India. In November 1971, responding to protests from India, Washington cancelled further shipments of arms to Pakistan. Then, early in December, India, after declaring war on Pakistan, proceeded to invade and free Bangladesh in a mercifully short clash of fifteen days. The United States, supporting the losing side, emerged from the episode looking rather foolish. Evidently seeking to counter a reported Soviet naval presence in the Indian Ocean and to display sympathy for its Pakistani ally, Washington hastily dispatched a powerful naval task force to the Indian Ocean. The transparent explanation given at the time was the necessity of evacuating a handful of U.S. citizens, most of whom had already left Bangladesh. This futile exhibition of old-fashioned "show the flag" gunboat diplomacy, with its "tilt toward Pakistan," probably gratified China, which was pro-Pakistan, but pleased neither the Soviets, the Indians, nor even the Pakistanis. Relations with India became frigid, especially after Washington cut developmental loans, charging that India was the "main aggressor" in the conflict. Nearly a year later, in November 1972, Pakistan withdrew from the SEATO alliance and in other ways indicated alienation from the United States. Thus, Bangladesh was born: a satellite of India, famine-ridden and impoverished.

In the meantime, leftist trends in Chile, once an outstanding democracy, had become especially worrisome to Washington. A left-wing coalition, which accused American copper mining and other interests of "milking" the country, won the 1970 election and elevated to the presidency Salvador Allende Gossens, a home-grown Marxist. As the first avowed Marxist to win a free election in the hemisphere, Allende posed an unusual problem for the United States. The dilemma intensified when he nationalized nearly $1 billion of American investment, opened diplomatic relations with the government of Fidel Castro, and signed a trade agreement with the Soviet Union. The United States retaliated by refusing to help Chile with trade or developmental programs. American banks and the Export-Import Bank cut credit. President Nixon secretly ordered the Central Intelligence Agency to follow a "get rougher" policy that encouraged anti-Allende demonstrations by middle-class Chileans. Kissinger wholeheartedly approved, in part because he was afraid that a successful radical left coalition might have contagious effects not only in Latin America but also in France and Italy. It was his own version of the domino theory.

Allende's inability to stop a rapid economic deterioration brought attacks from both conservatives and ultraleftists. In September 1973 a coup by army officers resulted in Allende's death and a right-wing military dictatorship. The United States quickly reopened its aid program; some property taken from American corporations was returned or paid for; and when the American ambassador protested the army's repression, which included torturing and imprisoning thousands of political opponents, Kissinger angrily told the ambassador "to cut out the political science lectures." By 1975 there was no longer any doubt that the United States had played a role in overthrowing the Allende government in Chile and replacing it with the ferociously right-wing General Augusto Pinochet.

U.S. POLICY IN AFRICA

American policy in Africa, although not so heavily involved, followed the same pattern. The dominant element after 1946 was opposition to communism and to the communist powers. As far as Africa was concerned, responsibility for pursuing these objectives was delegated to America's trusted allies—Britain, France, Belgium, and even Portugal—whose policies in the area were therefore broadly supported, despite minor disagreements that arose as American business became interested in Africa's potential. Inevitably, this placed the United States in opposition to an Africa seeking to win its independence from those same powers. However, when political freedom could be achieved peacefully, the United States was able to appear to Africa like a neutral bystander. In these cases the United States was able to adjust its policies and accept the new status of African sovereign states without any difficulty, although it continued to look at African affairs largely through anticommunist spectacles.

In southern Africa, practical support for the status quo continued unabated until after the Portuguese revolution in April 1974. Thus, despite America's verbal criticism of Portuguese colonialism, U.S. arms and equipment were used by Portugal in its military operations in Angola, Guinea-Bissau, and Mozambique. Despite verbal opposition to apartheid, American trade and investment in South Africa were expanded, and the United States opposed any effective United Nations demonstration of hostility toward the apartheid state. The United States also fought a hard and largely successful rearguard action against the demands for international intervention against South Africa's occupation of Namibia (South-West Africa). Regarding the British colony of Rhodesia, the United States trailed behind British opposition to the white-minority regime of Ian Smith, watered down the sanctions policies it had endorsed at the United Nations, and criticized black African regimes for the vehemence of their opposition to the Smith regime.

In Africa the superpowers nearly confronted each other in a crisis that typified the new Cold War that was developing in the 1970s. Throughout the anticolonial war in Angola (1960–1974), the United States supported Portugal, not any of the nationalist forces. Supplying the Portuguese-backed National Front for the Liberation of Angola (FNLA) with money and military and other equipment while decolonization finally took place was thus a rather blatant attempt to place "friends" in political power in the new state. But the more effective Popular Movement for the Liberation of Angola (MPLA) did not collapse. Instead, it asked for and received more arms from its supporters, including the Soviet Union, to meet a South African invasion of Angola in 1975. The MPLA also welcomed Cuban troops. When the FNLA demanded more help than the American administration could give without congressional approval, Congress—with the lessons of Vietnam still fresh in its mind—refused its support.

The Angolan debacle and other factors led toward a reassessment of traditional U.S. policies in southern Africa. Some Americans had long been urging support for the anticolonial struggle, and African Americans were beginning to take a greater interest in these matters. Also, trade with independent Africa had been growing and now included oil from Nigeria. The possibility that this trade might be jeopardized by pro–South African activities was no longer of merely academic interest to the United States. Moreover, guerrilla warfare in Rhodesia intensified after mid-1975, arousing fears of a repetition of the Angolan experience.

Black Africa welcomed Kissinger's Lusaka statement of 27 April 1976, which stipulated that majority rule must precede independence in Rhodesia and ruled out American material or diplomatic support to the Ian Smith regime. With some hesitation, Africa also cooperated with the Kissinger shuttle diplomacy later in the year. Africa hoped that "even at that late stage, the use of American power in support of majority rule could enable this to be attained in Rhodesia without further bloodshed." This Kissinger initiative forced Smith to shift his ground, but it did not succeed in its declared objective. Nor did it remove African uncertainty about the depth and the geographical limitations of the new American commitment to change in southern Africa.

HUMAN RIGHTS AS A CRITERION FOR SELF-DETERMINATION

With the election of President James E. Carter in 1976, the need to respect human rights became a focus of public attention and debate in the United States. This development reflected rising popular expectations around the world as individuals and groups expressed aspirations that included demands that government be more responsive to them. This trend appeared in many forms, from movements of national independence to devolution and demands for worker codetermination. In the United States, many saw the growing interest in the "human dimension" of world politics as a natural and healthy reaction to an overemphasis on great power diplomacy, elitist cynicism, and excessive secretiveness during the recent past.

The articulate and sympathetic stand adopted by the new administration on the question of human rights implied a distinct departure from the position of the Nixon and Ford administrations. The Carter administration's advocacy of respect for human rights and fundamental freedoms in the widest sense had an important implication for America's policy regarding national self-determination. First and foremost, it implied an insistence on effective guarantees to safeguard the position of individual citizens in the societies to which they belonged, and particularly to protect them against infringement of basic civil rights and liberties, such as freedom of expression, assembly, and movement—liberties inscribed in practically all modern constitutions, including those of the Soviet bloc. Second, to champion human rights involved supporting a long-established principle of international relations, reconfirmed in 1975 in the final act of the Conference on Security and Cooperation in Europe (CSCE); this so-called Helsinki Agreement recognized the collective rights of peoples to self-determination and equal status in the international community.

In the ensuing months, the Carter administration demonstrated its commitment to human rights and self-determination by seeking to reestablish normal relations with both Cuba and Vietnam, and withdrawing its opposition to Vietnamese membership in the United Nations. In his inaugural address President Carter said, "Because we are free, we can never be indifferent to the fate of freedom elsewhere."

In the African nations of Rhodesia (later Zimbabwe) and South Africa, Carter and his eloquent United Nations ambassador, Andrew Young, championed the oppressed black majorities. However, the president's most spectacular foreign policy achievement came in September 1978, when he invited President Anwar Sadat of Egypt and Prime Minister Menachem Begin of Israel to the presidential retreat at Camp David, Maryland, in an attempt to promote peace in the Middle East. Serving as a go-between, Carter persuaded them to sign an accord that month in which Israel agreed in principle to withdraw from Egyptian territory conquered in 1967, Egypt in return promised to respect Israeli borders, and both pledged to sign a formal peace treaty within three months. Carter also concluded two treaties designed to turn over complete ownership and control of the Panama Canal to Panamanians by the year 2000.

These dramatic accomplishments were overshadowed by the ominous reheating of the Cold War with the USSR. Détente fell into disrepute as thousands of Cuban troops, assisted by Soviet advisers, appeared in Angola, Ethiopia, and elsewhere in Africa to support revolutionary factions. The worst fears of the West, however, were not aroused until the Soviet army in December 1979 invaded Afghanistan, next door to Iran, and appeared to be poised for a thrust at the oil jugular of the Persian Gulf. Only a month before, a howling mob of rabidly anti-American Muslim militants stormed the United States embassy in Tehran, Iran, and took all of its occupants hostage. World opinion hotly condemned the diplomatic felony in Iran while Americans agonized over both the fate of the hostages and the stability of the entire Persian Gulf region. President Carter slapped an embargo on the export of grain and high-technology machinery to the USSR, called for a boycott of the upcoming Olympic Games in Moscow, and requested that young people be required to register for a possible military draft. Meanwhile, the Soviet army met unexpectedly stiff resistance in Afghanistan and became bogged down in a nasty guerrilla war that came to be called "Russia's Vietnam."

RONALD REAGAN: A COLD WARRIOR PURSUES DÉTENTE

Ronald Reagan, Carter's successor, took a hard-line stance toward the Soviet Union, characterizing the USSR as "the focus of evil in the modern world." He believed in negotiating with the Soviets, but only from a position of overwhelming strength. Reagan's view that self-determination was being

constantly threatened by what he saw as the revolutionary hand of the Soviet Union seemed to be clearly demonstrated in Poland. Challenged by a popular trade union movement called Solidarity, the government of Poland imposed martial law. Relations with the Soviet Union nosedived, with Reagan imposing economic sanctions on Poland and the Soviet Union alike.

In the backyard of the United States, Central America rumbled menacingly. A leftist revolution deposed the longtime dictator of Nicaragua in 1979. President Carter tried to ignore the anti-American rhetoric of the revolutionaries, known as the Sandinistas, and to establish good diplomatic relations with them, but Reagan took their words at face value and hurled back at them some hot language of his own. He accused the Sandinistas of turning their country into a forward base for Soviet and Cuban penetration of all of Central America, and more specifically of shipping weapons to revolutionary forces in tiny El Salvador. Reagan sent military "advisers" to prop up El Salvador's pro-American government. He also provided covert aid to the contra rebels opposing the Sandinista government. In the Caribbean, Reagan—convinced that a military coup in Grenada had brought Marxists to power—dispatched a heavy invasion force to that tiny island in October 1983.

In his second term, Reagan found himself contending for the world's attention with the charismatic new Soviet leader, Mikhail Gorbachev, installed in March 1985. Gorbachev was committed to allowing greater political liberty and the "restructuring" of the moribund Soviet economy by adopting many of the free-market practices of the capitalist West. Both these policies required great reductions in the size of the Soviet military that, in turn, necessitated an end to the Cold War. Gorbachev accordingly made warm overtures to the West. He sought without success the complete elimination of intermediate-range nuclear forces in Europe when he met Reagan at summit meetings in Geneva in November 1985 and Reykjavik, Iceland, in October 1986. However, it was at a third summit, in Washington, D.C., in December 1987, that they agreed on such a ban. Reagan, the consummate cold warrior, had been flexible and savvy enough to seize a historic opportunity to join with the Soviet chief to bring the Cold War to a kind of conclusion. History would give both leaders high marks for this.

The two most difficult foreign policy problems for Reagan were the continued captivity of a number of American hostages seized by Muslim extremist groups in civil war–torn Lebanon, and the continuing grip on power of the left-wing Sandinista government in Nicaragua. When Congress repeatedly rejected the president's request for aid to the contras, the administration grew increasingly frustrated, even obsessed, in its search for a way to help them. In 1985 American diplomats secretly arranged arms sales to the embattled Iranians in return for Iranian aid in obtaining the release of American hostages held by Middle Eastern terrorists. At least one hostage was eventually set free. Meanwhile, money from the payment for the arms was diverted to the contras. These actions brazenly violated a congressional ban on military aid to the Nicaraguan rebels, not to mention Reagan's repeated vow that he would never negotiate with terrorists.

In November 1986 news of these secret dealings broke and ignited a firestorm of controversy. President Reagan claimed that he was innocent of wrongdoing and ignorant about the activities of his subordinates, but a congressional committee condemned the "secrecy, deception, and disdain for the law" displayed by administration officials and concluded that if the president did not know what his national security advisers were doing he should have. The Iran-Contra affair cast a dark shadow over Reagan's record in foreign policy.

GEORGE BUSH AND THE END OF THE COLD WAR

George Herbert Walker Bush was inaugurated as president of the United States in January 1989 at a watershed moment in twentieth-century history. As with 1918 and 1945, 1989 was a year when the old great-power order collapsed and the United States stood as preeminent in world affairs. In the first months of the Bush administration, the world was astounded as democracy arose everywhere in the communist bloc. Long oppressed by puppet regimes propped up by Soviet guns, Eastern Europe was revolutionized in just a few startling months in 1989. The Solidarity movement in Poland led the way when it toppled Poland's communist government in August. In rapid succession, communist regimes collapsed in Hungary, Czechoslovakia, East Germany, and even hyper-repressive Romania. In December 1989 jubilant Germans danced atop the hated Berlin Wall, symbol of the division of Germany and all of Europe into two armed and hostile camps. The

two Germanys, divided since 1945, were at last reunited in October 1990, with the approval of the victorious allied powers of World War II.

But the changes that swept the heartland of world communism were the most startling of all. Mikhail Gorbachev's policies had set in motion a groundswell that surged out of his control. Waves of nationalistic fervor and long-suppressed ethnic and racial hatred rolled across the Soviet Union's constituent republics, overwhelming communist ideology. Old-guard hard-liners, in a last-gasp effort to preserve the tottering communist system, attempted to dislodge Gorbachev with a military coup in August 1991. With the support of Boris Yeltsin, president of the Russian Republic, Gorbachev foiled the plotters. But in December 1991, Gorbachev resigned as president and the Soviet Union dissolved into fifteen sovereign republics with Russia the most powerful state and Yeltsin the dominant leader. To varying degrees, all the new governments in the former Soviet republics repudiated communism and embraced democratic reforms and free-market economies.

By the time the Cold War came to an end, the international legal right of self-determination had been accepted in the context of decolonization. But it was not clear whether that right extended to noncolonial situations. Most scholars of government believed that the principle of political unity prevailed over any expression of self-determination within a state. However, events in the Soviet Union and Yugoslavia at the close of the Cold War forced the international community to cope with the demands of groups seeking to break off from existing states. International law, with its traditional rejection of such claims, provided little guidance. The United States and the international community scrambled to respond, with decidedly mixed results.

More then twenty months passed from the time the Baltic republics of the Soviet Union took their initial steps in March 1990 toward independence to the dissolution of the USSR. U.S. policy toward the Baltics set a pattern that would be followed until shortly before the Soviet Union's dissolution. The United States did not support steps toward sovereignty for the Soviet republics in general, or even on a case-by-case basis. Rather, it adopted a wait-and-see approach as a means to a larger object: the survival of Soviet president Mikhail Gorbachev in a mostly unified Soviet Union. The United States had diplomatic relations with Lithuania in the 1920s and 1930s and never recognized Stalin's annexation in 1940. Furthermore, it had permitted a Lithuanian diplomatic presence in Washington throughout the Cold War. Nonetheless, when Lithuania moved toward independence in 1990, the United States tilted toward Moscow.

American reluctance to move toward recognition of an independent Lithuania continued for nearly a year and a half. On 1 August 1991, weeks before the failed coup by communist hard-liners in Moscow, President Bush warned against "suicidal nationalism" in the republics and stated that the United States "would maintain the strongest possible relationship with the Soviet government." Even after the unsuccessful Soviet coup was launched and the three Baltic republics reasserted their independence, the United States stood back while European governments took the lead in responding to their claims.

With the breakup of the Soviet Union appearing more likely during the fall of 1991, the United States shifted its policy. Following Soviet president Gorbachev's resignation and the formal dissolution of the Soviet government on 25 December, the United States announced recognition of the twelve remaining Soviet republics as independent states. However, the United States proposed establishing full diplomatic relations with only six of the new states: Armenia, Belarus, Kazakhstan, Kyrgyzstan, Russia, and Ukraine, states that the administration claimed had made specific commitments to responsible security policy and democratic principles. However, Secretary of State James A. Baker's articulation of principles guiding the pace of U.S. recognition seemed governed more by political expedience than principle. Each of the four successor states that possessed strategic nuclear weapons—Belarus, Kazakhstan, Russia, and Ukraine—were among the first states to win U.S. recognition. This risked sending a dangerous message: that retaining nuclear weapons would offer the new states leverage with the West. Furthermore, the recognition of Armenia but not Azerbaijan may have exacerbated tension in the disputed territory of Nagorno-Karabakh—populated by Armenians but located in and administered by Azerbaijan—by undermining the U.S. neutral position regarding the conflict. Concern, however inflated, that a policy of selective recognition could prompt the Islamic republics of Tajikistan, Turkmenistan, and Uzbekistan in Central Asia and Azerbaijan in the Caucasus to turn toward Iran prompted the United States to quickly accept perfunctory promises of support for democratic principles and to establish diplomatic ties.

By the end of February 1992 the United States had granted formal diplomatic recognition to eleven of the twelve non-Baltic republics. It granted recognition to the final republic, Georgia, in March 1992, after its civil wars subsided and Eduard Shevardnadze, the former Soviet foreign minister, offered appropriate commitments.

POST–COLD WAR CONFLICTS

The end of the Cold War did not mean the end of all wars. In the middle of the apparent flood tide of democratization in Eastern Europe came Iraq's invasion and annexation of Kuwait in August 1990. Clearly, democracy was not the issue; neither in Iraq nor Kuwait could there be much hope of fostering self-determination. Nevertheless, by acting decisively Bush might give more shape to what he now called the New World Order that was to be crafted by American leadership. Most Americans cheered the rapid and enormously successful conclusion of the war against Iraq early in 1991. The war had nevertheless failed to dislodge Saddam Hussein from power. Moreover, the United States, for better or worse, found itself more deeply ensnared in the region's web of mortal hatred and intractable conflicts, from which no possibilities of self-determination seemed to emerge.

Caution, inconsistencies, and political expedience also characterized the American and, to a lesser degree, the European Community's initial response to Yugoslavia's self-determination crisis. Until hostilities broke out in mid-1991, the United States and the European governments asserted unconditional support for Yugoslav unity. That policy reflected, at least in part, concern that any splintering of Yugoslavia would be violent. When Serbia's strongly nationalist president, Slobodan Milosevic, began campaigning for a stronger Yugoslav federal center, calls among Slovenes, Croats, and Bosnians for a looser confederation or for outright secession multiplied. Slovenia, the most homogenous of the republics, had already taken its first steps toward independence in September 1989. In the fall of 1990 the Central Intelligence Agency reportedly predicted a breakup of Yugoslavia, probably involving civil war. Nevertheless, days after the May 1991 referendum in which Croatia's population voted overwhelmingly to secede, the United States remained firmly committed to the "territorial integrity" of Yugoslavia. Fighting erupted in June 1991 after Croatia and Slovenia formally declared their independence. As the war in Croatia escalated throughout the summer and fall of 1991, the issue of international recognition for the Yugoslav republics became more controversial. It was Germany that led the European Community to an agreement on a process for recognizing the republics of both the Soviet Union and Yugoslavia. In January 1992 the twelve EC countries, as well as several other European states and Canada, recognized both Slovenia and Croatia. The EC granted recognition to Bosnia-Herzegovina in April 1992, despite the fact that its referendum on independence had been largely boycotted by the Bosnian Serb minority.

U.S. policy evolved more slowly. In July 1991 Secretary Baker signaled a shift in policy when he indicated that the United States was prepared to accept any new political configuration negotiated by the republics. However, the United States was unwilling to grant separate recognition to any of the republics as long as the fighting continued.

UN Secretary General Javier Pérez de Cuéllar, along with the United States, opposed the European Community's moves toward recognition, fearing that such action would fatally undermine UN and EC peace initiatives. U.S. deputy secretary of state Lawrence Eagleburger warned EC members in December 1991 that early, separate recognition of Croatia and Slovenia would not only damage the prospect for peace but would "almost inevitably lead to greater bloodshed."

The issue was how best to prevent Serbian aggression while protecting the rights of the Serb minorities in Croatia and Bosnia-Herzegovina. After the EC announced its recognition guidelines, the United States reiterated four principles guiding its policies toward the republics of Yugoslavia, none of which acknowledged the prospect of secession, even though by December 1991 it could be fairly predicted as a strong possibility.

In April 1992 the United States recognized Slovenia, Croatia, and Bosnia-Herzegovina as independent states. Despite its recognition of Bosnia-Herzegovina and the pleas of that government for help against the onslaught of the Serb minority, the United States and the European Community were pitifully slow to initiate or support regional or international intervention to respond to aggression; "ethnic cleansing"; and other serious violations of international law, including international humanitarian law.

The war in Bosnia promoted a reappraisal of American foreign policy. Although President Bush had enunciated his support of a New World Order, in which weak countries would be free from fear of predation by the strong, American support for action against Saddam and his invasion of Kuwait rested on readily identifiable material interest, namely oil. Bosnia's misfortune was that it possessed nothing of vital interest or importance to Americans or other influential foreigners. Nevertheless, some who took the New World Order seriously believed that the United States would assist Bosnian Muslims despite Bosnia's lack of commercial commodities. Many of these likened the Serbs' ethnic cleansing to the Nazis' genocidal policies toward the Jews, and the failure of the United States and the other democracies to assist Bosnia to the failure to halt Hitler in the 1930s. Some Bosnia advocates called for direct American military intervention, even the introduction of ground troops. Others would have been content with the lifting of the international embargo of arms to the warring parties, claiming that it helped the better-equipped Serbs.

Opponents of American involvement in the Bosnia war pointed to the complexity of the Bosnian terrain and contended that military intervention would be costly and difficult—far more difficult, for instance, than intervention in the open desert of Iraq. They also insisted that only a political settlement could guarantee lasting peace between Serbs and Muslims (and Bosnian Croats), given the obvious determination of the Serbs; military intervention would be futile in the absence of a settlement. In addition, they even suggested that military intervention might be counterproductive, causing the war to spread beyond Bosnia.

Also, while the Gulf crisis had found the United States and the Soviet Union in agreement, the situation in Bosnia promised to be more divisive. Given Russia's long-standing role as the protector of the Slavic and Orthodox Serbs, it was difficult to predict how the Russian government would react to strong U.S. action. In any case, neither the Bush administration nor, beginning in January 1993, that of Bill Clinton could count on Moscow's cooperation. Finally, many Americans argued that the problems in the Balkans were Europe's problems. Throughout the Cold War, the United States had looked after Europe. It was now time, they said, for the Europeans to start looking after themselves. In fact, there was a resounding lack of popular enthusiasm for intervention. While both administrations supported UN initiatives to ease the plight of the Bosnians and pressure the Serbs politically to curtail their offensives, neither took the step of committing American combat troops directly to the battle.

The Cold War had provided the United States with the basic principles on which it had conducted foreign policy for nearly half a century; with the end of the Cold War, the Clinton administration groped for a diplomatic formula to replace anticommunism as the guiding mechanism in America's foreign affairs. The international environment was no longer one of great power confrontation, but of numerous global hot spots that periodically threatened to boil over into major regional conflagrations. The Clinton administration generally tried to persuade international agencies, especially the United Nations and NATO, to support multilateral peacekeeping efforts, but often the United States was left alone to try to keep the lid on these flare-ups.

The Middle East remained a major source of trouble. With Norway's help in 1993, Israel and the PLO negotiated the Oslo Accords, which involved mutual recognition and Palestinian autonomy in Gaza and parts of the West Bank. In 1994 Jordan joined the peace process. In 1998 Clinton brokered a new set of agreements between the two sides in marathon meetings at the Wye Plantation in Maryland. This was followed by the Barak-Arafat summit of 2000. However, by the turn of the century, all of these agreements, which promised some measure of self-determination for the Palestinians, had proved ineffective.

Despite the failure of various attempts to change Serb behavior, Congress in the autumn of 1994 forced the Clinton administration to end its efforts to prevent Bosnia from receiving weapons. This move strained U.S. relations with the rest of NATO, but did little to halt the Balkan war. Neither did NATO air attacks, starting in February 1994, against Serbian planes and artillery. Despite these actions and the formation of a Croat-Muslim federation, Bosnian Serbs continued to displace Muslims from much of Bosnia. When Bosnian Serbs in July 1995 seized the safe havens of Srebrenica and Zepa and massacred thousands of Muslims within sight of UN peacekeepers, Washington flashed a green light whereupon the Croatian army overran Serb-held territory in northwestern Bosnia and NATO intensified its air attacks. As new refugees fled into Serbia, Slobodan Milosevic asserted his authority over the Bosnian Serbs and agreed to a cease-fire in October 1995.

At a peace conference in Dayton, Ohio, Assistant Secretary of State Richard Holbrooke "cajoled, harassed, and pressured" the presidents of Serbia, Bosnia, and Croatia into an agreement. The Dayton Accords of December 1995 retained a Croat-Muslim federation and a Serb Republic within a single Bosnian state, with Sarajevo to remain a multi-ethnic capital. The United States agreed to contribute 20,000 personnel as part of a 60,000-member NATO implementation force that would separate the parties and assist in reconstruction. Four years later, some 8,000 U.S. troops remained in Bosnia, having sustained a fragile peace at a cost of more than $7 billion. Deadlines for removing U.S. peacekeeping troops in Bosnia were abandoned as it became clear that they alone could prevent new hostilities.

In 1999, Kosovo, a Serbian province whose population was overwhelmingly ethnic Albanian, became the next Balkan crisis to spark international consequences. There, President Milosevic ordered a brutal ethnic cleansing. After he rejected NATO demands to halt the persecutions and preserve Kosovo's autonomy, NATO in March began to bomb military and communication sites in Serbia. The bombing unleashed even more cruelties in Kosovo as the Serbs systematically moved against ethnic Albanians, massacring and raping them, burning their homes, and forcing 800,000 of them to flee as refugees to neighboring Albania and Macedonia. However, Milosevic—bombed, encircled, and embargoed—relented in early June under an agreement to withdraw his forces from Kosovo, permit the return of refugees, accept a NATO security presence, and grant greater autonomy to Kosovo. The International War Crimes Tribunal at The Hague indicted Milosevic and his top aides for atrocities against the people of Kosovo. The planned expansion of NATO in 1999 to include Poland, Hungary, and the Czech Republic increased incentives to prevent more fighting and to keep refugees from spreading into Eastern Europe.

ON THE VERGE OF THE TWENTY-FIRST CENTURY

At the beginning of the twenty-first century, the United States and the United Nations faced the fundamental question of how to manage demands for self-determination in a turbulent new world. The collapse of communism and the growing worldwide pressure for democracy had unleashed movements with broad public support. The number and variety of self-determination movements was growing, and bewildered governments and multilateral institutions tried to understand them and decide how to respond. Internal ethnic conflicts were proliferating, compelling national and international responses before considered policies could be developed. The United States and the world community faced the challenge of how to respond to the breakup of some nations and the restoration of others in ways that minimized violence and human suffering and maximized the chances for establishing democratic governments. The old assumption that the boundaries set after World War II were permanent had been shaken by events in the Soviet Union and Yugoslavia. Although bold conditions for U.S. recognition were imposed upon the successor states of the Soviet Union, they were hurriedly signed off in an attempt to reduce the danger of nuclear proliferation and to contain Islamic expansionism in Central Asia. Regarding Yugoslavia, U.S. policy remained focused on preserving it as a state while the European Community took the lead in recognizing the new states of Slovenia and Croatia.

The United States was slow to accept collective military intervention as a response in some situations such as preventing armed conflict, delivering humanitarian assistance, defending a new state, advancing the cause of self-determination in certain limited circumstances, occasionally guaranteeing compliance with the recognition criteria, and in some cases defending an existing government from limited insurgency. The American people were reluctant to take on new international responsibilities and resisted new commitments that might drain resources from domestic needs and that could involve the United States in a new quagmire.

BIBLIOGRAPHY

Bailey, Thomas A. *Woodrow Wilson and the Lost Peace.* New York, 1944. Contains a scholarly analysis of the implementation of Wilson's concept of self-determination.

Balzer, Harley D., ed. *Five Years that Shook the World: Gorbachev's Unfinished Revolution.* Boulder, Colo., 1991.

Barbour, Walworth. "The Concept of Self-Determination in American Thought." *Department of State Bulletin* 31 (1954). Presents an official view.

Barker, Sir Ernest. *National Character and the Factors in Its Formation.* London, 1948. A classic work originally published in 1927.

Birdsall, Paul. *Versailles Twenty Years After.* New York, 1941. Presents a "realistic" view of Wilson's efforts to implement the concept of self-determination at the Paris Peace Conference.

Carley, Patricia. *U.S. Responses to Self-Determination Movements.* Washington, D.C., 1997. A report of a roundtable by the United States Institute of Peace and the Policy Planning Staff of the U.S. Department of State on strategies for nonviolent outcomes and alternatives to secession.

Cassese, Antonio. *Self-Determination of Peoples: A Legal Reappraisal.* Cambridge and New York, 1995. A comprehensive legal account of the concept of self-determination.

Cobban, Alfred. *The Nation State and National Self-Determination.* New York, 1969. Presents the most nearly definitive history and political analysis of the general concept of national self-determination by means of a pragmatic approach.

Diesing, Paul. "National Self-Determination and U.S. Foreign Policy." *Ethics* 77 (1967). A provocative ethical analysis.

Eagleton, Clyde. "The Excesses of Self-Determination." *Foreign Affairs* 31 (1953). An excellent analysis of problems presented by the attempt to apply the concept of self-determination in the post–World War II period.

Emerson, Rupert. *Self-Determination Revisited in the Era of Decolonization.* Cambridge, Mass., 1964. A good synthesis, containing a fresh examination in a new nation-forming setting.

Gerson, Louis L. *The Hyphenate in Recent American Politics and Diplomacy.* Lawrence, Kans., 1964. Especially helpful on the role of East European hyphenates in promoting self-determination during the Wilson and Roosevelt administrations.

Halperin, Morton H., and David J. Scheffer. *Self-Determination in the New World Order.* Washington, D.C., 1992. Reviews U.S. and international claims during and after the Cold War.

Jessup, Philip C. "Self-Determination Today in Principle and in Practice." *Virginia Quarterly Review* 33 (1957). An evaluation by a first-rate scholar of international law.

Johnson, Harold S. *Self-Determination within the Community of Nations.* Leiden, Netherlands,

1967. Presents a careful analysis of conflicting interpretations of the great powers.

Lansing, Robert. *The Peace Negotiations: A Personal Narrative*. Boston and New York, 1921. Important for an understanding of Lansing's criticisms of national self-determination.

Link, Arthur S. *Woodrow Wilson: Revolution, War, and Peace*. Arlington Heights, Ill., 1979. Necessary for an appreciation of how Wilson's principles influenced his foreign policy.

May, Arthur James. *Contemporary American Opinion of the Mid-Century Revolutions in Central Europe*. Philadelphia, 1927. Essential for the mid-nineteenth-century outlook.

Mayer, Arno J. *Politics and Diplomacy of Peacemaking: Containment and Counterrevolution at Versailles, 1918–1919*. New York, 1967. Provides vital background for the Wilsonian position.

Musgrave, Thomas D. *Self Determination and National Minorities*. New York, 1997. Examines the historic and current status of self-determination in international law.

Sherwood, Robert E. *Roosevelt and Hopkins: An Intimate History*. Rev. ed. New York, 1950. Presents a glimpse of Roosevelt's efforts to secure support for self-determination from both Churchill and Stalin.

Shukri, Muhammad Aziz. *The Concept of Self-Determination in the United Nations*. Damascus, Syria, 1965. A scholarly study analyzing the attitudes of major powers.

Smith, Tony. *America's Mission: The United States and the World Wide Struggle for Democracy in the Twentieth Century*. Princeton, N.J., 1994. Emphasizes the role of the Wilsonian concept of self-determination in the twentieth century.

Unterberger, Betty Miller. "The United States and National Self-Determination: A Wilsonian Perspective." *Presidential Studies Quarterly* 26 (fall 1996): 926–942.

———. *The United States, Revolutionary Russia, and the Rise of Czechoslovakia*. College Station, Tex., 2000. Traces President Wilson's efforts to implement his concept of self-determination toward Austria-Hungary and Russia.

Wambaugh, Sarah. *A Monograph on Plebiscites, with a Collection of Official Documents*. New York, 1920. A classic work with an excellent introductory chapter on self-determination.

———. *Plebiscites Since the World War, with a Collection of Official Documents*. Washington, D.C., 1933. Presents a historical summary on matters of self-determination covering the years from 1914 to 1933.

See also ANTI-IMPERIALISM; HUMAN RIGHTS; IMPERIALISM; INTERVENTION AND NONINTERVENTION; REALISM AND IDEALISM; REVOLUTION; WILSONIANISM.

SPECIAL-INTEREST LOBBIES

★ ★ ★ ★

William Slany

Lobbies are generally recognized as those individuals or groups who seek to present the point of view of interest groups to members of Congress, generally with respect to specific legislation. But in the increasingly complicated American democracy of the late twentieth and early twenty-first centuries, lobbying must be seen as a wider and more dynamic phenomenon. Interest groups also lobby the executive branch, which has gained expanded discretionary authority from Congress; government officials lobby interest groups in the hope of generating grassroots support for policies and actions; and foreign governments lobby Congress to supplement traditional diplomacy. How and why these newer forms of lobbying arose and function is an important strand in the history of modern American foreign affairs.

The occasional lobbying on foreign affairs issues in the nineteenth century and the early decades of the twentieth century was largely by business and agricultural interests and was generally confined to trade and tariff issues. Until World War II, Congress generally met for short legislative sessions before members returned home; a handful of party oligarchs controlled the flow of legislation. They organized coalitions to adopt legislation and most of the deliberations of congressional committees took place in private. Foreign affairs very rarely rose above the level of inconsequential trade and tariff problems and Congress seldom faced the great pressure of international events that later became customary in World War II and the Cold War. For the greater part of the nation's history, members of Congress—whose constituents were very unlikely to come to Washington—had small staffs whose main task was answering mail, which was not very voluminous. There were few lobbyists and few interest groups in the capital.

By the middle of the nineteenth century Congress had begun in a rudimentary manner to regulate the influencing of legislation by outsiders, but attempts to control lobbyists systemat-

ically did not begin until the eve of World War I as a result of a congressional investigation of tariff lobbying by the National Association of Manufacturers (NAM). Nothing came of this initial probe, and a "control of lobbying" bill failed to win congressional approval in 1928. But Depression-era investigations of lobbying abuses by the utilities and Wall Street banks resulted in New Deal legislation that regulated public utilities, the merchant marine, and foreign agents and required registration and reporting for the first time in history.

After World War II, and particularly starting in the 1970s, lobbying in Washington expanded to a degree unimagined in previous generations. As the nation grew larger it also became more pluralistic. Interest groups multiplied and often were in conflict. Traditional isolationism or general indifference to foreign affairs was replaced by heightened awareness of the global involvement and reach of the United States. The dissident political movements of the 1960s demonstrated the possibilities of group political activities and prompted the rise of new groups that felt government was not being responsive to their needs and interests. The rapid evolution of efficient and cheap mass communication promoted grassroots advocacy far beyond previous levels.

Perhaps the most important change was the quiet revolution in the fundamental nature and rules of the legislative process in Washington: the fragmentation of the power of the political parties and party leaderships; the promotion of individual candidates with special agendas at odds with party preferences and priorities; and the restructuring of election campaign spending in ways that allowed groups to support particular candidates. Changes in Congress in the early 1970s, which some have described as a revolt of a new generation of younger politicians against old-guard traditional leaders, resulted in a reorganization of power within Congress, including a reduction in the power of party leaders and committee heads and an increase in the role of subcommittee heads and individual members. Instead of several dozen committees guided by the party leaderships, there were more than 200 subcommittees, often run by individual congressmen free of leadership control. Congressional staffs grew from 2,500 in 1947 to 18,000 in 2000.

These changes opened the door for interest groups, lobbyists, public relations experts, and political consultants of all kinds. The number of interest groups expanded steadily, growing by one measure from 10,300 in 1968 to 20,600 in 1988. The number of registered lobbyists in Washington grew from around 500 during World War II to more than 25,000 by the early 1990s. The number of political action committees (PACs) that financed many of the more powerful interest groups increased from a handful in 1970 to more than 4,000 in less than twenty years.

Changes in the 1970s in the regulations governing interest groups further facilitated the expansion of the legion of lobbyists. Congress adopted the Federal Regulation of Lobbying Act in 1946, the first comprehensive law controlling lobbying. It defined a lobbyist as one who has solicited or collected contributions, whose main purpose or the purpose of the contributions was to influence legislation, and whose method of influencing Congress was through direct communications with members of Congress. Lobbyists were required to register with the secretary of the Senate and the clerk of the House of Representatives and file quarterly financial statements listing receipts and expenditures and including detailed accounts of contributions over $500.

The Lobbying Act did not provide for enforcement, and there have been few investigations. Moreover, the law had major loopholes: it did not cover lobbies or industries that did not solicit funds but instead spent their own funds, and it did not apply to lobbying activities that sought to influence Congress indirectly by influencing public opinion. Nor did its provisions apply to the lobbying of the executive branch. Congress sought to close some loopholes with the Federal Election Campaign Act of 1971 (amended in 1974 and 1979), which compelled disclosure of contributions to and expenditures on behalf of candidates standing for election. The Supreme Court held that the provisions of the law did not apply to "issue groups," whose main purpose was not to elect candidates but to discuss public issues or influence public opinion. The legislation limited the amount of money, known as hard money,

that individuals or groups could contribute directly to any candidate in a federal election but not the amounts that could be spent indirectly on behalf of candidates and their electoral campaigns, the so-called soft money. The legislation of the 1970s and ensuing Supreme Court interpretations led to the growth of political action committees (PACs), which could spend unlimited amounts of money on behalf of candidates. They also allowed unlimited expenditures by political parties and interest groups in volunteer efforts to get out the vote and educate voters on election issues.

The congressional limitation on presidential war powers during the Nixon years gained for Congress an expanded share of the responsibility for foreign policy at the expense of the executive branch of government. This new codetermination of foreign policy, combined with the internal changes occurring within Congress, made Congress much more responsive to special interests and their lobbies, which on occasion became decisive players in shaping foreign policies. Lobbies operating outside the executive and legislative branches of government became the means for organizing information about foreign policy issues. They informed and galvanized public opinion regarding particular courses of action and coordinated the persuasion of lawmakers and policymakers to take the issues on board. At the same time, the political parties were less and less able to control and disseminate information about issues or give coordinated statements regarding urgent foreign policy goals and national interests. Moreover, the elaborate information security systems that were deployed within government in the last half of the twentieth century invested foreign policy with a secrecy shield that deprived the public of much in the way of meaningful information on diplomatic crises and commitments. Many Washington lobbyists found that members of Congress and their staffs were their best contacts for influencing foreign affairs or for obtaining unauthorized information. On the other hand, lobbyists and their PACs were—on issues that concerned them—great sources of information for members of Congress and for the public at large and frequently set the tone of the debate on current issues.

ECONOMIC LOBBIES IN THE MID-TWENTIETH CENTURY

Trade and Tariff Lobbies During the first century and a half of American history, trade was one of the few consistent issues in an essentially isolationist foreign policy. Most of the lobbying of Congress resulted from the clash between protectionists and supporters of moderate tariffs. However, the Reciprocal Trade Agreements Act adopted by Congress in 1934 signaled the end of Congress's attempts, in response to the pressure of economic lobbying groups, to determine the tariff on individual commodities. The act gave the president the authority to negotiate reciprocal agreements and set tariffs. It ended the period in which tariff making was essentially a domestic affair and changed it into a foreign policy matter in which Congress was only periodically involved when major enabling legislation came before it.

In the decades after World War II, the lobbies in Washington for industry, business, and farm groups focused on specific national, regional, or economic sector protectionist measures in response to the rising sentiment in support for or acquiescence to international trade liberalization. The United States took the lead in 1946 in convening a conference on multilateral trade negotiations that resulted in the 1947 General Agreement on Tariffs and Trade (GATT), dedicated to reducing tariffs and import quotas and achieving free trade. The GATT laid out a code of trade practices and schedules of tariff reductions for many of the commodities in international trade. By 1975 tariffs had been reduced worldwide from an average of about 40 percent to an average of 10 percent, and international trade had tripled. The periodic negotiations among nations under GATT during the rest of the century attracted protectionist lobbies, and industries and farmers were likely to lobby Congress and the executive branch regarding the "escape clause" exceptions to tariff levels that were managed by the executive branch and periodically reauthorized by Congress.

The United States also entered into multilateral trade agreements in the immediate postwar period for such major commodities as wheat and sugar. International arrangements for other commodities such as tea, wool, cotton, tin, and rubber arose, but resistance to joining such cartels was strong in the United States. Lobbyists for farmers and other agricultural interests worked tirelessly to influence executive branch agencies involved in the negotiations, and Congress had its own continuing role to play. The lobbying on specific commodities also came from foreign governments. Caribbean governments mounted lobbying campaigns aimed at Congress regarding the allocation of the annual quota of imported sugar. Success could mean the difference between prosperity and depression in those island nations.

The growth of foreign economic competition with American industries and farms over the decades caused lobbies for particular interest groups—oil producers, southern textile companies, and automobile makers, for example—to lobby insistently for tariff protection. The rising trend of trade liberalization of the postwar period reached a peak in the 1960s with the so-called Kennedy Round of the GATT negotiations (1962–1967) and the Trade Expansion Act adopted by Congress in October 1962. The 1962 legislation was strongly supported by the liberal trade lobby. It was led by the Committee for a National Trade Policy, representing large corporations with export interests, but which also included the AFL-CIO and the U.S. Chamber of Commerce. On the losing side in 1962 were such protectionist interest groups as the American Trade Council, representing big businesses, trade associations, and farm groups, and the Liberty Lobby, an ultraconservative group that opposed trade legislation as an unconstitutional delegation of tariff-making power to the president.

Under President Franklin D. Roosevelt, the authority to negotiate trade agreements had been in the State Department, but many farm and industry groups came to believe that State was unsympathetic with and unresponsive to domestic interests. The establishment under the terms of the Trade Act of 1962 of an independent Office of the Special Trade Representative located in the Executive Office of the president was largely attributable to the efforts of the lobbyists for those groups. The appointment of the trade representative was made by the president with the advice and consent of the Senate.

Military-Industrial Complex Another economic lobby resulted from the maintenance by the United States, from World War II onward, of a powerful and modern armed force based on the defense industries. This created a unique and troubling set of relationships between those industries and the government, particularly the Department of Defense (DOD). Also, the vast amount of U.S. military assistance to foreign countries became a major factor in American foreign affairs as well as in the domestic economy. The defense industries became the most consistently powerful of all interest groups. They developed and maintained vital relationships with the

Defense Department, which let contracts for the acquisition of arms, equipment, and services, as well as with members of Congress, particularly those whose districts were home to the corporations producing the arms. In his farewell address in 1960, President Dwight D. Eisenhower warned of the "grave implications" of the growing influence of the "military-industrial complex" in every city, statehouse, and federal agency. Eisenhower said that he had sought, without consistent success, to curtail military spending and the economic and political power of the complex.

One consequence of the recognition of the danger of the Congress-DOD-industry triumvirate was the rise in power, beginning with the Kennedy and Johnson administrations, of the national security adviser at the White House. This official could, better than the often unsatisfactory interagency resolutions within and outside the National Security Council system in the Eisenhower era, coordinate national security policy and insulate foreign policy decision making from the military-industrial interest groups.

IDEOLOGICAL LOBBIES IN THE MID-TWENTIETH CENTURY

Interventionism on the Eve of World War II
After World War I, most Americans remained isolationists well into the 1930s. By 1940, however, when Britain stood alone against the aggression of Germany and its Axis partners, a clear majority of Americans approved of providing assistance to those who resisted fascism, and many even favored armed intervention. But a large number of Americans still clung to their isolationist views, fearing the nation's involvement in war. A national debate during 1940 and 1941, punctuated by congressional legislation, gradually moved the United States from strict neutrality to near belligerency in the war against the fascist dictatorships.

Lobbies for and against neutrality were mobilized for the congressional votes on the Revised Neutrality Act in November 1939, the Selective Service Act in September 1940, the Lend-Lease Act in March 1941, the failed anticonvoy Senate resolution of April 1941, the renewal of Selective Service in August 1941, and the revision of the Neutrality Act in November 1941. President Roosevelt and some of his principal advisers maintained very close relationships with the pro-interventionist national interest groups in the lobbying

of Congress for the legislation needed to spur American rearmament and the more urgent task of aiding Britain (and the Soviet Union after it was invaded by Germany in June 1941).

The Non-Partisan Committee for Peace through the Revision of the Neutrality Law marshaled the support of prominent internationalists in 1939. The Committee to Defend America by Aiding the Allies, often called the White Committee after its chairman, William Allen White, became the leading interventionist mass pressure group until the outbreak of war in December 1941. Interventionists gained secret but significant support from the British government, which established the so-called British Security Coordination in New York City. This organization, which also headquartered British intelligence operations for the Western Hemisphere, had the approval of President Roosevelt and some assistance from FBI Chief J. Edgar Hoover in discrediting leaders of the isolationist America First Committee such as Charles Lindbergh. On the other side, the America First Committee was formed in September 1940 by pacifists and leading isolationist political and social leaders from all parts of the political spectrum. Some of them were anti-Semites. It had more than 800,000 members organized in more than 450 local chapters at its high point in mid-1941.

American isolationism largely disappeared after World War II, and President Harry S. Truman was successful in persuading Congress to support the Marshall Plan, aid to Greece and Turkey, and the establishment of NATO, all in the late 1940s. Nonetheless, in 1951 a great debate broke out as the remaining isolationist congressmen and senators sought legislation to restrict U.S. engagement in Europe and limit the president's authority to station troops abroad. A private, nonpartisan lobbying group, the Committee on the Present Danger, which included leaders from the Council on Foreign Relations, college and corporate presidents, and former government officials, successfully rallied support for an activist role for America abroad. The committee used radio extensively to help shape public opinion and influence Congress not to limit President Truman's authority to act abroad. By 1954 the perception among some that presidential direction of an ever more boldly internationalist foreign policy was totally escaping congressional control precipitated one last serious effort to invoke the Constitution to restrain the White House. Major efforts by coalitions of lobbying groups on both sides preceded a close vote in the Senate that repulsed Senator John Bricker's proposed legislation limiting the president's treaty-making authority.

Anticommunism and the China Lobby   In place of prewar isolationism, Americans in the postwar period accepted the nation's superpower status and generally embraced an assertive anti-communist ideology in foreign affairs. The struggle with the Soviet Union was the central theme of the Cold War, but the rise to power in China of a communist regime in 1949 gave rise to a noisy if small domestic claque demanding U.S. intervention into Asian affairs. The so-called China Lobby was a loose association of supporters of Chiang Kai-shek and his Nationalist Chinese regime both before and after it was overthrown by the communists. This pressure group counted among its active participants public relations and business leaders, newspaper editors, ultraconservative writers, wartime members of the Nationalist government, a number of American military figures who had served in China during World War II, and some prominent Republican members of Congress.

China Lobby activities included sponsoring articles in magazines and newspapers and providing research support for sympathetic politicians on such critical congressional committees as the House Un-American Activities Committee and the Senate committees used by Senator Joseph R. McCarthy to investigate communism in government and elsewhere. Many Republicans aligned themselves with the China Lobby in political attacks against the Truman administration and the Democratic Party. It aimed its sharpest criticisms at the president himself and at the State Department's policymakers—the so-called China hands—for their failure to save Chiang's government on the mainland and for allegedly favoring the communists. During the Eisenhower administration, Senator William Knowland of California, a leading proponent of strong ties with the Chinese Nationalists who had fled to Taiwan in 1949, was criticized for his acceptance of support and information from the China Lobby and was characterized as the "Senator from Formosa."

Nuclear Disarmament   Another postwar lobby emerged from the growth of antibomb and pro–nuclear disarmament sentiment. The development of this lobby, however, was slow and difficult in the face of the public's readiness to support military solutions to international problems, which were nearly always seen in Cold War terms. The antibomb movement in the United States drew upon the decades-old experience of traditional pacifists and antiwar groups in lobbying Congress. Nuclear disarmament issues, however, were not subjects for congressional legislation. Modern antiwar groups developed a unique mass movement and invented a new model of lobbying in the age of the "imperial presidency."

American scientists took the lead in warning of the dangers to humankind posed by nuclear weapons. The Federation of American Scientists (FAS), formed in late 1945, spearheaded the dissemination of information about the dangers of nuclear weapons and developed a program for seeking effective political controls over such weapons. However, antibomb activists, including the FAS, had only one early success: the lobbying effort in Congress in 1946 in support of creating the Atomic Energy Commission and legislation that removed the manufacture of weapons and further research in nuclear energy.

U.S. and Soviet development of hydrogen bombs in the 1950s, the proliferation of bomb-making technology to Britain and France, and nuclear weapons testing spurred another round of antibomb activities in the United States and elsewhere. However, the secrecy with which the government protected all aspects of nuclear weapons development placed a constraint on antibomb lobbying.

The dangers of radioactive fallout from the U.S. and Soviet bomb tests of the 1950s became an immediate, recognizable danger to people around the globe. Beginning in Pugwash, Nova Scotia, in July 1957, nuclear scientists from many nations met in a series of conferences over the next several decades that searched for a scientific basis for arms control, if not disarmament. The Pugwash movement laid the basis for later disarmament and arms control plans. The National Committee for a Sane Nuclear Policy (SANE) gave leadership to an emerging public consensus for an end to the testing of weapons and lobbied the government for action. SANE, founded in 1957, never numbered more than 25,000 members, but allied with such other groups as Women Strike for Peace, it soon convinced a majority of the population that nuclear fallout was a real public danger.

In the face of the secrecy and intensive security surrounding nuclear bomb development and testing and the absence of an effective dialogue with the government, antibomb activists resorted to civil disobedience. SANE and Women Strike for Peace were joined in these actions by the American Friends Service Committee, the Non-Violent Action Against Nuclear Weapons, and the Women's International League for Peace and Freedom. These groups conducted noisy demonstrations; protests at nuclear test sites, including intrusions by ship into Pacific test areas; prayer vigils outside the White House; and petition campaigns against testing.

The government, particularly during the Eisenhower presidency, denounced antiwar demonstrations as subversive and, wittingly or not, a boon to communism. The Federal Bureau of Investigation arrested and on occasion sought to prosecute demonstrators or movement leaders. The FBI's anticommunist infiltration program targeted antibomb and pacifist groups, while the Central Intelligence Agency intercepted and reviewed their mail. The Senate Internal Security Subcommittee and the House Un-American Activities Committee investigated antibomb organizations and accused many of them of being infected by communist sentiment to varying degrees.

The growing public awareness and anxiety regarding nuclear weapons testing that was stirred by the antibomb movement, combined with behind-the-scenes efforts of scientists to influence the government from within, finally moved the government toward arms control in the late 1950s and early 1960s. The Soviet Union adopted a unilateral testing moratorium in March 1958, and the United States followed suit later that year with its own moratorium, which lasted until 1961. President John F. Kennedy and his liberal advisers adopted a friendly attitude toward the disarmament and antibomb activists. SANE representatives lobbied sympathetic members of Congress to introduce legislation calling for an international test ban. President Kennedy used Norman Cousins, the president of SANE, as an intermediary with Soviet leader Nikita Khrushchev on partial test ban negotiations. After U.S., British, and Soviet representatives agreed to an atmospheric test ban treaty in July 1963, the Kennedy administration enlisted the antibomb movement in a lobbying effort with the Senate, and leaders of SANE and the United World Federalists worked with labor leaders to convince the Senate to confirm the test ban treaty by a large majority.

IDEOLOGICAL LOBBIES OF THE LATE TWENTIETH CENTURY

Vietnam Antiwar Movement The anti–nuclear bomb campaign, along with the civil rights movement, signaled the emergence of new and powerful ideological tendencies in the United States. The war in Vietnam in the 1960s and into the 1970s resulted in a steadily intensifying national debate and an antiwar movement of unprecedented scope and intensity. If the antiwar movement failed to conform to some of the more recognizable criteria of a lobby, its ultimate impact on American politics, on the organization of Congress, and on Americans' attitudes toward their government nevertheless precipitated an unprecedented engagement of the people with their government on foreign affairs issues that permanently changed the geography of foreign policy decision making.

The antiwar movement began on college campuses in the spring of 1965 with "teach-ins" and spread spontaneously later that year. Well-established peace groups like the SANE and traditional religious pacifist groups took up the movement. The November 1965 March on Washington brought together the largest antiwar protest seen in Washington in the postwar years and led to hearings on Vietnam before the Senate Foreign Relations Committee in February 1966. In 1967 the movement spread beyond the traditional arms control and pacifist groups to new specialized coalitions of activists from recently radicalized portions of the population. The new groups included Another Mother for Peace, Clergy and Laity Concerned About Vietnam, and the Student Mobilization Committee to End the War.

As the war continued, its domestic consequences included the shattering of the American consensus on foreign policy, skepticism about the veracity of the government, and a conviction of the need to petition the government directly and confrontationally. Antiwar demonstrations, although largely made up of middle-class and better-educated Americans, became increasingly strident and radical. In April 1967, 50,000 people in San Francisco gathered to protest the war and 200,000 demonstrated in New York. The October 1967 March on Washington drew 100,000 demonstrators to the Lincoln Memorial and 50,000 in a march on the embattled Pentagon.

President Richard M. Nixon's efforts to "Vietnamize" the war in Southeast Asia were frustratingly slow in bringing an end to the fighting. Continued bombing and new incursions outside Vietnam into Laos and Cambodia regenerated the antiwar movement. There were nationwide demonstrations in October 1969, along with mail campaigns aimed at Congress. Massive demonstrations in Washington in November 1969 included candle-carrying demonstrators circling the White House, which was protected behind a barricade of buses, and the massing of 325,000 marchers on the Mall. The demonstrations persisted into 1971 and 1972 as the war continued. The conflict ended formally in January 1973 after protracted negotiations in Paris, with the last U.S. personnel leaving Vietnam in 1975.

Frustrated at its inability to end American military involvement in Southeast Asia, Congress from 1973 to 1975 undertook a series of legislative actions focused on the president's war powers. These measures were aimed at limiting the initiative of the president in foreign affairs by insisting on congressional involvement in decisions concerning not only U.S. military engagement in other countries but in the rendering of military and economic assistance. The efforts of the anti–Vietnam War movement to halt American involvement in Vietnam thus served as the catalyst for a revolution in foreign policymaking. Moreover, the horrendous excesses of the Vietnam War aroused the sensibilities of the American people and confirmed their new attentiveness to humanitarian, social, and even environmental issues. This gave rise to the emergence of new and powerful foreign affairs lobbies based on previously unheard interest groups and constituencies.

Environmental Lobby   For Americans concerned about foreign policy, the anti–Vietnam War movement provided the model of how to influence and lobby policymakers. The environmental movement was one of the earliest outgrowths of the Vietnam experience. Millions were estimated to have participated in local activities during the first Earth Day, held in April 1970. Beginning that year the movement's more radical adherents employed the anticorporate rhetoric and civil-disobedience tactics developed by the Vietnam-era demonstrators. The mass action and confrontational model adopted by environmental advocates intersected with controversial foreign affairs issues in the 1990s to draw attention to the anti-environmental consequences of the North American Free Trade Agreement (NAFTA) and the decisions in support of economic globaliza-

tion made at meetings of the World Trade Organization (WTO) in Seattle in 1999 and the World Bank in Washington, D.C., in 2000.

Human Rights Lobby   In the first decades after the adoption by the United Nations of the Universal Declaration of Human Rights in 1948, the issue of human rights was overshadowed by the Cold War. The Friends Committee on National Legislation, a Quaker group founded in 1943, developed a reputation for lobbying activity on behalf of domestic civil rights and a humane foreign policy. It took a leading role in marshaling liberal political lobbies regarding the protection of human rights in the regional conflicts in Latin America. But the human rights lobby did not become important until the early 1970s. It was sparked in part by the civil rights movement of the 1960s but also by the fact that a major change occurred during the 1970s in the way American foreign policy was pursued. In that decade Congress acquired much more influence in the formulation of foreign policy. That was made possible particularly by the War Powers Act in 1973 but also by new measures for oversight of CIA operations, including creation of the permanent Joint Committee on Intelligence in 1976 and passage of the International Security Assistance and Arms Export Control Act of 1976, which regulated arms sales abroad.

Of signal importance was the revision in 1975 of the Foreign Assistance Act of 1961 to include a provision for congressional supervision of the application of human rights standards in decisions about economic assistance. The revision, called the Harkin Amendment, forbade for the first time the provision of assistance to "any country which engages in a consistent pattern of gross violations on internationally recognized human rights" unless the president determined that such aid would "directly benefit needy people" in the country.

Soon after the revision of the Foreign Assistance Act, human rights lobbies—much to the dismay of both the Ford and Carter administrations—began to intensify their efforts to halt or curb assistance to countries such as Chile, Argentina, Uruguay, Nicaragua, Uganda, and Ethiopia, whose governments were consistent human rights violators. The liberal human rights lobbying groups were soon matched by conservative human rights lobbies seeking to halt assistance to left-wing regimes in such countries as Angola and Mozambique. The Nixon and Ford administrations, Secretary of State Henry Kissinger, and the State Department sought to dissuade Congress with warnings of the negative impact that the withdrawal of aid would have on important relationships. The lobbyists could not persuade Congress to end or significantly scale back assistance to such strategically important nations as South Korea, Indonesia, Turkey, and the Philippines, even though their human rights records were poor. Human rights organizations did, however, become a primary source of legislative initiatives concerning U.S. policy on human rights issues in matters before the multilateral development banks, the International Monetary Fund, and the Export-Import Bank.

Nowhere were the post-1970 efforts of American human rights lobbies more vigorous than in the area of U.S. relations with Latin America. The human rights groups filled an information vacuum, providing sympathetic policymakers with information not accessible from government agencies. More importantly, in the 1970s ideologically liberal human rights groups developed more sophisticated, broadly based, and effective lobbying techniques. The Americans for Democratic Action (ADA) made U.S. support for repressive regimes in Latin America a major foreign policy issue. The ADA took the lead in opposing the oppressive regime of Augusto Pinochet in Chile in the mid-1970s by persuading Congress to limit assistance to that nation. The human rights lobby incited congressional action that ended military training for Argentina by exposing the brutality of the Argentine regime. In the 1980s the human rights lobby and its concerns about regimes with bad human rights records mobilized public opinion and contributed significantly to congressional action restraining President Ronald Reagan's policies for military and covert operations in Central America. To hamper opponents of military intervention, the Internal Revenue Service went so far as to challenge the tax-exempt status of the North American Congress on Latin America (NACLA), one of the main opponents of Central American policy.

While American business lobbies avoided taking a public stance against human rights lobbies, especially in the case of Latin America, they cultivated U.S. government support for regimes accused of repressive conduct and human rights violations. International Telephone and Telegraph was remarkably successful in promoting U.S. hostility to the Marxist government of Chile in the early 1970s. The successor right-wing government of Pinochet, in contrast, was supported by the business lobby.

Such key organizations as the Business Roundtable ensured that their members had personal meetings on foreign affairs issues with members of Congress and high-ranking executive branch officials, including the president. U.S. business interests in Latin America worked through organizations such as the Council of the Americas, a nonprofit association supported by more than two hundred corporations doing business in Latin America, and the Association of American Chambers of Commerce in Latin America. Neither organization opposed U.S. expressions of concern about human rights violations but sought to encourage the U.S. government to avoid actions that would disrupt normal lending policies of international financial institutions.

Amnesty International, which opened an office in Washington in 1976, and the International Commission of Jurists, based in Geneva, Switzerland, did not lobby Congress or the executive branch on human rights, but the authoritative information on human rights violations that these organizations provided made human rights lobbies more effective in Congress. In addition, the persistent lobbying by American groups of State Department officials responsible for human rights policy made the U.S. delegation to the United Nations Human Rights Commission the stalwart defender of human rights in nations around the world through the remainder of the twentieth century.

After the collapse of the Soviet Union at the beginning of the 1990s, Congress and the Clinton administration responded to a rising tide of lobbying on behalf of the victims, mostly Jewish, of fascist regimes in Europe, particularly Nazi Germany. The collapse of communism allowed for the revisiting of the unfinished history of the Holocaust era and a search for some final restitution to victims of Nazi aggression and genocide. In the United States, as in some European nations, Jewish organizations mobilized government support for a campaign against Switzerland, whose banks were alleged to hold the accounts of thousands of heirless victims of Nazi concentration camps. The U.S. and British governments took the lead in organizing an international effort to identify and recover what remained of monetary assets and gold looted by the Nazi regime. The lobbying effort expanded to other kinds of properties stolen from European Jews, such as art, insurance, and communal properties. By the end of the century it had extended its reach to the search for compensation for slave labor in Nazi Germany.

Anti-Apartheid Lobby   The founding of the Congressional Black Caucus in 1969 and TransAfrica in 1978 provided a focus for a remarkably effective lobby for African issues, particularly initiatives aimed at thwarting and overturning the apartheid policies of the white-minority government in South Africa. A coalition of anti-apartheid groups gathered under the umbrella of the Free South Africa Movement stirred public awareness of the consequences of South Africa's racist policies. These organizations provided information, not forthcoming from the executive branch of the U.S. government, for the debate over American policy toward Africa and the white-minority governments in Africa, particularly South Africa. They rallied around the so-called Sullivan Principles, formulated in the late 1970s by the Reverend Leon Sullivan and expressing basic requirements for the equal treatment of black workers in South Africa and for improving living conditions outside the workplace. These organizations lobbied members of Congress and, more effectively, the major corporations doing business in South Africa, which were persuaded to adopt the principles.

This remarkable effort to refashion American foreign policy by an alliance of black activists, corporations, and some members of Congress went forward in the absence of direction from the president and the State Department. The alliance decisively influenced the 1985 passage in Congress, over President Reagan's veto, of legislation imposing economic sanctions on South Africa and a ban on major investments in and exports to that country. This was the first time since 1973—when Congress overrode President Nixon's veto of the War Powers Act—that Congress overrode a presidential veto on a foreign affairs issue. Secretary of State George Shultz, who preferred a more restrained and studied effort to change South Africa's policies, deplored the action by Congress as a true erosion of the president's ability to conduct foreign policy.

Women's Issues and Lobbies   The vigorous involvement by women in the antibomb and anti–Vietnam War campaigns in the 1960s launched a new and powerful assertiveness by women in foreign affairs issues. This involvement coincided with the rapid evolution of the feminist movement. Observers have noted that no new domestic interest group rose more rapidly during the 1970s than organized feminism. One persistent demand of women's organizations from that time

forward was the appointment of more women to government positions. The Coalition for Women's Appointments, representing more than fifty women's organizations, made the first-ever independent effort by women's groups to lobby for the appointment of women to major posts.

The number of appointments of women to policymaking positions in the foreign affairs community slowly grew during the rest of the century but scarcely kept up with the rapidly strengthening international movement for women's rights. World conferences on women were convened at Mexico City in 1975, Copenhagen in 1980, and Nairobi in 1985, and women's rights were high on the agendas of the UN Conference on Environment and Development in Rio de Janeiro in 1992, the UN World Conference on Human Rights in Vienna in 1993, and the UN Conference on Population and Development in Cairo in 1994. Thousands of American women, most often organized in hundreds of nongovernmental organizations (NGOs), supported the advancement of women's issues in these and other international meetings and organizations. These women vigorously lobbied the U.S. government, particularly the State Department and the White House, beginning with the Carter presidency. The foreign affairs bureaucracy responded by appointing women to represent the United States on women's issues before the UN and other international organizations and to provide American leadership to international movements for women's rights.

ECONOMIC LOBBIES OF THE LATE TWENTIETH CENTURY

Panama Canal Treaty Lobbies   The enormous growth of lobbies beginning in the 1970s, the tendency of presidential administrations to emphasize the national security aspects of most crucial issues, and increasing American public awareness of environmental issues worldwide all made the public debate over major foreign economic policy issues increasingly complex. Ideological issues became deeply intertwined with economic issues and often brought ideological lobbies to the side of economic issues in major policy controversies. The run-up to the ratification by Congress of the Panama Canal Treaties in 1978 was marked by a national debate, the out lines of which were largely defined by two opposing groups of lobbies. Opponents of the treaties joined under an umbrella lobby called the Emergency Coalition to Save the Panama Canal. Included were the American Legion, Veterans of Foreign Wars, American Conservative Union, American Security Council, Young Americans for Freedom, Conservative Caucus, Citizens for the Republic, and National Conservative Political Action Committee. Richard Viguerie, at the time the leading direct mailer of lobbying literature, called the campaign surrounding the Panama Canal Treaties the largest grassroots lobbying effort ever mounted, estimating that up to ten million letters had been directed to Congress. Some liberal Senate supporters of the treaties attributed the failure of their 1978 reelection bids directly to the conservative lobbying campaign. President Jimmy Carter's White House mounted a vigorous educational and lobbying campaign in support of the treaties. A Committee of Americans for the Canal Treaties enlisted such prominent dignitaries as W. Averell Harriman, former CIA director William Colby, and AFL-CIO head George Meany. Leaders of the National Association of Manufacturers, the U.S. Chamber of Commerce, and the American Institute of Merchant Shipping testified on the benefits of the treaties for the United States. The AFL-CIO carried out a program for grassroots support of the treaties, and the White House urged Panamanian president Omar Torrijos to use professional lobbyists in approaching the Senate.

Business, Industrial, Aerospace, and Trade Lobbies

Congressional action to limit political contributions to individual members of Congress was a major factor behind the decision by corporations to increase lobbying expenditures in the 1970s as a substitute for the previous practice of creating "slush funds" for politicians. The Chamber of Commerce, with its 2,500 local chapters, 1,300 professional and trade associations, and nearly 70,000 corporate members, was the most important business lobbyist. The chamber did not engage extensively in foreign relations matters; it did, though, have a noteworthy record of rescuing foreign aid programs during the last quarter of the twentieth century. Ad hoc business organizations carried the burden of the business community in developing wide national support for various trade agreements such as the GATT, the International Trade Organization (ITO), and NAFTA.

No commodity in American trade is more heavily lobbied than sugar. Domestic growers of cane and beets persuaded New Deal officials that the trade liberalization then being strenuously

advanced by secretaries of state should not apply to sugar, which, they argued, should instead be protected from the uncertainties of international trade. The federal government, lobbied by highly effective organizations such as the American Sugar Alliance, continued until the end of the century legislative protections greatly limiting the import of sugar, despite the free-trade tide. By 2000, lobbyists for the American manufacturers of foods requiring large quantities of sugar were competing with the sugar-growing lobby to influence Congress regarding the future of programs limiting sugar imports and subsidizing domestic growers.

The oil and aerospace industries fielded the most important business lobbies. The American Petroleum Institute represented more than three hundred corporations, and major oil companies lobbied directly and retained costly legal and public relations firms. The oil industry lobbies were principally concerned with energy legislation and the administration of national energy policies, but they also acted to counter the efforts of the Israeli lobby to block arms sales to Israel's Arab neighbors.

The military-industrial complex continued through the end of the century to employ hundreds of former Defense Department officials as well as many former members of Congress. It appears, however, that the lobbyists in this area seldom united on foreign policy legislation; instead they simply competed with one another in securing contracts to supply the various branches of service.

Law of the Sea Agreement and Business, Fishing, and Environmental Lobbies

The negotiation of the UN Law of the Sea Treaty—a treaty aimed at ensuring broad fishing rights for maritime nations and assigning control of deep sea mineral rights to an international authority—greatly concerned American business interests and prompted vigorous lobbying on their behalf. A lobby representing the bulk of the U.S. fisheries industry, including the National Coalition for Marine Conservation, the Atlantic States Marine Fisheries Commission, the Maine Sardine Packers Association, and Yakima Tribal Council, persuaded Congress in 1975 to adopt a two-hundred-mile territorial zone from which foreign fishing was prohibited.

Joining in the lobbying effort were some of the newer public interest lobbies such as those mounted by the Sierra Club, National Audubon Society, and Friends of the Earth. Normally confined to domestic environmental issues, these organizations urged on Congress the need for strong national control of U.S. coastal zones in order to ensure high environmental and antipollution standards. American firms such as Kennecott Copper, Standard Oil of Indiana, Lockheed Missiles and Space, and Deepsea Ventures lobbied Congress for legislation to circumvent the international movement for the Law of the Sea Treaty and to allow American firms to exploit for profit seabed mineral resources. The proposals for the treaty, strongly supported by the many developing nations that had no means to reap the benefits of deep-sea mining, would establish an international authority with exclusive rights over the seabed. Nine years of intense international negotiations ended in 1982 with the adoption of the UN Convention on the Law of the Sea. The convention, which included definitions of international navigational rights, territorial sea limits, the legal status of the resources in the seabed, and the conservation of marine resources, came into force in 1994 with the ratification by sixty signatories including the United States.

North American Free Trade Agreement (NAFTA) In the lobbying over NAFTA and the Free Trade Agreement of the Americas (FTAA) during the 1990s, the older issues of tariff and investment policy intersected with the more recent issues of human rights and environmental protection. The precursor agreement, the bilateral U.S.–Canadian agreement of 1989, was the culmination of a century of intermittent discussion between the two countries. The extension of free trade to Mexico under NAFTA, signed by President George H. W. Bush in December 1992, required three years of intense diplomatic negotiation and almost frantic lobbying.

NAFTA was as much about the regulation and protection of transnational investments as it was about lowering tariffs and facilitating commerce; in addition, it sought to clarify immigration policies, consumer safety regulations, and environmental standards and practices. Most of the businesses that had lobbied for much of the century for lower tariffs embraced NAFTA, but some economic leaders felt the agreement posed grave dangers. Influential business leaders such as Ross Perot led the effort to persuade Congress to reject the agreement. Trade union lobbies joined those of environmental groups and human rights organizations in opposition. They feared that NAFTA would not protect Mexican workers from exploitation, would lead to the degradation of the environment in Mexico, and would cause job losses in the United States when businesses moved south of the border.

This collision of lobbies resulted in a fracture of party loyalties and the usual coalitions in Congress. President Bill Clinton became the principal and eventually the successful lobbyist for NAFTA. He bargained with various individual members of Congress with promises of amending the agreement to provide protection for various regional products in exchange for favorable votes. The Senate approved the treaty in November 1993 by 61 to 38. In April 2001, when leaders from nearly all of the Western Hemisphere nations met in Quebec to agree on the outlines for the FTAA, more than 20,000 human rights, labor rights, and environmentalist demonstrators took to the streets with a spirit reminiscent of the antiwar rallies to protest the globalization of the economy.

ETHNIC LOBBIES

Ethnic politics and lobbies began with the large waves of nineteenth-century immigration. Irish Americans were one of the more effective ethnic lobbies. But ethnic lobbying became much stronger in the last quarter of the twentieth century. With Congress gaining a larger role in making foreign policy during the 1970s, ethnic groups became more involved in the deliberations over foreign affairs matters in Washington.

Ethnic groups and their lobbies proliferated in the 1970s and 1980s. Greek, Armenian, Turkish, Irish, Hungarian, Romanian, Serbian, and Croatian issues were among the many that often roiled the political scene. Violent rhetoric, confrontations, and even physical clashes led to fractious controversy and bitter recrimination. Congressional leaders regretted the fractiousness of ethnic controversies and the danger they could pose to national interests, but could see no way around such primordial tendencies.

While the executive branch of government proved better able than Congress to insulate itself from ethnic lobbies, some members of Congress began to worry in the late 1970s about the "overall ethnicization of foreign policy." The frequently successful targeting of Congress by ethnic lobbies created fears among some in the executive branch that congressional involvement in the daily conduct of foreign affairs policy, combined with Congress's vulnerability to ethnic interest groups, was imparting an ethnic hue to American diplomacy.

493

Arab-Israeli Conflict   Among the ethnic lobbies, none were more vigorous—or more often successful—than those advocating American support for the state of Israel. The groups concerned with the fate of Israel were referred to at various times as the Zionist lobby, the Jewish lobby, or the Israeli lobby, a terminology that appears to have come into use in the 1970s, when lobbying both for and against support for Israel was most fierce. During World War II, Jewish groups united to advocate the establishment of a Palestinian state for the Jews at a time when outspoken appeals for the rescue of Jewish victims of nazism appeared politically unsound in the United States. They had, however, the support of Christian and labor groups and various public leaders. The American Zionist Council's Emergency Committee on Zionist Affairs, which evolved into the American Israeli Public Affairs Committee (AIPAC) in 1956, provided critical lobbying on behalf of U.S. recognition of Israel in 1948. President Truman acknowledged the importance of the lobbying, which, he observed, counterbalanced the pro-Arab sentiments prevailing in the State Department and the preferences of the oil companies. Pro-Israeli lobbying prevented congressional action mandating unconditional Israeli withdrawal from Egyptian territory following the 1956 Egyptian-Israeli war and also was successful in persuading Congress to suspend aid to Egypt until cargoes bound for Israel were allowed to pass through the Suez Canal.

AIPAC was among the most successful of the ethnic lobbies. By 1990 it represented the views of thirty-eight pro-Israeli organizations, had an annual budget of $12 million, a small but efficient staff supported by more than 10,000 dues-paying members, and an executive committee that included the heads of major American Jewish organizations. AIPAC, which confined its activities to advocating U.S. government policies in support of Israel (the Israeli government appears to have left to AIPAC the lobbying of Congress on important issues), gained the reputation for having outstanding intelligence about executive branch planning relative to Israel; often it was able to generate support for the Israeli government position by providing members of Congress with vital information sooner or more fully than could the State Department. AIPAC also generated grassroots lobbying by the many Jewish communities that deluged the State Department with telephone calls and other messages for or against American policies or actions.

AIPAC had some significant successes in lobbying for legislation that provided military and economic assistance to Israel and denied critical arms to its Arab neighbors. The tenacity of AIPAC was on occasion resented by both Republican and Democratic administrations, which wanted to measure American national interests in the Middle East by their own standards, and AIPAC occasionally failed to prevent actions opposed by the Israeli government. In 1978 the Carter administration pushed through Congress the sale of sixty F-15 planes to Saudi Arabia over the opposition of AIPAC. In 1981, Congress passed Reagan administration legislation for the sale of AWACS surveillance aircraft and other equipment to Saudi Arabia despite the strenuous lobbying of AIPAC, and during the senior Bush's presidency AIPAC unsuccessfully challenged White House opposition to a $10 million loan guarantee to Israel. The very vigor of AIPAC lobbying and its contribution to the electoral defeat of prominent congressional opponents of important pro-Israeli legislation stirred fear of renewed anti-Israeli and anti-Semitic sentiment in the United States.

In the absence of a substantial domestic constituency in the United States, Arab states countered the Israeli-AIPAC efforts with a combination of hired professional lobbyists and new advocacy groups. The National Association of Arab Americans (NAAA), formed in 1972, was never as successful as AIPAC, but it did attract attention in the media and in Congress among those who felt that the United States was not evenhanded in dealing with the Arab-Israeli conflict. NAAA became increasingly effective in influencing U.S. institutions as Americans grew more concerned about the plight of the Palestinians. Other groups included the Action Committee on American-Arab Relations, the American Palestine Committee, and the American Near East Refugee Committee. The rival lobbies tended to offset one another. They also intensified the debate around Middle East issues and often informed the outcome.

Jackson-Vanik Amendment   In 1973 ethnic and human rights concerns coalesced when Congress adopted legislation requiring that the Soviet government permit wider emigration to Israel in order to obtain most-favored-nation trade status. In working for the legislation—the so-called Jackson-Vanik Amendment to the 1974 Trade Act—Senator Henry Jackson gained critical support from the National Conference on Soviet Jewry, an umbrella organization representing major national and local Jewish organizations. The National Conference's grassroots campaign developed an expansive constituent appeal to Congress that generated more than 250 cosponsors for the amendment when Representative Charles Vanik introduced it in the House. The AFL-CIO, which lobbied Congress for special tariff protections for domestic industries impacted by cheap foreign imports, joined Jewish organizations in persuading Congress to adopt the Jackson-Vanik Amendment as well as to withdraw the United States from the International Labor Organization (ILO) because of that organization's recognition of "captive" labor unions in the USSR and the communist bloc generally. Despite an angry visit to Congress by Soviet politburo member Boris Ponomarev, efforts by President Nixon and Secretary of State Kissinger to negotiate a diplomatic compromise with the Soviet Union were thwarted by the lobbying campaign. Leaders in Congress afterward complained that the kind of lobbying evidenced by Jackson-Vanik made it impossible to conduct normal or effective foreign policy.

Greek-American Lobby In 1964 Greek-American organizations sought to persuade President Lyndon B. Johnson to deny Turkey the use of U.S. military aid to thwart the movement for independence by Greek Cypriots. The impact of the Greek-American lobby on U.S. foreign policy reached its peak in 1974, when it helped to foster congressional legislation that favored an independent Greek Cyprus and opposed Turkish intervention there. Although most observers blamed the Greeks for the fighting that broke out in 1974 in Cyprus between Greek and Turkish Cypriots after the Turkish invasion of the island, the Greek-American community and lobby persuaded Congress to deny U.S. arms to Turkey, a NATO ally. The American Hellenic Educational Progressive Association (AHEPA) and the American Hellenic Institute were instrumental in securing a law that amended foreign aid legislation to cut off assistance to nations using it for purposes other than national defense. In response to the congressional embargo of arms, an action strongly opposed not only by the Nixon administration but by the leadership of Congress itself, Turkey ordered the closing of American military installations on its soil.

A new, more professional lobbying organization, the American Hellenic Institute Public Affairs Committee (AHIPAC), arose in the 1970s; it pressed friendly members of Congress to repel

efforts to end the arms embargo against Turkey. AHIPAC—patterned after the successful, pro-Israeli AIPAC—and AHEPA carried on grassroots campaigns that generated large quantities of letters, telegrams, and telephone messages to Congress and the State Department whenever the administration initiated an effort to lift the embargo. The Greek-American community in the United States was not very large, and the effectiveness of its lobbies stemmed not from the number of senators and representatives they could influence but from their success in influencing those few members able to affect the work of Congress. Of course, the reorganization of power in Congress during the 1970s contributed to the potential effectiveness of lobbies like those pressing Greek concerns.

The Greek lobbies also increased their influence by cooperating with other ethnic lobbies, such as those advocating Armenian and Israeli issues. At the end of the 1970s, AIPAC supported the Greek lobby's effort to maintain the embargo against Turkey, while AHIPAC supported the lobbying effort to prevent the sale of aircraft to Saudi Arabia. The Turkish government then retaliated by breaking off relations with Israel, an example of the unintended and unexpected consequences for American foreign policy that these ethnic alliances could have. An alliance of groups—particularly American veterans' organizations—concerned about U.S. military security and strength, rallied in support of the government's eventually successful effort to lift the embargo against Turkey.

During the 1970s the Cyprus dispute not only ignited grassroots ethnic lobbying but also precipitated one of the early examples of direct lobbying by foreign governments with Congress. When in 1978 Congress had before it legislation aimed at removing the embargo on arms sales to Turkey, the leaders of all of the concerned governments—Turkish prime minister Bulent Ecevit, Greek prime minister Constantine Karamanlis, Turkish Cypriot leader Rauf Denktash, and Cypriot president Spyros Kyprianou—met with members of the House. Also, the Greek minister to the United States consulted frequently with the House staff preparing the legislation and apparently was able to mitigate the language removing the embargo.

Armenian American Lobby In the last several decades of the twentieth century, a small but passionate Armenian-American lobby made the public aware of alleged Turkish genocide in the massacre of Armenians—in estimated numbers ranging from hundreds of thousands to more than 1.5 million—between 1915 and 1923. The Armenian lobby in America and other major Western nations was able to obtain a resolution in 2000 from the House International Affairs Committee acknowledging the killing of Armenians as genocide. Only an urgent appeal by President Clinton to the House leaders, reminding them of the danger that Turkey would evict the United States from its Turkish bases if such a resolution were adopted, brought about a last-minute withdrawal of the resolution from consideration.

By the end of the twentieth century Armenian lobbyists, responding to the growing tendency of state governments to adopt positions on foreign policy issues important to their citizens, had pushed their campaigns to the individual states and obtained resolutions in fifteen state legislatures condemning the Turkish massacre of Armenians as genocide. By 2001 the increasingly powerful Armenian Assembly of America, the central Armenian lobby, had purchased a headquarters building two blocks from the White House. The Turkish side of the dispute had no natural constituency in the United States, but representatives of the Turkish embassy engaged in their own lobbying in Washington and in state capitols. An articulate Turkish lobby consistently succeeded in frustrating Armenian demands for resolutions regarding the massacres by reminding members of Congress of the importance of the U.S.–Turkish alliance.

Cuban-American Lobby   The waves of Cuban refugees to the United States in the last half of the twentieth century significantly impacted domestic politics in Florida and generated a foreign affairs lobby that was a virtual determinant in U.S. policy toward Cuba. The largest Cuban advocacy group, the Cuban-American National Foundation (CANF), led by Jose Mas Canosa until his death in 1997, was highly successful in pushing Congress and the executive branch into initiatives like the establishment of powerful U.S. broadcasting to Cuba by the Voice of America's Radio Martí (in 1985) and TV Martí (1990) and ensuring that the U.S. delegation to the annual meetings of the UN Human Rights Commission in Geneva took the lead in condemning and isolating the Castro regime. The U.S. sanctions regime against Cuba became a fixture of Washington's policy despite the general trend among America's friends and allies toward the end of the century—and espe-

cially after the collapse of the Soviet bloc—to seek to normalize diplomatic and economic relations. U.S. leadership in the UN on anti-Castro resolutions, whatever the cost to the overall American role in multilateral diplomacy, was a requirement of State Department policy in all administrations. None wished to arouse the anti-Castro lobby, which had no viable counter-lobby.

FOREIGN GOVERNMENT LOBBIES

Only in the last decades of the twentieth century did foreign governments find it necessary to go beyond traditional diplomatic practices to compete effectively in the often frenzied lobbying efforts surrounding important foreign affairs legislation in Washington. While retaining the usual contingent of consular and diplomatic personnel, foreign embassies increasingly turned to American firms and consultants to represent them with members of Congress, officials of the executive branch, and foreign affairs interest groups. By the early 1990s Japan, the United Kingdom, Canada, Germany, France, and Mexico were the biggest spenders on these kinds of activities in the United States. The Canadian government spent an estimated $40 million in seeking support for the U.S.–Canadian Free Trade Agreement and Mexico spent $40 million in promoting NAFTA. Nor did foreign governments rely exclusively upon paid lobbies; starting in the 1970s, foreign leaders began dealing directly with Congress. Visits of heads of state to Congress were initially ceremonial, but soon they became working sessions for negotiating with members of Congress and their staffs.

The first laws regulating lobbyists for foreign government were put in place on the eve of World War II, when Congress adopted the Foreign Agents Registration Act of 1938. The legislation was originally spurred by Nazi propaganda in the United States, but after the war its main target became the threat of communism. In 1966 the law was amended to deal more particularly with the lobbyists retained by friendly governments rather than with secret enemy agents. The revised law required every foreign agent engaged in political activity for a foreign government to register with the Justice Department and to make detailed reports of income, expenditures, and contributions. Although the law had enforcement and investigative provisions, it was not vigorously enforced, and compliance appears to have been only nominal. The Foreign Agents Registration Act was again amended later in the 1960s and in the 1970s to provide for the criminal prosecution of foreign agents and lobbyists making election campaign contributions.

By the late 1970s the number of registered foreign agents lobbying or otherwise working on behalf of foreign governments had grown to more than 600, compared to 160 in 1944, and observers noted that this was just the tip of the iceberg. Former high-ranking executive branch officials and members of Congress, including former secretaries of state and chairs of the Senate Foreign Relations Committee, registered as agents for foreign governments. They generally worked for nations of the eastern Mediterranean and the Middle East that would be affected by trade and military assistance legislation but whose governments knew little about the details of legislation or the workings of Congress. Many foreign governments maintained advocacy offices in Washington that were independent of their embassies. These generally sought to foster commerce by lobbying Congress directly or through sympathetic American business groups. Foreign governments funded fellowships and scholarly centers, which indirectly ensured that the governments' interests and concerns reached Congress through the advice and testimony of American scholars.

The emergence of vigorous human rights lobbies in the 1970s aimed at notoriously repressive governments in Central and South America and Asia caused some governments of the region to enlist Washington lobbyists to mitigate the loss or reduction of American economic or military assistance and counteract bad publicity resulting from human rights violations. In the 1970s the Argentine and Chilean lobbies spent hundreds of thousands of dollars but had little success in dissuading Congress from greatly reducing annual aid allotments. During the same decade, the Nicaraguan lobby was successful in gaining the confidence of some strategically placed members of Congress, who helped delay the withdrawal of American military assistance to General Anastasio Somoza's regime.

Lobbying on behalf of the South Korean government, which annually received about $200 million in military aid and $100 million in Food for Peace agricultural products, precipitated a major scandal in 1976 and 1977. Congress and various executive branch agencies launched investigations into Koreagate, in which the Korean Central Intelligence Agency (KCIA) was accused of bribery, espionage, influence peddling, and other illegal practices aimed at a number of members of Congress. The investigations concluded that as much as $750,000 may have been distributed to more than thirty members by KCIA agents. The KCIA-managed lobbying program apparently succeeded in warding off restrictions on South Korean aid because of human rights violations by the South Korean regime, but the investigations led to legal action against several former members of Congress and disciplinary action against some sitting members.

U.S. Government Response to Foreign Affairs Lobbying The heightened sensitivity and vulnerability of members of Congress to vocal and determined interest groups contributed to the structural changes in Congress in the 1970s and evolved over time further methods of interaction between legislators and lobbying groups. Where the multiplication of subcommittees failed to meet the needs of interest groups or ensure an effective hearing to their issues, so called "issue caucuses" outside the formal congressional committee structure were set up, allowing interested legislators to work together in responding in a far more focused way to interest groups and their lobbyists. The issue caucuses allowed complicated issues to be more fully delineated and provided venues for individual legislators to develop their positions. The issue caucuses worked so well in bringing together information about contentious matters that the executive branch often tended to favor them rather than dealing with the interest groups themselves, thereby providing an unintended but useful synergy in moving the government forward more quickly to respond to the expectations of interest groups.

As the lobbying of executive branch officials came to be recognized as legitimate, federal officials and lobbyists developed new ways to accomplish common goals. The White House and the State Department more frequently turned not to political parties but to particular interest groups and their lobbies when it was necessary to develop public support for treaties, agreements, and difficult foreign affairs initiatives. In 1978 the Carter White House established a public liaison office that, along with selected senior presidential advisers, had the task of gathering support from interest groups for administration policies and to ensure that the political needs and expectations of those groups were met as much as possible. This approach continued in following administrations. President Clinton drew criticism from political opponents for his extensive entertainment of business interests at the White House, but the practice resulted in important support for such foreign policy initiatives as NAFTA.

The Reagan administration developed a "public diplomacy" program aimed at lobbying public interest groups to counter the tide of public opinion and congressional action against counterinsurgency actions in Central America and the Caribbean. Public diplomacy was defined as government actions to generate support, through information and persuasion, for national security objectives. The State Department became the locus for this public diplomacy program, which over time consisted of numerous ad hoc working groups and task forces of officials drawn from various agencies. The program dealt with the public affairs aspects of each new crisis arising from the administration's Central American and, later, Middle East policies. Public diplomacy programs were carefully designed to allow the administration to skirt the legal constraints on executive branch lobbying of a Congress that sought to thwart the use of covert counterinsurgency actions. The State Department also sought to lobby the fragmented Congress, where individual members had acquired increased power to influence legislation. The liaison relationship between the State Department and Congress, previously funneled exclusively through a Congressional Relations Bureau, was decentralized, and State Department desk officers consulted with congressional staffs on a regular basis, something scarcely imaginable twenty years earlier. These mid-level policy officials also began to meet with interest group lobbyists as they developed policy proposals for the State Department leadership. Informing, persuading, or lobbying—everyone was doing it.

CONCLUSION

Foreign affairs experts have criticized the role and influence of domestic politics on the formulation and conduct of U.S. foreign policy. Former secretaries of state took no pleasure in the difficult task of conducting foreign affairs with other nations while simultaneously negotiating policies with Congress or, worse still, with powerful interest groups. Dean Acheson ruefully observed that the limitation imposed by democratic political practices made it difficult to conduct foreign affairs in what he saw to be the national interest, and Henry Kissinger and others complained of the near impossibility of effectively conducting foreign policy in an open society. George Shultz lamented when Congress, persuaded in large measure by public advocates, proscribed executive-branch diplomatic initiatives. It may be inevitable that practitioners of diplomacy, faced with the difficult task of reconciling U.S. national interests, as articulated by the president, with the demands and expectations of other nations, will view with distress and even horror the public airing by interest groups and their lobbies of facts or issues that can embarrass and constrain diplomatic relations. American negotiators, comparing their situation with the virtual autonomy often enjoyed by foreign diplomats, must often feel handicapped by the uninvited and unwelcome intrusions of interest groups and their lobbies.

Not only are lobbies recurrent obstacles to policymakers and negotiators, but they have gathered around them more than an aura of operating outside of traditional rules and roles. Gifts and favors from lobbies and interest groups to members of Congress and officials of the executive branch heighten the fear of corruption in the lobbying process. "Single-issue" groups convey a sense of narrow selfishness pursued at the expense of the larger good. On the other hand, the activities of lobbies regarding various aspects of foreign policy in the last quarter of the twentieth century made the policy process far more transparent than ever before. The need to protect the national security information that lay at the heart of foreign policy generated an elaborate security mechanism, but it also gave rise to its antithesis—growing public pressure for freedom of information and "government in the sunshine."

Lobbies, including those representing single-issue groups, are after all only giving necessary expression to an articulate and committed engagement with the democratic process. They have become another kind of check and balance to the branches of government beyond those provided by the Constitution. Lobbies and the government have been exploring various ways by which the rulers and ruled can get along. The public, for better or worse, has become interested and engaged in thinking and speaking about foreign policy. Many Americans, defining themselves in terms of economic, ideological, and ethnic loyalties and interests rather than the more traditional party preferences and geographic residences, have gravitated to those advocacy groups that allow them more effectively to inform elected and appointed officials about their particular views on foreign policy.

On the positive side, lobbies have contributed to the emergence of more durable foreign policies based on the interests and involvement of a broad range of people rather than those of a handful of top leaders. It can be argued that American foreign affairs officials blundered more often when they operated secretly than when they engaged interest groups and developed broader consensual policies that were more likely to have sustained understanding and support. At the least, lobbies present information and articulate issues in a manner that the executive branch cannot provide because of traditional political logrolling or concealment behind the shield of national security. They also reflect the interests of an increasingly well-informed American public more concerned with the moral and humanitarian concerns of foreign policy than with strategic considerations of traditional diplomacy, most of which faded with the end of the Cold War. Moreover, foreign powers have learned to live with the vagaries of American foreign policy as influenced and conditioned by frequent elections, ethnic group sensitivities, and an independent legislature.

Perhaps the balance of lobbies and government, however messy it can sometimes be, is the best sign of a vital democracy dealing with circumstances hardly envisaged by the Founders of our nation. The danger exists, of course, that one side or the other will gain an excessive advantage. The government, both the executive branch and Congress, is learning to cope with, and perhaps even exploit, the proliferating lobbies and interest groups. Surely the greater danger would be the stifling of full public debate of foreign policies in the name of narrowly or secretly defined national interests and national security. The challenge is for government to use the information and resources so willingly provided by the myriad lobbies operating in the foreign affairs field to make informed and wise decisions for the nation and the world.

BIBLIOGRAPHY

Cigler, Allan J., and Burdett A. Loomis, eds. "Interest Group Politics." *Congressional Quarterly.* Washington, D.C., 1995. The basic collection of essays by experts on the workings of interest groups and their lobbies.

Cohen, Bernard C. *The Public's Impact on Foreign Policy.* Boston, 1973. The classic description of how the activities of interest groups were seen by mid-level diplomats.

DeConde, Alexander. *Ethnicity, Race, and Foreign Policy: A History.* Boston, 1992. The best survey on the role of ethnicity in American foreign affairs.

Deese, David A. *The New Politics of American Foreign Policy.* New York, 1994. The impact of special interest groups and their lobbies appear in all of the aspects of the "new politics" that are closely examined by a group of experts.

Fisher, Louis. *Presidential War Powers.* Lawrence, Kans., 1995. The basic study of the origins and development of the congressional assertion of control of presidential war powers, a key element in the emergence of foreign affairs lobbies.

Franck, Thomas M., and Edward Weisband. *Foreign Policy by Congress.* New York, 1979. A close examination of how Congress came to share foreign policymaking with the executive branch and how human rights and other lobbies took advantage of this fact.

Holsti, Ole R. *Public Opinion and American Foreign Policy.* Ann Arbor, Mich., 1996.

Pastor, Robert A. *Congress and the Politics of U.S. Foreign Economic Policy, 1929–1976.* Berkeley, Calif., 1980. Provides valuable insights and examples of the role of interest groups in the evolution of American tariff and foreign economic policies.

Patterson, Mark. "The Presidency and Organized Interest Group Liaison." *American Political Science Review* 86 (September 1992): 612–625. An authoritative study of how presidents use interest groups.

Schoultz, Lars. *Human Rights and United States Policy Toward Latin America.* Princeton, N.J., 1981. Includes an extensive review and analysis of major human rights interest groups and their lobbies.

Small, Melvin. *Democracy and Diplomacy: The Impact of Domestic Politics on U.S. Foreign Policy, 1789–1994.* Baltimore, 1996. An outstanding historical summary and analysis of the domestic influences on foreign policy, including the role of interest groups.

Smith, Tony. *Foreign Attachments: The Power of Ethnic Groups in the Making of American Foreign Policy.* Cambridge, Mass., 2000.

Stalcup, Brenda, ed. *The Women's Rights Movement: Opposing Viewpoints.* San Diego, Calif., 1996.

Wittner, Lawrence S. *The Struggle against the Bomb.* 2 vols. Stanford, Calif., 1994, 1997. The indispensable guide to the rise and activities of a major interest group that changed everything.

See also AFRICAN AMERICANS; THE CHINA LOBBY; CONGRESSIONAL POWER; CONSORTIA; ENVIRONMENTAL DIPLOMACY; HUMAN RIGHTS; MULTINATIONAL CORPORATIONS; ORGANIZED LABOR; POWER POLITICS; THE PRESS; RACE AND ETHNICITY.

SUMMIT CONFERENCES

* * * *

Theodore A. Wilson

The practice of tribal heads, kings, emperors, and princes of the church meeting together has been the normal way of conducting diplomacy for most of recorded history. Identification of the interests of the state with the ruler's personal concerns dictated that rulers eschew the usual device of emissaries, and meet with their peers to deal with grievances, arrange dynastic marriages, proclaim wars, and enforce peace settlements. Chronicles are replete with examples, whether real or mythical, of personal diplomacy. The council of the Aegean leaders before the Trojan War, the confrontation of Moses and the pharaoh, Richard I's legendary encounter with Saladin in the Holy Land, and certainly the dramatic meeting of Holy Roman Emperor Henry IV with Pope Gregory VII at Canossa in 1077 might all be termed "summit conferences."

The meeting of Henry VIII of England and Francis I of France on the Field of the Cloth of Gold (1520) near Calais, France, however, was almost anachronistic. By the seventeenth century a system of diplomatic representatives was supplanting the personal diplomacy of secular and religious rulers. Thereafter, as permanent missions assumed responsibility for negotiations, the direct involvement of national leaders in diplomacy became quite unusual. For example, of the forty-two major international conferences that took place between 1776 and 1914 listed in Ernest Satow's *A Guide to Diplomatic Practice* (1957), only one, the Congress of Vienna, featured the presence of heads of state.

Before World War I, the American diplomatic style called for the president to delegate responsibility for negotiations to others: secretaries of state, ambassadors, and special agents. Of course, some chief executives, such as President James K. Polk during the Mexican War (1846–1848), did intervene decisively in foreign affairs, but their initiatives were implemented by special emissaries. Very early, a tradition was

established that a president not travel beyond the borders of the United States during his tenure in office. Theodore Roosevelt threw over this custom by visiting Panama in 1906. Another tradition appears to have discouraged official visits to the United States by foreign heads of state and heads of government, for just thirty such visits occurred prior to 1918. Thus, historical precedent alone made the exercise of personal diplomacy by the president unlikely.

All this changed when President Woodrow Wilson decided to attend the Paris Peace Conference in 1919. Since World War I every president except Warren G. Harding has traveled abroad, taking part either in formal conferences or in consultations with the leaders of other nations. The incidence of such conferences in the diplomacy of all nations has increased markedly. Certainly, since the beginning of World War II, the United States has led the way to the top-level conference table. Since 1940 American presidents have taken part in more than 200 international meetings, ranging from bilateral and informal conversations to highly organized multinational conclaves. One analysis claims that from 1953 to 2000, presidential visits abroad, ranging from a few hours to several days, total 314. President William Jefferson Clinton leads in personal diplomacy by a staggering margin, having spent 229 days abroad and visited seventy-four different countries (or entities) during his eight years in office.

In and of itself, the break with tradition, from minimal involvement by U.S. chief executives in the negotiation process to direct, repeated participation through personal diplomacy, was not unexpected. It paralleled the mushrooming American interest in world affairs and the increasing influence exerted by the United States in the international arena. What may be deemed surprising is the emergence of high-level personal diplomacy and its principal manifestation, the summit conference, as a major technique for the conduct of the nation's business abroad. "The summit conference," one observer wrote, "has become a vital part of the contemporary foreign relations system of the United States." Not only have post–World War II presidents relied extensively on this diplomatic technique; they have made it a test of the success or failure of ambitious initiatives in foreign affairs. Why have American leaders found the summit conference so appealing? What purposes have they believed summitry can accomplish that cannot be achieved by means of conventional diplomatic channels? Is the summit conference an inevitable result of the technological revolution in communication and transportation? A critical question is whether summit conferences are intended to deal with matters of substance or of style. Phrased bluntly, is the object of summit diplomacy the foreign leaders with whom a president confers or the American people? Last, what have been the significant effects, if any, of summitry on the course of U.S. foreign policy? Have these latter-day "religio-political circuses" benefited or harmed the United States?

CHARACTERISTICS OF A SUMMIT CONFERENCE

In order to treat at least some of these questions, it is necessary to identify the special characteristics of summit conferences and to ascertain which of the numerous international meetings American leaders have attended since 1950 were "summits" rather than "ordinary" high-level conferences. An impressive body of writing exists on this subject; but no precise, wholly satisfactory definition of "summit conferences" has been provided. *The Oxford Companion to American History*'s definition, which may be taken as typical, states: "Summit conferences, as the term has been used since World War II, applies to the meeting of heads of government of the leading powers in an effort to reach broad measures of agreement. The first such meeting took place (July 1955) at Geneva. . . . Although similar meetings have been proposed since then, none has taken place, since a fixed agenda prepared by lower-level conferences seems to be a necessary prerequisite." Not only is this definition self-contradictory (referring to the existence of the practice since World War II and then asserting that a summit conference first took place in 1955), it is also unduly restrictive and outdated. The stipulation that a summit conference be preceded by lower-level meetings to fix an agenda (which presumes that a summit must have an agenda) is unwarranted. From historical example and widespread usage, one may argue that any meeting sufficiently well organized to be termed a "conference" may also be called a summit conference. Indeed, the concept has become so widespread that just about any international convocation that includes one or more heads of government is labeled a "summit" conference.

The Oxford explication does, however, include certain other criteria that are essential to the construction of a working definition: for an international conference to be a summit meeting, heads of government must take part, "leading powers" must be involved, and it should represent "an effort to reach broad measures of agreement" rather than be merely a ceremonial visit. While admittedly unsophisticated, such a definition accurately reflects the present state of understanding. Elmer Plischke, whose *Summit Diplomacy: Personal Diplomacy of the President of the United States* (1958) was the first comprehensive study of the subject, simply refers to "the practice of chiefs of state and heads of government meeting in bipartite or multipartite gatherings." Clearly of most significance is the element of personal presidential involvement.

Application of the above criteria reveals that U.S. presidents have taken part in some eighty summit conferences since 1919. Among them would rank Versailles (1919); Franklin D. Roosevelt's nine wartime meetings with Allied leaders; Potsdam (1945); Geneva (1955); Camp David (1959); Paris (1959, 1960); Vienna (1961); Glassboro (1967); President Richard M. Nixon's visits to the Soviet Union and China; the participation of President Gerald R. Ford in the Helsinki summit and his trips elsewhere; the Group of Seven (G-7, but effectively G-8 since 1991) economic summits held annually since 1975; President James E. Carter's 1977 visit to London, the Sadat-Carter and Begin-Carter discussions in Washington, the Camp David Summit (1978), Carter's March 1978 trip to Egypt and Israel, and his Vienna meeting with Leonid Brezhnev to sign the SALT II Agreement; the participation of President Ronald Reagan in the Cancun Summit on International Cooperation and Development (1981), his visits to Europe (1982) and China (1984), the Reagan-Gorbachev summits at Geneva (1985), Reykjavik (1986), Washington (1987), and Moscow (1988), and the New York "mini-summit" with Gorbachev in December 1988; President George H. W. Bush's numerous consultations in Washington and abroad with world leaders, including six meetings with Gorbachev; and the seemingly nonstop recourse of President Bill Clinton to personal diplomacy.

It may be argued that all of these meetings followed the script written by Henry VIII and Francis I in 1520. That meeting certainly featured personal diplomacy. It was arranged for the purpose of reaching "a meeting of minds" between the principals rather than for the resolution of specific differences. It transpired in an atmosphere of opulence, informality, and artificial camaraderie. Last, its achievements typically were minimal. For the most part, any benefits were psychological, lying in the clearer understanding of one another's motives and motivations gained by the participants. The prototypical summit conference emphasized the "images" of progress rather than the realities of problems left unresolved.

WILSON AT VERSAILLES

The decision of President Woodrow Wilson to participate personally in the Paris Peace Conference ushered in the modern era of summit conferences. For the first time an American president was asserting the right to be present at negotiations affecting his nation's and the world's future security and to deal directly with his foreign counterparts, the heads of the Allied Powers. That the meeting to settle peace terms would be conducted by the principal political leaders of the allied nations was a logical continuation of wartime diplomatic experience. In almost every nation, the Allied Powers and Central Powers alike, elected leaders had assumed personal control of foreign policy. The British prime minister, David Lloyd George, had established a private diplomatic operation, bypassing even his foreign secretary, Lord Balfour. Similarly ignoring established channels and his secretary of state, President Wilson chose to use his friend and adviser, Colonel Edward House, as a personal representative, often communicating with other governments through him alone.

For the Allies, suspicion and dislike of the professional diplomats largely explained the direct intervention of heads of government. As Keith Eubank wrote: "Leaders of the Allied nations blamed secret diplomacy for World War I. Professional diplomats had secretly constructed entangling alliances which many thought had caused the war. Allied politicians were convinced that in the future they must control diplomacy to ensure peace. The professionals could not be trusted." In 1916 and 1917, meetings of allied premiers, with their chief assistants, had taken place. This practice was continued under the Supreme War Council, which brought together elected officials (or their representatives) and military spokesmen. During the final months of the war, the Supreme War Council assumed direct control over allied operations and also set in motion arrangements for the meeting of victorious governments to decide the terms of peace. All the major allied leaders planned as a matter of course to attend at least some planning sessions for the peace conference. For example, when President Wilson arrived in Paris, he immediately replaced Colonel House as U.S. representative to the Supreme War Council. By the time this body convened on 12 January 1919, to hear a report from Marshal Ferdinand Foch, allied commander in chief, on Germany's implementation of the armistice, the heads of the principal allied nations were in attendance. Thus, there existed precedents and procedures to make Versailles a true summit conference. Only the "spirit" of summit diplomacy was lacking, and Wilson soon provided a surfeit of that commodity.

President Wilson had not journeyed to Europe to exchange chitchat with obscure diplomats. From the beginning, the Supreme War Council (renamed the Council of Ten), which included the heads of government or foreign ministers of France, Great Britain, Italy, Japan, and the United States, dominated the proceedings. The great powers decided to meet separately "to find out their own minds before they entered into the process of the peace conference," thereby relegating the other delegates to a passive role. Conscious of his special status as a head of state and supremely confident about his powers of persuasion, Wilson willingly acceded to these arrangements. It appears that he was relying upon the enormous popular acclaim accorded him in Europe and the self-evident wisdom of the policies he advocated. He hoped to achieve an easy consensus within the "Big Five" and then to obtain quick ratification of his peace program by the full conference. It could then be offered to a jubilant world. President Wilson was counting on the powerful impact on American opinion should he return from Paris a modern Moses, carrying down from the summit the tablets of the Treaty of Versailles and the League of Nations Covenant that he and Europe's wise men had inscribed.

It did not work out as planned. The Versailles Conference lasted too long and grappled with too many specific, complicated issues for the tone of lofty detachment to be maintained. Although Wilson dealt personally with almost every problem brought before the conference, many proved too esoteric even for him, and he was forced to call upon the "experts" for advice. Even more important, Wilson simply did not possess the power to dictate terms to the other participants. His status as folk hero and senior statesman meant little to the shrewd, experienced leaders with whom he had to negotiate. These men had specific goals, and they forced President Wilson to compromise on such matters as reparations and the mandate system. Convinced that the League of Nations, if inaugurated, would soon correct the imperfections of the Treaty of Versailles, Wilson chose to sacrifice other points to ensure that the League Covenant got through intact.

His was to prove a meaningless victory, for the United States eventually rejected membership in the League of Nations. There were to be various causes of the rejection of Wilson's dream. Certainly, though, President Wilson's presentation of the Versailles Conference as heralding the approach of the millennium was pivotal. Having exaggerated the benefits to be gained from this convocation of global leaders, whom he described as the forces of righteousness, Wilson was vulnerable to attack from all sides. The Versailles Conference must be termed the first modern summit conference. It demonstrated many characteristics that later practitioners were to emulate and improve. But Wilson's plunge into personal diplomacy also served as a warning, for he had failed to orchestrate the episode so as to ensure favorable public reaction. One explanation for this failure was his foolish attempt to use a summit conference to deal with substantive issues. His successors would not repeat that particular error.

THE MUNICH CONFERENCE

Perhaps because of the contradictory results of Versailles, national leaders resisted the temptation to participate directly in the important diplomatic conferences of the interwar years. When they did attend, their role was formal and ceremonial. It required the emergence of personalities who recognized the propaganda benefits to be derived from dramatic confrontations with their political

opposite numbers to revivify the practice. Adolf Hitler was one such personality. It is now the accepted wisdom to characterize Munich, the infamous summit meeting of British Prime Minister Neville Chamberlain with the posturing, saber-rattling Hitler in April 1938, as a great blunder, the more tragic because Western diplomats should have recognized such efforts were futile and thus unnecessary. This ignores the climate that prevailed and the conviction (which Hitler, a dedicated advocate of personal diplomacy, cleverly fostered) that only direct discussions between political leaders could break through the paper barriers erected by professional diplomats. Hitler perceived that the summit conference preeminently offered an opportunity for publicity, the reiteration in dramatic circumstances of one's position, rather than serious negotiation. He was undoubtedly a master of the technique termed "spin doctoring" by a later generation.

ROOSEVELT'S SUMMITS

It is not surprising that Franklin D. Roosevelt, another political chief who was prone to personally engineered diplomatic fireworks, would find the summit conference a congenial tool. During his first term, Roosevelt concentrated on domestic problems. On the rare occasions he did involve himself in foreign affairs, his penchant for personal diplomacy, the dispatch of presidential agents, direct appeals to other heads of government, and proposals for top-level conferences offered a clear indication of his future course of action. After 1937, when Roosevelt assumed a more active role in foreign affairs, he based U.S. diplomacy largely on these techniques. Thoroughly distrusting the "striped-pants boys" in the Department of State and always on the lookout for opportunities to present issues to the American people in simple, dramatic terms, President Roosevelt loosed a torrent of midnight messages to European leaders and calls for general peace conferences. The purposes he assigned to these activities were less clearly formed, and in some ways more ambitious, than the cold assessment of potential results that underlay Hitler's fondness for summit conferences. While highly valuing the propaganda benefits, Roosevelt apparently also believed that leader-to-leader exchanges could bring about a personal rapport not possible via the ritualistic communications that typified traditional diplomacy. He also appears to have believed that mutual sympathy could lead to important breakthroughs. In retrospect, the emergence of the summit conference as a dominant instrument in the diplomacy of World War II appears to have been inevitable, given the leading role of Franklin D. Roosevelt.

Certainly, as compared with past eras, World War II witnessed a marked increase in meetings between national leaders. The assembling of presidents, premiers, and generalissimos became normal, even expected, events. On the American side, ten such summit conferences took place: the Atlantic Conference between President Roosevelt and British Prime Minister Winston Churchill in August 1941; the first Washington Conference (Roosevelt and Churchill) in December 1941–January 1942; Casablanca (Roosevelt and Churchill) in January 1943; the second Washington Conference (Roosevelt and Churchill) in May 1943; the first Quebec Conference (Roosevelt and Churchill) in August 1943; Cairo (Roosevelt, Churchill, and Generalissimo Chiang Kai-shek) in November 1943; Tehran (Roosevelt, Churchill, and Premier Joseph Stalin) in November–December 1943; the second Quebec Conference (Roosevelt and Churchill) in September 1944; Yalta (Roosevelt, Churchill, and Stalin) in February 1945; and Potsdam (President Harry S. Truman, Churchill [replaced by Clement Attlee], and Stalin) in July 1945. Although called for various reasons, these meetings shared common characteristics and together they made the concept of summit conferences, if not the term itself, familiar to anyone with the remotest awareness of foreign affairs.

The first of these conferences, the dramatic sea meeting off Argentia, Newfoundland, of Roosevelt and Churchill in August 1941, coming as it did before formal U.S. entry into World War II, was in many ways the most novel. The Atlantic Conference established the style and much of the agenda for subsequent wartime meetings. It was secret, occurred in unique circumstances, and—reflecting the purposes of summits to come—dealt more with personal relationships than substantive issues. The conference confirmed the program of U.S. military aid to Great Britain; produced a short-lived agreement on policy toward Japan; sanctioned a statement of high purpose, the Atlantic Charter; and, most important, brought together two members of the triumvirate that was to lead the Allies.

Roosevelt and Churchill had been corresponding on a regular basis since September 1939, when the president congratulated the British politician on his reappointment as first lord of the Admiralty and had invited him to "keep in touch personally with anything you want to know about." Churchill responded with alacrity, and thus began a momentous correspondence. Soon, however, the two men were expressing eager interest in a personal meeting, moved largely by curiosity and anxiety. Both leaders possessed tremendous confidence in their charm and persuasive powers, and wished to test them against a worthy opponent. This first confrontation, though "devoutly wished and gladly consummated," produced great concern on both sides. Roosevelt's confidant, Harry Hopkins, once predicted: "Bringing together President Roosevelt and the Prime Minister . . . would cause the biggest explosion ever seen." He was mistaken. Roosevelt and Churchill reached an amicable understanding at the conference. Deeply satisfied, Churchill informed the British war cabinet, "I am sure I have established warm and deep personal relations with our great friend." Roosevelt later told his wife that this personal encounter "had broken the ice," and he had been shown that Churchill was a man with whom he could work. Despite Churchill's boasts, however, political cooperation did not lead to true friendship.

Precisely what the Atlantic Conference achieved, other than the calming of anxious egos and the satisfaction of curiosity, is difficult to say. Roosevelt let pass the opportunity afforded by the postconference publicity to take bold action regarding American entry into the war. Looking back at this first summit, it appears that Roosevelt perceived the meeting as a way to avoid decisions. There was only the most rudimentary agenda, the president intentionally excluded Secretary of State Cordell Hull and other diplomatic officials, and the experts who did accompany him (mostly military figures) were given almost no time to prepare. As usual, the British were thoroughly briefed, and they took the lead in organizing the discussions. However, the environment in which the meeting occurred and Roosevelt's casual, often flighty approach to the weighty issues they raised proved a source of constant frustration to the British and to his own subordinates. The fact that there exists no official text of the Atlantic Charter, the conference's one clear achievement, is testimony to its chaotic and cursory nature.

The hopes and assumptions that Roosevelt assigned to this type of diplomatic initiative greatly influenced the summit conferences that followed at intervals during the war. The "conference" volumes in the Department of State's documentary series Foreign Relations of the United States reveal that subsequent meetings were vastly better organized than Roosevelt's meetings with Churchill off the coast of Newfoundland. But these documents also demonstrate that the procedures changed very little. Claiming that his meetings with Churchill (and the tripartite meeting at Tehran) dealt solely with military matters, President Roosevelt continued to exclude the professional diplomats. On several occasions he specifically forbade any member of his staff to take minutes of the talks with other political leaders. Only when the question of the final conference communiqué, the public announcement of the questions discussed and decisions taken, arose did the president participate fully in the discussion and ask for his advisers' recommendations.

It was not until Tehran, when issues affecting postwar problems were dealt with, that Roosevelt permitted thoroughgoing preparation, a more formal agenda, and the participation by subordinates in carefully organized discussions with their opposite numbers. Tehran perhaps was the only true "conference" out of all the wartime summit meetings. Much more than the meeting at Yalta—at which Roosevelt's participation, betraying ill health and mental exhaustion—was sporadic and confused, the Roosevelt-Churchill-Stalin conference at Tehran produced important decisions affecting the conduct of the war and the shape of the postwar world.

It is important to emphasize that the summit conferences of World War II treated vital issues: problems of grand strategy and logistics (the second front question being most important), policy regarding the vanquished enemies, creation of a viable international organization, and the political and economic conditions of the peace. Whether these issues could have been more successfully handled by means of traditional diplomacy is moot. Despite the baneful influences to which the participants in these meetings were subjected—interminable dinners and toasts, late night tête-à-têtes, the pressure to render crucial decisions on the basis of comradely pleadings and unsubstantiated information—one may argue that Roosevelt never reversed established policies of the United States while caught up in the "unreal atmosphere" of a summit conference. The decisions regarding the second front, German occupation zones, and the supposed "sellout" to Stalin at Yalta may have had little to do with summitry; and the most famous indictment of Roosevelt's participation in summit conferences, the

offhand announcement of the "unconditional surrender" policy at Casablanca, can be presented, as Warren Kimball and others have argued, as a logical, carefully prepared extension of accepted policy. In addition, the practice of traditional diplomacy continued and, indeed, greatly increased during the war. Summit diplomacy did not replace, but rather superimposed itself on, the normal diplomatic process, and the difficulties experienced by American diplomats in settling relatively minor disputes do not suggest that old-style laborious negotiation would have resolved the major issues dividing the wartime allies.

To the related question—whether the reliance on summit conferences best served the interests of the American people—a more definite answer is possible. Here the practice was clearly harmful. It gave rise to erroneous assumptions on the part of American leaders and public about the nature of wartime diplomacy and about the likelihood of harmonious adjustment of all international conflicts. A summit conference seems always to generate "an aura of unreality," because it brings together persons who perhaps hold diametrically opposed viewpoints, and compels them to smile and genuflect to each other and to the ideal of mutual understanding and goodwill. An individual such as Franklin Roosevelt, predisposed toward personal initiatives and the belief that, for example, "Uncle Joe" Stalin was basically a tough ward politician who happened to speak Russian, risked losing his sense of perspective. Roosevelt confused the appearance of progress fostered by the congeniality present at these meetings with the reality of the conflict between American, Soviet, and British goals. A rosy assessment of colleagues' good intentions manifestly colored Roosevelt's evaluation of their subsequent actions as set forth in the cables and memoranda that flooded into the White House map room. Further, the optimistic readings about the summit conferences offered by President Roosevelt stimulated popular euphoria about the era of universal peace that surely would ensue because of these highly publicized communions of world leaders.

HARRY S. TRUMAN

The death of President Roosevelt in April 1945 marked the beginning of a ten-year hiatus in American involvement with summit conferences. Roosevelt's successor, Harry S. Truman, did take part in the Potsdam Conference with his Russian and British counterparts; he hosted Clement Attlee and Canadian Prime Minister Mackenzie King in November 1945 for talks about sharing nuclear secrets; and he reluctantly welcomed Attlee again in December 1950, when the British prime minister insisted on personal discussions regarding a rumored American decision to use atomic weapons in Korea. But it was clear that Truman did not share his flamboyant predecessor's fondness for dramatic initiatives (such as summit conferences) in foreign affairs. Much more a team player, Truman preferred to find men whom he respected and trusted, then authorize them to carry on the business of diplomacy. President Truman's one major summit conference, Potsdam (which had been scheduled prior to his accession), was enlightening. He enjoyed meeting Stalin and Churchill on equal terms, and he gained a measure of confidence from the experience; but the methodical, straightforward Missourian was repelled by the frequent deviations from the agenda and the lapses of his fellow leaders into propaganda speeches. Truman's distaste for personal diplomacy and the deepening rift in Soviet-American relations temporarily banished the summit conference from the American diplomatic repertoire. By 1947 even the regular meetings of diplomatic chiefs, the Council of Foreign Ministers, had degenerated into self-serving rhetorical exercises. Thereafter, the Cold War inhibited communication of any kind between East and West. Only once, during the 1948 presidential election, did Truman seriously entertain the possibility of a personal meeting with Stalin.

DWIGHT D. EISENHOWER

It remained for a new president, one possessing a gregarious personality and enormous self-confidence, to break open the frozen channels of East-West communication and to restore the summit conference to preeminence. The epoch that began with the meeting of President Dwight D. Eisenhower and Soviet leaders at Geneva in July 1955 (the first "summit conference" so labeled) witnessed an astonishing return of popularity of the summit conference. It also produced significant changes in the functions of this diplomatic instrument. As Adam Ulam observed: "Negotiations as such were perhaps less important than the ability to assess your protagonists needs, fears, and goals." Thus, the dimension of personal understanding remained central. But in contrast with the wartime meetings, Geneva and a long list of successor conferences openly disavowed matters of substance in favor of the goodwill and rapport to be gained (or proclaimed). For example, the meeting in Panama in July 1956 of leaders from nineteen nations under the auspices of the Organization of American States was portrayed as a "hemispheric summit" to inaugurate a new era of cooperation. President Eisenhower attended but, aside from posed photographs, little was accomplished. From the American perspective, the effects of summitry on public opinion at home became more important than the chance for diplomatic breakthroughs. As noted, publicity always had been important. Now, however, the determination of American leaders to avoid any impression of weakness in dealings with the communists and, as well, to defuse popular anxieties produced modifications not just of emphasis but also of basic purpose. As Joan Hoff notes, when U.S. and Soviet leaders met in person, "it gave people a sense of reassurance that, even though there was the possibility of a terrible nuclear confrontation, . . . they were meeting and war was not going to happen."

The agreement to convene a summit conference in 1955 was especially noteworthy because of the previously intransigent attitude of President Eisenhower and his secretary of state, John Foster Dulles, toward the possibility of improved relations with the Soviet Union. It was forced upon them mainly by sentiment in Europe (where the Austrian peace treaty had finally been negotiated and the Warsaw Pact had been signed) and at home that, in Stephen Ambrose's cogent phrase, "some ground rules for the Cold War, of spirit if not of substance, were obviously needed." Worrying crises, such as the flare-up over the islands of Quemoy and Matsu off the China coast, demonstrated that the public would not support a long-term policy based on brinkmanship. Eisenhower himself was dedicated to peace, and he had been impressed by Churchill's argument for a summit. "It was only elementary prudence," the British statesman had written in the hopes of reviving the wartime habit of meetings between the United States, the Soviet Union, and Great Britain, "for the West to learn at firsthand what sort of men were now in charge in the Kremlin, and to let these new men gauge the quality and temper of Western leadership." Secretary of State Dulles at first opposed such a meeting. He argued that the Russians were eager for a conference to dramatize the Soviet Union's moral and social equality with the West and to enhance the legitimacy of Stalin's successors. Finally, Dulles bowed to the president's wishes, muttering that if the summit served "as an object lesson for deluded optimists," it would be worthwhile.

The meeting of Eisenhower, British Prime Minister Anthony Eden, and the new leaders of the Soviet Union, Nikita Khrushchev and Nikolai Bulganin, opened in Geneva on 18 July 1955. Each side brought a huge staff and a staggering amount of background data (the American delegation had prepared 20 "basic documents" and 150 "secondary papers"), and an elaborate agenda was agreed upon. The volume of documentation ensured that the conference would bog down in details, and this soon happened. The meeting's significance derived from the reopening of communication it symbolized. Perhaps, given the rigid stance of Soviet and American policy and the comparable frigidity of public attitudes, some such dramatic gesture was necessary. At any rate, it worked. Smiling genially, President Eisenhower posed for photographs with the beaming Bulganin and Khrushchev. Such incidents and the ingenuous statements by both sides about a possible future reduction of tensions sparked a wave of popular exhilaration. The conference had transpired in a blaze of publicity (some 1,500 reporters and such public figures as the evangelist Billy Graham were present), and almost everyone acclaimed the "spirit of Geneva" as inaugurating a new era. The "spirit of Geneva" did not end the Cold War and did not resolve any of the grave problems faced by the Soviet Union and the West. It did, however, provide a clear impression that neither side wanted a thermonuclear holocaust and recognition that a military stalemate existed.

As the Atlantic Conference had for the wartime summits, so the Geneva meeting of 1955 served as a model for the following period of conferences between national leaders. Indeed, the obvious psychological and political benefits of such affairs (Eisenhower's popularity index reached 79 percent shortly after Geneva) proved irresistible. Even the aborted Paris summit of 1960, at which Premier Khrushchev forced Eisenhower to admit publicly that he had authorized U-2 spy flights over Soviet territory, did not greatly diminish the luster of summitry.

KENNEDY AND JOHNSON

Anxious to prove his maturity to Khrushchev and the American people, President John F. Kennedy met the Russian leader at Vienna in 1961. Kennedy's apparent conviction that private discussions, avoiding bombastic public rhetoric, with someone such as Khrushchev would result in rational discourse foundered on the Soviet leader's desire to intimidate the young American president. Although Vienna proved a most unhappy experience, Kennedy's personal approach to diplomacy undoubtedly would have led to other such adventures had he lived. It is unlikely, however, that any repetition of the Vienna debacle would have occurred. With one notable exception, summit conferences from 1961 to the present have been carefully scripted.

President Lyndon Johnson was inclined toward face-to-face decision making. However, after a proposal in early 1965 for a U.S.–Soviet summit became enmeshed in Moscow's criticism of the U.S. bombing campaign against North Vietnam, Johnson, wary of possible political repercussions and unwilling to permit the Soviets a forum for attacking U.S. involvement in Vietnam, contented himself with one perfunctory meeting with the Russians, the so-called Glassboro Summit in New Jersey (1967). Even so, it appeared that some form of personal contact between national leaders had become an essential duty of office. If that was so, Richard Nixon elevated this ritual to something approaching high art.

RICHARD NIXON

All the elements of the modern-day summit conference were present in Nixon's personal diplomacy: the secret preparations; the dramatic announcement of the intended journey to Peking, Moscow, and Guam; the elaborate ceremonies and effusions of mutual regard; and the vague final communiqué. Whether Nixon's assorted trips abroad were "true" summit conferences or merely formal state visits, one leader journeying to another country to exclaim over scenic wonders, consume regional delicacies, acquire souvenirs, and proclaim admiration for the host nation's achievements, is open to question. The significant initiatives pursued by Nixon and his national security adviser Henry A. Kissinger to readjust U.S. foreign policy to the political and economic implications of a multipolar world owed little to Nixon's engagement with summitry. It may be that Nixon desired to use these affairs to achieve real breakthroughs. He certainly prepared for "conferences" rather than for ceremonial visits to the Great Wall of China and the Bolshoi Ballet. If that was the case, Nixon was disappointed, for his interventions in diplomacy followed the pattern established two decades earlier, and their effects were decidedly greater at home than abroad. Nixon, of course, emphasized the domestic political effects of a summit conference. Talking with Kissinger about his 1972 summit with Soviet leader Leonid Brezhnev, Nixon urged that no "final agreements be entered into" prior to his arrival in Moscow, for otherwise his critics "will try to make it appear that all of this could have been achieved without any summitry whatever."

Perhaps these frantic efforts proved unsuccessful because the usefulness of summit conferences now had been exhausted. Keith Eubank wrote: "Summit conferences ought not to be used as an antibiotic, believing that frequent doses will cure the patient. The summit conference can never be a quick cheap cure for international ills whose treatment requires time, labor, and thought." At some point, publicity stunts and presidential globe-trotting must give way to deliberate, serious analysis and negotiation. But diverting the public's attention may have been the point. Was it accidental that President Nixon visited ten countries and spent twenty-two days abroad during the eight months prior to his resignation on 9 August 1974?

THE BROKERED AND ECONOMIC SUMMITS

The summit conference as an instrument of U.S. diplomacy is marvelously exemplified by the Helsinki Conference in July 1975. There, President Gerald Ford and the leaders of some thirty other nations conferred in dignified surroundings and then signed a document that confirmed the political and territorial division of Europe that had occurred thirty years before. Convocation of a summit conference for such a blatantly propagandistic and shallow purpose appears to suggest, as Henry Kissinger wrote after the collapse of the Paris summit in 1960, that this technique, long put forward "as the magic solvent of all tensions," stood revealed as a "parody" of diplomacy. Nevertheless, summit conferences continued in favor, for they do offer political and propaganda benefits to participants. In November 1974, President Ford met with Leonid Brezhnev in Vladivostok to affirm their commitment to arms control, but SALT II was never implemented fully as a treaty.

Ford's visit to China in the fall of 1975 was billed a summit conference in order to improve his "image" as a statesman, thus enhancing his chances of reelection. Even though nothing of substance resulted from the trip, the president and his advisers considered the China summit a great success. President Jimmy Carter's triumphal tour of England in the spring of 1977, capped by a friendly but diplomatically insignificant meeting with European leaders in London, was clearly in the same tradition.

The Ford and Carter presidencies did witness the emergence of two new variants of the summit conference: the "economic summit" and the "brokered summit." The economic summit is perhaps best exemplified by the inauguration of an annual meeting of the heads of the seven most powerful economic states (the G-7). These meetings have many of the hallmarks and various defects of bilateral summits, though they have proved useful in highlighting such global problems as drugs, the information society, and energy. Such regional summits as the annual meeting of European Union heads and the so-called "Summit of the Americas" mirror this approach.

The brokered summit may appropriately be considered as a manifestation since the mid-1970s of the uniquely powerful role of the United States in international affairs. Seeking a way out of the quagmire in which Israel and its Middle East neighbors had been trapped for thirty years, a bog that threatened to drag in major powers and cause a global conflict, President Jimmy Carter decided to offer his good offices as a broker-mediator-matchmaker. Following the remarkable visit of the Egyptian president, Anwar Sadat, to Jerusalem in November 1977, Carter invited Sadat and the Israeli prime minister, Menachim Begin, to Washington for separate discussions about finding a way out of the quagmire. Next, the president arranged a joint meeting with the Egyptian and Israeli leaders at the presidential retreat, Camp David, Maryland. Originally planned as a three-day "meet-and-greet," this brokered summit went on for thirteen days (5–17 September 1978). By shuttling between cabins, soothing wounded feelings, and pushing the two adversaries to keep talking, Carter brokered the Camp David Accords, a framework for peace that, while never completely implemented, remains the basic document in the ongoing process to find a fair and equitable peace in the Middle East.

RONALD REAGAN AND
GEORGE H. W. BUSH

President Ronald Reagan brokered no peace settlements, and his first term saw a historic hiatus in the modern-day parade of summit conferences. Determined to rebuild America's power and prestige, Reagan and his advisers initially were hostile toward any dealings with that "evil empire," the Soviet Union. During his second term, however, there occurred a notable reversal of policies and attitudes. After Mikhail Gorbachev's accession to power in March 1985, Reagan met more frequently with his Russian counterpart than had any of his predecessors. Reagan and Gorbachev arranged a "meet-and-greet" in Geneva in November 1985; took part in a summit at Reykjavik, Iceland, in October 1986; were reunited in Washington in December 1987 to sign the Intermediate-Range and Shorter-Range Nuclear Forces (INF) Treaty; embraced in front of Lenin's Tomb at the Moscow Summit in June 1988; and met a final time in New York in December 1988.

The Reykjavik Summit was notable for its departures from the scripted agenda. President Reagan, eager for an attention-getting foreign policy feat prior to midterm congressional elections, agreed to a summit meeting without the usual lengthy preparations. The American delegation was stunned when Gorbachev proposed a 50 percent cut in intercontinental ballistic missiles (ICBMs) and their eventual elimination in return for U.S. abandonment of its missile shield, the Strategic Defense Initiative (SDI). Apparently convinced he was in a high-stakes poker game, Reagan offered to eliminate all American (and British and French) ICBMs within ten years if the Russians accepted deployment of SDI. This proposal confused Gorbachev, Reagan's aides, and, quite likely, the president himself. The Reykjavik summit broke up in disarray. Thereafter, summits have hewed closely to prearranged scripts.

The end of the Cold War and the disintegration of the Soviet Union brought neither the end of history nor the abolition of the summit conference as a favored tool in the American diplomatic and political arsenal. President George Bush met on six occasions with Gorbachev prior to the latter's transfer of power to Boris Yeltsin in December 1991, and he made numerous trips abroad.

ern era. He engaged in brokered summitry and also took part in conferences with Yeltsin (with whom he established warm relations), with the leaders of the European Union, and with Premier Zhu Rongji of the People's Republic of China. As well, between the spring of 1993 and the fall of 2000, Clinton made 133 visits to other nations, more than his predecessors Eisenhower, Kennedy, Johnson, and Nixon combined. Many of these trips were for political and psychological purposes, though Clinton also conducted presidential business. The itineraries and agendas of these visits were as carefully planned as were the summits Clinton attended. Both required enormous entourages. It has been estimated that more than 1,300 federal officials accompanied Clinton on his six-nation trip to Africa in 1998.

The technique of using the power and prestige of the president to bring adversaries to the bargaining table was used again by Clinton. Following a lengthy period of shuttle diplomacy by Secretary of State Warren Christopher, Clinton brought Israel's prime minister, Yitzhak Rabin, and the chairman of the Palestinian Liberation Organization, Yasir Arafat, to proclaim in a remarkable ceremony on the south lawn of the White House their commitment to mutual recognition, Palestinian self-rule, and a comprehensive peace settlement. Although Clinton did not personally oversee the tortuous negotiations that led to the Dayton Peace Accords in November 1995, the commitment of his prestige and the awesome power of the United States made Dayton yet another brokered summit. It may be that Clinton's greatly ballyhooed trips to Ireland—both Northern Ireland and the Republic—in December 1995 and September 1998, respectively, were intended to produce yet another brokered summit and public relations triumph. Unfortunately, Ireland's troubles were not so easily banished.

Although George W. Bush came into office as the least-traveled and perhaps least internationally minded of recent presidents, and waited some six months before taking part in his first summit (with the European Union leaders and Russian President Vladimir Putin in July 2001), Bush appeared to be prepared to conduct personal diplomacy much as did his predecessors.

BILL CLINTON AND GEORGE W. BUSH

President Bill Clinton proved to be the most enthusiastic exponent of personal diplomacy of the mod-

CONCLUSION

While the principal aims of the summit conference has changed little from the seventeenth to the twenty-first century, the environment in which summitry occurs has changed since the end of the Cold War. At present and for the foreseeable future, the "typical" summit conference, a bilateral meeting of national leaders, has been replaced by multilateral summits, reflecting the diverse circumstances and problems of an increasingly multipolar and interdependent world system.

BIBLIOGRAPHY

Ambrose, Stephen. *The Rise to Globalism: American Foreign Policy Since 1938.* 8th rev. ed. New York, 1997.

Ambrosius, Lloyd. *Wilsonian Statecraft: Theory and Practice of Liberal Internationalism During World War I.* Wilmington, Del., 1991.

Bailey, Thomas A. *Woodrow Wilson and the Lost Peace.* New York, 1944.

———. *Woodrow Wilson and the Great Betrayal.* New York, 1945.

Bischof, Gunter, and Saki Dockrill, eds. *Cold War Respite: The Geneva Summit of 1955.* Baton Rouge, La., 2000.

Brandon, Henry. *The Retreat of American Power.* Garden City, N.Y., 1973.

Burns, James MacGregor. *Roosevelt: The Soldier of Freedom.* New York, 1970.

Clemens, Diane S. *Yalta.* New York, 1970.

Dallek, Robert. *The American Style of Foreign Policy.* New York, 1983.

Eubank, Keith. *The Summit Conference, 1919–1960.* Norman, Okla., 1966.

Feis, Herbert. *Churchill, Roosevelt, Stalin.* Princeton, N.J., 1957.

Hankey, Maurice. *Diplomacy by Conference.* London, 1946.

Hoopes, Townsend. *The Devil and John Foster Dulles.* Boston, 1973.

Kemp, Arthur. "Summit Conferences During World War II as Instruments of American Diplomacy." In *Issues and Conflict: Studies in Twentieth Century American Diplomacy.* Edited by George L. Anderson. Lawrence, Kans., 1959.

Link, Arthur S. *Wilson.* 5 vols. Princeton, N.J., 1947–1965.

Mayer, Arno. *Politics and Diplomacy of Peacemaking.* New York, 1967.

Mee, Charles L., Jr. *Meeting at Potsdam.* New York and London, 1975.

Neustadt, Richard E. *Presidential Power.* New York, 1990.

Nicolson, Harold. *Peacemaking, 1919.* New York, 1965.

O'Connor, Raymond. *Surrender.* New York, 1973.

Parmet, Herbert S. *Eisenhower and the American Crusades.* New York, 1972.

Plischke, Elmer. "Recent State Visits to the United States—A Technique of Summit Diplomacy." *World Affairs Quarterly* 29 (1958).

———. *Summit Diplomacy: The Personal Diplomacy of the President of the United States.* College Park, Md., 1958.

Schlesinger, Arthur M., Jr. *The Imperial Presidency.* Boston, 1973.

U.S. Department of State. Supplement to *Foreign Relations of the United States: The Paris Peace Conference.* 13 vols. Washington, D.C., 1946–1952.

Walton, Richard J. *Cold War and Counterrevolution: The Foreign Policy of John F. Kennedy.* New York, 1972.

Walworth, Arthur. *Wilson and His Peacemakers.* New York, 1986.

Wilson, Theodore A. *The First Summit: Roosevelt and Churchill at Placentia Bay 1941.* Rev. ed. Lawrence, Kans., 1991.

See also AMBASSADORS, EXECUTIVE AGENTS, AND SPECIAL REPRESENTATIVES; THE MUNICH ANALOGY; PEACEMAKING; PRESIDENTIAL ADVISERS; PRESIDENTIAL POWER; PUBLIC OPINION; TREATIES.

SUPERPOWER DIPLOMACY

Vojtech Mastny

The concept of a superpower was a product of the Cold War and the nuclear age. Although the word appeared, according to Webster's dictionary, as early as 1922, its common usage only dates from the time when the adversarial relationship of the United States and the Soviet Union became defined by their possession of nuclear arsenals so formidable that the two nations were set apart from any others in the world. It came to be widely, though by no means universally, accepted that the very possession of these weapons, regardless of their actual use, made the two nations immensely more powerful than any other.

Superpower diplomacy is thus closely related to nuclear weapons. They gave the U.S.–Soviet diplomatic intercourse its distinct character. During the years when the United States and the Soviet Union were in superpower positions in relation to their allies and clients in different parts of the world, their respective relations with those countries were of a different order and are therefore usually not considered under the rubric of superpower diplomacy. These relationships nevertheless influenced the manner in which Washington and Moscow dealt with one another.

Superpower diplomacy was a product of particular historical circumstances, characterized by bipolarism—the domination of the international system by two exceptionally powerful states locked in an adversarial relationship. Historically, such circumstances were highly unusual. The age of the superpowers began in 1945 with the appearance of nuclear weapons and ended in 1991 with the disappearance of one of the superpowers, the Soviet Union. The subsequent survival of the United States as "the world's only superpower" evolved in a radically different international environment, where bilateralism had ceased to exist and the concept of superpower diplomacy therefore lost its original meaning.

Despite its uniqueness and limited life span, superpower diplomacy was important because it altered and distorted previously established diplomatic practices by making the conduct of diplomacy dependent, to an unaccustomed degree, upon a new kind of weaponry that carried with it the threat of universal annihilation. The dependence tended to impose oversimplification upon a profession traditionally known for its subtlety, sometimes raising questions about whether diplomacy may not have outlived its usefulness because of the limitations placed on it by the crudeness and excess of the new power it wielded. Although such predictions proved wrong, the overriding concern with the management of that power left indelible marks on diplomacy, making it difficult to adjust to an era in which nuclear weapons continued to exist but bipolarism no longer applied.

While the superpower status of the United States and the Soviet Union derived from what the two countries had in common, the understanding of their diplomatic interaction requires constant attention to the differences that distinguished them from each other. One was a pluralistic democracy with a government accountable to the people. The other was a one-party dictatorship ruled by a self-perpetuating oligarchy accountable only to itself. At the same time, both the United States and the Soviet Union defined themselves in different ways as outsiders to the traditional European system of power politics, which they regarded as alien to their respective values as well as detrimental to international order.

Twice in the twentieth century the United States attempted to reform the international system in accordance with its own, specifically American, model of a democratic federalism. It sought to ensure its primacy because of its superior economic power and presumably higher morality in an international system where the interests of all nations would be secured by generally accepted international institutions and procedures designed to mitigate and manage conflict.

Unlike the United States, the Soviet state in its early years sought to overthrow rather than reform what it regarded as an inherently destructive and ultimately doomed capitalist world order. Soviet leaders originally believed in a world revolution that would result in a community of states living in harmony because of their common dedication to Marxist principles, with the Soviet state as the first among equals. They hoped to conduct revolutionary diplomacy in conjunction with the management of congenial communist parties directed from Moscow.

Although both the United States and the Soviet Union had to adapt their utopian tenets to real life, the idealistic and ideological streaks never entirely disappeared from their foreign policies, making their diplomacy different from that of other countries, irrespective of their later superpower status. The United States, sobered by the rejection by its own Senate of the League of Nations designed during World War I by President Woodrow Wilson and the subsequent descent of Europe into another world war, subsequently attempted to build the United Nations on more realistic grounds, including a directorate of the main great powers. Once the concept of a directorate based on collaboration with the Soviet Union proved not realistic enough, American policymakers became more—though never entirely—receptive to European notions of balance of power based on the pursuit of national interest, as propagated by influential scholars of European origin such as Hans Morgenthau.

Under the dictatorship of Joseph Stalin, the Soviet Union likewise abandoned in practice its earlier revolutionary utopia in favor of a foreign policy that instead embraced many of the traditional goals of Russian imperialism. Under Stalin the Soviet Union became an opportunistic player in the international system, expanding its territory and sphere of influence first in collaboration with Nazi Germany, and, after Germany attacked it in World War II, in collaboration with the Western powers. To what extent Soviet foreign policy became traditional foreign policy despite the communist ideology of its practitioners became a tantalizing question for the United States once the Soviet Union emerged as its main rival and remains a contentious issue among historians and political scientists. The opening of former Soviet archives after the end of the Cold War has made more of them conclude that Marxist-Leninist ideological preconceptions continued to shape Soviet foreign policy in important ways until its

very end—not so much by determining its goals as by providing the conceptual framework through which policymakers viewed the outside world and interpreted the intentions and capabilities of their adversaries.

Accordingly, the Soviet Union was long reluctant to accept the notion that there were two superpowers, which implied commonality with its capitalist adversary as well as permanence of the hostile system presided over by the United States, with its superior resources. The notion is of Western origin and was always more popular with critics of the superpowers than with either of them. In any case, their superpower relationship had come into being before it was recognized and labeled as such, and neither of the two rivals was able to anticipate correctly what their future relationship would be like.

THE UNEXPECTED NEW WORLD, 1945–1947

The February 1945 Yalta conference between Stalin, President Franklin D. Roosevelt, and British Prime Minister Winston Churchill came to be regarded as the birthplace of superpower diplomacy. According to the Yalta myth, Stalin and Roosevelt, reluctantly assisted by Churchill, agreed to divide Europe into spheres of influence along the lines it would in fact be divided into three years later. In reality, no such agreement was concluded at the conference, whose main defect was instead the lack of any clear agreement about the potentially divisive effects of the respective visions of the postwar world. In its inattention to detail, its inability to distinguish the primary from the secondary issues, and its indulgence in wishful thinking, Yalta was characteristic of the excessively casual and highly personalized World War II coalition diplomacy—features that linked it with the later superpower diplomacy in style, if not in substance.

At issue in both the Soviet and the American visions of the postwar world was the choice between hegemony—domination by a single power—and condominium—predominance by several, not necessarily two, cooperating powers. Stalin's vision, now possible to reconstruct from Soviet archival documents, was that of a Europe in which the Soviet Union would have emerged, because of its overwhelming military victory, as the sole great power on the continent. He expected to achieve this hegemonic position by working with, rather than against, his American and British allies. But suspicious as he was of the motives of anyone he could not control, he sought to secure a particularly strong hold on the neighboring peoples of Eastern Europe, most of whom were traditionally hostile to Russia. Seeking absolute security, as dictators are predisposed to do, he could only achieve it at the cost of the absolute insecurity of those around him.

There has been a long-standing controversy about whether Stalin originally aimed at establishing communist regimes in Europe, as they were in fact later established under his auspices in its eastern part. No evidence of such a premeditated design has been found, although Stalin, as a communist, took it for granted that communism would eventually prevail in the world. In practical terms, at issue was the kind of control he considered necessary to satisfy his sweeping notion of security. In Eastern Europe it soon became evident that nothing short of the monopoly of power by the communist parties beholden to Moscow could ensure the attainment of Soviet security as Stalin understood it. This entailed the extension of the Stalinist system, whose record of arbitrary rule, disregard for human rights, and genocide justified apprehension about what Soviet hegemony meant.

The American vision of international order blended U.S. security interests more successfully with those of other nations. It was more innovative than Stalin's vision in that it did not rely on crude power: in the immediate aftermath of World War II, the United States reduced its formidable military machine much more drastically than the Soviet Union did. Americans were sufficiently confident in their economic power, democratic political system, and the international arrangements they had been instrumental in bringing about within the framework of the United Nations. U.S. hegemony, while liable to be resented as any hegemony would be, was incomparably more benign than the Soviet variety.

A school of American revisionist historians has challenged the traditional view, according to which Stalin's policies were primarily responsible for prompting the U.S.–Soviet rivalry that became known as the Cold War. Inspired by the writings of William Appleman Williams, the revisionists have regarded especially America's hegemonic economic diplomacy—the quest for an "open door" through which the United States would inevitably walk the tallest—as a prescription for conflict. Yet the Soviet Union, taking a Marxist

view, considered America's economic power to be resting on shaky foundations. Expecting the wartime boom to be followed by a crisis of overproduction, much on the order of the Great Depression, the Soviet Union expected to benefit from the capitalists' distress by being able to obtain U.S. economic assistance on its own terms.

Immediate post–World War II diplomacy had more in common with the traditional variety than with later superpower diplomacy. The July–August 1945 Potsdam conference of the Big Three—their first gathering after the victory in Europe and the last for another ten years—was about practical issues concerning treatment of the defeated Germany in anticipation of a later peace treaty. The London conference in September of that year inaugurated the Council of Foreign Ministers as what the three powers still believed would be their supreme coordinating body supervising the building of a new international order compatible with their respective interests. Although the incompatibility of those interests was becoming progressively evident, nothing yet pointed unequivocally to the emergence of a bipolar system dominated by the United States and the Soviet Union. For one thing, Great Britain still played an important role, often taking the lead over the United States in challenging the Soviet Union, and was for that reason regarded by Stalin as more dangerous a rival than the United States.

Despite their international ascendancy as a result of World War II, neither the United States nor the Soviet Union were superpowers in 1945. Later that year the United States exploded the first nuclear bomb, but it did not effectively link its atomic monopoly to diplomacy. According to Gar Alperovitz and other historians of U.S. foreign policy, the very possession of the superweapon gave Washington a powerful policy tool that could not fail to have a constraining effect on the policies of other countries, particularly the Soviet Union. Yet the United States showed an unwillingness to use the tool by proposing in June 1946 the Baruch Plan for the international control of atomic energy.

Nor did Stalin link nuclear weapons to diplomacy. Although he was prompted to accelerate the construction of the Soviet Union's own atomic bomb—the reason why the Soviet Union rejected the Baruch Plan—he notably failed to be constrained by the U.S. nuclear monopoly. As late as 1946 he was confident that he could secure Soviet primacy in Europe and pursue Soviet interests elsewhere in the world by besting the Western powers in the diplomatic game. The revealing secret exchanges between him and his foreign minister, Viacheslav M. Molotov, when the latter was attending the July–September 1946 Paris conference on peace treaties with Germany's former allies, show Stalin as being contemptuous of the Western statesmen's diplomatic skills as well as guts. The resulting peace treaties with Germany's former allies amounted to the reluctant recognition by the West of Soviet supremacy in Eastern Europe.

THE ONSET OF THE COLD WAR AND DECLINE OF DIPLOMACY, 1947–1953

Diplomacy failed to resolve disagreements among the occupation powers about the administration and future status of Germany. The disagreements reflected the conflict between the Soviet concept of a weak though undivided and not necessarily communist Germany, which would ensure its dependence on Moscow, and the U.S. concept of a Germany integrated in a unifying Europe, even at the cost of detaching the western-occupied part of the country from the Soviet occupation zone as a separate state. At the March 1947 Moscow conference of foreign ministers, Secretary of State George C. Marshall became convinced about the incompatibility of these respective approaches to the solution of the German question and the necessity of reviewing the overall U.S. policy toward the Soviet Union.

The result of the review was the adoption of the concept of containment, which remained, with different variations, the guiding principle of U.S. foreign policy until the Soviet Union's collapse ended the confrontation forty-four years later. Conceptualized by George F. Kennan, a historian, diplomat, and Russian expert who had served at the U.S. embassy in Moscow during the critical preceding years, containment was the most original, subtle, and successful foreign policy concept ever embraced by the United States. Anticipating long-term rivalry between the two future superpowers, Kennan grasped the fundamental systemic differences and conflicting interests that precluded their mutual accommodation, but concluded that America's superior political, economic, and moral assets could allow it to prevail without war until internal strains in the Soviet system brought about "either the break-up or the gradual mellowing of Soviet power." This is precisely what eventually happened.

Kennan believed that the Soviet Union posed a political rather than a military threat and was therefore critical of the later expansion of the U.S. military establishment as well as the application of containment to other nations on the questionable assumption that they were being manipulated from Moscow. In its original version, the containment doctrine assigned the primary role to diplomacy—including public diplomacy but not excluding covert action—while wielding enough military power to retain credibility. There had been successful U.S. attempts at using traditional diplomacy backed by force to prevent the expansion of Soviet power as an influence in peripheral areas, such as Iran and Turkey, as early as 1946. But the first example of containment in action motivated by Kennan's analysis was the Marshall Plan, announced by the secretary of state on 5 June 1947.

While the immediate goal of the plan was to provide extensive U.S. economic assistance to the European nations ravaged by the recent war, its larger purpose was to force a decision about the terms of the U.S.–Soviet rivalry. By offering assistance to any European state, including the Soviet Union, on conditions requiring openness, accountability, and cooperation among the recipients in pooling their resources—conditions incompatible with the system of imperial control Stalin was imposing on Eastern Europe—the United States shifted the decision onto him. He could either give up control by allowing the East Europeans to participate in the plan under American conditions or else reject it and let the Americans organize Western Europe under their auspices while he proceeded to organize Eastern Europe his own way. In either case the United States stood to win.

As the United States expected, the Soviet Union chose the partition of Europe, although the choice had not been predetermined in Stalin's mind. Scholars have discovered Soviet sources showing that he had hoped his negotiators could compel the Americans to give up their conditions and allow the Soviet Union to benefit from the Marshall Plan while preventing the consolidation of Western Europe—an illusion stemming from the dogmatic Soviet belief that U.S. capitalism was acting from a position of weakness because of its impending crisis. Once the illusion was exposed, the Soviet Union proceeded to tighten its hold on Eastern Europe by imposing full-fledged communist regimes—a policy that increased the West Europeans' willingness to rally behind U.S. leadership. The competition between the two nascent superpowers was henceforth determined by the contrast between what the Norwegian historian Geir Lundestad dubbed the American "empire by invitation" and the Soviet empire based on coercion.

The Soviet Union never developed a foreign policy concept comparable in intellectual subtlety and pragmatic utility to the U.S. concept of containment. Once the lines were drawn, its policy relied instead on what it considered an inevitable "general crisis of capitalism"—something beyond Soviet control that never came. The policy sought to precipitate the crisis by trying to foment instability in Western Europe and split it away from the United States, misjudging the extent to which West Europeans were ready to submit to American leadership as well as to overcome their differences in building new supranational structures. Although reputed for alleged realism and diplomatic skills, Stalin failed to achieve what mattered to him most. Having striven to ensure Soviet security as he understood it, he found himself in confrontation with the most powerful nation of the world, a situation he had neither wanted nor anticipated.

In 1949 two further developments prefigured the later superpower confrontation. The first was the militarization of the Cold War following the Berlin Blockade, in which Stalin vainly tried to dissuade the United States from proceeding with the proclamation of a separate West German state. By cutting overland supply lines to the western-controlled part of the city, Stalin ran the risk of a military clash should an attempt be made to force the blockade. Although the clash was avoided thanks to the West's ability to supply the city by air, the growing perception that the Soviet Union was not only a political but also a military threat persuaded the United States to support the establishment in April 1949 of the North Atlantic Treaty Organization (NATO) as its first peacetime military alliance. Created to reassure West Europeans about American support, the alliance was to become for the United States an essential military ingredient of superpower diplomacy.

The other crucial development was the successful testing of the first Soviet atomic bomb in August 1949, which ensured that the ingredient would be nuclear on both sides. Much as the end of the U.S. nuclear monopoly influenced perceptions of the balance of power, however, nuclear weapons did not yet critically influence the respective policies. They were particularly absent in the decision that brought U.S.–Soviet relations to a new level of hostility—the launching in June 1950 of the Korean War, initiated by the North Korean communists with Stalin's backing though without direct Soviet participation.

The Korean War further accelerated the decline of diplomacy as a casualty of the Cold War. After the negotiated end of the Berlin Blockade in May 1949, no important East-West negotiations took place; those that did occur, mainly within the framework of the United Nations, were notable for their futility. Once stalemated, the Korean War led in May 1951 to a conference of deputy foreign ministers at the Paris Palais Rose but it yielded no results. By 1952, Soviet-American diplomatic relations all but ceased to exist, as the relationship between the two countries deteriorated to little more than a mutual exchange of insults. The dawn of superpower diplomacy had to await Stalin's death, which came in March 1953.

THE ADVENT OF SUPERPOWER DIPLOMACY, 1953–1958

The aftermath of Stalin's death showed how difficult it was to establish a productive diplomatic relationship after years of intense hostility. There was a general feeling that the departure of the dictator, which coincided with the beginning of the Eisenhower administration, made negotiations both feasible and desirable. But neither side was ready for the kind of give and take that is the substance of diplomacy.

Soviet foreign policy, masterminded by Stalin's former aide Molotov, did not substantially depart from its previous strategy of driving wedges between the United States and Europe even though the strategy had been ineffective if not counterproductive. Churchill's efforts to reconvene another summit meeting foundered on both American and Soviet reluctance to address the many seemingly intractable issues that divided the two countries. The conference of foreign ministers that met in Berlin in January 1954 to address the German question failed to advance toward its resolution; significantly, their subsequent Geneva conference on Indochina, where U.S. and Soviet interests were less involved, proved more successful in achieving a political settlement there.

Secretary of State John Foster Dulles was readier than Molotov to draw new conclusions from the changing situation. But the conclusions he drew did not make him any more willing to engage the Soviet adversary in substantive negotiations. Dulles was particularly concerned about the growing Soviet nuclear arsenal and only wanted to negotiate after the United States had achieved a position of strength, by which he understood mainly military strength. He attached particular importance to equipping NATO with tactical nuclear weapons and ratifying the European Defense Community as NATO's subsidiary, through which West Germany could be rearmed.

A hallmark of U.S. superpower diplomacy was the critical importance it attached to the nuclear balance. Imputing to the Soviet Union a willingness to use or threaten to use nuclear weapons worked to its advantage by diverting attention from its weaknesses in other areas than military. Taking a narrowly military view in the assessment of the adversary limited U.S. options and made relations with America's allies more difficult. The European allies, while craving U.S. protection, no longer saw the Soviet threat in such stark terms as the Americans because of their position as the ultimate guarantors of Western security.

The different assessments of the Soviet threat led to the failure of the European Defense Community, regarded by Washington as the acid test of European willingness to stand up to the Soviet Union under U.S. leadership. During the debate that preceded the final rejection of the project in August 1954, Dulles in December 1953 threatened an "agonizing reappraisal" of U.S. foreign policy, implying a separate U.S.–Soviet arrangement over the heads of the Europeans and possibly at their expense. Yet a superpower deal did not materialize. An alternative way was found for making West Germany contribute to Western defense by admitting it into NATO.

The October 1954 Paris agreements, which reaffirmed U.S. commitment to the defense of Europe and provided for West Germany's subsequent admission into NATO, were a setback for the Soviet Union, to which its new leader, Nikita S. Khrushchev, responded by taking initiatives toward détente. According to the U.S. historian Marc Trachtenberg, the Soviet Union was ready for a European settlement whereby continued U.S. military presence on the continent would provide constraints on rising German power. But most other historians agree that the Soviet Union instead sought to weaken the American position in Europe. Rather than seeking a superpower deal, Khrushchev persistently if unsuccessfully pursued a plan for a European collective security

system from which the United States would be excluded, thus leaving the Soviet Union as dominant power on the continent.

The Geneva summit of July 1955 was the first since the onset of the Cold War and the last in which Great Britain and France participated as ostensibly equal partners together with the United States and the Soviet Union. But although Britain possessed nuclear weapons and France would soon acquire them, too, the two countries' potential was so far behind that of the superpowers that it did not translate into diplomatic clout at a time when the U.S.–Soviet nuclear standoff was becoming the key item on the international agenda. This was the result of technological rather than political developments, particularly the introduction into the superpower arsenals of hydrogen bombs, the destructive power of which was theoretically unlimited, and of intercontinental ballistic missiles capable of hitting with increasing precision any target on earth.

The unresolved question was whether what came to be known as the "balance of terror" enhanced stability by deterring each side from contemplating the use of the deadly weapons, or whether the incalculable balance made the U.S.–Soviet relationship more precarious by making it dependent on unpredictable changes in military technology, the effects of which could not be estimated with any certainty. Superpower relations remained tense as Khrushchev took advantage of the American preoccupation with military balance by pursuing a successful diplomatic offensive toward other Western nations as well as nonaligned countries of the Third World. The perception that the Soviet Union was gaining political ground thus kept delaying U.S. attainment of the position of strength that Dulles had made a precondition of negotiations with Moscow. And the Soviet Union awaited further weakening of the U.S. adversary before wanting to negotiate seriously.

Disarmament negotiations, conducted on a multilateral rather than bilateral basis within the framework of the United Nations, had made little progress as each of the superpowers made proposals known to be unacceptable to the other. The Soviet Union pleaded for "general and complete disarmament" at a time when the United States regarded the West's rearmament as being the priority. For its part, the United States insisted on controls of arms reductions so pervasive that, if implemented, they would have undermined the pillar of secrecy on which the closed Soviet society was resting.

A landmark in superpower relations was the launching in October 1957 of *Sputnik,* the first artificial Earth satellite, which showed that the Soviet Union was more advanced in the technology necessary for the delivery of nuclear weapons than had been generally believed. This demonstration of technological prowess encouraged Khrushchev to use his country's perceived nuclear might as an instrument of diplomacy. The calculation that the United States would be sufficiently impressed to consent to the settlement of the German question on Soviet terms underlay the demands he made that in November 1958 initiated the Berlin crisis—the first of the two major Cold War crises that tested the efficacy of the superpower diplomacy.

THE SUPERPOWER CRISES AND THEIR RESOLUTIONS, 1958–1963

Although the crisis over the status of West Berlin as an enclave within Soviet-controlled East Germany nominally involved all four powers responsible for Germany, it was in effect a crisis between the United States and the Soviet Union. The failed mission of British Prime Minister Harold Macmillan to Moscow in February–March 1959 to mediate between the superpowers was indicative of Britain's inability to be accepted by them as interlocutor. Only after the end of the Cold War did archival evidence come to light showing that the Berlin crisis was more dangerous than previously believed, and that its management by both superpowers left much to be desired.

In presenting the Western powers with demands for concessions amounting to the surrender of their positions in Berlin, Khrushchev acted on the assumption that the United States would not risk a military conflict that might escalate into nuclear war, but he did not entirely rule out that possibility either. When he met with President Dwight Eisenhower at Camp David in September 1959, he was given the wrong impression that the United States was willing to yield. This encouraged Khrushchev to subsequently moderate his demands, and when they were not met, resume pressure, staking his prestige on another meeting with the president. Yet just as the summit was about to take place in Paris in May 1960, following the shooting down over Soviet territory of the American U-2 spy plane that Eisenhower had been trying to cover up, the Soviet leader chose to humiliate the president and break up the talks that he had himself badly wanted.

The debut of superpower diplomacy was thus personal diplomacy at its worst—not because of the particular personalities involved, but because of the extent of discretion and improvisation it allowed the top leaders without adequate professional preparation. As a result, critical decisions were made that were excessively dependent on their personal beliefs and assessments of each other. The pattern continued during the disastrous June 1961 Vienna meeting between Khrushchev and Eisenhower's successor, John F. Kennedy, who, unlike Eisenhower, was ready to make substantive concessions to the Soviets in Berlin. Aware of this, Khrushchev again miscalculated by pressing too hard and leaving the new president with the impression that war might be inevitable. This in turn put Khrushchev into the position of having to decide whether he should make good on his threat to nullify the Western rights in Berlin by concluding a separate peace treaty with East Germany—as he led its leaders to believe he would do—or else back down. It is still not clear when and why he decided not to go ahead with the treaty. In any case, the building of the Berlin Wall in August 1961, which insulated the western part of the city from the surrounding communist territory, eventually defused the confrontation and provided a semblance of stability, without diplomacy having been substantially involved.

This did not prevent a far worse superpower crisis from developing in October 1962 over Cuba, after Khrushchev had surreptitiously tried to install nuclear-armed missiles on the island to protect its revolutionary regime from the perceived threat of an American invasion. At least the subsequent handling of the crisis, from which the allies and clients of both superpowers were notably excluded, showed that the superpowers were beginning to learn how to live with each other. On the one hand, the concentration of the decision-making power in Khrushchev and his docile Politburo and, on the other hand, the establishment of a special executive committee from which Kennedy prudently took and applied the advice, proved to be ways to avert a military showdown. Time and communication were of the essence, as were clarity of purpose and willingness to compromise while allowing the adversary to save face.

Even so, superpower diplomacy can only be credited for resolving a crisis that it had been responsible for creating in the first place. The management of the crisis bypassed established diplomatic channels, giving critical importance to persons whose primary responsibilities and expertise were elsewhere, such as the president's brother, Attorney General Robert F. Kennedy, and Georgi N. Bolshakov, a Soviet intelligence operative in Washington, who happened to have previously established a rapport. Diplomacy was thus made excessively dependent on chance.

Although the Cuban missile crisis has often been credited with establishing the "rules of the game" that allowed the superpowers to respect each other's interests while keeping their nuclear arsenals under control, the accomplishment was more apparent than real because of the absence of adequate institutional and procedural safeguards against capricious and arbitrary politics, particularly obvious on the Soviet side. The brush with disaster over Cuba prompted Washington and Moscow to establish in June 1963 the "hot line" connection—a technological communications gadget that was hailed at the time as a safeguard against another such emergency but which never played an important role in communication between the superpowers. More importantly, in the following month the two superpowers concluded the Limited Nuclear Test Ban Treaty—the first negotiated agreement between them that placed restrictions on the development of their nuclear arsenals.

Although the treaty has been rightly hailed in past years as a harbinger of détente, from a longer perspective it is more notable for its shortcomings. It banned nuclear tests above ground but not those under the ground, which both superpowers found it in their interest to continue to keep expanding their arsenals. Indeed, as late as 2000, the U.S. Senate voted down a treaty to ban all nuclear testing that had meanwhile been accepted by most other nations in the world. The 1963 agreement gave an air of permanence to the arms race by substituting the concept of disarmament with that of arms control. There were no more agreements for several years after the supreme practitioner of superpower diplomacy, Khrushchev, was forced out of office in October 1964.

ALLIANCES AND SUPERPOWER DOMINANCE, 1964–1968

The second half of the 1960s was a time of parallel crises for the two military alliances, NATO and the Warsaw Pact, in both of which superpower dominance was at issue. For the first time since the onset of the Cold War, the loosening of the Kremlin leadership in the aftermath of Khrushchev's ouster gave Soviet allies an opportunity to challenge the predominance of the Soviet superpower—as U.S. allies had always been able to do in regard to the U.S. superpower but had been more reluctant to do as long as the Soviet Union appeared threatening. Now the belief in the Soviet intention to attack Western Europe had all but disappeared, though not—after the Berlin and Cuban experiences—the fear that Europeans might still find themselves exposed to a devastating confrontation on their territories as a result of miscalculation or mismanagement of a crisis over which they would have no control.

The fear was all the more legitimate since the war plans of both alliances, elaborated under the impact of the Berlin crisis, envisaged extensive nuclear exchanges on European territory. In October 1963 the Romanian government secretly gave the United States assurances that in case of a military conflict between the superpowers, Romania would remain neutral—an act of flagrant disloyalty to the Soviet alliance. Poland had been preparing proposals for military disengagement between the two blocs, notably the Rapacki Plan for a nuclear-free zone in Central Europe, which, if implemented, would have restricted both U.S. and Soviet freedom of action in the area. Czechoslovakia, too, opposed the deployment of Soviet nuclear launchers on its territory.

U.S. leadership of NATO was challenged by French President Charles de Gaulle, who argued that the U.S. "nuclear umbrella" was no longer credible. In his opinion, shared by many Europeans, the United States would not risk the destruction of its cities by using its nuclear weapons to defend Europe against Soviet attack—an assessment retrospectively confirmed by the secretary of defense in the Kennedy and Johnson administrations, Robert S. McNamara. De Gaulle at first sought to replace superpower dominance by that of a larger consortium of powers, including France, which together would take the main responsibility for international security. When he did not succeed, in March 1966 he took France out of NATO's integrated command structure, though not out of the alliance itself, and proceeded to develop France's own small nuclear deterrent, which he believed sufficient to keep the Soviet Union and any other enemy at bay.

In 1962 the Kennedy administration proclaimed a "grand design" for interdependence that would heed the concerns of the European allies. But at the same time the administration pressed them to accept the new U.S. strategy of "flexible response," regarded by many of them as destabilizing and resolutely opposed by France. The strategy entailed widening military options in the event of war, including nuclear options, thus making the actual exercise of those options appear more likely. American ability to assert its superpower position in Europe was hampered by the deepening U.S. involvement in the Vietnam War, waged on the dubious and widely rejected assumption that fighting the Vietnamese communists was necessary to check the expansion of Soviet power.

The Johnson administration, though mired in the Vietnam War, managed the NATO crisis more deftly than the Kennedy administration had, helping the alliance overcome it once France's self-exclusion opened the door to its resolution. A compromise was found in the December 1967 Harmel Report, named after the Belgian foreign minister who prepared it, which set NATO the goals of both defense and détente—improvement of its military capabilities along with an effort to reduce the need to use them by improving relations with the Soviet enemy by diplomatic means. This was a new task for U.S. superpower diplomacy, invigorated by the reconfirmation of America's leading role in the alliance.

In 1966 the Soviet Union responded to Western overtures for détente and to the unrest within its own alliance by proposing to its members its reorganization for greater effectiveness. The difficult negotiations that followed were further slowed down by the communist reform movement in Czechoslovakia, which in August 1968 prompted a Soviet-led invasion of the country. The invasion reaffirmed the Soviet superpower prerogative to intervene militarily at will in any of the Warsaw Pact countries—the tenet of the "Brezhnev doctrine," named after the Soviet leader who succeeded Khrushchev. The suppression of the Czechoslovak heresy allowed the Soviet Union in 1969 to implement the reform of the alliance by introducing limited consultation with its members.

The reaffirmation of each superpower's primacy within its respective alliance facilitated their diplomatic rapprochement. Already, before the Czechoslovak intervention, the United States and the Soviet Union in July 1968 had succeeded in negotiating the conclusion of the Nonproliferation Treaty. This important agreement aimed at preventing further spread of nuclear weapons by committing countries that did not possess them to refrain from their acquisition in return for the promise by the existing nuclear powers to gradually reduce their nuclear potential and take measures for preventing its use. Precipitated by the recent development of China's nuclear capability, which both the United States and the Soviet Union found threatening, the treaty enshrined their own special status as superpowers—a fact that drew criticism but did not prevent most of the world's nations from signing the agreement. The treaty curbed the spread of nuclear weapons during the Cold War despite the superpowers' failure to live up to their promises to substantially reduce their arsenals, and in later years remained a substantial impediment to proliferation.

The restrained U.S. reaction to the advance of the Soviet troops into Czechoslovakia, reputedly characterized by President Lyndon B. Johnson as an "accident on the road to détente," showed how far the rapprochement between the United States and the Soviet Union had already advanced by the late 1960s. That rapprochement rested not on settlement of their differences but rather on the incipient perception of their military parity, defined primarily in terms of their nuclear capabilities and the notion that the military balance overshadowed the political imbalance. Accordingly, their common diplomatic goal consisted of perpetuating their superpower position while limiting the dangers posed by the continued growth of the nuclear arsenals upon which that position was based.

THE GOLDEN AGE OF SUPERPOWER DIPLOMACY, 1969–1975

For the United States, arms control dominated the superpower agenda. Washington regarded as its foremost priority an agreement that would limit the growth of strategic nuclear weapons, the destructive potential of which had reached a level that made them capable of wiping out human life on Earth. The Soviet Union, while agreeing in 1969 to the Strategic Arms Limitation Talks (SALT), was more prepared than the United States to assume that the doomsday weapons would never be used and therefore made an understanding on political issues a higher priority.

The Soviet campaign for a political settlement in Europe, initiated in 1969, took the form of the proposal for a security conference, including the United States and Canada, which would

THE HIGH POINT OF SUPERPOWER DIPLOMACY

On 29 May 1972, during President Richard M. Nixon's visit to Soviet party general secretary Leonid I. Brezhnev in Moscow, a U.S.–Soviet declaration of "basic principles" of mutual relations was adopted. Drafted by the Soviet Union and accepted by the United States without significant changes, the grandiloquent declaration papered over any of the conflicting interests that were at the heart of the superpower competition. Substituting appearance for substance, it was bound to bring disappointment. The following is a brief excerpt from the declaration.

> The USA and the USSR attach major importance to preventing the development of situations capable of causing a dangerous exacerbation of their relations. Therefore, they will do their utmost to avoid military confrontations and to prevent the outbreak of nuclear war. They will always exercise restraint in their mutual relations, and will be prepared to negotiate and settle differences by peaceful means. Discussions and negotiations on outstanding issues will be conducted in a spirit of reciprocity, mutual accommodation and mutual benefit.
>
> Both sides recognize that efforts to obtain unilateral advantage at the expense of the other, directly or indirectly, are inconsistent with these objectives. The prerequisites for maintaining and strengthening peaceful relations between the USA and the USSR are the recognition of the security interests of the Parties based on the principle of equality and the renunciation of the use or threat of force.

confirm the territorial, and by extension also political, status quo on the continent, thus certifying the position the Soviet Union had established there as a result of its victory in World War II. The proposal, addressed to the governments of all the countries concerned, gave impetus to multilateral diplomacy as a supplement to superpower diplomacy, though not a substitute for it. Europeans in both West and East welcomed it as an opportunity to increase their international weight, while the Soviet Union saw it as a way to gradually attain the supremacy in Europe that had eluded it at the end of World War II. This was to be achieved after the conclusion of a vaguely worded treaty on security and cooperation. Its fulfillment was to be reviewed and interpreted at periodic follow-up conferences that the Soviet Union could

expect to dominate, eventually acting as the arbiter of European security.

The United States, showing its greater concern with military matters, insisted on complementing the conference with negotiations that would address the asymmetry of the conventional forces in Europe favoring the Soviet Union. The United States was developing its bilateral relations with the Soviet Union with the goal of not only putting the arms race under control but also achieving a political understanding between the superpowers in terms of Realpolitik—a policy based on considerations of power and material interests rather than ethical considerations and ideals. The new trend was personified by Henry Kissinger, first the national security adviser and later secretary of state in the administration of President Richard M. Nixon.

Kissinger was the most influential of the foreign-born trio of America's most outspoken proponents of superpower diplomacy—the other two being President Jimmy Carter's national security adviser Zbigniew Brzezinski and President Bill Clinton's secretary of state Madeleine Albright. An admirer of the nineteenth-century European diplomacy that maintained peace and stability by reconciling conservative powers with post-revolutionary France, Kissinger developed a secretive and manipulative approach to foreign policy that enabled him to attain a degree of independence in its conduct that was rare in the American political system. He preferred to deal with the Soviet Union through the "back channel" he had established through the long-serving and congenial Soviet ambassador to Washington, Anatoly Dobrynin.

Kissinger's Soviet counterpart was the experienced and hard-driving foreign minister Andrei A. Gromyko, who was dedicated to the maintenance and further advancement of Soviet superpower status. He cogently described this status as meaning that there was no important issue in the world that could be decided without the Soviet Union anymore. Unlike his Stalinist predecessor, Molotov, Gromyko believed in the possibility of advancing Soviet power and influence amid low rather than high international tension, thus facilitating the growth of East-West détente.

Kissinger's greatest achievement concerned China rather than the Soviet Union. His secretive diplomacy was well suited to preparing the normalization of U.S. relations with China, which Washington had previously misjudged as being a greater threat to American interests than the

Soviet Union. By simultaneously improving relations with both the Soviet Union and China, a communist power hostile to the Soviet Union, the United States expanded the bilateral relationship with Moscow into a triangular relationship, which it was able to manipulate to its advantage. It did so better with China than with the Soviet Union, however.

Nixon's visit to Moscow in May 1972 resulted in a series of treaties that together represented the peak of achievement of superpower diplomacy. The United States and the Soviet Union initialed their first agreement limiting the growth of their strategic nuclear armaments (SALT I), agreed on precautions to prevent accidents arising from the movements of their naval and air forces, and concluded the Anti-Ballistic Missile Treaty (ABM), which banned for all time the deployment of missiles against nuclear attack.

Reflecting the concept of "mutual assured destruction," believed by U.S. theorists of deterrence as necessary for preventing the superpowers from attacking each other, the treaty incorporated the notion that the lack of defense against nuclear attack was the best protection against it. As such, it was an authentic product of the Cold War that tellingly reflected a bipolar international system dominated by superpowers unable to resolve their fundamental political differences. Once the Cold War ended and the bipolar system disappeared, the relevance of the treaty became doubtful, although it was still invoked at the beginning of the twenty-first century by both the opponents and the advocates of the U.S. plan for national missile defense (NMD).

The technical precision of the arms control measures adopted at the May 1972 summit contrasted with the ambiguity of the "basic principles" agreement, mistakenly hailed at the time as the framework that would allow the two superpowers to manage their relationship without generating unacceptable tension. The United States acknowledged the Soviet right to "equal security"—as if the reasons for the insecurity of the authoritarian Soviet system could possibly be the same as the reasons for the insecurity of a pluralistic Western democracy. Further, the two superpowers vowed not to seek advantage at the expense of each other—as if doing so were the cause rather than the effect of their competitive relationship. While Kissinger hoped to "enmesh" the Soviet Union in a growing web of relationships that would allow the United States to exercise a mitigating influence on its growing power,

the Soviet leaders regarded détente as an opportunity to enhance that power and influence without American interference.

The October 1973 Yom Kippur War—in which Moscow, in an attempt to deal a blow to the U.S. position in the Middle East, did not discourage its Arab clients from attacking Israel—revealed the different notions of détente while testing the efficacy of superpower diplomacy. The United States put in strategic nuclear forces at a high level of alert while the Soviet Union threatened to intervene in the war with its own forces. Yet since neither side wanted to go over the brink, preferring instead to curb its respective clients, the crisis passed, seemingly vindicating the efficacy of superpower diplomacy but shaking America's faith in détente.

Détente peaked in the conclusion of the August 1975 Helsinki agreement as a result of a new-style multilateral diplomacy defying the expectations of both superpowers. The Soviet Union, the architect of the Conference on Security and Cooperation in Europe (CSCE), in the end acquiesced in a treaty very different from the original Soviet concept in that the agreement embodied specific and detailed provisions for the protection of human rights as a matter of legitimate international concern. The Soviet Union signed the landmark treaty on the mistaken assumption that its paper provisions could not possibly gain political substance—an opinion shared by Kissinger, who, also mistakenly, regarded as more important Soviet consent to start negotiations on the "mutual and balanced" reductions of conventional forces (MBFR). The CSCE also encouraged the formation of nongovernmental organizations that challenged superpower diplomacy by the public advocacy of issues recently made relevant to foreign policy, such as human rights.

As a result of the unpopular Vietnam War and the scandals of the Nixon era, pressure increased for U.S. diplomacy to become more responsive to the public. While inevitable and potentially beneficial in a modern democracy, the pressure had the negative effect of increasing public and congressional expectations from the frequent superpower summits. Congenial to the authoritarian Soviet leaders, the summits were conducive to superficiality and improvisation. Rather than to finalize agreements previously negotiated and agreed upon, they often met without adequate preparation and yielded disappointing results.

By the mid-1970s, superpower diplomacy was thus challenged not only by the different notions of détente but also by alternative multilateral diplomacy as well as the pressure for more openness. At the same time, development of the nuclear arsenals, from which the superpowers derived their status, outpaced the political developments, making it more difficult for both the United States and the Soviet Union to apply their excessive stockpiles of weapons of mass destruction to any conceivable political purpose. Superpower diplomacy became increasingly divorced from political reality.

"COMPETITIVE DECADENCE," 1975–1980

The deterioration of superpower relations in the second half of the 1970s showed that nuclear balance was a precarious foundation for stable relations. There was a fundamental divergence of views about how the balance related to politics.

The United States tried to impress upon the Soviet Union the critical importance of strategic stability, with its corollary of political restraint by both superpowers. The Soviet Union, however, attached greater importance to what it called "military détente," understood as reductions of the strategic arsenals that would not alter the Soviet advantage in conventional forces, thus restricting political competition. Accordingly, only SALT negotiations were moving ahead while MBFR became stalled and CSCE proceeded in fits and starts.

The conduct of the superpowers was affected less by the development of military technologies, which evolved more and more independently of political developments than by their internal issues and their perceptions of those problems. By the end of the decade the terminal decline of the Soviet system had already begun, rooted in the inability of its command economy to ensure growth and the inability of its political system to accommodate the diversity of interests. On the American side the dispiriting legacy of the lost Vietnam War was magnified by the effects of its economic mismanagement amid spreading doubts about the merits of the American political system, leading to social unrest in the country and tensions with its allies.

The French political scientist Pierre Hassner characterized the resulting relationship between the superpowers as that of "competitive decadence," in which the issue for each was managing its mounting internal problems better than the other. The Soviet Union sought to use its military potential to offset its growing deficiencies in most other attributes of power. Its "arms diplomacy" consisted of both arms provision and outright military intervention by proxies in several countries of the Third World, where it managed to establish footholds, including Angola, Ethiopia, and Yemen. Such actions inevitably cast doubt on Soviet commitment to the principles of the 1972 agreement, causing alarm about Soviet intentions and harm to détente.

The initial U.S. response was equivocal. On the one hand, President Gerald Ford vowed publicly to erase the word "détente" from his vocabulary, implying that the United States no longer considered the Soviet Union a partner acting in good faith. On the other hand, the Ford administration proceeded with the strategic arms control negotiations to follow up SALT I with SALT II. Since Brezhnev, on the Soviet side, was personally committed to further reducing the growth of nuclear armaments as well, despite resistance by the Soviet military, the interim agreement signed in Vladivostok in November 1974 attested to the continued ability of superpower diplomacy to deliver results, at least in the limited area of arms control.

U.S.–Soviet relations took a turn for the worse after President Jimmy Carter took office. The new president sought to distance himself from what he regarded as an immoral and ineffective Nixon-Kissinger diplomacy, whose penchant for Realpolitik had not helped to prevent relations with the Soviet Union from deteriorating nor the specter of nuclear holocaust from persisting. Carter correctly anticipated the future in trying to deemphasize the importance of the Soviet Union within the larger global context and instead to emphasize the growing importance of the nonmilitary aspects of security, such as the safeguarding of human rights. But in trying to build what he wanted to be a satisfactory lasting relationship with the Soviet Union, his administration's diplomacy faltered.

In an attempt to improve on the Vladivostok agreement, Secretary of State Cyrus Vance surprised the Soviet Union by proposing arms reductions so radical that they amounted in Soviet eyes to repudiation by the United States of the more modest Vladivostok agreement on which Brezhnev had staked his prestige. Gromyko's peremptory rejection of the Vance proposals put the eventual approval of the SALT II Treaty by the U.S Senate in doubt. Moscow was further alarmed by the anti-Soviet reputation and rhetoric of the national security adviser, Brzezinski, whose influence in Washington increased after Vance's resignation. In September 1979, Washington raised an outcry about the presence of a Soviet "combat brigade" in Cuba, although the unit had been there for several years without arousing U.S. concern, thus adding to the impression of both hostility and incompetence.

The image of a U.S. administration that was talking loudly but carrying a small stick did little to discourage the Soviet Union from making the fateful decision to send troops to Afghanistan to intervene in the internal struggle there and put its protégés in power. This was the first instance of direct Soviet military intervention in a country outside its recognized sphere of influence, and adjacent to the Persian Gulf region that was vital to the West's security as its major supplier of oil. Thus, in U.S. eyes, the Soviet move amounted to a gratuitous challenge to mutual respect for each other's vital interests, a respect that had made superpower diplomacy possible.

The Afghanistan invasion sealed the fate of SALT II for the duration of the Cold War by destroying the chances of its approval by the U.S. Congress. The Carter administration increased U.S. defense spending and military preparedness. It pressed U.S. allies to reduce the many contacts with the Soviet bloc that had been the fruit of a decade of détente, adding tension to American-European relations that were already strained by Washington's insistence, abruptly reversed, on equipping NATO forces with controversial neutron radiation weapons, followed by abrupt reversal. The Carter administration ended its term in office in disgrace and humiliation as it proved helpless in trying to obtain the release of U.S. diplomats held hostage by the revolutionary regime in Iran.

Although the Soviet Union appeared to be better off in the superpower competition, the appearance was deceptive. It was being drawn deeper into the Afghanistan war, with diminishing prospects of victory. In 1980–1981 the rise of the opposition in Poland, spearheaded by the Solidarity labor movement, paralyzed the communist regime there, threatening the Soviet hold on the strategically crucial country. Attesting to the Kremlin's growing doubts about the political utility of its vast military power in dealing with its political problems, the Soviet leaders abstained from intervening in Poland by force, making the restoration of communist rule dependent on Pol-

ish generals. The imposition of martial law in the country outraged the United States, bringing superpower diplomacy to a standstill.

THE "SECOND COLD WAR," 1980–1985

President Ronald Reagan broke with the cardinal principle of superpower diplomacy by refusing to acknowledge the Soviet Union as a legitimate equal. He publicly referred to the Soviet Union as an "evil empire" and predicted that it would not last. Although these were fair estimates of the reality, they were hardly conducive to resuming businesslike relations between the two countries. Coupled with a massive U.S. armament program believed widely, if unjustly, to have been calculated to bankrupt the Soviet Union by forcing it into a ruinous arms race, the administration's posture evoked the specter of a "second Cold War," if not a real war.

In June 1982 the Soviet Union conducted an exercise simulating a several-hour, all-out nuclear strike against the United States. The president's "Star Wars" speech of March 1983, which announced the plan to abandon the strategy of deterrence based on mutual vulnerability in favor of defense behind an invulnerable missile shield, could be interpreted as being designed to make the United States capable of launching such an attack. Brezhnev's successor, Yuri Andropov, came to suspect the Reagan administration was preparing such an attack. In November 1983, the NATO exercise "Able Archer" practiced procedures for the release of nuclear missiles by using codes that made it indistinguishable from the real thing, prompting panic in Moscow, though no action to preempt the possible surprise.

The prudent Soviet behavior showed that fears of war precipitated by design or miscalculation were exaggerated but also that the susceptibility to uncontrollable accidents of the increasingly complex nuclear weaponry gave warranted concern. Yet by 1983 the only forum where the superpowers were negotiating with each other was the Geneva talks on intermediate-range nuclear forces (INF). The talks followed NATO's 1987 "dual track" decision, which provided for preparations, in the event of an attack by the Soviet Union, for the deployment of intermediate-range nuclear missiles in Western Europe to offset similar Soviet missiles that had already been deployed against it, unless an agreement had been reached to rectify the imbalance. So technical had the talks become that only experts understood the issues involved. The chief U.S. negotiator Paul Nitze and his Soviet counterpart, Iurii Kvitsinskii, nevertheless came to a tentative agreement during a "walk in the woods" outside Geneva. Yet the agreement was not approved by their superiors.

As long as the deployment of the "Euromissiles" intended to counter the Soviet intermediate-range missiles targeted on Western Europe remained uncertain because of the widespread opposition it faced there, neither superpower had the necessary incentive to compromise. As the crucial vote in the West German parliament was approaching, the Soviet Union increased pressure by threatening to walk out of the negotiations if the deployment were approved. And when it was approved in November 1983, the Soviet leaders had no choice but to make good on their word or else lose credibility.

The breakdown of the Geneva talks, which brought superpower diplomacy to the lowest point since Stalin's days, nevertheless heralded their more constructive later resumption. Rather than an aggressive design, the walkout reflected paralysis within the Kremlin leadership dating back to the last years of Brezhnev and continuing during the terms in office of his two infirm successors, Andropov and Konstantin Chernenko. Despite the presence and growing influence of the veteran diplomat Gromyko, the aging leadership was no longer willing and able to tackle the Soviet Union's mounting internal and external problems. Superpower diplomacy required strong leaders. In a tacit recognition of its own failure, the old guard in the Politburo in March 1985 selected as Chernenko's successor the Politburo's youngest member, Mikhail S. Gorbachev. With the Reagan line reconfirmed by his reelection to the presidency the year before, the stage was set for the last act of superpower diplomacy.

THE END OF THE SOVIET SUPERPOWER, 1985–1991

Gorbachev demonstrated his strength as well as courage by resuming the Geneva talks despite American failure to fulfill any of the conditions the Soviet Union had set for its returning to the negotiating table. By then he had gone farther than the U.S. administration in drawing conclusions from the futility of the arms race while remaining convinced of his ability to preserve the

Soviet Union as a superpower by ensuring its ascendancy through radical reforms of its political and economic system. Gorbachev understood that the West had reasons to fear the offensive Soviet military posture and acted to reassure it in order to break the spiral of the arms buildup.

As the Soviet Union began to set the pace of the Geneva negotiations by making unilateral concessions, the first meeting between Gorbachev and Reagan took place in Geneva in November 1985. The course of American policy at this critical juncture was in the hands of a president less attuned to the complexities of international politics, more beholden to an ideological view of the Soviet adversary, and less capable of sustained attention to the business of government than any U.S. president of the superpower era. Defying his own notion that the Soviet adversary was inherently untrustworthy, he intuitively decided that Gorbachev could be trusted—a decision that opened the door to the solution of problems previously regarded as insoluble and to the eventual termination of the Cold War.

The personal rapport established between the two leaders disrupted the pattern of superpower diplomacy. They both believed in the abolition of nuclear weapons—a convergence of views that foreshadowed the transformation of nuclear-based superpower diplomacy into a more normal kind. At the Reykjavik summit of October 1986, Reagan, not grasping the subtleties of deterrence, created confusion about whether he was willing to abolish all nuclear weapons or only some of them, thus putting in doubt the critical deterrent on which NATO had traditionally depended. Although the summit appeared to have failed, Gorbachev's readiness to give Reagan the benefit of the doubt allowed the Geneva talks to continue and bear fruit in the signing of the landmark treaty on intermediate-range nuclear forces (INF) in December 1987.

The treaty differed from previous arms agreements by providing for the complete elimination of a whole class of armaments, by reversing the arms race rather than merely slowing it down, and by introducing the kind of intrusive inspections that the Soviet Union had been consistently resisting to protect its secretive political system. By that time Gorbachev had already imposed upon the reluctant Soviet military a change of the country's strategic posture from offensive to defensive, precipitating the loosening and eventual disintegration of the Warsaw Pact. His unilateral reductions of Soviet conventional forces facilitated the negotiation of an agreement on deep reduction of conventional forces in Europe (CFE), previously regarded as all but impossible.

The CFE, which changed drastically the military landscape of Europe, had been negotiated between the two alliances rather than between the United States and the Soviet Union alone, thus signaling the demise of their superpower domination. In the last decisive stages of the Cold War, the nuclear balance that underlay that domination played a secondary role to the effects of the internal upheaval within the Soviet bloc, which led by the end of 1989 to the collapse of Soviet empire in Eastern Europe and, two years later, of the Soviet Union itself. Adaptation to these unexpected developments, which vindicated George F. Kennan's original design for containment, was a challenge comparable to that which the adoption of the policy of containment posed forty years earlier. This time the United States could at least rely on the expertise of a generation of academic specialists and career diplomats well versed in the workings of the Soviet system, such as ambassador Jack F. Matlock, Jr., in the sensitive Moscow post. In responding to the challenge, the administration of President George H. W. Bush, which inherited from its predecessor a dramatically improved U.S.–Soviet relationship, had a mixed record.

Even as the Soviet power was disintegrating, the Bush administration acted on the assumption that a reformed Soviet Union would remain America's superpower partner for the foreseeable future—an assumption confirmed at the December 1989 Bush-Gorbachev summit off Malta. The misjudgment led Washington to occasionally try to oppose the inevitable. When Romania threatened to descend into chaos amid the downfall of its dictator Nicolae Ceausescu, Washington sent signals that it would not mind Soviet intervention to restore order there, only to be rebuffed by Moscow. And when Ukraine showed a readiness to break away from the Soviet Union, Bush, on a visit to Kiev, publicly expressed U.S. displeasure.

Otherwise, however, in responding to the self-liberation of Central and Eastern Europe from Soviet domination, U.S. superpower diplomacy was at its best. It extended unqualified support to the postcommunist governments without trying to seek added advantage at Soviet expense—an attitude that facilitated the withdrawal of Soviet troops from the region and the emergence of Europe's new and safer security environment. The Bush administration wisely proceeded to unilaterally remove the tactical nuclear weapons that had been most prone to make Europe a nuclear battlefield, dismantle the intermediate-range missiles in accordance with the INF treaty, and begin to destroy, in collaboration with Moscow, the stockpile of strategic nuclear weapons as well. This was the most important legacy of superpower diplomacy for the post–Cold War era.

The United States was the first of the powers responsible for Germany to recognize the inevitability of its reunification and worked consistently toward that end together with the Soviet Union, once Gorbachev, too, had come to the same conclusion. Great Britain and France only reluctantly followed. The "two-and-four" agreement between the German states and the powers set the terms of the unification without antagonizing Moscow and ensured the integration of the potentially overwhelming German power into the European Community and NATO.

However, once the Soviet Union collapsed and a critically weakened Russia became its most important successor state, possessing the bulk of the Soviet nuclear arsenal, the United States continued to deal with the government of President Boris N. Yeltsin as if Russia still were a superpower. The likelihood of its irreversible descent to the ranks of secondary powers distorted America's priorities and its self-perception as the world's last remaining superpower.

THE UNITED STATES AS THE ONLY SUPERPOWER?

The self-image of the post–Cold War United States rested on the misconception that the disappearance of the Soviet Union left it the same kind of power it had wielded during the Cold War, when the possession of a vast nuclear arsenal was the measure of its special status in a bipolar international system. With the bipolar system gone, however, the U.S. nuclear potential became all but meaningless as a determinant of its status in the world. Instead, America's power in the new international system derived from its huge economic potential and unmatched cultural influence in addition to its military establishment, supported by defense spending that was greater than that of all other nations combined. America's new predominance thus was different from the superpower variety, as conveyed in the French-invented term "hyperpower," implying excess without clear purpose.

The legacy of the superpower era made it difficult for the United States to redefine its global role in the post–Cold War era and relate it to diplomacy. Americans also found it difficult to choose the proper ways of using their military power. On the one hand, they deployed it in some countries where their interests were not clearly involved. On the other hand, they placed self-imposed restrictions on its use by becoming beholden to the crippling concept of minimizing losses of their manpower and matériel and by insisting on the termination of their military involvements at a time of their choice.

Such restrictions made the involvements both controversial and less effective than suggested by America's military power. In the Gulf War of 1991 against Iraq—a conventional war against a regional aggressor—the United States showed a new sensitivity for multilateral diplomacy by being able to form a broad coalition in support of its intervention, but then abstained from trying to press for final victory, much as it had learned not to press the Soviet Union to the wall during their superpower competition. Similarly, it missed opportunities to prevent the descent of Yugoslavia into war by timely use of force sufficient to frustrate Serbian aggression. The Clinton administration, less attentive to foreign policy than most of its predecessors, suffered even more from belated and piecemeal deployment of military power, thus reducing America's ability to influence events. Its reluctance to commit itself militarily in the former Yugoslavia made the eventual American intervention in the Balkan wars more costly than it need have been. Secretary of State Madeleine Albright, misled by notions of deterrence dating from the superpower era, underrated Serb leader Slobodan Milosevic's aggressive intent, leading the United States and NATO to a war for which they were unprepared and only won at high political cost.

Looking back at the long rivalry with the Soviet Union, American officials tended to see rising security threats comparable to the old Soviet one. Some regarded Russia as one such potential threat despite the low probability of its recovery as a great power. Others viewed China as a future superpower because of its size and nuclear capability, regardless of its lack of an expansionist political culture and despite an extensive number of complementary interests between Americans and Chinese. Washington also came to regard otherwise minor "rogue states"—Libya, North Korea, Iran, Iraq—as potential threats on the order of the Soviet Union solely because of the conceivable acquisition of weapons of mass destruction by their dictatorial regimes.

In dealing with these real or imaginary threats, the United States showed the same predilection for regarding them as military rather than political problems that it had shown during its competition with the Soviet Union. In particular, the national missile defense (NMD) project, embraced tentatively by the Clinton administration and unconditionally by the George W. Bush administration, harked back to the Cold War days when the other superpower's inclination to attack unless deterred was taken for granted. The concept of NMD, which assumed that such an intent may develop in the future, was conducive to bringing about the very threat the project was intended to avert. Insufficient confidence in the susceptibility of such threats to diplomatic solutions divided the United States from its allies, thus undermining its leadership position among them.

Unilateralist tendencies threatened important accomplishments of American diplomacy after the end of the superpower rivalry. The United States took the lead in such achievements of multilateral diplomacy as the negotiation of the North American Free Trade Agreement, the establishment of the World Trade Organization, the provision of energy assistance to North Korea in return for the abandonment of its nuclear weapons program, and other international agreements recognizing the growing importance of dimensions of security other than military. As evidenced by the repudiation by the United States of the Kyoto Protocol to reverse global warming, of the International Criminal Court designed to deter crimes of genocide, and of the Comprehensive Nuclear Test Ban Treaty, those achievements proved liable to relapse to the obsolete superpower mentality. The United States had to recognize that, because of the increased relevance of economic and environmental as well as political constraints, the nation was in important ways less powerful than it had been as one of the two superpowers. America's transition from a superpower to the leading "normal" power marked the final demise of superpower diplomacy.

BIBLIOGRAPHY

Alperovitz, Gar. *Atomic Diplomacy: Hiroshima and Potsdam, the Use of the Atomic Bomb and the American Confrontation with Soviet Power.* New York, 1965. A passionate statement of what American diplomacy was not.

Bell, Coral. *Negotiation from Strength: A Study in the Politics of Power.* London, 1962. Enduring critique of the fallacies of power politics.

Beschloss, Michael R. *Mayday: Eisenhower, Khrushchev and the U-2 Affair.* Boston, 1986. A lively account of a major failure of superpower diplomacy by an able journalist-historian lent support by subsequently declassified documents.

Bischof, Günter, and Saki Dockrill, eds. *Cold War Respite: The Geneva Summit of 1955.* Baton Rouge, La., 2000. The first of the ambivalent Cold War summits thoughtfully analyzed by leading international historians.

Bozo, Frédéric. *Two Strategies for Europe: De Gaulle, the United States, and the Atlantic Alliance.* Lanham, Md., 2001. A perceptive French scholar does justice to the challenge to the U.S. superpower by the larger-than-life French president.

Brzezinski, Zbigniew. *Power and Principle: Memoirs of the National Security Adviser, 1977–1981.* Rev. ed. New York, 1985. The account by a respected academic specialist on the Soviet Union turned a controversial statesman in the Carter administration.

Dobrynin, Anatoly. *In Confidence: Moscow's Ambassador to America's Six Cold War Presidents (1962–1986).* New York, 1995. Self-promoting and conceited but well-informed memoir of the Soviet bureaucrat who served in Washington through the rise and fall of détente.

Freedman, Lawrence. *The Evolution of Nuclear Strategy.* New York, 1981. The classic sober and sobering account by Britain's leading expert.

———. *Kennedy's Wars: Berlin, Cuba, Laos, and Vietnam.* New York, 2000. On balance, Kennedy's accomplishments outweigh his deficiencies in this subtle assessment using up-to-date evidence.

Fursenko, Aleksandr, and Timothy Naftali. *"One Hell of a Gamble": Khrushchev, Castro, and Kennedy, 1958–1964.* New York, 1997. The first study based on extensive, if selective, Soviet documentation shows the web of misperceptions that made the Cuban missile crisis such a narrow escape from catastrophe.

Gaddis, John L. *Strategies of Containment: A Critical Appraisal of Postwar American National Security Policy.* New York, 1982. An indispensable examination of the crucial relationship between strategy and diplomacy.

———. *We Now Know: Rethinking Cold War History.* New York, 1997. Despite its title, a provisional, yet so far the most convincing assessment by the leading U.S. "postrevisionist" historian, benefiting from the wealth of new sources that surfaced after the end of the Cold War.

Garthoff, Raymond L. *Détente and Confrontation: American-Soviet Relations from Nixon to Reagan.* Washington, D.C., 1994. An experienced Washington analyst and staunch advocate of détente explores its course in painstaking detail.

Holloway, David. *The Soviet Union and the Arms Race.* New Haven, Conn., 1984. The standard account by a prominent U.S. academic expert.

Hutchings, Robert L. *American Diplomacy and the End of the Cold War: An Insider's Account of U.S. Policy in Europe, 1989–1992.* Washington, D.C., and Baltimore, 1997. A knowledgeable staff member of the National Security Council pays tribute to the management of the Soviet collapse by the Bush administration.

Kaplan, Lawrence S. *The Long Entanglement: NATO's First Fifty Years.* Westport, Conn., 1999. A spirited collection of essays by the dean of American NATO historians on the alliance that repeatedly complicated U.S. superpower diplomacy.

Kennan, George F. "The Sources of Soviet Conduct." *Foreign Affairs* 25 (1947): 566–582. The intellectual foundation of the policy of containment by its main architect.

Kissinger, Henry. *White House Years.* Boston, 1979. Self-serving but indispensable for understanding the achievements and limitations of America's foremost practitioner of superpower diplomacy.

Leffler, Melvyn P. *Preponderance of Power: National Security, the Truman Administration, and the Cold War.* Stanford, Calif., 1992. The most extensively documented critique of the U.S. policy, inclined to give the Soviet Union the benefit of the doubt.

Lundestad, Geir. *The American "Empire" and Other Studies of U.S. Foreign Policy in a Comparative Perspective.* Oxford, 1990. The concept of "empire by invitation," persuasively argued by a Norwegian historian.

Mastny, Vojtech. *The Cold War and Soviet Insecurity: The Stalin Years.* New York, 1996. New Soviet evidence on how Stalin's exaggerated notions of security challenged the United States without giving the Soviet Union the security he wanted.

Matlock, Jack F. *Autopsy of an Empire: The American Ambassador's Account of the Collapse of the Soviet Union.* New York, 1995. Memoir by the scholarly U.S. ambassador shows how U.S. policy facilitated the peaceful demise of the Soviet superpower.

May, Ernest R., and Philip D. Zelikow, eds. *The Kennedy Tapes: Inside the White House During the Cuban Missile Crisis.* Cambridge, Mass., 1997. Admirably interpreted record of the historic decision making that allowed the president to avert the Soviet threat he had inadvertently helped to precipitate.

Nye, Joseph S., Jr. *Bound to Lead: The Changing Nature of American Power.* New York, 1990. Harvard political scientist and former government official argues that, despite the changing nature of its power, the United States remains a superpower.

Pechatnov, Vladimir O. "'The Allies Are Pressing on You to Break Your Will': Foreign Policy Correspondence Between Stalin and Molotov and Other Politburo Members, September 1945–December 1946." *Cold War International History Project.* Working paper no. 25. Washington, D.C., 1999. Unique documentary material on highest-level Soviet decision making, interpreted by an able Russian historian.

Trachtenberg, Marc. *A Constructed Peace: The Making of the European Settlement, 1945–1963.* Princeton, N.J., 1999. An ambitious and subtle, yet often ambiguous, history of the superpower relations, giving due account to America's European allies though not its Soviet adversary.

Williams, William Appleman. *The Tragedy of American Diplomacy.* 2d rev. and enlarged ed. New York, 1972. The bible of the revisionist critics holding the United States responsible for provoking the Cold War.

See also ARMS CONTROL AND DISARMAMENT; BALANCE OF POWER; COLD WAR EVOLUTION AND INTERPRETATIONS; COLD WAR ORIGINS; COLD WAR TERMINATION; CONTAINMENT; DETERRENCE; INTERNATIONALISM; NUCLEAR STRATEGY AND DIPLOMACY; POST–COLD WAR POLICY; POWER POLITICS.

TARIFF POLICY

★ ★ ★ ★

Thomas W. Zeiler

The tariff has been a central issue throughout American history. Its importance evolved over the decades, involving politics, economics, diplomacy, and ideology. Long a source of national revenue, the tariff (or duty or customs)—a tax levied on goods imported into the United States—was critical to the domestic economy and at the center of debates over government intervention in the marketplace. Tariff policy was also embedded in the diplomacy of the United States from its birth. From independence to globalization, tariff policy indicated the direction of U.S. foreign policy toward a particular nation or bloc of countries. It could be used as a defensive tool, a coercive weapon, or as a facilitator of cooperation and unity.

Because one of the top concerns of the United States has been the preservation and expansion of commerce, debates over the nature and uses of tariff policy were considerations in economic diplomacy, which itself undergirded political, military, and ideological aspects of American foreign affairs. Yet a constant theme underlay tariff policy, whatever its target. The United States always pushed for trade liberalization, a tariff policy designed to lower duty rates moderately while protecting certain producers (as opposed to free trade, which aimed to remove all barriers to trade). This was carried out on behalf of the country's economic and political self-interests, but increasingly, through the decades, as a means to instill in the world America's capitalist, open-door ideology as well as to enhance global stability. Tariff policy served diplomacy.

It is evident that the use of tariff policy changed during the course of American history. Until the Civil War, tariffs defended the United States from European imperialism and protected infant industries. After 1865 until World War I, a transition occurred in which policymakers tied the tariff closer to expansionist, big-power diplomacy, although a protectionist Congress restrained these efforts. During the interwar period, the more assertive brand of protectionism had its last gasp, as the Great Depression brought attempts at freer trade to a halt. During World War II and the Cold War, the United States became the global leader of trade liberalization. Although protectionism did not disappear, a freer trade policy united the Western alliance against communism. Successive administrations promoted low tariffs to boost the prosperity, and hence political stability and loyalty, of allies. By the 1970s, tariff policy had dwindled in importance as duties themselves fell to negligible levels and nontariff barriers became more significant. Over the course of U.S. history, therefore, the role of tariff policy in the diplomatic arena progressively changed from being a tool of national survival to one of international integration.

TRADE INDEPENDENCE

Economic survival lay at the heart of America's earliest diplomatic initiatives, and thus the tariff, as an element of commercial policy, played a major role in the efforts of the Founders to build the nation and protect it from external aggressors. The country's founding coincided with the era of mercantilism, in which trade was subject to oftentimes irrational discrimination from abroad that threatened to choke off America's lifeblood. The new nation depended on exports and imports, so the Founders pushed for fair and equal access to markets overseas out of economic desperation as well as the desire for political independence. They were, in essence, trade liberalizers out of necessity (although they also promulgated a vision of a world of open and equitable commerce). Tariff policy was placed in the hands of Congress, not only to ensure an equitable system of taxation but as a means of uniting the disparate regions of the former thirteen colonies into a large and viable free-trade area with power to promote American foreign policy aims. The Constitution established a uniform, enforceable system of import duties (along with shipping rules and foreign treaties) that regulated the economies of the states into a national whole. This combination of a common external tariff with free trade among the states prevented each state from engaging in separate economic diplomacy with Europe. The country spoke with one voice in negotiations. Access to this tariff-free area was a card to be played in negotiations with the Europeans and, in particular, Great Britain.

Tariff policy, therefore, helped to build the economic infrastructure of the new nation while America engaged in great power diplomacy. The United States designed its customs policy with protection in mind; thus tariffs and protectionism became synonymous from the opening of the first Congress in 1789. Officials imposed duties mainly for revenue purposes but also to coax foreign nations to ease restrictions on U.S. shipping and trade. Thomas Jefferson, James Madison, and other foes of Britain had earlier proposed a schedule of additional duties on goods imported from those nations, namely England, that had no commercial treaty with the United States. Fearing retaliation, President George Washington sought a diplomatic solution with Britain, which made concessions and thereby confirmed to Jefferson that tariff policy could ensure America would not be pushed around by the Europeans.

The Tariff of 1789 represented America's first tariff legislation, designed by Alexander Hamilton primarily to raise revenue by setting up the bureaucratic machinery for administering duties. But it also attempted to undercut European commercial monopolies and expand overseas markets by insisting on equal treatment for nations that accorded U.S. goods the same nondiscriminatory access. As matters stood, nations without commercial treaties with the United States (Britain) stood on an equal footing with treaty powers (France). Federalists sought to stave off Jeffersonian trade retaliation policies that might jeopardize American security.

The effort at gaining reciprocal lowering of foreign restrictions in return for decreased U.S. protectionism did not work well during the succeeding wartime period in Europe; the United States found the threat of higher tariffs useless in protecting its neutral shipping from seizure on the seas. The nation was just too reliant on tariff revenue. To be sure, as the War of 1812 loomed, the Jefferson administration cut off trade with the

British and French but, recognizing U.S. dependence on customs duties, left commerce open with the rest of the world.

DEVELOPMENT AND DISCRIMINATION

At home, tariffs paid for the servicing of the public debt and the costs of defense and stimulated prosperity for farmers, merchants, and shipowners. Customs receipts multiplied five times during the 1790s. Imports for domestic consumption more than doubled, while the home market, protected by duties, experienced sizable gains from domestic exports. Some of the funds helped build a merchant marine independent from British shipping that boosted trade. Tariff policy of the late eighteenth century thus fueled economic prosperity, which, in turn, stimulated new settlements by a burgeoning population. Jefferson went to war to protect the rights of neutral shipping but also to retaliate against the embargo policies of Britain against U.S. merchants. The failed attempt convinced American diplomats that insulation from foreign conflict required building a domestic base of manufacturing through high-tariff protectionism. Tariff policy, in short, had evolved into an essential tool in American development and national security.

After the War of 1812 and the end of the Napoleonic wars, the protectionist approach to tariff policy dominated U.S. diplomacy; American leaders, on a nonpartisan basis, were convinced that without international peace and general commercial reciprocity, free trade was impossible. Thus, the Tariff of 1816 increased duties in order to pay for the wartime debt but also to promote the nascent production of textiles and iron. Protectionism of infant industries became standard practice. This was the thinking behind Henry Clay's American System. The United States would become Americanized, and less subject to the policy of the British Crown, by a tariff that developed the U.S. economy while it deemphasized diplomatic cooperation. This did not mean that overseas expansion into old and new markets would halt, but it did institutionalize a policy of higher tariffs.

The remarkable expansion of the United States before the Civil War was an outgrowth of this internally oriented approach, but it also necessitated an insistence on commercial reciprocity, or a mutual lowering of national tariff barriers. That is, America would lower its tariff on certain imports in return for a reduced rate abroad. The stimulation given to the U.S. economy by exports to industrializing Britain of cotton, grain, and other raw materials, and the simultaneous massive inflow of British manufactures, maintained the policy of seeking trade liberalization abroad in return for lower American duties. Although the United States was determined to be politically isolationist in regard to international affairs, its leaders also pressed onward with the mission to break down empires, liberalize the global system, and civilize underdeveloped areas of the world. Between 1820 and 1860, moreover, dependence on British trade (and investment) made American trade liberalization an imperative. Tariff policy served this multifaceted mission.

U.S. merchants wished to end the cycle of American-European retaliation that had emerged from 1789 to 1815. Mutual discrimination had led to a system of countervailing duties by each side. The Americans suffered most because their cargoes were bulky, while European ships entered U.S. ports and reexported to their colonies with compact cargoes of finished goods. Faced with additional maritime restrictions by the 1820s, and a European policy of easing mercantilist regulations in intercolonial commerce through reciprocal accords, American officials wielded tariff policy once again in self-defense. The United States had no colonies and thus could not make similar deals. Left only with a policy of insisting on completely unrestricted free trade, the Americans linked a diplomatic stance of anticolonialism to a reciprocal tariff policy.

They failed in their objectives. While Europeans gradually abolished countervailing duties in return for the termination of U.S. discriminatory tariffs, American merchants still faced commercial monopolies in the European colonies. In the British West Indies, for instance, the United States's tariff reciprocity policy capitulated to the British principle of imperial preference. The other European powers, including Russia, extended such discriminatory tariff networks into their colonies. Meanwhile, American imperialists who sought similar preferential arrangements in U.S.-dominated territories in the Pacific and Latin America were rebuffed by anticolonial and latent trade liberalization sentiment at home. America sought open doors abroad but tariff policy, once again, accomplished little in this regard.

Commercial liberalization, always a hallmark of American diplomacy, drove U.S. tariff policy before the Civil War, but not for the entire country. Therein lay the linkage of tariff policy to sectionalism and the Civil War. At home, manufacturers struggled with British competition, while on the seas and in foreign ports merchants experienced French and British mercantilism and colonial restrictions. Western farmers found themselves excluded by tariffs in Europe; southern planters faced higher taxes abroad on their cotton. They blamed foreign producers and their governments for the 1819 panic and subsequent depression. Britain closed off the West Indies to U.S. vessels, and France imposed protective tariffs. American merchants demanded that the government negotiate reciprocity treaties to open foreign markets, or seek retaliation. Secretary of State and then President John Quincy Adams took up this cause, but he faced determined resistance both inside the country and out.

LIBERALIZATION OR PROTECTIONISM?

American manufacturers and westerners, convinced of Britain's intention to destroy the growing (though suffering) U.S. economy, pursued the nationalistic American System, designed to provide Americans with independent control over their economy. High-tariff protectionism, the antithesis of Adams's reciprocal tariff policy, would build the American System. Economic defense drove this conception of tariff policy, but advocates also argued that it would achieve the same goal as that pursued by the trade liberalizers. Protectionism would catalyze the production of raw materials at home while promoting increased surplus of manufactured goods for export. U.S. producers and labor would be the beneficiaries. European powers, prevented from further monopolizing the U.S. and Latin American markets, would be the losers. A high-tariff policy would result in economic independence for the United States, whose diplomats could then use the leverage of their closed market to pry open European colonies and markets. Clay believed tariff mercantilism would benefit the American economy, and thus serve as a weapon in diplomacy that could bring greater national security and even lead to U.S. imperial expansion. Of course, such a tariff policy was anathema to merchants, southerners, and others concerned about American diplomacy. The former noted that expansion into Latin America could never compensate for Britain's likely retaliation against U.S. exports. In addition, the revolutions then erupting across Latin America meant that the region would not be a reliable buyer of American products. And angering Spain by supporting the rebels might hurt U.S. trade with Cuba, to the benefit of other European powers. Southerners argued that protectionism would prompt Britain to turn to Latin America and away from the United States, thereby depleting the latter of manufactures that were traded for cotton. Latin America would become Britain's economic colony. Beyond the favoritism that high tariffs gave to northern manufacturers over western and southern farmers, low-tariff advocates warned that U.S. prosperity and expansion were at stake.

This debate led to considerations of tariff policy and diplomacy. President James Monroe supported revolutionaries in Latin America, but he also worried that Europeans would intervene to rescue their regional compatriot, Spain, against the forces of republicanism. He sought caution. Meanwhile, though siding with the northern merchants in their quest for profits, John Quincy Adams pushed for trade liberalization mostly on the principles of the open door and competition in global markets. He was determined to destroy European colonialism and impose an ideology of American-led trade liberalization that would boost U.S. commerce. He feared that without this course, not only would the United States continue to suffer deprivation from foreign mercantilism but that Latin American rebels would sign agreements for special trade privileges with the Europeans. Thus, the Monroe Doctrine of 1823, based on commercial diplomacy and drawing support from both liberal traders and protectionists, warned Europe not to extend its "system" to the Western Hemisphere.

Another significant consensus was reached when John Quincy Adams became president in 1825, for by then he and Clay had accepted the basic foundations of each other's approaches. Adams committed to the American System and lived with Clay's protective tariff of 1824, which raised rates from the 1816 levels. Even liberal traders supported the notion of incidental protection for industry. For his part, Clay, the new secretary of state, attended to commercial reciprocity, even though he was skeptical that pleasing foreigners would lessen their protectionism. He negotiated a trade treaty with new Central American republics that served as a model of tariff liberalization. The tariff policy consensus was also served by the political alignments over the tariff of 1824, in which Westerners joined with divided

northerners to back protectionism, but this result turned out to be temporary.

The culmination of the protectionist campaign was the so-called Tariff of Abominations of 1828, which enacted the highest tariffs in U.S. history. This law emerged after the celebrated debates between Clay and New England Representative Daniel Webster, who called the American System destructive to international commerce. Webster noted, for instance, the striking development of England's gradual phasing out of trade restrictions. He lost the day in 1828, yet the revision of 1833 reduced protectionism. A depression three years later led to the return to power of the Whigs and to a higher tariff in 1842. The West had turned to local needs, however, and flipped to the liberal trade side. Indeed, until the Civil War, tariffs slowly fell, although they remained high relative to the pre-Napoleonic period.

Regardless of the tariff, or tariff policy, scholars generally accept that neither tariffs nor the effort to forge commercial treaties with Latin America had much effect on U.S. growth, overseas expansion, or trade with the Europeans from 1820 to the Civil War. This conclusion satisfies scholars who support freer trade. They conclude that the high-tariff era came at an opportune time when American diplomacy focused more on continental rather than overseas expansion, and thus protectionism did not excite foreign concerns. But backers of the protectionist cause also are satisfied, for they argue that a protective tariff did not impede the nation's growth. Rather, it might have aided that growth.

The way of thinking that forged the American System faded away, with low-tariff Democrats asserting that the tariff should be for revenue only, and not for protection of industries. By the mid-1850s, the Democrats declared themselves in favor of "progressive" liberal trade the world over. They cut duties in 1857 and continued to negotiate reciprocity treaties with other nations. In 1854, the United States and Canada agreed to free trade in certain goods (although Congress abrogated the pact because it was not reciprocal). Canada gained from cuts in raw materials but raised its tariffs on U.S. manufactured goods. The expansionists also forged accords with China (1844) and Japan (1854), although these were one-sided arrangements that privileged American exports in those markets. These treaties represented the continued interest in reciprocity in tariff policy. But it was growing sectionalism, not the impact of tariff policies, that had the greatest bearing on American diplomacy. Thus, trade liberalism—a pursuit of freer trade tempered by protectionism—remained the general approach in tariff policy.

GOLDEN AGE OF TRADE

Foreign trade in manufactures yoked U.S. diplomacy and economics together after the Civil War. This was a period of tremendous economic growth in the country, and in U.S. and European expansion overseas. American production of industrial goods gradually replaced raw materials in significance as exports, and imports of manufactures slowly declined. This pattern, as the United States moved into markets controlled by Britain and other commercial powers by the 1890s, lent tariff policy a new and important dimension. The country's dynamic domestic economy, combined with its emerging rapprochement with Great Britain and increasing reach abroad, transformed tariff policy into a diplomatic tool geared toward enhancing American competition. Before this time, the aim of tariff policy was to defend U.S. interests through reciprocity treaties. After the sectional conflict, tariff policy was an indicator of American economic and political muscle that projected the nation's power abroad, although it still remained enmeshed in domestic politics.

From the 1870s onward, more farmers and manufacturers had a stake in overseas trade than ever before, and more producers were devastated by recurrent bank panics and depressions. These caused gluts on domestic markets and thus dropped prices repeatedly throughout the Gilded Age. Producers pushed the government to expand U.S. foreign trade with appropriate trade policies. Historians, led by Marxist scholars, have emphasized the "glut theory" as the driving force behind tariff diplomacy of this time. They argue that policymakers sought to unload surpluses at home on world markets by creating an informal empire of commerce and investment throughout Latin America and into the Pacific and Asia. In this view, tariffs were part of a foreign economic policy that served the purposes of American business, which sought to dominate economies at home and abroad. Opponents of such economic determinism point out that U.S. business support for a lower tariff was not consistent or uniform. Some manufacturers sought exports as their salvation to overproduction but most focused on the home market. It is more evident that the executive branch managers of diplomacy saw great advantages to a tariff policy based on trade liberalization, and so acted accordingly to make this policy amenable to America's emerging foreign interests.

The debate over the tariff did not cease, by any means. Tariffs began to rise as early as 1861, as the southern coalition exited Congress, leaving the Republican Party, long a supporter of protectionism, in control of the presidency and at least one house of Congress for most of the period until 1913. In addition, powerful northern manufacturers demanded protection from imports. Farmers in particular campaigned against high duties, which forced them to buy in a pricey domestic market but sell in an unprotected one. By the 1890s, the Populists had taken up the cause of trade liberalization, focusing their wrath on the tariff as a punitive instrument to farmers and labor. But protectionist views were politically appealing. In addition, the tariff was a highly complex issue, buffeted by many interest groups, each seeking a slight revision in rates or valuation methods to gain an edge in cutthroat competition in the various fields over their equivalents abroad.

The low-tariff advocates in the business and diplomatic community tried to bypass the entrenched interests in Congress by taking up the cause of a tariff policy fashioned to bolster America's international power. Liberal traders lobbied for tariff reform (lower customs rates) as part of a package of foreign policy initiatives, although they just as strongly appealed on economic grounds by denouncing protectionist monopolies that operated behind a wall of tariffs while workers and farmers were exposed to free-trade winds. These liberal traders included in their calculations for lower customs duties the expansion of overseas commerce, the construction of U.S.-dominated transportation systems (with priority given to building a trans-isthmian canal through Central America), and a bigger, updated, and stronger navy. Liberal trade advocates, including southern legislators, diplomats, and presidents, welcomed British commercial prowess as confirmation that freer trade brought riches and diplomatic leverage. A rising power like the United States, they argued, should follow the British lead in liberalizing tariff restrictions. Richard Cobden, Britain's chief opponent of the protectionist Corn Laws, had successfully crusaded for a free-trade strategy on the notion that increased commerce would boost prosperity and peace. American liberal traders agreed. Besides, a protectionist tariff policy would merely provoke retaliation from Europe. Such a response would not only lead to political and even military conflict abroad, but it would hurt American producers.

In what became the traditional State Department approach, bureaucrats in the diplomatic branch of the government, such as Worthington C. Ford of the Bureau of Statistics, promoted the idea that a liberal tariff policy would help Americans export production surpluses by encouraging Europeans to treat U.S. commerce on a reciprocal basis. The State Department no doubt suffered from the passivity of presidents of this time; Congress was the dominant branch, with the result that tariff policy remained pointed in a protectionist direction. Still, trade expansion—and thus tariff liberalization—held sway over the State Department, the agency responsible for negotiating international tariff treaties. Thus, duties, although of secondary interest to Secretary of State William Seward, nonetheless played a role in his ambition for territorial annexation across the Pacific, for he stressed that political expansion succeeded trade expansion. Tariff reciprocity accords promoted the latter. James G. Blaine attempted in 1881 to combat Britain's dominant position in major trade items in the hemisphere by creating a hemispheric customs union on the model of the German Zollverein, but the Latin Americans rejected him in 1889 during his service as secretary of state. He turned instead to reciprocity treaties to promote commerce. Later secretaries of state advocated trade growth abroad; most adopted reciprocity as the best means to accomplish this end.

TARIFF RECIPROCITY

Reciprocity treaties became the cause célèbre for the liberal traders. Between 1860 and 1898, nearly a dozen reciprocity treaties or other types of executive agreements were in effect. These bilateral accords, negotiated between the United States and another nation, usually took the form of modest agreements to reduce or eliminate duties on certain goods. The goal was to promote more trade. The reciprocity treaties of this era covered more than one-third of U.S. imports. But, unlike the agreements reached with Europeans in the early national period, these reciprocity treaties were forged with the Western Hemisphere and Pacific regions. Canada was the first target. The Elgin-Marcy Reciprocity Treaty, which lasted until 1865, made the Canadians dependent on U.S. markets. Ottawa thus pressed for tariff reciprocity thereafter, which itself gave way to advocacy by the 1870s of a commercial union that would eliminate border customhouses. The planned free-trade area gained much backing but died in 1890, as American protectionists jacked duties under the McKinley Tariff and nationalists on both sides belittled the idea as a danger to sovereignty. The North American Free Trade Agreement (NAFTA) realized the dream one hundred years later.

Wary of European tariff wars, the United States turned elsewhere for reciprocal trade accords. The second reciprocity treaty was forged with Hawaii, beginning in 1878. Domestic sugar producers protested, but they could not overcome the much more powerful support for the treaty from industrial sugar refiners, which gained immeasurably from the sudden increase in sugar production, American land-ownership, and island trade with the United States. Once renewed in 1887, the treaty's effect of tying Hawaii to the United States led to discussion of a coaling station for American warships near Honolulu, a port created in 1898 and named Pearl Harbor. Annexation attempts also resulted from the reciprocity treaty, which so stimulated the American-run Hawaiian economy that emboldened U.S. businessmen and landowners entered the imperial game by overthrowing the queen of the islands in 1893. This caused a diplomatic stir and such disgust at home that the Cleveland administration withdrew an annexation treaty from Congress. (Territorial annexation of Hawaii was finally achieved in 1898, marking the end of the reciprocity treaty.)

In Latin America, tariff agreements did not endure, or failed to be ratified by Congress, because of lobbying from U.S. protectionists. The influence of the U.S. domestic wool lobby hindered deals with South American countries, for which wool was a chief export. Mexico and a few nations in the Caribbean did enjoy reciprocity treaties, because their goods did not compete with American-made products. But Congress rejected most of the treaties reached by Secretary of State Frederick T. Frelinghuysen in the early 1880s as threats to the American domestic economy.

Reciprocity was a compromise between free trade and protectionism. This weakened its cause because both sides could attack it. Diplomats were wary of foreign—namely British and German—commercial influence in the Western Hemisphere and also were mindful that growth and power overseas depended on negotiation of treaties. Thus, diplomats sought the middle way of trade liberalization. The State Department insisted that the treaties confer only conditional most-favored-nation status (MFN) on another nation. Most other countries granted MFN on an unconditional basis, which meant that any tariff concessions the United States earned from the nation with which it had negotiated a treaty could be given by that nation to other countries, including America's competitors. Conditional treatment compelled the third nation to grant an equivalent concession in return or not receive the benefits of the reciprocity treaty to which the United States was a party. Europeans ignored this State Department proclamation (which the Supreme Court supported), eventually compelling America, in 1923, to adopt the unconditional form of MFN status.

Conditional MFN treatment indicated the intensifying interrelationship of tariff policy with diplomacy after the Civil War, as the United States became a player in the big-power scene. During the early 1880s, France and Germany banned American pork and pork products. This was a protective maneuver designed to help their farmers, cloaked in the excuse that U.S. meat was tainted by trichinae that the Germans claimed was the result of inadequate inspection at American meatpacking plants. American meatpackers protested, as did U.S. diplomats, to little effect until the McKinley Tariff Act passed Congress in 1890. German Chancellor Otto von Bismarck refused to accede to American demands against the embargo. He did so for reasons of domestic politics but also because he wished to limit U.S. overseas influence, especially in the Pacific, where the division of the Samoan Islands remained a sore point until a German-American accord in 1899. The McKinley law contained a provision giving the president the authority to levy a retaliatory duty on German beet sugar imported into the United States. Congress, meanwhile, also passed meat inspection legislation. Recognizing that the two countries needed to ease tensions, for they had nearly come to blows over Samoa, American and German diplomats quickly agreed that U.S. pork would be admitted (after paying a duty) while German sugar would be kept on the American duty-free list. The United States and France also reached an agreement. The episode revealed how tariff policy wielded considerable clout in international political relations.

Reciprocity accords with Latin American nations also had diplomatic implications. Essentially, the State Department negotiated these accords to bind smaller nations to the American economy and keep them out of the hands of the Europeans. But the refusal by the House of Representatives to implement the reciprocity treaty of 1883 with Mexico (after Senate passage) was an affront to America's neighbor. The arrangement would have placed Mexican sugar, tobacco, and some other goods on the tariff-free list in return for Mexico cutting some of its duties. Later tariff hikes against silver-lead ores further strained relations, and, overall, U.S. protectionism was one cause among many that prompted Mexican revolutionaries to seek economic independence from the United States. The McKinley tariff, moreover, scuttled further attempts at reciprocity treaties, although a short-lived one with Brazil proved successful. Still, it was the United States's rather heavy-handed treatment of Latin Americans—in the *Baltimore* affair, Venezuelan boundary dispute, seizure of the Canal Zone, and Cuban revolutions—that combined with the very limited tariff reciprocity policies to shape American responses in the region.

PRESIDENTIAL REFORM

The tepid approach to trade liberalization, or a low-tariff policy, continued into the new century, but change was afoot. Congress still blocked major downward revisions of the tariff because politics dictated that reducing duties also reduced votes. Yet as the national Progressive movement took hold in the early 1900s, market-seeking trade associations such as the National Association of Manufacturers and the U.S. Chamber of Commerce lobbied vigorously for a tariff policy conducive to export expansion. Their case was strong, as imports of manufactured goods continued their steady decline—from 14 percent of consumption of industrial products in 1869 to just under 6 percent by 1914, and the case of the protectionists became weak. They failed to persuade Congress to grant large-scale tariff cuts but sowed the ground for economic liberalization and expansion in foreign policy. Consular branches became active promoters of U.S. goods, the Department of Commerce provided necessary information on foreign markets, and the Federal Reserve Act of 1913 authorized foreign branch banking. Furthermore, export expansion had made its mark abroad, as American goods carved such inroads into European markets that the British, by the turn of the century, began to protest U.S. competition. The presidents of the times thought systematically about foreign affairs, of which tariff policy was increasingly deemed a part.

President William McKinley, noted for the high tariff in his name, actually pursued moderate customs policies. Like his successor, Theodore Roosevelt, he had denounced free trade as a threat to prosperity and even morality. Indeed, the champion of the Republican Party's high-tariff policy, Representative and Senator Justin Morrill of Vermont, had equated protectionism with patriotism. McKinley preached Republican-style tariff nationalism, as GOP leaders did until 1932, by arguing that duties were simply fees to be paid by foreigners to have the privilege of competing in the U.S. market. Tariffs protected wages, guarding the country from invasion and plunder from abroad. Yet McKinley also became a believer in reciprocity.

Backing trade liberalization, McKinley vowed to boost exports without surrendering domestic markets. Thus, the president welcomed a provision of the Dingley Tariff of 1897 that included European nations, along with Latin Americans, in reciprocity treaties. Including Europe indicated America's new confidence abroad and willingness to negotiate as an equal with the great powers and, in particular, lay aside more than a century of bitterness toward England. Consistent with the temper of the post–Civil War period, McKinley appointed a former congressman, now an elderly diplomat, John Kasson, to negotiate treaties with the European powers. Kasson's treaties were controversial, as many industries protested that production at home was sacrificed to the interests of exporters who would benefit from lower duty rates in Europe. Neither McKinley nor Roosevelt actively promoted the treaties in a protectionist-run Congress, and the agreements died in the Senate. There was more success with the commercial treaty that bound Cuba to the United States after the Spanish-American War. In return for a guaranteed sugar and tobacco market in the United States, American business, as well as the military, persuaded Congress to liberalize trade. The result, unfortunately for Cuba, was American domination of the island for a half century afterward.

Regardless of the imperial nature of the Cuban arrangement, tariff policy turned toward internationalism. The Republicans considered tariff revision, realizing that protectionism undercut American power abroad and led to conflict with the Europeans. Just before his assassination in

September 1901, McKinley proclaimed that nations could no longer be indifferent toward each other. He urged reciprocity treaties and cuts in unnecessary tariffs. The new president, Theodore Roosevelt, who viewed reciprocal arrangements as "the handmaiden of protection," let the Kasson treaties die in the Senate but pursued preferential agreements with Cuba and the Philippines. Such a tariff policy would not only bind them economically to the United States but also promote political stability. Roosevelt advocated reciprocity as a form of aid to Cuba, a nation strategically located close to America and within the approaches to the Panama Canal, then under construction. Reciprocity, he believed, would encourage its independence from Europe. In regard to the Philippines, Roosevelt pushed tariff reciprocity to ensure that this territory, so essential to American trade and security interests along the route to the China market, remained hinged to the United States. He stood pat at first in 1905 when Germany threatened a tariff war over America's unwillingness to grant unconditional MFN status to the nation's exports. Recognizing Germany's importance in the European balance of power, the president backed the eventual accord in 1907 that rejected protectionism and allowed for reductions in tariffs of concern to Germany.

The Taft administration showed even less concern than Roosevelt for the tariff's effect on domestic politics and more sensitivity to foreign concerns. Such neglect of protectionism helped William Howard Taft lose his reelection bid in 1912. This former governor of the Philippines had backed tariff-free treatment for that territory's sugar and tobacco. The Republican Congress aided him by enacting the Payne-Aldrich Tariff of 1909, which facilitated reciprocal tariff bargaining with other nations by giving Taft discretionary authority to impose a minimum duty rate if he found no evidence of discrimination. The State Department discovered that the new authority was no inducement to France and Germany to relax restrictions against the United States. But Taft did forge a reciprocity treaty with Canada in 1911, only to be rebuffed by his own party, despite his argument that Canada would become a neocolonial "adjunct" of the United States, dependent on U.S. manufactures and banking while assuming the role of mere commodity supplier. The GOP rejected this argument of self-interest, retreating to traditional protectionism. Canadians did, however, buy the view, and as a result, they turned the Liberal Party from power out of a fear that U.S. continental expansion, fueled by freer trade, would overtake the British Empire in Canada.

Protectionism was on the defensive, however. As an antimonopolist and internationalist, Democratic candidate Woodrow Wilson won election in 1912 on a low-tariff policy. He counseled that Americans could compete effectively abroad but that a high-tariff policy hamstrung the State Department in its ability to conclude reciprocity treaties. The Underwood-Simmons Tariff Act of 1913 sharply reduced duties and added a provision that gave the president authority to forge reciprocity treaties. The act did not lead to equal treatment for American exports, but it did confirm Wilson's intention of using trade liberalization as a panacea to economic distress and a means to maintain peace. World War I delayed Wilson's tariff internationalism.

FITS OF LIBERALISM

Throughout World War I, Wilson strove to have the United States play a lead role in planning the peace, which, in an economic sense, he based on an open world economy of free-flowing trade and investment. Such a structure would boost American power and profits (exports of manufactures skyrocketed from 1913 to 1920), yet Wilson looked beyond realism to the ideological elements of a new world order of democracy and liberal capitalism. A major element of his Fourteen Points involved accessible and expanded commercial relations. In this plan, tariffs would be reduced. Without cuts in duties, claimed businessmen, bankers, and the administration, U.S. imports of European products would flag, preventing European recovery from the war. Without economic revival, the Europeans would never stabilize their exchange rates or pay off their debts. The downward economic spiral not only would make them feeble trade partners but also render them susceptible to vicious cycles of political instability caused by economic uncertainties. That would jeopardize the peace and Wilson's grand scheme of internationalism. Lower duties became a general foreign policy objective for international stability, a watershed in thinking about tariff policy.

That was not the view of Congress, in which protectionists, farmers, and small business demanded a higher tariff wall. Once Congress rejected the Versailles Treaty, turning aside Wilson's internationalism, legislators then responded to the postwar recession in 1920 by trying to boost commodity prices for farmers. Wilson vetoed emergency tariff legislation to jack duties on agricultural products as a violation of his ideological crusade for trade liberalization, but in May 1921, his successor, President Warren Harding, signed a similar law into effect, placing the prosperity of American producers before that of foreigners. This pleased farmers and small manufacturers who feared an influx of cheap European chemical goods, and particularly stiff competition from German producers. The emergency tariff set the tone for the rest of the decade: reluctance to overhaul tariff (and loan) policies in the direction of liberalism. Tariff policy remained a part of more general strategic and economic interests, but not the impetus to a shift to internationalism in foreign policy. Higher tariffs, like the rejection of the League of Nations, indicated that domestic priorities still won out over foreign policy objectives.

During the 1920s and into the Great Depression, the United States searched for export markets while Congress maintained high tariffs. This posed a paradox in that the nation sought freer trade overseas but frowned on more imports at home. Foreign trade expansion became a cardinal aim of Secretary of Commerce Herbert Hoover, who viewed commerce as "the lifeblood of modern civilization." Thus, while the Fordney-McCumber Tariff of 1922 raised duty rates back to their prewar levels, Hoover recognized that peace and prosperity were interlocked. Administration leaders viewed the world economy as an interdependent network of American, European, small-power, and colonial needs and interests. It was no surprise, then, that the Republican leaders who ran the country did not shy away from the rise in imports. The inflow only enhanced American exports abroad and made it easier to solve thorny issues like reparations and debt repayments that poisoned international political affairs. Yet the paradox remained: the aspiration to spread capitalist liberal principles worldwide did not match policy, as protectionism remained strong. Small industry and farmers still clashed with international bankers and diplomats over the tactics of protecting American markets but expanding in global markets. Until 1934, this deadlock prevented the trade liberalization necessary for world economic recovery. America's actions did not live up to its potential of global leadership.

On the internationalist side of the ledger, several positive steps pleased U.S. officials but fell short of their goals. First, the acceptance of unconditional most-favored-nation status for America's trade partners ensured foreigners that their goods would be treated equally in every nation that had an agreement with the United States. Washington abandoned its preferential treatment in Brazil, for example, for equality of treatment in all other markets. Frank W. Taussig, the first chairman of the new Tariff Commission, had urged Wilson to push this approach as one way to open up foreign markets. Although the commission did not rule on revising conditional MFN status at the end of the war, it set the stage for further pressure toward this end. Using Fordney-McCumber's provision for retaliating against foreign discrimination, the State Department switched to unconditional MFN in 1923 in order to dampen antagonism in trade relations. Fairness, rather than special concessions, would avoid diplomatic misunderstandings and help assure American exports of equal treatment.

But this revolution in tariff policy coincided with growing discriminatory policies in Europe. By 1930, the State Department had inserted unconditional MFN status provisions into nearly half of its commercial treaties with forty-three nations. Fifteen additional executive agreements with trade partners included the equality-of-treatment principle. Yet countries in Europe and Central America maintained their unfair protectionism. In addition, the British Empire continued to advance its imperial preferential system of tariffs, showing Europe's embrace of restrictive trade principles and practices. In America's most important markets—Canada, Britain, and France—discrimination remained, preventing market openings for U.S. exports. These nations insisted on holding to protectionism until they received reciprocal concessions in the huge American market. Thus, the late-nineteenth-century vogue for reciprocity treaties returned a quarter century later.

A second liberal policy involved successfully lobbying in Congress to strengthen the Tariff Commission, the nonpartisan body of experts created in the Wilson years that advised the president on the height of tariffs. Under the urging of Hoover and Tariff Commissioner William Culbertson, Congress also accepted a flexible tariff policy and "scientific" protectionism, giving the president authority to adjust customs according to production costs in America and overseas. These measures, embodied in the Fordney-McCumber Tariff Act, attempted to take tariff-setting out of the hands of the logrolling Congress

and place it with the unbiased Tariff Commission, which would act according to national and international economic needs. But the commission did not avail itself of the flexible tariff policy, and duties increased. The Republican presidents of the 1920s refused to confront Congress on protectionism. Their pursuit of international stability and trade expansion through the efficacy of private market forces came up lame.

PROTECTIONIST BACKSLIDING

Fordney-McCumber coincided with a general rise in tariffs worldwide, as new nations formed out of the Austro-Hungarian empire sought to protect their industries. America, Britain, and other big powers called several international conferences—in Brussels in 1920 and Genoa two years later—to stop the increase in protectionism. But when these nations looked to the United States for leadership, they found—with passage of the Fordney-McCumber duty hikes—that America still elevated its domestic economy over foreign considerations in tariff policy. When the law passed, America was the world's creditor but, ironically, possessed the world's highest tariffs. Unable to negotiate down U.S. customs rates, European and Latin American nations revised their tariffs upward between 1926 and 1929. Three of the major British dominions—Australia, New Zealand, and Canada—responded likewise.

This tariff war alarmed the League of Nations, which called a world economic conference in Geneva in 1927. The representatives, including an American, resolved to terminate all prohibitions on imports. This was too bold for many nations, which attached reservations and loopholes. The U.S. delegate railed against high tariffs but focused on those in Europe, not in America. The Geneva meeting failed to stop the climb in tariff levels. Germany and Italy immediately raised tariffs against imported wheat, thereby escalating the world tariff war. In this context, the infamous Smoot-Hawley Tariff Act of 1930 (proposed in 1929) culminated the cycle of protectionism that liberal traders had feared for decades. The fallout was positive, however, for it transformed tariff policy into an internationalist instrument.

The initial trade-policy response to the Great Depression pointed in a protectionist direction under the Smoot-Hawley tariff. Historians continue to debate whether or not Smoot-Hawley represented the highest tariff in American history, worsened the Depression, or sent chills into the stock market. The large majority of twentieth-century economists, politicians, diplomats, and students of international affairs believed the worst, but there is reason to believe this perspective exaggerates the case. Research reveals that earlier tariff levels on dutiable goods regularly exceeded those of Smoot-Hawley. The Tariff of Abominations raised the average ad valorem rate (set on a percentage of value) on dutiable imports to a higher level than the 1930 legislation. Scholars should be skeptical of weighing the effect of tariff levels too heavily when trying to show their impact on the Great Depression; demand and supply conditions and currency rates had much more influence. And a close reading of stock market fluctuations and the battle over Smoot-Hawley in Congress shows no correlation between the law and the bear market. Thus, a "myth" of Smoot-Hawley arose, perpetuated by free-trading economists and Democrats seeking to wrest control of the White House by blaming the Depression—and the rise of militarism in Europe and Asia—on selfish, shortsighted, and provocative Republican tariff policy.

Still, such conclusions were beyond commentators and policymakers at the time. In reality, perception was critical, and the tariff act indicated to foreign observers that America had chosen the path of economic nationalism. In short, Smoot-Hawley's timing was atrocious. World trade, both exports and imports, plummeted in value by 40 percent and by a quarter in volume from 1929 to 1933. That spooked U.S. investments, which, along with any hopes of loans to Europe, dried up. In a vicious economic cycle, the resulting defaults by foreigners holding U.S. loans led to further instability and slumps in Europe, which were echoed in America.

Journalists exaggerated the intensity and number of protests abroad regarding Smoot-Hawley, but governments did rally against the legislation. France, Argentina, Japan, and others assailed the law as it wended its way through Congress. Thirty-eight nations urged the Senate to reject it, while American liberals warned that the high tariff was a threat to peace. Switzerland, which exported almost all of its watch and clock production, suffered a 48 percent decline in sales to the United States as a result of Smoot-Hawley rates. The Swiss called for a consumer boycott of U.S. cars and typewriters as a response. Mussolini's Italy criticized the high tariffs on agricultural imports and, in retaliation, mounted a campaign against American autos that fizzled when the Italians realized that reprisals would jeopardize their olive oil and tomato exports to the United States. Spain imposed higher duties on bicycles and wine from France, in reaction to the unconditional MFN treatment given to third countries. In effect, although there was less foreign retaliation following passage of Smoot-Hawley than claimed at the time, the impact of American protectionism came in the form of uncooperative commercial relations in the international arena.

For example, the British Commonwealth did not directly retaliate against Smoot-Hawley when it forged the Ottawa Agreement of 1932, but the discriminatory duties and quotas against non-empire sources, especially the United States, were deemed a natural outgrowth of the measure for nations seeking a quid pro quo. Under the agreement, free trade flowed between Britain and its dominions but high tariffs faced America. In 1930, nearly three-quarters of U.S. exports entered Britain free of duties, but two years later, about one-fifth enjoyed such status. Smoot-Hawley prompted the British nations to circle their wagons around imperial preferences that the United States then spent the next three decades trying to eliminate in extensive tariff negotiations. Also, Canadians erupted over American tariff hikes on farm goods during their national election. Running for reelection, Prime Minister Mackenzie King issued countervailing duties in May 1930 to bolster his image as a protector of Canadian economic interests. The international trade situation was begging for a peaceful resolution.

HULL'S REVOLUTION

At this low ebb in the world economy, the administration of Franklin Roosevelt entered office. The president's secretary of state, Cordell Hull, determined to lower tariff and trade barriers. From his first speech in Congress in 1908, this Tennesseean crusaded against the protective tariff. Hull became a near-fanatical champion of liberal trade, arguing that American prosperity depended on trade expansion encouraged by a reciprocal lowering of tariffs. The Democrats forged an export-based coalition of producers, workers, business, and bankers to support Franklin D. Roosevelt's New Deal agenda and numerous reelection bids. Yet materialism and politics were only one part of Hull's agenda. A low-tariff policy, or freer trade, promoted lasting peace. Tariff wars were part of economic rivalries that led to political tensions, he argued. Expanded and mutually prosperous trade brought economic well-being and, therefore, political stability and cooperation. Furthermore, reduced duties freed the economy from governmental intrusion. Regimentation and control of markets, as seen in Stalin's communist Soviet Union and Hitler's fascist Germany, threatened liberty and democracy.

The secretary of state pushed for mutual tariff concessions under reciprocal trade treaties and close adherence to the unconditional most-favored-nation policy. He attacked Smoot-Hawley as detrimental to U.S. interests and security. Liberal trade dovetailed with peace, he declared, and high tariffs with war. Hull labored to remove tariff-making policy from the clutches of self-interested congressmen and place it in the executive branch, namely with the freer-trade State Department and president. Using the lure of the large American market, he pursued reciprocity agreements with the revolutionary trade legislation that accomplished his agenda: the Reciprocal Trade Agreements Act (RTAA) of 1934.

Although Roosevelt was at first a lukewarm liberal trader, preferring instead nationalistic and unilateral solutions to the Great Depression, the president endorsed the RTAA. This began a new relationship of the tariff to diplomacy. The legislation, renewable every three years or so, amended the Smoot-Hawley Act, giving the president authority to negotiate bilateral agreements that raised or lowered tariff rates up to 50 percent on the condition that the other nation grant U.S. products reciprocal access to its markets. Each agreement included the unconditional MFN clause so that the concessions would apply to third parties. Congress would renew the RTAA but would not vote on any agreement, thus eliminating lobbying in the tariff process.

Protectionists were not routed, however. The president would seek advice from the Tariff Commission, as well as the departments of state, commerce, and agriculture, before engaging in commercial negotiations. The public would be given opportunities to be heard. The president could not transfer goods between the free and dutiable lists. And the preferential relationship of exclusive trade arrangements with Cuba would stand. Hull would not depart from previous tariff policies that granted cautious concessions and pushed nationalism to the fore. For instance, he ignored Australian requests to enter negotiations for months, and then protested when Canberra

adopted certain restrictive measures. To many Latin American nations, the Hull program seemed bent more on U.S. export expansion than mutual, reciprocal benefits. An RTAA pact signed with Cuba just after dictator Fulgencio Batista came to power in 1934 did not stimulate the island's economy but instead tied the nation closer to the United States in a dependent relationship.

But Hull's philosophy represented a major shift in tariff policy. Protectionists railed that the RTAA meant unilateral economic disarmament on the part of the United States. The RTAA accord with Cuba, for instance, pursued political stability through economic dependence with the United States. In 1935, Hull signed an agreement with Belgium, offering the maximum 50 percent reduction in tariffs on many competitive products, including steel and cotton textiles. The goal was to open up Belgium's market for American automotive products, apples, and wheat flour. In fact, the accord gave one-sided benefits to Belgium, even allowing the nation to rescind some of its concessions. This pattern of sacrificing domestic industry for the imperatives of export expansion and, overall, for foreign policy goals, became a basic pattern that remained in RTAA negotiations well into the 1970s. Even though government experts found substantial discrimination abroad against U.S. goods, Hull decided to negotiate reciprocal trade pacts with as many nations as possible, except for aggressors like Germany and Japan. The State Department took a conciliatory position toward RTAA countries, oftentimes allowing imports into the United States to surge past, and even damage, home interests. The reason for such sacrifices lay in foreign policy objectives.

By the end of the twentieth century, many commentators lamented Hullian liberal trade logic as self-destructive, naive, or unwise. They accused tariff liberals of economic appeasement and of trading away American interests for illusive foreign policy goals. Yet the RTAA did not dismantle trade barriers, nor did they produce anything more than modest export expansion for U.S. farmers and manufacturers. Imperial preferences remained in force. But Hull was satisfied, for he had world politics, not economics, in mind as he negotiated agreements. He agreed that international affairs, and specifically matters of democracy, security, and peace, lay at the heart of the RTAA and American tariff policy. By 1937, in a policy enduring into the next millennium, officials elevated internationalism above domestic economic well-being. By doing so, they transformed tariff policy from its protective guise to one of expansion and liberalism. As the world headed for another war, the Roosevelt administration used tariff policy to group together a coalition of democracies to confront militarist aggressors in Europe and Asia.

TARIFF DIPLOMACY

Under an RTAA bilateral accord with Britain in 1938, the Americans initially sought to curb the imperial preference system to outsiders but acquiesced to the maintenance of this discriminatory network. For example, the United States allowed the British to reduce American apple exports deemed competitive with dominion produce. The payoff, however, lay in the political arena. The British, Canadians, and Americans lauded the accord as representing Anglo-American solidarity in the face of fascism. With the tensions brought on by the Munich Pact a few months after the trade agreement, the State Department stressed that a conciliatory tariff policy was significant for it diplomatic impact.

Tariff reduction agreements appeared in rapid succession as war loomed. The Roosevelt administration successfully renewed the RTAA in 1937 and used the law to forge an agreement with Turkey in 1939, the first with a nation in the Middle East and the twenty-first since the RTAA had become law five years before. This accord, in which the United States granted an inordinate number of concessions relative to Turkey's offers, helped keep the nation out of Nazi Germany's grasp. The State Department signed bilateral pacts with several Latin American nations to turn them from German influence, and agreements with Iceland in 1943 kept that country in the Allied fold. No RTAA agreements were signed with Russia and China, two of America's closest allies during the war, providing evidence that Hull was selective in his wielding of the RTAA and that political partnership was not always conditioned upon economic cooperation. Yet it was just as evident that signatories stayed friendly to the United States during the war. Of the twenty-seven RTAA nations, only Finland fought an Allied power. (And for good reason: It had been invaded by the Soviet Union.) Sixteen countries sided with the United States, six had broken relations with the Axis, and four remained neutral. Placing the tariff in the service of wartime diplomacy helped deter aggressors.

Doing so also deterred the communist threat during the Cold War. Just as important as wartime liberalization was the postwar planning agenda dealing with duties. The war prevented major concessions, slowing down trade negotiations to a trickle. And protectionism did not disappear, either during or in the decades after the war. But State Department planners took Cordell Hull's vision of freer trade to the conference table and fashioned multilateral agreements (with several nations signing on under the unconditional MFN principle) designed to reduce tariffs and other commercial barriers as a basis for peace and stability. These more general ideological hopes changed once the Cold War began and the policy of containment was instituted in the late 1940s, first by economic means and then by military responses.

GATT AND THE COLD WAR

Early in World War II, Anglo-American planners addressed tariffs, especially the British imperial system of discrimination and America's high duty rates. They agreed to negotiate down such protection and include as many nations as possible in the exercise of tariff liberalization. The planners thus launched bargaining talks in the first round of the General Agreement on Tariffs and Trade (GATT) in 1947 between twenty-three nations, and simultaneously formulated a blueprint for a trade organization, replete with rules and principles to guide future commercial policies on tariffs as well as related issues such as cartels, employment, and development. The organization itself never came into existence because of a lack of political will power in the United States (it would finally be born under the guise of the World Trade Organization, or WTO, in 1995), but tariff negotiating rounds of GATT continued into the 1990s, until the WTO absorbed GATT.

The first Geneva Round of GATT bogged down over imperial preferences, but the State Department placed greater importance on British economic problems than British intransigence in the negotiations. Maintaining free world unity took precedence over reducing foreign tariffs, which might undermine foreign recovery efforts and thus play into Soviet hands. This was an era in which aid proved more effective than trade in addressing the economic crises facing western Europe. Once the Marshall Plan period ended in the early 1950s, however, GATT rounds gradually lowered tariffs to the point that, by the early

LEMONS AND DIPLOMACY

The idea of placing tariffs in the service of diplomacy during the Cold War was so prevalent that it can be applied in the most esoteric of cases, such as lemons. At the second round of GATT in 1949, America and Italy disputed U.S. tariffs on lemons, a key Italian export. But timing was everything. Moscow had initiated a blockade of Berlin to chase out the Western powers. Czechoslovakia had fallen to the Soviets, while the Marshall Plan had been rushed to Western Europeans struggling to recover from the war and against popular socialist parties tied to Stalin. Communists were poised for triumph in China as the Russians exploded an atomic device, shocking the United States. In these dire circumstances, the State Department sided with Italy, warning that without a cut in the U.S. import duty on lemons, the result would be a failing economy, a peasant revolt in Sicily, and Italy's defection from NATO, which would have devastating effects on America's containment policy. California and Arizona lemon growers, however, lobbied the Truman administration against a concession. They noted, and even the State Department agreed, that Italian lemons competed effectively in the U.S. market, and so a tariff decrease was unnecessary. Furthermore, domestic producers accused the diplomats of trying to bribe Italy with a U.S. tariff decrease to remain at the GATT discussions as a show of Western unity against communism. President Harry Truman weighed their complaints alongside foreign policy objectives, and decided the matter on the latter's merits. America could absorb Italian lemons; growers would survive. Even if they were hurt, however, their sacrifice did not match the potential for Italy's economic and political instability, which would only cause diplomatic strife at a time of great tension in the Cold War. Subsuming tariffs under the containment doctrine ruled trade policy for decades thereafter.

1970s, industrial tariffs fell to minimal levels. Tariffs dropped about 80 percent under the RTAA, providing a boon to foreigners and many U.S. exporters, although the American merchandise trade surplus dwindled away by the early 1970s. By that time, nontariff forms of protection emerged as issues, and so it was difficult to separate tariffs from other barriers.

Postwar U.S. tariff policy also succeeded in molding an anticommunist alliance of solvent nations, bound together by integrated economies. Although protectionism reared up periodically during the half century after World War II, the battle over tariffs shifted to arguments over how much tariff slashing would boost America's Cold War allies. The State Department encouraged U.S. imports oftentimes more strenuously than exports. This was particularly the case during the early Cold War, in light of Japanese and western European recovery needs, but that approach persisted for decades. Repeatedly, the Eisenhower administration turned back protests from domestic producers for import restrictions on items ranging from clothespins to lemons. The Kennedy, Johnson, and Nixon administrations preferred side agreements, or special tariff hikes designed to help certain politically powerful interest groups in Congress, as they maintained an overall strategy of liberal trade for the accomplishment of foreign policy goals. Richard Nixon and Congress, however, restored the old emphasis on reciprocity abroad by adding retaliatory authority into trade legislation, although under subsequent presidents this amounted mostly to muscle flexing with lax enforcement against foreign discrimination. And by this time, tariffs were little involved; when protectionism against automobile imports became a cause célèbre in the 1980s, for example, the backlash from Congress and administrations came in the form of quotas and other nontariff restraints.

Trade liberalization succeeded in its diplomatic objectives: strengthening the alliance, integrating western Europe into a dynamic bloc of nations, attaching Japan to the U.S. side, and luring Third World countries into the free world fold. So successful was the RTAA that it had a large part in fueling growth in the West to the point that the Soviet Union and its satellites tried to compete but bankrupted themselves in the process, thereby ending the Cold War.

At home, by the 1970s and into the next decade there were renewed calls for tariff barriers. The ascendance of Japan in particular sparked protectionism. The advent of the WTO, with its supranational powers over global commerce, and the revolution of globalization spurred a loose coalition of protective-minded groups, among them labor, environmentalists, and populist politicians, to crusade at the turn of the new century for barriers, including tariffs, that would enhance national livelihoods. For example, labor sought restrictions on the ability of corporations to shift production overseas, as well as safeguards for fellow overseas workers. Environmentalists sought to impose U.S. protections for the environment on other nations. One notable case was in the type of nets used by foreign (Mexican) fishing interests; their nets were not dolphin-safe, while U.S. nets were. Populists opposed America's joining international organizations that supposedly undermined U.S. national sovereignty, which was part of the neo–Fortress America mentality, linked, for example, to Patrick Buchanan's crusade against immigration from Mexico.

The days of the high protective tariff had long passed, but it remained to be seen, after Cold War strictures had ended and America was released from its obligation to provide foreigners with profits at U.S. expense, whether reciprocity and protection for domestic producers would flourish anew. Yet clearly, more than two centuries of history pointed to the possibility of tariff and trade policy accounting for domestic needs, as it increasingly met diplomatic imperatives along the way.

BIBLIOGRAPHY

Bauer, Raymond A., Ithiel De Sola Pool, and Lewis Anthony Dexter. *American Business and Public Policy: The Politics of Foreign Trade*. 2d ed. Chicago, 1972. Classic political science study testing pluralist theory, with a focus on the 1950s.

Becker, William A., and Samuel F. Wells, Jr., eds. *Economics and World Power: An Assessment of American Diplomacy Since 1789*. New York, 1984. Excellent survey of all economic diplomacy, including tariffs.

Butler, Michael A. *Cautious Visionary: Cordell Hull and Trade Reform, 1933–1937*. Kent, Ohio, 1998.

Capie, Forrest. *Tariffs and Growth: Some Insights from the World Economy, 1850–1940*. New York, 1994. An economist weighs in on the side of freer trade.

Culbertson, William S. *Reciprocity: A National Policy for Foreign Trade*. New York, 1937. A government official champions the RTAA.

Dobson, John M. *Two Centuries of Tariffs*. Washington, D.C., 1976.

Eckes, Alfred E., Jr. *Opening America's Market: U.S. Foreign Trade Policy Since 1776*. Chapel Hill, N.C., 1995. Emerging classic that criticizes State Department liberal trade policy as a digression from traditional protectionism.

Eichengreen, Barry. "Did International Economic Forces Cause the Great Depression?" *Contemporary Policy Issues* 6 (April 1988): 90–113.

Gardner, Richard N. *Sterling-Dollar Diplomacy: The Origins and Prospects of Our International Economic Order*. 2d ed. New York, 1969.

Hody, Cynthia A. *The Politics of Trade: American Political Development and Foreign Economic Policy*. Hanover, N.H., 1996. Examining tariff policy from the early 1900s onward, this political scientist finds that policymakers usually lagged behind dynamic economic change.

Hull, Cordell. *The Memoirs of Cordell Hull*. New York, 1948.

Jones, Joseph M., Jr. *Tariff Retaliation*. Philadelphia, 1934. A proponent of liberal trade who takes aim at protectionism.

Kaplan, Edward S. *American Trade Policy, 1923–1995*. Westport, Conn., 1996.

Kaplan, Edward S., and Thomas W. Ryley. *Prelude to Trade Wars: American Tariff Policy, 1890–1922*. Westport, Conn., 1994.

Kaufman, Burton I. *Efficiency and Expansion: Foreign Trade Organization in the Wilson Administration, 1913–1922*. Westport, Conn., 1974.

———. *Trade and Aid: Eisenhower's Foreign Economic Policy, 1953–1961*. Baltimore, 1982.

Kottman, Richard N. *Reciprocity and the North Atlantic Triangle, 1932–1938*. Ithaca, N.Y., 1968.

Lake, David A. *Power, Protection, and Free Trade: International Sources of U.S. Commercial Strategy, 1887–1939*. Ithaca, N.Y., 1988. Argues that tariff policy arose from international sources rather than conflict among domestic groups.

Merrill, Milton R. *Reed Smoot: Apostle in Politics*. Logan, Utah, 1990.

Pastor, Robert A. *Congress and the Politics of U.S. Foreign Economic Policy, 1929–1976*. Berkeley, Calif., 1980. A useful analysis of tariff policymaking and its impact.

Rhodes, Carolyn. *Reciprocity, U.S. Trade Policy, and the GATT Regime*. Ithaca, N.Y., 1993.

Rowland, Benjamin M. *Commercial Conflict and Foreign Policy: A Study in Anglo-American Relations, 1932–1938*. New York, 1987.

Schattschneider, Elmer E. *Politics, Pressures, and the Tariff*. New York, 1935. Classic study of Smoot-Hawley logrolling.

Setser, Vernon G. *The Commercial Reciprocity Policy of the United States, 1774–1829.* Philadelphia, 1937.

Stanwood, Edward. *American Tariff Controversies in the Nineteenth Century.* New York, 1903.

Steward, Dick. *Trade and Hemisphere: The Good Neighbor Policy and Reciprocal Trade.* Columbia, Mo., 1975.

Strackbein, O. R. *American Enterprise and Foreign Trade.* Washington, D.C., 1965. Protectionist tract by a lobbyist.

Tarbell, Ida M. *The Tariff in Our Times.* New York, 1911. A Progressive-era crusader against protectionism.

Tasca, Henry J. *The Reciprocal Trade Policy of the United States.* Philadelphia, 1938.

Tate, Merze. *Hawaii: Reciprocity or Annexation.* New Haven, Conn., 1965.

Taussig, Frank W., ed. *Tariff History of the United States.* 8th ed. New York, 1931.

Terrill, Tom E. *The Tariff, Politics, and American Foreign Policy, 1874–1901.* Westport, Conn., 1973.

Wolman, Paul. *Most Favored Nation: The Republican Revisionists and U.S. Tariff Policy, 1897–1912.* Chapel Hill, N.C., 1992.

Younger, Edward A. *John A. Kasson: Politics and Diplomacy from Lincoln to McKinley.* Iowa City, Iowa, 1955.

Zeiler, Thomas W. *American Trade and Power in the 1960s.* New York, 1992. Explores side agreements common in the Cold War to preserve liberal trade.

———. *Free Trade, Free World: The Advent of GATT.* Chapel Hill, N.C., 1999.

See also CONGRESSIONAL POWER; ECONOMIC POLICY AND THEORY; GLOBALIZATION; MOST-FAVORED-NATION PRINCIPLE; RECIPROCITY.

TELEVISION

★ ★ ★ ★

Chester Pach

Under the cover of darkness on 9 December 1992, U.S. forces went ashore at Mogadishu, Somalia, and got an unexpected reception. The night suddenly turned bright, as television lights illuminated the landing area and temporarily blinded marines and navy SEALs equipped with night vision goggles. At the water's edge were hundreds of journalists who had been waiting to film the beginning of Operation Restore Hope, a humanitarian mission to distribute food and other vital supplies to starving Somalis. The news media had turned the beach into a kind of outdoor television studio, much to the distress of the troops.

The advance guard of Operation Restore Hope did not know that television journalists would complicate their landing. Yet the reporters were there because Pentagon officials had alerted them. Military officials hoped for favorable publicity from news stories about the beginning of a mission that they thought would win widespread approbation. But while they notified reporters, Pentagon authorities forgot to tell marine and navy commanders to expect a reception of lights and cameras.

This incident illustrates the complex relationship between the news media—and particularly television journalists—and those who plan and implement U.S. foreign policy. Journalists depend on government officials for information and access—to conferences, briefings, crisis areas, and war zones. Yet they often chafe under the restrictions that policymakers or military commanders impose. Those who formulate or carry out foreign policy depend on TV news to provide them with favorable publicity as well as information about international affairs or channels for building public support. Yet these officials also worry about the power of cameras and reporters to transform events as well as to frame issues, expose secrets, or challenge official policies. Cooperation and mutual dependence is the flip side of tension and conflicting interests.

Since the middle of the twentieth century, television has been closely connected to U.S. foreign policy. What makes TV important is that it is a visual medium that commands large audiences. Continuing technological improvements, including live broadcasting of international events as they take place, have made television a powerful instrument for conveying information, molding public attitudes, and influencing government policies. Yet it is easy to exaggerate or misunderstand the power of television to shape foreign policy. Beginning in the late twentieth century, the U.S. government had to deal with twenty-four-hour news cycles, "real-time" reporting of "breaking" news, and extensive coverage of international events with large significance, such as the terrorist attacks on New York City and Washington, D.C., on 11 September 2001, or with dramatic appeal, such as whether Elián Gonzalez, the six-year-old refugee, should remain with relatives in Miami or return to his father in Cuba. Television has affected the ways that the U.S. government has made foreign policy and built public support for it. Yet presidents and other high officials with clear objectives and sophisticated strategies for dealing with the news media—for example, George H. W. Bush's administration during the Persian Gulf War and the international crisis that preceded it—have maintained control of foreign policy and commanded public backing for their international agenda.

Yet even before it had such immediacy or reach, television played a significant—and sometimes controversial—role in shaping government actions and popular understanding of international affairs. The Vietnam War was a critical event. It began, at least, as an American war, just when television had become the principal source of news for a majority of the U.S. public. It offered lessons—controversial, to be sure—about the role of TV in shaping public attitudes toward international affairs. And it occurred at a time of significant changes in journalism. Despite their devotion to objectivity, balance, and fairness, TV reporters would no longer insist, as Edward R. Murrow had in 1947, on a contract provision that limited his right to express opinion in his stories. Vietnam, in short, marked a major transition in the relationship between television and foreign policy.

TV NEWS AND THE EARLY COLD WAR

Although it was a novelty in the United States at the end of World War II, television became an important part of American life during the first postwar decade. Fewer than one out of ten American homes had television in 1950. Five years later the proportion had grown to two-thirds. New stations quickly took to the air and usually affiliated with one of the networks: the National Broadcasting Company (NBC), the Columbia Broadcasting System (CBS), the American Broadcasting Company (ABC), or the short-lived DuMont Television Network.

Even when the networks consisted of a handful of stations, government officials showed keen interest in using television to build public support for U.S. foreign and military policies. Public affairs officers in the State Department said they favored television because it did "a better job than any other medium at depicting foreign policy in action." The department worked with both networks and independent producers to create shows about foreign policy and world affairs or make available for telecast films that it produced itself. Among the most popular series was *The Marshall Plan in Action,* which premiered on ABC in June 1950 and continued under the title *Strength for a Free World* until February 1953. Other shows were the interview program *Diplomatic Pouch* (CBS) and, during the Korean War, *The Facts We Face* (CBS) and *Battle Report—Washington* (NBC). In these early days of broadcasting, the networks were eager for programming to fill up their time slots. They also took advantage of opportunities to demonstrate support for American Cold War policies, especially during the McCarthy era.

Evening newscasts became regular features during the late 1940s and early 1950s. Each network aired fifteen-minute programs. CBS and NBC expanded their shows to thirty minutes in September 1963; ABC did not do the same until January 1967. John Daly anchored the ABC broadcast during most of the 1950s. Douglas

Edwards held the same position at CBS until Walter Cronkite replaced him in April 1962. The most popular news program in the early 1950s was NBC's *Camel News Caravan,* with host John Cameron Swayze. With a carnation in his lapel and zest in his voice, Swayze invited viewers to "go hopscotching the world for headlines." After this brisk international tour, there might be stops at a beauty pageant or a stadium for the afternoon's scores. Chet Huntley and David Brinkley succeeded Swayze in October 1956. Anchors and journalists rather than hosts, as Swayze had been, they brought greater depth to the NBC newscasts without making them solemn. They also attracted viewers because of the novelty of their pairing, the contrast in their personalities, and the familiarity of their closing—"Good night, Chet;" "Good night, David." They led the ratings until the late 1960s.

International news was important on each of these programs, yet there were difficulties in covering distant stories, especially on film. Fifteen minutes (less time for commercials, lead-in, and closing) allowed coverage of only a few stories and little time for analysis. Cumbersome and complicated cameras and sound equipment made film reports difficult. Before the beginning of satellite communication in the 1960s, it might take a day or two for film from international locations to get on the air. Despite these limitations, the audience for these newscasts grew steadily. By 1961 surveys showed that the public considered television the "most believable" source of news. Two years later, for the first time, more people said that they relied on television rather than newspapers for most of their news.

Many viewers watched in utter astonishment on 22 October 1962, when President John F. Kennedy informed them about Soviet missiles in Cuba and the possibility of nuclear war. Soviet diplomats got a copy of the speech only an hour before Kennedy went before the cameras. The president's decision to make his demand for the removal of the missiles on television made compromise on this fundamental issue all but impossible. Kennedy spoke directly to Soviet premier Nikita Khrushchev, calling on him to step back from the nuclear brink. It was an extremely skillful use of television as a medium of diplomatic communication. The crisis dominated TV news coverage until its end six days later. The reporting surely influenced public attitudes, but it probably had little direct effect on Kennedy's advisers. Secretary of Defense Robert S. McNamara later revealed that he did not watch television even once during the thirteen days of the Cuban Missile Crisis. Yet during the growing difficulties in Vietnam, Kennedy, his advisers, and those who succeeded them in the White House paid close attention to television news.

THE FIRST TELEVISION WAR

Vietnam did not become a big story on American television until 1965, but it was a controversial one from the time that U.S. military personnel began to play a significant role in combat in the early 1960s. Officials of both the U.S. and South Vietnamese governments were extremely concerned about coverage of the war. Their criticism at first centered on reporting in newspapers and magazines and on wire services, as these news media began sending full-time correspondents to Vietnam several years before NBC's Garrick Utley became the first television journalist based in Saigon, beginning in mid-1964. Yet even though their assignments were brief and their numbers few, TV journalists still found that South Vietnamese authorities scrutinized their reporting and sometimes objected to it, as Utley's colleague, Jim Robinson, learned during one of his occasional trips to Saigon while stationed in NBC's Hong Kong bureau. Offended by one of Robinson's stories, President Ngo Dinh Diem expelled the correspondent from the country in November 1962, despite protests from both the U.S. embassy and journalists in Saigon.

The Kennedy administration used less heavy-handed methods to manage the news from Vietnam. Administration officials tried to play down U.S. involvement in what it described as a Vietnamese war, even as the president sharply increased U.S. military personnel from several hundred to more than sixteen thousand. Yet Kennedy and his advisers rejected the military censorship of news reporting that had prevailed in previous twentieth-century wars, lest such restrictions call attention to a story whose significance they wished to diminish. Instead, U.S. officials in Saigon mixed patriotic appeals "to get on the team" with upbeat statements about South Vietnamese military success and misleading information about what were ostensibly U.S. military advisers who in reality participated in combat operations.

The administration's efforts at news management collapsed during the Buddhist crisis of 1963, as horrifying images of the fiery suicides of monks protesting government restrictions on religious expression appeared in American television news reports and on the front pages of newspapers. What the U.S. embassy called the "press problem" worsened, as reporters not only mistrusted official sources because of their manipulation of information, but contributed to a public debate about whether the Diem government's liabilities were so great that it might not be able to prevail in the war against the National Liberation Front. In important televised interviews in September with Cronkite of CBS and Huntley and Brinkley of NBC on the day that each of those newscasts expanded to thirty minutes, Kennedy reaffirmed the U.S. commitment to South Vietnam while publicly delivering the message that diplomatic emissaries privately conveyed: that the Diem government should make changes to reclaim popular support so it could more effectively prosecute the war. Kennedy also quietly tried to dampen public criticism of Diem, even as his advisers debated how to step up the pressure on the South Vietnamese leader and whether to encourage a coup, by suggesting that the *New York Times* remove correspondent David Halberstam, whose critical reports had questioned the administration's backing of Diem. The publisher of the *Times* refused to buckle to presidential pressure; Halberstam remained in Saigon to cover the coup that ousted Diem on 1 November.

The administration of Lyndon B. Johnson in many ways followed its predecessor's pattern of news management as it expanded U.S. involvement in the war in Vietnam in 1964 and 1965. Johnson and his principal advisers believed that domestic support was critical to the U.S. war effort, but worried "that our public posture is fragile." Like its predecessor, the Johnson administration ruled out censorship of the news in favor of a system of voluntary cooperation in withholding certain kinds of military information. "Because we are fools" was the explanation that the president gave one group of journalists for this choice. Yet administration policymakers repeatedly considered censorship and rejected it for fear of damage to official credibility. They also hoped that an ambitious program of public relations would ensure favorable coverage of the U.S. war effort.

Yet the "information problem" continued, even after U.S. policy became "maximum candor and disclosure consistent with the requirements of security." Many reporters distrusted the daily official briefings in Saigon, which they derisively

✦ ✦ ✦ ✦

FRIENDLY PERSUASION: LBJ, TV NEWS, AND THE DOMINICAN REPUBLIC

On 28 April 1965, President Lyndon B. Johnson ordered U.S. marines to the Dominican Republic to protect U.S. citizens during political violence and to prevent communists from seizing power. Johnson was extremely concerned about news coverage of the intervention. He tried unsuccessfully to get CBS to remove television correspondent Bert Quint, whose reports from Santo Domingo cast doubt on whether there was a significant communist threat. But Johnson found other ways to affect television reporting. In an oral history interview, NBC correspondent John Chancellor revealed the following about events of 2 May 1965: "We had a program, a television program on a Sunday afternoon. . . . I had gone down . . . to stand in front of the White House and speak a little essay into the camera on what the President's reaction was. . . . As I stood out there waiting for the program to begin, what I didn't know was that the President was upstairs. . . . He was alone and looking at me out the window, and he got very curious about what I was doing. . . . And the guard in the West Wing came out and got me, and I went inside. He said, 'There's a telephone call for you,' and it was the President."

According to the tape of the telephone conversation, Johnson said:

> John, . . . I don't want to be quarrelsome, but I want you to know the facts. . . . If we don't watch out, the bellyachers are going to run the country and we'll lose our democracy.

. . . Our mission down there [in the Dominican Republic], evacuation, is not half-way through.. . . . [U.S. Ambassador John Bartlow Martin] says that the Latin American . . . ambassadors, generally, are very favorable to us because we've saved their hide. . . . While they can't come out and say we're against mother or we support marines in Latin America, . . . they're very happy. . . . And . . . he's [Martin] going to point out [at a press conference] some of . . . them that have been imported and are known Castro leaders. . . . Fifty are identified as of last night. . . . I have to be very careful because I don't want to say a guy [who] disagrees with me is a Communist, or I'm a McCarthy. . . . The point, though, that I want to get over with you is those on the ground . . . are very happy that their lives have been spared and we're there. . . . Number two—the mission is not completed or about to be completed.

Chancellor replied, "All right, I have that clearly in mind," and Johnson said, "Okay, partner."

Chancellor recollected: "And I went out and stood out there—it didn't sound right, what he had told me, but nonetheless . . . I put it into the piece I'd written. . . . Then I went back and the following day I was able to determine pretty accurately that what he'd told me was an absolute fabrication, a big lie! I've rarely been as angry. I really was just furious! Presidents use all kinds of tools on reporters to do their work. . . . . I've never really told this to anybody before except a few close friends because you don't go around calling the president a liar. In this case, he was."

called "The Five O'clock Follies." While some journalists considered these briefings a mixture of spin, exaggeration, and half-truths, others concluded that the information officers told "outright lies." Evidence for this darker interpretation came from Arthur Sylvester, the assistant secretary of defense for public affairs, who turned an innocuous social occasion in Saigon in July 1965 into a nasty confrontation when he sneered at reporters, "Look, if you think that any American official is going to tell you the truth, you're stupid."

Some White House officials worried about "fragmentary" reports lacking "perspective" on TV newscasts as the networks rapidly increased their news operations in South Vietnam in 1965. Their fears about what TV cameras might reveal became acute when the *CBS Evening News*

showed correspondent Morley Safer's sensational film report about U.S. marines using cigarette lighters to burn civilian huts in a search-and-destroy operation in the village of Cam Ne in August. Pentagon officials charged Safer with staging the incident and tried unsuccessfully to get him removed from his assignment because his Canadian nationality supposedly made it impossible for him to report fairly on what they now called an "American" war.

Safer's story was exceptional. Few reports on TV newscasts in 1965 and 1966 directly questioned U.S. objectives or methods of warfare. Most concentrated on combat that involved what anchors commonly called "our" troops or pilots. Many of these "bang-bang" stories lauded the sophisticated military technology that gave U.S.

forces advantages in firepower and mobility or the scale of the U.S. war effort, as troops and supplies poured into South Vietnam. Television news often entertained as it informed by providing many appealing human interest stories about American war heroes or ordinary GIs. Reporters and anchors usually accorded commanders in the field and high policymakers in Washington deferential treatment. Critics of the war—especially those in the more radical organizations—often got skeptical or patronizing coverage, if they got any at all.

Yet TV news also showed the difficulties, dilemmas, and horrors of Vietnam, if only occasionally, from the time that the Johnson administration committed large numbers of U.S. combat troops to the war in 1965. Some reporters quickly recognized fundamental strategic problems, as when ABC's Lou Cioffi asserted in October 1965 that "the United States has brought in a fantastic amount of military power here in Vietnam. But so far we've not been able to figure just exactly how to use it effectively in order to destroy the Vietcong." There were stories about the persistent troubles with pacification programs and the many ways that the war was distorting—and destroying—the lives of Vietnamese civilians. The difficulties and dangers of filming heavy fighting, along with the "queasy quotient" of network production staffs that edited reports for broadcast at the dinner hour, ensured that TV news programs would not show daily, graphic scenes of human suffering. But the newscasts did provide glimpses of severely wounded soldiers, as in Charles Kuralt's report for CBS about an artillery sergeant who clenched a cigar and grimaced as medics dressed the wounds in a leg that surgeons later amputated. A few stories also concerned atrocities, as when CBS's Don Webster described how U.S. troops severed ears from enemy corpses. And some stories could be unsettling, even if they contained no graphic images, as when the *CBS Evening News* showed a soldier's widow, baby in arms, reading one of her husband's last letters from Vietnam. Such stories were infrequent, yet their power came from what NBC News executive Reuven Frank said television journalism did best, which was the transmission of experience.

Johnson was concerned about the impact of dramatic images and the simplification inherent in half-hour newscasts. He also knew that television audiences were increasing; more than half the American people said they got most of their news from TV. The president's thinking was an example of what sociologist W. Phillips Davison has called "the third-person effect," a belief that mass communications have their greatest influence "not on 'me' or 'you,' but on 'them'" and a tendency to exaggerate the impact "on the attitudes and behavior of others." Johnson, who frequently watched the newscasts on banks of monitors tuned simultaneously to all three major networks, worried about the effects of even a single critical story and sometimes expressed his dismay directly to network news executives, anchors, or reporters. He also repeatedly found what he considered evidence of one-sidedness, unfairness, and bias.

As the war became more controversial and public support for his Vietnam policies declined, Johnson made more extreme charges. He told the president of NBC News in February 1967 that "all the networks, with the possible exception of ABC, were slanted against him," that they were "infiltrated," and that he was "ready to move on them if they move on us." The following month, he alleged that CBS and NBC were "controlled by the Vietcong," and later that year he insisted, "I can prove that Ho [Chi Minh] is a son-of-a-bitch, if you let me put it on the screen—but they [the networks] want me to be the son-of-a-bitch."

When many reporters began to describe the war as a stalemate in mid-1967, the Johnson administration launched a new public relations campaign aimed at persuading the American people that the United States was indeed making progress in achieving its goals in Vietnam. Believing that the "main front" of the war was "here in the United States," Johnson urged his advisers "to sell our product," since he insisted that "the Administration's greatest weakness was its inability to get over the complete story" on Vietnam. The Progress Campaign produced increased public support for Johnson's Vietnam policies. The improvement in the polls reflected the hopeful statements of high officials, including General William C. Westmoreland's famous declaration in a speech at the National Press Club in November 1967 that "we have reached the point when the end begins to come into view."

Such assertions of progress contributed to public disbelief and confusion and to further decline in the president's credibility when the Tet Offensive began in January 1968. TV showed startling scenes of South Vietnam under "hard, desperate, Communist attack," in the words of NBC's Brinkley, as fighting occurred in Saigon as well as in more than one hundred other locations. Some of the film was the most spectacular of the war, including footage on NBC and ABC of General Nguyen Ngoc Loan, the chief of the South Vietnamese police, executing a captured NLF officer after a street battle. Several disturbing reports showed TV journalists suffering wounds on camera.

Some observers have been highly critical of the news coverage of Tet. "The dominant themes of the words and film from Vietnam," wrote Peter Braestrup, "added up to a portrait of defeat for the allies. Historians, on the contrary, have concluded that the Tet offensive resulted in a severe military-political setback for Hanoi in the South." Yet historians continue to debate the results of the Tet fighting; there is no scholarly consensus, despite Braestrup's assertion. Moreover, TV journalists who assessed the battles did not find allied defeat. The most famous evaluation came from Walter Cronkite, who declared in a special, prime-time program on 27 February that "the Vietcong did not win by a knockout, but neither did we." "We are mired in stalemate," he concluded, and the time had come for negotiations to end U.S. involvement in the war.

"If I've lost Cronkite, I've lost the country," Johnson said gloomily. Cronkite's call for disengagement did influence the president, but only in combination with many other indications of deep divisions within the public, the Congress, the Democratic Party, and even his own administration over the war. Fearing that he could not govern effectively for another term, Johnson made his dramatic announcement to millions of stunned television viewers on the evening of 31 March 1968 that he sought negotiations to end the war and would not run again for president.

President Richard M. Nixon believed that he faced even greater opposition than Johnson from the news media in general and television journalists in particular, especially over his handling of the Vietnam War. Nixon usually read daily news summaries rather than watching the newscasts themselves. His marginal comments frequently indicated his displeasure and instructed assistants to "hit" or "kick" a particular correspondent or network for a story that he considered inaccurate or unfair. Presidential aides also maintained lists of journalists—mainly network anchors, White House correspondents, and syndicated columnists or commentators—ranked according to their friendliness toward the administration and that could be used for inflicting retaliation or providing "a special stroke."

Nixon followed a two-pronged strategy to deal with the alleged hostility of television news and to build public support for his Vietnam policies. One part involved direct, often hard-hitting, attacks on the networks. Beginning with his famous speech in Des Moines on 13 November 1969, Vice President Spiro T. Agnew tried to channel popular frustration with the war toward the networks by charging that the executives who ran them were "a tiny and closed fraternity" who "do not represent the views of America." The second part of the strategy was to use television as a medium of direct communication with the American people in order to bypass as much as possible critical reporters, editors, and commentators. As he withdrew U.S. forces from South Vietnam, Nixon urged his aides to use public relations initiatives—increasingly centered on television—to create an image of him "as a strong leader of boldness, courage, decisiveness, and independence" who would settle for nothing less than "peace with honor."

Television coverage of the war diminished as U.S. troops came home and U.S. casualties declined. Those stories that did air gave more attention to the social, political, and economic dimensions of a war that was again becoming mainly a Vietnamese conflict, one that to many Americans lacked the significance of earlier years, one that had simply gone on too long. In a report on the *CBS Evening News* about fighting in Quang Tri province in April 1972, the camera showed the crumpled bodies of children, refugees who died when their truck hit a land mine. There would be more fighting, correspondent Bob Simon declared, and more that generals, journalists, and politicians would say about those battles. "But it's difficult to imagine what those words can be," Simon concluded. "There's nothing left to say about this war. There's just nothing left to say."

Some critics blamed the extensive, uncensored television coverage for U.S. failure in Vietnam. Robert Elegant, who reported about Vietnam for the *Los Angeles Times,* insisted that partisanship prevailed over objectivity as journalists "instinctively" opposed the U.S. government and "reflexively" supported "Saigon's enemies." The television screen rather than the battlefield, according to Elegant, determined the outcome of the war by creating a "Vietnam syndrome" that "paralyzed American will" during Saigon's final crisis and that may have led to further troubles in Angola, Afghanistan, and Iran. Elegant offered little evidence to support these inflammatory charges, and Daniel C. Hallin, who carefully studied news media coverage of Vietnam, found many compelling reasons to conclude that television did not somehow lose the war. Hallin argued in *The "Uncensored War": The Media and Vietnam* (1986) that public opinion had turned against Johnson's handling of the war by early 1967, during a time that TV news coverage was most favorable to administration policies. Moreover, public support for the Korean War diminished even more quickly, yet "television was in its infancy, censorship was tight, and the World War II ethic of the journalist serving the war effort remained strong."

Hallin had the stronger argument, but Elegant's point of view had a greater effect on U.S. policy. Military officials resented the portrayal, as time went on, of the Vietnam War as part of what Hallin called the "sphere of legitimate controversy." Their belief that TV coverage undermined popular support for the war led to new restrictions on reporting when U.S. troops invaded Grenada in October 1983. Military commanders refused to transport reporters to the combat zone and barred them from the island for several days. Most journalists simply did not believe the official explanation that their exclusion was mainly to ensure their safety. ABC correspondent Steve Shepard was one of several reporters who chartered a boat, only to be turned away by the U.S. Navy as he approached Grenada. The Pentagon provided TV news programs with the only available video of the military operations in Grenada, but it did not include any scenes of combat. Walter Cronkite, who had retired in March 1981 as CBS anchor, deplored the abridgment of the public's right to know. Yet these protests did little to detract from the main story, which closely followed the Reagan administration's position—that U.S. forces had conducted a successful military operation against a potential Cuban-Soviet satellite. The restrictions on the reporting of the Grenada operation were an indication that in government-media relations, there would be no more Vietnams.

THE IRANIAN HOSTAGE CRISIS

No international story other than war dominated television news for as long as the Iranian hostage crisis. The seizure of the staff of the U.S. embassy in Tehran on 4 November 1979 marked the beginning of fourteen months of concentrated, dramatic, and controversial news coverage that affected both public understanding of the hostage crisis and government efforts to resolve it.

TV's treatment of the Iranian hostage crisis invites comparison with its reporting about a similar event—the seizure of the USS *Pueblo* on 23 January 1968 and the imprisonment of its crew of eighty-two (another crew member died of wounds incurred during the ship's capture). The North Korean capture of this intelligence ship got extensive coverage for several days on all three networks. Yet even when it led the news, the *Pueblo* seizure seemed to be related to the biggest continuing story at the time—the Vietnam War. Some reporters, such as ABC's diplomatic correspondent John Scali, told viewers that senior U.S. officials believed that the North Koreans had coordinated their action with the North Vietnamese, who were massing troops around the U.S. marine base at Khe Sanh. The beginning of the Tet Offensive a week later eclipsed the *Pueblo* story, although newscasts occasionally reported about the negotiations to free the crew. No one, at least on TV, counted the days (335) that the sailors remained in captivity. No Western journalist could go to Pyongyang to interview government officials or gauge popular attitudes toward the United States. Without such film reports, the *Pueblo* story simply could not hold a prominent, continuing position on TV newscasts. Film of some crew members did occasionally appear on the evening news programs. But the North Korean government approved its release; it contained confessions of wrongdoing and apologies, and the network journalists who narrated it made clear that the film was highly suspect. A few interviews with family members dwelled less on their distress or outrage than on whether the face or voice in the film was really their relative's and whether he appeared any different since being imprisoned. The *Pueblo* was an important story, but in 1968—a year of "horrors and failures," according to CBS's Harry Reasoner—it was not nearly as sensational or shocking or troubling as the assassinations of Martin Luther King Jr. and Robert F. Kennedy, the violence at the Democratic Convention in Chicago, the Soviet invasion of Czechoslovakia, or the war in Vietnam.

The Iranian hostage crisis, by contrast, became a dominant story quickly and remained so throughout its duration, even during the 1980 presidential election campaign. Some journalists did not imagine that it would become a news event of such magnitude. Ted Koppel, who covered the State Department for ABC, thought that this incident, like the detention of U.S. diplomats during an earlier invasion of the embassy in

Tehran on 14 February 1979, would be over in hours. Yet the Sunday evening edition of ABC's *World News Tonight* on the first day of the crisis showed some of the images that did much to stoke public outrage: glimpses of hostages in handcuffs and blindfolds, the burning of an American flag, and a photograph of the Ayatollah Ruhollah Khomeini, who reportedly approved the takeover of the embassy.

Network competition had a notable effect on ABC's coverage of the crisis. In 1977 ABC News, traditionally third in ratings and reputation, got a new president, Roone Arledge, who also headed the network's highly successful sports division. Arledge considered expanding *World News Tonight* to a full hour as a way of giving it more prominence, but local affiliates were unwilling to cede to the network an additional—and highly profitable—half hour. Arledge then experimented with late night news programming by airing half-hour specials with increasing frequency at 11:30 P.M. (EST). The hostage crisis gave Arledge the opportunity to secure permanent hold of that time slot. ABC, however, did not show its first late-night special until 8 November 1979 nor make it a nightly offering until six days later. The title of the show was both revealing and influential: *America Held Hostage.*

On 24 March 1980 the program got a new, permanent host, Koppel, and a new name, *Nightline.* It continued to provide daily coverage, even if the hostage crisis sometimes was not the lead story. Koppel hoped to use the growing capabilities of satellite technology and his skills as an interviewer to create "intercontinental salons" on live TV. Yet the discussion on the debut program was hardly genteel, as Dorothea Morefield, wife of a hostage, asked Ali Agah, the Iranian chargé in Washington, how his government could "continue to hold these innocent people." Some critics found such verbal confrontations contrived and mawkish, with news taking a back seat to show business. Yet television newscasts have long been a mixture of entertainment and information; *Nightline* expanded the limits of an established genre. And like ABC, the other networks covered the hostage crisis as a human drama as well as an international event, devoting considerable time both to interviews with family members and to the diplomatic efforts to secure the hostages' release. While ABC may have provided the hostage crisis with a melodramatic title, CBS's Walter Cronkite, television's most respected journalist, popularized what became the standard for

measuring its duration. He added to his famous sign-off—"and that's the way it is"—a count of the days, eventually 444, that the fifty-two hostages endured captivity.

The Carter administration at first welcomed the heavy news coverage. Administration officials had many chances to explain to viewers that they were taking strong, but measured action—diplomatic initiatives, economic sanctions—to try to resolve the crisis without resorting to military force. Jimmy Carter could concentrate on his role as president, rather than as candidate facing a vigorous challenge for his party's presidential nomination from Senator Edward M. Kennedy of Massachusetts. Indeed, Carter conspicuously refrained from campaign travel in favor of a Rose Garden strategy that played up his responsibilities as national leader. Carter's approval rating surged from 30 to 61 percent during the first month of the hostage crisis. Never before had the Gallup Poll recorded such a sharp improvement.

Yet administration officials soon deplored the extensive television coverage. Hodding Carter, the State Department spokesperson, complained that news reports were complicating negotiations. White House officials found considerable evidence that Iranian demonstrators were playing to the cameras. Yet their efforts to shift public attention away from the hostage crisis simply would not work because of what presidential counsel Lloyd Cutler called "the constant drumbeat of TV news." Deputy Secretary of State Warren Christopher believed that television intensified public anger and frustration as it reported about the failed rescue effort in April 1980, described diplomatic initiatives that seemed ineffective, and relentlessly counted the days. Press secretary Jody Powell expressed his frustration at the end of one long day when there had been demonstrations across from the White House by two antagonistic groups that had shouted and scuffled. He crossed Pennsylvania Avenue late at night, walked into Lafayette Park, and unexpectedly encountered CBS reporter Jed Duvall. The reason for these prolonged difficulties, Powell blurted out, was "the networks with their nose up the Ayatollah's ass."

CENTRAL AMERICA AND THE LEGACIES OF VIETNAM

"No more Vietnams" was a popular slogan in the late 1970s and early 1980s, but there were strong disagreements about the meaning of that simple phrase. Some people wanted to avoid another long, costly, and—most important—unsuccessful war. Like Ronald Reagan's first secretary of defense, Caspar Weinberger, they believed that the United States should use its military forces only to achieve clear objectives that commanded public support and that would lead to victory. Others wanted to refrain from intervention in Third World revolutions or civil wars where no outside power could hope to impose a lasting settlement. Some counseled against a major effort, even to stop the spread of communism, in a peripheral area. Still others were wary of situations in which limited measures—military aid, the dispatch of advisers, covert action—might create pressures for progressively deeper involvement culminating in the commitment of combat troops.

Television viewers often learned about these perspectives as their advocates addressed a major, recurring question: Would Central America become "another Vietnam"? On the evening newscasts, the range of views on this issue—and, more generally, on U.S. policy toward Nicaragua or El Salvador—was much greater than in the early 1960s when television covered the expanding U.S. involvement in Vietnam. Changes in broadcast journalism did not account for this difference. Reporters still relied heavily on official sources of information. Quantitative studies of television newscasts show that officials of the Carter or Reagan administrations and members of Congress most frequently appeared in stories about Central America. What was different was that the sphere of legitimate controversy was broader, in large measure because of the legacy of Vietnam.

Television reporting did occasionally have a notable effect on public attitudes or U.S. policy concerning Central America. One shocking example involved ABC correspondent Bill Stewart, who was reporting about the civil war in Nicaragua. Carrying a white flag and media credentials, Stewart approached a National Guard roadblock in Managua on 20 June 1979. A guard officer ordered him to lie on the ground and then shot him and his interpreter. Stewart's crew filmed the killings from its van; the tape ran not just on ABC but on CBS and NBC as well. The footage was uniquely horrifying; the only comparable incidents that TV had shown were Jack Ruby's shooting of Lee Harvey Oswald and General Loan's execution of the NLF prisoner during the Tet Offensive. Speaking the next day to the Organization of American States, Secretary of State Cyrus Vance deplored

"the mounting human tragedy" in Nicaragua. "This terror was brought home vividly to the American people yesterday with the cold-blooded murder . . . of an American newsman." Vance then issued the Carter administration's first public call for the resignation of Nicaraguan president Anastasio Somoza and his replacement with a "government of national reconciliation."

Eight years later in very different circumstances, television focused on another individual who affected public views about U.S. policy toward Nicaragua. Colonel Oliver North, fired from his position with the National Security Council, testified for several days in July 1987 during televised congressional hearings into the Iran-contra scandal. Dressed in marine uniform, North was poised and passionate. He admitted that he had misled Congress, but was unrepentant. He presented himself as a patriot who had served his country and his president by maintaining the contras, "body and soul." Polls revealed a significant shift in public attitudes toward continued U.S. military aid to the contras, with opponents outnumbering supporters by a margin of more than two to one before North's testimony but opinion almost equally divided after his appearance. Television, however, helped focus attention more on North's personality than on public issues. Polls showed that many Americans agreed with Ronald Reagan, who called North "a national hero." "Olliemania," as some journalists called the phenomenon of his sudden celebrity, helped launch North on a new career as radio talk show host after appeals overturned three felony convictions.

THE GREAT COMMUNICATOR ON THE WORLD STAGE

President Ronald Reagan became known as the Great Communicator, a distinction that earned him both plaudits and derogation. Reagan's speeches moved, inspired, and reassured millions of people. Critics, however, insisted that Reagan was an acting president, a performer who brought to the White House the theatrical skills that he had learned in Hollywood and who followed scripts that he had done little, if anything, to create. Reagan, like most contemporary presidents, usually read texts that speechwriters had prepared. Yet sometimes the words and often the ideas were his own. Opponents deplored the troubling oversimplifications in his folksy anecdotes and uplifting stories. Yet many viewers found an authenticity that came from the president's sincerity and conviction. Reagan was extraordinarily successful at using the White House and, indeed, the world, as a stage—or perhaps, more accurately, a studio—as he exploited the medium of television to build public support for his presidency.

White House aides planned Reagan's public appearances with meticulous care as television events. They chose the best camera angles, chalked in toe marks so the president would know exactly where to stand, and positioned reporters to minimize opportunities for unwanted questions. The preparations reflected what the president's assistants called the "line of the day," the story that they wanted to lead the news in order to advance their legislative or international agenda. What viewers saw, Reagan's communications experts thought, was more important than what they heard. When the *CBS Evening News* ran a critical story in October 1984 about Reagan's use of soothing images to obscure unpopular policies, reporter Lesley Stahl was astounded when White House aide Richard Darman telephoned to congratulate her. "You guys in Televisionland haven't figured it out, have you?" Darman said. "When the pictures are powerful and emotional, they override if not completely drown out the sound. Lesley, I mean it, nobody heard you."

Televised images mattered so much to the Reagan White House partly because of changes in TV news. By the early 1980s about two-thirds of the American public said that television was their primary source of news. Viewers could watch a growing number of news programs, including morning and midday shows as well as the traditional evening broadcasts. During prime time there were popular magazine programs, such as *60 Minutes* (CBS) and *20/20* (ABC), as well as brief updates called "newsbreaks." And at the end of the day, there was *Nightline*. Cable TV, which reached 20 percent of television households in 1981 and more than twice that proportion in 1985, offered more choices. On 1 June 1980 the Cable News Network became the first 24-hour news channel. Greater competition and corporate pressures made network news executives more concerned with ratings and willing to try to increase them by altering the balance between information and entertainment. At CBS, for example, when ratings plunged after Cronkite's retirement, the news director urged the new anchor, Dan Rather, to dress in a sweater to appear friendly and informal and insisted on more

"feel-good" features. CBS producers dropped a report about State Department reaction to Israeli bombing in Lebanon to open a slot on the evening news of 30 November 1982 for a story about singing sheep. On all the networks, lighter features, striking visuals, and ten-second sound bites increasingly became ways to attract and hold viewers who had more choices, remote controls, and seemingly shorter attention spans. The communications experts in the White House exploited these trends, packaging presidential appearances to fit the changes in TV news.

Reagan's international trips produced many dramatic and memorable television scenes. The advance planners created public occasions, often in striking surroundings, where the president would be in the spotlight. For example, on the rocky coast of Normandy, Reagan gave a magnificent speech in which he commemorated the fortieth anniversary of D-Day on 6 June 1984 by saluting "the boys of Pointe du Hoc . . . the champions who helped free a continent . . . the heroes who helped end a war." White House aide Michael Deaver made sure that the French scheduled Reagan's address so it would air live during the network morning news programs. In another stirring scene, Reagan expressed his fervent anti-communism and his commitment to freedom when he stood before the Brandenburg Gate in West Berlin on 12 June 1987 and cried, "Mr. Gorbachev, tear down this wall." Other trips produced less exalted, but nonetheless effective events. During a trip to South Korea in November 1983, Reagan attended an outdoor service at a chapel within sight of the North Korean border. One military police officer explained that a nearby armored personnel carrier was there for "backdrop." In one notorious case, advance planning failed. Presidential assistants did not learn that SS troops were buried at Bitburg cemetery in West Germany before the White House announced Reagan's visit. The president refused to change his plans, but he also went to Bergen-Belsen, the site of a Nazi concentration camp, where he gave one of his most moving addresses.

Reagan's summits with Mikhail Gorbachev were international media events with considerable symbolic significance. At their first meeting in Geneva in November 1985, Reagan said that he recognized from Gorbachev's smile that he was dealing with a different kind of Soviet leader. Televised images of their close and friendly relations symbolized the international changes that were occurring as the Cold War began to wane.

At their summit in Washington, D.C., in December 1987, the most important substantive achievement was the signing of the Intermediate-Range Nuclear Forces treaty. But what mattered as well was what the news media called "Gorby fever," which the Soviet leader stoked by stopping his limousine and plunging into welcoming crowds in downtown Washington. When Reagan reciprocated by traveling to Moscow in May 1988, he followed a schedule that was the result of elaborate planning, including the use of polling and focus groups to test the themes of his speeches. Cameras followed Reagan and Gorbachev as they strolled through Red Square answering questions that appeared to be spontaneous, but some of which had been planted. When a reporter asked about the "evil empire," as Reagan had described the Soviet Union in a famous speech in March 1983, the president replied, that was "another time, another era." The televised scenes beginning in late 1989 of revolutions in Eastern Europe and the opening of the Berlin Wall confirmed Reagan's pronouncement.

THE PERSIAN GULF WAR

On 16–17 January 1991, viewers around the world watched the beginning of a war for the first time ever on live television. As allied bombs and cruise missiles hit targets in Iraq, CNN reporters described what they saw from their hotel in Baghdad during the first hours of the Persian Gulf War. The explosions had severed communications with other U.S. network reporters in the Iraqi capital. Using the telephone, CNN correspondents Peter Arnett, John Holliman, and Bernard Shaw acted much like radio reporters, since they were unable to transmit pictures of what they saw. "Now there's a huge fire that we've just seen," Holliman exclaimed. "And we just heard—whoa. Holy cow. That was a large air burst that we saw. It was filling the sky." "Go for it, guys," a CNN producer told the reporters. "The whole world's watching." One of those viewers was President George H. W. Bush, who said with relief that the war had begun, "just the way it was scheduled."

The reporting on that first night from Baghdad was exceptional, in part because government restrictions did not impede it. But Iraqi authorities established censorship within twenty-four hours after the start of the bombing and U.S. military officials imposed a system of restraints on the news media that had been years in the making.

Its outlines emerged in 1984, when the Pentagon responded to complaints about the exclusion of reporters from Grenada by creating a committee chaired by General Winant Sidle, who had served as a military information officer during the Vietnam War. The Sidle panel recognized that technological innovations—portable satellite antennas that made possible live broadcasting from the battlefield—might jeopardize the security of U.S. military operations or the safety of U.S. troops. It called on journalists to refrain from reporting sensitive information as a condition of their accreditation. If commanders decided that military considerations required limited access to combat areas, the Sidle panel recommended that small groups of journalists be allowed into battle zones and then share their reporting with their colleagues.

This pool system got its first test when U.S. troops invaded Panama in December 1989. Military transports carried reporters to base areas, but kept them sequestered during the first days of Operation Just Cause. Complaints about a system that seemed to keep reporters away from military action rather than to facilitate their access to it led to extended discussions between news organizations and military authorities during the buildup of U.S. forces in Saudi Arabia during late 1990. On the eve of Operation Desert Storm, the Pentagon announced new guidelines, which required journalists to participate in pools, exclude restricted information from their articles and broadcasts, and submit their reports to military officials for security review.

The legacies of Vietnam exerted a powerful influence on the Bush administration as it prepared for war. General Colin Powell, the chair of the Joint Chiefs of Staff, believed that Vietnam had shown that the American public simply would not tolerate a prolonged, televised war with heavy casualties. Bush thought that Vietnam had also proven other lessons. He insisted that the United States and its coalition partners must use overwhelming military force that would produce decisive results. The president did a masterly job of building public support for his demand that Iraqi troops withdraw from Kuwait and his determination to use force, if necessary, to achieve that goal. He portrayed Saddam Hussein as a kind of Middle Eastern Hitler—a dictator who brutalized Iraqis, an outlaw who defied fundamental principles of international order, and an aggressor who wanted weapons of mass destruction to threaten other nations. TV news provided other viewpoints, other voices, including Hussein's, as the Iraqi president granted interviews to several Western journalists, including news anchors Peter Jennings of ABC and Rather of CBS. The newscasts also covered the debate over the use of force, which Congress authorized on 12 January 1991. Polls showed that substantial majorities favored military action and endorsed Bush's handling of the crisis. Once the war began, the president enjoyed overwhelming public support for his policies.

TV's war coverage in some ways resembled a miniseries. The networks had distinctive titles—"War in the Gulf," " Showdown in the Gulf"—and accompanying music. A good deal of the coverage emphasized the drama of war—the danger of a sudden attack of Iraqi Scud missiles, the risks of flying into hostile fire, the heroism of U.S. troops and the sacrifices of their relatives at home.

Yet in all this reporting about war, TV provided an extremely limited view of the fighting. The Defense Department supplied most of the video of the air war. Recorded with night vision equipment, it seemed fantastic and futuristic, something that reminded many viewers of a video game. The pool system ensured that reporters would have few unregulated opportunities to cover combat. A handful of correspondents, like CBS's Bob Simon, went out into the Saudi desert without escorts. Simon's first such excursion produced a report from Khafji, near the border with Kuwait, where U.S. marines were under attack. On his next unescorted trip, Iraqi troops captured him; Simon and his crew remained prisoners until the end of the war. Although network newscasts ran several reports about what they bluntly called censorship, there was little public dissatisfaction with the Pentagon's restrictions. Viewers were far more interested in seeing the briefings of General H. Norman Schwarzkopf, commanding and apparently authoritative performances that made the general the greatest hero of the Gulf War.

The television journalist who got the most attention—much of it unwelcome—was CNN's Peter Arnett. When most reporters decided to put personal safety ahead of the story, Arnett decided to stay in Baghdad. When Iraqi authorities decided to expel the remaining Western TV correspondents during the first week of fighting, they excepted CNN, mainly because producer Robert Wiener had spent months building cooperative relations with government officials in Baghdad. Arnett had no competition, but he did have "minders," information officials who limited his move-

ments and censored his reporting. Repeatedly Arnett pushed against those limits, for example, by arguing that his reports would have greater credibility if he could respond more freely to questions from CNN anchors during live broadcasts. His stories about civilian casualties during allied bombing raids—at a baby milk formula factory and an air raid shelter—stirred enormous controversy in the United States. The most extreme of many attacks on the alleged impropriety of reporting from behind enemy lines came from Republican representative Lawrence Coughlin of Pennsylvania, who denounced Arnett as "the Joseph Goebbels of Saddam Hussein's Hitler-like regime." Arnett disliked becoming part of the story, yet he stayed in Baghdad until the end of the ground war.

Arnett's reporting notwithstanding, Bush administration officials were pleased with television coverage of the Gulf War. Pete Williams, the Pentagon's chief public affairs officer, concluded that the news media had provided "the best war coverage we've ever had." Secretary of State James A. Baker spoke more candidly when he described "that poor demoralized rabble—outwitted, outflanked, outmaneuvered by the U.S. military. But I think, given time, the press will bounce back."

THE CNN EFFECT

By the early 1990s many people had concluded that television news possessed formidable powers to influence the U.S. government's foreign policy. The "CNN effect," as it is usually called, actually has several dimensions. The first is providing a new channel of diplomatic communication, one that allows governments to transmit proposals or engage in dialogue, sometimes with extraordinary speed. Officials in the Bush administration, for example, sometimes used TV to send messages to Saddam Hussein after the invasion of Kuwait, hoping that a public channel might increase the pressure on the Iraqi leader to accede to U.S. demands. Government leaders, however, have long used the news media as channels of diplomacy. Radio, for example, carried Woodrow Wilson's Fourteen Point Address of 8 January 1918 to an international audience.

The second dimension of the "CNN effect" is setting the foreign policy agenda—giving certain issues urgency or importance through news reports that capture the interest of millions of viewers and elicit a strong response. The ability to provide live reports from almost anywhere in the world, to transmit dramatic, emotional images, and to show them repeatedly seems to provide television with powers that exceed the other news media to alter the priorities that the government gives to international issues. The third dimension is accelerating official action. Even before the advent of CNN and other twenty-four-hour news channels, Lloyd Cutler, a counsel to President Carter, found that TV news had led to "foreign policy on deadline," as White House officials hurried to take action—to make a statement, to announce a new initiative—before the next newscast.

The final—and most controversial—dimension of the "CNN effect" is forcing government action. George F. Kennan, the foreign service officer who was an architect of containment during the early Cold War, summarized this perspective in a diary entry about U.S. intervention in Somalia in December 1992. Kennan maintained that television pictures of starving Somali children had produced "an emotional reaction, not a thoughtful or deliberate one," but one strong enough to take control of foreign policy decisions from "the responsible deliberative organs of our government."

A closer look at U.S. involvement in Somalia, however, suggests different conclusions than Kennan's about the effects of televised images on government policy decisions. Quantitative studies show that extensive coverage of the famine and fighting in Somalia followed the policy initiatives of the Bush administration in 1992 rather than preceded them. Television coverage surely affected the views of administration officials and gave them confidence that what they thought would be a limited, low-risk humanitarian intervention would have considerable public support. But television pictures of suffering Somalis did not determine the president's decision to dispatch troops. Television had a more decisive effect on President William Jefferson Clinton's decision to terminate Operation Restore Hope when newscasts showed shocking tape in early October 1993 of a crowd in Mogadishu desecrating the corpse of a U.S. soldier who had been killed in a firefight. The U.S. casualties took the president by surprise, and he was not prepared to appeal to angry members of Congress for the continuation of a mission that had suddenly grown dangerous. Instead, Clinton announced that U.S. forces would come home by 31 March 1994.

Television showed the horrors of ethnic cleansing and civil war in Bosnia, and those reports were influential but not decisive in shaping U.S. government action. Scenes of Serb camps with emaciated Muslim and Croat prisoners in August 1992 produced condemnations from the Bush administration. Yet the president and his principal advisers were unwilling to take military action, as they believed that there was no clear exit strategy. Clinton, too, reacted intensely to graphic TV reports of atrocities, such as the casualties that occurred when a mortar shell exploded in a Sarajevo marketplace on 5 February 1994. But he followed no consistent policy. Not until mid-1995 did the Clinton administration approve strong measures, including continuing NATO air strikes, to bring the Bosnian war to an end. Available evidence suggests that the president acted to eliminate a major problem that burdened U.S. foreign policy and that threatened his political prospects. Almost four years later, in March 1999, the United States and its NATO allies again used military force in an air war against Yugoslavia to persuade President Slobodan Milosevic to halt ethnic cleansing in Kosovo. News reports, including many on TV, of brutality against Kosovars contributed to public support for this war. But concern about popular reaction to potential U.S. casualties led Clinton to rule out the use of ground troops, except for peacekeeping.

The "CNN effect" influenced U.S. interventions in Somalia, Bosnia, and Kosovo. TV reports helped set the agenda; at times, officials of the Bush and Clinton administrations had to react—sometimes quickly—to events that dominated the newscasts. But the "CNN effect" was variable, and it was only one of many factors in the process of formulating foreign policy.

THE TWENTY-FIRST CENTURY

The new millennium began with televised celebrations on every continent, hopeful events that suggested that modern communications were bringing closer the creation of Marshall McLuhan's global village. Yet the twenty-first century also brought almost unimaginable scenes of horror and suffering when terrorists flew hijacked airplanes into the twin towers of the World Trade Center and the Pentagon on 11 September 2001. Enormous audiences in the United States and around the world relied on television for news about these disasters. Even government officials watched television because it provided more information more quickly than other available sources. Round-the-clock coverage on the broadcast as well as the cable news channels quickly spread the disbelief, outrage, grief, and uncertainty about the future that were immediate products of these startling events.

Technological changes—especially greater Internet access and the increasing convergence of the computer and the television—may alter viewing habits and change sources of news and information. But for the immediate future, at least, during conflicts, crises, and other important international developments, both public officials and citizens will turn to television news.

BIBLIOGRAPHY

Arlen, Michael J. *Living-Room War.* New York, 1982.

Arnett, Peter. *Live from the Battlefield: From Vietnam to Baghdad, 35 Years in the World's War Zones.* New York, 1994. A superb memoir by a reporter who covered the Vietnam War for the Associated Press and the Persian Gulf War for CNN.

Barnouw, Erik. *Tube of Plenty: The Evolution of American Culture.* 2d rev. ed. New York, 1990.

Baughman, James L. *The Republic of Mass Culture: Journalism, Filmmaking, and Broadcasting in America Since 1941.* 2d ed. Baltimore, 1997.

Bernhard, Nancy E. *U.S. Television News and Cold War Propaganda, 1947–1960.* New York, 1999.

Braestrup, Peter. *Big Story: How the American Press and Television Reported and Interpreted the Crisis of Tet 1968 in Vietnam and Washington.* 2 vols. Boulder, Colo., 1977.

Cannon, Lou. *President Reagan: The Role of a Lifetime.* New York, 2000.

Cutler, Lloyd N. "Foreign Policy on Deadline." *Foreign Policy* no. 56 (fall 1984): 113–128.

Davison, W. Phillips. "The Third-Person Effect in Communication." *Public Opinion Quarterly* 47 (spring 1983): 1–15.

Dennis, Everette E., et al. *The Media at War: The Press and the Persian Gulf Conflict.* New York, 1991.

Elegant, Robert. "How to Lose a War." *Encounter* 57 (August 1981): 73–90. A harsh and often polemical critique of reporting of the Vietnam War.

Halberstam, David. *War in a Time of Peace: Bush, Clinton, and the Generals.* New York, 2001.

Hallin, Daniel C. *The "Uncensored War": The Media and Vietnam.* New York, 1986. The best analysis of news media reporting of Vietnam.

———. *We Keep America on Top of the World: Television Journalism and the Public Sphere.* New York, 1994. A collection of excellent essays.

Hammond, William M. *Public Affairs: The Military and the Media, 1962–1968.* Washington, D.C., 1988.

———. *Public Affairs: The Military and the Media, 1968–1973.* Washington, D.C., 1996.

Isaacs, Arnold R. "The Five O'Clock Follies Revisited: Vietnam's 'Instant Historians' and the Legacy of Controversy." *The Long Term View* 5 (summer 2000): 92–101. Explains how Vietnam created lasting distrust of the news media among military officers.

Kimball, Jeffrey P. *Nixon's Vietnam War.* Lawrence, Kans., 1998.

Koppel, Ted, and Kyle Gibson. *Nightline: History in the Making and the Making of Television.* New York, 1996. Contains an insider account of the birth of the ABC news show *Nightline* during the Iranian hostage crisis.

MacArthur, John R. *Second Front: Censorship and Propaganda in the Gulf War.* New York, 1992. A scathing critique of the pool system and the news media's cooperation with it.

Maltese, John Anthony. *Spin Control: The White House Office of Communications and the Management of Presidential News.* 2d ed. Chapel Hill, N.C., 1994.

Mermin, Jonathan. "Television News and American Intervention in Somalia: The Myth of a Media-Driven Foreign Policy." *Political Science Quarterly* 112 (autumn 1997): 385–403.

Neuman, Johanna. *Lights, Camera, War: Is Media Technology Driving International Politics?* New York, 1996.

O'Neill, Michael J. *The Roar of the Crowd: How Television and People Power Are Changing the World.* New York, 1993.

Pach, Chester J., Jr. "And That's the Way It Was: The Vietnam War on the Network Nightly News." In David Farber, ed. *The Sixties: From Memory to History.* Chapel Hill, N.C., 1994.

———. "Tet on TV: U.S. Nightly News Reporting and Presidential Policymaking." In Carole Fink, Philipp Gassert, and Detlef Junker, eds. *1968: The World Transformed.* New York, 1998.

———. "The War on Television: TV News, the Johnson Administration, and Vietnam." In Marilyn Young and Robert Buzzanco, eds. *Blackwell Companion to the Vietnam War.* Malden, Mass., 2002.

Small, Melvin. *Covering Dissent: The Media and the Anti-Vietnam War Movement.* New Brunswick, N. J., 1994.

Stahl, Lesley. *Reporting Live.* New York, 1999.

Strobel, Warren P. *Late-Breaking Foreign Policy: The News Media's Influence on Peace Operations.* Washington, D.C., 1997. Includes excellent analysis of TV coverage of military interventions in Somalia, Haiti, and Bosnia.

Tallman, Gary C., and Joseph P. McKerns. "'Press Mess:' David Halberstam, the Buddhist Crisis, and U.S. Policy in Vietnam, 1963." *Journalism and Communication Monographs* 2 (fall 2000): 109–153.

Utley, Garrick. *You Should Have Been There Yesterday: A Life in Television News.* New York, 2000. A highly informative memoir by one of television's most important international affairs correspondents.

Woodward, Bob. *The Commanders.* New York, 1991.

Wyatt, Clarence. *Paper Soldiers: The American Press and the Vietnam War.* New York, 1993.

See also DISSENT IN WARS; THE NATIONAL INTEREST; THE PRESS; PUBLIC OPINION.

TERRORISM AND COUNTERTERRORISM

Brian Michael Jenkins

Terrorism was a matter of growing international concern during the last three decades of the twentieth century, but following the 11 September 2001, attacks on New York City and Washington, D.C., it became the paramount issue of U.S. foreign policy. On that day Middle Eastern terrorists hijacked four U.S. commercial airliners. They seized the controls and crashed two of the planes into the World Trade Center and one plane into the Pentagon. Passengers fought to regain control of the fourth plane, which then crashed in Pennsylvania, missing any symbolic targets but killing all those on board. These attacks, unprecedented in the annals of terrorism and unparalleled in American history in the magnitude and concentration of casualties, provoked an equally unprecedented declaration of war against terrorism.

Terrorist tactics themselves are nothing new. Political intrigues and wars throughout history have involved murder, hostage taking, and sabotage. Deliberately savage and cruel, even by eighth-century standards, Viking berserkers spread terror throughout the British Isles. Muslim assassins provoked terror among Christian crusaders and Arab leaders in the twelfth century. Julius Caesar, King Richard the Lionhearted, and Miguel de Cervantes were all held for ransom.

The word "terror" entered the political lexicon during the French Revolution's "reign of terror" and in the twentieth century was associated with oppression by totalitarian governments. The term "terrorism" emerged in the nineteenth century when bomb-throwing revolutionaries who wanted to obliterate property and terrorize the ruling classes acknowledged themselves to be terrorists. Revolutionary terrorism continued into the early twentieth century and reemerged following World War I. From the late 1940s to the early 1960s, terrorism often accompanied armed struggles for independence, especially in Algeria and Palestine.

THE EMERGENCE OF INTERNATIONAL TERRORISM

Terrorists continued to use the tactics of their historical predecessors: setting off bombs in public places, assassinating officials, kidnapping individuals to demand political concessions or ransom payments. But a new phenomenon, international terrorism, began with a series of spectacular attacks in the late 1960s. In 1968, Palestinians hijacked an El Al jetliner and flew it to Algeria, where they demanded the release of Palestinian prisoners. This began a wave of hijackings to obtain political concessions. In 1969 urban guerrillas in Brazil kidnapped the U.S. ambassador, later releasing him in return for the release of fifteen comrades imprisoned in Brazil. The tactic quickly spread throughout the world. In the following twelve months, diplomats were kidnapped in Uruguay, Argentina, Bolivia, Guatemala, the Dominican Republic, and Jordan.

In February 1970 members of the Popular Front for the Liberation of Palestine (PFLP) sabotaged a Swissair flight to Tel Aviv, killing all forty-seven persons on board. In September 1970 the same group hijacked three airliners bound for Europe and diverted them to Jordan. In May 1972 three members of the Japanese Red Army, a group allied with the PFLP, attacked passengers at Israel's Lod Airport, killing twenty-five and wounding seventy-six. And in September of that year, members of Black September, another Middle Eastern group, seized nine Israeli athletes at the Munich Olympics. Five of the terrorists and all nine of the hostages were killed in a disastrous rescue attempt by German police. The three surviving terrorists were traded for hostages aboard a Lufthansa flight hijacked the next month.

International terrorism emerged from a confluence of political circumstances and technological process. In the Middle East, Israel's defeat of the Arab armies in the Six-Day War of

1967 and the inability of Palestinians to mount an effective resistance movement in the territories newly occupied by Israel pushed them toward the use of terrorist tactics. Their mentors were the Algerian revolutionaries who in the fight for independence had carried their own terrorist campaign to France itself. For the Palestinians, anyone anywhere in the world who supported Israel's continued existence became a potential target, greatly broadening the theater of operations.

Inspired by the success of the Cuban revolution but unable to replicate its success, Latin America's guerrillas moved their struggle from the countryside into the cities. They replaced traditional guerrilla warfare with bombings, assassinations, and kidnappings, which guaranteed them national and international attention. Spectacular action took the place of patient political mobilization. At the same time, the Vietnam War sparked a new wave of revolutionary fervor that spread through the universities of Europe, Japan, and the United States. Mass protest movements spawned small groups on their extremist fringes that were determined to pursue a more violent struggle. These extremist groups emulated the tactics of their ideological counterparts in Latin America and the Middle East.

Changes in the technological environment during the 1970s also facilitated international terrorism. Jet air travel offered terrorists worldwide mobility and, with it, opportunities to strike targets anywhere. Television and the deployment of communications satellites offered terrorists almost instantaneous access to a global audience. By choreographing dramatic incidents of violence and hostage situations in which human life hung in the balance, terrorists could guarantee worldwide press coverage for their acts and their causes. The diffusion of small arms around the world and of increasingly powerful explosives and sophisticated detonating devices took terrorists far beyond the capacity of the early bomb throwers. Modern technology-dependent societies offered numerous vulnerabilities, from power grids to jumbo jets.

The relationship of all these incidents to one another was not self-evident at the time. Beyond the similarity in tactics, there was no obvious connection between a kidnapping in Uruguay, a bombing in Germany, and a hijacking in Africa. Why should actions carried out by persons who called themselves Tupamaros, Montoneros, the Red Brigades, or the Japanese Red Army be addressed within the same analytical and policy framework? International terrorism was an artificial construct useful for policy purposes. While recognizing the diversity of the terrorists and their causes, it identified their actions in the international domain as a mutual problem for all nations.

THE TARGETING OF AMERICA

Concern about international terrorism on the part of the U.S. foreign policy community was driven by two overlapping issues: the use of tactics that fell outside the accepted norms of diplomacy and armed conflict and the spillover of terrorist violence into the international domain. The latter was particularly important, since the prominence of the United States in world affairs and its involvement in many contentious areas made Americans and American interests frequent targets. Hundreds of terrorist attacks have been directed against the United States, its diplomats, and its diplomatic facilities.

Major incidents have included the kidnappings of U.S. diplomats in Latin America in the late 1960s and early 1970s; the multiple hijacking to Jordan's Dawson Field in 1970; the attack on arriving American passengers at Israel's Lod Airport in 1972; the terrorist seizure of the Saudi Arabian embassy in Khartoum, Sudan, and the subsequent murder of two American diplomats in 1973; the terrorist takeover of the U.S. consulate in Kuala Lumpur, Malaysia, in 1975; the 1979 takeover of the American embassy in Tehran; the suicide bombings of the American embassy and U.S. marine barracks in Beirut in 1983; the bombing in 1983 of the American embassy in Kuwait; the kidnappings of Americans and the protracted hostage crisis in Lebanon, which lasted from 1984 to 1991; the hijackings of TWA flight 847 and of the cruise ship *Achille Lauro* in 1985; the Libyan terrorist campaign in 1986; the sabotage and crash of PanAm flight 103 in 1988; the assassination plot against former President George H. W. Bush in 1993; the bombing of the World Trade Center in 1993; the suicide bombing of the American military residential facility in Dhahran, Saudi Arabia, in 1996; the bombings of the American embassies in Kenya and Tanzania in 1998; the suicide bombing of the destroyer USS *Cole* in 2000; and the attacks in 2001 on the World Trade Center and the Pentagon.

The attacks in the 1980s increasingly involved truck bombs, huge amounts of explosives on wheels, often driven by suicide drivers. These attacks manifested a fundamental change in terrorism. Traditionally, terrorists wanted a lot of people watching, not a lot of people dead. Wanton violence was seen as counterproductive. But with the replacement of ideological causes by ethnic hatreds and religious fanaticism, large-scale, indiscriminate violence became the reality. Terrorists wanted a lot of people dead. But while truck bombs increased death tolls, they could not easily push the number of victims above several hundred. The terrorist solution was multiple attacks. In 1994 terrorists plotted to sabotage twelve U.S. airliners in the Pacific, and the 1998 attacks on the American embassies in Africa as well as the 2001 attacks on the World Trade Center and the Pentagon involved multiple targets. These large-scale operations have also led to fears that terrorists will incorporate chemical, biological, or possibly even nuclear weapons in future attacks.

DEFINING TERRORISM

It is clear that efforts to combat terrorism depend on international cooperation, but international politics has complicated attempts even to define international terrorism. Discussions in international forums have inevitably bogged down in futile debate. Some see terrorism as an alternative mode of warfare used by nations or groups that lack the conventional means of waging war, not as something to be outlawed. Some, believing that the ends justify the means, seek to exclude from the definition anything done by those engaged in wars of liberation. Others have wanted to broaden the definition to include acts of violence and other repressive acts by colonial, racist, and alien regimes against peoples struggling for liberation.

The United States has tried to define terrorism objectively on the basis of the quality of the act, not the identity of the perpetrators or the nature of their political cause. The rationale is that all terrorist acts are crimes, and many would also be war crimes or "grave breaches" of the rules of war even if one accepted the terrorists' assertion that they wage war. Terrorist acts involve violence or the threat of violence, sometimes coupled with explicit demands and always directed against noncombatants. The perpetrators are usually members of an organized group whose purposes are political. And the hallmark of terrorism—actions that are carried out in a way that will achieve maximum publicity and cause major alarm—introduces a distinction between the victims of the violence and the target audience. Indeed, the identity of the victims may be secondary or even irrelevant to the terrorist cause. "Pure terrorism" is entirely indiscriminate violence.

The U.S. position never won universal endorsement, but ultimately, the international community has come to achieve a rough consensus on terrorism. Although the community of nations could not reach an agreement on a precise definition, it did denounce terrorism as a form of political expression or mode of armed conflict and managed to construct a corpus of conventions that identified and outlawed specific tactics: airline hijacking, the sabotage of commercial aircraft, attacks on airports, attacks on diplomats and diplomatic facilities, the taking of hostages, bomb attacks on civilian targets, and so on. This tactic-by-tactic approach gradually extended to cover virtually all the manifestations of international terrorism.

CRIME OR WARFARE?

A continuing U.S. policy issue has been whether terrorism should be considered as a crime or a mode of war. The question is not merely one of a choice of words. The two are different concepts with entirely different operational implications. If terrorism is considered a criminal matter, the appropriate response is to gather evidence, correctly determine the culpability of the individual or individuals responsible for the incident, and then apprehend and bring the perpetrators to trial. This has been the primary approach taken by the United States, and it has received wide international acceptance. To enhance this approach, the United States extended the jurisdiction of American courts to cover all terrorist acts against U.S. citizens and facilities anywhere in the world, thereby giving the Federal Bureau of Investigation legislative authority to investigate terrorist crimes and apprehend terrorists anywhere. Although not all nations accept this assertion, a number of terrorists have been turned over to U.S. authorities for prosecution in the United States.

Public trials of terrorists keep terrorism firmly in the realm of crime, strip terrorists of their political pretensions, and allow the United States to make a public case against those terrorists still at large. Dealing with terrorism strictly as a criminal matter, however, presents a number of problems. Evidence is extremely difficult to gather in an international investigation where some countries might not cooperate, and apprehending individual terrorists is extremely difficult. Moreover, the criminal approach does not provide an entirely satisfactory answer to a continuing campaign of terrorism waged by a distant group, and it does not work against a state sponsor of terrorism.

If, on the other hand, terrorism is viewed as war, there is less concern with individual culpability; only proximate responsibility—for example, the correct identification of the terrorist group—need be established. Evidence does not have to be of courtroom quality; intelligence reporting will suffice. The focus is not on the accused individual but on the correct identification of the enemy.

The United States has at different times taken both approaches, and recently began to orchestrate the criminal and military approaches, combining conventional evidence gathering and intelligence reporting to indict and prosecute terrorists, then combining that with information gained at trial to support further indictments, which were then utilized to justify military action.

THE DEVELOPMENT OF COUNTERTERRORIST POLICY

U.S. policy on terrorism has been largely driven by events. Indeed, policy is rarely created in the abstract. It responds to events that create a requirement to do something. Policy is reactive, an accumulation of statements and actions that then become precedents. And it is constantly evolving. Ask some official to explain the reasoning behind a certain policy and, if he knows his history well enough, he will cite the exact incident that prompted the reaction. This is especially true of a diverse, multifaceted phenomenon such as terrorism.

Much of the early U.S. counterterrorist policy focused on dealing with hostage incidents—hijackings and kidnappings. In addition to increasing security at airports, the United States sought to improve international cooperation in returning passengers and aircraft and prosecuting or extraditing the hijackers. Gradually, use of this

tactic became less frequent, but it never disappeared. In the cases of kidnappings of American diplomats by urban guerrilla organizations in Latin America, the United States initially took the position that the host country must do whatever is necessary, including yielding to the kidnappers' demands. As kidnappings continued, however, resistance grew and the policy moved toward one of no concessions. That policy was sealed in blood in March 1973 with the murder of two American diplomats by members of Black September who demanded, among other things, the release of the convicted assassin of Senator Robert F. Kennedy. The no-concessions policy has remained one of the pillars of the U.S. response to terrorism, although at times creative ways to bend it have been sought.

The same hard-line policy was applied to embassy takeovers. Improved security made such takeovers more difficult and governments were increasingly willing to use force. Faced with declining prospects of achieving their demands and growing risks of capture or death, terrorists gradually abandoned the tactic in the 1980s.

American presidents have learned that hostage situations can be politically perilous. Frustration over the inability of the United States to rescue or negotiate the release of American hostages held for more than a year in Iran probably contributed to President James Earl Carter's defeat in the 1980 presidential elections. Six years later, the revelation that the United States, in contradiction to its own no-concessions policy, had secretly sold weapons to Iran in return for the release of American hostages in Lebanon deeply embarrassed the Reagan administration.

Since the late 1970s, the question of how to deal with state sponsors of terrorism has been a major policy issue. Under pressure from Congress, the U.S. Department of State identified Iran, Syria, Libya, Iraq, Sudan, North Korea, and Cuba as state sponsors of terrorism, a list that has changed little in the past quarter century. In 2000, the National Commission on Terrorism recommended that Afghanistan be added to the list and that both Pakistan and Greece be identified as countries that were not fully cooperating with the United States, a suggestion that provoked howls of protest.

Middle East conflicts have motivated most of the major terrorist crises, and most of the states identified by the United States as state sponsors of terrorism are in that part of the world. The region's secular extremists and, increasingly, its religious fanatics have seen themselves as being at

* * * *

KIDNAPPED

On 9 September 1969 a small team comprised of members of two leftist urban guerrilla organizations—the October 8 Revolutionary Movement and Action for National Liberation—kidnapped Charles Burke Elbrick, the recently arrived U.S. ambassador to Brazil, the first of many kidnappings of diplomats. They selected him as their target because, in their words, "If we had selected the Turkish ambassador, nobody would have paid any attention." The kidnappers' communiqué gave more details. "Mr. Elbrick represents in our country the interests of imperialism, which . . . maintain the regime of oppression and exploitation." Elbrick's kidnappers never told him that in return for his safe release they had demanded the release of fifteen prisoners, mostly student and labor leaders, one old Communist Party leader, and several of those allegedly involved in the earlier assassination of American diplomat. It was a deliberately mixed group chosen to inspire unity among Brazil's revolutionaries.

The United States urged the government of Brazil to do everything necessary to ensure the ambassador's release. In fact, the triumvirate of military officers ruling Brazil during the president's illness had already decided to meet the kidnappers' demands, not because of U.S. pressure, but because they saw it as an opportunity to make a humanitarian gesture and give Brazil the chance to disprove accusations of widespread torture. This line of reasoning did not win unanimous approval through the Brazilian armed forces, and one local commander briefly ordered his forces to surround the airport where the prisoners had been assembled to be flown to political exile in Mexico, but higher-ranking officers intervened and the exchange plan proceeded.

Once the prisoners arrived in Mexico, Elbrick was released in good condition. His captors had washed and pressed his bloodstained shirt and tie (he had been hit on the head with a pistol during the abduction), and they gave him a copy of a book on revolution by Ho Chi Minh, in which they had inscribed, "To our first political prisoner, with the expression of our respect for his calm behavior in action."

In the following months the guerrillas kidnapped the Japanese consul general in Sao Paulo and the ambassadors of Germany and Switzerland. In each case the government freed prisoners in exchange for release of the diplomats but subsequently cracked down hard and brutally, ultimately destroying the urban guerrilla groups. But the tactic of kidnapping diplomats spread to other countries. Local governments and the governments of the diplomatic representatives became increasingly resistant to meeting the demands of those holding hostages. The term "terrorist" increasingly replaced the more neutral term "urban guerrilla."

---

war with America. America's steadfast support for the State of Israel has angered many, but even U.S. attempts to broker agreements between Israel and the Palestinians have provoked reactions by hardliners who oppose any accord. America's close relationship with the shah of Iran, overthrown by Islamic revolutionaries in 1979, was a further source of antagonism. Some Muslim fanatics have come to see the American commitment to the principles of freedom, democracy, and equality and what they regard as a subversive and libertine American popular culture as a dangerous influence to be eradicated. The fanatic terrorists' beliefs require them to strike violently at the American presence and influence, and no reconciliation is in sight. One continuing foreign policy challenge for the United States has been to keep efforts to combat terrorism from appearing to be a war on the Arab world or Islam. The United States opposes the violent tactics of terrorism, not any system of beliefs.

Countries identified as state sponsors of terrorism are subject to economic sanctions that deny U.S. assistance and prohibit trade with the United States, but sanctions are only effective if they are universally enforced. International compliance has been patchy at best, although Syria's blatant involvement in a 1986 plot to plant a bomb aboard an airliner departing London led to further European sanctions against that country. Largely to appease an angry United States, Europe went along with some sanctions against Libya in 1986, and suspected Libyan involvement in the sabotage of PanAm 103 in 1988 and a French airliner in Africa in 1989 resulted in more stringent sanctions being imposed until Libya agreed to turn over two Libyans suspected of involvement in the PanAm incident to a tribunal in The Hague. U.S. sanctions on Libya remained in effect for other reasons. To ensure more universal compliance, the United States has sought to have the United Nations impose sanctions. In 2000 Afghanistan became subject to UN sanctions for its refusal to turn over known terrorists.

Additional sanctions were imposed on Iraq as a consequence of that country's invasion of Kuwait in 1990 and the subsequent Gulf War. However, the issue transcends Iraqi sponsorship of terrorism and involves that country's suspected secret efforts to manufacture chemical, biological, and nuclear weapons. Sudan entered into productive discussions with the United States in mid-2000 and became a possible candidate for removal of American sanctions.

Sanctions, however, have been criticized as blunt, ineffective instruments—the modern economic equivalent of medieval siege warfare. They inflict more suffering on ordinary people than on the governments in which the people have no say, and efforts have been initiated to develop more precisely targeted sanctions that hurt rulers, not the general populace. Nonetheless, economic sanctions have stunted economic development in these countries and probably have moderated, if not reversed, the behavior of their governments, although that would be hard to prove.

MILITARY FORCE AND ITS LIMITS

The United States has used military force in response to terrorism on a number of occasions. U.S. forces bombed Libya in 1986 in response to a Libyan-sponsored terrorist attack in Germany and indications of further attacks being planned; an Iraqi intelligence facility was bombed in 1993 in response to Iraqi involvement in the thwarted assassination attempt on former President Bush during a visit to Kuwait; and, in response to terrorist attacks on American embassies in Africa in 1998, U.S. forces bombed terrorist training camps in Afghanistan and a pharmaceutical plant in Sudan suspected of manufacturing chemical weapons.

While terrorists themselves offer few lucrative targets for conventional attack, military action may still be useful. It can disrupt the terrorists' operations, forcing them to move their camps, tend to their own security, and worry about the possibility of further strikes. It can also

be used to reinforce diplomacy. Military force serves as a warning to states that sponsoring terrorism is not without serious risks. It demonstrates resolve and it clearly signals that the country initiating it regards terrorism as a very serious issue. It also carries with it an invitation to states to cooperate.

Military force may also be viewed in some cases as necessary for domestic political purposes, not as a cynical ploy to garner political support or distract the public from other issues, but as a way to demonstrate to an alarmed public that something is being done. The British suffered terribly during the Battle of Britain, and their ability to take the punishment without a complete collapse of morale depended in part on the fact their British forces were fighting to destroy the enemy. The absence of military action could reinforce feelings of national impotence that could, in turn, lead to popular support for draconian measures to ensure security that might imperil civil liberties.

The opportunities for military action against terrorism, however, are limited. It is necessary to focus and carefully calibrate the response; otherwise, the use of force becomes capricious. A military response, moreover, must be delivered soon after the terrorist incident that provokes it. It has been difficult to sustain military operations beyond the first strike. The United States may have wanted the terrorists to fear that it might attack them again, but in fact it never did. That may change in light of the attacks on New York City and Washington, D.C.

QUESTIONABLE ALTERNATIVES

There were possible alternatives to the policies that have been chosen. The United States might have tried to pay less attention to the issue of terrorism, putting it lower on the foreign policy agenda, deliberately adopting a more phlegmatic posture and using less bellicose rhetoric. But given the spectacular nature of terrorist attacks and the public outrage they provoke, it would have been extremely difficult to sustain a deliberately phlegmatic policy.

The United States could have followed a more flexible policy in dealing with hostage situations, as did some European nations. However, the private sector's practice of routinely paying ransom for company executives kidnapped abroad suggests that compliance only encourages further kidnappings. And research suggests that it is the ability of the local government to apprehend, convict, and punish kidnappers and destroy their gangs, whether they are politically motivated or common criminals, that determines the frequency of kidnappings. Politically motivated kidnappings have declined. The United States could have adopted a policy of assassinating foreign terrorist leaders, as Israel did in 1972. While this policy may have led to the removal of some effective terrorist leaders, it has had little discernible effect on the level of terrorism aimed against Israel.

The United States did not have to officially designate state sponsors of terrorism and automatically impose sanctions, thus depriving itself of more flexible forms of diplomacy. As noted earlier, the record of sanctions is at best a mixed one. The United States could have rejected the use of military force altogether, relying instead exclusively on a criminal justice approach. However, few other nations extend the jurisdiction of their courts and send law enforcement officials abroad to investigate terrorist crimes against their citizens.

Persuading other nations to support sanctions, America's use of military force, and the rendition of foreign terrorists to the United States for trial have all required vigorous American diplomacy. The willingness to impose sanctions and use military force, as well as offer assistance in other areas, has in turn reinforced that diplomacy.

THE FRUITS OF AMERICAN POLICY

American policy has historically been pragmatic. Efforts to combat terrorism were just that. American diplomats paid little attention to root causes and conflict resolution, lest counterterrorism efforts become mixed up with judgments of causes. At the same time, the United States has devoted considerable effort to resolving the Middle East conflict, helping to bring about an end to the violence in Northern Ireland, and intervening to prevent ethnic cleansing and other atrocities in the Balkans that, if left to fester or produce vast new semi-permanent populations of refugees, could have become new sources of terrorist violence.

Progress has been made. Intelligence has improved through unilateral efforts and improved liaison with other intelligence services. An international legal framework has been created and international cooperation has increased.

Countries would rather not be identified as state sponsors of terrorism. The volume of international terrorism, as it is defined by the United States, has declined, and certain tactics have declined significantly. All this could have been seen as a measure of success on 10 September 2001. However, the terrorist attacks on the following day—attacks on American soil that caused far more casualties than all of the previous terrorist incidents put together—overshadowed any sense of achievement.

11 SEPTEMBER 2001

The 11 September 2001 attacks have provoked a more formal expression of belligerency—a presidential declaration of war on those responsible for the attacks. The declaration clearly indicates the intention of the United States to use military force again and again at times and places and with means it deems appropriate. More terrorist attacks against Americans, abroad and in the United States, are possible. Exactly how the continuing campaign will be conducted, whether allies of the United States will participate, and what effect it will have are unknown at this time. Whether the counterattack will divide the nation politically remains to be seen.

Within the shadow of this tragedy, however, lie opportunities for even greater international determination and cooperation, if not to end terrorism once and for all—an unrealistic objective—at least to significantly reduce its practice. Whether such determination and cooperation materialize will depend on whether the rest of the world sees this event as an attack on the United States or as a threat to the international system as it exists.

BIBLIOGRAPHY

Bass, Gail, et al. *Options for U.S. Policy on Terrorism.* Santa Monica, Calif., 1981.

Evans, Ernest. *Calling a Truce to Terror: The American Response to International Terrorism.* Westport, Conn., 1979.

Heymann, Philip B. *Terrorism and America: A Commonsense Strategy for a Democratic Society.* Cambridge, Mass., 1998.

Hoffman, Bruce. *Inside Terrorism.* New York, 1998.

Jenkins, Brian Michael. *International Terrorism: A New Mode of Conflict.* Los Angeles, 1975.

————. *International Terrorism: The Other World War.* Santa Monica, Calif., 1985.

————. *Terrorism: Policy Issues for the Bush Administration.* Santa Monica, Calif., 1989.

Lesser, Ian O., et al. *Countering the New Terrorism.* Santa Monica, Calif., 1999.

Long, David E. *The Anatomy of Terrorism.* New York, 1990.

Pillar, Paul R. *Terrorism and U.S. Foreign Policy.* Washington, D.C., 2001.

Simon, Jeffrey D. *The Terrorist Trap: America's Experience with Terrorism.* Bloomington, Ind., 1994.

U.S. Department of State. *Patterns of Global Terrorism.* Washington, D.C. Published annually.

See also COVERT OPERATIONS; EMBARGOES AND SANCTIONS; INTELLIGENCE AND COUNTERINTELLIGENCE.

TREATIES

* * * *

J. B. Duroselle and Ian J. Bickerton

Tracing the history of treaties entered into by the United States provides an illuminating insight into the changing nature, concerns, and direction of United States foreign relations. Given that the Constitution provides that the Senate must be advised and give consent before their ratification, treaties also provide a revealing insight into the ever-changing relationship between the executive and legislative branches of the U.S. government, as well as domestic politics and foreign relations.

Thus we see the Republic in its early years enter a series of treaties of amity and trade with European powers, followed in the nineteenth century by further commercial treaties (with their corollaries, freedom of the seas in time of war, provision for the safety of shipwrecked sailors, access to major communication routes), and treaties delineating the nation's expanding boundaries as well as defining its legal relations with indigenous Americans. Despite its own successful interventionist policy of military and economic expansion—especially in Central America and the Pacific—in the first half of the twentieth century the United States was reluctant to enter the most destructive conflict Europe had yet seen, and the Senate succeeded in limiting American involvement in international legal arrangements designed to prevent its recurrence. Following a second round of world war, in the latter half of the twentieth century, and reflecting a widespread American fear created by a ideologically polarized and increasingly militarized world, the United States entered a series of collective security alliances and arms—especially nuclear arms—limitation treaties. Reflecting renewed American efforts to establish global hegemony, the United States also embarked upon a number of economic agreements in the latter part of the twentieth century to break down what Washington regarded as restrictive trade barriers.

With the transformation of numerous former European colonies in Africa and Asia into independent states and a tremendous increase in the world's population in the second half of the twentieth century, the changed nature of international relations and the role of the United States in world affairs can be traced in the appearance of new kinds of treaties dealing with such matters as human rights, ecology and the environment, and the utilization of outer space. As the twenty-first century began much of U.S. foreign relations and domestic politics was taken up with determining how to respond to these new challenges.

DEFINITIONS

In the broad sense, a treaty is an accord concluded between members of the international community. These are generally states, although sometimes they are political entities seeking to become states (for example, Britain's American colonies in 1776). In the latter case, signing a treaty with the entity gives it the character of a state. According to this broad definition, a treaty is neither a law, which is internal as opposed to international, nor a contract, which is private (or is concluded between a state and a person or an organization). This was the case in the Lake Success Accord of 26 June 1947 between the United Nations and the United States, regarding the location of the permanent headquarters of the United Nations.

In the strict sense, a treaty is an international accord in which the parties involved abide by the constitutional or legal rules that, in a given state, establish treaty-making power. This is clearer in the United States than in Europe, where terminology tends to be ambiguous (the terms in use include "treaty," "convention," "pact," "charter," "statute," "act," "declaration," "protocol," "arrangement," "accord," and "modus vivendi").

In the United States the word "treaty" refers to a procedure defined in the Constitution. The president, the Constitution states, "shall have power, by and with the Advice and Consent of the Senate, to make Treaties, provided two thirds of the Senators present concur." Accordingly, regardless of how they are described in ordinary language (the "Covenant" of the League of Nations, the "Charter" of the United Nations, or the Atlantic "Pact"), all international accords concluded according to this procedure are "treaties," and all others are "agreements." For the first half century after independence, all treaties, once ratified by Congress, were regarded as, in the words of the Constitution, the (supreme) Law of the Land, super-added to the laws of the land and creating individual rights and duties in all states and upheld by federal courts. Today not all treaties are so highly regarded.

The distinction between treaties and agreements is clearer in the United States than elsewhere. In the latter category it is necessary to distinguish several types. An executive agreement is an accord not approved by Congress, either before or after its signing. An example is the Korean War armistice. A congressional executive agreement is an international accord concluded by the president in accordance with a law (and, as a law, enacted by a simple majority vote of the Congress), or approved after the fact by a simple majority. Examples are the Reciprocal Trade Agreements Acts of 1934 and 1962, along with the lend-lease agreements and the European Recovery Program agreements. A joint congressional-executive action is an accord passed by joint resolution of Congress requiring only a simple majority of both houses of Congress. Examples are the annexation of Texas in 1845 and American guarantees concerning Taiwan in 1955.

The president can avoid the constitutional requirement of submitting an international accord to the Senate for approval through the use of an executive agreement. While such an agreement may concern important matters, it can take as simple a form as an exchange of letters. Sometimes it derives from the president's powers as commander in chief of the armed forces. Or it may result from a law voted by Congress giving the president the power to conclude certain accords (for example, those pertaining to the Lend-Lease Act and to the European Recovery Program, as well as postal accords and certain tariff agreements since 1934). The scope of an agreement also can extend to the recognition of states and of governments, and to the provisional or preliminary accords drawn up prior to the signing of definitive treaties.

Executive agreements were unknown in the days of George Washington, only being recognized as constitutional by the Supreme Court in 1936 and 1937. It was not until January 1972 with the Case Act (Public Law 92-403, 1 USC 112b) that Congress accepted executive agreements as constitutional, a journey begun by Senators William Knowland of California and Homer Ferguson of Michigan in 1954. The distinction between treaties and executive agreements has only domestic significance, as both are regarded as binding in international law. But there has been a vast increase in executive agreements since World War II, in part at least because of the difficulty of obtaining two-thirds Senate approval.

The increase in executive agreements also reflects the increased volume of American business with other countries, a constant and accelerated growth of governmental responsibilities imposed on all nations by technological progress, an enormous increase in the amount of power exerted throughout the world by the United States, and congressional legislation authorizing the executive branch to conclude agreements in such areas as agriculture, trade, and foreign aid. The combined necessities of skill and speed in increasingly diversified international politics have made the president of the United States, more so than was formerly true, the most important person in the world. The following statistics speak for themselves. Between 1789 and 1840, there were 60 treaties and 27 executive agreements (a ratio of 2 to 1). Between 1789 and 1940, there were 841 treaties and 1,200 executive agreements (a ratio of 2 to 3). Between 1940 and 1955, there were 139 treaties and 1,950 executive agreements (a ratio of 1 to 14). Between 1960 and 1963, there were 30 treaties and 1,132 executive agreements (a ratio of 1 to 37). A 1984 Senate study revealed that approximately 88 percent of international agreements reached between 1946 and 1972 were based on statuary authority, 6 percent were treaties, and 6 percent solely executive agreements. By the end of the twentieth century the United States was a party to more than 5,000 executive agreements and more than 950 treaties.

Treaties include all types of international agreements among sovereign states. Those agreements may be referred to as "conventions" (usually multilateral agreements), "protocols" (which expand an agreement), "charters," or even "letters." Treaties may be bilateral or multilateral, binding or nonbinding, self-executing or requiring implementing legislation. A treaty enters into force when it is deposited with an international organization or exchanges ratification with another country.

Treaties have existed for centuries, but an internationally acceptable law of treaties was not codified until the Vienna Convention on the Law of Treaties of 1969, which came into force in 1980. The United States, although not a party to the convention (it has been signed but not ratified), accepts it as setting out international law on the subject. Historically, treaties were used as instruments by states to transfer territory, settle disputes and execute other foreign policy matters (for example, to make peace). In recent history treaties have been concluded to regulate economic activities such as trade, commercial relations and intellectual property, and, increasingly, to protect international human rights, regulate pollution and protect the environment, and facilitate transnational litigation.

In the United States, the Founders gave the Senate a share of the treaty power to check presidential power. They also saw Senate involvement as a means of safeguarding the sovereignty of the states by giving each state an equal vote in the treaty-making process. The relationship between the executive branch and the Senate in the making of treaties has remained a controversial issue in U.S. foreign relations. While many presidents have sought the advice of the Senate before entering treaties or conventions, some have not. During the nineteenth century the Senate considerably extended its influence over the treaty-making process by exercising its power to amend treaties—a process begun with an amendment to Jay's Treaty in 1803—and, by the mid to late nineteenth century, requiring a simple majority vote.

Senate amendment may include reservations, understandings, interpretations, declarations, and other statements as conditions for the Senate recommendation of approval. Forty-three treaties never entered force because Senate reservations made them unacceptable to the executive or the other party(s) to the treaty, and eighty-five were withdrawn because of Senate failure to take final action on them. President William McKinley, hoping to avoid Senate rejection, which had become increasingly frequent, named three senators to negotiate the peace treaty with Spain in 1898, thereby facilitating Senate approval. Woodrow Wilson's failure to include any senators in negotiations over the Treaty of Versailles ending World War I and establishing the League of Nations was widely believed to have contributed to the Senate defeat of that treaty. Warren G Harding included senators in negotiations leading to the 1922 Washington Arms Limitation Treaty. Senators assisted in drawing up the United Nations Charter following World War II, and there were only two Senate votes against ratification.

The Senate has rejected relatively few of the treaties it has considered. It sought, with not much success, to have its deliberations kept secret. The Senate approved more than 1,500 treaties—around 90 percent of those submitted to it—in its first two hundred years. The first treaty rejected was with the Wabash and Illinois Indians in 1794, and in 1825 the Senate rejected by a vote of 40 to 0 a convention with Colombia for the suppression of the slave trade.

The flexibility of the system derives from the wide range of options it provides. In a few major instances the treaty method is required constitutionally. In the vast majority, however, the president has the principal prerogative of deciding which method will be used or attempted. Over the vast network of events, times, ideas, attitudes, and strength relationships of the political parties, a decision on the preferred method in all given types of instances rests upon calculations virtually approaching infinity.

CREATING A FRAMEWORK FOR MAKING TREATIES

During and immediately following the war of independence, Benjamin Franklin, John Jay, John Adams, and the other American negotiators found their dealings with the French, Spanish, Dutch and other European powers extremely harrowing. Accordingly, they sought to avoid becoming involved in the intricacies of European politics. American leaders were determined to follow an independent foreign policy and to avoid all treaties other than those promoting (free) commerce and manufactures. In 1776, John Adams drew up a "Model Treaty," and it became the basis for the Americans' first treaties, the U.S.–French treaties signed by Benjamin Franklin and French Foreign Minister Charles Gravier, count of Vergennes, on 6 February 1778.

Negotiations between the American colonists and France began at Passy and resulted in two treaties. The first was a treaty of military alliance, the object of which was "to establish the liberty, sovereignty, and absolute and unlimited independence of the United States, in affairs of government as well as in affairs of commerce." It was asserted that the treaty "is based on the most perfect equality and reciprocity." The second treaty was a treaty of amity and commerce, under which each nation granted most-favored-nation status to the other.

On 4 May 1778, Congress unanimously ratified the two treaties, with the exception of a few secondary clauses. Under the Articles of Confederation, Congress had responsibility for conducting foreign policy, and every treaty had to be approved by at least nine of the thirteen states. Thus, through these first two treaties in American history, the United States was "introduced among the nations." It should be noted that these treaties dealt simultaneously with alliance, commerce, and the creation of international law, or "treaty law"—reciprocity of treatment, freedom of the seas, and the rights of neutral powers.

Peace negotiations between Britain and the Americans, already under way, proceeded apace following the American military success at Yorktown on 19 October 1781. The American delegates, Jay and Adams in particular, demanded more than independence; they also wanted the Newfoundland fisheries, the area west of the Alleghenies as far as the Mississippi River, the cession of Canada, and a war indemnity. Jay opened secret negotiations with England that led to British acceptance of the Mississippi frontier, of the Great Lakes frontier, and of a northeast boundary line at the St. Croix River. Although it was customary in the eighteenth and nineteenth centuries for the loser to pay the winner a cash indemnity for its costly victory, the British refused to consider paying an indemnity.

A treaty—considered as only preliminary, in conformity with European usage—was signed at Paris on 30 November 1782. France and Spain followed the American example and on 20 January 1783 also signed preliminary treaties with England. The definitive treaties were signed on 3 September 1783, at Paris, between the United States and England, and a few days later, at Versailles, between France and England.

The first article of the 1783 Treaty of Paris states: "His Britannic Majesty acknowledges the United States, viz. [here follows a list of the thirteen colonies], to be free, sovereign and Independent States; that he treats with them as such, and for himself, his Heirs and Successors, relinquishes all Claims to the Government Propriety and Territorial Rights." Thus, following France (1778) and the Netherlands (1782), England extended recognition to its former colony. At first, the new nation's dealings with other nations tended to lack direction. Each state wished to be consulted about international affairs. A consular convention signed with France in 1784 was not accepted by Congress until 1788, after the elimination of a clause treating each of the thirteen states as sovereign. And when commercial and territorial negotiations with Spain produced the Jay-Gardoqui Treaty in 1786, its ratification was blocked by the southern states, which felt that their interests had been neglected. However, commercial treaties were signed with Sweden in 1783 and Prussia in 1785, as well as a treaty of peace and friendship with Morocco in 1786.

The situation of drift persisted until the adoption of the Constitution. When the Constitution came into force in 1788, it brought with it a more precise definition of "treaty-making power." On the question of the role the Senate would play in the negotiation of treaties, the Founders did not wish to see the Senate play the dominant role in foreign affairs that had been the prerogative of the Roman Senate, whose exploits in this domain were known and appreciated by such cultivated leaders as Jefferson. From the beginning, George Washington established the tradition of presidential designation of negotiators. (In 1778 and 1782 negotiators had been chosen by Congress.) The president was required, however, to obtain the "advice and consent" of the Senate (with a two-thirds majority) in the appointment of the secretary of state and of ambassadors.

TO ENTER TREATIES OR NOT TO ENTER TREATIES?

Whether because of fear of entrapment, abandonment, or exploitation by European powers, for the next century and a half the United States was wary of signing treaties of military alliance as a means of guaranteeing its own security. Concern over being drawn into the war between revolutionary France and England undoubtedly influenced President George Washington to exhort Americans to avoid entangling alliances in his Farewell Address of 1796, a warning repeated by Jefferson as president four years later. In relation to Europe, treaties were seen by the United States as too "open," too "anarchic" in character. As each party to a treaty retains substantial decision-making capabilities, the risks were too great in a region where the United States was not likely to be the dominant party in any treaty arrangement. The United States did not sign another treaty of alliance until 1947 (the Rio Treaty) and 1949 (the NATO alliance).

This does not mean that the United States was not engaged in or active on the world stage. It simply means that the nation regarded unilateral action as in its best interests. The costs of cooperation—either in economic or military terms—were regarded as too high or the returns insufficient to warrant the risks involved in cooperation. This was not the case in continental America, where the United States was dealing with indigenous Americans and Mexico and Canada—although both those countries were integrated into the European state system. In this instance the United States readily entered into—and broke—treaty arrangements. In the Western Hemisphere the United States also felt it could best protect its interests unaided. Successive administrations felt that the issuance of the Monroe Doctrine—establishing Latin America as a sphere of interest, if not a protectorate—rendered treaties unnecessary.

In the Pacific and East Asia, on the other hand, American attitudes to treaties varied, although the major motivation remained commercial expansion. Although the United States was too late to participate in the "great game of empire" played out there by the European powers, it participated with the Western powers in the unequal treaty system they forced upon China following the Opium Wars. Following British success in the Treaty of Nanking in 1842, the United States, in the Treaty of Wanghia (July 1844), extorted similar concessions from China—most-favored-nation status, the opening of five ports, the imposition of extraterritorial rights for Americans (legal trials for foreigners in special courts of their own nationality)—that lasted until 1942. Also, although no treaty of alliance had been entered into, a U.S. navy warship acted in concert with British, French, and Dutch ships during 1863–1864 to punish Japan for harassment of merchant shipping, and the United States shared an indemnity that Japan was forced to pay to the Western powers.

Throughout the nineteenth and the first half of the twentieth centuries, the two poles of American treaty making were territorial acquisition and amity and commerce, with its various corollaries.

TREATIES ACQUIRING TERRITORY

After the critical phase of revolution and gaining independence, American policy began to focus on the possibilities of the vast North American continent. In the category of territorial politics alone, the United States made fourteen major attempts to annex territory between 1800 and 1869. Four were unsuccessful (Cuba, the Dominican Republic, the Hawaiian Islands, and the Virgin Islands); one (the annexation of Texas in 1845) was settled not by a treaty but by a joint resolution. Eight of the remaining nine resulted in major treaties: four purchase treaties (Louisiana, Florida, parts of Arizona and New Mexico, and Alaska); three partition treaties concerning Oregon (1846); and a single peace treaty (Guadalupe Hidalgo in 1848). Another, earlier peace treaty, that of Ghent (1814) did not involve territorial annexation.

The drafters of the Treaty of Ghent (December 1814), which ended the divisive war with the British begun two years earlier, were satisfied simply to restore the territorial status quo. News of the treaty did not reach Washington until February 1815, a delay that permitted General Andrew Jackson to prevent the capture of New Orleans in the meantime (8 January 1815). The Senate immediately approved the treaty, one of the most popular ever negotiated by Americans.

Territorial questions played a dominant role in American politics both before and after the Civil War. The territories in question were generally located on the North American continent and contiguous to previously annexed territories. (Alaska in 1867 and the Midway Islands seized in the same year were exceptions to this general rule.) Thus, the attempts or plans to acquire island territories—Hawaii, the Virgin Islands, Santo Domingo, even Cuba—were considered by many as immoral and not in accord with American tradition. Once the territories were acquired, generally by treaty, it was still necessary to occupy them, which often meant fighting and then negotiating with the indigenous inhabitants.

TREATIES AND NATIVE AMERICANS

One purpose of the new Constitution was to organize an effective army to deal with issues surrounding the "western lands." The western lands, were, of course, occupied by Native Americans. The history of U.S. relations with Native Americans during the nineteenth century is long and complicated because of the number of different Native American peoples involved, but fundamentally simple in terms of the process that was repeated hundreds of times across the continent. The U.S. government deployed military garrisons on the edge of Indian (Native American) territories, and when conflict arose, as it invariably did, the army reacted by invading the Indian nations and attacking the Native Americans.

At the time of the American Revolution, however, Americans viewed the Indians as distinct peoples, and they viewed their nations as distinct nations, even if other countries did not. Both the Articles of Confederation and the Constitution of the United States reflected this reality. One of the first acts of the Continental Congress was the creation in 1775 of three departments of Indian affairs: northern, central, and southern. Among the first departmental commissioners were Benjamin Franklin and Patrick Henry. Their job was to negotiate treaties with Indian nations and obtain their neutrality in the coming revolutionary war. Among the first treaties presented to the Senate by George Washington—in August 1789—dealt with U.S. relations with various Native American tribes.

While the many accords reached with the Native Americans were sometimes called treaties, in reality the treaties were fictions. On 9 July 1821, Congress gave the president authority to appoint a commissioner of Indian affairs to serve under the secretary of war and have "the direction and management of all Indian affairs, and all matters arising out of Indian relations." From 1824, Native Americans were subject to the jurisdiction of the Bureau of Indian Affairs, newly established as a division of the War Department. After 1849 they were subject to the Home Department (later the Department of the Interior), which, within a century, controlled virtually every aspect of Indian existence.

International law in the nineteenth century did not consider as true treaties accords concluded with indigenous tribes that were not constituted in the form of genuine states. In 1831 the Supreme Court under Chief Justice John Marshall in *Cherokee Nation* v. *Georgia* ruled that Indian nations were not foreign nations but "domestic dependent nations," although the following year in *Worcester* v. *Georgia,* in a ruling that was defied by President Andrew Jackson and ignored by Congress, he ruled that they were capable of making treaties that under the Constitution were the supreme law of the land.

Between 1789 and 1871 the president was empowered by the Senate to make treaties with the Native American tribes or nations in the United States. These treaties ostensibly recognized the sovereignty of Native Americans. Many of the very early Native American treaties were ones of peace and friendship, and a few included mutual assistance pacts, or pacts to prevent other tribes from making hostile attacks. The majority of Native American treaties, however, dealt with trade and commerce, and involved Indians ceding land. Native title was effectively extinguished by treaties of evacuation and removal of the Native American population. Most were signed under coercion. During the two terms of the presidency of Andrew Jackson (1828–1836), when removal of Native Americans from their lands reached almost a frenzy, ninety-four Indian treaties were concluded under coercion. Interestingly, one feature that all Native American treaties share with foreign treaties is that the courts will not inquire into the validity of the signatories. Just as a court will not inquire into whether a foreign dignitary was bribed or forced into signing a treaty, the courts will not inquire into whether a Native American tribe was properly represented during negotiation of a ratified treaty or whether such a treaty was acquired by fraud or under duress.

The president's authority to make treaties with Native Americans was terminated by the Indian Appropriations Act of 3 March 1871, which declared that no Indian tribe or nation would be recognized as an independent power with whom the United States could contract by treaty. However, this statute did not alter or abrogate the terms of treaties that had already been made. Native American treaties are still enforced today and continue to constitute a major federal source of Native American law.

In later years, Congress made provisions to permit Native Americans to recover monetary damages for treaty violations by the federal government. Prior to 1946 Congress enacted numerous special statutes permitting tribes to recover damages through the court of claims, and in 1946 Congress established the Native American Claims Commission to settle claims.

NINETEENTH-CENTURY COMMERCIAL TREATIES

In addition to the territorial treaties, the United States signed a number of trade treaties during its first half century. In realizing these treaties, as was also the case with the treaties annexing overseas territories, the navy was the chief instrument utilized. Chief among these were the Commercial Convention of 1815 with England (extended in 1818) and treaties of commerce with Russia (1832), Siam (1833), China (1844, 1858, and 1867), the Hawaiian Islands (1849 and 1875), and England (the Marcy-Elgin Treaty of 1854). Of a rather different nature were the treaties concerning possible canals linking the Atlantic and the Pacific. In 1846 a treaty was concluded with New Granada (later Colombia) guaranteeing the United States transit across the Isthmus of Panama, as well as the neutrality of the canal zone. In 1850 England and the United States signed the Clayton-Bulwer Treaty regarding the isthmus. Each of the countries undertook not to establish exclusive control over and to guarantee the neutrality of any canal that might be built across Central America. In 1867 a treaty signed with Nicaragua gave the United States the right to build a canal across that country.

Another economic treaty, which subsequently proved to be of great importance, was the Treaty of Kanawaga (Yokohama) with Japan (31 March 1854). Commodore Matthew C. Perry, bearing a letter from President Millard Fillmore requesting the opening of the archipelago to world trade and seeking provision for the safety of shipwrecked American sailors (mainly whalers), led an expedition that reached Japan in July 1853 and returned in February–March 1854 to receive Japan's answer. This treaty was supplemented by the Harris Treaties of 18 June 1857 and 29 July 1858, the latter of which established diplomatic relations between the two countries. In 1883 the Treaty of Chemulpo, negotiated the year before by Commodore Robert Shulfeldt, which provided for American diplomatic representation in Seoul and opened Korea to American trade, passed the Senate.

The Treaty of Washington of 8 May 1871 between Great Britain and the United States should also be mentioned. The Confederate privateer *Alabama,* one of several constructed in British shipyards, had been involved in destructive attacks on the merchant fleet of the North. The United States demanded that London reimburse the damages incurred, with compound interest, as well as the cost of the two additional years of war supposedly rendered possible by this naval activity. The Senate had rejected an earlier treaty proposal (the Johnson-Clarendon Conven-

tion) on 13 April 1869. After international arbitration at Geneva, the Alabama Claims were settled by payment of an indemnity of $15.5 million.

Few treaties were signed in the next quarter century. From the time of the Alabama Claims until around 1890, the United States, preoccupied with its internal expansion, pursued a reserved foreign policy, being satisfied to formulate or recall the basic principles unilaterally, without concluding any important treaties. And, although after 1890 the United States did embark upon an imperialist foreign policy, replete with overseas conquests or interventions, this development came relatively late and was not as extensive as the colonial activities of the European powers, being limited geographically to the Caribbean, Central America, and the Pacific.

In addition, American annexation methods (whether purchase and partition, or through treaty or joint resolution) had been brought to a high degree of refinement and had only to be applied to colonial or occupied insular territories. The occupation of a territory depended, moreover, not on treaty-making power but on the power of the president as commander in chief and did not, therefore, provide occasions for making treaties.

COLLECTIVE TREATIES AT THE TURN OF THE TWENTIETH CENTURY

During the period 1880–1910, two new phenomena appeared that were to have great significance. The first was American participation in the vast collective treaties negotiated in Europe that dealt with such matters as the rules of warfare at sea and other issues important to American overseas commercial activities. Whereas the United States had been absent from the congresses of Vienna (1814–1815), of Paris (1856), and of Berlin (1878), as well as from the ambassadorial conferences of the Concert of Europe (an obvious consequence of the Monroe Doctrine), in 1880 it participated in the Madrid Conference on Morocco (treaty approved by the Senate on 5 May 1881) and in 1884 and 1885 in the Berlin Conference on equatorial Africa. In July 1890 the United States signed an international agreement on the suppression of the slave trade in Africa (approved by the Senate on 11 January 1892).

The United States also participated in the 1888–1889 Pan-American Conference in Washington, D.C., which created the Pan American Union; it had refused to take part in the attempt to create such a union in 1826. Later it took a seat at the Pan-American conferences in Mexico City (1901–1902), Rio de Janeiro (1906), and Buenos Aires (1910), as well as at the First International Peace Conference at The Hague (1899), which created the Permanent Court of Arbitration, and at the Second International Peace Conference at The Hague (1907). The United States also was represented at the Algeciras Conference (1906) on Morocco. On this occasion the Senate accepted the resulting agreement (in December 1906), but with the reservation that its approval did not signify a break with the traditional policy of noninvolvement in Europe.

The second new development was that for the first time in its history, the United States assumed the role of mediator between two great powers, Russia and Japan, then at war. President Theodore Roosevelt had been anxious to maintain the balance of power in the Far East. He knew that the United States possessed an effective means of putting pressure on the victorious Japanese, that is, the possibility of helping them obtain funds to revive their bankrupt economy. Consequently, as early as April 1905, before the decisive Russian naval defeat at Tsushima, he secretly agreed to serve as a mediator. Japan accepted mediation on 31 May, after the battle of Tsushima, for it realized that it was better to limit its ambitions than to risk provoking a coalition against it. The resulting Treaty of Portsmouth, in part a product of American initiatives, dissatisfied Japanese ultranationalists. The United States also was mediator (without being a signatory) at the Central American Peace Conference held in November–December 1907 in Washington, D.C.

TREATIES ACQUIRING OVERSEAS TERRITORY

It is not surprising that the most important acts of American foreign policy during this period involved territorial acquisitions, the only difference being that, with the disappearance of the frontier, the object was overseas territory, and the instrument employed was the navy rather than the army. This change was influenced by the great colonial expansion undertaken by the Europeans since 1881, as well as by Alfred Thayer Mahan, the apostle of seapower. The major motivation for U.S. expansion was the search for markets in a world (Indochina, Africa, and China) being closed off by Europeans. Nevertheless, the American approach

retained its versatility: treaties remained but one among several methods of annexation.

On 17 January 1878 the United States signed the Samoan Treaty with a number of tribal chiefs, thereby receiving the right to use the strategic port of Pago Pago on the island of Tutuila. The Senate gave its approval on 30 January. The Berlin Conference of 1889, involving the Americans, the British, and the Germans, resulted in an accord establishing a tripartite protectorate over the islands (14 June). On 2 December 1899 a new treaty reallocated the islands among the three powers. It was ratified by the Senate on 16 January 1900.

In the Hawaiian Islands, after numerous futile negotiations during the nineteenth century, Queen Liliuokalani was deposed in 1893 in favor of a provisional revolutionary government. The latter (composed mainly of Americans) proposed a treaty of annexation by the United States (14 February 1893), which was rejected by President Grover Cleveland. The Republic of Hawaii was proclaimed on 4 July 1894 and recognized by Cleveland on 7 August. Cleveland was hostile to the annexation of the archipelago, but his successor, William McKinley, signed a treaty of annexation on 16 June 1897. In the Senate, however, a coalition of Democrats and anti-imperialist Republicans delayed ratification. During the Spanish-American-Cuban-Filipino War, in order to ensure uninterrupted reinforcements to Admiral Dewey in Manila, McKinley asked Congress for a joint resolution, which required only a simple majority in both houses. The resolution was passed on 7 July 1898.

The most important actions taken in this decade were linked to the war against Spain, declared on 25 April 1898. As in the war with Mexico half a century earlier, the Americans were assured of victory. French mediation paved the way for a provisional protocol, signed on 12 August. The peace conference opened on 1 October in Paris, and the peace treaty was signed on 10 December. The final treaty added the annexation of the Philippines to that of Puerto Rico, provided for in the earlier protocol. The proposed annexation of the Philippines, which had become the symbol of U.S. imperialism, provoked heated debate in the Senate. Democrats, Populists, and anti-imperialist Republicans (numerous in New England) opposed the treaty. The imperialists based their argument on national prestige and the strategic necessity of a base in the area. The Senate did not approve the Treaty of Paris until 6 February 1899. The vote was 57 to 27; a change of two votes would have made it impossible to attain the necessary two-thirds majority. Guam was also acquired from Spain along with the Philippines and was important for logistical support of the army as a means of suppressing the Philippine Insurrection. Senate approval was not sought when Wake Island was similarly annexed as a war measure on 17 January 1899.

THE CARIBBEAN AND CENTRAL AMERICA

With the Spanish-American War ended, the United States manifested a striking disregard for British naval power (still the greatest in the world) in the strategically critical zone of the Caribbean and Central America. The only two feasible trans-isthmian routes went through Panama, which belonged to Colombia, and Nicaragua. The Frelinghuysen-Zavala Treaty of 1884 (not ratified), which gave the United States exclusive rights to build a canal across Nicaragua, was complemented and made official by the Bryan-Chamorro Treaty of 1914. Panama was the scene of considerable upheaval. In the wake of the scandal-ridden bankruptcy of the Compagnie Française du Canal de Panama (1893), its liquidator, Philippe Bunau-Varilla, made a concerted effort to persuade the United States to purchase the concession that the French had obtained from Colombia.

President Theodore Roosevelt, who was very interested in the project, sought to revive an old idea by forcing the British (at a disadvantage, because of their involvement in the Boer War) to relinquish their share of the control of the canal through the Hay-Pauncefote Treaty. As early as 1880, James G. Blaine had called for replacement of joint Anglo-American control of the canal, provided for in the Clayton-Bulwer Treaty of 1850, by exclusive American control. Blaine was supported by Congress, but the British had refused to agree. The first Hay-Pauncefote Treaty (5 February 1900), approved by the Senate, gave the United States exclusive rights but forbade it to fortify the canal zone. A second Hay-Pauncefote Treaty (signed on 18 November 1901 and approved by the Senate on 16 December) eliminated this restriction.

The United States thereupon entered into negotiations with Colombia to obtain the concession for the canal. This was the object of the Hay-Herran Treaty of 22 January 1903, which was approved by the Senate but rejected by Colombia. Rather than seize the zone by force, Roosevelt preferred to encourage Panama's secession from Colombia. Coordinated by Bunau-Varilla, this action was taken on 3 November 1903; and by 6 November the United States, which had sent warships to the area, recognized the new republic. Bunau-Varilla was sent as Panamanian minister to Washington; and on 18 November he signed the Hay–Bunau-Varilla Treaty, whereby the United States was accorded the concession in perpetuity of a zone ten miles wide, with complete sovereignty and fortification rights. The Senate accepted the treaty on 23 February 1904.

In order better to protect the Canal Zone (the canal itself was completed in 1914), the United States set out to maintain order in the Caribbean. With Cuba there was initially only a unilateral decision made in 1901 (in the form of an amendment by Senator Orville H. Platt to the Army Appropriations Bill) according itself the right to intervene there. The Cubans were obliged to incorporate the Platt Amendment into their constitution. A treaty of 22 May 1903 later confirmed the amendment. This interventionist policy in Latin America, which President Woodrow Wilson greatly extended, gave rise to unilateral actions by the United States (based on the Roosevelt Corollary to the Monroe Doctrine, on 6 December 1904). Referred to as the "big stick" policy, it ultimately resulted in the landing of U.S. marines in Nicaragua on 14 August 1912. However, the Senate refused to ratify a treaty giving the United States a naval base in Nicaragua.

THE TREATY OF VERSAILLES

Woodrow Wilson, elected president in 1912, introduced what would be known as the New Diplomacy. His conception of this policy evolved gradually as the Great War in Europe progressed. Convinced that the European balance of power, from which the United States was excluded by the Monroe Doctrine, was the main cause of the war, Wilson envisioned international relations based on "a world safe for democracy." For him this meant equality of rights between states both large and small, replacement of an equilibrium based on violence by maintenance of peace through the creation of a league of nations, and abolition of secret treaties in favor of "open covenants openly arrived at" (the first of the Fourteen Points of 8 January 1918). In his eyes, the mission of the American people, which he considered morally superior to other peoples by its composition and its democratic tradition, was the establishment of a lasting peace.

When Germany resumed its unrestricted submarine war on 1 February 1917, thereby violating the rights of neutral parties, Wilson, on 2 April, proposed to Congress that the United States enter the war. From this moment it became clear that the greater their role in the war, the more Americans would be in a position to impose the New Diplomacy on their associates, with whom they were careful not to link themselves by alliance.

Subsequently, Wilson exerted considerable influence on the negotiation and conclusion of a number of treaties, most notably the Treaty of Versailles (28 June 1919). Regarding the negotiation of that treaty, Wilson imposed several important breaks with tradition on the Europeans. He announced that he would lead the American delegation himself, a step that caused a delay in the opening of discussions until 18 January 1919. He demanded that the Allies, following Germany, adopt the Fourteen Points before the signing of the armistice of 11 November 1918. He stipulated that the Covenant of the League of Nations must be drawn up before territorial, military, and economic issues were dealt with. Finally, Wilson wanted the Allies and associate powers to reach an agreement among themselves before imposing the treaty on Germany (a step that gave the treaty the appearance of a diktat).

When it was time to conclude the treaty, Wilson, supported by British Prime Minister David Lloyd George, obliged France to renounce permanent military occupation of the Rhineland in exchange for two treaties (one Franco-American and the other Anglo-French) guaranteeing France's national boundaries. Wilson also delayed indefinitely the satisfaction of Italy's claims to Austrian territory and colonies. On the other hand, he had to yield to Japanese demands to acquire Germany's rights in China. The Japanese had threatened, first, to insert an article on racial equality in the Covenant of the League of Nations and, then, not to join the organization. Finally, Wilson and French Premier Georges Clemenceau forced Lloyd George, who was sympathetic to German objections and would have wanted to soften the terms of the treaty draft, to agree to keep it much as it had been presented on 7 May 1919 to the German delegation.

But Wilson failed to obtain ratification in the U.S. Senate. He made the error of not inviting any senators to participate in the negotiations. Since November 1918 the Senate membership had included forty-nine Republicans and forty-seven Democrats. The chairman of the Senate Foreign Relations Committee, Henry Cabot Lodge, was a personal enemy of Wilson's. The Senate was bitterly divided on the issue of support for the Treaty of Versailles and U.S. membership in the League of Nations. In a vote, which had to approve the treaty by a two-thirds majority, Wilson could count on a maximum of only fifty-eight votes, while a two-thirds majority required sixty-four. It was clear that the Senate would accept the treaty only with major amendments.

Wilson refused to seek a compromise. He overestimated the support of world public opinion for the league as well as his own influence in the Senate. From 3 September to 29 September, Wilson traveled across the United States in order to arouse public support. The exertion was too much for him, and he became seriously ill. Sheltered from contact with the world by his wife and his physician, who withheld bad news, he obstinately refused any compromise, even though he was advised to do so by the Allies themselves. The Foreign Relations Committee agreed to condense all its objections into fourteen reservations, known as the Lodge Reservations. These were mostly aimed at denying the league the right to impose any obligations or restrictions on the United States (such as military sanctions), at rejecting any intervention of the league in internal affairs, and at exempting the Western Hemisphere—the area covered by the Monroe Doctrine—from sanctions of any kind. The text finally submitted to the Senate on 19 December was not the treaty but the treaty plus the Lodge Reservations. On 18 March 1920, in a surprise move, a fifteenth reservation, calling for the independence of Ireland, was added. On 19 March a final vote was held on the treaty plus the Lodge Reservations plus the fifteenth reservation. With only forty-five in favor, the two-thirds majority was not reached and the treaty was definitively rejected. The new president elected in 1920, Warren G. Harding, was a nationalist hostile to the League of Nations.

UNILATERALISM OR MULTILATERALISM?

Following World War I, the United States reaffirmed unilateralism as its preferred modus operandi on the world stage. From 1921 to 1941 the debate between Harding-style nationalism and Wilsonian internationalism continued. Nationalism held sway for twenty years, transforming itself in the 1930s into the doctrine of isolationism. Foreign policy was nationalist in the sense that important matters were settled not by treaties but by the unilateral acts of the United States (either declarations by the executive branch or, more commonly, laws passed by Congress). In 1921 and 1924 laws settled the immigration question through the institution of quotas (a matter normally involving relations with the other countries concerned). Laws were passed to raise tariff rates (Fordney-McCumber Tariff of 1922 and Smoot-Hawley Tariff of 1930). A law announcing U.S. adherence to the Permanent Court of International Justice was voted on 27 January 1926, but it was accompanied by so many reservations that the World Court ultimately rejected America's candidacy.

The United States acted unilaterally in Asia in the case of the Stimson Doctrine. Following the Japanese invasion of Manchuria in late 1931, Secretary of State Henry L. Stimson issued identical notes to Japan and China on 7 January 1932, asserting that the United States would not recognize any impairment of American treaty rights in China and morally condemning Japanese aggression. The Stimson Doctrine was later (March 1932) endorsed by the League of Nations. Other unilateral decisions included the Neutrality Acts (1935–1937), which imposed embargoes on arms and munitions destined for all belligerents, whether aggressors or victims. A promise of independence for the Philippines took the form of a law (Tydings-McDuffie Act of 1934). There were declarations broadening the application of the Monroe Doctrine. An exchange of letters sufficed for recognition of the Soviet Union in 1933. Everything seemed to indicate that Americans, after having rejected the greatest treaty of the century, had become suspicious of treaties, especially of collective ones. Nonentanglement no longer extended to alliances only, but also to numerous other types of treaties.

However, despite rejection of the multilateral Versailles approach, the United States under certain conditions was very willing to sign collective agreements. The clearest cases emerged from the Washington Conference of 1921–1922: the Five-Power Naval Disarmament Treaty (6 February 1922), the Nine-Power Treaty on China (6 February 1922), the Four-Power Treaty on the Pacific (13 December 1921), and the London Naval Conference agreements (1930 and 1935). The United States also forced Japan to renounce its claims to German rights in the Shantung Peninsula and in Siberia.

Another illustration of American willingness to act in concert with other nations was the Pact of Paris (the Kellogg-Briand Pact) of 27 August 1928, signed by an unprecedented sixty-three nations. This pact had originated in the useless, romantic proposal by French Foreign Minister Aristide Briand on the tenth anniversary of U.S. entry into the war (April 1927) that France and the United States undertake never to wage war on each other. At the urging of the chairman of the Senate Foreign Relations Committee, William Borah, Secretary of State Frank Kellogg proposed that the pact be expanded to include all nations. War "as an instrument of national policy" was to be renounced (thereby leaving open the possibility of military sanctions voted by the league). In this way it was possible to satisfy American pacifists like Salmon Levinson, who rejected the League of Nations but called for "the outlawry of war," as well as men like James Shotwell and the Carnegie Endowment for International Peace, who sought an alternative to collective security. There was no provision for enforcement or sanctions, however, and the Japanese violated the pact in Manchuria as early as 16 September 1931, leaving Stimson with little to fall back on except the moral condemnation contained in his "doctrine."

This was also the period of Pan-Americanism. Whereas the United States made few treaties with Europe or the Far East during these years, it concluded a fairly large number with Latin American republics. Matters such as evacuation of occupied Caribbean nations were generally settled by executive agreements (Dominican Republic, 1922; Nicaragua, 1927); but many pacts were signed at the conferences of Havana (1928), Montevideo (1933), Buenos Aires (1936), and Lima (1938). The most important were those of Montevideo, stipulating that "No State has the right to intervene in the internal or external affairs of another," and Lima, providing for consultations between ministers of foreign affairs whenever there was danger of war.

WORLD WAR II AND SECURITY AGREEMENTS

World War II brought American isolationism to an end. The first steps moving the United States

★ ★ ★ ★

ON TREATIES

"He [the President] shall have Power, by and with the Advice and Consent of the Senate, to make Treaties, provided two thirds of the Senators present concur; and he shall nominate, and by and with the Advice and Consent of the Senate, shall appoint Ambassadors, other pubic Ministers and Consuls."

— From Article 2, Section 2
of the U.S. Constitution —

"Do Americans want, or are they ready for world government?. . .That is what government by treaty will do, sooner or later. . . . Government by treaty is a dangerous approach, and if we wish to retain our freedom, and maintain our American concept of government we have got to abandon that approach."

— Subcommittee of the
Senate Committee on
Foreign Relations, Genocide
Convention Hearings, 1950 —

"The Internationalists in this country and elsewhere really proposed to use the United Nations and the treaty process as a law-making process to change the domestic laws and even the Government of the United States and to establish a World Government along socialist lines."

— Frank Holman, president of the
American Bar Association,
November 1955,
on human rights treaties —

"Only one overriding factor can determine whether the U.S. should act multilaterally or unilaterally, and that is Americans' interests. We should act multilaterally when doing so advances our interests, and we should act unilaterally when that we serve our purpose. . . . What works best."

— Anthony Lake, assistant to
President Bill Clinton for national
security affairs, September 1993 —

away from neutrality took the form of executive agreements (such as the destroyers-for-bases accord of 3 September 1940) permitting increased aid to England. But it was the crucially important Lend-Lease Act (11 March 1941) that, even prior to Pearl Harbor, introduced the United States into the front stage of world diplomacy and at the same time gave the latter an entirely new form. Franklin Roosevelt's bold initiatives, combined with the enormous growth of American economic power, yielded a new and unprecedented diplomatic form, that of foreign aid. While traditional diplomacy had been conducted between great and small powers, and Wilsonian diplomacy had established the principle of equality, diplomacy after lend-lease assumed a dual nature. On the one hand, relations between nations deemed to be equals continued to be conducted by ambassadors. On the other hand, there emerged a new form of relationship between two countries, whereby one became the aid donor and the other the aid recipient. Assistance, which could be economic, military, or technical, was administered by government officials who were not ambassadors

and generally were dependent on them only nominally. Aid accords tended to evolve in the following manner: first, voting of a general law by Congress; second, voting of appropriations; third, aid accords concluded with the beneficiaries.

Many programs, each involving a set of accords, were elaborated in this fashion: lend-lease (11 March 1941–21 August 1945); bilateral aid accords (1945–1948); the Marshall Plan (5 June 1947), leading to the European Recovery Program (April 1948); Point Four (aid to underdeveloped countries, 20 January 1949); and the Mutual Security Program (replacing the European Recovery Program). These programs led to the signing of hundreds of accords, some of which were treaties. Occasionally, an accord has been considered an agreement by the United States and a treaty by the other party. This was the case, for example, with the Franco-American Mutual Aid Accord of 27 January 1950.

President Franklin D. Roosevelt took considerable precautions so that the Senate would not refuse American participation in the new international organization whose principles he had outlined as early as 1941 in the Atlantic Charter. The conferences at Tehran (28 November–1 December 1943), Dumbarton Oaks (August–October 1944), and Yalta (4–11 February 1945) had elaborated the underlying principles of the United Nations. Roosevelt constantly consulted with the Senate, endeavoring to make his collective security policy a bipartisan affair. The founding conference of the United Nations was held in San Francisco from 25 April to 26 June 1945. Forty-six nations signed the charter, which the United States was the first to adopt, the Senate approving it on 29 July 1945 with near unanimity.

It should be noted that the right of veto held by the five permanent members of the Security Council protected the United States, in the last resort, against any obligations imposed by the council. At the same time, the locating of the UN headquarters in the United States (Lake Success Accord of 26 June 1947, between the United Nations and the United States) contributed to the popularity of the organization in America. Thereafter, actively involved in the life of the international organization, the United States found that it had adopted Wilsonian "internationalism," which constituted a break with tradition.

The main preoccupation of American treaties following World War II was security cooperation in a postwar climate characterized by ideological conflict with the Soviet Union, bipolarization of the world between these two powers, destruction of the colonial empires and the emergence of nearly ninety new nations, economic inequality, and reliance on atomic weapons as a deterrent. The United States, therefore, could no longer pursue its traditional (moderate and reserved) policy of treaty making. Indeed, since 1945 it has concluded more treaties (not counting agreements) than any other nation, and almost all have been of a new type. They have included aid accords, participation in the United Nations, peace treaties, treaties of alliance, treaties linked to deterrence, and treaties dealing with a far wider range of issues than had traditionally been the case: human rights, ecology, the environment and resources, global warming, the outlawing of chemical and other weapons of mass destruction, access to and the future use of outer space, copyright and the protection of intellectual property, and biotechnology and human cloning.

The existence of fundamental disagreements between the Soviet Union and the United States prevented the conclusion of a peace treaty with Germany. The creation of the Federal Republic of Germany in September 1949 was facilitated by the fact that the three Western occupying powers had unified their zones economically and had made procedural provisions for the reconstitution of a German nation (the London convention regarding Germany, June 1948). Having also defined the respective areas of responsibility for the future state and the occupiers (the Washington accords regarding Germany, April 1949), they began transferring an increasingly important role to the former. Finally, a simple peace protocol, the Treaty of Paris (October 1954), ended the occupation, replacing it with the presence of "security forces." The treaty was approved by the Senate on 1 April 1955.

For similar reasons it proved impossible to sign a common peace treaty including both Japan and the Soviet Union, despite the efforts of John Foster Dulles in 1947. Although formal surrender ceremonies had been held aboard the USS *Missouri* on 2 September 1945, it was not until 8 September 1951 that the United States and forty-eight other countries concluded a peace settlement with Japan, the San Francisco Peace Treaty. The Soviet Union, although it attended the San Francisco meeting, abstained. The Senate gave its consent with reservations on 20 March 1952 by a vote of 66 to 10.

In the case of Austria, which the victors intended to keep permanently separate from Germany, it required ten years of negotiations before the Soviet Union decided, in exchange for a guarantee of the country's neutrality, to join the other occupying powers in signing the Austrian State Treaty. Following Senate approval, President Dwight D. Eisenhower ratified it on 24 June 1955.

All of the above was accomplished outside the procedural framework provided for by the Potsdam Conference of 1945. On that occasion, a council of foreign ministers (of the United States, the Soviet Union, the United Kingdom, France, and China) was created for the purpose of negotiating the various peace treaties, on the understanding that of the five countries, only those that had signed armistice agreements with the defeated nations would participate in treaty negotiations (France being considered as having signed an armistice with Italy). In principle, this should have excluded the United States from the peace treaty with Finland. In fact, however, all the treaties with the "Axis satellites" were discussed by the Big Four (China being absent). Many meetings of the council took place in 1945 and 1946. They produced five peace treaties, signed by the

American secretary of state in Washington and by the other countries (Italy, Finland, Romania, Bulgaria, and Hungary) on 10 February 1947 in Paris. The Senate approved them on 4 June 1947.

Two further meetings of the council took place, in Moscow (10 March–24 April 1947) and London (25 November–December 1947). These negotiations were brought to a halt by U.S. adoption of containment policy (the Truman Doctrine of 12 March 1947 and the Marshall Plan of 5 June 1947), the creation of the Kominform by the Soviet Union, and the increasing tensions of the Cold War in 1948 (the Berlin Blockade). While such diplomacy did revive sporadically, beginning with the Paris conference of 23 May–20 June 1949, which ended the Berlin Blockade, and including several summit meetings, it did not bring about any peace treaties.

Nor were peace treaties enacted—only armistice agreements—after the Korean War (27 July 1953), after French withdrawal from Indochina (the Geneva Accords of 20 July 1954 were rejected by the United States), or after the war in Vietnam. In the latter case, after five years of negotiations involving the United States, North Vietnam, South Vietnam, and the National Liberation Front, an accord was finally reached on 28 January 1973. Although it had the breadth and scope of a peace treaty, it was simply an executive agreement that, on the American side, went into effect with its signing by Secretary of State Henry Kissinger, and not after approval by the Senate.

As soon as World War II ended, American officials sought to give new form to Pan-Americanism. They began with a provisional alliance, excluding Argentina, that was signed at Chapultepec, Mexico, in March 1945. The signatories undertook to consult with one another in the event of aggression or the threat of aggression. At the inter-American conference "for the maintenance of continental peace and security" at Rio de Janeiro (15 August–2 September 1947), the twenty-one republics (except Nicaragua, which was absent) signed a reciprocal inter-American assistance treaty, which contained essentially the same provisions as the Pact of Chapultepec. Sanctions could be voted collectively against aggressors. Finally, on 30 April 1948, the Charter of the Organization of American States was signed, making the Pan American Union a regional organization within the framework of the United Nations. The United States did not ratify the charter until June 1951. Despite their innovative elements, these alliances invariably fell within the tradi-

tional perspective of the Monroe Doctrine. The same was not the case with later alliances.

The Atlantic Pact of 4 April 1949, which created NATO, was a reaction to the Cold War. The five European signatories of the treaty of alliance of Brussels (17 March 1948) gave the premier of France (Georges Bidault) and the foreign minister of England (Ernest Bevin) the task of requesting the American secretary of state, George C. Marshall, to secure his country's participation. The necessity of defending western Europe seemed so critical that on 11 June 1948 the Senate adopted, by a vote of 64 to 4, the Vandenberg Resolution, authorizing the president to conclude peacetime alliances outside the Western Hemisphere. This represented a break with prior American foreign policy, which had avoided alliances since the end of the eighteenth century. Negotiations were prolonged, since it was necessary to await the outcome of the presidential elections, in which Harry S. Truman was the victor.

A preliminary draft of 28 December was followed on 15 March 1949 by the version ultimately signed by the five (France, the United Kingdom, Belgium, the Netherlands, and Luxembourg), the United States, and Canada. They then invited Norway, Denmark, Iceland, Portugal, and Italy to participate. The treaty, published on 18 March, before it had been signed, provided for consultation in the event of threatened or actual aggression and for military assistance, which was not to be absolutely automatic. (In the event of aggression in the North Atlantic region, each party would undertake "immediately, individually and in accord with the other parties, whatever action it shall judge necessary, including the use of armed force.") The signing by the twelve members took place in Washington, D.C., on 4 April 1949. The following day, the U.S. government granted a request for military aid, which was voted by the Congress on 14 October, a few days after the first Soviet atomic explosion.

The treaty was supplemented by the creation of the North Atlantic Council (18 May 1950) and of an integrated command in Europe known as Supreme Headquarters Allied Powers in Europe (SHAPE, 19 December 1950). Greece and Turkey joined the alliance in February 1952 and the Federal Republic of Germany in May 1955. On 13 September 2001, two days into the crisis created by the horrific suicide attacks by Islamic terrorists on the World Trade Center towers in New York City and the Pentagon outside Washington, D.C., NATO Secretary General Lord

Robertson (of Scotland) announced in Brussels that NATO (numbering nineteen members by 2001) stood ready to back U.S. military retaliation to the terror attack described by President George W. Bush as "an act of war." For the first time in its fifty-two-year history, NATO was invoking Article 5 of the alliance's charter, which states that "an armed attack against one or more of the nations in Europe or North America shall be considered an attack against them all," and if such an armed attack occurs, each of them will take the necessary action to assist the party so attacked, "including the use of armed force.

At the same time as the Japanese peace treaty, the United States concluded three new alliances: the Pacific Security Pact with Australia and New Zealand (ANZUS) on 1 September 1951, an alliance with the Philippines on 30 August 1951, and a security treaty with Japan on 8 September 1951. Provisions of ANZUS were invoked for the first time in September 2001, by Australian Prime Minister John Howard, in response to the attack on the World Trade Center and the Pentagon. Later, the United States joined the Southeast Asia Treaty Organization (SEATO), created by the Treaty of Manila of 8 September 1954. The other signatories of this collective defense treaty for Southeast Asia were the United Kingdom, France, Australia, New Zealand, the Philippines, Thailand, and Pakistan. Article 4 guaranteed the political independence and territorial integrity of South Vietnam, Laos, and Cambodia, although there was no formal alliance with these three states.

The United States also concluded bilateral mutual defense treaties with South Korea (1 October 1953), Pakistan (19 May 1954), and the Republic of China, or Taiwan (2 December 1954). This last treaty gave rise to a curious situation. Anxious to dramatize the danger presented by the People's Republic of China to Taiwan and its dependencies, the administration, without waiting for Senate approval (ultimately obtained in February 1955), had the two houses of Congress vote a joint resolution on 25 and 28 January, respectively (the votes were 409 to 3 in the House of Representatives and 95 to 3 in the Senate), authorizing the president to protect Taiwan against attack.

Thus, the United States, hostile to all military alliances for a century and a half, had enmeshed itself in the most extensive system of alliances in the history of the world, incorporating, at its peak, forty-four allies: twenty American

republics, Canada, Australia, New Zealand, thirteen European nations in NATO, Japan, and seven Asian nations (including Iraq).

NUCLEAR ARMS LIMITATION TREATIES

Among the most important treaties signed in the postwar years by the United States, despite their inadequacies, were those seeking to ban nuclear testing and to limit the proliferation of nuclear arms. It also became apparent in the years following World War II that national security would extend to activities in outer space. At first, in the face of obvious Soviet satellite superiority, the United States was determined to act unilaterally to assure its security from attack. But NATO had created a situation whereby Europe was dependent upon U.S. nuclear protection, and these obligations placed restraints upon the U.S. capacity to act unilaterally in relation to nuclear defense. Public opposition at home and in Europe to the threat of nuclear destruction forced the United States and the Soviet Union to stabilize the balance of their nuclear strategic weapon systems through some form of treaty arrangement. The first such treaty, the Treaty of Moscow, known as the Limited Nuclear Test-Ban Treaty (the United States, the Soviet Union, the United Kingdom), banning nuclear tests in space, in the atmosphere, and underwater, was signed on 5 August 1963. It was approved on 24 September by the Senate, 80 to 19. As of 2001, more than 100 nations had signed it.

A treaty regarding the nonproliferation of nuclear arms was signed on 1 July 1968. It had been presented to the Geneva disarmament conference on 11 March by the United States and the Soviet Union. A resolution recommending the signing of the treaty was voted on 12 June 1968 by the General Assembly of the United Nations, 95 to 4, with 21 abstentions. As with the Test Ban Treaty, France and China refused to endorse it.

In June 1968 the United States and the Soviet Union began disarmament negotiations aimed at restricting the construction of launching devices for nuclear and thermonuclear projectiles. Such was to be the objective of the Strategic Arms Limitation Talks (SALT). On the occasion of President Richard M. Nixon's trip to the Soviet Union (22–30 May 1972), many economic and technical accords were signed. Among the most important was an Anti-Ballistic Missile (ABM) Treaty limiting the number of missiles and launchers each side could deploy. The Senate approved the ABM treaty by a vote of 88 to 2. A further major accord concerning the prevention of nuclear war was signed on 22 June during Leonid Brezhnev's visit to Washington, D.C. (16–25 June 1973). A number of agreements curbing nuclear testing were signed (3 July 1974) during Nixon's Moscow visit to meet with Brezhnev for the third time.

SALT bogged own, but negotiations on European cooperation and security came to fruition. In July 1975, President Gerald Ford traveled to Helsinki to attend a summit meeting of thirty-five nations and signed an accord that recognized Europe's boundaries as inviolable and provided vaguely for improvement of human rights, such as emigration and access to information, even in communist bloc countries. President Jimmy Carter made clear subsequently that arms control and the issue of the human rights element in the Helsinki Accords was at the core of relations with the Soviet Union. When Secretary of State Cyrus R. Vance visited Moscow late in March 1977 hoping to conclude a SALT II agreement, the Soviets flatly rejected his proposals, indicating that Washington's rhetoric on human rights displeased them as meddling in their internal affairs. However, a new SALT II agreement was reached in 1979 placing a ceiling on intercontinental ballistic missiles (ICBMs). Although not ratified, the United States and the Soviet Union more or less honored its terms.

In 1983 Republican President Ronald Reagan announced the Strategic Defense Initiative (SDI), a space-based defense system against nuclear attack. SDI would not only have destabilized the nuclear balance with the Soviet Union, it would certainly have violated the spirit if not the letter of the 1972 ABM treaty. In 1985 Reagan initiated the Strategic Arms Reduction Talks (START) with Soviet leader Mikhail Gorbachev, but no treaty resulted in the ensuing summit meetings because of Reagan's adherence to the highly controversial SDI. Of special concern were intermediate-range land-based cruise and ballistic missiles (range of 500 to 1,000 kilometers). Finally, Reagan and Gorbachev signed the Intermediate-Range Nuclear Forces (INF) Treaty in 1987, which aimed to reduce and eliminate rather than, as in previous arms agreements, limit a class of weapons. The Senate ratified the treaty, with conditions, on 27 May 1988, by a vote of 93 to 5. The treaty was to stay in effect until 2001. Reagan's successor, George H. W. Bush, signed a START agreement with Gorbachev in Moscow in

1991, and in 1993, after the breakup of the Soviet Union, he signed a START II treaty with Russian President Boris Yeltsin.

Following the adoption of a resolution calling for a comprehensive nuclear test ban treaty (CTBT) in the United Nations General Assembly in December 1993, negotiations on a CTBT began in the Conference on Disarmament in Geneva in January 1994. On 10 September 1996 the UN General Assembly approved the CTBT by an overwhelming vote of 158 to 3, with five nations abstaining. On 24 September 1996, President Bill Clinton became the first national leader to sign the treaty, and the White House submitted it to the U.S. Senate for ratification in September 1997. Despite overwhelming public support, after a long delay the Senate rejected it on 13 October 1999 by a vote of 51 to 48.

More than 160 nations had signed the CTBT by 2001, but of the original five nuclear powers (Britain, China, France, Russia, and United States), only Britain, France, and Russia had ratified it. The treaty required the ratification of forty-four specific countries, including the United States. These were nations that had nuclear power reactors or nuclear research facilities; all were members of the Conference on Disarmament. This group included India and Pakistan, both of which tested nuclear devices in May 1998. India and Pakistan (and China) were thought unlikely to ratify the treaty unless the United States did so first.

The Clinton administration supported a CTBT that would contain the usual clause permitting a state to withdraw from the treaty for reasons of "supreme national interest." (The maintenance of a safe and reliable nuclear stockpile was considered to be a supreme national interest of the United States.) President Bush declared a moratorium on the testing of nuclear weapons in 1992 and, by 2001, the United States had not conducted a nuclear test since that time. The disappearance of Cold War bipolarity brought an end to the strategic world it created and sharply reduced the sense of mutual vulnerability experienced by the two superpowers. The basic philosophy behind the 1972 ABM treaty, which banned the deployment of nationwide defenses against missile attacks, was that no nation would risk launching a missile attack if it was left defenseless against a retaliatory strike. After the Gulf War of 1991, however, the United States argued that the spread of missile technology required advanced nations to erect defenses against at least the handful of missiles that could one day be launched against them by terrorists or rogue states. This, of course, would mean that the ABM treaty would have to be adjusted to accommodate a new strategic reality.

President Clinton pushed for unilaterally constructing a partial missile defense system, which he claimed would protect the United States against the new threat. Russia objected, claiming that this would violate the ABM Treaty and start the major nuclear powers on a new, defensive dimension of the arms race. Yeltsin's successor, Russian President Vladimir V. Putin, argued that mutual reduction was the path to stability. There were good political reasons to cooperate with Russia, and in May 2001, President George W. Bush offered Russia a package to broaden the scope of missile defense technology to enlist Russian support for the new system.

By the early twenty-first century there was a broad consensus emerging in the United States that it was in the American national security interest to develop a limited missile defense commensurate with the emergence of real threats and the technology available. The politics of missile defense internationally would require cooperation with allies and Russian involvement. In relation to China, the other major concern for American policymakers, missile defense would also have to be handled as a part of the overall U.S.–China relationship.

The move toward cautious cooperation with Russia at the end of the Cold War was also evident in the peaceful use and exploration of outer space. For thirty years after World War II, the United States had primarily regarded space as an area of competition. Tentative steps toward cooperation had been taken in the 1970s, symbolized by the 1975 Apollo-Soyuz docking. In 1988 the Reagan administration signed an agreement with ten European nations, Canada, and Japan to undertake technological collaboration in space and human space flights, but little came of the collaboration until Russia joined in 1993.

HUMAN RIGHTS TREATIES

Although American attitudes to treaties entered a new phase following World War II, the unilateralist impulse so dominant before the war continued in certain areas. The Senate opposed the ratification of multilateral UN treaties, particularly in relation to human rights issues. In the 1950s human rights became a major political issue in the United States, focusing on domestic racial segregation and civil rights. The civil rights movement and the Cold War were the domestic and international elements in a broad debate over the future of America. Conservatives believed human rights treaties conflicted with important national domestic interests. To them, desegregation at home and American participation in human rights treaties abroad were tools of the communists. Conservatives also regarded human rights treaties as a mechanism whereby the federal government would expand its powers over the rights of states and individuals, thereby destroying the constitutional rights of states and citizens. They believed the federal government would use treaty-making authority to make domestic and local law for the people of the various states, dismantling segregation and the property, marriage, and education laws associated with segregation. UN human rights treaties were seen as threatening the American way of life and introducing communist or socialistic government. The Soviet explosion of a nuclear device, the Korean War, and the success of the communist regime in China confirmed American fears of the threat and spread of communism. A further element in Senate opposition to human rights treaties was a strong chauvinistic belief in the superiority of the United States.

The principles of the Universal Declaration of Human Rights (UDHR) drawn up by the UN Human Rights Commission, chaired by Eleanor Roosevelt, were formally codified in the treaty known as the Human Rights Covenant completed in 1954. The United States supported the adoption of the declaration in the United Nations. Although not binding in legal terms, it was regarded by many legal scholars as a statement of customary international law. The Genocide Convention, linked to the proposed declaration and drafted in response to the atrocities of the Third Reich, was the first postwar treaty on human rights. It grew out of the Charter of the International Military Tribunal signed in London on 8 August 1945 by the United States, the United Kingdom, and the Soviet Union. Adopted by the UN General Assembly on 9 December 1948, its purpose was to make genocide an international crime. President Truman transmitted the convention to the Senate on 16 June 1949 with a recommendation of ratification, but because of Senate opposition led by the American Bar Association (ABA), it was not ratified for almost forty years. The ABA was the main body influencing the Senate. In the early 1950s as many as 60 percent of senators were lawyers and had a professional relationship with the organization. Of the membership of 41,000, only thirteen were African Americans—the ethnic group that, aside from Native Americans, had been the primary object of an American variant of genocide. The Genocide Convention was unsuccessful because of legal arguments used against it by opponents in the Senate. It is clear that many senators feared that the southern system of discrimination and segregation of African Americans—especially incidents of lynching and race riots—fell within the definition of genocide under the Genocide Convention. They did not appear to have the same awareness in relation to indigenous Americans. The Senate repeatedly held hearings on the Genocide Convention between 1950 and 1985, and it was finally approved with numerous reservations, understandings, and declarations (after passage by the House as the Proxmire Act) on 14 October 1988. The act was signed by President Ronald Reagan on 4 November 1988 and lodged with the United Nations on 15 November.

The opposition to human rights treaties is odd in a way because there is a rich history of the use of human rights precepts in U.S. history—especially U.S. domestic history. In the late eighteenth century, such precepts came under the rubric of "the rights of man," and, as noted by Alexander Hamilton in 1775, they could "never be erased or obscured by a mortal power." By 1789 human rights precepts were an established part of U.S. courts, although the vast majority of Supreme Court decisions referring to human rights have occurred only since the 1950s. John Adams stated in 1781 that the United States stood for "reason, justice, truth, the rights of mankind and the interests of the nations of Europe." Thomas Jefferson used the phrase the "rights of man" in presidential addresses in 1805–1806 to acknowledge the rights of Native Americans and African American slaves. Presidents John Quincy Adams, Andrew Jackson, and Abraham Lincoln were among many who reaffirmed these rights in the decades preceding the Civil War. Human rights was the plank many in the Senate used to argue for the abolition of slavery. They argued that slavery was a violation of the rights of man, and that "the Constitution of the United States confers no power on Congress to deprive men of their natural rights and inalienable liberty." Some senators went even further. Charles Sumner argued in 1863, for example, that intervention in foreign countries was permissible if "on the side

of Human Rights." In a treaty with China signed in 1868 the United States affirmed the "inherent and inalienable right of man to change his home and allegiance."

Despite the Supreme Court decisions supporting segregation in the late nineteenth century and the Senate rejection of the Covenant of the League of Nations, by the second decade of the twentieth century there was a clear movement to further human rights. Women were given the vote, the civil rights of Native Americans as citizens were recognized, and Americans began to contemplate incorporating a Declaration of Universal Human Rights into the law of the land. Woodrow Wilson's Fourteen Points and Franklin Roosevelt's Four Freedoms were perhaps the clearest expressions of America's commitment to human rights. Indeed the impulse to further human rights had reached such a point by mid-century that the career diplomat and leading architect of the American policy of containment of the Soviet Union, George F. Kennan, felt obliged to warn that the moral legalistic thread running through American foreign policy seriously threatened its vital national interests abroad. Nevertheless, nongovernmental organizations have been highly critical of the selective manner in which the United States has applied its foreign policy in relation to human rights.

The United Nations Universal Declaration of Human Rights, however, broadened the definition of human rights to include not only the traditional, classic, political, and civil rights such as the rights to property, the right to a fair trial, freedom of movement, freedom of expression and religion, and so on, but also formalized the prohibition of slavery, torture, arbitrary arrest, and such social and economic rights as the right to work, right to an adequate standard of living, right to an education, right to seek asylum—rights formerly not included in the jurisdiction of international treaties. Cultural rights—the right to participate in the cultural life of one's community, the right to share in scientific advancement, and the protection of the moral and material interests resulting from one's scientific, literary, or artistic production—were also recognized and codified in the International Covenant on Civil and Political Rights and the International Covenant on Economic Social and Cultural Rights adopted as legally binding treaties by the UN General Assembly in 1966.

These broad definitions gave many senators pause. President Carter signed the two human rights treaties in 1978 and recommended their adoption, but the Senate only ratified the International Covenant of Civil and Political Rights in 1992, and then with a number of reservations, understandings, and declarations. The most important of these was that the treaty could not be invoked before American courts, and that the provisions of the treaty relating to, for example, "cruel and unusual punishment" (like the death penalty) must be interpreted as it is under the U.S. Constitution. These reservations have been rejected by many parties to the International Covenant of Civil and Political Rights, including the United Kingdom, Sweden, and the Netherlands, under the Vienna Convention on the Law of Treaties.

During the Nixon administration Congress added an amendment to the Foreign Assistance Act prohibiting U.S. assistance to any government that consistently, grossly violated internationally recognized human rights, and in 1976 it extended the prohibition to security assistance and arms sales, except under "extraordinary circumstances." This loophole enabled Washington to continue to support such governments as that of President Ferdinand Marcos of the Philippines and President Suharto of Indonesia despite their gross human rights violations. President Carter, who regarded human rights as a major element of foreign policy, did terminate military assistance to a number of Latin American countries because of their human rights policies, although Presidents Reagan and George H. W. Bush did not pursue Carter's policies. By the late twentieth century the State Department was required to report to Congress annually on the human rights records of those countries receiving U.S. economic and military assistance, some 190 nations. China's violations of human rights were a particular target of the Bush administration, although President Clinton came under strong criticism for renewing China's most-favored-nation status in 1993 and 1994. Increasingly, U.S. support of Israel was being criticized by international nongovernmental organizations such as Amnesty International because of Israel's alleged human rights violations in its treatment of Palestinians.

ENVIRONMENTAL TREATIES

The number and range of international agreements on environmental practices and policies have grown tremendously since the 1970s. Some estimates suggest that there were around 900 agreements in force in 1992, including regional and bilateral treaties. Major accords reached on issues related to global environmental change include the Montreal Protocol on Substances that Deplete the Ozone Layer (1987), the United Nations Framework Convention on Climate Change (1992), the Convention on Biological Diversity (1992), and the various agreements forged as part of the United Nations Conference on Environment and Development in 1992.

The United States, like many other countries, came to the realization that solutions to shared environmental problems would occur only through cooperation among states. Successful cooperation, in turn, would require effective international institutions to guide international behavior toward sustainable development. Treaties and agreements are among the more important of these institutions. Environmental scientists identified seven major international environmental problems: oil pollution from tankers, acid rain, stratospheric ozone depletion, pollution of the North and Baltic seas, mismanagement of fisheries, overpopulation, and misuse of agricultural chemicals.

Responding to concerns that human activities were increasing concentrations of greenhouse gases (such as carbon dioxide and methane) in the atmosphere, most nations of the world joined together in 1992 to sign the United Nations Framework Convention on Climate Change (UNFCCC). The United Nations Conference on Environment and Development (UNCED) was held in Rio de Janeiro in June 1992 and was the world's most comprehensive organized response to international environmental degradation. UNCED delegates sought to adopt conventions on greenhouse gases and biodiversity; to enunciate in an Earth Charter the principles by which humans should conduct themselves in relation to the environment; to adopt a program of action, called Agenda 21, to implement the Earth Charter; and to develop a set of institutional and financial arrangements to support such measures.

The Framework Convention on Climate Change was one of two binding treaties opened for signature at UNCED in 1992. The treaty, also known as the Climate Convention, addressed potential human-induced global warming by pledging countries to seek "stabilization of greenhouse gas concentrations in the atmosphere at a level that would prevent dangerous anthropogenic interference with the climate system."

Although stated only in general terms, the Climate Convention parties agreed to attempt to limit emissions of greenhouse gases, mainly carbon dioxide and methane.

Although signed at UNCED, the Climate Convention was negotiated through a separate process under the Intergovernmental Negotiating Committee for the Framework Convention on Climate Change. The text was adopted at New York on 9 May 1992 and opened for signature at Rio de Janeiro from 4 to 14 June 1992 and thereafter at United Nations Headquarters from 20 June 1992 to 19 June 1993. By that date the convention had received 166 signatures.

The United States was one of the first nations to ratify this treaty. It included a legally nonbinding, voluntary pledge that the major industrialized, developed nations would reduce their greenhouse gas emissions to 1990 levels by the year 2000. However, as it became apparent that major nations such as the United States and Japan would not meet the voluntary stabilization target by 2000, parties to the treaty decided in 1995 to enter into negotiations on a protocol to establish legally binding limitations or reductions in greenhouse gas emissions. These negotiations were completed at a meeting held in Kyoto, Japan, 1–10 December 1997. There was wide disparity among key players especially on three items: (1) the amounts of binding reductions in greenhouse gases to be required, and the gases to be included in these requirements; (2) whether developing countries should be part of the requirements for greenhouse gas limitations; and (3) whether to allow emissions trading and joint implementation, which allow credit to be given for emissions reductions to a country that provides funding or investments in other countries that bring about the actual reductions in those other countries or locations where they may be cheaper to attain.

The Kyoto Protocol committed the industrialized nations to specified, legally binding reductions in emissions of six greenhouse gases. The treaty was opened for signature on 16 March 1998 through 16 March 1999, and the United States signed the protocol on 12 November 1998. The treaty committed the United States to a target of reducing greenhouse gases by 7 percent below 1990 levels during a "commitment period" between 2008 and 2012. By February 2000, eighty-four countries had signed the treaty, including the European Union and most of its members, along with Canada, Japan, China, and a range of developing countries. Some twenty-two countries were reported by the UNFCCC Secretariat to have ratified the treaty. Following completion of the protocol in December of 1997, details of a number of the more difficult issues remained to be negotiated and resolved. At a fourth Conference of the Parties (COP-4) held 2–13 November 1998 in Buenos Aires, Argentina, it became apparent that these issues could not be resolved as had been expected during this meeting. Instead, parties established a two-year "Buenos Aires action plan" to deal with these issues, with a deadline for completion by the sixth Conference of the Parties (COP-6) held in The Hague, Netherlands, 13–24 November 2000.

More than 7,000 participants from 182 governments, 323 intergovernmental and nongovernmental organizations, and 443 media outlets attended the COP-6 meeting. COP-6 sought to reduce differences among member countries over the following issues: the transfer of technology to assist developing countries and countries with economies in transition; the adverse effects of climate change and the impact of implementation of response measures; best practices in domestic policies and measures to address greenhouse gas emissions; the mechanisms outlined under the Kyoto Protocol; a compliance system for the protocol; and issues relating to the land use, land-use change, and forestry (LULUCF) sector. Despite the best efforts of COP-6 president Jan Pronk (of the Netherlands), by 23 November negotiations had stalled. Two days later, Pronk announced that delegates had failed to reach agreement. Delegates agreed to suspend COP-6 and expressed a willingness to resume their work in 2001.

President Clinton voiced strong support for the Kyoto Protocol but criticized it for not including commitments for developing countries. The United States signature was criticized by several members of Congress who opposed the treaty on a number of grounds, including questions about the scientific justification for it and about the likely economic impacts that might occur if the United States were to attempt to meet its emission reduction commitments. In recognition of the opposition to the protocol expressed in the Senate by Resolution 98 (which passed 95–0), President Clinton indicated that he would not submit the treaty to the Senate for advice and consent until meaningful developing-country participation had been achieved, thereby delaying indefinitely any possibility of ratification.

House and Senate delegations served as observers on the U.S. delegation to the Kyoto meeting, as well as to other COP meetings, including Buenos Aires. Supporters and opponents of the protocol were included in these delegations. A number of committees held hearings on the implications of the protocol for the United States—its economy, energy prices, impacts on climate change, and other related issues. While the Clinton administration stated that the treaty could be implemented without harm to the United States economy and without imposing additional taxes, a number of questions related to how its goals could be achieved, and at what cost, continued to be of interest to Congress.

In a major setback for the environmental movement, in April 2001, President George W. Bush, responding to pressure from domestic business interests, announced that the United States no longer regarded itself bound by the Kyoto Protocol. This decision represented the triumph of U.S. economic interests over the realistic preservation of the natural global environment, and reflected the force of economic motives in the United States regardless of any detrimental impact on the world.

POST–WORLD WAR II COLLECTIVE TRADE AGREEMENTS

The determination of the United States to spread "free" market capitalism can be seen in the multilateral economic agreements and treaties entered into by the United States in the last decade of the twentieth century. Following World War II, Washington sought cooperative ways to rebuild the world economy and create a more coherent institutional framework within which the United States might best utilize its economic strength. This restructuring was to be based on the law of comparative advantage and free trade.

The first steps were taken at Bretton Woods, New Hampshire, where forty-four nations met from 1 July to 22 July 1944 and created the International Monetary Fund (IMF) to oversee the world's monetary and exchange-rate systems. The Bretton Woods Conference also established the World Bank to rebuild western Europe utilizing Marshall Plan funds. Congress passed the Bretton Woods Agreement Act in July 1945 (House 345 to 18; Senate 61 to 16). In 1946 the first session of the Preparatory Committee of the UN Conference on Trade and Employment created the General Agreement on Trade and Tariffs (GATT), to which the United

States became a party. The trade rules in the GATT were part of the International Trade Organization (ITO) agreed to in the Havana charter in 1948. Interestingly, because the rules governing world trade set out in the GATT were so ambiguous, flexible, and loosely framed, Congress refused to ratify U.S. membership in the International Trade Organization. So the United States joined through an executive agreement, using power given to the president under the Reciprocal Trade Agreements Act of 1934. Congress has never recognized the GATT, but in the Trade Expansion Act of 1962, it extended the power given to the president in the 1934 act to negotiate tariff-cutting agreements.

The initial purpose of the GATT was to negotiate tariff concessions among members and to establish a code of conduct and procedures for the resolution of trade disputes by negotiation. The core assumption underlying American participation in these efforts to encourage multilateral trade arrangements was that international cooperation in trade and investment created harmonious political relations and reduced tensions between nations. The GATT was founded on the principles of nondiscrimination and multilateralism in international trade. Nondiscrimination was expressed through unconditional most-favored-nation status for all contracting parties. By this convention, if tariffs on imports from one country were lowered, the tariff on all imports of the same goods from other GATT members must also be reduced. Most-favored-nation treaties had been the preferred device for the United States in dealing with China in the nineteenth century, when the United States gained access to the China market on the back of British imperialism. Indeed, most-favored-nation treaties were favored throughout U.S. history, and the GATT was just the latest embodiment of this mechanism of extending commercial opportunities. Multilateralism in the 1950s and 1960s favored the expansion of U.S. corporations across the globe, but by the 1970s and 1980s free trade meant that the United States faced stiff competition from the revitalized economies of western Europe and Japan. At first Washington sought to maintain its advantage by promoting the expansion of the GATT rules into nontraditional areas. GATT sponsored a series of multinational trade negotiations (called rounds) to progressively lower tariffs and eliminate unfair trade practices. At the Uruguay Round (1986–1994), in which 117 countries participated, the GATT agreement was extended to include such areas as services, patents, trademarks, copyright, and, most importantly, agriculture. At its final meeting (held in Marrakesh, Morocco, on 7 April 1994), the Uruguay Round also created the World Trade Organization, which, from 1 January 1995, would take over the administrative functions formerly conducted by GATT. Congress legislated to implement the agreement on 7 December 1994.

Under President Reagan the United States adopted protectionist measures. It attempted to stem the hemorrhage of its traditional areas of comparative advantage through "managed" trade and ending European subsidies on agriculture. When members of GATT resisted, Washington reverted to a unilateral policy—falling back on Section 301 of the 1974 Trade Act, which allowed for more effective (punitive) measures on goods entering the United States. The United States also entered bilateral arrangements with Canada.

As the twentieth century came to an end the world economy was in turmoil. Macroeconomic failures across countries had created staggering levels of unemployment in rich and poor countries alike. American protectionist practices, along with the programs dictated by the International Monetary Fund and World Bank, helped increase the gap between rich and poor countries. Mexico, one of the countries whose economy was most at risk because of foreign-owed debt—primarily to American-owned banks—had signed the GATT in 1986, and in response to International Monetary Fund demands, began to restructure its economy along lines acceptable to U.S. economic and financial interests. These requirements included elimination of fetters on the free market, privatizing areas of the economy that were previously under public control, and eliminating restrictions on foreign investment. Mexico set in motion a series of tariff-reduction and other economic liberalization measures. It also indicated that it would be interested in securing a "Canadian" deal with the United States.

The United States, once the defender of multilateralism and free trade, sought regional solutions to its economic woes. One such initiative was the North American Free Trade Agreement (NAFTA), signed with Canada and Mexico. Designed to create a free trade zone in the North American continent, it came into effect on 1 January 1994. NAFTA was an executive agreement reached on 12 August 1992. It was approved by the Congress after a vigorous national debate in late 1993.

In its own words, one of the main objectives of NAFTA was "the elimination of tariffs between Canada, Mexico, and the United States on 'qualifying' goods by the year 1998 for originating goods from Canada and for originating goods from Mexico by the year 2008." It also sought to promote fair competition, increase investment in the territories, protect and enforce intellectual property rights, and establish a framework for further cooperation between the countries.

Critics argued that NAFTA had only a limited relation to free trade. They pointed out that a primary U.S. objective was increased protection for "intellectual property," including software, patents for seeds and drugs, and so on. Such measures were designed to ensure that U.S.-based corporations controlled the technology of the future, including biotechnology, which, it was hoped, would allow protected private enterprise to control health, agriculture, and the means of life generally, locking the poor into dependence and hopelessness. Nevertheless, NAFTA provided Mexican exporters with additional market access and helped attract foreign direct investment into Mexico, in services as well as in the industrial export sector. At the end of 1999, Mexico was the eighth largest export economy in the world, with $280 billion in exports. By the end of 2000, Mexico ranked as the fifth largest export economy in the world (up from twenty-sixth at the beginning of the 1990s) with an estimated $300 billion in exports. Between 1993 and 1999, Mexico's exports to the United States rose a remarkable 160 percent. The U.S. International Trade Commission estimated that American companies stood to gain $61 billion a year from the Third World if U.S. protectionist demands were satisfied by NAFTA. Opponents further pointed out that NAFTA included intricate "rules of origin" requirements designed to keep foreign competitors out. Moreover, the agreements went far beyond trade. A prime U.S. objective was liberalization of services, which would allow supranational banks to displace domestic competitors and thus eliminate any threat of national economic planning and independent development .

The treaty was also thought likely to have harmful environmental effects, encouraging a shift of production to regions where enforcement was lax. Increasingly in the global economy, production could be shifted to high-repression, low-wage areas and directed to privileged sectors. In 1996, General Motors, for example, planned to close almost two dozen plants in the United States and Canada even as it became the largest private employer in Mexico. Critics charged that the agreement overrode the rights of workers, consumers, and the future generations who cannot "vote" in the market on environmental issues, and that the goal was to provide a business environment unfettered by government interference. Package and labeling requirements and inspection procedures to protect consumers, for example, would not be required.

NAFTA did set up an institutional framework to address regional environmental issues. The North American Agreement on Environmental Cooperation (NAAEC) and the Commission for Environmental Cooperation (CEC) were two such steps to promote the effective enforcement of environmental law. Mexico attempted to enforce its environmental laws for new companies, thereby diminishing any incentive for firms to relocate to Mexico to avoid environmental enforcement. The Mexican government began to enforce more effectively its environmental laws by imposing sanctions against the more visible polluters and, more importantly, developed a program of voluntary environmental audits. One institution set up to help deal with the extensive environmental problems on the U.S.–Mexico border was the Border Environment Cooperation Commission (BEEC). The BEEC was an autonomous, binational organization that supported local communities and other project sponsors in developing and implementing environmental infrastructure projects related to the treatment of water and wastewater and the management of municipal solid waste.

CONCLUSION

The meaning, nature, and purpose of treaties changed significantly over two centuries, reflecting the greater complexity of international relations. Several developments contributed to this phenomenon. Among the more obvious changes that occurred in the second half of the twentieth century were the unprecedented rise in the world's population, the emergence of ethnic awareness around the world, an increase in the number of independent states, and developments associated with inventions in weapons systems, communications, and science, especially biochemistry. Treaties came to address not only the needs met by the relatively simple military security alliances and trade arrangements of the eighteenth and nineteenth centuries; they became also instruments for organizing and structuring the tremendously complex demands of an interdependent global geopolitical economic system. Treaties now dictated the conduct of nations in matters of global importance such as human rights, resource use and allocation, pollution, protection of the environment and animal species, intellectual property rights, and a whole host of hitherto unthought-of areas of national behavior. Despite the objections of individual nations, these international arrangements were proving remarkably successful in shaping international and domestic performance, and whether they liked it or not, most nations were linked into a complex international treaty system.

In this interdependent, international environment, the United States found itself in an anomalous position. It could no longer continue to enter—or refuse to enter—into treaty arrangements based solely upon domestic political considerations or an entirely independent assessment of whether or not unilateral action is preferable to multilateral action. The United States, although by some measures the world's most powerful military and economic power and free of the crippling shackles of the Cold War, could not ignore the responsibilities and restraints imposed by such institutions as the United Nations, the World Bank, or the International Monetary Fund, acting through a global, multilateral, treaty system. Nor could it ignore world opinion while seeking to take advantage of its membership in that treaty system.

Treaties came to impinge upon almost all aspects of the lives of Americans as well as the lives of most of the world's population. Perhaps the most dramatic change in respect to treaties was that they came to reflect the interests of global institutions as much as individual nations or their populations. This was as true of the United States as it was of other nations. A little over two centuries later, the worst fears of the Founders appeared to have been realized: the United States was involved in a series of world entanglements they could not have imagined.

Despite these views, it was not clear at the turn of the twenty-first century that the United States would accept the new order. President George W. Bush and his administration appeared to want to return to the nonentanglement envisioned in the days of the early Republic, and in their desire to do so they struck a resonant chord in the American people.

BIBLIOGRAPHY

Bemis, Samuel F. *John Quincy Adams and the Foundations of American Foreign Policy.* New York, 1949.

———. *Pinckney's Treaty: America's Advantage from Europe's Distress.* New Haven, Conn., 1960.

———. *Jay's Treaty: A Study in Commerce and Diplomacy.* New Haven, Conn., 1962. All three Bemis books provide an excellent background to the early treaties.

Byrd, Elbert M. *Treaties and Executive Agreements in the United States, Their Separate Roles and Limitations.* The Hague, 1960. Good on the treaty-making process.

Caldwell, Lynton Keith. *International Environmental Policy: Emergence and Dimensions.* 2d ed. Durham, N.C. 1990.

DeConde, Alexander. *Entangling Alliance: Politics and Diplomacy Under George Washington.* Westport, Conn., 1958.

———. *The Quasi-War: The Politics and Diplomacy of the Undeclared War With France, 1797–1801.* New York, 1966. Both DeConde works clearly set out the issues that shaped early attitudes toward treaties.

DeConde, Alexander, ed. *Isolation and Security: Ideas and Interests in Twentieth-Century American Foreign Policy.* Durham, N.C., 1957. Examines the domestic factors at work between the wars.

Duroselle, Jean Baptiste. *From Wilson to Roosevelt: Foreign Policy of the United States, 1913–1945.* Cambridge, Mass., 1963. Helpful for World Wars I and II.

Ferrell, Robert H. *Peace in Their Time: The Origins of the Kellogg-Briand Pact.* New Haven, Conn., 1952. Careful and scholarly.

Fisher, Louis. *Constitutional Conflicts Between Congress and the President.* 4th ed. Lawrence, Kans., 1997. A survey that contains useful material on treaty ratifications.

Jackson, John H. *The World Trading System: Law and Policy of International Economic Relations.* Cambridge, Mass., 1997. An introduction to trade law and policy by a supporter of GATT and the WTO.

Kaufman, Natalie Hevener. *Human Rights Treaties and the Senate: A History of Opposition.* Chapel Hill, N.C., 1990. Forceful attack on Senate opposition to human rights treaties, including the Genocide Convention.

Kimball, Warren F. *The Most Unsordid Act: Lend-Lease, 1939–1941.* Baltimore, 1969. Indispensable on the turning point toward cooperation.

Lake, David A. *Entangling Relations: American Foreign Policy in Its Century.* Princeton, N.J., 1999. A political scientist examines the tension that surrounded the question of whether the United States should act unilaterally or cooperatively through treaties in twentieth-century foreign relations.

Leopold, Richard. *The Growth of American Foreign Policy: A History.* New York, 1962. Although it does not go beyond the 1950s, this survey provides helpful structural details on the relationship between treaties and foreign relations.

Malloy, William M., comp. *Treaties, Conventions, International Acts, Protocols, and Agreements Between the United States and Other Powers, 1776–1909.* 2 vols. Holmes Beach, Fla., 1996. A comprehensive collection of nineteenth-century treaties.

Paterson, Thomas G., J. Garry Clifford, and Kenneth J. Hagan. *American Foreign Relations: A History.* 2 vols. Boston, 2000. A particularly useful survey of United States foreign relations for this topic.

Pletcher, David M. *The Diplomacy of Annexation: Texas, Oregon, and the Mexican War.* Columbia, Mo., 1973. Remains the classic examination of these episodes.

Prucha, Francis Paul. *The Great Father: The United States Government and the American Indians.* 2 vols. Lincoln, Neb., 1984. Traces the stages of government policy toward Native Americans.

Rosenne, Shabtai. *Developments in the Law of Treaties, 1945–1986.* Cambridge, 1989. Technical lectures on legal aspects of how treaties have developed since World War II.

United States Department of State. *Treaties in Force: A List of Treaties and Other International Agreements.* Washington, D.C., annually since 1950. The most up-to-date list (by topic and country) of treaties to which the United States is a signatory.

United States Senate, Committee on Foreign Relations. "Implications of the Kyoto Protocol on Climate Change." Hearings Before the Committee on Foreign Relations, 105th Congress, 2d Session, 11 February 1998 (Washington D.C., 1998). One of a series of congressional publications on hearings before Congress on the Kyoto Protocol.

Van Cleave, William R., and S. T. Cohen. *Nuclear Weapons, Policies, and the Test Ban Issue.* New York, 1987. Critical of test ban treaties.

Zupnick, Elliott. *Visions and Revisions: The U.S. in the Global Economy.* Boulder, Colo., 1999. A strong defense of the U.S. role in globalization.

See also AMBASSADORS, EXECUTIVE AGENTS, AND SPECIAL REPRESENTATIVES; ARMS CONTROL AND DISARMAMENT; COLLECTIVE SECURITY; CONGRESSIONAL POWER; THE CONSTITUTION; ECONOMIC POLICY AND THEORY; ENVIRONMENTAL DIPLOMACY; HUMAN RIGHTS; INTERNATIONAL LAW; PRESIDENTIAL POWER; NUCLEAR STRATEGY AND DIPLOMACY; TARIFF POLICIES.

THE VIETNAM WAR AND ITS IMPACT

★ ★ ★ ★

Larry Berman and Jason Newman

On 2 September 1945 at Hanoi's Ba Dinh Square, Ho Chi Minh issued the historic Vietnamese proclamation of independence with words borrowed from the American Declaration of Independence: "We hold the truth that all men are created equal, that they are endowed by their Creator certain unalienable rights, that among these are life, liberty and the pursuit of happiness." Ho Chi Minh—who four years earlier had founded the League for Revolution and Independence, or Vietminh—had been preparing his entire life for the opportunity to rid Vietnam of colonial rule, both Japanese and French. Crowds marched from one end of Saigon to the other chanting, "Do Dao de quoc, Do Dao thuc dan phap." (Down with the Imperialists, Down with the French Colonialists.) Throughout Vietnam banners proclaimed "Vietnam for the Vietnamese."

Ho Chi Minh requested support for his cause from nations that recognized the principles of self-determination and equality of nations. President Franklin D. Roosevelt seemed to favor an international trusteeship for Vietnam to be followed by independence, but new pressures would soon change the situation for Ho and the Vietnamese. As the Cold War developed, Washington became more sensitive to the colonial interests of its allies than to the decolonization of Indochina. Ho was defined as being pro-Moscow. U.S. Cold War policy was guided by the containment of a perceived Soviet aggression. Containment was composed of economic, political, and military initiatives that sought to maintain stability in the international arena. The bitter recriminations in the United States over "who lost China?" after 1949 led the Truman administration to do what it could to prevent a Vietminh victory in Vietnam or anywhere else in Indochina. Vietnam was valued not for its own merit, but was seen rather as a test of America's global position and credibility. In December 1950, the United States joined France and the French-controlled governments of Viet-

nam, Cambodia, and Laos in signing the Mutual Defense Assistance Agreement. The United States agreed to provide military supplies and equipment through a military advisory group. This small contingent of U.S. advisers provided limited logistical services; all supplies and equipment were dispensed through the French Expeditionary Corps. U.S. aid to the French military effort mounted from $130 million in 1950 to $800 million in 1953.

In May 1953 the French government appointed General Henri Navarre commander in Vietnam and charged him with mounting a major new offensive against the Vietminh. One of Navarre's first moves, late in 1953, was to dispatch French troops to Dien Bien Phu, the juncture of a number of roads in northwestern Indochina about 100 miles from the Chinese border. On 7 May 1954 the French forces were defeated there. Shortly thereafter the Geneva Conference was held, bringing together representatives of Vietminh-controlled territory and Bao Dai's French-controlled government—which would later evolve into North and South Vietnam, respectively—the other emerging Indochinese states of Laos and Cambodia, and the major powers of France, Britain, the United States, the Soviet Union, and the People's Republic of China. The Geneva Accords, formally known as the Final Declaration of the Geneva Conference on the Problem of Restoring Peace in Indochina, essentially settled military but not political issues.

The Vietminh controlled most of Vietnam and sought a political settlement at Geneva that would lead to the withdrawal of French forces and the establishment of an independent government led by Ho Chi Minh. But at the Geneva Conference, Anthony Eden of the United Kingdom, Pierre Mendès-France of France, Vyacheslav Molotov of the Soviet Union, and Chou En-lai of China pressured the Vietminh, through its representative, Pham Van Dong, to accept much less than it had won in battle. Under great pressure in particular from the Chinese and Soviets, who feared American military intervention under Secretary of State John Foster Dulles, Ho made two major concessions—a provisional demarcation line drawn at the seventeenth parallel and free nationwide elections for unifying the country supervised by an international commission scheduled for 1956. The election was intended to settle the question of political control over Vietnam. Externally, the accords provided for a neutral Vietnam, meaning that no military alliances were to be made by either side.

Three months after Dien Bien Phu, President Dwight D. Eisenhower convened the National Security Council (NSC) to review U.S. policy in Asia. The president was already on record as claiming that

> strategically South Vietnam's capture by the Communists would bring their power several hundred miles into a hitherto free region. The remaining countries in Southeast Asia would be menaced by a great flanking movement. The freedom of 12 million people would be lost immediately and that of 150 million others in adjacent lands would be seriously endangered. The loss the Republic of Vietnam, or South Vietnam, would have grave consequences for us and for freedom.

Eisenhower had also articulated the line of reasoning that came to be known as the domino theory, that the fall of one state to communism would lead to the next and the next being knocked over. Not losing Southeast Asia thus became the goal of the United States.

In an October 1954 letter to the president of South Vietnam, Ngo Dinh Diem, President Eisenhower was exceedingly clear:

> I am, accordingly, instructing the American Ambassador to Vietnam to examine with you in your capacity as chief of Government, how an intelligent program of American aid given directly to your Government can serve to assist Vietnam in its present hour of trial, provided that your Government is prepared to give assurances as to the standards of performance it would be able to maintain in the event such aid were supplied. The purpose of this offer is to assist the government of Vietnam in developing and maintaining a strong, viable state, capable of resisting attempted subversion or aggression through military means.

By 1961 Vietnam loomed as a test of President John F. Kennedy's inaugural commitment "to pay any price, to bear any burden, in the defense of freedom." But Diem's government had evolved

★ ★ ★ ★

THE LESSONS OF 1954

There is an important historical caveat worth noting. Richard Nixon was vice president of the United States at the time of the Geneva Conference of 1954 and Pham Van Dong headed the DRV delegation. By 1970 both men would be the leaders of the United States and the Democratic Republic of Vietnam, respectively. Both drew lessons from the Geneva experience that would influence how each approached the final phase of negotiations in Paris nearly two decades later. Dong always believed that the Vietminh had been betrayed by its friends and was wary of a repetition. Therefore, he was determined that the Soviet Union and China not use their interest in improved relations with the United States to leverage a quick settlement. For Nixon the lessons from Geneva were just as clear. He would again try to use Hanoi's friends, the Soviets and Chinese, to force concessions that would lead to a political settlement advantageous to the United States. Nixon would insist that President Thieu remain in office as part of any negotiated settlement. Once that goal was accomplished, there would be no need to hold elections until the North Vietnamese troops went home. After all, with American support, Diem had called off the elections of 1956. Such was Nixon's view of Geneva's lessons.

into a family oligarchy that ruled through force and repression. Opposition grew from a wide range of political, social, and religious groups. Protests raged, including the quite dramatic self-immolations by Buddhist monks. On 1 November 1963, Diem was removed from office and murdered in the back of a U.S.-built personnel carrier. The coup was planned and implemented by South Vietnamese military officers; U.S. ambassador Henry Cabot Lodge and the Central Intelligence Agency (CIA) were involved. Kennedy, given the opportunity to instruct Lodge that the coup be stopped, issued no such order.

Diem's death was followed by a period of great political instability in Saigon, while three weeks after the coup Kennedy was assassinated in Dallas. His successor, President Lyndon B. Johnson, assumed office with the belief that the United

States had to ensure the stability and security of South Vietnam. Momentum was building in favor of action that might reverse the disintegrating political conditions in South Vietnam, which was under military pressure from the North Vietnamese–backed National Liberation Front (NLF), or Vietcong (VC). One form of new activity involved U.S. Navy patrols up the Gulf of Tonkin for intelligence-gathering purposes. On 2 August 1964 the destroyer *Maddox* was returning from one of these DeSoto electronic espionage missions when North Vietnamese torpedo boats fired on the ship. Rather than withdrawing U.S. ships from the danger zone, the president ordered another destroyer, the *C. Turner Joy,* to join the *Maddox* in the Gulf of Tonkin. On 4 August both the *Maddox* and the *C. Turner Joy* reportedly came under attack. The president later met with congressional leaders and sought assurance that his response would be supported.

On 10 August 1964, Congress passed the Southeast Asia Resolution, also known as the Tonkin Gulf Resolution, which authorized Johnson "to take all necessary measures to repel any armed attack against the forces of the United States and to prevent further aggression." The president later used the resolution to justify his escalation of American involvement in Vietnam. With the 1964 presidential election against Republican conservative Barry Goldwater less than three months away, however, he had no desire to be portrayed as planning for war. Instead, he left the rhetoric of war to Goldwater and the planning to his military advisers. "Peace candidate" Johnson won the election in a landslide.

AMERICANIZING THE WAR

Rolling Thunder, the commitment of marines in March 1965, and the deployment of other troops all before June 1965 provided ample evidence that the war was already on the road to being Americanized. Throughout June and July of 1965, the question of "Americanizing" the war was at the center of all foreign policy discussions. Undersecretary of State George Ball tried to warn Johnson of the dangers ahead. In an 18 June memo titled "Keeping the Power of Decision in the South Vietnam Crisis," Ball argued that the United States was on the threshold of a new war:

> In raising our commitment from 50,000 to 100,000 or more men and deploying most of the increment in combat roles we were beginning a new war—the United States directly against the VC. The president's most difficult continuing problem in South Vietnam is to prevent "things" from getting into the saddle—or, in other words, to keep control of policy and prevent the momentum of events from taking command.

The president needed to understand the effect of losing control:

> Perhaps the large-scale introduction of U.S. forces with their concentrated firepower will force Hanoi and the VC to the decision we are seeking. On the other hand, we may not be able to fight the war successfully enough—even with 500,000 Americans in South Vietnam we must have more evidence than we now have that our troops will not bog down in the jungles and rice paddies— while we slowly blow the country to pieces.

Ball tried to review the French experience for Johnson, reminding the president that

> the French fought a war in Vietnam, and were finally defeated—after seven years of bloody struggle and when they still had 250,000 combat-hardened veterans in the field, supported by an army of 205,000 South Vietnamese. To be sure, the French were fighting a colonial war while we are fighting to stop aggression. But when we have put enough Americans on the ground in South Vietnam to give the appearance of a white man's war, the distinction as to our ultimate purpose will have less and less practical effect.

Ball's arguments had little influence on policymakers. On 26 June, Secretary of Defense Robert McNamara circulated his "Program of Expanded Military and Political Moves with Respect to Vietnam." McNamara argued that North Vietnam was clearly winning the war and "the tide almost certainly cannot begin to turn in less than a few months and may not for a year or more; the war is one of attrition and will be a long one." McNamara defined winning as "to create conditions for a favorable settlement by demonstrating to the VC/DRV that the odds are against their winning. Under present conditions, however, the chances of achieving this objective are small—and the VC are winning now—largely because the ratio of guerrilla to antiguerrilla forces is unfavorable to the government." The secretary recommended that ground strength be increased to whatever force levels were necessary to show the VC that they "cannot win."

The Joint Chiefs of Staff (JCS) urged Johnson to call up the Reserves and the National Guard and seek public support on national security grounds.

National Security Adviser McGeorge Bundy proposed that the president go before a joint session of Congress or make a statement in the form of a fireside address. But Johnson decided that there would be no public announcement of a change in policy. Instead, he simply called a midday press conference for 9 July. The content as well as the forum of Johnson's presentation downplayed its significance. The expected call-up of the Reserves and request for new funds were absent. In announcing a troop increase, Johnson did not fully reveal the levels he had now authorized: 175,000 to 200,000. Instead, he noted only the immediate force increment of fighting strength from 75,000 to 125,000. Nor did he tell the U.S. people that just a few days earlier, Clark Clifford had privately warned against any substantial buildup of U.S. ground troops. "This could be a quagmire," the president's trusted friend had warned. "It could turn into an open-ended commitment on our part that would take more and more ground troops, without a realistic hope of ultimate victory." Instead, Johnson chose to walk a thin line of credibility. "Additional forces will be needed later, and they will be sent as requested," Johnson observed at his afternoon press conference. His seemingly passing remark correctly indicated that the U.S. commitment had become open-ended: "I have asked the Commanding General, General Westmoreland, what more he needs to meet this mounting aggression. He has told me. We will meet his needs."

Having made the fateful decision, Johnson traveled in February 1966 to Honolulu for a first-hand assessment of the war's progress and to secure additional commitments for political reform from South Vietnam. Johnson utilized his favorite exhortation, telling Westmoreland to "nail the coonskin to the wall" by reaching the crossover point in the war of attrition by December 1966. This so-called light at the end of the tunnel was to be achieved primarily by inflicting losses on enemy forces. Johnson and his advisers expected the enemy to seek negotiations when this ever-elusive crossover point was reached. A fixation on statistics led to use of such terms as "kill ratios," "body counts," "weapons-loss ratios," "died of wounds," and "population-control data" to show that progress was being made. The computers could always demonstrate at least the end of the tunnel; statistically, the United States was always winning the war. In the words of Senator J. William Fulbright, the Great Society had become the "sick society." Disenchantment with the war manifested itself in the growing anti-war movement that began organizing massive protests and moratoriums against U.S. policy.

THE TET OFFENSIVE

While the American people had been told repeatedly that there was a light at the end of the tunnel in Vietnam, the deployment of some 525,000 troops had brought the United States no closer to achieving its limited political goals, and there would soon be a call for major new increases in troop deployments. In effect, the United States faced a stalemate in Vietnam because the enemy controlled the strategic initiative. During the early morning hours of 31 January 1968, the Vietnamese New Year, known as Tet, approximately 80,000 North Vietnamese regulars and NLF guerrillas attacked more than one hundred cities in South Vietnam. The military goal was to spark a popular uprising and, as captured documents revealed, "move forward to achieve final victory." This final victory was not achieved, but psychological and political gains were made. The front page of the 1 February *New York Times* showed a picture of the U.S. embassy in Saigon under assault. Guerrillas had blasted their way into the embassy and held part of the embassy grounds for nearly six hours. All nineteen guerrillas were killed, as were four MPs, a marine guard, and a South Vietnamese embassy employee.

The enemy sustained major losses at Tet, from which it would take years to recover. But Tet also demonstrated the enemy's great skill in planning, coordination, and courage. North Vietnamese regulars and NLF forces had successfully infiltrated previously secure population centers and discredited Saigon's claims of security from attack.

On 27 February, Johnson received JCS chairman Earle Wheeler's report on military requirements in South Vietnam. The document contained a request for 206,000 additional troops. To some, this was proof of the bankruptcy of the army's strategy in Vietnam. Despite the large enemy losses during Tet, the United States was no closer to achieving its goal in Vietnam than it had been in 1965. There appeared to be no breaking point in the enemy's will to continue the struggle indefinitely. The new reinforcements would bring the total American military commitment to three-quarters of a million troops. It was becoming increasingly evident that no amount of military power would bring North Vietnam to the conference table for negotiations.

That same evening CBS news anchorman Walter Cronkite told the nation that the war was destined to remain deadlocked:

> We have been too often disappointed by the optimism of the American leaders, both in Vietnam and Washington, to have faith any longer in the silver linings they find in the darkest clouds. . . . For it seems now more certain than ever that the bloody experience of Vietnam is to end in a stalemate. To say that we are mired in stalemate seems the only realistic, yet unsatisfactory, conclusion.

BOMBING HALT

The president appointed a task force, under the direction of Secretary of Defense Clark Clifford, to evaluate a request for 206,000 troops. The president's final instructions to Clifford were "give me the lesser of evils." For weeks Johnson wavered between a bombing halt and sending another 206,000 troops. Within the White House, Clifford led the cabal to convince their president that he ought to stop the bombing and thereby start negotiations that might end the war. "Is he with us?" a phrase from the French Revolution, became the code for those working toward a bombing halt.

Johnson's instincts told him that the North Vietnamese could not be trusted, and his fears made him worry that a bombing halt would be exploited by domestic political opponents. Still, in the end Johnson listened to those who urged that he stop the bombing. Addressing the nation on 31 March 1968, the president spoke of his willingness "to move immediately toward peace through negotiations." Johnson announced that "there is no need to delay talks that could bring an end to this long and this bloody war." He was "taking the first step to deescalate the level of hostilities" by unilaterally reducing attacks on North Vietnam, except in the area just north of the demilitarized zone, known as the DMZ. "The area in which we are stopping our attacks includes almost 90 percent of North Vietnam's population and most of its territory," said Johnson. "Even this very limited bombing of the North could come to an early end if our restraint is matched by restraint in Hanoi."

Johnson called on North Vietnam's leader, Ho Chi Minh, to respond favorably and positively to these overtures and not to take advantage of this restraint. "We are prepared to move immediately toward peace through negotiations." The United States was "ready to send its representatives to any forum, at any time, to discuss the means of bringing this ugly war to an end." To prove his sincerity, Johnson named the distinguished American ambassador-at-large W. Averell Harriman as his "personal representative for such talks," asking Harriman to "search for peace."

Then, in a dramatic gesture toward national unity, the president announced that he would not seek reelection, declaring, "I do not believe that I should devote an hour or a day of my time to any personal partisan causes or to any duties other than the awesome partisan causes of this office—the presidency of your country. Accordingly, I shall not seek and I will not accept the nomination of my party for another term as your president."

Three days later, Radio Hanoi broadcast the news that the DRV had accepted Johnson's offer and would agree to establish contact with representatives of the United States. This was the first time that Hanoi had said publicly that it was willing to open talks with the United States. Hanoi was careful to stipulate that these initial contacts would focus first on bringing about the unconditional end to American bombing and other acts of aggression against Vietnam.

On 3 May 1968 President Johnson announced that both sides had agreed to hold preliminary talks in Paris, but he cautioned that "this is only the first step. There are many, many hazards and difficulties ahead." The talks were scheduled to begin on 10 May. President Johnson knew that the government of South Vietnam (GVN), headed by President Nguyen Van Thieu, opposed any bilateral discussions with the North Vietnamese on issues that would effect the South. Thieu believed that North Vietnam would use these initial contacts to demand direct negotiations between the GVN and the NLF in the hope of creating the conditions for a coalition government. Thieu also feared the election of Vice President Hubert Humphrey, a Democratic president hopeful, who was slowly distancing himself from Johnson's position.

President Thieu believed that a Humphrey victory would bring a coalition government and a U.S. withdrawal. "A Humphrey victory would mean a coalition government in six months. With Nixon at least there was a chance," recalled Thieu. This view was shared by Vice President Nguyen Cao Ky, who remembered that "we had little desire to sit down with the communists at all, and no intention of sitting down with, and thereby recognizing, the National Liberation Front." Thieu thus decided he would not go to Paris even if there were a bombing halt.

President Thieu had two contacts in Washington: Anna Chennault, the widow of Flying Tigers hero General Claire Chennault, and Bui Diem, the respected South Vietnamese ambassador. Chennault was a central figure in the China lobby, a vehement anticommunist, and chair of Republican Women for Nixon. During the 1968 campaign Nixon, the Republican candidate for president, asked her to be "the sole representative between the Vietnamese government and the Nixon campaign headquarters." With Nixon's encouragement, Chennault encouraged Thieu to defy Johnson. The latter knew all about it, but his information had been obtained from illegal wiretaps and surveillance, so he could not do much with it.

NIXON'S PEACE WITH HONOR

Prior to 5 May 1968, Nixon spoke of seeking a "victorious peace" in Vietnam. But on that day, speaking in New Hampshire, the nation's first primary state, he used the term "honorable peace" for the first time. Crucial to his plan was the concept of linkage—using the Soviet Union to get the North Vietnamese to negotiate seriously.

In what Nixon believed was an off-the-record discussion with southern delegates at the 1968 Republican Convention, the nominee described another way to end the war:

> How do you bring a war to a conclusion? I'll tell you how Korea was ended. We got in there and had this messy war on our hands. Eisenhower let the word get out—let the word go out diplomatically to the Chinese and the North Koreans that we would not tolerate this continued round of attrition. And within a matter of months, they negotiated.

When Nixon took office in January 1969, the United States had been involved in combat operations in Vietnam for nearly four years. U.S. military forces totaled 536,040, the bulk of which were ground combat troops. More than 30,000 Americans had lost their lives to then and the war cost $30 billion in fiscal year 1969. In 1968 alone, more than 14,500 U.S. troops were killed.

Richard Nixon was determined that Vietnam would not ruin his presidency, as had been the case with Lyndon Johnson. The Nixon plan was to "de-Americanize" the war, an approach

that became known as Vietnamization. It involved building up the South Vietnamese armed forces so that they could assume greater combat responsibility while simultaneously withdrawing U.S. combat troops. The U.S. military role would shift from fighting the DRV and VC to advising the South Vietnamese and sending in a massive influx of military equipment and weaponry. Perhaps most important, Nixon changed the political objective of U.S. intervention from guaranteeing a free and independent South Vietnam to creating the opportunity for South Vietnam to determine its own political future. Vietnamization along with negotiation were Nixon's twin pillars for achieving an honorable peace.

During the first weeks of his presidency, Nixon also began to consider options for dealing with Cambodia, including the feasibility and utility of a quarantine to block equipment and supplies coming from that nation into South Vietnam. Under code name MENU, B-52 strikes began on 18 March 1969 against enemy sanctuaries in that country. They were kept secret from the American public, in part because Cambodia was a neutral country, but even more important because Nixon had not been elected to expand the war after just three months in office.

Halfway through Nixon's first year in the White House, President Thieu requested that a meeting be held in Washington, D.C., but Nixon, fearful of demonstrations, selected Honolulu, which the Vietnamese rejected because they did not want to meet on a U.S. resort island. Nixon next suggested the remote island of Midway, where Nixon won Thieu's public acquiescence for Vietnamization. When Nixon proposed that secret or private contacts be started between Washington and Hanoi in an effort to secure a negotiated settlement, Thieu asked that he be kept fully informed on the details of these meetings and that he be consulted on any matters internal to South Vietnam. He received assurances that this would most certainly be the case. By January 1972 the United States had conceded on almost every major point, including, at least implicitly, that any cease-fire would be a cease-fire in place, which meant that North Vietnamese troops then in the South would stay there. What came next was predictable: The North Vietnamese could not get the United States to dispose of Thieu for them. They did not intend to stop fighting until they regained the South. Thus, they had one obvious strategy: stall the peace, pour forces into the South, and strike a deal only when a ccase-fire in place virtually amounted to a "victory in place." In an announcement made on national television on 25 January 1972, President Nixon revealed that Henry Kissinger had been holding private talks with the North Vietnamese starting in August 1969 and that every reasonable American proposal to end the war had been turned down. Nixon offered the details of a secret proposal made on 11 October 1971 that called for internationally supervised free elections in which the communists would participate and before which President Thieu would resign.

On 30 March 1972, Easter Sunday, the North Vietnamese began their biggest attack of the Vietnam War. It was a conventional military assault, designed to inflict a crippling blow against the army of the Republic of Vietnam (ARVN) and would last six months. On 8 May, President Nixon met with the NSC and told of plans for mining Haiphong harbor and resuming the bombardment of Hanoi and Haiphong. He also told the council that he would inform the public of his decision in a televised speech that evening.

After the NSC meeting Nixon brought his cabinet together and stated frankly, "We've crossed the Rubicon." As Nixon would put it to Kissinger the next day, he wanted to "go for broke" and "go to the brink" to "destroy the enemy's warmaking capacity." He wanted to avoid the previous mistakes of "letting up" on the bombing that he and Johnson had made in the past. "I have the will in spades," he declared. Nixon was determined not to repeat LBJ's mistakes. "Those bastards are going to be bombed like they've never been bombed before," gloated Nixon. What followed, starting in May, was the most successful use of airpower during the Vietnam War and one of the largest aerial bombardments in world history—Operation Linebacker. Targeting roads, bridges, rail lines, troops, bases, and supply depots, the attack was the first large-scale use of precision-guided laser bombs in modern aerial warfare.

In the short term, the offensive was clearly a military defeat for the North Vietnamese and would cost General Vo Nguyen Giap his job as chief strategist. On the other hand, although Hanoi never retained control over a provincial capital, the North Vietnamese did gain ground along the Cambodian and Laotian borders and the area just south of the DMZ. Hanoi remained in control of this territory for the rest of the war, and in 1975 would use it to launch a successful attack on Saigon.

A week before the 1972 presidential election, Kissinger stated that "peace is at hand," but again the talks stalled and Nixon turned to "jugular diplomacy." Nixon decided that no treaty would be signed until after the November 1972 election, when his position would be strengthened by what most observers expected to be an overwhelming election victory over Democratic challenger and antiwar leader George McGovern. Reelected by just such a landslide, Nixon moved swiftly against North Vietnam.

On 13 December the peace talks broke down, and on the following day Nixon ordered that the bombing be resumed. Now his only goal was to bring Hanoi back to the bargaining table. On 18 December, Linebacker II—widely known as the Christmas bombing—began with B-52 bomber sorties and fighter-bomber sorties on the Hanoi-Haiphong area. The day prior to the start of the Christmas bombing, Nixon told Admiral Thomas Moorer, chairman of the Joint Chiefs of Staff, "I don't want any more of this crap about the fact that we couldn't hit this target or that one. This is your chance to use military power effectively to win this war, and if you don't, I'll consider you responsible." Admiral Moorer called for expanded air attacks with an objective of "maximum destruction of selected military targets in the vicinity of Hanoi/Haiphong." He ordered that B-52s carry maximum ordnance with preapproved restrikes of targets. Kissinger wrote later that "the North Vietnamese committed a cardinal error in dealing with Nixon, they cornered him." The B-52s were his last roll of the dice.

THE PEACE AGREEMENT

The basic elements of the Agreement on Ending the War and Restoring Peace in Vietnam—signed at the International Conference Center in Paris on 27 January 1973—provided for the end of the fighting and the withdrawal of American forces. The United States committed itself to ending all air and naval actions against North Vietnam and to dismantling or deactivating all mines in the waters of North Vietnam. Within two months after the signing of the agreement, all forces of the United States and of U.S. allies would depart Vietnam. The United States was barred from sending new war materials or supplies to South Vietnam and was required to dismantle all military bases there. The armed forces of the GVN and the NLF were allowed to remain where they were, but the cease-fire barred the introduction of new troops, military advisers, military personnel—including technical military personnel—armaments, munitions, and war material from North Vietnam or anywhere else. The disposition of Vietnamese armed forces in South Vietnam would be determined by the two South Vietnamese parties in a spirit of "national reconciliation and concord." In addition, the accord required the return of all captured military personnel and foreign civilians during the same two-month period. The two South Vietnamese parties would handle the return of Vietnamese civilians. The United States and North Vietnam promised to uphold the principles of self-determination for the South Vietnamese people, which included free and democratic elections under international supervision.

Even more unusually, the treaty called for a Four-Party Joint Military Commission to be constituted by the four signatories for implementing and monitoring compliance with the provisions on withdrawal, cease-fire, dismantling of bases, return of war prisoners, and exchange of information on those missing in action. An International Commission of Control and Supervision (ICCS), consisting of Canada, Hungary, Indonesia, and Poland, would oversee the agreement and report violations. In *No Peace, No Honor* (2001), Larry Berman utilized recently declassified records to show that Nixon had little faith in the Paris accord and expected that the accord would be violated, which would trigger a brutal military response. Permanent war (air war, not ground operations) at acceptable political cost was what Nixon expected from the signed agreement. President Thieu received repeated assurances that when the communists violated the accord, the B-52s would return to punish Hanoi, but the Watergate scandal prevented such a retaliation.

Not a moment of peace ever came to Vietnam. Following the return of the American POWs, there was little adherence to the Paris agreements from either North or South Vietnam. The U.S. troops departed Vietnam sixty days after the Paris agreement was signed, but the level of violence had not significantly declined. Watergate was about to destroy the Nixon presidency and a new antiwar Congress had little interest in continuing economic support to the South. Faced with funding a $722 million supplement to stave off a collapse of South Vietnam, Congress refused to act. For many Americans, the last image of Vietnam was that of ambassador Graham Martin carrying a folded American flag during the final

---

★ ★ ★ ★
TAPES, BLACKMAIL, AND PEACE TALKS

The Watergate tapes revealed that in January 1973, when the Democratic-controlled Congress was investigating the Watergate break-in, Nixon devised a bizarre scheme of pressuring former President Lyndon Johnson to call his Democrat friends in Congress and request that they stop the Watergate investigation. Nixon threatened Johnson with a public disclosure that Johnson had bugged the Nixon and Agnew planes and campaign offices during the 1968 campaign, thus embarrassing Johnson and also proving that Nixon was not the first to illegally wiretap those suspected of leaking information. On a 9 January 1973 tape, Nixon says, "LBJ could turn off the whole Congressional investigation." But Johnson trumped Nixon by threatening to release the complete National Security Agency (NSA) Chennault files showing that the Nixon campaign had "illegally interfered with the Paris peace talks by convincing Saigon to stay away until after Nixon came to office."

---

evacuation. This bitter aftermath left Americans searching for explanations as to what had gone wrong and who was responsible for failure.

LESSONS AND LEGACIES

There may be no phrase more overused in foreign policy discussions and analyses since the 1960s than "the lessons of Vietnam." Nonetheless, exactly what those lessons are have been hotly debated. The debate has also been played out in the larger field of American politics, splitting the Democratic Party for more than two decades and fueling the political appeal of Ronald Reagan in 1980. It has framed U.S. policy toward a number of other countries, most notably Central America in the late 1970s and the 1980s and later in the Persian Gulf, where the Vietnam analogy was invoked with regularity. And time and again the debate has come back to heated arguments about the Vietnam War itself, as scholars and former policymakers have continued to reflect, lecture, and write about it. Former Defense Secretary Robert S.

McNamara, in his *In Retrospect: The Tragedy and Lessons of Vietnam* (1995), broke his own long silence on the subject with the provocative admission that while "we acted according to what we thought were the principles and traditions of this nation . . . we were wrong, terribly wrong."

In 1975 the Vietnamese economy lay in shambles and it would take decades to rebuild. Most of the population of fifty-five million was unemployed, impoverished, and suffering from the emotional and physical ramifications of the war. Over two million had been killed and 300,000 were reported missing and presumed dead. The number of Vietnamese who lost loved ones and family members was many times more. The loss of so many adults made Vietnam by the 1990s one of the youngest nations on earth.

Lacking an industrialized base and highly lucrative mineral or agricultural products, Vietnam found one immediate solution by exporting over $1 billion in abandoned American military equipment and scrap metal. The new regime also sold rice and other essential goods at below market prices for ten years. But a war against Cambodia beginning in December 1978 strained the economy. Large defense expenditures to fight the Khmer Rouge and conduct a war with the People's Republic of China in 1979, along with low consumer prices, combined to unleash widespread famine and hyperinflation that lasted into the 1980s.

Economic reforms improved conditions in Vietnam beginning in the mid-1980s. The benefits of peace with Cambodia after 1989 were balanced by the loss of economic aid from the declining Soviet Union. Impatient at the slow pace of economic change and heartened by the collapse of communism in Eastern Europe, over seventy-five thousand Vietnamese fled the nation in 1989 for Australia, the United States, and other nations willing to accept them. Vietnam continued privatization reforms, known as *dau man hade,* that transformed it into the third-largest rice producer in the world.

Another long-term impact of the Vietnam conflict entailed the presence of toxic chemicals in the soil and water. Between 1961 and 1970 the United States sprayed over nineteen million gallons of herbicides containing hazardous dioxins over the forests and farmlands of Vietnam, poisoning the people and contaminating the soil to the present day. A special U.S. Air Force program known as Operation Ranch Hand employed a fleet of C-123 airplanes to spread defoliants across the inland and coastal areas of South Vietnam in order to reduce tree cover and render crops unfit for consumption by North Vietnamese troops. Hundreds of thousands of Vietnamese suffered a range of illnesses from varying levels of chemical poisoning, in some cases leading to cancer and birth defects that have passed through three generations.

Many species of animals disappeared from heavily sprayed regions, while others adapted to a new environment and returned to their former habitats slowly over time. By the late 1980s the inland forests had recovered, but the more delicate mangrove coastal zone still had not returned to its former health. Today, the vestiges of chemical pollution are still apparent in altered vegetation patterns and cancer clusters in some areas of Vietnam. Although it became accepted scientific fact by the late 1960s that herbicides and dioxin were harmful to humans and the environment, the spraying of chemicals like Agent Orange continued until 1971, when the United States and the Soviet Union agreed to stop using biological weapons.

A large number of returning veterans on both sides of the war developed cancer and unknown illnesses during the 1970s as a result of contact with dioxins in Vietnam. When the last herbicides were destroyed by the U.S. military in 1977, veterans were already mounting a vigorous campaign to make the government more aware of their plight; some even sued the chemical industry. In 1984 the Dow Chemical Company and other chemical companies that had manufactured Agent Orange made a $180 million out-of-court settlement with veterans and their families (for an average payment of $1,000 per veteran). The following year the federal government funded $1 billion to conduct research on the chemical poisoning of veterans. In 1992 the Department of Defense declared that Vietnam veterans exhibiting Hodgkin's disease, non-Hodgkin's lymphoma, soft-tissue sarcoma, chloracne, and birth defects could claim contamination by herbicides in Vietnam.

The economy of Vietnam revived in the early 1990s when political relations with the United States began to thaw. In February 1994 the United States lifted a twenty-year embargo of Vietnam, enabling American companies to resume business with the communist nation. Incentives for companies to invest in Vietnam included cheap wages and abundant natural resources. The Vietnamese welcomed this development. By 1996 foreign investment, most of it from neighboring Asian "tiger" nations, had topped $20 billion. American holdings in Vietnam also had increased from a few million into billions of dollars. But policies by the Vietnamese government slowed foreign investment by 1997, making some analysts cautious about Vietnam's economic turn toward the West. Foreign investment took a downward spiral from $2.8 billion in 1997 to a mere $500 million by 1999. Tourism, however, continued to increase, as did student and cultural exchange programs that funneled foreign influences and dollars into Vietnam.

Improved relations with Vietnam also enabled more Vietnamese Americans to reunite with family members. When college-educated Vietnamese granddaughters met their elderly Vietnamese grandmothers living in rural villages for the first time, emotional healing, cultural exchange, and an improved financial situation for some Vietnamese were the consequences. Reflecting the impact of the war on so many different groups of people, American and Vietnamese veterans and war widows from both nations traveled thousands of miles to Vietnam to participate in private and officially sponsored exchange groups. They often searched for missing remains, shared their pain, and tried to understand the loss of their loved ones in the devastating conflict.

The communist government memorialized the war primarily through several public museums, as at the hidden Vietcong southern base within the Cu Chi tunnels outside of Ho Chi Minh City, or at Dien Bien Phu, where the French were finally defeated in 1954. Both have become major tourist destinations for war-fixated foreigners and patriotic and proud Vietnamese. To some extent the government utilized the successful prosecution of the war as propaganda to keep Vietnam a socialist state. The hero worship of Ho Chi Minh reflects a conscious decision on the part of the government to create a cult of personality for the father of modern Vietnam at a time when the overwhelming majority of the Vietnamese population was born after his death.

VIETNAMESE VETERANS

For Vietnamese veterans on both sides of the conflict, the violence of war remained firmly with them for the rest of their lives. For the victorious communist troops, the end of the war meant a return home to participate in village life and the rebuilding of a united nation. Compared to South Vietnamese veterans, many northern veterans suf-

fered long isolation from their families whom they had not seen in some cases since the mid-1960s. The communist government forbade the returning veterans to fully take part in village politics due to fears that ex-soldiers would take on increased power through their enhanced status as war heroes. Over the next two decades the veterans fared poorly and received paltry rations of rice, meat, and cigarettes in compensation for their war service. Even more so than for American veterans, Vietnamese veterans were largely forgotten by the government, and the service of women was utterly ignored. Only near the end of the twentieth century did the Vietnamese government fully honor the women who fought as frontline troops during the war.

The five million ARVN veterans (including 500,000 disabled vets) faced difficult choices at the war's end. Of the 145,000 Vietnamese refugees who fled Vietnam in 1975, approximately 33 percent were South Vietnamese veterans who, with their families, chose to immigrate to the United States. Most South Vietnamese veterans who fought with the Vietcong were, along with their families, forced into land redevelopment projects, or New Economic Zones, established in the rural countryside to increase land productivity. They comprised nearly half of the one million Vietnamese detailed to the rural projects. Those who survived malaria and malnutrition drifted back to major southern cities when food supplies dissipated. There, many reentered Vietnamese urban society as cab drivers. In the late 1970s and early 1980s, many of these veterans and their families swelled the tide of "boat people" seeking refuge in the United States. Approximately 100,000 South Vietnamese veterans entered the United States in this fashion, though an unknown number perished at sea.

Other South Vietnamese veterans deemed more dangerous were sent to reeducation camps located in rural areas. The estimate of the number sent to the camps was over 300,000 and included army officers, civil servants, teachers, Catholic clergy, journalists, doctors, engineers, and political activists. The system of reeducation involved regular confessions of "crimes" against Vietnam, coupled with readings on American imperialism and Vietnamese socialism. Higher officials and those who resisted were sometimes tortured. Terms of service ranged from a few months to several years. Those prisoners viewed as the most threatening were sent to camps in northern Vietnam, where slave labor was not uncommon. Some of these prisoners were held until 1989, when the camps finally disbanded. The United States estimated that at least fifty camps existed in the 1970s and 1980s, with an average population of four thousand people each. An unknown number of the war veterans perished from disease, starvation, and overwork. Family members who attempted to smuggle food to the prisoners endured great suffering by having to support themselves while they made long trips to the camps. American and Vietnamese efforts led to the release of most of the sixty thousand veterans by 1990.

Vietnamese veterans who fought for South Vietnam and immigrated to the United States secured political asylum beginning in 1988 through the official Orderly Departure Program. By 1997 tens of thousands of veterans had used the program. Many remained bitter, however, over alleged abandonment by Vietnamese and American officials, who failed to provide adequate financial support once the veterans arrived in the United States. Many Vietnamese veterans suffered from substance abuse, joblessness, and underemployment.

REFUGEES AND "BOAT PEOPLE"

The immigration of thousands of people from Southeast Asia in the 1970s and 1980s impacted American-Vietnamese relations and gave rise to new communities of Vietnamese, Cambodian, Laotian, and Hmong Americans in the United States. Known as boat people for escaping Southeast Asia by sea, the exodus of hundreds of thousands of Southeast Asians (predominantly Vietnamese) generated a political and humanitarian firestorm for the international community, the United States, and Vietnam.

The first wave in 1975 included 140,000 South Vietnamese, mostly political leaders, army officers, and skilled professionals escaping the communist takeover. Fewer than a thousand Vietnamese successfully fled the nation. Those who managed to escape pirates, typhoons, and starvation sought safety and a new life in refugee camps in Malaysia, Thailand, Singapore, Indonesia, the Philippines, and Hong Kong. For many, these countries became permanent homes, while for others they were only waystations to acquiring political asylum in other nations, including the United States.

During the administration of President James Earl Carter, Vietnamese immigration to the United States became a prominent political issue. The number of refugees fleeing Vietnam by sea increased to nearly six thousand in 1976 and twenty thousand the following year. Officials estimated that nearly one-third of this total perished at sea from starvation, drowning, and pirates, problems that increased when some Asian countries began turning away boat people.

The Vietnamese government began to institute socialist reforms by the late 1970s, including the confiscation of businesses and farmland. Many ethnic Chinese business owners who had lived in southern Vietnam for generations came under attack. The Chinese, or Hoa as the Vietnamese called them, were suspected of sympathizing with China, profiting from the poverty of the Vietnamese people, and betraying Vietnam during the conflict with the United States. As a result, they were officially encouraged to leave the country. Adults could pay a bribe and a departure fee to arrange their deportation. In at least one case, a Hoa man paid for the passage of himself and his large family with a bag of gold bars obtained from the liquidation of his estate. Other Vietnamese took advantage of the black market trade in selling passage outside of the country, which developed into a lucrative business in Vietnam between 1977 and 1979.

International attention to the plight of Vietnamese immigrants escalated in 1979, when the human tide of boat people increased to an unprecedented level of 100,000. Public alarm outside of Asia increased when Thailand, Malaysia, Singapore, Indonesia, Hong Kong, and the Philippines (known as ASEAN countries) declared that they could no longer accept immigrants into their overcrowded camps. But from ten thousand to fifteen thousand immigrants were still leaving Vietnam each month. United Nations secretary general Kurt Waldheim called a conference in response to the impending catastrophe. Sixty-five nations attended the meeting in Geneva, voting to increase funding to the United Nations High Commissioner for Refugees. Utilizing an executive order to raise immigration quotas, President Carter doubled the number of Southeast Asian refugees allowed into the United States each month. Agreements were also reached with Vietnam to establish an orderly departure program. These developments combined to slow the exodus of refugees in 1980 and 1981. By 2000, more than two million Vietnamese had left the nation of their birth to start new lives in foreign lands.

Ethnic minorities in Vietnam confronted difficult choices in the wake of the Vietnam conflict. Hundreds of thousands of Hmong and Montagnard people, who supported the United States and South Vietnam during the conflict, migrated to refugee camps in the late 1970s to evade the violence and instability left in the wake of American withdrawal. Many of the Hmong, natives of Laos, became political refugees and finally settled in communities in California and Minnesota, where they continued to practice their culture and adjust to new circumstances as hyphenated Americans. Until 1990 many Hmong funded attempts to retake Laos from communist control. Many Montagnards, who inhabited the Central Highlands of Vietnam, continued resisting the Vietnamese until the close of the Cold War in the early 1990s. By then, most of the one-half million Montagnards had either fled to refugee camps in Cambodia or resettled in the United States.

The political plight of Amerasian children embodies one of the most fundamental and lasting legacies of the Vietnam conflict. The offspring of American men and Vietnamese women, Amerasian children could not immigrate to the United States until the late 1980s. Following the end of the war in 1975, the Vietnamese government refused to meet with American officials to arrange for the immigration of these children. In turn, the United States refused to deal directly with the new communist regime. The children languished in uncertainty, held political hostage by two nations over a war long over.

Although the children were viewed as halfcastes, they were not officially targeted for discrimination. But the Vietnamese government viewed their mothers as traitors and called the children *bui doi* (dust of life). Local officials often targeted Amerasian families for forced migration to New Economic Zones, where the surplus urban population resettled. Some Amerasian children suffered abandonment by families that did not want them for the shame and fear it brought upon their families. As a result, the children were sent to orphanages, and many became street urchins in Hanoi and Ho Chi Minh City. For children of African-American soldiers and Vietnamese women, ethnic discrimination was even more intense.

The children allowed to leave between 1975 and 1982 included those who could prove U.S. citizenship. Vietnamese mothers and refugee organizations attempted to contact the fathers, who would be in a position to arrange for the immigration of the children through government agencies in their home nation. Yet citizenship itself did not guarantee safe passage. Bribes and exit fees were necessary to leave Vietnam legally during the era of massive emigration from 1977 to 1980.

Amerasian children received renewed hope in 1982 when Congress passed the Amerasian Immigration Act, which applied to children throughout Southeast Asia, not just Vietnam. The act had substantial limitations and only a small number of children successfully immigrated. The Vietnamese government announced in 1986 that over twenty-five thousand cases still awaited processing; it then stopped the processing of new cases, causing a steep decline of Amerasian immigration by 1987.

Abandoned and unwanted by the Vietnamese and American governments, the struggle of Amerasian children received widespread publicity, prompting renewed congressional action. The Amerasian Homecoming Act of 1988, sponsored by U.S. Representative Robert Mrazek, facilitated the immigration of Vietnamese Amerasians and certain members of their families. The act successfully broadened Amerasian immigration so that by 1994, refugee watch groups had declared that only a few thousand Amerasian children remained in Vietnam. The by-then grown children and their families had adapted to life there and had chosen to stay.

Despite setbacks and challenges, many Amerasian children became prosperous. Those who adjusted most successfully were usually children who accompanied their Vietnamese mothers to America. Some of these children received assistance through the Big Brother and Big Sister programs. By 1995, however, all Amerasian children had reached adulthood, and all federal programs to assist their assimilation and adjustment were terminated.

Another group of children from Vietnam also grew to adulthood in the United States. As communist forces closed on Saigon in early April 1975, President Gerald Ford began Operation Babylift, the evacuation of 2,600 Vietnamese orphans for adoption by American parents. Twenty years later, many of the children had adjusted successfully to living in the United States. Some became part of the tide of temporary migration back to Vietnam to find missing relatives.

By 1995 over 480,000 Vietnamese had chosen to immigrate to the United States. Another 210,000 lived in other countries around the world. But 46,000 still remained in the refugee camps in ASEAN nations. Many of these countries began to close the camps, forcing dislocated refugees to contemplate returning to Vietnam. By early 1996 more than 39,000 Vietnamese still remained in the camps. That year the United Nations began to withdraw funding of the refugee installations, and soon after closed the camps. Most of the Vietnamese refugees, including children who had never seen Vietnam, returned to an uncertain fate in their home country.

VIETNAM AND THE UNITED STATES

Foreign relations between the United States and Vietnam soured after 1975. They did not fully recover until the mid-1990s, when economic, political, and cultural ties revived, leading to a vibrant period of political reconciliation by the year 2000. Following North Vietnam's victory in 1975, the U.S. attitude toward Vietnam was antagonistic. In the Paris Peace Accords, the United States had agreed to provide $3.3 billion over five years to help rebuild the shattered infrastructure of Vietnam. Rather than meeting its obligations, the United States extended to all of Vietnam the trade embargo against communist North Vietnam that had been ratified under the Trading with the Enemy Act passed during the early years of the conflict. The United States further marginalized Vietnam by halting credits and loans from monetary institutions such as the World Bank, the International Monetary Fund, and the Asian Development Bank. Seeking acceptance in the international arena, Vietnam attempted several times to join the United Nations, only to be halted by American vetoes.

Relations with the United States began to soften during the first year of the Carter administration, though war wounds still ran too deep to permit a relationship of cooperation and agreement between the two nations. President Carter and Congress indicated that relations could be normalized if the vexing issues surrounding prisoners of war (POWs) and soldiers missing in action (MIAs) were resolved. Approximately 2,500 U.S. service personnel continued to be reported as missing in the jungles of Vietnam, and Americans desperately wanted an accurate assessment of their numbers and of whether any of them were still alive in Vietnamese camps. Optimism grew in 1977 and 1978 as the two nations discussed preliminary issues.

President Carter sent Assistant Secretary of State Richard Holbrooke in May 1977 to meet with Vietnamese officials. The talks broke down, however, when Vietnam demanded several billion dollars in payment for war damages, which the United States rejected because the Vietnamese had allegedly violated the 1975 Paris Accords by invading South Vietnam. President Carter indicated that the United States would provide aid, but that funding could not be linked to normalization or the POW-MIA issue.

When the Vietnamese finally relented on their demands for reparations, they failed to receive a corresponding overture from the United States. This stemmed from official and public alarm over Vietnamese immigration, a Vietnamese invasion of Cambodia, and an increasingly powerful Soviet presence in the region (epitomized by the Soviet base at Cam Ranh Bay, the largest military installation of the USSR outside of its borders). After the Vietnamese invasion of Cambodia, the United States sent covert aid to noncommunist Cambodian guerrillas who were fighting Vietnam.

Meanwhile, as relations between China and Vietnam worsened, U.S.–Chinese relations improved, culminating in the establishment of full diplomatic ties between the two nations in 1978. This development, combined with Vietnam's invasion of Cambodia in 1978, its treaty of alliance with the Soviet Union the same year, and a border war with China in 1979 gave more impetus to American hostility toward Vietnam. During the final years of the Cold War, Vietnam found itself strongly aligned with anti-American forces that helped offset billions of dollars lost from the American trade embargo.

At the heart of the inability of American and Vietnamese leaders to reconcile national interests in the 1970s and 1980s lay the troublesome POW-MIA issue. Although the number of MIAs in World War II and the Korean War (80,000 and 8,000, respectively) was much greater than MIAs in the Vietnam War, the small number of missing American soldiers in the latter conflict (1,992 in all of Southeast Asia, 1,498 in Vietnam) captured the national psyche. They became the focus of a national crusade that retained its fervor into the twenty-first century. The plight of MIAs received much greater attention in the aftermath of the conflict as national leaders and the media fed public alarm over the fate of missing veterans. Although the Department of Defense declared the MIAs deceased, it could not stop the issue from growing to national importance. Unconfirmed public sightings of U.S. soldiers in Vietnam by refugees and others led to expeditions by American veterans to find their missing comrades. As of 2001 no sightings had been confirmed, although human remains were repatriated from Vietnam to the United States as part of an ongoing plan of cooperation between the two nations. More than $5 million were spent annually by the United States on attempts to find and return the remains of missing servicemen in Southeast Asia.

During the 1980s President Ronald Reagan kept the MIA issue at the forefront of American relations with Vietnam. Supported by the National League of POW/MIA Families, Reagan harnessed a national crusade to hinge the normalization of relations with Vietnam on the fate of the MIAs. In July 1985 Vietnam finally allowed an American inspection team to visit alleged MIA burial sites. The return of the remains of several dozen pilots that year eased tensions and led to further investigations. In 1987 and 1989 Vietnam allowed General John Vessey, former chairman of the Joint Chiefs of Staff, to visit with Vietnamese leaders as an emissary of Presidents Reagan and George H. W. Bush.

Realizing that further concessions would help improve a stagnant economy, Vietnam assisted in returning the remains of more than two hundred American soldiers between 1985 and 1990 and also provided access to archives, war files, and cemetery records. They also allowed the United States to establish a Hanoi office to oversee MIA investigations. Between 1993 and 2001, joint ventures by the United States and Vietnam generated thirty-nine official searches that yielded 288 sets of remains and the identification of another 135 American servicemen previously unaccounted for in Vietnam. In a move to further pacify American political leaders, Vietnam announced in 1995 that its continuing cooperation regarding American MIAs and POWs did not depend on an accurate accounting by the United States and its allies of the whereabouts of the 330,000 Vietcong and North Vietnamese MIAs.

Kindled by the MIA issue, relations between the United States and Vietnam grew closer during the 1990s. As the Cold War came to a close in 1989, Vietnam finally agreed to withdraw all of its troops from Cambodia, ending its long and costly period of isolation from the United States. The Cold War's termination also improved relations by ending the Soviet-Vietnamese partnership. To further ease foreign antagonism toward Vietnam and to increase foreign investment, the communist government removed from the Vietnamese constitution unflat-tering characterizations of Western countries.

Other agreements between Vietnam and the United States centered upon the issue of Vietnamese political refugees. To improve relations with many of its southern people, the Vietnamese government in September 1987 released more than six thousand military and political prisoners, many of them senior officials in the former government of South Vietnam. Under the Orderly Departure Program in 1990, Vietnam agreed to assist the United Nations in helping refugees utilize official channels rather than leaky boats to immigrate to America. Another agreement, signed in 1990, enabled former South Vietnamese officials and army officers to immigrate to America.

Under the administration of President William Jefferson Clinton during the 1990s, Vietnamese-American relations continued to improve. With the lifting of the U.S. trade embargo in 1994, economic relations opened and American companies increased their investments in Vietnam. Clinton fostered educational and cultural exchange, enabling veterans, students, and the expatriate sons and daughters from Vietnam to cement family ties. Humanitarian aid to Vietnam from the American government and private associations increased and tourism became a vibrant element of the national economy. In a sign of growing political ties, Vietnamese officials in January 1995 signed an agreement with the United States providing for an exchange of diplomats and other officials as a prelude to full normalization of relations. As expected, President Clinton overrode Republican conservative critics and MIA stalwarts to extend full recognition to Vietnam in July 1995.

One month later the American flag was raised over the new U.S. embassy in Hanoi while Secretary of State Warren Christopher looked on. Over the next two years, President Clinton established the diplomatic structures necessary to bring the two nations closer together. He nominated U.S. Representative Douglas "Pete" Peterson, a former POW, to represent the United States as the first envoy to a united Vietnam. Soon after Peterson took up his post in the summer of 1997, Secretary of State Madeleine K. Albright visited Vietnamese officials in both Hanoi and Ho Chi Minh City. The first U.S. secretary of state to visit Vietnam since the end of the war, Albright participated in ceremonies dedicating a new site for an American consulate.

Beginning in the late 1990s a number of steps further enhanced economic relations between the United States and Vietnam. After Vietnam joined the Asia Pacific Economic Cooperation (APEC) forum in 1998, the United States jettisoned the Jackson-Vanick Amendment that had capped U.S. investment programs in Vietnam. In 1999 the two nations finally agreed on the outlines of a trade agreement to help Vietnam open its markets to world investors. American investment support programs then poured in, reversing the decline of world economic interest in Vietnam that had begun to worry investors in 1997, when the Vietnamese government enacted political and economic policies of retrenchment that retarded the growth of capitalism and capital investment in Vietnam. President Clinton further thawed U.S.–Vietnamese relations during the waning days of his administration. In July 2000 the two countries signed an unprecedented bilateral trade agreement reached between the two nations. The agreement mandated that Vietnam halt quotas on all imported goods over the following seven years, cut tariffs, and handle American imports in the same manner as domestic products.

Four months later President Clinton traveled to Vietnam, the first president to do so since President Nixon touched down in South Vietnam in 1969. The visit closed a sad chapter of violence and strained political relations between the two nations, and ushered in a new era of economic boom in Vietnam that was unparalleled in its tragic history of successful resistance against foreign military intervention. Vietnamese analysts predicted that Vietnamese exports to the United States, hovering near the $800 million mark in 2001, could top $3 billion in 2005 and $11 billion by 2010. U.S. investment in Vietnam had already increased from $4 million in 1992 to $291 million in 1999, providing hope that this trend would continue well into the twenty-first century. In late July 2001, Secretary of State Colin L. Powell, who had been a soldier in Vietnam, returned there for the first time in thirty years in an historic attempt to put the past to rest.

During the first six months of his administration in 2001, President George W. Bush pledged to continue Clinton's policy of economic liberalization toward Vietnam, and took active steps to support the American diplomatic mission based in Hanoi. In one of his first actions as president, Bush reappointed as ambassador Pete Peterson, who in the Clinton years had been instrumental in helping to negotiate the bilateral trade agreement. Although Bush was associated with a conservative Republican bloc that in the past had voiced criticism of American reconciliation with Vietnam, the new administration recognized the potential economic windfall awaiting U.S. investors in Vietnam.

AMERICAN VETERANS

The Vietnam conflict impacted veterans in a variety of ways. Most combat soldiers witnessed violence and lost friends to the horrors of war. The dedication of eight new names to the Vietnam War Memorial on 28 May 2001 brought the American death toll to 58,226, a number that will continue to rise as the classified casualties of the covert war in Laos and Cambodia continue to surface. Some American veterans bore emotional and physical injuries that they would carry for the rest of their lives. Most remained proud of their service and of the role of the United States in the conflict. During the war approximately twenty-seven million American men dealt with the draft; 11 percent of them served in some fashion in Vietnam. As a consequence of college deferments, most U.S. soldiers in Vietnam came from minority and working-class backgrounds. The average age of U.S. soldiers in Vietnam, nineteen, was three years lower than for American men during World War II and Korea.

In contrast to World War II, American soldiers in Vietnam served individualized tours of duty rather than remaining attached to their units throughout the war. This sometimes produced difficulties in adjusting to life back at home. A minority of soldiers in Vietnam also became drug addicts who continued their self-medication because of the difficulties of transitioning to a peacetime existence, the availability of drugs in the United States, and the lack of federal programs to help veterans cope with postwar life at home.

Whether or not they felt proud of their service or sustained war injuries, returning Vietnam veterans received a lukewarm welcome for their service. A vocal section of the public vented its frustration with racism, the federal government, and the war on the returning veterans. While most Americans viewed World War II as the "good war," a majority of the American public viewed the Vietnam conflict as a disaster. Only the POWs generated postwar sympathy for the suffering they endured.

Some veterans wrote about their war experiences to educate the nation as well as improve their own understanding of their participation in the conflict and the public reception they

611

received. Ron Kovic, a disabled veteran who served two tours of duty in Vietnam with the marines, wrote *Born on the Fourth of July* (1976), which explained his participation in the war and the difficulties of coming home in a wheelchair to an angry and hostile American public. Oliver Stone transformed the book into a successful film in 1989. Stone, who served in Vietnam, also produced the film *Platoon* (1986).

Despite the myth of the chronically impaired Vietnam veteran, most vets married, found jobs, and successfully reintegrated into American society. Many became successful businessmen and politicians whose experiences in the war shaped subsequent U.S. policy toward Vietnam. They became the point men leading the nation to a complex but more hopeful phase of Vietnamese-American relations. Yet veterans like Senator Bob Kerrey continued to face the fallout from their actions in Vietnam, revealing that the American people were still unable to unburden themselves from the political context of the conflict. Reminiscent of many veterans who have come under fire for their participation in the war, Kerrey rationalized his participation in a firefight that left twelve women and children dead as a response to orders followed in a chaotic and unconventional military engagement.

Although most veterans were not permanently damaged by the war, some 15 to 25 percent of Vietnam veterans (between 500,000 and 700,000) suffered from a stress-related impairment known as post-traumatic stress disorder (PTSD), a psychological disease brought on by acute combat experience. Some of the 11,500 women who served in the war—90 percent of them as nurses—also returned exhibiting PTSD. This condition can occur in combat soldiers or other individuals suffering from violent trauma and can manifest itself years after the initial experience. Also known as shell shock or combat fatigue, the disorder is vaguely defined and was overused in diagnosing the psychological reactions to war of Vietnam veterans. Some of the 11,500 women who served in the war (90 percent as nurses) also returned exhibiting PTSD.

Reflecting the changing mood of the American public toward both the war and the veterans, memorials and other commemorations of the Vietnam conflict began to surface in the mid-1980s. They revealed a national desire to "welcome home" vets who had not received domestic support when they most needed it—immediately after the war.

THE POW AND MIA CRUSADE

A national obsession over the fate of the approximately two thousand American soldiers missing in Southeast Asia became one of the most unexpected and permanent legacies of the war. To many Americans, perpetuation of the search for the POWs and MIAs provided the opportunity to extend belated thanks and honor to all Vietnam veterans.

The return of POWs became a heated political and military issue during the Paris peace talks that culminated in 1973. Both sides attempted to use it to their advantage over the next two years. The Americans claimed that the freeing and returning of the veterans was taking too long, though most of the men were later returned. During the administration of President Jimmy Carter in 1977, more than one thousand of the two thousand listed as MIA were reclassified as killed in action, although no credible reports existed that any missing service personnel not declared prisoners of war were still alive.

In the late 1970s the POW-MIA issue resurfaced as a result of lobbying by the National League of Families of American Prisoners and Missing in Southeast Asia. In 1979 Congress reclassified the fate of the soldiers killed in action as POW-MIA. President Ronald Reagan kept the issue alive three years later by stating publicly that he felt some Americans were still being held in Vietnam. His belief was supported by international humanitarian workers and Vietnamese immigrants who reported seeing Americans still held under guard.

Public passion for the return of MIAs increased following a spate of films in the mid-1980s, such as *Rambo: First Blood Part II* (1985), starring Sylvester Stallone as a lone American freeing American POWs under intense enemy fire. MIA supporters soon began wearing bracelets and dog tags that listed a missing American veteran as a hero to be remembered and located. During his failed bid for the presidency in 1992, Ross Perot also fueled the MIA cause by declaring that he not only believed that Americans were still held, but that he had funded covert forays to locate and free the missing men. Because of contradictory and late-arriving information from the Vietnamese and U.S. governments, many Americans remained suspicious of the POW-MIA issue and came to believe it had declined as an issue of national importance.

Furthering national support for the controversial cause, President Reagan in 1988 ordered a black and white POW-MIA flag designed by the National League to fly one day each year at the White House. It stands as the only other flag besides the Stars and Stripes that has ever been hoisted at the White House. A Massachusetts state law passed in 1990 mandated that the flag be flown above one or more public buildings in every Massachusetts town. In April 2001, the state of Virginia passed similar legislation. Senator John Kerry of Massachusetts organized the Senate Select Committee on POW-MIA Affairs in 1992. Congressional prodding soon led the Postal Service to issue a POW-MIA stamp. Eventually, all fifty states officially recognized National POW-MIA Recognition Day to commemorate the missing veterans.

COMMEMORATING THE WAR

The Vietnam Memorial, like the POW-MIA flag, stands as the physical embodiment of the desire of the American people to understand the meaning of the Vietnam conflict and remember the men and women who took part in it. During the late 1970s both public and private efforts began to congeal around the idea of establishing a monument to the 58,000 American dead in Vietnam. Influenced by the film *The Deer Hunter* (1978), Jan Scruggs, a Vietnam veteran, teamed up with two other servicemen in 1979 to create a nonprofit organization known as the Vietnam Veterans Memorial Fund.

The location and design of the memorial generated intense political controversy over an issue still raw in the American national consciousness. Maya Lin, a young Chinese-American architectural student at Yale University, won the competition with a design based on a sunken 500-foot, V-shaped wall of polished black granite bearing inscriptions on fourteen panels of all the names of the American men and women who died in Vietnam between 1959 and 1975.

Controversy immediately erupted over the political message conveyed by the wall. Some detractors saw it as a thinly veiled criticism of American motives in the war. Lin, who was also attacked by American racists who saw her Chinese heritage as implicated in her interpretation of the war and design of the memorial, effectively kept critics at bay and successfully preserved the inclusion of a chronological listing of the names of the deceased. Conservative critics influenced Secretary of the Interior James Watt to delay construction,

---

★ ★ ★ ★

DIFFERENT SHAPES, DIFFERENT LANGUAGES

The Soviet ambassador to France made a recommendation for the Paris peace talks: use a round table and two opposite rectangular tables off the round table for secretaries with no flags or plates for names. That way, the parties could speak of either a two- or four-sided conference, depending on their view. The United States would call the talks two-party, the communists would call them four-party. The United States called them the Paris peace talks, Hanoi the Paris talks. For months, nobody spoke the same language.

---

however, until agreement was reached adding three life-sized bronze casts of American soldiers in more heroic form near the wall. This new addition reflected the desires and needs of a more conservative segment of the American population, personified by Ross Perot, who felt that the memorial should also recognize the positive aspects of the war and American service in Southeast Asia.

The wall, once unveiled, induced some veterans to feel guilt about surviving a conflict that their friends had not. Others discovered friends had not perished, and reconnected with former friends in the armed services who were at the wall to do the same. Thousands of flowers, cards, and other mementos have been left at the wall, a tradition that serves as a constant reminder that the conflict remains firmly imbedded in the memories of most Americans. A sacred shrine to many, over 2.5 million people visit the wall each year; it is the most visited memorial in Washington, D.C. The Korean War Veterans Memorial, established in 1995, owes its existence in part to a heightened sense of sympathy toward veterans by the American people in the wake of the Vietnam conflict.

On Veterans Day 1993 the Vietnam Women's Memorial Project unveiled a monument to the participation of women in the Vietnam War. Diane Evans, a Vietnam veteran who served as a nurse in hospitals and transport planes along with thousands of other women, pushed the project forward with tireless effort. In ways similar to the inclusion of a black male soldier in a bronze statue installed near the Vietnam Memorial in

1984, the women's memorial—built by sculptor Glenna Goodacre—reflected the inclusiveness of the war and the shared experiences of participants across race and ethnicity. The statue depicts two female nurses (one black and one white) assisting a fallen soldier. The Vietnam War elevated the visibility of military women within the armed services, leaving a lasting legacy that helped later women achieve even greater gains in rank, job participation, and benefits.

POLITICAL LESSONS

The meaning of the Vietnam War for American foreign policy remains a hotly contested and unresolved issue. Most aspects of the war remain open to dispute, ranging from the wisdom of U.S. involvement to the reasoning behind continued escalation and final withdrawal.

The political legacies of the war began to surface even before North Vietnam's victory in 1975. A powerful domestic antiwar movement that arose in the mid-1960s influenced a bipartisan group of U.S. congresspersons who by 1970 began to question openly the commitment of American troops to conflicts of uncertain national importance. Their doubts were enhanced by the fact that Presidents Kennedy, Johnson, and Nixon sent U.S. forces into Vietnam with little regard for congressional approval. Passage of the War Powers Resolution by both houses of Congress and over President Nixon's veto in 1973 signaled that American politicians and the public would no longer allow presidents to single-handedly dictate military policy as commander in chief of the armed forces.

The War Powers Resolution mandated that U.S. presidents inform Congress within forty-eight hours of a troop commitment in the absence of a declaration of war. If Congress does not declare war within sixty days of the commitment, the president must terminate the use of U.S. military forces, unless he has sought in writing a thirty-day extension of the deadline. Since its passage, however, the War Powers Resolution has made little impact on presidential warmaking because creative ways have been found to circumvent its limitations.

More important as a brake on presidential war policy is the Vietnam syndrome, a catchall phrase that describes the public's impatience for protracted American wars based on vague policy goals. Most pronounced from the American withdrawal in 1973 to the Gulf War in 1991, the Vietnam syndrome congealed after the war as the public mood slid toward isolation and the belief that troops should be committed only in cases of national invasion. This sentiment handcuffed President Jimmy Carter's ability to use military force to free American hostages in Iran in 1979 and 1980, and deterred President Ronald Reagan from seeking congressional approval to fund the Nicaraguan contras in the early 1980s.

During his first term in office, President Ronald Reagan assured the nation that there would be "no more Vietnams," a refrain also echoed by George H. W. Bush during his presidency. To conservatives, this meant that U.S. troops would never again fight a war without the necessary full political support to win it. To others, it meant that popular opinion would now limit any extensions of American military power across the globe. The public would not support a troop commitment to another war against communists, even in the Western Hemisphere. Mistrust spawned by the Vietnam conflict led Reagan's foreign policymakers to cover up arms deals during the Iran-Contra affair.

American invasions of Grenada and Panama in the 1980s were short-lived partly because of executive fears of escalating military involvement without strong public support. The deaths of more than two hundred marines at a base in Beirut, Lebanon, in 1983 threatened to rekindle the nightmare of Vietnam once again. But the victorious Gulf War of 1991 did much to remove the enormous burden of the Vietnam conflict from the back of American foreign policy.

In the invasion plan to oust the Iraqi forces occupying Kuwait, General Norman Schwarzkopf, a Vietnam veteran, remembered lessons of Southeast Asia. He helped to limit the information released about the conflict (to prevent another "living-room" television war) and patiently built up his forces to maximum strength before attacking Iraqi troops. The architects of the Gulf War also relied on precision bombing rather than ground troops in order to minimize casualties and preserve public support for the war. President Bush successfully mollified the public's post-Vietnam fears of wasteful wars fought by poor men by pledging to do away with college draft deferments, if the draft was reinstated, and by calling for unqualified patriotic support to honor the 500,000 servicemen sent to the Gulf.

Following the Persian Gulf War the American public showered returning troops with a level of adulation not witnessed in the United States since 1945, and cracks became visible in the Vietnam syndrome. But hesitation in committing troops to Bosnia and the withdrawal from Somalia stemmed in part from Clinton administration fears that the conflicts there would escalate and damage American credibility, as with Vietnam. Strong domestic support for a precision bombing campaign over Kosovo in 1999, however, demonstrated how far the American public had drifted from the antiwar fervor of the early 1970s.

As time healed the wounds of violence and bloodshed, the impact of the Vietnam conflict still lingered for the Vietnamese and American people. But a new phase began, characterized by hope, new friendships, and cultural and political exchange unprecedented in the history of two nations once at war.

BIBLIOGRAPHY

Andrade, Dale. *Trial by Fire: The 1972 Easter Offensive, America's Last Vietnam Battle.* New York, 1995. Using official records, interviews with participants, and captured North Vietnamese documents, this important book covers the entire scope of the Easter offensive.

Berman, Larry. *Planning a Tragedy: The Americanization of the War in Vietnam.* New York, 1982. A detailed archival-based account of the crucial July 1965 decision that Americanized the war in Vietnam.

———. *Lyndon Johnson's War: The Road to Stalemate in Vietnam.* New York, 1989.

———. *No Peace, No Honor: Nixon, Kissinger, and Betrayal in Vietnam.* New York, 2001. Drawing on new declassified documents, the case is presented that Nixon and Kissinger viewed the Paris accords as a vehicle for prolonging indefinitely American involvement in Southeast Asia.

Brigham, Robert K. *Guerrilla Diplomacy: The NLF's Foreign Relations and the Viet Nam War.* Ithaca, N.Y., 1999. The very best account of the NLF's activities during the war. The author utilizes many primary source documents from Hanoi archives and interviews with many Vietnamese leaders.

Bundy, William P. *A Tangled Web: The Making of Foreign Policy in the Nixon Presidency.* New York, 1998.

Butler, David. *The Fall of Saigon.* New York, 1985.

Chanoff, David, and Doan Van Toai. *Vietnam: A Portrait of Its People at War.* New York, 1986.

Clodfelter, Mark. *The Limits of Air Power: The American Bombing of North Vietnam.* New York, 1989. The most comprehensive account on the subject of U.S. airpower and strategy during the war.

Diem, Bui, and David Chanoff. *In the Jaws of History.* Boston, 1987. Diem, the former Vietnam ambassador to the United States, offers a gripping personal and political account of his life and the struggle for democracy in Vietnam.

Dillard, Walter Scott. *Sixty Days to Peace: Implementing the Paris Peace Accords, Vietnam 1973.* Washington, D.C., 1982.

Don, Tran Van. *Our Endless War: Inside Vietnam.* San Rafael, Calif., 1978.

Engelmann, Larry. *Tears Before the Rain: An Oral History of the Fall of South Vietnam.* New York, 1990. A stunning series of more than seventy oral history interviews with those who were there for the fall of South Vietnam.

Gaiduk, I. V. *The Soviet Union and the Vietnam War.* Chicago, 1996. A seminal contribution that draws on Soviet archives to advance understanding of Soviet ideology and policy during the war.

Gardner, Lloyd C. *Pay Any Price: Lyndon Johnson and the Wars for Vietnam.* Chicago, 1995.

Herring, George C. *LBJ and Vietnam: A Different Kind of War.* Austin, Tex., 1994.

Hung, Nguyen Tien, and Jerrold L. Schecter. *The Palace File.* New York, 1986. Based on more than thirty previously unpublished letters between South Vietnam's President Thieu and U.S. Presidents Nixon and Ford, the book documents the broken promises that resulted in the fall of South Vietnam.

Isaacs, Arnold R. *Without Honor: Defeat in Vietnam and Cambodia.* Baltimore, 1983.

Karnow, Stanley. *Vietnam: A History.* New York, 1991. This monumental narrative clarifies and analyzes the many facets of the Vietnam War.

Kimball, Jeffrey. *Nixon's Vietnam War.* Lawrence, Kans., 1998.

Kutler, Stanley I., ed. *Abuse of Power: The New Nixon Tapes.* New York, 1997.

Logevall, Fredrik. *Choosing War: The Lost Chance for Peace and the Escalation of War in Vietnam.* Berkeley, Calif., 1999. The first truly comprehensive examination of the making of the war in Vietnam from 1963 to 1965.

Develops an international context for the author's analysis and documents that at every step American decision makers chose war over disengagement.

Loi, Luu Van, and Nguyen Anh Vu. *Le Duc Tho–Kissinger Negotiations in Paris.* Hanoi, 1996. Vietnam diplomats who participated in the negotiations offer an invaluable Vietnamese perspective with documents and analysis.

McNamara, Robert S. *In Retrospect: The Tragedy and Lessons of Vietnam.* New York, 1995.

———. *Argument Without End: In Search of Answers to the Vietnam Tragedy.* New York, 1999. Provides a new view of the Vietnam conflict by offering the assessments of what went on in the minds of decision makers in Hanoi and Washington as they confronted one another. The Vietnamese perspectives are especially valuable for the historical record.

Record, Jeffrey. *The Wrong War: Why We Lost in Vietnam.* Annapolis, Md., 1998.

Shawcross, William. *Sideshow: Kissinger, Nixon and the Destruction of Cambodia.* New York, 1979.

Sheehan, Neil. *After the War Was Over: Hanoi and Saigon.* New York, 1992.

Snepp, Frank. *Decent Interval: An Insider's Account of Saigon's Indecent End.* New York, 1977.

Sorley, Lewis. *A Better War: The Unexamined Victories and Final Tragedy of America's Last Years in Vietnam.* New York, 1999. Draws on many previously unavailable documents and provides a valuable interpretation for American strategy and policies during the war.

Tang, Truong Nhu. *A Viet Cong Memoir.* New York, 1985.

Tin, Bui. *Following Ho Chi Minh: The Memoirs of a North Vietnamese Colonel.* Honolulu, 1995.

Zhai, Qiang. *China and the Vietnam Wars, 1950–1975.* Chapel Hill, N.C., 2000. In examining China's conduct toward Vietnam, Zhai provides important insights into Mao Zedong's foreign policy and the ideological and geopolitical motives behind it.

See also COLD WAR EVOLUTION AND INTERPRETATIONS; COLD WAR ORIGINS; COLD WAR TERMINATION; CONTAINMENT; DOMINO THEORY; INTERVENTION AND NONINTERVENTION; POST–COLD WAR POLICY.

WILSONIANISM

★ ★ ★ ★

Tony Smith

Defining a term like "Wilsonianism" presents the same sort of difficulties one finds in attempting to define virtually any "ism" in world affairs. On the one hand, aspects in U.S. foreign policy of what we currently call Wilsonianism handily predate Woodrow Wilson's tenure in office (1913–1921), while on the other, aspects of what came to define the term appeared later in fuller or different form than Wilson himself could ever have imagined. Given the multitude of connotations the term consequently bears, at times it may appear that everyone is to some extent Wilsonian, while at other moments it seems that Wilsonians may differ among themselves over how best to proceed in world affairs, as if their compass lacks the sure points of reference an "ism" should rightly give them.

These concessions made, no other American president has had his name used to define a foreign policy orientation. Given the importance of the set of ideas introduced by America's twenty-eighth president, it is widely agreed that using the term "Wilsonianism" is meaningful, even if just what the word means may be open to some disagreement. Surely the best way to proceed is to look at the sets of policies Woodrow Wilson advanced for world order, then to place them within earlier and later American foreign policy initiatives so as to see a family resemblance from which a group of concepts may be said to emerge that, taken together, is the substance of Wilsonianism.

The first (and for some the only) defining element of Wilsonianism is the conviction that a leading priority of U.S. foreign policy should be the promotion of democratic government the world around—"national self-determination," as Wilson put it. Original as this conviction was with Wilson, we should be careful to see it more as a development out of an American tradition rather than as a wholly new departure. For as Wilson himself said, what he was calling for was the "globalization of the Monroe Doctrine." Put differently, international order should be based on a politically plural world, a situation where national self-determination (a phrase Wilson used constantly after 1914) would be the rule of the day. As the evocation of the Monroe Doctrine (1823) indicates, and as the Open Door Notes with respect to China confirmed at the turn of the century, Wilson understood that his call to dismember the Ottoman, Austro-Hungarian, and Russian empires in 1918–1919 was long-standing U.S. policy. This same reliance on globalizing the Monroe Doctrine would be reflected later, during and after World War II, when the administrations of Franklin D. Roosevelt and Harry Truman denounced great power spheres of influence and so supported the decolonization of European empires and criticized the expansion of Soviet influence in Eastern Europe by use of the Red Army.

If Wilson's dedication to a politically plural world was in the established tradition of American foreign policy, his call for the democratization of this political plurality most certainly was not. Here was this president's single most important contribution to the American foreign policy tradition—the notion that in an era of nationalist passion, the blueprint for state construction should be of a liberal democratic sort.

At the time, most diplomats were astonished—or amused—at Wilson's ambition. Only today, nearly a century after Wilson's dramatic appeals, can we fully appreciate how momentous his suggestions actually were. For nationalism—the ideologically based demand of a "people," defined in terms of a collective history and purpose, for a state based on popular participation—came to be one of the politically most volatile forces of the twentieth century. The problem was that while nationalist passions excelled at destroying authoritarian and imperial regimes, they were less good at establishing new forms of the state, modern regimes based on radically different principles of legitimacy and different structures of state power and mass mobilization.

In sum, to be "for nationalism" and "against imperialism," as U.S. policy was prior to Wilson, turned out not to be enough. Once the old order was destroyed, what would go in its place? Into this hornets' nest Wilson stepped with his blueprint for liberal democracy, first for Latin America (his intervention in the Mexican Revolution in 1914 and the U.S. occupations of various countries, of which the most ambitious was the Dominican Republic in 1916), and later, and with far more consequences, for eastern Europe, in a design presented to the Paris Peace Conference in 1919.

With the notable exception of Czechoslovakia, Wilson's hopes came to naught. Many blame Wilson himself for the demise of his plans, pointing to his personal rigidity at home and abroad as the source of his undoing. But surely a better explanation was the tenor of the times. The Bolshevik Revolution (1917), Mussolini's seizure of power in Rome (1922), the Great Depression that started in 1929, and Hitler's assumption of power in Berlin in 1933 combined with the U.S. Senate's refusal to let the United States join the League of Nations so as to make Wilson's policies seem impractical in the interwar years. The United States had played a determining role in winning the Great War but Wilson could not win the peace that followed.

Still, seeds had been planted. When the United States confronted the task of winning the peace after it won the war against fascism in 1945, the Roosevelt and Truman administrations found themselves returning to Wilsonianism as the basis for at least a part of U.S. policy for world order. Thus, in occupation policy for Italy, Germany, and Japan, U.S. intentions were that these countries be democratized—purged of their militaristic elites and converted by institutional and ideological means into pacific, constitutional polities. In eastern Europe, the United States called on Joseph Stalin to respect national self-determination for the peoples liberated from Nazi control by the Red Army (an appeal Stalin agreed to in the Declaration on Liberated Europe at Yalta in 1945). In Latin America, too, there was for a brief moment hope that democracy would take root.

Nevertheless, even before the Cold War obliged Washington to work with authoritarian friends against local communist takeovers, the United States recognized that in many parts of the world in which it had an interest after 1945—Iran and China, for example—the prospects for democratic government were decidedly dim. Roosevelt had seen the failure of Wilson's efforts in the Caribbean as a warning signal as to how much change the United States could actually introduce into agrarian, authoritarian lands. As a result, Roosevelt might be called a "realistic liberal," ready to push for a Wilsonian world where the ground appeared promising, but careful not to engage American power in quagmires from which it could not easily extricate itself.

Still, the dream of promoting democracy elsewhere did not die with occupation policy. During the Eisenhower years, Washington continued to call for democratic national self-determination in Eastern Europe so as to undermine the rule of "puppet" governments in "captive nations" controlled by Moscow. So, too, the Kennedy administration saw American security in Latin America helped by that region's democratization and authored the Alliance for Progress. Jimmy Carter's important innovation in the Wilsonian tradition was to craft a "human rights" policy that called not so much for democratization as for the liberalization of authoritarian regimes (constitutional restraints on the government's power), a policy that might be seen as a prelude to eventual democratization.

Ronald Reagan's foreign policy continued in the Wilsonian tradition through innovations of its own. For example, "constructive engagement" was designed to ease authoritarian allies of the United States into the construction of liberal democratic regimes, an initiative that had impact in lands as different as the Philippines, South Korea, South Africa, Central America, and the Soviet Union. Also, the deregulation and privatization of the economy Reagan called for was seen as a socioeconomic facilitator of a democratic political order.

Promotion of democracy in Central America and Eastern Europe remained an appeal of the Bush administration, but George H. W. Bush famously commented that he did not "have the vision thing." Under President Bill Clinton, Wilsonianism became the centerpiece of administration policy early on, when it was announced that "the containment of communism" would be replaced by "the enlargement of democracy."

In sum, the best short definition of what it means to be Wilsonian is that American security interests are well served by promoting liberal democratic governments internationally. When most people casually refer to Wilsonianism, this is what they usually mean to summon up: the notion that promoting democracy for others should be "a," if not "the," leading goal of U.S. foreign policy.

EXPANDING THE DEFINITION OF WILSONIANISM

It can well be argued, however, that Wilsonianism has critical elements besides fostering democracy in its framework for global order. For a politically plural world, one opposed to great power imperial spheres of influence, would rather obviously need mechanisms to stitch together regional and global consensus on any number of matters. One of Wilson's leading concerns, consequently, was to get international affairs past balance-of-power politics. His solution was "collective security," the notion that all peace-loving states (a category he at first reserved only for democratic countries) should pledge themselves to joint action to keep the peace. Wilson recognized early on that a world composed of a large number of independent states, an order explicitly committed to anti-imperialism in the name of national self-determination, would by its very nature be forced to create a set of multilateral institutions to maintain the peace. Hence, he proposed the Pan American League (today the Organization of American States) and, most important of all, the League of Nations (the prototype of what became the United Nations). In short, a second element of Wilsonianism is multilateralism: the conviction that a range of international institutions based on the rule of law could keep the peace among states pledged domestically to the same principles.

Wilson's hopes for multilateral institutions may be said to have come to fruition in the five years between 1944 and 1949, the period that saw the creation of the Bretton Woods system for the world economy, the establishment of the United Nations, the Marshall Plan for the reconstruction of Europe, and the setting up of the North Atlantic Treaty Organization (NATO). Here were the instruments for Washington to pursue two goals—a two-track policy—at the same time: the containment of communism and the construction of a democratic fraternity with special emphasis on western Europe and Japan.

International economic openness was a third element of Wilsonianism. Following the British example, Wilson championed liberalism in world economics, the notion that states should not claim special privileges for themselves in economic matters (a position that often led to political imperialism) but instead let market forces operate, treating all comers equally through what are called "most-favored-nation treaties." The result would contribute not only to a more prosperous, but also to a more peaceful, international system. The concern to foster such a system stretches back in American history to the American Revolution itself, with its hatred of British mercantilist practices.

Nevertheless, Wilson's ideas on this score were not highly developed. By comparison, the efforts at Bretton Woods in 1944 to set up an open postwar international economic system were far more ambitious than anything he had ever conceived. Yet whatever these earlier and later considerations, Wilson certainly embraced international economic openness and saw it as an ingredient in his liberal internationalist package, one that tied in rather neatly with his call for strong multilateral institutions to regulate world affairs.

The fourth element of Wilsonianism was the conviction that the United States had to be deeply involved in international affairs if "the world was to be safe for democracy." Whatever the fear of "entangling alliances" warned against by George Washington, the United States simply could no longer stand aloof. By Wilson's lights, the United States had stepped onto the world stage in the War with Spain (1898), which had made it a Pacific power and the dominant presence in the Caribbean. By entering the European war in 1917 and presiding at the Paris Peace Conference in 1919, the United States had committed itself to being a European power as well. Henceforth, matters of political moment in most parts of the globe necessarily had to be the concern of Washington.

As with other elements of Wilsonianism, the notion that the United States was necessarily committed to internationalism became more widespread with World War II and the Cold War that followed. To be sure, in the aftermath of the collapse of Soviet communism, both public and elite opinion in the United States began to become relatively more concerned with domestic issues than had been the case before. Nevertheless, the Republican commitment to "unilateralism" rather than multilateralism, vexing as it may be to Wilsonians who fear that neo-isolationism might follow if the Republican penchant should be confirmed, does not necessarily mean that U.S. involvement in world affairs will noticeably diminish in the twenty-first century.

Thus, while Wilsonianism is most commonly identified as human rights and fostering democracy for others, in fact, it is necessarily a commitment as well to multilateralism, open markets, and U.S. leadership in world affairs. An interest in an open international economic system and a politically plural world may predate Wilson's tenure as president, and all aspects of what we call Wilsonianism may have evolved with time, without putting in doubt the utility of keeping the term.

Perhaps the most significant change since Woodrow Wilson's time in liberal democratic internationalism is the conviction that for democracy to occur, changes in other domains of a people's life must be involved. For example, while Wilson himself did not envision socioeconomic change as a constituent part of the democratizing process, his successors who oversaw the democratization of Germany and Japan were New Dealers, who most certainly did. So, too, the Alliance for Progress linked the democratization of Latin America to socioeconomic change, and especially to land reform. And again, Ronald Reagan had an economic dimension to his call for democratization when he stressed the importance of deregulation and privatization along with economic openness as essential for political change. Neither Jimmy Carter nor George H. W. Bush gave much attention to the socioeconomic character of political change, yet each could nonetheless be called Wilsonian, given their commitment to human rights and promotion of democracy abroad.

With respect to later innovations, Jimmy Carter's call for the respect worldwide of human rights emerges as especially important. The character of virtually all these "rights" dealt with restraints on governments in their relationship with society. Such rights were thus part of the liberal heritage of the West and were basic to the emergence of constitutionally limited government there. But as Carter himself understood, human rights were not synonymous with democracy. Nonetheless, a government that respected human rights as defined by the Western tradition almost necessarily was setting into motion forces that could lead to democratic government.

As this example of Carter's human rights appeal indicates, Wilsonianism is a multifaceted concept, constantly in evolution. Differences may well appear among Wilsonians as to the proper cast of U.S. foreign policy, and changes are sure to be introduced that today we can see only dimly. But such is the lot of any general approach to world events and not a reason to conclude that Wilsonianism is too vague, too internally contradictory, or too subject to change to be worthy of being considered a distinctive approach to answering the question of how the United States should orient itself, at least in part, with respect to the challenges posed by international affairs.

Perhaps most important of all, Wilsonianism should be seen as a U.S. bid to structure a world order on American terms. It is an essential part of the framework for American hegemony, designed to win the peace after winning three wars: the two world wars and the Cold War. Foreign critics of the United States have generally grasped this truth about Wilsonianism more clearly than many Americans, including those who think of themselves as Wilsonians. Wilson would make the world safe for democracy. But critics of Wilsonianism sometimes have understandably been concerned that in these circumstances democracy might not be safe for the world, that it might become the rallying call for an international crusade, waging war in the name of peace and bringing American domination in the guise of national self-determination. What is certainly the case is that Wilsonianism is part of an American bid for international hegemony, and it should be more widely recognized as such by those who might otherwise treat the doctrine as more altruistic and less self-interested than it actually is.

WHY WILSONIANISM?

Wilsonianism came into being not because of American "innocence" and "religiosity," as its critics often like to claim, so much as because the program was based on deep-seated American interests, values, and institutions, and, equally important, because the doctrine found a response in social and political forces the world around that sensed its global relevance. The source of the doctrine's strength thus lies in powerful material forces, some domestic, others foreign, which must be appreciated if we are to free ourselves from the notion that Wilsonianism is simply ideology without substance, a form of "social work" best performed by Mother Teresa, as one critic called it, devoid of an ability to express and serve the national interest. Let us then focus on each of the doctrine's analytically distinct material bases in turn, first the domestic and then the international.

The origins of an American belief that democracy, open markets, and multilateralism might serve as a framework for the construction of the country's foreign policy grew from the interests, values, and institutions of this country itself. Thus, the American Revolution stemmed from many sources, but one was the colonists' objection to British mercantilism, the feeling that the colonies would be better off if they were able to buy and sell on the world market without London's interference. What was true for London was equally true for Madrid; hence, U.S. sympathy with the independence of Latin America in the early nineteenth century. As the United States grew into an industrial power in the second half of the nineteenth century, its commitment to open markets was confirmed. Thus, the Open Door Notes for China, predicated on the assumption that an independent China was good for American commerce, expressed essentially the same interests at the end of the nineteenth century that the Monroe Doctrine had expressed at its opening.

Antimercantilism meant anti-imperialism. From the Monroe Doctrine to the Open Door Notes, the United States favored a politically plural world for economic reasons. With the coming of Franklin D. Roosevelt to the presidency, the American preference for open markets for the first time became an appeal for free (or freer) trade, an ambition institutionalized in the Bretton Woods system created in 1944, which has evolved and expanded significantly since. As the world's dominant economic power, the United States could only gain, on balance, from open economic arrangements, and it could easily be maintained, as it had been by the British in the nineteenth century, that the political dividends of international accord on open markets would be the dampening of competition, and hence the likelihood of war, among the great powers. In short, Wilsonianism's call for a plural political world of countries engaged in an open international economic network corresponded with the interests of powerful social and political domestic forces.

But there were critical security considerations as well. Protected by mighty oceans and weak neighbors, the United States was able to indulge the belief of its founders that standing armies were a menace to the health of republican institutions and values. Anti-imperialism thus meant that the United States need maintain only a small armed force—at the time of the Spanish-American War in 1898, there were fewer than 50,000 men in the army and navy combined, an astonishingly small number by comparative measures. The fear, however, was that other great powers might somehow endanger the United States by their imperial expansions, developments

Washington was determined to keep at bay in the Western Hemisphere (the Monroe Doctrine) and was concerned to see limited in northeast Asia (the Open Door Notes and later support for China) and in Europe as well after 1914.

In addition to economic and military reasons to oppose great power imperialism, the United States put forth arguments that were political as well. As a democracy, the country was not interested in annexing foreign peoples to participate in its government—especially when these people were numerous, poor, dark-skinned, and Roman Catholic, as was the case in the Caribbean, Mexico, and the Philippines, where American power bulked large after the victories over Mexico in 1848 and over Spain in 1898. Nor did controlling these people through military proconsuls seem appealing, for there was concern that such practices might endanger republican institutions at home. The character of the country's values and institutions thus melded with security and economic considerations to allow the United States to respect the nationalist ambitions of other peoples and to applaud the destruction of foreign empires when they occurred.

Now that some account has been made of why Wilsonianism originated in the United States for reasons apart from Woodrow Wilson's personal genius, we turn to the international reception of liberal democratic internationalism. Too often, U.S. foreign policy is explained "from the inside out," as if the context in which Washington's ambitions are operationalized is of second-order importance (if even that) in understanding a policy's logic. Yet, if we set U.S. policy within a global framework, our perspective changes, because we can see the correspondence, the synchronization, the "fit" between American hopes and global realities and better appreciate how U.S. policy often succeeded (so that the Wilsonian ambition was confirmed) by working in tandem with global forces of modernization in ways that secured a range of U.S. interests. Simply put, there were powerful reasons why large parts of the globe might respond to Wilsonianism—just as there were reasons why parts might respond instead to the contemporary doctrines of Marxism-Leninism or fascism or national socialism.

From a historical perspective, the ideologies of communism, fascism, and liberal democracy that dominated politics in the twentieth century were relatively recent responses to economic, social, and political changes whose most immediate origins lie in the eighteenth century but whose pedigree can be traced farther back by the careful historian. A competitive European state system gave rise as early as the late sixteenth century to forms of nationalism and mass mobilization that would be accentuated as time progressed. The coming of the Industrial Revolution meant the empowerment or despoliation (the middle class on the one hand, the peasantry on the other, for example) of social forces new and old. The Renaissance and the Reformation engendered forms of thought that implicitly questioned a host of practices, from the basis of social order to the character of state legitimacy. Ultimately, the Enlightenment allowed the articulation of radically novel concepts of the nature of citizenship, the state, and the basis of international peace that were as troubling to domestic, regional, and global order as the challenges produced by a competitive state system and economic change.

In the process of what might be termed "the crisis of modernity," authoritarian and imperial states came one by one to their day of reckoning. It was not so much that these states were corrupt, immoral, decadent, and the like (although, of course, they typically were, from our current perspective) as that they were weak relative to states based on mass mobilization. In short order, a law of international life obliged other peoples in contact with the states where modern nationalism and economic development began either to imitate these new political forms or to perish. The result was a host of efforts at defensive modernization—undertakings by the Young Turks from central and eastern Europe to East Asia whose nationalist passion to modernize by reforming the state and society called forth tremendous domestic upheavals that quickly found their parallels in international life.

How were states and the international order to be restructured in an era of unprecedented economic and social change and modern nationalism? The American and French revolutions (as well as the evolution of Great Britain) initially suggested a natural affinity between liberal democracy and modernization. But the problems France later had in consolidating constitutional government, the failure of the "springtime of nations" in 1848, the deliberate attempts of conservative governments such as those in Japan, Russia, and Turkey to modernize without liberalizing or democratizing (although the former sometimes made headway without the latter), and the authoritarian aftermath of the Mexican Revolution (1910–1917) all indicated the difficulties

in many lands of founding constitutional government with a liberal democratic base. Ultimately, World War I revealed that the progressive optimism of the fin de siècle was altogether mistaken in its confident assurances that nationalism and liberal democracy necessarily had much in common.

Both communism and fascism were born of the conflagration of 1914–1918, the most momentous period of that terrible century. Each of these ideologies answered the crisis of modernity by setting forth ways of organizing society, the state, and state-society relations, and each came to be championed by great powers and to appear to be a viable alternative to liberal democratic government, which was despised by both of these forms of totalitarianism.

For the communists, the state would be structured as "the dictatorship of the proletariat," dominated by a "vanguard party" working through the Third International (the Comintern) to liberate the wretched of the earth—oppressed peasantries and working classes especially. Fascism would counter communist mass mobilization by mass parties of its own, parties devoted to defending the traditional order (as they mythologized it), including property, royalty, and established religion (where these institutions existed), while raising popular support with brands of nationalism that were racist and militarist. Different as communism and fascism were from each other and from liberal democracy, what all three had in common was their modernity, their ability to deal with new ideas of citizenship, state power, and world order in ways that were decisively different from any ideologies or organization of power that had preceded them and that promised new forms of state power to those who embraced their blueprints. As a consequence, each of these ideologies came to be championed by class, ethnic, and political interests not only in their lands of origin but virtually everywhere in the world. As the Spanish Civil War (1936–1939) revealed, a three-way contest thus was joined from which few could stand apart.

This overly brief review of twentieth-century politics indicates that the stark elegance of realist theory about international relations, which holds that there is a universal dynamic to states' behavior, based on their calculation of their relative power position with respect to other states, needs to be augmented by historical and domestic analysis of the great changes of our times. While there may well be eternal verities about the human condition that we should honor whatever the differences of time and place (let us read and reread Thucydides and Machiavelli, by all means), these arguments should not give a license to overlook those verities that are specific to time and place, especially when they are of the fundamentally transformative kind we witnessed in the century just past. For what was occurring in the twentieth century was the birth pangs, on an international level, of the modern state, where more power was accumulated than ever before but where political actors often had opposing ideas as to the proper structuring of domestic and international life. In these circumstances, Wilsonianism, or liberal democratic internationalism, represented interests and values in fundamental opposition to those of communist and fascist regimes. The epochal struggle of World War II was over purpose as well as power, as Stalin's remark to the Yugoslav communist Milovan Djilas in April 1945 reveals: "This war is not as in the past. Whoever occupies a territory also imposes on it his own social system. Everyone imposes his own system as far as his army can reach. It cannot be otherwise."

To be sure, ideologies were also camouflages in the age-old struggle for power that concerned personalities as well as states. Still, the reason to take ideological contests seriously is that these idea sets represented large groupings of interests that gave them a material base in the struggle for supremacy in the twentieth century. In the event, it is not at all simplistic to maintain that it was not so much the United States and its European allies that triumphed in the struggles against fascism and communism as that what triumphed (at least by the end of the century) was liberal democratic internationalism, a set of ideas on the proper organization of the state, state-society relations, social structures from the family to the relative place of ethnic and religious minorities, and the structure of economic production.

Here, then, is a second persuasive reason why Wilsonianism should be taken seriously: it is not simply an American project for world order favorable to U.S. interests; it is also a formula (incomplete, vague, contradictory, and in constant evolution though it may be) that corresponds to the interests, values, and institutions of many other peoples around the globe. As Wilsonians realize, regime type matters. That is, it may well be a matter of concern for Washington whether powerful foreign governments are liberal democracies, for the historical evidence is clear

that when they are, then the likelihood of stable, cooperative relations is significantly increased.

The evidence of the uniquely complicated agenda of social and political reorganization in the modern era is apparent in the early twenty-first century, when liberal democratic capitalism is the only game in town. This monopoly of design should not disguise the fear and hatred that many around the world feel for it. Still, no other general form of political and social life has yet been devised that is as effective at the local and international level as the one enjoyed by the international liberal democratic community today—a system kept in place, it might be underscored, largely by the terms set out by a hegemonic America.

Of course, the set of ideas that we call liberal democratic has never been either fully coherent or static. It has shown itself to possess numerous internal contradictions and to evolve dramatically according to time and place. American hegemony is complicated, therefore, not simply by its external rivals but also by its internal organization, which ceaselessly works to bedevil the problems of leadership.

As we have seen, by the early twentieth century—the time Wilson was elected president—it was becoming increasingly apparent that nationalism itself was no guarantee that a stable political order would be born either locally or regionally. In these circumstances, liberal democratic government could be proposed for others as a tried and proven formula perhaps of universal applicability. Perhaps Wilson was ahead of his time for most of Latin America and eastern Europe. But it is noteworthy at the beginning of the twenty-first century that whatever the troubles these regions experienced in the twentieth century, the promise of liberal democratic government remains as relevant today as ever. Fascism and communism have not worked as models of government in these areas. Hence, the continuing promise of Wilsonianism as the form of organization most likely to provide peace and well-being.

Nevertheless, many parts of the world rejected the Wilsonian premise in the twentieth century. In the early twenty-first century, the anarchy of much of Africa, the hostility of much of the Muslim world, and the cultural pride of China suggest clear limits to the appeal of liberal democratic government. Such countries and regions must nonetheless be worked with by Washington in a search for mutual interest that a well-nigh religious fervor for human rights and democratic government may fail to perceive at all adequately.

The record of the Clinton administration (1993–2001) suggests the limits of the Wilsonian argument. Initially, the administration believed that "the containment of communism would be replaced by the enlargement of democracy," that a "muscular multilateralism" would prevail, and that the intensified globalization of the world economy not only would lead to general prosperity but also would help to integrate the world politically while fostering democratic governments in areas like China, where the future of regime types seemed up for debate.

In short order, the Clinton administration was chastened to learn how limited a Wilsonian policy could be. China successfully rebuffed efforts to link trade negotiations to its human rights conduct. The U.S. intervention in Somalia for human rights purposes backfired, stymieing efforts to duplicate such action in Haiti, Rwanda, and Bosnia. Later, Clinton oversaw a U.S. occupation of Haiti and an attack on Serbia so as to end its human rights abuses in Kosovo, but as the prospects for democratic government appeared stark in both regions, a certain soberness set in as to the centrality of Wilsonian thinking in the making of U.S. foreign policy.

In sum, Wilsonianism is a tried and proven formula for advancing U.S. interests in the world because of its correspondence both to the character of America as a country and to the needs of peoples around the world. But it is far from a complete or foolproof guide to what American foreign policy should be. The task for the future, as it was for the past, is to know when and how to make use of its recommendations, but also when and why to be skeptical of its relevance.

WHITHER WILSONIANISM?

Arguing the strength and the success of Wilsonianism in American foreign policy does not necessarily predict its role in the framework for American policy in the new century. The so-called realist critics of Wilsonianism have been cogent in the analysis of the shortcomings they see in liberal democratic internationalism. To realists such as George Kennan, Hans Morgenthau, Walter Lippmann, and Henry Kissinger, Wilsonianism is "idealistic," "utopian," and "moralistic" for two essential reasons.

First, not all the world is ready for liberal

democratic government. The social, economic, cultural, and political preconditions for such a regime type are in many instances so lacking that for the United States to pursue global democratization is to engage upon a quixotic crusade sure to damage the national interest. From this point of view, Wilsonians may fail to cooperate with authoritarian governments when this is necessary for security reasons; indeed, they may raise tensions with such regimes by their hectoring, superior, self-righteous posturing. Or Wilsonians may intervene, trying to bend local conditions to their recipes, in the process overextending American power and confusing national priorities.

Realists are thus correct to suggest that Wilsonians may suffer from a failure to recognize the objective limits to American power, to set clear priorities regarding American goals, to see the United States with the modesty that a reading of the country's history should reveal, and to sup with the devil when expediency demands it. Liberal democratic internationalists should learn from these counsels when they consider how to promote their agenda abroad.

In many parts of the world (China, many Muslim countries), cultures hostile to the West or proud of ancient traditions equate democratization with Westernization, and any such process with cultural decadence and national disintegration. Like Slavophiles, Germanophiles, or groups of Japanese, Turkish, or Chinese reformers in the late nineteenth and early twentieth centuries, the hopes of many in these lands are to duplicate the power of the West but in terms of local ways. Elsewhere, as in much of Africa, hostility toward the West may be less marked, but anarchy undermines every effort toward democratic consolidation.

The second criticism offered by realists is that even were the world to be dominated by liberal democratic states, the anarchy of international relations would soon pit them against one another. Consider, for example, that in world affairs both India and France rather consistently distance themselves from American policy. In other words, from the point of view of war and peace, whether governments are democratic or not is not of great moment.

Here, however, realists are on far weaker ground than in their first objection to Wilsonianism, or so liberal internationalists believe. Since the early 1990s, a compelling amount of data have been produced demonstrating that liberal democratic regimes are in fact more cooperative and less conflictual in their relations with one another than other regime types would be. This literature argues the existence of a "democratic peace," maintaining that there is strong historical evidence that liberal democratic states do not go to war with one another, are likely to make superior economic partners, and are remarkably successful at making common institutions work. The Princeton political scientist Michael Doyle was the first to present empirical findings in this direction in the early 1980s, but with the fall of the Berlin Wall in 1989 and the implosion of the Soviet Union two years later, Doyle's articles became subject to closer attention. The result was a string of empirical confirmations of the existence of the democratic peace and a variety of efforts to explain why it held true.

Seen from this perspective, the emergence of liberal democratic government in Russia, Turkey, and Mexico—to cite three examples of nations where such transitions seem possible in the early twenty-first century—could be argued to be of genuine importance to the national interests of the United States and its co-democracies in the European Union. Indeed, the character of the European Union is the most dramatic evidence of the kind of positive effects democratization may bring. Thanks to the democratization of Germany, European integration became a possibility. As the European Union grew in power, it drew into its institutions the countries of southern Europe, where the prospects for liberal democratic government had been relatively weak. The result was the consolidation of democratic regimes throughout this region, a development that would have been inconceivable without the European Union's insistence on democracy as a prerequisite for membership. The same process seems evident in central Europe, from Poland to Slovenia especially, where the prospect of joining the European Union offers a fillip for democratic forces and institutions there. And behind the integration of Europe on these terms stands the spirit of Woodrow Wilson, who was the first to maintain that this epochal event could occur only if Germany were democratized and Germany and France were to join together, creating what today is called the "engine of European unity."

Much the same positive outcome, so far as promotion of democracy and U.S. interests are concerned, can be said to have occurred with the expansion of the North Atlantic Treaty Organization. NATO's basic security mission should not conceal the fact that it has also been associated with the liberalization of those countries that are members. To take but one example, civilian control of the military is obligatory on all member countries, and the reforms that this rule has entailed have contributed directly to the stability of democratic life in southern and central Europe. In these circumstances, it is worth noting that the most outspoken Wilsonian on European affairs at the turn of the century was Czech President Václav Havel.

To what extent have the lessons of history, as they are taught by Wilsonians, captured the mind of the American political elite? The vagaries of American political life are such that some individuals and parties stress the importance of liberal democratic internationalism more than others. Traditionally, the Democratic Party has been more Wilsonian than the Republican Party, but one should be careful not to overstate the differences. Republican Ronald Reagan was especially strong in his efforts to promote democratic government worldwide, while the dominant wing of the Republican Party has long favored open international markets and an active role for the United States in world affairs. Nevertheless, at the beginning of the twenty-first century, the Democratic Party is far more likely to call for promotion of human rights and democracy abroad and to be concerned about U.S. participation in multinational institutions of a variety of sorts. The Republicans, by contrast, tend to be suspicious that promotion of democracy and excessive commitments to international organizations could muddle the priorities for the national interest while imprudently overextending the United States in situations where it has little at stake.

One problem for Wilsonians in the early twenty-first century is that public opinion polls show little interest in fostering human rights and democracy for others among the public at large. Meanwhile, powerful voices representing the working class warn of possible income decline among poorer Americans should economic globalization proceed apace. And a neo-isolationist sentiment, a concern about entanglements abroad where the United States has no evident stake, makes leadership in a host of multinational institutions difficult to assert.

In these circumstances, some liberal internationalists began to call themselves "national security liberals," meaning they argued that the promotion of Wilsonianism constituted what Arthur Link called a "higher realism," a way of defending vital U.S. interests around the world.

These modern Wilsonians stress that it is not only the degree of its power that allowed the United States to emerge as the world's leader at the beginning of the twenty-first century; there was a style to this power as well, a character that allowed it to create a security alliance and a world economic order unprecedented in history. They worry that lack of understanding of the purpose behind American power may cause this power to lack direction and confidence. But they comfort themselves with the notion that the package of programs liberal democratic internationalism calls for corresponds both to deep-set U.S. interests and to the needs of many foreign people. The result is that Wilsonian features of American foreign policy should remain an inescapable part of its character into the foreseeable future.

BIBLIOGRAPHY

Auchincloss, Louis. *Woodrow Wilson.* New York, 2000.

Brown, Michael, ed. *Debating the Democratic Peace.* Cambridge, Mass., 1996.

Carothers, Thomas. *Aiding Democracy Abroad.* Washington, D.C., 1999.

Doyle, Michael W. "Kant, Liberal Legacies, and Foreign Affairs." *Philosophy and Public Affairs* 12 (summer 1983) and (fall 1983).

——. *Ways of War and Peace.* New York, 1997.

Gowa, Joanne. *Ballots and Bullets.* Princeton, N.J., 1999.

Human Rights Watch. *Human Rights Watch World Report.* New York, annual publication.

Ikenberry, G. John. *After Victory: Institutions, Strategic Restraint, and the Rebuilding of Order After Major Wars.* Princeton, N.J., 2000.

Kennan, George. *American Diplomacy.* Enlarged ed. Chicago, 1984.

Kissinger, Henry. *Diplomacy.* New York, 1994.

Knock, Thomas. *To End all Wars: Woodrow Wilson and the Quest for a New World Order.* New York, 1995.

Link, Arthur S. *Woodrow Wilson and the World of Today.* Edited by Arthur P. Dudden. Philadelphia, 1957.

Maoz, Zeev. "The Controversy over the Democratic Peace." *International Security* 22 (summer 1997).

Morgenthau, Hans. *In Defense of the National Interest: A Critical Examination of American Foreign Policy.* New York, 1951.

Owen, John M., IV. *Liberal Peace, Liberal War.* Ithaca, N.Y., 1997.

Pearlmutter, Amos. *Making the World Safe for Democracy: A Century of Wilsonianism and Its Totalitarian Challengers.* Chapel Hill, N.C., 1997.

Risse-Kappen, Thomas. *Cooperation Among Democracies: The European Influence on U.S. Foreign Policy.* Princeton, N.J., 1999.

Risse-Kappen, Thomas, Stephen C. Ropp, and Kathryn Sikkink. *The Power of Human Rights: International Norms and Domestic Change.* New York, 1999.

Ruggie, John Gerard, ed. *Multilateralism Matters: The Theory and Praxis of an International Form.* New York, 1993.

Smith, Tony. *America's Mission: The United States and the Worldwide Struggle for Democracy in the Twentieth Century.* Princeton, N.J., 1994.

——. "Making the World Safe for Democracy." In Michael Hogan, ed. *The Ambiguous Legacy: U.S. Foreign Relations in the "American Century."* New York, 1999.

Steigerwald, David. "The Reclamation of Woodrow Wilson." *Diplomatic History* 23 (1999).

See also ECONOMIC POLICY AND THEORY; HUMAN RIGHTS; MOST-FAVORED-NATION PRINCIPLE; THE NATIONAL INTEREST; REALISM AND IDEALISM; SELF-DETERMINATION; WILSONIAN MISSIONARY DIPLOMACY.

WILSONIAN MISSIONARY DIPLOMACY

★ ★ ★ ★

Roger R. Trask

"Missionary diplomacy" is a descriptive label often applied to the policies and practices of the United States in Mexico, Central America, and the Caribbean during the presidency of Woodrow Wilson (1913–1921). According to Arthur S. Link in *Wilson: The New Freedom* (p. 278), "[Secretary of State William Jennings] Bryan and Wilson were both fundamentally missionaries of democracy, driven by inner compulsions to give other peoples the blessings of democracy and inspired by the confidence that they knew better how to promote the peace and well-being of other countries than did the leaders of those countries themselves." Wilson related both missionary diplomacy and the New Freedom, his domestic program, to his concepts of morality and democratic government. Despite Wilson's admirable ideas and objectives, missionary diplomacy was a disaster. Perhaps some of the historians who have placed Wilson high in the presidential pantheon have not given enough consideration to the failure of missionary diplomacy.

FOUNDATIONS OF WILSONIAN FOREIGN POLICY

Woodrow Wilson came to the presidency with little knowledge of or interest in foreign affairs. His well-known remark to a Princeton friend, "It would be the irony of fate if my administration had to deal chiefly with foreign affairs," seemed to emphasize his concentration on domestic questions. But from the start of his term, Wilson saw close relationships between domestic and foreign policies. The New Freedom envisaged a return to free competition in the United States. The monopolistic interests had to be destroyed at home and their influence in foreign policy dispelled, and thus Wilson's initial rejection of "dollar diplomacy." Although he was not unqualifiedly hostile to business interests, he believed that their activities ought to serve, rather than dominate, the public interest.

Wilson's ethical and religious beliefs also profoundly influenced his foreign policy. Nations, like individuals, should adhere to high ethical and moral standards. Democracy, Wilson thought, was the most Christian of governmental systems, suitable for all peoples. The democratic United States thus had a moral mandate for world leadership. At the end of World War I, the president saw the League of Nations as an instrument for the application of Wilsonian democracy on an international scale.

WILSON'S INITIAL POLICY FOR LATIN AMERICA

When Wilson took office in March 1913, the immediate problems he faced in Mexico, Central America, and the Caribbean gave him opportunities to apply these concepts to Latin American policy. He promptly presented a draft Latin American policy statement to his cabinet. Most of the cabinet thought Wilson's proposal hasty and radical; it had not been discussed with Bryan or other advisers, or with Latin American diplomats in Washington. D.C. Wilson held firm, arguing that the change in administration in Washington could not be the occasion for a wave of irresponsible revolutions in Latin America. His statement appeared in the press on 12 March 1913.

Wilson said that his administration desired the "most cordial understanding and cooperation" with Latin America. "As friends . . . we shall prefer those who act in the interest of peace and honor, who protect private rights, and respect the restraints of constitutional provision." Wilson concluded by extending "the hand of genuine disinterested friendship." The statement was a curious mixture of Wilson's commitment to democracy and constitutionalism, a profession of neighborly friendship, and a threat against revolutionists. He put forward a significant change in United States recognition policy: de facto governments would have to be constitutionally legitimate in order to gain recognition. Otherwise, Wilson's statement did not really change Latin American policy.

Wilson's address to the Southern Commercial Congress at Mobile, Alabama, on 27 October 1913 presumably did. He predicted improved and closer relations between the United States and its southern neighbors. The United States would seek a "spiritual union" with Latin America and the freeing of those nations from the exploitative nature of foreign concessions. Referring to the Panama Canal, then under construction, he noted, "While we physically cut two continents asunder, we spiritually unite them. It is a spiritual union which we seek." The canal would "open the world to a commerce . . . of intelligence, of thought and sympathy between north and south." Wilson deplored the exploitative nature of foreign concessions in Latin American nations. "I rejoice in nothing so much as in the prospect that they will now be emancipated from these conditions, and we ought to be the first to take part in assisting that emancipation." In conclusion, Wilson emphasized his commitment to "constitutional liberty."

As Wilson's first term progressed, the promise of the Mobile address disintegrated. United States intervention in Latin America escalated to heights perhaps beyond the comprehension of earlier practitioners of "big stick" and dollar diplomacy. Missionary diplomacy created seemingly permanent hostility between the United States and Latin America. This was especially true in Mexico, Nicaragua, Haiti, and the Dominican Republic, which experienced Wilsonian interventionism in its most virulent forms.

INTERVENTION IN MEXICO

Wilson first tested his Latin American policy in Mexico. In February 1913, Mexico entered a new stage in the epic revolution that had begun in 1910 against the dictator Porfirio Díaz. Francisco Madero, the leader of the rebels, was a moderate revolutionist who eventually aroused the ire of radicals like Emiliano Zapata, who demanded redistribution of land to peasants, as well as Francisco (Pancho) Villa, Pascual Orozco, and Felix Díaz, nephew of the deposed dictator.

President William Howard Taft, although unenthusiastic, had recognized Madero as president of Mexico in November 1911. Ambassador Henry Lane Wilson, concerned about threats to U.S. business interests in Mexico, maintained cool relations with the Madero government. In the "Pact of the Embassy" (19 February 1913), Ambassador Wilson joined with Victoriano Huerta, Madero's top general, and Felix Díaz in a plan to replace Madero: Huerta as provisional president, and Díaz as a candidate in a later presidential election. Huerta assumed the presidency after pressuring Madero and Vice President José Maria Pino Suárez to resign. Apparently some of Huerta's men assassinated Madero and Pino Suárez, although they had been assured of safe conduct on 22 February. Taft left the problem of recognizing Huerta to the incoming Wilson administration. Wilson believed that Huerta had gained power by undemocratic and unconstitutional means, and the Madero–Pino Suárez murders shocked him. Furthermore, the president had deep suspicions about Ambassador Wilson, who flooded Washington with dispatches lauding Huerta and asserting that the new Mexican leader would cooperate with United States interests. President Wilson, however, applied the tough tests of constitutional legitimacy to the Mexican regime.

The president sent a friend, the journalist William Bayard Hale, to Mexico in June 1913 to get firsthand information. Hale was unenthusiastic about Huerta, describing him as "an ape-like old man" who "may almost be said to subsist on alcohol." With Hale's views in mind, President Wilson continued to shun the new Mexican government, even though Ambassador Wilson virtually insisted that Huerta be recognized. Acting on the president's orders, Bryan recalled Wilson and accepted his resignation.

In August 1913, Wilson sent another personal representative, John Lind, to Mexico. Previously both a representative and governor of Minnesota, Lind had no diplomatic experience. His instructions put forth terms for a Mexican settlement: an immediate cease-fire, an early and free election, a promise from Huerta not to be a candidate, and pledges that all Mexican factions would respect the election results. Huerta flatly rejected these proposals, as well as a subsequent offer of a large private loan if he would agree to an election in which he was not a candidate. On 27 August, Wilson told a joint session of Congress that the United States would wait patiently until the Mexican civil strife had run its course, meanwhile embargoing arms sales to all sides. Unfortunately, Wilson did not consistently adhere to this policy of "watchful waiting."

In the fall of 1913, Venustiano Carranza, Huerta's main opponent, announced that his Constitutionalist Party would boycott the presidential election scheduled for 26 October. When Huerta arrested more than 100 opposition deputies in the Mexican congress, Wilson announced that the United States would ignore the election results. After an inconclusive election, Mexico's congress reappointed Huerta provisional president until balloting scheduled for July 1914. Wilson now abandoned "watchful waiting." As Secretary Bryan wrote to United States diplomats in Latin America, President Wilson considered that "it is his immediate duty to require Huerta's retirement," and that the United States would "proceed to employ such means as may be necessary to secure this result." At this point, Wilson sympathized with the Carranza group. The president's struggle with Huerta had become personal as well as national.

Wilson, feeling that Great Britain's role was crucial, put special pressure on London to repudiate Huerta. Although the British fleet depended somewhat on Mexican oil, Britain's problems in Europe dictated rapprochement with the United States. Britain withdrew recognition of Huerta in mid-1914, after negotiations with the United States that included a satisfactory settlement of the controversy over a U.S. law providing discriminatory tolls on the Panama Canal.

In February 1914, in a further attempt to strengthen Carranza and the Constitutionalists, Wilson lifted the embargo on arms to Mexico, but Huerta continued to hold out. A new crisis developed on 9 April 1914, when Mexican authorities mistakenly arrested eight U.S. sailors at Tampico. Within an hour, Huerta's commanding general in the port released the men and apologized to Rear Admiral Henry T. Mayo, the commander of the U.S. squadron at Tampico. Mayo gave Huerta twenty-four hours to make a more formal apology, punish the arresting officer, and fire a twenty-one-gun salute. Wilson backed Mayo and ordered an increase in U.S. forces in Mexican waters. Congress gave him permission to take punitive action against Mexico. These acts presumably were on behalf of constitutionality and democracy.

Before these plans could be implemented, the United States consul at Veracruz reported the imminent arrival of the German steamer *Ypi-*

★ ★ ★ ★

PRESIDENT WILSON'S ADDRESS AT MOBILE, ALABAMA, 27 OCTOBER 1913

"The future . . . is going to be very different for this hemisphere from the past. These States lying to the south of us, which have always been our neighbors, will now be drawn closer to us by innumerable ties, and, I hope, chief of all, by the tie of a common understanding of each other. Interest does not tie nations together; it sometimes separates them. But sympathy and understanding does [*sic*] unite them, and I believe that by the new route that is just about to be opened, while we physically cut two continents asunder, we spiritually unite them. It is a spiritual union which we seek. . . .

"What these States are going to see, therefore, is an emancipation from the subordination, which has been inevitable, to foreign enterprise and an assertion of the splendid character which, in spite of these difficulties, they have again and again been able to demonstrate. The dignity, the courage, the self-possession, the self-respect of the Latin American States, their achievements in the face of all these adverse circumstances, deserve nothing but the admiration and applause of the world. . . .

"We must prove ourselves their friends, and champions upon terms of equality and honor. You cannot be friends upon any other terms than upon the terms of equality. You cannot be friends at all except upon the terms of honor. We must show ourselves friends by comprehending their interest whether it squares with our own interest or not. . . .

"I want to take this occasion to say that the United States will never again seek one additional foot of territory by conquest. She will devote herself to showing that she knows how to make honorable and fruitful use of the territory she has, and she must regard it as one of the duties of friendship to see that from no quarter are material interests made superior to human liberty and national opportunity."

---

ranga with a cargo of guns and ammunition for Huerta's forces. Wilson decided to seize the customhouse at Veracruz and impound the cargo. When this occurred on 21 April, the Mexicans resisted, precipitating a battle in which 126 Mexicans were killed and 200 were wounded. Huerta severed diplomatic relations after U.S. forces occupied the city.

The bloodshed appalled President Wilson, who had not expected Mexican resistance. Thus, he welcomed the offer of Argentina, Brazil, and Chile to mediate; and Huerta also accepted. Wilson intended to use the mediation conference, which began in Niagara Falls, Canada, on 20 May 1914, to get rid of Huerta and bring the Constitutionalists to power. But Carranza, who had denounced the U.S. aggression at Veracruz, instructed his delegation, which never really participated in the conference, to refuse a cease-fire and to deny the right of the mediators to discuss the Mexican situation. The conference adjourned on 2 July without positive results. But the United States intervention and heightened conflict with his enemies forced Huerta to resign on 15 July. Venustiano Carranza soon entered Mexico City. Although earlier an advocate of Carranza, Wilson now rejected him and initiated negotiations with his chief rival in northern Mexico, Pancho Villa, who then had a favorable image in the United States. Carranza, who retained the support of Alvaro Obregón and other leading generals, refused to give in to Villa. As the months passed, Wilson's policy became more threatening; but Carranza insisted that he would fight until victory over his opponents.

At this juncture, Wilson proposed a meeting of the United States and six Latin American nations (Argentina, Brazil, Chile, Bolivia, Uruguay, and Guatemala), anticipating joint intervention to remove Carranza; but by the time the conference convened at Washington in August 1915, Wilson had changed his mind. Secretary of State Robert Lansing, worried about German activity in the hemisphere, thought it necessary to improve relations with Mexico in the face of this external threat. Although the conferees offered to act as mediators in Mexico, Wilson ignored them and extended de facto recognition to Carranza on 19 October 1915.

Even if Wilson wished to concentrate on problems other than Mexico, Pancho Villa was unwilling to let him. Unable to defeat Carranza with his army, Villa apparently decided to provoke U.S. intervention as an alternative way to achieve his goal. On 10 January 1916, Villa forces murdered sixteen U.S. mining engineers and technicians in Chihuahua. On 7 March, the U.S. Congress responded with a resolution advocating armed intervention. Two days later, Villa raided the border town of Columbus, New Mexico,

killing seventeen Americans. Wilson immediately ordered troops into Mexico. General John J. Pershing's force never caught Villa but clashed with Carranza's army. Unsuccessful in his efforts to extort concessions from Carranza, and embroiled in a serious crisis with Germany, Wilson withdrew the troops from Mexico in February 1917.

Mexican-American relations followed a less spectacular course for the rest of Wilson's presidency. The Mexican constitution of 1917 contained several provisions threatening to foreign concessionaires, but Wilson extended de jure recognition to Carranza in August 1917, after assurances that such interests would be respected. A potentially serious dispute developed in 1918, after Mexico decreed taxes on oil property, rents, royalties, and production based on contracts effective before 1 May 1917. United States oil companies refused to register their land titles, arguing that to do so would be recognition of Mexican claims to subsurface deposits. Carranza ignored State Department protests, but he did not enforce the decrees until June 1919, when Mexican troops moved into the oil fields to halt unapproved drilling operations. Secretary of State Lansing, backed by the Association for the Protection of American Rights in Mexico, urged Wilson to be more aggressive. But in January 1920, Wilson wisely rejected Lansing's recommendations, and the oil producers arranged a satisfactory modus vivendi with Carranza. After Obregón ousted Carranza in May 1920, a Senate subcommittee recommended that the United States delay recognition until U.S. citizens gained exemption from certain articles of the Mexican constitution. Wilson and Secretary of State Bainbridge Colby favored this approach, but negotiations failed and the United States did not recognize Obregón until 1923.

INTERVENTION IN NICARAGUA

When Wilson used missionary diplomacy elsewhere, it led to the same legacy of failure and ill will as in Mexico. In Nicaragua, Wilson inherited from the Taft administration a military intervention and an extensive effort at dollar diplomacy. Taft broke relations in 1909 with Nicaraguan President José Zelaya and encouraged the latter's enemies to revolt when he menaced the nearby Central American nations, threatened the ouster of United States financial interests, and mortgaged his country to European interests. When his successor, Adolfo Díaz, faced a revolt in 1912, Taft sent in U.S. marines, who were still there when Wilson became president. In 1911 the two countries signed the Knox-Castrillo Convention, providing for a large loan from United States bankers to re-fund the Nicaraguan debt and U.S. administration of the customs services. The U.S. Senate rejected this plan, but a new treaty signed early in 1913 gave the United States an option on a canal route, naval base rights on the Gulf of Fonseca, and leases on the Corn Islands in the Caribbean, in return for a payment of $3 million. Bryan favored this glaring example of dollar diplomacy and persuaded President Wilson to accept it.

The Senate demurred, partly because of an amendment (patterned after the 1901 Platt Amendment for Cuba) allowing the United States to intervene to maintain internal order. Bryan then suggested to Wilson that the United States should be a "modern example of the Good Samaritan"—the government should make direct loans to Latin American nations by issuing bonds at 3 percent and lending the proceeds at 4.5 percent, with the profit used for debt retirement. Wilson rejected the proposal, leaving private loans as the only alternative. In October 1913, the U.S. firms of Brown Brothers and J. and W. Seligman, by buying stock in the Pacific Railroad and the National Bank of Nicaragua, purchasing Treasury bills, and lending money to the railroad, provided Nicaragua with more than $2.5 million. Bryan consulted Wilson before approving this formal act of dollar diplomacy.

In August 1914, the United States and Nicaragua signed the Bryan-Chamorro Treaty, a restatement of the 1913 proposals without Platt Amendment provisions. Because of questions about the role of U.S. business interests in Nicaragua, charges that the United States was dealing with a puppet regime, and protests from several Central American countries, the Senate delayed approval of the treaty until February 1916. El Salvador, Honduras, and Costa Rica, by raising critical questions about U.S. motives, exposed the bankruptcy of missionary diplomacy. Costa Rica argued that the canal concession violated its rights in the area; El Salvador and Honduras claimed that establishment of a naval base would violate their equal rights in the Gulf of Fonseca. In 1916, Costa Rica and El Salvador brought charges against Nicaragua in the Central American Court of Justice. Both the United States and Nicaragua argued that the court had no jurisdiction and refused to accept its decisions in favor of Costa Rica and El Salvador. This reaction made

it clear that the court, which the United States had helped to establish in 1907, was useful only when it did not tread on the toes of the United States. Impotent to enforce its decisions, the court soon ceased to exist.

After ratification of the Bryan-Chamorro Treaty, the United States moved to control Nicaraguan politics and finance. Political and economic pressures and a naval demonstration helped to ensure the election of the conservative Emiliano Chamorro as president in 1916. The United States also dictated the disbursement of the $3 million Bryan-Chamorro fund, handed over after adoption of the Financial Plan of 1917. The plan limited the monthly budget of Nicaragua, provided for a high commission dominated by U.S. citizens to monitor government spending, and established a schedule for payment of the Nicaraguan debt to British bondholders and U.S. bankers. Another financial plan in 1920 increased the government's monthly allowance, but the presence of U.S. marines and continued financial and political control tainted this progress.

INTERVENTION IN THE DOMINICAN REPUBLIC

As in Nicaragua, the Wilson administration inherited a difficult situation in the Dominican Republic. Political instability and nonpayment of debts threatened U.S. business interests and invited European intervention in the country as early as 1904. These problems influenced President Theodore Roosevelt to announce a corollary to the Monroe Doctrine that assumed a unilateral right for the United States to intervene in Latin America. After the Taft administration intervened in a civil war in the Dominican Republic in 1912, Archbishop Adolfo A. Nouel became president; he resigned in late March 1913, however, giving up the almost impossible task of pacifying the various political factions.

The Dominican situation demanded astute action by the Wilson administration; but Secretary of State Bryan replaced a competent minister, William W. Russell, with James M. Sullivan. Sullivan was associated with New York financiers who controlled the National Bank of Santo Domingo, an institution hoping to become the depository of funds collected by the receiver general of Dominican customs. Sullivan later resigned after a State Department investigation disclosed his deficiencies. Another bad appointment was that of Walter

C. Vick as receiver general. Bryan's choices inevitably led to inaccurate, biased reports from the Dominican Republic.

In September 1913, when a new revolt broke out against the provisional government in Santo Domingo, Bryan announced that the United States would not recognize any revolutionary regime, thus invoking Wilsonian constitutional legitimacy. After an armistice, the United States supervised elections in December 1913 for a constituent assembly, even though the Dominican government resented the outside pressure. With less than gentle prodding by Minister Sullivan, President José Bordas Valdés agreed to the appointment, in June 1914, of Charles W. Johnston as financial expert, with power to control Dominican expenditures. Following a U.S. electoral plan, the Dominicans held a presidential election in late 1914. The candidates, Juan Isidro Jiménez and Horacio Vásquez, represented the two strongest political factions in the country. Jiménez won and took office on 5 December 1914; the United States immediately pressed for more financial control and intervention privileges. Jiménez resisted these demands, but he could not overcome the continued opposition of his rivals, including Desiderio Arias, whom he dismissed as minister of war in May 1916. After Arias's forces took the city of Santo Domingo and Jiménez resigned, the United States intervened. Admiral William B. Caperton demanded that Arias withdraw and occupied the city. Fearing that Arias would come to power, President Wilson proclaimed full military occupation of the Dominican Republic on 26 November 1916. He cited political and fiscal disorder and the Dominican government's refusal to reform as reasons for the intervention. Undoubtedly, another factor was State Department concern about possible war with Germany and the influence of pro-German elements in the Dominican Republic.

Until 1924 a U.S. military government ruled the Dominican Republic. Although there were noticeable improvements—highway construction, establishment of the constabulary, expansion of the schools, and a better internal revenue collection system—the opposition to U.S. domination steadily increased. When the troops finally left late in 1924, a new treaty continued U.S. financial control.

INTERVENTION IN HAITI

Events in Haiti followed a familiar path. When Wilson became president, political and economic instability and threats of foreign intervention existed there. United States citizens owned perhaps 40 percent of the stock in the National Bank of Haiti, half the stock in the national railroad, and a smaller portion of the German-dominated Central Railroad. Loans from foreign sources contributed to the financial crisis and increased the threat of intervention. By 1915, Haiti's public debt stood at $32 million.

In January 1914 a revolution brought Oreste Zamor to power. The United States recognized him as president on 1 March 1914, even though he declined to accept a customs receivership and to pledge that no foreign power other than the United States would secure a naval station at Môle St. Nicholas. President Zamor later rejected a similar proposal, strengthened perhaps by German and French demands to share in the customs receivership; President Wilson objected, in effect invoking the Monroe Doctrine.

In October 1914, when Davilmar Theodore ousted Zamor, Secretary of State Bryan notified him that recognition would be extended only after agreement on a customs convention, settlement of disputes between the government and the railroads and the national bank, and guarantees against leases of coaling or naval stations to any European country. Theodore rejected these demands. Domestically, he became involved in a serious controversy with the national bank. His government printed a large quantity of paper currency and seized $65,000 of the bank's gold supply. To prevent further raids, the bank transferred $500,000 in gold to New York aboard the USS *Machias.* Although Bryan denied Haitian claims that armed intervention on behalf of U.S. business interests had taken place, U.S. investment in the national bank was extensive.

Theodore resigned in February 1915, and General Vilbrun Guillaume Sam assumed the presidency. Wilson sent a special agent to Haiti to press a treaty upon Sam's government as a condition for recognition. Failing to achieve his mission, the agent suggested that U.S. marines be used to impose a settlement. Although the State Department did not overtly accept this recommendation, the revolutionary situation in Haiti made its implementation possible. President Sam apparently ordered the murder of 167 political opponents at the prison in Port-au-Prince on 27 July. Although he took asylum in the French legation, he was dragged out by a mob that dismembered him in the streets. As these events occurred, the USS *Washington,* under Admiral Caperton, landed forces in Port-au-Prince. Caperton occupied the major coastal towns and took charge of customs collections.

After some confusion, the Haitian congress designated Caperton's choice, Sudre Dartiguenave, as the new president. The State Department soon presented Dartiguenave with a draft treaty providing for United States control of Haiti's finances, creation of a U.S.-officered constabulary, appointment of U.S. engineers to supervise sanitation and public improvement, a pledge not to transfer territory to any power other than the United States, and an article giving the United States the right to intervene to enforce the treaty and preserve Haitian independence. Dartiguenave's government signed the treaty after the United States refused to discuss substantive changes and threatened to establish a full military government. To implement the pact, the signatories set up five treaty services—a customs receivership, the financial adviser, the public works service, the public health service, and the constabulary. Although each except customs was subordinate to the Haitian government, the president of the United States nominated the top officials, who at first were all naval officers.

Late in 1917, the State Department proposed a draft constitution for Haiti (this was the document that Assistant Secretary of the Navy Franklin D. Roosevelt later claimed he had written). The Haitian congress resisted, but President Dartiguenave proclaimed it after a plebiscite (with a low vote and opponents abstaining) endorsed it. The constitution incorporated the 1915 treaty and validated acts of the military government. As in the Dominican Republic, there were improvements in Haiti under U.S. occupation. The constabulary, a well-trained force, maintained peace in the country; prisons improved; and the road-building program greatly extended the internal transportation and communications system. The courts and public schools did not receive the attention they needed, however, and Haiti's financial problems remained unsolved. When President Wilson left office, resentment against continued military occupation and the financial adviser's complete control of government expenditures was high.

MISSIONARY DIPLOMACY: NEGATIVES AND POSITIVES

This account of missionary diplomacy suggests that there was no significant change from earlier (1898–1913) United States policy in Latin America. If anything, missionary diplomacy meant "missionaries" (U.S. diplomats, military and naval officers, and businessmen) sometimes working in distasteful and ill-conceived ways, certainly not destined to ensure the voluntary "conversion" of the flock. Woodrow Wilson's objectives for Latin America, emphasizing democracy and constitutionalism, were admirable in the abstract; but they did not accord with reality in the nations affected. Furthermore, Wilson's methods were paradoxical: he did not use democratic and constitutional means to achieve his objectives. As on other occasions during his service in higher education and government, personal combat consumed Wilson; his struggles with Huerta, Carranza, and Villa ultimately became tests of personal strength and honor. On such occasions he lost his sense of perspective and the ability to see varieties of opinion and alternative approaches.

Missionary diplomacy was not devoid of positive effects. The negotiation of a treaty with Colombia in 1914 to resolve the deep resentment over that nation's loss of Panama in 1903 is an example. In the treaty, the United States expressed "sincere regret that anything should have occurred to interrupt or to mar the relations of cordial friendship that had so long subsisted between the two nations" and proposed to pay Colombia $25 million. Partly because of opposition from Theodore Roosevelt, the Senate ignored the treaty while Wilson was president but approved it in 1921 after removing the expression of regret. Wilson's support for the settlement appears to have been based on a conviction that U.S. actions in 1903 were wrong, that the whole affair had contributed substantially to Yankeephobia, and that an apology and reparations were long overdue. But Wilson could take this stand because the Colombian treaty did not interfere with his basic objectives for Latin America.

Some historians, especially Mark T. Gilderhus, have pointed to Wilson's support for a "Pan American pact" beginning in 1914 as another effort to put United States–Latin American relations on the basis of "equality and honor," as promised in the Mobile address. The draft pact was a multilateral agreement to guarantee territorial integrity, political independence, republican government, arbitration of disputes, and arms control. Presumably, the United States would forgo the unilateral right of intervention in Latin America. Edward M. House, who did much of the planning for the proposal, saw it as a way to promote hemispheric peace, just as Wilson later envisaged the world role of the League of Nations. Efforts to secure agreement on the pact failed. Some of the larger countries, such as Chile, rejected the idea of guaranteeing territorial integrity before the settlement of existing boundary disputes; and, given the contemporary United States interventions, it was difficult to see the pact as anything other than a cloak for established policy. In fact, neither Wilson nor his advisers were willing to renounce the practice of intervention.

SCHOLARLY VIEWS ON MISSIONARY DIPLOMACY

Recent works by scholars demonstrate the varying views they hold about Wilsonian missionary diplomacy in Latin America. Many of these scholars are more critical of Wilson's diplomacy in their books and articles than earlier historians. Walter LaFeber in *The American Age* (p. 261) observes that Wilson, "Determined to help other peoples become democratic and orderly, . . . himself became the greatest military interventionist in U.S. history." The works of Frederick S. Calhoun strongly back this point of view. "More than any other president," Calhoun writes in *Power and Principle* (p. ix), "Woodrow Wilson defined the various ways armed interventions could support foreign policy." In another work, *Uses of Force and Wilsonian Foreign Policy* (p. 9), Calhoun defines five categories for the use of force, all of which he argues Wilson used in Latin America: "force for protection," to defend specific national interests; "force for retribution," military action against a government that has violated international law; "force for solution," to oppose a nation's policies in a third nation; "force for introduction," military intimidation to persuade a government to enter negotiations to settle a dispute; and "force for association," military action in accordance with alliance regulations.

Lester D. Langley writes in *America in the Americas* (p. 111) that "the record of Woodrow Wilson, who condemned the interventionism of his predecessor [Taft] and chastised the economic imperialists," was "among the ironies of the Latin American policy of the United States." He added, "Three-quarters of a century later, the United States has yet to shake off the cultural paternalism he grafted onto the Pan-American tissue."

In an astute analysis, *Ideology and U.S. Foreign Policy* (pp. 17–18), Michael H. Hunt identifies three enduring components of the U.S. worldview in place early in the twentieth century:

> The capstone idea defined the American future in terms of an active quest for national greatness closely coupled to the promotion of liberty. . . . A second element . . . defined attitudes toward other peoples in terms of a racial hierarchy. . . . The third element defined the limits of acceptable political and social change overseas in keeping with the settled conviction that revolutions, though they might be a force for good, could as easily develop in a dangerous direction.

Hunt applies these elements in his account of Wilson's policy in Mexico, Haiti, and the Dominican Republic, as well as elsewhere in the world.

Walter A. McDougall in *Promised Land, Crusader State* (p. 129) contends that Wilson intensified the so-called progressive imperialism that had become prominent in U.S. foreign policy by the turn of the twentieth century. Wilson made clear, according to McDougall, that the United States (the "Crusader State") would cooperate with its Latin American neighbors, but only "when supported at every turn by the orderly processes of just government based on law." When order collapsed, the United States would use "influence of every kind" to reestablish it. He discusses "Wilsonianism, or liberal internationalism (so called)" in reference to U.S. policy in Mexico, Haiti, and Nicaragua.

Jules R. Benjamin's revisionist interpretation of Wilson's policy in the article "The Framework of U.S. Relations with Latin America in the Twentieth Century" (p. 99) emphasizes his uses of military intervention as well as the promotion of U.S. economic interests. As Benjamin puts it, "Although Wilson protested that neither Mars nor Mammon would be a part of his liberal hemisphere, he found no way to improve Latin America that did not include entrepreneurs and policemen. . . . [H]is principal legacy was to add to the older punishment of sins against order the punishment of sins against progress."

In the article "'An Irony of Fate': Woodrow Wilson's Pre–World War I Diplomacy," based mainly on *The Papers of Woodrow Wilson*, volumes 27–30, John Milton Cooper Jr. takes a more favorable view of Wilson's diplomacy in Latin America, especially in Mexico. He rejects the argument that Wilson aimed to promote U.S. economic interests in Mexico, and argues that "Mexico provides the clearest application of Wilson's political ideals to a diplomatic solution and offers . . . the best test of the effects of his ideals on his diplomacy" (p. 434).

Wilson's use of military force in Veracruz was a "blunder," according to Cooper, the result of his "interventionist impulses" temporarily determining his course of action. Cooper also argues that the "irony of fate" viewpoint associated with Wilsonian diplomacy has little relevance. Wilson, he says, "embarked on leadership in foreign affairs willingly and confidently" (p. 429) and clearly led his administration in foreign policy.

Kendrick A. Clements's article "Woodrow Wilson's Mexican Policy, 1913–15" reaches similar conclusions. After Veracruz, "Wilson's policy . . .was to support the [Mexican] revolution, avoid intervention, and attempt to influence the rebel leaders into the path of justice and moderation by means of diplomatic influence" (p. 135). Neither Cooper nor Clements mentions Pershing's 1916 punitive expedition into Mexico; this event needs to be considered in evaluating their views on Wilson's policy.

MISSIONARY MOTIVES: DEMOCRACY, CONSTITUTIONALISM, SECURITY, ECONOMICS

How, in the final analysis, can missionary diplomacy be explained? What were Wilson's motives and objectives? No single explanation will suffice, although there were unquestionably occasions when one consideration carried more weight than others. First, Wilson's concern about democracy and constitutionalism was genuine, and this was probably the main component of his Latin American policy when his administration began. What makes acceptance of this point difficult is that from the beginning, Wilson apparently assumed that the United States might have to use a heavy hand, to act undemocratically to install democracy. It was hard to see his commitment to constitutionalism in the midst of the bombardment of Veracruz or the U.S. marines' occupation of Santo Domingo, but it was there. Revolutions were unconstitutional and had to be prevented; illegitimate governments could not be recognized.

There is a second explanation for Wilson's policy that became clearer as World War I progressed—concern about the security of the hemisphere. Potential enemies, such as Germany, became of increasing concern. State Department documents illustrate the point clearly. What more startling example than the 1917 Zimmerman telegram, in which the German foreign minister invited Mexico to ally with Germany against the United States in the event of a German-American war? Security considerations were not always the primary explanation for missionary diplomacy, but they were constant concerns for Wilson, the State Department, and diplomats in the field. With a world war being fought during most of the Wilson presidency, and with the United States a belligerent by 1917, the situation was understandable.

There are also economic explanations for missionary diplomacy. As had long been the case, American entrepreneurs hoped to increase trade, find new markets and raw materials, and expand investment fields. Clearly these goals were applicable to Latin America during the Wilson administration. The available evidence does not prove conclusively that Wilson's central objective, as some scholars insist, was to advance U.S. economic interests. But facilitating the work of these interests, and giving them diplomatic protection, was important to Wilson and the State Department. Some diplomats, such as Henry Lane Wilson in Mexico and James Sullivan in the Dominican Republic, were dominated by their personal economic interests.

Missionary diplomacy contributed enormously to the Yankeephobia that had been building steadily in Latin America since the late nineteenth century. The task of the interwar presidents and the State Department was to dispel this aura of hostility. Considerable progress came with what came to be known as the Good Neighbor Policy, which reached its peak in the late 1930s. Whether the Good Neighbor Policy represented substantive change or merely a shift in rhetoric and tactics is debatable. Whatever the case, Woodrow Wilson, the practitioner of missionary diplomacy, made the Good Neighbor Policy, or something similar, a necessity.

BIBLIOGRAPHY

Benjamin, Jules R. "The Framework of U.S. Relations with Latin America in the Twentieth Century: An Interpretive Essay." *Diplomatic History* 11 (1987): 91–112.

Calder, Bruce J. *The Impact of Intervention: The Dominican Republic During the U.S. Occupation of 1916–1924.* Austin, Tex., 1984.

Calhoun, Frederick S. *Power and Principle: Armed Intervention in Wilsonian Foreign Policy.* Kent, Ohio, 1986.

———. *Uses of Force and Wilsonian Foreign Policy.* Kent, Ohio, 1993.

Calvert, Peter. *The Mexican Revolution, 1910–1914: The Diplomacy of Anglo-American Conflict.* London and New York, 1968. Emphasizes England's role in the U.S.–Mexican conflict.

Clements, Kendrick A. "Woodrow Wilson's Mexican Policy, 1913–15." *Diplomatic History* 4 (1980): 113–136.

Cooper, John Milton, Jr. "An Irony of Fate: Woodrow Wilson's Pre–World War I Diplomacy." *Diplomatic History* 3 (1979): 425–437.

Gilderhus, Mark T. *Pan American Visions: Woodrow Wilson in the Western Hemisphere, 1913–1921.* Tucson, Ariz., 1986.

———. "Wilson, Carranza, and the Monroe Doctrine: A Question in Regional Organization." *Diplomatic History* 7 (1983): 103–115.

Healy, David. *Drive to Hegemony: The United States in the Caribbean, 1898–1917.* Madison, Wis., 1988. Covers Cuba, the Dominican Republic, Haiti, Nicaragua, and Panama.

Hunt, Michael Hy. *Ideology and U.S. Foreign Policy.* New Haven, Conn., 1987. A valuable study that applies three elements helping shape the U.S. vision of the world to Wilson's policies and actions in Latin America and elsewhere.

Katz, Friedrich. *The Secret War in Mexico: Europe, the United States, and the Mexican Revolution.* Chicago, 1981. A detailed volume suggesting that Wilson's policy was designed to promote U.S. capital interests.

LaFeber, Walter. *The American Age: United States Foreign Policy at Home and Abroad Since 1750.* New York and London, 1989.

Langley, Lester D. *America in the Americas: The United States in the Western Hemisphere.* Athens, Ga., 1989. An interpretive survey of the history of U.S.–Latin American relations.

Levin, N. Gordon, Jr. *Woodrow Wilson and World Politics: America's Response to War and Revolution.* New York, 1968. Emphasizes economic motives in Wilson's foreign policy.

Link, Arthur S. *Wilson: The New Freedom; Wilson: The Struggle for Neutrality, 1914–1915; Wilson: Confusion and Crises, 1915–1916; Wilson: Campaign for Progressivism and Peace, 1916–1917.* Princeton, N.J., 1956–1965. Volumes 2–5 in Link's monumental biography. Traces in detail the story of missionary diplomacy, of which Link is critical.

Link, Arthur S., et al., eds. *The Papers of Woodrow Wilson.* 69 vols. Princeton, N.J., 1966–1993. Vols. 27–30 present documents on Wilson's diplomacy in Latin America.

McDougall, Walter A. *Promised Land, Crusader State: The American Encounter with the World Since 1776.* Boston and New York, 1997. A thoughtful survey and interpretive history of U.S. foreign policy.

Schmidt, Hans. *The United States Occupation of Haiti, 1915–1934.* New Brunswick, N.J., 1971. Argues that Wilson's policy was ill conceived and economically motivated.

Trask, David F., Michael C. Meyer, and Roger R. Trask, eds. *A Bibliography of United States–Latin American Relations Since 1810: A Selected List of Eleven Thousand Published References.* Lincoln, Neb., 1968. Meyer, Michael C., ed. *Supplement to A Bibliography of United States–Latin American Relations Since 1810.* Lincoln, Neb., 1979. These two volumes present an exhaustive list of books, articles, and documents.

Ulloa, Berta. *La revolución intervenida: Relaciones diplomáticas entre México y los Estados Unidos (1910–1914).* Mexico City, 1971.

See also DOLLAR DIPLOMACY; INTERVENTION AND NONINTERVENTION; OIL; WILSONIANISM.

EDITORS AND ADVISERS

Richard Dean Burns   Professor emeritus and former chair of the Department of History at California State University, Los Angeles. Burns has designed and edited a number of award-winning projects, including *A Guide to American Foreign Relations Since 1970;* the three-volume *Encyclopedia of Arms Control and Disarmament;* and, as general editor, the War/Peace Bibliography Series and the Twentieth Century Presidential Bibliographical Series. He has authored, coauthored, or edited more than a dozen books and two dozen articles covering arms control, diplomatic history, international law, and American foreign policy. He is the founder and publisher of Regina Books.

Elizabeth Cobbs Hoffman   Dwight Stanford professor of U.S. foreign relations at San Diego State University. Her first book, *The Rich Neighbor Policy: Rockefeller and Kaiser in Brazil* (1992), received the Allan Nevins Prize of the Society of American Historians and the Stuart Bernath Award of the Society for Historians of American Foreign Relations. She is also the author of *All You Need Is Love: The Peace Corps and the Spirit of the 1960s* and *Major Problems in American History, 1865 to the Present.* Cobbs Hoffman has received fellowships from the Woodrow Wilson International Center for Scholars and the Organization of American States, is a member of the Historical Advisory Committee to the U.S. Department of State, and has served on the editorial board of *Diplomatic History.*

Nick Cullather   Associate professor of history at Indiana University. He is the author of *Illusions of Influence: The Political Economy of United States–Philippine Relations, 1942–1960* and *Secret History: The Classified Account of the CIA's Operations in Guatemala.* He is also the coauthor of *Making a Nation: The United States and Its People.*

Alexander DeConde   Professor emeritus of American history at the University of California,

Santa Barbara, has also taught at Stanford University, Whittier College, Duke University, and the University of Michigan. He has also lectured and taught in Europe and Asia and written essays and books on American foreign relations, covering topics from the colonial era to the present. He was editor in chief of the first edition of the *Encyclopedia of American Foreign Policy.* His books include the two-volume *History of American Foreign Policy; Entangling Alliance; The Quasi-War; Half-Bitter, Half Sweet; This Affair of Louisiana; Ethnicity, Race, and American Foreign Policy; Presidential Machismo;* and *Gun Violence in America.*

Louise B. Ketz   President of Louise B. Ketz Book Producing and Literary Agency in New York City. She was a senior editor at Charles Scribner's Sons (1970–1983) and publisher of Prentice Hall Press (1985). She was editor of the *Dictionary of American History, Revised Edition,* and executive editor of the *Concise Dictionary of Scientific Biography, 2d Edition.* She was also coeditor of the three-volume *Encyclopedia of the American Military* and has contributed essays to various encyclopedias, including the *Scribner Encyclopedia of American Lives* and *Violence in America.*

Fredrik Logevall   Associate professor of history and codirector of the Cold War History Group at the University of California, Santa Barbara. Logevall is the author of *Choosing War: The Lost Chance for Peace and the Escalation of War in Vietnam* (1999), which won the Warren F. Kuehl Prize from the Society for Historians of American Foreign Relations. In 1998 he received the University of California at Santa Barbara Academic Senate Distinguished Teaching Award.

Chester Pach   Faculty associate of the Contemporary History Institute at Ohio University. He is author of *Arming the Free World: The Ori-*

gins of the United States Military Assistance Program, 1945–1950, The Presidency of Dwight D. Eisenhower, Revised Edition, and *The First Television War: TV News, the White House, and Vietnam.* He has received grants from the National Endowment for the Humanities and the Fulbright Program. He has been a member of the board of editors of *Diplomatic History* and a member of the council of the Society for Historians of American Foreign Relations.

William O. Walker III   Professor of history and international relations at Florida International University, where he is also chair of the History Department. He is the author or editor of six books on U.S. drug control policy, including *Drug Control in Americas, Opium and Foreign Policy: The Anglo-American Search for Order in Asia, 1912–1954,* and *Drugs in the Western Hemisphere: An Odyssey of Culture in Conflict.* He is a recipient of an SSRC-MacArthur Foundation Fellowship in Peace and Security.

CONTRIBUTORS

Michael R. Adamson. MOST-FAVORED-NATION PRINCIPLE

David Gray Adler, Idaho State University. THE CONSTITUTION

David L. Anderson, University of Indianapolis. DEPARTMENT OF STATE

Thom M. Armstrong, Citrus College. NEUTRALITY

Burton F. Beers, North Carolina State University. PROTECTION OF AMERICAN CITIZENS ABROAD

Edward M. Bennett, Washington State University. COLONIALISM AND NEOCOLONIALISM; MANDATES AND TRUSTEESHIPS

Larry Berman, University of California Washington Center. THE VIETNAM WAR AND ITS IMPACT

Barton J. Bernstein, Stanford University. CONTAINMENT

Ian J. Bickerton, University of New South Wales. TREATIES

Albert Bowman,† University of Tennessee, Chattanooga. PRESIDENTIAL ADVISERS

William R. Braisted, University of Texas at Austin. NAVAL DIPLOMACY

H. W. Brands, Texas A&M University. THE NATIONAL INTEREST

Kinley Brauer, University of Minnesota. CIVIL WAR DIPLOMACY

Richard Dean Burns, California State University, Los Angeles. ARMS CONTROL AND DISARMAMENT; BALANCE OF POWER; CHRONOLOGY OF AMERICAN FOREIGN POLICY

Robert Buzzanco, University of Houston. ANTI-IMPERIALISM

A. E. Campbell, University of Alabama at Birmingham. BALANCE OF POWER

Berenice A. Carroll, Purdue University. PEACEMAKING

Charles Chatfield, Wittenberg University. PACIFISM

Inis L. Claude, Jr., University of Virginia. INTERNATIONAL ORGANIZATION

Warren I. Cohen, University of Maryland Baltimore County. THE CHINA LOBBY; CONSORTIA

David Coleman, Miller Center of Public Affairs, University of Virginia. DETERRENCE

Paolo E. Coletta, U.S. Naval Academy. RECOGNITION

Jerald A. Combs, San Francisco State University. EMBARGOES AND SANCTIONS

Nick Cullather, Indiana University. DEVELOPMENT DOCTRINE AND MODERNIZATION THEORY

Roger Daniels, University of Cincinnati. IMMIGRATION

Jules Davids,† Georgetown University. EXTRATERRITORIALITY

Calvin D. Davis, Duke University. ARBITRATION, MEDIATION, AND CONCILIATION

Alexander DeConde, University of California, Santa Barbara. PRESIDENTIAL POWER

Robert A. Divine, University of Texas at Austin. PRESIDENTIAL ADVISERS

Ronald E. Doel, Oregon State University. SCIENCE AND TECHNOLOGY

Justus D. Doenecke, University of South Florida. MOST-FAVORED-NATION PRINCIPLE

639

Kurk Dorsey, Horton Social Science Center, University of New Hampshire. ENVIRONMENTAL DIPLOMACY

Michael Dunne, University of Sussex. ASYLUM

J. B. Duroselle, University of Paris. TREATIES

Raymond A. Esthus, Tulane University. PROTECTORATES AND SPHERES OF INFLUENCE

Thomas H. Etzold,† Naval War College. POWER POLITICS

Robert H. Ferrell, Indiana University. BLOCKADES; PEACE MOVEMENTS

James A. Field, Jr., Swarthmore College. PHILANTHROPY

Francis J. Gavin, University of Texas at Austin. INTERNATIONAL MONETARY FUND AND WORLD BANK

Jessica C. E. Gienow-Hecht, Harvard University. CULTURAL IMPERIALISM

Doris A. Graber, University of Illinois at Chicago. INTERVENTION AND NONINTERVENTION

Norman A. Graebner, University of Virginia. REALISM AND IDEALISM

Kenneth J. Grieb, University of Wisconsin Oshkosh. AMBASSADORS, EXECUTIVE AGENTS, AND SPECIAL REPRESENTATIVES

Terrence R. Guay, Syracuse University. JUDICIARY POWER AND PRACTICE

Kenneth J. Hagan, Naval War College at Monterey. NUCLEAR STRATEGY AND DIPLOMACY

David Healy, University of Wisconsin–Milwaukee. IMPERIALISM

Alan K. Henrikson, Fletcher School of Law and Diplomacy, Tufts University. ELITISM

Walter L. Hixson, Buchtel College of Arts and Sciences. COLD WAR EVOLUTION AND INTERPRETATIONS

Valerie M. Hudson, Brigham Young University. DECISION MAKING

James A. Huston. THE MILITARY-INDUSTRIAL COMPLEX

Akira Iriye, Harvard University. CULTURAL RELATIONS AND POLICIES

Jerry Israel, University of Indianapolis. DEPARTMENT OF STATE

Brian Michael Jenkins, RAND Corporation. TERRORISM AND COUNTERTERRORISM

T. Christopher Jespersen, North George College and State University. HUMAN RIGHTS

Robert David Johnson, Brooklyn College. CONGRESSIONAL POWER

Manfred Jonas, Union College, Schenectady, New York. ISOLATIONISM

Christopher C. Joyner, Georgetown University. INTERNATIONAL LAW

William Kamman, University of North Texas. MILITARISM

Lawrence S. Kaplan, Georgetown University. NATIONALISM

Thomas L. Karnes, Arizona State University. PAN-AMERICANISM

Burton I. Kaufman, Miami University, Oxford, Ohio. MULTINATIONAL CORPORATIONS

Louise B. Ketz, Louise B. Ketz Book Producing and Literary Agency, New York. CHRONOLOGY OF AMERICAN FOREIGN POLICY

Warren F. Kimball, Rutgers University, Newark. ALLIANCES, COALITIONS, AND ENTENTES

Michael T. Klare, Hampshire College. ARMS TRANSFERS AND TRADE

Warren F. Kuehl,† University of Akron. INTERNATIONALISM

Klaus Larres, Queens University Belfast. INTERNATIONAL ORGANIZATION; NORTH ATLANTIC TREATY ORGANIZATION

Roger Launius, National Aeronautics and Space Administration. OUTER SPACE

Mark Atwood Lawrence, University of Texas at Austin. OPEN DOOR POLICY

Thomas M. Leonard, University of North Florida. PAN-AMERICANISM

Ralph B. Levering, Davidson College. THE PRESS

Louis W. Liebovich, University of Illinois, Urbana-Champaign. THE PRESS

Fredrik Logevall, University of California, Santa Barbara. PARTY POLITICS

Thomas R. Maddux, California State University, Northridge. COLD WAR TERMINATION

Vojtech Mastny, Woodrow Wilson Center and National Security Archive. SUPERPOWER DIPLOMACY

James I. Matray, New Mexico State University. REPARATIONS

Tim Matthewson, The Patent Company of Arlington, Virginia. PHILANTHROPY

Trevor B. McCrisken, Cartmel College, Lancaster University. EXCEPTIONALISM

Laura McEnaney, Whittier College. GENDER

Elizabeth McKillen, University of Maine. ORGANIZED LABOR

Richard A. Melanson, National War College. POST–COLD WAR POLICY

Frank J. Merli,† Queens College. BLOCKADES

Robert L. Messer, University of Illinois at Chicago. POWER POLITICS

Edwin Moïse, Clemson University. DOMINO THEORY

Ian Mugridge, The Open University. ARMED NEUTRALITIES

Anna Kasten Nelson, American University. NATIONAL SECURITY COUNCIL

Jason Newman. THE VIETNAM WAR AND ITS IMPACT

Jonathan C. Nielson, Columbia College. EXTRATERRITORIALITY

Kenneth A. Osgood, Florida Atlantic University. PROPAGANDA

Gary B. Ostrower, Alfred University. INTERNATIONALISM

Chester Pach, Ohio University. TELEVISION

David S. Painter, Georgetown University. OIL

Carl P. Parrini, Northern Illinois University. REPARATIONS

David S. Patterson, Office of the Historian, Department of State. DISSENT IN WARS

David M. Pletcher, Indiana University. CONTINENTAL EXPANSION

Brenda Gayle Plummer, University of Wisconsin–Madison. AFRICAN AMERICANS

John Prados, National Security Archives. COVERT OPERATIONS; INTELLIGENCE AND COUNTERINTELLIGENCE

Armin Rappaport,† University of California, San Diego. FREEDOM OF THE SEAS

Steven L. Rearden, Joint History Office, Department of Defense. DEPARTMENT OF DEFENSE

David M. Reimers, New York University. REFUGEE POLICIES

Leo P. Ribuffo, George Washington University. RELIGION

Darlene Rivas, Pepperdine University. HUMANITARIAN INTERVENTION AND RELIEF

Andrew J. Rotter, Colgate University. COLD WARRIORS

T. Michael Ruddy, St. Louis University. NEUTRALISM

David F. Schmitz, Whitman College. DICTATORSHIPS

Jennifer W. See, University of California, Santa Barbara. IDEOLOGY

Marc Jay Selverstone, Miller Center of Public Affairs, University of Virginia. DOCTRINES

David Shreve, Miller Center of Public Affairs, University of Virginia. ECONOMIC POLICY AND THEORY

Katherine A. S. Sibley, St. Joseph's University. FOREIGN AID

J. David Singer, University of Michigan. THE BEHAVIORAL APPROACH TO DIPLOMATIC HISTORY

Joseph M. Siracusa, University of Queensland. LOANS AND DEBT RESOLUTION; THE MUNICH ANALOGY

Elizabeth Skinner, Naval Postgraduate School. NUCLEAR STRATEGY AND DIPLOMACY

William Slany, Department of State. SPECIAL-INTEREST LOBBIES

Melvin Small, Wayne State University. PUBLIC OPINION

Geoffrey S. Smith, Queens University, Kingston, Ontario. NATIVISM

Robert Freeman Smith, University of Toledo. RECIPROCITY

Tony Smith, Tufts University. WILSONIANISM

John Snetsinger, California Polytechnic State University. RACE AND ETHNICITY

Anders Stephanson, Columbia University. COLD WAR ORIGINS

Roland N. Stromberg, University of Wisconsin–Milwaukee. COLLECTIVE SECURITY

Jeremi Suri, University of Wisconsin. REVOLUTION

Athan G. Theoharis, Marquette University. REVISIONISM

Eugene P. Trani, Historical Office, Office of the Secretary of Defense. DOLLAR DIPLOMACY

Roger R. Trask, Historical Office, Office of the Secretary of Defense. WILSONIAN MISSIONARY DIPLOMACY

Betty Miller Unterberger, Texas A&M University. SELF-DETERMINATION

Richard W. Van Alstyne,† Callison College, University of the Pacific. LOANS AND DEBT RESOLUTION

William O. Walker III, Florida International University. NARCOTICS POLICY

Zuoyue Wang, California Polytechnic State University. SCIENCE AND TECHNOLOGY

William Earl Weeks, Frostburg State University, Maryland. FREEDOM OF THE SEAS

Russell F. Weigley, Temple University. DISSENT IN WARS

William Appleman Williams,† Oregon State University. OPEN DOOR INTERPRETATION

Theodore A. Wilson, University of Kansas. SUMMIT CONFERENCES

Randall Woods, J. William Fulbright College of Arts and Sciences, University of Arkansas. BIPARTISANSHIP

Marvin R. Zahniser, The Ohio State University. THE CONTINENTAL SYSTEM

Thomas W. Zeiler, University of Colorado at Boulder. GLOBALIZATION; TARIFF POLICY

Index

Boldface indicates essay titles and page numbers and volume numbers.

A

King, Rufus, 3:333
Kipling, Rudyard, 1:416, 463
Kirkland, Lane, 3:58
Kirkpatrick, Jeane, 1:241, 308,
    501–502, 536; 2:124, 181,
    452; 3:189
Kissinger, Henry A., 1:36, 39, 141,
    241, 362, 451, 458, 459, 471,
    488, 532; 2:247, 607
    and ABM Treaty, 2:617
    and Africa, 3:474
    American hegemony, 3:153
    on balance of power, 1:137
    and Chile, 2:182; 3:473
    and China, 1:190; 3:351
    and détente, 1:216; 2:556
    and elitism, 2:24–25
    on European cooperation, 2:584
    on foreign policy, 3:101, 498
    and human rights, 2:45, 178, 179
    on intervention, 3:161
    as national security adviser, 1:44
    and National Security Council,
        2:504, 505–506, 507
    and new world, 1:138, 164, 166
    and Nixon's China trip, 2:505
    and nuclear war, 1:473
    and nuclear weapons negotia-
        tions, 1:90–91
    and oil embargo of 1973, 3:176
    and power politics, 1:166
    as presidential adviser,
        3:187–188
    on revolution, 3:438
    and superpower diplomacy,
        3:522–523
    and Vietnam War, 3:106–107
Kistiakowsky, George, 3:186
Kitchin, Claude, 1:55; 2:393
Klopsch, Louis, 2:155; 3:144
Knaplund, Paul, 3:26
Knickerbocker, 1:411
Knight, Frank, 2:6
Knights of Labor, 3:46
Knowland, William F., 1:241, 185,
    189, 301; 2:449; 3:487, 572
Knowlton's Rangers, 2:235
Know-Nothing (or American) Party,
    2:512, 516; 3:376, 377
Knox, Henry, 3:180
Knox, Philander C., 1:68, 313, 314,
    315, 316, 544, 546–547; 2:38,
    244; 3:132, 283
    and China, 3:270
    and Nicaragua, 2:368
Knox-Castrillo Convention (1911),
    1:545
Koch, Robert, 3:144
Koen, Ross Y., 1:190
Kogoro, Takahira, 3:37
Kohl, Helmut, 2:586, 589

Kohlberg, Alfred, 1:185, 187, 188,
    189, 190
Kohn, Hans, 2:485
Kolchak, Aleksandr Vasiliyevich,
    1:299
Kolko, Gabriel, 1:401; 2:387, 397;
    3:101,416, 417
Koppel, Ted, 3:553, 554
Korea
    as Japan protectorate, 3:268
    missionaries in, 3:380
    and naval diplomacy, 2:530–531
    and Point Four program, 1:480
    relief assistance, 2:164
    and Soviet occupation, 1:348
    special envoys to, 1:43
    and United Nations, 2:254
Koreagate, 3:497
Korean Airlines Flight 007,
    1:218, 262
Korean Americans, 3:302
Korean Central Intelligence
    Agency, 3:497
Korean War (1950–1953), 1:211,
    247–248, 468; 2:409,
    569, 579, 598–600;
    3:207, 208, 517
    armistice, 3:121
    and asylum, 1:119
    and bipartisanship, 1:163
    and blockade, 1:181; 2:119
    and China, 1:185, 186, 252
    and Congress, 1:301
    and containment doctrine,
        1:357–358
    dissent during, 1:505, 515–516
    and military-industrial complex,
        2:406
    and Munich analogy, 2:447–449
    and national interest, 2:479
    and nationalism, 2:396
    and NATO contribution, 1:23
    and navy, 2:536
    and party politics, 3:105
    prisoners of war, 1:358
    propaganda, 3:248
    reparations, 3:403
    and Soviet Union, 1:245
    and trade restrictions, 2:436
    and United Nations, 1:277
    and warmaking power,
        1:333–334
Korematsu (1944), 2:176
Kornai, Janos, 2:6
Kosovar refugees, 3:367
Kosovo war (1999), 1:111,
    279–280, 310, 449, 518, 519;
    2:46, 170, 183; 3:108, 161,
    191, 218, 297, 326–327, 479
    and NATO, 2:590

Kossuth, Lajos, 2:340, 516, 530;
    3:150, 319–320, 359–360,
    429, 462
Kosygin, Aleksei, 1:89; 2:606
Krauthammer, Charles, 1:137, 139
Krenn, Michael L., 1:400; 2:177
Krige, John, 3:70
Kristallnacht, 2:444
Krueger, Anne, 2:295
Kuala Batu, Sumatra, incident, 3:199
Kubek, Anthony, 3:414
Kubitschek, Juscelino, 3:94
Kuchel, Thomas H., 1:189–190
Kuhn, Fritz, 2:524
Kuhn, Loeb and Company, 1:313
Kuisel, Richard F., 1:404
Kuklick, Bruce, 3:416, 417
Ku Klux Klan, 2:494, 523, 525
Kultur (high culture), 1:399,
    400, 405
Kun, Bela, 2:159
Kung, H. H., 1:188
Kuomintang, 2:88
Kuralt, Charles, 3:551
Kurds, 2:167
Kurtz, Stephen G., 1:508
Kurz, Robert J., 3:224
Kuwait
    arms transfers to, 1:105
    Gulf War, 1:280, 309, 517–518;
        2:167, 274, 333
    military sales to, 1:115
    oil, 3:6
    and self-determination, 3:477
Kuznets, Simon, 2:14
Kvitsinskii, Iurii, 3:526
Kyoto Protocol (1997), 1:341; 2:27,
    60–61, 148, 184, 255, 278,
    310; 3:233

L

labor, see organized labor
Labor Division, 3:55
labor internationalism, 3:57–58
Lacan, Jacques, 2:511
Ladd, William, 2:242; 3:130
Ladies Greek Committee, 2:152
Ladies' Soldiers Aid Societies, 2:154
LaFeber, Walter, 1:289; 3:27, 101,
    416, 417, 431, 432, 456, 634
La Follette, Robert, 1:55, 56, 298
Lage, William, 3:412, 413
Laird, Melvin B., 1:446; 2:608
laissez-faire economic theory, 2:2
Lake, Anthony, 2:509; 3:158–159,
    160, 162, 191, 582
Lake Mohonk Conference on Inter-
    national Arbitration (1895),
    2:242

arms transfers to, 1:105
CIA covert operations, 1:394-395
and dollar diplomacy, 1:545–546;
2:368–369
and drugs, 2:468
earthquake relief, 2:165
and human rights, 2:181–182
interventions in, 1:299, 545;
2:368; 3:550, 630–631
liberation movement in, 1:56
and peace groups, 3:77
and Reagan Doctrine, 2:273
sanctions against, 2:44
and Sandinista rebels, 1:218
Stimson mission to, 1:37
as U.S. protectorate, 3:267
Nicaraguan lobby, 3:497
Nicaraguans
and asylum, 3:364
Nicholas II of Russia, 1:65, 68, 81;
3:433
Nicolson, Harold, 3:113
NIE 11/3-8 series, 2:229
Niebuhr, Reinhold, 1:241;
3:386, 387
Nigeria
aid to, 2:102–103
Nightline, 3:554
Nike Company, 2:147
Niles, David, 3:304
Nine-Power Naval Treaty (1922),
1:19; 2:87, 249, 251, 534;
3:40, 270, 349
Ninkovich, Frank, 1:402; 2:349
Nitze, Paul H., 1:91, 236, 241, 265,
356, 441, 468, 473; 2:397,
447, 598, 609; 3:526
Nixon, Richard M., 1:39, 44, 45,
531–533; 2:24; 3:104, 276
on biological and chemical
weapons, 1:95
and bipartisanship, 1:164, 166
and Cambodia, 1:307; 3:279
and Chile, 1:394, 500; 3:473
and China, 1:190, 216, 253, 341;
2:43, 348, 505; 3:289, 351
and civil rights, 2:178
and Cold War, 1:212
and containment, 1:360
covert operations, 1:393
and currency float, 2:438
and détente, 1:216, 223; 2:556
and dollar-gold convertibility,
2:292
and domino theory, 1:557, 558
drug policy, 2:455, 466–467
and economic policy, 2:584
and Guatemala, 2:97
House Un-American Activities
Committee, 1:302

imperial presidency of, 1:59;
2:179
and Kissinger, 3:187
and media, 3:552
mining of North Vietnam ports,
2:120
and National Security Council,
2:499, 504–506
Nicaragua aid, 2:165
and nuclear strategy, 1:473;
2:606–608
and nuclear test bans, 1:88
and oil-producing countries,
3:13
and party politics, 3:107
and the press, 3:226
and presidential power,
3:212–213
and propaganda, 3:251
and reciprocity, 3:340
and revolution, 3:438
and space program, 3:64
summit conferences, 3:508–509
and superpower diplomacy,
3:522–523
and tariffs, 3:340–341, 544
and Vietnam War, 2:357, 452,
480, 538; 3:106–107,
212–213, 281, 472, 602–604
and War Powers Act, 2:358
see also Nixon Doctrine
Nixon administration
and covert operations, 1:394
and Europe, 2:584–585
and intelligence collection, 2:228
and most-favored-nation principle, 2:427
and NATO, 2:584
and nuclear weapons, 1:90–91
and Persian Gulf, 1:111
and Vietnam, 1:164, 166
Nixon Doctrine, 1:111, 278,
531–533, 535; 2:272, 318,
585; 3:472
Noah, Mordecai, 3:376
Nobel, Alfred, 3:131–132
no-first-use doctrine, 1:356
nonalignment, 2:543, 545–546
nongovernmental organizations
(NGOs), 1:422–423, 489;
2:108
and aid, 2:104
and environment, 2:49, 58
and pacifism, 3:78
and women's issues, 3:491
nonimportation, 2:34
Nonimportation Act of 1806,
2:35, 36, 563
Nonintercourse Act of 1808, 2:340
Nonintercourse Act of 1809, 1:382;
2:36–37, 563

nonintervention, 2:269, 315–318,
323, 334
and self-determination, 3:462
see also intervention and nonintervention
Non-Partisan Committee for Peace,
3:486
nonproliferation, 1:87
Non-Proliferation Treaty (1968),
1:88; 2:613
non-quota immigrants, 1:121
nonrecognition, 1:496; 2:325;
3:103, 350
nonrefoulement principle, 1:124
nonresistance, 3:73–74
non-tariff barriers (NTBs), 2:426
Non-Violent Action Against Nuclear
Weapons, 3:488
nonviolent direct action, 3:77, 78
nonviolent resistance, 3:78
Noonan, Peggy, 1:536
Nordlinger, Eric, 2:349
Noriega, Manuel Antonio, 1:309;
2:44, 182, 273, 330, 466, 469;
3:107, 215, 266
Norman, Henry, 1:414
Norris, George, 1:56; 2:343. 394
Norstad, Lauris, 2:601
North, James H., 1:202
North, Oliver, 1:255, 261; 2:508;
3:189, 555
North Africa oil, 3:13
North American Congress on Latin
America, 3:489
North American Free Trade
Agreement (NAFTA) (1993),
1:42, 169, 309, 403; 2:53,
103, 270, 426, 440; 3:58,
96, 341–342, 489
North American Rockwell, 2:407
North Atlantic Alliance, 1:23; 1:25
North Atlantic Cooperation Council, 2:590
North Atlantic Station, 2:531
North Atlantic Treaty (1949), 1:23,
24, 247
North Atlantic Treaty Alliance,
1:528
North Atlantic Treaty Organization
(NATO), 1:23, 26, 162, 211,
301, 355–356, 441; 2:22, 303,
348, 573–593
and arms aid, 1:109
and Balkans wars, 2:333; 3:479
and collective security, 1:278,
279; 2:254
covert operations, 1:392
enlargement of, 3:108
and France, 1:24; 2:604
humanitarian intervention in
Kosovo, 2:170

Stennis, John, **1**:304, 307
Stephanson, Anders, **2**:64, 66, 73, 195, 199
Stephen, James, **1**:381
Stephens, Alexander H., **1**:204, 510
Stephenson, Sir William, **1**:388
Stettinius, Edward R., **1**:246; **2**:384; **3**:137
Stevens, John L., **3**:265
Stevens, Sylvester K., **3**:26
Stevens, Ted, **3**:165
Stevenson, Adlai, **1**:249; **2**:450
stewardship theory of the presidency, **3**:203
Stewart, Bill, **3**:555
Stieglitz, Joseph, **2**:293; **3**:156
Stillwell, Joseph W., **2**:462
Stimson, Henry L, **1**:33, 186, 231, 245, 452, 453, 457–458, 465, 497; **2**:21, 40, 249, 250, 345
  and arms control, **1**:83, 84, 85
  and Japan, **3**:41
  Manchurian crisis, **2**:251
  and naval diplomacy, **2**:534
  and Nicaragua, **1**:37
  and Open Door policy, **3**:21
  and recognition policy, **3**:348, 349
  and Soviet Union, **1**:347
  and World War I debts, **2**:373
  see also Hoover-Stimson Doctrine
Stimson Doctrine, **1**:33; **2**:251; **3**:349, 581
  see also Hoover-Stimson Doctrine
Stoddard, Lothrop, **2**:522
Stoeckle, Edouard de, **1**:194
Stohl, Rachel, **2**:107
Stone, I. F., **1**:57
Story, Joseph, **3**:117
Stouffer, Samuel A., **2**:395
Stowell, Ellery C., **2**:246
Straight, Willard D., **1**:544, 546, 547, 548; **3**:38
Strategic Air Command (SAC), **1**:466; **2**:536, 600
strategic arms limitation talks (SALT), **1**:90, 445, 446, 473; **2**:228, 607
Strategic Arms Limitation Treaty of 1972 (SALT I), **1**:39, 90–91, 98, 216–217; **2**:556; **3**:523
Strategic Arms Limitation Treaty of 1979 (SALT II), **1**: 91, 92, 98, 217, 306; **2**:228, 608–609
strategic arms reduction talks and treaties (START I and II), **1**:92, 98, 266, 267, 474; **2**:228, 611, 613, 617
Strategic Defense Initiative (SDI), **1**:92, 218, 219, 254–256, 258, 262, 263, 266–267, 444–447,

448, 474, 538; **2**:408, 482, 587, 609; **3**:138
Strategic Hamlet Program (Vietnam), **2**:74
Strategic Petroleum Reserve, **2**:378; **3**:15
Strategic Services Unit (SSU), **1**:390
Street, Cyrus, **2**:245
Streibert, Theodore C., **3**:250
Streit, Clarence, **2**:250, 253
Strong, Caleb, **1**:508
Strong, Josiah, **2**:493, 494, 518, 519; **3**:379, 431–432, 437
structural adjustment program, **1**:490; **2**:293
structuralism, **1**:489
structuralist theories and underdevelopment, **1**:481
Stuart, J. Leighton, **1**:185
Studds, Gerry E., **1**:111
Student Mobilization Committee to End the War, **3**:488
Student Non-violent Coordinating Committee, **1**:9
Student Peace Union, **3**:76
Students for a Democratic Society, **1**:58
Student Volunteer Movement for Foreign Missions, **3**:143, 379
Suarez-Lamont agreement (1942), **1**:321
Sub-Commission on Prevention of Discrimination and Protection of Minorities, **1**:6, 7
submarine-launched ballistic missiles (SLBMs), **1**:91
submarines
  nuclear-powered, **2**:599
Sudan, **2**:167
  aid to, **2**:106
  and human rights, **2**:173
  refugees, **3**:367
Suez crisis (1956), **1**:24, 529; **2**:42; **3**:11, 209
sugar lobby, **3**:492
Sukarno, Achmad, **3**:209
Sullivan, Leon, **3**:491
Sullivan and Cromwell, **1**:453
Sullivan Principles, **3**:491
Sully, duc de, **3**:130
Summers, Harry, **3**:418–419
Summers, Lawrence H., **3**:156
Summit Conferences, **3**:501–511
  and superpower diplomacy, **3**:514–515
Summit of the Americas, **3**:509
Sumner, Charles, **1**:63–64, 296, 297; **2**:204
Sumner, William Graham, **3**:318
Sun Tzu, **3**:241
Sun Yat-sen, **1**:249, 250, 417, 478; **3**:40–41

Sunday, Billy, **3**:383
supercarriers, **2**:536, **2**:599
Super NAFTA, **3**:342
Superpower Diplomacy, **3**:513–530
Support for East European Democracies Act (1994), **2**:103, 104
supremacy clause, **1**:323, 324, 325–326, 327
Supreme Court
  on blockade, **1**:177
  on commander in chief clause, **1**:335
  and constitutional power, **1**:324–325
  and foreign affairs, **2**:353
  and political questions, **2**:359
  on treaty-making power, **1**:334
  on war, **1**:331
  on war powers, **1**:329; **2**:354, 355–356
Supreme War Council, **3**:503
Sussex, **2**:566
sustainable development, **1**:490
Sutherland, George, **1**:324–325, 335, 341; **2**:355, 360; **3**:205
Suttner, Bertha von, **3**:131
Suzuki, Ichiro, **2**:148
Swanson Resolution (1926), **2**:344
Swayze, John Cameron, **3**:548
Sweden
  and maritime principles, **2**:112
  and neutrality, **2**:545, 546, 548, 550
  and neutral rights, **1**:75, 76
  and Vietnam War, **2**:556
Sweeney, John, **3**:58
Sweetser, Arthur, **2**:251
Swift, John Franklin, **2**:89
Switzerland
  and most-favored-nation principle, **2**:421
  and neutrality, **1**:73; **2**:545, 546, 548, 550
Swope, Herbert Bayard, **1**:224
Sylvan, Donald A., **1**:429
Sylvester, Arthur, **3**:550
Sylvis, William, **3**:46
Symington, Stuart, **1**:305
Synar, Mike, **1**:307, 309
Syria, **3**:162
  sanctions against, **3**:567
  and Soviet Union, **1**:214
Szilard, Leo, **1**:57

T

Taepo Dong-1 missile, **2**:614; **3**:165
Taft, Robert A., **1**:57, 162, 163, 301, 302, 333–334, 350, 514–515; **2**:94, 253, 347–348, 394, 398; **3**:104

ISBN 0-684-80660-6

90000